COMPARATIVE HEALTH SYSTEMS

SECOND EDITION

A Global Perspective

Edited by

James A. Johnson, PhD, MPA, MSc
Medical Social Scientist and Professor
School of Health Sciences
Central Michigan University
Mount Pleasant, Michigan
and
Visiting Professor
St. George's University
Grenada, West Indies

Carleen H. Stoskopf, ScD, MS
Professor and Chair
Health Management and Policy
San Diego State University
San Diego, California

Leiyu Shi, DrPH, MBA, MPA
Professor
Bloomberg School of Public Health
Johns Hopkins University
and
Director
Johns Hopkins Primary Care Policy Center
Baltimore, Maryland

JONES & BARTLETT
LEARNING

World Headquarters
Jones & Bartlett Learning
25 Mall Road
Burlington, MA 01803
978-443-5000
info@jblearning.com
www.jblearning.com

Jones & Bartlett Learning books and products are available through most bookstores and online booksellers. To contact Jones & Bartlett Learning directly, call 800-832-0034, fax 978-443-8000, or visit our website, www.jblearning.com.

Substantial discounts on bulk quantities of Jones & Bartlett Learning publications are available to corporations, professional associations, and other qualified organizations. For details and specific discount information, contact the special sales department at Jones & Bartlett Learning via the above contact information or send an email to specialsales@jblearning.com.

Copyright © 2018 by Jones & Bartlett Learning, LLC, an Ascend Learning Company

All rights reserved. No part of the material protected by this copyright may be reproduced or utilized in any form, electronic or mechanical, including photocopying, recording, or by any information storage and retrieval system, without written permission from the copyright owner.

The content, statements, views, and opinions herein are the sole expression of the respective authors and not that of Jones & Bartlett Learning, LLC. Reference herein to any specific commercial product, process, or service by trade name, trademark, manufacturer, or otherwise does not constitute or imply its endorsement or recommendation by Jones & Bartlett Learning, LLC and such reference shall not be used for advertising or product endorsement purposes. All trademarks displayed are the trademarks of the parties noted herein. *Comparative Health Systems: A Global Perspective, Second Edition* is an independent publication and has not been authorized, sponsored, or otherwise approved by the owners of the trademarks or service marks referenced in this product.

There may be images in this book that feature models; these models do not necessarily endorse, represent, or participate in the activities represented in the images. Any screenshots in this product are for educational and instructive purposes only. Any individuals and scenarios featured in the case studies throughout this product may be real or fictitious, but are used for instructional purposes only.

This publication is designed to provide accurate and authoritative information in regard to the subject matter covered. It is sold with the understanding that the publisher is not engaged in rendering legal, accounting, or other professional service. If legal advice or other expert assistance is required, the service of a competent professional person should be sought.

Production Credits
VP, Executive Publisher: David D. Cella
Publisher: Michael Brown
Associate Editor: Danielle Bessette
Production Manager: Carolyn Rogers Pershouse
Director of Vendor Management: Amy Rose
Vendor Manager: Juna Abrams
Senior Marketing Manager: Sophie Fleck Teague
Manufacturing and Inventory Control Supervisor: Amy Bacus
Composition: Integra Software Services Pvt. Ltd.

Project Management: Integra Software Services Pvt. Ltd.
Cover Design: Kristin E. Parker
Director of Rights & Media: Joanna Gallant
Rights & Media Specialist: Wes DeShano
Media Development Editor: Shannon Sheehan
Cover Image: © Matvienko Vladimir/Shutterstock
Printing and Binding: LSC Communications
Cover Printing: LSC Communications

Library of Congress Cataloging-in-Publication Data
Names: Johnson, James A., 1954- editor. | Stoskopf, Carleen H. (Carleen
   Harriet), 1953- editor. | Shi, Leiyu, editor.
Title: Comparative health systems : a global perspective / [edited by] James
   Johnson, Carleen Stoskopf, Leiyu Shi.
Other titles: Comparative health systems (Johnson)
Description: Second edition. | Burlington, MA : Jones & Bartlett Learning LCC,
   [2018] | Includes bibliographical references and index.
Identifiers: LCCN 2016054758 | ISBN 9781284111736 (paper back)
Subjects: | MESH: Delivery of Health Care—organization & administration |
   Health Policy | Internationality | Cross-Cultural Comparison
Classification: LCC RA441 | NLM W 84.1 | DDC 362.1—dc23 LC record available at https://lccn.loc.gov/2016054758

6048

Printed in the United States of America
26 25   10 9 8 7

To Elizabeth

June 19, 1989 – March 29, 2014

Drawing by Elizabeth Johnson, University of Montevallo, '13

-J.A.J.

Contents

Acknowledgments vii
Foreword by Drs. David and Kathleen Jordan viii
Foreword by Dr. Ted Karpf ix
Preface by Dr. James A. Johnson x
Contributors xii
About the Editors xv

PART I Global Health and Health Systems   1

Chapter 1 Introduction to Health Systems ... 3
Introduction...3
Conclusion 16

Chapter 2 Global Health and Disease 21
Introduction..21
Burden of Disease 22
Noncommunicable/Chronic Diseases..................23
Zoonotic Infections.................................39
Public Health and Healthcare Services 44

Chapter 3 Global Health Systems Politics, Economics, and Policy........... 49
Introduction..49
How to Think About Health Policymaking—Micro and Macro Models 50
Possible Responses to the Convergence of Policy Problems..........................52
The Nature of National Health Tradeoffs, Ideology, and Ethics 57
Conclusion: Health Policymaking Around the World—Uncertain Times and Futures 60

Chapter 4 Role of International Organizations in Health Systems 65
Introduction..65

Intergovernmental Organizations..................65
Nongovernmental Organizations 68

PART II Health Systems by Country   75

The Americas Region

Chapter 5 United States 77
Country Description 77
Brief History of the Healthcare System 84
Description of the Current Healthcare System......85
Evaluation of the Healthcare System 89
Conclusion 94

Chapter 6 Canada 97
Country Description 97
Brief History of the Healthcare System 103
Description of the Current Healthcare System.... 106
Evaluation of the Healthcare System 111
Current and Emerging Issues and Challenges 114
Conclusion 117

Chapter 7 Mexico........................ 121
Country Description 121
Brief History of the Healthcare System 126

Chapter 8 Peru......................... 133
Country Description 133
Brief History of the Healthcare System 140
Description of the Current Healthcare System.... 141

Chapter 9 Brazil........................ 149
Country Description 149
Brief History of the Healthcare System 154
Description of the Current Healthcare System.... 158

Evolution of the Healthcare System in Brazil...... 160
Current and Emerging Issues and Challenges.... 163

European Region

Chapter 10 United Kingdom 169
Country Description 169
Brief History of the Healthcare System 174
Description of the Current Healthcare System.... 179
Evaluation of the Healthcare System 182
Current and Emerging Issues and Challenges.... 184

Chapter 11 France...................... 187
Country Description 187
Brief History of the Healthcare System 195
Description of the Current Healthcare System.... 200
Evaluation of the Healthcare System 205
Current Issues in Healthcare 209

Chapter 12 Germany.................... 215
Country Description 215
Brief History of the Healthcare System 222
Description of the Current Healthcare System.... 232
Evaluation of the Healthcare System 233
Quality 236
Access.. 237
Current and Emerging Issues and Challenges.... 238

Chapter 13 Ireland 245
Country Description 245
Brief History of the Healthcare System 254
Evaluation of the Healthcare System 256

Chapter 14 Russia 263
Country Description 263
Brief History of the Healthcare System 267
Description of the Current Healthcare System.... 269
Evaluation of the Health System 271
Current and Emerging Issues and Challenges.... 276

Middle East and Africa

Chapter 15 Turkey..................... 281
Country Description 281
Brief History of the Healthcare System 285

Description of the Current Healthcare System 288
Evaluation of the Health System 292
Emerging Challenges............................ 294

Chapter 16 Jordan...................... 297
Country Description 297
Brief History of the Healthcare System 302
Description of the Current Healthcare System.... 302
Evaluation of the Healthcare System 305
Current and Emerging Issues and Challenges.... 308

Chapter 17 Israel...................... 313
Country Description 313
History of Country 315
Size and Geography 316
Government and Political System 316
Macroeconomics 318
Demographics................................... 318
Healthcare System in Israel: Organization, Financing, and Delivery....................... 319
Emerging Challenges and Opportunities......... 326
An Integrated Healthcare System 328
Israeli Leadership in Global Health 329
Summary....................................... 330

Chapter 18 Ghana 335
Country Description 335
Brief History of the Healthcare System 338
Description of the Current Healthcare System.... 341
Evaluation of the Healthcare System 343
Current and Emerging Issues and Challenges.... 348

Chapter 19 Nigeria 353
Country Description 353
Brief History of the Healthcare System 358
Description of the Current Healthcare System.... 359
Evaluation of the Current Healthcare System...... 363
Current and Emerging Issues and Challenges.... 366

Chapter 20 Botswana................... 371
Country Description 371
Brief History of the Healthcare System 376
Description of the Current Healthcare System.... 377

Evaluation of the Healthcare System 379
Current and Emerging Challenges 381

Asia and Pacific Region

Chapter 21 Bangladesh 383
Country Description 383
Brief History of the Healthcare System 392

Chapter 22 India 401
Country Description 401
Brief History of the Healthcare System 412
Description of the Current Healthcare System.... 413
Evaluation of the Healthcare System 418
Current and Emerging Challenges
   and Opportunities........................... 420

Chapter 23 China...................... 425
Country Description 425
Brief History of the Healthcare System 433
Description of the Current Healthcare System.... 439
Evaluation of the Current Healthcare System..... 444
Current and Emerging Issues and Challenges 448

Chapter 24 Japan 453
Country Description 453
Brief History of the Healthcare System 458
Description of the Current Healthcare System.... 459
Evaluation of the Healthcare System 461
Current and Emerging Issues and Challenges 468

Chapter 25 Korea...................... 473
Country Description 473
Introduction................................... 475
Brief History of the Healthcare System 478
Description of the Current Healthcare System.... 479
Evaluation of the Healthcare System 483
Current and Emerging Issues and Challenges 487

Chapter 26 Australia................... 491
Country Description 491
Brief History of the Healthcare System 496

Description of the Current Healthcare System.... 497
Evaluation of the Healthcare System 499
Current and Emerging Issues and Challenges 504

PART III Challenges, Innovations, and Opportunities 509

Chapter 27 Small Country Innovations 511
Introduction................................... 511
Cuba 512
Singapore 516
Taiwan 521
The Netherlands................................ 524
Costa Rica 529
Concluding Commentary........................ 533

Chapter 28 Health Systems in Crisis and Disaster.................. 541
Introduction................................... 541
Geophysical Disasters........................... 542
Biological Events................................ 543
Climate Events.................................. 546
Health Systems Response....................... 548
Conclusion 549

Chapter 29 Comparative Global Challenges and Opportunities............ 553
Introduction................................... 553
International Health Policy, Globalization,
   and Privatization............................ 554
Decentralization 555
Health Care as an Increasing Portion of GDP 556
Injuries and Violence............................ 556
Mental Illness.................................. 557
Aging Population............................... 557
Environmental Impact/Climate Change.......... 558
Refugees, Displaced People, and Humanitarian
   Crises...................................... 559

Glossary of Health Systems Terms 565
Index 587

Acknowledgments

We would like to thank all of the authors from around the world for their invaluable and insightful contributions to this book. We also want to thank Danielle Bessette for her exceptional job and hard work as associate editor. Danielle brought her own perspectives and much appreciated professionalism to this project, often serving in the valued role of fourth editor. We also want to thank George Jacob and Athena Lakri for their valuable and skillful input. Additionally, we thank Michael Brown of Jones & Bartlett Learning for his support as we worked our way through this multifaceted international undertaking.

Foreword

Drs. David and Kathleen Jordan

As we write this foreword, we are viewing a world with global climate change, income inequalities, gaps in educational opportunities for girls, societal unrest, and an unprecedented number of refugees who are seeking personal and economic safety from war-torn regions from around our world. Any of these social determinants has a direct effect upon the health of individuals in every corner of the globe—from the remote steppes of Mongolia to the bourgeoning urban settings in South America and Asia. Health care is no longer a local or even a national phenomenon; it is a global network of disparate groupings of practitioners, systems, facilities, governmental funding approaches, non-governmental organizations, shamans, midwives, technological wonders, and cultural beliefs. To attempt to understand the myriad aspects of global health care is akin to unraveling the untold mysteries of human DNA and the very essence of what makes us human.

Understanding global health systems, outcomes, and practices is a complex and multidimensional exercise worthy of social scientists capable of grasping both the balcony views and the ground-level realities of the social determinants that affect the health of the world's 7.4 billion men, women, and children. Dr. James Johnson is one such individual who has spent a lifetime attempting to make sense of the multiple metrics which contribute to our understanding of global health systems. This latest edition of *Comparative Health Systems* provides an important reference for practitioners, scholars, academics, researchers, and students whose work rests in understanding global health care.

We are social entrepreneurs, college educators, and health and human service executives and are deeply invested in addressing economic, social, and healthcare outcomes in underresourced countries around the world. We work in areas of the developing world where natural and child mortality rates are frustratingly high.

The second edition of *Comparative Health Systems*, edited by James Johnson, Carleen Stoskopf, and Leiyu Shi, offers one of the few comprehensive sources of both statistical information and anecdotal narrative behind the data. This new edition will replace our current dogged-eared copy of the first edition and will gain its new place in our library bookshelf in the years to come. It is—much like James himself—a treasure to us both. He has been an invaluable mentor, former professor, and trusted friend over the years.

If you are a student trying to broaden your understanding of global health, a practitioner researching information on a country in which you may work, or a researcher attempting to understand the dynamics associated with health care around the globe, this is the text you need in your backpack, your office, or in the hands of your students.

—Dr. David A. Jordan and Dr. Kathleen M. Jordan
Founder/President (David) and
Executive Vice President (Kathleen)
Seven Hills Foundation

Foreword

Dr. Ted Karpf

This is a most timely book. Drs. Johnson, Stoskopf, and Shi have anticipated and documented the core concerns faced by nations. Health and health care are at the forefront of international concern, especially in a time of global financial turmoil and insecurity. This book is absolutely essential to understanding what's at stake and to charting a path through the maze of issues confronting healthcare planners and healthcare recipients, healthcare professionals and financing managers, politicians, and bureaucrats. It's more than a matter of systems and approaches; it is about the security of the global community. According to Dr. Margaret Chan, director-general of the World Health Organization:

> Healthy human capital is the very foundation for productivity and prosperity. Equitable distribution of health care and equity in the health status of populations is the foundation for social cohesion. Social cohesion is our best protection against social unrest, nationally and internationally. Healthy, productive, and stable populations are always an asset but they must especially be so during a time of crisis.

The recipients of health care must be heard above the din of competing claims of equity and effectiveness:

> The people have the right and duty to participate individually and collectively in the planning and implementation of their health care. Primary health care… requires and promotes maximum community and individual self-reliance and participation in the planning, organization, operation, and control of primary health care, making fullest use of local, national, and other available resources; and to this end develops through appropriate education the ability of communities to participate." (Declaration of Alma-Ata International Conference on Primary Health Care, Articles IV and VII, Alma-Ata, Khazakhstan, USSR, September 6–12, 1978)

Obtaining decent care, which acknowledges the voice of the people through the values of agency and dignity, interdependence and solidarity, subsidiarity and sustainability, raises the ante a bit higher. Political and healthcare leaders, financial managers, and medical and healthcare professionals must be reminded amidst the policy debate that when the people are invested in their own care, the formulas for success and sustainability change. When the people are engaged in determining the levels and resource allocations for care, there is also more decision latitude than those charged with determining formulas can imagine.

The healthcare debate must finally factor in the people who it claims are to be served and sustained with improved health. Then the various financial models and healthcare systems will still not bring us the long-needed satisfaction and support we need today. Nobel Laureate and former U.S. president Barack Obama stated repeatedly that "health care is a right." This notion, enshrined three decades ago at Alma-Ata, changes the rules and reorganizes the lines of accountability along with our thinking and expectations. Where health is a right, social responsibility will lead to an enhanced commitment to improved health. The formula ceases to be about "those people" or "their problems" and becomes about us!

As we proceed through these pages it will be important to ask how this approach will help ensure that the people are heard and heeded.

—Dr. Ted Karpf
International health advocate (retired),
World Health Organization, and author of
the book *Restoring Hope: Decent Care
in the Midst of HIV/AIDS*

Preface

Dr. James A. Johnson

Over the past two decades, I have taken graduate students to Geneva, Switzerland, each summer to study global health. While there, we always spend time at the World Health Organization (WHO), which is receiving updates on global health and interacting with senior scientists, health practitioners, and leaders in the mission of "health for all." In addition to being spellbound by descriptions of the many initiatives and great successes of the WHO, we repeatedly hear of one major limitation that continues to impede even the greater progress. That is the poor state of health systems in many parts of the world. There are models of success as well as models of failure. Most health systems are oriented toward disease care, and many are underfunded and understaffed, whereas some countries expend large portions of their national resources on health. Some health systems are operated by governments, and others are more involved in the private sector. Regardless of scope or scale, every program, every initiative, every policy, and every course of treatment are imbedded within a particular country-specific health system.

Several years ago, my friend and colleague Dr. Carleen Stoskopf joined me on one of the trips to Geneva. While there, we discussed the need for a book that would describe a range of health systems so that students could better understand the limitations and opportunities offered in the diversity that we had each seen in our own international work. We felt that one of the best ways for students to learn about the range of systems would be through comparative study. As with many invigorating sidewalk café conversations in Europe (and elsewhere), we set this idea aside and returned to the busy activities of our academic positions at the time—Carleen, a department chair at the School of Public Health at the University of South Carolina in Columbia, South Carolina, and myself, a department chair at the Medical University of South Carolina in Charleston. A few years later, however, at a meeting of the American Public Health Association in Boston, in a conversation with publisher Michael Brown, the topic came back up and momentum for such a book grew quickly.

We conceptualized the book as a text to be used in courses in international health, comparative studies, global health, international affairs, health administration, and public health. In an increasingly interconnected and interdependent world comprised of wide variations in health delivery systems, practices, and policy, the book was developed to offer students some understanding through comparative study.

In seeking to achieve this goal, we enlisted contributors from many countries to write about the systems that they had worked in and were familiar with. Thus, every chapter that describes a health system is written by at least one person from that country. Chapters also ended up having U.S.-based coauthors because we used our own professional networks in schools of public health, medicine, administration, and policy to identify chapter contributors. Needless to say, the book project emerged as a significant multicultural undertaking involving authors from every continent and from the largest possible range of health system types. This led to the publication of the first edition of *Comparative Health Systems: Global Perspectives* in 2010.

Over five years later, we were asked by the publisher to write the *Second Edition*. For this undertaking, I asked another friend and colleague that goes back to our South Carolina days to join Carleen and me. This third editor is Leiyu Shi, now at Johns Hopkins University. He brought his usual high energy and global viewpoint to the project.

Following the conceptual structure of the *First Edition*, we continued to use the framework Carleen and I had previously developed. This framework for each chapter allows students to compare and contrast such divergent systems as Canada, India, Japan, Nigeria, Germany, Australia, Mexico, and many others. The framework used to develop each chapter country focused includes the following:

Country Description

- History
- Size and geography
- Government and political system

- Macroeconomics (GDP, OECD)
- Demographics (including religion, gender, and poverty)

Brief History of the Healthcare System
- Description of healthcare system
- Facilities
- Workforce
- Technology and equipment

Evaluation of the Healthcare System
- Cost
- Quality
- Access
- Current innovations and emerging challenges

Although these chapters were developed by in-country authors and their collaborators, additionally, working with colleagues, we developed other chapters that are overarching. This includes a chapter that describes health systems and one that provides an overview of disease. Dr. Walter Jones contributed a very useful chapter discussing health policy and economics. My son, Dr. Allen Johnson, and coauthors contributed a chapter describing the role of nongovernmental organizations (NGOs) as an important, though sometimes overlooked, component to health systems and global health. Dr. Caren Rossow and I also added a chapter on health systems in crisis and disaster response. Additionally, Carleen and I included a chapter that outlines future challenges. There is also a glossary of health systems terms that should be useful to students and professors.

Having worked in or traveled to over 45 countries myself, I can say with great confidence that this book will serve to broaden the reader's understanding. It will also likely change their perspectives on global health. They will learn that although highly developed countries continue to offer profound breakthroughs in medical science and technology, as well as reform and continuous improvement of health systems, the best solutions do not always emerge in the wealthiest countries. In the *Harvard International Review*, Dr. Vanessa Kerry, founder and CEO of Seed Global Health, stated "I think the most important thing is for people to realize that to be in global health, you can come from any field or background. In order to have an impact on global health, we need to, again, realize that there is a fundamental breakdown of the system on any number of levels in different countries."

As stated by Dr. Barry Bloom, former dean of the Harvard School of Public Health, the huge disparities in health that exist between countries remain some of the great moral and intellectual problems of our time. This book can serve as one tool among many that will be needed to empower students to become change agents in this ongoing challenge.

—Dr. James A. Johnson

Contributors

Musah Sugri Alhassan, MSA
Ghana National Association of Teachers—GNAT
Tamale, Ghana

Stephanie Baiyasi, DVM
University of Denver
Denver, Colorado, United States

Antonio Pires Barbosa, PhD, MD
Universidade Nove de Julho
São Paulo, Brazil

Steven D. Berkshire, EdD, MHA, FACHE
Central Michigan University
Mt. Pleasant, Michigan, United States

Raul Chiquiyauri, MD, MPH, PhD
Centro de Investigación de Enfermedades Tropicles
Instituto Nacional de Salud
Sede Iquitos, Peru

Omur Cinar Elci, MD, PhD
St. George's University School of Medicine
True Blue, Grenada

Maria Creavin, RD, SM, MAS
Central Michigan University
Mount Pleasant, Michigan, United States

Mark Anthony Cwiek, JD, MHA
Central Michigan University
Mount Pleasant, Michigan, United States

Gary E. Day, DHSM, MHM, RN, EM, FGLF, FCHSM
School of Medicine, Griffith University
Southport, Queensland, Australia

José Delacerda-Gastelum, PhD, MILR
ITESO University
Guadalajara, Mexico

Linda F. Dennard, PhD
Auburn University Montgomery
Montgomery, Alabama, United States

James E. Dotherow IV, MPA
So They Can (NGO)
Babati, Tanzania

Mazwell Droznin, BA
Rollins College
Winter Park, Florida, United States

R. Paul Duncan, PhD, MS, BA
University of Florida
Gainesville, Florida, United States

Sharon R. Elefant, DHAc,
Central Michigan University
Mt. Pleasant, Michigan, United States

Harry Flaster, MD
University of Washington Medical Center
Seattle, Washington, United States

Leonard Friedman, PhD, FACHE
George Washington University
Washington, DC, United States

Lesego Gabaitiri, PhD, ScM, MSc, BA
University of Botswana
Gaborone, Botswana

Sheyna Gifford, MD, M.Sc., MA, MBA
St. Louis Science Center
St. Louis, Missouri, United States

Octavio Gomez-Dantés, MD, MPHA
Carso Health Institute
Mexico City, Mexico

Mikiyasu Hakoyama, PhD
Central Michigan University
Mt. Pleasant, Michigan, United States

Whiejong M. Han, PhD
University of South Carolina
Columbia, South Carolina, United States

Umar Haruna, PhD, MPhil
University for Development Studies
Upper West, Ghana

Kuo-Cherh Huang, DrPH, MBA
Taipei Medical University
Taipei, Taiwan

Manzoor Hussain, MBBS, FRCP, FRCPCH
Bangladesh Institute of Child Health
Dhaka, Bangladesh

Styn M. Jamu, DHA, MPA
Stepping Stones International
Gaborone, Botswana

Allen Johnson, DrPH, MPH
Rollins College
Winter Park, Florida, Untied States

Walter J. Jones, PhD, MHSA, MA
Medical University of South Carolina
Charleston, South Carolina, United States

Kalu Kalu, PhD, MBA
Auburn University Montgomery
Montgomery, Alabama, United States

Bernard J. Kerr Jr., MHA, MBA, MPH, MIM, EdD, FACHE
Central Michigan University
Mt. Pleasant, Michigan, United States

Sophie Kobouloff, DHA, MBA, EDHEC MBA
Saddle Implant Technologies
Geneva, Switzerland

Hailun Liang, MS
Johns Hopkins School of Public Health
Baltimore, Maryland, United States

Gerald Ledlow, PhD, MHA, FACHE
University of Texas Health Science Center Northeast
Tyler, Texas, United States

Osnat Levtzion-Korach, MD, MHA
Hadassah Medical Center
Jerusalem, Israel

Marcus Longley, PhD
Welsh Institute for Health and Social Care
University of South Wales
Pontypridd, Wales, United Kingdom

John Lopes, Jr., DHSc, PA-C
Central Michigan University
Mt. Pleasant, Michigan, United States

Ning Lu, PhD, MPH
Governors State University
University Park, Illinois, United States

Hala Madanat, PhD, MS
San Diego State University
San Diego, California, United States

Linda A. McCarey, MS, BSN, RN
Haliburton, Kawartha, Pine Ridge Health Unit
Haliburton, Ontario, Canada

John E. McDonough, DrPH, MPA
Harvard University
Cambridge, Massachusetts, United States

Hani Michel Samawi, PhD, MS
Georgia Southern University
Statesboro, Georgia, United States

Amal K. Mitra, MD, MPH, DrPH
Jackson State University
Jackson, Mississippi, United States

Michael E. Morris, PhD, MPH, MPA
University of Florida
Gainesville, Florida, United States

Adrienne Nevola, MPH
University of Arkansas
Fayetteville, Arkansas, United States

Marcia Cristina Zago Novaretti, PhD, MD
Universidade Nove de Julho
São Paulo, Brazil

Qwolabi Ogunneye, MD, FRCP, FASN
Covenant Healthcare
Saginaw, Michigan, United States

Yetunde Ogunneye, MD, DHAc, MPH
Central Michigan University
Mt. Pleasant, Michigan, United States

Elena A. Platonova, PhD, MHA
University of North Carolina, Charlotte
Charlotte, North Carolina, United States

Hugo Rodriguez, MD, MPH
Hospital Iquitos
Iquitos, Peru

Caren Rossow, DHA, MSA, RN, FACHE
Indiana University
South Bend, Indiana, United States

Alexander V. Sergeev, MD, PhD, MPH
Ohio University Department of Social and Public Health
Athens, Ohio, United States

Neelam Sharma, MD
Newark-Wayne Community Hospital
Newark, New Jersey, United States

Hatice Simsek, MD, PhD
Dokuz Eylül University School of Medicine
İzmir, Turkey

Douglas A. Singh, PhD
Indiana University, South Bend
South Bend, Indiana, United States

James H. Stephens, DHA, MHA
Georgia Southern University
Statesboro, Georgia, United States

Reyhan Ucku, MD, MPH
Dokuz Eylül University School of Medicine
Izmir, Turkey

Stalin Vilcarromero, MD, MPHc
Naval Medical Research
Iquitos, Peru

Matthew W. Walker, DrPH, MPH
U.S. Food and Drug Administration
Silver Spring, Maryland, United States

Sudha Xirasagar, PhD, MBBS
University of South Carolina
Columbia, South Carolina, United States

Kapil Yadav, MD
Tulane University
New Orleans, Louisiana, United States

About the Editors

James A. Johnson, PhD, MPA, MSc, is a medical social scientist and professor of health administration and international health at the Dow College of Health Professions, Central Michigan University, and visiting professor at St. George's University, Grenada, West Indies. He was previously chairman of the Department of Health Administration and Policy at the Medical University of South Carolina. Dr. Johnson teaches courses in health organization development, international health, systems thinking, and comparative health systems. His publications include over 100 journal articles, most of which are peer reviewed, and 15 books on a wide range of healthcare and organizational issues. His most recent books include *Public Health Administration: Principles of Population-Based Management*; *Introduction to Public Health Management, Organizations, and Policy*; *Multisector Casebook in Health Administration, Leadership, and Management*; and *Organizations: Theory, Behavior, and Development*. He is also coeditor of the widely used *Handbook of Health Administration and Policy*. Dr. Johnson has also served as editor of the *Journal of Healthcare Management*, published by the American College of Healthcare Executives; editor of the *Journal of Management Practice*; and founding editor of the *Carolina Health Services and Policy Review*. He is a contributing editor for the *Journal of Health and Human Services Administration*. He has served on the Board of Directors for the Association of University Programs in Health Administration and the Scientific Advisory Board of the National Diabetes Trust Foundation. Dr. Johnson has worked and traveled in 45 countries, including Tanzania, Zimbabwe, South Africa, Nepal, China, Belize, Peru, Ethiopia, Turkey, and Mexico and has lectured at Oxford University (England), University of Dublin (Ireland), Beijing University (China), and University of Colima (Mexico). He also works on projects with the WHO and the Belize-based NGO, Heart to Heart and is active in the Organization Development Institute. He completed his PhD in 1987 at the Askew School of Public Policy and Administration at Florida State University and his MPA in health administration at Auburn University.

Carleen H. Stoskopf, ScD, MS, is Professor of Health Management and Policy and Division Head in the Graduate School of Public Health at San Diego State University, where she also served as School Director for 7 years. Dr. Stoskopf held academic appointments at the Arnold School of Public Health at the University of South Carolina for 19 years, advancing to Chair of the Department of Health Services Policy and Management. Dr. Stoskopf has served as a Fellow of the Commission on Accreditation of Health Management Education and served as a site visitor for the Council on Education in Public Health reaccreditation process. Her areas of teaching include finance, health insurance, and reimbursement. At the University of South Carolina, she was Director of Doctoral Programs and developed two additional doctoral programs in Taiwan and South Korea. Prior to entering her career in academics, Dr. Stoskopf served in the U.S. Navy as an Environmental Health Office with the Third Marine Aircraft Wing at El Toro, California and as Chief of the Preventive Medicine Service at the Naval Regional Medical Center in Okinawa, Japan. She was honorably discharged as a Lieutenant, USN, MSC in 1982. She was also a Registered Sanitarian with the State of California.

Internationally, Dr. Stoskopf has worked extensively for USAID and a variety of agencies in countries such as Haiti, Kenya, South Africa, the United Arab Emirates, Oman, Kuwait, Jordan, People's Republic of China, the Republic of China, Republic of South Korea, Republic of Georgia, Kazakhstan, Ukraine, and Russia. Dr. Stoskopf's activities have ranged from lecturing, providing healthcare management training, healthcare management curricular reviews and development, policy and curriculum consultations with new schools of public health, public health assessments, HIV/AIDS research, and hospital management consultations.

Dr. Stoskopf has been an active researcher conducting studies in access, utilization, and outcomes of healthcare services. Specific areas of research include disparities in vulnerable populations such as persons living with HIV/AIDS, living with mental illness, in poverty, older persons, and African Americans living in the southern United States. Dr. Stoskopf's research has been funded from such sources as the National Institutes of Health, Centers for Disease Control and Prevention, the Health Resources and Services Administration, as well as a number of state and local agencies and foundations. Dr. Stoskopf has authored or co-authored over 50 peer-reviewed publications in academic journals. She completed her doctor of science (ScD) degree from The Johns Hopkins University Bloomberg School of Public Health in 1989 in the Department of Health Policy and Management, and earned her MS degree from the University of Minnesota School of Public Health in 1977 in environmental health biology.

Leiyu Shi, DrPH, MBA, MPA, is professor of health policy and health services research in the Department of Health Policy and Management, Bloomberg School of Public Health at Johns Hopkins University. He is also director of The Johns Hopkins Primary Care Policy Center. Prior to his academic positions, Dr. Shi worked in the public health field focusing on community-based primary care and vulnerable populations. He received his doctoral education from the University of California, Berkeley, majoring in health policy and services research. He also has a master's in business administration focusing on finance. Dr. Shi's research focuses on primary care, health disparities, and vulnerable populations. He has conducted extensive studies about the association between primary care and health outcomes, particularly on the role of primary care in mediating the adverse impact of income inequality on health outcomes. Dr. Shi is also well known for his extensive research on the nation's vulnerable populations, in particular community health centers that serve vulnerable populations, including their sustainability, provider recruitment and retention experiences, financial performance, experience under managed care, and quality of care. Dr. Shi is the author of 9 textbooks and more than 150 scientific journal articles.

PART I
Global Health and Health Systems

CHAPTER 1　Introduction to Health Systems

CHAPTER 2　Global Health and Disease

CHAPTER 3　Global Health Systems Politics, Economics, and Policy

CHAPTER 4　Role of International Organizations in Health Systems

CHAPTER 1
Introduction to Health Systems

James A. Johnson and **Carleen H. Stoskopf**

Introduction

A health system as described by the World Health Organization (WHO) is the sum total of all the organizations, institutions, and resources whose primary purpose is to improve health. A health system needs staff, funds, information, supplies, transport, communications, and overall guidance and direction. Furthermore, it needs to provide services that are responsive and financially fair, while treating people decently.[1]

Within this definition, there are several concepts that need to be understood before one embarks on the task of studying health systems. First and foremost, an agreed-on definition of health is paramount. Health is too often seen as a concept that applies only to physical well-being or the absence of disease; however, the most widely accepted definition of health is the one first published by the WHO in 1948.

> Health is a state of complete physical, mental, and social well-being and not merely the absence of disease or infirmity[2]

This comprehensive concept of health is the one used in this book and serves to inform discussions on health systems.

The other key word that needs to be explored here is the word "system." The human body is a system composed of many physiological subsystems that are interconnected in a holistic way. The subsystems, including respiratory, circulatory, neurological, endocrine, and musculoskeletal systems, communicate and are interdependent. They work together for the purposes of survival, adaptation, growth, and development. They also interact with the environment and respond to feedback from within and outside the system. In many ways, the interconnectivity of the various subsystems and its extension as a whole into the environment form the building blocks of larger systems, such as family, community, and nation. Thus a natural (biological) system, such as a human being, is also a participant in and a creator of larger social systems. The human-created systems have many of the same attributes of biological systems. Additionally, it can be said that these larger systems are characterized by

- A structure that is defined by its parts and processes.
- Generalizations of reality.
- A tendency to function in the same way, involving the inputs (material, human resources, finances, etc.) and outputs (products and services) that are then processed, causing them to change in some way.
- A system's various parts, which have functional as well as structural relationships.

Human-created systems can be small, as in the three-person family, or quite large, as in a nation-state such as India with a billion people. The most widely dispersed human-created systems are organizations. As with the other examples described previously, organizations share the same attributes and adapt accordingly to their environments. In fact, organizations are complex human systems that have evolved over time and continue to do so.[3] The natural emergence of human-created systems, such as organizations and communities, probably grew out of instinct for survival. In the hostile world of early humankind, food, shelter, and safety needs usually required cooperative efforts. In turn, cooperative efforts typically require some form of organization.[4] This is no less true in the case of providing health. In order to meet the criteria of health as a state of complete physical, mental, and social well-being, individuals, communities, organizations, and nation-states have worked together to form elaborate and diverse health systems throughout the world.

As with any system, a health system has inputs. These include financial, material, and human resources that differentiate one health system from another. The data in TABLE 1-1 clearly demonstrate some of these differences.

One of the major "inputs" into any healthcare system is patients. Patients present with a variety of symptoms/diseases/injuries; however, they also come with a myriad of characteristics, such as personality, life experiences, knowledge, attitudes, cultural norms, education level, income level, intellect, prejudice, religious and other belief systems, emotions, biological strengths and weaknesses, and genetic makeup. In addition, patients may or may not be plugged into society's infrastructure, such as having access to transportation, childcare, or health insurance. The complexity these many factors create cannot be overlooked by healthcare systems nor should they be overlooked by health policymakers. It has been well established that income is perhaps one of the best predictors of health. The income gradient within a population is highly associated with health status of individuals or groups in that population, and the per capita incomes and the GDP of nations are also highly correlated with the health status of that country's population. Taken from this perspective, health policy makes us also be

TABLE 1-1 Select Health System Financial Input Data, 2015 (in U.S. dollars)

Total global expenditure for health	$6.5 trillion plus
Total global expenditure for health per person per year	$948
Country with highest total spending per person per year on health	United States ($8,362)
Country with lowest total spending per person per year on health	Eritrea ($12)
Country with highest government spending per person per year on health	Luxembourg ($6,906)
Country with lowest government spending per person per year on health	Myanmar ($2)
Country with highest annual out-of-pocket household spending on health	Switzerland ($2,412)
Country with lowest annual out-of-pocket household spending on health	Kiribati ($0.02)
Average amount spent per person per year on health in countries belonging to the Organisation for Economic Co-operation and Development (OECD)	$4,380
Percentage of the world's population living in OECD countries	18%
WHO estimate of minimum spending per person per year needed to provide basic, life-saving services	$44
Countries where total health spending was lower than $50 per person per year	34
Countries where health spending was lower than $20 per person per year	7

Data from World Health Organization. (2014).

concerned with poverty and lifting populations out of poverty through social policies designed to improve education, housing, infrastructure, job creation, and the environment.

Health systems arise within a social, cultural, political, and economic context. As with all human constructed systems, there is considerable diversity in size, scope, and form. As a result, health systems have structure, processes, and outcomes that vary considerably. TABLE 1-2 shows some of the variation along these three dimensions for the countries selected for this book. As you will see here and in subsequent chapters, financial and human resource inputs do interrelate with health outcomes.

TABLE 1-2 Healthcare Resources for Selected Countries

		Spent per capita on health		% of total health expenditure			
	Percent of GDP	US $	PPP $	Government	Private	Out-of-pocket	% of total government expenditures spent on health
Australia	9.4	6,110	4,991	66.6	33.4	57.1	18.7
Bangladesh	3.7	32	95	35.3	64.7	93.0	7.8
Botswana	5.4	397	851	57.1	42.9	12.7	8.8
Brazil	9.7	1,085	1,454	48.2	51.8	57.8	6.9
Canada	10.9	5,718	4,759	69.8	30.2	50.1	18.5
China	5.6	367	646	55.8	44.2	60.3	12.6
DR Congo	3.5	16	26	53.1	46.9	69.8	12.9
France	11.7	4,864	4,334	77.5	22.5	32.9	15.8
Germany	11.3	5,006	4,812	76.8	23.2	55.6	19.4
Ghana	5.4	100	214	60.6	39.4	91.9	10.6
India	4.0	61	215	32.2	67.8	85.9	4.5
Ireland	8.9	4,233	3,867	67.7	32.3	52.1	14.1
Israel	7.2	2,599	2,355	59.1	40.9	64.5	10.5
Japan	10.3	3,966	3,741	82.1	17.9	80.2	20.0
Jordan	7.2	336	761	66.0	34.0	69.1	13.5
Korea	7.2	1,880	2,398	53.4	46.6	78.6	11.5
Mexico	6.2	664	1,061	51.7	48.3	91.5	15.4
Nigeria	3.7	109	206	23.9	76.1	95.8	6.5

(continues)

TABLE 1-2 Healthcare Resources for Selected Countries (*continued*)

	Percent of GDP	Spent per capita on health		% of total health expenditure			% of total government expenditures spent on health
		US $	PPP $	Government	Private	Out-of-pocket	
Peru	5.3	354	626	58.7	41.3	84.6	14.7
Russia	6.5	957	1,587	48.1	51.9	92.4	8.4
Turkey	5.6	608	1,053	77.4	22.6	66.3	8.7
United Kingdom	9.1	3,598	3,311	83.5	16.5	56.4	16.2
United States	17.1	9,146	9,146	47.1	52.9	22.3	20.4

Data from World Health Organization. Violence and injury prevention: Country profiles. http://www.who.int/violence_injury_prevention/road_safety_status/country_profiles/en/. n.d.; Central Intelligence Agency. The World Fact Book, 2016. https://www.cia.gov/library/publications/resources/the-world-factbook/.

Building Blocks of Health Systems

Even though every health system is unique in its given social and cultural environment, all health systems have common elements that are necessary for functionality. These building blocks not only help us to understanding health systems better but they also provide opportunities for system improvement. The WHO, the World Bank, and various governments around the world have a common understanding of these key elements. Some would describe them as critical success factors that are essential to a health system's survival (**TABLE 1-3**).

One widely accepted way of measuring the building blocks or the overall functioning of a health system is through the lens of cost, quality, and access. The cost, quality, access triangle is shown in **FIGURE 1-1**.

In the era of rapid globalization and change, it is becoming increasingly prudent to add a fourth dimension, innovation. This results in a cost, quality, access, innovation diamond as shown in **FIGURE 1-2**.

Furthermore, as shown in **BOX 1-1** countries must embrace the notion of incorporating health in all policy arenas, such as transportation, agriculture, education, and others. There is considerable overlap of interest and purpose that can benefit societies.

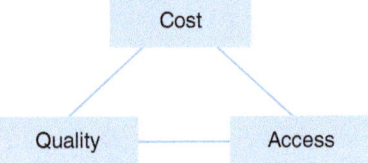

FIGURE 1-1 The Cost, Quality, Access Triangle

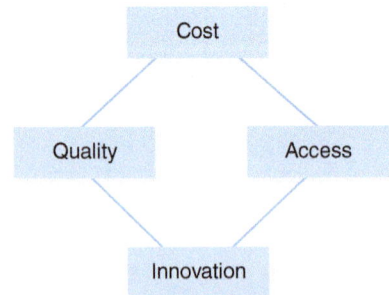

FIGURE 1-2 The Cost, Quality, Access, Innovation Diamond

Health Systems Within Larger Social Systems

In 2013 at the Helsinki Conference, the WHO adopted and began to promulgate a Health in All Policies approach. This is based on the understanding that all

TABLE 1-3 Health Systems Building Blocks (Critical Success Factors)

Service delivery	Medical technology
Good health services are those that deliver effective, safe, quality personal and non-personal health interventions to those who need them, when and where needed, with minimum waste of resources.	A well-functioning health system ensures equitable access to essential medical products, drugs, vaccines, and technologies of assured quality, safety, efficacy, and their scientifically sound and cost-effective use.
Health workforce	**Health financing**
A well-performing health workforce is one that works in ways that are responsive, fair, and efficient to achieve the best health outcomes possible, given available resources and circumstances (i.e., there are sufficient staff, fairly distributed; they are competent, responsive, and productive).	A good health financing system raises adequate funds for health, in ways that ensure people can use needed services and are protected from financial catastrophe or impoverishment associated with having to pay for them; it provides incentives for providers and users to be efficient.
Health information	**Leadership and governance**
A well-functioning health information system is one that ensures the production, analysis, dissemination, use of reliable and timely information on health determinants, health system performance, and health status improvements.	Leadership and governance involve ensuring that strategic policy frameworks exist and are combined with effective oversight, coalition building, regulation, attention to system design, and accountability.

Data from World Health Organization. The WHO Health Systems Framework. http://www.wpro.who.int/health_services/health_systems_framework/en/. 2016.

sectors of a society must work together to promote health and support the health system. The statement of this approach follows.

Ron Andersen proposed a model in the 1960s that sought to identify some of the factors that influence whether a patient even accesses healthcare services.[5] His model identifies three main components: predisposing factors, enabling factors, and need factors. Predisposing factors include family characteristics, social structure, and health beliefs. Enabling factors include family resources and community resources. Need factors include illness and the response to illness. This work was expanded into the Behavioral Model for Vulnerable Populations. This model is presented in **FIGURE 1-3**. Understanding the characteristics of the population that a health system serves is key to designing the system processes, providing adequate and appropriate resources, and having clear expectations for the right outcomes.

The notion that one's social circumstances, or socioeconomic status, can influence one's health was a notion coming into its own. In recent decades, social science researchers have laid the groundwork for further exploration of this relationship. It is thought that social circumstances lead to disease in individuals and populations via three pathways: behavioral, material, and psychological. The premise is that social circumstances, such as socioeconomic status based on income and education, influence behaviors. For example, smoking is a behavior more often found in people with low socioeconomic status. Smoking, then, has a direct impact on health status because the incidences of lung cancer, emphysema, asthma, and other respiratory illnesses are higher among smokers. Other behaviors that are believed to be associated with lower socioeconomic status are under study and include such behaviors as drinking, risky sexual behavior, drug use, and violence.

BOX 1-1 Health in All Policies

Health in All Policies is an approach to public policies across sectors that systematically takes into account the health implications of decisions, seeks synergies, and avoids harmful health impacts in order to improve population health and health equity. It improves accountability of policymakers for health impacts at all levels of policymaking. It includes an emphasis on the consequences of public policies on health systems, determinants of health and well-being.

Reproduced from World Health Organization. *Health in all policies: Training manual.* Geneva: Author; 2015.

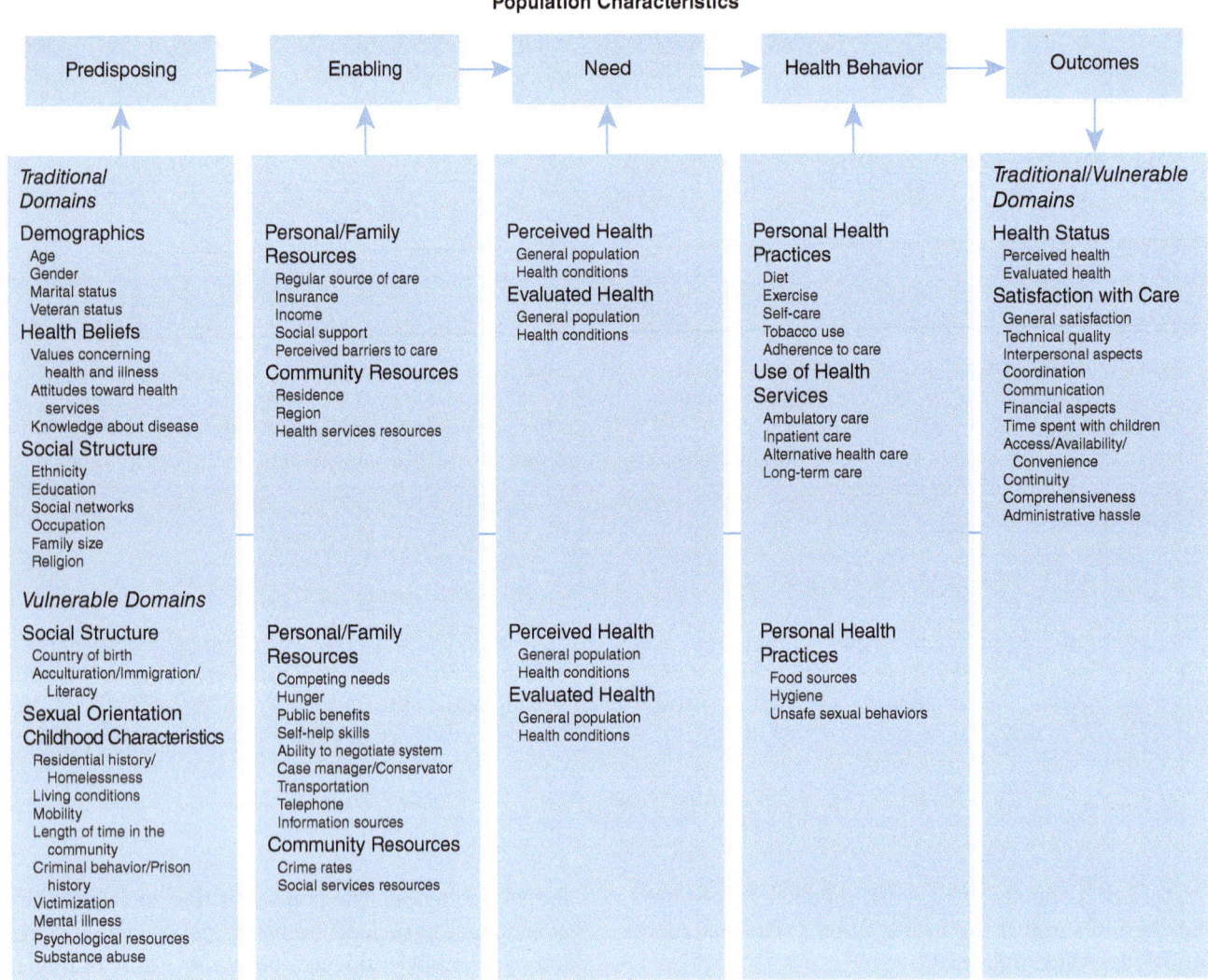

FIGURE 1-3 The Behavioral Model for Vulnerable Populations

Reproduced from Gelberg L, Andersen RM, Leake BD. The behavioral model for vulnerable populations: Application to medical care use and outcomes for homeless people. *Health Serv Res*. 2000;34(6):1278. Health services research: HSR by Association for Health Services Research; Association of University Programs in Health Admin; Hospital Research and Educational Trust. Reproduced with permission of Blackwell Publishing, Inc.

A second pathway is material circumstances associated with deprivation. People living with a substantially lower income are unable to provide for the most basic needs, such as adequate food, shelter, and safety. As a result, some segments of the population suffer from malnutrition, inadequate home heating and warm clothing, and environmental exposures and are more exposed to community violence. These factors in turn result in lower health status through increased exposure to infectious diseases due to overcrowding, malnutrition, limited access to appropriate medical care, exposure to pollutants both in the community and in substandard housing, and an increased risk of being a victim of violence.

The third pathway, the psychosocial pathway, is more complex. This pathway requires a connection between social structure and health. Extensive research has resulted in establishing mechanisms that make connections among social structures, stress, and biology, or the "psychobiological stress response."

Although stress can be an important factor in survival in a "fight or flight" scenario, if prolonged stress occurs and the body no longer can return to homeostasis quickly, long-term effects on health can occur, including cardiovascular disease, cancer, infection, and cognitive decline.

A number of social determinants and social conditions have been studied to ascertain whether there is an association between these factors and health statuses of both individuals and populations. **TABLE 1-4** summarizes some of the major findings in the literature and **BOX 1-2** provides a more detailed example.

There is great interest in the fields of public health and medicine to better understand these contributors to population health status. In fact, it is now estimated that 60% of health status is based on a person's address.[6] The definition of social determinants of health, according to the U.S. Centers for Disease Control and Prevention (CDC) is:

TABLE 1-4 A Summary of Some of the Social Determinants of Health

Social determinant	Mediating factor(s)	Health status > Increased < Decreased	Reference
Unemployment		< Health status	5–7
Employment		> Health status	8
Unemployment	Financial stress	< Health status	9, 10
Unemployment	Psychological stress	< Health status	11–13
Unemployment	Health-damaging behavior	< Health status	14–16
Poor work environment		Ill health Poor health status	17, 18
Psychosocial work environment	Job demand/control (low efficacy)	< Health status	19, 20
Psychosocial work environment	Effort-reward imbalance (low self-esteem)	< Health status	21
Psychosocial work environment		Social gradient of ill health	22–29
Transportation	Traffic-related accidents	< Health status	30
Transportation	Air pollution	> Respiratory illnesses	31
Transportation	Noise	< Health status	32
Social support		> Health status < Health status	33, 34
Social support	Moderating effects	> Health status	35–38
Inadequate nutrition		< Health status	39, 40
Proper nutrition		> Health status	41
Poor nutrition		> Obesity	42, 43
Poverty		< Health status > Mortality	44–46
Poverty	Material deprivation	< Health status	47–50
Poverty	Social deprivation	< Health status	51–53
Poverty	Unemployment	< Health status	54
Poverty	Inequity	< Health status	51, 55, 56

(continues)

TABLE 1-4 A Summary of Some of the Social Determinants of Health (*continued*)

Social determinant	Mediating factor(s)	Health status > Increased < Decreased	Reference
Poverty	Social exclusion	< Health status	57
Poverty	Minorities and/or refugees	< Health status	20, 58–60
Poverty	Homelessness	< Health status < Mental health status	61–63
Ethnic groupings		< Health status > Health status > Mortality < Mortality	64–71
Ethnicity	Income	> Health status < Health status	72
Ethnicity	Maternal education	> Health status < Health status	64
Ethnicity	Education level	> Health status < Health status	73–75
Ethnicity	Experience of racial harassment and discrimination	< Health status	76–78
Neighborhood environment		> Health status < Health status	79–81
Neighborhood environment	Physical environment	> Health status < Health status	82–86
Social environment		> Health status < Health status	87–89
Neighborhood environment	Amenities	> Health status < Health status	90, 91
Sexual behavior		< Health status > Health status	92, 93
Sexual behavior	Increased rate of partner change	< Health status	94
Sexual behavior	Increased variation in sexual behavior	< Health status	92
Sexual behavior	Demography	Demography	95, 96
Sexual behavior	Social disruption (war)	Social disruption (war)	97

BOX 1-2 Social Determinants of Health: Birth and Infancy as an Example

Research has shown that early life circumstance is one of the more important predictors of health status. In the 1970s, it was established that malnutrition in a pregnant woman has a direct impact on the health and well being of her fetus and hence its susceptibility to low birth weight. Further research has demonstrated that undernutrition for a fetus results in long-term changes in physiology, metabolism, and structure. Research has shown that poor nutrition, smoking, alcohol consumption, atmospheric pollution, and infections associated with a pregnant mother are also associated with low birth weight. Low birth weight in turn is related to poor growth in children and is eventually associated with poor adult health. The accumulation of risk occurs when both poor growth and poor socioeconomic status interact to create a lifetime of poor social and health statuses, or when adverse circumstances and health in early life, coupled with a negative health event at an older age, result in poor adult health.

Some studies have found that although poor growth in early childhood is associated with poor health in adulthood, mitigating circumstances can overcome some of these effects. Improvement in social conditions can result in better health and performance later in life. When parents improve their social condition and attain higher levels of education, their low-birth-weight children have less association with poor health and other types of attainment as adults and achieve higher levels of cognitive development. These results may be due to improved nutrition or parental stimulation.

The phenomenon of *social accumulation* is also important in understanding the complexity of inputs into the health system. Social accumulation is due to the fact that both disadvantage and advantage tend to accumulate throughout a lifetime and can even be transgenerational. For example, a mother of lower social economic status is more likely to have a low-birth-weight baby, who in turn is more likely to be exposed to more environmental hazards, have poorer nutrition and less education, attain less in school, and emerge as an adult with poorer health status and the same disadvantages as those that he or she experienced in childhood. This disadvantage is then experienced by their children. The same is true for those who are advantaged. It is further found that when a person crosses social economic boundaries, his or her health status changes in accordance with the direction of change.

The complex, integrated, and overlapping social structures and economic systems that are responsible for most health inequities. These social structures and economic systems include the social environment, physical environment, health services, and structural and societal factors. Social determinants of health are shaped by the distribution of money, power, and resources throughout local communities, nations, and the world.[6]

The *Healthy People 2020* initiative also includes social determinants among its goals, including the following:

- biology and genetics (examples: sex, age, genetic predispositions)
- individual behavior (alcohol use, injection drug use, unprotected sex, and smoking)
- social environment (discrimination, income, education, and gender)
- policymaking, i.e., making policies that improve living conditions in society (traffic laws, zoning laws, environmental protection laws, including enforcement)
- health services (access to quality health care and having or not having health insurance)
- The CDC includes physical environment (where a person lives, crowding conditions, quality of housing, environmental pollution, work safety).

This research over the past 45 years has demonstrated the huge importance of social determinants of health and the impact that they have on the health of individuals and populations. It started a dialogue about the importance of these determinants and has taken some focus off the traditional healthcare delivery system, seeing it as just one cog in the wheel that leads to good health.

As shown in **FIGURE 1-4**, it is generally accepted that a person's genetic makeup and biology, as well as personal behaviors and choices, account for only about 25% of population health status. The remaining factors, the social environment, physical environment/total

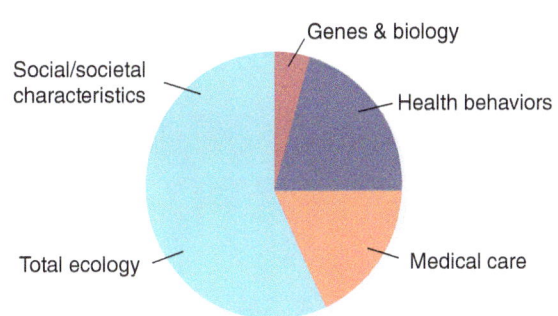

FIGURE 1-4 Estimates of How Each of the Five Major Determinants Influence Population Health

Reproduced from Tarlov AR. Public policy frameworks for improving population health. *Annals of the New York Academy of Sciences*. 1999; 896(1): 281–293.

TABLE 1-5 Global Health and Disease

Indicator	Behavioral health				Other social indicators			Vaccination rates (% complete)						
	Adult HIV prevalence rate (%)	Adult obesity rate (%)	Underweight children <5 years old (%)	Infectious disease risk	Adult smoking rate (%)	Literacy rate (% of adult population)	Unemployment rate (% age 15–24) (data year)	BCG, ≤1 year old	DPT, ≤1 year old	Hep B, ≤1 year old	Hib (3) ≤1 year old	MEV (measles) ≤1 year old	PAB (tetanus) neonatal (at birth)	Pol (3) ≤1 year old
Australia	0.17	29.9	0.2	—	16.0	—	11.7 (12)	—	92	91	92	93	—	92
Bangladesh	0.10	3.3	35.0	Intermediate	21.8	61.5	9.3 (05)	99	95	95	95	89	96	96
Botswana	25.00	19.5	11.0	High	—	88.5	36.0 (15)	98	95	95	96	97	92	96
Brazil	0.55	20.1	2.2	Very High	16.1	92.6	15.4 (11)	99	93	96	94	97	93	99
Canada	—	30.0	—	—	16.2	—	14.3 (12)	—	96	75	95	95	—	92
China	0.10	7.3	3.4	Intermediate	25.9	96.0	—	99	99	99	—	99	—	99
DR Congo	1.04	3.7	23.0	Very High	18.5	64.0	—	95	90	90	79	80	85	77
France	—	25.7	—	—	28.1	—	23.9 (15)	—	99	82	98	90	—	98
Germany	0.15	22.7	1.1	—	30.7	—	8.1 (12)	—	96	87	94	97	—	95
Ghana	1.47	10.9	13.4	Very High	6.3	77.0	12.0 (15)	99	98	98	92	92	88	92
India	0.26	4.7	43.5	Very High	12.4	71.0	10.7 (12)	91	83	70	—	83	87	69

Ireland	0.28	27.0	—	—	23.2	—	24.0 (12)	74	96	95	95	93	—	93
Israel	—	26.0	—	—	30.4	98.0	12.1 (12)	—	94	87	94	96	—	94
Japan	—	3.5	—	—	22.8	—	7.9 (12)	93	98	—	—	98	—	98
Jordan	—	28.0	3.0	—	38.4	95.0	29.3 (12)	95	98	98	98	98	90	98
Korea	—	6.3	0.6	NA	27.4	—	9.0 (12)	99	99	99	—	99	—	92
Mexico	0.23	28.0	2.8	Inter-mediate	14.5	95.0	9.4 (12)	96	87	84	99	97	88	96
Nigeria	3.17	9.7	31.0	Very High	8.9	60.0	—	74	66	66	10	51	55	60
Peru	0.36	20.4	3.5	Very High	—	95.0	9.5 (11)	94	88	88	95	89	85	93
Russia	—	26.0	—	Inter-mediate	39.5	100.0	14.8 (12)	96	97	97	18	98	—	98
Turkey	—	29.0	1.9	—	27.0	95.0	17.5 (12)	95	96	96	95	94	90	96
United Kingdom	0.33	29.8	—	—	20.3	—	21.0 (12)	—	95	—	95	93	—	92
United States	—	35.0	0.5	—	18.1	—	17.3 (11)	—	94	90	94	91	—	94

ecology, and health services/medical care account for 75% of health status. The role of public policy is critical in addressing and improving social determinants of health and in understanding the role of social determinants and their interaction with behavioral choices.

TABLE 1-6 summarizes some of the major published findings that have led health and public health professionals to refocus energy in the area of improving population health through understanding and improving social determinants of health.

TABLE 1-6 A Summary of Some of the Social Determinants of Health Status Identified in Literature

Social determinant	Mediating factor(s)	Health status > Increased < Decreased	Literature reference
Unemployment		< Health status	10–12
Employment		> Health status	13
Unemployment	Financial stress	< Health status	14, 15
Unemployment	Psychological stress	< Health status	16–18
Unemployment	Health-damaging behavior	< Health status	19–21
Work environment	Poor quality	< Health status	22, 23
Psychosocial work environment	Job demand/control (low efficacy)	< Health status	24, 25
Psychosocial work environment	Effort-reward imbalance (low self-esteem)	< Health status	26
Psychosocial work environment	Unhealthy social dynamic	< Health status	27–34
Transportation	Traffic-related accidents	< Health status	35
Transportation	Air pollution	> Respiratory illnesses	36
Transportation	Noise	< Health status	37
Social support		> Health status < Health status	38, 39
Social support	Moderating effects	> Health status	40–43
Nutrition	Inadequate	< Health status	44, 45
Nutrition	Proper	> Health status	46
Nutrition	Poor	> Obesity	47, 48
Poverty		< Health status > Mortality	49–51
Poverty	Material deprivation	< Health status	52–55

TABLE 1-6 A Summary of Some of the Social Determinants of Health Status Identified in Literature (*continued*)

Social determinant	Mediating factor(s)	Health status > Increased < Decreased	Literature reference
Poverty	Social deprivation	< Health status	56–58
Poverty	Unemployment	< Health status	59
Poverty	Inequity	< Health status	56, 60, 561
Poverty	Social exclusion	< Health status	62
Poverty	Minorities and/or refugees	< Health status	25, 63–65
Poverty	Homelessness	< Health status < Mental health status	66–68
Ethnic groupings		< Health status > Health status > Mortality < Mortality	69–76
Ethnicity	Income	> Health status < Health status	77
Ethnicity	Maternal education	> Health status < Health status	69
Ethnicity	Education level	> Health status < Health status	78–80
Ethnicity	Experience of racial harassment and discrimination	< Health status	81–83
Neighborhood environment		> Health status < Health status	84–86
Neighborhood environment	Physical environment	> Health status < Health status	87–91
Social environment		> Health status < Health status	92–94
Neighborhood environment	Amenities	> Health status < Health status	95, 96
Sexual behavior		< Health status > Health status	97, 98
Sexual behavior	Increased rate of partner change	< Health status	99
Sexual behavior	Increased variation in sexual behavior	< Health status	97

(*continues*)

TABLE 1-6 A Summary of Some of the Social Determinants of Health Status Identified in Literature (*continued*)

Social determinant	Mediating factor(s)	Health status > Increased < Decreased	Literature reference
Sexual behavior	Demography	> Health status < Health status	100, 101
Sexual behavior	Social disruption (war)	< Health status	102

▸ Conclusion

As health systems continue to evolve in every country in the world, we will see many variations. Some will follow predictable pathways that reflect local government structure, and others will form uniquely according to cultural and social forces. All systems, regardless of locale, will be challenged by changes in economics and pressures to provide services based on measures of cost, quality, and access. As indicated in the last section of this chapter, health systems do not exist in a vacuum because they are profoundly influenced by a range of social determinants health. and future events and trends as indicated in **BOX 1-3**. The determinants shape demand on services and the range of options that need to be provided within the system. They also influence the kinds of medical practitioners needed, as well as appropriate levels of education. Finally, in the context of growing populations and diverse demands, health systems will need to find

BOX 1-3 Select World Health Trends and Health Systems Implications

Population Aging

A demographic revolution is under way throughout the world. Today, there are around 600 million people in the world aged 60 years and older. This total will double by 2025, and by 2050, it will reach 2 billion, the vast majority of whom will be in the developing world. Such accelerated global population aging will increase economic and social demands on all countries.

Although the consequences of population aging in the areas of health and income security are already at the center of discussions by policymakers and planners in the developed world, the speed and impact of population aging in the less developed regions are yet to be fully appreciated. By 2025, in countries such as Brazil, China, and Thailand, the proportion of elderly people will be above 15% of the population, whereas in Colombia, Indonesia, and Kenya, the absolute numbers will increase by up to 400% over the next 25 years—up to 8 times higher than the increases in already aged societies in western Europe, where population aging occurred over a much longer period of time.

Population aging is related to two factors: a decline in the proportion of children, reflecting declines in fertility rates in the overall population, and an increase in the proportion of adults 60 years of age and older as mortality rates decline. This demographic transition will bring with it a number of major challenges for health and social policy planners.

Improving health systems and their responses to population aging makes economic sense. With old-age dependency ratios increasing in virtually all countries of the world, the economic contributions and productive roles of elderly people will assume greater importance. Supporting people to remain healthy and ensure a good quality of life in their later years is one of the greatest challenges for the health sector in both developed and developing countries.

The Burden of Mental Illness

A large proportion of individuals do not receive any health care for their conditions because (1) the mental health infrastructure and services in most countries are grossly insufficient for the large and growing needs and (2) widely prevalent stigma and discrimination prevent them from seeking help. As of 2015, a policy for mental health care is lacking in 40% of countries, and 25% of those with a policy assign no budget to implement it. Even where a budget exists, it is very small: 36% of countries devote less than 1% of their total health resources to mental health care. Although community-based services are recognized to be the most effective, 65% of all psychiatric beds are still in mental hospitals—cutting into the already meager budgets while providing largely custodial care in an environment that may infringe patients' basic human rights.

> **BOX 1-3** Select World Health Trends and Health Systems Implications (Continued)
>
> Cost-effective healthcare interventions are available. Recent research clearly demonstrates that disorders, such as depression, schizophrenia, alcohol problems, and epilepsy can be treated within primary health care. Such treatment is well within the reach of even low-income countries and will reduce substantially the overall burden of these disorders. Interventions rely on inexpensive medicines that are commonly available and, for the most part, free of patent restrictions and that require only basic training of health professionals.
>
> **Injuries—A Hidden Epidemic of Young Men**
>
> Injuries, both unintentional and intentional, primarily affect young adults, often resulting in severe, disabling consequences. According to the 2015 *Global Status Report on Injuries* published by the WHO, overall, injuries accounted for over 15% of adult disease burden in the world. In parts of the Americas, Eastern Europe, and the Eastern Mediterranean region, more than 30% of the entire disease burden among male adults aged 15 to 44 years is attributable to injuries.
>
> **Air and Water Quality**
>
> Millions of families in the world exist in environmental hazards. They are exposed to harsh weather, poor ventilation, little light, and the need for constant repair. These conditions are especially oppressive for children—their bodies, their growth and development, and their dreams. We need to find ways to strengthen links between health and environment and to integrate health systems and policies to improve quality of life worldwide.
>
> Contributed by Dr. DaNita Weddle.

ways to adapt to globalization and meet the push for greater sustainability.

In 2015, world leaders from 193 countries came together at the United Nations to adopt a new agenda for sustainable development. The outcome was a 17-goal agenda known as Sustainable Development Goals designed to end poverty, promote well-being, and protect the planet. Goal 3 focuses on health, calling for dramatic and inspiring achievements, including ending the epidemics of AIDS, tuberculosis, and malaria and achieving universal health coverage. All will require significantly greater investments in global health concurrent with improvements in health systems to gain more effectiveness and greater efficiency, along with equity and access for all.

References

1. Marmot M. Social determinants of health inequalities. *Lancet*. 2005;365:1099–1104.
2. Preamble to the Constitution of the World Health Organization as adopted by the International Health Conference, New York, June 19–22, 1946; signed on July 22, 1946 by the representatives of 61 states (official records of the World Health Organization, no. 2, p. 100) and entered into force on April 7, 1948.
3. Andersen RM. *Families' Use of Health Services: A Behavioral Model of Predisposing, Enabling, and Need Components*. Purdue, IN: Purdue University; 1968.
4. Gelberg L, Andersen RM, Leake BD. The behavioral model for vulnerable populations: application to medical care use and outcomes for homeless people. *Health Serv Res*. 2000;34(6):1273–1302.
5. Andersen R, Smedby B, Anderson OW. *Medical Care Use in Sweden and the United States: A Comparative Analysis of Systems and Behavior*. Chicago: Center for Health Administration Studies, University of Chicago, Research Series No. 27; 1970.
6. Centers for Disease Control and Prevention. Social determinants of health: definitions. http://www.cdc.gov/nchhstp/socialdeter-minants/definitions.html. Published March 21, 2016. Accessed September 21, 2016.
7. Commission on Social Determinants of Health. Closing the gap in a generation: health equity through action on the social determinants of health. Final report of the Commission on Social Determinants of Health. Geneva: World Health Organization; 2008.
8. World Health Organization. About WHO: leadership priorities. The World Health Organization has placed the issues of social determinants of health as one of its six priority areas. http://www.who.int/about/agenda/en/. Published 2016. Accessed September 21, 2016.
9. *Healthy People 2020*. Foundation health measures: determinants of health. https://www.healthypeople.gov/2020/about/foundation-health-measures/Determinants-of-Health. Published September 21, 2016. Accessed September 22, 2016.
10. Korpi W. Accumulating disadvantage: longitudinal analyses of unemployment and physical health in representative samples of the Swedish population. *Eur Sociol Rev*. 2001;17(3):255–274.
11. Warr P. Reported behaviour changes after job loss. *Br J Soc Psychol*. 1984;23(3):271–275.
12. Montgomery SM, Cook DG, Barley MJ, Wadsworth ME. Unemployment predates symptoms of depression and anxiety resulting in medical consultation in young men. *Int J Epidemiol*. 1999;28(1):95–100.
13. Jenkins R, Lewis G, Bebbington P, Brugha T, Farrell M, Gill B. The National Psychiatric Morbidity surveys of Great Britain—initial findings from the household survey. *Psychol Med*. 1997;27(4):775–789.
14. Heady P, Smyth M. *Living Standards During Unemployment*. London: HMSO; 1989.
15. Kressler RC, Turner JB, House JS. Intervening processes in the relationship between unemployment and health. *Psychol Med*. 1987;17(4):949-961.
16. Isaksson K. Unemployment, mental health and the psychological functions of work in male welfare clients in Stockholm. *Scand J Soc Med*. 1989;17(2):165–169.

17. Jahoda M. The impact of unemployment in the 1930s and the 1970s. *Bulletin of British Psychological Medicine*. 1979;32:309–314.
18. Fryer D. Monmouthshire and Marienthal: sociographies of two unemployed communities. In: Fryer D, Ullah P, eds. *Unemployed People*. New York: Open University Press; 1987.
19. Cook DG, Cummins RO, Bartley MJ, Shaper AG. Health of unemployed middle-aged men in Great Britain. *Lancet*. 1982;1(8284):1290–1294.
20. Power C, Estaugh V. Employment and drinking in early adulthood: a longitudinal perspective. *Br J Addict*. 1990;85(4):487–494.
21. Morris JK, Cook DG, Shaper AG. Non-employment and changes in smoking, drinking, and body weight. *BMJ*. 1992;304(6826):536–541.
22. Schilling RSF. Health protection and promotion at work. *Br J Ind Med*. 1989;6:683–688.
23. Morris JN, Heady JA, Raffle PAB, Roberts CG, Parks JW. Coronary heart disease and physical activity of work. *Lancet*. 1953;II:1053–1057.
24. Karasek R, Theorell T. *Healthy Work: Stress, Productivity, and the Reconstruction of Working Life*. New York: Basic Books; 1990.
25. Marmot MG, Shipley MJ, Rose G. Inequalities in death: specific explanations of a general pattern. *Lancet*. 1984;323:1003–1006.
26. Siegrist J. Adverse health effects of high-effort/low-reward conditions. *J Occup Health Psychol*. 1996;1:27–41.
27. Kohn M, Schooler C. Occupational experience and psychological functioning: an assessment of reciprocal effects. *Am Sociol Rev*. 1973;38:97–118.
28. Gardell B. Alienation and mental health in the modern industrial environment. In: Levi L, ed. *Society, Stress and Disease: The Psychosocial Environment and Psychomatic Disease*. London: Oxford University Press; 1971.
29. Karasek RA. Job demands, job decision latitude and mental strain: implications for job redesign. *Adm Sci Q*. 1979;24:285–308.
30. Belkic KL, Landsbergis PA, Schnall PL, Baker D. Is job strain a major source of cardiovascular disease risk? *Scand J Work Environ Health*. 2004;30(2):85–128.
31. Hemingway H, Marmot M. Psychosocial factors in the primary and secondary prevention of coronary heart disease: a systematic review. In: Yusuf S, Cairns J, Camm J, Fallen E, Gersch B, eds. *Evidence-Based Cardiology*. London: BMJ Publishing Group; 1998.
32. Schnall P, Belkic K, Pickering TG. Assessment of the cardiovascular system at the workplace. *Occup Med*. 2002;15(1):189–212.
33. Kuper H, Singh-Manoux A, Siegrist J, Marmot M. When reciprocity fails: effort-reward imbalance in relation to coronary heart disease and health functioning within the Whitehall II study. *Occup Environ Med*. 2002;59(11):777–784.
34. Marmot MG, Davey Smith G, et al. Health inequities among British civil servants: the Whitehall II study. *Lancet*. 1991;337:1387–1393.
35. Peden M, Scurfield R, Sleet D, et al., eds. *World Report on Road Traffic Injury Prevention*. Geneva: World Health Organization; 2004.
36. Schwartz J. Health effects of air pollution from traffic: ozone and particulate matter. In: Fletcher T, McMichael AJ, eds. *Health at the Crossroads: Transport Policy and Urban Health*. London: John Wiley and Sons; 1997.
37. Stansfeld SA, Haines MM, Burr M, Berry B, Lercher P. A review of environmental noise and mental health. *Noise Health*. 2000;2(8):1–8.
38. Pahl R. Some sceptical comments on the relationship between social support and well-being. *Leisure Studies*. 2003;22(4):357–368.
39. Cohen S, Syme SL, eds. *Social Support and Health*. London: Academic Press; 1985.
40. Cobb S. Presidential address–1976. Social support as a moderator of life stress. *Psychosom Med*. 1976;38:300–313.
41. Cornman JC, Goldman N, Glei DA, Weinstein M, Chang MC. Social ties and perceived support: two dimensions of social relationships and health among the elderly in Taiwan. *J Aging Health*. 2003;15:616–644.
42. Coyne JC, Downey G. Social factors and psychopathology: stress, social support, and coping processes. *Annu Rev Psychol*. 1991;42:401–405.
43. Fuhrer R, Stansfeld SA, Hudry-Chemali J, Shipley MJ. Gender, social relations and mental health: prospective findings from an occupational cohort (Whitehall II study). *Soc Sci Med*. 1999;48(1):77–87.
44. Brunner EJ, Rayner M, Thorogood M, et al. Making Public Health Nutrition relevant to evidence-based action. *Public Health Nutr*. 2001;4(6):1297–1299. PMID: 11820206
45. Nelson M. Nutrition and health inequalities. In: Gordon D, et al., eds. *Inequalities in Health: Studies in Poverty, Inequality and Social Exclusion*. University of Bristol: Policy Press; 1999.
46. Irala-Estévez JD, Groth M, Johansson L, Oltersdorf U, et al. A systematic review of socio-economic differences in food habits in Europe: consumption of fruit and vegetables. *Eur J Clin Nutr*. 2000;54(9):706–714.
47. Martinez JA, Kearney JM, Kafatos A, et al. Variables independently associated with self-reported obesity in the European Union. *Public Health Nutr*. 1999;2(1a):125–133.
48. Pan American Health Organization. *Obesity and Poverty: A New Public Health Challenge*. PAHO Scientific Publications, no. 576, Washington, DC; 2000.
49. Kunst AE, Geurts JJM, van der Berg J. International variation in socioeconomic inequalities in self reported health. *J Epidemiol Community Health*. 1995;49(2):117–123.
50. Mackenback JP, Huisman M, Andersen O, et al. Inequities in lung cancer mortality by the educational level in 10 European populations. *Eur J Cancer*. 2004;40(1):126–135.
51. Davey Smith G, Dorling D, Shaw M, eds. *Poverty, Inequality and Health in Britain, 1800–2000: A Reader*. Bristol: The Policy Press; 2001.
52. Ineichen B. *Homes and Health: How Housing and Health Interact*. London: Chapman and Hall; 1993.
53. Davey Smith G, Blane D, Bartley M. Explanations for socio-economic differentials in mortality: evidence from Britain and elsewhere. *Eur J Public Health*. 1994;4(2):131–144.
54. Shaw M, Dorling D, Gordon D, Davey Smith G. *The Widening Gap: Health Inequalities and Policy in Britain*. Bristol: Policy Press; 1999.
55. Shaw M. Housing and public health. *Annu Rev Public Health*. 2004;25:397–418.
56. Davey Smith G, Dorling D, Mitchell R, Shaw M. Health inequalities in Britain: continuing increases up to the

57. Blackburn C. *Poverty and Health: Working with Families*. Buckingham: Open University Press; 1991.
58. Graham H. Cigarette smoking: a light on gender and class inequality in Britain? *J Soc Policy*. 1995:24(4):509–527.
59. Bartley M, Plewis I. Accumulated labour market disadvantage and limiting long-term illness: data from the 1971–1991 Office for National Statistics' Longitudinal Study. *Int J Epidemiol*. 2002;31(2):336–341.
60. McLoone P, Boddy FA. Deprivation and mortality in Scotland, 1981 and 1991. *BMJ*. 1994;309(6967):1465–1470.
61. Phillimore P, Beattie A, Townsend P. Widening inequality of health in northern England, 1981–1991. *BMJ*. 1994;308(6937):1125–1128.
62. White P. Urban life and social stress. In: Pinder D, ed. *The New Europe: Economy, Society and Environment*. Chichester: Wiley; 1998.
63. Corvalan CF, Driscoll TR, Harrison JE. Role of migrant factors in work-related fatalities in Australia. *Scand J Work Environ Health*. 1994;20(5):364–370.
64. Trovato F. Violent and accidental mortality among four immigrant groups in Canada, 1970–1972. *Soc Biol*. 1992; 39(1-2): 82–101.
65. Nazroo J. The racialization of ethnic inequalities in health. In: Dorling D, Simpson S. *Statistics in Society*. London: Arnold; 1998.
66. Darbyshire JH. Tuberculosis: old reasons for a new increase? *BMJ*. 1995;310:954–955.
67. Gill B, Meltzer H, Hinds K, Petticrew M. *OPCS Surveys of Psychiatric Morbidity in Great Britain, Report 7: Psychiatric Morbidity Among Homeless People*. London: HMSO; 1996.
68. Folsom D, Jeste DV. Schizophrenia in homeless persons: a systematic review of the literature. *Acta Psychiatr Scand*. 2002;105(6):404–413.
69. Pamuk E, MaKuc D, Heck K, Reuben C, Lochner K. *Socioeconomic Status and Health Chartbook. Health, United States, 1998*. Hyattsville, MD: National Center for Health Statistics; 1998.
70. Williams DR, Neighbors H. Racism, discrimination and hypertension: evidence and needed research. *Ethn Dis*. 2001;11(4):800–816.
71. Harding S Maxwell R. Differences in the mortality of migrants. In: Drever F, Whitehead M, eds. *Health Inequalities: Decennial Supplement*. Series DS no. 15. London: The Stationery Office; 1997.
72. Sorlie PD, Backlund E, Keller JB. US mortality by economic, and social characteristics: the National Longitudinal Mortality Study. *Am J Public Health*. 1995;85(7):949–956.
73. Erens B, Primatesta P, Prior G. *Health Survey for England 1999: The Health of Minority Ethnic Groups*. London: The Stationery Office; 2001.
74. Sidiropoulos E, Jeffery A, Mackay S, et al. *South Africa Survey 1996/1997*. Johannesburg, South Africa: South African Institute of Race Relations; 1997.
75. Pan American Health Organization. *Equity in Health: From an Ethnic Perspective*. Washington, DC: Pan American Health Organization; 2001.
76. McLennan W, Madden R. *The Health and Welfare of Australia's Aboriginal and Torres Strait Islander Peoples*. Commonwealth of Australia: Australian Bureau of Statistics; 1999.
77. Nazroo JY. *The Health of Britain's Ethnic Minorities: Findings from a National Survey*. London: Policy Studies Institute; 1997.
78. Jaynes GD, Williams RM. *A Common Destiny: Blacks and American Society*. Washington DC: National Academy Press; 1989.
79. Orfield G. The growth of segregation: African Americans, Latinos, and unequal education. In: Orfield G, Eaton ES, eds. *Dismantling Desegregation: The Quiet Reversal of Brown v. Board of Education*. New York: The New Press; 1996.
80. Wilson WJ. *The Truly Disadvantaged*. Chicago: University of Chicago Press; 1987.
81. Virdee S. *Racial Violence and Harassment*. London: Policy Studies Institute; 1995.
82. Krieger N, Sidney S. Racial discrimination and blood pressure: The CARDIA Study of young black and white adults. *Am J Public Health*. 1996;86(10):1370–1378.
83. Chahal K, Julienne L. *We Can't All Be White! Racist Victimization in the UK*. London: York Publishing Services; 1999.
84. Humphreys K, Carr-Hill R. Area variations in health outcomes: artefact or ecology. *Int J Epidemiol*. 1991;20(1):251–258.
85. Martikainen P, Kauppinen TM, Valkonen T. Effects of the characteristics of neighbourhoods and the characteristics of people on cause specific mortality: a register based follow up study of 252,000 men. *J Epidemiol Community Health*. 2003;57(3):210–217.
86. Wiggins RD, Barley M, Gleave S, Joshi H, Lynch K. Limiting long term illness: a question of where you live or who you are? A multilevel analysis of the 1971–1991 ONS Longitudinal Study. *Risk Decision and Policy*. 1998;3:181–198.
87. Cummins S, Staffor M, Macintyre S, Marmot M, Ellaway A. Neighbourhood environment and its association with self rated health: evidence from Scotland and England. *J Epidemiol Community Health*. 2005;59(3):207–213.
88. Weich S, Blanchard M, Prince M, et al. Mental health and the built environment: cross-sectional survey of individual and contextual risk factors for depression. *Br J Psychiatry*. 2002;180:428–433.
89. Schwartz J. Air pollution and daily mortality: a review and meta analysis. *Environ Res*. 1994;64(1):36–52.
90. Maheswaran R, Elliott P. Stroke mortality associated with living near main roads in England and Wales: a geographical study. *Stroke*. 2003;34(12):2776–2780.
91. Blane D, Mitchell R, Barley M. The "inverse housing law" and respiratory health. *J Epidemiol Community Health*. 2000;54:745–749.
92. Buka SL, Brennan RT, Rich-Edwards JW, Raudenbush SW, Earls F. Neighborhood support and the birth weight of urban infants. *Am J Epidemiol*. 2003;157(1):1-8.
93. Wen M, Browning CR, Cagney KA. Poverty, affluence, and income inequality: neighborhood economic structure and its implications for health. *Soc Sci Med*. 2003;57:843–860.
94. Lochner KA, Kawachi I, Brennan RT, Buka SL. Social capital and neighborhood mortality rates in Chicago. *Soc Sci Med*. 2003;56(8):1797–1805.
95. Boreham R, Stafford M, Taylor R. *Health Survey for England 2000: Social Capital and Health*. London: The Stationery Office; 2002.

96. Yen IH, Kaplan GA. Poverty area residence and changes in depression and perceived health status: evidence from the Alameda County Study. *Int J Epidemiol*. 1999;28(1):90–94.
97. Rothenberg RB, Long DM, Sterk CE, et al. The Atlanta Urban Network Study: a blueprint for endemic transmission. *AIDS*. 2000;14(14):2191–2200.
98. Buvé A, Caraël M, Hayes RJ, et al. The multicentre study on factors determining differences in rate of spread of HIV in sub-Saharan Africa: summary and conclusions. *AIDS*. 2001;15(Suppl 4):S127-S131.
99. Fenton KA, Mercer CH, Johnson AM, et al. Reported sexually transmitted disease clinic attendance and sexually transmitted infections in Britain: prevalence, risk factors, and proportionate population burden. *J Infect Dis*. 2005;191 (Supp 1): S127-S138.
100. Fenton KA, Mercer CH, McManus S, et al. Sexual behavior in Britain: ethnic variations in high-risk sexual behavior and STI acquisition risk. *Lancet*. 2005;359:1246–1255.
101. Johnson AM, Wadsworth J, Wellings K, Field J. *Sexual Attitudes and Lifestyles*. Oxford: Blackwell Scientific Press; 1994.
102. Adler MW. The terrible peril: a historical perspective on the venereal diseases. *BMJ*. 1980;281(6234);206–211.

CHAPTER 2
Global Health and Disease

Carleen H. Stoskopf and James A. Johnson

▶ Introduction

In the development and management of a country's healthcare system, an essential component is an understanding of the environment or national context in terms of (1) the social and cultural beliefs and behaviors; (2) the physical environment, such as exposures to environmental hazards, levels of sanitation, and food and water supply safety; (3) the political climate, including legal issues that impact the provision of health care; (4) the design for financing health care and the distribution of health resources; (5) economic development, including poverty levels, distribution of wealth, types of industry, and agriculture; (6) other social structures, such as the education and judicial systems; and finally, (7) the types of diseases that are present in the population (morbidity) and rates of mortality, the disease burden. Assessment of the population's health needs in light of the national profile should drive how medical resources are distributed and health services are provided. Healthcare systems are called on to do disease prevention, primary treatment, secondary treatment, and tertiary treatment. Integration of the healthcare system with the public health system is essential for effective intervention in the cycles of disease that plague many populations.

Public health systems can provide a variety of nonmedical services, such as sanitation improvements, environmental hazard control, vector control, health promotion, community interventions to improve health and well-being, and setting health policy for the financing and distribution of health services. The public health systems are also responsible for the surveillance of disease in populations. The activity of disease surveillance is vitally important to healthcare systems that are often called on to decide how few and precious resources are to be deployed. Understanding the disease profile of a population and the burden of disease that exists in that population is essential to planning and implementation of health programs. For example, in the case of malaria, healthcare providers must rapidly identify and treat specific types of malaria, as well as asymptomatic cases, to prevent further transmission. The public health system must work to eliminate vectors through destruction of breeding sites and use of safe and effective pesticides. Equally important is the role of health educators who work with the community to change behavior by encouraging use of bed nets at night and emptying local water receptacles. Simultaneously, researchers must continue the search for safe and cost-effective new treatments, for methods to quickly identify asymptomatic individuals, and for a new vaccine. No campaign to eliminate or substantially reduce malaria will be successful without all of these components; therefore, it is incumbent on healthcare systems to understand the populations they serve and to work with their communities through public health efforts and other social institutions to effect change. **BOX 2-1** identifies the 10 essential public health functions.

> **BOX 2-1** Ten Essential Public Health Functions
>
> Monitor health statuses to identify and solve community health problems.
>
> Diagnose and investigate health problems and health hazards in the community.
>
> Inform, education, and empower people about health issues.
>
> Mobilize community partnerships to identify and solve health problems.
>
> Develop policies and plans that support individual and community health efforts.
>
> Enforce laws and regulations that protect health and ensure safety.
>
> Link people to needed personal health services and assure the provision of health care when otherwise unavailable.
>
> Assure a competent public and personal healthcare workforce.
>
> Evaluate effectiveness, accessibility, and quality of personal and population-based services.
>
> Research for new insights and innovative solutions to health problems.
>
> Reproduced from Centers for Disease Control and Prevention. The public health system and the 10 essential public health services. http://www.cdc.gov/nphpsp/essentialServices.html. March 2014.

No healthcare system can be successful without a close working relationship with the public health system. In an ideal world, they would blend seamlessly.

▸ Burden of Disease

Disease is measured in many ways. In public health, the term *prevalence* is used to measure the number of individuals with a disease in a specific population at a discrete point in time. *Incidence* is the number of new cases of a disease in a population over a specified period of time.[1] A vast amount of data are available on the incidence and prevalence of diseases (morbidity data) by country, states, regions, and cities and by population demographics, such as age, gender, and race/ethnicity. Disease severity is commonly measured by disease-specific mortality for that disease. Disease-specific mortality is the number of deaths due to a given disease per time, usually expressed per 1,000 or 100,000 people per year. An example is the mortality from prostate cancer (25 per 100,000 in 2000 in Germany).

To communicate the magnitude of a disease in different populations, it can also be reported as a case fatality rate, that is, the rate of death among those who have the disease reported per 1,000 or 100,000 people with the disease. For example, 720 out of 1,000 men with prostate cancer that has spread to other areas of the body will die within 5 years. Mortality rates are often reported based on age groups or other demographic variables.[1] A list of commonly used health indicators can be found in **TABLE 2-1**.[2]

The burden of disease is expressed by statistics that attempt to determine the impact of disease on a population through measuring disability and healthy-life years lost. The World Health Organization (WHO) initiated the Global Burden of Disease study in 1992 that continues to the present. The study selected disability-adjusted life years for its measurement.[3,4] Other measures include quality-adjusted life years, health expectancies, and healthy life years.[1] Implicit in these measures is the idea that one can apply cost-benefit analyses in terms of the cost to a population to prevent and treat diseases versus the cost that population pays for years lived with disability and/or early mortality from those same diseases. Healthcare providers who avail themselves of these types of measures as applied to their populations can make better decisions in appropriating scarce resources. National health policymakers can use the economic data applied to loss of healthy life years to understand better the impact of diseases upon their nation's population and therefore its productivity as measured in gross domestic product (GDP). An understanding of the burden of disease results in better decision making in terms of allocation of resources for specific programs for prevention, treatment, eradication, and control of specific diseases that severely impact their populations and ultimately the economic viability of the country. A good example of this is the burden that malaria places on populations where it is endemic.

The collection of health statistics is difficult and complicated, even in countries with well-developed health systems like the United States. Collection of these statistics requires standardized definitions of diseases, consistent standards for diagnosis of these diseases, and a well-defined population at risk for these diseases. For developing countries struggling to provide the most basic healthcare needs of their communities, the collection of useful statistics can be a daunting but nevertheless vital task. **TABLE 2-2** illustrates the burden of disease, both communicable and noncommunicable, for the countries presented in this book, allowing a comparison across counties.

TABLE 2-1 Commonly Used Population Health Indicators

Indicator*	Definition**
Crude birth rate	Number of live births per 1,000 people in a population during a specific period of time
Crude death rate per 100,000 people	Number of deaths per 100,000 people in a population during a specific period of time
Specific death rate per 100,000 people (age, gender, cause)	Deaths by age, gender, or per 100,000 people in a population during a specific period of time
Infant mortality rate per 1,000 live births	Deaths under one year of age per 1,000 live births in a population
Neonatal mortality rate per 1,000 live births	Deaths < 28 days of age per 1,000 live births in a population
Maternal mortality rate per 100,000 women	Deaths from maternal causes per 100,000 women of childbearing age
Proportionate mortality	Percentage of deaths that can be attributed to a particular disease, calculated out of all deaths within that population
Incidence rate	New cases for a condition per 1,000 or 100,000 people in a population during a specific period of time
Prevalence (point in time)	Number of cases of a condition at a specific point in time per 100,000 people in a population
Disease-specific mortality rate	Number of deaths from a specific condition in a defined population group per 1,000 or 100,000 people during a specified period of time
Case fatality rate	Number of deaths among those with a specific condition per 1,000 people suffering from that condition

* All indicators are per year.
** All definitions are per a defined population.

Data from Basch PF. *Textbook of International Health*. 2nd ed. New York: Oxford University Press; 1999, pp. 80, 81; World Health Organization. WHO Global Health Observatory Data. https://www.cia.gov/library/publications/resources/the-world-factbook/CIA. Accessed June 8, 2016.

▸ Noncommunicable / Chronic Diseases

As we enter the second decade of the 21st century, we are also facing a growing prevalence of noncommunicable chronic disease. As shown in **EXHIBIT 2-1**, this trend is expected to be even more dramatic in coming years. Diseases such as heart disease, stroke, cancer, chronic respiratory disease, mental illness, and diabetes have reached epidemic status in low- and middle-income countries, as well as in high-income countries.[5] In fact, of approximately 60 million deaths worldwide each year, over half are the result of chronic disease. Cardiovascular disease is now the leading cause of death in the world and is the number one cause of death in all regions except sub-Saharan Africa, where the combination of HIV/AIDS and malaria are the culprits. Communicable, or infectious, diseases are caused by a pathogen or infectious agent spread from person to person or from animal to person, whereas noncommunicable diseases are in many ways the opposite, as they do not spread from person to person by an infectious agent. Chronic diseases also tend to last a long time

TABLE 2-2 Major Causes of Death per 100,000 Population, 2016, in Selected Countries

Country	All causes of death	Communicable diseases	Noncommunicable diseases	Injuries
Australia	345	14	303	28
Bangladesh	847	235	549	64
Botswana	1,255	555	612	88
Brazil	687	93	514	80
Canada	372	23	318	31
China	668	41	576	50
DR Congo	1,782	920	724	137
France	369	21	313	35
Germany	410	22	365	23
Ghana	1,222	476	670	76
India	1,051	253	682	116
Ireland	397	22	344	32
Israel	363	31	311	21
Japan	319	34	244	41
Jordan	746	53	640	54
Mexico	589	57	468	63
Nigeria	1,685	866	674	146
Peru	533	121	453	58
Korea	389	34	302	53
Russia	967	74	790	103
Turkey	638	44	555	39
United Kingdom	409	29	359	22
United States	488	31	413	44

Data from World Health Organization. Global Health Observatory Data Repository. http://www.who.int/gho/en/. Accessed July 5, 2016.

EXHIBIT 2-1 Chronic Disease Worldwide

Prevalence of diabetes worldwide

Year	2000	2030
Diabetics in the world	171 million	366 million

7.4 million: the number of people who died from cancer worldwide in 2004. Today, cancer causes one death in every eight, which was almost 7 million in 2015.

15 years: the deficit in average life expectancy for men in Eastern Europe compared with those living elsewhere in Europe in 2015. Almost half of this excess mortality was due to cardiovascular diseases with a further 20% due to injuries.

150 million: the number of people globally experiencing financial catastrophe due to the costs of chronic disease care and disability.

Data from World Health Organization. World Health Statistics 2008. http://www.who.int/whosis/whostat/EN_WHS08_Full.pdf?ua=1. 2008.

and can be disabling or cause death if not treated. The WHO says the worldwide threat is growing. They predict that deaths from infectious diseases will decline by about 3% until about 2025, whereas deaths caused by chronic diseases are projected to increase by 17%. This means that of the 65 million deaths in 2016, over 40 million died of chronic diseases. To understand chronic disease fully, one must use the multicausation model, as illustrated in **FIGURE 2-1**.

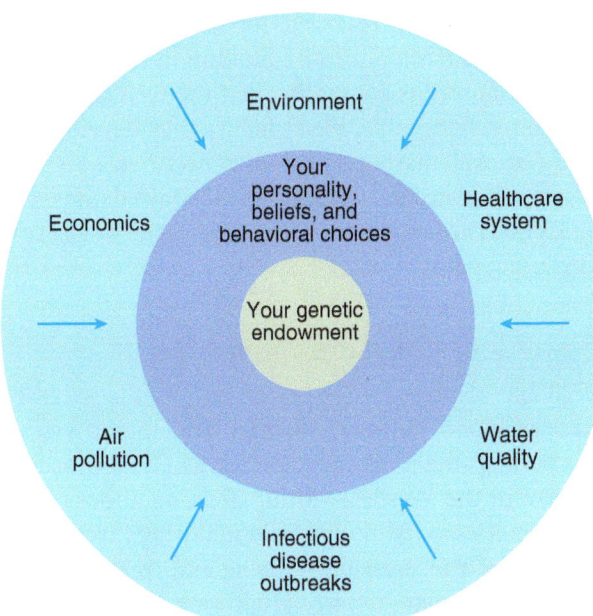

FIGURE 2-1 Multicausation Disease Model

As demonstrated in the diagram, chronic disease relates to lifestyle and the environment in which a person lives. The WHO asserts that there are common, modifiable risk factors that underlie the major chronic diseases. These risk factors explain the vast majority of chronic disease deaths at all ages, in women and men, and in all parts of the world. They include the following:

- Unhealthy diet
- Physical inactivity
- Tobacco use

These causes are expressed through the intermediate risk factors of high blood pressure, high glucose levels, abnormal blood lipids, and obesity. Each year at least

- 6 million people die as a result of tobacco use.
- 5 million die as a result of being overweight or obese.
- 5 million die as a result of raised total cholesterol levels.
- 8 million die as a result of raised blood pressure.

Of course, there are many more risk factors for chronic disease. Harmful alcohol use is a significant contributor to injury, disability, liver cirrhosis, pancreatitis, and various cancers. Other risk factors for chronic disease include infectious agents that can lead to cervical cancer (human papillomavirus) and liver cancer (hepatitis). There are also many environmental factors—such as air pollution, water pollution, and radiation—that contribute to a range of chronic diseases. Finally, we cannot underestimate the impact of psychosocial and genetic factors.

The top 10 leading causes of death worldwide are as follows:

1. Heart disease
2. Cerebrovascular disease
3. Respiratory infections
4. HIV/AIDS
5. Chronic pulmonary disease
6. Perinatal conditions
7. Diarrheal disease
8. Tuberculosis
9. Malaria
10. Respiratory tract cancers

The various infectious diseases on this list are discussed in a later section of this chapter. Several of the chronic diseases along with diabetes, cancer, and mental illness will be discussed here.

Cardiovascular Disease

Cardiovascular disease, or coronary heart disease, is the number one killer, accounting for approximately 25 million deaths worldwide. This represents nearly

60% of all deaths in Europe and Central Asia and approximately 30% of all deaths in East Asia and the Pacific, but only 10% of deaths in sub-Saharan Africa. Cardiovascular disease includes three common conditions: ischemic heart disease, stroke (cerebrovascular disease), and congestive heart failure. As described by the Mayo Clinic, cardiovascular disease is a broad term that is used to describe a range of diseases that affect the heart or blood vessels. The various diseases that fall under the umbrella of cardiovascular disease include coronary artery disease, heart attack, heart failure, high blood pressure, and stroke.

Although cardiovascular disease can refer to many different types of heart or blood vessel problems, it is used most often to describe damage caused to the heart or blood vessels by atherosclerosis. Over time, too much pressure in the arteries can make the walls thick and stiff—sometimes restricting blood flow to organs and tissues; however, some forms of cardiovascular disease are not caused by atherosclerosis. Those forms include diseases such as congenital heart disease, heart valve diseases, heart infections, or disease of the heart muscle (called cardiomyopathy).

The cardiovascular system consists of your heart and all the blood vessels throughout your body. Diseases ranging from aneurysms to valve disease are types of cardiovascular disease. A person may be born with some types of cardiovascular disease (congenital) or may acquire others later on, usually from unhealthy habits, such as smoking.

Coronary Artery Disease

This is a common form of cardiovascular disease. Coronary artery diseases are diseases of the arteries that supply the heart muscle with blood. Sometimes known as CAD, coronary artery disease is the leading cause of heart attacks. It generally means that blood flow through the coronary arteries has become obstructed, reducing blood flow to the heart muscle. The most common cause of such obstructions is a condition called atherosclerosis, a largely preventable type of vascular disease. Coronary artery disease and the resulting reduced blood flow to the heart muscle can lead to other heart problems, such as chest pain (angina) and heart attack (myocardial infarction).

Heart Attack

A heart attack is an injury to the heart muscle caused by a loss of blood supply. The medical term for heart attack is myocardial infarction. A heart attack usually occurs when a blood clot blocks the flow of blood through a coronary artery, a blood vessel that feeds blood to a part of the heart muscle. Interrupted blood flow to your heart can damage or destroy a part of the heart muscle.

Congenital Heart Disease

Congenital heart disease refers to a form of heart disease that develops before birth (congenital). Congenital heart disease is a broad term and includes a wide range of diseases and conditions. These diseases can affect the formation of the heart muscle or its chambers or valves. Some congenital heart defects may be apparent at birth, whereas others may not be detected until later in life.

Aneurysm

An aneurysm is a bulge or weakness in a blood vessel (artery or vein) wall. Aneurysms usually get bigger over time. Because of that, they have the potential to rupture and cause life-threatening bleeding. Aneurysms can occur in arteries in any location in the body. The most common sites include the abdominal aorta and the arteries at the base of the brain.

Heart Failure

Heart failure, often called congestive heart failure, is a condition in which the heart cannot pump enough blood to meet the needs of the body's organs and tissues. It does not mean that your heart has failed and cannot pump blood at all. With this less effective pumping, vital organs do not get enough blood, causing such signs and symptoms as shortness of breath, fluid retention, and fatigue. "Congestive" heart failure is technically reserved for situations in which heart failure has led to fluid buildup in the body. Not all heart failure is congestive, but the terms are often used interchangeably. Heart failure may develop suddenly or over many years. It may occur as a result of other cardiovascular conditions that have damaged or weakened the heart, such as coronary artery disease or cardiomyopathy.

High Blood Pressure

High blood pressure (hypertension) is the excessive force of blood pumping through your blood vessels. It is perhaps the most common form of cardiovascular disease in the Western world, affecting about one in four Americans. Although potentially life threatening, it is one of the most preventable and treatable types of cardiovascular disease. High blood pressure also causes many other types of cardiovascular disease, such as stroke and heart failure.

Stroke

A stroke occurs when blood flow to the brain is interrupted (ischemic stroke) or when a blood vessel in the brain ruptures (hemorrhagic stroke). Both can cause the death of brain cells in the affected areas. Stroke is also considered a neurological disorder because of the many complications it causes. Other forms of cardiovascular disease, such as high blood pressure, increase your risk of stroke.

Arrhythmias

Heart rhythm problems (arrhythmias) occur when the electrical impulses in your heart that coordinate your heartbeats do not function properly, causing your heart to beat too fast, too slow, or irregularly. Other forms of cardiovascular disease can cause arrhythmias.

Cancer

The WHO says that dramatic increases in risk factors such as tobacco use and obesity are contributing to a worldwide rise in cancer rates, particularly in low- and middle-income countries, where more than 70% of all cancer deaths occur. Worldwide, 84 million people will die in the next 10 years if action is not taken, the WHO estimates. Preventable risk factors include many environmental carcinogens. In addition, nearly half of cancer incidences can be prevented by a healthy diet, physical activity, and avoiding tobacco. Cancer refers to any one of a large number of diseases characterized by the development of abnormal cells that divide uncontrollably and have the ability to infiltrate and destroy normal body tissue. Cancer also has the ability to spread throughout your body. Cancer is a leading cause of death worldwide, but survival rates are improving for many types of cancer thanks to improvements in cancer screening and cancer treatment. Cancer is caused by damage (mutations) to the DNA within cells. DNA contains a set of instructions for your cells, telling them how to grow and divide. Normal cells often develop mutations in their DNA, but they have the ability to repair most of these mutations. If they cannot make the repairs, the cells often die; however, certain mutations are not repaired, causing the cells to grow and become cancerous. Mutations also cause cancer cells to live beyond their normal cell life span. This causes the cancerous cells to accumulate. In some cancers, accumulating cells form a tumor, but not all cancers form tumors. For example, leukemia is a cancer that involves blood, bone marrow, the lymphatic system, and the spleen, but it does not form a single mass or tumor.

Genetic makeup, forces within the body, lifestyle choices, and the environment can all set the stage for cancer or help complete the process once it has started. For instance, if you have inherited a genetic mutation that predisposes you to cancer, you may be more likely than other people to develop cancer when exposed to a certain cancer-causing substance. The genetic mutation begins the cancer process, and the cancer-causing substance could play a role in further cancer development. Likewise, smokers who work with asbestos are more likely to develop lung cancer than smokers who do not work with asbestos. That is because tobacco smoke and asbestos both play roles in cancer development.

Factors known to increase the risk of cancer include the following:

- Age: Cancer can take decades to develop. That is why most people diagnosed with cancer are age 55 or older. Although it is more common in older adults, cancer is not exclusively an adult disease; cancer can be diagnosed at any age.
- Lifestyle: Certain lifestyle choices are known to increase your risk of cancer. Smoking, drinking more than one drink a day (for women) or two drinks a day (for men), excessive exposure to the sun or frequent blistering sunburns, and having unsafe sex can contribute to cancer.
- Family history: Only about 10% of cancers are due to an inherited condition. If cancer is common in your family, it is possible that mutations are being passed from one generation to the next.
- Health conditions: Some chronic health conditions, such as ulcerative colitis, can markedly increase the risk of developing certain cancers.
- Environment: The environment may contain harmful chemicals that can increase the risk of cancer. Even if people do not smoke, they might inhale secondhand smoke or other indoor pollutants. Chemicals in the home or workplace, such as asbestos and benzene, also are associated with an increased risk of cancer.
- Globalization: Globalized markets and urbanization are leading to rising consumption of tobacco; processed foods high in fats, sugars, and salt; declining consumption of fruit and vegetables; and more sedentary activity levels. As a consequence the incidence of cancer and other chronic diseases is increasing.

The WHO has proposed a global goal of reducing death rates for all chronic diseases by 2% per year. Achievement of this goal would avert over 8 million of the projected 84 million deaths caused by cancer in the next decade.

Diabetes

The International Diabetes Federation estimates that more than 245 million people around the world have diabetes. This total is expected to rise to 380 million within 20 years. Each year a further 7 million people develop diabetes.

Diabetes is a disease in which the body does not produce or properly use insulin. Insulin is a hormone that is needed to convert sugar, starches, and other food into energy needed for daily life. The cause of diabetes continues to be a mystery, although both genetics and environmental factors, such as obesity and lack of exercise, appear to play roles.

There are 24 million children and adults in the United States, or about 8% of the population, who have diabetes. Although an estimated 18 million have been diagnosed with diabetes, unfortunately, 6 million people (or nearly one quarter) are unaware that they have the disease.

Type 1 Diabetes

This results from the body's failure to produce insulin, the hormone that "unlocks" the cells of the body, allowing glucose to enter and fuel them. It is estimated that 5%–10% of people diagnosed with diabetes have type 1 diabetes.

Type 2 Diabetes

This results from insulin resistance (a condition in which the body fails to properly use insulin), combined with relative insulin deficiency. Most people worldwide who are diagnosed with diabetes have type 2 diabetes.

Gestational Diabetes

Immediately after pregnancy, 5%–10% of women who had gestational diabetes are found to have diabetes, usually type 2. Diabetes often predates the birth and often continues postpartum.

Prediabetes

Prediabetes is a condition that occurs when a person's blood glucose levels are higher than normal but not high enough for a diagnosis of type 2 diabetes. There are 57 million Americans who have prediabetes. This number is even higher in Mexico, India, China, and the Middle East.

The International Diabetes Federation anticipates the following:

- By 2025, the number of people with diabetes is expected to rise to 380 million worldwide, with 80% living in the developing world.
- Each year, another 7 million people develop diabetes, while 3.8 million die of diabetes-linked causes.
- In many countries in Asia, the Middle East, and the Caribbean, diabetes already affects 15%–20% of the adult population.
- India now has the largest number of diabetics (over 40 million) in the world, followed by China (nearly 40 million), the United States (about 24 million), and Russia (about 10 million).
- Diabetes increasingly affects the young and middle aged, with more than half of diabetics in developing countries between the ages of 40 and 59 years.

Mental Illness

Neuropsychiatric conditions account for 14% of the global burden of disease. Within noncommunicable diseases, they account for 28% of the disability-adjusted life years, more than cardiovascular disease or cancer. The most important contributions to this number are depression, alcohol abuse, schizophrenia, and dementia. Up to 30% of all people worldwide have a mental disorder, and although interventions for the treatment of mental disorders are available, the proportion of those people with mental disorders who need treatment but who do not receive mental health care is very high. This treatment gap is estimated to reach about 76%–85% for low- and middle-income countries and remain at 35%–50% for high-income countries.

Mental illnesses are medical conditions that disrupt a person's thinking, feeling, mood, ability to relate to others, and daily functioning. Just as diabetes is a disorder of the pancreas, mental illnesses are medical conditions that often result in a diminished capacity for coping with the ordinary demands of life.

Mental illnesses can affect people of any age, race, religion, or income. Mental illnesses are not the result of personal weakness, lack of character, or poor upbringing. Mental illnesses are treatable. Most people diagnosed with a serious mental illness can experience relief from their symptoms by actively participating in an individual treatment plan.

In addition to medication treatment, psychosocial treatments—such as cognitive behavioral therapy, interpersonal therapy, peer support groups, and other community services—can also be components of a treatment plan and assist with recovery. The availability of transportation, diet, exercise, sleep, friends, and meaningful paid or volunteer activities contribute to overall health and wellness, including mental illness recovery.

Here are some important facts about mental illness and recovery:

- The World Health Organization has reported that 4 of the 10 leading causes of disability in the United States and other developed countries are mental disorders. By 2020, major depressive illness will be the leading cause of disability in the world for women and children.
- Mental illnesses usually strike individuals in the prime of their lives, often during adolescence and young adulthood. All ages are susceptible, but the young and the old are especially vulnerable.
- Without treatment the consequences of mental illness for the individual and society are staggering: unnecessary disability, unemployment, substance abuse, homelessness, inappropriate incarceration, suicide, and wasted lives. The economic cost of untreated mental illness is more than 100 billion dollars each year in the United States.
- The best treatments for serious mental illnesses today are highly effective. Between 70% and 90% of individuals have significant reduction of symptoms and improved quality of life with a combination of pharmacological and psychosocial treatments and supports.
- With appropriate, effective medication and a wide range of services tailored to their needs, most people who live with serious mental illnesses can significantly reduce the impact of their illness and find a satisfying measure of achievement and independence. A key concept is to develop expertise in developing strategies to manage the illness process.
- Early identification and treatment is of vital importance. By ensuring access to the treatment and recovery supports that are proven effective, recovery is accelerated, and the further harm related to the course of illness is minimized.
- Stigma erodes confidence that mental disorders are real, treatable health conditions. Nearly all cultures of the world have allowed stigma and an unwarranted sense of hopelessness to erect attitudinal, structural, and financial barriers to effective treatment and recovery.

Infectious Disease

Infectious diseases are illnesses that are spread from person to person, either directly, or indirectly. They may spread in a variety of ways. Some require an intermediary host, such as diseases that are vector borne (yellow fever virus, West Nile virus, Lyme disease, and most recently Zika virus) and diseases that require zoological hosts for part of their life cycles and development (malaria, schistosomiasis). Others are spread through direct contact (impetigo, gonorrhea, syphilis, Ebola), contact with infected surfaces or fomites (*Staphylococcus aureus* infection, rhinovirus), ingestion of contaminated water (cholera, giardiasis), infection via the blood, (hepatitis B and C, HIV), ingestion of fecal material (hepatitis A, *Escherichia coli*), intake via the respiratory system (tuberculosis, severe acute respiratory syndrome [SARS]), or in some cases, direct contact with infected animals themselves (tularemia). Many diseases can be spread in more than one way.

Infectious diseases have experienced a major comeback in the last four decades. In the 1970s, many public health and medical professionals believed that the age of infectious disease was mostly over because of successful vaccination development, a reduction of potential disease vectors through pesticide use, vast increases in basic public health sanitation, and identification and knowledge about infectious disease life cycles and modes of transmission. Most health professionals living in industrialized nations thought little of infectious diseases and turned their attention to chronic disease and its management. Within this environment of complacency appeared a newly recognized pathogen in the 1980s, the human immunodeficiency virus (HIV). HIV turned out to be the first of many new emerging and reemerging infectious diseases that caught us unprepared. Since the early 1980s, public health and healthcare systems have faced a number of new infectious diseases and new challenges with some diseases thought conquered.

The report of a new sexually transmitted disease whose infection led to almost certain death was a concept that shocked everyone from professionals in the medical community to the average person on the street. How could this occur? The emergence of HIV was quickly followed by other infectious diseases, including Ebola virus, SARS, avian flu, and most recently the Zika virus. In addition, some infectious diseases began to spread to new areas of the world, such as West Nile virus introduction into North America from Africa, Ebola spreading out from West Africa, and SARS from Asia to Canada. Contributing to this situation further, the role of commercial airline traffic in spreading disease throughout the world changed from being a theoretical concern to a public health reality. And more importantly, we came to realize that the infusion of healthcare workers into endemic areas of some diseases created new fears in their home countries. As Ebola outbreaks in Africa appeared on our television screens, we were stunned to learn that this disease jumped from other primates to humans. Now we nervously watch for new cases of avian flu for the same reason. HIV in Africa reminds us of those historical plague epidemics that changed the basic population structure of societies as vast numbers of people died within short time periods. Those old infectious diseases that we thought were under control suddenly started to reappear or grow in prevalence. Malaria, for instance, is on the rise. Some infectious agents have now developed resistance to treatment. A virulent new form of tuberculosis has appeared that is also resistant to most treatments. Nature seems to thwart us at each turn. Those in the business of providing healthcare services and those who conduct disease surveillance must very seriously assess the burden of infectious diseases on the populations they serve and be prepared to address them through prevention, early detection, and treatment. Countries with healthcare resources who reach out as responders in emergency outbreaks around the world must prepare their own people with the knowledge and equipment necessary to prevent transmission to themselves and to those at home when they return.

As we progress through the early 21st century, developed countries are becoming increasingly aware of the health problems and needs of developing countries. This is not just because the developed countries are concerned that diseases endemic to developing countries may pose a hazard for their own citizens, but it is also out of a sense of justice and social responsibility. Because of real-time communication through technology such as the Internet and dedicated 24-hour news programming, an increase in international travel to developing countries, and demographic changes caused by immigration, people from all over the world are more aware of the conditions under which many people live. As our global awareness has increased, so has our sense of interconnectedness to those beyond our borders.

Global awareness has motivated governments, private organizations, and international organizations to come to the aid of people and nations with large burdens of illness. Unfortunately, special interests, politics, international corruption, and incompetence have thwarted many of these well-meaning efforts. Conditions in developing countries often contribute to the disease burden caused by infectious diseases. Many developing countries not only lack adequate healthcare services but also lack many of the public health advancements and infrastructure that developed countries experienced and enjoyed in the early part of the 20th century. Conditions of many developing countries include poverty, undernutrition, poor sanitation, lack of potable water, little or no access to healthcare services, and low levels of education.

Recent studies have shown that undernutrition is a leading contributor to childhood deaths by infectious disease. Of the estimated 10 million children who die each year, the majority die from preventable causes: pneumonia and diarrhea, followed by malaria, AIDS, and measles.[6]

It is essential for healthcare delivery systems to provide effective interventions for infectious diseases, including both prevention and treatment. These systems must also work to collect and provide timely and accurate health statistics for both the planning and monitoring of the use and provision of health services by the populations they serve. It is further incumbent on healthcare services to work with their communities to reach out with interventions to those in the population who cannot or will not access services. It is equally important for countries to develop plans for improvement of infrastructure, community education, and economic development, which have been shown to significantly improve the health statuses of populations.

Vector-Borne Diseases

Of great concern to epidemiologists worldwide is the resurgence of vector-borne diseases. This resurgence is due to a number of factors, including resistance to pesticides, poor environmental and ecosystem management, resistance to drugs used for treatment, the shifting of health policy from prevention to emergency response, genetic changes in pathogens, climate change, deforestation, and changes in agricultural practices.[7] The newest of these is the Zika virus that was endemic in Africa and Asia in humans in the early 1950s but first caused an outbreak in the South Pacific in 2007 among populations with no resistance. Suddenly this virus came to our awareness through its teratogenic properties in South America. The idea of globalization and interconnectedness took on a whole new meaning as people from around the world gathered in Brazil for the Olympics. Many athletes risked their safety to attend. We would never have imagined in the 1970s that the Olympics in 2016 would be impacted by an infectious disease. It is changing the world and requires a different type of thinking to manage infectious diseases. Health systems must be prepared for these diseases, the old and the new.

Vector-borne diseases are those that require a blood-sucking agent (arthropod) to transmit the pathogen among vertebrate hosts. These diseases can be grouped according to three types of pathogens: parasitic, bacterial, and viral. Until World War II, vector-borne diseases were the number one cause of morbidity around the world. Since the early 1990s, it has been clear that vector-borne diseases continue to contribute significantly to the burden of disease in most areas of the developing world and continue to spread to the developed world. TABLE 2-3 provides a summary of three categories of major vector-borne diseases and their geographical distribution in the world today.

Malaria

The vector-borne disease of greatest concern worldwide is malaria. Malaria is caused by a protozoan parasite that invades the red blood cells of humans. It is spread by mosquitoes in the genus *Anopheles*; after biting one infected person, they go on to a bite someone else, thus transmitting the disease. It is important to note that part of the life cycle of the parasite occurs in the mosquito and is required for disease transmission. Common symptoms include malaise, febrile episodes with cerebral damage, hypoglycemia, respiratory distress, anemia, chronic debilitation, malnutrition, and neurological syndromes. Malaria in endemic areas presents itself in two basic forms. For those under the age of five years and travelers without previous exposure, the parasitemia results in acute symptoms and can eventually lead to death. In Africa, the majority of deaths from malaria are among children.[6] People who live in endemic areas and who have survived early childhood episodes of malaria often develop a level of immunity. In this case, malaria may present itself with mild symptoms, including general malaise, general debilitation, and periods of low fever. Frequently, adults with malaria may be completely asymptomatic.

TABLE 2-3 Geographic Distribution of Major Vector-Borne Diseases by Type of Pathogen

Country	Parasitic disease	Bacterial disease	Arboviral disease
North America	Malaria	Tularemia, tick-borne relapsing fever, Lyme disease	Encephalitis types: eastern equine, La Crosse, Venezuelan equine, St. Louis, West Nile virus, dengue, Zika virus (emerging)
South American and Central America	Malaria	Plague	Venezuelan eastern equine encephalitis, St. Louis encephalitis, dengue fever, yellow fever, Zika virus
Europe	—	Lyme disease, tularemia	Sindbis, tick-borne encephalitis, Dengue fever, Crimean-Congo hemorrhagic fever
Africa	Malaria, leishmaniasis, African trypanosomiasis	Louse-borne typhus, plague	Rift Valley fever, Kyasanur Forest disease, dengue fever, yellow fever, Crimean-Congo hemorrhagic fever, chikungunya
Asia	Malaria, leishmaniasis	Plague	Chikungunya, dengue, Japanese encephalitis, California encephalitis, Sindbis, Crimean-Congo hemorrhagic fever, tick-borne encephalitis
Australia	—	—	Dengue, Japanese encephalitis, Murray Valley encephalitis, Ross River hemorrhagic fever

Data from Centers for Disease Control and Prevention. List of VHF diseases. http://www.cdc.gov/vhf/diseases.html. June 6, 2016. Accessed August 8, 2016; Centers for Disease Control and Prevention. Division of Vector-Borne Diseases. www.cdc.gov/ncezid/dvbd/. April 2, 2016. Accessed July 20, 2016; Centers for Disease Control and Prevention. Technical Fact Sheet Eastern Equine Encephalitis. http://www.cdc.gov/EasternEquineEncephalitis/. April 5, 2016. Accessed August 8, 2016; Centers for Disease Control and Prevention. La Crosse Encephalitis. http://www.cdc.gov/lac/. April 11, 2016. Accessed August 8, 2016; Centers for Disease Control and Prevention. Arboviral Diseases, Neuroinvasive and Non-neuroinvasive 2015 Case Definition. https://wwwn.cdc.gov/nndss/conditions/arboviral-diseases-neuroinvasive-and-non-neuroinvasive/case-definition/2015/. n.d. Accessed August 8, 2016; Heymann DL. *Control of Communicable Disease Manual*. Washington, DC: American Public Health Association; 2015: 33–43.

Untreated mild or asymptomatic cases preserve a reservoir of parasites for transmission to others via mosquito vectors because the symptoms may be so mild that adults do not seek treatment. This asymptomatic pool of people poses the biggest obstacle to eradicating malaria. In order to eradicate malaria, it is necessary to find and treat these individuals and use new drugs and treatment regiments that eliminate the parasites from the blood of humans. The call to public health is surveillance, finding asymptomatic cases, and treating those cases quickly and effectively. This also calls for the development and use of highly sensitive diagnostic tools. Treating a population as a whole prophylactically has been controversial.

Treatment of malaria has become complicated over time, as some of the species of malaria (*P. malariae*, *P. falciparum*, *P. vivax*, and *P. ovale*) have developed resistance to more commonly used treatment drugs. As of now, there are no vaccines for malaria.[6] Long-term chemoprophylaxis with malaria-preventing drugs is not a viable option, as it can result in further resistance and poses other risks and side effects to the individual. The current recommendation is to provide targeted groups (pregnant women and small children) in endemic areas with intermittent therapeutic doses of malaria treatment.[1] Other options include programs to eliminate mosquito breeding sites and to educate people in the use of bed nets, which can weaken the chain of infection, but only the successful treatment of asymptomatic people will move us further toward eradication of malaria globally.

Of all the vector-borne diseases, malaria is believed to cause the greatest morbidity burden around the world. A worldwide campaign that started in 1955 and operated through the mid-1960s resulted in a substantial reduction in malaria in areas where it was endemic.[6] As efforts abated, a resurgence of malaria occurred. This was primarily caused by the ban of DDT and the discontinuation of programs to reduce mosquito breeding areas resulting in a decrease in vector control. The initial successful efforts show how public health measures, when appropriate, can have a significant impact on vector-borne diseases and can result in less reliance on treatment. Perhaps most importantly, as many sub-Saharan countries earned independence in the 1950s and 1960s, the ensuing political instability, escalation of foreign debt, and decrease in international aid resulted in the collapse of the public health and healthcare systems in many countries. The result of these multifaceted factors is that malaria has returned with a vengeance. Not until 1998 were efforts once again renewed to reduce malaria levels by introducing the Roll Back Malaria program. The Roll Back Malaria program is a partnership with WHO, UNICEF, UNDP, and the World Bank that had a goal of reducing the number of cases of malaria by one half by the year 2010. This program has had limited success in great part because of lack of adequate funding.[8] Recently renewed efforts to bring the disease under control have been funded by new organizations, such as the Bill and Melinda Gates Foundation[9] and The Global Fund to Fight AIDS, Tuberculosis, and Malaria.

The population at risk for malaria increased significantly during the 20th century. The at-risk population grew from 0.9 billion to 3.0 billion people from 1900 to 2002, with 48% of the world's population currently at risk.[10] Of all cases, 90% occur in sub-Saharan Africa, although malaria exists in more than 100 countries. It resulted in over 600,000 deaths in 2012, 77% of which were children under the age of 5 years, while 207 million people remained infected. Martens and Hall report that migration of populations caused by urban relocation and the flight of refugees increases the distribution of malaria regionally into areas that were previously malaria free. This type of population migration results from crises, such as environmental changes, economic necessity, war and conflict, and natural disasters, all of which result in populations moving to neighboring areas to escape these conditions.[12] Often this results in people moving into city shanty towns without any services, such as potable water, electricity, or sanitation. These conditions are more likely to exist in areas where poverty is common and where malaria is endemic.[11] To complicate matters more, the surveillance, treatment, public health interventions, and disease reservoirs vary from one region to another, making efforts in eradication all the more difficult.

Because of the debilitating nature of malaria, the disease has a major impact on the economies of the regions and countries where it is endemic, reducing productivity, lowering rates of economic growth, impeding development, and discouraging savings and investment.[13] Control of malaria mostly has a clear association with economic development, although up until now malarial control has mostly occurred outside of Africa. After an area becomes malaria free, the growth in the economy over the next five years is significantly higher than neighboring countries for which malaria remains a significant problem. A study of the association between malaria and economic growth looked at the years between 1965 and 1990 and found that in areas with high incidence and prevalence of malaria, the economy grew 1.3% less per person per year, but a reduction in malaria by 10.0% is associated with a 0.3% increase in GDP growth.[14]

Zika Virus

Over the past two decades, we have experienced a number of emerging or reemerging infectious diseases, posing new threats in new places, for example, West Nile virus becoming endemic in North America. While we have eradicated smallpox and hope to soon have eradicated polio, many new diseases are vector-borne, making eradication highly unlikely, if not impossible. An excellent example of an emerging virus is the Zika virus that was brought to prominent attention in 2015.[15]

Zika virus, of little significance throughout equatorial African and Asia between 1960 and 1980, emerged in the South Pacific as an epidemic on Yap Island in 2007 in a mild form. In 2013 to 2014, it emerged again in a number of South Pacific Island nations, and for the first time its association with birth defects was noted. In March of 2015, Brazil detected its first case, and by January 2106, it was in 18 additional countries in South America and in the Caribbean. In July of 2016, the United States announced its first case and found an endemic area in north Miami.[16]

This disease, spread primarily by the *Aedes aegypti* and *Aedes albopichis* mosquitoes, has no treatment or vaccination. Furthermore, the virus can also be spread from pregnant mothers to their fetuses, through sexual contact with partners, and theoretically through blood products, although there are no recorded cases of this type of transmission to date. These mosquitoes are commonly found throughout the world in certain climate zones, including the southern United States and Europe. These zones are expanding each year with climate change and global warming. These same mosquitoes transmit dengue and chikungunya disease. Our efforts today are left to reducing mosquito populations in infected areas. Unfortunately, widespread spraying of insecticides results in its own problems of toxic exposure for wildlife. In many areas of the world, populations are left to reduce standing water, which serves as breeding sites. These mosquitoes are both daytime and nighttime biters, so the use of bed nets is limited in its impact. Only three insecticides for personal use are effective and include DEET, IR 3535, and icaridin.[17]

The emergence of Zika on the world stage is an excellent example of "one health." This new discipline looks at the entire environment, physical and social, and the interaction and interconnectedness of all things in the environment that contribute to human health. In the case of Zika, climate changes and increasing temperatures have increased the zones where these two mosquitoes can live and breed. Global travel has moved the virus from Africa and Asia to Central and South America, the Caribbean, and North America. Pesticide use is limited and may contribute to further deterioration of other species' habitats and may harm humans. Social and environmental systems in many countries are not prepared to develop and enforce policies that might contain the virus' spread. Healthcare systems are not prepared to test for and treat the disease nor are they set up to deal with the terrible consequences of the microcephaly associated with the transmission of the virus from mother to fetus. The concept of one health is to understand the complete interconnectedness of all human, social, and physical systems on the planet and its impact on human health and well-being.[18]

Waterborne Diseases

Waterborne diseases generally invade the gastrointestinal system, although some parasitic forms found in water can enter the body through the skin, such as schistosomiasis (blood fluke/trematode), and cause damage to other areas of the human body. Of particular importance are those infections that are caused by viruses (rotaviruses), bacteria (*Vibrio cholerae, E. coli*), and parasites (*Entamoeba histolytica*), to name a few. In addition, water is critical in the reproduction and development of a number of insect vectors that contribute to disease burden. Finally, water is a place where a number of toxins, chemicals, and metals concentrate, such as arsenic, mercury, and chromium.[19]

These pose health hazards as they enter the food chain, as well as through direct exposure to skin during water activities close to sources of these contaminants. In the developing world, many of the infections result in diarrhea that can often be life threatening because of loss of fluids and salts. Chronic diarrheal infections can lead to poor absorption of nutrients, malnutrition, malaise, stunted growth, and chronic disability. The impact on children of waterborne diseases in developing countries can be devastating and is a leading cause of death among children worldwide. In all regions of the world, flooding and contamination of water systems can cause disease, especially with climate change and an increase in the number, duration, and severity of storms and flooding.[20]

Diarrheal Disease

Each day over 2,000 children die from diarrheal illness worldwide. Approximately 11% of child deaths are due to diarrheal illness globally, and 1 in every 9 children under the age of 5 dies of this disease. For children with HIV/AIDS, the mortality rate is 11 times greater. Diarrheal illness in children leads to poor growth and to disabilities associated with cognitive development. In addition, diarrheal illness is a major contributor to malnutrition. In reverse, malnutrition contributes to the susceptibility of children to the pathogens that cause diarrhea. Although there are many causes of diarrheal illness, the most prevalent cause is rotaviruses.[21]

The most common mode of transmission of all diarrheal illnesses is through contaminated water (88%), water contaminated with feces. The most common cause in children is the rotavirus, which is present in contaminated water sources. Around 5% of all deaths in children under the age of 5 years are caused by this specific virus. In diarrheal episodes seen in outpatient clinics in developing countries, up to 35% of them are caused by rotaviruses.[22] As a cause of death, the rotavirus is estimated to cause 440,000 deaths per year, 2 million hospitalizations per year, and over 110 million visits to clinics.[23-25] A specific vaccine for rotavirus is available and has been determined to be highly effective. Vaccination programs for rotavirus infection, however, face the numerous challenges other vaccinations face in developing countries, many of which are underfunded, poorly organized, and have limited access to needed supplies.

The chain of infection for nearly all diarrheal illness is through fecal contamination of water or food, although more commonly water; and the level of sanitation present in most developing countries remains a major obstacle to relieving this burden. Today, nearly 1.1 billion people do not have access to a clean and sustainable water source,[26] and 84% of those people live in rural areas. In these areas, the lack of potable water for cleaning and preparing food, hand washing, and bathing, not to mention drinking, results in a continuous cycle of diarrheal diseases. This problem is compounded by the fact that 2.6 billion people in the world have no access to a sanitary toilet facility and must defecate in uncontrolled areas. This contributes to the problem in many ways, as uncovered excrement can contaminate food and water supplies, and an inability to wash your hands properly can facilitate the spread of pathogens from person to person. In developed countries, the 20th century saw the introduction of clean water sources for the bulk of their populations, as well as municipal wastewater disposal. This single achievement is cited as one of the major reasons developed countries saw a substantial drop in infectious diseases in the early part of the 20th century.[27]

There are a number of efforts to reduce this disease, starting with an active vaccination program for rotaviruses. Secondly, there is promotion of exclusive breastfeeding of infants for the first 6 months of life.[28] UNICEF estimates that 13% of all under-five deaths in developing countries could be prevented by exclusive breastfeeding, making it the most powerful means of preventing child mortality. In terms of the importance of healthcare systems, mortality from diarrheal diseases can also be prevented through the use of oral rehydration therapy (ORT). It is estimated that the lives of 50 million children have been saved by the use of ORT over the last 25 years and that ORT therapy is a significant factor in the reduction of yearly mortality from diarrheal diseases from over 5 million per year in the 1980s to just under 2 million a year.[29] Finally, the improvement of water supplies for drinking and the improvement of hygiene and sanitation are vital to bringing an end to this illness.[30]

Cholera

Cholera is caused by the bacteria, *Vibrio cholerae*, and is one of three diseases that is required to be reported to the WHO.[1] In 1992, the WHO organized the Global Task Force on Cholera Control to reduce the number of outbreaks and to address the social and economic conditions that lead to periodic epidemics.[31] Cholera is endemic to parts of India and Bangladesh, but periodic outbreaks occur in South America and Africa as well. This is a disease that can spread quickly, especially during natural or man-made disasters that disrupt water and sewage treatment systems. Like other etiological agents that cause diarrheal illness, cholera is spread through contaminated water, exposure to feces, and person-to-person contact, especially between patients and caregivers. Cholera takes advantage of crisis and overcrowding.

Cholera is an extremely virulent disease and can cause death in both children and adults within hours of onset of diarrhea, causing severe dehydration. Of those with cholera, 75% are asymptomatic but continue to shed the bacteria for 7 to 14 days, making transmission to others more likely. During periods of environmental stress due to disasters, healthcare workers and first responders should be aware of water and sewage treatment systems that have been compromised, as well as be vigilant for signs of the disease.

Following the earthquake in Haiti, a serious outbreak of cholera occurred. Politically, this has become a point of contention between the government of Haiti and the United Nations. It is believed that U.N. healthcare workers from Nepal, who came to Haiti to respond to this emergency, were responsible for bringing cholera with them and contaminating the water supply in Haiti.[32]

Respiratory Infections

Respiratory infections are generally categorized as upper or lower respiratory infections. Those of the upper respiratory tract include the common cold, viral and group A streptococcal pharyngitis, and middle ear infections. Upper respiratory infections are found worldwide and in all populations regardless of socioeconomic status or general living conditions. Generally, when indicated, treatment of upper respiratory infections is successful, and as a result, they do not contribute to mortality. Many of these types of infections require only supportive care.

Lower respiratory infections, however, can often be very serious and lead to death, especially among children.[33] Lower respiratory infections are caused by viruses and bacteria, often simultaneously. The most common viral causes of lower respiratory infection are influenza, parainfluenza, syncytial virus, and adenovirus. Bacterial causes include *Streptococcus pneumoniae, Haemophilus influenzae,* and *Staphylococcus aureus*. It is estimated that over 2 million children die from pneumonia and other lower respiratory infections each year, making it the number one killer of children less than 5 years old. Worldwide, the mortality of children under the age of 5 years from pneumonia is 12%, not including neonatal deaths with pneumonia-related etiology. Most of these deaths are in poorer countries; however, children who live in poverty in industrialized countries are at greater risk of dying from pneumonia than those not living in poverty.[34] Children from low-income groups are exposed to a number of risk factors, including indoor air pollution, cigarette smoke, poor housing and nutrition, and limited access to health care for proper diagnosis and treatment.

Respiratory infections are spread from person to person through aerosols (coughing and breathing) when close, through person-to-person contact such as with the face and hands, and through inanimate objects that have been touched or used for eating and drinking and then used by others. The campaign for handwashing and coughing in your arm is an effort in the United States to reduce transmission of these types of respiratory illnesses. In addition, the widespread use of hand wipes and disinfectants is the result of trying to reduce respiratory illnesses in developed countries.

Tuberculosis

Tuberculosis is caused by *Mycobacterium tuberculosis*, spread through aerosol exposure from an infected person, and is considered a problem for every low-income country in the world. It is estimated that nearly one-third of the world's population is infected.[1] The immune systems of healthy people successfully keep this organism in check, even while the bacteria remain alive in their systems; however, with a compromised immune system, often associated with circumstances such as poverty, poor nutrition, and stress, the infection may become active and create a clinical case. In such circumstances, the immune system can no longer protect the body from the organism. Other conditions in developing countries that contribute to the transmission of tuberculosis are close living conditions, due to overcrowding, and lack of healthcare services that could successfully identify and treat new cases of tuberculosis. Even in developed countries, the public health systems must be vigilant for new cases of tuberculosis, especially among those with impaired immune systems, including people living with HIV, and those infected with drug-resistant strains of the bacteria.

The treatment recommended for tuberculosis is multiple drug therapy. Success in limiting the spread of tuberculosis is dependent on rapid detection and treatment of active cases in this manner. Some industrialized countries have historically treated asymptomatic infected individuals with daily doses of the drug isoniazid for up to one year, but this approach has led to drug resistance. In developing countries, the strategy for treatment has been a "directly observed short-course therapy," which has proved to be more effective in circumstances where constraining factors would otherwise result in noncompliance with a daily regimen.[35] Also, in many low-income countries, infants are given a BCG (bacilli Calmette-Guérin) vaccination. This has been successful in reducing tuberculous meningitis but has had limited success in treating pulmonary tuberculosis. Currently, the biggest concern in controlling tuberculosis is antimicrobial drug resistance.

Multidrug-resistant tuberculosis (MDR TB) became increasingly more prevalent in all areas of the world, developing and developed, in the mid-1980s. Treatment of TB with antibiotics started in 1947 and had a dramatic effect in reducing TB in industrialized countries. Until the advent of antibiotic treatment, the mortality rate for people with TB was 50%. In 1985, MDR TB appeared. This new development is believed to be the result of patients not taking their medication properly (i.e., not completing doses over time). In the 1990s, new strains appeared that are resistant to virtually all antituberculosis drugs, and the mortality rate returned to 50% among those infected with these new strains, which are referred to as extensively drug-resistant tuberculosis, or XDR TB. These fast-paced events have taken us nearly full circle, back to pre-1947. Tuberculosis is once again a major fixture of concern among public health and medical personnel.[36(p152-153)]

New concerns for tuberculosis have emerged as people living with HIV have become increasingly at risk for contracting tuberculosis because of the compromised nature of their immune systems. In sub-Saharan Africa, it is estimated that 60% of tuberculosis patients are also living with HIV/AIDS.[37] Among infected people in general, only 10% develop active cases of tuberculosis, but among those living with HIV, 50% develop active cases.[38] In addition, increases in homelessness, incarceration, and even urban hospitalization have contributed to the transmission and increase of TB. Internationally, the movements of people through immigration and as refugees of war make the control of this disease more complex, as well as more urgent.

Influenza

There are three general viruses that cause seasonal influenza: viruses A, B, and C. In addition, there are subtypes of virus A. Virus C causes a mild form of influenza. Seasonal and sporadic outbreaks of influenza are generally caused by viruses A and B. Influenza has a nasty history, causing pandemics in 1918 (Spanish flu H1N1), 1957 (Asian flu, H2N2), and 1968 (Hong Kong flu, H3N2). Because there are multiple strains of influenza and these strains experience genetic shifts from time to time, new strains can appear with new characteristics and infect populations that may have been exposed previously but now are at risk. Since 1977 eight new strains have appeared and caused outbreaks in various locations. Of particular interest is the strain H5N1 that is found in birds and pigs and makes the jump to humans during close contact. See **TABLE 2-4** for influenza outbreaks and variations in strains.

There are a limited number of antiviral drugs to combat influenza. In addition, replication of the viruses often results in genetic shifts through coding mutations, making it difficult for public health professionals to determine which virus subtype will be responsible for illness in any given season or global location. Each year, a vaccine is made with the best guess for what the flu season will bring; sometimes it is on the mark, and other times it results in an ineffective vaccine for that season's influenza. The most common reservoir for influenza viruses is aquatic birds. Bats have also been implicated. People at greatest risk are generally children, older adults, and people with compromised immune systems. Immunity for some may exist based on prior exposure to a specific strain earlier in life. Since influenza is spread through airborne droplets, droplets on surfaces, and direct person-to-person contact, good hygiene is basic to preventing transmission.

Sexually Transmitted Diseases

Until the advent of HIV in the early 1980s, little time or interest was spent on sexually transmitted infections (STIs), especially from a global perspective. Given the nature of HIV with its high mortality rate and extensive comorbidities, HIV infection and STIs have taken on lives of their own in the collective minds of governments. Rates of more common STIs, such as syphilis and gonorrhea, are often predictors of previously undetected HIV infections. Because of this relationship, surveillance of STIs is an important part of public health, as is disease prevention through education, provision of barrier prophylaxes, family planning, and treatment. Most recently, the emergence of the Zika virus raises further concerns because it is a disease that causes flu-like symptoms, is generally spread by mosquitoes, and is now found to pass between sex partners and ultimately between mother and fetus, with potentially catastrophic results.[40]

STI control has many obstacles. STIs are often asymptomatic. There are few treatments that are easy to administer in a single dose, and worldwide, there is a dearth of easy and inexpensive laboratory tests available for detection. In addition, social and cultural practices often aid in the transmission process. This includes practices of polygamy, attitudes toward sexual conquests among young men, the wide use of sex workers around the world, beliefs regarding the use of condoms, taboos surrounding the teaching of sex education and family planning, and limited access to health care for women.

The primary etiologic agents of STIs are bacteria and viruses. Tracking of STIs is complicated by the fact that some—including syphilis, gonorrhea, HIV/AIDS, and hepatitis B—can also be transmitted by blood products, whereas other STIs, like chlamydia, can be transmitted through physical contact between mother and newborn child (see **TABLE 2-5**).

TABLE 2-4 Influenza Epidemics and New Strains in Humans

Year	Influenza virus	Impact
Epidemics		
1918	Spanish flu, H1N1	Worldwide: 20–50 million infected, 500,000 deaths
1957/1958	Asian flu, H2N2	Worldwide: 70,000 deaths
1968	Hong Kong flu, H3N2	Worldwide: 34,000 deaths
1976	Swine influenza, U.S.	4 infected, 1 death
New strains in humans		
1977	H1N1	Emerged in northern China: children and young adults susceptible
1997	Avian flu, H5N1	Hong Kong: 18 infected, 6 deaths * first influenza virus transmitted directly from birds to people
1999	H9N2	Hong Kong: 2 children infected
2002	H7N2	Virginia: 1 poultry worker infected
2003	H5N1	Hong Kong: 2 hospitalized, 2 deaths ** family with recent travel to China
2003	H7N7	Netherlands: 89 poultry workers infected
2003	H7N2	New York: 1 infected
2003	H9N3	Hong Kong: 1 child infected
2004	H5N1	Thailand and Vietnam: 47 infected, 34 deaths
2004	H7N3	Canada: 2 poultry workers infected
2004	H10N7	Egypt: 2 children of a poultry worker infected
2005	H5N1	Cambodia: 4 deaths Indonesia: 7 infected, 4 deaths
2005	H5N1	Worldwide: 142 infected, 74 deaths
2006	H5N1	Turkey: 2 infected, 2 deaths China: 20 infected, 7 deaths Iraq: 1 infected, 1 death Azerbaijan: 7 infected, 5 deaths Djibouti***: 115 infected, 79 deaths *** First new strain in Africa
2007	H5N1	Indonesia, Cambodia, China, Laos, Myanmar, Nigeria, Pakistan, Vietnam: 88 infected, 59 deaths

(*continues*)

TABLE 2-4 Influenza Epidemics and New Strains in Humans (continued)

Year	Influenza virus	Impact
2007	H7N7	United Kingdom: 1 poultry worker infected
2008	H5N1	Bangladesh, Cambodia, China, Egypt, Indonesia, Vietnam: 40 infected
2009	H1N1	Mexico, and spread rapidly to other countries; new strain of Spanish flu.

Modified from Heymann DL. *Control of Communicable Disease Manual*. Washington, DC: American Public Health Association; 2015: 306–309.

The link in now well established between human papillomaviruses and various cancers, including cervical, vulvar, vaginal, penile, anal, and oropharyngeal. The availability of a vaccination for these viruses has brought this issue to the forefront of public health policy. The vaccination holds out hope for reducing the incidence of some types of cancer, but at the same time, it comes with problems of cost, distribution in poor countries, and ethical issues surrounding the use of this vaccine in girls and boys as young as 11 years old. Professionals believe that in order for the vaccination to be successful, it must be administered early before the chance of being sexually active is real. Given that the total mortality for cervical cancer worldwide was estimated to be over 300,000 in 2013,[48] the decision of whether to vaccinate against HPV highlights

TABLE 2-5 Principle Sexually Transmitted Diseases of Interest to Global Public Health

Etiological agent	Disease	Transmission to newborns	Transmission through blood products
Treponema pallidum (spirochete)	Syphilis	yes	yes
Neisseria gonorrhoeae (bacteria)	Gonorrhea, pelvic inflammatory disease	yes	yes
Chlamydia trachomatis (bacteria)	Cervicitis, urethritis, lymphogranuloma venereum, pelvic inflammatory disease	yes	no
Human immunodeficiency virus	AIDS	yes	yes
Herpes simplex virus	Genital herpes	yes	no
Human papillomavirus	Genital warts, cervical dysplasia, cervical carcinoma	unknown	no
Hepatitis B virus	Acute and chronic hepatitis, cirrhosis, hepatocellular carcinoma	yes	yes
Zika virus	Flu-like symptoms	yes	Unknown

Data from Merson MH, Black RE, Mills AJ. *International Health: Diseases, Programs, Systems, and Policies*. 2nd ed. Sudbury, MA: Jones and Bartlett Publishers, 2006; Centers for Disease Control and Prevention. Zika Virus: What you need to know. http://www.cdc.gov/zika/about/needtoknow.html. August 4, 2016. Accessed August 20, 2016; Heymann DL. *Control of Communicable Disease Manual*. Washington, DC: American Public Health Association; 2015: 99–101, 237–241, 257–264, 275–282, 287–294, 298–301, 595–600.

the difficult dilemma faced by healthcare providers when deciding how to allocate funds. In contrast, the measles vaccination, which cost under US $1 for a full series, is still underused in many countries around the world. Measles has been responsible for over 700,000 deaths annually, all of which could have been prevented by properly administered vaccinations. In the United States and other developed countries, the wisdom of paying for this vaccine is evidence-based, and most healthcare insurance now pays for this inoculation.[41(p298-301)]

HIV/AIDS

When HIV emerged in the early 1980s, the developed world was not prepared for a new infectious disease. Many healthcare professionals were surprised and were caught unprepared. However, the onset of this epidemic inspired efforts worldwide not only to confront HIV but also to put renewed emphasis on all infectious diseases and their identification, control, and treatment. In addition, the emergence of HIV and its rapid spread around the world, as well as its diffusion to different types of populations through sexual contact, have served to identify the potential for rapid changes in disease patterns. Factors contributing to these changes include globalization, cultural and social contexts, resource availability, and the increasing ease of international transportation. The emergence of HIV/AIDS provided a new infectious disease challenge for all of public health and healthcare delivery.[42]

In 2015, 1.1 million people died of AIDS, while 37.6 million continued to live with HIV/AIDS, of which 25.6 million lived in sub-Saharan Africa. During that time, there were 2.1 million new cases. Although since 2000 there has been a 35% reduction in new cases, the challenges remain. Only 54% of those infected know their status. One of the most powerful ways to control new infections is to find and confirm new infections and engage in counseling on transmission and treatment. It goes back to the old public health practice of case finding. A rapid diagnostic test is available, and results can be obtained within one day. Globally, however, many areas of the developing world do not have these tests available, and determination of infection is either not done or it is time consuming and expensive. Many are unable to gain cooperation for testing due to social and cultural factors. The advent of treatment is making an impact for those who can obtain the antiretrovirals (ARVs). At the end of 2015, it was reported that 17.0 million people living with HIV/AIDS were under treatment with ARV. Foundations such as the Bill and Melinda Gates Foundation seek to find vaccines and to develop long-acting prevention measures, as well as to expand and simplify HIV treatments. Their focus has been in the worst-hit areas of sub-Saharan Africa. They have provided more than US $3.0 billion to the cause and have partnered with The Global Fund to Fight AIDS, Tuberculosis, and Malaria.[43] The Global Fund is directly responsible for ensuring that 9.2 million people, of the total 17.0 million who take ARVs, receive ARVs through their partnerships with local experts in areas with the most need around the globe. The fund brings donors together to make a major impact on HIV/AIDS, as well as tuberculosis and malaria.[44] The importance of health care and public health systems meeting the challenge of HIV/AIDS is vital for success in limiting this terrible disease.

Transmission of HIV is primarily through exchange of bodily fluids during unprotected sex, sharing needles, and through blood transfusion. Having another STI puts a person at higher risk of being positive for HIV. The importance of diagnosing, treating, doing partner/contact follow-up, counseling, encouraging male circumcision, and getting people on ARV cannot be underestimated. This disease, left unchecked, can have long-term social consequences. In some areas of Africa, nearly an entire generation has succumbed to AIDS, leaving societies without workers, parents, or incomes, creating a myriad of other problems. The good news, as stated previously, is that the number of new cases decreased by 35% between 2000 and 2015, indicating that the constant and tireless work of scientists, healthcare providers, and public health professionals can, and does, make an impact.[41(p287-294)]

▶ Zoonotic Infections

Zoonosis is "an infection or infectious agent transmitted under natural conditions from vertebrate animals to humans."[41(p706)] The interaction between people and animals can lead to diseases, some common, such as salmonella (*Salmonella enterica*) from uncooked or undercooked turkey or chicken, or direct handling of infected animals. Other less prevalent diseases include hantavirus disease, a hemorrhagic disease contracted through contact with rodent urine and feces; *Campylobacter enteritis* (*C. jejuni*) that is contracted through ingestion of undercooked meat or directly handling puppies, kittens, or farm animals; tularemia (*Francisella tularensis*) a bacterial zoonotic infection contracted through handling infected animals, especially during hunting and dressing small game such as rabbits and hares; and trichinellosis (*Trichinella spiralis*), an intestinal nematode caused by ingestion of uncooked infected pork.[41]

Avian Influenza

There are seven types of influenza (type A) viruses that can be transmitted directly to humans from animals and cause illness, but the one of most concern is H5N1, which causes avian flu. Avian flu surfaced in Southeast Asia in 1997 with the first case of bird-to-person transmission of H5N1. It is now considered to be endemic in poultry in Southeast Asia, posing a serious hazard for people routinely handling poultry in processing, markets, and in farming. There have been only a few cases that have demonstrated direct transmission from one human to another and only between a severely ill patient and close caregivers. Outbreaks of avian flu among poultry and migratory birds is carefully monitored, as are any incidences of human cases. The case fatality rate of this disease in humans is high (30%–50%). In addition to birds, H5N1 can be transmitted from sick pigs to humans who are in direct contact with them, although this is rare, especially in developed countries where agricultural practices reduce the risk of disease. In 1976 at Fort Dix, four soldiers became infected with swine flu, which was transmitted from person to person, creating a panic and subsequent vaccination program for swine influenza in the United States. This was a rare incident.[41(p314–317)]

In the case of these types of diseases, it is incumbent upon the public health surveillance systems and laboratories to quickly identify cases and confirm them through laboratories. The Laboratory Response Network (LRN) maintains a global system of laboratories that work together to help rapidly identify pathogens. The LRN was created in 1999 between the Federal Bureau of Investigation and the Association of Public Health Laboratories. It joins state and local public health laboratories, federal and military laboratories, and international laboratories in Canada, the United Kingdom, Australia, Mexico, and South Korea. The federal laboratories in the United States include those at the Centers for Disease Control, Food and Drug Administration, and the U.S. Department of Agriculture, which can do animal testing.[45]

Ebola Virus

Ebola virus was first identified in 1976 in the Congo with 318 cases, of which 280 died. As the virus was researched, it was found that the reservoir in nature is among several species of bats. It was also found that the virus infects a variety of primate species, resulting in die-offs of primate populations in local areas. The spread to humans is the result of contact between humans and infected primates, alive or dead. Monkey meat, for example, is commonly prepared and eaten in sub-Saharan Africa, and if not cooked thoroughly, Ebola can be transmitted; it can also be contracted simply by handling a primate.

Including the first outbreak, there have been 17 outbreaks between 1976 and 2014. The last outbreak was in the West African nations of Guinea, Liberia, Sierra Leone, Nigeria, and Senegal, resulting in 3,707 cases and 1,848 deaths. Due to the huge international response, sending in nurses, doctors, public health professionals, lab workers, and the military, two cases were imported to the United States, of which one person died and two additional healthcare workers were infected in U.S. hospitals.[46]

Once humans are infected with Ebola virus, person-to-person transmission is quick and aggressive. Any contact with infected blood, urine, vomit, feces, secretions, organs, or semen can cause infection. Given that the symptoms of patients include diarrhea, vomiting, and bleeding from body orifices, caregivers are at immediate and high risk. Proper care for healthcare workers is to use full-barrier protection, including respirators, face shields, and nonporous garments and gloves while caring for patients. There is no antiviral known to cure Ebola at this time.[41(p173–178)]

Because of the ease of transmission and the high mortality rate, Ebola outbreaks, especially the one in 2014, raise major concerns for containing outbreaks, managing patients and healthcare workers, and providing supportive health services. These issues are paramount in the minds of national leaders around the world and especially among international healthcare agencies and workers. In order to address these types of outbreaks, emergency preparedness is essential, not only for those health and public health systems and healthcare workers in country, but for all governments and healthcare workers. The ability to bring diseases, such as Ebola (easily transmitted to other humans and with high mortality rates), to other countries was demonstrated in 2014. As a result, the United States and many developed nations have structured new policies and made preparations to engage in containing these outbreaks both at home and abroad. Unfortunately, countries in sub-Saharan Africa are some of the poorest in the world, have the worst infrastructure, especially for healthcare services, to deal with a disease as devastating as Ebola. In addition, there are many local, cultural, religious, and social customs that increase the likelihood of transmission. Ebola has served to demonstrate the need for all nations to come together and work on solutions to diseases that diminish human life.[36(p140–144)]

The Future of Infectious Disease

Infectious disease clearly demonstrates the need for good public health and healthcare systems globally. Prevention, early diagnosis, and treatment are the cornerstones of disease control. The 10 essential services of public health mentioned in the introduction of this chapter begin to come into focus as critical to limiting the impact of infectious disease.

The challenges we are facing today are great, and all impact the emergence, reemergence, and transmission of communicable disease. These challenges include climate change, violence/war, population migration, rapid global transportation and communication, declining infrastructure, poverty, antibiotic resistance, and viral and bacterial mutations.

Climate Change

Climate change has an impact on all countries. The United States has suffered an inordinate number of serious storms that have brought flooding and destruction, as well as extreme drought that threatens water supplies and results in serious fires.[47] These types of events are also seen worldwide. Droughts cause many to migrate to other areas. Floods increase breeding areas of disease vectors and increase waterborne diseases; sea levels rising causes disruption to coastal communities; and the pollution associated with climate change and the warming of the earth are clearly linked to many diseases. These diseases include asthma (increased allergens), cardiovascular disease, insufficient food resources, and increases of stress. The importance of climate change cannot be underestimated.[48]

Population Migration

Migration of populations is a critical issue in infectious disease. Bringing populations together introduces new disease agents, and many new migrants live in close quarters, have poor sanitation and water sources, and limited access to health care. Populations move for many reasons, and today we find that war and anarchy (no government) are principle reasons. The 2016 estimate of the number of forcibly displaced people on a global basis was 65.3 million. More than 21.0 million people were in refugee status, and 10.0 million people were considered stateless (denied a nationality). Each day, 34,000 more people are displaced.[49]

Countries with the highest number of refugees have a high burden put on their own resources. The countries with the most refugees are Turkey (2.5 million refugees), Pakistan (1.6 million), Lebanon (1.1 million), Iran (980,000), Ethiopia (736,000), and Jordan (665,000). In addition, drought moves farming families into urban areas, as does perceived economic opportunity through the mechanism of "urbanization." Concentrations of displaced people in urban areas have the same environmental characteristics as found in refugee situations: crowding, poor sanitation, inadequate drinking water, lack of health care, poor nutrition, and exposure to vectors.

Poverty

Poverty takes its toll as poorer people in all countries experience lower health status than their wealthier counterparts, and wealthier nations consistently experience better health status among their citizens, as compared to poorer countries. Although the millennium goal of cutting the poverty rate in half from 1990 to 2015 was actually met in 2010, 12.7% of the world's population (896.0 million) live at or below US $1.90 per day, and 2.1 billion people live at or below $3.10. Poverty contributes to the infectious disease burden because of substandard housing, poorer educational systems and opportunities, less access to quality healthcare services, crumbling infrastructure (roads, water systems, wastewater systems), increased pollution, and often more violence. Lifting people out of poverty improves health status, and improving economic opportunities for all is an important part of improving health at all levels and reducing communicable diseases and noncommunicable diseases.[50]

Drug-Resistant Infectious Bacteria

Drug-resistant etiological agents are on the rise and are already contributing to an increase in morbidity and mortality. As discussed previously in the section on tuberculosis, its reemergence as a disease to be reckoned with is due to the development of resistance to common treatments by the bacteria itself. For 70 years healthcare professionals have successfully relied upon a wide choice of antibiotics to cure a number of infectious diseases, but over time, a number of these "miracle drugs" have become less effective as the bacteria has found ways to resist the effects of the antibiotics.[51]

The Centers for Disease Control and Prevention has identified 18 bacteria that are resistant to antibiotics. **TABLE 2-6** outlines these 18 organisms and puts them into the three categories outlined by the CDC: urgent threat, serious threat, and concerning threat.

TABLE 2-6 Eighteen Drug-Resistant Bacteria, Threat Level, and Disease/Symptoms

Organism	Disease/symptoms
Urgent threat	
Clostridium difficile	Diarrhea associated with hospital stays
Carbapenem-resistant Enterobacteriaceae	Bloodstream infection associated with hospital stays, 50% mortality rate
Neisseria gonorrhoeae	Common STI, gonorrhea
Serious threat	
Multidrug-resistant (MDR) *Acinetobacter*	Pneumonia and bloodstream infections among the critically ill
Drug-resistant (DR) *Campylobacter*	Fever, diarrhea
Fluconazole-resistant *Candida*	Fungus, on skin or in bloodstream
Extended-spectrum β-lactamase–producing Enterobacteriaceae	Extended-spectrum β-lactamase: enzyme that allows bacteria resistance to various penicillins and cephalosporins
Vancomycin-resistant *Enterococcus*	Surgical sites, bloodstream infections
MDR *Pseudomonas aeruginosa*	Associated with hospitals; can attack numerous sites
MDR *Salmonella enterica* serotype Typhi	Typhoid fever
DR Nontyphoidal *Salmonella*	Diarrhea, fever, associated with foodborne illness
DR *Shigella*	Diarrheal illness with fever and cramps
Methicillin-resistant *Staphylococcus aureus*	Skin and wound infections
DR *Streptococcus pneumoniae*	Leading cause of pneumonia and meningitis
DR tuberculosis	Tuberculosis
Concerned	
Vancomycin-resistant *Staphylococcus aureus*	Found on skin and associated with surgical sites and use of catheters and ventilators
Erythromycin-resistant group A *Streptococcus*	Associated with pharyngitis, toxic shock syndrome, necrotizing fasciitis (flesh-eating bacteria), scarlet fever, rheumatic fever, and impetigo
Clindamycin-resistant group B *Streptococcus*	Bloodstream infections, pneumonia, meningitis, and skin infections

Data from Centers for Disease Control and Prevention. Antibiotic/Antimicrobial Resistance: Biggest Threats. https://www.cdc.gov/drugresistance/biggest_threats.html. September 8, 2016. Accessed August 18, 2016.

Lack of Infrastructure

Many countries lack the infrastructure needed to reduce the number of infectious diseases in their region. Most important of these is providing drinkable water to populations, as well as improving sanitation (wastewater treatment). Globally, in 2016, 780.0 million people lived without improved water resources and 2.5 billion people lived without improved sanitation. Seven out of 10 of these people lived in rural areas. It is estimated that for every US $1 invested in improving these most basic life-assuring systems, the economic benefit is between $5 and $46. In the early part of the 20th century in the United States, infectious diseases were rampant, but with the building of water treatment facilities and wastewater management systems, infectious disease rapidly declined. It is expected that the improvement of water resources and sanitation in many areas of the developing world will see many of the same benefits, reducing waterborne, soil-transmitted, and hygiene-related diseases.[52]

Globalization

In a world of rapid transportation and communication, the spread of infectious disease has become a concern to all public health and healthcare workers worldwide. As demonstrated by the Ebola outbreak in 2014 in West Africa, the introduction of West Nile virus to the United States, and the spreading of the new Zika virus to Florida in a matter of months, developed countries cannot rest on their past achievements. People living in developed countries can no longer turn a blind eye to poverty, violence, political strife, and diseases that plague people around the world. Globalization leads us to know and understand the injustices suffered by others, just as rapid communication brings a glimpse of the developed world to all others on the planet. This interconnectedness of us all may lead to improvements in health status for everyone. Today, the phrase "no man is an island" is exceedingly poignant. **TABLE 2-7** indicates some of the most recent outbreaks of infectious disease and transmission.

TABLE 2-7 Examples of Emerging Infectious Disease

Disease (agent)	Source of emergence/reemergence	Transmission	Comments	Prevention
West Nile virus[53,54]	Uganda 1937; New York 1999, 59-patient outbreak; now a U.S. endemic	Mosquitoes; birds are intermediary hosts	Severe cases have 1 in 150 fatalities; no specific treatment; no vaccination	Prevent mosquito bites; survey migratory bird die-offs; monitor domestic flocks for disease; reduce standing water
Severe acute respiratory syndrome[1,55] SARS-associated coronavirus	Southern China 2002, from animal reservoir (civet)	Person to person by respiratory droplets	Overall case fatality rates are 14%–15%, but over 50% in those 64 or older; severe pneumonia symptoms	Identify and isolate patients; quarantine exposed people; restrict air travel
Ebola hemorrhagic fever virus[56,57]	Zaire 1976; probably caused by primate contact; from the *Filoviridae* family of RNA viruses	Person to person through blood and secretions	44% to 88% mortality rates	Diagnose early; implement hemorrhagic fever isolation and barrier nursing care techniques; sterilize equipment; avoid contact with blood and secretions

(continues)

TABLE 2-7 Examples of Emerging Infectious Disease (continued)

Disease (agent)	Source of emergence/reemergence	Transmission	Comments	Prevention
Avian influenza[58,59]	Thailand 2004; Vietnam 2005, first human-to-human cases; Azerbaijan 2006; Indonesia 2006; Vietnam 2006	Healthy wild birds; domestic birds (poultry); person to person in small family groups, especially caregivers	50% human mortality rate; 90% mortality in bird flocks	Early case finding and diagnosis; monitor for future virus mutation; resistant to antiviral drugs amantadine and rimantadine
Methicillin-resistant *Staphylococcus aureus*[60-62] Vanco mycin-intermediate/resistant *Staphylococcus aureus*		Person to person; contact with contaminated surfaces; healthcare personnel who may spread infection among patients	20% mortality rate for invasive infection	Identify early; increase sanitation in healthcare settings; address community reservoirs in health clubs; resistant to methicillin, oxacillin, penicillin, amoxicillin, vancomycin
Multidrug-resistant tuberculosis[61,63] Extensively resistant tuberculosis		Person to person through the air; people with HIV particularly susceptible	Not available, varies significantly between countries and people with and without HIV	Identify and treat active tuberculosis cases early; stress importance of complete treatment; resistant to isoniazid, rifampicin, fluoroquinolone, amikacin, kanamycin, capreomycin
Zika virus	South Pacific 2007–2014; Brazil 2015; United States 2016.	Person to person via *Aedes aegypti* and *Aedes albopichis* mosquitoes; sexual contact; healthcare blood products	Not generally fatal and with many subclinical infections; infection during pregnancy can lead to microcephaly; no specific antiviral or vaccine	Prevent mosquito bites; spray pesticides on infected regions; use personal insecticides, DEET; eliminate mosquito breeding sites; abstain from sexual contact with infected people for 6 months

Data from European Center for Disease Prevention and Control. Zika virus infection: factsheet for health professionals. http://ecdc.europa.eu/en/healthtopics/zika_virus_infection/factsheet-health-professionals/pages/factsheet_health_professionals.aspx. Published June 23, 2016. Accessed November 15, 2016; Center for Infectious Disease Research and Policy. Estimates of SARS death rates revised upward. http://www.cidrap.umn.edu/news-perspective/2003/05/estimates-sars-death-rates-revised-upward. Published May 7, 2003. Accessed November 15, 2016.

▶ Public Health and Healthcare Services

The challenges of infectious disease and disease transmission seem overwhelming. The successful intervention of these diseases depends on the good practice of public health and healthcare services. It requires all public and healthcare professionals to be vigilant and well prepared for their jobs. It is incumbent on countries to ensure adequate training, access to appropriate equipment and medication, and good policies related to disease transmission (e.g., providing healthcare workers with barrier protection and knowledge of its proper use, or having adequate vaccine).

Of particular importance in meeting the challenges of infectious disease is the constant surveillance for disease. This requires that public health professionals collect and maintain health records and information and means of quick communication of information throughout the country and the world. It requires that healthcare professionals are well educated, are prepared for rapid and accurate diagnosis, have the means for proper treatment, and work with good policies to prevent further transmission.

Community health workers need the skills to investigate outbreaks, understand the dynamics of the diseases they confront, and be prepared to educate the public about how to protect themselves from transmission. It is vital that public and healthcare professionals are able to link people to the proper healthcare services and treatments as quickly as possible.

Countries must be able to assess their infectious disease burdens, develop policies that address public education, provide proper training for professionals, and have a plan for emergency preparedness and acute intervention. Governments need to prepare communities to help with the intervention of infectious diseases and need to support community efforts. Laws and regulations should be enforced to limit the spread of disease and protect the population, for example, require vaccination of school-aged children, quarantine infected people if appropriate, and require the use of safety products, such as seatbelts or helmets.

Finally, all nations must engage in new research to find new treatments, cures, and innovative solutions to limit these diseases. They must also engage in constant evaluation of the services people receive and the systems that support those services. An example of this is shown in **BOX 2-2**. As evidenced in this section, public and healthcare professionals, politicians, and citizens cannot afford to "drop the ball" when infectious disease is concerned.

BOX 2-2 Neglected Tropical Diseases: Lymphatic Filariasis Elimination Program

The microscopic threadlike worm (*Wuchereria bancrofti*) invaginates the lymphatic nodes and vessels where it reproduces, creating millions of microfilariae. Microfilariae are transmitted from person to person via mosquito bites. The worms become adults in approximately 6 months, and the adult worms live for approximately 6 years. When the adult worms die, the person's bodily response causes inflammation of the vessels, resulting in lymphedema (swelling), of limbs, legs, breasts, or the genitalia. According to the Centers for Disease Control (CDC), lymphatic filariasis (LF) is "one of the world's neglected tropical disease (NTDs), affecting more than 1 billion people" (2011). Although most infected people are asymptomatic, 30% of infected people develop debilitating manifestations, which affect their ability to be productive.

Current statistics indicate that LF affects over 120.0 million people in 73 countries worldwide. However, this is a neglected tropical disease that can be eliminated. In 2000, the World Health Organization launched the Global Lymphatic Filariasis Elimination Program with a target elimination deadline of 2020. In the Americas, 11.3 million people are at risk for acquiring the disease. Mass public health efforts reduced the transmission in Costa Rica, Suriname, and the Republic of Trinidad and Tobago. However, there is still active transmission in four countries in the Americas: Brazil, the Dominican Republic, Haiti, and Guyana.

The public health strategy to interrupt transmission requires the health agency to map the endemic areas, administer drugs to break the transmission cycle, and reduce microfilaraemia.

Mapping

Statistics generated by the Ministry of Health indicates the prevalence of the LF antigen in 7 of the 10 geographic regions in Guyana.

Administering the Drugs

In 2003, the Ministry of Health collaborated with the Pan American Health Organization/World Health Organization (PAHO/WHO) to implement phase one of the Transmission Interruption Plan. This phase included social mobilization, distribution, promotion and use of diethylcarbamazine-fortified (DEC-fortified) salt, and monitoring and evaluating the progress at sentinel sites. The scientific efficacy of DEC-fortified salt to reduce microfilaraemia is well established and documented in pilot studies in Brazil, Haiti, India, and the United Republic of Tanzania. In fact, the DEC-fortified salt causes few or no adverse reactions when compared with the DEC tablet (2007). As such, officials in Guyana launched a national program that introduced DEC-salt into the competitive market. This was accompanied by social marketing activities to increase consumer demand. These included television ads, health education seminars, appearances at health expositions, and door-to-door counseling.

Challenges with implementing the program

Guyana is classified as the second poorest country in South America and the Caribbean with per capita GDP of US $800 in 999 (2001). All of the healthcare initiatives are coordinated by the minister of public health and his/her ministry. Some of the challenges with this program were:

1. The lead agency for health promotion is the Division of Health Sciences Education, which is involved in training health staff and NGOs. However, the Ministry of Health lacked sufficient health staff to coordinate mass countrywide drug/salt marketing education activities. As such, a partnership with PAHO/WHO resulted in a project launch funded by PAHO/WHO for training and development of a team specifically geared toward countrywide health education, DEC-fortified salt promotion, and active marketing and sales of the salt.
2. DEC-fortified salt needed to be imported and sold not as a drug but as a food product. As such, the MoH partnered with the salt producers and importers to facilitate the ease of importation regulations.
3. The sales of salt decreased with disruptions to the salt supply and reduced consumer confidence after the salt became discolored (turned blue over time). The MoH increased quality control and collaborated with PAHO/WHO on a second social mobilization campaign to restock the retail suppliers and quell the concerns of the population.
4. DEC-fortified salt competed with cheaper alternatives, which were not fortified with DEC or iodine. The MoH and government partnered with importers and salt producers to increase the supply and consumer demand for the salt, as this targeted both the iodization and LF programs.

The production of DEC-fortified salt for mass treatment stopped in 2007 after the importation of approximately 900 tons of salt from the time the program launched in July 2003. In 2008, The MoH embarked on phase two, which included evaluation of phase one, identification of *hotspots* using surveillance information, Mass Drug Administration with tablets (DEC-fortified salt and albendazole) and monitoring and evaluation of sentinel sites. Once again the Ministry of Health partnered with PAHO/WHO and the Inter-American Development Bank (IDB) for support. The MoH has even indicated that this LF elimination program is integrated with the Georgetown Sanitation Improvement Program, which was supported by both the IDB and Guyana Water Incorporated. The healthcare system in Guyana is able to achieve successful results because of its public/private partnerships. These partnerships offset not only the financial and human resource constraints of the country's healthcare system but also strengthen the health system's ability to reduce the burden of diseases, especially neglected tropical diseases that can be eliminated.

Contributing author: Gabrielle Walcott-Bedeau MD, MMSci, PGCME

References

Center for Disease Control and Prevention, Center for Global Health, Division of Parasitic Diseases and Malaria. Lymphatic filariasis: elimination in the Americas. https://www.cdc.gov/globalhealth/ntd/resources/lf_americas_at_a_glance.pdf Published September 2011. Accessed October 20, 2016.

Commonwealth Health Online. Health systems in Guyana. http://www.commonwealthhealth.org/americas/guyana/health_systems_in_guyana/. Published 2016. Accessed October 20, 2016.

Lammie P, Milner T, Houston R. Unfulfilled potential: using diethylcarbamazine-fortified salt to eliminate lymphatic filariasis. *Bulletin of the World Health Organization*. http://www.who.int/bulletin/volumes/85/7/06-034108/en/. Published July 2007. Accessed October 20, 2016.

Pan American Health Organization. Health systems and services profile of Guyana. http://www.paho.org/hq/dmdocuments/2010/Health_System_Profile-Guyana_2001.pdf. Published December 14, 2001. Accessed October 20, 2016.

Persaud S. Tenth Regional Lymphatic Filariasis Elimination Program. www.pancap.org/NTD_%20Guyana.pptx

World Health Organization. Country cooperation strategy at a glance: Guyana. http://www.who.int/countryfocus/cooperation_strategy/ccsbrief_guy_en.pdf. Published. May 2013. Accessed October 20, 2016.

References

1. Merson MH, Black RE, Mills AJ. *International Public Health: Diseases, Programs, Systems, and Policies.* 2nd ed. Sudbury, MA: Jones and Bartlett Publishers; 2006.
2. Basch PF. *Textbook of International Health.* New York: Oxford University Press; 1999.
3. Lopez AD, Murray CC. The global burden of disease, 1990–2020. *Nat Med.* 1998; 4(11):1241–1243.
4. Murry CJL. Quantifying the burden of disease: the technical basis for disability-adjusted life years. *Bull World Health Organ.* 1994;72(3):429–445.
5. Skolnick RS. *Essentials of Global Health.* Sudbury, MA: Jones and Bartlett Publishers; 2008.
6. Moorthy VS, Good MF, Hill AV. Malaria vaccine development. *Lancet.* 2004;363(9403):150–156.
7. McKenzie JF, Pinger RR, Kotecki JE. *An Introduction to Community Health.* Sudbury, MA: Jones and Bartlett Publishers; 2005.
8. Sachs JD. A new global effort to control malaria. *Science.* 2002;298(5591):122–124.
9. Bill and Melinda Gates Foundation. http://www.gatesfoundation.org/What-We-Do/Global-Health/Malaria. Accessed July 13, 2016.
10. Yamey G. Roll back malaria: a failing global health campaign. *BMJ.* 2004;328:1086. doi: http://dx.doi.org/10.1136/bmj.328.7448.1086
11. Hay SI, Guerra CA, Tatem AJ, Noor AM, Snow RW. The global distribution and population at risk of malaria: past, present, and future. *Lancet Infect Dis.* 2004;4(6):327–336.
12. Martens P, Hall L. Malaria and the move: human population movement and malaria transmission. *Emerg Infect Dis.* 2000;6(2):103–109.
13. Sachs J, Malaney P. The economic and social burden of malaria. *Nature.* 2002;415(6872):680–685.
14. U.S. Centers for Disease Control and Prevention. Impact of Malaria. http://www.cdc.gov/malaria/malaria_worldwide/impact.html. Published March 26, 2014. Accessed July 22, 2016.
15. World Health Organization. Health topics: Zika virus. www.who.int/topics/zika/en. Published 2016. Accessed August 8, 2016; Fact sheet. www.who.int/emergencies/zika-virus/en. Published 2016. Accessed August 8, 2016; U.S. Centers for Disease Control and Prevention. Zika virus: information about the virus and current updates. www.cdc.gov/zika. Published 2016. Accessed August 8, 2016.
16. World Health Organization. Zika virus and complications. www.who.int/emergencies/zika-virus/en. Published 2016. Accessed August 15, 2016; World Health Organization. History of the Zika virus. www.who.int/emergencies/zika-virus/en. Published August 2016. Accessed August 1, 2016; World Health Organization. Zika situation report. www.who.int/emergencies/zika-virus/en. Published August 2016. Accessed August 1, 2016.
17. U.S. Centers for Disease Control and Prevention, 2016. What you can do to protect yourself. www.cdc.gov/zika/prevention/. Updated August 31, 2016. Accessed August 15, 2016; World Health Organization. Dispelling rumors around Zika complications. www.who.int/emergencies/zika-virus/articles/rumors/en. Accessed August 15, 2016.
18. One Health Initiative. www.onehealthinitiative.com/. Accessed August 14, 2016; U.S. Centers for Disease Control and Prevention. Global One Health Activities. www.cdc.gov/onehealth/. Accessed August 14, 2016.
19. U.S. Centers for Disease Control and Prevention. Arsenic.cdc.gov/healthywater/disease/az.html. Published 2016. Accessed August 2016, 2016.
20. World Health Organization. Climate Change and Health. www.int/mediacentre/factsheets/fs280/en. Published 2016. Accessed August 16, 2016.
21. U.S. Centers for Disease Control and Prevention. Global water, sanitation and hygiene (WASH). http://cdc.gov/healthywater/global/diarrhea-burden.html. Published December 2015. Accessed August 17, 2016.
22. Fontaine O, Garner P, Bhan MK. Oral rehydration therapy: the simple solution for saving lives. *BMJ.* 2007;334(Suppl 1):s14.
23. Parashar UD, Hummelman EG, Bresee JS, et al. Global illness and deaths caused by rotavirus disease in children. *Emerg Infect Dis.* 2003;9(3):565–572.
24. Bern C, Martines J, de Zoysa I, Glass RI. The magnitude of the global problem of diarrhoeal disease: a ten-year update. *Bulletin of the World Health Organization.* 1992;70(6):705–714.
25. Kosek M, Bern C, Guerrant RL. The global burden of diarrhoeal disease, as estimated from studies published between 1992 and 2000. *Bulletin of the World Health Organization.* 2003;81(3):197–204.
26. World Health Organization and UNICEF. *Meeting the MDG Drinking Water and Sanitation Target: The Urban and Rural Challenge of the Decade.* Geneva, Switzerland: WHO Press. http://www.childinfo.org/areas/water/pdfs/jmp06final.pdf. Published 2006. Accessed March 25, 2008.
27. Epidemiology Program Office, Office of the Director, CDC. Achievements in public health, 1900–1999: changes in the public health system. *JAMA* (online). 2000;283:735–738.
28. Bryce J, Pinto-Boschi C, Shibuya K, Black RE. WHO estimates of the causes of death in children. *Lancet.* 2005;365:1147–1152.
29. UNICEF. *Progress for Children: A World Fit for Children Statistical Review.* 6th ed. New York: UNICEF Division of Communication. http://childinfo.org/areas/childmortality/Progress_for_Children.pdf. Published 2007. Accessed March 21, 2008.
30. World Health Organization. Manary M, et al. Systems review of the cause of children with diarrhea in community-based management of severe acute malnutrition. http://www.who.int/nutrition/publications/guidelines/updates_management_SAM_infantandchildren_review4.pdf?ua=1. Published February 2012. Accessed August 16, 2016.
31. World Health Organization. Cholera. www.who.int/cholera/en/index.html. Published June 2015. Accessed October 20, 2016.
32. World Health Organization. Global Task Force on Cholera Control: Prevention and control of cholera outbreaks: WHO policy and recommendations. http://www.who.int/cholera/technical/prevention/control/en/#, Published 2016. Accessed August 17, 2016.
33. Graham NM. The epidemiology of acute respiratory infections in children and adults: a global perspective. *Epid Rev.* 1990;12:149–178.
34. Murray CJ, Lopez AD. Global and regional cause-of-death patterns in 1990. *Bull World Health Organ.* 1994;72(3):447–480.
35. Dye C, Garnett GP, Sleeman K, Williams BG. Prospects for worldwide tuberculosis control under the WHO DOTS strategy. *Lancet.* 1998;352:1886–1891.
36. Schneider, MJ. *Introduction to Public Health.* 5th ed. Burlington, MA: Jones and Bartlett Learning; 2017.
37. Williams BG, Dye C. Antiretroviral drugs for tuberculosis control in the era of HIV/AIDS. *Science.* 2003;301:1535–1537.

38. Gill B, Okie S. China and HIV: a window of opportunity. *N Eng J Med.* 2007;356(18):1801–1806.
39. National Institutes of Health, National Institute of Allergy and Infectious Diseases 2011. Timeline of human flu pandemics. http://www.niaid.nih.gov/topics/flu/research/pandemic/pages/timelinehumanpandemics.aspx. August 20, 2016.
40. U.S. Centers for Disease Control and Prevention. Zika virus: what you need to know. http://www.cdc.gov/zika/about/needtoknow.html. Published August 4, 2016. Accessed August 20, 2016.
41. Heymann DL. *Control of Communicable Diseases Manual.* Washington, DC: American Public Health Association. 2015:298–301.
42. World Health Organization. HIV/AIDS. http://www.who.int/mediacentre/factsheets/fs360/en/. Published July 2016. Accessed August 20, 2016.
43. Bill and Melinda Gates Foundation. What we do: Global Health Division. http://www.gatesfoundation.org/What-We-Do/Global-Health/HIV. Accessed August 20, 2016.
44. The Global Fund to Fight AIDS, Tuberculosis, and Malaria. What We Do: HIV/AIDS. http://www.theglobalfund.org/en/hivaids/ Published July 2016. Accessed August 20, 2016.
45. U.S. Centers for Disease Control and Prevention. Facts about the Laboratory Response Network. https://emergency.cdc.gov/lrn/factsheet.asp. Published September 30, 2104. Accessed August 21, 2016.
46. U.S. Centers for Disease Control and Prevention. Ebola: outbreaks. http://www.cdc.gov/vhf/ebola/outbreaks/history/summaries.html. Published April 14, 2106. Accessed August 21, 2016.
47. U.S. Centers for Disease Control and Prevention. Climate and effects on health. http://www.cdc.gov/climateandhealth/effects. Published July 26, 2016. Accessed August 21, 2016.
48. National Institutes for Environmental Health Science. Health Impacts of Climate Change. http://www.niehs.nih.gov/research/programs/geh/climatechange/health_impacts/index.cfm. Published September 9, 2015. Accessed August 21, 2016.
49. United Nations High Commission on Refugees. http://www.unhcr.org/en-us/figures-at-a-glance.html. June 20, 2016. Accessed August 21, 2016.
50. World Bank: Poverty overview. http://www.worldbank.org/en/topic/poverty/overview. Published April 13, 2016. Accessed August 22, 2016.
51. U.S. Centers for Disease Control and Prevention. Drug resistance. https://www.cdc.gov/drugresistance/about.html. Published July 14, 2016. Accessed August 12, 2016.
52. U.S. Centers for Disease Control and Prevention. Global water, sanitation, and hygiene (WASH). http://www.cdc.gov/healthywater/global/wash_statistics.html. April 11, 2016. Accessed August 14, 2016.
53. Huhn GD, Sejvar JJ, Montgomery SP, Dworkin MS. West Nile virus in the United States: an update on an emerging infectious disease. *Am Fam Physician.* 2003;68(4):653–670.
54. U.S. Centers for Disease Control. West Nile virus activity—United States, January 1–December 1, 2005. *MMWR.* 2005;54(49):1253–1256.
55. U.S. Centers for Disease Control. Severe Acute Respiratory Syndrome (SARS). Fact sheet: basic information about SARS. http://www.cdc.gov/ncidod/sara/factsheet.html.
56. U.S. Centers for Disease Control. Ebola hemorrhagic fever information packet. Special Pathogens Branch, Division of Viral and Rickettsial Diseases, National Center for Infectious Diseases. Published 2002.
57. U.S. Centers for Disease Control. Ebola hemorrhagic fever: known cases and outbreaks of Ebola hemorrhagic fever, in chronological order. www.cdc.gov.
58. U.S. Centers for Disease Control. Key facts about avian influenza (bird flu) and avian influenza A (HN1) virus. http://www.cdc.gov/flu/avian/gen-info/facts.html. Published 2007.
59. U.S. Centers for Disease Control. Avian influenza: current H5N1 situation. http://www.cdc.gov/flu/avian/outbreaks/current.html. 2008.
60. U.S. Centers for Disease Control. Healthcare-associated Methicillin-resistant *Staphylococcus aureus* (HA-MRSA). http://www.cdc.gov/ncidod/dhqp/ar_mrsa.html. Published November 16, 2007.
61. U.S. Centers for Disease Control. Invasive MRSA. http://www.cdc.gov/ncidod/dhqp/ar_mrsa_Invasiv_FS.html. Accessed October 17, 2007.
62. U.S. Centers for Disease Control. VISA/VRSA: Vancomycin-intermediate/resistant *Staphylococcus aureus.* http://www.cdc.gov/ncidod/dhqp/ar_fisavrsa.html. Published 2004.
63. U.S. Centers for Disease Control. Multidrug- resistant tuberculosis (MDR TB) fact sheet. http://www.cdc.gov/tb/pubs/tbfactsheets/mdrtb.html. Accessed January 22, 2008.

CHAPTER 3

Global Health Systems Politics, Economics, and Policy

Walter J. Jones

▸ Introduction

The Worldwide Challenge of Health Policymaking in the 21st Century

Health care is one part of society that has always been subject to varying degrees of public scrutiny and regulation, and thus there is health policymaking, in one guise or another. Since medicine originated thousands of years ago within such important social institutions as religion, societies have recognized that healthcare organization and practice have a social dimension that needs to be monitored.[1] Governments, or other social/community organizations, have intervened in health care because the nation's society has viewed it to be at least partly a social service, not an economic good. Government intervention often takes place because of market imperfections or failure, or due to political imperatives that override the prerogatives of the healthcare market.[2–4]

As will be discussed later, the biggest policymaking challenges faced by nations around the world are broadly similar, and they represent efforts to manage a medical/scientific revolution that has positively transformed the life prospects of humanity. Using almost any metric of performance, there is no area of human endeavor that has been more successful in the last 150 years than health care. In that very success lie the worldwide problems we now face. Physician and social theorist William Schwartz notes:

> Even the prospect of dependable and sustained progress against disease—let alone the achievement of a medical utopia—emerged only after World War II .... [At the end of] the hundred-year span ... beginning with ... the 1950s and ending in the year 2050 ... it seems conceivable that most of today's debilitating and fatal diseases will be preventable or curable. ... That is the utopian vision for medicine that now, for the first time, appears to have a scientific foundation. The critical question is at what price—economically, politically, and ethically—that vision will be realized.[5(pp2–3)]
>
> Schwartz, WB. *Life without Disease: The Pursuit of Medical Utopia*. Berkeley, Cal.: University of California Press; 1998.

All nations now have problems controlling costs, providing effective access to care, ensuring a reasonable level of quality of care, controlling the introduction and use of technology, and validly measuring individual and community health outcomes. However, at the same time, nations are attempting to address these common health system aspects while possessing widely varying national cultures, governmental structures, economies, political systems, and population/subpopulation health statuses and lifestyles.[6] Not surprisingly, then, what U.S. policymakers are considering with respect to health system reform differs considerably from that contemplated by their counterparts in nations such as the United Kingdom, Brazil, Russia, and China.[7,8,9]

It will be argued here that, despite these differences, the general range of policymaking issues and options faced by nations can be productively analyzed and compared by using well-defined models of what can be called *micro* and *macro* health policymaking. To consider health policymaking issues and activities around the world, we must first understand how to think about health policymaking.

▸ How to Think About Health Policymaking—Micro and Macro Models

It must be remembered that, in the most fundamental way, health policymaking (like any other area of policymaking) is a political process. There may be varying technical and clinical issues at stake in any given action, and the particular actors in the policy process may differ markedly. Most policymaking (whether it is taking place within a democratic or nondemocratic framework) usually involves both governmental and nongovernmental individuals and organizations. Nevertheless, all policy activities are critically determined by the interactions of individuals and interest groups within the society over the distribution of its resources. It is, at bottom, politics—in the words of Harold Lasswell, "who gets what, when, how."[10]

As suggested previously, health policymaking can be usefully analyzed using both micro and macro frameworks. In some ways, these policy frameworks are analogous to microeconomics (the study of economic interactions at the level of individual producers and consumers) and macroeconomics (the analysis of economic activity at the sector, regional, national, and international levels). For the purposes of policy analysis, they are interrelated and should both be used if the dynamics, substance, and outcomes of health policymaking are to be fully understood.

Micro Policymaking—The Policy Marketplace Model

The marketplace model of policymaking is outlined most completely in the work on health legislative policymaking done by Paul J. Feldstein.[11] As the term indicates, it is adapted from economic theory, with suppliers and demanders, as in the economic marketplace. The policy marketplace model has the following characteristics:

- Like its economic counterpart, the policy marketplace model assumes that individuals and groups are constantly interacting to satisfy their needs. All policy actors are both suppliers and demanders, since they must exchange some commodity in the marketplace to purchase the other goods that they want. For example, politicians supply favorable policies. In democratic states, these usually include financial subsidies, regulations, and additional health-related services for constituency groups, such as senior citizens, hospitals, and medical schools. In exchange, the politicians receive political support, which could include financial contributions, votes, and other desirable commodities.[11] In dictatorships such as Zimbabwe, the exchanged goods could also include such items as access to basic health services in exchange for support from armed groups, including the nation's military and police forces, used to suppress the mass public.[12]

- As in the economic marketplace, the policy marketplace around the world features disparities in power.[13] Individuals and groups that can supply more can demand more in exchange. In the United States, physicians, senior citizens, hospitals, pharmaceutical and insurance companies, and academic health centers are among the "haves," since they are politically organized, particularly through interest groups and professional associations, such as the American Hospital Association, the American Medical Association, and the AARP. Members of these groups receive relatively generous government services and legal protections. On the other hand, politically unorganized groups in nations as diverse as the United States and India are often less educated, less politically powerful, and poorly situated geographically, and as a consequence they receive substandard or no medical services.[14,15]

- In the policy marketplace, the currency used in exchanges can be money, but it can also include superior leadership, more effective organization, access to and greater articulation through communications media, and greater group-member intensity, or willingness to exert great efforts to advance the interests of the group.[16,17] The latter is evident in U.S. health policymaking with disease-specific and victim groups, such as family members of the mentally ill and as people with HIV/AIDS,[18,19,20] and it is evident in the post–World War II development of the Japanese health insurance system.[21] Money matters, but power in the policy marketplace involves much more than money.

- To gain control over their relevant areas of the marketplace, nongovernmental groups will attempt to forge enduring alliances with governmental agencies. For example, disease-specific groups in the United States lobby for more federal government funding for research via the National Institutes of Health in their area of disease. In the distinctive policy marketplaces of the United States, Canada, the United Kingdom, and France, pharmaceutical companies attempt to influence regulation by interacting differently with the relevant national health policymakers.[22] More politically powerful groups will be more successful at this than the "have-nots." Often, these groups will engage in their activities via enduring *iron triangles* or more transient *issue networks* of power and influence.[23] As a result, it cannot be assumed that government in any given policy system will protect "the little guy." Indeed, more often than not, governmental regulations reinforce power disparities in health policymaking.[11]

Macro Policymaking—The Policy Systems Model

In contrast to the marketplace of micro policymaking, the *macro* level of policymaking can be best conceived of as the continual evolution of a complex system. Systems theory was developed in the disciplines of engineering and ecology. It was first applied to political systems by Easton[24] and has been modified to describe health policymaking by Longest.[14] As applied to policy systems, systems theory has the following characteristics:

- *Complexity*—Numerous influences interact to produce a system that is continually in flux while generally attaining some level of equilibrium or stability. Individuals, social groups, and organizations are all actors in the policy process.
- *Interrelatedness*—Most significant activities are connected to one another by feedback loops and both direct and indirect impacts. All policy actions create reactions within the system, some perhaps modifying the system itself.
- *Cyclical process*—With complexity and interrelatedness, the policy process does not have a definite beginning or end; it continues on as long as organized society continues to exist. There are no permanent policy successes or failures.

As noted, the system's model is cyclical, so strictly speaking, there is no start or finish—just a continual cycle in which any beginning is arbitrary. In Longest's model, the policy process has the following stages:

1. *Recognition of inputs.* There are numerous elements of feedback from previous policy decisions (health outcomes, budgets, programs, elections, and so forth). These include support and opposition to current policies and include demands for modifications of these policies. These inputs are recognized by policy actors (including elected officials, interest group leaders, and regulators) and lead to their reactive efforts to engage in further policy activities.
2. *Policy formulation.* Significant policy actors attempt to develop new policies to address these new inputs. In advanced nations, these efforts usually center on formal policymaking structures, such as executive, legislative, judicial, and regulatory institutions. Executive orders are issued, legislation passes through Congress or a similar assembly, and lawyers bring cases for consideration before judicial bodies or regulatory agencies take up issues brought before them. As with the other stages of policymaking, the actions of policy formulation cannot be separated from politics and political considerations. As suggested in a study of health policymaking in advanced, industrial democracies, there is no such thing as apolitical policy formulation.[25]
3. *Policy outputs.* Efforts at formulation can result in a variety of policy outputs. The most obvious and conventional include statutory laws and regulatory directives (passed by legislatures but subsequently implemented by regulatory agencies). These actions can also contain subsidy and taxation provisions, thus redistributing wealth from one area of society to another. One output can in fact be a *nondecision*—a phenomenon first described by Crenson[26] and defined as a decision to do nothing, which itself creates political and policy impacts,

such as when the U.S. Congress blocked Bill Clinton's Health Security Act in 1994 without ever holding any formal hearings or votes.[27,28]

Many policy outputs also intentionally provide some element of political symbolism. As described by Edelman, symbolic politics is virtually inseparable from policymaking because it provides both policymakers and the mass public with threatening and/or reassuring images that emotionally condense often complex arguments into easily accessible reactions.[29] Often these symbols include evocative legislative titles, such as the Medicare Modernization Act of 2003, which not only added a prescription drug benefit for seniors in the United States but also multibillion-dollar subsidies for the U.S. health insurance and pharmaceuticals industries. Who could oppose "modernization"? Similarly, the Patient Protection and Affordable Care Act of 2010 (ACA), which was enacted by the Obama administration in the teeth of determined Republican party opposition, has a title that implies the victory of the average American over the costly medical/industrial complex. However, the legislation actually includes considerable financial concessions to the health insurance and pharmaceutical industries, providing them with additional subsidized customers for their products.[30] As Edelman notes, symbols can often be used in policymaking to distract the public from policy details that powerful and focused interest groups have worked out for their own benefit (if not the general public's).[29]

4. *Implementation.* Any policy output that is not a nondecision has to be implemented to have a social impact, and that implementation can be highly variable.[31,32] Government agencies must often work through nongovernmental elements of society to implement policies, and the values, political skills, and preferences of leaders in these organizations often determine whether or not (and, if so, how) a new governmental policy is realized through implementation.[14] Due to the vagaries of implementation, the actual impacts of policies are often unanticipated.[33,34]

5. *Outcomes.* Policies create individual, group, and social impacts. In health policy, the most obvious outcome may involve changes in individual, group, and social health resource consumption and health status. Usually, however, health policies have non-health outcomes that may be equally important politically. There are always winners and losers. Some individuals and groups get more resources while others pay. Some have their needs attended to while others' needs are neglected. Policy outcomes may also have profound long-range impacts that were unanticipated, such as the creation of new ethical issues (for example, in the case of new technological development resulting from the Human Genome Project), and the need for explicit resource rationing (for example, when government research funding leads to useful but costly new medical technologies and procedures).[35]

6. *Feedback and subsequent modification.* As previously mentioned, the outputs and outcomes of policy cycles include reactions in society and related efforts to further develop policy. In policy cycles, outputs and outcomes create the reactions in society mentioned earlier, and related further efforts at policy development. The policy agenda is refreshed, and the cycle continues onward. Often the success of a previous cycle (say, the enactment of Medicare and Medicaid to address the lack of healthcare access for seniors and some low-income categories) leads to the challenges faced in a subsequent cycle (for example, how to cope with the unsustainable healthcare demands and cost inflation triggered by events such as the introduction of large government health insurance programs such as Medicare and Medicaid).[36,37] Health policymaking does result in great benefits for individuals and society, but it also seems a compounding hassle when viewed in terms of day-to-day activities.

▶ Possible Responses to the Convergence of Policy Problems

Since the rise of modern medicine in the 19th and 20th centuries, national variations in health organization, practice, and policies have been gradually affected by a growing convergence due to technological change and social globalization.[38,39] Recent international surveys of health systems changes emphasize that nations are all coping with some of the same major problems, including cost containment, access barriers to large population subgroups, the impact of rapidly developing new technologies, ensuring a reasonably high-quality standard for care, and measuring health outcomes.[6]

1. *Cost containment.* All nations face the problem that the cost of providing modern health care with currently accepted standards and technologies is outrunning the patients' abilities to generate the wealth to pay for it. Nations that do not have true healthcare systems, such as the United States, may be racing toward the cliff of runaway healthcare costs faster than most European nations, which have historically possessed national structures for healthcare organization and delivery.[40] But all nations are being forced to confront the issue of allocating scarce healthcare resources. It is estimated that, by 2020, world healthcare spending will triple in real dollars from the level seen in 2010, to $10 trillion, taking 21% of U.S. GDP and 16% of GDP in other Organisation for Economic Co-operation and Development (OECD) nations—essentially, the economically advanced nations in North America, Europe, Asia, and Australia.[6]

   The need for cost containment entails consideration of the cost-effectiveness of health technologies and procedures.[41] Frequently, the most cost-effective technology is not the most recently developed, particularly in areas where it appears that healthcare research and development are approaching, or have reached, the "flat of the curve."[42] Cost containment requirements also include the imperative to sometimes say *no*, even when the added consumption of health resources might benefit individual and/or population health in some way.[43] The removal of "waste" in health services delivery is certainly desirable, but the ultimate challenge in cost containment is controlling and limiting the application of potentially useful health services. As the PWC world leaders' survey suggests, this will require a "quest for common ground" so as to provide "basic health benefits within the context of societal priorities."[6(p6)]

2. *Access to care.* Whether they are economically advanced and wealthy or relatively poor and less developed, all nations have at least some subpopulations that are relatively disadvantaged in their access to necessary health services. However, it is often difficult to address these needs since they usually require the expenditure of additional resources (clearly limited, as noted earlier). In addition, the redistribution of national resources to "have-not" groups is often administratively and technically difficult (it is hard to reach vast rural populations in nations such as China, for example), and politically divisive (politically active and articulate "have" groups in all nations usually want to keep their share of national wealth rather than having a significant part of it taken away and given to others).[44]

   Often, poorer citizens in nations such as Bolivia, Vietnam, and Moldova have to rely on under-the-table payments (often constituting bribery) to get even the most essential healthcare services from underpaid and overworked providers.[45] In extreme situations of political instability and repression, healthcare institutions can break down entirely, as was the case in Zimbabwe in early 2008. Life expectancy in Sub-saharan Africa has plummeted, HIV-AIDS has affected one fifth of the population, and three-quarters of health professionals have emigrated to other countries.

   An equally horrifying medical disaster has taken place in Syria during a civil war that began in 2011 and has continued to the present (2016), with 60% of hospitals destroyed or damaged, and almost half of the physicians fleeing the country. "The few remaining facilities struggle to cope with the large number of patients who need treatment, and clinics no longer have the personnel, equipment, or sanitary conditions in which to treat patients (especially children)."[47]

   At the same time, wider access to basic health services would save hundreds of millions of people worldwide from death and disability and would serve as a powerful tool in antipoverty efforts.[48,49,50] The case for greater access to health care is therefore both sensible from the standpoint of national interests and urgent as a global moral imperative.[51,52] When the wealthiest nations in the world help the poorest and sickest people in the world, they wind up doing well for themselves by doing good for others. (Indeed, if this was not the case, the outlook for the poorest and the sickest would be even worse than it is now.)

3. *Impact of new technologies.* Health technologies have continuously and rapidly evolved in the last century, usually becoming more complex and costly. These technologies, in areas as varied as assistive technologies, pharmaceuticals, and surgical techniques, often provide major health benefits to their recipients.[53] But all nations, facing cost containment difficulties, have to balance the use of limited resources with these new technologies against older but cheaper services (often in the realm of primary care) that may help larger numbers of people, but less dramatically or visibly. This leads to both economic and ethical conflict, since such decision making inevitably does involve "playing God," often with life and death consequences.[54] All nations do have to decide, at least at some level, who lives and who dies.

4. *Quality of care considerations.* As healthcare technologies become more complex, the issue of quality assurance looms larger. Health professionals often cannot monitor technologies through simple observation—detailed technologies are required to provide constant readings.[55] In addition, there have been breakthroughs in data collection and analysis during the last two decades, particularly with respect to the development of computerized data entry and aggregation (often via Internet-based means). For the first time in history, it is possible to aggregate large numbers of patient encounters and detect variations in care quality, along with their consequences, such as medical errors. Major studies that have been done in the United States, the United Kingdom, Canada, and Australia constitute the first steps in defining and understanding the level of medical errors.[55-58] However, as noted in the PWC report, "no one really knows how many errors or adverse events occur because of gaps in reporting processes and differences in definition."[6(p33)]

The revolution in health information technology means that nations can consciously guide healthcare quality assurance and improvement, with enormous benefits accruing to both patients and providers. Of course, to benefit from these technologies, nations must also develop the necessary data collection systems, along with the trained professionals to administer and utilize them. As with other aspects of health technologies, this can pose major challenges for less economically developed nations, such as India.[59]

5. *Measuring health outcomes.* In the long run, the greatest potential benefit from new health information technologies is that they increase the likelihood that health status and outcomes can be measured and related back to health services utilized, as well as individual and community lifestyles and practices. The *health outcomes movement* has the potential to make health services delivery much more cost-effective, as well as to reduce medical errors and to clarify which aspects of health care and behavior are more or less important.[60]

It must be noted that an important part of this is showing to what extent health services and new technologies cannot substitute for improved individual and community health lifestyles. For example, whatever funding the nation of China puts into its health system for treatment of lung cancers, it is clear that the funding cannot substitute for a concerted effort to reduce the rapid increase in national tobacco consumption, which will result in the deaths of tens of millions over the next few decades.[61] A 2015 report by the National Research Council at the National Academies of Science suggested that 50% of premature deaths in the United States can be accounted for by one or more quantified lifestyle and environmental risks.[62] Unfortunately, as follows, it is also true that nations differ in their abilities to afford and apply the systems needed for effective health outcomes research, as well as the subsequent systems reforms driven by research results, with poorer nations being especially hampered.

Internationally, there is a growing general consensus over the existence of the previously mentioned healthcare system problems. Within each country, there has also been some debate (if only at the upper policymaking level) over how the nation should respond to these challenges. China, a rapidly developing but still relatively low-income nation that has never really had a structured national health system, is discussing how one might be set up and how the costs might be borne.[44] Developed nations with existing national health systems, such as Australia and Japan, are talking about to what extent (and if so, how) private sector components should be introduced and integrated to improve provider responsiveness to consumer demands.[63,64]

The United States is unique internationally in that it is a very wealthy nation with a lavishly funded healthcare sector but lacks an effective structure to direct spending and system restructuring. So, while the U.S. system can produce some of the best high-technology health care in the world and leads in research and development spending, it wastes money on an epic scale and suffers from glaring disparities in health insurance coverage and access to care.[43] With the highest proportion of GDP devoted to health care, and with cost inflation generally recognized as unsustainable, health reform has been and will continue to be a major item on the nation's policy agenda. Reform proposals have been put forth by political liberals (such as the introduction of a *single payer system* like that in Canada and such as enhanced employer coverage within existing insurance structures) and conservatives (such as the increased use of individual healthcare purchasing through Health Savings Accounts, HSAs).[65,66]

In the international study done by PriceWaterhouseCoopers,[6(p11)] three clear findings emerge:

- No nation's study respondents are confident that their nation's healthcare system can be sustained, given current trends. Cost inflation is outrunning available resources everywhere, with nations such as the United States and France looking at possible system-wide breakdowns in the next 10–20 years. Entirely government-run and mixed public/private sector systems alike face financial ruin in coming decades, while developing nations' efforts to construct effective basic healthcare systems are threatened by enormous budgetary and taxation burdens.
- The most important attribute of reformed national healthcare systems in coming years will be sustainability. "To be sustainable, health executives will need information, metrics, and transparency to support decision making …. Transparency enables a comparative focus on access as well as the cost and quality of care."
- Increasingly, with ever-growing global communication between national health policymakers, it appears that *convergence* will characterize policy reform efforts. In the words of the PWC study, "global convergence, as best practices are shared, and industry-wide convergence, as the barriers among pharmaceuticals, providers, clinicians, biotech, and payers melt away. Sustainability requires an understanding of the blended nature of health. It requires leadership to integrate and balance the need of individual sectors for their own sustainability while creating an overall model that will support itself beyond 2020."

If sustainability is the key objective for health policymakers around the world, what aspects of reform do they need to focus on to get there? Like most others who have considered the issue, the PWC analysts believe that there are some critical factors. The PWC list includes these:

1. *A quest for common ground.* Essentially, this is an effort to develop national political consensus on the public/private sector division of healthcare responsibilities, along with social agreement about some basic level of guaranteed access to basic health services for all citizens.
2. *A digital backbone.* This refers to the use of nationwide integrated clinical and administrative information systems to increase the efficiency of the healthcare system, as well as to provide data that can be utilized for program evaluation and outcomes research efforts.
3. *Incentive realignment.* This feature centers on the nation's citizens who are healthcare recipients and contends that a sustainable national system must "ensure and manage access to care while supporting accountability and responsibility for healthcare decisions."[6(p15)]
4. *Quality and safety standardization.* This feature focuses on provider accountability and responsibility, suggesting that there needs to be transparent quality and safety standards so that consumer trust can be established and maintained in the nation's healthcare services.
5. *Strategic resource deployment.* This is more vaguely defined in the PWC study, since it suggests the need for resource allocation that "appropriately satisfies competing demands on systems" to balance cost containment and access requirements without being able to provide any real definition of what might constitute *appropriate satisfaction.*[6(p15)] This indicates the contingent nature of this feature, since it will most clearly be determined by the political balance of power within each society.
6. *Climate of innovation.* This feature suggests that nations need to embrace innovation in both technology and processes in order to improve the functioning of the healthcare system.

7. *Adaptable delivery roles and structures.* The PWC report calls for patient-centered care that is maximized in varying circumstances by the adoption of variable care practices and clinical roles.

Surveying the current state of national health systems around the world, what can be concluded with respect to the progress being made in policymaking in these areas?

Two of the previously mentioned sustainability features are primarily technological in nature and can be assessed fairly easily. Some nations have moved materially toward a true *digital backbone* (#2), but only a few. The Netherlands has pioneered in using health information systems to improve healthcare quality within a constrained national budget.[67] Both Canada and the United Kingdom have also worked toward developing national integrated electronic medical records.[68] However, these nations already have truly integrated national health systems; the Netherlands has a national employer-based system, the United Kingdom has a National Health Service, and Canada has a single payer system administered by its provinces.[65] There may be significant problems with national health systems, but it is easier to implement uniform technical and structural reforms within them. In all of these nations, the policy marketplace has been dominated by forces (particularly the government and organized labor, along with general public opinion) in favor of national health care. As will be discussed later, if that decision is made (or not made), choices concerning structure, including of information systems, are significantly affected.

In contrast, the United States is very wealthy, and spends an enormous amount on health care, but lacks such a national governing structure. In the policy marketplace, there is bitter political controversy over the structure and functioning of the ACA, and industry groups tend to further system fragmentation through their own interests in controlling market share. Consequently, U.S. health care has failed to produce a viable health information system through market mechanisms.[69] Smaller providers in the United States, particularly home health agencies and skilled nursing facilities, have clearly lagged behind larger private and public sector health systems in adopting health information technologies.[70]

In recent years, the need for national health information integration has become so evident that it has united conservatives like Newt Gingrich and liberals like Hillary Clinton in support of national policy initiatives.[71] A conservative Republican president, George W. Bush, followed through on this call by supporting the establishment of a National Health Information Infrastructure (NHII), which is supposed to be a "comprehensive knowledge-based network of interoperable systems of clinical, public health, and personal health information."[72] In the case of the United States, the policy marketplace has shifted to support for national health information system restructuring due to growing concerns by payers (that a lack of a national information infrastructure is not cost-effective) and patients/consumers (primarily due to desires for increased quality improvement and safety and for easier personal access to care information).

Since they usually lack the funds and technical expertise, most poor and less developed nations are far from attaining the digital backbone sustainability goal put forth by PWC. For example, in Mexico, the Ministry of Health is responsible for overall health system functioning, but provider funding is very fragmented (much of it coming from patient self-payment), and there is essentially no functioning national information system. The nation's healthcare problems are so great, and government funding so limited, that it will be many years before the system will be sufficiently coherent to permit a digital backbone.[73] For these nations, sustained economic growth will be necessary to generate the required capital for health systems upgrades.

Some of the same conclusions are reached in a global examination of quality and safety standardization (#4). In Europe and Canada, physicians have taken a leadership role in forwarding these causes. In the U.S. policy marketplace, the prominence of patient advocacy groups has provided a different avenue to advance demands for quality and safety assurance.[6] The Health and Medicine Division (formerly the Institute of Medicine) of the National Academies of Science has provided a reasonably clear blueprint as to how the United States can cross the quality chasm.[74] Generally, in economically advanced nations, there are important and increasingly influential groups that are effectively demanding higher quality standards, although there are still debates about the extent to which these standards should be dictated by the government, as opposed to the private sector.[75]

As with the digital backbone, less economically advanced nations generally do not yet have the funds or organizational structure to provide system-wide quality and safety standards, whatever the political preferences might be. A study of practice quality in Indonesia, Tanzania, India, Paraguay, and Mexico suggests substantial variation within each country and different factors leading to each country's pattern of variation. As the study's authors conclude, "questions relating to practice quality [in low-income countries] remain unanswered in the literature, because the quality of health care in low-income countries is difficult to measure."[77(p297)] Until data collection and database development related to the quality of care are improved in these nations, they will not have the necessary inputs to even begin developing and monitoring system-wide quality standards.

The same thing can be said for safety standards. Many poorer nations do not have well-established and effective regulatory structures for overseeing medical safety. China has been particularly visible with respect to safety problems. It is the largest supplier of pharmaceutical ingredients in the world, and there have been major problems reported with some medical products.[78] China's chief food safety watchdog has said that almost 20% of products made for consumption in China were found to be substandard.[79] It appears that neither government nor voluntary private sector safety guidelines and agreements are effective in China, where there is high turnover in manufacturers and their executives.[80] The severity of the problem (and, to a significant degree, of the nature of government in China) can be gauged by the fact that China executed its former State Food and Drug Administration head, Zheng Xiaoyu, in July 2007 for approving untested medicines in exchange for cash bribes.[79] These ongoing problems resulted in the United States and China signing a Memorandum of Agreement on December 11, 2007, to establish a bilateral mechanism to ensure the safety of drugs, excipients, and medical devices exported from China to the United States.[81] This has resulted in a permanent FDA presence in China as a condition for continued exports to the United States.

Beyond the two previously described factors, a digital background and system-wide quality and safety standards, it should be noted that the others listed in the PWC report ("a quest for common ground," "incentive realignment," "strategic resource deployment," "climate of innovation," and "adaptable delivery roles and structures") are fundamentally political in nature. Their definition within each nation depends on ideological decisions that in turn will come from widely varying political systems and structures. These varying decisions made by each will reflect tradeoffs between multiple valued objectives. So, to understand the nature of what nations will be doing in health care in the coming decades, we must understand the nature of tradeoffs, and how these tradeoffs relate to national systems of ideology and ethics in health and non-health areas.

The Nature of National Health Tradeoffs, Ideology and Ethics

In policymaking, tradeoffs come from the inescapable fact that all policy decisions involve the use of finite resources, and to use them in one area means that they may not be available to be deployed in alternative areas. As the great economist Arthur Okun suggested, "Tradeoffs are the central study of the economist. 'You can't have your cake and eat it too' is a good candidate for the fundamental theorem of economic analysis."[3(p1)] But resources in policy analysis can also be intangible and involve such value-laden tradeoffs as individual choice versus government dictation, or political equity versus economic efficiency. That means that tradeoffs must involve ideology and ethics as well as economics.

The importance of tradeoffs in health policymaking—and differing decisions on tradeoffs—have been widely recognized, both within and among nations. Dervaux, Leleu, and Valdmanis conducted an expanded Data Envelopment Analysis of World Health Organization (WHO) and individual national rankings of five health objectives: life expectancy, health distribution, health system responsiveness, responsiveness distribution, and financial contribution fairness. The authors agreed with the WHO Commission for Macroeconomics and Health that any global perspective on health policy priorities needs to be complemented by individual national health policy priority analyses and choices.[82]

When it comes to tradeoffs between economic efficiency and political equity, some researchers have attempted to provide tools that contain explicit criteria. Focusing on developing nations, James et al. suggest that more explicit analysis can aid efforts to attain social justice. "Expenditures on health in many developing countries are being disproportionately spent on health services that have a low overall health impact, and that disproportionately benefit the rich. Without explicit consideration of priority setting, this situation is likely to remain unchanged: resource allocation is too often dictated by historical patterns and maintains vested interests."[83(p33)]

In their work, the researchers list and explain a number of efficiency and equity criteria to guide priorities, including cost-effectiveness, horizontal equity, and vertical equity. They point out that "prioritizing interventions solely on the basis of efficiency [cost-effectiveness] criteria is unlikely to optimize the welfare of society, because of peoples' concerns for equity and the potential tradeoffs between efficiency and equity."[83(p37)]

Particularly in wealthy nations with expensive healthcare systems, policymakers and clinicians are following the researchers and starting to develop guidelines for tradeoffs in healthcare decision making. New York State health officials have now developed protocols for the allocation of ventilators in the event of an H5N1 influenza pandemic. The lead author of their study, Dr. Tia Powell, calls for the public to confront such triage issues, so that such decisions reflect community views as well as ethical and clinical standards. "It's not really a technical solution. ... It's values. And the people are the experts on that."[84] Another example of this is in cancer treatment. According to *The New York Times*, medical groups such as the American Society of Clinical Oncology are now recommending that physicians weigh the costs as well as the effectiveness of treatments when making cancer care decisions. The Society is developing a scorecard to evaluate drugs on cost and value as well as efficacy and side effects.[85]

There are clear political obstacles to explicit tradeoff analysis in health policymaking. The public in most nations does not have a clear understanding of the inescapability of tradeoffs, especially if they suspect that they entail rationing of popular services.[86] As some have observed, all Americans ask for is cheap, fast, and high-quality health care, but they do not understand that they can never get health care with more than two out of those three characteristics in a real-world healthcare system with limited resources and potentially unlimited demands. Research on public response to possible cost-quality tradeoffs in clinical decisions indicates that reactions are unpredictable and not necessarily clinically or economically logical.[87] On the other hand, their findings suggest that a significant portion of the public (at least in the United States) would be willing to accept cost-quality tradeoffs, if they are provided with clear information on the cost-effectiveness of specific treatments.

At the global level, it is just as difficult to analyze tradeoffs. In research conducted for the WHO Advisory Committee on Health Research, Schunemann et al. reviewed available literature on "determining which outcomes are important for the development of guidelines" and found "limited relevant research evidence." The authors offered the general recommendation that methods to examine tradeoffs and their impact on outcomes should employ "systematic and transparent methods involving key stakeholders, including consumers and people from different cultures, to help ensure that all important outcomes are considered."[88(p4)] Of course, this recommendation only addresses procedural issues and does not touch on the substance of which choices should be made. And the division and debate over the substance of health reform is the primary challenge facing national publics and their policymakers.

As noted earlier, there is a convergence of opinion (at least, at the policy elite level) that current national health systems are unsustainable because of growing cost, access, and quality problems. In the ongoing global discussion about tradeoffs and possible health system reforms, it is equally clear that there is no current consensus—only a diversity of ethical perspectives and ideological positions.

One thing is clear: national deliberations over health reform policymaking cannot take place without recognizing that there are ethical and ideological disagreements at the heart of the debates. Unfortunately, all too often, policymakers do engage in *de facto* social experiments without ethical review and debate, both among themselves and with their nation's citizens.[89] In an analysis of the role of justice and solidarity in priority setting in health care, two ethicists point out that

> The outcomes of decisions on in- or exclusion of healthcare services in a benefit package need not necessarily be the same in the various countries. This is not only caused by local, regional, or national differences in approach or different ideas about health, disease, and quality of life but also by different normative judgments. Concrete decisions in different countries can be based on different models of distributive justice, and the weight given to these normative considerations can be different. Also humanitarian considerations have an influence on healthcare package decisions.[90(pp325-326)]
>
> Hoedemaekers R, Dekkers W. Justice and solidarity in priority setting in health care. *Health Care Anal.* 2003; 11(4): 325–343.
> Copyright 2003 with permission of Springer.

Globally, one major reason for this is that some nations do not have the ideologies or institutions of inclusive social participation and modern economics that provide the foundation for a balanced debate over tradeoffs in health systems reform. One analyst contends that "in a political process, where reforms are implemented by democratically controlled agencies, the analogy to informed consent is democratic oversight of the reform process. Unfortunately, this analogy is problematic wherever democratic control of institutions is weak ... and wherever powerful external agencies offer large incentives and are not themselves held accountable for the reforms they impose."[91(p450)]

Scholars have developed a variety of perspectives related to this. The economist Hernando de Soto has contended that many poor nations, particularly in the "post-communist" world, have not developed the social habits of the rule of law that permit widely accepted policies for resource use. Absent these, decisions on resource allocation in all areas of society—including health care—are made largely on the basis of "might makes right." The less powerful are largely disenfranchised and simply attempt to evade the rule of the powerful (usually through governments) by the use of black markets.[92] According to the social philosopher John Rawls, "One may think of a public conception of justice as constituting the fundamental charter of a well-ordered human association."[93(p5)] In societies with volatile political and social systems in transition (including nations experiencing rapid economic and social growth, such as China and India), the principles of justice and popular participation are often not well established or widely shared, which means that health policymaking may be essentially the imposition of the will of political elites. In the long run, such policymaking may contribute to rather than reduce social and political instability.

Justice has both individual and social components. Ethical health policymaking implies an acceptance of *individual autonomy*—the belief that individuals have the right to their own beliefs and values and to related decisions and choices with respect to the use of health services. Some of the most politically charged policy debates occur when the principle of autonomy clashes with social/communal welfare principles of treatment, as in the case of Terri Schiavo in the United States.[94] "Whose Life Is It Anyway?" is a noted play and movie that considers the dilemma of which set of priorities should prevail over life and death decisions—that of the individual whose life is at question or that of a society which has to put forth and defend laws regulating medical treatment.

In health policymaking, the social component is reflected primarily in the debate over *distributive justice,* or the fairness in the distribution of health benefits and burdens in society.[14] In most nations, the question of fairness is debated endlessly by the various participants in the policy marketplace. The economist Thomas Rice, criticizing the United States in 1998 for its unique status as the only economically advanced nation without some system of national health insurance, articulated the egalitarian view of justice, in which equal access to health services (at least to an essential minimum package of services) for all citizens, regardless of income or class, is of central importance. He made the ethical case for U.S. adoption of national health insurance as follows:

> The case for a national health insurance program is strong. Universal coverage is consistent with prevailing notions of fairness; people should not be penalized for circumstances—such as their sociodemographic background or their current health—over which they have little control… [In addition] unlike other characteristics, good health is instrumental in people's capabilities to achieve their personal goals. Financial barriers to obtaining care are doubly unfair: They not only result in poorer health, but they also frustrate people's ability to attain the other things that they value. Furthermore, most people draw pride from being part of a society in which the well-being of others is an important part of the welfare of all members. That nearly every developed nation is committed to providing health insurance to its population, regardless of the individual's ability to pay, is not surprising.[95(p314)]
>
> Rice TH. *The Economics of Health Reconsidered.* 3rd ed. Chicago, Ill.: Health Administration Press; 2009.

In most Western nations (particularly in the United States), there is also a libertarian perspective of fairness that would argue that Rice's preferences are decidedly unfair. Libertarians (who adhere to a mix of beliefs found both on the political left and right) tend to believe that individual freedom is the most important social value. *Fairness* means that individuals have the freedom to choose to do what they wish with their own resources, and that the best set of policies rests on the belief in a minimal state, enforcing basic laws and regulatory "rules of the game" but not attempting to dictate economic outcomes or to engage in large scale redistribution of wealth.[96,97] In contrast to Rice, libertarian health economists prescribe individual choice and responsibility as the best way to *reform* U.S. health care.

Health policymaking is certainly a matter of data collection and analysis, of research and forecasting, of power struggles within national policy marketplaces. Like other aspects of public policy, it is also an "inescapably moral enterprise."[98] Because of that, health policymaking and analysis will be sterile and ultimately ineffective if the policymakers and analysts do not realize—whether they want to or not—that "policy and ethics both ask the same question: 'what is the good, and how do we achieve (create, protect, cultivate) it?'"[98(p247)]

Conclusion: Health Policymaking Around the World—Uncertain Times and Futures

It is not at all clear how the nations of the world, with greatly differing political, economic, healthcare, and social systems, are going to meet the health system challenges in the next 20 years. Most wealthy countries, with aging populations, are going to hit the financial wall with unpredictable consequences. In the United States, any reasonably balanced investigation of the numbers—rising demand for more (and more technologically intensive) health care, an aging population, declining employer-based insurance, increasing number of uninsured individuals, and, above all, a healthcare cost inflation rate that outruns economic growth by a significant margin—will reveal that, sometime between 2020 and 2030 when almost all of the *baby boomers* will have retired and expect to get all of the health care they want and "deserve" from Medicare, financing the U.S. healthcare system as it is currently structured will not add up. Something will have to give.

In the absence of the establishment of a true national healthcare system, the supply/demand imbalance is already creating *de facto* rationing, with insured individuals waiting longer and longer and paying more and more to get ever more tightly limited care. If the U.S. healthcare system hits the financial wall, many individuals who cannot afford to even make co-payments on ACA insurance purchased through state exchanges will fall completely through the cracks, since the *ad hoc* public and charity healthcare system will come apart at the seams. This is a profoundly depressing vision for anyone who believes that access to some effective level of basic health care should be a right that all citizens possess.

U.S. reformers who want to avoid these dire straits generally advocate increased cost controls on health system expenditures and/or increased taxes on upper-income citizens. Some advocate eliminating private health insurance and moving to a single payer system ("Medicaid for all").[99] They will experience major political difficulties in getting any post–ACA proposal enacted. Most efforts to enact national health reform, including the ACA, are sold to the public as giving everyone the right to relatively easy access to comprehensive health services, with only modest costs. As was seen in 1993–1994, the largely insured public reacted badly when they found out that they would actually have to adjust their own healthcare arrangements and pay out themselves to provide insurance for those fellow citizens who were going without.

There has also been a significant backlash against the ACA, with claims of decreased access, with health providers withdrawing from markets, and with employers eliminating jobs or reducing work hours to reduce their obligations to fund expanded health insurance.[100] Access was further reduced when the U.S. Supreme Court, in its *National Federation of Independent Business v. Sebelius* decision in 2012, made a key element of the ACA, state Medicaid expansion, optional rather than mandatory.[101] Many states with Republican-dominated government immediately pronounced that they would not expand their state Medicaid systems. Most Republicans in Congress still advocate "repeal and replace" for the ACA while being extremely vague on what exactly the replacement might be.[102] On the other hand, as time has gone by, more and more states (31 plus the District of Columbia, as of July 2016) have expanded Medicaid as part of the ACA, including states led by Republican governors.[103] Yet even the ACA does not squarely confront the dilemma of a continuing large gap between healthcare demand and affordable supply and ongoing cost inflation exceeding the economic growth required to pay for care.

The problems of cost containment and access in the United States have continued to mount. There is no question of maintaining the current "system"—it is visibly coming apart before our eyes. Something major beyond the ACA, perhaps the development of a U.S. single payer system, will happen one way or the other in the next 10–20 years. Either we shape the future healthcare system now, or we will inherit the disorder of our old healthcare system as it collapses in the near future.

Any examination of the experiences of those nations that do have comprehensive national health systems, such as the National Health Service in the United Kingdom, shows that national health insurance means national health rationing, like it or not, with real consequences for patient health and well-being.[43] In any event, European nations, with rapidly aging populations and relatively expansive social expectations for public health and welfare spending, will have their own political conflicts. However, with structured healthcare systems, they appear to have the potential to develop some political consensus over providing health care within tighter financial limits.

The situation in many developing nations will be incomparably more difficult. It is hard to see how most African nations, with their unstable political systems and desperately poor populations, could afford to even approach "advanced nation" healthcare provision anytime in the foreseeable future. Some of the Asian "tigers," like South Korea, Singapore, and Taiwan, have already reached very high economic development levels and so can afford the most modern health care. But China and India, with strong but declining economic growth rates in the last decade, will continue to face the prospect of rapidly growing (and potentially politically explosive) social inequities, with growing numbers of relatively well-off urban populations, and hundreds of millions of very poor people in their rural hinterlands.

So the world approaches what will undoubtedly be a turbulent period, with national healthcare systems everywhere requiring major overhauls of one form or another. There is no past template that nations can employ to respond to this challenge. However, it is very important to remember that any response to escalating healthcare costs must recognize that health care has never been, and can never be, treated as a purely market good. There is clearly a role for competition and economic incentives in providing and selecting health care. At the same time, any long-range response that brings healthcare supply and demand into a sustainable balance—by regulatory fiat or by market competition—will have to recognize that, as citizens, community members, and human beings, we must all care enough about each other to insure that none of us lacks the essential healthcare services that we can afford to provide.

To end on a note of optimism, it is important that we do not lose sight of the ongoing achievements of modern health care that have transformed the lives of citizens in wealthy nations and are now doing the same for a majority of the poor in the rest of the world. A renewed sense of economic limits in health care need not be in opposition to this worldwide trend. In fact, recognizing the limits is almost certainly a requirement for continuing to make progress. Here it is appropriate to conclude with another quotation from the scholar and visionary cited at the beginning of this chapter, Dr. William Schwartz:

> Where does all this leave us as we try to sort out the challenges that face us at the beginning of a new century? We are enticed by visions of triumph over disease but disturbed by the near-term prospect of denying useful care to some patients .... The next 25 years will be especially challenging and possibly divisive ones, but it is important that we not lose sight of the utopian visions that are emerging. The possibility of mastery over a broad range of illnesses is no longer the sole property of philosophers and science fiction authors. Our challenge will be to tackle the ethical and social issues that accompany medical progress with the same rigor that we apply to the scientific challenges themselves. Above all, we must ensure that in the sacrifices required to realize our visions, especially in the critical area of healthcare rationing, we do not compromise fairness and equity, without which the conquest of disease would be a hollow victory.[5(pp157-159)]
>
> Schwartz, WB. *Life without Disease: The Pursuit of Medical Utopia*. Berkeley, Cal.: University of California Press; 1998.

References

1. Porter R. *The Cambridge History of Medicine*. Cambridge, England: Cambridge University Press; 2006.
2. Rawls J. *A Theory of Justice*. Cambridge, MA: Harvard University Press; 1971.
3. Okun A. *Equality and Inefficiency: The Big Tradeoff*. Washington, DC: The Brookings Institution; 1975.
4. Rice T. *The Economics of Health Reconsidered*. Chicago, IL: Health Administration Press; 1998.
5. Schwartz WB. *Life without Disease: The Pursuit of Medical Utopia*. Berkeley, CA: University of California Press; 1998.
6. PriceWaterhouseCoopers. *HealthCast 2020: Creating a Sustainable Future*. Washington, DC: Health Research Institute, PWC; 2005.
7. World Economic Forum. *Future of Healthy: How to Realize Returns on Health*. Geneva, Switzerland; January 2016.
8. Anderson OW. *The Health Services Continuum in Democratic States*. Ann Arbor, MI: Health Administration Press; 1989.
9. Capital Health and the Global Strategy Initiative. Crisis response: global health care strategy in the 21st Century. Report on Symposia. Washington, DC and Paris, France; 2004.
10. Lasswell H. *Politics: Who Gets What, When, How*. New York, NY: World Publishing Co; 1951.
11. Feldstein PJ. *The Politics of Health Legislation: An Economic Perspective*. Chicago, IL: Health Administration Press; 2006.
12. Gande C. Zimbabwean government triples army officer pay ahead of elections. *VOA News.Com*. February 21, 2008. Available at http://www.voazimbabwe.com/a/a-13-56-74-2008-02-21-voa45-68976302/1470185.html. Accessed February 24, 2008.
13. Blank RH, Burau V. *Comparative Health Policy*. New York, NY: Palgrave Macmillan; 2004.
14. Longest BB. *Health Policymaking in the United States*. 6th ed. Chicago, IL: Health Administration Press; 2015.
15. Das J, Hammer J. Location, location, location: residence, wealth, and the quality of medical care in Delhi, India. *Health Aff*. 2007;26(3):w338–w351. doi: 10.1377/hlthaff.26.3.w338

16. Olson M. *The Logic of Collective Action.* Cambridge, MA: Harvard University Press; 1965.
17. James C, Carrin G, Savedoff W, Hanvoravongchai P. Clarifying efficiency-equity tradeoffs through explicit criteria, with a focus on developing countries. *Health Care Analysis.* 2005;13(1):33–51.
18. Denenberg R. The community: mobilizing and accessing resources and services. In: Cohen FL, Durham JD, eds. *Women, Children, and HIV/AIDS.* New York, NY: Springer Publishing Co; 1993.
19. Foreman C. Grassroots victim organizations: mobilizing for personal and public health. In: Cigler AJ, Loomis BA, eds. *Interest Group Politics.* 4th ed. Washington, DC: Congressional Quarterly Press; 1995.
20. Koyanagi C Bevalacqua JJ. Managed care in public mental health systems. In: Hackey RB, Rochefort DA, eds. *The New Politics of State Health Policy.* Lawrence, KS: University Press of Kansas; 2000:186–206.
21. Steslicke WE. Development of health insurance policy in Japan. *J Health Polit Policy Law.* 1982;7(1):197–226.
22. Wiktorowicz ME. Emergent patterns in the regulation of pharmaceuticals: institutions and interests in the United States, Canada, Britain and France. *J Health Polit Policy Law.* 2003;28(4):615–658.
23. Weissert CS, Weissert, WG. *Governing Health.* 2nd ed. Baltimore, MD: Johns Hopkins University Press; 2002.
24. Easton D. *A Systems Analysis of Political Life.* Chicago, IL: University of Chicago Press; 1979.
25. Wilsford D. States facing interests: struggles over health policy in advanced, industrial democracies. *J Health Polit Policy Law.* 1995;20(3):571–613.
26. Crenson MA. *The Unpolitics of Air Pollution.* Baltimore, MD: Johns Hopkins University Press; 1971.
27. Yankelovich D. The debate that wasn't: the public and the Clinton plan. *Health Aff.* 1995;14(1):7–23.
28. Skocpol T. The rise and the resounding demise of the Clinton Plan. *Health Aff.* 1995;14(1):66–85.
29. Edelman, M. *The Symbolic Uses of Politics.* Urbana, IL: University of Illinois Press; 1964.
30. Starr P. *Remedy and Reaction.* New Haven, CT: Yale University Press; 2013.
31. Brown LD. Getting there: the political context for implementing health care reform. In: Brecher C, ed. *Implementation Issues and National Health Care Reform.* Washington, DC: Josiah Macy, Jr. Foundation; 1992:13–46.
32. Thompson FJ. The evolving challenge of health policy implementation. In: Litman TJ, Robins LS, eds. *Health Politics and Policy.* 3rd ed. New York, NY: Delmar Publishers; 1997:155–175.
33. Pressman JL, Wildavsky A. *Implementation.* Berkeley, CA: University of California Press; 1973.
34. Sparer MS, Brown LD. States and the health care crisis: limits and lessons of laboratory federalism. In: Rich RF, White WD, eds. *Health Policy, Federalism and the American States.* Washington, DC: Urban Institute Press; 1996:181–202.
35. Wenk E. *Margins for Survival: Overcoming Political Limits in Steering Technology.* New York, NY: Pergamon Press; 1979.
36. Moon M. *Medicare Now and in the Future.* 2nd ed. Washington, DC: Urban Institute Press; 1996.
37. Oberlander J. *The Political Life of Medicare.* Chicago, IL: University of Chicago Press; 2003.
38. Torrens PR. Historical evolution and overview of health services in the United States. In: Williams SJ, Torrens PR, eds. *Introduction to Health Services.* 5th ed. New York, NY: Delmar Publishers; 1999:chap 1.
39. Friedman TL. *The World Is Flat.* New York, NY: Farrar Straus & Giroux; 2005.
40. Davis K, Anderson GF, Rowland D, Steinberg EP. *Health Care Cost Containment.* Baltimore, MD: Johns Hopkins University Press; 1990.
41. Gold MR, Siegel JE, Russell LB, Weinstein MC. *Cost-Effectiveness in Health and Medicine.* New York, NY: Oxford University Press; 1996.
42. Lee RH. *Economics for Healthcare Managers.* Chicago, IL: Health Administration Press; 2015.
43. Aaron H, Schwartz WC. *Can We Say No? The Challenge of Rationing Health Care.* Washington, DC: Brookings Institution; 2005.
44. Anonymous. Health care in China: losing patients. *Economist.* 2008;386(8568):58.
45. Lewis M. Informal payments and the financing of health care in developing and transition countries. *Health Aff.* 2007;26(4):984–997.
46. Anonymous. Coming to a crunch. *Economist.* 2008; 386(8572): 51–53.
47. The Syrian healthcare system's collapse. Global Law Initiatives for Sustainable Development. http://www.glawcal.org.uk/index.php/books/9-news/276-the-syrian-healthcare-systems-collapse.html. Accessed August 2, 2016.
48. World Bank. *Global Monitoring Report 2005, Millennium Development Goals: From Consensus to Momentum.* Washington, DC: World Bank; 2005.
49. Sachs JD. *The End of Poverty.* New York, NY: Penguin Press; 2006.
50. Martin G, Grant G, D'Agostino M. Global health funding and economic development. *Global Health.* 2012;8(8). doi: 10.1186/1744-8603-8-8
51. Brower J, Chalk C. *The Global Threat of New and Reemerging Infectious Diseases.* Santa Monica, CA: RAND Corp; 2003.
52. Roychoudhuri O. The end of poverty: an interview with Jeffrey Sachs. *Mother Jones.* May 6, 2005. http://www.motherjones.com/news/qa/2005/05/jeffrey_sachs.html. Accessed January 28, 2008.
53. Newman PJ, Weinstein MC. The diffusion of new technology: costs and benefits to health care. In: Gelijns AC, Halm EA, eds. *The Changing Economics of Medical Technology.* Washington, DC: National Academy Press; 1991:21–34.
54. Ubel PA. *Pricing Life: Why It's Time for Health Care Rationing.* Cambridge, MA: MIT Press; 2001.
55. Wilson RM, Runciman WB, Gibberd RW, Harrison BT, Newby L, Hamilton JD. The quality in Australian health care study. *Med J Aust.* 1995;163:458–471.
56. Kohn L, Corrigan JM, Donaldson MS, eds. *To Err Is Human: Building a Safer Health System.* Washington, DC: National Academy Press; 2000.
57. Vincent C, Neale G, Woloshynowych M. Adverse events in British hospitals: preliminary retrospective record review. *BMJ.* 2001;322(7285):517–519.
58. Baker GR, Norton PG, Flintoft V, Blais R, et al. The Canadian adverse events study: the incidence of adverse events among hospital patients in Canada. *CMAJ.* 2004;170(11):1678–1686.

59. Anonymous. India's fake doctors: Quackdown. *Economist.* 2008:386(8568):58–59.
60. Epstein, AM. The outcomes movement: will it get us where we want to go? *N Engl J Med.* 1990;323:266–270.
61. China's cigarette threat. BBC News. http://news.bbc.co.uk/1/hi/health/216998.stm. November 19, 2007. Accessed January 8, 2008.
62. *Measuring the risks and causes of premature death: Summary of a workshop.* Institute of Medicine, National Academy of Sciences, 2015. Available at https://www.nap.edu/catalog/21656/measuring-the-risks-and-causes-of-premature-death-summary-of. Accessed October 25, 2016.
63. Hall J. Incremental change in the Australian health care system. *Health Aff.* 1999;18(3):95–110.
64. Ikegami N, Campbell JC. Health care reform in Japan: the virtues of muddling through. *Health Aff.* 1999;18(3):56–75.
65. White J. *Competing Solutions: American Health Care Proposals and International Experience.* Washington, DC: Brookings Institution; 1995.
66. Cogan JF, Hubbard RG, Kessler DP. *Healthy, Wealthy, and Wise.* Washington, DC: American Enterprise Institute Press; 2005.
67. Grol R. *Quality Development in Health Care in the Netherlands.* Commonwealth Fund report, commission on a high performance health system, Pub. 910. Available at http://www.commonwealthfund.org/~/media/files/publications/fund-report/2006/mar/quality-development-in-health-care-in-the-netherlands/grol_qualitynetherlands_910-pdf.pdf. Accessed 10/25/16.
68. Anderson GF, Frogner KK, Johns RA, Reinhardt UE. Health spending and use of information technology in OECD countries. *Health Aff.* 2006;25(3):819–831.
69. Kleinke JD. Dot-gov: market failure and the creation of a national health information technology system. *Health Aff.* 2005;24(5):1246–1262.
70. Kaushal R, Bastes DW, Poon EG. Functional gaps in attaining a national health information network. *Health Aff.* 2005;24(5):1281–1289.
71. Donald B. *Newt Gingrich pushing "wired" hospitals.* Associated Press; June 22, 2004.
72. U.S. Department of Health and Human Services. FAQs about NHII. http://aspe.hhs.gov/sp/NHII/FAQ.html. Accessed January 29, 2008.
73. Barraza-Llorens M, Bertozzi S, Gonzalez-Pier E, Gutierrez JP. Addressing inequity in health and health care in Mexico. *Health Aff.* 2002;21(3):47–56.
74. Institute of Medicine. *Crossing the Quality Chasm.* Washington, DC: National Academy Press; 2001.
75. Schoenbaum SC, Audet AJ, Davis K. Obtaining greater value from health care: the roles of the U.S. Government. *Health Aff.* 2003;22(6):183–190.
77. Das J, Gertler PJ. Variations in practice quality in five low-income countries: a conceptual overview. *Health Aff.* 2007;26(3):w296–w309. doi: 10.1377/hlthaff.26.3.w296
78. Harris G, Bogdanich W. Drug tied to China had contaminant, F.D.A. says. *New York Times.* March 6, 2008. http://nyti.ms/2dO4GIn. Accessed March 10, 2008.
79. Associated Press. China executes former FDA chief amid product safety crisis. CBC News. July 10, 2007. http://www.cbc.ca/world/story/2007/07/10/china-tainted-products.html. Accessed January 10, 2008.
80. More disturbing news about contaminated imports. Consumer Reports. http://www.consumerreports.org/cro/news/2007/06/more-disturbing-news-about-contaminated-imports/index.htm. Accessed October 26, 2016.
81. FDA-SFDA China, agreement on the safety of drugs and medical devices. U.S. Food and Drug Administration. http://www.fda.gov/InternationalPrograms/Agreements/Memorandaof Understanding/ucm107512.htm. Published December 11, 2007. Accessed October 26, 2016.
82. Dervaux B, Leleu H, Valdmanis V. Estimating tradeoffs among health care system's objectives. *Health Serv & Outcomes Res Method.* 2004;5:39–58.
83. James M, Hoff T, Davis J, Graham R. Leveraging the power of the media to combat HIV/AIDS. *Health Aff.* 2004;24(3):854–857.
84. Dean C. Guidelines for epidemics: who gets a ventilator? *New York Times.* http://nyti.ms/1OPpFRR. March 25, 2008. Accessed March 25, 2008.
85. Pollack, A. Cost of treatment may influence doctors. *New York Times.* http://www.nytimes.com/2014/04/18/business/treatment-cost-could-influence-doctors-advice.html. Accessed October 25, 2016.
86. Baily, MA. "Rationing" and American health policy. *J Health Polit Policy Law.* 1984;9(3):489–501.
87. Beach MC, Asch DA, Jepson C, Hershey JC, Mohr T, McMorrow S, Ubel PA. Public response to cost-quality tradeoffs in clinical decisions. *Med Decis Making.* 2003;23:369–378.
88. Schunemann HJ, Oxman AD, Fretheim A. Improving the use of research evidence in guideline development: determining which outcomes are important. *Health Policy Res and Sys.* 2006;4(18). doi: 10.1186/1478-4505-4-18
89. Daniels N. Toward ethical review of health system transformations. *Am J Public Health.* 2006;96(3):447–451.
90. Hoedemaekers R, Dekkers W. Justice and solidarity in priority setting in health care. *Health Care Analysis.* 2003;11(4):325–343.
91. Daniels N. Toward ethical review of health system transformations. *Am J Public Health.* 2006;96(3):447–451.
92. de Soto H. *The Mystery of Capital.* New York, NY: Basic Books; 2003.
93. Rawls J. *A Theory of Justice.* New York: NY: Oxford Paper backs; 1971.
94. Goodnough A, Hulse C. Feeding-tube case roils Washington and Florida. *New York Times.* http://hdl.handle.net/10822/982594. March 18, 2005. Accessed August 5, 2016.
95. Rice TH. *The Economics of Health Reconsidered.* 3rd ed. Chicago, IL: Health Administration Press; 2009.
96. Friedman M, Friedman R. *Free to Choose: A Personal Statement.* New York, NY: Manner Books; 1990.
97. Nozick R. *Anarchy, State, and Utopia.* New York, NY: Basic Books; 1974.
98. Kenny N, Giacomini M. Wanted: a new ethics field for health policy analysis. *Health Care Anal.* 2005;13:247.
99. Gaffney AW, Verhoef PA, Hall JB. Should pulmonary/ICU physicians support single payer health care reform? Yes. *Chest.* 2016;150(1):14–15.
100. Antos J, White J. Can we afford four more years of Obamacare? *Inside Sources*, American Enterprise Institute. http://www.aei.org/publication/can-we-afford-four-more-years-of-obamacare/. 2016. Accessed August 5, 2016.
101. Kaiser Family Foundation. A guide to the Supreme Court's decision on the ACA's Medicaid expansion. *Focus on*

Health Reform. https://kaiserfamilyfoundation.files.wordpress.com/2013/01/8347.pdf. August 2012. Accessed August 8, 2016.

102. KHN Morning Briefing. Repeal? Replace? Repair? GOP lawmakers contemplate health law strategy. *Kaiser Health News.* http://khn.org/morning-breakout/repeal-replace-repair-gop-lawmakers-contemplate-health-law-strategy/. February 9, 2015. Accessed August 7, 2016.

103. Kaiser Family Foundation. Status of state action on the Medicaid expansion decision. *State Health Facts.* http://kff.org/health-reform/state-indicator/state-activity-around-expanding-medicaid-under-the-affordable-care-act/. July 7, 2016. Accessed August 1, 2016.

CHAPTER 4
Role of International Organizations in Health Systems

Allen Johnson, Matthew W. Walker, and **Maxwell Droznin**

▸ Introduction

Although national health systems have an important role in providing health services, they are not the only entities that are tasked with improving and ensuring the health of individuals and populations. There is a spectrum of organizations that directly and indirectly contributes to global health that include foundations, development banks, nongovernmental organizations, bilateral agencies, and intergovernmental organizations. Myriad organizations and agencies that are independent from governments or larger health systems work to provide conditions conducive for good health. Additionally, partnerships among nation-states have been ever present in global health through collaborative efforts to prevent conflict, famine, and disease. The focus of this chapter is on organizations beyond national health systems that broadly fall into one of two categories: intergovernmental organizations and nongovernmental organizations.

▸ Intergovernmental Organizations

Intergovernmental organizations (IGOs, also referred to as international governmental organizations) are organizations composed primarily of sovereign states, referred to as member states. IGOs are established by treaty among member states, and the treaty acts as a charter for creating the group. Although formally established by treaty, IGOs are distinct agencies and differ from organizations of sovereign states unified by treaties like the North American Free Trade Agreement (NAFTA). IGOs are also distinguished from informal groupings or coalitions of states, such as the Group of Eight (G8). IGOs vary in function, membership, membership criteria, goals, and scope, which are often outlined in the treaty or charter that established the organization. IGOs are developed to carry out mutual interests with unified aims to resolve conflict and improve international relations, promote international cooperation on matters such as environmental protection, promote human rights and social development (education, health), render humanitarian aid, and foster economic development. Some are more general in scope, whereas others may have specific missions. The largest IGO is the United Nations (UN).

The United Nations System

After World War I, the League of Nations was created in 1920 as the first IGO with the purpose of achieving world peace.[1] At its height, the League was composed of 58 member states.[2] However, the start of World War II made it apparent that the League of Nations had failed at its primary goal. In 1941, Franklin Roosevelt and Winston Churchill signed a "Declaration by United Nations" as a pact to fully cooperate in the war against the Axis powers. In addition, the declaration outlined the necessity to defend life, liberty, religious freedom, and human rights.[3] Later, 47 additional states, including the Soviet Union and China, signed the pact.[4,5] In 1945, a delegation of representatives from 50 governments met in San Francisco for the United Nations Conference on International Organization. It was the culmination of a process that started in 1944 to create a new IGO that would formally replace the now defunct League of Nations. On October 24, 1945, the United Nations Charter was ratified and the UN was officially established.[6]

The UN is composed of 193 member states and is divided into 6 main branches: General Assembly, Security Council, Economic and Social Council, International Court of Justice, Secretariat, and Trusteeship Council. Each branch has its own unique role and function within the UN to help achieve the mission of world peace, friendly relations among nations, and international cooperation on economic, social, environmental and humanitarian issues.[7,8] In addition to the 6 main branches, the UN system includes 11 funds and programs, 15 specialized agencies, and many other affiliated groups.[9] To ensure effective communication among its members, Arabic, Chinese, English, French, Russian, and Spanish are official languages of the UN with documents presented in all 6 languages.[10] The UN headquarters is located in New York City. Although it is situated in the United States, the land occupied by the UN headquarters is under the sole administration of the UN and not the U.S. government. The UN has 3 additional headquarters, located in Geneva, Switzerland; Vienna, Austria; and Nairobi, Kenya. Each site is considered international territory and is exempt from the jurisdiction of local law.[11]

The General Assembly is the main representative arm of the UN. The General Assembly oversees the UN budget, receives reports from various UN system organizations, and makes policies and recommendations for resolutions. The General Assembly also has the power to appoint or dismiss nation-states from various roles within the UN, including Security Council roles and UN membership. Member states are equally represented in the General Assembly, with all 193 given one vote per state. An appointed president of the General Assembly, the secretary-general, presides over its annual meetings. Resolutions pass with a simple majority vote among those present and voting. However, if the membership deems an issue to be critical, then the issue must pass with a two-thirds majority. Such issues are usually matters of budget, appointments, dismissals, peace, and security.[7] The General Assembly may also be called to meet outside of its regularly scheduled meetings for emergency special sessions. Such sessions may be convened either at the request of the Security Council or at the request of a majority of the member states. If the Security Council is at an impasse on resolution, they may hold an emergency special sessions to deal with a breach of peace. In such an event, the General Assembly has the power, with a two-thirds majority vote, to recommend use of armed forces.[12] Special sessions may also be called to confront a range of humanitarian issues, such as the one called in 2001 to discuss the HIV/AIDS pandemic.[13]

According to the UN Charter, the role of the Security Council is to maintain international peace and security. Additionally, the Council has the power to add new members to the UN as well as to alter the UN Charter. All UN member states must comply with resolutions of the Security Council charged with establishing peacekeeping operations, sanctions, and authorizing military action. The 15-member council is composed of 10 appointed, nonpermanent member states and 5 permanent members.[7] The 5 permanent members include the United States, United Kingdom, France, Russia (replacing the Soviet Union in 1991), and China.[14] All Security Council decisions must pass with a 9-member assenting vote. However, a negative vote by one of the 5 permanent members on any resolution is an effective veto.[15]

The Economic and Social Council has the primary role of UN economic, social, and environmental policy review and implementation. Composed of 54 member states, 14 specialized agencies of the UN system, and over 3,200 partner nongovernmental organizations, the Council coordinates the effort of agreed-upon development goals. The Economic and Social Council is elected by the General Assembly for 3-year terms.[7,16]

The International Court of Justice is the judicial branch of the UN. Its primary responsibilities are to settle disputes among member states in accordance with international law and to give legal counsel on questions referred by other UN departments and specialized agencies.[7] The Court is composed of 15 judges elected to 9-year terms by the General Assembly and Security Council.[17] All 193 members of the UN must comply with the court's decisions, and its orders are enforced by the Security Council.[18] Situated in The Hague (the seat of the Dutch government), the Netherlands, the Court is the only primary organization of the UN not headquartered in New York City.[7]

The UN Secretariat is composed of the secretary-general as well as 44,000 civil servants. Its primary purpose is to carry out the mandates of the other 5 main branches, including day-to-day operations, peacekeeping operations, research and communication with non-state participants. The secretary-general is the head of the Secretariat and is appointed to a renewable 5-year term by the General Assembly after a recommendation from the Security Council.[7,19]

Working together with the UN main body, its funds, programs, and specialized agencies are integral to the achievement of the UN mission.

Funds and Programs

Throughout its history, the UN General Assembly has established a number of programs and funds to address particular humanitarian and development concerns. Each of the funds and programs is headed by an Executive Director and is governed by an Executive Board. These bodies report to the General Assembly through the Executive Board. Following are a few notable funds and programs.

United Nations Children's Emergency Fund In 1946, the General Assembly created the United Nations Children's Emergency Fund (UNICEF) to provide food and health care for children of countries that were ravaged by World War II. Since then the goal of the organization has expanded to the development of sustainable community-based systems that provide for the well-being of all children. UNICEF currently operates in 190 countries and relies on member state contributions as well as private donations. For its efforts and achievements, UNICEF was awarded the Nobel Peace Prize in 1965.[20]

United Nations Development Programme Founded in 1965, the United Nations Development Programme (UNDP) serves as the global development network of the UN. Funded entirely by member states, the UNDP works to help 170 countries reach their development goals. The focus of the UNDP is broad and includes the reduction of poverty, inequality, and HIV/AIDS, as well as the creation of sustainable environmental, energy, and crisis prevention projects. To measure their progress, the UNDP releases an annual Human Development Report.[21]

United Nations High Commissioner for Refugees Founded in 1950, the United Nations High Commissioner for Refugees (UNHCR) is a UN agency focusing on the protection and well-being of refugees. It strives to make sure that all peoples have the ability to seek safe asylum in another country when necessary. It also works to protect the ability of refugees to voluntarily integrate into the society of the host country, relocate to another country, or return home. For its efforts, the UNHCR was awarded the Nobel Peace Prize in 1954 and again in 1981.[22]

World Food Programme Considered the largest humanitarian organization focused on hunger in the world, the goal of the World Food Programme (WFP) is to ensure every person has sustained access to food necessary for a healthy life. Founded in 1961, the WFP works in 75 countries and provides food assistance to an estimated 80 million people each year. In addition to food aid, the WFP works on community-level projects that help reduce the risk of food shortage and malnutrition. It is funded by a combination of member-state support and private donations.[23]

Specialized Agencies

Specialized agencies are autonomous organizations working with the UN and each other through the coordination of the United Nations Economic and Social Council. Specialized agencies may or may not have been originally created by the UN, but they are incorporated into the UN system. Although they are part of the UN system, specialized agencies typically have their own member states separate from UN member states. Following are a few notable specialized agencies.

International Monetary Fund The International Monetary Fund (IMF) is composed of 189 member states working to foster global monetary cooperation, secure financial stability, facilitate international trade, promote high employment and sustainable economic growth, and reduce poverty around the world. The IMF promotes international cooperation, trade, exchange-rate stability and sustainable economic growth. The IMF collects money from member states to create a monetary reserve. Countries may borrow from the IMF reserve to stabilize their economy or invest in development projects. Additionally, the IMF may assist in the management of international payment difficulties and financial crises.[9,24,25]

World Bank The World Bank's primary goals are to reduce poverty by providing grants, low-interest loans, and interest-free credit to developing countries and to promote foreign investment and international trade. Founded in 1944, two of the main branches, the International Bank for Reconstruction and Development and the International Development Association, now have 188 and 173 member states, respectively. To become a member of the World Bank, a country must first join the IMF. Although not a UN agency, the World Bank coordinates with the UN on a number of economic development projects.[9,26]

World Health Organization Founded in 1948, the World Health Organization (WHO) is a specialized agency of the UN focused on global public health.[27] Its overall mission is "the attainment of all people to the highest level of health."[28] Through research, health policymaking, education initiatives, and disease monitoring and intervention, the WHO seeks to stop the spread of communicable diseases and lessen the burden of chronic disease. Currently involved in the fight against HIV/AIDS, malaria, and tuberculosis, the WHO is also a major partner in the Global Polio Eradication Initiative. Its *World Health Report* publication highlights health concerns relating to each of its member states.[27]

A Look at Other Intergovernmental Organizations

Although the UN is the largest IGO with great influence and participation around the world, it is by no means the only one. The following section summarizes a few of the world's largest and most influential non-UN IGOs.

African Union

Formed in 2002, the African Union is composed of 54 member states (every country on the African continent except for Morocco). It aims to foster international cooperation, peace, and economic and social development among African peoples. The African Union functions with its own Secretariat; Assembly; Economic, Social, and Cultural Council; Peace and Security Council; and peacekeeping force. Its highest decision-making body, the Assembly of the African Union, is composed of the heads of state of all 54 of its member states.[29]

International Criminal Court

Founded in 2002 as part of the Rome Statute and located in The Hague, the International Criminal Court (ICC) is an international tribunal whose purpose is prosecuting individuals for international war crimes, crimes against humanity, and genocide. The ICC initiates prosecution, following investigations and requests by individual states or by the UN Security Council. The ICC may also take up an investigation when a country's national courts are unwilling to prosecute an individual. Currently, 124 countries are members of the ICC.[30]

Organisation for Economic Co-operation and Development

Originating in 1948 as the Organisation for European Economic Co-operation to help administer the Marshal Plan, it was reformed in 1961 as the Organisation for Economic Co-operation and Development (OECD). The mission of the OECD is to implement policies that improve the economic and social well-being of people around the world. Most of the 34 states that comprise the OECD have high-income economies and a high Human Development Index score. Through government collaboration and analysis of successful strategies and underlying global issues, the OECD provides a forum for implementing quality of life improvement for every country.[31]

World Trade Organization

The World Trade Organization (WTO) was founded in 1995 and currently is composed of 162 member states with the explicit purpose of regulating international trade. The WTO oversees the implementation of trade deals and serves as a forum for its member states to settle trade disputes. It provides assurance among consumers and producers that international markets will remain open to them. The philosophy of the WTO is that by removing trade barriers, it also removes barriers among peoples and nations. Although not formally a UN specialized agency, the WTO has cooperative agreements with the UN.[32]

▸ Nongovernmental Organizations

The term *nongovernmental organization* (NGO) remains vaguely defined. In general, NGOs are broadly defined as "legal entities created by private individuals, private organizations, publicly traded organizations, or in some combination where governmental influence, supervision and management are removed, or at least greatly minimized, from the NGO's strategic and operational mission."[33] The term came into currency in 1945 because of the need for the UN to differentiate in its charter between participation rights for intergovernmental specialized agencies and for international private organizations. At the UN, virtually all types of private bodies can be recognized as NGOs. They only have to be not-for-profit, noncriminal, independent from government control, and not seeking to challenge governments either as a political party or by a narrow focus on human rights.[34] The definition generally used by the U.S. Peace Corps to define an NGO is "a specific type of organization that is not part of government and that possesses the following four characteristics:

- Works with people to help them improve their social and economic situations and prospects
- Was formed voluntarily
- Is independent, controlled by those who have formed it or by management boards representing the organization's stakeholders
- Is not-for-profit; although NGOs engage in revenue-generating activities, the proceeds are used in pursuit of the organization's aims."[35]

NGOs serve in a wide and varied spectrum of advocacy and operations around the globe. From locally based groups meeting in private homes to global giants with budgets in the hundreds of millions of U.S. dollars, NGOs make significant contributions to global health based on their unique missions. NGOs engage in a wide array of activities involving political advocacy, the environment, health care, women and children's rights, economic development, and many other issues. By definition, NGOs are independent from government influence, and therefore they are often in a unique position to address issues that governments do not. Operating in milieu, lacking constraints by bureaucratic or political considerations, NGOs are often able to provide leadership and resources for producing and advocating public policy when government agencies are unable or unwilling to do so. The efficiency of NGOs is, in part, attributed to their grassroots approach. According to the UN, the strength of NGOs lies in their "proximity to their members or clients, the flexibility and the high degree of people's involvement and participation in their activities, which leads to strong commitments, appropriateness of solutions and high acceptance of decisions implemented."[36]

NGOs are not formally part of the UN system; rather, some NGOs work closely with the UN in consultative capacities. Having participated in the work of the UN from its inception, NGOs first took a role in formal UN deliberations through the Economic and Social Council in 1946. Initially, 41 NGOs were granted consultative status by the Council, and by 1992, more than 700 NGOs had attained that level of credibility. The number has been steadily increasing ever since, and today, 2,921 NGOs hold consultative status with the UN.[37]

There are over 1.5 million NGOs operating in the United States alone.[38] The amount of resources controlled and distributed by these organizations vary greatly and can be quite extensive. For instance, one of the largest in terms of budget and scope, World Vision, had annual expenses for 2015 of over US $993 million,[39] as much as 20 times the gross domestic product (GDP) of some of the smaller countries around the world.[40] Based on firm financial growth, the largest NGOs continue to expand in both funding and mission.

Classifying NGOs

Nationally and internationally, the broad range of NGOs has become so expansive that the establishment of a single classification system is exceedingly difficult. The World Bank classifies NGOs into two categories: operational and advocacy.[41] According to the WHO definition, the primary purpose of an operational NGO is the design and implementation of development-related projects, as opposed to advocacy NGOs which assert a primary purpose to defend or to promote a specific cause. NGOs can be further classified as either relief oriented or development oriented by the development status of the countries in which they work, by the nature of their work, and whether they are faith based or secular or any combination thereof. Due to extensive variation among NGOs, a list of acronyms has been developed to aid in the classification of such organizations. Some examples of these include the following:

- FONGO—Funder-Organized NGO
- RINGO—Religious International NGO
- PVO—Private Voluntary Organization
- CBO—Community-Based Organization
- CSO—Civil Society Organization
- BONGO—Business-Organized NGO
- TANGO—Technical Assistance NGO

A Look at Some of the Largest International NGOs

The following section summarized the NGO "global giants," who have hundreds, even thousands, of employees and budgets in the hundreds of millions of dollars. This list, although certainly not exhaustive, represents some of the largest and most established NGOs working in the world today.

Acumen

Acumen is a nonprofit global venture fund that uses entrepreneurial approaches to address the problems of poverty. Headquartered in New York City, with regional offices in India, Pakistan, Kenya, and Ghana, it aims to help build financially sustainable organizations that deliver affordable goods and services to improve the lives of the poor. Acumen raises charitable donations that allow it to make long-term debt or equity investments in early-stage companies providing reliable and affordable access to agricultural inputs and markets, quality education, clean energy, healthcare services, formal housing, and safe drinking water to low-income customers. Founded in 2001, Acumen has approved US $88 million in investments and has invested in 82 enterprises, creating over 60,000 jobs.[42]

Amnesty International

Amnesty International (commonly known as Amnesty) was founded in 1961 in London. It was originally established to facilitate the release of political prisoners. Amnesty has since grown into an organization aimed at upholding the whole spectrum of human rights, including abolishing the death penalty, protecting sexual and reproductive rights, combatting discrimination, and defending refugee and migrant rights. It draws attention to human rights abuses, and it campaigns for compliance with international laws and standards. The organization was awarded the Nobel Peace Prize in 1977. Amnesty currently has over 7 million members and supporters worldwide.[43]

BRAC

BRAC (formally Bangladesh Rural Advancement Committee) is an international development organization based in Bangladesh. Established in 1972 as a small-scale relief and rehabilitation project to help returning war refugees, today BRAC is the largest NGO in the world in terms of number of employees. BRAC employs over 100,000 people, roughly 70% of whom are women. The organization's activities involve economic development, education, public health, and gender equality. BRAC's Economic Development Programme includes the use of microcredit. It provides collateral-free loans to mostly poor, landless, rural women, enabling them to generate income and improve their standards of living. Reaching nearly 4 million borrowers, BRAC has provided loans to those who, due to extreme poverty, have been otherwise unable to secure other financial sources. BRAC's microcredit program has funded over US $1.9 billion in loans with 95% of its borrowers being women. According to BRAC, the repayment rate is over 98%.[44,45]

CARE International

Founded in 1945 to provide relief to World War II survivors, CARE is committed to promoting social change and ending global poverty. CARE currently works in 95 countries around the world. A leading humanitarian organization fighting global poverty, CARE's philosophy is that women are essential in regard to helping families and communities escape poverty. Women are at the heart of CARE's community-based efforts to improve basic education, prevent the spread of HIV, increase access to clean water and sanitation, expand economic opportunity, and protect natural resources. CARE also provides emergency aid to survivors of war and natural disasters.[46]

Human Rights Watch

The largest human rights organization based in the United States, Human Rights Watch conducts fact-finding investigations into human rights abuses around the world. Founded in 1978 as Helsinki Watch to monitor human rights in the former Soviet Union, Human Rights Watch publishes numerous books and reports every year, generating extensive coverage in local and international media. Human Rights Watch also meets with government officials to urge changes in policy and practice. In extreme circumstances, Human Rights Watch presses for the withdrawal of military and economic support from governments that egregiously violate the rights of their people.[47]

International Committee of the Red Cross

The International Committee of the Red Cross (ICRC) is based in Geneva and is a three-time Nobel Prize Laureate. The ICRC is mandated to protect victims of international and internal armed conflicts. Such victims include prisoners, refugees, civilians, and other noncombatants. The ICRC is part of the International Red Cross and Red Crescent Movement, which—along with the ICRC—includes the International Federation of Red Cross and Red Crescent Societies consisting of 190 national societies. The ICRC is the oldest and most honored organization within the Movement and one of the most widely recognized humanitarian organizations in the world. Today, the ICRC is based in around 80 countries and has a total of more than 12,000 staff.[48]

Médecins Sans Frontières (Doctors Without Borders)

Médecins Sans Frontières (MSF) is an independent humanitarian medical aid agency that is committed to two objectives: providing medical aid wherever needed, regardless of race, religion, politics, or gender, and raising awareness of the plight of the people they help. Founded in 1971, MSF has 20 country offices and provides emergency medical aid in more than 60 countries. MSF teams are composed of doctors, nurses, and other professionals, medical and nonmedical, working alongside locally hired staff. In 2014, MSF teams working in 63 countries around the world provided around 8.3 million outpatient consultations, admitted more than 511,800 patients for inpatient care, and helped deliver more than 194,000 babies.[49]

Oxfam International

The name *Oxfam* comes from the British group Oxford Committee for Famine Relief, founded in 1942 during World War II. Oxfam International is a confederation of 18 independent NGOs working with thousands of partner organizations in more than 90 countries with the common goal of ending global poverty and related injustice. Oxfam works with communities, allies, and partner organizations undertaking long-term development, emergency work, research, and advocacy. Oxfam focuses on a broad range of issues, including trade, conflict, debt and aid, and education.[50]

Partners in Health

Partners in Health (PIH) was founded in 1987 in Boston, Massachusetts, United States, to deliver health care to the poorest areas of Haiti. Today, PIH has programs in nine countries on four continents. With a mission to provide a preferential option for the poor in health care, PIH works globally to bring the benefits of modern science to those most in need through service delivery, training, research, and advocacy.[51]

Save the Children International

Save the Children International promotes children's rights, provides relief, and helps support children in developing countries. Headquartered in the United Kingdom, it aims to improve the lives of children through better education, health care, and economic opportunities, as well as to provide emergency aid in natural disasters, war, and other conflicts. The organization includes 29 national organizations who are members of Save the Children International, providing a global network of organizations supporting local partners in over 120 countries around the world.[52]

World Vision International

World Vision International is a Christian humanitarian organization that is dedicated to working with children, families, and communities worldwide to reach their full potential by tackling the causes of poverty and injustice. World Vision began caring for orphans and other children in need first in South Korea in 1950, and then it expanded throughout Asia. Today, World Vision International works in nearly 100 countries around the world and has expanded its mission to include community development and advocacy for the poor. World Vision International's child sponsorship program has been popular in attracting donors who send funds each month to provide support for sponsored children and projects.[53]

NGO Diversity by Country

NGOs have become increasingly influential in world affairs. They often impact the social, economic, and political activities of communities and countries as a whole. In numerous countries, NGOs have led the way in democratization, combatting diseases and illnesses, promoting and enforcing human rights, and increasing standards of living. It is difficult to estimate the comprehensive value of NGOs over the past 60 years (since the establishment of the UN Charter); however, it is clear that NGOs will continue to play an important role into the future considering the varied nature of their work. **TABLE 4-1** lists examples of NGOs actively working in countries discussed in this book. A diverse sample of NGOs was chosen to present an overview of the broad range of work they perform on a global scale.

TABLE 4-1 Select Operational and Advocacy NGOs with Country-Specific Missions

Country	NGO	Example activity	Country	NGO	Example activity
Australia	OzGREEN	Water conservation in the Murray Darling river basin	Israel	Magan David Adom	Distributing and storage services of blood plasma
Bangladesh	BRAC	Train community health workers	Japan	Kokkyo naki Kodomotachi	Video workshops for children
Botswana	Direct Relief International	Medical assistance programs	Jordan	Islamic Relief Worldwide	Seasonal Ramadhan and Qurbani projects
Brazil	Oiyakaha	Protect the Amazon rainforest	Korea	Korean Association for Suicide Prevention	National Suicide Prevention Day
Canada	Coaching Association of Canada	Improve the effectiveness of coaching through national certification	Mexico	CORECO	Conflict resolution workshops
China	Zigen Fund	Rural village development	Nigeria	Girl Power Initiative	Educational programs for young women
France	Ligue des droits de l'Homme	Observe, defend, and promulgate human rights	Peru	Peruvian Hearts	Empower young women through education and mentorship to become leaders within their communities
Germany	Deutscher Musikrat	Support improvements in the social situation of musicians	Russia	No to Alcohol and Drug Abuse	Prevention and recovery programs
Ghana	International Trachoma Initiative	Dedicated to the elimination of blinding trachoma	Turkey	AÇEV	Early childhood education
India	Operation Smile	Repair cleft lips and cleft pallets	United Kingdom	Parkinson's Disease Society	Fund medical care and support groups
Ireland	Crisis Housing Caring Support	Support people who are at risk for homelessness	United States	American Red Cross	Disaster relief

The NGO Code of Conduct for Health Systems Strengthening is a response to the recent growth in the number of international NGO's associated with the health sector worldwide. The code serves as a guide to encourage NGO practices that contribute to building public health systems and discouraging harm. The primary areas of focus include the following:

1. employee hiring;
2. employee compensation;
3. continuous training and support;
4. minimizing burdens on government due to multiple NGO projects in their countries;
5. helping connect communities to the formal health systems; and

6. providing support to governments through policy advocacy.

The Code is administered by Health Alliance International and can be viewed in detail at http://ngocodeofconduct.org/

References

1. Tomuschat C. *The United Nations at Age Fifty: A Legal Perspective*. Martinus Nijhoff Publishers; 1995:77.
2. United Nations. Chronology of the League of Nations. http://www.unog.ch/80256EDD006B8954/(httpAssets)/3DA94AAFEB9E8E76C1256F340047BB52/$file/sdn_chronology.pdf. Accessed May 12, 2016.
3. Foreign Relations of the United States. The Conferences at Washington, 1941-1942 and Casablanca, 1943. Washington, DC: Government Printing Office; 1968.
4. Roll D. *The Hopkins Touch: Harry Hopkins and the Forging of the Alliance to Defeat Hitler*. Oxford University Press; 2013:172–175.
5. Osmańczyk E, Mango A. *Encyclopedia of the United Nations and International Agreements* 4. Taylor & Francis; 2004.
6. United Nations. 1945: The San Francisco Conference. http://www.un.org/en/sections/history-united-nations-charter/1945-san-francisco-conference/index.html. Accessed May 12, 2016.
7. United Nations. Main Organs. http://www.un.org/en/sections/about-un/main-organs/index.html. Accessed May 12, 2016.
8. United Nations. The Charter of the United Nations. http://www.un.org/en/sections/un-charter/chapter-i/index.html. Accessed May 12, 2016.
9. United Nations. Funds, Programmes, Specialized Agencies and Others. http://www.un.org/en/sections/about-un/funds-programmes-specialized-agencies-and-others/index.html. Accessed May 12, 2016.
10. United Nations. Official Languages. http://www.un.org/en/sections/about-un/official-languages/index.html. Accessed May 12, 2016.
11. Fomerand J. *The A to Z of the United Nations*. Lanham, Maryland: Scarecrow Press; 2009:149–151.
12. United Nations. Emergency Special Sessions. http://www.un.org/ga/sessions/emergency.shtml. Accessed May 12, 2016.
13. United Nations. General Assembly Special Session on HIV/AIDS. http://www.un.org/ga/aids/coverage /. Accessed May 12, 2016.
14. United Nations. United Nations Security Council. http://www.un.org/en/sc/members/. Accessed May 12, 2016.
15. Fasulo L. *An Insider's Guide to the UN*. New Haven, Connecticut: Yale University; 2004:40–41.
16. United Nations. United Nations Economic and Social Council. http://www.un.org/en/ecosoc/about/index.shtml. Accessed May 12, 2016.
17. Harris D. *Cases and Materials on International Law*. 7th ed. London, England: Sweet & Maxwell; 2012:39.
18. United Nations. Chapter XIV of the UN Charter (Articles 92-96). http://www.un.org/en/sections/un-charter/chapter-xiv/index.html. Accessed May 12, 2016.
19. United Nations. Secretariat. http://www.un.org/en/sections/about-un/secretariat/index.html. Accessed May 12, 2016.
20. United Nations Children's Emergency Relief Fund. About. http://www.unicef.org/about/. Accessed May 12, 2016.
21. The United Nations Development Programme. A World of Development Experience. http://www.undp.org/content/undp/en/home/operations/about_us.html. Accessed May 12, 2016.
22. United Nations High Commissioner for Refugees. About us. http://www.unhcr.org/pages/49c3646c2.html. Accessed May 12, 2016.
23. World Food Programme. About us. https://www.wfp.org/about. Accessed May 12, 2016.
24. International Monetary Fund. About the IMF. https://www.imf.org/external/about.htm. Accessed May 12, 2016.
25. Lipscy P. Explaining institutional change: policy areas, outside options, and the Bretton Woods Institutions. *American Journal of Political Science*; 2015:59(2):341–356.
26. World Bank. About. http://www.worldbank.org/en/about. Accessed May 12, 2016.
27. World Health Organization. History. http://www.who.int/about/history/en/. Retrieved May 12, 2016.
28. World Health Organization. Constitution of the World Health Organization. http://www.who.int/governance/eb/who_constitution_en.pdf. Accessed May 12, 2016.
29. East African Center for Law and Justice. The AU: Mission, Goals, Organs and Objectives. http://eaclj.org/general/24-general-east-africa/103-the-au-mission-goals-organs-and-objectives.html. Accessed May 12, 2016.
30. International Criminal Court. About. https://www.icc-cpi.int/about. Accessed May 12, 2016.
31. Organisation for Economic Co-operation and Development. About. http://www.oecd.org/about/. Accessed May 12, 2016.
32. World Trade Organization. The WTO… in Brief. https://www.wto.org/english/thewto_e/whatis_e/inbrief_e/inbr00_e.htm. Accessed May 12, 2016.
33. Duke University. NGO Database. http://library.duke.edu/research/subject/guides/ngo_guide/ngo_database. Accessed May 09, 2016.
34. Willetts P. What is a Non-Governmental Organization? http://www.staff.city.ac.uk/p.willetts/CS-NTWKS/NGO-ART.HTM. Accessed May 9, 2016.
35. Peace Corps. An NGO training guide for Peace Corps Volunteers. Peace Corps Information Collection and Exchange; 2003. Publication number MOO7O. http://files.peacecorps.gov/multimedia/pdf/library/M0070_all.pdf. Accessed April 2, 2008.
36. United Nations Department of Economic and Social Affairs. http://esa.un.org/coordination/ngo/new/index.asp?page=intro.
37. United Nations. Department of Economic and Social Council. List of nongovernmental organizations in consultative status with the Economic and Social Council as of September 1, 2013.
38. Bureau of Democracy, Human Rights and Labor. Fact Sheet: Non-Governmental Organizations (NGOs) in the United States. US Department of State. http://www.humanrights.gov/dyn/2016/01/fact-sheet-non-governmental-organizations-ngos-in-the-united-states/. January 16, 2016. Accessed May 16, 2016.
39. World Vision. Letter from the CFO: Financial Results for 2015. http://www.worldvision.org/sites/default/files/2015-letter-from-cfo.pdf. Accessed March 28, 2007.
40. International Monetary Fund. World Economic Outlook Database. Data for 2015. New York, NY: IMF; May 2016.
41. World Bank. Guidelines for Non-Government Organizations. http://www.worldbank.org/afr/ik/guidelines/ngoguides.pdf. Accessed May 9, 2016.
42. Acumen. About Acumen. http://acumen.org/about/. Accessed May 16, 2016.
43. Amnesty International. Who we are. https://www.amnesty.org/en/who-we-are/. Accessed May 16, 2016.
44. BRAC. Brac at a glance. http://www.brac.net/sites/default/files/BRAC-at-a-glance-december-2012.pdf. Accessed May 16, 2016.

45. BRAC. What we do. http://www.bracuk.net/. Accessed May 16, 2016.
46. CARE. Where we work. http://www.care.org/work/where-we-work. Accessed May14, 2016.
47. Human Rights Watch. About us. https://www.hrw.org/about. Accessed May 14, 2016.
48. International Federation of Red Cross and Red Crescent Societies. Annual Report 2014. http://www.ifrc.org/Global/Documents/Secretariat/201601/1296700-IFRCAnnualReport2014-EN_LR.pdf. Accessed May 14, 2016.
49. MSF. About us. http://www.doctorswithoutborders.org/about-us/faq. Accessed May 14, 2016.
50. Oxfam. FAQ. https://www.oxfam.org/en/frequently-asked-questions#1. Accessed May 14, 2016.
51. Partners in Health. Countries. http://www.pih.org/countries. Accessed May 14, 2016.
52. Save the Children International. About us. https://www.savethechildren.net/. Accessed May 14, 2016.
53. World Vision. Our impact. http://www.worldvision.org/our-impact. Accessed May 14, 2016.

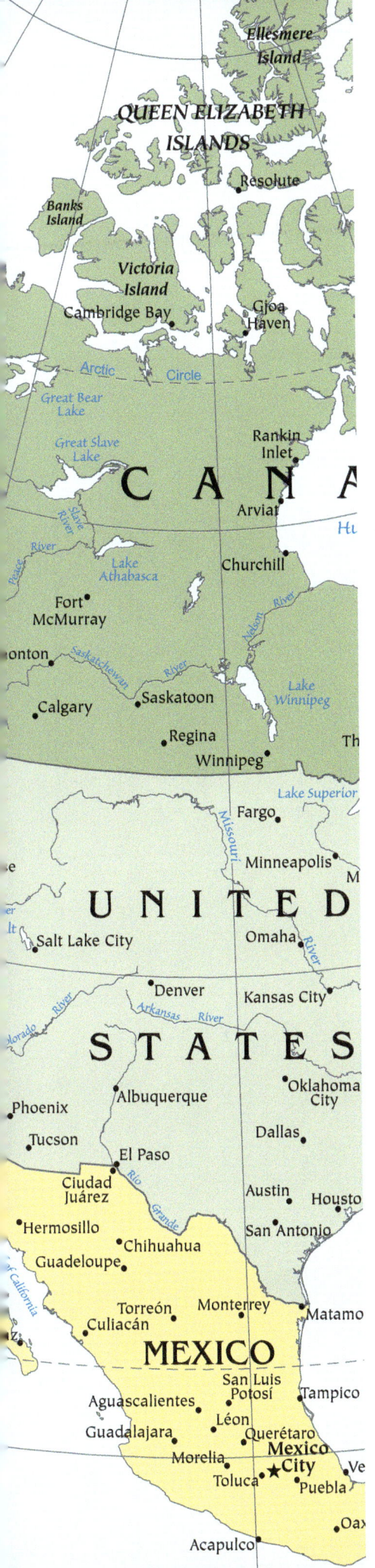

PART II

Health Systems by Country

The Americas Region

CHAPTER 5	United States
CHAPTER 6	Canada
CHAPTER 7	Mexico
CHAPTER 8	Peru
CHAPTER 9	Brazil

European Region

CHAPTER 10	United Kingdom
CHAPTER 11	France
CHAPTER 12	Germany
CHAPTER 13	Ireland
CHAPTER 14	Russia

Courtesy of the Central Intelligence Agency

Middle East and Africa

CHAPTER 15 Turkey

CHAPTER 16 Jordan

CHAPTER 17 Israel

CHAPTER 18 Ghana

CHAPTER 19 Nigeria

CHAPTER 20 Botswana

Asia and Pacific Region

CHAPTER 21 Bangladesh

CHAPTER 22 India

CHAPTER 23 China

CHAPTER 24 Japan

CHAPTER 25 Korea

CHAPTER 26 Australia

CHAPTER 5

United States

Leiyu Shi, Douglas A. Singh, and **Hailun Liang**

▸ Country Description

TABLE 5-1 United States	
Nationality	Noun: American(s) Adjective: American
Ethnic groups	White 77.1%, black 13.3%, Asian 5.6%, Amerindian and Alaska native 1.2%, native Hawaiian and other Pacific islander 0.2%, two or more races 2.6%, Hispanic or Latino 17.6%* (2015 est.)
Religions	Protestant 46.5%, Roman Catholic 20.8%, Mormon 1.6%, other Christian 1.7%, Jewish 1.9%, Buddhist 0.7%, Muslim 0.9%, Hindu 0.7%, other or unspecified 1.8%, unaffiliated 22.8%, don't know/refused 0.6% (2014 est.)
Language	English 78.5%, Spanish 13.3%, other Indo-European 3.7%, Asian and Pacific Island 3.5%, other 1.0% (2015 est.)
Literacy	Definition: age 15 and over and can read and write Total population: 99% Male: 99% Female: 99% (2003 est.)
Government type	Constitution-based federal republic; strong democratic tradition
Date of independence	July 4, 1776 (from Great Britain)
Gross Domestic Product (GDP) per capita	$17,947 billion (2015 est.)
Unemployment rate	5.2% (2015 est.)

(continues)

TABLE 5-1 United States (continued)

Natural hazards	Tsunamis, volcanoes, and earthquake activities around the Pacific Basin; hurricanes along the Atlantic and Gulf of Mexico coasts; tornadoes in the Midwest and Southeast; mud slides in California; forest fires in the West; flooding; permafrost in northern Alaska a major impediment to development
Environment: current issues	Air pollution resulting in acid rain in both the United States and Canada; carbon dioxide from the burning of fossil fuels; water pollution from runoff of pesticides and fertilizers; careful management of limited natural freshwater resources in much of the West; desertification
Population	321,418,820 (2015 est.)
Age structure	0–14 years: 18.99% (male 31,171,623/female 29,845,713) 15–64 years: 66.13% (male 106,043,437/female 106,477,846) 65 years and over: 14.88% (male 21,129,978/female 26,700,267) (2015 est.)
Median age	Total: 37.8 years Male: 36.5 years Female: 39.2 years (2015 est.)
Population growth rate	0.78% (2015 est.)
Birth rate	12.49 births/1,000 population (2015 est.)
Death rate	488 deaths/100,000 population (2016 est.)
Disease burden	**Communicable disease deaths:** 31/100,000 population **Noncommunicable disease deaths:** 413/100,000 population **Injury deaths:** 44/100,000 population (2016 est.)
Net migration rate	3.86 migrant(s)/1,000 population (2015 est.)
Gender ratio	At birth: 1.1 male(s)/female (2014 est.) Under 15 years: 1.05 male(s)/female 15–64 years: 1 male(s)/female 65 years and over: 0.79 male(s)/female Total population: 0.97 male(s)/female (2015 est.)
Infant mortality rate	Total: 5.87 deaths/1,000 live births Male: 6.37 deaths/1,000 live births Female: 5.35 deaths/1,000 live births (2015 est.)
Life expectancy at birth	Total population: 79.68 years Male: 77.32 years Female: 81.97 years (2015 est.)
Total fertility rate	1.87 children born/woman (2015 est.)
HIV/AIDS adult prevalence rate	0.4–0.9% (2012 est.)
Number of people living with HIV/AIDS	1,200,000 (2016 est.)
HIV/AIDS deaths	6,955 (2013 est.)

*Hispanics may be of any race, so they also are included in applicable race categories.

Data from Central Intelligence Agency. The World Fact Book, 2016: United States. https://www.cia.gov/library/publications/the-world-factbook/geos/us.html. Accessed April 14, 2016.

Introduction

The United States has a unique system of healthcare delivery. Unlike other developed countries where health care is perceived as a right and almost all citizens are entitled to receive at least basic healthcare services, the United States still has a significant number of people who are without health insurance despite recent healthcare reform effort (i.e., the Affordable Care Act, nicknamed Obama Care). The United States also witnesses significant disparities in health status across racial/ethnic and socioeconomic groups and between those insured and uninsured. The U.S. healthcare delivery "system" is not a system in the true sense, even though it is called a system when reference is made to its various features, components, and services. The system is fragmented because there are numerous private insurance plans and tax-supported public programs. The system has periodically undergone incremental changes, mainly in response to concerns about cost, access, and quality. In spite of these changes, providing at least a basic package of health care at an affordable price to every American remains an unrealized goal. People outside the United States sometimes wonder why Americans do not have a national healthcare system. The answers lie in the way American culture was shaped by a history that resulted in self-reliance, an aversion to excessive taxes, and a preference for limited government. Also, within the country today, sentiments about health care are paradoxical. Influenced by the American media, Americans have come to believe that the healthcare system may be in need of major reform, but at an individual level, they are mostly satisfied with their own care.

The main objective of this chapter is to give a general overview of the United States as a nation and to furnish a broad understanding of the healthcare delivery system. For a more in-depth understanding and systematic analysis of U.S. healthcare, readers may wish to consult additional textbooks, including those by the authors.[1,2]

History

The first Americans are believed to be people who crossed from Asia to North America over a narrow land strip that connects Siberia to Alaska and that is now submerged below the Bering Strait.[3] This migration likely occurred millennia before the Whites arrived from Europe. Gradually, many of these American Indians and Alaskan Natives, as we call them today, migrated southward. By the time the Europeans arrived, the indigenous population had spread throughout the North American continent.

In the 15th century, European sailors began exploring new routes to India by sailing west from Spain and Italy. The modern history of the Americas begins with the voyage of Christopher Columbus, who crossed the Atlantic and reached the Bahamas in 1492.[3] In subsequent expeditions, he discovered other islands in the Caribbean Sea. Although Columbus is credited with discovering the New World, he never reached the continent of North America[4]; however, after the New World had been discovered, other explorers, such as Juan Ponce de León and John Cabot, reached North America's eastern shores. The voyage of John Cabot, an Italian, was commissioned by the British king. Cabot's voyage to North America later provided the basis for England's claim over the continent. Later, King Francis I of France sent Giovanni da Verrazano, an Italian adventurer, and subsequently Jacques Cartier, a French explorer, to lay claims on parts of North America on behalf of France. The Dutch hired Henry Hudson, an English navigator, who also reached North America. However, America was named after another Italian explorer, Amerigo (Americus in Latin) Vespucci, who likely explored the American coast further than any navigator of his time in at least two voyages; the accounts of his voyages were published in Europe.[5]

The first European colony in what would become the United States was established by neither England nor France but by the Spanish forces of Pedro Menéndez in what is now Florida. Menéndez destroyed a group of French settlers in northern Florida in 1565. The British sent Walter Raleigh, who in 1585 established the first British colony, on Roanoke Island off the coast of North Carolina. Although this colony did not last long, the British finally succeeded in establishing a colony in Jamestown, Virginia, in 1607. This was the first permanent English settlement in what later became the United States. Virginia soon became prosperous by growing tobacco on plantations. These plantations required a labor force in excess of the available supply. In 1619, a Dutch ship brought the first African slaves to Virginia. By the 18th century, slavery became an integral part of the economic and social composition of Virginia.[6] Around 1795, the rapid increase in cotton cultivation brought slaves to other parts of the South.[7]

The early 1600s saw the beginning of a great tide of emigration from Europe to North America. Between 1620 and 1635, economic difficulties swept England. Many people could not find work. Even skilled artisans could earn little more than a bare living. Poor crop yields added to the distress. Other European emigrants left their homelands to escape political oppression, to seek freedom to practice their religions, or to find opportunities denied them at home. Britain continued to establish colonies in Plymouth (now Massachusetts), Maryland, Rhode Island, Connecticut, the Carolinas, New Jersey, and Pennsylvania. The New England colonies flourished from profits gained through commerce in fishing. The French established their settlements in what is now Quebec, Canada, and in Alabama and Louisiana. The Dutch established some scattered footholds, but theirs was never a strong colony in terms of political power or stability.[6] The Spaniards also established settlements mainly in the southern parts of North America. Around 1732, Britain founded a colony in Georgia to avert any threats of Spain's expansion into South Carolina.[6] In 1664, under the threat of an armed conflict, the Dutch surrendered New Amsterdam to the British, and the colony was renamed New York.[3] The French lost control of their colonies after they were defeated by the British. The British then had 13 colonies, all located east of the Mississippi River, that were secure for the first time in almost a century from attack by another power.[6]

A chain of events led to the War for American Independence. The Anglo-French wars were fought in both America and Europe and had dragged on from 1689 to 1763. The British wanted the colonies to bear part of the burden of new taxes. The American Revenue Act (Sugar Act) of 1764 and the Stamp Act of 1765 were passed by the British Parliament as means of raising revenues from Americans. The Currency Act of 1764 prohibited the American colonies from issuing paper currency. The Townshend Revenue Act of 1767 imposed taxes on tea, lead, paper, glass, and paint imported into the colonies.[6] The Americans bitterly resented these taxes. Boycotts, protests, and skirmishes between the citizens and British troops posted in Boston brought on the Boston Massacre of 1770 in which three Bostonians were killed and two were mortally wounded. The incident inflamed public opinion.[6] The Tea Act of 1773 gave the British East India Company monopoly status to sell tea to the colonies. This action resulted in what is referred to as the Boston Tea Party in which American radicals boarded the ships carrying prime tea and dumped about 350 chests of tea into Boston harbor as a gesture of protest. Retaliation from Britain brought on the Coercive Acts of 1774. Although these acts were designed to coerce the Massachusetts colony into submissiveness, they had the opposite effect.[6] The American Revolution was born as a result of what Americans generally believed to be tyranny under Great Britain. Later, the framers of the Constitution were careful to place limits on the government's power over individual freedoms.

Not surprisingly, the Revolutionary War began in the Boston area with fighting between armed citizens and British forces in 1775. On June 10, 1776, the Continental Congress appointed a committee under the leadership of Thomas Jefferson to draft the Declaration of Independence. On July 4 of that year, Congress approved the Declaration of Independence, according to which the 13 colonies in North America were "free and independent states" and became the United States of America. The Revolutionary War came to an end on October 19, 1781, when the American army, under the command of George Washington and with the help of the French, defeated the British forces at Yorktown, Virginia. In 1783, the Treaty of Paris endorsed the independence of the colonies from Great Britain. In 1789, George Washington became the first president of the United States.

When the population of a state reached 60,000 free inhabitants, it was eligible to join the union (the United States). During Washington's tenure as president, Vermont, Kentucky, and Tennessee were added to the union. In later years, the country acquired land from France, Spain, Great Britain, Mexico, and Russia and annexed the Republic of Texas and the Republic of Hawaii. In 1959, Alaska and Hawaii became the 49th and 50th states, respectively, to join the union. The United States also has a number of territories, all islands or groups of islands, that are under the jurisdiction of the federal government. The main territories are Puerto Rico, U.S. Virgin Islands, American Samoa, Guam, and Northern Mariana Islands. The nation's capital is Washington, DC (District of Columbia), which is a federal district.

Size and Geography

The total area of the United States is 3.79 million square miles (9.83 million square kilometers). Of this area, 93.0% is land (**FIGURE 5-1**).[8] The estimated population in July 2015 was 321.4 million.[9] The United States occupies roughly 6.5% of the world's surface (about the same as China, and a little over half as much as Russia) and has about 4.4% of the world's population.

Forty-eight states and the District of Columbia are situated between Canada and Mexico and between the Atlantic and Pacific oceans. Alaska and Hawaii are physically separate from the rest of the country (see the U.S. map). Alaska occupies the northwestern corner of the North American continent, with Canada to its east and Russia to the west across the Bering Strait. Hawaii consists of 8 major islands and over a 100 small ones. The main Hawaiian islands are located approximately 2,400 miles (3,900 kilometers) southwest of the U.S. mainland in the mid-Pacific.

FIGURE 5-1 Map of the United States
© Bardocz Peter/Shutterstock

The 50 states have significantly different sizes. Alaska is the largest state and is about 425 times bigger than the smallest, Rhode Island. The three largest states, Alaska, Texas, and California, make up about 30% of the entire country. The most populous states are California (39.1 million), Texas (27.5 million), and Florida (20.3 million). Wyoming (586,107), Vermont (626,042), and North Dakota (756,927) have the least number of people.[9]

Government and Political System

The United States is a representative republic in which those who govern are popularly elected by those who are governed. All U.S. citizens who have attained the age of 18 have the right to vote. As the supreme law of the land, the Constitution of the United States (adopted on September 17, 1787) incorporates several key principles of government: (1) government by the people, which means that it is the people who form the government; (2) limited government, which means that government can only do what the people allow it to do through exercise of a duly developed system of laws[10]; (3) federalism, according to which the central government shares sovereign powers with the state governments[10]; (4) separation of powers, which divides political power among the three branches of government: the legislative, the executive, and the judicial; (5) checks and balances that emanate from separation of powers and enable inspection and restraint of one part of the political system by another[7]; (6) respect for individual worth, a principle that was first embraced in the Declaration of Independence and that has been used as a measure of the value of social institutions to individuals[7]; and (7) equal opportunity, which stresses individual worth by making available to each individual the opportunity to develop his or her abilities and interests[7]; and (8) a Bill of Rights that protects individual liberties against violations by the government. These rights were added to the Constitution in the form of 10 amendments that were ratified by all states in 1791. The First Amendment protects the right to freedom of religion and freedom of expression from government interference.

The federal government has three branches: legislative (the Senate and House of Representatives), executive (the president and cabinet departments), and judicial (federal courts and the U.S. Supreme Court). Each of the states also has its own constitution and its own legislative, executive, and judicial branches. In general, the states can do anything that is not prohibited by the U.S. Constitution or that is contrary to federal policy. The major reserved powers of the state include the authority to regulate commerce within the state and to exercise police powers. The latter refer to the state's right to pass and enforce laws that promote health, safety, welfare, and morality.[10]

Two political parties have traditionally dominated the political process. Other minor party groups have appeared on the political scene, but none has succeeded in replacing the two major parties,[7] currently the Republican and Democratic parties.

In response to issues that politicians believe their constituents face, the government makes decisions and takes actions that are broadly referred to as public policy. Policies can take the form of new laws; repeals of existing laws; and interpretations and implementations of laws, executive orders, and court rulings. Throughout the policymaking process, the system of constitutional checks and balances prevails. The president often plays an important leadership role in key policy issues.

The Constitution grants Congress the power to make laws. The legislative process is often cumbersome as a bill (before it becomes law) goes through both houses of Congress and various committees and subcommittees. Numerous organizations, called interest groups, which represent common objectives of their members, try to influence policymakers to protect their members' interests. In the end, if the president signs the approved bill, it becomes law. The president also has the power to veto (overturn) a bill passed by Congress. Unless a presidential veto is overruled by a two-thirds majority of Congress, it fails to become law. Even after a law has been passed, policymaking continues in the form of interpretation and implementation by the federal agency responsible for implementing the law. For example, the Department of Health and Human Services oversees more than 300 programs related to health and welfare services. It is responsible for 12 different agencies that deal with such diverse areas as issues related to public health, approval of new drugs, healthcare research, services for the elderly, and substance abuse.

Macroeconomics

America is called a "land of plenty." The nation is richly blessed with natural resources. In large part, the nation's spectacular economic growth has been credited to the enterprising way in which Americans have used the nation's resources.[7] The seeds of American capitalism are found in the Constitution. At the foundation of American capitalism is the belief that individuals know best what is in their self-interest. Americans believe that their market economy and its political system provide avenues for individuals to act in their own interest and realize achievement limited only by one's own potential and motivation. The economic system in the United States is based largely on the principles of free market, open competition, profit motive, and private ownership of the means of production. These forces unleash human potential to maximize productivity and innovation and to produce and distribute goods and services that people value. A significant majority of Americans believe that the marketplace provides people with the opportunity to succeed and that hard work is the ticket to success.[11]

The United States has the largest and most technologically advanced economy in the world. Components of the gross domestic product (GDP) in 2015 are shown in **TABLE 5-2**. Even though the service sector of the economy has grown, the United States has a thriving manufacturing sector in industries such as petroleum, steel, aerospace, defense, telecommunications, computers, chemicals, electronics, mining, pharmaceuticals, and consumer goods.

U.S. residents enjoy one of the highest standards of living in the world. The labor force is among the most productive, and unemployment is relatively low (4% to 9%). Roughly one-third of the civilian labor force has college degrees. Both full- and part-time workers work 38.3 hours per week on average. In 2010, the median weekly earning for full-time workers was $747. Among employed civilians, approximately 13% worked for various levels of government; the remaining 87% were employed in the private sector.[8] In 2015, the size of the average American family was 3.1, and the median annual family income (inflation adjusted) was $55,775.

TABLE 5-2 Components of the U.S. GDP, 2015

	Billions of Dollars	Percentage
Total GDP	17,947	100.0
Consumption	12,258	68.3
Goods	3,985	22.2
Services	8,273	46.1
Private investment	3,015	16.8
Government spending	3,194	17.8
Federal	1,220	6.8
State and local	1,974	11.0
Exports minus imports	−520	−2.9

Data from US Bureau of Economic Analysis. Natioanl Data. 2015. http://www.bea.gov/iTable /iTable.cfm?ReqID=9&step=1#reqid=9&step=3&isuri=1&903=5. Accessed October 20, 2016.

Demographics

America is a nation of immigrants and minority groups. In 2013, 12.7% of the total population was foreign born. Between 2000 and 2013, more than 15.8 million foreign-born individuals entered the country. Hispanics/Latinos represent the largest number of foreign-born residents (TABLE 5-3).

The fertility rate per 1,000 U.S. women residents has declined from 70.9 in 1990 to 62.5 (estimated) in 2015. Age-adjusted death rates have also declined from 939 per 100,000 residents in 1990 to 729.5 in 2015. Hence, immigration is a critical factor in determining the nation's labor force. According to the data from Migration Policy Institute, the number of new U.S. legal permanent residents was 1,016,518 in 2014.[13]

TABLE 5-4 provides the racial/ethnic mix, age categories, and gender mix of the U.S. resident population. In 2014, life expectancy at birth was 78.8 years (81.2 years for females; 76.4 years for males; 79.0 years for whites; 75.6 years for blacks). A person aged 65 years could expect to live to an age of 84.3 years, and a person aged 75 years could expect to live to an age of 87.2 years.[14]

In 2014, 14.8% of the U.S. population lived in poverty (annual income of less than $24,230 for a family of 4). The poverty rate was higher among blacks (26.2%) and Hispanics (23.2%).[15] In 2014, 82.0% of the population lived in urban areas. Poverty rates vary by rural versus urban residence. In 2014, 18.1% of the rural population and 15.1% of the urban population was poor.[16]

The religious makeup of the U.S. population in 2014 was 46.5% Protestant, 20.8% Roman Catholic, 1.6%

TABLE 5-3 Foreign-Born Population, 2013

Region	Population (thousands)	Percentage
Total resident population	40,107	100.0
Latin America (The Caribbean, Central America, South America)	21,047	52.5
Asia	11,763	29.3
Europe	4,441	11.1
Other (from Africa, Oceania, Northern America, and born at sea)	2,856	7.1

Data from US Census Bureau. Current Population Survey, Annual Social and Economic Supplement, 2013. http://www2.census.gov/programs-surveys/demo/tables/foreign-born/2013/cps2013/2013-asec-tables-year-of-entry.pdf. Accessed October 20, 2016.

TABLE 5-4 Racial/Ethnic Mix, Age Categories, and Gender Mix of the U.S. Resident Population, 2015

Race/Ethnicity	Population (thousands)	Percentage
Total resident population	321,419	100.0
White	247,785	77.1
Black/African American	42,633	13.3
Asian	17,982	5.6
American Indian/Alaskan Native	4,011	1.2
Native Hawaiian/Pacific Islander	760	0.2
Two or more races	8,248	2.6
Hispanic or Latino origin	51,294	16.0
Age categories		
5–14	41,110	12.8
15–29	66,310	20.6
30–49	83,119	25.9
50–64	63,212	19.7
65–74	27,551	8.6
75–84	13,923	4.3
85 and over	6,287	2.0
Gender mix		
Male	158,229	49.2
Female	163,190	50.8

Data from US Census Bureau. Annual Estimates of the Resident Population. 2015. http://factfinder.census.gov/faces/tableservices/jsf/pages/productview.xhtml?src=bkmk.

Mormon, 1.7% other Christian, 1.9% Jewish, 0.7% Buddhist, 0.9% Muslim, 0.7% Hindu, 1.8% other or unspecified, 22.8% unaffiliated, and 0.6% do not know/refused.[17]

▸ Brief History of the Healthcare System

Pre–World War II

Medical Services in Preindustrial America

From colonial times to the beginning of the 1900s, medical education and practice were far more advanced in Great Britain, France, and Germany than they were in the United States. The practice of medicine in the United States had a strong domestic rather than a professional character because medical procedures were primitive. Medical education was not grounded in science. Consequently, medical practice was more a trade than a profession. The nation had only a handful of hospitals that existed in very large cities, such as New York, Boston, and Philadelphia. There was no health insurance—private or public.

Since World War II

Medical Services in Postindustrial America

The postindustrial era is marked by the growth and development of a medical profession that benefited from urbanization, new scientific discoveries, and reforms in medical education. American physicians became professionally organized and to this day have been a powerful force in resisting proposals for a national healthcare program.

The system for delivering health care in America took its current shape during this period. Private practice of medicine became firmly entrenched as *physician* became a cohesive profession and physicians opted for specialization and gained power and prestige. The hospital emerged as a repository for high-tech facilities and equipment.

History of Health Insurance

The first broad-coverage health insurance in the United States emerged in the form of workers' compensation. It was originally designed to make cash payments to workers for wages lost because of job-related injuries and diseases. Later, compensation for medical expenses and death benefits to survivors were added.

Health insurance began in the form of disability coverage that provided income during temporary disability caused by bodily injury or sickness. During the early 1900s, medical treatments and hospital care became socially acceptable; however, they were also becoming increasingly more expensive, and people could not predict their future needs for medical care or the costs. These developments pointed to the need for some kind of insurance to spread an individual's financial risk over a large number of people. Between 1916 and 1918,[16] state legislatures, including New York and California, attempted to enact legislation compelling employers to provide health insurance, but the efforts were unsuccessful.

Health insurance became a permanent feature of employment benefits during World War II. During this period, wages were frozen, and employees accepted employer-paid health insurance to compensate for the incremental losses from their salaries. Thus, health insurance became an important component of collective bargaining between unions and employers. Subsequently, employment-based health insurance expanded rapidly, and private health insurance became the primary vehicle for the delivery of healthcare services in the United States. It is estimated that private health insurance grew from a $1.0 billion industry in 1950 to an $8.7 billion industry by 1965.

Before 1965, private health insurance was the only widely available source of payment for health care, and it was available primarily to middle-class working people and their families. The elderly, the unemployed, and the poor had to rely on their own resources, on limited public programs, or on charity from hospitals and individual physicians. In 1965, Congress passed the amendments to the Social Security Act that created the Medicare and Medicaid programs. The government thus assumed direct responsibility for insuring two vulnerable population groups—the elderly and the poor.

Although adopted together, Medicare and Medicaid reflected sharply different traditions. Medicare was upheld by broad grassroots support and, being attached to Social Security, had no class distinction. Medicaid, on the other hand, carried the stigma of public welfare. Medicare had uniform national standards for eligibility and benefits; Medicaid varied from state to state in terms of eligibility and benefits. Medicare covered anyone at or over the age of 65 years. Medicaid became a means-tested program, which confined eligibility to people below a predetermined income level. Consequently, many of the poor did not qualify because their incomes exceeded the means-test limits.

The creation of Medicare and Medicaid had a drastic impact on both federal and state budgets, but the federal government bore the greatest brunt. Federal healthcare expenditures increased at an average annual rate of 30.0%, whereas total federal expenditures increased at a rate of only 11.3%. To curb inflation, president Richard Nixon implemented the

Economic Stabilization Program in 1971. Under this program, wages and prices were frozen, including those in the healthcare industry. The Health Maintenance Organization (HMO) Act of 1973 was passed during the Nixon administration after price controls had failed to be effective. The main rationale behind the new law was to create competition in the healthcare marketplace. The law required employers with more than 25 workers to offer an HMO plan as an alternative to the standard health insurance plans which were already in wide use.

During the 1990s, managed care was largely credited with containing double-digit inflation in healthcare costs. The beginning of the 21st century, however, has once again been marked with an increase in healthcare spending.

▸ Description of the Current Healthcare System

Facilities

Health care is the largest industry in the United States. From a technological standpoint, the nation has a highly developed infrastructure for the delivery of medical services. The nation has ultramodern healthcare facilities, high-caliber medical schools, university-based curricula to prepare healthcare managers and public health professionals, research organizations, a large pharmaceutical industry, manufacturers of medical devices, and providers of long-term care and rehabilitation services. The private sector owns most of the infrastructure. The government, however, plays a critical supportive role. The public health infrastructure, for example, is in the public domain. The government is also a major financier of health services research and medical education. It operates the military and veterans health systems (discussed later). It supports the delivery of care for certain vulnerable populations (discussed later) and funds the Indian Health Service (IHS) for American Indians and Alaska Natives. By having state-of-the-art technology, the United States offers medical services by highly trained physicians in its world-renowned facilities that are the envy of the world. On the other hand, this focus on high technology and specialization has certain negative effects. It raises the cost of medical care, which produces imbalances in access to health insurance. It also influences medical education, practice of medicine, and technology-driven competition among hospitals.

Workforce

In 2013, there were 854,698 professionally active doctors of medicine in the United States, which amounted to 27.6 physicians per 10,000 civilian population. Roughly 74.0% of the physicians work in private office-based practice; the rest work in hospitals or other professional settings related to teaching, research, or administration.[18] Approximately 25.5% of all practicing physicians are graduates of foreign medical schools; however, they must take rigorous examinations and undergo further training before they can practice in the United States. Compared with most European nations, the United States has a greater aggregate supply of physicians, but their distribution shows certain imbalances. A lopsided focus on technology has over time caused the supply of medical specialists to far outpace the supply of primary care physicians. For example, in 2012, 38.0% of the physicians worked in primary care, 11.7% in family medicine and general practice, 14.3% in internal medicine, 4.8% in obstetrics and gynecology, and the remaining in various medical specialties.[19] Besides a specialty-oriented medical education, disparities in income offer another reason why the majority of medical students in the United States opt for specialty training. For example, according to data from the American Medical Association, general surgeons can make 40.0% to 80.0% more than physicians in family practices. A high proportion of specialists in medicine drive up the use of technology and the cost of health care. Besides imbalances in primary and specialty care, locations outside metropolitan areas experience shortages of physicians. About 17.0% of the U.S. population lives in nonmetropolitan areas, but only 9.0% of the physicians practice in these areas.[18] People needing medical care in these areas may experience increased travel time to see a physician, which can deter timely and appropriate healthcare. Scarcity of physicians may result in higher caseloads, so patients face increased time to get appointments and wait longer in physicians' offices before they receive care.

Nurses constitute the largest group of healthcare professionals. Like physicians and other healthcare professionals, nurses must be licensed to practice in their respective states of employment. Depending on their level of education and competency assessment, nurses can be licensed as registered nurses (RNs) or as licensed practical/vocational nurses (LPNs/LVNs); 77% of all nurses are RNs. RNs must complete a 4-year bachelor's degree, a 4-year diploma, or a 2-year or 3-year associate's degree. Nurses can also specialize beyond their RN training to become advanced practice nurses.

Dentists, optometrists, psychologists, podiatrists, pharmacists, and chiropractors must complete doctoral-level education to qualify for licenses in their respective fields. Audiologists and speech/language pathologists must have master's level preparation. Healthcare professionals who generally are required to complete a 4-year bachelor's degree include physical therapists, occupational therapists, clinical laboratory technologists, and dietitians. Educational requirements for numerous other types of allied health professionals vary from one state to another and require between one and 4 years of training.

Inpatient Institutions

Depending on patient needs, institutional care that requires overnight stays is delivered in general acute care hospitals, specialty hospitals (including rehabilitation hospitals and psychiatric facilities), and long-term care facilities. The construction and operation of these institutions is governed by federal laws; state regulations; city ordinances; standards of the Joint Commission on Accreditation of Healthcare Organizations; and national codes for building, fire protection, and sanitation. The Joint Commission on Accreditation of Healthcare Organizations is a private, nonprofit organization that sets standards and accredits various types of healthcare facilities for ongoing verification of compliance with the standards.

The military medical care system and the Veterans Administration (VA; described later) operate federal hospitals that are largely inaccessible by the general public. Most of the remaining hospitals in 2013 were community hospitals, accessible to the general public; there were almost 5,000 in operation with over 800,000 beds. In 2013, the United States had 2.5 community hospital beds per 1,000 population residents,[18] far fewer than what most developed countries have. Hospitals in the United States come under three main types of ownership: private nonprofit, private for profit, and government owned. Private nonprofit organizations, such as community associations and churches, operate nonprofit hospitals. By law, these hospitals must reinvest the profits in the hospitals' operations and must not distribute them to any individuals. For-profit hospitals are proprietary or investor owned. They are operated for the financial benefit of the stockholders; however, hospitals operate in a competitive environment, and they must often compete on the basis of high-quality, cost-efficient services. In 2013, 68.4% of the nation's community hospital beds were operated as nonprofit, 16.9% were operated as for profit, and 14.7% were operated by state or local governments.[18] Approximately 400 teaching hospitals (including 64 VA medical centers) belong to the Council of Teaching Hospitals and Health Systems. These hospitals generally have substantial teaching and research programs, are affiliated with medical schools of large universities, and train the majority of physician residents in the United States.

Specialty hospitals in the United States are establishments that primarily treat specific types of medical conditions (such as cardiac or orthopedic), provide specialized rehabilitation care, or specialize in treating certain types of patients (such as women or children). The exact number of such hospitals is unknown, but their numbers are increasing. In addition, in 2014, there were nearly 3,000 mental health institutions (over 212,000 beds) that provide 24-hour hospital and residential treatment. Approximately 15,700 nursing homes with over 1,693,000 beds delivered 24-hour long-term care to mostly elderly patients.[18] Nursing homes mainly provide skilled nursing care, which is medically oriented care, approved by physicians and provided by and under the direction of licensed nurses, for complex chronic conditions and often includes rehabilitation therapies. In addition to these nursing homes, there are a large number of assisted living and personal care facilities that mainly provide assistance with activities of daily living.

Outpatient Settings

Outpatient (ambulatory care) services are delivered in a variety of settings, depending on factors such as the type of care needed, location, and whether the person has health insurance. Development of new technology and innovations in payment methods to providers have led to a decline in the utilization of inpatient hospitals and an expansion of outpatient services in both volume and scope. Many procedures that previously required a hospital stay are now performed on an outpatient basis. In the United States, an average of 2.6 community hospital beds per 1,000 population residents and an average length of stay of 5.4 days are among the lowest in the world. Consequently, many hospitals provide both inpatient and outpatient services to remain profitable. In 2011, 10.1% of all ambulatory visits occurred in hospitals' outpatient units (an increase from 6.2% in 1992). Of course, most outpatient visits take place in physicians' offices (79.0% in 2011).[18] Hospital emergency rooms, however, are commonly used by the insured and the uninsured alike for both urgent and nonurgent conditions. Heavy use for nonemergencies results in overcrowding and waste of resources. For nonurgent care, emergency rooms are often used by those who do not have routine access to primary care. In 2013–2014, 3.8% of children under the age of 18 and 18.2% of adults did not have a usual source of care.[18] Since the creation of the State Children's Health Insurance Program (SCHIP; discussed later), the proportion of children who do not have a usual source of care declined from 7.7% in 1993–1994 to 3.8% in 2013–2014.

Home health has been among the fastest growing sectors in U.S. healthcare. Over 70% of home health patients are elderly. Home health commonly includes part-time or intermittent nursing care, rehabilitation services, nutritional consultations, and assistance with activities of daily living. Since the early 1980s, specialized high-technology home therapies have proliferated. They include intravenous antibiotics, oncology therapy, hemodialysis, nutrition, ventilator care, and telehome health technologies for remote in-home patient monitoring. Overall, home health has proven to be cost effective because it decreases the use of hospitals, emergency departments, and nursing homes.

Other main outpatient settings in the United States include walk-in clinics that provide the convenience of evening and weekend hours with no prior appointments, urgent care centers that operate 24 hours a day 7 days a week, free-standing surgicenters that perform outpatient surgeries, laboratories, imaging centers, dialysis centers, pharmacies, and rehabilitation centers. Retail medical clinics have started to open in major stores where people commonly shop for everyday things.

The federal government provides funding for more than 1,300 community health centers. These centers are located in defined, medically underserved areas where they provide primary care, mental health care, and dental care to mostly low-income and uninsured populations.

Public Health

Public health services in the United States are typically provided by local health departments, and the range of services offered varies greatly by locality. The programs are generally limited in scope. They include well-baby care, venereal disease clinics, family planning services, screening and treatment for tuberculosis, and outpatient mental healthcare.

The Subsystems of U.S. Healthcare Delivery

The United States does not have a well-integrated and coordinated healthcare delivery system enjoyed by everyone. Instead, there are multiple subsystems developed either through market forces or as a result of policy initiatives to address the needs of certain population segments. The major subsystems are described later in this chapter.

The Managed Care System

Managed care is a system of healthcare delivery that (1) seeks to achieve efficiencies by integrating the basic functions of healthcare delivery, (2) employs mechanisms to control (manage) utilization of medical services, and (3) determines the price at which the services are purchased and consequently how much the providers get paid. It is the most dominant healthcare delivery system in the United States today and is available to most Americans.

The primary financiers of the managed care system are employers and the government; however, it is not a private–public partnership. Employers purchase insurance for their own employees, but they do so voluntarily. As a result, many small employers do not provide health insurance to their employees. On the other hand, because employer-based health insurance requires cost sharing, many workers choose not to participate even when the employer pays the bulk of the premium costs. Because of variations in the government programs, beneficiaries are either required to obtain healthcare services through a managed care organization (MCO) or through alternative mechanisms. There are two main types of MCOs: HMOs and preferred provider organizations (PPOs). An MCO functions like an insurance company and promises to provide healthcare services contracted under the health plan to the enrollees of the plan.

The terms *enrollee* and *member* refer to the individual covered under the plan. The contractual arrangement between the MCO and the enrollee—including the array of covered health services that the enrollee is entitled to—is referred to as the health plan (or *the plan*, for short). The health plan generally uses selected providers from whom the enrollees can choose to receive routine services. HMOs typically require in-network access—that is, the enrollees must receive services from the providers selected by the HMO. PPOs, on the other hand, allow out-of-network access—that is, the enrollees can choose to receive services either from providers that participate in the PPO's selected network or from providers that are not part of the network. The enrollee incurs higher out-of-pocket costs when out-of-network providers are used. Nevertheless, because of the option to choose one's providers, PPO plans have been more popular than HMO plans. Particularly in HMOs, primary care providers or generalists manage routine services and determine the appropriateness of referrals to higher level or specialty services. In these plans, generalists are often referred to as gatekeepers. Some HMOs may deliver services partially through the plan's own hired physicians, but most services are delivered through contracts with providers, such as physicians, hospitals, and diagnostic clinics.

Although the employer finances the care by purchasing a plan from an MCO, the MCO is the one responsible for negotiating with providers. HMOs typically use capitation arrangements to pay providers. Under capitation, a negotiated fixed amount per enrollee is paid each month to the provider. This fixed amount is commonly referred to as the per-member-per-month rate. Risk is shared between the HMO and the provider who receives the per-member-per-month rate, because in exchange for this payment the provider is obligated to deliver whatever contracted services the enrollees might need. PPOs commonly pay the providers a discounted fee that has been negotiated between the PPO and the provider. Providers are willing to discount their services in exchange for being included in the PPO's network and being guaranteed a patient population. As insurers, health plans must make actuarial projections of the expected cost of healthcare utilization. They bear the risk that the cost of services delivered could exceed the premiums collected. By underwriting this risk, a plan assumes the role of insurer.

The Military and Veterans Systems

The military medical care system is available free of charge to active-duty military personnel. It is a well-organized and highly integrated system operated by the U.S. Department of Defense. Comprehensive services cover prevention as well as treatments provided by salaried healthcare personnel. Routine ambulatory care is often available at a dispensary, sick bay, first-aid station, or medical station located close to the military personnel's workplace. Routine hospital services are provided in dispensaries located in military bases, in sick bays aboard ships, and in small base hospitals. Complicated hospital services are provided in regional military hospitals. Dependents of service members, retirees and their dependents, and survivors of deceased members can receive medical care through an insurance program called TriCare. This program permits the beneficiaries to receive care from military as well as private medical care facilities. Although patients have little choice regarding how services are provided, in general, the military medical care system provides high-quality health care.

War veterans are entitled to receive a wide array of medical and long-term care services through facilities operated by the VA. The VA system provides a broad spectrum of medical, surgical, and rehabilitative care. It is one of the largest, oldest formally organized healthcare systems in the world. The VA, predecessor to the current Department of Veterans Affairs, was established in 1930. In addition to medical care, its mission includes education, training, research, and contingency support and emergency management for the Department of Defense medical care system. The VA system operates 155 medical centers, with at least one located in each state, Puerto Rico, and the District of Columbia. VA facilities also include 1,400 sites of care (such as outpatient clinics, nursing homes, and rehabilitation centers). In 2014, almost 9.1 million people received care in VA facilities. The VA delivery system is organized under 22 geographically distributed Veterans Integrated Service Networks. Healthcare spending for 2013 was $65.6 billion.[20]

The System for Vulnerable Populations

In 1965, the U.S. Congress passed two major amendments to the Social Security Act that created the Medicare and Medicaid programs, and the government assumed direct responsibility to pay for some of the health care on behalf of two vulnerable population groups—the elderly and the poor.[21] Medicaid and Medicare are prime representations of the public sector in the amalgam of private and public approaches for providing access to health care in the United States. Originally created for the elderly, the Medicare program now covers 55 million Americans that also include low-income disabled individuals below the age of 65 and people who have end-stage renal disease. The Medicaid program finances healthcare services for the indigent who qualify based on assets and income below the threshold levels established by each state. The program serves nearly 70 million poor Americans. In 1997, the SCHIP was enacted to provide health insurance to children living in low-income families that did not qualify for Medicaid. Of the 77 million children in the United States, about 45% are enrolled in either Medicaid or SCHIP. In the three main public programs, the government finances the insurance, but healthcare services are received mainly through private providers. Medicaid and SCHIP enrollees incur little out-of-pocket costs, but Medicare enrollees pay for approximately half of their healthcare costs. This is mainly due to high deductibles, co-payments, and certain noncovered services—such as dental, vision, hearing aid—and gaps in prescription drug coverage (coverage was added to the program in 2005). Poor enrollees can qualify for both Medicaid and Medicare, in which case Medicaid pays for the gaps in Medicare coverage. Most other enrollees purchase private health insurance called Medigap to pay for noncovered Medicare expenses.

Other vulnerable populations—especially uninsured minorities, immigrants, and those living in geographically or economically disadvantaged communities—receive care from safety net providers, including community health centers, physicians' offices, hospital outpatient departments, and emergency rooms, of which community health centers are expressly designed for the underserved. Consistent with their unique role and mission, safety net providers offer comprehensive medical and enabling services (e.g., language interpretation, transportation, outreach, and nutrition and social support services) that address the needs of vulnerable populations.

For over 50 years, federally funded health centers have provided primary and preventive health services to rural and urban underserved populations. The Bureau of Primary Health Care, within the Department of Health and Human Services' Health Resources and Services Administration, provides federal support for community-based health centers that include programs for migrant and seasonal farm workers and their families, homeless people, public housing residents, and school-age children. In addition to essential primary care and preventive services, health centers provide enabling services, such as case management, transportation, health education, language translation, and childcare. These services facilitate regular access to care for predominantly minority, low-income, uninsured, and Medicaid patients. By the end of calendar year 2014, the nationwide network of 1,278 reporting health centers delivered essential primary and preventive care at more than 9,000 sites serving 22.9 million users, which is more than 30% of the nation's 63.0 million underserved people.[22] Health centers have contributed to significantly improved health outcomes for the uninsured and Medicaid populations and have reduced disparities in health care and health status across socioeconomic and racial/ethnic groups.[23,24]

America's safety net, however, is by no means secure, and the availability of safety net providers varies from community to community. Vulnerable populations residing in communities without safety net providers have to forgo care or seek care from hospital emergency rooms, if such services are available in the areas where they live. Safety net providers face enormous pressures due to high demand, particularly in communities that have an increasing number of uninsured and poor. The inability to shift costs for uncompensated care onto private insurance has become a significant problem because revenues from Medicaid, the primary source of third-party financing for core safety net providers, are inadequate because of funding constraints.

The Indian Health System

American Indians and Alaska Natives are the only ethnic groups for which the federal government has taken direct responsibility for healthcare. Also, as citizens of the United States, these groups are eligible to participate in all public, private, and state health programs available to the general population. The Indian Health Service (IHS), an agency of the federal government, is the principal healthcare provider and health advocate for these groups. The agency provides health services to approximately 2.2 million people who belong to more than 566 federally recognized tribes in 35 states. The policy of self-determination underlies healthcare services for these citizens. Accordingly, the tribes have three options for receiving health care: (1) directly from the IHS, (2) through contracting with the IHS to have the administrative control, operation, and funding for health programs transferred to American Indian and Alaska Native tribal governments, or (3) through contracting with the IHS and assuming even greater control and autonomy for the provision of tribes' healthcare services. The IHS operates 46 hospitals and over 600 health centers, clinics, and health stations.[25]

Integrated Delivery Systems

An integrated delivery system (IDS) may be defined as a network of organizations that provides, or arranges to provide, a coordinated continuum of services to a defined population and is willing to be held clinically and fiscally accountable for the outcomes and health status of that population. For over a decade now, organizational integration to form IDSs has been the hallmark of the U.S. healthcare industry. Integration in the U.S. healthcare delivery system has occurred in response to cost pressures, development of new alternatives for the delivery of health care, the growing power of MCOs, and the need to provide services more efficiently to populations spread over large geographic areas. An IDS represents various forms of ownership and other strategic linkages among major participants, such as hospitals, physicians, and insurers. The objective is to achieve greater integration of healthcare services along the continuum of care.

▸ Evaluation of the Healthcare System

The healthcare system of a nation is influenced by external factors, including the political climate, economic development, technological progress, social and cultural values, the physical environment, and population characteristics, such as demographic and health trends. The combined interaction of these forces influences the course of healthcare delivery in the United States. In the following sections, we summarize the basic characteristics that differentiate the U.S. healthcare delivery system from that of other countries.

No Central Governing Agency and Little Integration and Coordination

The U.S. healthcare system provides a conspicuous contrast to the healthcare systems of other developed countries. The centrally controlled universal healthcare systems of most developed countries authorize financing and delivery of health care for all residents. The U.S. system is not centrally controlled and has a very complex structure of financing, insurance, delivery, and payment mechanisms. Private financing, which is predominantly through employers, accounts for approximately 54% of total healthcare expenditures; the government finances the remaining 46%.

The main characteristics of U.S. healthcare system are as follows:

- No central governing agency and little integration and coordination
- A technology-driven delivery system focusing on acute care
- High cost, unequal access, and average outcome
- Delivery of health care under imperfect market conditions
- Government as subsidiary to the private sector
- Market justice versus social justice, pervasive throughout health care
- Multiple players and balance of power
- Quest for integration and accountability

The less complex structure of a centrally controlled healthcare system improves efficiency by managing total expenditures through global budgets and by governing the availability and utilization of services through central planning. Because the United States has such a large private system of financing, insurance, and delivery, the majority of insurers and providers are private businesses, independent of the government. Nevertheless, the federal and state governments play an important role in healthcare delivery. They finance healthcare services for publicly insured patients, such as those covered under Medicare and Medicaid. They also determine public sector expenditures and establish reimbursement rates for services delivered to Medicare and Medicaid patients. The government uses various payment mechanisms for providers. Currently, almost all inpatient and home healthcare services delivered to Medicare and Medicaid patients are reimbursed according to a variety of prospective payment methods. Physician reimbursement rates are derived using complex formulas that take into account factors such as time, skill, and intensity of physician work; beginning in 1983, a gradual departure occurred from the previous cost-based reimbursement methods. The government also formulates standards of participation through health policy and regulation and requires providers to comply with the standards and receive federal certification in order to deliver care to Medicare and Medicaid patients. Certification standards are also regarded as minimum standards of quality in most sectors of the healthcare industry.

The insurance and delivery functions are separated in the main government programs (Medicare, Medicaid, and SCHIP) because the government provides insurance but services are delivered through the private sector. Even in the military and VA systems, some services are contracted through the private sector.

A Technology-Driven Delivery System Focusing on Acute Care

The United States has been the hotbed of research and innovation in new medical technology. Because of its cost implications, almost all nations try to limit the diffusion and utilization of technology through central planning and control. Lack of such controls in the United States promotes innovation, rapid diffusion, and utilization of new technology. Growth in science and technology often creates demand for new services despite shrinking resources to finance sophisticated care. Other factors contribute to increased demand in expensive technological care: patients assume that the latest innovations offer the highest quality, physicians want to try the latest gadgets, and competition among hospitals is often driven by the acquisition of technology. After organizations acquire new equipment and facilities, they are often under pressure to recoup the capital investments. Legal risks for providers and health plans alike may also play a role in discouraging denial of new technology.

Although technology has ushered in a new generation of successful interventions, the negative outcomes resulting from its overuse are many. For example, the expense of highly technical interventions increases insurance payments to providers. Insurance premiums rise, and it becomes more difficult for employers to expand coverage. Broad exposure to technology early in medical training affects not only clinical preferences but also future professional behavior and practice patterns. Because medical specialization revolves around technology, an oversupply of specialists in the United States has compounded the rate of technology diffusion. In this technology-driven environment, the healthcare system suffers from inadequate resources and mechanisms to address the growing needs of people with chronic conditions and co-morbidities. Given the rising number of elderly in the U.S. population, the system that is primarily driven by the acute care model will be overburdened unless appropriate steps are taken to shift resources from acute to chronic care.

High Cost, Unequal Access, and Mixed Outcomes

Although data on healthcare spending in various countries are not always comparable because of differences in accounting for the expenditures, experts generally agree that compared with any other developed country in the world, the United States spends the most. For example, in 2014, U.S. healthcare spending was $9,523 per capita, or 17.5% of the GDP.[26] The average annual healthcare cost inflation between 2011 and 2015 was 6.8% compared with an average annual increase of 3.3% in the nation's GDP. High cost of health care has ramifications for the expansion of health insurance to the uninsured, the long-term solvency of publicly financed programs, and other issues of equity and health disparities that remain unaddressed.

Access means the ability of an individual to obtain healthcare services when needed. In the United States, access is restricted to (1) those who have health insurance through their employers, (2) those covered under a government healthcare program, (3) those who can afford to buy insurance out of their private funds, and (4) those who are able to pay for services privately. Health insurance is the primary means for ensuring access, although some uninsured Americans receive care through the safety net. In early 2015, 29 million Americans of all ages (9.2% of the population) were uninsured—that is, they were not covered under a private or public health insurance program.[27]

For consistent, basic, and routine primary care, the uninsured are unable to see a physician unless they can pay the physician's fees. Those who cannot afford to pay generally wait until health problems develop, at which point they may be able to receive services free of charge in a hospital emergency department. The Emergency Medical Treatment and Labor Act of 1986 requires screening and evaluation of every patient, necessary stabilizing treatment, and admitting when necessary, regardless of ability to pay. Uninsured Americans therefore are able to obtain medical care for acute illness. Hence, one can say that the United States does have a form of universal catastrophic health insurance even for the uninsured.[28]

It is well acknowledged that absence of insurance inhibits the patients' ability to receive well-directed, coordinated, and continuous health care through access to primary care services and, when needed, referral to specialty services. Experts generally believe that inadequate access to basic and routine primary care services is the main reason that the United States, in spite of being the most economically advanced country, lags behind other developed nations in measures of population health such as infant mortality and overall life expectancy. This belief, however, remains largely unsubstantiated, mainly in view of the fact that the health status of a population is based on many factors, including individual lifestyles and behaviors.

Delivery of Health Care Under Imperfect Market Conditions

Under national healthcare programs, patients have varying degrees of choice in selecting their providers; however, true economic market forces are virtually nonexistent. In the United States, even though the delivery of services is largely in private hands, health care is only partially governed by free market forces. The delivery and consumption of health care in the United States do not quite meet the basic tests of a free market, as described later in this chapter. Hence, the system is best described as a quasi-market or an imperfect market.

These are some key features characterizing free markets. In a free market, multiple patients (buyers) and providers (sellers) act independently. In a free market, patients should be able to choose their provider based on price and quality of services. If it were this simple, patient choice would determine prices by the unencumbered interaction of supply and demand. Theoretically at least, prices are negotiated between payers and providers; however, in many instances, the payer is not the patient but a managed care organization, Medicare, or Medicaid. Because prices are set by agencies external to the market, they are not freely governed by the forces of supply and demand.

For the healthcare market to be free, unrestrained competition must occur among providers on the basis of price and quality. Generally speaking, free competition exists among healthcare providers in the United States. The consolidation of buying power into the hands of private health plans, however, has forced providers to form alliances and integrated delivery systems on the supply side. In certain geographic sectors of the country, a single giant medical system has taken over as the sole provider of major healthcare services, restricting competition. As the healthcare system continues to move in this direction, it appears that only in large metropolitan areas will there be more than one large integrated system competing to get the business of the health plans.

A free market requires that patients have information about service options. Free markets operate best when consumers are educated about the products they are using. Patients, however, are not always well informed about the decisions that need to be made regarding their care. Choices involving sophisticated technology, diagnostic methods, interventions, and pharmaceuticals can be difficult and often require physician input. Acting as advocates, primary care providers can reduce this information gap for patients. Recently, healthcare consumers have taken more initiative to educate themselves using Internet resources for gathering medical information. Also, pharmaceutical product advertising is having an impact on consumer expectations and is increasing awareness of available medications.

In a free market, patients have information on price and quality for each provider. Current pricing methods for healthcare services further confound free market mechanisms. Hidden costs make it difficult for patients to gauge the full expense of services ahead of time. Item-based pricing, for example, refers to the costs of adjunct services that often accompany major procedures such as surgery. Patients are usually informed of the surgery's cost ahead of time but cannot anticipate the cost of anesthesiologists, pathologists, and hospital supplies and facilities, thus making it extremely difficult to ascertain the total price before services have actually been received. Package pricing and capitated fees can help overcome these drawbacks by providing a bundled fee for a package of related services. Package pricing covers services bundled together for one episode, which is less encompassing than capitation. Capitation covers all services an enrollee may need during an entire year.

In recent years, care quality has received much attention. Performance rating of health plans has met with some success; however, apart from sporadic news stories, the public generally has scant information on the quality of healthcare providers.

In a free market, patients must directly bear the cost of services received. The purpose of insurance is to protect against the risk of unforeseen catastrophic events. Because the fundamental purpose of insurance is to meet major expenses when unlikely events occur, having insurance for basic and routine health care undermines the principle of insurance. Health insurance coverage for minor services, such as colds, coughs, and earaches, amounts to prepayment for such services. There is a moral hazard that after enrollees purchase health insurance, they will use healthcare services to a greater extent than if they had to pay for such services themselves. If the patient has to bear the full cost, the patient may even forgo certain referrals.

Moral hazard can be contained by a new type of health insurance arrangement that seems to be gaining some initial momentum. Under certain qualifying conditions, individuals can have a Health Savings Account (HSA), which is a tax-sheltered trust account that the individual owns for the purpose of paying qualified medical expenses. The HSA account works in conjunction with a high-deductible health plan. In order to have an HSA, the individual must enroll in a high-deductible health plan. Healthcare expenses are paid out of the HSA. Insurance kicks in once the annual deductible is met. The minimum annual deductibles for 2015 were $1,300 for an individual plan and $2,600 for a family plan.

In a free market for healthcare, patients as consumers make decisions about the purchase of healthcare services. In addition to the factors discussed earlier, at least two more factors limit the ability of patients to make decisions. First, decisions about the utilization of health care are often determined by need rather than price-based demand. Need has generally been defined as the amount of medical care that medical experts believe a person should have to remain or become healthy.[29] Second, the delivery of health care can result in creation of demand. This follows from self-assessed need, which, when coupled with moral hazard, leads to greater utilization. This creates an artificial demand because prices are not taken into consideration. Practitioners who have a financial interest in additional treatments also create artificial demand,[30] commonly referred to as provider-induced demand.

Government as Subsidiary to the Private Sector

In most other developed countries, the government plays a central role in the provision of health care. In the United States, the private sector plays the dominant role. This can be explained to some degree by the American tradition of reliance on individual responsibility and a commitment to limiting the power of the national government. As a result, government spending for health care has been largely confined to filling in the gaps left open by the private sector.

These gaps include environmental protection, support for research and training, and care of vulnerable populations.

Market Justice Versus Social Justice Pervasive Throughout Health Care

Market justice and social justice are two contrasting theories that govern the production and distribution of healthcare services in the United States. The principle of market justice ascribes the fair distribution of health care to the market forces in a free economy. Medical care and its benefits are distributed on the basis of people's willingness and ability to pay.[31] In contrast, social justice emphasizes the well-being of the community over that of the individual; thus, the inability to obtain medical services because of a lack of financial resources would be considered unjust. A just distribution of benefits must be based on need, not simply one's ability to purchase it in the marketplace. In a partial public and private healthcare system, the two theories often operate side by side; however, market justice principles tend to prevail. Unfortunately, market justice results in the unequal allocation of healthcare services, neglecting critical human concerns that are not confined to the individual but that have broader negative impacts on society.

Multiple Players and Balance of Power

The U.S. healthcare system involves multiple players. The key players in the system have been physicians, administrators of health service institutions, insurance companies, large employers, and the government. Big business, labor, MCOs, insurance companies, physicians, and hospitals make up the powerful and politically active special interest groups represented before lawmakers by high-priced lobbyists. Each player has a different economic interest to protect. The problem is that the self-interests of each player are often at odds. For example, providers seek to maximize government reimbursement for services delivered to Medicare and Medicaid patients, but the government wants to contain cost increases. The fragmented self-interests of the various players produce countervailing forces within the system. In an environment that is rife with motivations to protect conflicting self-interests, achieving comprehensive system-wide reforms is next to impossible, and cost-containment remains a major challenge. Consequently, the approach to healthcare reform in the United States is characterized as incremental or piecemeal.

Quest for Integration and Accountability

The use of primary care as the organizing hub for continuous and coordinated health services was recognized in the United States. It was envisioned that through primary care, other healthcare services would be integrated in a seamless fashion. Although this model gained popularity with the expansion of managed care, its development stalled before it could reach its full potential. The large-scale transition of healthcare delivery to the managed care system in the 1990s was met with widespread criticism, which turned into backlash from consumers, physicians, and legislators. As a result, various compromises were reached. The HMO model that was based on primary care and gatekeeping became less popular than was initially foreseen by its proponents. A compromised PPO model has become dominant in U.S. healthcare delivery; however, current political debates seem to exhibit the need for a model of healthcare delivery that is based on primary care. The PPO model also emphasizes the importance of the patient–provider relationship and how it can best function to improve the health of each individual; however, such a system would fall short of meeting any population-wide objectives without universal access to basic health care.

In 2007, the state of Massachusetts implemented a program that promises to achieve nearly universal health coverage in the state. Under legal penalties, the program calls for all residents to obtain health insurance and for all employers to offer a basic insurance plan that workers can buy with pretax dollars. Government subsidies are made available to low-income individuals to buy insurance; the indigents have their premiums paid by the state. A central clearinghouse brokers the purchase of insurance and establishes rules and procedures. After six years of implementation, the reform initiative has demonstrated the potential for expanding coverage and improving access to care by embracing a model of shared responsibility. With the lowest rate of uninsured in the country, the Massachusetts experience became a model for federal health reform;[32] the Affordable Care Act (ACA) was passed by Congress and then signed into law by the president on March 23, 2010.[33]

The ACA was enacted to increase the affordability of health insurance, to lower the uninsured rate by expanding public and private insurance coverage, and to reduce the costs of healthcare. It introduced mechanisms like mandates, subsidies, and insurance exchanges.[34] Since the ACA was enacted, the U.S. healthcare system has taken important steps toward providing all Americans with quality, affordable healthcare. About 16.4 million uninsured people have gained health insurance coverage. As of January 2015, approximately 11.2 million more Americans were covered under Medicaid and SCHIP than compared to the start of October 2013. During open enrollment for 2015, nearly 11.7 million Americans selected plans or were automatically reenrolled in coverage through the marketplaces.[35]

Integral to the relationship between patients and providers is the concept of accountability. For providers, accountability means delivery of care that is efficient, ethical, and of a high quality. From the patient's standpoint, it means taking individual responsibility to safeguard one's own health and to use available resources sensibly.

▸ Conclusion

The United States does not have a well-integrated healthcare delivery system for all citizens. Instead, there are multiple subsystems developed either through market forces or through public initiatives to address the needs of certain population segments. The subsystems include managed care, the military and VA systems, the system for vulnerable populations, and the emerging integrated delivery system. The basic features that characterize the unique healthcare delivery system in the United States include the absence of a central agency to govern the system, little integration and coordination, a technology-driven delivery system focusing on acute care, a costly system that produces unequal access and average outcomes, delivery of health care under imperfect market conditions, government as subsidiary to the private sector, the conflict between market justice and social justice, multiple players and balance of power, and quests for integration and accountability.

References

1. Shi L, Singh DA. *Delivering Health Care in America: A Systems Approach.* 6th ed. Burlington, MA: Jones and Bartlett Learning; 2015:649.
2. Shi L, Singh DA. *Essentials of the US Health Care System.* 3rd ed. Burlington, MA: Jones and Bartlett Learning; 2013.
3. Bedford HF, Colbourn T. *The Americans: A Brief History to 1877,* part 1. New York: Harcourt Brace Jovanovich; 1972.
4. Konstam A. *Historical Atlas of Exploration: 1492–1600.* New York: Checkmark Books; 2000.
5. Bryant WC, Gay SH, Brooks N. *Scribner's Popular History of the United States.* New York: Charles Scribner's Sons; 1897.
6. Bradley HW. *The United States 1492–1877.* New York: Charles Scribner's Sons; 1972.
7. Karlen HM. *The Pattern of American Government.* 2nd ed. Beverly Hills, CA: Glencoe Press; 1975.
8. US Census Bureau. *Statistical Abstract of the United States, 2012.* Washington, DC: US General Printing Office; 2012.
9. US Census Bureau. QuickFacts. Statistics for all states and counties. https://www.census.gov/quickfacts/table/PST045215/00. January 2016. Accessed April 14, 2016.
10. Sidlow E, Henschen B. *America at Odds: An Introduction to American Government.* 2nd ed. Belmont, CA: Wadsworth/Thomson Learning; 2000.
11. Gosling JJ. *Economics, Politics, and American Public Policy.* Armonk, NY: ME Sharpe; 2008.
12. Migration Policy Institute. Annual Number of U.S. Legal Permanent Residents, Fiscal Years 1820-2014. http://www.migrationpolicy.org/programs/data-hub/us-immigration-trends#history. Accessed October 24, 2016.
13. US Department of Homeland Security. U.S. Lawful Permanent Residents: 2014. https://www.dhs.gov/sites/default/files/publications/Lawful_Permanent_Residents_2014.pdf. Accessed October 24, 2016.
14. Kochanek KD, Murphy SL, Xu JQ, Tejada-Vera B. Deaths: Final data for 2014. National vital statistics reports; vol 65 no 4. Hyattsville, MD: National Center for Health Statistics. 2016.
15. DeNavas-Walt C, Proctor BD, Smith J. *Income, Poverty, and Health Insurance Coverage in the United States: 2014.* Washington, DC: US Government Printing Office; 2015.
16. US Department of Agriculture. Rural America at a glance. 2015 ed. http://www.ers.usda.gov/media/1952235/eib145.pdf. Accessed April 15, 2016.
17. Pew Research Center. America's changing religious landscape. http://www.pewforum.org/2015/05/12/americas-changing-religious-landscape/. Accessed October 21, 2016.
18. National Center for Health Statistics. Health, United States, 2015. Hyattsville, MD: US Department of Health and Human Services; 2016.
19. Bureau of Labor Statistics, US Department of Labor. Occupational Outlook Handbook. Physicians and surgeons. http://www.bls.gov/ooh/healthcare/physicians-and-surgeons.htm. Accessed April 14, 2016.
20. Department of Veterans Affairs. Fact sheet. Facts About the Department of Veterans Affairs. Washington, DC: VA Office of Public Affairs; 2016.
21. Potter MA, Longest BB. The divergence of federal and state policies on the charitable tax exemption of nonprofit hospitals. *Journal of Health Politics, Policy and Law.* 1994; 19(2):393–419.
22. Bureau of Primary Health Care. *BPHC-UDS Annual Report.* Washington, DC: BPHC; 2014.
23. Politzer RM, Schempf AH, Shi L, Starfield B. The future role of health centers in improving national health. *Journal of Public Health Policy.* 2003;24(3):296–306.
24. Shi L, Politzer R, Regan J, Lewis-Idema D, Falik M. The impact of managed care on vulnerable populations served by community health centers. *Journal of Ambulatory Care Management.* 2001;24(1):51–66.
25. Indian Health Service. IHS fact sheets. https://www.ihs.gov/newsroom/factsheets/. January 2016. Accessed April 15, 2016.
26. Centers for Medicare and Medicaid Services. National Health Expenditure Fact Sheet. https://www.cms.gov/research-statistics-data-and-systems/statistics-trends-and-reports/national healthexpenddata/nhe-fact-sheet.html. Accessed October 24, 2016.
27. Cohen RA, Martinez ME. Division of Health Interview Statistics, National Center for Health Statistics. Health insurance coverage: estimates from the National Health Interview Survey. http://

www.cdc.gov/nchs/data/nhis/earlyrelease/insur201508.pdf. January–March 2015. Accessed April 15, 2016.
28. Altman SH, Reinhardt UE. Introduction: where does health care reform go from here? An uncharted odyssey. In: Altman SH, Reinhardt UE, eds. *Strategic Choices for a Choices for a Changing Health Care System*. Chicago: Health Administration Press; 1996:xxi–xxxii.
29. Feldstein PJ. *Health Care Economics*. 4th ed. New York: Delmar Publishing; 1993.
30. Hemenway D, Fallon D. Testing for physician-induced demand with hypothetical cases. *Medical Care*. 1985;23(4):344–349.
31. Santerre RE, Neun SP. *Health Economics: Theories, Insights, and Industry Studies*. Chicago: Irwin; 1996.
32. Kaiser Family Foundation. Massachusetts health care reform: six years later. https://kaiserfamilyfoundation.files.wordpress.com/2013/01/8311.pdf. May 2012. Accessed April 15, 2016.
33. Patient Protection and Affordable Care Act, 42 U.S.C. § 18001. 2010.
34. Kaiser Family Foundation. Summary of the Affordable Care Act. http://files.kff.org/attachment/fact-sheet-summary-of-the-affordable-care-act. April 2013. Accessed April 15, 2016.
35. The Domestic Policy Council. Accomplishments of the Affordable Care Act: a 5th year anniversary report. https://www.whitehouse.gov/sites/default/files/docs/3-22-15_aca_anniversary_report.pdf. May 2015. Accessed April 15, 2016.

CHAPTER 6

Canada

R. Paul Duncan, Michael E. Morris, Linda A. McCarey, and Adrienne Nevola.

▸ Country Description[1]

TABLE 6-1 Canada	
Nationality	Noun: Canadian(s) Adjective: Canadian
Ethnic groups	Canadian 32.2%, English 19.8%, French 15.5%, Scottish 14.4%, Irish 13.8%, German 9.8%, Italian 4.5%, Chinese 4.5%, North American Indian 4.2%, other 50.9%* (2011 est.)
Religions	Catholic 40.6% (includes Roman Catholic 38.8%, Orthodox 1.6%, other Catholic 0.2%), Protestant 20.3% (includes United Church 6.1%, Anglican 5.0%, Baptist 1.9%, Lutheran 1.5%, Pentecostal 1.5%, Presbyterian 1.4%, other Protestant 2.9%), other Christian 6.3%, Muslim 3.2%, Hindu 1.5%, Sikh 1.4%, Buddhist 1.1%, Jewish 1%, other 0.6%, none 23.9% (2011 est.)
Language	English (official) 58.7%, French (official) 22.0%, Punjabi 1.4%, Italian 1.3%, Spanish 1.3%, German 1.3%, Cantonese 1.2%, Tagalog 1.2%, Arabic 1.1%, other 10.5% (2011 est.)
Literacy	Definition: Age 15 and over can read and write. Total population: 99% Male: 99% Female: 99% (2003 est.)
Government type	Federal parliamentary democracy (Parliament of Canada) under a constitutional monarchy; a Commonwealth realm

(continues)

TABLE 6-1 Canada (continued)

Date of independence	July 1, 1867 (union of British North American colonies); December 11, 1931 (recognized by the United Kingdom per Statute of Westminster)
Gross Domestic Product (GDP) per capita	$45,900 (2015 est.)
Unemployment rate	6.9% (2015 est.)
Natural hazards	continuous permafrost in the north is a serious obstacle to development; cyclonic storms form east of the Rocky Mountains as a result of the mixing of air masses from the Arctic, Pacific, and North American interior, and they produce most of the country's rain and snow east of the mountains; volcanism is possible, but the vast majority of volcanoes in Western Canada's Coast Mountains remain dormant
Environment: current issues	metal smelting, coal-burning utilities, and vehicle emissions impacting on agricultural and forest productivity; air pollution and resulting acid rain severely affecting lakes and damaging forests; ocean waters becoming contaminated due to agricultural, industrial, mining, and forestry activities; shrinking polar ice cap
Population	35,099,836 (July 2015 est.)
Age structure	0–14 years: 15.46% (male 2,781,043/female 2,644,008) 15–24 years: 12.39% (male 2,236,425/female 2,111,681) 25–54 years: 40.69% (male 7,239,027/female 7,041,886) 55–64 years: 13.74% (male 2,389,423/female 2,433,621) 65 years and over: 17.73% (male 2,766,909/female 3,455,813) (2015 est.)
Median age	total: 41.8 years male: 40.6 years female: 43.1 years (2015 est.)
Population growth rate	0.75% (2015 est.)
Birth rate	10.28 births/1,000 population (2015 est.)
Death rate	850 deaths/100,000 population (2016 est.)
Disease burden	**Communicable disease deaths**: 23/100,000 population **Noncommunicable disease deaths:** 318/100,000 population **Injury deaths:** 31/100,000 population (2016 est.)
Net migration rate	5.66 migrant(s)/1,000 population (2015 est.)
Gender ratio	at birth: 1.06 male(s)/female 0–14 years: 1.05 male(s)/female 15–24 years: 1.06 male(s)/female 25–54 years: 1.03 male(s)/female 55–64 years: 0.98 male(s)/female 65 years and over: 0.8 male(s)/female total population: 0.98 male(s)/female (2015 est.)

TABLE 6-1 Canada (continued)	
Infant mortality rate	total: 4.65 deaths/1,000 live births male: 4.97 deaths/1,000 live births female: 4.3 deaths/1,000 live births (2015 est.)
Life expectancy at birth	total population: 81.76 years male: 79.15 years female: 84.52 years (2015 est.)
Total fertility rate	1.59 children born/woman (2015 est.)
HIV/AIDS adults prevalence rate	NA
Number of people living with HIV/AIDS	NA
HIV/AIDS deaths	fewer than 400 (2013 est.)

*Percentages add up to more than 100% because respondents were able to identify more than one ethnic origin.

Data from Central Intelligence Agency. The World Fact Book, 2016: Canada. https://www.cia.gov/library/publications/the-world-factbook/geos/ca.html. Accessed May 2, 2016.

History

Archeological records indicate that Canada has some of the first lands in North America to be inhabited by humans. Aboriginal people settled the area roughly 10,000 years ago. At the time of Columbus's voyage, there had been a highly developed and flourishing society in Canada for over a thousand years.[2]

It is now widely held by historians that the Norse, led by Leifur Eiriksson, were the first Europeans to set foot on Canadian soil, around the year 1000 CE. Eiriksson's and the subsequent Norse ventures to North America were short lived and yielded little lasting sway over the development of Canadian society.[3,4]

In contrast, a new era of European arrivals was initiated in 1497 with the voyage of Englishman John Cabot, the first post-Columbian explorer to land upon the shores of Canada. Although the English conducted the earliest exploration of the region, it was not until 1605 that the French founded the first large-scale permanent European colony. For the ensuing century and a half, rivalries between the colonial powers of France and England were to be the hallmark of the Canadian experience.[3,5]

The Treaty of Paris, 1763, represents a critical turning point in Canadian history. With the English victory in the Seven Years' War, the dual colonial structure of Canada was at an end. In its place arose an English hegemony over the Canadian colonies that would be sustained for the next century.[3,5]

Although the direct power of the French colonial presence ceased, the social and cultural influence was to endure, particularly in the region of Quebec. At the close of the American Revolution, there was a significant migration of English loyalists from the lower 13 colonies into the southeastern regions of Canada. These new residents were committed Anglophiles and staunchly supportive of the British Empire. As a result of the cultural divergence between these new immigrants and the existing French-Canadians, the area was divided, and two separate colonies were formed. One colony reflected the French heritage of Canada and the other, the English heritage. These two regions would eventually become what are now the provinces of Quebec and Ontario. The multicultural origins and heritage of Canada continue into the 21st century to be a characteristic trait of the nation and a pivotal element in many policy areas.[3,4]

During the period of English colonial rule, the colonies that comprised what is now Canada operated as semiautonomous entities under the leadership of their respective lieutenant governors. The high degree of independence of action enjoyed by the Canadian colonies under English rule served to ingrain an ethos of local reliance.[5] This identity as independent colonies and this focus on local self-reliance laid the foundations for the structure of strong provinces that emerged with the formation of the Canadian nation-state in the last half of the 19th century.[3,5]

With its inauguration on July 1, 1867, the British North America Act established the Dominion of Canada. The foundations of a nation were thus laid with the unification of the Canadian colonies as a single entity.[5] Under the terms of confederation, the provinces were granted authority over broad areas of governance, and thus, they represented a powerful force within the new nation. From the outset, the issue of balancing the delegation of authority between the national government and the provinces was contentious.

The period of Dominion, 1867 to 1982, represented a slow transition toward a progressively greater degree of autonomy from England. During this era, Canada underwent three pivotal events that were to influence greatly the complexion of the contemporary nation-state: the westward expansion of the nation, the Great Depression, and World War II.[5,6]

During the last half of the 19th century and the early years of the 20th, Canada began to expand westward, extending the nation fully across the North American continent. As the newly formed provinces were added to the Dominion, a stronger and more prosperous nation-state grew. This expansion also served to reinforce the Canadian ethic of communal action, as the challenges of inhabiting the vast rural territory made local and regional coordination essential for successful settlement.[5]

Canadians suffered greatly during the Depression. The enormity of the economic disaster overwhelmed the resources of individuals and local governments. Because of the scale of the crisis, Canadians began to focus more on communal action and on an expanded role for the state in the lives of their citizens. As a result, many of Canada's social welfare programs at the provincial and national levels can trace their origins to this time period.[7] This era also provided the catalyst for the evolution of the modern Canadian healthcare system.[8]

World War II had three primary effects on Canadian society. First, it served to further galvanize the national identity of Canada, among its own citizenry and in the international community.[5] A second influence of the war was the substantial increase in population that came in the wake of the Allied victory. This rise was fueled by a spike in birth rates and by a wave of immigration from around the world.[9] The third significant result of World War II, specifically of the fighting efforts, was the shift in taxation powers among the various levels of the Canadian government. During the war years, the provincial governments ceded considerable powers to the federal government to assess and collect taxes. This expansion of the federal tax base became a pivotal issue in future years, particularly regarding the financing of health and social services.[8]

With the patriation of the British North America Act in 1982, Canada formally became a fully independent nation. It is recognized as a world leader in peacekeeping and as an influential actor in the international economy. The nation has experienced and responded to numerous short-term challenges over the past several decades, and it has also continued to deal with issues of a more fundamental nature. Two of the more prominent long-standing areas of contention that merit mention are constitutional matters related to power sharing under the nation's federal structure and conflicts arising from the dual ethnic heritage of the nation, particularly regarding the issue of greater autonomy for the province of Quebec. Both issues are germane to health and health care.

Size and Geography

Canada is geographically the second largest nation in the world and the largest on the North American continent, covering 9.9 million square kilometers (3.8 million square miles; see **FIGURE 6-1**).

Spanning the width of the continent, Canada has a varied environment ranging from its coastal regions, to the arid plains of the interior, to the polar cap of the north.[9]

Although some population centers are spread across the nation's land mass, roughly two-thirds of the population reside along the southern border. The population density of Canada is 3.7 people per square kilometer, but this figure is misleading because more than 80% of the population resides in relatively dense urban areas.[10] In metropolitan areas, the population concentration is 2,250 people per square kilometer, roughly comparable with that of England. The rural areas in the west and north are very sparsely populated.[9]

Government and Political System

It is often said that the essence of the Canadian perspective on government and society is captured in one brief phrase from the Constitution Act of 1867, "Peace, Order and Good Government." These few words, often noted in counterpoint to the United States' "life, liberty, and the pursuit of happiness," convey the Canadian dedication to the practical application in government of communally held values and

FIGURE 6-1 Map of Canada
© Bardocz Peter/Shutterstock

collective action. Equality represents the foundation on which the civil union in Canada is constructed, and this core value is infused throughout government policy actions and debates at the federal, provincial/territorial, and local levels, particularly regarding health policy.[11]

As established under the British North America Act, 1867, and subsequently patriated on April 17, 1982, the governmental structure of Canada is a constitutional monarchy. Under this system, Queen Elizabeth II of Great Britain and the United Kingdom rules as monarch of Canada but does not govern. The functional government of Canada is an English-style parliamentary democracy with a federal structure. The federal system of rule that exists in Canada delegates governing authority to the national and provincial governments; thus, the provincial governments are sovereign entities in their own right and not merely extensions of the national government.[11]

The national government, based in the city of Ottawa, is led by the prime minister, the elected leader of the political party that garnered the largest number of parliamentary seats in the previous parliamentary elections. Parliament is a bicameral body consisting of the 105 members of the Senate who are appointed by the Queen's representative, the governor general, and the House of Commons, whose 338 members are elected by popular vote of the citizenry.[12] Among the varied levels of government in Canada, taxation authority is broadest for the national government, which holds constitutional authority to levy personal/corporate income taxes, value-added taxes on goods and services, and the exclusive power to impose excise taxes and duties on imported goods.[13]

The 10 provincial and 3 territorial governments are headed by their respective premiers, who are elected by the predominant party in the provincial assemblies. In all 13 jurisdictions, the legislatures are unicameral assemblies. The breadth of provincial and territorial taxation authority is roughly equivalent to that of the national government. The exception is excise taxes and duties, which are solely the purview of Ottawa.[13]

Political parties emerged in Canada during the 1830s and were, in essence, a colonial reflection of the British two-party system, composed of the Liberal party and the Conservative party. This approach to a political system continued in Canada until the time of World War I, when conflicts over the draft ignited a rift within Canadian parties and forever changed the nation's political landscape. By 1921, the Progressive party had established a tradition of a multiparty system within Canada.[14] Over the following decades, three to five substantial political parties have existed in Canada, and minor and regional parties have played pivotal roles in many elements of Canadian governance, particularly in relationship to the development of national health insurance.[15,16]

Macroeconomics

Canada, a member of the Group of 8, is recognized as one of the leading market-based economies in the world. Government estimates place the total gross domestic product (GDP) for 2014 at $1.785 trillion, a per capita GDP of $35,540 based on 2014 population estimates.[17]

Other indicators of the health of the economy include the rate of inflation and the unemployment rate. In January 2016, the core consumer price index measured at 2.0%, a level safely within the target range of the Bank of Canada.[18] The unemployment rate as of April 2016 was 7.1%.[19]

Since the turn of the 20th century, the Canadian economy has evolved from its predominately natural resource-driven origins to encompass a richly diverse array of market sectors. The service sector is the largest element of the Canadian economy, comprising roughly 70% of GDP in the year 2016, up from 49% in the years immediately after World War II. Manufacturing accounted for less than 15% of GDP in 2016.[20]

Key industries include trade, health care and social services, finance and insurance, machinery and auto manufacturing, production of natural gas and oil, mining, and agriculture. As is true with the population of Canada, all sectors of the economy—with the exclusion of the gas, oil, and mining—are heavily concentrated along the southern border. Agricultural production is primarily found in the central and western provinces. The financial and insurance industries are disproportionately headquartered in the provinces of Ontario and Quebec.

Canada has a highly developed infrastructure, with a national system of roads and highways covering 1.4 million kilometers. An extensive rail system exists providing 72,093 kilometers of track covering all areas of Canada. Air travel is available throughout the country from a system of 10 international airports located in the major metropolitan cities and 300 smaller terminals spread across the nation. Extensive maritime port facilities are located on both the Atlantic and Pacific coasts as well as along the Great Lakes, which border Canada's primary trade partner, the United States.

Public schools, administered by the local and provincial governments, are provided at no direct cost to students throughout the nation for elementary and secondary education.[21] In 2008, education spending at all levels of government totaled over $48 billion.[22] Attendance is mandatory for children under certain ages, although the age varies by jurisdiction. Private schools are also allowed under the educational system.[21] Canada possesses a world-class postsecondary educational system. Universities in Canada not only educate Canadians but also attract students from Asia, Europe, the United States, and around the world. In 2012, international students accounted for 9 percent of students enrolled in tertiary education.[23]

Demographics

As of January 1, 2016, Canada's population slightly exceeded 36 million people.[24] As is true for most industrialized nations, the population of Canada is aging. In 1985, the median age was 31.0 years, but by 2015, the median age rose to 40.5 years. It is striking that in 2015, for the first time, the proportion of people over age 65 (16.1%) was greater than the proportion under age 15 (16.0%). The number of people 0–14 years old has remained relatively constant during this time: 5,974,508 in 1995 compared with 5,749,396 in 2015. It is the increase in the over-65 population causing the population shift; there were 3,506,480 people over 65 years old in 1995 compared with 5,780,926 in 2015.[25] Comparing racial and ethnic characteristics of the total population, we can see that only the Aboriginal people present a significantly younger demographic distribution, with an average age of 27 years. Nearly half of the Aboriginal population in 2006 was younger than 24 years of age. Aboriginal peoples—Inuit, Métis, or First Nation heritage—represented 3.8% of the population in 2006.[26]

Data from the 2011 census indicate that 64.1% of Canadians aged 25–64 years had some level of education beyond secondary schooling. People in this age range holding university degrees accounted for 25.9% of the population, whereas people having less than a secondary education represented 12.7% of Canadians. A high school diploma was the highest level of educational attainment for just under 24.0% of the population aged 25–64 years.[27]

The median after-tax income of individuals was $32,020 in 2013. For families of two or more, the median was $76,550 in after-tax earnings.[28] As measured by the Gini coefficient, income distributions across families indicate that from the late 1970s to 2015 there was a slight widening of the income gap among Canadians. The coefficient for income inequality increased from 0.29 to 0.32 during this period.[28,29] Comparing these figures with other industrialized nations, Canada has a more equitable distribution of income than the United States and the United Kingdom but a slightly less evenly distributed income base than the central European and Scandinavian nations.[28,29]

Followers of various denominations of the Christian faith comprise the majority (67.3%) of Canadians. In 2011, Roman Catholics represented the most prevalent group (39.0%), whereas Protestants accounted for 19.0% of the population. Other Christian faiths accounted for an additional 9.2%. Canadians reporting no religion represented 23.9% of the population. Muslims were the most prominent non-Christian religion, representing 3.2% of Canadians. Adherents of the Jewish, Buddhist, Sikh, and Hindu faiths each accounted for approximately 1.0% of the population. The remaining 0.6% of the population represented a variety of religious beliefs.[30]

Patterns of morbidity and mortality in Canada have changed greatly since the turn of the 20th century. As in every other Western industrialized nation, the predominance of infectious disease processes has been supplanted by chronic and lifestyle-related pathologies.[15] Cancer is the leading cause of mortality in the nation, accounting for 29.6% of deaths in 2008, followed by heart disease, accounting for 21.3% of deaths.[31] It has been found that 85.0% of adult men and 60.0% of women have at least 1 modifiable risk factor for cardiovascular disease.[31] Hypertension, a significant risk factor for cardiovascular disease, was found in 19.2% of the adult population in 2007, with 18.6% of men and 19.8% of women being diagnosed with the condition.[31]

Diabetes, another known risk factor for cardiovascular disease, has been steadily rising in the Canadian population. Among the overall population, the prevalence of diabetes was 6.8% in 2008–2009, with men (7.2%) slightly more likely than women (6.4%) to be diagnosed with the condition.[33] Diabetes prevalence increases with age, from about 2.0% in Canadians in their 30s, to about 23.0% in those aged 75–79 years.[31]

Obesity has been repeatedly linked in medical literature to cardiovascular disease, diabetes, and hypertension. In 2007, 34.0% of Canadians were reported overweight, with 16.9% reported obese.[31] The trend toward greater levels of obesity is clearly demonstrated among adolescents; between 1970 and 2004 the rate of overweight among 12- to 17-year-olds increased from 14.0% to 29.0%. The rate of increase in obesity among this age group is even more striking—it rose from 3.0% in 1970 to 9.0% in 2004.[31] The observation that physical activity helps to moderate obesity is demonstrated by the fact that 27.0% of sedentary Canadian men were found to be obese, compared with 19.0% of active men.[31] A hopeful sign for the future is that the levels of physical activity among the population in Canada appear to be rising. In 2005, 51.6% of Canadians reported being either active or moderately active, whereas in the year 2000, 43.0% were.[32]

Cancer continues to be the leading cause of mortality in the country. Estimates for 2015 indicate that 196,900 cases of cancer were diagnosed, and 78,000 people died from the disease. Breast cancer and prostate cancer were, respectively, the most common forms of cancer for women and men. Lung cancer remains the most common cancer-related cause of death in both genders, with 52.8 deaths per 100,000 men and 36.1 deaths per 100,000 women reported in the year 2010.[31] The rate of lung cancer death among men has been falling since 1988, but among women, it has been increasing, reflecting changes in the historical trend of smoking patterns. However, in a hopeful trend beginning in 2005, the lung cancer mortality rate for women leveled off and has remained approximately stable since then.[34]

The prevalence of illness and chronic conditions is considerably higher in certain subpopulations, such as the First Nations. In 2012, 49% of First Nations people aged 15 years and older living off reserve reported excellent or very good health, compared with 62% (age standardized) of the total population of Canada.[35]

▸ Brief History of the Healthcare System

Historical and sociocultural factors play a fundamental role in the evolution of a nation's health system.[36] To understand better the structures and performance of the current Canadian healthcare system, some context is valuable. As will become clear, the steps leading toward Canada's contemporary healthcare financing and delivery system do not dramatically differ from those observed in most of the Western democracies.

Pre–World War II

From the earliest era of European influence and continuing until the beginning of the 20th century, health care in Canada was focused on the relationship between a physician and a patient. Independent physicians and surgeons, practicing in the private sector, provided services to patients predominantly in the physician's offices or the patient's homes. The fiscal dimension of this type of care would be characterized as a private mercantile exchange. Hospitals, until the late 19th century, were viewed as places to be avoided as the level of care was sadly lacking. Socially, hospitals were stigmatized through their association with the poor.[15]

Through the 19th century, government's role in health care was limited. Some support was given for the establishment of facilities to care for the poor, but for the most part, this service was provided by religious orders. It should be noted that Canada's first hospital opened in Quebec in the year 1639, and that hospitals proliferated more rapidly in Canada than in other areas of North America.[15]

Other areas of governmental involvement in health care before the 20th century were primarily sanitation, quarantine during times of epidemics, and medical licensure. Infectious disease was the primary pathological process of concern during this period. As late as 1849, a single cholera outbreak was responsible for the deaths of 2% of the population of Quebec. Although there are records of some limited licensing activities in Quebec during the 18th century, it was not until well into the 19th century that any concerted effort was made in Canada to standardize certification procedures for physicians.[15]

Throughout the 19th century and into the turn of the 20th century, the status of the physician began to ascend within Canadian society. Advances in medical knowledge allowed the provision of more effective care. As occurred in the United States and western Europe, this resulted in improved social and financial standing for physicians. Changes in the setting of medical education and patient care also began to take shape. As early as 1819, with the opening of Montreal General Hospital, the care of patients and the education of physicians began to shift to the hospital setting. This trend was further intensified throughout the 19th and into the 20th centuries by the rapid advance of medical technology and clinical knowledge.[15]

As Canada emerged from World War I, infectious disease remained the predominant challenge. Public hygiene, the Spanish Influenza, and other population health issues catalyzed the development of the public health infrastructure under the direction of the provincial governments. In 1919, the federal government began to provide a coordinating hand to the provincial public health efforts and created the national hygiene grants program to fund these efforts. The first school of public health was opened in Canada in 1920 to provide the trained workforce needed to pursue the aims of infectious disease control.[15]

During this same time frame, changes also occurred in the financing and delivery of clinical health services. Beginning in 1916, rural regions of Saskatchewan developed the Municipal Doctor Plans to recruit and retain physicians in these remote areas.[37] Instead of patients paying for their services, local governments paid the physicians a salary, thus guaranteeing their income.[8]

The concept of communal resource pooling again rose in Saskatchewan in 1920 when Union Hospital Districts were formed among adjacent rural towns to fund the construction and operation of hospitals. These collective actions, though limited to the rural areas of Canada, are viewed by some as the seeds of what would become the nation's modern healthcare system.[37]

The Great Depression of the 1930s served to galvanize the transformation of Canadian health care by fostering a new environment that embraced an active role for government. As economic hardships befell the nation, patients began to have difficulties in paying physicians and hospitals for their services. This was particularly true in the province of Saskatchewan, where the impact of the depression was especially severe in an economy based on the production of commodities such as wheat. In 1928, Saskatchewan had the fourth leading per capita income in Canada; by 1933, the province was the poorest in the nation.[5] Physicians and hospitals were financially strained by the economic downturn and more open to government intervention in health care. The extent to which this position took hold is demonstrated by the Saskatchewan Medical Association openly endorsing a public health insurance program in 1933; however, the momentum for change was slowed as the economy improved and Canada entered World War II.[8]

With the provincial election of 1944, the process of reorganizing health care reemerged. The Cooperative Commonwealth Federation (CCF) party came to power in Saskatchewan under the banner of progressive reformation of government and its role in society. A socialist leaning party, the CCF vigorously promoted the agenda of "socialized health services."[37]

Since World War II

At the close of World War II, the national environment seemed ripe for the establishment of a national health insurance program. A bill was drafted in Ottawa for such a program, but because of a conflict over the allocation of taxation powers between the federal and provincial governments, the bill failed to pass.[8] From this debate, it became clear that the provinces were divided in their opinions based on their level of prosperity. The wealthier provinces, especially Ontario, wanted to trim the federal government's power to levy taxes, which had been expanded during the war. The poorer provinces, such as Saskatchewan, were in favor of keeping tax policies in place as they were, in exchange for federal cash transfers to support social programs at the provincial level.[8]

In the wake of this stalemate at the federal level, the provincial governments once more provided the impetus for change. In 1946, Saskatchewan's government, led by the CCF, implemented the Hospital Services Plan. This program provided payment for all hospital-based services rendered in the province. Initially reimbursement was based on a per diem system, but this was soon recognized as contributing to an unwarranted increase in utilization. Subsequently, a prospective global budget was developed in which the hospital was paid a flat monthly rate for the care of all patients treated at the facility. The rate was based on an estimated 90% occupancy rate for the hospital.[37] This method became a hallmark of hospital service financing throughout Canada.

For 10 years healthcare reform continued to be relegated to the provincial level, but in 1957, the federal government, under the leadership of the Liberal party, enacted the National Hospital and Diagnostic Services Act. This program established a 50/50 funding scheme, in which the federal government would match dollar-for-dollar provincial expenditures for providing hospital services to their residents. These matching funds were contingent on the provinces meeting certain requirements about the scope of services and universal coverage. Other provinces soon adopted Saskatchewan's Hospital Services Plan as the template for hospital payment plans developed under the new federal legislation. By 1961, all 10 provinces were participating in the federal match program, providing near-universal coverage for hospital services. The experience of the National Hospital and Diagnostic Services Act served to establish the constitutionality of a federal role in health care, which, under the British North America Act, was ostensibly a provincial matter.[37,38] The resulting program of insurance for medical care (both diagnostic and therapeutic) was popular and perceived as a success by the federal government, the provincial governments, and the vast majority of Canadians.

In 1962, Saskatchewan once more took the national lead in Canada's healthcare and health policy conversation, enacting the Medical Care Insurance Act. Under the provisions of this legislation, universal coverage was provided in the province for services provided by physicians. In response, physicians declared a strike in July 1962. For 23 days, physicians refused to treat patients in the province. The settlement allowed for the continuation of universal health insurance within the province, administered under government control, but in exchange, physicians were allowed to balance bill patients for any charged amounts above the government fee schedule. Initially, 12% of physicians took advantage of this balance billing procedure, but because of market pressures, by 1974, only 2% continued the practice.[37] Other provinces soon began to consider programs comparable to Saskatchewan's.

The federal government once more capitalized on the innovations of the provinces, and in 1966, the Medical Care Act was passed by the national parliament. This act established universal coverage for physician services under provincially administered programs. Financing of the plan was a mixed model similar to that of the National Hospital and Diagnostic Services Act, with the federal government matching provincial expenditures at roughly a 50% rate for physician services.[39] This part of the system was quickly labeled Medicare (sometimes causing terminology confusion when Canada–United States comparisons are pursued).

As was the case for the National Hospital and Diagnostic Services Act, provinces had considerable latitude in developing their health plans under the Medical Care Act. Many of the provinces adopted a more rigid stance than Saskatchewan on dealing with physician balance billing. While the practice continued to exist in principle, physicians who wanted to pursue balance billing were required to opt out of the government-sponsored plan. The physician could either accept the government fee schedule rate as payment in full for all services rendered to patients, or they could practice outside of the insurance program entirely, receiving no payments from the government. Given the consistent stream of revenue the government program offered, few physicians were willing to opt out.[37] The Medical Care Act had the effect of creating near-universal coverage for office and clinic-based physician care and all closely related diagnostic services.

After enactment of the two federal programs, the National Hospital and Diagnostic Services Act and the Medical Care Act, utilization and costs were observed to rise across the country. In response, the Federal-Provincial Fiscal Arrangements and the Established Programs Financing Act were passed in 1977 to provide a stronger incentive for the provinces to control escalating costs of health care by exposing them to more of the risk for such cost increases in their programs. Under the terms of the legislation, the original 50/50 expenditure-matching formula for both of the jointly financed programs was revised in order to reduce the federal fiscal obligations. Through a system of block grant transfers, the federal government's contributions were reduced in 1977 to a figure that equaled roughly 25% of provincial hospital and physician expenditures.[38] Block grants effectively severed any direct connection between the costs of health care provided and the amount of the federal government's contributions to support the care.[37,40]

The Canada Health Act of 1984 served to integrate the three previously enacted pieces of federal legislation into one national framework for health insurance. This unified system of insurance/financing has come to be known as Medicare, adopting the common name previously used to denote insurance provided under the 1966 Medical Care Act. Provisions of the Act stipulated that the provinces would continue to devise and administer the health insurance system under guidelines set out by Ottawa and known as the five principles (TABLE 6-2), which outline the framework within which provinces develop their own unique health insurance systems.

One notable change brought about by the Canada Health Act was the virtual end of balance billing by physicians. One component of the act provided that the amount of match funds provided to the provinces would be reduced by the estimated amount of revenue collected by physicians through balance billing their patients. As a result, every province in Canada passed legislation restricting the practice of balance billing.[37]

During the 1990s, stress within the economy triggered a key policy issue. In response to escalating levels of national debt, Ottawa imposed significant reductions in federal expenditures. At the federal level, these cuts were successful in reining in both the growth in spending and the debt. From 1998 to 2009, there was a 1.9% increase in revenue and a 2.9% reduction in debt charges; however, this trend has not continued in the wake of the 2008 global recession.[42]

Since 1996, the Canada Health and Social Transfer and its successor, the Canadian Health Transfer block grant system, have been the primary method used to provide federal financial support for health programs, including Medicare. In its first year, this system reduced federal cash transfers to the provinces by $2.5 to $7.0 billion, depending on the estimate. Block grants ostensibly allow for great flexibility at the provincial and territorial level. Given the climate of budgetary restraint that has been consistent in Ottawa over the past decade, many at the provincial level see the Canada Health and Social Transfer system as simply a method to reduce federal support for provincially administered programs like Medicare. This has served to create tension within the federal structure of Canada, as the provinces felt excluded from the initial decision process for the creation of the Canada Health and Social Transfer system and continue to feel that the financing arrangements place a disproportionately heavy burden on them to operate the Medicare program with insufficient resources.[40,43,44]

▸ Description of the Current Healthcare System

The contemporary healthcare system in Canada is characterized by a system of mixed sources of funding, delivery, and administration of services. The sources

TABLE 6-2 Five Principles of the Canada Health Act

Public administration	The plan must be administered and operated on a nonprofit basis by a public authority.
Comprehensiveness	Province/territorial health insurance plans must cover all medically necessary health services provided by hospitals and physicians. They must also cover hospital-based dental surgeries.
Universality	All insured residents must be entitled to all the insured health services provided by the provincial/territorial healthcare plan on equal terms.
Portability	Residents moving from one province/territory to another are entitled to continued coverage under their original health insurance plan until any waiting periods required by the new jurisdiction are met. The waiting periods may not exceed three months.
Accessibility	Insured people must have uniform and reasonable access to hospital, physician, and dental surgery services available in that location.

Data from Health Canada. Canada Health Act Annual Report 2006–2007. http://www--.hc-sc.gc.ca/hcs-sss/alt_formats/hpb-dgps/pdf/pubs/chaar--ralcs-0607/chaar-ralcs-0607_e.pdf. Accessed March 3, 2008.

vary depending on the nature of the services being rendered and the person being treated. Hospital and physician services for approximately 97% of Canadians are covered under Medicare, the jointly funded federal/provincial health insurance system whose emergence was described in the previous section and that will be the focus of the remainder of this chapter.[45]

Health services for people of First Nation and Inuit descent are solely the purview of the federal government and are handled outside of the Medicare framework. Similarly, healthcare services for veterans, members of the armed forces, and members of the Royal Canadian Mounted Police fall under the sole auspices of the federal government.[45] Together, these segments of the population totaled roughly 1 million people in.[46]

For both the joint programs and the federal-only programs, a number of services are not covered, including portions of dental care, residential care, and pharmaceutical costs. They are funded outside of the national health insurance plans, either directly by the individual or through private sector insurance.[45]

In recent years, the Canadian health system has begun to face the repercussions of the policy decisions made in the 1980s and 1990s. With decreased financial support for the Medicare program, particularly from the federal level, investment in the maintenance and expansion of the healthcare infrastructure declined, creating a number of problems. At the core of these issues is a concern over physical access to healthcare services. Waiting times for services, particularly technologically complex or procedure-oriented services, have repeatedly been presented by critics as a problem point for the healthcare system. Concern over a lack of infrastructure, such as computed tomography (CT) and magnetic resonance imaging (MRI) scanning machinery, as well as a shortage of physicians and other healthcare professionals, has garnered considerable attention both in the public eye and among policy circles.

The delivery of health care in Canada involves both public and private transactions. Physicians and residential care facilities are mostly nongovernmental entities. The hospital sector is substantially composed of facilities operated by local and provincial governments. In addition, not-for-profit private sector hospitals, particularly religiously affiliated institutions, constitute a smaller yet highly significant source of hospital-based care.[45]

The governmental component must be seen in context. As noted, a long history of geographic dispersion and independent local action created a federal structure characterized by strong provincial governments and created an interest in local (municipal) autonomy where appropriate. This tradition, coupled with well-documented innovation by provincial governments in the healthcare arena, contributed to the development of the observed structure and to the considerable latitude of action.[47] The provinces have adopted a wide variety of approaches for their health insurance plans; thus, it is frequently argued that Canada has (at least) 13 healthcare systems, not one.

The observed variations among provinces encompass many elements of medical care and the healthcare system. The generosity of coverage (e.g., the inclusion of outpatient pharmaceuticals) is one example of this variation. In British Columbia and Alberta, premiums are charged to individuals to augment tax revenues for coverage under Medicare; although premiums are assessed, the law does not provide for the withholding of services in response to nonpayment of premiums. A greater number of and more significant differences exist between the province of Quebec and the remaining 12 provinces and territories.

Although the healthcare system in Quebec has always had distinct elements, the divergence has become more pronounced in recent years. In 1999, Quebec declined to sign the Social Union Framework Agreement and thus distanced itself from some elements of Ottawa's influence.[40] More than any other jurisdiction's, the healthcare system of Quebec is based on an integrated health and social services model with an increased concentration on the coordination of primary care and public health services.[48] Medical licensure requirements are uniform and fully transferable across all of the provinces and territories of Canada except Quebec, which administers its own system for licensing physicians.[37]

Facilities

Canada operates an extensive physical infrastructure for health care. Primary care services are provided in a variety of settings. Private physician offices constitute by far the most common venue for the delivery of primary care.[49] Primary health services are also delivered in ambulatory care clinics and in community health centers.[45]

In another example of this recurring theme, community health centers emerged as a result of provincial innovation—Quebec's. The concept spread to Ontario and then across the nation.[49] Although community health centers provide a significant amount of care, they continue to represent a much smaller provider source when compared with private physician practices. In 2010 there were approximately 300 community health centers, with the majority located in Quebec and Ontario.[50]

There were 720 hospitals operating an estimated 93,525 beds in Canada during the year 2012. Of these hospitals, 712 were publicly owned, including by federal, municipal, provincial, and regional/district entities.[51] The number of acute care hospital beds in Canada has declined significantly since reaching a peak of 179,256 beds in 1989. Between 1986 and 1995, the number of hospitals decreased from 1,224 to 978; public hospitals decreased from 1,053 to 901, and private hospitals declined by almost two-thirds (from 59 to 22). A significant portion of these closures was among smaller hospitals, particularly those located in rural areas. Saskatchewan, for instance, witnessed the closure of 52 of its rural hospitals during the early 1990s.[52,53]

In summary, these closures reduced the number of acute care beds from 178,137 in 1986 to 156,547 by 1995.[54] Some of this decline in the number of hospitals and beds reflects the transition of a number of hospitals to residential care facilities and also reflects the reclassification within other facilities of a portion of their acute care beds for long-term care use.[55] In the mid-1990s, 14,000 beds were reclassified for residential care use in the provinces of Alberta and Quebec alone.[55] In 2013, Canada had 270 acute care hospital beds per 100,000 population, down from 400 per 100,000 in 1990. This mirrors the trend among other nations in the Organisation for Economic Co-operation and Development (OECD), where the average rate of acute care beds dropped from 510 per 100,000 people to 480 beds per 100,000 residents.[56]

In 2009–2010, there were 4,633 residential care facilities operating in Canada with 265,220 approved beds. Of these, 2,136 (46.1%) were designated for the care of the elderly population; 2,202 (47.5%) were mental health institutions; and the remaining 295 facilities were dedicated to an array of different specialties, including care of the physically disabled and the delinquent youths. The distribution of facilities yields 212,948 beds staffed and in operation for the care of the elderly population, 39,644 for mental health patients, and 9,353 for the other types of institutions.[57]

Long-term care facilities in Canada are distributed somewhat differently than hospitals in terms of ownership, with the private for-profit sector representing a far more substantial component of the mix. In 2009–2010, out of 4,633 total residential care facilities, 1,914 were proprietary ownership, 253 were religious ownership, 1,746 were lay ownership, 144 were municipal ownership, 442 were provincial or territorial ownership, 15 were federal ownership, and 119 were other ownership. Out of 2,136 homes dedicated to the care of the elderly, 1,145 were proprietary ownership (93,308 beds in operation), 157 were religious ownership (15,622 beds in operation), 314 were lay ownership (30,197 beds in operation), 132 were municipal ownership (18,878 beds in operation), 291 were provincial or territorial ownership (25,255 beds in operation), none were federal ownership, and 97 were of other ownership (29,688 beds in operation).[57]

Recent studies indicate that there are notable differences between the for-profit facilities and those operated under other modes of ownership. For-profit elderly care facilities have lower staff-to-patient ratios than other institutions. In 2009–2010 the number of accumulated paid hours per resident-day, a measure of the level of staffing of long-term care facilities, was found to be 5.2 for all facilities, and 4.9 in facilities for the elderly.[58]

Public health in Canada is, for the most part, a distinct entity from the delivery of medical care. The focus of public health activities in Canada is not on supporting the delivery of healthcare services as it is in many nations, but rather on population health issues, such as community health assessment, disease surveillance, health promotion, disease and injury prevention, and health protection. In Quebec, the boundary between population health and individual medical care is somewhat more blurred, as the system relies on greater integration of health services.[48]

Under the Canadian system, public health departments are the purview of provincial and local governments. The roles between the two levels of government vary from province to province, with Ontario being the most reliant on local government funding and administration. In recent years, reports by the Krever Commission and the Auditor General of Canada have raised concerns over the existing funding and infrastructure for the support of public health functions.[48]

The federal government's public health role has traditionally been limited. Implementing processes of the Quarantine Act and various pieces of health protection legislation have, for the most part, constituted the core of the Public Health Agency of Canada's functional role in the past. Since the outbreak in 2003 of severe acute respiratory syndrome, a restructuring of public health efforts at the federal level has been undertaken. A more active role for Ottawa appears to be taking form, more in line with the position held by the Centers for Disease Control in the United States.[48]

Workforce

Human resources are a critical element of any healthcare system. Canada has focused considerable attention on this area, particularly since the 1990s, when it was perceived that the numbers of physicians and nurses were declining. The First Ministers Accord of 2003 designated healthcare human resources planning a high priority in the Canadian health policy sphere. Beyond its inherent importance in the delivery of care for patients, health care is among the nation's largest sources of employment, with over 1 million direct employees, representing 6.0% of the workforce. In 2010, 24.8% of healthcare costs were directly attributable to human resource costs.[59]

As of 2013, there were 79,905 physicians practicing in Canada, a ratio of roughly 224 physicians per 100,000 people in the population.[60] This is comparable to that of the United States—260 per 100,000 people—and the United Kingdom—280 per 100,000 people—but is below the OECD average of 330 physicians per 100,000 people.[56] Canada has seen more than a 2.0% increase in the number of physicians each year since 2007.[60]

Slightly more than half (51.0%) of practicing Canadian physicians in 2014 were in the primary care field of family medicine. Medical specialists other than surgeons accounted for 36.7% of physicians, whereas surgeons accounted for 12.2%. The remaining fraction of physicians is classified as medical scientists.[61] The percentage of primary care physicians in the workforce is notably higher than the 36.0% observed in the United States but lower than the 56.0% found in Australia.[62]

Of physicians, 74.0% were educated in one of the 17 accredited Canadian medical schools, whereas 25.4% were trained in other countries—most notably the United Kingdom, South Africa, and India—and the remaining 0.6% had unknown places of MD graduation.[61,63] Physicians are required to hold the Medical Doctor (MD) degree. To practice in Canada, foreign medical school graduates must first pass the Medical Council of Canada's Qualifying Examinations Parts I and II. This is followed by fulfilling a required residency in a Canadian medical program and completing any pertinent examinations required by the provincial or territorial medical board.[59]

Demographically, the population of Canadian physicians has changed in recent years. From 2010 to 2014, the percentage of female physicians rose from 36.1% to 39.0% of the workforce. The proportion was higher among family medicine physicians (43.8%) and lower among specialists (34.0%).[60] Between 1997 and 2011, the number of female residents grew by 113.0% compared with 42.0% for their male counterparts.[59]

Due to the increasing number of younger physicians entering the workforce, the average age of physicians has remained relatively stable from 2010 to 2014 (50.0 and 50.1 years, respectively). In 2014, the proportion of physicians under age 40 (24.5%) was approximately equal to the proportion of physicians age 60 and over (25.2%).[60]

The change in the demographics of the physicians presents a challenge for the future, as research indicates that both female physicians and older physicians on average work fewer hours per week and see fewer patients than their younger male counterparts. Unlike the general Canadian workforce, with whom part-time work has remained constant, from 1997 to 2011 the percent of general practitioners working part time has increased from 9% to 11%. Interestingly, this is in contrast to the decline in part-time work seen across all health professionals, from 26% to 22%.[59]

A 2002 study conducted by the Canadian Institute for Health Information determined that in the period between 1993 and 2000 the "real" physician-to-population ratio decreased 5.1%. The "real" physician ratio was determined by adjusting the proportion of physicians per population unit by modifiers, and it reflects the changing pattern of patients' demand for medical services and the changing composition of the physician workforce over the time period. The findings indicate that there has been a functional decrease in the number of physicians in Canada. It is further hypothesized that perhaps another component to the perception of a physician gap is that the expectations of the Canadian population, which rose in recent years, are in conflict with the actual capacity of the current supply of physicians.[63]

In 2011, there were 270,724 registered nurses (RNs) in Canada, or 885 RNs for every 100,000 people. In addition, there were 277 licensed practical nurses (LPNs) per 100,000 people in the population. The overall ratio of roughly 1,162 practicing nurses per 100,000 population puts Canada above the 977 per 100,000-person average of G8 countries (excluding Russia) in 2010.[59]

Between 1997 and 2011, the number of practicing nurses rose 16.3%. The average age of nurses also rose slightly during this period: from 43 to 45 years old for registered nurses, and from 41 to 42 years old for licensed practical nurses. In 2011, registered nurses and licensed practical nurses who were over the age of 55 represented 26.0% and 20.0% of the workforce, respectively.[59] As was seen with their physician counterparts, the nursing workforce is growing older at the same time as the general population ages and demands greater access to healthcare services.

The educational requirements for entry-level positions for registered nurses have recently undergone a transition in Canada. The Atlantic provinces were the first to institute the new policy requiring a 4-year baccalaureate degree for nursing licensure. Alberta enacted this policy in 2009, followed by Ontario. Previously, nurses could be licensed through 2- and 3-year diploma programs.[59] When fully enacted across the nation, there will be an increased lag time in bringing newly trained nurses into practice. This may produce a short-term exacerbation of the existing nursing shortage. As with physicians, foreign nursing graduates fill a considerable portion, 7.5% in 2013, of nursing positions in Canada (see **TABLE 6-3**).[51]

Technology and Equipment

Canada's healthcare system possesses a considerable infrastructure of advanced medical imaging and diagnostic equipment. The CT scan machine was introduced in Canada in 1973. In 2012, there were 510.0 machines located throughout the country.[65] This represents 14.7 CT scan machines per million people in the population. The United Kingdom in 2013 reported 7.9 per million, and the United States had 43.5 per million. The OECD average for 2013 was 24.4 CT scan machines per million.[56] Between 2003 and 2012, 185.0 new CT scan units were installed in Canada, representing a 57% increase. Utilization of CT scans in 2011–2012 was at the rate of 125.5 scans per 1,000 people in the population. MRI technology was first introduced in Canada in 1982. There were 308.0 MRI machines in Canada in 2012[65], reflecting 8.8 machines per million. This total is similar to the 6.1 per-million rate observed in the United Kingdom but is much lower than the 35.5 MRI machines per million people found in the United States. The OECD average in 2013 was 14.1 MRI machines per million.[56] In the period between 2003 and 2012, 159.0 new MRI units were installed in Canada, representing a 107% increase. Utilization totals for 2011–2012 reflect a rate of 49.3 MRI scans per 1,000 Canadians.[65]

Since 2000, there has been a considerable growth in freestanding private sector imaging facilities offering CT and MRI scans. In 2003, there were 9 CT machines in freestanding clinics. That number rose to 25 by 2012, which represented 5% of CT machines in the country. Similarly, there were 26 MRI machines located in freestanding clinics in 2003; by 2012, there were 66, which represented 21% of the nation's scanners.[65] Interestingly, the funding for these freestanding facilities is different than for hospital-based machines. For hospitals, the primary source of revenue is the government's health insurance plan; for the freestanding facilities, the primary sources of revenue are private insurance and out-of-pocket payment.

Imaging capacity (whether public or private, hospital-based or freestanding) is largely an urban phenomenon. In Toronto, Montreal, Vancouver, and other large urban settings, the availability of such technology is comparable to, in some cases slightly less than, other industrialized nations. Access to advanced imaging technology in the more sparsely populated areas, such as the Northwest Territories, Newfoundland, and Labrador, is considerably more limited (see **TABLE 6-4**).[65]

TABLE 6-3 Number of Health Professionals per 100,000 Canadians, 2013

Health profession	Number per 100,000 population
Optometrists	15
Chiropractors	25
Respiratory therapists	31
Dietitians	31
Psychologists	49
Physiotherapists	55
Dentists	62
Occupational therapists	41
Pharmacists	101
Social workers	125
Physicians (excluding residents)	221
Registered nurses (including nurse practitioners)	788
Licensed practical nurses	266
Nurse practitioners	10

Data from Canadian Institute for Health Information. Canada's Health Care Providers: Provincial Profiles, 2013. https://secure.cihi.ca/estore/productFamily.htm?pf=PFC3045&lang=en&media=0. November 26, 2015. Accessed May 10, 2016.

TABLE 6-4 Medical Imaging Technology per Million Canadians, 2012

Imaging technology	Number per million population
CT scanners	14.7
MRI scanners	8.9
Nuclear medicine cameras	16.7
PET scanners	0.3
PET/CT scanners	1.0
SPECT/CT scanners	4.1

Data from Canadian Institute for Health Information. MIT 2012 Data Release—Static Figures & Tables. https://www.cihi.ca/en/types-of-care/specialized-services/medical-imaging#_Highlights; CIHI Report Medical Imaging Technologies in Canada, 2012.

▸ Evaluation of the Healthcare System

Cost

Overall spending on the healthcare system in 2013 was estimated to be $209.4 billion, approximately $4,569 per Canadian. This was an increase of 2.0% over 2012 expenditures. It was estimated that in 2015 total expenditures totaled $219.1 billion or approximately $6,105 per Canadian. Expenditures are projected to vary by province within a 7%–15% range about the mean. Quebec is projected to have the lowest per capita spending at $5,665, and Newfoundland and Labrador to have the highest at $7,036 per person. Expenditures in the territories were projected to be considerably higher in 2015 with Nunavut being the highest at $14,059 per capita. This is primarily due to the small populations and vast geography of the territories. The relationship pattern for provincial and territorial spending has been consistent over the recent past.[42]

Trends in overall healthcare expenditures have varied significantly since 1975. From 1975 until 1991, healthcare costs in Canada rose at a rate of 2.7% per year. As the effect of budget cuts during the 1990s took hold, spending on health decreased dramatically. From 1991 to 1996, healthcare expenditures declined at 0.5% per year, a value less than the overall rate of inflation in the economy, thus representing real dollar cuts in resources. As budgetary restraints were loosened in the late 1990s and early 2000s, the rate of spending began to increase once more. Between 1996 and 2010, the rate of increase in spending rose to 3.3% per year. From 2010 to 2013, spending has decreased by an average of 0.6% per year.[42]

As a percentage of economic output, healthcare expenditures in 2013 represented 10.7% of the nation's GDP, 38.0% of the budget. By province, Nova Scotia and Manitoba had the highest spending in relation to the budget, estimated to be 46.0%. Quebec spent the lowest, 30.0% of the budget. Among the territories, the range varied from Yukon, which spent 18.0% of the budget in 2013, to Nunavut, which is estimated to have spent 29.0%.[42]

Growth in healthcare expenditures as a percentage of GDP displays a trend quite similar to overall spending. In 1975, spending on health care represented 7.0% of GDP. During recession periods, such as that experienced in Canada during the early 1980s, the rate of healthcare spending as a percentage of GDP rose sharply from 6.8% in 1979 to 8.3% in 1983. This reflected the steady rise in healthcare costs as national production slipped. A similar effect was witnessed with the recession in the early 1990s, and for the first time, healthcare expenditures as a percentage of GDP reached 10% in 1992. The effects of government spending cuts lowered health expenditures during the mid-1990s, and as the economy began to expand during the post-recession period, the percentage of GDP consumed by health care dropped to 8.7% in 1997. Between 1998 and 2010, healthcare spending expanded slightly faster than the overall economy, reaching 11.6% of GDP in 2010. Subsequent to the 2009 recession, health spending growth has been slower than growth in the overall economy, declining to 10.9% of GDP in 2013.[42]

Financing of the Canadian healthcare system is achieved through the convergence of multiple streams of funding. The three primary sources of financing are the Medicare system, out-of-pocket payments by individuals, and private insurance. Since 1997, the division of spending on health care has been relatively set with the public sector contributing roughly 70.0% of funding and the private sector generating 30.0% from out-of-pocket payments, private insurance payment for services not covered under Medicare, and nonconsumption revenue.[66] In 2013, the overall per capita spending of $4,569 consisted of $4,214 from public sources and $1,744 from private sector funds. Among private sector funding, there has been a significant shift in recent years in the mix of out-of-pocket payment and private health insurance coverage. In 1988,

29.2% of private sector spending was contributed by private insurance; by 2013, that percentage had risen to 41.3%.[42]

In 2013, hospital costs represented the single largest expense item, constituting 29.5% of healthcare spending. Pharmaceuticals were the second largest cost item, consuming 15.7% of every healthcare dollar, followed by physician services at 15.5%. The pattern of spending since 1975 has shifted dramatically, attributable to hospital spending falling while pharmaceutical costs were rising sharply until recently. The reduced growth in pharmaceutical expenditures in recent years is at least partially the result of generic pricing control policies, patent expirations, and fewer new drugs emerging on the market. The growth per capita of physician expenditures has outpaced that of hospitals or drugs since 2007, due in part to more rapid growth in the supply of physicians and the increases in fees.[42]

Medicare spending represents the majority of healthcare spending in Canada. Funding for Medicare is derived from tax revenues collected at both the federal and provincial levels. Federal support is delivered through Canada Health Transfer per-capita block grants to the provinces.[42,66,67] Prior to 2014, block grants were composed of two components: actual cash transfers, and tax point transfers. Beginning in 2014/2015, Health Transfers converted to cash only, to provide comparable treatment for all residents regardless of where they live.[68] The actual percentage of expenditures under Medicare that the federal government pays compared with what the provinces pay has varied considerably over time. In 1980, the federal government contributed 30.6% of public funds allocated to health care; this figure dropped to 21.5% by 1996.[69]

The mechanism of funding Medicare has created a degree of tension between the federal and provincial governments. Under the Constitution Act of 1867, the provinces officially hold authority over health care and most other social welfare issues[13]; however, in practical application, the federal government holds considerable influence in these ostensibly provincial-level policy matters through the power derived from financial transfers of tax revenues.[40]

Payment systems for healthcare services vary by provider type and the nature of the service being rendered. Hospitals, regardless of ownership status, are paid through the provincial government based on a global budget for the year. Physician services, in most cases, are handled on a fee-for-service basis. The fee schedule is negotiated annually between the provincial government and the province's medical association.[42,69] Physicians may also be paid under a blended system of fee-for-service and incentive-based payments. This is particularly common with those working in large group practices and community health centers. Some physicians are salaried employees.[42]

Pharmaceuticals are paid for under a mixed method that varies considerably by province. Quebec has a comprehensive prescription drug plan that is financed through tax revenues and that covers the cost of most outpatient drugs. In the majority of Canadian provinces, some portion of outpatient drug costs are supplemented by the government at least for specific segments of the population, such as low-income people and the elderly. For the remainder of the population, the bulk of outpatient prescription drug costs are paid for either through private insurance or out-of-pocket payments. This issue is complicated by the fact that provincial laws prohibit the marketing of insurance products for services covered under public health insurance.[42]

The reimbursement structure for long-term care is primarily made through a per diem system. Payments for this care represent a blend of funding streams from both the public and private sector. The public sector paid 71% of the costs for care in "other institutions" (besides hospitals) in 2013. The remaining 29% was paid primarily out-of-pocket, although there is a limited market for private sector long-term care insurance.[42]

Quality

The quality of a healthcare system can be measured in numerous dimensions. Three measures are population health, system efficiency, and patient perception/satisfaction. Several clinical measures are routinely used for the comparative assessment of healthcare systems. These include infant mortality rates, life expectancy, and immunization rates. Efficiency measures refer to wait times for procedures or services.

The overall infant mortality rate in Canada in 2013 was 4.8 infant deaths per 1,000 live births. This rate has remained virtually unchanged since 2002. The rates differed by gender with deaths among male infants occurring at a rate of 5.1 per 1,000 live births and among female infants at a rate of 4.6 deaths per 1,000 live births.[70] This is close to the OECD national average of 3.8 infant deaths per 1,000 live births in 2013. Infant mortality rates are higher in the United States, 5.0 deaths per 1,000 live births, and lower in the United Kingdom at 3.5 infant deaths per 1,000 live births.[56] The overall rates do not fully relate the picture as the infant mortality rate is significantly higher in some subpopulations. Residents of rural Nunavut Territory had an infant mortality rate in 2012 of 21.4, which is more than four times the national average that year.[70] Similarly, members of the First Nations have been found to have infant mortality rates upward of three times that of the nation as a whole. Disparities also exist in infant mortality rates between people in the top quartile of income and those in the bottom quartile.[71]

Life expectancy at birth has been rising among Canadians. In 2013, the overall life expectancy was 81.5 years. Between 2007 and 2009, men had an expected longevity of 79.0 years compared with women who lived on average 83.0 years.[56] Each of these longevity markers is significantly above the OECD averages and surpasses those of both the United Kingdom and the United States.[72] Disparities in life expectancy do, however, continue to exist within certain subpopulations. Men of Aboriginal heritage live on average 7.0 years less than the national average. Likewise, Aboriginal women live an average of 5.0 years less than the Canadian average.[71]

Another significant reflection of the performance of a healthcare system is the longevity of people after reaching the age of 65.0 years. Overall, Canadians can expect to live 20.3 years after reaching 65.0 years of age. For men, that figure is slightly less at 19.0 years, and for women, the expected additional lifespan is 22.0 years. Both averages surpass those observed for men and women of OECD nations.[56]

Immunization rates in Canada are high across the population. In 2014, 89% of children received an immunization for measles, mumps, and rubella by their second birthday. Similarly, 90% of children received an immunization for polio by age 2. Other internationally recommended childhood vaccination rates are also high. Approximately three-quarters of girls aged 12–14 years were immunized for HPV, and by age 17, almost 90% of children were immunized for Hepatitis B.[73]

Waiting time for appointments is an issue that has garnered considerable attention in the Canadian healthcare system. A 2010 survey indicated that Canadians waited longer to see a physician than did their counterparts in 10 other countries, including the United States, the United Kingdom, Germany, and Australia. Only 45% of Canadians were able to see a physician on the same day or the next day that they attempted to obtain an appointment, compared with more than 57% in the United States, more than 70% in the United Kingdom, and more than 60% in both Germany and Australia. Among Canadians, 33% reported that it took more than 6 days to see a physician regarding a health condition. When attempting to see a specialist, 41% of Canadians waited less than one month, and another 41% waited for two months or more, the lowest and highest proportions, respectively, of the 11 countries surveyed.[74] Similarly, wait times for diagnostic testing varied among the provinces. For example, median wait times for MRIs ranged from 32 to 55 days.[75] Wait times are a significant issue with Canadians, although only about one-fifth of the population considers the current circumstances "unacceptable."

Overall, Canadians are quite satisfied with their healthcare system. In 2005, 84.4% of Canadians rated their satisfaction with health services as "very satisfied" or "somewhat satisfied." These results have been stable since the year 2000.[32] Modest variations across subpopulations have been observed. For example, males are generally more pleased with the system than are females, with 85.1% of men rating healthcare services positively versus 83.8% for women. For the most part, Canadians are satisfied with their system and, in some studies, are noted to be proud of its fundamental attributes, especially the degree of equity it achieves. It is a subtle but important point that can easily be lost in cross-national comparisons; Canadians are particularly proud of the perceived fairness of their system. Changes or advances that are not experienced in an equitable manner would not be viewed as improvements.

Access

Universal coverage is one of the five core principles of the Canadian healthcare system. All residents of Canada not specifically designated as being covered under another federal health insurance program are entitled to coverage for hospital and physician services under the national health insurance plan, Medicare. The cornerstone of the Canadian philosophy of health care is equality among people.[43] Since the introduction of Medicare, it has been an expressed intent that a two-tiered system of health care not only be avoided but actively prevented from developing in Canada. It is felt that need, not financial position, should be the basis on which the allocation of healthcare resources is decided. Although disparities in health care do exist in Canada, they are based on processes that are not rooted in strictly defined financial access to physician and hospital services.[42]

Health insurance coverage substantially reduces financial barriers to obtaining care, but it does not eliminate all. Other expenses (e.g., transportation to the site of care and the costs of uncovered services) are also impediments. The influence of such costs is disproportionately felt by people with lower incomes, creating differential impacts on access to care.

Beyond financial issues, access to care can also be constrained by geographic, social, cultural, psychological, and other attributes of both the potential recipient of care and the potential provider of services. In Canada, the wide expanses of rural areas and the resulting travel times are a significant barrier to access. Similarly, harsh winter weather and language issues have been cited as impeding access to care. For the most part, the Canadian population views access to care in much the same way that it views other elements of the system, strongly emphasizing questions of equity and fairness.

Virtually all Canadians are covered by one of the varieties of health insurance programs sponsored by some level of government; however, a small number of people do remain uninsured. The few people who fall into this category are primarily recent immigrants and refugees to Canada.[76]

Current and Emerging Issues and Challenges

Canada will face several healthcare challenges as the 21st century proceeds. Among the more prominent issues facing the Canadian system are the financial sustainability of the system as currently structured, questions about access to care (generally focused on system capacity), concerns about outpatient pharmaceuticals, debates about the appropriate role of the private sector, and continuing conversations about the importance of equity in assessing system performance.

In recent years, there has been considerable discussion regarding the sustainability of the Canadian healthcare system.[77,78] If considering solely the financial capacity of the nation as a whole to shoulder the rising costs of health care, international comparisons of health expenditures as a percentage of GDP indicate that Canada is operating well within a supportable and sustainable range.[56,77-79] Annual federal budget surpluses also indicate that the nation remains in a solid position to sustain the healthcare system[18] and to manage any unexpected events in the relatively near future.

The 2002 Commission on the Future of Health Care in Canada, commonly referred to as the Romanow Commission, considered this topic and determined that the real issue was not the actual financial burden but rather the willingness of the Canadian people and their governments to accept and bear the expense of universal health care. In respect to this, the commission found that Canadians were resolved to the preservation of their healthcare system in the face of increased costs of health care as long as the system was responsive to the needs and expectations of the people.[77] From this perspective, the financial sustainability of the system is intimately tied to its performance in terms of meeting the requirements of the Canadian people. The terminology is noteworthy—needs, requirements, and expectations are not the same as demand in the sense that the latter term is employed in orthodox economic terminology. Thus, it seems clear that the central element of Canadian health policy conversations in the coming years will be bending the cost curve while maintaining access to timely high-quality health care.[77,80]

Achieving these diverse aims will be particularly challenging given the ever-changing political landscape of a democratic nation and the shift that has occurred over the last decade in the health policy dynamic between Ottawa and the provinces. Since 2011 the central government has attempted to divest itself of much of the guidance and administrative responsibilities for the healthcare system. This shift has placed an even greater level of reliance on the provincial and territorial governments. This expands the traditional role of the provinces as the incubators of innovation, making them now drivers in bending the cost curve while addressing issues of access and quality.

Problems with access to care in the Canadian context do not refer to the same financial access (insurance coverage) issues that exist in the United States and in many other nations. Rather, the focal concerns in Canada are primarily questions of availability (including distance, travel times, and wait times, coupled with social, psychological, demographic, and similar elements of use and access, all noted by Andersen[81] and many other analysts of healthcare utilization).[82] In recent years, this part of the access conversation has focused heavily on waiting times and on a general perception that waiting times can and should be reduced by increasing service capacity.

It is reasonably well documented that waiting times for a significant number of services and procedures are longer in Canada than in comparable nations.[83] This international comparison, however, is less significant than the emerging perception among a substantial number of Canadians that some wait times, especially for appointments with primary care doctors, specialty referrals, some imaging procedures, and a relatively specific list of surgical interventions, are simply too long.[84]

In general, wait times for services can be attributed to both supply and demand factors, and given the evolving circumstances of the Canadian healthcare sector, it would seem likely that wait times will lengthen without some alteration in the status quo. Changes in the supply of and demand for health care caused by the shifting demographics of both the general population and the healthcare professions represent one of the most significant factors related to access to care that Canadians will have to face in the coming years. As the population continues to age, greater demands will be placed on the healthcare system. The human resources necessary to meet the evolving needs of the population must be identified, trained, and placed. This will be a challenge as the physician workforce transitions into a cohort that is older and more evenly distributed in terms of gender. Both older physicians and female physicians on average work fewer hours than their younger male colleagues.[59] This presents a situation in which either the number of physicians per population must be increased or steps must be taken to increase the productivity of the existing physician supply or to provide for a comparable set of services from other professionals. One such step that is currently taking form in Canada is the integration of nurse practitioners into the healthcare setting. While in 2000 only 7 jurisdictions in Canada permitted the licensure of nurse practitioners,[59] now all 13 provinces and territories have licensing statutes in place.

The overall supply of physicians is not the only concern related to healthcare availability. Access to primary care physicians also continues to be an issue in many areas of Canada. Although physicians practicing in the primary care fields of family medicine and general practice comprise more than 51% of Canadian physicians, it has been observed that getting appointments with them can be difficult.[59] Efforts to increase the availability and accessibility of primary care practitioners to meet the demands of the Canadian people (especially those residing in rural sparsely populated areas) will certainly be a significant policy focus of the next decade.[77]

As a result of budget cuts in the 1980s and 1990s, the infrastructure for providing many technologically advanced services has not expanded at a rate that aligns with the growth in demand for these services.[65] This gap in the available supply of physical infrastructure has compounded issues arising from the decline in the real number of physicians practicing in Canada. Similarly, the construction of new hospital capacity, additional long-term care beds, assisted-living facilities, and other capital-intensive projects lagged over the same period. While efforts to increase and enhance primary prevention and other public (population) health initiatives may serve to mitigate this downward trend in the availability of some medical services, the gap between capacity and demand will remain a significant policy issue.

Achieving an increased capacity requires at least four things. First, there must be a clear specification of the target—the optimal numbers of medical professionals, beds, scanners, etc., given the population. Such a target must be determined in a manner that reflects the best available data and technical analyses of the needs for service that are manifested in any particular population, as well as in a manner that addresses the wishes of that population. Second, there must be a reasonable level of agreement as to the target. Third, the investment capacity necessary to produce that amount of service must be available, despite competition with other societal needs that have their own constituencies. Fourth, there must be sufficient time allocated for the investment decisions to reach fruition. It takes several years to train professional healthcare personnel. It is entirely possible for several years to pass between the moment when it is determined that a particular community needs a new full-service hospital and the moment when the first patient is treated in that new setting.

In the five decades since Canada's Medicare program was introduced in the 1960s, there have been considerable changes in the manner in which medical services are provided. Fifty years ago, hospital costs were overwhelmingly the "big-ticket" component of total costs. Physician services were a somewhat distant second. Long-term care was a far distant third, and pharmaceuticals were just barely part of the picture. In 2014, outpatient pharmaceuticals constituted the second leading cost among national health expenditures,[42] accounting for $33.9 billion, 15.7% of total healthcare spending. This figure does not include expenditures on many of the most expensive drugs (such as cancer treatment drugs) that are delivered only in inpatient settings as a part of hospital care. Under the federal legislation that enacted Medicare, outpatient drugs are not a required item of the provincial plans. Many provinces do offer coverage for certain segments of the population, but the scope varies greatly by province, ranging from a low in 2008 of 9.0% of the population receiving either direct coverage or premium supplements in Manitoba to 43.0% in Quebec. Over 75.0% of Canadians have some form of prescription drug coverage, primarily private sector insurance.[85] Estimates from 2014 suggest that 42.0% of outpatient pharmaceutical spending was paid for through public sector sources with the remaining 58.0% coming from private insurance (35.8%) and out-of-pocket funds (22.2%).

In a nation where there is virtually universal insurance coverage for major medical expenses from hospitalization and physician services, having nearly a quarter of the population be without coverage for the second leading source of medical expenses represents a significant issue. This issue is compounded by the wide variation in the degree of coverage provided under both public and private sector drug plans. These geographic variations in coverage foster significant concerns over the equity of the system. Compounding the concerns over equity is the view held in many circles that by having such a fragmented system of insurance for pharmaceuticals, the system is forfeiting the opportunity to leverage scale to negotiate better pricing with manufacturers. Addressing cost and equity issues in outpatient pharmaceuticals is likely to be a pressing issue in the coming years whether it continues to be addressed at the provincial level or through a national effort. In a different vein, outpatient drugs also present another challenge for the Canadian healthcare system: cross-border sales to citizens of the United States. Because of the regulation of prices for patented medicines in Canada, the consumer costs are lower for some brand-name medications than in the United States. As a result, at least since the 1990s, there has been a growing business—legal in Canada, but perhaps not in the United States—in the sale of prescription drugs to Americans both in traditional over-the-counter sales and through Internet pharmacies. Some estimates place the total upward of $1.2 billion in annual sales. If accurate, this would account for roughly 10% of Canadian retail pharmaceutical sales.[86]

There has been a growing concern in recent years over the potential of this cross-border industry to jeopardize drug availability in Canada or to prompt U.S. drug manufacturers to either withhold sale of medications to Canada or to greatly increase their wholesale prices. There is some anecdotal evidence to support the proposition that localized drug shortages in Canada are attributable to the international resale of pharmaceuticals.[86] The 2003 granting of prescription drug coverage for U.S. Medicare participants in the United States may serve to decrease the total demand for medications from Canada. In the years to come, this friction point in Canadian-U.S. relations will need to be addressed.

There has also been some movement in Canada toward developing private health insurance products to support the financing of services that are also covered under Medicare. In a widely reported 2005 decision, the Canadian Supreme Court struck down Quebec's statute prohibiting the sale of insurance products that would provide payment for any services covered under the provincial Medicare plan.[87] Technically, this decision is germane only to Quebec, but other similar cases are under consideration in courts across Canada. In response to this judicial direction, some political forces are being marshaled to accomplish whatever constitutional change is necessary to effectively overturn the court's ruling.

At the core of the Supreme Court's ruling is that the government has a responsibility to provide the services covered under Medicare in a timely fashion to prevent undue pain and risk of death. If the government fails to meet these obligations, the statutory prohibition of people going outside the public system to obtain care is unconstitutional under the laws of Quebec.[88] Although the long-term consequences of the movement toward privatization and the Supreme Court's decision are not clear at present, this certainly will be a central element in the future health policy debate in Canada.

Beyond these questions of supply, the changing composition of medical care, and some unique relationship issues that arise because of proximity to the United States, Canada faces an ongoing, perhaps perpetual, review and reconsideration of a fundamental philosophical question. Since the inception of publicly financed health insurance in Canada, the nation's healthcare and health policy conversations have included a delicate balancing act with three core values: (1) a respect for and commitment to communal action; (2) a faith in the abilities and power of free market economics, competition, and the private sector; and (3) a belief that the distribution of services, perhaps especially health services, should be achieved in a manner that is equitable, fair, and just. Balancing these three core values led to the development of a system that uses community orientation for financing and making major capital decisions; leaves the individual medical care transaction in the private realm of the patient, the family, and the provider; and expects everyone to play the same game, on the same field, and by the same rules. This conversation can perhaps be best understood by returning to the question of waiting times.

In 1978, Canadians were the most satisfied nation in the world with regard to their healthcare system. By 2001, a significant majority of Canadians felt "fundamental changes" needed to be made.[89] Much of this continuing conversation has been focused on waiting lists and a public perception that waiting lists for care in Canada were creating a migration of patients to the United States to receive healthcare services. Some estimates placed the expenditures outside Canadian borders in the range of $1 billion per year.

It is clear that some degree of this phenomenon is witnessed. In fact, a few Canadian provinces have standing agreements with providers in the United States to handle overflow demand for certain services at their facilities. Indeed, some such agreements are reciprocal. Canadian hospitals located near the international border are part of emergency surge plans and offer other capacity management support to their U.S. colleagues. There is no question that a quantity of cross-national service delivery occurs. Some are contractually sanctioned. Some reflect the capacity of wealthy individuals to obtain whatever care they seek in whatever setting they prefer and at whatever time meets their priorities, presuming that they have the resources necessary to implement those decisions. Despite the publicity, when taken together, all such instances sum to a relatively infrequent phenomenon. A 2002 study indicates that the majority of healthcare expenditures by or on behalf of Canadians in the United States are the result of incidental occurrences while traveling on vacation or business and are not due to some form of medical tourism.[90]

The question of waiting times will continue to be a central part of Canada's healthcare conversation. In part, this derives from the simple fact of proximity to the United States and the perception (on both sides of the border) that care can be obtained more quickly in the United States. For an individual patient, that fact may be all the discussion that is required. Of course, at the societal level, there is no consensus as to the optimal waiting time, especially for diagnosis or therapeutic procedures that are relatively elective and not urgently time sensitive. Most thoughtful analysts recognize that establishing the quantity and distribution of capacity necessary to obtain a zero or near-zero waiting time for most people most of the time would require that same expensive capacity to sit idle for extensive periods. Such idle time would be unacceptably wasteful and would consume resources extracted from other components of the system.

Of course, the Canadian conversation about waiting times has been influenced by activities emanating from the United States, including academic assessments, news stories, advocacy positions, mass media portrayals, and other devices. It is not unreasonable to consider whether the issues of waiting time in Canada would be viewed in the same way if there was no ongoing and sometimes rancorous health policy conversation in the United States about universal coverage and closely related questions.

Until quite recently, most Canadians appeared to view waiting times as a necessary constraint deriving from communitarian needs for fiscal responsibility and system solvency. As long as there was a perception that the wait times were within reasonable bounds of medical prudence and were fairly and equitably distributed, they were of only modest concern. The cliché was that Canadians did not care if they had to wait in line, as long as they knew the line was moving at a reasonable pace and that everyone was in the same line together. At least some portion of the current discussion reflects new questions about the absolute duration of the wait and nagging concerns about cross-border health care in which some people are unfairly buying shorter wait times—in the vernacular, "jumping to the head of the line."

Concern about waiting times has given rise to renewed consideration of whether Canadians would, in general, prefer that the system continues under its current form, guided by the five principles of the Canada Health Act, or that it be modified to embrace a greater degree of privatization in the organization and financing of health services. Although there are, and have always been, some advocates who argue for a greater private role in Canadian health care, the momentum behind the current discussion can be traced back to a perception of increased difficulties in obtaining services that began during the 1990s.[91]

At the crux of this privatization agenda is the view that the current system is failing to meet the needs of the population in terms of timely health services and that the rigors of market opportunities and constraints might be valuable in providing more services. Given the historical commitment of the nation to free market principles, it certainly should be no surprise that this proposition would be considered. It is seen by many as an obvious way to bolster the infrastructure for the delivery of high-technology services, which are perceived as being in short supply.[88] Such proposals, however, are quickly extended to a discussion about if any newly developed "private" capacity would be universally accessible or available only to some subset of the population who would be willing and able to use the new services by virtue of their private economic circumstances. Opponents of increased privatization assert that private capacity would violate the "just, fair, and equitable principle" that is a hallmark of the Canada Health Act.[43] Proponents of market initiatives contend that new, private capacity, even if it is available only to some, would "free up" public capacity and hence make access better for all. This stance has not gained much traction to date.

▶ Conclusion

During the 1980s and 1990s, Canada made political and fiscal decisions that curtailed the development of the nation's physical healthcare infrastructure and perhaps its supply of healthcare personnel. The consequences of these decisions are particularly evident in the areas of diagnostic technology and complex procedures. Waiting times for these services continue to range beyond those of comparable nations. Privatization initiatives have taken place for these services, including an increase in the number of private imaging service delivery sites (freestanding CT and MRI clinics). For proponents of some privatization, there is considerable hope that the approach taken to imaging might be extended to include such services as complex procedural interventions and appointments with specialists. For those opposed to any privatization that is not universally accessible, the same outcome is viewed with concern.[43]

Canadians still overwhelmingly support their healthcare system, and this support is indicated by favorable satisfaction rates. Their satisfaction with the system includes giving it very high marks for fairness and its achievement of community obligations, but concerns over individual access to certain areas of care are pervasive. Canadians are an affluent, well-educated population. Their needs and expectations in terms of health care reflect that status and are compounded by geographic, economic, and cultural proximity to the United States. To preserve the essential features of their healthcare system will require that the nation confront and meaningfully address the needs and expectations experienced at both the individual and community levels.[77] In the near term, it appears that efforts to overcome the challenges and reach the health system's multifaceted objectives will be driven by and played out in the provinces and territories.

References

1. Central Intelligence Agency. *The World Fact Book*. 2016. https://www.cia.gov/library/publications/the-world-factbook/geos/ca.html. Accessed May 2, 2016.
2. Dickason O. *Canada's First Nations: A History of Founding Peoples from Earliest Times*. 3rd ed. Toronto, ON: Oxford University Press; 2002.
3. Bumsted J. *The Peoples of Canada: A Pre-Confederation History*. 2nd ed. Toronto, ON: Oxford University Press; 2003.
4. Brune N. A history of Canada online. http://canadachannel.ca/2/2Avikings.php. Accessed February 15, 2008.
5. Morton D. *A Short History of Canada*. 6th ed. Toronto, ON: McClelland & Stewart; 2006.
6. Bumsted J. *The Peoples of Canada: A Post-Confederation History*. 3rd ed. Toronto, ON: Oxford University Press; 2007.
7. Horn M. The Great Depression of the 1930s in Canada. The Canadian Historical Association. 1984;39. http://www.collectionscanada.gc.ca/cha-shc/008004-119.01-e.php?&b_id=H-39ψnbr=1&brws=y&&page_id=H-39-EN-4671406&&&&&PHPSESSID=bgbuuv4ucgkg1rs6rt0dpq1267. Accessed October 25, 2016.
8. Ostry A. The roots of North America's first comprehensive public health insurance system. *Hygiea Internationalis*. 2001;2(1):25–44. http://www.ep.liu.se/ej/hygiea/ra/007/paper.pdf. Accessed October 16, 2016.
9. Statistics Canada. *Portrait of the Canadian Population*. 2011 Census. Statistics Canada Catalogue no. 98-316-XWE. Ottawa. http://www12.statcan.gc.ca/census-recensement/2011/dp-pd/prof/index.cfm?Lang=E. Released October 24, 2012. Accessed October 16, 2016
10. Statistics Canada. Population, urban and rural, by province and territory. http://www.statcan.gc.ca/tables-tableaux/sum-som/l01/cst01/demo62a-eng.htm. Accessed May 11, 2016.
11. Government of Canada. Canadians and their government: a resource guide. Published 2008. http://publications.gc.ca/collections/collection_2009/pc-ch/CH4-70-2008E.pdf. Accessed October 25, 2016.
12. Elections Canada. The electoral system of Canada. 4th edition. http://www.elections.ca/content.aspx?section=res&dir=ces&document=index&lang=e. 2015. Accessed October 16, 2016.
13. Government of Canada. The Structure of the Canadian Govern-ment. http://canada.gc.ca/howgoc/glance_e.html. Published 2007. Accessed February 25, 2008.
14. Underhill FH. Canadian political parties. The Canadian Historical Association. 1974;8. http://www.collectionscanada.gc.ca/cha-shc/008004-119.01-e.php?&b_id=H-8ψnbr=1&brws=y&&PHPSESSID=bgbuuv4ucgkg1rs6rt0dpq1267. Accessed October 25, 2016.
15. Bernier J. Disease, medicine, and society in Canada: a historical overview. The Canadian Historical Association. 2003;63. http://www.collectionscanada.gc.ca/cha-shc/008004-119.01-e.php?&b_id=H-63ψnbr=1&brws=y&&PHPSESSID=bgbuuv4ucgkg1rs6rt0dpq1267. Accessed October 25, 2016.
16. Maioni A. Parting at the crossroads: the development of health insurance in Canada and the United States, 1940–1965. *Comparative Politics*. 1997;29(4):411–431.
17. The World Bank. Data by country, Canada. http://data.worldbank.org/country/canada. Accessed May 12, 2016.
18. Statistics Canada. Consumer Price Index, January 2016. http://www.statcan.gc.ca/daily-quotidien/160219/dq160219a-eng.htm. Accessed May 12, 2016.
19. Statistics Canada. Labour force characteristics, seasonally adjusted, by province (monthly) (Newfoundland and Labrador, Prince Edward Island, Nova Scotia, New Brunswick). http://www.statcan.gc.ca/tables-tableaux/sum-som/l01/cst01/lfss01a-eng.htm. Accessed May 12, 2016.
20. Statistics Canada. Gross domestic product at basic prices, by industry (monthly). http://www.statcan.gc.ca/tables-tableaux/sum-som/l01/cst01/gdps04a-eng.htm. Accessed May 12, 2016.
21. Council of Ministers of Education, Canada. *The development of education*. Report of Canada by the Council of Ministers of Education. http://www.cmec.ca/Publications/Lists/Publications/Attachments/122/ICE2008-reports-canada.en.pdf. Published 2008. Accessed October 26, 2016.
22. Statistics Canada. School boards revenue and expenditures by province and territory. http://www.statcan.gc.ca/tables-tableaux/sum-som/l01/cst01/govt43a-eng.htm. Published 2008. Accessed May 5, 2016.
23. Statistics Canada. Education Indicators in Canada: An International Perspective 2015. http://www.statcan.gc.ca/pub/81-604-x/81-604-x2015001-eng.htm. Published 2016. Accessed October 26, 2016.
24. Statistics Canada. Quarterly demographic estimates. October–December, 2015;91-002-X. http://www.statcan.gc.ca/pub/91-002-x/91-002-x2015004-eng.htm. Accessed May 5, 2016.
25. Statistics Canada. Annual demographic estimates: Canada, provinces and territories. 2015;91-215-XR. http://www.statcan.gc.ca/pub/91-215-x/91-215-x2015000-eng.htm. Accessed May 5, 2016.

26. Statistics Canada. Aboriginal peoples in Canada 2006: Inuit, Métis, and First Nations. 2006 Census. 2007;97-558-XIE. http://www12.statcan.ca/english/census06/analysis/aboriginal/pdf/97-558-XIE2006001.pdf. Accessed April 1, 2008.
27. Statistics Canada. Education in Canada: Attainment, field of study and location of study. 2011 Census. 2013; 99-012-X2011001. http://www12.statcan.gc.ca/nhs-enm/2011/as-sa/99-012-x/99-012-x2011001-eng.pdf. Accessed May 5, 2016.
28. Statistics Canada. Household, family and personal income. 2015;111-0008 and 111-0009. http://www.statcan.gc.ca/tables-tableaux/sum-som/l01/ind01/l3_3868_2812-eng.htm?hili_famil107. Accessed May 5, 2016.
29. The World Bank. *World development indicators*. http://databank.worldbank.org/data/reports.aspx?frmsrc=search&CNO=2&country=&series=SI.POV.GINI&period=. Published 2013. Accessed May 5, 2016.
30. Statistics Canada. *Canada (Code 01) (table). National Household Survey (NHS) Profile*. 2011 National Household Survey. 2013:99-004-XWE. Ottawa. http://www12.statcan.gc.ca/nhs-enm/2011/dp-pd/prof/index.cfm?Lang=E. Accessed May 6, 2016.
31. Pan American Health Organization. Health in the Americas. 2012 County Volume. http://www.paho.org/salud-en-las-americas-2012/index.php?option=com_content&view=article&id=9%3Aedicion-2012&catid=36%3Apublication&Itemid=124&lang=en. Accessed May 7, 2016.
32. Health Canada. Healthy Canadians: a federal report on comparable health indicators. http://www.hc-sc.gc.ca/hcs-sss/pubs/system-regime/2006-fed-comp-indicat/index-eng.php. Published 2006. Accessed February 15, 2008.
33. Public Health Agency, Canada. Diabetes in Canada: highlights from the National Diabetes Surveillance System 2004–2005. dicndss-04-05-eng.pdf. Accessed October 16, 2016.
34. Government of Canada. Canadian Cancer Statistics, 2015. http://www.cancer.ca/en/cancer-information/cancer-101/canadian-cancer-statistics-publication/?region=on. Accessed May 12, 2016.
35. Statistics Canada. Aboriginal Peoples Survey, 2012. Social determinants of health for the off-reserve First Nations population, 15 years of age and older, 2012. http://www.statcan.gc.ca/pub/89-653-x/89-653-x2016010-eng.htm. Accessed May 12, 2016.
36. Starr P. *The Social Transformation of American Medicine*. New York: Basic Books; 1982.
37. Roemer M. *National Health Systems of the World Volume I: The Countries*. New York: Oxford University Press; 1991.
38. Vayda E. The Canadian health care system: an overview. *J Public Health Policy*. 1986;7(2):205–210.
39. Iglehart J. Revisiting the Canadian health care system. *N Engl J Med*. 2000;342:2007–2012.
40. Rocher F, Smith M. Federalism and health care: the impact of political-institutional dynamics on the Canadian health care system. Commission on the Future of Health Care in Canada. Discussion Paper No. 18. https://qspace.library.queensu.ca/bitstream/1974/6884/23/discussion_paper_18_e.pdf. Published 2002. Accessed February 22, 2008.
41. Health Canada. Canada Health Act Annual Report 2006–2007. http://www.hc-sc.gc.ca/hcs-sss/alt_formats/hpb-dgps/pdf/pubs/chaar-ralcs-0607/chaar-ralcs-0607_e.pdf. Published 2007. Accessed October 16, 2016.
42. Canadian Institute for Health Information. National health expenditure trends 1975–2015. https://secure.cihi.ca/free_products/nhex_trends_narrative_report_2015_en.pdf. Published 2015. Accessed October 26, 2016.
43. Premont M. The Canada Health Act and the future of health care systems in Canada. Commission on the Future of Health Care in Canada. Discussion Paper No. 4. http://www.hcsc.gc.ca/english/pdf/romanow/pdfs/4_Premont_1E.pdf. Published 2002. Accessed February 25, 2008.
44. Marmor T, Maioni A. One issue, two voices health care in crisis: the drive for health reform in Canada and the United States. Woodrow Wilson International Center for Scholars. 2008;9. https://papers.ssrn.com/sol3/papers.cfm?abstract_id=1259253. Accessed April 20, 2008.
45. Health Canada. Canada's Health Care System. http://www.hc-sc.gc.ca/hcs-sss/pubs/system-regime/2011-hcs-sss/index-eng.php. Published 2012. Accessed October 27, 2016.
46. Health Canada. First Nations and Inuit Health. http://www.hc-sc.gc.ca/fniah-spnia/index-eng.php. Accessed October 27, 2016.
47. Kohn R, Radius S. Two Roads to Health Care: US and Canadian Policies 1945–1975. *Medical Care*. 1974;12(3):189–201.
48. Canadian Institutes of Health Research. The future of public health in Canada: developing a public health system for the 21st century. http://rnao.ca/sites/rnao-ca/files/Future_of_Public_Health_in_Canada_2003.pdf. Published 2003. Accessed March 7, 2008.
49. Hutchinson B, Abelson J, Lavis J. Primary care in Canada: so much innovation, so little change. *Health Aff*. 2001;20(3):116–131.
50. National Association of Community Health Centers. Landmark International Conference to Focus on Community Health Centers. http://www.nachc.com/magazine-article.cfm?MagazineArticleID=182. Accessed May 12, 2016.
51. Organisation for Economic Co-operation and Development Health Statistics 2015. http://stats.oecd.org/index.aspx?DataSetCode=HEALTH_STAT. Accessed May 12, 2016.
52. Barer M, Morgan S, Evans R. Strangulation or rationalization? Costs and access in Canadian hospitals. *Longwoods Review*. 2003;4:10–419.
53. Liu L, Hader J, Brossart B, White R, Lewis S. Impact of rural hospital closures in Saskatchewan, Canada. *Social Science & Medicine*. 2001;52:1793–1804.
54. Tully P, Saint-Pierre E. Downsizing Canada's hospitals, 1986/87 to 1994/95. *Health Reports*. 1997;8(4):33–39.
55. Canadian Institute for Health Information. Hospital trends in Canada—results of a project to create a historical series of statistical and financial data for Canadian hospitals over twenty-seven years. https://secure.cihi.ca/free_products/Hospital_Trends_in_Canada_e.pdf. Published 2005. Accessed April 9, 2008.
56. Organisation for Economic Co-operation and Development. *Health at a Glance 2015: OECD Indicators*. Paris: OECD Publishing. doi:10.1787/health_glance-2015-en.
57. Statistics Canada. Residential care facilities, 2009/2010. Residential care facilities by ownership, facility characteristics and geography—Canada. http://www.statcan.gc.ca/pub/83-237-x/2012001/t001-eng.htm. Accessed May 10, 2016.
58. Statistics Canada. Accumulated paid hours during year1 per resident-day in operating residential care facilities by facility characteristics and geography—Canada. http://www.statcan.gc.ca/pub/83-237-x/2012001/tablesectlist-listetableauxsect-eng.htm. Accessed May 12, 2016.
59. Canadian Institute for Health Information. *Canada's Health Care Providers, 1997 to 2011: A Reference Guide*. https://secure.cihi.ca/estore/productFamily.htm?pf=PFC2161&lang=en&media=0. Published 2013. Accessed May 8, 2016.

60. Canadian Institute for Health Information. Physicians in Canada, 2014: Summary Report. https://secure.cihi.ca/free_products/Summary-PhysiciansInCanadaReport2014_EN-web.pdf. Published 2015. Accessed May 8, 2016.
61. Canadian Institute for Health Information. Supply, Distribution, and Migration of Canadian Physicians, 2014. https://secure.cihi.ca/estore/productFamily.htm?locale=en&pf=PFC2964. Accessed May 10, 2016.
62. Bindman A, Forrest C, Britt H, Crampton P, Majeed A. Diagnostic score of and exposure to primary care physicians in Australia, New Zealand and the United States: cross sectional analysis of results from three national surveys. *British Medical Journal.* https://www.ncbi.nlm.nih.gov/pmc/articles/PMC1892467/. Published May 15, 2007. Accessed April 2, 2008.
63. Chan B. From Perceived surplus to perceived shortage: what happened to Canada's physician workforce in the 1990s. https://secure.cihi.ca/free_products/chanjun02.pdf. Published 2002. Accessed February 15, 2008.
64. Canada Institute for Health Information. Canada's health care providers: provincial profiles, 2013. https://secure.cihi.ca/estore/productFamily.htm?pf=PFC3045&lang=en&media=0. Accessed May 10, 2016.
65. Canada Institute for Health Information. MIT Selected medical imaging equipment in Canada, MIT 2012 data release – static figures and tables. https://www.cihi.ca/en/types-of-care/specialized-services/medical-imaging/mit-selected-medical-imaging-equipment-in-canada. Accessed May 10, 2016.
66. Canadian Institute for Health Information. Exploring the 70-30 split: how Canada's health care system is financed. https://secure.cihi.ca/estore/productSeries.htm?pc=PCC292. Published 2005. Accessed March 28, 2008.
67. Department of Finance, Canada. History of health and social transfers. https://www.fin.gc.ca/fedprov/his-eng.asp. Published 2008. Accessed March 3, 2008.
68. Department of Finance, Canada. Canada Health Transfers. https://www.fin.gc.ca/fedprov/cht-eng.asp. Accessed October 27, 2016.
69. Naylor C. Health care in Canada: incrementalism under fiscal duress. *Health Aff.* 1999;18(3):9–26.
70. Statistics Canada. Infant mortality rates, by province and territory, 2012. http://www.statcan.gc.ca/tables-tableaux/sum-som/l01/cst01/health21a-eng.htm. Accessed May 11, 2016.
71. Public Health Agency, Canada. Reducing health disparities—roles of the health sector: discussion paper. http://www.phac-aspc.gc.ca/ph-sp/disparities/pdf06/disparities_discussion_paper_e.pdf. Published 2005. Accessed April 3, 2008.
72. Statistics Canada. Life expectancy at birth, by sex, by province, 2012. http://www.statcan.gc.ca/tables-tableaux/sum-som/l01/cst01/health21a-eng.htm. Accessed May 11, 2016.
73. Government of Canada. Vaccine coverage in Canadian children: Highlights from the 2013 childhood National Immunization Coverage Survey (cNICS). http://healthycanadians.gc.ca/publications/healthy-living-vie-saine/immunization-coverage-children-2013-couverture-vaccinale-enfants/index-eng.php. Accessed May 11, 2016.
74. The Commonwealth Fund. 2010 International Health Policy Survey in Eleven Countries, November 2010. http://www.commonwealthfund.org/~/media/files/publications/chartbook/2010/pdf_2010_ihp_survey_chartpack_full_12022010.pdf. Accessed May 11, 2016.
75. Canada Institute for Health Information. Health Care in Canada, 2012: A Focus on Wait Times. https://secure.cihi.ca/free_products/HCIC2012-FullReport-ENweb.pdf. Accessed May 11, 2016.
76. Caulford P, Vali Y. Providing health care to medically uninsured immigrants and refugees. *CMAJ.* 2006;174(9):1253–1254.
77. Romanow R. Commission on the future of health care in Canada—final report. http://www.cbc.ca/healthcare/final_report.pdf. Published 2002. Accessed February 15, 2008.
78. Dhalla I. Canada's health care system and the sustainability paradox. *CMAJ.* 2007;177(1):51–53.
79. Evans R. Economic myths and political realities: the inequality agenda and the sustainability of Medicare. Published 2007.
80. Stolberg H. The Canadian health care system: past, present, and future. *J Am Coll Radiology.* 2004;1(9):659–670.
81. Andersen R. Revisiting the behavioral model and access to medical care: does it matter? *J Health Soc Behav.* 1995;36(1):1–10.
82. Baxter N. Equal for whom? Addressing disparities in the Canadian medical system must become a national priority. *CMAJ.* 2007;177(12):1522–1523.
83. Health Council of Canada. Fixing the foundation: an update on primary care and home care renewal in Canada. http://publications.gc.ca/collections/collection_2008/hc-sc/H174-14-2008E.pdf. Published 2008. Accessed April 14, 2008.
84. Soroka S. A report of the health council of Canada: Canadian perceptions of the health care system. Health Council of Canada. http://www.queensu.ca/cora/_files/PublicPerceptions.pdf. Published 2007. Accessed April 9, 2008.
85. Demers V, Melo M, Jackevicius C, et al. Comparison of provincial prescription drug plans and the impact on patient's annual drug expenditures. *CMAJ.* 2008;178(4):405–409.
86. Voelker R. Northern exposure US Canada clash on cross-border medication sales. *JAMA.* 2003;290(22):2921–2925.
87. Ouellet R. The Chaoulli decision: a debate in which physicians must be heard. *CMAJ.* 2005;173(8):896.
88. Steinbrook R. Private health care in Canada. *N Engl J Med.* 2006;354(16):1661–1664.
89. Tuohy C. The cost of constraint and prospects for health care reform in Canada. *Health Aff.* 2002;21(3):32–46.
90. Katz S, Cardiff K, Pascali M, Barer M, Evans R. Phantoms in the snow: Canadians' use of health care services in the United States. *Health Aff.* 2002;21(3):19–31.
91. Kenny N, Chafe R. Pushing right against the evidence: turbulent times for Canadian health care. *Hastings Center Report.* 2007; September–October:24–26.

CHAPTER 7

Mexico

Steven D. Berkshire, José DelaCerda-Gastelum, and **Octavio Gomez-Dantés**

▶ Country Description

TABLE 7-1 Mexico	
Nationality	Noun: Mexican(s) Adjective: Mexican
Ethnic groups	Mestizo (Amerindian-Spanish) 62%, predominantly Amerindian 21%, Amerindian 7%, other 10% (mostly European) (2012 est.)
Religions	Roman Catholic 82.7%, Protestant 8.0% (Pentecostal 1.4%, Jehovah's Witness 1.1%, other 3.8%), other 1.9%, none 4.7% (2010 census)
Language	Spanish only 92.7%, Spanish and indigenous languages 5.7%, indigenous only (includes various Mayan, Nahuatl, and other regional languages) 0.8%, unspecified 0.8% (2005)
Literacy	Definition: Age 15 and over can read and write. Total population: 95.1% Male: 96.2% Female: 94.2% (2012)
Government type	Federal republic
Date of independence	September 16, 1810
Gross Domestic Product (GDP) per capita	$17,500 (2015 est.)

(continues)

TABLE 7-1 Mexico (continued)

Unemployment rate	4.4% plus underemployment of perhaps 25% (2015 est.)
Natural hazards	Tsunamis along the Pacific coast; volcanoes and destructive earthquakes in the center and south; and hurricanes along the coasts of the Pacific, Gulf of Mexico, and Caribbean
Environment: current issues	Scarcity of hazardous waste-disposal facilities; rural to urban migration; scarcity of natural freshwater resources, water pollution in the north, and water inaccessibility and poor quality in the center and extreme southeast; raw sewage and industrial effluents pollution in rivers in urban areas; deforestation; widespread erosion; desertification; deterioration of agricultural lands; serious air and water pollution in the national capital and urban centers along the U.S.-Mexico border; and land subsidence in the Valley of Mexico caused by groundwater depletion. The government considers the lack of clean water and deforestation national security issues.
Population	123,166,749 (July 2016 est.)
Age structure	0–14 years: 27.26% (male 17,167/female 16,402,301) 15–24 years: 17.72% (male 11,049,818/female 10,770,843) 25–54 years: 40.69% (male 24,174,900/female 25,938,909) 55–64 years: 7.41% (male 4,187,644/female 4,944,802 65 years and over: (3,827,870/female 4,702,026) (2016 est.)
Median age	Total: 28 years Male: 26.9 years Female: 29.1 years (2016 est.)
Population growth rate	1.15% (2016 est.)
Birth rate	18.5 births/1,000 population (2016 est.)
Death rate	589 deaths/per 100,000 population (2016 est.)
Disease burden	Communicable disease deaths: 57/100,000 population Noncommunicable disease deaths: 468/100,000 population Injury deaths: 63/100,000 population (2016 est.)
Net migration rate	−1.7 migrant(s)/1,000 population (2016 est.)
Gender ratio	At birth: 1.05 male(s)/female Under 15 years: 1.05 male(s)/female 15–24 years: 1.03 male(s)/female 25–54 years: 0.93 males(s)/female 55–64 years: 0.85 male(s)/female 65 years and over: 0.82 male(s)/female Total population: 0.96 male(s)/female (2016 est.)
Infant mortality rate	Total: 11.9 deaths/1,000 live births Male: 13.3 deaths/1,000 live births Female: 10.4 deaths/1,000 live births (2016 est.)

TABLE 7-1 Mexico (continued)	
Life expectancy at birth	Total population: 75.9 years Male: 73.1 years Female: 78.8 years (2016 est.)
Total fertility rate	2.25 children born/woman (2016 est.)
HIV/AIDS adult prevalence rate	0.24% (2015 est.)
Number of people living with HIV/AIDS	198,200 (2015 est.)
HIV/AIDS deaths	4,000 (2015 est.)

Data from Central Intelligence Agency. The World Fact Book, 2016: Mexico. https://www.cia.gov/library/publications/the-world-factbook/geos/mx.html. Accessed January 12, 2017.

History

Mexico is the largest Spanish-speaking country in the world and is the nation with the largest indigenous population in the Americas (10.2 million). Around 5,000 years ago, ancient Mesa-American Indians domesticated corn.[1] This agricultural revolution, among other things, allowed for the construction of advanced civilizations, which were then conquered by the Spaniards in 1519. Independence from Spain was achieved in 1821. A war with the United States from 1846 to 1848 ended with Mexico losing half of its territory.[2] In 1864, the French invaded Mexico and ruled until 1867. A major revolt against a long-standing dictatorship produced the Mexican Revolution in 1910, which resulted in the death of 10% of the nation's population.[3]

Size and Geography

Mexico covers 1.9 million square miles of land, 13% of which is arable.[4] To the north, it borders the United States and to the south Guatemala and Belize (see **FIGURE 7-1**).

Government and Political System

Mexico is a federation with a presidential representative, democratic republic whose government is based on a congressional, multiparty electoral system. The president of the country is both head of state and head of government. The federal government is divided into three branches: executive, legislative, and judicial, as established by the Constitution published in 1917. The 32 constituent states of the federation also have a republican form of government based on a local congressional system.[5]

Business and Economic Environment

Mexico, like many other emerging economies, has been experiencing major changes in social and economic variables that have unfolded the potential for development since the beginning of the 21st century. Democracy has ensued, and the political system is stable. The central bank (Banco de México) has complete autonomy to enhance monetary and fiscal policies, and macroeconomic policies have prioritized fiscal discipline, increasing confidence in the Mexican economy all over the world. Improvements in the industrial base have made Mexico a very competitive manufacturing country with strong exports, and Mexico has embraced free trade with conviction. It is now one of the most open countries in the world.

Mexico is now a predominantly urban country. Most of its 125 million population are still relatively young, with a median age of 27 years old. The educational level in Mexico is more than 8 years of formal education, with significant growth in enrollment in more advanced levels (middle and higher education).

But there are still huge challenges in supporting potential and future development of this country, such as raising education quality, reducing government corruption, controlling drug-related

FIGURE 7-1 Map of Mexico
© Bardocz Peter/Shutterstock

crime, assuring public safety, catching up on infrastructure backlogs, and above all, relieving poverty and achieving well-being for a large majority of Mexicans.

An economic output of more than US $2.1 trillion (power purchasing parity) in 2015 ranked Mexico among the 15 largest economies in the world. Located in a multilateral free trade area, the Mexican economy has been advancing firmly by developing manufacturing capabilities oriented toward intensive exports, mainly to the U.S. markets. In fact, according to the Office of U.S. Trade Representative, U.S.-Mexico bilateral trade reached a total of $583.6 billion in 2015; exports were $267.2 billion; and imports were $316.4 billion, meaning a U.S. trade deficit with Mexico of $49.2 billion. In 2015, Mexico was the United States' second largest export market and third largest supplier of goods imports.[6]

In terms of annual growth rate, the Mexican economy averaged 2.6% during a period of twenty years, 1995–2015, of which the last five had an average of 2.9%.[6] These growth rates are not impressive compared to what China, India, Brazil, South Africa, and other emerging economies achieved in a similar period of time. However, in favor of Mexico, its economy was singularly resilient to the "reverse gear" trend observed in many emerging countries since. In addition, Mexico managed to keep annual inflation rates under control, well below 5% since the beginning of the century, with an average of 2.5% in 2014–2015. A burden in other times, national debt averaged a reasonable 25% of GDP during the 1990s through 2010, climbing to about one-third of GDP for 2014–2016, as reported by the Minister of Finance.[7]

With a labor force of 52.91 million, an unemployment rate of 4.4%, national reserves of $178 billion, and an industrial production growth rate of 0.9% in 2015, among other relatively positive economic indicators, the Mexican economy looks healthy and promising for future opportunities.[8] As put by *The Economist*:

> Once dependent on oil, [Mexico] has Latin America's largest and most sophisticated industrial base, exporting more cars than any country except Germany, Japan, and South Korea. For two decades its macroeconomic

management has been impeccably orthodox. Recently, it has thrown open its oil industry to private investment, and has tackled private monopolies. A vibrant Mexican middle class prospers along an industrial corridor running from the American border down to Mexico City. Its political system is essentially stable.[9]

But there is a dark side of this story: economic inequality. According to the food-based definition of poverty, more than 50% of the total Mexican population of 120 million was living below the poverty line in 2012.[8] The benefits of economic progress have been distributed abundantly for the few rich Mexicans at the top of the income structure and miserably for the poor: for the disadvantaged, per capita income has registered an annual growth rate of barely 1% since the mid-1990s when Mexico started its economic strategy of market liberalization and free trade agreements. *The Economist* furthers the "Two Mexicos" argument with "Mexico's duality shows that getting macroeconomic policy right is necessary to success, but not sufficient."[9]

According to *The Economist*, the three lessons behind Mexico's dual economy are: (1) the ineffective centrality of urbanization attracting millions of migrants to large cities from the countryside, but without providing the necessary public services and protection against drug-related crime and exploitation of poor urban communities; (2) the need to double the revitalization of the country's infrastructure—mostly railroads and highways—to efficiently connect industrial cities with the rest of the country, ports, and the northern border; and (3) the failure to bring the informal sector of the economy out of the low-value-added, vicious circle that submerges this huge component of the domestic economy into chronic distrust and low productivity.[9]

Poverty and Economic Equality in Mexico

The limits of minimum economic well-being in Mexico are established by the Consejo Nacional de Evaluación de la Política de Desarrollo Social (CONEVAL, the National Council for the Evaluation of Social Development Policy), which keeps track of the changes in prices of food and nonfood products using the National Consumer Price Index. For instance, the limits in March 2016 were US $1,338 pesos monthly for minimum well-being per person and $2,714 pesos for well-being (about $78 and $159).[10]

The General Law for Social Development in Mexico determined that to measure poverty and well-being, all of the following indicators need to be included: income per capita, access to health services, educational backlog, access to social security, quality of housing and utilities, access and quality of food, and degree of social cohesion. In the analysis of poverty, significant deprivation from any of these indicators are considered social deficiencies. Most recent measurement and evaluation of poverty and well-being by CONEVAL refers to the years 2010–2014 (see **TABLE 7-2**).[11]

Mexico has an estimated population of 123 million as of July 2016 with approximately 46% of the population living below the poverty line.[8] This is the most important challenge facing Mexico's social and economic development. Although this percentage kept stable for nearly a decade, the absolute number of people living in poverty increased from 53.0 million in 2010 to more than 55.0 million in 2014. Behind the disappointing figures, there was some relative progress in the fight against poverty: the reduction of the population living in "extreme" poverty was 13.0 million in 2010 and 11.4 million in 2014. Therefore, it was the population in "moderate" poverty that made the overall number of poor grow from 2010 to 2014.

According to the 2014 evaluation by CONEVAL, there were 40.0 million additional people, apart from those already in moderate and extreme poverty, who have some level of vulnerability to poverty. Table 7-2 shows the reasons for vulnerability under indicators of backlogs and lack of well-being. There were 22.4 million with educational backlogs, 21.8 million with compromised well-being due to poor access to health services, 70.1 million without access to social security services, 14.8 million without adequate housing, 25.4 million without some sort of access to urban services and utilities, and 28.0 million who suffer without quality food and adequate nutrients. Summing up, there were 26.5 million people in Mexico, about 22.0% of its total population, suffering from three or more backlogs in well-being, and 86.9 million, 72.4% of the total population, with at least one backlog in well-being.[11]

Education

Education is compulsory in Mexico through the 9th grade. In 2012, 25.7 million students were enrolled in elementary school and another 4.2 million were enrolled in secondary schools. The postsecondary level (colleges and universities) enrolled 3.5 million students. The youth literacy rate in 2009 was at 98.5% and adult literacy was 93.4%. However, according to OEDC only 53.0% of youth between

TABLE 7-2 Mexican Poverty, 2010–2014

Indicators	Percentage			Population (millions)		
	2010	2012	2014	2010	2012	2014
Poverty						
Population in poverty	46.1	45.5	46.2	52.8	53.3	53.3
Due to poor well-being	28.1	28.6	26.3	32.1	33.5	31.5
Due to income	5.9	6.2	7.1	6.7	7.2	8.5
Social well-being						
Lack of access to educational services	20.7	19.2	18.7	23.7	22.6	22.4
Lack of access to health services	29.2	21.5	18.2	3.5	25.3	21.8
Lack of access to social security	60.7	61.2	58.5	69.6	71.8	70.1
Lack of access to quality housing	15.2	13.6	12.3	17.4	15.9	14.3
Lack of access to urban services and utilities	22.9	21.2	21.2	26.3	24.9	25.4
Lack of access to food and nutrients	24.8	23.3	23.4	28.4	27.4	28.0

Data from CONEVAL. Poverty measurement. http://www.coneval.org.mx/Medicion/MP/Paginas/Pobreza_2014.aspx.

the ages of 15 and 19 are actually enrolled in school on an ongoing basis.[12]

Brief History of the Healthcare System

Formal health care in Mexico probably dates to 1791 when the Archbishop of Guadalajara founded the Hospicio Cabañas in the city of Guadalajara. The original hospital is still functioning and may be the oldest continuously operating hospital in the Americas.[12]

The origins of the modern Mexican health system dates back to 1943, when three important institutions were created: the Ministry of Health (MoH), the Mexican Institute for Social Security (IMSS), and Mexico's Children Hospital. The MoH now consists of 12 National Institutes of Health, charged with tertiary care, training of specialists, and performing scientific research. The IMSS was created to tend to the needs of the industrial workforce, and in 1960 a similar institution for federal civil servants was created, the Institute for Security and Social Services for Government Employees (ISSSTE). The MoH was assigned the responsibility of caring for the urban and rural poor.[13]

The prevailing model of healthcare delivery, which was mostly hospital based and specialty oriented, produced a dramatic increase in the costs of health care. In addition, health services were not reaching an important proportion of the rural poor. Furthermore, many households had to mobilize their own resources to access care in an unregulated private market.

Mortality and Morbidity

The increase in life expectancy and the growing exposure to risks related to unhealthy lifestyles are modifying the main causes of disease, disability, and death. Mexico is going through an epidemiological transition characterized by an increasing predominance of noncommunicable diseases and injuries. In 1950, around 50% of all deaths in the country were due to common infections, reproductive events, and ailments related to malnutrition. Today, these diseases represent less than 15% of total deaths.[18] Noncommunicable diseases and injuries are now responsible for more than 85% of total deaths (see TABLE 7-3).

TABLE 7-3 Selected Major Causes of Death, 2005–2015

Disease or condition	2005 rank order	2015 rank order
Infectious and parasitic	1	6
Diarrheal	2	13
Respiratory	3	7
Perinatal	4	9
Cardiovascular	5	1
Ill-defined	6	14
Injuries	7	4
Malignant	8	3
Malnutrition	9	8
Chronic	10	5
Genitourinary	11	10
Neuropsychiatric	12	11
Congenital	13	12
Diabetes	14	2
Maternal	15	15
Ill-defined	16	16

Data from Mexico Institute of Health Metrics. http://www.healthdata.org/mexico

In contrast to other developing countries, Mexico's posttransitional ailments coexist with pretransitional diseases. Noncommunicable diseases are increasingly dominating the epidemiological profile, but common infections, reproductive ailments, and diseases related to malnutrition are still affecting a large number of Mexicans, especially those living in poverty. In the central state of Mexico, for example, mortality rates for acute respiratory infections are 11 times higher than those in the northern state of Durango. Maternal mortality figures in the southern state of Guerrero are two times higher than those for the country as a whole and four times higher than those in the northern state of Coahuila. Finally, malnutrition, although decreasing in the general population, is still common among poor children. Mortality rates in 2006 caused by malnutrition in children under 5 years old were 12 times higher in the southern state of Puebla than in the northern state of Nuevo Leon, and stunting, which affected 1.2 million Mexican children under 5 years of age, was five times more frequent in the rural areas of the southern part of Mexico than in the urban communities in the north of the country. Poor populations are also being affected by emerging risks and noncommunicable diseases. The southern state of Yucatan, for example, shows higher mortality rates because of cardiovascular diseases than Mexico City, both in women and men (see **TABLE 7-4**).[15]

New Approaches and Change

As noncommunicable diseases and injuries experienced a sharp increase, there was a perceived need for

TABLE 7-4 Some 2012 Population Health Indicators	
Life expectancy	76 years
Life expectancy at age 60	22 years
Crude birth rate	18.80 per 1,000
Crude death rate	5.00 per 1,000
Fertility rate	2.22 per female
Under 5 mortality rate	16.00 per 1,000 live births
Infant mortality rate	14.00 per 1,000 live births

Data from Ministry of Health Mexico and World Health Organization

changes that could adapt the health system to the new health conditions and meet the demands for equitable and cost-effective services. The response to this situation was an effort to extend basic health care to underserved populations through two programs, one for the rural poor and the other for poor urban communities. The economic crisis of the early 1980s, however, limited their prospects.[16]

In the search for new approaches to extend access and improve the efficiency and quality of care, healthcare reform was launched in 1983.[17] A constitutional amendment establishing the right to the protection from health problems was introduced. A new health law was published, replacing an old-fashioned sanitary code. Health services for the uninsured population were decentralized to state governments. Finally, limited coverage of health services resulted in a program that included the construction of health centers and district hospitals. The force guiding this program was the primary healthcare model, which implied a greater emphasis on first-level care, a proper mix of technologies, and the promotion of community participation. However, the possibility of extending comprehensive health services to all was not reached until the initial years of the new millennium. Funding of the system comes from a combination of tax dollars at both federal and state levels and employer and employee contributions.[18]

In the 1990s, several national health studies revealed that more than half of total health expenditures in Mexico were out of pocket. This was due to the fact that half of the population lacked health insurance. The high levels of out-of-pocket expenditure exposed Mexican families to catastrophic financial episodes. In fact, in 2000, nearly 3 million Mexican households suffered catastrophic health expenditures.[19(p57)] Not surprisingly, Mexico performed poorly on the international comparative analysis of fair financing developed by the World Health Organization as part of the *World Health Report 2000*.[20] The poor results motivated the development of additional analysis which showed that impoverishing health expenditures were concentrated within the poor and uninsured households.

While access to health care is guaranteed in the Mexican Constitution, prior to the passage of the Segura Popular law in 2003, approximately 47% of the population was enrolled in one of the existing programs and another 3% had private insurance. There was also inequality in access because only 50% of the population had coverage. In 2003, the Mexican Congress passed the Social Protection in Health.[17] This system mobilized public resources by a full percentage point of GDP for a period of 7 years and continues to provide health insurance through Segura Popular to all of those ineligible for social security. These include the self-employed, those out of the labor market, and those working in the informal sector of the economy.[17]

Organizations

The Mexican health system includes two sectors, public and private.[21] The public sector is composed of the social security institutions (IMSS, ISSSTE, the social security institutions for oil workers [PEMEX], the armed forces [SEDENA and SEMAR]), Segura Popular, and institutions offering services to the uninsured population, including the MoH, the State Health Services (SESA), and the IMSS-Oportunidades Program. These institutions own and run their health facilities and employ their own staff, except for Segura Popular, which buys services for its affiliates from the MoH and the SESA. The private sector includes facilities and providers offering services mostly on a for-profit basis. The states often provide separately funded health care for residents of the state funded by state budgets and through agreements with the Social Security system. TABLE 7-5 illustrates the organizational structure of the healthcare system.

Social security institutions are financed with contributions from the government, the employer (which includes the government in its role as employer, as is the case for ISSSTE and the social security institutions for oil workers and the armed forces), and the employee. The MoH and the SESA are financed with federal and state government resources, coming from general taxation and small contributions that users pay when receiving care. The IMSSOportunidades program, which is directed to the rural poor of 17 states, is financed with federal resources, although the

TABLE 7-5 Components of the Healthcare System			
	Public sector components		**Private sector**
	Seguridad social	**SESA**	
How funded	Government Employer Contributions Worker Contributions	Federal contributions State government contributions Individuals*	Individuals Employers Private health insurance
Provider organizations	IMSS ISSSTE PEMEX SEDENA MARINA	Secretaría de Salud y SESA IMMS-Opportunidades	Private hospital Private physicians and other qualified providers
Services	Hospital care, clinics and physician services, outpatient and ambulatory services**		Dependent on coverage
Eligible to participate	Employees and their families, retirees***		Population in general who have insurance or resources

* Seguro Popular de Salud is funded by individuals in the private sector electing to participate and by state governments.
** Services are usually all within the system.
*** Not all employers are part of IMSS. Employees not eligible for IMSS, unemployed, and individuals are in Seguro Popular de Salud.
Data from Gomez-Dantes O, Sesma S, Becerril VM, Knaul FM, Arreola H, Frenk J. The health system of Mexico. *Salud pública de México.* 2011;53(suppl 2): S220–S232.

program is operated by IMSS. Finally, Segura Popular is financed with federal and state government contributions and family contributions, with total exemption for those families in the bottom 20% of income distribution.

The services of the private sector are financed mostly with out-of-pocket payments. A small portion of private health expenditure in Mexico comes from private insurance premiums. The Social Security system provides more than health coverage; it also provides pharmaceuticals and medications. Also included are unemployment insurance, disability insurance, life insurance, and retirement benefits.

Facilities

The Mexican health system as of 2015 had 23,269 health service units, not counting the medical offices of the private sector; 4,103 were hospitals and the remainder were ambulatory care clinics.[20] Of the total number of hospitals, 1,121 were public and 3,082 were private, for a rate of 1.1 hospitals per 100,000 population; however, there were regional differences. The Mexican state of South Baja California had 3.2 hospitals per 100,000, whereas the state of Mexico had only 0.5 per 100,000. Of the total number of public hospitals, 628 belonged to social security institutions, and the remainder belonged to those institutions that care for the population without social security; 86% were general hospitals, and the rest were specialty hospitals.

In terms of size, public hospitals are classified as either hospitals with 30 beds or less or as hospitals with more than 30 beds. In 2005, around 64.0% of social security hospitals, and 54.0% of hospitals for the population without social insurance, had more than 30 beds. In the private sector, most hospitals are small maternity clinics. Around 69.0% of private hospitals had less than 10 beds and only 6.2% had more than 25 beds. There were 78,643 beds in the public sector; 53.7% belonged to social security hospitals, and the remainder belonged to the MoH, the SESA, and the IMSS-Oportunidades Program. This means that there were 0.74 beds per 1,000 population in the public sector. Public institutions also counted around 19,000 public ambulatory units and 2,990 operating rooms. The number of operating rooms per 1,000 population in the public sector was 2.7, with important differences among states and institutions. No reliable figures for the private sector are available.[23(p57)]

Cost of Health Care

According to the World Bank and OEDC, the total healthcare expenditures in Mexico was 6.3% in 2014 and per capita expenditure on health was US $1,048. This was below the 9.0% of GDP for OEDC countries and the per capita expenditure of $3,450. Public spending on health care is approximately 51.1% of all healthcare expenditures.[22,24]

OEDC reports that there were 2.2 physicians per 1,000 population in 2014, which was still below the average for OECD countries. The distribution of physicians is not equal among the regions of the country. There were 2.4 nurses per 1,000 in 2014, a slight increase from 2005 but still well below the OEDC average of 9.1 nurses per 1,000. There was a decline in the number of medical school graduates in 2014 from a previous average of 11.1 graduates per 1,000 population to 9.9 graduates. The OEDC average is 11.1. For nursing, the graduation rate is 10.8 graduates per 1,000 compared to the OEDC rate of 46 per 1,000.[24]

In 2014, Mexico had 1.6 hospital beds per 1,000 population compared to the OEDC average of 4.8 (the U.S. average was 2.6). The MRI rate was 2.1 per 1,000 while the OEDC rate was 14.3, and the ratio of CT scans was 5.3 per 1,000 while to the OEDC rate was 24.6 per 1,000. Hospital discharges were 4,779 with an average length of stay of 4.0 days.[24]

Quality

Quality of health care has been a permanent challenge of the Mexican health system. A quality assessment conducted between 1997 and 1999 in more than 1,900 public health centers and 214 general public hospitals documented serious problems with waiting lists and waiting times, with drug supply in both ambulatory settings and hospitals, and with medical equipment and medical records. Historically, public health agencies have operated as monopolies with little consumer choice, poor responsiveness to consumer needs, and lack of concern for quality. Furthermore, few health facilities, public or private, were subjected to a formal accreditation process, although the MoH has made great strides in reviewing hospitals and clinics in recent years, especially the public hospitals and major private hospitals. A number of hospitals have sought Joint Commission on Accreditation of Healthcare Organizations International (JCAHO) accreditation.

Several initiatives have been recently implemented to improve technical and interpersonal quality of care. These initiatives have been designed to improve standards of quality in service delivery while enhancing the capacity of citizens to demand accountability. A central component of these initiatives was the strengthening of the certification process for public and private health units, which is now coordinated by the National Health Council, an institution created in 1917 as the highest policymaking body in the sector. In 2006, 223 public hospitals (19.9%) were certified. The institution with the highest percentage of certified hospitals was IMSS, with 42.0%. The National Health Council also certified 304 private hospitals in 2006. This process was reinforced by a disposition incorporated into the General Health Law in 2003 requiring the accreditation of all units providing services to Segura Popular. In 2006, 38 hospitals and 1,408 ambulatory clinics, all from the SESA, had completed the accreditation process.

Initiatives to improve the availability of basic inputs have also been designed. A regular external measurement of the availability of drugs in public institutions was implemented by the government as a monitoring tool designed to improve access to essential drugs in the public sector. In 2002, these measurements showed that only 55.0% of prescriptions in ambulatory clinics of the MoH were fully filled. By 2006, this figure had increased to 79.0% in ambulatory clinics of the MoH and to 89.0% in ambulatory clinics of the MoH that serve Segura Popular beneficiaries.[25] Percentages in ambulatory clinics of social security institutions in 2006 were consistently above 90.0%. A national system of indicators was also implemented to monitor quality of care by state and institution. This monitoring system includes indicators for waiting times for ambulatory and emergency care, waiting times for elective interventions, and distribution and dispensing of pharmaceuticals.

Regarding overall satisfaction, the National Health and Nutrition Survey conducted in 2006 indicates that 81.2% of health service users consider healthcare services "good" or "very good." Social security institutions providing services to oil workers and the armed forces show the highest satisfaction levels (96.6%), followed by private services (91.1%).

According to this same survey, waiting times tended to be too long. IMSS is the institution with the highest average waiting time in ambulatory settings (91.7 minutes), followed by ISSSTE (78.7 minutes). In contrast, average waiting time in the private sector is only 29.2 minutes.

One of the most frequent complaints in the public services sector is related to waiting times for elective surgeries and their cancellation. A national responsiveness survey implemented in 2004 indicates that the percentage of canceled surgeries in public hospitals was 18.2%, with similar figures for all public institutions.[25] Almost half of these canceled surgeries were canceled after the patient had been hospitalized. The main causes of cancellation were related to problems in health services, including lack of surgery rooms and medical personnel.

Access

The mobilization of additional public resources for Segura Popular created the financial conditions to expand the coverage of health insurance in Mexico. As a result, the proportion of the population with social protection for health increased by 20% between 2003 and 2007. According to Article 4 of the Mexican Constitution, the protection of health is a social right; however, not all Mexicans have been equally able to exercise it. In 2003, half of the population, by virtue of its occupational status, enjoyed the legislated protection of social security, whereas the other half was left without access to any form of health insurance. A very large fraction of this population received health care at units of the MoH, which implies the transfer of health benefits to vulnerable populations under a public charity scheme.

The Mexican health system is a segmented system with three broad categories of beneficiaries: (1) workers of the formal sector of the economy and retired people and their families; (2) self-employed, workers of the informal sector of the economy, and unemployed and their families; and (3) the population with the ability to pay.[25]

The workers of the formal sector of the economy and their families are the beneficiaries of social security institutions, which in 2000 covered 45.6 million people. IMSS covered 80% of this population, ISSSTE another 18%, and social security institutions for oil workers and the armed forces covered the remainder. The second category (self-employed, workers of the informal sector of the economy, and unemployed and their families) was covered until 2003 by services of the MoH, the SESA, and the IMSSOportunidades Program. In 2000, this population amounted to 48.9 million people. The third category is the users of private health services, mostly upper- and middle-class individuals. However, the poor and those affiliated with social security institutions also use them on a regular basis. According to the National Health and Nutrition Survey in 2006, around 25% of beneficiaries of social security institutions regularly used private health services, mostly ambulatory care.[23(p57)]

The System of Social Protection in Health has extended public health insurance. As mentioned previously, in 2000 only 45.6 million Mexicans (45.4% of the total population) had access to social insurance. In 2006, this figure reached 48.9 million. By 2013, around 55.6 million people were enrolled in Segura Popular.

In general terms, those affiliated with social security institutions have access to a broad, but not an explicitly defined, package of health services. This includes ambulatory and hospital care, as well as drugs. Those affiliated with the Segura Popular have access to 255 essential interventions and the respective drugs. In addition, they have access to a package of 18 high-cost interventions for the treatment of acute neonatal conditions, cancer in children, cervical and breast cancer, and HIV/AIDS, among others. The uninsured population has access to a limited package of benefits that vary considerably depending on the population. Uninsured individuals living in large urban areas have access to a relatively large package of services, in contrast with the uninsured rural poor, who tend to have access only to limited ambulatory care on an irregular basis.

Public Health Services

Public health services are provided by the MoH to the entire population, regardless of affiliation with any particular health institution. These services include health promotion, risk control, and disease prevention activities, including vaccination and epidemiological surveillance.

The MoH is also responsible for the generation of information on health conditions and health services and for the evaluation of the national and state health systems, health institutions, health policies, programs, and services. Salient among the monitoring and evaluation activities are the annual publication of *Salud: Mexico,* a report on the performance of state health systems and health institutions, and the *Observatory on Hospital Performance,* which monitors the performance of public hospitals. The Federal Commission for Protection against Health Risks was created in 2001 with the mission of regulating products and services related to health, including drugs and medical equipment, occupational and environmental exposures, basic sanitation, food safety, and health-related advertisements.

Challenges Facing Mexico

Improvements continue to be made in increasing the access and availability of health care in Mexico and in improving the quality of the available services. Evidence shows that the recent reforms are expanding access to comprehensive health care, with the promise of extending it to all. Mexico, however, continues to face difficulties, mostly related to the challenges posed by emerging diseases. Efforts in controlling common infections and dealing with reproductive problems and malnutrition have yielded significant progress. However, after certain benchmarks were reached, such as increased vaccination coverage and reductions in deaths caused by diarrhea and acute respiratory infections, the prevalence of noncommunicable diseases began to increase, creating enormous pressures on the health system. Salient among the challenges related to the new epidemiological profile is a critical need for additional public funding to extend access to costly interventions for noncommunicable ailments, such as cardiovascular and cerebrovascular diseases, cancer, mental illness, and the complications of diabetes. Another challenge facing the reformed health system is to achieve the right balance between additional investments in public health activities and personal curative health services. Finally, additional improvements in the quality of care are still expected. To accomplish this goal, several areas must be strengthened: technical quality of care; availability of drugs in hospital settings; availability of care during evenings and weekends; and reduction in waiting times for ambulatory, emergency care, and elective interventions.

Narrowing health gaps also remains a challenge. These gaps are concentrated in rural, dispersed, and indigenous communities, especially in the southern states of the country. The main cause of gaps in health care and access is poverty. Its final solution depends on the possibility of improving the general level of well-being in these populations. Nevertheless, the experience of 20 plus years of consistent investments in public health in Mexico shows that, despite the existence of extended poverty, it is possible to reduce the burden of communicable diseases through highly effective and accessible interventions.

References

1. Covarrubias M. *The Eagle, the Jaguar, and the Serpent: Indian Art of the Americas*. New York: Alfred A. Knopf; 1954.
2. Gonzalez L. El periodo forrnativo. In: *Historia Mínima de México*. Cosio-Villegas D, coordinator. Mexico City: El Colegio de México; 1994:75–118.
3. Blanquel E. La revolucion mexicana. In: *Historia Mínima de México*. Cosio-Villegas D, coordinator. Mexico City: El Colegio de México; 1994:119–156.
4. Aguayo Quezada S. *El Almanaque Mexicano 2008*. Mexico City: Aguilar; 2008.
5. Gómez Dantés O, Sesma S, Becerril VM, et al. Sistema de salud de México. *Salud pública de México*. 2011;53(Suppl 2):S220–S232.
6. World Bank. GDP growth (annual%). http://data.worldbank.org/indicator/NY.GDP.MKTP.KD.ZG. Accessed April 26, 2016.
7. Secretaría de Hacienda (minister of finance). México. http://www.shcp.gob.mx/POLITICAFINANCIERA/FINANZASPUBLICAS/Estadisticas_Oportunas_Finanzas_Publicas/Paginas/unica2.aspx. Accessed April 28, 2016.
8. *The World Factbook*, Central Intelligence Agency. Accessed December 5, 2016.
9. *The Economist*. The two Mexicos: with its combination of modernity and poverty, Mexico provides lessons for all emerging markets. http://www.economist.com/news/leaders/21665027-its-combination-modernity-and-poverty-mexico-provides-lessons-all-emerging. Published September 19, 2015. Accessed April 27, 2016.
10. CONEVAL. Medición de la pobreza: Evolución de las líneas de bienestar y de la canasta alimentaria. http://www.coneval.org.mx/Medicion/MP/Paginas/Lineas-de-bienestar-y-canasta-basica.aspx. Accessed July 4, 2016.
11. CONEVAL—Evolución de las líneas de bienestar y de la canasta alimentaria. http://www.coneval.org.mx/Medicion/MP/Paginas/Lineas-de-bienestar-y-canasta-basica.aspx. Accessed July 4, 2016.
12. World Education News and Reviews. An overview of education in Mexico. http://wenr.wes.org/2013/05/wenr-may-2013-an-overview-of-education-in-mexico. Published May 1, 2013. Accessed May 26, 2016.
13. UNESCO. http://whc.unesco.org/archive/advisory_body_evaluation/815.pdf. Accessed May 26, 2016.
14. Organisation for Economic Co-operation and Development. *OECD Reviews of Health Systems: Mexico*. http://www.borderhealth.org/files/res_839.pdf. OECD Publishing; 2005. Accessed May 26, 2016.
15. Secretaría de Salud. *Programa Nacional de Salud 2007–2012*. Mexico City: Secretaría de Salud; 2007.
16. Frenk J, Sepúlveda J, Gómez-Dantés O, Knaul F. Evidence-based health policy: three generations of reform in Mexico. *Lancet*. 2003;362(9396):1667–1671.
17. Knaul FM, Frenk J. Health insurance in Mexico: achieving universal coverage through structural reform. *Health Aff*. 2005;24(6):1467–1476. doi: 10.1377/hlthaff.24.6.1467.
18. Dantes OG, et al. Sistems de salud de Mexico. *Salud Publica de México*. January 2011;53(2). http://dx.dol.org/1-.1590/S0036-36342011000800017.
19. Secretaría de Salud. Programa Nacional de Salud 2001–2006. *La democratización de la salud en Mexico: Hacia un sistema universal de salud*. Mexico City: Secretaría de Salud; 2001.
20. World Health Organization. *World Health Report 2000. Health Systems: Improving Performance*. Geneva: World Health Organization; 2000.
21. Gómez-Dantés O, Sesma S, Becerril V, et al. Sistema de salud de México. http://www.observatori delasalud. Accessed August 20, 2008.
22. World Bank 2015 and Organisation for Economic Co-operation and Development. http://www.oecd.org/els/health-systems/health-data.htm. Accessed May 26, 2016.
23. Secretaría de Salud. Programa Nacional de Salud 2001–2006. *La democratización de la salud en Mixico. Hacia un sistema universal de salud*. Mexico City: Secretaría de Salud; 2001.
24. Organisation for Economic Co-operation and Development. Health Statistics 2014. www.oecd.org/health/health data.
25. Secretaría de Salud. *Observatorio del Desempeño Hospitalario 2005*. Mexico City: Secretaría de Salud; 2006.

CHAPTER 8

Peru

Raul Chuquiyauri, Hugo Rodriguez, and **Stalin Vilcarromero**

The views expressed in this article are those of the authors and do not necessarily reflect the official policy or position of the Department of the Navy, Department of Defense, or the United States government.

▸ Country Description

TABLE 8-1 Peru	
Nationality	Peruvian
Ethnic groups	Amerindian (45%); mestizo* (37%); European (15%); Japanese, Chinese, and African (3%) (2016)
Religions	Roman Catholic (81.3%), Evangelical (12.5%), other (6.0%) (2016)
Language	Spanish (84.1%); native peoples also speak Quechua (13.0%), Aymara (1.7%), and others (2016)
Literacy	Definition: Age 15 and over can read and write. Total population: 94.5% Male: 97.3% Female: 91.7% (2015)
Government type	Constitutional republic
Date of independence	July 28, 1821 (from the Spanish)
Gross Domestic Product (GDP) per capita	$12,200 (2015, PPP)

(continues)

TABLE 8-1 Peru (continued)

Unemployment rate	8.8% for ages 15 to 24 years (2016 est.)
Natural hazards	Earthquakes, tsunamis, flooding, landslides, mild volcanic activity (2016)
Environment: current issues	Deforestation, overgrazing, desertification, air pollution in Lima, pollution of rivers and coastal waters due to municipal waste and mining (2016)
Population	30,741,062 (2016)
Age structure	0–14 years: 26.62% (male 4,164,681/female 4,019,436) 15–24 years: 18.63% (male 2,868,743/female 2,859,476) 25–54 years: 39.91% (male 5,892,065/female 6,377,681) 55–64 years: 7.62% (male 1,135,938/female 1,205,579) 65 years and over: 7.21% (male 1,049,409/female 1,168,054) (2016 est.)
Median age	27.7 years (2016)
Population growth rate	0.96% (2016)
Birth rate	18 births/1,000 population (2016)
Death rate	533 deaths/100,000 population (2016 est.)
Disease burden	Communicable disease deaths: 121/100,000 population Noncommunicable disease deaths: 453/100,000 population Injury deaths: 58/100,000 population (2016 est.)
Net migration rate	−2.4 migrants/1,000 population (2014)
Gender ratio	At birth: 1.05 male(s)/female 0–14 years: 1.04 male(s)/female 15–24 years: 1 male(s)/female 25–54 years: 0.92 male(s)/female 55–64 years: 0.94 male(s)/female 65 years and over: 0.9 male(s)/female Total population: 0.97 male(s)/female (2016 est.)
Infant mortality rate	19 deaths/1,000 live births 21.1/1000 males 16.7/1000 females (2016 est.)
Life expectancy at birth	73.7 years 71.7 male 75.9 female (2016 est.)
Total fertility rate	2.15 children born/woman (2016 est.)
HIV/AIDS adult prevalence rate	0.33% (2015 est.)
Number of people living with HIV/AIDS	62,200 (2015 est.)
HIV/AIDS deaths	1,600 (2015 est.)

* Peruvian mestizos are individuals who are part Amerindian and part Caucasian.
Data from Central Intelligence Agency. The World Factbook, 2016. https://www.cia.gov/library/publications/resources/the-world-factbook/geos/pe.html.

History

The ancient Republic of Peru was inhabited by several prominent Andean civilizations, most notably that of the Inca Empire, which was invaded and conquered by the Spanish conquistadors in 1533.[1] The Republic of Peru declared its independence in 1821 and defeated the residual Spanish forces around 1824. From 1879 to 1883 the Pacific War between Chile and Peru took place. Then, after nearly a decade of military rule (1968–1975), the Republic of Peru established a system of democratic leadership in 1980. At that time the country experienced economic problems while a violent insurgency grew in the country. The period between 1985 and 1990 was chaotic and included the biggest economic slump in Peru's history. Simultaneously, the country experienced a huge increase in terrorist guerrilla activities. The political insecurity and economic crisis accelerated the emigration of professionals, which was a significant loss of human resources for the country. Moreover, Peru was excluded from international financial agencies as a result of the decision not to pay the external debt taken by the government at that time.

From 1990 to 2000, the Republic of Peru experienced a decade of dramatic turnaround in the economy and significant progress in curtailing terrorist guerrilla activity. Nevertheless, the president at the time, Alberto Fujimori, became increasingly reliant on authoritarian measures, and another economic slump in the late 1990s generated mounting dissatisfaction with his regime, which led to his ouster in 2000. In 2001, there was a transitional caretaker government that oversaw new elections in the spring of 2001, which ushered in the first democratically elected president of Amerindian ethnicity in modern times, Alejandro Toledo. The presidential election of 2006 saw the return of Alan Garcia who, after a disappointing presidential term from 1985 to 1990, returned to the presidency with promises to improve social conditions and maintain fiscal responsibility; he oversaw a robust macroeconomic performance. In June 2011, a former army officer, Olanta Humala Tasso was elected president and continued the market-oriented economic policies of the three preceding administrations, resulting in a reduction of poverty and unemployment. As of July 2016, Peru's elected president and head of state is Pedro Pablo Kuczynski Godard. The president selects his own cabinet, the Council of Ministers.[2]

Size and Geography

The Republic of Peru is located in the central western region of South America, bordering the South Pacific Ocean to the west, Ecuador to the northwest, Colombia to the northeast, Brazil to the east, Bolivia to the southeast, and Chile to the south. Peru is 1,285,216 square kilometers in size with only 3% of this area being arable. There are 1,279,996 square kilometers of land, and 5,220 square kilometers of water (**FIGURE 8-1**).[1,3] Due to the presence of the Andean Mountains, the largest in the world at 8,900 kilometers, and the Humboldt Sea Current, Peru has a complex weather pattern with a wide variety of climates: from tropical in the east to dry desert in the west, and temperate to frigid in the Andes. The Andes divide the country into three geographical units or natural regions: the coast, the Andes, and the Amazon forest.

The Coast is a thin longitudinal area that extends 2,250 kilometers and runs from Chile to Ecuador and from the Andes to the Pacific Ocean, representing 11% of the country's area. Its relief is almost uniform, forming an extensive barren plain, with alternating small valleys and mountains of low elevation. The southern coast has a median annual temperature of 18°C (64°F), and despite high atmospheric humidity, it has a very low rainfall. In the northern coast, the annual median temperature is 24°C (75°F) with high atmospheric humidity and regular rains during the summer season. Throughout all the coastal valleys, human settlements remain totally dependent on the waters that flow from the Andes along canals and aqueducts. Here, uncontrolled and unplanned urban growth competes directly with scarce and vitally needed agricultural land, steadily removing it from productive use.

The Andes are the commanding feature of Peru's territory, located between the coast and the Amazon forest, with an area that represents approximately 35.0% of the country and that reaches heights up to 6,768 meters. Its relief is markedly irregular with inter-Andean valleys along the rivers, and different weathers patterns correspond to the different altitudes. The world's highest navigable lake is Lake Titicaca, located at 3,812 meters and shared by the Andean Department of Puno (Peru) and Bolivia. Although rich in mineral resources—such as copper, lead, silver, iron, and zinc—which are mined at altitudes as high as 5,152 meters, the Andes are endowed with limited usable land. Only 4.5% of the land in the Andes (19,665 square kilometers) is arable and constitutes more than half the nation's productive land. About 93,120 square kilometers of the Andean region is natural pasture at altitudes higher than 4,000 meters, too high for agriculture. Therefore, the 4.5% of arable land has fairly dense populations, particularly in Puno, Cajamarca, Junín, and Ancash. The torrential rains of the winter months frequently cause severe landslides and avalanches throughout the Andean region, damaging irrigation canals, roads, and even destroying villages and cities.

Chapter 8 Peru

FIGURE 8-1 Map of Peru
© Rainer Lesniewski/Shutterstock

The Amazon forest, located to the east of the Andes, occupies 57% of the country but contains only about 11% of the country's population, with two well-defined areas: the high forest where the relief is irregular, with mountains and deep gorges, and the Amazon forest, which is uniformly flat and contains abundant tropical vegetation, furrowed by the Amazon River and its tributaries. The climate of the forest is warm and humid with abundant precipitation throughout the year, but it is accentuated January through April. The zone with heavier rains is the low forest. The annual average temperature fluctuates between 16°C and 35°C, low in the high forest and high in the low-lying Amazon forest. The Amazon River is the longest in the world and runs 6,762 kilometers. This region is an important potential source of new discoveries in the medical field, fuel resources, and mineral fields. Petroleum and gas reserves have been known to exist in several areas but remain difficult to exploit.

Population Centers: Urban Versus Rural

The Republic of Peru has a population of 30,741,062 (July 2016), with approximately one third of those living in the capital city of Lima.[4,5] In Peru 78.60% of all people live in urban areas, primarily along the western coastal region. The urbanization rate each year is 1.69% (TABLE 8-2).

The change in distribution from rural to urban living has been profound: the urban population rose from 35% in 1940 to 47.0% in 1961, to 70.0% in 1990, to 76.0% in 2007, and 78.6% in 2016.[4] Peru's population has reached a point where its configurations are substantially different than they were a generation ago, largely because of the enormous growth of metropolitan Lima. The migrant's dynamism, powered by a will to progress and modernize, helped build Lima from a quaint seaside town of 4,200 residents in 1940, to 296,000 in 1990, and to nearly ten million (9,886,647) in 2015.[6,7]

Departments with the highest proportion of urban population are Lima (97.1%), Tacna (90.8%), Arequipa (87.2%), and Tumbes (88.9%), while departments with the lowest proportion of urban population are Cajamarca (27.1%), Huancavelica (28.5%), Huánuco (42.5%), and Apurimac (37.9%)[4,5]

Government/Political System

The Peruvian government type is a constitutional republic with a unitary, representative, and decentralized government, organized according to the principle of separation of powers (executive, legislative, and judicial) with a multiparty political system. The country is divided into 24 departments, 188 provinces, and 1,793 districts. The executive branch is led by the president and the Council of Ministries. Members of the Council of Ministries are appointed by the president. The legislative branch is a unicameral congress with 120 seats. The judicial branch consists of the Supreme Court of Justice, and members are appointed by the National Council of the Judiciary. There are over 10 political parties, and most of

TABLE 8-2 Total Population and Annual Average Growth Rate in Peru, 1940–2016

Year	Total population	Intercensus growth	Annual growth	Annual growth rate (%)	Urban annual growth rate (%)	Rural annual growth rate (%)
1940	7,023,111	3,397,246	161,774	1.9	3.7	—
1961	10,420,357	3,701,207	336,473	2.8	5.1	1.20
1972	14,121,564	3,640,667	404,519	2.6	3.6	0.50
1981	17,762,231	4,877,212	406,434	2.0	2.8	0.80
1993	22,639,443	5,581,321	398,666	1.6	2.1	0.90
2007	28,220,764	—	—	—	—	0.01
2016	30,741,062	—	—	0.96%	1.69%	—

Data from National Institute of Statistics and Informatics (INEI), Peru; Central Intelligence Agency. The World Factbook, 2016. Peru. https://www.cia.gov/library/publications/the-world-factbook/geos/pe.html. Accessed October 3, 2016.

them have been founded recently. Presidential and congressional elections are held together at the same time by popular vote for a five-year term. The president cannot be reelected for a consecutive term, but congress members can be. Regional and municipal elections are held every four years.

Each municipality is autonomous and is composed of a municipal council, a provincial council, and a district council. Municipalities have jurisdiction over their internal organization, and they administer their assets and income, taxes, transportation, local public services, urban development, and education systems. Yet, the autonomy of municipalities may be reduced by their financial dependence on the central government. Resource constraints substantially limit the ability of municipal governments to implement independent activities. The central government transfers funds and assets, such as state sector enterprises to the regions, but the central government tends to be focused on Lima. Lima is composed of 33 municipalities, each with its own plaza, elected mayor and council, and municipal functions. The government of the province of Lima unites them and coordinates the metropolis as an urban entity.

In an effort to take power away from Lima and distribute it more among the many regions, in 1987, a decree to reorganize the regions was put forth as an effort to empower these areas and decentralize the overwhelming power of Lima. The plan was to regroup the 24 departments into 12 regions with legislative, administrative, and taxing powers, thereby consolidating power and increasing the power of each region. However, because of the political and economic instability at that time, both the congress and the government decided to postpone these changes.

Macroeconomics

Peru's economy draws from its varied geography: from abundant mineral resources found in the mountainous areas to excellent fishing grounds in coastal waters. Agriculture and textiles are also main economic activities.

During the 1980s and 1990s, Peru suffered serious structural problems in its economy; the 1980s were characterized by hyperinflation and the progressive loss of the productive capacity of the country, while during the first half of the 1990s, orthodox economic measures were applied to control inflation and stimulate liberalization of the markets, which contained the economic inflation and brought transitory economic growth from 1993 to 1997. Up until 1997, economic growth was sustained in the setting of restructuring of public expenditures, reintegration to the international economy, and incentives for private investment, stimulated by the significant reduction of violence in the country and by deregulation of the market. After 1998, the economic activity was reduced due to internal problems to which the eruption of external factors was added, such as abrupt withdrawal of capital associated with international financial crises, the phenomenon of "El Niño" which affected agriculture, and price variations of the main exports. From 1998 to 2001, Peru entered into a persistent recession period that only started to revert in 2002.

The Peruvian economy grew by more than 4.0% per year between 2002 and 2006, with a stable exchange rate and low inflation. Growth jumped to 9.0% per year in 2007 and 2008, driven by higher world prices for minerals and metals and the government's aggressive trade liberalization strategies, but then it fell by 1.0% in 2009 in the face of the world recession and lower commodity export prices. Between 2009 and 2013, the Peruvian economy grew by an average of 5.6% with a stable exchange rate and low inflation. The growth was due partly to high international prices for Peru's metal and mineral exports, which account for almost 60.0% of the country's total exports. Peru's economy reflects its varied topography from the coastal region to the Andes to the dense forest of the Amazon, the tropical lands bordering Colombia and Brazil. A wide range of important mineral resources are found in the mountainous and coastal areas, and Peru's coastal waters provide excellent fishing grounds. Peru is the world's second largest producer of silver and the third largest producer of copper. However, too much dependence on mineral and metal exports subjects the economy to fluctuations in world prices, and poor infrastructure precludes the spread of growth to Peru's noncoastal areas. Growth slipped in 2014 and 2015 due to weaker world prices for these resources.[8]

Since 2006, Peru has been negotiating free trade agreements with Canada and the European Union. In November 2009 it ratified an agreement with China. The United States and Peru completed negotiations on the implementation of the United States–Peru Trade Promotion Agreement, which started February 1, 2009. Peru's free trade policy has continued under the HUMALA administration. Since 2006 Peru has signed trade deals with the United States, Canada, Singapore, China, Korea, Mexico, Japan, the European Union, the European Free Trade Association, Chile, Thailand, Costa Rica, Panama, and Venezuela; has concluded negotiations with Guatemala and the Trans-Pacific Partnership; and has begun trade talks with Honduras, El Salvador, India, Indonesia, and Turkey. Peru also signed a trade pact with Chile, Colombia, and Mexico called the Pacific Alliance, which seeks integration of services, capital, investment, and movement of people. Since the United States–Peru Trade Promotion Agreement entered into force in February 2009, total trade between Peru and the United States has doubled.[8]

Peru's rapid expansion coupled with cash transfers and other programs have helped to reduce the national poverty rate by 28% since 2002, but inequality persists and continues to pose a challenge. The administration, through the spring of 2016, championed a policy of social inclusion and a more equitable distribution of income. However, poor infrastructure hinders the spread of growth to Peru's noncoastal areas. Several economic stimulus packages were initiated in 2014 to bolster growth, including reforms to environmental regulations to spur investment in Peru's lucrative mining sector, a move that was opposed by some environmental groups. In 2015, however, mining investment fell as global commodity prices remained low and social conflicts plagued the sector.

The Gross Domestic Product (GDP) per capita (PPP) in 1991 was US $1,922. By 2008, it was $3,104.[5,9] Remarkably, by 2015, GDP per capita (PPP) had risen to $12,200. The structure of GDP in 2015 is primarily services (58.5%) followed by agriculture, fishing, and mining at 34.5% of GDP, of which agriculture represents 7.0% of GDP.

In terms of unemployment, the country rate estimated for 2015 was 6.1%, which reflects the Lima area. There is widespread unemployment in rural areas. In 2012, the poverty level was 26.0%, showing steady improvement over 2007, when the rate was 39.0% of the population living below the poverty level.[8]

Infrastructure

In terms of availability of consistent electricity, as of 2013, 91% of the population is covered, 98% of urban residents, and 73% of rural residents. Communication has consistently improved over the past two decades, with nearly three million land lines and with more than 34 million subscribers to cell phone plans. There are 10 major networks, and 13 broadcast stations countrywide. It is estimated that in 2015, 41% of the population had access to the Internet.[10]

Peru has 59 airports with paved runways, and nearly 140 airports with unpaved runways in rural and remote locations. There are 140,000 kilometers of roads in Peru, but only 19,000 kilometers of those are paved, primarily in urban areas. There are 8,800 kilometers of navigable waterways in the tributaries of the Amazon River system in eastern Peru. There are three major sea ports, Callao, Matarani, and Paita, with two of them having oil terminals. And Peru has three major river ports in the Amazon, Iquitos, Pucallpa, and Yurimiaguas.[11]

In terms of public health infrastructure, 82.5% of the urban population, and 53.2% of the rural population have access to improved sanitation. Approximately 91.0% of the urban population has access to improved drinking water sources, as opposed to 69.2% of rural populations.[12]

Peru spends 3.7% of its GDP on education and has a literacy rate of 94.5%. Slightly more males (97.3%) than females (91.7%) are literate. The average school expectancy is 13 years, but females get 14 years of education on average. There is disparity in achieved education levels between children in urban areas versus those raised in rural and remote areas of the country, with poorer levels of literacy and educational achievement in rural areas. Working against school attendance is the fact that child labor rates (ages 5 to 14 years) is 34.0%. Young adults (ages 15 to 24) experience an 8.8% unemployment rate.[12]

Demographics

The annual average growth rate of the population has been declining for the last 48 years. From 1981 to 1993 the annual average growth rate was 2.00%, and from 1972 to 1981 it was 2.60%. The estimated growth rate for 2016 is 0.96%. This decreasing trend in population growth could be explained by increased urbanization (reaching 78.60% of the population in 2015), which has been changing at a rate of 1.69% annually between 2010 and 2015, as well as better educational level attainment for women. Around 75.00% of women use contraception, and the age of first birth for a woman is 22 year. The birth rate is 18 per 1,000 live births, and the death rate is 6 per 1,000. In addition, the net migration for Peru is −2.40 per 1,000 estimated for 2016.[12]

Age and Sex Distribution of the Population

When analyzing the age distribution of the population, we can look at it as a population pyramid. How the pyramid has changed over time reflects the overall health and growth of the population. In 1993, the population pyramid had a wide base, representing high birth rates, with a thin apex, representing a small population progressing to old ages. Today we observe a reduced base with a progressive widening of the center and apex, which reflects three processes: fewer births, more population living to adulthood, and a larger proportion of the elderly surviving. Over the past 40 years, the population of those over age 60 has tripled, while the annual growth for the population as a whole is now 0.96%.[4]

Religion

The major religious groups are Roman Catholic (81.3%) and Evangelical (12.5%), with 3.3% of the population professing other religions and 2.9% who do not profess any religion. Comparing 2007 and 1993, there has been a 7.7% decrease in the number of Catholics, a 5.7% increase in the number of Evangelicals, and a 0.5% and 1.5% increase in the number of people professing other or no religion, respectively. Moreover, there are differences in religion by area of residency, with 82.3% and 77.9% of the urban and rural populations being Catholics, respectively, and 11.5% and 15.9% of the urban and rural population being Evangelicals, respectively. Finally, 50.6%, 53.9%, and 52.2% of women profess to be Catholic, Evangelical, and other religion, respectively. On the contrary, the population with no religion is predominantly male (61.5%).[5]

▸ Brief History of the Healthcare System

In 1935, the Ministries of Education, Public Health, and Social Forecast were created, and the last one included the Directorate of Salubrity, Work, Social Forecast, and Indigenous Matters, having as a base the General Directorate of Salubrity, created in 1903.[13] In 1940, with 8 million inhabitants, Peru was basically a rural country, with a mainly agricultural and miner population, and an epidemiological profile of a poor, rural country.

The Allied victory in World War II reinforced the relative democratic trend in Peru, as Prado's presidential term came to an end in 1945. José Luis Bustamante y Rivero (1945–1948), a liberal and prominent international jurist, was elected president and practiced more reform- and populist-oriented politics, moving Peru away from the strictly orthodox, free market policies that had characterized his predecessors' terms. Increasing the state's intervention in the economy in an effort to stimulate growth and redistribution, the new government embarked on a general fiscal expansion, increased wages, and established controls on prices and exchange rates. The policy was neither well conceived nor efficiently administered and came at a time when Peru's exports, after an initial upturn after the war, began to sag. This resulted in a surge of inflation and labor unrest that ultimately destabilized the government. In 1948, Social Security for Employees was established with the creation of the Hospital of the Employee. The National Medical Union opposed this at the time out of concern that it would lead to privatization of medical services.[13,14] At that time, there was only one school of medicine dedicated to treating illness but little emphasis on prevention.

The 1960s was a period of growth for Peru in many realms, including industrialization, education, social insurance, increased home ownership, and sanitary infrastructure. The National Hospital Plan oversaw the modernization of the sanitary infrastructure and the expansion of these measures to more areas of the country. In 1969, the Sanitary Code was enacted and constituted the legal framework of the actions in the health sector, and simultaneously, the Organic Law of the Health Sector was put forth.[13] It was also at this time that the health system started to closely follow the international health policies of the Panamerican Health Organization, United Nations Fund for Children, and the United Nations Population Fund. Governments of Latin American countries were also advancing health care by setting up family planning programs and improving access to contraceptive methods, but all these activities stopped in the first phase of the military government (1968–1975).[14]

During the 1970s, continued progress in health care was made with the establishment of free maternity services. In addition, it became mandatory for graduates from the schools of medicine, nursing, and dentistry to do civil service to get their professional diplomas.[15] In 1974, rapid population growth became a problem, and population health policies were defined and approved as Lineaments of Population Policies in the second phase of the military government (1976–1980).[13] The expansion of the government-run social services ended with the beginning of the fiscal crisis that was triggered by the external debt and the general economic crisis of 1975. From this time on, the government neglected social responsibilities, mainly those of health and education. It is important to highlight that even with the expansion of the public services during 1963–1975, there was always a great proportion of the population with no access to health services and social insurance.[13]

The 1980s, now called "the lost decade," were led by two democratic governments: the first was a weak government whose leadership resulted in daily monetary devaluation and disorganization of the health sector, and the second caused chaos characterized by huge increases in terrorism, continuous monetary devaluation, and hyperinflation. The health sector faced several problems related to the health establishments in bankruptcy due to limited economical resources and the lack of credibility in the sector.[1] The fiscal crisis in the 1980s seriously affected the resources of the health sector, and as a consequence, the per capita expenditure of the Ministry of Health (MINSA) and of the Social Insurance Peruvian Institute (which was the Peruvian Institute of Social Security, IPSS, until 1996 and is currently EsSalud) decreased by 50%. Regarding coverage, only 25% of the population had some kind of health insurance, and the other 75% of the population did not have any provisional coverage.[16(pp 23–29)]

In the 1990s the Peruvian government was in an intense crisis because of the political violence, its waning authority, and its declining legitimacy in the eyes of society.[16,17] A new government (Alberto Fuimori's) took the responsibility of solving the hyperinflation. Since then, a neoliberal policy has been applied, noting an increase in the globalization of information and economies and the disappearance of socialist regimes, bringing about a redefinition of many theories and concepts in public health and health policies.[18] It is important to also mention the cholera epidemic in 1991 that left in total crisis the most excluded of society: the poor people.[18] It also generated one of the biggest loans from the World Bank to fight against cholera. After this, the Fujimori administration also enacted the Social Emergency Program, an objective created to reduce the social cost of the crisis.[1]

In this global context, health policies were formulated with the goal of reforming the health system through regionalization and decentralization as strategies to obtain change and reorient the model to obtain greater coverage of the population.[14] This reform process was guided by the principles of fairness, universality, solidarity, quality, effectiveness, and efficiency. It sought to build a new legal framework for the development of health actions, to expand government capacities, to establish a new system for individual health care and attending to collective health, and to create a new system for health care funding and health service administration.[16]

Since 1994, the government has budgeted US $88 million per year for the program Basic Health Program for All. Later, projects began with international funding of $202 million total: the Program of Fortification of Health Services was supported with $98 million, the Health and Basic Nutrition Project of the World Bank with $44 million, and Project 2000 with $60 million. It was equivalent to a per capita expenditure of $42.06 dollars per year.

With the movement from rural life to city life, impoverished medium-socioeconomic class layers have appeared, and the lifestyles of many people have changed from living in close contact with nature to the stressful world of the city. People went from the unhealthiness of rural deficiencies to the relative unhealthiness of urban deficiencies as healthcare changed from the meager hospital services of years past to the current system of massive services. Consequently, Peru currently has a very heterogeneous epidemiological profile.

▸ Description of the Current Healthcare System

The current health system is composed of two sectors: public and private. The first consists principally of MINSA and EsSalud and the Armed Forces and Police health units. The private sector is composed of doctor's offices, private clinics, local companies, and nongovernmental organizations (NGOs) providing health services. MINSA is in charge of issuing policy guidelines as well as the technical standards and procedures to regulate sectoral activity. In practice, the health sector is highly fragmented and inequitable.[19] Regional governments and municipalities play an important role in providing public health services, first through the regional health directorates (which are extensions of MINSA and are in the process of decentralization and therefore have some autonomy) and the second by partially subsidized public hospitals that provide health services to the general population (for example, in Lima these hospitals are known as Hospitals of Solidarity).

In order to evaluate health spending, one must consider two factors: the type of insurance coverage an individual has and the type of health facility where an individual receives medical attention. If a person has Comprehensive Health Insurance (SIS), theoretically the patient would receive 100% coverage with a few exceptions; this option was created to serve the poor and extremely poor who have no ability to pay and have no other health insurance. MINSA is currently trying to expand the availability of the option to the entire population with pilot projects in the poorest departments of Ayacucho, Apurimac, and Huancavelica, with the hope of reaching all departments by 2012.[20,21] The second option is a partially subsidized insurance called SISALUD, for which participants make monthly contributions ranging from US $3.30 to $10.00, depending on whether coverage is for the individual or for a family and on the eligibility of the patient for SIS coverage. The third option is for individuals with no public insurance coverage, who must pay for the services directly at rates set by each health establishment, the cost of which is much lower than in EsSalud or private offices or clinics because the financing of MINSA facilities is subsidized. In the case of some cities, such as Lima, people have an additional option, public hospitals run by local municipalities that are equipped with specialized equipment and care offered at lower cost than in the private sector. There are also some civil associations, NGOs, that provide healthcare services through clinics and diagnostic laboratories at a cost significantly lower than private clinics but slightly higher than in MINSA facilities.

EsSalud serves salaried and contract employees from both the public and private sectors as part of their employee benefits; employers are required to pay 9% of a person's base salary each month for healthcare coverage for the employee and family. EsSalud also offers insurance coverage that can be purchased by independent workers for a monthly premium, and although this represents a minority of those affiliated with EsSalud, many continue to use this modality and receive the same benefits as those affiliated through their employers.

Members of the national police and military and their families receive health care from the Armed Forces and Police Force health services, each with a flagship hospital in Lima, the capital of Peru, as well as other health facilities in the country. These services are subsidized by the central government through the Ministry of Defense and provide 100% and partial coverage to members and their families, respectively.

A relatively small percentage of the population, usually with moderate to high income, has private insurance offered by a group of officially authorized Health Maintenance Organizations (EPS), such as RIMAC, PERSALUD, and PACIFICOSALUD, and MAPFRE PERU.[20] These EPSs have their own financial support and either their own health facilities or agreements with well-recognized private clinics, usually located in major cities.

Facilities

The infrastructure of the health sector ranges from primary care facilities, such as health posts headed by nurses and health centers headed by physicians, to larger hospitals and institutes, which are staffed with specialty physicians and, in some cases, provide tertiary care. These facilities are distributed among the different health institutions: MINSA, EsSalud, Armed Forces, National Police, and the private sector (private clinics), but the facilities in the public sector, specifically MINSA facilities, account for the vast majority of them. Excluding informal private practices, in 2005, public facilities accounted for 85% of the health infrastructure, and private sector facilities accounted for 7% (TABLE 8-3).[22-24]

In 2009, the National Institute of Statistics and Informatics reported 485 hospitals, 2,049 health centers, and 6,016 health posts managed by MINSA or EsSalud.[3] In 2015, the number of beds per 1,000 population was 1.5.[12] The distribution of these health facilities, however, was uneven. In 2002, MINSA and EsSalud reported 42 hospitals in the Department of Lima, compared to 2 in Huancavelica, one of the poorest departments in Peru.[20,23] The distribution of health centers throughout Peru remains unequal, with most located in Lima.

Overall, there has been very slow growth of MINSA infrastructure; observed growth, however, has generally been in response to local efforts by community leaders and local governments that are sharing in healthcare costs through the implementation of decentralization policies. The bulletin published by the MINSA Office of Statistics and Informatics shows a slight increase in health facilities in Peru between 1996 and 2005. In 2009, EsSalud had an institutional initiative to improve

TABLE 8-3 Number of Health Facilities by Institution in Peru, 2006

Institution	Total	Hospital	Health center	Health post
Total	8,055	453	1,932	5,670
Ministry of Health	6,821	146	1,203	5,472
EsSalud	330	78	252	0
National Police of Peru	280	5	77	198
Peruvian Army	60	16	44	0
Private clinics	564	208	356	0

Data from Peru Ministry of Health. http://www.minsa.gob.pe/

both primary health and hospital care. Under this initiative, by February 2010, EsSalud had constructed 48 of 100 projected primary care facilities and 11 of 18 projected tertiary hospitals located throughout Peru. Large numbers of professional and nonprofessional staff had been contracted to work in these health facilities.[25] The impact of this rapid growth has yet to be evaluated, but EsSalud serves less than 30% of Peru's population, so it is unlikely to be of great impact. Only if the Peruvian government is able to establish a unified national health system will the situation improve.

Workforce

In 2005, the health workforce included 139,231 workers distributed among MINSA, EsSalud, and health maintenance organizations, which together serve more than 80% of the population.[26] Similarly, in 2007, there were 1.48 physicians per 1,000 inhabitants, and in 2015, the ratio was 1.13 per 1,000, indicating a significant decline in a short period of time. The number of nurses and/or midwives per 1,000 population was 1.50 in 2012.[27]

To add to the problem, like with health facilities, the distribution of health workers is unequal. For example, in 2005, Lima had 1.86 physicians per 1,000 inhabitants, 3 times that observed in the department of Huancavelica.[24] The gap between Lima and poorer departments continued to increase. In reports from 1992, 2004, and 2006, the numbers of physicians per inhabitants continued to also show a consistent inverse correlation with poverty levels, and this situation continues into 2016.[21]

The primary barriers to the improvement of the health infrastructure fall into two major categories: human resources and an increased demand on the health sector. Issues surrounding human resources are complex and include a worrying decline in the quality of medical and nursing education for those entering the field and those seeking further educational opportunities. The impact of underemployment leads to many healthcare professionals migrating out of underserved communities or Peru altogether. Only 2 of the 29 medical schools have international accreditation, and scores in the national medical boards have been consistently low.[28] In spite of this, between 1992 and 2003, the number of medical schools increased from 13 to 28 and nursing schools from 34 to 44. In turn, this increased the number of graduates in medicine. Health professionals continue to migrate to better served areas or outside the country.

Precarious employment opportunities further complicate this situation, often leading to low and unequal wages, lack of regular employment benefits, kickbacks to obtain employment, and labor disputes. All of these factors lead to worker dissatisfaction and subsequent reductions in the quality of care delivered. There has been a lack of consistent government policy or regulation on wages for health personnel, especially between different institutions. Perhaps more important has been the increased demand on the healthcare system overall, and more specifically on the public sector due to the SIS system, designed to provide free healthcare access to traditionally underserved populations, primarily those in poverty and extreme poverty. The supply of human resources, including salaries and health facilities, has failed to keep up with the demand, which far exceeds the capacity of existing facilities and personnel.

Technology and Equipment

Although communication infrastructure continues to increase, in rural areas telephone service and electricity are often unavailable or unreliable. Radio communication is critical, especially because many of these facilities are extremely isolated and many days of travel from the nearest city. The service is efficient because operating costs are minimal and coordination with the administrative headquarters can be carried out to solve problems, and the service allows information transfer and sharing. Impact is highest in the case of emergencies and disasters. In 2002, the Hispano American Health Link Foundation (Enlace Hispano Americano de Salud), a nonprofit institution that promotes the appropriate use of new information and communication technologies applied to health services in remote rural areas in developing countries, started a pilot project for telemedicine in Yurimaguas city, and later it extended the project to Iquitos and Cuzco. According to the Census of Sanitary Infrastructure and Health Resources, the number of radios in use increased from 625 in 1996 to 2,621 in 2005 (most radios are high frequency). The role of telemedicine for remote areas of Peru continues to expand in 2016.

In 2012, MINSA reported 24,055 available hospital beds, distributed in 2,512 health facilities; 31.1% are in health centers or posts, which usually treat births and uncomplicated illnesses with short hospital stays. Larger hospitals and institutes treat 68.9% of patients with medium and severe medical problems. In 2012, Peru had 1.5 beds per 1,000 population countrywide. Hospital beds in MINSA facilities are distributed predominantly in the departments of Lima, Cusco, Arequipa, Puno, and Junin. At the institutional level, 57.3% of hospital beds are with MINSA, 15.8% with EsSalud, 9.0% with Armed Forces and National Police health units, and 17.9% with private institutions.[22]

Evaluation of the Healthcare System
Cost

The GDP per capita in 1991 was US $1,992; in 1995 it was $2,505; and in 2000 there was a significant drop to $2,180.[29] In 2005 GDP rose to over $2,500 per capita; in 2007 it reached $3,766; and in 2008 it increased to $4,422 per person per year.[30,31] Total expenditures on health, out of the total Peruvian budget, in 2013 was 14.7%. In 2015 GDP per person had risen to $12,200 (PPP). In 2014 and 2015, the real growth rate was 2.4% and 3.3%, respectively. As of 2016, health expenditures are 5.3% of GDP.[8,27]

The per capita health expenditure from 1995 to 1996 was US $102, then it increased to in 1997 and 1998 to $107, and then it decreased in 1999 to $100 and in 2000 to $99.[32] In 2002 it was $104, in 2004 $113, and 2005 $130.[32] In 2013, the WHO reported per capita health spending in Peru as $354, representing a PPP of $626.[27]

According to expenditure by lenders, throughout the period of 1995–2005, the highest spending was from EsSalud, which increased during that period, while MINSA expenditures, Police and Military Departments of Health, and the private sector expenditures remained constant. Drugstore expenditures reduced yearly. The three main centers of expenditure in 2005 were the one managed by MINSA nationwide (27.2%), EsSalud (26.7%), and the private lucrative sector including the EPS (23.8%).[31]

Mechanisms of healthcare financing include taxes, premium contributions, and out-of-pocket payments. The government financed 25.2% in 1995, 24.1% in 2000, and 30.7% in 2005, and in 2013 the government's proportion of total healthcare financing rose to 58.7%, while the private proportion of the total healthcare financing expenditure in Peru was 41.3%. Out-of-pocket financing by individuals and families represented 84.6% of the private proportion, continuing to be the main source of financing: 45.6% in 1995, 37.9% in 2000, and 34.2% in 2005. This proportion has stayed fairly constant over the last decade, with out-of-pocket spending representing 34.7% of the total healthcare expenditure in 2013. The remaining funding (6.6%) comes from external funders, internal donations, and others (3.4% in 1995, 3.7% in 2000, 4.6% in 2005, and 6.6% in 2013).[27]

Between 1995 and 2015, Peru consistently increased its proportion of funding. Especially since 2005, Peru has observed a very important increase in financing on the part of the government, with increased reliance on resources from the national treasury, from 25.2% to 60.4% through 2014. At the same time there was a decreased reliance on out-of-pocket financing from 45.8% to 34.7%. The most probable explanation of this trend is that this effect was due to the presence of SIS.[31] Personal resources are used mostly to buy pharmaceuticals (most of the time without support from the Peruvian public health service), as well as to pay the bill for private or public care.[19]

Studies about the breakdown of health expenses according to levels of care suggest that approximately 40% of the MINSA public allowance in health (defined as the payment of health expenses minus the payment of the fees paid per user minus the expenses of the central administration of MINSA) is sent to the hospital level, while the remaining 60% goes to primary care facilities (health centers and health posts).[33] The distribution of the MINSA public allowance for health by income quintiles has shown a clear decreasing pattern in hospital expenses, especially in rural areas, while there is a meaningful increasing pattern in the expenses of urban health centers and urban health posts.[3]

Quality
Mortality and Life Expectancy

The infant mortality rate for 1972–1976 was 96 per 1,000 live births. This rate went down to 83 for 1977–1981, to 77 for 1982–1986, to 57 for 1987–1992, to 38 for 1993–1997, to 30 for 1998–2002, and to 19 for 2003–2008.[34,35] In 2015, the CIA reports that the infant mortality rate had remained steady at 19 per 1,000 live births.[12]

The child mortality rate (deaths of children under the age of 5 per 1,000 live births) was 227 per 1,000 in 1960, 53 for 1993–1997, 39 for 1998–2002, 27 for 2003–2007 and by 2015 had reached a new low of 17 per 1,000.[35,36] The reduction in neonatal mortality has also consistently improved since 1990 when the neonatal mortality rate was 28 per 1,000 live births. The rates were 19 for the period 1993–1997, 17 for 1998–2002, 10 for 2003–2008, and in 2015 the rate was 8 per 1,000 live births.[35,36] The area of residency makes a significant difference in both neonatal mortality rates and mortality rates for children under 5 years of age. For 2003–2008, infant mortality was 12 per 1,000 live births in urban areas, but in rural areas the rate was 30 per 1,000 live births.[35] Child mortality also showed a major difference by area of residency, with 17 per 1,000 deaths in urban area and 43 child deaths per 1,000 live births in rural areas. Neonatal mortality was noticeable but less significant at 8 per 1,000 deaths in urban areas and 14 per 1,000 in rural areas. In Lima, the infant mortality rate was a low as 2 per 1,000 live births, indicating the advantage to population living in the capital city.[35,36]

The mothers' level of education (as a feature related to infant mortality) for 2003–2008 showed one of the most important inequities, reaching rates of 30 and 29 deaths per 1,000 per live births in mothers with no education or who went to primary school only, respectively. On the other hand, for mothers with high levels of education or with secondary school education only, infant mortality rates were as low as 6–15 per 1,000 live births. These differences are also observed for both child mortality and neonatal mortality.

Infant and child mortality rates are highly correlated with wealth. During the period 2003–2008, the distribution of wealth by quintiles also revealed significant differences in child mortality with only 2 deaths per 1,000 live births in the highest quintile of income, and 50 per 1,000 in the lowest quintile. This difference is also observed for child mortality with a rate of 9 per 1,000 live births in the highest quintile and 59 per 1,000 in the lowest quintile. For neonatal mortality, 1 per 1,000 live births was recorded in the upper quintile of income and 20 per 1,000 in the lowest quintile.[35]

The general mortality rate in Peru has shown a decreasing trend since 1950, and most notably in the last 40 years. In 1990, the gross mortality rate was 7.2 per 1,000 inhabitants.[37] For 2000–2005 it was estimated at 6.0 deaths per 1,000 inhabitants, where it has remained steady into 2016.[38] By 2015, life expectancy had risen to 73.1 years for males, and to 78.0 years for females. Life expectancy, like other measures, varies by region of the country, with higher life expectance in urban areas versus rural areas.[12] The top 10 major causes of death in Peru per 100,000 population are presented in **TABLE 8-4**. In Peru there is also a high risk for infectious diseases, especially in rural areas. These include bacterial diarrhea, hepatitis A, and typhoid fever, as well as vector-borne diseases such as dengue fever, malaria, and the Zika virus. In terms of lifestyle factors, 20.4% of adults are considered obese. Peru reports a moderate level of alcohol and tobacco use.

Fertility Rate

The overall fertility rate in Peru has changed from 3.50 children born per woman in 1996 to 3.00 in 2000, 2.40 in 2007, and 2.15 in 2016. In the last few years important differences have been observed according to area of residence, with the highest birth rates in rural areas, the Amazon forest region, the Andes, and in the lower quintiles of wealth. Contraception is reported to be at 75.5% (2012) for all women of child bearing age. Maternal mortality rate is at 68.00 deaths per 100,000 live births (2015). Consistent with other health statistics, the fertility rate is going down while mortality statistics are going down over time.[12]

TABLE 8-4 Top 10 Causes of Death per 100,000 Population in Peru in 2014

Cause of death (2014)	Number per 100,000 population
Influenza and pneumonia	73.15
Coronary heart disease	56.73
Stroke	37.12
Prostate cancer	19.89
Liver disease	18.89
Road traffic accidents	16.86
Kidney disease	16.13
Stomach cancer	15.34
Other injuries	13.59
Cervical cancer	13.06

Data from World Health Rankings. Health Profile: Peru. www.worldlifeexpectancy.com/country-health-profile/peru. 2014. Accessed October 19, 2016.

Malnutrition

In 2014, 3.1% of children in Peru under the age of 5, were underweight. Chronic malnutrition, according to *Encuesta Demográfica y de Salud Familiar*, 2007–2008, was 27.8% for children under five years, which showed a slight decrease in relation to 2000 and 2005, with rates of 31.0% and 29.5%, respectively. Malnutrition affected mainly children living in rural areas (44.7%) compared to urban areas (16.0%). Huancavelica (located in the Andes) was the department with the highest proportion of malnourished children (56.6%), and Tacna (located in the coast) had the lowest proportion with 9.1%. Mothers with no education had malnourished children at a proportion of 61.4%, while mothers with more advanced education had the lowest proportion levels at 8.9%. Acute malnutrition at the country level was 0.8%, while for children under age five it was 4.2%.[35]

Vaccination

The proportion of children aged 18 to 29 months who were fully vaccinated was 66.0% in 2000 and 56.9% in the period 2004–2006.[35] Improvement was made in the vaccination rates over the following decade. **TABLE 8-5** shows the level of vaccination for children one year or less in age for the major vaccines. It should be noted that studies have consistently found that the level of vaccination rates vary by location and the education of the mother. Vaccination rates are higher in urban areas as compared to rural areas of the country, and the rates are higher among better education women.[35]

Access

Equity/Universality

Peru shows a skewed distribution of income: while 20% of the population with the highest income concentrates 47.5% of the national income, 20% of the population with the lowest income concentrates only 6% of the national income.[39] The Gini coefficient for distribution of income by population deciles was 0.51 in 2003,[40] 0.510 in 2005, 0.507 in 2007, 0.479 in 2008, 0.453 in 2012, and 0.441 in 2014.[41] This decline in the Gini coefficient, although slow, is consistently going in the direction of better equity in terms of income.[8,42]

TABLE 8-5 Vaccination Rates for Children ≤ 1 Year of Age in Peru, 2014

Vaccine	Completion rate (%)
BCG (bacillus Calmette-Guérin for tuberculosis)	94
DPT (diphtheria, pertussis, tetanus)	88
Hepatitis B	88
Hib (*Haemophilus influenza* type b, 3 in series)	95
MEV (measles)	89
PAB (tetanus, at birth)	85
Polio (3 in series)	93

Data from World Health Organization. Global Health Observatory Data: Peru. http://www.who.int/gho/en/. 2016. Accessed May 31, 2016.

The number of doctors in Peru was 1.1 per 1,000 population in 2012. Like other resources in Peru, the number of physicians is poorly distributed, with a higher concentration in urban areas than in rural areas such as the Andes and the Amazon.[3] Better living conditions, access to services, and better pay draw healthcare professionals away from the most needy and vulnerable populations. For nurses/midwives, there are only 1.5 per 1,000 population nationally. Access to health care also depends on transportation, availability of clinics, and cost. Theoretically, everyone has access to healthcare services in government-run facilities and/or is covered by SIS, but actually only 73% of the population has some form of health insurance. In addition, the numbers of services and quality of services available varies considerably across Peru geographically and by income.[12]

Uninsured Population

There are four ways in which to receive health insurance: Comprehensive Health Insurance (SIS), Social Health Insurance (EsSalud), Public Health of Military and Police Institutions insurance, and private insurance companies. SIS has evolved as a public insurance, funded publicly, with a focus on poor and vulnerable populations.[31] EsSalud provides health, social, and economic services, which complements its insurance role. Workers of the formal sector of the economy and their direct relatives are mainly affiliated with EsSalud, which is financed mainly by contributions from the payroll of the employee's institution.[31] Employers calculate the equivalent of 9% of the monthly wage of their workers, and the number of contributors depends on the evolution of the formal economic sector. In addition to dependent workers, social security has looked for ways to expand this service to workers who are not salaried, but this has resulted in scarce results.[43]

The public insurance of military and police institutions exclusively covers its workers and direct relatives, and it is financed by public treasury funds. Private health insurances are usually taken by families, less often directly by employers. The main differences between the services given by the SIS and the EsSalud insurances are the gratuity of the care and the medication required by the insured ones. EsSalud insurance keeps the services for all its members unified regardless of the level of income/contribution and type of affiliation (there are regular affiliated members and special affiliated members) until early 2000. Since then, EsSalud has developed health plans with different levels of coverage for the special affiliated members, the independently insured members (also known as facultative members) and their families.[43] In 2005, the proportion of the population receiving any type of health insurance was 35.9%, but by 2012, 73.0% of the population was enrolled in one of these four types of health insurance. The proportion of the population receiving SIS has increased continuously, and Peru is inspired to continue expanding this insurance so that there is universal coverage, which is a national priority. Peru's strategic initiative is to increase the level of funding as a percentage of GDP, improve access to high-quality care, improve disease monitoring activities for chronic and infectious diseases, and develop inclusive approaches focused on human rights, gender, intercultural aspects, primary health care, families and communities, life course, and determinants of health status.[44]

References

1. *The World Factbook*. Washington, DC: Central Intelligence Agency. http://www.cia.gov/library/publications/the-world-factbook/geos/pe.html. 2008. Accessed February 2, 2010.
2. *The World Factbook*. Peru. Washington, DC: Central Intelligence Agency. cia.gov/library/publications/resources/the-world-factbook/geos/pe.html. September 25, 2016. Accessed October 1, 2016.
3. Instituto Nacional de Estadística e Informática. *Perú: Compendio Estadístico 2009*. Peru 2009.
4. Instituto Nacional de Estadística e Informática. *Perfil Sociodemografico del Peru*. 2008.
5. Instituto Cuánto. *Anuario estadístico: Perú en números*, 2009.
6. *Peru: Estimaciones y Proyecciones de Poblacion Total por Sexo de las Principales Ciudades 2013–2015*.
7. World Population Review. Peru population 2016. www.worldpopulationreview.com/countries/peru-population/. Published August 6, 2016. Accessed October 2, 2016.
8. *The World Factbook*. Peru. Economy. Washington, DC: Central Intelligence Agency. cia.gov/library/publications/resources/the-world-factbook/geos/pe.html. September 25, 2016. Accessed October 18, 2106.
9. Instituto Nacional de Estadística e Informática. *Compendio de Estadísticas Sociodemográficas 1998–2009*.
10. *The World Factbook*. Peru. Communication. Washington, DC: Central Intelligence Agency. CIA.gov/library/publication/resources/the-world-factbook/geos/pe.html. September 25, 2106. Accessed October 14, 2016.
11. *The World Factbook*. Peru. Transportation. Washington, DC: Central Intelligence Agency. CIA.gov/library/publication/resources/the-world-factbook/geos/pe.html. September 25, 2106. Accessed October 14, 2016.
12. *The World Factbook*. Peru. People and Society. Washington, DC: Central Intelligence Agency. CIA.gov/library/publication/resources/the-world-factbook/geos/pe.html. September 25, 2016. Accessed October 13, 2016.
13. Lip C. Los Cambios en la profesión médica y sus implicancias. El caso del Perú. *Educ Med Salud*. 1994;28(1):96–101.
14. Estrada MV, Godoy RM. Genero y políticas de salud de la mujer en America Latina: caso Peru. Parte 2. *Rev Esc Enfermagem*. USP, São Paulo. 1996;30(1):204–208.
15. Yong EM. Seminario internacional reforma del sector salud. Lima, 1996. Discurso del Ministro de Salud de Perú.
16. Aguinaga AR. *Situación de la salud en Perú y sus tendencias: la reforma sectorial*. Lima: Ministério de Salud del Perú. Lima. 1996.
17. Ministerio de Salud del Perú. Oficina General de Epidemiología. *Situación de salud del Perú*. Lima; 1998.
18. Gonzales RIC, Rojas VC, Villa TCS. Vision panoramica de la situacion de salud en el Peru. *Rev Latino-Am Enfermagem*. Ribeirão Preto. 2000;8(6):7–12.
19. Organización Panamericana de la Salud. Programa de Organización y Gestión de Sistemas y Servicios de Salud División de Desarrollo de Sistemas y Servicios de Salud. *Perfil del Sistema de Servicios de Salud de Perú*. 2001.
20. Barboza-Tello M. El aseguramiento universal en el Perú: La Reforma del financiamiento de la salud en perspectiva de derechos. *Rev Perú Med Exp Salud Pública*. 2009;26(2):243–247.
21. Organización Panamericana de la Salud. Organización Mundial de la Salud. Cuarto curso internacional de desarrollo de Sistemas de Salud en Latinoamérica. Nicaragua: 29 abril–15 de mayo 2009.
22. Ministerio de Salud del Perú. *Boletín Estadístico No. 5: Infraestructura Sanitaria en el Perú. Oficina Estadística e Informática*. Vol. 5, 2005.
23. Ministerio de Salud del Perú. Oficina General de Epidemiología. *Informe Análisis de la Respuesta Social*. 2002.
24. Organización Mundial de la Salud. *La Salud en las Américas 2007, Vol. 2: países*.
25. Establecimientos de Salud (EsSalud). Oficina Central de Planificación y Desarrollo. Gerencia de Planeamiento Corporativo.
26. Del Carmen Sara J. *El rol de las políticas y los planes: Objetivos de salud y Políticas de Recursos Humanos*. Toronto, Canadá: Reunión Regional de los Observatorios de RHUS; Octubre 2005.
27. World Health Organization. World Global Health Observatory data. Peru. http://www.who.int/gho/en/. 2015. Accessed June 22, 2016.
28. *Boletín Electrónico de Asociación Peruana de Facultades de Medicina*. Vol. 123. 2008 Disponible en: http://www.aspefam.org.pe/boletin_elec/Boletin%20123/Boletin%20123.htm.
29. Instituto Nacional de Estadística e Informática. Elaborado sobre la base de: a) Cuanto S.A. Anuário estadístico. Peru en números 2000. Cuadros 18.5; 17.2; 30.18; 30.37, b) MINSA—OPS. Cuentas Nacionales de Peru. Lima 2001.
30. Luis Carranza Ugarte. *Presentación Situación y Perspectivas de la Economía Peruana*. Banco Central de Reserva, Ministerio de Economía y Finanzas—Perú. Ministro de Economía y Finanzas, Setiembre 2009.
31. Ministerio de Salud del Perú. Cuentas nacionales de salud. Perú, 1995–2005. Oficina General de Planeamiento y Presupuesto/Consorcio de Investigación Económica y Social. *Observatorio de la Salud*. Lima: Ministerio de Salud del Perú; 2008.
32. Mejoras metodologicas de la información de cuentas nacionales de salud, 1999–2000.
33. MINSA-SEPS-OPS. *Equidad en la Atención de Salud 1997*. Lima: septiembre 1999.
34. Instituto Nacional de Estadística e Informática. *Encuesta Demográfica y de Salud Familiar IV*.
35. Instituto Nacional de Estadística e Informática. *Encuesta Demográfica y de Salud Familiar (ENDES) 2007–2008*.
36. UN Inter-agency Group for Child Mortality Estimation. Mortality rate, children < 5. http://data.worldbank.org/indicator/SH.DYN.MORT. 2016. Accessed November 24, 2016.

37. Instituto Nacional de Estadística e Informática. *Perú: Estimaciones y Proyecciones de la Población por Años Calendario y Edades Simple 1970–2025*. Lima: INEI; 1995.
38. Ministerio de Salud. *Análisis de la Situación de Salud de Perú 2005: Dirección General de Epidemiología*. Lima, Perú. Julio 2006.
39. Instituto Cuánto. Anuario estadístico: Perú en números, 2005.
40. Instituto Nacional de Estadística e Informática. *La Pobreza en el Perú 2003–2004*. 2005.
41. Organización Panamericana de la Salud. *Perú: Perfil de País. Salud en las Américas*. 2007.
42. World Bank. 2014. World Bank indicators: Peru. The poverty level in 2012 was 25.8% of the population. www.data.worldbank.org/indicator/SI.POV.GINI. Accessed October 20, 2016.
43. Instituto Nacional de Estadística e Informática. Encuesta Nacional de Hogares (ENAHO Continua 2006, 2007, 2008).
44. World Health Organization. *WHO Country Cooperation Strategy: Peru at a Glance*. www.who.int/iris/bitstream/10665/246214/1/ccbrief_per_en.pdf. Geneva: WHO; 2016. Accessed October 20, 2016.

CHAPTER 9

Brazil

Marcia Cristina Zago Novaretti, Mark Anthony Cwiek, and **Antonio Pires Barbosa**

▸ Country Description

TABLE 9-1 Brazil

Nationality	Noun: Brazilian(s) Adjective: Brazilian
Ethnic groups	White 47.7%, Mulatto (mixed white and black) 43.1%, Black 7.6%, Asian 1.1%, Indigenous 0.4% (2010 est.)
Religions	Roman Catholic 64.6%, other Catholic 0.4%, Protestant 22.2% (includes Adventist 6.5%, Assembly of God 2.0%, Christian Congregation of Brazil 1.2%, Universal Kingdom of God 1.0%, other Protestant 11.5%), other Christian 0.7%, Spiritist 2.2%, other 1.4%, none 8%, unspecified 0.4% (2010 est.)
Language	Portuguese (official and most widely spoken); English and Spanish (most focused on by second-language learners; less common: German, Italian, Japanese, many minor Amerindian languages
Literacy	Definition: Age 15 and over can read and write. Total population: 92.6% Male: 92.2% Female: 92.9% (2015 est.)
Government type	Federal presidential republic
Date of independence	September 7, 1822 (from Portugal)
Gross Domestic Product (GDP) per capita	$15,600 (2015 est.)

(continues)

TABLE 9-1 Brazil (continued)

Unemployment rate	9.0% (2015 est.)
Natural hazards	Recurring droughts in northeast; floods and occasional frost in south
Environment: current issues	Amazon Basin deforestation destroys habitat and endangers a multitude of local indigenous plants and animals; lucrative illegal wildlife trade; air and water pollution in Rio de Janeiro, São Paulo, and several other large cities; land degradation and water pollution from improper mining activities; wetland degradation; severe oil spills
Population	205,823,665 (July 2016 est.)
Age structure	0–14 years: 22.79% (male 23,905,185/female 22,994,222) 15–24 years: 16.43% (male 17,146,060/female 16,661,163) 25–54 years: 43.84% (male 44,750,568/female 45,489,430) 55–64 years: 8.89% (male 8,637,011/female 9,656,370) 65 years and over: 8.06% (male 7,059,944/female 9,523,712) (2016 est.)
Median age	Total: 31.6 years Male: 30.7 years Female: 32.4 years (2016 est.)
Population growth rate	0.75% (2016 est.)
Birth rate	14.3 births/1,000 population (2016 est.)
Death rate	687 deaths/100,000 population (2016 est.)
Disease burden	**Communicable disease deaths:** 93/100,000 population **Noncommunicable disease deaths:** 514/100,000 population **Injury deaths:** 80/100,000 population (2016 est.)
Net migration rate	−0.1 migrant(s)/1,000 population (2016 est.)
Gender ratio	At birth: 1.05 male(s)/female 0–14 years: 1.04 male(s)/female 15–24 years: 1.03 male(s)/female 25–54 years: 0.98 male(s)/female 55–64 years: 0.89 male(s)/female 65 years and over: 0.74 male(s)/female Total population: 0.97 male(s)/female (2016 est.)
Infant mortality rate	Total: 18 deaths/1,000 live births Male: 21.2 deaths/1,000 live births Female: 14.7 deaths/1,000 live births (2016 est.)
Life expectancy at birth	Total population: 73.8 years Male: 70.2 years Female: 77.5 years (2016 est.)
Total fertility rate	1.76 children born/woman (2016 est.)

TABLE 9-1 Brazil (continued)	
HIV/AIDS adult prevalence rate	0.58% (2015 est.)
Number of people living with HIV/AIDS	826,7000 (2015 est.)
HIV/AIDS deaths	15,300 (2015 est.)

Data from Central Intelligence Agency. The World Fact Book, 2014: Brazil. https://www.cia.gov/library/publications/the-world-factbook/geos/br.html. Accessed October 5, 2014. The United Nations: UNAIDS. http://www.unaids.org/en/regionscountries/countries/brazil/. Accessed October 5, 2014. EU Business School. The languages spoken in Brazil. http://www.studycountry.com/guide/BR-language.htm. 2016. Accessed October 27, 2016.

History

Brazil was discovered in 1500 by Portuguese explorer Pedro Cabral, more or less by accident, as part of a journey to find India by traveling west on the Atlantic Ocean to secure trade and treasure and to advance the Catholic faith.[1] For more than three centuries it remained a colony of Portugal. In 1882 Brazil gained its independence and maintained a monarchical form of government until slavery was abolished in 1888, and then in 1889 the formation of a republic was proclaimed by the military.[2] Political control of Brazil was dominated by its coffee growers and exporters until populist leader Getulio Vargas ascended in 1930 to power.[3] Populist and military government existed for greater than a half century until 1985, when the military regime peacefully ceded power to civilian rulers.[4] Brazil continues to this day to be governed in the federal republic model.

Size and Geography

Brazil is by far the largest and most populated country in South America, bordering the Atlantic Ocean for 7,491 kilometers and sharing land borders with Argentina, Bolivia, Colombia, French Guiana, Guyana, Paraguay, Peru, Suriname, Uruguay, and Venezuela. It enjoys the fifth largest area mass in the world; with over 8.5 million square kilometers, it is the largest country in the southern hemisphere.[3] There are now over 202 million people living in Brazil, and nearly 85% of the population lives in urban areas. With nearly 20 million people, São Paulo is the largest urban area in Brazil, followed by Rio de Janeiro with about 12 million inhabitants. Brasilia, the nation's capital, has approximately 3.8 million citizens. Urbanization has been occurring at the rate of approximately 1.15% per year.[3] The climate is mostly tropical, including the Amazon rain forest, but it is more temperate in the southern part of the country.

Brazil continues to be the net recipient of immigrants, with the Southeast region being the prime relocation area (Brazil officially has five Major Regions; see **FIGURE 9-1**). In the mid-19th century the importation of African slaves was made illegal, and Brazil sought Europeans to work in agriculture—particularly in the coffee growing business, including Italians, Portuguese, Spanish, and Germans—and later, Japanese. More recently, immigrants have come from Argentina, Chile, and the Andean countries (many as unskilled illegal migrants) or are returning Brazilian nationals.[3]

While Brazil has a growing middle class (estimated to be more than half of the population), poverty and unequal income levels remain high. This is particularly true in the Northeast, North, and Central-West regions, and disproportionately so for women, blacks, mixed-race, and indigenous populations. These disparities lead to a sense of social exclusion and contribute to Brazil's high crime rate, with violent crime found in densely populated urban areas and favelas (slums).[3]

Government and Political System

The conventional long-form name of the country of Brazil is *República Federativa do Brasil*, and in English, this is translated as *Federative Republic of Brazil*. As the long-form name implies, Brazil is a federal republic, which means that the powers vested in the central government through the Brazilian constitution are restricted, and in which the component parts (states and municipalities) retain a degree of self-government. The constitution of Brazil is considered the supreme law of the country, and health care is guaranteed as a constitutional right. The ultimate sovereign power remains with the voters, who retain the ability to choose their governmental representatives in the voting process.[3]

There are 26 states and a federal district (Brasilia) represented in the federal Brazilian government, and

FIGURE 9-1 Map of Brazil
© Bardocz Peter/Shutterstock

each state has its own governor and legislature. The 1988 constitution (as amended over time) extends broad powers to the federal government, made up of executive, legislative, and judicial branches. The president is the head of the executive branch, holds office for 4 years—with the right to reelection for an additional 4-year term—and appoints the cabinet. The president may unilaterally intervene in state affairs, and the president serves as both head of the state and head of the government.[5]

There is a bicameral legislature consisting of an upper Federal Senate and a lower Chamber of Deputies. The 81 senators are elected for 8 years, and the 513 deputies are elected for 4 years. Each state is eligible for a minimum of 8 seats in the chamber, the largest state delegation (São Paulo's), and it is capped at 70 seats.[6] The main political parties include the Brazilian Democratic Movement, the Democrat, the Democratic Labor, the Brazilian Social Democracy, the Workers, and the Progressive.[7]

The third branch of government is the Judiciary, and the highest court is the Supreme Federal Court, with 11 justices. There are various subordinate courts, including the Federal Appeals Court, the Superior Court of Justice, the Superior Electoral Court, regional federal courts, and the state court system.[6]

Macroeconomics

Major Industries and Where They Are Located

Brazil enjoys several well-developed economic sectors, including agricultural, manufacturing, mining, and service industries, as well as the development of its vast interior. Brazil has abundant natural resources, a large labor pool, and a growing middle class. Brazil's economy is very large in comparison to all of the other South American countries, and it is becoming an even greater presence in the world markets.

Since 2003, Brazil has steadily enhanced its macroeconomic stability, reducing its debt burden by shifting it toward real denominated and domestically held instruments and by building up foreign reserves. In 2008, Brazil became a net external creditor, and two ratings agencies awarded investment-grade status to its debt. After strong growth in 2007 and 2008, the global financial crisis rocked Brazil. Brazil experienced two quarters of recession as global demand for Brazil's commodity-based exports constricted and external credit withered. On the other hand, Brazil was one of the first emerging markets to begin recovering. In 2010, consumer and investor confidence revived, and GDP growth reached 7.5%, the highest growth rate in the past 25 years. Rising inflation led the authorities to take measures to slow down the economy. These steps and the world's economic slowdown affected Brazil's growth potential in 2011–2013.

Brazil's traditionally high level of income disparity has declined for each of the last 14 years. Brazil is an attractive location for foreign investors because of its historically high interest rates. The unemployment in recent years has been at historic lows, but it began rising again, to over 9%, in 2015.[3] The government has been compelled to intervene in foreign exchange markets and raise taxes on some foreign capital inflows, as large capital inflows over the past several years have contributed to the appreciation of the currency, which has harmed Brazilian manufacturing to an appreciable extent. Dilma Rousseff, president from 2011 to 2016, retained the previous administration's commitment to a floating exchange rate, fiscal restraint, and inflation targeting by the central bank.[3]

The 10 main export destinations for Brazilian products in 2012 were China (41.2%), United States (26.7%), Argentina (18.0%), Netherlands (15.0%), Japan (8.0%), Germany (7.3%), India (5.6%), Venezuela (5.1%), Chile (4.6%), and Italy (4.6%). The 10 main countries from where Brazil imported products in 2012 were China (34.2%), United States (32.4%), Argentina (16.4%), Germany (14.2%), South Korea (9.1%), Nigeria (1.2%), Japan (1.1%), Italy (1.1%), France (1%), and India (1.0%). Brazil is the largest exporter of soybean and soybean oil to China, and it exports iron ore in large quantities for Chinese steel production. The main products Brazil imports from China are electric equipment, machines, and mineral fuels. The main products exported to the United States are mineral fuel, oil, iron, steel, machinery, and beverages. The top import categories are machinery, mineral fuel, aircraft, electrical machinery, and optic and medical instruments.[8]

Infrastructure and Transportation

As of 2010, there were over 1.58 million kilometers of roadways in Brazil.[3] The Brazilian-paved highway system is one of the largest in the world, but it is seen as inadequate for the growing needs of the country. Great efforts were made to improve the roadways for the 2014 FIFA World Cup and for the 2016 Olympic Games and to better connect the industrial parts of the nation with the less developed areas. An estimated 1.2 billion people travel the highways in Brazil each year.[9] Railways were nationalized in Brazil in the past, but today rail services are under the control of various public and private operators. There are approximately 50 major commercial airports in the country, with more than 115 million air passengers yearly.[9]

Approximately 90% of Brazil's power is secured from hydroelectric plants, and fossil fuel and nuclear plants have met the remainder of the power needs. By law, only state-owned power companies can produce power in Brazil, and this has proven a fairly reliable system to date.[9] Brazil is blessed with approximately 50,000 kilometers of navigable waterways. There are 15 or so major seaports and harbors along the coast and the Amazon and Paraguay Rivers.[9]

Demographics

Age Distribution of the Population

Brazil is the sixth most populated country in the world at just over 205 million people in 2016, representing approximately 2.8% of the world's overall population. It was not until the year 2013 that Brazil first exceeded a population of 200 million, and it continues rising faster than previously estimated largely due to its expanding middle class that enjoys a longer lifespan than their parents' generation.[10] As of 2016 there was favorable age distribution in Brazil, with nearly 40% of the population under 25 years of age and with just over 8% of the population 65 years and over.[3]

Like many industrialized countries, Brazil has experienced a decline in fertility rate since the 1970s, when women had an average of 4 children. The birth rate in 2016 was estimated to be 1.76 children per woman, largely attributed to more women entering the workforce and electing to wait longer before having offspring. It is estimated that the birth rate will decline to 1.5 by 2034 and will remain approximately at that level through 2060.[10] It is projected that the current favorable age structure will begin to shift around 2025, with the labor force shrinking somewhat and the elderly starting to represent an increasing share of the total population. Poverty among the elderly has been nearly eliminated due to funded public pensions, and Bolsa Familia and other social programs have lifted tens of millions out of poverty.[3]

Education Levels of Population

The literacy rate in Brazil (age 15 and over who can read and write) in 2016 was 92.6%.[3] The federal government of Brazil regulates education through the Ministry of Education, which sets forth guiding principles for education programs throughout the country. Federal funding is used to develop state and local education programs. The national budget for education in 2006 was 4.3% of GDP, and the federal government intends to increase this number over time to 7.0%.[6] The compulsory level of education in Brazil is 9 years, compared to 12 years in the United States, Great Britain, and Peru; 13 years in Germany and Argentina; and 8 years in Turkey and Bolivia.[11] Approximately 11.0% of the working-age population has a university degree, and college graduates earn on average 2.5 times as much as those without degrees and 5.0 times as much as the majority who never complete secondary school. There are approximately 2,400 universities or colleges of further education in Brazil, the majority of which are private institutions.[12]

Religion

In census data, approximately 90% of the Brazilian population has revealed that they subscribe to some religious ideal, making it more religiously inclined than any other South American country.[9] Brazil is, and has historically been, made up largely of members of the Catholic faith (nearly 65% of the population identifies itself in this manner), and another 22% of the population identifies itself as Protestant Christian.[3] Today, there are more Catholics in Brazil than in any other county of the world. Only about 1% of the population identifies itself today as not believing in God or a supreme being.[9]

The Catholic faith was brought to Brazil when Portuguese and other European settlers arrived with the aim of "civilizing" the local native people. Churches, schools, and hospitals were built, all buttressing the doctrines of the Catholic faith. In the 19th century, Catholicism was made the official religion of Brazil, which meant that Catholic priests were paid a salary by the government, and the Catholic hierarchy was included in the political affairs of the country. As such, Catholicism became an integral part of the administration of Brazil and of its people, and many of the Brazilian festivals are based on the Catholic religion.[9]

Protestant denominations in Brazil include Methodist, Episcopal, Pentecostal, Lutheran, Baptist, and nondenominational Protestant. Non-Christian religions include Judaism, Islam, Buddhism, Shintoism, Rastafarianism, Candomblé, Umbanda, and Spiritism.[9]

Distribution of Major Morbidity in the Country

The following top 10 causes of death in Brazil as of 2014 are provided here, per 100,000 population, with the World Health Ranking of each cause: coronary heart disease 74.74 (World Health Ranking 117); stroke 66.71 (113); influenza and pneumonia 43.59 (73); diabetes mellitus 39.74 (51); hypertension 33.67 (18); violence 30.53 (13); lung disease 24.52 (51); road traffic accidents 24.13 (42); prostate cancer 22.52 (47); and breast cancer 16.91 (81).[13]

▸ Brief History of the Healthcare System

The story of the Brazilian healthcare system is connected deeply to the political, economic, demographic, and social changes that occurred through the centuries. Brazil was a colony of Portugal from 1500 until 1822, when it gained political independence. During these centuries, gold, gemstones, and many other natural resources were transferred to Portugal, and Portugal left Brazilian natives and most of its immigrants in extreme poverty. Slavery persisted in Brazil for more than two centuries. During this period, raw materials were also used for payment to the English who intermediated slave trade worldwide. In 1888 slavery was abolished. Brazil turned into a federal republic in a relatively peaceful process in 1889, and this remains the political form of government to the present time.

Healthcare in the Colonial Period (1500–1808)

In the colonial period, Brazil was under the political, economic, and cultural control of Portugal. The first news that arrived in Europe about Brazil was description of a new land characterized by naïve native Indians and exuberant tropical flora and fauna, resembling an idyllic paradise. Based on these reports, countless expeditions sailed to the New Continent with the purpose of finding gold and securing rapid wealth. These adventurous men were soldiers, beggars, fugitives, and people with financial problems in their homeland. They brought with them numerous diseases, such as tuberculosis, syphilis, malaria, gonorrhea, and measles. Pestilent diseases and local wars contributed enormously to the extermination of many native Indian tribes. Smallpox was brought to Brazil by slaves and became the main cause of death in the colony.[14]

The combination of indigenous conflict, disease, and inadequate sanitation led Portugal to deploy, as early as the sixteenth century, people appointed to positions of chief physician and chief surgeon. However, few doctors chose to venture across the ocean to work in Brazil. In 1746, there were only six medical doctors who had graduated in Europe and who were available in all of Brazil. Healers and traditional healers, although prohibited by law to act as medical doctors, were frequently consulted and were respected by the population.[14]

The organization of health care during this period was in its most primal form. During the colonial period, there were no hospitals in Brazil that were similar to those that existed in Europe. There were only the so-called *santa casas*, large infirmaries maintained by the Jesuits. The first *santa casa* was installed in Olinda (Northeast region) in 1539. After that, they were installed in Santos (1543), Bahia (1549), São Paulo (1560), Rio de Janeiro (1582), and Belem (1619). Today there are *santa casas* in almost all cities in Brazil, many of them in small cities. It is relevant that the *santa casa* system in many ways led to future government-sponsored healthcare assistance in Brazil.[15]

Healthcare During the Imperial Phase (1808–1888)

Napoleon invaded Portugal in 1808, necessitating Dom João VI, King of Portugal, and his entourage to transfer royal activities to Brazil. The king established the first schools of medicine in Brazil, in the state of Bahia and then in Rio de Janeiro. The opening of ports to other countries allowed an increase of commerce and economic prosperity in the country. Cultural and social life flourished, and Rio de Janeiro was brought into a golden age. International artists, scientists, engineers, architects, and lawyers visited Rio de Janeiro, and some of them moved to Brazil.

Health-related programs and structures were developed to provide better health care to the Portuguese court, including vaccination against smallpox and sanitary control of ports and epidemics. In spite of this, from 1820 to 1840 yellow fever, smallpox, measles, and typhoid fever epidemics devastated Rio de Janeiro, leaving more than 4,000 dead in a single year (1849). The imperial government established the first Public Health Care Commission, with the purpose of developing sanitation policies and epidemic control procedures. Soon thereafter, a Central Public Hygiene Joint Commission started controlling medical activities, vaccinations, food handling, pharmacies, and public health planning.

The general public's access to health care improved during the imperial phase. However, these new programs and strategies did not effectively control the epidemics of that time. Tuberculosis was not the focus of sanitary vigilance during the imperial phase because it was more commonly found among slaves. Yellow fever caused more deaths among Europeans, and it was easier to control yellow fever, so yellow fever was emphasized in terms of medical attention. Hospitals were created specifically to isolate tuberculosis patients in an attempt to control the dissemination of this disease.[15]

Healthcare in the Old Republic Period (1889–1930)

The Old Republic period can be characterized as the time of a "liberal oligarchic state." The federal government emphasized immigration to bolster the economy's agricultural workforce after the abolition of slavery. Consequently, efforts were necessary to control pestilential diseases and other widespread diseases (tuberculosis, syphilis, and rural endemic diseases) that were common in the imperial phase. This was especially true for protection of the coffee farms and for the incipient industries that were developing.

Rio de Janeiro and São Paulo developed effective measures against yellow fever, smallpox, and typhoid fever, but there was a lack of focus on the fight against tuberculosis.[14] At the end of 19th and the beginning of the 20th centuries, Dr. Clemente Ferreira from São Paulo initiated a philanthropic action, Leagues Against Tuberculosis, that spread all over Brazil. These leagues provided epidemiological data and economic analysis and promoted an effective interaction with the government. Public institutes for healthcare research and assistance were launched in São Paulo (Butantan Institute, Emilio Ribas Institute, Biological Institute) and in Rio de Janeiro (Oswaldo Cruz Institute).

A Federal Law in 1904 established a healthcare crusade to eradicate yellow fever through mandatory vaccination, which then precipitated the Vaccination Revolt. Large parts of the population resisted the exposure of women's arms to strangers for vaccination, as well as the mandatory forced entry into homes by police and health workers to conduct vaccination. There were physical confrontations, looting, and civil disobedience, culminating in the deaths of several civilians. The government was considered responsible for the mayhem, and subsequently it repealed the mandatory vaccine program, instead settling on a more acceptable optional vaccination approach.

In 1920, a new concept of sanitary vigilance was implemented that introduced sanitary education and specific departments for the vigilance and control of other diseases, such as leprosy and venereal diseases. Hospital assistance, pediatric care, and endemic rural diseases—such as Chagas disease, schistosomiasis, malaria, filariasis, trachoma infection, and leishmaniasis—gained attention with specific programs. The Special Strategic Health Care Service was created during the Second World War with the mission to provide health care in a strategic manner, and it continued after the war to provide services to underrepresented areas.[15]

Healthcare During the Vargas Dictatorship (1930–1945)

During the time that Getulio Vargas was in control, known as the "authoritarianism period," the president governed through federal decrees until 1934, when a new Federal Constitution was published. Reforms institutionalized public health through the Ministry of Education and Public Health and institutionalized social security and occupational health through the Ministry of Labor, Industry, and Commerce. Intensification of public health campaigns against yellow fever, tuberculosis, rural endemic diseases, and nutritional deficiencies reached most of the Brazilian states. Pension institutes extended insurance security to the majority of urban workers.[14,16]

Healthcare in the Post-Vargas Era to 1988

After the Vargas deposition, there was a period of democratic instability until 1964 that was characterized by rapid urbanization, immigration, and the first arrival of the automobile industry in Brazil. Although the creation of the Ministry of Health (1953) allowed a better organization of health assistance, the public health system was fragmented and made up of several unconnected programs. During this period, there was an expansion of hospital care and an emergence of the private healthcare sector.

During the time of the military dictatorship (1964–1985), the public health budget reductions resulted in the recrudescence of dengue, meningitis, and malaria. Public health care was chaotic, and the Brazilian quality of life stagnated. Nevertheless, during the 1970s Brazil experienced impressive economic growth with disproportional improvement of quality of life for the most privileged in society. Significant advances for the general population occurred only in 1983 when an interministerial project, Integrated Actions in Health, simultaneously incorporated prevention, therapeutics, and education in health care. The National Social Security Healthcare Institute funded states and municipalities to expand healthcare coverage. The period of military government was hallmarked by a number of political interventions that provided privileges to the private medical sector.[16]

Healthcare in the Era of Democracy (1988–Present)

At the end of the 1980s and the beginning of the 1990s, an economic crisis engulfed Brazil and contributed to a great loss of income and hyperinflation. Fernando Collor de Mello, the president elected in 1990, facilitated policies that expanded importation of goods and that generated significant unemployment—with loss of almost 920,000 jobs in a single fiscal year. He was impeached in 1992 with allegations of corruption.

The Brazilian Federal Constitution (BFC) published in 1988 drove the country toward a completely new health system beyond major political and social changes. The insertion of health as a "citizen's right and duty of the state," earlier in the Eighth National Health Conference in 1986 and reinforced in BFC (art. 196), established a new dynamic to the social welfare model in the country.[17,18] It made possible the creation of the Universal Health System (SUS), composed of the core traits of equity, comprehensiveness, universality, and decentralization of health care.[17] SUS brought important developments in organization of health care, cooperation between public and private sectors, and social participation in control of policies and services.[18,19] Consequently, health care in Brazil was segmented into two large nuclei of assistance: SUS, directed to the whole population and emphasizing primary care, and the private healthcare (or supplemental) system, for that portion of the population insured with private health plans. Since then, the evolution of the Brazilian health system has shown substantial differences, mainly due to an inability of the government to meet and to guarantee Federal Constitution healthcare principles. TABLE 9-2 shows the key differences between SUS and private health care in Brazil.

Brazil began the process for acquiring and distributing free antiretroviral drugs (medications that hinder the multiplication of HIV) in 1988, and it is recognized as one of few countries that provide free treatment for all HIV-infected individuals. In 1994, Brazil set a course for economic stability after the institution of the Plano Real, a currency and monetary reform model. Incomes began to recover, although in a sporadic fashion. The Family Health Program also was set up in 1994, but it is not yet fully implemented in all Brazilian cities, even though it is considered a key component of the SUS.[18]

The SUS has gone through several phases since its inception. In the initial years (1990–2002), management focused on role differentiation among the federal, state, and municipal levels. The federal Ministry of Health served in the regulatory and policy-making function, delegating to the states and municipalities the responsibilities for activities related to high- and intermediate-complexity healthcare levels.[19] During this period, the basis of regulation consisted of establishing operational mechanisms for financial transfers for three levels of care (primary care, medium complexity care, and high-complexity care) on a productivity basis, similar to the "fee-for-service" model. Simultaneously, the private sector cost-control actions focused on the more expensive clinical procedures and the requirement for prospective authorizations for high-complexity cases.

In 1999, the National Health Surveillance Agency was formed with the responsibility of surveillance and control of healthcare services and products in Brazil.[20] A few months later, the Supplementary Health Care Agency was established to regulate and oversee private healthcare plans.[21] The generic drug program in Brazil, based on the American and Canadian models, was launched in 1999 and allowed access to medications

TABLE 9-2 Major Differences Between Public (SUS) and Private Health Care in Brazil After 1988

	Public Health Care (SUS)	Private Health Care
Population coverage	All individuals on Brazilian soil (citizens or not)	Exclusively for healthcare plan subscribers
Focus	Primary care, including hospital care	Both outpatient and hospital care
Funding	Federal fiscal resources	Individual and employer payments
Management	Federal, state, and municipal	Targeted by functions (providers and payers)
Sanitary and health vigilance activities	Yes	No
Pharmaceutical assistance	Yes, for primary care	Only for inpatient care
Scope	Entire liability of high-cost therapeutics, procedures, and transplants	Restricted to therapeutics on a list of treatment and procedures; revised periodically
Investments in infrastructure	Low	High
Investments in technology	Low	High
Compensation for health professionals	Low—causing reduced efficiency and high personnel rotation	Adequate for market changes

for large portions of the population. The generic drug program gained rapid popularity and support from employers and the general population.[22]

A constitutional amendment was passed in 2000 that defined the duties of federal, state, and municipal governments as related to SUS financing, and it determined the minimum percentage allocation of public budgets for health care. In the second phase (2002–2006), there was an expansion of SUS services among the Brazilian states. A National Mobile Emergency Care system (similar to 911 in the United States) was set up in Brazil in 2003, effectively reducing deaths and severe injuries.

In 2006, the Pact for Health Act established within the SUS prioritized health prevention and promotion standards. This program was originally conceived in 1998, and it progressively became an effective health policy reaching over 55% of Brazilians in 2012. The Pact for Health also expanded the Family Health Program and its multiprofessional family health support teams to all Brazilian states. In 2006, the Health Promotion Program, the National Primary Care Policy, and the National Oral Health Policy provided substantial advances in health care, especially for underprivileged populations. At the same time, new legal requirements went into place to protect consumer rights and to promote changes in the private sector, with the purpose of ensuring mechanisms for access to private hospitals and for the maintenance of financial reserves for the third-party payer market.

From 2008 to the present, the Brazilian public health system has been incorporating the concept of service networks. There are five Healthcare Service Networks: (1) an Urgent and Emergency Network, designed for acute events of trauma, cardiovascular diseases, stroke, and acute complications of chronic and other disorders; (2) a Maternal Infant Network (or "stork network," *rede cegonha*), focused on women's pediatric and perinatal care; (3) a Chronic Diseases Network, focused on chronic hypertension, diabetes mellitus, and oncology; (4) a Psycho-Social Network, focused on mental health care and alcohol and drug addiction; and (5) a Special Needs People Network, focused on rehabilitation and social reintegration of individuals, post-acute events.[19] In the private sector, the implementation of quality programs (ISO, National Organization Certification) and international accreditation (Joint Commission) in hospitals and clinics became more common, and it validated a commitment to excellence in patient care and safety. Recently, there has been a merging of clinics, hospitals, and healthcare insurance providers under large employee pension plans.

The present system is now well in place, and it is a source of national pride because of the steady improvement in access to healthcare services and the overall improvement in healthcare status and quality indicators. These gains, however, are not exclusively a consequence of the Brazilian healthcare model. Over the last few years, Brazil also has stabilized economically, and it has evolved toward the preservation of democratic values and the search for equity and justice for all of its citizens, today and into the future.

▸ Description of the Current Healthcare System

A poll in 2013 showed that health care is the top priority for Brazilians.[24] The majority of the population, almost 74%, has depended exclusively on the Brazilian public healthcare (SUS) system. SUS is a hierarchized, universal, and integrated system. Although the Brazilian public healthcare plan requires universality of coverage, it is still not a reality. Brazilian health care is available to every person who needs health care in the country, whether or not the individual happens to be a Brazilian citizen. This kind of healthcare system generates an immigration influx from other Latin American countries, especially when people from afar are presented with a diagnosis of a severe and/or complex disease (cancer, cardiac surgery, or brain surgery, for example). There are no reimbursement compacts for health care among the Latin American countries. Consequently, even though Brazil has spent more on health care in the last decade, it does not reflect necessarily that it has yet to achieve the highest level of healthcare services and outcomes.

The Brazilian public healthcare system provides a wide range of services, from primary care to highly complex surgical procedures. However, these broad-scoped services are not yet fully available in all Brazilian states. In some states, where the public healthcare services are well organized, internal immigration from other Brazilian states are a daily reality. Located in the state of São Paulo (in the Southeast region of the country), Clinicas Hospital Complex, with 2,200 inpatient beds in 2016, it has been the largest university hospital in Braziland. Almost 3% of all admissions relate to patients from other Brazilian states.[25] Therefore, it is very difficult to develop a comprehensive strategic plan for public healthcare services due to intensive internal and external immigration realities and funding restrictions.

Facilities

The Brazilian healthcare system has been marked by inequity. In October 2016, total beds available for both public and private settings were 438,623, which represented 2.1 beds per 1,000 inhabitants. According to the National Standards, the minimum of beds available should be of 2.5 to 3.0 per 1,000, so in 2016 there was a gap of 75,936 to 178,848 beds throughout the country. There has been a slow decline in the number of total hospital beds in Brazil since 2004.[26] Of total existing beds in October 2016, 129,727 were exclusively for non-SUS individuals, resulting in 2.5 beds per 1,000 inhabitants. However, bed distribution varied from state to state in number and in complexity of health care. Despite the efforts made by the federal government in the last 10 years, there still has been a lack of beds, particularly for intensive care, neonatal intensive care, oncology, and emergency care for the public healthcare sector. In intensive care (adults, pediatric, neonatal, and burns), there were 41,559 total beds available, or 2.02 beds per 10,000 inhabitants in October 2016. However, while there were 1.32 intensive care beds per 10,000 inhabitants for public care, there were 4.11 intensive care beds per 10,000 for nonpublic care. In the state of Maranhão (Northeastern region) there was only 1.00 intensive care bed per 10,000 inhabitants in two hospitals, far less than the state of Rio de Janeiro (Southeastern region), which had 3.54 intensive care beds per 10,000 inhabitants in 47 hospitals.[27]

There were 269,708 healthcare facilities registered in Brazil in 2013, 28.8% of them public. Of this total, 104,316 provided medical consultation for spontaneous demand, and of these, 37.4% were public institutions. The Brazilian healthcare system consisted of approximately 5,208 general hospitals, 1,096 specialized hospitals, 1,524 day-hospitals, 1,214 general emergency care units, and 127 specialized emergency care units. About 61.3% of healthcare facilities were designed for patients referred from primary or emergency care. A total of 133,683 medical offices were distributed throughout Brazil, mainly in the Southeast region (52.7%).[28]

In May 2014, there were 45,045 public primary care units registered, 29.9% in the Southeast region; 23 fluvial mobile healthcare units provided primary care in remote areas, mainly in the Amazon region, and 368 healthcare clinical locations were provided to Brazilian natives. There were 4,338 mobile emergency units interspersed throughout the country. In Brazil, there were 4,326 blood testing sites, and 39.3% of them were found in the Southeast region in 2014.

According to the Brazilian Institute of Geographics and Statistics, almost 42.1% of all Brazilians lived in the Southeast region during that time. In 2012 and 2013, there were 163 public centers for obesity care developed as a result of the substantial percentage of overweight (50.8%) and obese (17.5%) people living in Brazil.[28]

Pharmaceutical assistance in Brazil is composed of a generic drug program, free medication distribution at public primary care units, and an agreement with pharmacies throughout the country to promote the free distribution of subsidized medicines. The Brazilian Generic Drugs Program, based on similar programs found in the United States and Canada, was initiated 25 years ago with the goal to increase access to medications and maintain low cost. Today, there are more than 21,000 generic drugs in the formulary for treatment of almost 80% of most common diseases in the country. The number of pharmacies was the highest in the world, with 91,000 in 2014, resulting in a proportion of 1 pharmacy per 2,088 inhabitants—substantially higher than that recommended by the World Health Organization of 1 pharmacy per 10,000 inhabitants.[29] This huge number of pharmacies brings about inspection difficulties, especially in towns located far from large urban centers.

Workforce

More healthcare personnel are needed in Brazil, and in a better dispersion pattern throughout the nation. According to the Brazilian Demographic Study 2013, Brazil had 1.86 practicing physicians per 1,000 population, which was far below that of Argentina (3.1 per 1,000).[30] The physician distribution in Brazil has been unequal and markedly concentrated in larger cities. In the North region there were only 1.01 physicians per 1,000, while in the Southeast there were 2.67 per 1,000 inhabitants in 2013. In Maranhão state (Northeastern region), the density of physicians was only 0.70 per 1,000. The number of physicians overall has increased over the past 30 years, especially due to the opening of private medical schools.[30]

The Brazilian physician profile has been changing dramatically. Since 2009, the number of female doctors graduated surpassed males, and by 2013 female doctors represented 54.50% of practicing physicians under 29 years of age.[31] In 2013, the average age of all physicians in active practice in the country was 46.20 years, including non-specialists, generalists, and specialists. In 2013, it was estimated that there were in Brazil 415,265 physicians (57.18% men and 42.82% women).[32] Approximately 215,640 physicians

(55.50%) worked in government settings at federal, state, and municipal levels. The number of generalist physicians was approximately 180,136 (43.50%), but they were not heterogeneously distributed. Although 56.40% of physicians worked in the Southeast region, there were 1.09 generalists per 1,000 inhabitants in this region in 2013. Specialists represented 53.60%, and of these 29% had two or more Brazilian board certifications. The North and Northeast regions had fewer specialist than generalists with ratios of 0.81 and 0.92, respectively.[32]

Brazil had the largest number of dentists in the world in 2013, in proportion to the overall population, with approximately 219,575 in active practice. However, the distribution of dentists has been marked by inequity. About 59% of all Brazilian dentists worked in the Southeast region. Two-thirds of them were active in private clinics, and there was ongoing difficulty in getting dentists to work regularly in small cities. Consequently, the majority of Brazilians have not had access to ongoing dental care because they depend exclusively on public health care.[32]

The Brazilian Federal Board of Nursing estimated that there were 1.7 million health professionals (excluding physicians and dentists) in Brazil in 2012. The number of registered nurses reported was 1.43 per 1,000 inhabitants, which is below the minimum recommended by WHO of 2.00 per 1,000 inhabitants.[33] Approximately 53.5% of nurses were actively working in the Southeast region. During that time, there were also 6.30 practical nurses per 1,000 inhabitants. The majority of nursing professionals was 26–45 years old (71.2%) and female (87.2%).[34]

Technology and Equipment

There have been substantial efforts made to increase the availability of diagnostic capabilities in Brazil. Even though federal regulation, Portaria 1101, recommended one magnetic resonance imaging (MRI) unit per 500,000 inhabitants, the proportion of MRI units in use in Brazil in October 2016 was approximately 1.0 per million population. In comparison, at that time, the Organisation for Economic Co-operation and Development (OECD) average was 9.80 MRI units per million. For nonpublic health care, there were 1.57 MRI units per million population in Brazil, while in public setting care there were only 0.59 MRI units per million. Unfortunately, the distribution of MRI units has been unequal among Brazilian states and between the public and private sectors. The Southeast region accounted for 51.9% of total MRI units available in Brazil and 36.9% were exclusively for the private sector in 2016.

According to the National Standards, the number of computed tomography (CT) scanners was adequate at 1.95 per million population as of October 2016; however, there were 2.90 times more of these CT units available to the non-SUS population. The data shown here demonstrate how the National Standards for healthcare equipment is outdated. It was published in 2002, and medical therapies and diagnostics have progressed dramatically since then.[31]

▸ Evolution of the Healthcare System in Brazil

Cost Approach

Unlike the health systems from other OECD member countries, the Health System in Brazil (called Sistema Unico de Saude, SUS) was defined in constitutional principles and specific legislation.[17] Also established was the contribution of fiscal resources from the central government, the federal states, and the municipalities. The Brazilian Federal Constitution (BFC) also allowed for the involvement of private resources in the provision of services to Brazilian citizens.[17,20]

The system to finance and fund health assistance was organized in two categories: a public system, theoretically responsible for providing universal coverage to the population of 205 million people, and a private (supplementary) system, providing care to 49 million users who are covered by health insurance.[35] The private system is financed by individuals/families (approximately 48% of the total) or companies (approximately 52% of the total), provided as an employment benefit to employees.[27]

The coverage provided to the user of the public system contemplates three areas of direct care and areas of technical support, as follows[19]:

- Primary care—in extensive modalities to the whole population
- Care of medium and high complexity—in outpatient and inpatient forms
- Pharmaceutical assistance, with free-of-charge medications, by component:
    - *Basic component*—primary care medication, including for maternal and infant care and for some chronic illnesses.
    - *Strategic component*—medication for endemic illnesses that have an economic impact. Among these, the most important items include biopharmaceuticals, blood products, and medication for the treatment of HIV/AIDS, tuberculosis, and leprosy.

- *Speciality component*—high-cost medication for the care of special pathologies; regulated by protocols and clinical-therapeutic guidelines.

Furthermore, the public system sets aside resources from its budget for sanitary and epidemiological surveillance, investments in replacement of medical technology facilities, and training of human resources and management in its three levels.

The coverage provided by the private system is organized by means of assistance networks, integrated by clinics and private practices, outpatient diagnostic centers, hospitals, and day (day care) hospitals. The suppliers of care, in general, adhere to the following models: (1) units owned by health insurance companies; (2) units owned by philanthropic or not-for-profit organizations; (3) private units; (4) clinics, practices, and units of autonomous physicians or other healthcare professionals. Access to these units is regulated according to the degree of complexity of care and restricted to those covered by health insurance. Generally, these units are able to perform consultations, diagnostic tests, hospital admissions and procedures, and—depending on the contract format—between service providers and health plan companies.[36]

The public healthcare system can arrange for services and procedures of high complexity from non-profit organizations. These services and procedures are regulated by a system of information and central authorization, for example the execution of procedural diagnoses by MRI and CT scanners, cancer treatment, organ and bone marrow transplantation, invasive vascular procedures, physical rehabilitation, and the dispensing of high-cost medications.[37,38]

Total Expenditure for Health Care in Brazil and Its Evolution

Like in other parts of the world, the expenditures for health care in Brazil have increased at a rate higher than the economic growth rate. According to data from the National Congress and the National Agency for Supplementary Health, the budget for SUS grew 95.0% in real terms between 2001 and 2011, with greater impact on the resources of federal states and municipalities.[39] For instance, between 2006 and 2011, the budget (adjusted for inflation rates) of the public system increased by 41.7%, which corresponds to a variation of US $51.6 billion to $95.4 billion. In the meantime, the covered population increased from 174.0 million to 193.5 million citizens.[40] Among the most important causes of this growth are the increased frequency of chronic degenerative diseases, a reflection of the aging population, and external causes (especially trauma), a result of the incorporation of a substantial portion of the covered population.

The total expenditure for health care in Brazil varied between 8.0% and 8.5% of the GDP from 2005–2014, with budget growth typically above inflation. In 2009, 8.5% of the GDP was the total expenditure for health care. Of this, 57.6% was spent by the private sector. Similarly, spending within the private funding system has evolved with the incorporation of a large contingent of citizens as a result of decreased unemployment rates found in the country. Data from the National Agency for Supplementary Health demonstrate that between 2001 and 2013, the population with health care financed by families and companies (by the private system) leaped from 31 million users to the current 49 million users.[42]

In 2011, the annual per capita expense from the public system reached approximately US $511, with SUS having provided more than 11.3 million hospitalizations, 3.3 million surgeries, 11.3 thousand transplants, 531.0 million consultations, and 3.7 million ambulatory procedures. In the same year, the per capita expense of the private system reached $1,029, having produced 6.6 million hospitalizations and 255.0 million consultations and ambulatory procedures.[43]

Structure of the Public Services

It is the consensus among managers and healthcare professionals in Brazil that the implementation of SUS considerably increased the access to primary care and to emergency services. As a result, for instance, there has been a greatly improved rate of prenatal care and immunization.[44] Many changes have taken place to make SUS more effective in providing healthcare assistance. There are considerable efforts being made to improve the quality of primary care as well as to reduce the rate of hospitalizations. The introduction in 2011 of a federal program to measure the performance of primary care units is one adopted approach that has already shown promising results.[45]

As a trend, the Brazilian federal government also decided to become less dependent on the importation of strategic medicines. A federal plan was initiated with the installation of public companies devoted to producing blood derivatives. For example, to support federal healthcare programs that provide free medication to all AIDS positive and hepatitis C positive people, as well as other high-cost medicines and vaccines, publicly held pharmaceutical laboratories (including Farmanguinhos, Fundação para o Remédio Popular, São Paulo's Instituto Butantan) were modernized and received substantial grants.

In 2006, SUS initiated a series of changes to promote improvement in the operations at local and state levels, with the institution of decision-making boards and the emphasis on primary care. These changes brought about an intense program of medical and health education and the implementation of family health teams (which include 1 general physician, 1 nurse, practical nurses, and community agents) responsible for the care of communities of up to 1,000 families and the management of the use of health resources in each segment. As of 2012, there were 33,404 teams in the Family Health Program and 257,265 community agents, reaching 54.8% of the national population.

Another important initiative took place in 2011 with the creation of Healthcare Service Networks, which were based on conditions that required integrated services of several units and specialized equipment. The networks were coordinated by a unique information, communication, and control system. Throughout 2012 and 2013, some networks were implemented, including networks for urgent and emergency care, networks for perinatal care, networks for chronic conditions, and networks for psychosocial care. These networks provide care and rehabilitation programs for conditions such as cardiovascular and cerebrovascular emergencies and trauma, the cycle of pregnancy to birth to one year of life, hypertension, diabetes, cancer, and mental disturbances including addiction.[46]

Quality

Between 1990 and 2010, there were a few indicators of improvement in the health of the population, such as a decrease in maternal mortality from 143.2 to 68.2 per 1,000 inhabitants and a decrease in infant mortality from 45.3 to 16.0 per 1,000 live births.[48] This improvement seems to be related to improvements in sanitation and drinking water—both determinants of health but not directly within the scope of action coordinated by SUS—as well as the development of health programs related to maternal and infant health, perinatal care, breast feeding, oral rehydration, and vaccine campaigns.[27] In addition, in the South and Southeast, regions that concentrate the greatest share of population and the greatest volume of industrial production, infant mortality rates range between 9.0 and 13.0 deaths per 1,000 live births. When one considers the first 5 years of life, the child mortality rate was 17.7 per 1,000 children in general, and in industrialized areas it was 16.0 per 1,000, during this time frame.[47]

Infant Mortality

The main causes of childhood mortality in Brazil are associated with perinatal conditions and respiratory diseases. For people between 15 and 40 years of age, mortality is due mainly to external causes (traffic accidents, chiefly), and for people older than 40, mortality is due to cancer and cardiovascular and cerebrovascular diseases. With the implementation of the Networks of Care, the levels of morbidity and mortality have dropped appreciably. For example, the implementation of the Maternal Infant Network, between 2010 and 2013 in the North and Northeast regions, produced a 56% decrease of maternal mortality in these regions.[48]

Other Health Indicators

Immunization program coverage rates for children are high, and they are improving for the elderly. The vaccination rate varies between 83% and 97% for the population at risk. Recently, the immunization against hepatitis B, HPV in preadolescent girls, and influenza gained more attention.[49] It is hoped that in the end, there will be a decrease in demand for hepatic transplants, fewer cervix cancer cases, and a reduction of influenza complications for populations at risk.

Another point that deserves attention relates to the increase of Family Health Program coverage (PSF) for the population users of SUS. Between 1998 and 2012, the proportion of the population covered by PSF decreased from 6.58% to 54.40%.[48] The degree of coverage varied by region and municipality. In 1998 only 9.41% of the population residing in municipalities with less than 20,000 inhabits were covered by the program, and in 2010, the coverage for this group reached nearly 80.00%.[42] One of the positive observations from the program is that the higher the coverage within PSF in a group of municipalities, the greater the decrease in postneonatal infant mortality—associated with a decrease in the number of deaths due to diarrhea and respiratory infections.[50] Other studies suggest a reduction of 15% of avoidable hospitalizations in the years following 1999.[51]

Access

Equity/Universality

The coverage of the public healthcare system in Brazil, as mentioned before, is universal and includes also the population otherwise covered by health insurance plans. The main differences between the two models relate to available structures in terms of hospitality, readiness, and assertiveness. Due to a lack of coordination between supply and demand within the system, the concept of "systemic regulation" emerged. That is, it has developed that access to available resources is largely free, and access to resources that are more complex requires special authorization. Often, because of a lack of generally agreed-upon protocols and therapeutic guidelines, one can observe the installation of mechanisms for managing resources that do not meet the real needs of users in terms of availability, time, and quality. One of the consequences has been an observed increase in lawsuits by disgruntled users pursuing fulfilment of their perceived constitutional rights.[52]

Despite these issues, there have been substantial improvements in standards of care, with new models of procurement of public services by nongovernmental organizations and with installation of the system of regulatory mechanisms that are based on scientific evidence and/or protocols for economic evaluation of healthcare activities.

The supply of healthcare services has been impacted by changes in demographic characteristics, educational and cultural levels, economic production, and industrial and urban concentrations in different regions of the country. One of the consequences is the concentration of resources of greater complexity in large cities and states in the South and Southeast regions. The distribution of users of health insurance plans is similar, with large participation in the South and Southeast regions, where some cities have over 45% of their populations with health insurance coverage. Wide dispersions in health insurance coverage exist in other states and regions. In one capital of the North region, for example, about 20% of the population maintains a health plan or private health insurance.[17]

▸ Current and Emerging Issues and Challenges

As in other developed countries, Brazil is witnessing important demographic and epidemiological transitions that are at the root of national healthcare system problems. Brazil faces rapid aging of the population and consequent increases in the prevalence of chronic degenerative diseases. Coupled with this, there is growth in morbidity and mortality in younger populations due to external causes. Projections from IBGE, the National Geographic and Statistic Institute, estimate a stabilization of population around 217 million between 2030 and 2035.[53] These issues will require deep changes in the profile of health facilities, especially in the public sector.

The following issues in Brazilian health care are in need of resolution:

- Addressing the financial and allocation alternatives for provision of resources that complement the current cost models, even if this means an increase in overall spending;
- Restructuring healthcare facilities so as to treat more effectively chronic diseases and their complications;
- Incorporating new medical technologies;[54]
- Implementing a rigorous approach to ensure high standards of quality and safety for users and patients in outpatient and inpatient settings, especially in mid- and high-complexity care;
- Reviewing medical education programs, with an eye on the use of evidence-based care protocols and assessments of economical approaches;[54]
- Promoting outpatient and home care;
- Implementing a national electronic health registry that allows the system to identify and evaluate major situations of overspending and off-protocol therapeutic treatments and procedures;[54]
- Reviewing the role of health boards, currently responsible for local health control and political influence in determining spending on municipal and state levels;
- Reviewing and restraining the judiciary, with the goal to reduce interference in the determination of not-scientifically-proven therapeutic procedures, such as in dubious and experimental treatments of cancer; and
- Preventing and controlling emerging epidemics, such as those caused by dengue, Zika, and chikungunya viruses.

Solutions to these issues will require the cooperation of multiple stakeholders and interest groups in both the public and private sectors. Indeed, one must understand that the Federal Constitution was enacted in a peculiar historical moment at the end of the military period during the transition to full democracy.[17] At that time, many of the approved platforms of the constitutional body included the incorporation of citizen rights and obligations, for which the government had not identified financial resources. As a consequence of this movement, the system now exhibits a series of malfunctions and process failures to which health managers and planners devote much time and effort. For example, investments in new beds and adding new critical care units have been virtually stymied in the public system since the 2000s.

The private system, in turn, has seen important conflicts arise among payers, hospitals, and physicians related to standards of compensation. The private sector, together with some nonprofit organizations, has been largely responsible for the implementation of newer medical technologies and in "making their case" through clinical/economic evaluation studies. Competition continues between funds and payers in this area, as the natural result of entities wishing to attract and increase their number of users in the system.

An emerging epidemic caused by the Zika virus has spread in Brazil. It is thought that the Zika virus infection was brought onto Brazilian soil in 2013 during the Confederation Soccer Championship. This virus has been rapidly transmitted to different Brazilian states because its vector, the *Aedes aegypti* mosquito, is highly prevalent in Brazil. As of April 2016, Zika virus infection has been reported throughout all of Brazil. Approximately 80% of adult-infected individuals are asymptomatic. The most common symptoms are fever, joint pain, rash, and conjunctivitis. In those who develop symptoms, the disease is usually mild and lasts from several days to a week.[55] There are reports of Guillain-Barré syndrome in adults also affected by Zika virus infection. In fetuses, Zika virus can be devastating. The Brazilian Secretary of Health has confirmed over 2,063 newborns with microcephaly due to Zika virus, and more than 3,505 were under investigation from November 2015 to October 2016.[56] It has been suggested that Zika virus infection can also cause arthrogryposis, brain calcifications, excessive and redundant scalp skin and arthrogryposis in newborns, so some researchers use the term "congenital Zika syndrome."[57] Pregnant women are advised to use appropriate insect repellents and long clothing.

The following represent the myriad health care actors, interests, associated problems, and possible resolution alternatives that can be identified for Brazil's foreseeable future:

- *Customers/patients* are individuals who expect immediate access and positive clinical results in the system. There is widespread overuse of the healthcare system, especially when individuals are not satisfied with the treatment that has been rendered and then they simply go elsewhere for additional and/or different treatment. Amelioration may occur with the implementation of the Brazilian National Electronic Health Records that will allow for monitoring of public health actions in real time.
- *Public system providers* (including public hospitals and public ambulatory care units) are caregivers who often are perceived as not as accountable as providers in the private system. Payments to public sector providers are often substantially less than payments in the private sector, so public sector productivity is often not as high, and complacency is often seen as more acceptable than what is typically found in the private sector. Improvements are contingent on the establishment of new contractual relationships that reward productivity and eliminate ineffective practices. Improvements may also depend on important changes in legislation dealing with organized labor in the public sector, in terms of curtailing certain worker rights.
- *Private system providers* (including private hospitals and clinics) generally seek to optimize mark-up and profitability margins for healthcare services rendered, and they face strong pressure on prices based on negotiations with third-party payers. In Brazil, physicians are considered part of the private system, in terms of offering private services to clinic outpatients and hospital inpatients.
- *Third-party payers* are important in the private sector and predominantly represent insurance companies and health plans. Third-party payers depend on the performance of the economy as a whole and therefore are vulnerable to periods of economic downturn and low production. Third-party payers need to develop funding mechanisms to help weather economic slumps and to allow smaller carriers to avoid closure or merging.
- *Federal government* provides a major regulatory element of the system and is responsible for the administration of budgetary resources for the public system. The federal government faces ongoing problems with the changing epidemiological profile and the transitioning geodemographic and structural aspects of the system. A major point of discussion is the need for more resources from the social security budget and the pressure to expand scope of assistance. For example, an argument has surfaced in recent times that even diapers should be covered by the public system. The federal government generally has guided its healthcare activities toward overall equity of access and universal coverage.
- *The judiciary and legal systems* interpret the Federal Constitution healthcare mandates and strive to balance the need for protections of individual rights. At times, the courts have been a factor of imbalance in overall health planning as they consider coverage claims in both the private and public healthcare systems, often without sufficiently evaluating technical issues of healthcare assistance on a scientific basis. To remedy this, the courts should defer to an administrative mechanism

that verifies a priori the effectiveness of clinical modalities based on best evidence and outcomes research grounded in scientific methodology.

- *The medical technology and pharmaceutical industries* are greatly affected by infusion of foreign capital. There is a predominance of launching products that have higher markups. The sector underwent a major overhaul recently with the introduction of the production of essential and strategic items (e.g., generics) within Brazil in order to reduce the dependence on imported medicines.

The political situation in Brazil took an extraordinary turn in May 2016, when Brazil's Senate voted to convene a presidential impeachment trial of Dilma Rousseff, who then was suspended from her executive duties and was replaced by Michel Temer, who stepped up from vice president to acting president. The Senate voted overwhelmingly in favor of conviction of Rousseff, so Temer will serve the remainder of Rousseff's term until January 1, 2019.[3] In the meantime, there has been great uncertainty as to what may occur next in the political arena in Brazil, including the possibility of further corruption investigations and prosecutions of other political office holders.[58] An ongoing federal investigation called Operation Car Wash (Operação Lava Jato) has implicated officials at all levels in Brazilian government, and many prosecutions have resulted.[59] The full impact of all this on health care in Brazil remains uncertain.

There are many aspects of the Brazilian healthcare experience that are worthy of being benchmarks in other countries, particularly as related to overall coverage of the population and conceptual innovation. There are many opportunities to extend and improve quality of care, both in the public and private systems. In essence, the Brazilian healthcare system has been a unique construction of Brazilian society, and one can expect that the following will be maintained into the future: the pursuit of equity, universal access, community-level participation in its control, and broad collaboration from all players in the planning and design of the model.

References

1. Smith A. *A History of Brazil*. New York: Routledge; 2013.
2. Fausto B. *A Concise History of Brazil*. Cambridge, UK: Cambridge University Press; 1999.
3. Central Intelligence Agency. *The World Factbook*. Brazil. https://www.cia.gov/library/publications/the-world-factbook/geos/br.html. Published and updated March 1, 2016. Accessed October 27, 2016.
4. Levine R. *The History of Brazil*. Westport, CT: Greenwood; 1999.
5. Michigan State University. globalEDGE: Brazil. http://globaledge.msu.edu/countries/brazil/government. Published 2016. Accessed October 27, 2016.
6. Farlex. The Free Dictionary: Brazil. http://encyclopedia2.thefreedictionary.com/Brazil. Published 2016. Accessed October 27, 2016.
7. Mello J. The Brazil Business. Political parties in Brazil. http://thebrazilbusiness.com/article/political-parties-in-brazil. Published and updated October 11, 2013. Accessed October 27, 2016.
8. Farah A. The Brazil Business. Largest trading partners for Brazil. http://thebrazilbusiness.com/article/largest-trading-partners-of-brazil. Published and updated October 24, 2013. Accessed October 27, 2016.
9. Brazil.org. http://www.brazil.org.za. Published and updated March 23, 2016. Accessed October 27, 2016.
10. World Population Review: Brazil. http://worldpopulationreview.com/countries/brazil-population/. Published and updated March 2016. Accessed October 27, 2016.
11. Nation Master. Compulsory education duration: countries compared. http://www.nationmaster.com/country-info/stats/Education/Compulsary-education-duration. Published 2012. Accessed October 27, 2016.
12. *The Economist*. Higher education in Brazil: the mortarboard boom. http://www.economist.com/node/21562955/print. Published September 15, 2012. Accessed October 27, 2016.
13. WorldLifeExpectancy. World Health Rankings. http://www.worldlifeexpectancy.com/country-health-profile/brazil. Published and updated May 2014. Accessed October 27, 2016.
14. Bertolli Filho C. *História da Saúde Pública no Brasil*. São Paulo. 11th ed. Atica, Brazil; 2008.
15. Rosemberg AMF. Breve historia da saúde pública no Brasil. In: Rouquayrol MZ & Gurgel M. *Epidemiologia & Saúde*. 7th ed. Medbook, Rio de Janeiro; 2013.
16. Paim J, Travassos C, Almeida C, Bahia L, Macinko J. The Brazilian health system: history, advances, and challenges. *Lancet*. 2011;377(9779):1778–1779.
17. Mendes A, Marques RM. Saúde e Sociedade. Democracia, saúde pública e universalidade: o difícil caminhar. *Saúde e Sociedade*. 2007;16(3):35–51.
18. Agência Nacional de Vigilância Sanitária. Registros de medicamentos. http://www.anvisa.gov.br/medicamentos/registro/index.htm. Published September 2016. Accessed November 1, 2016.
19. Brasil - Ministério da Saude. Norma operacional da assistência à Saude - NOAS - SUS. http://bvsms.saude.gov.br/bvs/saudelegis/gm/2002/prt0373_27_02_2002.html. Published February 27, 2002. Accessed April 4, 2016.
20. Brasil. Lei 9961 de 28 janeiro de 2000. Cria a Agencia Nacional de Saude Suplementar e dá outras providencias. http://www.planalto.gov.br/ccivil_03/leis/L9961.htm. Published and updated 2004. Accessed March 25, 2016.
21. Brasil. Emenda Constitucional n.º 29 de 13 setembro de 2000. Altera os arts. 34, 35, 156 e 198 da Constituição Federal de 1988 e dá outras providências. http://www.planalto.gov.br/ccivil_03/constituicao/Emendas/Emc/emc29.htm. Published September 14, 2000. Accessed March 25, 2016.
22. Brasil. Lei 9.787, de 10 de fevereiro de 1999. Altera a Lei n.º 6.360, de 26 de setembro de 1976, que dispõe sobre a vigilância sanitária, estabelece o medicamento genérico, dispõe sobre a

23. Barbosa EC. 25 Anos do Sistema Único de Saúde: Conquistas e Desafios. *Revista de Gestão em Sistemas de Saúde*. 2013;2(2):85-102.
24. Nielsen. Saúde é a maior preocupação do brasileiro, aponta pesquisa da Nielsen. Pesquisa de Confiança do Consumidor do 1.º trimestre de 2013.http://www.nielsen.com/br/pt/press-room/2013/saude-e-a-maior-preocupacao-do-brasileiro-aponta-pesquisa-da-nielsen.html. Published 2013. Accessed April 04, 2016.
25. Bassette F. Número de pacientes de outros Estados cresce 89% no HC. http://www1.folha.uol.com.br/fsp/cotidian/ff3105200611.html. Published May 31, 2006. Accessed April 12, 2016.
26. World Bank. Brazil data. http://data.worldbank.org/country/brazil. Published and updated 2016. Accessed March 25, 2016.
27. Portaria n.º 1101/GM. (2002, 12 de junho). Parâmetros de cobertura de assistência do Sistema Único de Saúde. http://www1.saude.ba.gov.br/regulasaude/2009/PN%20PORTARIAS%202009/nvos%20pdfs%202009/PT%20GM%201101%2012.06.2002.pdf. Published 2012. Accessed April 4, 2016.
28. Vigitel 2014 Vigilância de fatores de risco e proteção para doenças crônicas por inquérito telefônico. http://www.abeso.org.br/uploads/downloads/80/553a243c4b9f3.pdf. Published 2014. Accessed November 1, 2016.
29. Folha De S. Paulo, Datafolha / Instituto de Ciência, Tecnologia e Qualidade [internet]: Censo Demográfico Farmacêutico. http://folha.com/no1399934. Published January 20, 2014. Accessed March 25, 2016.
30. World Health Organization. Global Health Observatory data repository. http://apps.who.int/gho/data/node.main.A1444. Published 2013. Accessed March 25, 2016.
31. CREMESP. Demografia médica no Brasil. http://www.cremesp.org.br/pdfs/DemografiaMedicaBrasilVol2.pdf. Published February, 2013. Accessed March 25, 2016.
32. Demografia Médica no Brasil 2: Cenários e Indicadores de Distribuição (PDF). Conselho Federal de Medicina (CFM) Tabela 7—Distribuição de médicos registrados (CFM) por 1.000 habitantes, segundo Unidades da Federação. Brasil; 2013:256.
33. World Health Organization. Working together for health. *World Health Report 2006*. Geneva, Switzerland: WHO; 237.
34. A Enfermagem. Perfil da enfermagem. http://aenfermagem.com.br/materia/perfil-da-enfermagem/. Published 2012. Accessed November 1, 2016.
35. ANS - Agencia Nacional de Saude Suplementar. - Cadernos de informação em Saude. http://www.ans.gov.br/index.php/a-ans/sala-de-noticias-ans/numeros-do-setor/1485-ans-publica-caderno-de-informacao-da-saude-suplementar-. Published December, 2013. Accessed March 25, 2016.
36. Agencia Nacional de Saude Suplementar. Guia ANS de Planos de Saude. http://www.ans.gov.br/index.php/planos-de-saude-e-operadoras/contratacao-e-troca-de-plano. Published 2013. Accessed March 25, 2016.
37. Agencia Nacional de Saúde Suplementar. Nova listagem de coberturas obrigatórias entra em vigor. http://www.ans.gov.br/sala-de-imprensa/releases/consumidor/1268-nova-listagem-de-coberturas-obrigatorias-entre-em-vigor-?highlight=WyJjYZXNvbHVcdTAwZTdcdTAwZjVlcyIsInNvYnJlIiwicm9sIiwiZGUiLCJwcm9jZWRpbWVudG9zIiJ3Byb2NlZGltZW50b3MiLCJzb2JyZSByb2wiLCJzb2JyZSByb2wgZGUiLCJyb2wgZGUiLCJyb2wgZGUgcHJvY2VkaW1lbnRvcyIsImRlIHByb2NlZGltZW50b3MiXQ. Published 2011. Accessed November 1, 2016.
38. Associação Nacional de Hospitais Privados. Observatório, 2015. http://anahp.com.br/produtos-anahp/observatorio/observatorio-anahp-ingles-2015. Published 2016. Accessed November 1, 2016.
39. Brasil. Câmara dos Deputados. Consultoria de Orçamento e Fiscalização Financeira. Nucleo de Saude, 2011. http://www2.camara.leg.br/a-camara/estruturaadm. Published and updated 2016. Accessed March 25, 2016.
40. Brasil - Ministério da Saude - Indicadores e Dados Básicos - IDB - 2012 - E - Indicadores de Recursos. http://tabnet.datasus.gov.br/cgi/tabcgi.exe?idb2012/e0601.def. Published 2012. Accessed March 25, 2016.
41. Brasil. MS. Indicadores e Dados Básicos - IDB - 2009 - E - 4 - Indicadores de recursos - Gasto com consumo percentual em saude sobre PIB ajustado, por setor. http://tabnet.datasus.gov.br/cgi/idb2012/e04.htm. Published 2012. Accessed March 25, 2016.
42. ANS - Agencia Nacional de Saude Suplementar - ANS - Caderno de informaçaõ da saude suplementar - 2011. http://www.ans.gov.br/images/stories/Materiais_para_pesquisa/Perfil_setor/Caderno_informacao_saude_suplementar/2013_mes12_caderno_informacao.pdf. Published December, 2013. Accessed March 25, 2016.
43. Brasil. MS. Informações de Saude - Indicadores de produção assistencial 2015.http://www2.datasus.gov.br/DATASUS/index.php?area=0202&id=19451&VObj=http://tabnet.datasus.gov.br/cgi/deftohtm.exe?sih/cnv/qr. Published 2015. Accessed November 1, 2016.
44. Bahia L. A privatização no sistema de saúde brasileiro nos anos 2000: tendências e justificação In: Santos NR, Amarante PD, orgs, *Gestão Pública e Relação Público Privado na Saúde*. Rio de Janeiro: Cebes; 2011.
45. Marins M, Daher DV. O programa nacional de melhoria do acesso e qualidade da atenção básica (PMAQ-AB). Relato de experiência. *Revista Enfermagem Profissional*. 2014;1(2), 331–337.
46. Brasil. Indicadores de transição do Pacto pela Saude e Contrato Organizativo da Ação Pública de Saude (COAP); 2012. http://tabnet.datasus.gov.br/cgi/pacto/2012/pactmap.htm. Published February 27, 2015. Accessed March 25, 2016.
47. Brasil - Ministério da Saude - Indicadores e Dados Básicos - IDB - 2012-3 Indicadores epidemiológicos - Taxas de mortalidade infantil. http://tabnet.datasus.gov.br/cgi/idb2012/matriz.htm#mort. Published 2016. Accessed March 25, 2016.
48. Brasil. Portal da Saude. Rede Cegonha - Indicadores de impacto sobre a assistencia integrada. http://dab.saude.gov.br/portaldab/ape_redecegonha.php. Published 2012. Accessed March 25, 2016.
49. Brasil. Portal da Saude. Programa Nacional de Imunização. http://pni.datasus.gov.br/sipni/documentos/Protocolo_MRC_vers%E3o_27-01-2015.pdf. Published 2015. Accessed April 07, 2016.
50. Rasella D, Aquino R, Barreto ML. Impact of the Family Health Program on the quality of vital information and reduction of child unattended deaths in Brazil: an ecological longitudinal study. *BMC Public Health*. 2010;10:380. doi:10.1186/1471-2458-10-380
51. Guanais F, Macinko J. Primary care and avoidable hospitalizations: evidence from Brazil. *J Ambul Care Manage*. 2009;32:114–121.

52. Diniz D, Machado TRC, Penalva J. A judicialização de saude no Distrito Federal, Brasil. *Ciência e Saude Coletiva*. 2014;19(2): 591–598. doi: 10.1590/1413-81232014192.23072012
53. Instituto Brasileiro de Geografia e Estatística - Projeção da população do Brasil por sexo e idade: 2000–2060. http://www.ibge.gov.br/home/estatistica/populacao/projecao_da_populacao/2013/. Published 2015. Accessed April 4, 2016.
54. Vecina Neto G. Malik AM - Gestão em Saude - Rio de Janeiro: Guanabara Koogan; 2011.
55. de Carvalho NS, de Carvalho BF, Fugaça CA, Dóris B, Biscaia ES. Zika virus infection during pregnancy and microcephaly occurrence: a review of literature and Brazilian data. *The Brazilian Journal of Infectious Diseases*. 20(3):282–289.
56. Saúde. http://combateaedes.saude.gov.br/images/pdf/informe_microcefalia_epidemiologico48.pdf. Published 2016. Accessed November 1, 2016.
57. Rasmussen SA, Jamieson DJ, Honein MA, Petersen LR. Zika virus and birth defects—reviewing the evidence for causality. *N Engl J Med*. 2016;374:1981–1987. doi: 10.1056/NEJMsr1604338
58. Anderson JL. A way forward for Brazil. *The New Yorker*. http://www.newyorker.com/news/daily-comment/a-way-forward-for-brazil. Published June 1, 2016. Accessed October 27, 2016.
59. Alves L. Brazil's former Speaker arrested on corruption charges. *The Rio Times*. http://riotimesonline.com/brazil-news/rio-politics/brazils-former-speaker-arrested-on-corruption-charges/. Published October 20, 2016. Accessed November 1, 2016.

CHAPTER 10

United Kingdom

John Lopes and **Marcus Longley**

▸ Country Description

TABLE 10-1	United Kingdom
Nationality	Noun: Briton(s), British (collective plural) Adjective: British
Ethnic groups	White 87.2%, Black/Afro-Caribbean 3.0%, Indian 2.3%, Pakistani 1.9%, Mixed 2.0%, Other 3.7% (2011 est.)
Religions	Christian (includes Anglican, Roman Catholic, Presbyterian, Methodist) 59.5%, Muslim 4.4%, Hindu 1.3%, other 2.0%, unspecified 7.2%, none 25.7% (2011 est.)
Language	English Recognized regional languages: Scottish (about 30% of the population of Scotland), Welsh (about 20% of the population of Wales), Irish (about 10% of the population of Northern Ireland), Cornish (2,000–3,000 in Cornwall) (2012 est.)
Literacy	Definition: Age 15 and over can read and write. Total population: Male: Female:
Government type	Parliamentary constitutional monarchy, a Commonwealth realm
Date of independence	April 12, 1927 (Royal and Parliamentary Titles Act established the name United Kingdom of Great Britain and Northern Ireland)*

(continues)

TABLE 10-1 United Kingdom (continued)	
Gross Domestic Product (GDP) per capita	$41,200 (2015 est.)
Unemployment rate	5.4% (2015 est.)
Natural hazards	Winter windstorms, floods
Environment: current issues	Continuing to reduce greenhouse gas emissions; by 2005 the government reduced the amount of industrial and commercial waste disposed of in landfill sites to 85% of 1998 levels and recycled or composted at least 25% of household waste, increasing to 33% by 2015
Population	64,430,428 (2016 est.)
Age structure	0–14 years: 17.44% (male 5,761,3411/female 5,476,649) 15–24 years: 12.50% (male 3,997,150/female 3,830,268) 25–54 years: 40.74% (male 43,367,242/female 12,883,674) 55–64 years: 11.77% (male 3,760,020/female 3,820,525) 65 years and over: 17.90% (male 5,710,542/female 6,363,047) (2016 est.)
Median age	Total: 40.5 years Male: 39.3 years Females: 41.7 years (2016 est.)
Population growth rate	0.53% (2016 est.)
Birth rate	12.1 births/1,000 population (2016 est.)
Death rate	409 deaths/100,000 population (2016 est.)
Disease burden	Communicable disease deaths: 29/100,000 population Noncommunicable disease deaths: 359/100,000 population Injury deaths: 22/100,000 population (2016 est.)
Net migration rate	2.5 migrant(s)/1,000 population (2016 est.)
Gender ratio	At birth: 1.05 male(s)/female Under 15 years: 1.05 male(s)/female 15–24 years: 1.04 male(s)/female 25–54 years: 1.04 male(s)/female 55–64 years: 0.98 male(s)/female 65 years and older 0.81 male(s)/female Total population: 0.81 male(s)/female (2016 est.)
Infant mortality rate	Total: 4.3 deaths/1,000 live births Male: 4.7 deaths/1,000 live births Female: 3.9 deaths/1,000 live births (2016 est.)
Life expectancy at birth	Total population: 80.7 years Male: 78.5 years Female: 83.0 years (2016 est.)

TABLE 10-1 United Kingdom (continued)

Total fertility rate	1.89 children born/woman (2016 est.)
HIV/AIDS adult prevalence rate	0.33% (2013 est.)
Number of people living with HIV/AIDS	126,700 (2013 est.)
HIV/AIDS deaths	< 600 (2013 est.)

*Earlier dates related to independence are 927 CE when minor English kingdoms united; March 3, 1284 when the Statute of Rhuddlan was enacted, uniting England and Wales; 1536 when the Acts of Union formally incorporated England and Wales; May 1, 1707 when Acts of Union formally united England and Scotland as Great Britain; January 1, 1801 when Acts of Union formally united Great Britain and Ireland as the United Kingdom of Great Britain and Ireland; December 6, 1921 when Anglo-Irish Treaty formalized partition of Ireland—six counties remain part of the United Kingdom and Northern Ireland.

Data from Central Intelligence Agency. The World Fact Book, 2008: United Kingdom. https://www.cia.gov/library/publications/the-world-factbook/geos/uk.html. Accessed November 18, 2008.

History

The United Kingdom is a sovereign nation composed of the four constituent countries of England, Scotland, Wales, and Northern Ireland. It is also commonly referred to as Great Britain and Northern Ireland. In the past, England was the dominant country, controlling all aspects of U.K. governance. However, Scotland, Wales, and Northern Ireland now have significant autonomy. As a result of the devolution of powers, each country is responsible for providing health care for its citizens. Because England is the largest of the countries, this chapter will concentrate on England's National Health Service (NHS).

The U.S. Central Intelligence Agency's *The World Factbook* has been collecting geographical, political, and demographic information on all countries of the world for almost two decades. The following demographic, economic, and political information regarding the United Kingdom has been extracted from the 2015 edition of the *The World Factbook*.[1]

At the height of its economic and political power in the 19th century, it was said that the sun never set on the British Empire. In the beginning of the 20th century, however, two world wars seriously diminished the Empire's political and economic hold on its territories. During the second half of the 20th century and continuing into the 21st, the United Kingdom rebuilt itself into a modern and prosperous European nation.

As one of the five permanent members of the United Nations Security Council, a founding member of the North Atlantic Treaty Organization, and the Commonwealth of Nations, the United Kingdom pursues a global approach to foreign policy. Although a member of the European Union, the United Kingdom chose to remain outside the Economic and Monetary Union and maintain its own currency. In 2016, the Conservative government scheduled a referendum on the United Kingdom's continued membership in the European Union, known as the Brexit (*British + exit*) referendum,[2] and although the vote was close, the United Kingdom is now prepared to exit the European Union. The vote was generally split between the young who wished to stay and the elderly who wished to exit. Further demographics indicate that Scotland and the areas around London were strongly in favor of staying. This change in the United Kingdom's relationship with the European Union will take a number of years to occur and will bear watching. The NHS is not expected to be directly influenced by this change.

Constitutional reform is also a significant issue in the United Kingdom. The Scottish Parliament, National Assembly for Wales, and the Northern Ireland Assembly were established in 1999, affording these countries a greater role in self-rule. In 2014, the United Kingdom survived a vote for Scottish independence.[3]

The United Kingdom has played a huge role in shaping the democratic political structure of many Western societies. As a country steeped in tradition and institutionalism, the United Kingdom does not have a common set of governing documents similar to the United States' Declaration of Independence, Constitution, or Bill of Rights. It is one of the few countries of the world without a written constitution. Rather, the English system of government traces many of its roots back to the Magna Carta of 1215, which outlined and protected certain individual rights. These rights were later validated and augmented through various Acts of Parliament over the subsequent 900 years. The result is a highly evolved democratic country in respect to certain individual freedoms while maintaining certain expectations from the government for what Americans might call socialized practices. Among one of these expectations is free and universal health care for all citizens.

Size and Geography

The United Kingdom is 241,590 square kilometers in size. This is equivalent to the U.S. state of Oregon. The bulk of the land is in agricultural use with 25% in crops and 46% in pasture. Natural resources include coal, petroleum, natural gas, tin, limestone, iron ore, and salt.

As an island nation, the United Kingdom is located at the northwest corner of Europe. With weather primarily influenced by the warm waters of the Gulf Stream, the climate is temperate despite the United Kingdom's relatively northern latitude. The average high temperature is approximately 17°C (63°F) with an average low of 3°C (37°F). Approximately 50% of days are overcast.

Population Centers

Approximately 64.00 million people inhabit the United Kingdom with just over 10.30 million people residing in the Greater London area (2015 estimate). Other larger urban centers include Manchester (2.65 million), Birmingham (2.56 million), and Glasgow (1.22 million). Approximately 82% of the population resides in areas classified as urban as illustrated in **FIGURE 10-1**.

Government or Political System

The United Kingdom's government is a constitutional monarchy. The chief of state is the monarch, currently Queen Elizabeth II. She holds her position by birthright, but she has no real governing role. The head of government is the prime minister (PM), the leader of the political party with the largest share of parliamentary seats. In 2016, Theresa May became PM, leader of the Conservative Party. The PM appoints cabinet members to run various government departments. Members of the cabinet are department heads and must be members of Parliament. The legislative branch is a bicameral parliament that consists of the House of Lords and House of Commons. The House of Lords currently has 760 seats, the vast majority held by life peers with members appointed by the monarch on advice of the PM. The House of Commons has 650 members popularly elected from single-seat constituencies; they serve five-year terms.

The judicial branch of government is the Supreme Court, established by the Constitutional Reform Act of 2005. The court consists of 12 justices selected by a judicial commission and appointed by the monarch upon the PM's recommendation.

At the last national election in 2015, the Conservative (Tory) Party won 36.8% of the popular vote, the Labour Party 30.5%, the Independence Party 12.7%, and the Liberal Democrats 7.9%.[4] This result gave the Conservatives a 12-vote majority in the House of Commons and control of the government.

In September 1997 a majority of voters in Scotland and Wales voted to establish a Scottish Parliament and a National Assembly for Wales. A semiautonomous government in Northern Ireland was established under what is commonly referred to as the Good Friday Agreement and was affirmed by voters in 1998. One area of responsibility that devolved under legislation passed by the U.K. Parliament was control over the delivery of healthcare services within each of the countries.[5] Each country has its own structure for planning, monitoring, and delivering healthcare services within its boundaries.

Macroeconomics

The United Kingdom has enjoyed one of the most prosperous periods of sustained growth in all of Europe. For its relatively small geographic size and relative scarcity of natural resources, the United Kingdom has the third largest economy in Europe, after Germany and France. As with many first-world economies, services are the primary drivers of the economy, particularly banking, insurance, and business services. Manufacturing still accounts for about 10% of economic output.

During the global economic downturn beginning in 2008, Gross Domestic Product (GDP) fell by 6.1% and did not return to pre-2008 levels until mid-2013.[6] The 2015 estimate for GDP was US $2.86 trillion with an estimated real growth rate of 2.5%. Nevertheless, government budgets remain in deficit with a number of austerity measures begun under the Conservative-Liberal Democrat coalition government in 2010 continuing under David Cameron's Tory-led government. The current government under Theresa May, estimates balancing the budget by 2020.

FIGURE 10-1 Map of the United Kingdom
© Bardocz Peter/Shutterstock

Major Industries, Ports and Airports, and Infrastructure and Transportation Development

Employed in the service sector are 8 out of 10 working Britons. About 1% work in agriculture, with the remainder in manufacturing. Major industries include aircraft/aerospace, railroad equipment, machine tools, electronics, chemicals, automobiles, and natural gas.

The United Kingdom is serviced by major airports located in London and Birmingham. There are 9 major seaports with container facilities located at Felixstone, London, and Southampton. There are 5 oil terminals and 1 liquefied natural gas terminal. Ground transportation is served by 395,000 kilometers of paved roads (3,519 kilometers of expressways) and 30,858 kilometers of railways. The United Kingdom maintains 3,200 kilometers of waterways (canals and rivers).

The United Kingdom boasts an advanced communications infrastructure with phone services provided by a mix of buried cable, microwave, and fiber-optic systems. The British Broadcasting Corporation (BBC) is the largest broadcasting system in the world, operating international, national, and local broadcasting operations. The BBC operates radio, television, and streaming services.

Demographics

Age Distribution of the Population

The estimated population of the United Kingdom in 2015 was 64,088,222.[1] The median age is 40.4 years (male 39.2, female 41.6). Annual growth rate of the population is 0.54% reflecting a birth rate of 12.70 per 1,000, a death rate of 9.35 per 100,000, and an immigration rate of 2.54 per 1000. The dependency ratio is 55.10%.

Education Levels of the Population

The United Kingdom has a literacy rate of 99%. This outcome is a result of state-funded education policy that mandates primary school attendance through age 16. The primary school population has been rising since 2009, but is projected to stabilize due to lowering birth rates.[7] As a result, attendance in secondary education (ages 11–18) is expected to increase as well. Approximately 47% of students elect to enter higher education (university).[8]

Major Religious Groups

For those citizen who profess a religious affiliation, the United Kingdom is predominantly Christian: about three-quarters Protestant and one-quarter Roman Catholic. There are also significant populations of Muslim, Sikh, and Hindu. The growth of these religions is due to increasing numbers of descendants of immigrants from countries formerly part of the British Empire and due to the expansion of the European Union.

▸ Brief History of the Healthcare System

Pre–World War II

The National Health Service (NHS) of the United Kingdom was established by Act of Parliament in 1946.[9] This action followed years of study and consideration by the government. The greatest changes in health care would be the nationalization of the hospital system, payment for care by the government, and universal coverage for all residents of the United Kingdom. By 1948, all of the pieces were in place for implementation, and on July 5, 1948, the NHS was born.

Before the establishment of the NHS, hospital services were provided by a combination of private *voluntary hospitals*, tax-supported public hospitals, and *cottage hospitals* in smaller communities and rural areas.[10] Specialty care was provided by hospital-based outpatient departments; primary care was delivered by community-based general practitioners (GPs).

Hospitals were established to provide medical care for sick, poor people. The wealthier classes were generally attended at home by their physicians. To provide this care, altruistic individuals might organize into charitable groups to raise the necessary funding for a hospital, or individuals might endow an established facility or the development of a hospital. Providing care free of charge initially, financial constraints generally led these hospitals to ask patients to voluntarily pay what they could toward the provision of care.

In the hospitals, appointed physicians and surgeons managed patient care. This staff provided general care for all conditions that were admitted. These staff appointments were few in number and were particularly prized. It was the goal of many resident medical officers to achieve an appointment to the attending staff. These staff positions did not pay well, if at all, and attending physicians supported themselves with fees from private patients and from medical students and resident medical officers who paid the attending physician or surgeon for training. In smaller cities, the hospital might be staffed with resident medical officers (trainees) overseen by local GPs and with regular visitations by out-of-town specialists. The voluntary hospitals saw themselves as providers of care for the acutely ill who would benefit from a short stay and treatment or surgery, and in many cases, patients with chronic illness and infectious diseases were turned away.

Public hospitals generally developed separately from the voluntary hospitals and infirmaries associated with workhouses.[10] Initially, the workhouses were intended for the able-bodied who were temporarily without work, but they increasingly became final destinations for the chronically ill, the elderly, and the mentally ill. In many instances, the number of infirmary beds quickly outnumbered the beds available for the indigent. These infirmaries were also facilities to which the voluntary hospitals would refer or transfer infected and chronically ill patients. In the early 20th century, local county governments took over the operation of the workhouses and infirmaries with some financial support from the central government, and the rest was made up by local taxes. Under the new arrangements, the counties could separate the hospital section of these institutions and assign them to public health committees for operation. Many local general hospitals in operation today began their existence as workhouse infirmaries, and some of these hospitals still use their original infirmary buildings.

Cottage hospitals were small rural facilities, generally established and attended by a local GP. A number of these hospitals are still in operation. Advantages to the cottage hospital are care closer to home and medical staff familiar with the health histories of the patients. Visiting consultants from the local general hospital or teaching hospital held specialty outpatient clinics.

Before the NHS, general practice was provided by apothecaries and physicians who were trained in the teaching hospitals and had returned to their communities to establish a practice or who failed to receive an appointment to a hospital staff position. Apothecaries traced their lineage to herb merchants who compounded and sold medicine preparations.[11] In the Rose decision of 1704, the House of Lords decided that apothecaries could both prescribe and dispense medicine for the treatment of illness, establishing apothecaries as the forefathers of the modern GP. In 1815, the apothecary society was given statutory authority to administer examinations and license doctors in England and Wales. In addition to seeing patients in surgery, GPs also visited patients in their home and attended deliveries at the request of midwives.

Before the establishment of the NHS, health care was paid for mostly out of pocket by those who could afford to. Voluntary and public hospitals provided inpatient care and some outpatient care to the poor for free or for whatever the patient could afford to pay toward their care. Beginning in the 19th century, trade unions, fraternal societies, and other groups established provident dispensaries, providing free medical care to their members and sometimes their families.[9] In most cases, primary care and prescriptions were paid for by the society; inpatient care was generally not covered because services were generally free at the local charitable or public hospital. Some societies also provided coverage for worker families for an additional fee. In the mid- to late 19th century, worker participation in these programs became compulsory. These provident societies collected a regular contribution from their members (essentially the forerunner of the prepaid health plan).

Government payment for health services was established in the United Kingdom when David Lloyd George introduced the Liberal Welfare Reforms between 1906 and 1914. One of these provisions was the 1911 National Health Insurance Act.[9] This act provided payment for workers' medical care, funded by employee, employer, and government contributions. Eligibility for care was subject to income limits. As with the provident society, payment through the National Insurance Act covered payment for GP services and drugs; hospital services were still provided by public and private hospitals for free. Dental and other services were not covered. It was after the 1911 Act that GPs generally chose to be paid under capitation arrangements with local insurance committees.

Post–World War II

The Department of Health

Each country in the United Kingdom (England, Wales, Scotland, and Northern Ireland) has a cabinet-level secretary or minister for health who makes political decisions on health care in general and on the NHS in particular. An individual country's health ministers are accountable to their respective legislative bodies. Some policies are generated from the central government in London and then implemented via the United Kingdom Department of Health (DH), the Scottish Executive Health Department, the Department of Health and Social Services in Wales, and the Department of Health, Social Services, and Public Safety of Northern Ireland. There are some differences in the structure and delivery of services in each of the four countries, but they are all based on the English system; thus, this chapter concentrates on the English NHS.

Government control of health care in the United Kingdom resides in the DH.[12] The DH has control over the NHS in England, and matters affecting health care are reserved under the devolution agreements.

The U.K. Parliament funds the DH and provides block grants to fund health services in the other countries. Each country's legislature is then responsible for allocating funds for their respective health services. England's responsibilities include:

- Creating national policies
- Providing long-term vision
- Providing funding for delivery and continuity of services
- Championing innovation and improvement
- Promoting honesty, openness, and transparency

BOX 10-1 lists the DH's priorities from 2016 to 2017. The DH is a ministerial department. It is headed by the secretary of state for health (also known as the health secretary). The secretary is appointed by the prime minister and is a sitting member of Parliament. The secretary is also assisted by a cabinet of ministers and under secretaries. See BOX 10-2 for a list of these offices and their responsibilities. Ministers and under secretaries are political appointees drawn from members of the House of Commons or the House of Lords.

The senior civil servant of the DH is the permanent undersecretary of state for health (permanent secretary) responsible for the day-to-day operation of the department.[12] The permanent secretary is also the chief accounting officer for the department and is responsible to the Parliament for how the department spends it appropriations. The permanent secretary chairs the Department Board. The Department Board is made up of department ministers and nondepartmental members responsible for setting departmental standards, establishing the framework for management of the department, assurance and management of risk and advising on the general budgeting in support of accomplishing the department's strategies. Board subcommittees further advise the Board on individual issues. The permanent secretary heads a management team of senior civil servants with specific duties. BOX 10-3 lists the DH management team.

The DH has seven key strategic objectives[13]:

- To improve local and national health outcomes through better commissioning and particularly by addressing poor outcomes and inequalities
- To help create the safest, highest quality health and care services
- To balance the NHS budget and improve efficiency and productivity
- To improve the NHS's ability to prevent ill health and to support people in living healthier lives
- To maintain and improve performance at or beyond care standards
- To improve care not provided in hospitals
- To support research, innovation, and growth

The DH is supported by and collaborates with a number of government agencies and partner organizations in the development and delivery of health and social care in the United Kingdom. A list of these bodies is shown in BOX 10-4.

The National Health Service

NHS England is an arm's length body (funded by the government to deliver a public service but operates independently from the government) that sets the priorities and direction of the NHS. NHS England is the commissioning body for primary care, pharmacy, dental, and other specialized services.[14] In contrast, the national health services of Wales and Scotland are more directly involved in the provision of both primary and secondary care.

The NHS was established by Act of Parliament in 1947 and was realized in 1948.[15] The NHS was the result of the tireless efforts of the minister of health at that time, Aneurin Bevan, and was based on three core principles:

- That it met the needs of everyone
- That it be free at the point of delivery
- That it be based on clinical need, not ability to pay

These three principles remain the core of the NHS as it delivers healthcare services to the citizens of the United Kingdom. In 2011, the DH published the NHS Constitution.[16] Within this document are seven key principles that guide the NHS in everything it does.

BOX 10-1 Department of Health Priorities, 2016–2017

- Improving out-of-hospital care
- Creating the safest, highest quality healthcare services
- Maintaining and improving performance against core standards while achieving financial balance
- Improving efficiency and productivity of the health and care system
- Preventing ill health and supporting people to live healthier lives
- Supporting research, innovation, and growth
- Enabling people and communities to make decisions about their own health and care
- Building and developing the workforce
- Improving services through the use of digital technology, information, and transparency

Reproduced from Department of Health. About us: Our priorities. https://www.gov.uk/government/organisations/department-of-health/about. n.d. Open Government License available at https://www.nationalarchives.gov.uk/doc/open-government-licence/version/3/.

BOX 10-2 Ministers and Parliamentary Under Secretaries

Parliamentary Under Secretary of State for NHS productivity[15]

- NHS and DH financing
- NHS financial performance
- Clinical Commissioning Group allocations
- Budgets for arm's length bodies (budgets at lower levels of government)
- NHS England
- NHS operation and performance
- NHS estates and facilities

Parliamentary Under Secretary of State for Life Sciences[16]

- Cancer Drugs Fund
- Data and technology
- Genomics
- Medicines and industry
- National Institute for Health and Care Excellence
- Medication and Healthcare products Regulatory Agency
- Regenerative medicine
- Research and development
- Specialized commissioning
- Uptake of new drugs and medical technology

Parliamentary Under Secretary of State for Public Health[17]

- Antimicrobial resistance
- Cancer
- Dementia
- Diabetes
- Fertility and embryology
- Health improvement
- Health protection
- Long-term conditions
- Prevention measures
- Sexual health

Parliamentary Under Secretary of State for Care Quality

- End-of-life care
- Failing hospitals
- Hospital care
- Maternity care
- Pathology and death certification
- Patient experience
- Patient safety
- Prison health services
- Secondary care commissioning policy
- Workforce

Minister of State for Community and Social Care[19]

- Adult social care
- Autism
- Integration
- Local government
- Elderly people
- Physical and learning disabilities
- Allied health professions
- Primary care, including dentistry and ophthalmic services

Data from Department of Health. https://www.gov.uk/government/organisations/department-of-health. n.d. Open Government License available at https://www.nationalarchives.gov.uk/doc/open-government-licence/version/3/.

BOX 10-3 Department of Health Management Team

Director General of Innovation, Growth and Technology
Director General for Social Care, Local Government and Care Partnerships
Director General of Finance at the Department of Health
Director General for Public and International Health
Director General for Group Operations and Chief Operating Officer
Department of Health Chief Scientific Adviser
Director General for Strategy and External Relations
Chief Medical Officer

Data from Department of Health. https://www.gov.uk/government/organisations/department-of-health. n.d.

These principles are listed in **BOX 10-5**. The Constitution also outlines rights and responsibilities of the NHS to the public and its staff as well as responsibilities of the public and staff to the NHS.

The NHS cares for more than 64 million people in the United Kingdom and 54.3 million in England alone.[17] The NHS in England sees more than 1 million patients every 36 hours and covers everything from prenatal care to routine checkups, long-term care for chronic conditions, emergency treatment, and end-of-life care.

The NHS in England is led by a chief executive who leads a management team consisting of a chief nursing officer; a national medical director; and national directors for commissioning operations, commissioning strategy, transformation, and corporate operations; and a chief financial officer.[18] In addition, chief professional officers (CPOs) provide

BOX 10-4 Supporting and Collaborating Agencies and Public Bodies

Executive Agency
- Medicines and Healthcare products Regulatory Agency
- Public Health England

Executive Nondepartmental Public Body
- Care Quality Commission
- Health Education England
- Health Research Authority
- Health and Social Care Information Centre
- Human Fertilization and Embryology Authority
- Human Tissue Authority
- Monitor
- NHS Blood and Transplant
- NHS Business Services Authority
- NHS England
- NHS Litigation Authority
- NHS Trust Development Authority
- National Institute for Health and Care Excellence

Advisory Nondepartmental Public Body
- Administration of Radioactive Substances Advisory Committee
- Advisory Committee on Clinical Excellence Awards
- British Pharmacopoeia Commission
- Commission on Human Medicines
- Committee on Mutagenicity of Chemicals in Food, Consumer Products and the Environment
- Independent Reconfiguration Panel
- NHS Pay Review Body
- Review Body on Doctors' and Dentists' Remuneration

Other
- Accelerated Access Review
- Morecambe Bay Investigation
- National Data Guardian
- National Information Board
- Porton Biopharma Limited

Reproduced from Department of Health. Departments, agencies, and public bodies. https://www.gov.uk/government/organisations. n.d. Open Government License available at https://www.nationalarchives.gov.uk/doc/open-government-licence/version/3/.

---

expert clinical advice to the NHS management team. These CPOs are the heads of their respective professions and include the chief scientific officer, chief dental officer, chief therapeutic officer, and chief health professions officer.

In 2012, Parliament passed the Health and Social Care Act.[19] The Act took effect in 2013 and instituted significant changes to the organization of the NHS in England. Primary changes included:

- Moving to clinically led commissioning
- Increasing patient involvement in the NHS
- Renewing focus on the importance of public health
- Streamlining of arm's length bodies
- Allowing healthcare market competition in the best interest of patients

Prior to the implementation of the Act, a wide range of NHS trusts managed and/or provided care in England. Previously, commissioning was done by Primary Care Trusts and specialized commissioning groups. Under the Act, the majority of hospital services are provided by foundation trusts and NHS trusts providing ambulance, emergency, or mental health services. Arranging for, or commissioning, of services is conducted by NHS England and clinical commissioning groups (CCG). NHS England commissions primary care services as well as services for the military and corrections facilities. In addition, NHS England is responsible for commissioning low-volume, specialized health care. In 2015, NHS England had a budget of about £95 billion, of which it spent about £30 billion directly. The majority was allocated to CCGs, which are meant to be led by GP practices in the geographic area for which they have responsibility. Currently there are 211 CCGs serving

BOX 10-5 NHS Key Principles

1. The NHS provides a comprehensive service available to all.
2. Access to NHS services is based on clinical need, not an individual's ability to pay.
3. The NHS aspires to the highest standards of excellence and professionalism.
4. The NHS aspires to put patients at the heart of everything it does.
5. The NHS works across organizational boundaries and in partnership with other organizations in the interest of patients, local communities, and the wider population.
6. The NHS is committed to providing best value for taxpayers' money and the most effective, fair, and sustainable use of finite resources.
7. The NHS is accountable to the public, communities, and patients that it serves.

Data from NHS. About the NHS. http://www.nhs.uk/NHSEngland/thenhs/about/Pages/nhscoreprinciples.aspx. 2015.

an average of 250,000 people each (the range is 61,000 to 860,000). CCGs are responsible for arranging the provision of urgent and emergency care, elective hospital care, community health services, maternity and newborn care, mental health care, and care for those with learning disabilities. Services may be provided through voluntary and private sectors. CCGs replaced primary care trusts and strategic health authorities who were previously responsible for planning and commissioning care for defined geographic areas.[20]

Description of the Current Healthcare System

Primary Care

The first point of contact with the NHS is typically the general practice (GP) surgery. GPs act as gatekeepers for secondary care. In 2013, there were 40,236 GPs in 7,962 practices.[21] There was an average of 7,000 patients per practice and 1,500 patients per GP. About half of GPs are made up of five or more surgeons; only 1,400 are solo practices. Residents of England who are eligible for health care are required to register with a general practice. While patients nominally have their choice of GP, choice may be limited because GPs reach their patient limits and stop accepting new patients.

About two-thirds of GPs are private contractors, and a similar proportion of GPs operate under the nationally negotiated general medical services contract. The contract covers payment for services using a combination of capitation, fee-for-service, and pay-for-performance schemes. GPs are paid by capitation for essential medical services such as acute illness and injury, general management of patients who are terminally ill, and management of chronic diseases. In addition, GPs are expected to provide what are considered additional services. These include cervical cancer screening, contraceptive services, vaccinations and immunizations, child health surveillance, and maternity care. If the practice opts out of providing these additional services, a portion of the global payment is withheld in order for the CCG to commission for these services by another provider. Enhanced services such as screening for alcohol abuse, certain minor surgery procedures, and early detection of dementia are paid on a fee-for-service basis. Performance related payments are made under the Quality and Outcomes Framework (QOF). Payments under the QOF can account for up to a quarter of practice income for meeting certain evidence-based clinical benchmarks. Some of the bonus is linked to the operation of the organization and patient experience. **BOX 10-6** lists the domains, indicators, and improvement areas for the QOF for 2016/2017. The amount allocated to QOF payments is being decreased and redirected to the capitation payments. Payments are made to the practice monthly, based on its registered patients and on information about the enhanced services that it provides. The new GMS contract also allows GPs to list patients from outside their geographic area who do not require home visits or emergency follow-up, as long as the patient is made aware of these exceptions.

GPs are no longer responsible for directly providing out-of-hours (OOH) care for their patients. They are, however, required to ensure that arrangements for provision of OOH care are in place. Most GPs have opted out and instead have a portion of their payments retained by the CCG for contracting those services. Most OOH care is provided by GP cooperative and private services. The GP is responsible for providing scheduled visits for 10 sessions per week (in-hours care). A session is a three- to four-hour block during which the GP will schedule appointments. The workday typically starts at 9 AM and ends at 7 PM, although hours may vary if there are early morning, late evening, or weekend sessions. The GP will see patients from 9 AM to 12 PM and then again from 3 PM to 6 PM. The time between sessions is often used for making house calls and attending meetings. If a GP will be absent for any reason, locum tenens coverage must be arranged or another GP in the practice must pick up the extra session to ensure availability of care.

A second form of primary care contract arrangement is the primary medical service (PMS) contract. In contrast to the GMS, PMS is a local arrangement between NHS England and the practice. In this setting, the practice does not have to be a traditional GP; it could be a nurse-led service with a salaried GP or other primary care professionals. PMS was introduced to provide greater freedom for practices to address the specific needs of their patients. PMS also allowed the option of GPs being salaried rather than practice owners. GPs benefit from more assured income, and offering a salary enhances the ability for practices to recruit providers into underserved areas. Around 40% of GPs in England operate under PMS contracts.

Alternative provider medical service contracts allows NHS England to enter into agreements with any individual or organization who meets the provider conditions under the rules. This includes the independent sector, voluntary sector, not-for-profit organizations and NHS trusts. These agreements give NHS England the flexibility to provide services that are not available from GP practices and to improve access and responsiveness to the specific needs of patient populations.

BOX 10-6 List of Outcomes and Indicators in the NHS Outcomes Framework for 2016/2017

Domain 1: preventing people from dying prematurely

Overarching indicators

1a. Potential years of life lost from causes considered amenable to health care
- Adults
- Children and young people

1b. Life expectancy at 75
- Males
- Females

1c. Neonatal mortality and stillbirths

Improvement areas

- Reducing premature mortality from major causes of death
- Reducing premature mortality in people with mental illness
- Reducing mortality in children
- Reducing premature death in people with learning disability

Domain 2: enhancing quality of life for people with long-term conditions

Overarching indicators

2. Health-related quality of life for people with long-term conditions

Improvement areas

- Ensuring people feel supported in managing their conditions
- Improving functional ability in people with long-term conditions
- Reducing time spent in hospital by people with long-term conditions
- Enhancing quality of life for caregivers
- Enhancing quality of life for people with mental illness
- Enhancing quality of life for people with dementia
- Improving quality of life for people with multiple long-term conditions

Domain 3: helping people to recover from ill health or injury

Overarching indicators

3a. Emergency admissions for acute conditions that do not usually require hospital admission

3b. Emergency readmissions within 30 days of discharge from hospital

Improvement areas

- Improving outcomes from planned treatments
- Preventing lower respiratory infections in children from becoming serious
- Improving recovery from injuries and trauma
- Improving recovery from stroke
- Improving recovery from fragility fractures
- Helping elderly people to recover independence after illness or injury
- Improving dental health

Domain 4: ensuring that patients have positive care experiences

Overarching indicators

4a. Patient experience of primary care
- GP services
- GP *out-of-hours* services
- NHS dental services

4b. Patient experience of hospital care

4c. Friends and family test

4d. Patient experience characterized as poor or worse
- Primary care
- Hospital care

Improvement areas

- Improving people's experience of outpatient care
- Improving hospitals' responsiveness to personal needs
- Improving people's experience of accident and emergency services
- Improving access to primary care services
- Improving women's and their families' experience of maternity services
- Improving the experience of care for people at the end of their lives
- Improving experience of health care for people with mental illness
- Improving children and young people's experience of health care
- Improving people's experience of integrated care

Domain 5: treating and caring for people in a safe environment and protecting them from avoidable harm

Overarching indicators

5a. Deaths attributable to problems in health care
5b. Severe harm attributable to problems in health care

Improvement areas

- Reducing the incidence of avoidable harm
- Improving safety of maternity services
- Improving the culture of safety reporting

Data from NHS Commissioning Board. NHS outcomes framework and CCG outcomes indicators: Data availability table. https://www.england.nhs.uk/wp-content/uploads/2012/12/oi-data-table.pdf. December 2012.

In addition to medical services provided by GPs, community-based services are also provided by a number of other health professionals. These include dental, pharmacy, and optometry services. District nursing in the NHS is the equivalent of U.S. home health nursing. District nurses visit patients in their homes and provide wound care and chronic disease monitoring services. Community midwives provide services for pregnant women in GP surgeries or maternity clinics. Health visitors are specially trained nurses who provide care for newborns, infants, and children. Health visitors provide developmental screening and vaccination services for preschool-age children.

Secondary Care

Almost all specialty physicians and surgeons are employed by NHS hospitals. Physicians and surgeons are paid salaries by the hospital. Consultant physician and surgeons who are employed full time usually work a set schedule of 10 programmed activities. These are four-hour blocks of time during which the consultant provides patient services in either the outpatient department, operating theater, or hospital ward. The schedule may be adjusted for on-call time and emergency work arising from on-call status and time spent teaching. As with GPs, locum coverage must be arranged in the absence of the consultant by either additional hours or by a colleague or a locum tenens. Unlike with GPs however, arrangements for locum coverage is the responsibility of the hospital. Physicians and surgeons are allowed to engage in private practice as long as it doesn't interfere with their hospital duties. Payments for consultations and procedures are made by CCGs to the hospitals at nationally determined rates. Under the current scheme, patients are able to select the hospital and even the specialist they wish to provide the service.

Hospitals have been under public ownership since the establishment of the NHS in 1948. Hospitals are either organized as an NHS trust, accountable to the DH, or as a foundation trust, regulated by Monitor, the government agency that regulates public and private providers. There are currently 147 foundation trusts and 102 NHS trusts. The DH aims to have all hospitals become foundation trusts in the near future. Foundation trusts are not under the direct control of the DH and have more freedom to make strategic and financial decisions. Foundation trusts were introduced in 2004 and are organized as independent public benefit corporations. Foundation trusts are able to do the following:

- Access capital on the basis of affordability instead of the being under central financial management
- Invest surpluses in developing new services for local people
- Tailor new governance arrangements to the individual circumstances of their community

This freedom from central government comes with a price: foundation trusts must operate under balanced budgets and cannot expect the government to cover any shortfalls. Foundation trusts are reimbursed for services based on a national tariff or fee schedule, with payments following the patient. Foundation trusts are required to provide care under the core principles of the NHS: free care based on need and not the ability to pay.

Other Care

NHS services are also delivered by a number of other organizations. Ambulance trusts provide emergency and nonemergency transport. Inpatient and outpatient mental health services are provided by mental health trusts. Mental health services are commissioned and paid for by CCGs. Community health services such as home nursing visits, health visitor services, school nursing, and NHS walk-in centers are provided by community health trusts.

Nursing home services are provided by the public sector and are regulated by the government. Care is usually paid for privately, subject to asset limitations. State support for nursing home care is provided on a sliding scale basis. Patients below a certain asset threshold are eligible for government supported care.

Facilities

There are approximately 778 hospitals providing services in the NHS. This is divided into 221 acute care hospitals, 268 community hospitals, 173 specialty hospitals, and 116 multiservice hospitals.[19] These hospitals host just under 150,000 beds, mostly for acute care. This number has been declining steadily over the past quarter century. Much of the decline is due to improved medical care leading to shorter lengths of stay and to a transition to more out of hospital care.[23] As a result of the decline in number of beds, the occupancy rates have increased. Hospital utilization has increase over the last five years.[24] Emergency admissions have risen 2%, accident and emergency visits have risen 3%, and first outpatient appointments have risen 5%. Factors such as population growth and the aging of the population account for some of the increase; however, the same changes in technology and medical care likely combine with the previous factors to explain the increases.

Technology and Equipment

NHS trusts are also responsible for providing access to diagnostic technology. Laboratory services and diagnostic radiology are commissioned by CCGs. In 2013 there were an estimated 6.1 MRI scanners per 1,000,000 people.[25] There were an estimated 7.9 CT scanners per 1,000,000 people in 2013. This equates to a total of 384 MRI and 506 CT scanners throughout the NHS. This does not include scanners available through the private system.

Private Versus Public Components

In addition to healthcare coverage under the NHS, people residing in the United Kingdom have access to private medical insurance (PMI).[26] PMI is also called voluntary insurance because the purchaser participates voluntarily. The most commonly offered type of PMI is supplementary PMI, which provides insured access to privately delivered care. There is considerable overlap in the services covered, duplicating many services available to the purchaser through the NHS, to which the purchaser retains access. Benefits to PMI include faster access to treatment, a wider choice of specialists, more comfortable care treatment environment, and more convenient timing of treatment.

PMI is available as a perquisite of employment or through the individual market. PMI is offered at three levels of coverage: comprehensive, standard, and budget. The widest range of services is covered by more expensive comprehensive policies. Budget policies are cheaper but may cover fewer services or have conditions on usage. As of 2006 there were 27 insurers offering PMI in the United Kingdom. They are roughly evenly divided between provident and commercial companies. Of these 27 insurers, 4 insurers comprise about 88% of the private market.

Workforce

The NHS employs more than 1.5 million people making it the largest employer in the United Kingdom and one of the top 5 employers in the world. With 1.2 million employees, the NHS in England is the largest component of the system. Clinical staff include 45,400 consultants; 52,592 doctors in training; 40,584 general practitioners; 314,966 nurses and health visitors; 25,400 midwives; 18,862 ambulance staff; and 111,127 hospital and community health service medical and dental staff.

Medical Education

By July 2014, there were 31 universities offering medical degrees in the United Kingdom.[27] Entry into medical education can take two paths. The first, or traditional method, is entry directly from secondary education, culminating 5–6 years later in the undergraduate medical degree of bachelor of medicine and bachelor of surgery (or chirurgy). The second method is after receiving a first bachelor's degree, in which care medical education may be completed in four years. Some universities require the first bachelor's degree to be in a science, while others have no specific requirements. Upon graduation students are awarded a primary medical qualification.

After graduation from undergraduate training, new graduates complete a two-year foundation training program. This is equivalent to a rotating internship with trainees rotating through different specialties every three or four months. Successful completion of the first foundation year leads to registration with the General Medical Council (GMC). The GMC is one of two medical licensing agencies in the United Kingdom. After the second year, the trainee can apply to specialty training programs as either a GP or as a physician or surgeon. Training can take up to eight years for some specialties. In 2013 the government required Health Education England to achieve a rate of 50% of graduates entering GP training by 2015.

▶ Evaluation of the Healthcare System

Cost

Almost 99% of NHS funding comes from general tax collections (80%) and National Insurance (19%) contributions.[28] The balance is collected each year in user fees, mainly from prescription and dental co-payments. The budget for the NHS overall was £116.4 billion (£101.3 for England) in 2015–2016.[29] The NHS budget has increased steadily despite attempts by the government to reduce its budget deficit. Despite this, the United Kingdom ranks only 16th among OECD nations in spending.

Budgets are usually set on a three-year schedule.[1] CCGs and other commissioning groups are provided their allocation with NHS England providing oversight and monitoring to ensure that these groups avoid overspending. The economic downturn of 2008 resulted in relatively flat national budgets, and the NHS budget was similarly affected with the 2010/2011 fiscal year showing a decrease in spending. The subsequent improvements in the economy and rising demand for services resulted in an increase in the NHS budget to £107 billion in 2012/2013. Of this figure £96 billion was appropriated to NHS England (£30 billion used for direct commissioning) and the remainder distributed to CCGs and other commissioning groups.

In 2014 the United Kingdom spent about 9.1% of GDP on health care, a total of US $3,289 per capita. Spending is growing at a rate of around 2.7%. Of this figure, public expenditure accounted for about 84%. Most private expenditure is for over-the-counter medications and other medical products and private medical insurance.

Quality

The Care Quality Commission (CQC) is responsible for regulating health and social care for adults in England.[1] This includes care provided by the NHS, local authorities, and the private and voluntary sectors. All providers must be registered with the CQC which applies national quality standards and does investigation of consumer complaints.

The National Institute for Health and Clinical Excellence (NICE) is responsible for development of treatment guidelines for common conditions across primary and secondary care. NICE is also responsible for determining which pharmaceutical are approved for use in the NHS in England and Wales. NHS Choices publishes information on quality at the organization, department, and physician levels.

Average life expectancy at birth for citizens (2016 est.) was 80.7 years.[5] Infant mortality was 5 per 1,000 live births and maternal mortality was 8 per 100,000 live births, compared to European rates of 10 per 1,000 and 17 per 100,000 respectively.[29] The diphtheria/tetanus/pertussis vaccination rate in the United Kingdom in 2015 was near 98% among 1-year-olds, and 95% of 1-year-olds are vaccinated against measles. All of the population have access to improved water and sanitation.

Ischemic heart disease was the leading cause of death in the United Kingdom in 2012. This was followed by stroke, respiratory cancers, and dementia (including Alzheimer disease). Lower respiratory tract infections, chronic obstructive lung disease, and cancers of the colon, breast, prostate, and esophagus round out the top 10 causes of death. Of these, the numbers of deaths from lower respiratory tract infection, chronic lung disease, colon cancer, and breast cancer have been on the decline.

Patient Satisfaction

The NHS enjoys broad support among the citizens of the United Kingdom. However, about a third of the public feels that fundamental changes have to be made and two-thirds feel that the system works well with only minor changes required.[1] A very small minority feels that the system needs to be completely revised.

Access

One of the major issues with the NHS has been waiting times for urgent and elective care. The NHS sets target waiting periods for a variety of conditions. In the English NHS 94.7% of patients were seen within two weeks of an urgent referral by a GP for a suspected cancer. In the fourth quarter (January–March) of 2015/2016,[30] approximately 93% of women were seen within two weeks of referral for breast symptoms, and 97% of patients met had their cancer treatments started within 31 days of receiving their diagnosis.

Around 52% of patients were able to get a same day appointment with their GP when sick, and 69% reported that it was very easy or somewhat easy to get care after hours. Only 7% reported waiting more than two months for a specialist appointment.

Innovation

In 2015, the NHS introduced a new care delivery model, the vanguard site.[31] There are five types of vanguard sites: integrated primary and acute care systems, enhanced health in care homes, multispecialty community provider, urgent and emergency, and acute care collaborations. Integrated primary and acute care systems aim to integrate GP, hospital, community, and mental health services. Multispecialty community providers aim to move specialist care out of the hospital and into the community. Enhanced health in care homes will integrate health, care, and rehabilitation services. Urgent and emergency care vanguards are designed to improve coordination of services and reduce demand on emergency departments. Acute care collaborations are intended to link local hospitals to improve their clinical and financial viability.

The NHS is committed to improving access to primary care through GP surgeries.[32] The government published the *General Practice Forward View* in 2016. The document outlines a multibillion dollar effort to increase access to GP care to meet growing demand. The plan calls for doubling the number of doctors entering GP training in the next 5 years. This is in addition to increased support for practice nurses, physician assistants, practice managers, mental health therapists, and pharmacists. The government will also increase funding for infrastructure to renovate or replace GPs and invest in practice technologies to improve appointment systems, consultation referrals, and better record sharing.

Current and Emerging Issues and Challenges

The NHS is facing many of the same challenges as other health systems in industrialized countries. A growing and aging population is increasing demand on the systems. As noted above, the NHS is addressing this by enhancing primary care services and making significant investments in GPs.

However, there is significant pressure on the government to erase a budget deficit as well as control spending. The government has charged the NHS with reducing its spending by 2%–3% per year with a total 10%–15% delivery in efficiencies by 2021.[13] Despite this, spending levels are projected to increase, just at a slower rate.

This call for budget restraint is being made difficult by financial challenges facing NHS trusts and foundation trusts.[34] For 2014/2015, 52% of foundation trusts were in deficit and 35% of NHS trusts were in deficit. These percentages have been increasing since the 2011/2012 fiscal year. NHS trusts reported budget surpluses for the early years of the decade, but by 2014 the sector was running a deficit of £467 million. Foundation trusts reported operating surpluses as well during the early years of the decade but deficits began accumulating in the fiscal year 2013/2014.

The King's Fund produced a report in early 2015 titled *The NHS Under the Coalition Government*.[35,36] The report was released ahead of general elections in 2015. The report concludes that the:

- Coalition government reforms have resulted in greater marketization of the NHS, but claims of mass privatization are exaggerated.
- Reforms have resulted in top-down reorganization of the NHS, and this has been distracting and damaging.
- New systems of governance and accountability resulting from the reforms are complex and confusing.
- Absence of system leadership is increasingly problematic when the NHS needs to undertake major service changes.
- Care Act 2014 has created a legal framework for introducing a fairer system of funding of long-term care.
- NHS performance held up well for the first three years of the 2010–2015 Parliament but has since come under increasing strain.
- Patient experience generally remains positive; public confidence is close to an all-time high; and there have been some improvements in outcomes, safety and quality.
- There are concerns over the quality of mental health services and challenges in achieving parity of esteem between mental and physical health.
- Most of the NHS is working close to or beyond its limits, and staff morale is a growing concern.

Since the publication of this report, the Conservatives achieved an outright majority in the Parliament and now head the government. The passage of the Health and Care Act of 2016 lays the groundwork for improvement in the healthcare system of the UK. Only time will tell if it will be successful.

References

1. *The World Factbook*. United Kingdom. Washington, DC: Central Intelligence Agency. https://cia.gov/library/publications/the-world-factbook/geos/print_uk.html. Accessed May 3, 2016.
2. Hunt A, Wheeler B. Brexit: All you need to know about the UK leaving the EU. *BBC News*. http://www.bbc.com/news/uk-politics-32810887. November 10, 2016. Accessed May 22, 2016.
3. Scottish referendum: Scotland votes "no" to independence. *BBC Newsround*. http://www.bbc.co.uk/newsround/29272574. September 19, 2014. Accessed May 22, 2016.
4. Election 2015: Results. Conservatives win 12-seat majority. *BBC News*. http://www.bbc.com/news/election/2015/results. Accessed May 22, 2016.
5. Cylus J, Richardson E, Findley L, et al. United Kingdom: Health system review. *Health Systems in Transition*. 2015;17(5):1–125.
6. United Kingdom Government. HM Treasury. Economic Assessment Team. *Forecasts for the UK Economy: A Comparison of Independent Forecasts. No. 349*. https://www.gov.uk/government/uploads/system/uploads/attachment_data/file/523954/PU797_forecasts_for_uk_economy_349_may_2016.pdf. May 2016. Accessed May 22, 2016.
7. United Kingdom Government. Department for Education. *National Pupil Projections—Future Trends in Pupil Numbers: July 2015*. https://www.gov.uk/government/uploads/system/uploads/attachment_data/file/478185/SFR24_2015_Projections_Text.pdf. July 22, 2015. Accessed May 22, 2016.
8. United Kingdom Government. Department for Business and Innovation Skills. *Participation Rates in Higher Education: Academic years 2006/2007–2013/2014 (Provisional)*. https://www.gov.uk/government/uploads/system/uploads/attachment_data/file/458034/HEIPR_PUBLICATION_2013-14.pdf. September 2, 2015. Accessed June 13, 2016.
9. Roemer MI. National health systems throughout the world. *Annual Review of Public Health*. 1993;14(1):335–353.
10. Rivett G. The development of the London hospital system, 1823–2015. www.nhshistory.net. Accessed May 22, 2015.
11. The Worshipful Society of Apothecaries of London. History. Origins. http://www.apothecaries.org/charity/the-archives. Accessed May 22, 2016.
12. United Kingdom Government. Department of Health. https://www.gov.uk/government/organisations/department-of-health. Accessed May 22, 2016.

13. United Kingdom Government. Department of Health. The Government's Mandate to NHS England for 2016–17. https://www.gov.uk/government/uploads/system/uploads/attachment_data/file/494485/NHSE_mandate_16-17_22_Jan.pdf. Published January 2016. Accessed May 3, 2016.
14. NHS Choices. The NHS structure explained. http://www.nhs.uk/NHSEngland/thenhs/about/Pages/nhsstructure.aspx. Accessed May 3, 2016.
15. NHS Choices. About the NHS. Principles and values that guide the NHS. http://www.nhs.uk/NHSEngland/thenhs/about/Pages/nhscoreprinciples.aspx. Accessed May 3, 2016.
16. United Kingdom Government. Department of Health. The NHS Constitution for England. https://www.gov.uk/government/publications/the-nhs-constitution-for-england/the-nhs-constitution-for-england. Updated October 14, 2015. Accessed May 3, 2016.
17. United Kingdom Government. Department of Health. About the National Health Service (NHS). http://www.nhs.uk/NHSEngland/thenhs/about/Pages/overview.aspx. Accessed May 3, 2016.
18. NHS England. Senior management structure. https://www.england.nhs.uk/about/structure/. Accessed May 22, 2016.
19. NHS England. *Understanding the New NHS*. https://www.england.nhs.uk/wp-content/uploads/2014/06/simple-nhs-guide.pdf. Published June 26, 2014. Accessed May 22, 2016.
20. Timmins N. The UK's four national health services: Time to learn the difference? The King's Fund, 2013.
21. Mossialos E, Wenzl M, Osborn R, Sarnak D, eds. *2015 International Profiles of Health Care Systems*. The Commonwealth Fund. http://www.commonwealthfund.org/~/media/files/publications/fund-report/2016/jan/1857_mossialos_intl_profiles_2015_v7.pdf. Published January 2016. Accessed May 3, 2016.
22. Health and Social Care Information Centre. Hospital estates and facilities statistics. http://hefs.hscic.gov.uk/ReportFilterConfirm.asp?FilterOpen=&Year=2014%2F2015±01&Level=T&Section=T±01&SHA=&Org_Type=&Foundation=&Site_Type=&PFI=&getReport=Get±Report. *Accessed May* 22, 2016.
23. The King's Fund. The number of hospital beds. http://www.kingsfund.org.uk/projects/nhs-in-a-nutshell/hospital-beds. Published March 25, 2015. Accessed May 22, 2016.
24. The King's Fund. Hospital Activity. http://www.kingsfund.org.uk/projects/nhs-in-a-nutshell/hospital-activity. Accessed May 22, 2016.
25. OECD Data. Health equipment. https://data.oecd.org/health.htm. Organisation for Economic Co-operation and Development. Accessed May 22, 2016
26. Foubister T, Thomson S, Mossialos E, McGuire A. *Private Medical Insurance in the United Kingdom*. Copenhagen: WHO Regional Office for Europe; 2006.
27. *The State of Medical Education and Practice in the UK Report: 2015*. http://www.gmc-uk.org/Chapter_1_SOMEP_2015.pdf_63501394.pdf. Accessed May 22, 2016.
28. The King's Fund. How the NHS is funded. http://www.kingsfund.org.uk/projects/nhs-in-a-nutshell/how-nhs-funded. Accessed May 22, 2016.
29. World Health Organization. *United Kingdom: WHO Statistical Profile*. http://www.who.int/gho/countries/gbr.pdf?ua=1. Updated January 2015. Accessed May 22, 2016.
30. NHS England. *Cancer Waiting Times, January to March 2016—Provider Based*. https://www.england.nhs.uk/statistics/wp-content/uploads/sites/2/2016/05/Cancer-Waiting-Times-Press-release-Q4-2015-16-Provider-based.pdf. Accessed may 22, 2016.
31. NHS England. New care models. Vanguard sites. https://www.england.nhs.uk/ourwork/futurenhs/new-care-models//. Accessed May 17, 2016.
32. NHS England. General practice forward view. https://www.england.nhs.uk/ourwork/gpfv/. Accessed May 17, 2016.
33. Lord Carter of Coles. *Operational Productivity and Performance in English NHS Hospitals: Unwarranted Variations*. United Kingdom Government. Department of Health. https://www.gov.uk/government/uploads/system/uploads/attachment_data/file/499229/Operational_productivity_A.pdf. First published June 11, 2015. Accessed May 3, 2016.
34. The King's Fund. Trusts in deficit. http://www.kingsfund.org.uk/projects/nhs-in-a-nutshell/trusts-deficit. Accessed May 22, 2016.
35. Ham C, Baird B, Gregory S, et al. *The NHS Under the Coalition Government. Part One: NHS Reform*. London: The King's Fund. 2015.
36. Appleby J, Baird B, Thompson J, Jabbal J. *The NHS Under the Coalition Government. Part Two: NHS Performance*. London: The King's Fund. 2015.

CHAPTER 11

France

Sophie Kobouloff and Stephanie Baiyasi

▶ Country Description

TABLE 11-1 France

Nationality	Noun: Frenchman (men) Frenchwoman (women) Adjective: French
Ethnic groups	Celtic and Latin with Teutonic, Slavic, North African, Indochinese, Basque minorities Overseas departments: black, white, mulatto, East Indian, Chinese, Amerindian
Religions	Christian (overwhelmingly Roman Catholic) 63.0%–66.0%, Muslim 7.0%–9.0%, Jewish 0.50%–0.75%, Buddhist 0.50%–0.75%, other 0.5%–1.0%, none 23.0%–28.0% (2015 est.)*
Language	French 100%, rapidly declining regional dialects and languages (Provencal, Breton, Alsatian, Corsican, Catalan, Basque, Flemish) Overseas departments: French, Creole patois
Literacy	Definition: Age 15 and over can read and write. Total population: 99% Male: 99% Female: 99% (2003 est.)
Government type	Semi-presidential republic
Date of independence	No official date of independence**

(continues)

TABLE 11-1 France (continued)

Gross Domestic Product (GDP) per capita	$41,200 (2015 est.)
Unemployment rate	10.1% (2015 est.)
Natural hazards	Metropolitan France: flooding; avalanches; midwinter windstorms; drought; forest fires in south near the Mediterranean Overseas departments: hurricanes (cyclones); flooding; volcanic activity (Guadeloupe, Martinique, Reunion)
Environment: current issues	Some forest damage from acid rain; air pollution from industrial and vehicle emissions; water pollution from urban wastes, agricultural runoff
Population	66,836,154 (2016 est.)***
Age structure	0–14 years: 18.59% (male 6,354,241/female 6,070,971) 15–24 years: 11.8% (male 4,035,407/female 3,853,153) 25–54 years: 38.04% (male 12,799,923/female 12,625,781) 55–64 years: 12.44% (male 4,011,853/female 4,303,261) 65 years and over: 19.12% (male 5,510,337/female 7,271,227) (2016 est.)
Median age	Total: 41.2 years Male: 39.5 years Female: 42.9 years (2016 est.)
Population growth rate	0.41% (2016 est.)
Birth rate	12.3 births/1,000 population (2016 est.)
Death rate	369 deaths/100,000 population (2016 est.)
Disease burden	Communicable disease deaths: 21/100,000 population Noncommunicable disease deaths: 313/100,000 population Injury deaths: 35/100,000 population (2016 est.)
Net migration rate	1.1 migrant(s)/1,000 population (2016 est.)
Gender ratio	At birth: 1.05 male(s)/female 0–14 years: 1.05 male(s)/female 15–24 years: 1.05 male(s)/female 25–54 years: 1.01 male(s)/female 55–64 years: 0.93 male(s)/female 65 years and over: 0.75 male(s)/female Total population: 0.96 male(s)/female (2016 est.)
Infant mortality rate	Total: 3.3 deaths/1,000 live births Male: 3.6 deaths/1,000 live births Female: 2.9 deaths/1,000 live births (2016 est.)

Life expectancy at birth	Total population: 81.8 years Male: 78.7 years Female: 85.1 years (2016 est.)
Total fertility rate	2.07 children born/woman (2016 est.)
HIV/AIDS adult prevalence rate	—
Number of people living with HIV/AIDS	—
HIV/AIDS deaths	1,500 (2013 est.)

* France maintains a tradition of secularism and has not officially collected data on religious affiliation since the 1872 national census, which complicates assessments of France's religious composition; an 1872 law prohibiting state authorities from collecting data on individuals' ethnicity or religious beliefs was reaffirmed by a 1978 law emphasizing the prohibition of the collection or exploitation of personal data revealing an individual's race, ethnicity, or political, philosophical, or religious opinions; a 1905 law codified France's separation of church and state.

** In 486 CE, Frankish tribes unified under Merovingian kingship; on August 10, 843 CE, Western Francia was established from the division of the Carolingian Empire; on July 14, 1789, the French monarchy was overthrown; on September 22, 1792, the First French Republic was founded; on October 4, 1958, the Fifth French Republic was established.

*** This population figure is for metropolitan France and five overseas regions; the metropolitan France population is 62,814,233 (July 2015 est.).

Data from Central Intelligence Agency. The World Factbook, 2016: France. https://www.cia.gov/library/publications/the-world-factbook/geos/fr.html. Accessed May 23, 2016; IndexMundi. France: Literacy. www.indexmundi.com/france/literacy.html. June 2015. Accessed November 13, 2016.

History

France's history started a million years ago with the first tribes. The Neanderthals created the first organized habitats, and around 8,000 BCE the *Homo sapiens* developed the first industries, and later they evolved from hunters/gatherers and established village communities. At the beginning of the third millennium BCE, there were around 2 million people[1] living off agriculture, hunting, and fishing. Metallurgy started to develop with the use of copper and tin, and during the second millennium, communities were organized societies with warriors, merchants, and trade agents looking for metals. By the first millennium, civilizations were highly evolved and had mastered the art of metal, and their mortuary rites and funeral art were sophisticated. Gaul—the territory of the Celtic Gauls between the Rhine River, the Alps, and the Mediterranean Sea—was born during this time.

From 58 to 51 BCE to the 5th century, Rome dominated the country, and a brilliant Gallo-Roman culture developed until the Barbarians ended Rome's domination and spread chaos. In the 500s CE, Clovis and the Germanic tribes, called the Franks, pushed the invaders out, and the land of Francie (the archaic name of France) became a mosaic of kingdoms ruled by several kings and one Emperor, Charlemagne (768–814), who expanded his kingdom from the Ebro River (Spain) to the Elbe River (Czech Republic). When this vast empire broke into pieces, the western part of it became France in 843.

Throughout the Middle Ages, until 1483, kings set the basis of the French society: feudalism, power of the religious orders (crusades, chivalry), economic development, creation of major urban centers, development of a bourgeoisie, major artistic and cultural expansion, and reinforcement of the royal administration. The country was constantly expanding through invasions and conquests.

During the Renaissance (from 1483), France was ruled by a succession of conquering kings who increased their power over France and the world while shaping their futures. The highlights of the expansion of this colonial empire include the conquest and annexation of northeast Italy, parts of Spain, Germany, and Holland; the signature of perpetual peace with Swiss regions; and the creation of France's first colonial empire in Canada. By the 18th century, France was the cradle of intellectual and philosophical movements that spread all over the world (e.g., the Enlightenment) and became one of the most powerful countries economically, politically, and culturally.

The constant wars took a heavy toll on the French population already living in poverty. The demographic and commercial expansion of the country did not balance the increasing financial difficulties of the state, and intellectuals and philosophers started to undermine the king's authority. France lost part of its colonial empire to the benefit of England in 1763. While the French helped secure American independence in 1783, King Louis XVI was powerless to solve the financial, economic, and social crisis of the 1780s in France, which lead to the 1789 revolution.

In June 1789, France was given a constitutive National Assembly. Feudalism and privileges for elite classes were abolished, and the Declaration of Human Rights was published. The monarchy was banished in 1792, and the First Republic was proclaimed. Terror and chaos reigned as coalitions fought for power until 1799, when Napoleon Bonaparte became France's first consul after a coup d'état. He brought back peace and set the basis of the French state: centralization of the state powers, creation of the Bank of France, organization of the judiciary system, and publication of the Civil Code. In 1804, Bonaparte became Emperor Napoleon I and set out to conquer a vast empire from Spain to Russia. Defeated in Russia and Germany, Napoleon abdicated power and went into exile in 1814. He returned for one hundred days in 1815, only to be defeated at Waterloo, and France's monarchy was restored for a second time.

During 1815–1848 France was back under royal leadership and saw the development of a wealthy bourgeoisie class. In 1848, the Second Republic was proclaimed. Freedom of the press, freedom of meeting, and direct universal suffrage were institutionalized. That same year, Napoleon Bonaparte's nephew, Louis-Napoleon Bonaparte, was elected president. In power from 1852 to 1870, Emperor Napoleon III established the Second Empire, took over parts of Italy, and attached them to France. French troops were present in China and Crimea and annexed Cochin-China (a part of Vietnam).

The 1870 war against Germany saw the defeat of France and the end of the Second Empire. France was now under the Third Republic. The peace this afforded came at a high price: two French provinces, Alsace and part of Lorraine, were reattached to Germany.

The end of the century brought a deterioration of the economy, expansion of the colonial conquests in Africa and Asia, and political instability. The 20th century started with a rise of leftist parties. Under their influence, the separation of church and state was officially declared in 1905. The poor state of the economy led to social unrest and resentment toward a threatening Germany.

World War I (1914–1918) gave France back its two lost regions. The frontiers of France were definite, but France was weakened. The economic and social situations were difficult, and socialism began to rise. With the 1929 crisis, social movements, strikes, and demonstrations multiplied. In 1936, a lack of stable political leadership brought to power the Popular Front (Front Populaire), a coalition of Communist and Radical parties. The Popular Front passed social reforms that shaped the face of the French labor policy (40-hour weeks, paid holidays, etc.).

World War II, which began in 1939, ended in 1940 for occupied France. The French Resistance and the intervention of the Allies brought victory, and for France, this was the beginning of the Fourth Republic, which lasted until 1958. This period of economic development was also favorable for the creation of social legislation that is still in use today.

The year 1958 saw the birth of the current Fifth Republic. The major milestones of the past 50 years were the entrance of France into the European Community and the major economic transformation under President Charles de Gaulle. The beginning of the 1970s focused on the industrial and commercial development of the nation, and the second half of the decade emphasized France's European commitment. In 1981, the Socialists were brought to power. They put an end to centuries of central ruling and gave more power to the regions. They abolished the death penalty and nationalized many companies. In 1995, the President Jacques Chirac's liberal government aimed to reduce public spending and adopted a rigorist political stance that triggered popular unhappiness, notably plans regarding the reform of social security. This brought Socialism back to power at the ministerial level, and they passed several social reforms, including the 35-hour workweek and universal healthcare coverage (1999).

In 2007, Nicolas Sarkozy was elected president. In a difficult economic context, he tried to tackle the problems of public spending and huge deficits. Navigating between the many economic rules dictated by the European Union, and while the world was facing a major economic crisis, Sarkozy pushed back retirement age to 62 (it used to be 65 and had been lowered to 60 under Socialist ruling). His reforms made him very unpopular and he lost the next presidential elections to Socialist Francois Hollande, who became president in 2012. Since his election, the economic situation in France has been plummeting and unemployment has risen to unseen numbers, with 5,459,700 unemployed people in January 2016 (all categories included) versus 4,935,900 a year before.[2] In 2016, the president's popularity, as well as that of the Socialist government, reached an all-time low. Despite a few reforms (marriage for all, health care, judiciary system, etc.) that aimed at contenting his electors, Hollande succeeded in alienating most of the French people who consider their future with gloom. His successor's task is daunting: sky rocketing unemployment numbers, public deficits, terrorist threats, fiscal pressure that strangles the country's many small businesses, brain exodus, refugee intake, and European rules. France's government faces strong union unrest and strikes at every attempt to reform a system that has proven its limits. However, the country remains today one of the most modern countries in the world and a leader among European nations.[3]

Size and Geography

France is commonly referred to as a hexagon. Metropolitan France is in western Europe, north of Spain and Andorra, with the Bay of Biscay to the west and the Mediterranean Sea to the southeast. Belgium, Luxembourg, Germany, Switzerland, Italy, and Monaco lie on its eastern boundary, and the English Channel lie to the north. Covering an area of around 551,500 square kilometers, France is slightly smaller than Texas.[3] Refer to **FIGURE 11-1**.

France is also comprised of various territories around the globe. These include French Guiana in northern South America, bordering the North Atlantic Ocean; Guadeloupe and Martinique, Caribbean islands between the Caribbean Sea and the North Atlantic Ocean; the Reunion, an island in the Indian Ocean east of Madagascar; Saint Pierre and Miquelon in the Atlantic Ocean, right off the Canadian shores; Mayotte, one of the Comoros Islands; Wallis and Futuna, New-Caledonia, and French Polynesia, all located in the Pacific Ocean; and many other territories around the globe. These remains of the

FIGURE 11-1 Map of France
© Bardocz Peter/Shutterstock

former French colonies double the area of France (over 559,000 square kilometers) and provide the country with a political presence in those parts of the world as well as total control over an exclusive economic maritime zone of more than 10 million square kilometers, the third largest in the world.[4]

With a current population of 64.50 million people in Metropolitan France (66.60 million including the overseas territories),[5] it is the second largest country by population in the EU, right after Germany. Around 13% of the approximately 507.00 million Europeans live in France.[6] If average density is 104 inhabitants per square kilometers, the French population is not evenly distributed. The French population is 79.5% urban[3] and lives mainly in medium-sized cities. Paris, with a population of almost 2.23 million (the extended Paris area includes more than 12.00 million), is the only city with over 1.00 million people. Marseilles comes next with a population of 855,393, and Lyon comes third with a population of only 500,715.[7] Half of the population of Metropolitan France is concentrated in little more than 10% of the territory, mainly in Paris, in a few other cities, and on the southern Mediterranean. Agricultural areas, forests, and nonagricultural lands represent 87.0% of the territory, with 25.0% being forests. Urban zones represent 8.5% of the country.

France acts as a junction between northern and southern Europe, and it is also a European isthmus that points toward the Atlantic Ocean. France is a reduction of Europe by itself, presenting all the climates and the landscapes of Europe condensed in its tiny space. France is the crossroads of western Europe and a major player in Europe since its creation.

Government and Political System

The government of the French Republic is a semi-presidential system, which means that both the president and the prime minister actively participate in the daily operations of the state. This form of government was determined by the French Constitution of the Fifth Republic. The Constitution provides for a separation of powers and proclaims France's "attachment to the Rights of Man" and the principles of national sovereignty as defined by the Declaration of 1789. The national government of France is divided into an executive, a legislative, and a judicial branch.

The legislative power is in the hands of Parliament, which is composed of the National Assembly and the Senate. It passes statutes and votes on the budget, and it controls the action of the executive through formal questioning on the floor of the houses of Parliament and by establishing enquiry commissions. The constitutionality of the statutes is checked by the Constitutional Council, whose members are appointed by the president of the Republic, the president of the National Assembly, and the president of the Senate. The National Assembly can revoke the entire government, including the prime minister, through a "censure motion," ensuring that the prime minister is always supported by a majority of the House.

The independent judiciary branch is based on a civil law system that evolved from the Napoleonic codes and is divided into the judicial branch, which deals with civil law and criminal law, and the administrative branch, which deals with appeals against executive decisions. Each branch has its own independent supreme court of appeals: the Cour de Cassation for the judicial courts and the Conseil d'Etat for the administrative courts. The French government includes various bodies that check abuses of power and independent agencies.

France is a unitary state, but the administrative subdivisions (the regions, departments, and communes) have various legal functions, and the national government is prohibited from intruding into their normal operations. Each entity is headed by elected assemblies with their own competences and autonomy.

As a founding member of the European Coal and Steel Community, which later became the European Union, France has had to transfer part of its sovereignty to European institutions, something that has been included in the country's Constitution. This means that the French government must adopt and follow all European treaties, directives, and regulations.

Macroeconomics

France ranks among the leading European countries and is one of the most modern countries in the world. Formerly the fourth strongest economy in the world, it now ranks 11th in the world (7th in 2010), with an estimated GDP of US $2.647 trillion for 2015.[2] GDP only increased by 0.2% in 2014, after a 0.7% increase in 2013.[8] The unemployment rate rose to 10.2% at the end of Q1 2016,[9] right above the European Union's 9.1% average, ranking 21st among the 28-member European Union.[10] Meanwhile "lower-than-expected growth and high spending have strained France's public finances. The budget deficit rose sharply from 3.3% of GDP in 2008 to 7.5% of GDP in 2009 before improving to 4.0% of GDP in 2014 and 2015, while France's public debt rose from 68.0% of GDP to more than 98.0% in 2015, and may hit 100% in 2016."[2]

France is the 6th largest exporter of goods in the world. It ranks 4th for services[11] and 7th for agriculture.[12] Around 66% of the country's commercial exchanges take place with EU countries, China, and

Russia. France is a less appreciated country by foreign investors because in 2008 it dropped from second place (after the United States)[2] to 19th place in the world for foreign investments.[13] In general, foreign investors are attracted by the quality of the work population, the high level of research, the development of advanced technologies, and good management of production costs.

The structure of the French economy has evolved much during the past decades. The primary and secondary sectors have declined in favor of the services industries, the country's assets. France's major industries are machinery and transportation equipment, aircrafts, plastics, chemicals, pharmaceutical products, agribusiness, transformation of raw materials, space and aeronautics, and luxury industries (cosmetics, perfumes, fashion, wine, and liqueurs). Many French companies excel in their areas and rank among the top five in the world. This is the case for Michelin, one of the top producers of tires in the world, and Saint-Gobain, which is number one in glass production. The space and aeronautic industry is one of France's poles of excellence, and France has been recognized as a world leader for many programs. Agribusiness is France's number one industry. The country ranks sixth in the world after the United States, even though it is only barely the size of Texas. Machinery and transportation equipment are the first export sector, accounting for 38.36% of the country's exports, followed by chemical products that represent 18.89% of exports, and agribusiness at 13.45%.[14]

Agriculture and fishing are the other main poles of production. With agricultural production of €74.6 billion in 2015,[15] France ranks first in Europe. In 2015, 27,739,000 hectares representing 50% of the French territory were dedicated to agriculture.[16] Around 18% of Europe's agricultural output comes from France.[17] France is the number one European producer of cereals (fifth in the world), beef, poultry, sugar beet, and number two for milk (fifth in the world). It is the number one producer of wine in the world.

In the services area, France's expertise is recognized in banking, insurance, and of course, tourism. French insurance companies occupy the fifth position in the world. As far as tourism is concerned, France is the most visited country in the world, with 83.8 million visitors in 2014, which was 9 million more than the United States had.[18] The tourism industry generates receipts of €43.2 billion.[19]

As of the beginning of 2008, 99.85% of French companies were mostly small- to medium-sized, from 20 to 499 employees, with 93.13% employing fewer than 9 employees.[20] The French workforce is an asset for the country. Its quality can be explained by the high level of qualifications; 6.33% of the GDP was attributed to education in 2011.[21] R&D is also an asset for the country. In 2013, public spending for R&D was €49.424 million, 2.34% of the GDP.[22] Public spending concentrates on the current functioning of the National Centers for Scientific Research. Research financed by these companies focuses on technological branches, such as pharmaceuticals.

Capitalism à la Française

Although France belongs to the liberal world, it does not adopt all of its characteristics. If France's economy relies on the capitalist system, its singularity comes from the role and importance of the state as the defender of public interest, which preempts private interests. The state controls, stimulates, and regulates the economy. It is present in all the spheres of economic and social life of the country. The leaders of France remain committed to maintaining social equity within a capitalist economy. They do this by means of laws, social spending, and tax policies that reduce disparity between incomes and the impact of free markets on public health and welfare.[2] The state plays a major social role as the "providential state." Among its actions are the creation, maintenance, and management of social security and national insurance, the motors of France's health care and workers' social protection. In France, all workers have a right to a *social salary* owed by society at large. It is the counterpart workers receive for being part of the workforce. Social security pays for most of people's healthcare expenditures, disability, and pensions. It is financed by employees' and employers' contributions.

As a result of the state's many actions in the social area, France's tax burden—nearly 50% of GDP—is one of the highest in Europe. The country's public debt increased from 95.5% of the GDP in 2014 to over 98.2% of the GDP in 2015.[2] In that context, Hollande's government tried to reform some social services in order to cut public expenditures. The pension system and health care have been some of the leads for this action.

Demographics

As of January 1, 2016, the total population of metropolitan France and French overseas departments was estimated at 66.628 million.[23] In 2014, 818,600 children were born and 559,300 people died, putting the natural increase at 259,300. Net migration is estimated at 47,000.[24] France's demographic increase is today one of the most dynamic of the European Union. In 2015, the Total Fertility Index was just slightly below

2 children per woman (1.99). France is, along with Ireland, the EU country with the highest fertility rate. Women are having children at ever older ages. The mean age at childbearing is 30.3 years,[25] which is 2 years older than in the late 1980s. This trend is common to all of Europe except the eastern European countries that have recently joined the EU.

Life expectancy is increasing as well. The age-specific mortality rate for a boy born in 2015 is expected to be 80.0 years and for a girl, 85.6 years.[26] Life expectancy in France is comparable to the EU average when excluding eastern European countries. A few years ago, female life expectancy in France was one of the highest in the European community, a fact directly linked to the easy access to health care that French people enjoy.[27] Today the gap has been narrowed for most European countries.

The slowdown in France's birth rate experienced in the past decades and the simultaneous increase in life expectancy have led to an aging of the population. 18.8% of the population was over 64 at the beginning of 2016,[27] which represents 1 out of 6 people; the ratio was 1 out of 8 thirty years ago. This trend is likely to continue with the aging of the baby boomers born after World War II, a phenomenon known as the *papy-boom*. According to statistical forecasts, in 2020, there will be more people over 60 years old in France than below 20. In 2050, around one-third of the French population is expected to be over 60 years old.[28] However, there is a slight increase of the young population, with 18.5% of the population under 15 at the beginning of 2016.[28]

Employment rates are 75.5% for men and 67.5% for women, respectively.[29] Around 48.0% of employed workers are women. Some 76.8% of workers are in services and 2.8% in agriculture.[30]

Poverty

The National Institute of Statistics and Economic Studies (INSEE) defines the relative poverty threshold as 50% of the nation's median living standard, while a value of 60% is used for comparisons within the EU by Eurostat, INSEE's European counterpart.

In 2013, France had an average per capita living standard of €23,150. One-half of its population had a living standard of under €20,000, while the other half had a living standard of over €20,000.[31] The poverty threshold was €833 per month using the 50% value and €1,000 using the 60% value.[32] This means that 8% and 14% of the French population were living under the poverty thresholds, respectively, which represents between 4.953 and 8.648 million people.[33]

Religion

Since 1905, church and state have been officially separated, and secularity is a notion strongly defended. Religion is a private matter, and on principle, the French state does not conduct any religious poll or census. Therefore, information about religions in France can only be based on estimates and extrapolations of nongovernment polls.

Although France is a traditionally Catholic country whose history has been molded in part by the church, the influence of the church has enormously diminished. Only 51%–60% of the population is baptized, and a large part of the population claims to be agnostic or atheist. In 2006–2007 a nonofficial survey among the French people gave a picture of a country with a majority of Christians, with 51% of the people claiming to be Catholics. The rest of the population was divided as follows: 31% atheist, 4% Muslim, 3% Protestant, and 1% Jewish. According to the CIA *World Factbook*, around 9% of the French population claims to be Muslim.

Health Status of the Population

An assessment of the health of the French population is enviable at first sight. Infant mortality is only 3%, a figure that keeps decreasing. This is lower than the European average of 3.44%.[27] Besides very high life expectancy, the French also enjoy very high ratios of healthy-life years; a French woman born in 2011 can expect 63.5 years of healthy life, and a French man can expect 61.8.[34] However, the current trend shows a decrease since 2009 (64.6 for a woman and 62.8 for a man in 2009). Technical progress explains part of the constant increases that France experienced until that time. Today's decrease is preoccupying because it occurs in a time when technical progress is made daily, a factor that should push the limits even further.

However, if the French die on average later than most, they die mostly at an age when they should not die, especially men, with a premature mortality rate in 2014 of 252 per 100,000 people, compared to 125 for women.[35] These deaths are mainly linked to the consumption of tobacco and alcohol. In France, the main causes of premature death are circulatory diseases, which account for 33.3% of deaths, cancers, which cause more than 25.0%, followed by violent death (accidents, suicides, and other causes) at about 7.7%, and respiratory diseases, 6.7%.[36] Dietary risks, tobacco smoking, and high blood pressure are France's main risks factors that account for most disease burden. As people die prematurely more frequently in some regions of France than others, it seems that there are some marked regional inequalities regarding health in France. Regional eating and living habits that are culturally linked do not fully explain these disparities. Healthcare availability seems to be unequal throughout the territory, and prevention campaigns do not seem effective enough. Finally, the level of vaccination of children in France is unsatisfactory according to the WHO standards. Only 72% of children under two were vaccinated against measles in 2014.[37]

▸ Brief History of the Healthcare System

France's current health system is the product of a long history. The oldest French hospital is reputedly Paris's hôtel-Dieu, which, according to tradition, was founded by Saint Landry in the year 650. Admittedly, the notion of the hospital really appeared during the 12th and 13th centuries. Managed by the church, the hôtels-Dieu were financed by contributions from wealthy nobles and bourgeois. At the time, their main goal was to provide shelter, food, and care for the destitute. The first hospital in the modern-day sense is the *maison royale de santé*, founded in 1607 by Henri IV—also located in the capital, known today as the Hôpital Saint-Louis. The first example of rationalization of the public health organization, it was built on the outskirts of the city for sanitation reasons.[38] In 1662, Louis XIV ordered the creation of an hôtel-Dieu and a hospice in every important city of the French kingdom to welcome and seclude the poor, the elderly, the tramp, and the orphan.

The French Revolution

With the 1789 French Revolution, the church-linked notion of charity was replaced by that of assistance. Although impossible to apply at the time, the basic principles of modern health care were articulated for the first time: the human body is not a commodity, public health is the responsibility of the state, and society must ensure the subsistence of the poor either through the supply of work or by sustaining them if they are unable to work. Public aid is part of the guaranteed rights of the citizen, and social help is a social debt owed to everyone. In 1794, hospitals were nationalized, and their administration was put in the hands of the municipalities in 1796, thus returning the management of public health under the responsibility of the state through a highly decentralized system.

From the 19th Century to 1945: Public Health at the Heart of the System

During the 19th century and the first half of the 20th century, the regulation of public health problems and the development of a real health organization brought stability to the French healthcare system. The evolution of medical and sanitary practices as well as social development concomitantly transformed the face of health care. Medical progress and discoveries led to the adoption of laws and rules to address sanitary problems and improve people's health. These included laws on sanitary practices to contain epidemics (1822), laws on treatments and procedures for mental diseases (1838), spring water management and water sanitation (1856), mandatory vaccinations, disinfection procedures, mandatory reports of transmissible diseases, and regulation of new constructions (1902).[39] By the beginning of the 20th century, the 1902 law compiled all past legislation and put the responsibility of its application in the hands of the mayors who officially became the protectors and defenders of public health. However, the management of public health can be difficult to enforce when it is solely in the hands of local authorities. Therefore, in 1920 the creation of the Ministry of Health in charge of hygiene, assistance, and social planning put health care back under the authority of the central state. In 1941, the hospital law further enforced the weight of the central state in health care by putting most of the hospital management under direct control of the Ministry of Health, as opposed to the former exclusively communal management of the hospitals voted for in 1796.

Financing Through Mutual Benefit Companies as Opposed to Public Assistance

While sanitary legislation was developing on the one hand, on the other hand rose the question of financial resources for health care. From the beginning, health care in France was self-paid by the people who used it. You called the doctor, and you paid for the service. Then, at the beginning of the 19th century, the notion of social protection began to develop under the form of provision for the future. Everyone had to be able to pay their own health expenses and had to plan for them. That was the funding concept for the mutual benefit movement. In 1852, a decree allowed the creation of mutual benefit companies under state control. Their goal was to provide temporary aid for their members when sick, injured, or disabled and to cover for their funeral expenses. Mutual companies with a certain number of honorary members were also allowed to provide pension funds. In 1898, mutual benefit companies were freed from state control, and a mutuality code was published to define their roles and missions. By 1900, the number of mutual benefit associations had reached 13,000, with 2.5 million members. They continued to develop in the early decades of the 20th century, and in 1940 these associations had nearly 10 million members.[40] They are still an important force in French political life.

However, those mutual benefit companies provided care for their members only. Penniless people still had to rely on charity. Although public aid has been a recognized right since the French Revolution, it remained poorly developed, and it was only in 1893 that this fundamental right became officially enforced through the free medical assistance law. Through the creation of the Office of Assistance, anyone without resources was guaranteed free help, at-home medical assistance, or hospitalization in the city where he or she lived, from the department or the state. In 1904 this law was extended to children, then to the elderly, disabled, and incurable in 1905, and finally to pregnant women in 1913. Thus the hospital became the place of reference for health care, a first-time status for this institution.

Transition to the Notion of Insurance

The beginning of insurance for health matters is linked to the notion of worker accidents. Until 1898, the victim of a work-related accident had to prove that the employer was at fault in order to get coverage for his medical expenses. In 1898, a new legislation stated that in a case of a work accident, the employer was systematically personally responsible and would therefore have to support all of the related expenses for the employee. To protect themselves against this risk, employers called upon insurance companies to cover their employees. The insurance company's logic is different from that of the mutualist philosophy because there is a direct link between damage and premium, and it is important for evaluating the potential risk for individuals or groups of people.

The 1898 law covered only industry workers. In 1930, an Act on Social Insurance was signed for "the emergence of a statutory insurance system." This legislation created a system of compulsory protection for employees in industry and business whose earnings fell below a certain level. It provided insurance in five areas: illness, maternity, disability, old age, and death. By the outbreak of World War II (in 1939), two-thirds of the French population was covered for illness, with free choice of the organization providing coverage.[45] However, this social protection applied only to employed people, leaving a large part of the French population without coverage. Moreover, social protection remained highly unorganized, as people could choose from a multitude of organizations.

The institutionalization of the insurance system further developed the role of the hospital, which through a 1943 decree, became a sanitary and social establishment destined to treat the sick, the elderly, the disabled, the incurable, and pregnant women, as well as those whose treatment was in charge of the public collectivities and of insurance companies.

All of these laws and decrees set the basis for the future evolution of the healthcare system that would take place after World War II.

La Sécurité Sociale

The present system of social security, including statutory health insurance, was established in 1945, at the end of World War II. The founding principle of social security was to give everyone the guarantee that under any circumstances they would be given the necessary means to insure their subsistence and that of their family under decent conditions. Its creation also called for the development of a vast nationwide mandatory mutual aid organization that would be useful only by being extremely general and open in terms of the people it covered and of the risks it guarded against. Therefore, the 1945 ruling replaced the many insurance organizations that had developed during the past century with a single network of coordinated insurance departments. The goal was to extend coverage to all individuals, regardless of their employment status, and to provide everyone with similar rights.

The conditions covered by social security in 1945 were sickness, maternity, disability, old age, and death. A 1946 addition included a child benefit and protection for work-related accidents. Today, social security covers four areas of risk: sickness-maternity-disability-death, family, old age, widowhood, and work accidents or profession-related sickness.

When social security was funded, it was based on the work insurance system created in 1898 and on the 1930 Social Insurance act. Thus it concerned only industry workers and their families. To give protection to everyone, the legislation progressively extended coverage to different categories of the population. Statutory health insurance was extended to state employees in 1947, to farmers in 1961, and to self-employed nonagricultural workers in 1966. In 1948, industrial and commercial professionals, artisans, and other workers were given their own social cover scheme. This process of expanding coverage was recognized in the statutes of 1974, which established a system of personal insurance for those who did not fall into any of the categories already covered. To obtain this insurance, individuals had to pay a contribution, or if they had insufficient means, to request that the department contribute on their behalf. In practice, however, access to health insurance remained problematic for certain population groups.[45]

Universal Health Coverage

The year 1999 was a milestone in French health care with an act that passed on June 1999 establishing universal statutory health coverage, CMU, for any person with permanent residence in France. For people whose income was below a certain level, this access to medical coverage was free, emphasizing the French philosophy of national solidarity.

Together with the CMU, the legislator created Complementary Universal Health Coverage, or CMU-C, with the goal of helping people receive voluntary health insurance to cover all expenses not included in the basic social security scheme. This meant that people with an income below a certain level were exempted from most of the expenses that normally remained at the charge of the patient and for which most people subscribed to a voluntary health insurance contract: hospital daily charge, moderating ticket for consultations and medicines, dental care, optics, etc.

Despite those measures, the system still excluded people whose income was just slightly over the minimum income level defined to become a CMU and CMU-C recipient. Therefore, in 2004 the Complementary Health Aid (ACS) was created. People with resources between the CMU level and the CMU level plus 15.0% could benefit from a government-fixed reduction for voluntary health insurance premiums. This measure further increased the development of mutual companies, the purveyors of voluntary health insurance. By the end of 2007, 7.4% of the population benefited from the CMU and the CMU-C.[41] Finally, for destitute people who were ineligible for the CMU for lack of proof of stable or regular residency in France, the State Medical Aid (Medicaid or AME) was established, putting all their medical care expenses under the responsibility of the state.

To summarize, in 2004, the old system of individual insurance involving contributions financed by income scales (which varied throughout the system) was replaced by a system based on a citizen's right to health insurance. There was then a situation of social protection through insurance rather than state aid. The Universal Health Coverage Act further shifted the balance of the health insurance system away from a work-based system toward a system of universal health coverage.[45]

Financing and Regulating Health Care

In 1945, the founders of the system hoped that the better access to health care provided to all through social security would help keep the population in good health, thus reducing the need for care and health expenditures. However, the ever-increasing demand and offer of health care have led to a constant increase of healthcare expenditures. In the 1960s, healthcare consumption expanded tremendously, while revenues did not. With the 1970s and the beginning of economic difficulties, financial constraints became a main driver of healthcare policies.

Social security was funded on the principle of employees' and employers' contributions as a proportion of wages and salaries. Later, coverage was extended to those on benefits (retired, those on early retirement benefit, and the unemployed). The contribution rates for health insurance have steadily increased to cover spending on health care. Between 1992 and 1997, contribution rates remained stable at 12.8% of gross earnings for the employer and 6.8% for the employee.[45] A law voted on in 1990 introduced the notion of taxing all income in order to provide health care. The goal was to widen the social security system's financial base. Called the General Social Contribution (CSG), it is still paid today by every French fiscal resident and represents around 7.0% of salaries, 8.0% of personal assets revenues, and 9.0% of gaming gains. This contribution is, in fact, a tax on total income. Health insurance funds' revenue has therefore been partially disconnected from earnings, making it less vulnerable to wage and employment fluctuations. While this change has widened the revenue base of health insurance, it has not increased the actual amount of revenue collected.

Confronted with the impossible task of increasing revenue for health care and balancing the accounts of the health insurance system, governments have implemented a succession of cost containment policies in the past 30 years. However, in a system characterized by a fee-for-service payment for doctors, retrospective reimbursement, and unrestricted freedom of choice for patients, it is not easy to implement cost control policies.

Regulating Demand

In an attempt to contain the demand for health care, governments and voluntary insurance companies have tried several times to lower the reimbursement rate of some health expenditures. The goal was to make people contribute more to their health expenses in a direct way and to increase public awareness of health costs. The hospital daily charge and the moderating ticket have increased over the years. Dental treatments, optics, some prostheses, and many prescribed medicines have seen their reimbursement rates drastically reduced, if not brought back to zero for many medicines. However, these policies have met great resistance from the general public and have not yielded the expected results. Since 1998, the debate has shifted toward steering demand and organizing channels of treatment to limit free choice. In 1998, the notion of doctor referral was introduced, with general practitioners becoming gatekeepers, with voluntary registration of patients. In 2004, the referring doctor became an obligation for patients. Reimbursement rates by social security were from then on lowered to 60% instead of 70% if patients did not have a prescription from their referent when consulting another specialist and to 30% instead of 70% when consulting a GP who was not their referent. Since 2004, a patient must pay €1 directly out of pocket for every consultation without insurance coverage. In 2008, deductibles were introduced for the first time.

Curbing Supply

Policies relating to the supply of treatment have targeted capacity as well as professional practices and charges for goods and services. Control of capacity was one of the first instruments introduced after 1970. Limiting supply rapidly came to be seen as an essential mechanism on the basis of the potential for *supplier-induced demand* in health care, with which patients have a low level of information and do not have to bear the full cost of treatment. This type of control has been exercised in two ways: by the medical map, which until 2003 made the provision of hospital beds and certain kinds of equipment subject to authorization and limited them on the basis of an agreed ratio of beds and equipment per head of population, and by the *numerus clausus* system, which regulates access to medical training.[45]

Regarding professional practices, since the 1970s, measures have been put in place to influence the behavior of healthcare providers. Medical guidelines and evaluations have had a significant and lasting impact on prescribing patterns without, however, having a clear macroeconomic impact.

There have been significant attempts at keeping the price of health care low through negotiations with healthcare professionals on the level of charges plus administrative regulation of the price of reimbursable drugs. In terms of global comparisons, both overall drug prices and payments to physicians have been relatively low in France for a considerable period of time. The evolution of prices for medical services and goods has been moderate in relation to inflation in the long term; between 1978 and 2000 the consumer price index rose by 280% (210% for ambulatory treatment and 150% for pharmaceuticals). France's high volume of consumption, particularly where pharmaceuticals are concerned, may be linked to the relatively low level of prices.[45] Since 1960, the government has controlled medical fees by imposing ceilings on charges and setting out the conditions under which these ceilings might be exceeded. As a result, medical fees in France today are extremely low, with a medical consultation costing €23 for a GP (2016 tariffs). It was €22 in 2010.

As a possible solution to the price/volume dilemma, restrictive budgets were introduced in different sectors of the healthcare system in the 1980s and 1990s. From 1984 to 1985 onward, the system of funding public hospitals using a per diem rate was replaced by a system of global budgets. At the beginning of the 1990s, targets for limiting the expenditure of a whole sector were negotiated with laboratories, private for-profit hospitals, and freelance nurses. If these targets are not met, corrective mechanisms, such as lowering levels of charges and claiming refunds (as penalties) from practitioners, may be applied. Most healthcare professionals have remained fiercely opposed to both the principle and practice of a restrictive total framework for expenditure ex ante. The 1996 Juppé reform clearly included doctors among those subject to the principle of such restrictive budgets, with refunds in cases of noncompliance with budget targets.[45]

The 2010–2012 Hospital, Patients, Health, and Territories Bill[42]

Hospitals, Patients, Health, and Territories was the official name of the bill presented on October 22 by the minister of health Roselyne Bachelot, which passed in June 2009. The bill was the first stage of the Hospital 2012 Plan, launched by then president Nicolas Sarkozy. It aimed to revamp the French healthcare system as a whole by addressing the main healthcare stake: guaranteeing better and equal access to care for all French people and legal residents, whatever their geographic location. This meant fighting against geographical *medical deserts*, a decompartmentalization between ambulatory, hospital, and medico-social care, a better management of chronic diseases and of youth health, as well as a better coordination of the healthcare system in general.

The bill contained four main points:

- Reinforcement of the *prevention* against all addictions, especially for young people and women.
- *Access to healthcare* thanks to a better repartition of health professionals throughout the country and a regional organization of healthcare provision.
- *Modernization of hospitals* with the end of the frontiers between hospital and city medicine. Hospitals were to merge, reconvert, or specialize in a certain type of care. Resources and technical means would be polarized in major hospitals, while small structures would be encouraged to find other orientations and to specialize, notably in the rehabilitation of the disabled and care for the elderly. Private organizations would have to provide care to everybody, acting as a public service.
- *Territorial organization* and the implementation of regional health agencies would centralize the powers currently exercised by health agencies, such as regional hospital agencies, or health insurance. Led by the regional prefects, they would oversee the overall delivery of care, whether private, hospital, or medico-social.

The Fourcade Law passed in August 2011 partly amended some of the major articles of the HPHT bill, hence undermining its possible benefits for French health care. The HPHT bill has been a success to some extent in terms of prevention, modernization of hospitals, and territorial organization. However, access to quality health care has not been successfully implemented. There are still medical deserts in some parts of France. Even worse, as collateral consequences of the territorial reorganization of health supply, some regions saw medical services reduced when some local hospitals closed in order to regroup regionally.

La Loi Santé—January 2016

During his presidential election campaign in 2012, François Hollande promised to further reduce the disparities that still prevent the fair and universal access to health care for the French people. La Loi Santé, much criticized by medical professionals, was passed in January 2016 to address three major challenges: adapting to the aging of the population, accounting for the increase of chronic diseases, and addressing the social and territorial disparities for healthcare access over the country.

As France's population is aging and people live longer, patients' needs are shifting. More than 20% of the population is over 65, and it is expected that by 2040, 10 million people will be over 75. People live on average 2 years longer than they did 10 years ago. Therefore, this longer living and ever growing population must be taken care of for longer. This older population also suffers from long and chronic diseases: more than one out of four people present a chronic condition, which implies that care usually involves different health providers, a major challenge to coordinate for a complex and compartmentalized system. Finally, disparities, whether social or geographical, still weight heavily on life expectancy. In 2012, life expectancy at birth varied by almost 5 points for males and 3 points for females, depending on the region where they lived. Social factors like income level, education, profession, and life and work conditions also have a direct impact on people's health: there are 10 times more obese children in blue-collar families than in higher income or white-collar families. Also, in kindergarten, 80.0% of children from blue-collar families had dental cavities and 50.0% of children from higher income or white-collar families had cavities. In 2010, 51.0% of unemployed people were daily smokers. This number drops to 33.4% for the active population of the same age.[43] The healthcare system must develop a solution to level these disparities.

La Loi Santé is organized around three axes: innovation as prevention, innovation for proximity, and innovation to promote patients' rights and safety.

- *Innovation as prevention:* prevention is the heart of the health system with key measures to enhance the fight against smoking, alcoholism, and drugs; to develop nutritional awareness; and to prevent STDs. Children are at the core of the measures because they are tomorrow's adults. An attending physician will be designated for each child and will follow him from 0 to 16 years old to detect any risk factor early on.
- *Innovation for proximity:* ambulatory and local care becomes the priority, and the GP is reinforced as the heart of the healthcare network. Consultation costs will be paid directly to the GP from *securité sociale*, ensuring that everyone can visit his/her doctor even if they cannot offer to put the money upfront and get reimbursement later. Patient information about local medical services and their opening hours is emphasized; some medical professions are given more competences to deliver public services (e.g., a nurse or a dental surgeon can prescribe smoking substitutes), and the electronic medical file is once again envisaged to ensure that the patient's medical information is available anytime anywhere.

- *Innovation to promote patients' rights and safety:* patients' rights are reinforced, and new rights are instituted, like the possibility to file class action suits in case of medical wrongdoings. Some heavy pathologies do not need to be declared after a certain lapse, a real progress for insurance purposes. Access to abortion becomes easier. Medicine traceability is reinforced. Medical data becomes accessible, under conditions of anonymity, to develop new services and facilitate research and innovation.

This new law was projected to come into application during 2016. The medical profession is totally against payment for services being passed onto *sécurité sociale* and the complementary insurances. The fear that this will make them mere employees of insurance companies, which would therefore impose conditions onto physicians, both in terms of tariffs and of working conditions (number of patients seen, prescriptions, etc.) Whether this new law will help improve health care in France or not remains to be seen.

Also, effective January 1, 2016, employers in France must provide each employee compulsory private complementary health insurance.

- The French health and social protection system is original in several ways, largely due to its history. The early public assistance and welfare systems were progressively replaced with a social insurance system, introduced at the end of the 19th century and continued throughout the first half of the 20th century. However, social protection in its current form was only introduced shortly after World War II. From 1946, the right to social protection was recognized in the preamble of the French Constitution. Even if they have been adapted over time, the basic principles of the French social protection system, progressively put in place since the end of World War II, still apply today:
- *Universality*: all nationals and residents are covered by the system, and it is compulsory to sign up with the social protection organizations.
- *All-encompassing*: the French system covers every possible eventuality in life (health, parenthood, old age, disability, industrial accidents and professional illnesses, family benefits and dependency, as well as unemployment).
- *Solidarity*: the French social protection system stems from the professional insurance schemes introduced before World War II. Today, however, it combines this insurance-based approach—particularly with contributions deducted from employment income—with measures reliant on solidarity and collective financing.[44]

Description of the Current Healthcare System

When studying the French healthcare system, one must keep in mind that social security is the main framework and that all the actors, decisions, implementations, and policies relate to social security. In describing the current health system, one must begin by looking at the care supply, which includes hospitals and health professionals.

Facilities

In France, hospitals are core to the healthcare system.[45] Hospitals are planned using a medical map (quantitative) and the regional strategic health plan (qualitative).[45] The medical map divides each section into healthcare regions and psychiatric regions. The Ministry is required to authorize expensive equipment and specialized care. French medical institutions can be roughly divided into three categories: public hospitals, private not-for-profit hospitals, and private for-profit hospitals and clinics.[46]

In 2013, there were 3,192 hospitals in operation in France.[47] There were approximately 4,000 in 2008.[48] The 1,458 public hospitals tend to be larger in size than private hospitals and account for about 25% of all hospitals (i.e., 1,000 in 2008). These public hospitals provide for research and training of medical students and personnel and are generally well equipped. Nonprofit private hospitals number 712 (i.e., 22.0%), down from 1,400, or about one-third of all French hospitals in 2008. Private for-profit hospitals that used to be most numerous, at 1,750, specialized most often in medical, surgical, or obstetric procedures and are now down to 1,022 (i.e., 32%). Although all hospitals receive a per diem payment, the services covered in that rate vary based on hospital type. Public hospitals receive a single per diem rate that covers all services provided, while private for-profit hospitals bill medical fees and other items, such as prostheses, separately. Patients also contribute 20% of the cost of hospital stays per day.

The number of hospital beds has decreased in recent years. There are roughly 6.3 beds per 1,000 inhabitants,[49] which is over the European average, with a slight decrease of inpatient care beds and acute care beds and, as in many other European countries, a notable increase in beds in long-term nursing care homes. Every year, the regional courts of auditors identify most hospitals for their low occupancy rates. Some maternities have an annual occupancy rate under 60%, and this can go down to 27% for the smaller ones. This abundance of hospital beds explains in part why hospital expenses weigh so heavily in the global health expenditures of the country. Hospital costs represent 38% of France's total health expenditures, whereas the European average is 31%. France has closed 32,000 hospital beds over the past 20 years but has not yet succeeded in overcoming strong public resistance. Closure of small, local hospitals is underway in many remote regions to promote bigger structures around the main cities. But to align with international standards, 98,000 beds out of the existing 414,000 should be closed. At the end of 2013, the court of auditors declared that 18,000 hospital beds were to be closed. Ambulatory care is clearly designated as the preferred mode of hospital care whenever possible, but France does not seem ready to step away from its tradition of hospitalized care. Neither is it ready to part with small local structures, even when their size and lack of the latest medical technology impair efficiency and safety.[50]

Public hospitals have specific obligations, such as ensuring the continuity of care, teaching, and training. The budgets they receive are largely based on history and on the number of patients they treat. Private for-profit hospitals concentrate on elective surgeries and obstetrics and rely financially on fee-for-service remuneration. Proprietary hospitals, typically smaller than public hospitals, have traditionally emphasized elective surgery and obstetrics, leaving more complex cases to the public sector. However, although there has been no change in its relative share of beds over the past 15 years, the proprietary sector has consolidated, and many proprietary hospitals have developed a strong capacity for cardiac surgery and radiation therapy.

There is no significant difference in the quality of care between public and private hospitals. A uniform information system has been implemented to monitor activity from the various establishments. Gradually, all private and public establishments will switch to diagnosis-related group payment systems.[50]

The number of non-physician personnel per bed is higher in public hospitals than in private hospitals; in the aggregate, it is 67% lower than in U.S. hospitals. This difference in hospital staffing may reflect a more technical and intense level of service in U.S. hospitals. It also reflects differences between a national health insurance system and the U.S. health system, which is characterized by large numbers of administrative and clerical personnel whose main tasks focus on billing many hundreds of payers, documenting all medical procedures performed, and handling risk management and quality assurance activities.[51]

Healthcare personnel and associated enterprises and organizations for ambulatory care are mostly in the private sector in France. Outpatient care is provided by generalists, specialists, and outpatient departments of hospitals. Competition among GPs and between GPs and specialists appears to be fierce. However, over the past 15 years, the trend has been for GPs and specialists providing outpatient care to regroup in medical posts, conveniently located in industrialized and commercial areas with access to modern facilities and parking spaces. Other suppliers of medical support services, like pharmacies and optical services, are often nearby. As this geographical synergy provides efficiency and convenience for patients, those medical posts could become more attractive than hospital outpatient facilities, which are often overloaded and more often than not deliver services in aging facilities.

Specialized medicine increasingly concentrates on the use of high technology diagnostic techniques, while general medicine focuses more on geriatric care. Consultation of physicians is frequent in France. On average, ambulatory patients consulted a doctor 6.4 times per year.[54] There are also about 1,000 municipal health centers where salaried doctors provide primary and preventive care, usually in urban areas. They are operated by municipalities, mutual benefit organizations, and other groups, and they play an important role in providing services for the poor.

France has established a nationwide system to oversee prenatal and early childhood health care. The care team includes nurses, physicians, social workers, and psychologists. This system is geared to identify health problems early and thereby reduce complications and expenditures later.

Workforce

Doctors and other healthcare professionals can work in both public hospitals and private practices, or they can choose to work in only one type of structure. They are mostly self-employed and paid on a fee-for-service basis. The number of general practitioners and specialists in France is almost evenly split: of the 222,150 physicians in France in 2015, 58.8% were specialists, and 46.2% provided primary care. Around 50.0% of specialists and 67.0% of general practitioners work in private practice, some working part time in the hospital setting.[52] Notably, private general practitioners in France still make home visits, which account for about 12.0% of their care activities. Those visits are billed at the same rate as an office appointment, €23, plus a flat €10 fee for transportation. Night visits are billed between €35 and €48 more. About 41.0% of physicians work in public hospitals or establishments only, and their salary is determined by the government. The majority of practicing medical doctors is concentrated in metropolitan France, and they operate essentially as independent practitioners. Today, many physicians feel that the prestige of working in a hospital does not compensate for the difficult working conditions. Around 56.0% of physicians work in private practices and are paid on a fee-for-service basis.

Providers receive full or partial payment from patients at the time of service, or they can be paid part of the fee directly by social security within 10 days. Experts set the relative weight of the procedures, and the prices are negotiated by physicians' unions and public health insurance funds.

Physicians represent 18.25% of total health employment. Physicians play a key political role in the healthcare system. As of 2015, there were 222,150 physicians licensed to practice in France. In the last 30 years, the number of physicians has tripled, but the rate of increase is now very slight. Since 1971, the Ministry of Health has limited the number of medical students, which has resulted in a decrease in the number of physicians today and in the near future, since many currently active doctors will soon retire. As of 2015, there were 3.37 physicians per 1,000 people, even lower than in 2009 when there were 3.39 physicians per 1,000 people. There is a considerable shortage of nurses, as nursing is a fairly unpopular career in France.

Since the creation of social security, the relationship between private practice physicians and the state and public insurance funds has been strained. Experts set the relative price of procedures that are then negotiated by physicians' unions and public health insurance funds. Around 99% of practitioners conform to the *Tarif de convention* (tariff references), which sets prices. Tariff references are the fixed rates to be used by doctors, and rates are set according to national convention for all health services. A contract (*convention*) that sets the general regulatory framework and the remuneration of the profession is supposed to be signed every five years by physicians' unions. Subsequent *conventions* allowed some physicians to charge more than social security tariffs (1980), limited this right (1990), and implemented official medical practice guidelines (*Références médicales opposables*) in 1993. The negotiations between doctors' unions and the funds are usually strained. The root of the problem is that private practice physicians are strongly opposed to the setting of caps on outpatient expenditures. They have always had a great deal of freedom over when they set up shop, how they practice, and what they prescribe (compared to their counterparts in other countries). Yet the bulk of their income is paid by public funds. This contradiction has become more glaring as concerns about soaring health expenditures grow. Medical practitioners and clinics/hospitals who are not *conventions* (complying with the tariff references) must display their prices. In some situations, certain medical practitioners (such as surgeons with extra qualifications or experience) can charge more than the *Tarif de convention*. The extra fee is called a *dépassement*,[53] and it is not reimbursed by social security.

The last tariff convention was signed in July 2011. It sets a milestone in the relationship between physicians and the legal social insurance entities. Fee-for-service remains the core of physician remuneration, but physicians can also get remuneration based on the Realization of Public Health Objectives (Rémunération sur Objectifs de Santé Publique). Those objectives are the computerization of physicians' offices with, among other things, an increase of the tele-transmission of at least two-thirds of billing documents and the improvement of medical practices regarding prevention, chronic diseases, and prescriptions content.

French physicians earn substantially less than their American colleagues. Some rural general practitioners barely make a living, working long hours for barely minimum wage. On average, a physician earns approximately twice the average income of fellow citizens. Refer to **TABLE 11-2** for statistics. Medical school is free, but competition is fierce—only 20,000 out of 60,000 students are selected after the first year. Attending an expensive and prestigious prep school before and during the first year of medical school has become the norm. Because malpractice suits are much less common in France, healthcare providers pay modest premiums for liability insurance. However, this trend is changing fast, and lately premiums have been increasing alarmingly.

Physicians today complain that they collapse under administrative work that prevents them from doing their real jobs. The ever-growing administrative part of their daily workload makes the profession much less attractive for new generations, as this administrative overload consumes so much time for physicians that they end up barely making a living. This is especially true for general practitioners. Consequently, there is a real shortage of them in France, and waiting times have dramatically increased for patients to get an appointment. GPs work extremely long hours, hardly have a family life, and see their revenues drop. The profession is pursued less and less, and doctors who retire are

TABLE 11-2 Healthcare Professions in France, 2012–2015[54]

	2012	2013	2014	2015	Density for 100,000 inhabitants* (January 1)
Medical and pharmaceutical professions					
Doctors	216,762	218,296	219,834	222,150	337
General practitioners	101,896	101,803	102,140	102,485	155
Private practice doctors	64,638	63,595	62,986	62,211	94
Salaried doctors	32,447	32,597	32,914	33,475	51
"Mixed" physicians**	4,811	5,611	6,240	6,799	10
Specialized doctors	114,866	116,493	117,694	119,665	181
Private practice doctors	47,387	46,386	45,688	45,142	68
Salaried doctors	54,594	55,593	56,625	58,226	88
"Mixed" physicians**	12,885	14,514	15,381	16,297	25
Dental surgeons	40,599	40,833	41,186	41,495	63
Midwives***	19,535	20,235	20,772	21,632	148
Pharmacists	72,811	73,670	73,598	74,345	113
Medical assistants					
State certified and authorized nurses	567,564	595,594	616,796	638,248	967
Masseuses-physiotherapists	75,164	77,778	80,759	83,619	127
Pedicurists-podiatrists	12,085	12,430	12,850	13,250	20
Speech therapists	21,220	21,902	22,744	23,521	36
Orthopedists	3,655	3,826	4,016	4,185	6
Opticians	25,010	27,340	29,071	32,245	49
Psychomotor experts	8,385	8,891	9,516	10,252	16
X-ray technicians	30,201	31,242	32,316	33,464	51

(continues)

TABLE 11-2 Healthcare Professions in France, 2012–2015 (continued)

	2012	2013	2014	2015	Density for 100,000 inhabitants* (January 1)
Occupational therapists	8,079	8,539	9,122	9,691	15
Hearing-care professionals	2,625	2,768	2,920	3,090	5

* number of professionals in activity per 100,000 inhabitants.
** "Mixed" physicians are self-employed, but some of them may be hospital physicians as a secondary activity.
*** the density of midwives was calculated in relation to the female population of ages 15 to 49.

Reproduced from National Institute of Statistics and Economic Studies. Healthcare Professions in 2015. http://www.insee.fr/en/themes/tableau.asp?reg_id=0&ref_id=NATTEF06103. Accessed May 26, 2016.

almost never replaced. This is a recurring problem in remote parts of France that attract even fewer candidates compared to more attractive places like the Riviera or big cities. Even there, the shortage of doctors, and of GPs in particular, becomes preoccupying.

Technology and Equipment

Medical technology is one of the most innovative industries in the world, improving and saving lives every day. Data on the European medical technology industry show that in 2014, the medical technology market in Europe was estimated at roughly €100 billion. France is the second largest market in Europe for medical equipment and represents 16.00% of the market. Average expenditure on medical technology as a percentage of total expenditure in health care was estimated at 5.00% to 10.00% (between 0.52% and 1.04% of the GDP). Expenditure on medical technology per capita in Europe is at around €195 (weighted average), compared with €380 in the United States.[55] The data also reveal that the European medical technology industry invests some €5.8 billion in R&D and employs nearly 575,000 highly skilled workers.[56]

The country hosts 2,500 manufacturers of medical equipment, who produced €11 billion in gross sales in 2010. This market shows a continuous annual growth of about 7% per year and shows an even greater potential with the aging population.[57]

In comparison to other European countries, France is the sixth largest exporter of medical technology, exporting about €9 billion in 2014. France is the third largest importer of medical technologies in Europe, with €11 billion, so there is a trade deficit.[60]

The French medical technology industry can be proud of its dynamic international profile since several major innovations are credited to its very dynamic R&D sector.[58] Over 20% of the projects supported by the French national council for the promotion of research in industry (Oséo-ANVAR) concern breakthrough innovations (i.e., global or European firsts). French cutting-edge medical technology has now placed the country in the forefront of quality health care.

France is a leader in several medical fields. Cardiovascular medicine entered a new era with the advent of drug-eluting medical devices (prostheses that also release a drug). The new generation of coronary stents is a typical example: these metal mesh tubes not only preserve arterial patency but also release an active substance that prevents restenosis (recurrence of arterial lumen narrowing). Parkinson's disease is now treated at a deep-brain level using electric neurostimulation, with electrodes implanted in the brain and connected via a subcutaneous wire to a small pulse generator inserted just below the clavicle.

Surgical robots coupled to 3-D simulators allow surgeons to practice and refine the most complex surgical procedures. The main innovations involved in this system are an artificial wrist and 3-D camera. Sitting at a workstation, the surgeon uses a set of finger controls to manipulate the surgical instruments and perform virtual surgery. His or her motions are analyzed and, after any hand tremor has been filtered out, these motions are translated to the robot's articulated arms in contact with the patient. Today Rosa, a robot manufactured by a southern French company, assists many surgeons worldwide during surgeries.

In the field of disabilities, industrial innovation is enhanced by medical partnerships. For instance, the technological innovation center of the Garches Hospital provides manufacturers with clinical expertise and evaluation protocols to help them develop new technical solutions (stair-climbing wheelchairs, puff-controlled alarm devices, etc.). Interventional radiology has changed radiologists into therapists. In this broad field, their role ranges from nodule aspiration (biopsy, sampling) to the complex treatments of vascular or tumoral lesions in various organs. These imaging-guided procedures use minimally invasive techniques and are usually performed under local anesthesia. Also, breast cancer is now treated using ultrasounds, a recent French protocol.

Telemedicine is a new approach that improves diabetic retinopathy screening and optimizes cardiac-patient monitoring and follow-up. Neonatology uses increasingly sophisticated and efficient equipment in varied fields, including heating and humidifying devices or nosocomial infection prevention technologies for incubators and pediatric transport. On December 8, 2013, the first artificial heart was implanted at the Georges Pompidou hospital in Paris. This is an emblematic example of medical innovation made in France.

France's commitment to advancing the healthcare industry—from regenerative medicine for neurodegenerative diseases to vaccines and vaccinotherapy—is noteworthy. Since 2005, France has established eight official innovation clusters that focus solely on biotechnology and health care. Projects within these clusters are selected for funding by the French government following a biannual request for project proposals.[59] The minister of health recently announced that €340 million would be allocated to Fabs, a public fund that was specially created to help and sponsor French start-ups in the medical technologies.[60]

Evaluation of the Healthcare System

Cost

Existing data—whether they come from surveys or are byproducts of the administrative system—consistently indicate that the French, in comparison to Americans, consult their doctors more often, are admitted to the hospital more often, and purchase more prescription drugs. Yet health expenditures per capita are lower in France, since the average prices of physician services, prescription drugs, and hospital services are significantly lower than in the United States.

Since 2008 there have been indications that welfare spending as a percentage of GDP is decreasing in France, but people have generally complained because of the original actions taken. For years, costs have exceeded the money coming into the system. Explanations for the crisis are numerous: the aging population, the increasing cost of the technology created for this aging population, the demand for higher standards, and the laid back, lazy attitude that a high level of welfare appears to engender. However, the signs of a decrease in state expenditure on welfare, plus more controls to ensure more efficient use of medical facilities, are everywhere, and France is no exception. Indeed, in 2005 France spent more on health care than any other country except Switzerland, reporting figures of health care as a percentage of GNP to the European Commission, including the United States, as outlined in Figure 11-2. In 2015, France still spent more on the health of its population, as a percentage of GNP, than most other countries of the OECD; nevertheless, it ranked after Germany, the Netherlands, and Sweden, as can be seen in **TABLE 11-3**.

The growth of health spending came to a halt in 2009 mainly because of the global financial and economic crisis, and the trend quickly reversed in 2013. However, France's health expenditure growth rate remains well below pre-crisis levels (0.9 for 2009–2013 vs. 1.5 for 2005–2009). In fact, at 1.2% in 2013, the increase in health spending was a little over the overall economic growth of the country, and therefore health expenditure as a share of GDP remains more or less stable.[61]

Health prices in France for goods and services are only slightly higher than in most European countries. On average, prescriptions and hospitalization times are the same in most European countries. These are not the explanatory factors for the rise of health expenditures in France. However, the rapid rise in the costs of new medications and technology strains the health budget. For example, French physicians and their patients have remarkable access to the latest chemotherapy, even experimental agents that may be unavailable to EU patients. Many of these drugs are budget-busters that may cost the equivalent of thousands of dollars per year. Also, managing the *sécurité sociale* is quite expensive. In 2010, administrative costs represented an average of 4% of total health expenditures, a percentage that France cannot seem to be able to lower.[62]

TABLE 11-3 Health Expenditures in OECD Countries in 2013

OECD country	GDP%
Germany	11.0
Australia	8.8
Austria	10.1
Belgium	10.2
Canada (2)	10.2
Chile	7.4
South Korea	6.9
Denmark	10.4
Spain	8.9
Estonia	6.0
United States	16.4
Finland	8.6
France	10.9
Greece	9.2
Hungary	7.4
Ireland	8.1
Iceland	8.7
Israel (2)	7.5
Italy	8.8
Japan	10.2
Luxemburg (1)	6.6
Mexico	6.2
Norway	8.9
New Zealand	9.5
Netherlands	11.1
Poland	6.4
Portugal (2)	9.0
Czech Republic	7.1
United Kingdom	8.5
Slovakia	7.6
Slovenia	8.7
Sweden	11.0
Switzerland	11.1
Turkey	5.1

Data from OECD. Health at a Glance 2015: OECD Indicators. http://www.oecd.org/els/health-systems/health-at-a-glance-19991312.htm. November 4, 2015.

The French system is much more generous to its entire population than the United States is to its seniors.[27] Unlike with Medicare, there are no deductibles. French citizens have only modest co-payments, which are dismissed for the chronically ill. In addition, most French people buy supplemental insurance to reduce any out-of-pocket expenses on extras such as eyeglasses, dental work, and private hospital rooms. Interestingly, in France, the sicker you get, the less you pay. Diabetes and other such chronic diseases, as well as critical surgeries (e.g., coronary bypass), are reimbursed at 100%. Cancer patients are not charged for their treatment. For medications the situation is also better for patients who are seriously ill. Patients suffering from colon cancer, for example, can receive Genentech Inc.'s Avastin at no charge. In the United States, a patient could pay US $48,000 a year for the same medication.

France also excels in prenatal and early childhood care. Since 1945, there has been a widespread network of thousands of healthcare facilities, called Protection Maternelle et Infantile, to make sure that every mother and child receive basic preventive care. Mothers are paid for attending prenatal and postnatal appointments. Children are evaluated by a team of private-practice pediatricians, nurses, midwives, psychologists, and social workers. When parents fail to bring their children in for regular checkups, a social worker will make a visit to the family home. This is all made affordable because the French government reimburses its doctors at a lower rate than U.S. physicians receive. This is more acceptable, in part, because medical schools in France are paid for by the state, so there are no exorbitant student loans to pay back, nor is malpractice insurance a crushing cost to French doctors. Physicians in the United States pay roughly between US $20,000 annually in low-cost states to $200,000 annually in high-cost states for malpractice insurance, and French doctors pay only a very small fraction of this. The average yearly net income for French doctors is around $106,000 ($82,000 for a GP, $133,000 for a specialist), a half to a third of the $230,000 that their American counterparts earn. The French government also pays two-thirds of the social security tax for most French physicians. This social security tax is typically 40% of the annual income.

The government's Assurance Maladie has a kind of monopoly both on the healthcare system and as France's largest buyer of medical services. This gives it the power to keep the fees charged by doctors low. About 90% of general practitioners in France have an agreement with Assurance Maladie specifying that they can't charge more than €23 (about US $28) for a consultation. For house calls they can add €10 to the bill. By comparison, under U.S. Medicare, doctors are paid around $92 for a first visit and $125 for a moderately complex consultation, according to the American College of Physicians (2009 data). If a specialist has spent at least 4 years practicing in a hospital, that specialist is free to charge what he or she wants, sometimes upward of $675 for a single consult, but American-style compensation is rare. There is an unspoken and undefined limit to what you can charge.

So far France has been able to keep the cost burden of patients low through a combination of price controls and increased government spending, but the latter effort has led to higher taxes for both employers and workers. Around 7% of healthcare expenditures were financed out of general revenue taxes in 1990, and the rest came from mandatory payroll taxes. By 2003, the general revenue figure had grown to 40%, and this was still not enough. Since 1985, the French national insurance system has been running constant deficits, which have mushroomed to over €13.5 billion in 2009. The French government has worked hard to reduce this deficit and has taken measures despite strong citizen resistance. It already required patients to register with a general practitioner before visiting a specialist or else to agree to a lesser reimbursement, similar to the arrangement present with many U.S. insurance plans. The past two reforms have focused on the following measures: developing ambulatory care to decrease the number of hospitalizations and to shift part of health care to outpatient facilities, encouraging the use of generic medicines by reimbursing a lesser part on brand medicines when a generic option is available, and decreasing the number of healthcare workers in the public sector by improving efficiency and closing hospital beds that are not fully occupied. As a result of those actions, the general deficit of the *sécurité sociale* has been lowered to €13.2 billion in 2014, and it is expected to drop to €10.6 billion for 2015. The NHS part of this deficit is expected to decrease from €9.7 billion to €6.6 billion in the same period (remember that there are three branches for the *sécurité sociale*: NHS, unemployment, and retirement funds).

In fact, the French approach to the problem is a combination of measures that can be summed up as follows:

1. to reduce waste by the introduction of controls on the national habit of shopping around for treatment and medicines
2. to improve the health of the nation by better planning of routine preventive treatment
3. to enlist the cooperation of the medical establishment and the health insurance industry in the control and management of the NHS system
4. to increase the patient's participation in the cost of treatment. French residents may consume as much health care as they like; however, to increase their price sensitivity they do not receive full reimbursement.

Quality

In 2000, the World Health Organization ranked France first in a one-time study of the healthcare services of 191 countries. The United States placed 37th.

On the basis of life expectancy and infant mortality indicators, France comes out ahead of the United States and relatively high in comparison to the rest of Europe. A girl born in France in 2015 could expect to live 85.6 years, in comparison to 81.9 years in the United States. As for infant mortality, in 2015 there were 3 deaths for every 1,000 live births in France, in contrast to 5 per 1,000 in the United States. These indicators are hardly complete enough to draw inferences on the relative health status of the French and American populations because they do not account for other dimensions of health, such as functional autonomy and well-being. However, they are the only comparable data available. In terms of patient satisfaction, although polls in

France have found different results depending on the nature of the questions posed, a 1990 comparative survey suggested that France ranked high in comparison to the United States. In the United States, 60% of the population felt that fundamental changes were needed; in France, 42% of the population shared this feeling.[63] In a 2014 report from the Commonwealth Fund, the U.S. healthcare system ranked lowest among 11 countries when comparing data on expenditures, delivery, and access to healthcare services, as did France. France was found to perform low in areas concerning quality of care, with a total lack of effectiveness, coordination, and patient-access centered care. Access encompasses ability to pay, timeliness of care, efficiency, and equity. However, France ranked first for healthy lives, whereas the United States ranked last, and France ranked second for safe care, with the United States in 7th place.[64] Therefore, although the new reforms have allowed the country to start to bring healthcare expenditures under control, this comes with a cost. The perceived quality of the system has dropped dramatically over a very short period. Apart from the quality of life and the safety of the care delivered, all indicators show areas that need to be reassessed in order to balance savings and quality of care.

Access

The French enjoy free choice among a panoply of services in primary and secondary medical care. There is no limitation on doctors' or patients' freedom of choice and no GP gatekeeping role for hospital services. Healthcare consumption is highly concentrated among a small group of people, with a high level of medical care being consumed in the first year of life and beyond the age of 50. In addition, utilization differs significantly between social classes.

The supply of French hospitals and medical technologies is generally adequate enough to avoid the problem of wait times that is common in other nations. However, in rural areas there are fewer hospitals and providers, and wait times can increase tremendously. If it takes an average of 19 days to get an appointment with an ENT specialist in France, regional disparities can bring this delay up to 168 days in some remote regions. For dental surgeons, delays vary from an average of 28 days up to 81 days. For an appointment with a cardiologist, average wait time is 53 days, and for an ophthalmologist delays go from 11 days in Paris up to 327 days the Loire region.[65] There is a marked increase in wait times all over the country, and this phenomenon can become preoccupying in some areas designated as medical deserts. This has become an issue for those regions.

Along the same lines, a recent survey showed that most French people are satisfied with the proximity of available health services: slightly more than a third of those living in rural areas stated that specialist services were not located close enough. Despite universal coverage, there is considerable inequality in the availability of health care in France. For example, in 2014 there were on average 335 physicians per 100,000 inhabitants. But there were three times as many specialists per person in the Greater Paris region than in the region of Eure.

Social Disparity

Although French national health insurance has effectively eliminated significant financial barriers to medical care, and despite universal coverage of the population, there remain wide disparities among social classes in patterns of medical care use. The distribution of health resources is also highly skewed in favor of urban areas and well-to-do regions. Moreover, as in other systems in which health outcome indicators have been compared with measures of socioeconomic status, in France there are significant inequalities. With regard to patterns of use, the most well-to-do and educated French people rely more on office-based private practice, particularly the services of specialists and dentists. The more disadvantaged groups, including laborers, make greater use of general practitioners and public hospitals. From 1960 to 1980 these disparities diminished, but since 1980 they have been exacerbated. These disparities are matched by equally flagrant disparities in life expectancy. For example, from 1980 to 1989 the life expectancy of an engineer at age 35 was an additional 45.0 years of age. This was 9.0 years (25%) more than that of a manual labor worker, who was only expected to live an additional 35.8 more years. For the years 2009–2013, disparities have improved. Life expectancy of a 60-year-old male was an additional 25.5 years for an executive as compared to an additional 21.1 years for a manual labor worker.[66] Of course, differences in life expectancy reflect such factors as education, housing, and working conditions and cannot be attributed solely to differential access to medical care. But it is important to note that the medical system has been unable to compensate for these and other inequalities.[69]

The coordination of the various healthcare providers is clearly insufficient. The system encourages competition and discourages cooperation: there is friction between the public and private sectors, between outpatient facilities and hospitals, and between the many healthcare professions. Concern is growing among patients, providers, and regulating agencies. Incentives have been initiated to increase the development of managed-care networks, but progress has been rather slow.

There was a reform in July of 2005 that put a process of coordinated care in place. Patients now have control over which primary doctor they choose to see, but they need a GP to refer to specialists in order to receive reimbursement. The patient first visits his/her *médecin traitant* (general practitioner), which is the physician that has been previously registered at the *caisse d´assurance maladie* as the one in charge of the coordination of care for the patient. The *médecin correspondant* (correspondent doctor) is the physician to whom the patient has been referred and is usually a specialist. With the authorization of the patient, this physician sends the relevant information to the *médecin traitant* in order to follow up and coordinate care. Several specialists have direct authorization for passing on information relevant to care, such as gynecologists, ophthalmologists, dentists, pediatricians, and psychiatrists, and the services of these specialists are covered by the state without a referral by a *médecin traitant* (the patient does not have to go to his/her GP first). Patients visiting physicians and dentists pay full price and are later reimbursed for costs by public health insurance and complementary insurance. For other services, such as pharmaceutical costs, they do not have to pay. Payment is made directly by la *sécurité sociale* and the complementary insurance to the provider through the use of the *carte vitale*. Patients are exempt from paying if they receive public assistance (CMU) or if they visit a procedure-oriented specialist. Patients who consult a specialist outside of the referring system see their reimbursement reduced tremendously.

In the French system, patients carry social security cards containing microchips that store basic information about the patient, and more importantly information about his/her coverage by social security and the complementary insurance. Thus the card allows patients to be almost immediately reimbursed for their medical care. When it is scanned at a healthcare facility, electronic funds are quickly deposited into the patient's bank account as reimbursement for the appropriate portion of any fees associated with the visit, usually within a ten-day period. The patient has to present his card called *Carte Vitale*, which transmits all transactions to the *caisse d' assurance maladie* where he/she is registered. All medical procedures (hospitalization, laboratory tests, X-rays, etc.) have to take place in the locality of his/her *caisse d´assurance*. However, the patient can buy medicines anywhere in France without advancing any money. Payment is made directly through the *carte vitale*, and the pharmacy receives payment directly from the administration and the complementary insurance organisms. Administrative costs are significantly reduced by this nationwide system of electronic billing and payment.

Originally, the *carte vitale* was supposed to contain on its chip a patient's comprehensive medical information, allowing physicians immediate access to a patient's record. However, although the system has been experimentally in place for patients with diabetes in some parts of France, there has yet to be national use of the *carte vitale* as personal medical records storage.

To make consumers price sensitive at the time the service is provided, most patients pay the full cost of services out of pocket and request reimbursement from the statutory plan, with the exception of those requiring hospitalization and low-income beneficiaries under the Universal Health Care Act. Typically, patients receive only partial reimbursement and thus pay the equivalent of a co-payment for services. Patients without supplementary insurance typically receive a reimbursement rate of 70% for physician and dentist services and 60% for auxiliary and laboratory services. Reimbursements are on average 95% for a major surgery, 80% for minor surgery, 95%–100% for pregnancy and childbirth, and 70% for X-rays, routine dental care, and nursing care at home. Reimbursements for prescribed medicines depend on the type of medication, ranging from 15% to 65%. A patient can receive 100% coverage under certain conditions, such as having a chronic or acute medical condition (including cancer, insulin-dependent diabetes, heart disease, etc.), requiring long-term care, having a long-standing condition, or requiring a hospital stay of more than 30 days.

Expanded Coverage

Although France provided nearly all of its residents with health insurance prior to 2000, the Universal Health Care Act (Couverture Maladie Universelle) expanded coverage to all French residents. Single residents whose taxable income falls below a certain amount per year are entitled to free coverage. For a list of some of the covered benefits, see **BOX 11-1**.

Because the system is quite liberal, in that patients may choose to see their licensed practitioner at any time without limit, the French average 6.9 contacts with a general practitioner or a specialist each year, while Americans typically have 3.8 appointments, according the OECD in 2010.

▸ Current Issues in Healthcare

The French health system has some strong characteristics: a satisfactory level of access to care and service utilization, an abundant availability of choice without

> **BOX 11-1** Statutory Health Insurance Benefits
>
> - Hospital services for health care, rehabilitation, or physiotherapy
> - Outpatient care from GPs, specialists, dentists, and midwives
> - Prescribed diagnostic services and care
> - Prescribed eligible pharmaceutical drugs and devices
> - Prescribed healthcare-related transport
> - Certain preventive care practices
>
> Data from Chevreul K, Berg Brigham K, Durand-Zaleski I, Hernández-Quevedo C. France: Health system review. Health Systems in Transition. 2015;17(3): 1–218. http://www.euro.who.int/__data/assets/pdf_file/0011/297938/France-HiT.pdf. Accessed January 12, 2017.

any significant waiting lists, and high life expectancy. Indeed, the *World Health Report 2000* ranked France as having the best healthcare system in the world. Yet not many people in France took particular pride in this ranking despite a general recognition of the distinctive role played by the mixed public and private system. The health system faces numerous challenges, many of which are common to neighboring countries.[67] The 2010–2012 Hospital, Patients, Health, Territories Bill and the 2016 Loi Santé (currently in application) aim to address some of these problems.

The first challenge that the last two reforms are supposed to address is the likely significant decrease in the number of doctors per head of the population that France has started to experience due to medical school quota systems. Coupled with the persistent unequal distribution of existing medical professionals across the country, this starts to create tensions in respect to the supply of care, as equal access to care remains a core system objective. The aging population also contributes to uncertainties over future healthcare workforce needs.

Less talked about, though not the least of the challenges for French health authorities, is the continuous need not only to maintain but also to improve the quality of care and ensure access to innovative medicines. The introduction of global budgeting for hospitals appears partially successful in limiting growth in this area of expenditure. However, the government moved to control the growth of primary care spending, which has been ardently opposed by public and independent medical professions. The various plans to curb spending in ambulatory care by (1) setting national targets with collective and individual sanctions for overshoot, (2) linking physician fees with the levels of prescriptions, and (3) reducing overall spending, have not proven efficient.

Recent developments, for example hospice care, partial hospitalization, and day surgery care, have increased the role for alternatives to inpatient hospitalization in France. However, there is still a significant shortfall of long-term care, which is not keeping pace with the growing needs of an aging population, leading to serious financial burdens. Other current issues in the French healthcare system are medical guidelines and medical references, medical dossiers, and the development of computerized management tools. The introduction of patient records aims to limit recourse to multiple practitioners and thereby avoid redundant prescriptions.

To tackle these challenges, several major reforms have been introduced and two laws adopted in 2004: The Public Health Policy Act and the Health Insurance Reform Act, followed in 2005 and 2011 by new agreements between the national health insurance funds and medical trade unions on rules governing private practice. In 2006, a new strategic plan was also introduced to foster health workforce development, reinforcing measures announced in previous years.[71] According to Xavier Bertrand, then French minister of health, the main objectives of those reforms were to improve health system organization and management. They placed a special emphasis on the monitoring of healthcare expenditure by healthcare professionals. The reforms focused both on the renewal of the organization and management of the health system on one hand, and financial measures and incentives on the other. Moreover, they were intended to have strong implications for health information systems. Elsewhere, the Health Insurance Reform Act permits more flexibility and relative internal organizational freedom to public hospitals, despite relatively strict controls on hospital management. The organization and planning of healthcare facilities has also been simplified. Hospital regulatory power was shifted, to some extent, from the central to regional level. The controlling role of regional hospital agencies in charge of defining targets through contracts with individual hospitals has been reinforced. At a higher level, a strategic plan for health workforce development promotes group practice and also experiments with the transfer of tasks away from doctors to paramedical staff. Another crosscutting, albeit less obvious, feature of these reforms is the general need for robust information systems at every level. The creation of a comprehensive electronic patient record, coupled with the preferred doctor system in primary care, is presented as a core component of the Health Insurance Reform Act, while quantitative targets and indicators are the backbone of the Public Health Policy Act.[74] However, these reforms did not fully answer those many challenges, which led to the adoption of the 2010–2012 Hospital, Patients, Health, Territories Bill which started to address those many problems.

This bill also aimed to emphasize medical awareness, prevention of addictions, and general education of the population in terms of health care, another major challenge. Given the excessively high rates of mortality in those under 65, there is an urgent need to develop preventive actions within a coherent public health framework. Research shows that 39% of premature deaths of men and 24% of premature deaths of women could have been avoided and are related to primary prevention: these deaths are mostly linked to risky behaviors, such as smoking, drinking, and dangerous driving. Tobacco is the number one cause of death in France (60,000 deaths per year), followed by alcohol (45,000 deaths). The number of suicides has increased by 25% between 1970 and 1991.[41] In 2012 there were 27 deaths by suicide per day and 80,000 yearly hospitalizations, double the average numbers in European countries.

The current Loi Santé that was voted on in January 2016 is the logical extension of the 2010–2012 bill. The goal is to go further than the 2010–2012 bill in terms of prevention of chronic diseases that are still the cause of more than 25% of deaths in France in 2016. The new law also emphasizes the fight against the geographical and social disparities that prevent the fair distribution and access of care for all French people. Finally, the major challenge for the government remains the aging of the population and its many consequences.

Through the fight against chronic diseases, disparities, and the adaptation of health care to an aging population, there remains one major daunting challenge that the successive governments have not really succeed in addressing: the financial deficit of the healthcare system and its sustainability in the future. France has experienced a substantial slowdown in contributions due to low economic growth and an increase in unemployment. Also, as the nation's population ages, there are progressively fewer citizens of working age who pay into the national system. Meanwhile, health expenditures continue to increase, mainly due to the progress of technologies and the aging of the population, leading to sizeable budget deficits for the social security fund. Despite a net decrease in recent years, the deficit of la sécurité sociale still represents today half of the country's public debt. Many people believe that the drop in healthcare expenditures that has been experienced lately is not sustainable if France wants to maintain quality and universal access. Economies have been made, but there is little chance that they will follow an exponential curve.

So far, measures taken have been directed toward the restriction of health services in the health plans and control of the diffusion of high technology. But today's problems need more aggressive measures. Ensuring equilibrium between various healthcare schemes has become a high priority in France. It will necessitate a deeper reform of the system in general and a total change in the French mentalities. In a country with extremely high levels of taxation, new taxes cannot be the answer indefinitely, and reducing expenditures can only go to a certain point. In a conference held in August 2009, Sarkozy explained that one solution would be increased cost participation by patients, directly out of pocket or through secondary insurance. Many medicines have been put outside of the reimbursement list of the sécurité sociale. Optical and dental procedures and equipment also necessitate an important direct financial contribution from the patient or his/her private insurance. But those measures raise concerns as some people cannot always afford good private insurance. Figures show that a certain part of the population foregoes some dental and optical treatments for lack of complementary coverage, and lately the number of people who sacrifice dental and eye care for lack of means has increased tremendously. In a country where "free access to as much health care as you want" is ingrained in the population's mind and considered an absolute right of the people, measures like those are highly unpopular and often lead to social unrest. Many governments have renounced efforts to touch this fundamental right. Sarkozy's idea of lowering payments by the sécurité sociale has therefore been met by criticism and cries that this was a disguised privatization of the system as well as the beginnings of two-tiered medicine, one tier for the rich and one tier for the poor. Therefore, raising cost participation can only be a small part of the problem solving, not the major funder of the situation. However, this additional financial burden to the patient is a path the current government must follow.

The other solution the government has been working on since 2010 is reaching deeper into the system. It concerns social security at large and calls for a major reform of French society: reforming the age of retirement. In 2005, France was one of the countries with the lowest average retirement age: 58.5 for men and 59.2 for women.[68] As the population ages and as life expectancy increases, this means that there will soon be more retired people to consume retirement and healthcare funds than active people to pay and provide those funds. If these people keep on working longer, they do not use funds for retirement and those funds can be used otherwise, since sécurité sociale manages both health care and retirement. Moreover, working people pay for their own health care through their salary taxes. Finally, the CSG tax (general social contribution used to partly finance health care) paid by workers is higher than that paid by retired people; the taxation rate applied is higher for workers, and the taxed revenues of working people are also usually more significant than pensions. Therefore, raising the retirement age should help contain, if not reduce, healthcare deficits by reducing the immediate number of nonpaying beneficiaries and increasing the amount of funds available for health care. Even if the debate on retirement age is geared toward improving the situation of pension funds and ensuring the pensions of future generations, the side effects of the reform on healthcare funds could be tremendous.

In 2010, Sarkozy raised the retirement age by two years. Highly unpopular for this major step, he was not reelected in 2012. The debate is still steaming and is sure to continue to be for future presidential candidates, and healthcare access and financing as well as retirement are likely to remain at the heart of reform proposals for some time. Sarkozy once again suggested pushing retirement age even further. Some other candidates have talked about universal access to comprehensive medical care, including full reimbursement for dental and eye care. Everybody has suggestions for financing, decreasing, and curbing medical costs, and retirement is always part of the debate.

The road to the final reform is still long and promises to be chaotic. Everybody agrees that the pension system must be saved, but there is much more at stake: the future of the healthcare system, so dear to the heart of the French. Of course, this alone will not be enough to tackle the problem of healthcare deficits definitely. After the pensions reform, France will have to imagine new ways to solve the universal problem of healthcare financing. The French health system is indeed one of the best in the world: universal access, reasonable unit costs of the services, honorable health outcomes, and all this seems rather inexpensive for its users.

While most people find this fantastic, we can ask the question "Isn't the system too good for its own good?" Because it seems so inexpensive on an individual basis, health care is overconsumed in France. Maybe the system was skewed from the beginning because of the impression of free access consumers have, when in fact the bill is out of control. There is no such thing as a free lunch. Everything comes at a price, and the French are realizing that.

References

1. Larousse. *Le Petit Larousse Illustré: France*. Paris, France: Editions Larousse; 2003.
2. Juritravail. Chiffres du chômage 2016 en France. http://www.juritravail.com/chiffres-et-indices/chiffres-chomage.html. Accessed May 23, 2016.
3. *The World Factbook*. Central Intelligence Agency. https://www.cia.gov/library/publications/resources/the-world-factbook/geos/fr.html. Accessed May 23, 2016.
4. Cleach JY, Le Morvan J, Steck B. *La France, Histoire et Géographie Economiques*. Rosny, France: Editions Bréal; 2000.
5. Institut National de la Statistique et des Etudes Economiques. Evolution de la population. http://www.insee.fr/fr/themes/document.asp?reg_id=0&ref_id=T16F031. Accessed May 23, 2016.
6. Institut National de la Statistique et des Etudes Economiques. La France en bref, France in Figures. 2015 ed. http://www.insee.fr/fr/pdf/france-en-bref-2015.pdf. Accessed May 23, 2016.
7. Institut National de la Statistique et des Etudes Economiques. Taille des communes les plus peuplées en 2013. http://www.insee.fr/fr/themes/tableau.asp?reg_id=0&ref_id=NATTEF01214. Accessed May 23, 2016.
8. Institut National de la Statistique et des Etudes Economiques. Principaux indicateurs économiques. http://www.insee.fr/fr/themes/document.asp?reg_id=0&ref_id=T16F111. Accessed May 23, 2016.
9. Institut National de la Statistique et des Etudes Economiques. Taux de chômage stable au premier trimestre 2016. http://www.insee.fr/fr/themes/info-rapide.asp?id=14&date=20160519. Accessed May 23, 2016.
10. Eurostat. Euroindicateurs. http://ec.europa.eu/eurostat/documents/2995521/7121207/3-07012016-AP-FR.pdf/aafaf15c-2ac1-4d05-814a-5f6b4d0282e1. March 2016. Accessed May 23, 2016.
11. World Trade Organization. *Statistiques du commerce international 2014*. https://www.wto.org/french/res_f/statis_f/its2014_f/its2014_f.pdf. Accessed May 23, 2016.
12. BSI Economics. La place de l'agriculture française et européenne dans le monde. http://www.bsi-economics.org/408-agriculture-francaise-europeenne-dans-le-monde. Accessed May 23, 2016.
13. CNUCED. *Rapport sur l'investissement dans le monde 2015*. Vue d'ensemble. http://unctad.org/fr/PublicationsLibrary/wir2015overview_fr.pdf. Accessed May 23, 2016.
14. Perspective Monde. France 2013. Commerce des marchandises. http://perspective.usherbrooke.ca/bilan/servlet/BMImportExportPays?codePays=FRA. Accessed May 23, 2016.
15. Institut National de la Statistique et des Etudes Economiques. Production et valeur ajoutée de l'agriculture en 2015. http://www.insee.fr/fr/themes/tableau.asp?reg_id=0&ref_id=NATTEF10104. Accessed May 23, 2016.
16. Institut National de la Statistique et des Etudes Economiques. Exploitations et superficie agricole utilisée dans quelques pays de l'Union Européenne en 2013. http://www.insee.fr/fr/themes/tableau.asp?reg_id=98&ref_id=CMPTEF10204. Accessed May 23, 2016.
17. Institut National de la Statistique et des Etudes Economiques. Production agricole de l'Union Européenne en 2015. http://www.insee.fr/fr/themes/tableau.asp?reg_id=98&ref_id=CMPTEF10113. Accessed May 23, 2016.
18. Institut National de la Statistique et des Etudes Economiques. Arrivée de touristes aux frontières en 2014. http://www.insee.fr/fr/themes/tableau.asp?reg_id=98&ref_id=CMPTEF13511. Accessed May 23, 2016.
19. Institut National de la Statistique et des Etudes Economiques. Recettes du tourisme international en 2014. http://www.insee.fr/fr/themes/tableau.asp?reg_id=98&ref_id=CMPTEF13503. Accessed May 23, 2016.

20. Institut National de la Statistique et des Etudes Economiques. Principales caractéristiques des entreprises par catégorie en 2012. http://www.insee.fr/fr/themes/tableau.asp?reg_id=0&ref_id=ESANE033. Accessed May 23, 2016.
21. Institut National de la Statistique et des Etudes Economiques. Dépenses d'éducation dans l'Union Européenne en 2011. http://www.insee.fr/fr/themes/tableau.asp?reg_id=98&ref_id=CMPTEF07305. Accessed May 23, 2016.
22. Institut National de la Statistique et des Etudes Economiques. Financement de la dépense nationale et exécution de la dépense intérieure de R&D en 2013. http://www.insee.fr/fr/themes/tableau.asp?reg_id=0&ref_id=NATTEF09512. Accessed May 23, 2016.
23. Institut National de la Statistique et des Etudes Economiques. Evolution de la population jusqu'en 2016. http://www.insee.fr/fr/themes/tableau.asp?reg_id=0&ref_id=NATnon02145. Accessed May 25, 2016.
24. Institut National de la Statistique et des Etudes Economiques. Composantes de la croissance démographique jusqu'en 2016. http://www.insee.fr/fr/themes/tableau.asp?reg_id=0&ref_id=NATnon02151. Accessed May 25, 2016.
25. Institut National de la Statistique et des Etudes Economiques. Fécondité totale, fécondité selon le groupe d'âges de la mère et âge moyen des mères à l'accouchement jusqu'en 2015. http://www.insee.fr/fr/themes/tableau.asp?reg_id=0&ref_id=bilandemo3. Accessed May 25, 2016.
26. Institut National de la Statistique et des Etudes Economiques. Espérance de vie, taux de mortalité et taux de mortalité infantile dans le monde en moyenne de 2015 à 2020. http://www.insee.fr/fr/themes/tableau.asp?reg_id=98&ref_id=CMPTEF02216. Accessed May 25, 2016.
27. Institut National de la Statistique et des Etudes Economiques. Population par sexe et groupes d'âges quinquennaux au 1er janvier 2016. http://www.insee.fr/fr/themes/tableau.asp?reg_id=0&ref_id=NATnon02150. Accessed May 25, 2016.
28. Institut National de la Statistique et des Etudes Economiques. Projection de population par grand groupe d'âge en 2060. http://www.insee.fr/fr/themes/tableau.asp?reg_id=0&ref_id=NATTEF02164. Accessed May 25, 2016.
29. Institut National de la Statistique et des Etudes Economiques. Population active et taux d'activité selon le sexe dans l'Union Européenne en 2014. http://www.insee.fr/fr/themes/tableau.asp?reg_id=98&ref_id=CMPFPS03138. Accessed May 25, 2016.
30. Institut National de la Statistique et des Etudes Economiques. Emploi total par grand secteur dans l'Union Européenne en 2014. http://www.insee.fr/fr/themes/tableau.asp?reg_id=98&ref_id=CMPTEF03136. Accessed May 25, 2016.
31. Institut National de la Statistique et des Etudes Economiques. Niveau de vie des individus en 2013. http://www.insee.fr/en/themes/tableau.asp?reg_id=0&ref_id=natsos04207. Accessed May 25, 2016.
32. Institut National de la Statistique et des Etudes Economiques. Seuils de pauvreté mensuels en 2013. http://www.insee.fr/fr/themes/tableau.asp?reg_id=0&ref_id=NATSOS04401. Accessed May 25, 2016.
33. Institut National de la Statistique et des Etudes Economiques. Taux de pauvreté et nombre de personnes pauvres selon le seuil en 2013. http://www.insee.fr/fr/themes/tableau.asp?reg_id=0&ref_id=NATTEF04415. Accessed May 25, 2016.
34. Institut National de la Statistique et des Etudes Economiques. Evolution de l'espérance de vie et de l'espérance de vie en bonne santé dans l'Union Européenne. http://www.insee.fr/fr/themes/tableau.asp?reg_id=98&ref_id=CMPECF02228. Accessed May 25, 2016.
35. Institut National de la Statistique et des Etudes Economiques. Taux de mortalité prématurée selon le sexe en 2014. http://www.insee.fr/fr/themes/tableau.asp?reg_id=0&ref_id=NATnon06228. Accessed May 25, 2016.
36. Fantino B., Ropert G. La santé des français: *Le Système de Santé en France. Diagnostic et Propositions* Paris, France: Editions Dunod; 2008.
37. Mes Vaccins.net. Couverture vaccinale en France en 2014: un bilan contrasté. https://www.mesvaccins.net/textes/rapport_mesure_couverture_vaccinale_France.pdf Accessed May 25, 2016.
38. GIP SPSI. The French health care system. http://www.gipspsi.org/GIP/layout/set/print/le_systeme_francais_de_sante/presentation. Accessed March 25, 2010.
39. Comiti V.P. Que sais-je? *Histoire du droit sanitaire en France*. Paris: Presses Universitaires de France; 1994.
40. Sandier S, Paris V, Polton D. *Health Care Systems in Transition. France*. E-book. WHO Regional Office for Europe on behalf of the European Observatory on Health Systems and Policies. Copenhagen; 2004. http://www.irdes.fr/EspaceAnglais/Publications/IrdesPublications/HealthCareSystemsInTransition.pdf. Accessed May 25, 2016.
41. Institut National de la Statistique et des Etudes Economiques. Population couverte par la CMU (assurés et ayants droits) au 30/12/2007. http://www.insee.fr/fr/themes/tableau.asp?reg_id=20&ref_id=revopte1032. Accessed March 25, 2010.
42. Ministère de la santé, de la jeunesse, des sports et de la vie associative. Présentation de projet de loi "Hôpital, patients, santé et territoires." Un projet de santé durable pour nos citoyens. Conférence de presse du 22 octobre 2008. http://www.sante-sports.gouv.fr/IMG/pdf/Dossierdepresse.pdf. Accessed March 25, 2010.
43. Ministère des affaires sociales et de la santé. Loi de modernisation de notre système de santé. http://social-sante.gouv.fr/grands-dossiers/loi-de-modernisation-de-notre-systeme-de-sante/. Accessed May 25, 2016.
44. GIP SPSI. Health and Social Protection. International expertise. The French health and social protection system, renowned expertise. http://www.gipspsi.org/GIP/layout/set/print/content/download/4971/55291/version/2/file/GIPSI_plaquette_savoir_faire_GB.pdf. Accessed March 25, 2010.
45. Couffinhal A. The French health care system: a brief overview. October 2001. http://www.irdes.fr/EspaceAnglais/DocumentationCentre/Documents/FrenchHealthCareSystem.pdf. Accessed April 30, 2010.
46. The Henry J. Kaiser Family Foundation. International health systems: France. http://www.kaiseredu.org/topics_im_ihs.asp?imID=4&parentID=61. Accessed April 30, 2010.
47. Institut National de la Statistique et des Etudes Economiques. Etablissements de santé en 2013. http://www.insee.fr/fr/themes/tableau.asp?reg_id=0&ref_id=NATTEF06116. Accessed May 25, 2016.
48. Schabloski AK. *Health Care Systems Around the World*. 2008. http://www.itup.org/Reports/Fresh%20Thinking/Health_Care_Systems_Around_World.pdf. Accessed April 30, 2010.
49. Organisation for Economic Co-operation and Development. OECD-Health Statistics 2015. Frequently requested data. http://www.oecd.org/fr/sante/statistiques-sante-2014-donnees-frequemment-demandees.htm. Accessed May 25, 2016.
50. Fargues L. La vérité sur la fermeture de lits d'hôpitaux. *Challenges*. http://www.challenges.fr/economie/20150205.CHA2834

/pourquoi-la-france-n-arrive-pas-a-reduire-le-nombre-de-lits-d-hopitaux.html. Feb. 8, 2015. Accessed May 26, 2016.

51. Rodwin VG. The healthcare system under French national health insurance: Lessons for health reform in the United States. *Am JPublic Health*. http://www.ncbi.nlm.nih.gov/pmc/articles/PMC1447687/. 2003 January; 93(1): 31–37. Accessed May 25, 2016.

52. Institut National de la Statistique et des Etudes Economiques. Médecins suivant le statut et la spécialité en 2015. http://www.insee.fr/fr/themes/tableau.asp?reg_id=0&ref_id=NATTEF06102. Accessed May 26, 2016.

53. Brunner S. The French healthcare system. *Medical News Today*. http://www.medicalnewstoday.com/articles/9994.php. June 8, 2009. Accessed May 26, 2016.

54. Institut National de la Statistique et des Etudes Economiques. Healthcare professions in 2015. http://www.insee.fr/en/themes/tableau.asp?reg_id=0&ref_id=NATTEF06103. Accessed May 26, 2016.

55. MedTech Europe. The European Medical Technology industry in figures. http://www.ub.edu/medicina/grauEB/2014%20The%20European%20medical%20technology%20industry%20in%20figures.pdf. January 2014. Accessed May 26, 2016.

56. Eucomed Medical Technology. http://www.eucomed.be/abouttheindustry.aspx. Accessed May 4, 2010.

57. Medtec go French/Medtec a l'heure francaise/Bei Medtec stehen die Zeiger auf Frankreich. *Eurotec* 363 (2009): 44+. *General OneFile*. http://find.galegroup.com.ezproxy.delta.edu:2048/gps/infomark.do?&contentSet=IACDocuments&type=retrieve&tabID=T003&prodId=IPS&docId=A198994208&source=gale&srcprod=ITOF&userGroupName=lom_deltacoll&version=1.05 Accessed May 5, 2010.

58. Snitem. French medical technology industry the vanguard of innovation. FTPO North America Product Releases. http://www.infotechfrance.com/cgi-local/affichage_signet_secteur.pl?UNI_ID=13&RUB_ID=74&SS_ID=9163&SEC_ID=73. April 28, 2006. Accessed May 4, 2010.

59. Invest in France Agency. November 19, 2009. French's new stem cell research projects make opportunities for U.S. companies. FTPO North America Product Releases. http://www.infotechfrance.com/cgi-local/affichage_signet_secteur.pl?UNI_ID=13&RUB_ID=74&SS_ID=12650&SEC_ID=73. Accessed May 4, 2010.

60. Bajos S, Haus H. La France en super-forme dans l'innovation médicale. *Le parisien Economie*. http://www.leparisien.fr/economie/business/sante-la-france-en-pointe-dans-l-innovation-medicale-21-03-2016-5644609.php#xtref=http%3A%2F%2Fwww.google.fr%2Furl%3Fsa%3Dt%24rct%3Dj%24q%3D%24esrc%3Ds%24source%3Dweb%24cd%3D1%24ved%3D0ahUKEwjh5KqanfjMAhVL1ywKHZxoARkQFggcMAA%24url%3Dhttp%253A%252F%252Fwww.leparisien.fr%252Feconomie%252Fbusiness%252Fsante-la-france-en-pointe-dans-l-innovation-medicale-21-03-2016-5644609.php%24usg%3DAFQjCNFQMvj8UtxzLjes1Y5hyME5bQNGHA. Accessed May 26, 2016.

61. Organisation for Economic Co-operation and Development. OECD. Health statistics 2015. Focus on health spending. http://www.oecd.org/health/health-systems/Focus-Health-Spending-2015.pdf. Accessed May 30, 2016.

62. Institut de Recherches Economiques et Fiscales. Réforme du système de Santé—Comparaison européenne. *Etudes et monographies*. http://fr.irefeurope.org/Reformer-et-ameliorer-le-systeme-de-Sante-grace-au-prive-et-a-la-concurrence,a2586. October 16, 2013. Accessed May 30, 2016.

63. Rodwin VG, Sandier S. Health care under National Health Insurance. http://www.nyu.edu/projects/rodwin/french.html. Accessed May 30, 2016.

64. Figer J. U.S. health care system ranks lowest in international survey. *CBS News*. http://www.cbsnews.com/news/u-s-health-care-system-ranks-lowest-in-international-survey/. Accessed May 30, 2016.

65. SudOuest. Ophtalmos, cardiologues, radiologues ... Des délais d'attente très disparates. *SudOuest.fr*. http://www.sudouest.fr/2015/10/10/rendez-vous-medicaux-des-delais-d-attente-disparates-selon-les-specialites-2150712-4696.php. October 11, 2015. Accessed May 30, 2016.

66. Institut National de la Statistique et des Etudes Economiques. Espérance de vie à 60 ans par sexe et catégorie socioprofessionnelle en 2009–2013. http://www.insee.fr/fr/themes/tableau.asp?reg_id=0&ref_id=espvie60ansparcs. Accessed May 30, 2016.

67. Cases C. French health system reform: Recent implementation and future challenges. *Eurohealth*. 2006;12(3): 10–11. http://www.Euro.who.int/Document/Obs/Eurohealth12_3.pdf. Accessed April 30, 2010.

68. Centre d'Analyse Stratégique. *L'Europe dans la mondialisation. Recueil de données*. http://www.strategie.gouv.fr/IMG/pdf/EuropedanslaMondialisation-RecueildedonneesCAS221107-FINAL.pdf. Accessed May 31, 2016.

CHAPTER 12

Germany

Katherine H. Leith, PhD, LMSW; and **Gerald (Jerry) Ledlow, PhD, MHA, FACHE**

▸ Country Description

TABLE 12-1 Germany	
Nationality	Noun: German(s) Adjective: German
Ethnic groups	German 91.5%, Turkish 2.4%, other 6.1% (largely Greek, Italian, Polish, Russian, Serbo-Croatian, and Spanish)
Religions	Protestant 34.0%, Roman Catholic 34.0%, Muslim 3.7%, unaffiliated or other 28.3%
Language	German (Deutsch) Official minority languages: Danish, Frisian, Sorbian, and Romany Regional languages recognized under the European Charter for Regional or Minority Languages: Low German, Danish, North Frisian, Sater Frisian, Lower Sorbian, Upper Sorbian, and Romany
Literacy	Definition: Age 15 and over can read and write. Total population: 99% Male: 99% Female: 99% (2014 est.)
Government type	Federal parliamentary republic
Date of independence	No independence day. Unification of eastern and western Germany, 1990.
Gross Domestic Product (GDP) per capita	$46,900 (2015 est.)

(continues)

215

TABLE 12-1 Germany (*continued*)

Unemployment rate	7.7% (2014 est.)**
Natural hazards	Flooding
Environment: current issues	Air pollution from coal-burning utilities and industries; acid rain from sulfur dioxide emissions damaging forests; pollution in the Baltic Sea from raw sewage and industrial effluents via rivers in eastern Germany; hazardous waste disposal; government ending the use of nuclear power by 2022; government identifying nature preservation areas in line with EU's Flora, Fauna, and Habitat directive
Population	80,722,792 (July 2016 est.)
Age structure	0–14 years: 12.83% (male 5,317,183/female 5,040,664) 15–24 years: 10.22% (male 4,203,985/female 4,044,789) 25–54 years: 40.96% (male 16,721,667/female 16,345,911) 55–64 years: 14.23% (male 5,695,117/female 5,788,493) 65 years and over: 21.76% (male 7,709,799/female 9,855,184) (2016 est.)
Median age	Total: 46.8 years Male: 45.7 years Female: 47.9 years (2016 est.)
Population growth rate	−0.16% (2016 est.)
Birth rate	8.5 births/1,000 population (2016 est.)
Death rate	11.6/1000 population (2016 est.)
Disease burden	Communicable disease deaths: 22/100,000 population Noncommunicable disease deaths: 365/100,000 population Injury deaths: 23/100,000 population (2016 est.)
Net migration rate	1.5 migrant(s)/1,000 population (2016 est.)
Gender ratio	At birth: 1.06 male(s)/female Under 15 years: 1.05 male(s)/female 15–24 years: 1.04 male(s)/female 25–54 years: 1.02 male(s)/female 55–64 years: 0.98 male(s)/female 65 years and over: 0.78 male(s)/female Total population: 0.78 male(s)/female (2016 est.)
Infant mortality rate	Total: 3.4 deaths/1,000 live births Male: 3.7 deaths/1,000 live births Female: 3.1 deaths/1,000 live births (2016 est.)
Life expectancy at birth	Total population: 80.7 years Male: 78.4 years Female: 83.1 years (2016 est.)
Total fertility rate	1.44 children born/woman (2016 est.)

TABLE 12-1 Germany (continued)	
HIV/AIDS adult prevalence rate	0.15% (2013 est.)
Number of people living with HIV/AIDS	77,500 (2013 est.)
HIV/AIDS deaths	400 (2013 est.)

*The German Empire unified on January 18, 1871. In 1945 after World War II, Germany was divided into four zones of occupation (the United Kingdom, the United States, the USSR, and later, France). The Federal Republic of Germany (West Germany) was proclaimed May 23, 1949, and included the former British, American, and French zones. The German Democratic Republic (East Germany) was proclaimed on October 7, 1949, and it included the former USSR zone. Unification of West Germany and East Germany took place on October 3, 1990. All four powers formally relinquished rights on March 15, 1991.

**This is the International Labor Organization's estimated rate for international comparisons. Germany's Federal Employment Office estimated a seasonally adjusted rate of 10.1% for 2012.

Data from Central Intelligence Agency. The World Fact Book, 2016: Germany. https://www.cia.gov/library/publications/the-world-factbook/geos/gm.html. Accessed April 19, 2016.

History

The origin of what is known today as the Federal Republic of Germany lies not in the ancient Germanic forests but in the Holy Roman Empire, which at one point covered the entire midsection of the European continent. By the year 1400, several areas of this empire—including (although nominally) North Italy, Savoy, Burgundy, and the Swiss Confederations, along with Lorraine and Brabant—were considered *Teutsche Lande* (German Country).[1]

As a result of the Napoleonic war, the German Empire was replaced by the Confederation of the Rhine. Prussia and Austria remained outside the Confederation. At the Vienna Congress in 1815, the German Confederation, a loose conglomerate of states in Germany that included Prussia and Austria, was founded. After the Prussian-Austrian War in 1867, the German Confederation was re-formed into the North German Confederation, without Austria and Bavaria.[1]

In 1862, Otto von Bismarck became prime minister (*ministerpräsident*) of Prussia. He ardently pursued German unity, not through "speeches and majority decisions" (*reden und majoritätsbeschlüsse*) but through "blood and iron" (*blut und eisen*).[2] In other words, Bismarck favored war over diplomacy. The foundation for the second German Empire was laid on January 18, 1871, when Wilhelm I was crowned Emperor of the new constitutional monarchy, in the Room of Mirrors (Spiegelsaal) in the Palace of Versailles in Paris.[2] Only five years later, in 1876, the German Empire was created from above, with the merger of the German states, Austria not included. Under the chancellorship of Otto von Bismarck, Germany transitioned into a socially advanced state, with the stepwise introduction of a federal system of social insurance. Although the German political leadership loathed social democracy and sought to weaken social democratic movements by passing antisocialist laws, even Bismarck himself agreed that the social reforms he implemented—although he did so primarily to win workers for his political ideals—would not have been possible without social democracy.[2] Despite his fervent efforts to maintain a conservative empire, Bismarck was not able to find common ground with Wilhelm II, and he eventually resigned. Wilhelm followed a much more aggressive stance on foreign policy, and in the following decades, Germany played a central role in setting the stage for World War I and II.

The immediate trigger for the First World War was the assassination of Archduke Francis Ferdinand of Austria-Hungary by a Serbian nationalist in 1914. Also known as the Great War, it was fought by two rival sets of powers—Germany and Austria-Hungary on one side, and Russia, France, Serbia, and Great Britain on the other—and ended in late 1918 as one of the deadliest conflicts in human history. What emerged in the aftermath became known as the Weimar Republic (Weimarer Republik), a "sort-of" democracy with a new constitution that had to contend with hyperinflation, political and paramilitaristic extremism, and a very contentious relationship with the victors of World War I. The continued tensions, in large part, allowed the rise of national socialism and Adolf Hitler; both held the promise of a better social and political future.

Hitler and his Nazi party began to systematically eliminate all political opposition and to consolidate power, with the coordinated and methodical extermination of the Jewish race, via extermination camp or concentration camps (*Konzentrationslager*) as a central feature. In 1939, Hitler's army invaded Poland and thereby set off World War II, believed by many to be to single-most deadliest conflict in human history. For example, the Battle of Stalingrad, fought between August 23, 1942 and February 2, 1943 resulted in 1.25 million casualties, although some estimates are as high as 1.8 million.[3] After the end of World War II in May 1945, Germany experienced a slow but steady rebuilding of its war-torn economy (more is discussed about this period in the chapter section about the history of the healthcare system). East and West Germany, two separate blocs since the end of World War II, were officially reunified in 1990, and Germany has since become a leader in the formation and advancement of the European Union.

Size and Geography

Today, the Federal Republic of Germany (*Bundesrepublik Deutschland*) is located in Central Europe and is bordered by the Netherlands, Belgium, Luxembourg, and France to the west; Switzerland and Austria to the south; the Czech Republic and Poland to the east; and Denmark to the north. The territory of Germany covers about 357,093 square kilometers (about 137,846 square miles),[4] making it slightly smaller than the state of Montana. The longest distance from north to south is 876 kilometers; from west to east, it is 640 kilometers. With a population of 82.2 million inhabitants at the end of 2015, it is the largest country by population in the European Union and the second largest in Europe after Russia.[4] The number actually reflects the highest population growth since 1992 and is the result of a high net immigration. At an average of 591.0 inhabitants per square mile, the population density in Germany is about 7 times higher than in the United States, which has an average of 85.5 inhabitants per square mile. At the same time, only two German cities, Hamburg and the national capital of Berlin, had more than 1.0 million inhabitants in 2015, with 1.8 million and 3.5 million, respectively.[4]

Much like in the United States, Germany's population is not evenly distributed. More than three-quarters of inhabitants (76%) live in cities: 13% in small cities/towns, 28% in large cities, and 35% in medium-sized cities.[4] The largest proportion of Germany's total land area, about 53%, is used for agriculture; another 30% consists of forests. A much smaller land area, about 12%, is dedicated to settlements, including roads and railroads.[5]

Government and Political System

As its name implies, Germany is a federal republic that is composed of 16 federal states (*Bundesländer*) (see **TABLE 12-1** and **FIGURE 12-1**). The country's political system seeks to implement the republican, democratic and socialist principles embodied in the federal constitution, known as the Basic Law (*Grundgesetz*). The Basic Law establishes Germany as a parliamentary democracy with separation of powers and 3 branches: executive, legislative, and judicial. Amendments to the Basic Law require a two-thirds majority in both houses of parliament. The constitutionally defined bodies which have primarily legislative functions are the lower and upper houses of parliament, namely the Federal Assembly (Bundestag, lower house) and the Federal Council (Bundesrat, upper house). Simply put, the Federal Assembly represents the German people, while the Federal Council represents the 16 federal states.[6,7]

Members of both the Bundestag and the Bundesrat meet in the national capital of Germany, Berlin. The head of state is the federal president (*Bundespräsident*), who has mostly ceremonial duties. The second highest official in the German order of precedence is the president of the Bundestag, and the third-highest official is the federal chancellor (*Bundeskanzler*), who is the head of government and handles day-to-day politics.[6] Each of the 16 federal states has a constitution which also must be consistent with the republican, democratic, and socialist principles embodied in the federal constitution. Each state is represented in the Bundesrat and, through this medium, participates in federal lawmaking.[8] In Germany, the highest judicial body is the supreme constitutional court, the Federal Constitutional Court (*Bundesverfassungsgericht*). Its sole purpose is to ensure that the Basic Law is respected and obeyed. Decisions of the Federal Constitutional Court are final, and all other legal and governmental bodies are required to follow its rulings.[9] In addition to ordinary law, Germany also has four specialized jurisdictions: the Federal Administrative Court (*Bundesverwaltungsgericht*), the Federal Labor Court (*Bundesarbeitsgericht*), the Federal Social Court (*Bundessozialgericht*), and the Federal Tax Court (*Bundesfinanzhof*). A fifth specialized court is the Federal Patent Court (*Bundespatentgericht*).[10] Like the ordinary courts, these specialized courts are organized hierarchically with the state court systems under a federal appeals court.

Germany in the European Union

In recent history, the most important characteristics of the German foreign policy have been its Western

FIGURE 12-1 Map of Germany
© Bardocz Peter/Shutterstock

political orientation as well as its integration in Europe. In the period between 1945 and 1959, the European Union was formed by the six founding countries, Belgium, France, Germany, Italy, Luxembourg and the Netherlands, with the purpose to unite European countries economically and politically in order to secure lasting peace. Today, the European Union has 28 member states.[11] Germany joined the North Atlantic Treaty Organization (NATO) in 1955, thereby laying the foundation for its Western political affiliation, and it signed the Treaty of Rome in 1957, which created the European Economic Communities. In addition to its membership in NATO, Germany is also a member of the United Nations, the Organisation for Economic Development and Co-operation (OECD), the Organization for Security and Cooperation in Europe, and the Group of Seven, a governmental political forum that includes the United States, Canada, France, Germany, Great Britain, Italy, and Japan, (although it has been suspended since 2014).

During the second half of the 20th century, Germany has become a leader in the European Union in its attempts to create a common, effective system of European foreign and security policy. Since then, two major events have prompted it to take a much more assertive role on the world stage. First, as a result of the September 11, 2001, attacks and the subsequent War on Terror, Germany, under the leadership of Angela Merkel (Germany's *Bundeskanzler* since 2005) has been one of the United States' strongest allies in the effort to combat terrorist and radical movements, although this alliance has not remained without discord. Second, with the emergence of the European refugee crisis in 2015, during which more than a million migrants and refugees crossed into Europe in that first year alone, a bitter controversy arose in the European Union about how best to cope with the influx of millions of people from the war-torn Middle East seeking asylum and holding hope for a better life elsewhere. In Germany, which received the highest number of new asylum applications in 2015 (almost 500,000), the crisis has begun to polarize society. While thousands of Germans are volunteering to help refugees, many have begun to voice their frustration over what they perceive to be an indifferent political leadership that does nothing to address their concerns of a slowly changing Germany.

Macroeconomics

Major Industries and Where They Are Located

Since Germany is comparatively poor in raw materials, the country's economy focuses on industrial manufacturing and on the service sector. Although only 2%–3% of the population is employed in agriculture, about half of the total land area is used for agrarian purposes. With an estimated gross domestic product (GDP) of US $3,355.77 billion in 2015, the German economy represents 5.41% of the world economy.[4] The German economy is heavily export-oriented; therefore, the country has been called the export champion of the world. Germany is the third largest exporter in the world, with $1.31 trillion in goods and services exported in 2015.[13] Its top 10 exports are vehicles, machineries, chemical goods, electronic products, electrical equipment, pharmaceuticals, transport equipment, basic metals, food products, and rubber and plastics.[13]

Infrastructure, Transportation, Road Development, Airports, and Ports

The first paved roads were constructed during Roman times. The first large highways were built in the 18th century. With the invention of the automobile, the importance of road construction increased dramatically. The AVUS roadway in Berlin was the first motorway in the world when it was completed in 1921. During the economic recovery of the 1950s, roads replaced railways as the most important means of transportation. Today Germany has one of the most dense road grids in the world, with about 650,000 kilometers of roads.[14] In 2013, the federal highway grid (autobahn) had almost 13,000 kilometers of highways, making it one of the longest systems in the world. At the same time, the grid also has almost 40,000 kilometers of federal roads (*Bundesstraßen*), 90,000 kilometers of state roads (*Landesstraßen*), 92,000 kilometers of country roads (*Kreisstraßen*), and more then 400,00 kilometers of local roads (*Ortsstraßen*).[14] The German railway system had approximately 43,468 kilometers of tracks in 2016,[13] down from 40,981 in 1990.[15] The network accommodates 27,196 passenger trains and 4,674 freight trains each day.[16]

Because of the extensive network of roads and railways, along with relatively short distances to be traveled, air travel is less popular in Germany. In fact, Germans like to walk: one in four trips is on foot. Nevertheless, 187 million Germans traveled by plane in 2014, the majority of the trips (87.7%) were to destinations outside of Germany. The most important of the more than 100 civilian German airport is Frankfurt/Main, which is the hub for Lufthansa, the major German airline. Germany also has about 30 military airports.[14,17]

With its focus on foreign trade, Germany is also heavily dependent on maritime trade. In 2011, almost 300 million tons of goods were shipped overseas.[17] Although a number of modern seaports exists in Germany, a large portion of German trade is shipped overseas through ports in neighboring countries, especially the Netherlands. By far the most important German seaport is Hamburg. The most important Baltic seaport is Lübeck. In contrast, although Germany has a highly developed network of almost 7,000 kilometers of inland waterways,[17] inland water transportation has struggled since 2011 due to frequent low water levels that year. The most important inland waterway is the Rhine River (*Rhein*), which connects Germany with the major seaports of Antwerp, Rotterdam, and Amsterdam in the Netherlands, but the Rhine was closed for some time due to a major ship wreck.[18]

Demographics

Birth Rates

Like most industrialized countries in the 21st century, the Federal Republic of Germany has been experiencing low birth rates and an aging population. Although birth rates in the formerly divided West Germany and East Germany were similar up until the 1960s, they developed quite differently after the mid-1970s. In the former West Germany (Federal Republic of Germany), it fell to its lowest mark by the mid-1980s, when less than 1.30 children were born to each woman. In contrast, in the former East Germany (the German Democratic Republic), spurred by government policy, the birth rate rose to 1.94 children per woman in the 1980s and then has declined somewhat since then. After the reunification in 1990, the decline first accelerated dramatically, when the overall birth rate fell from 1.52 children to 0.77 children per woman.[13] Since then it has risen again slightly; in 2016, the total fertility rate in Germany is estimated to be 1.44 children per woman,[13] up slightly from 1.42 children per woman in 2013.[19]

Nevertheless, Germany's birthrate continues to be the lowest in the world, with 8.2 babies born each year per 1,000 people, even lower than Japan's birthrate, and by 2060, Germany's population could drop from about 81 million today to a possible low of 68 million. Such a precipitous change in the population may lead to a decline in the proportion of working-age Germans from 61% to 54% of the total population, resulting in fewer workers paying into Germany's social security system that is to provide for the rising number of older Germans.[20] In fact, the old-age dependency ratio, the percentage of people ages 65 and older per 100 people in the labor force (i.e., people ages 15 to 64), which is assumed to be reflective of the economic burden due to rising health and pension expenditures, is currently hovering around 35% and is expected to rise to over 50% by 2030—the highest in Europe apart from the small Baltic state of Latvia.[21]

Life Expectancy and Age Distribution

Concurrent with the declining birth rate, life expectancy has been increasing, and consequently, the age distribution in Germany has been shifting upward. The declining birth rate has been of concern for several decades. For 2050, male life expectancy at birth is projected to reach 83.5 years, while female life expectancy is projected to reach 88.0 years, an increase of 7.6 and 6.5 years, respectively, from 2003/2004.[4] In fact, by 2010, life expectancy at birth in Germany had reached 78.1 years for men and 83.1 years for women. However, although it has remained below the European average, the difference has been cut in half since 1990.[22] Today, Germany has more people ages 65 or older than people ages 15 years and younger. As Germany's 2015 population pyramid in **FIGURE 12-2** shows, more than one-third of the population is aged 55 years and older, and more than one-fifth is 65 and older.[13]

In keeping with most industrialized nations, Germany's population is almost evenly split between male and female residents, at 49.3% and 50.7%, respectively. In 2015, there were total of 20.4 million couples residing in Germany. There were 40.8 million households, with 41.4% being single households. Of the 8.0 million families, 20.5% were headed by a single parent. A total of 209,000 households were made up of three or more generations.[23]

Educational System

In Germany, the 16 federal states are responsible for the organization of the educational system. Superordinate control, up to a certain degree, is provided via the nationwide Conferences of Ministers of Education (*Kultusministerkonferenzen*).[24] Pupils are required to attend school for 9 years to obtain a general education. Subsequently, they may choose to start vocational training or to continue their schooling to prepare them for higher education. Most federal states have a three-pronged school system beyond primary education: *Hauptschule* (lowest level secondary school; up to 9th or 10th grade), *Realschule* (lower level secondary school), and *Gymnasium* (equivalent to the American high school). Only a high school diploma from a *Gymnasium* affords pupils an opportunity to continue their studies at a traditional university. The general qualification required for university entrance is 12 or 13 years of schooling, depending on the state. Students graduating from *Hauptschule* usually continue on with vocational training. This form of training is typically a combination of practical skills training or work at a business or factory with theoretical instruction at a vocational school (*Berufsschule*). It usually last for 2 to 3 years. Institutions of higher education are divided into universities (103) and universities of applied sciences (176).[13] The latter are practice-oriented professional schools.

Culture and Religion

Freedom of religion is guaranteed in Germany as a fundamental right. The area that today is Germany has

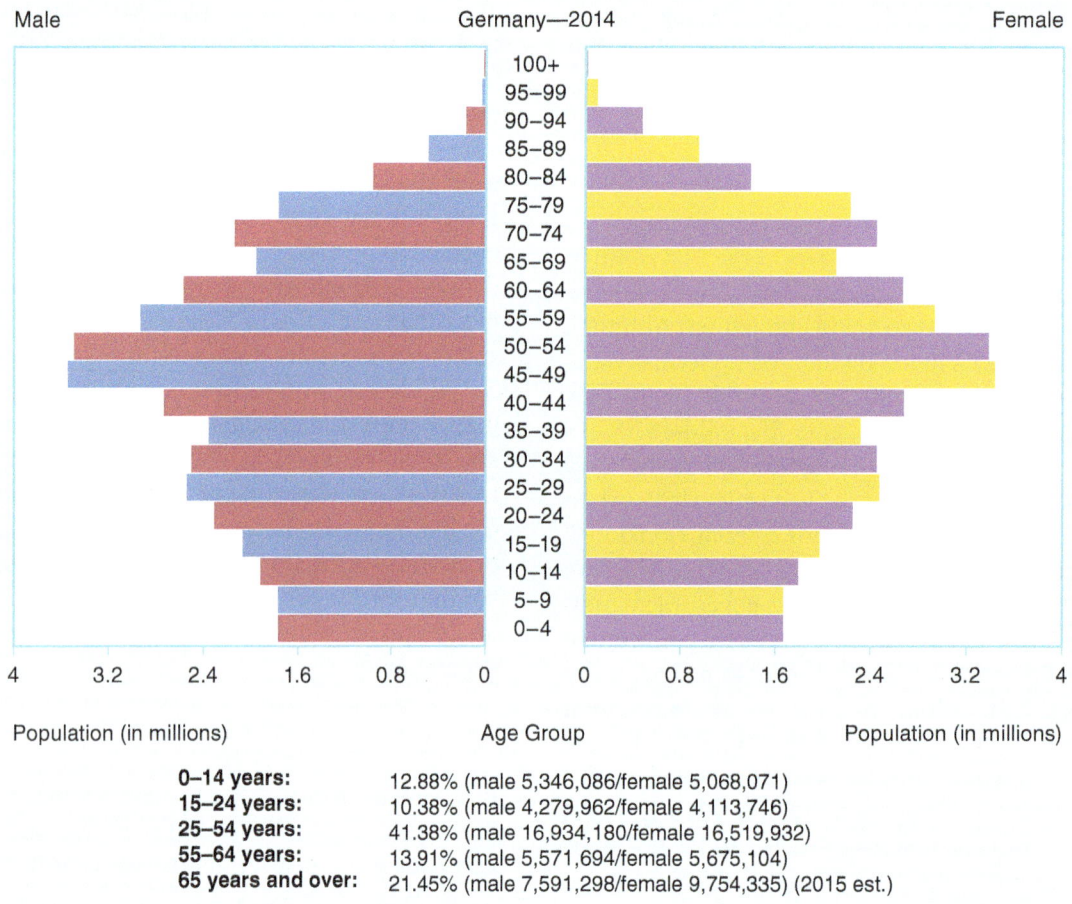

FIGURE 12-2 Germany Age Distribution, 2014
Reproduced from Central Intelligence Agency. The World Factbook, 2016: Germany. https://www.cia.gov/library/publications/the-world-factbook/geos/gm.html

been Christianized since the early Middle Ages. Consequently, Christianity is the largest religion in Germany, with an estimated 61.0% of the country's population. The two largest churches are the Roman Catholic Church and the Protestant Evangelical Church. In 2016 the Catholic Church accounted for 34.0% and the Evangelical Church for 34.0% of the population. At the same time, 28.3% of the country's population are not affiliated with any church or religion.[25] The second largest religion is Islam, with between 2.1 and 4.0 million adherents; smaller religious groups include Judaism, Hinduism, and Buddhism. Church membership has drastically fallen in recent years. In part due to a recent change in the compulsory tax law that requires all Germans who were baptized as children and are therefore automatically members of the church and obliged to pay the tax, some 200,000 German Protestants renounced their church membership, while 178,000 Catholics renounced their membership in 2013.[26]

Mortality and Morbidity in the Country

In 2014, a total of 868,356 people died in Germany, of whom 48.6% were male. During that year, the number of deaths decreased by 2.8% from the number of deaths in the year before. The increase in life expectancy has coincided with an increase in the average age of death, up by nearly 2.0 years to 78.1 years in the last decade.[27] The five most common causes of death in Germany in 2014 remained cardiovascular diseases (38.9%), followed by cancer (26.6%), illnesses of the respiratory system (6.7%), illnesses of the digestive system (4.4%), and mental and behavioral illnesses (4.1%).[27] Although numbers of deaths for each of these five causes has been steadily increasing over time, there was a slight decline in 2014 from the year before.

▸ Brief History of the Healthcare System

The story of the German healthcare system is one of political compromise and of successful implementation of communitarian values. The system has remained relatively intact over time, even in the face of governmental change and recent reforms.[28] In fact,

Germany is widely regarded as the first country to have introduced a national system of social and health insurance. As mentioned earlier, the first mandatory health insurance requirement was introduced by Otto von Bismarck in 1883; during the following years and decades, it was further expanded to cover occupational accidents and disease (1884), old age and disability (1889), unemployment (1927), and long-term care (1994).[22] The legal basis of these five branches has been established in the German Social Code (*Sozialgesetzbücher*) to guarantee all German citizens a minimum of life with dignity (*Menschenwürdiges Existenzminimum*).[29] In the past 50 to 60 years, and as shown in **TABLE 12-2**, the system has undergone several major reform.[30,31]

Today, Germany's healthcare system can be described as a mixed public and private system. It is not only one of the world's oldest social insurance health systems but also one that offers near universal healthcare coverage that includes about 95% of the country's residents via enrollment in one or more of the 120 government-regulated public health insurances (*Gesetzliche Krankenversicherung*, GKV, or sickness funds), or in one or more of the 40 private *substitutive* health insurances (*Private Krankenversicherung*) from a German or international insurance company, or a combination of the two kinds. The system has been described as the most restriction-free and consumer-oriented healthcare system in Europe, one that permits patients to look for the best service provider of state health insurance or for the most suitable coverage from a private health insurer while still at a competitive rate.[28,31] Access to such high-quality comprehensive healthcare services is stipulated via the GKV, and the majority of Germans, about 70 million (85%), are insured that way. The GKV provides an organizational framework for the delivery of public health care that has shaped the roles of payers, sickness funds, and providers, physicians, and hospitals since major reforms in the system took place under Otto von Bismarck. At the time, the system was designed as statutory health insurance for low-income, blue-collar workers and certain government employees; over the next century, it was gradually expanded to cover virtually the entire population.[22]

The German healthcare system can be described as a mixed public and private system. As shown in **TABLE 12-3**, it has several key strengths and weaknesses: although access to services is available to almost all German citizens and although care is virtually free, generous benefits and an ability to select providers freely have led to overconsumption and rising healthcare costs. Although direct healthcare transaction cost is nearly free, the high tax rate and burden on the German population is significant; tax-based subsidy and support for the healthcare system contributes to the high individual tax rate, given that it is a socialist-leaning system. Membership is compulsory; contributions are based on income, and fees for the system have always been paid for almost entirely through the labor market. Perhaps the system's most significant strength is that its member contributions are based on a person's ability to pay, which essentially makes it a fund rather than an insurance (into which members pay risk-equivalent premiums). The system is characterized by three fundamental principles, solidarity, subsidiarity, and corporatism.[31-33] Because of the principle of subsidiarity (i.e., decentralized governance, with implementation of policy by the smallest feasible political and administrative units in society), which has in fact been written into the Basic Law, German government neither finances nor pays for the provision of healthcare services, nor does it run the system per se. It has continued to subsidize costs for unemployed Germans and to partially reimburse costs for low-income workers; however, it primarily serves a legislative and regulatory role, much like the Health Care Financing Administration in the United States. Among other things, it regulates drug prices, sets guidelines for private health insurances, and stipulates the rules under which employers are to provide coverage to their employees. In general, it does not involve itself in the daily management of the system, which results in greater flexibility, better understanding of local needs, and less bureaucracy.[22,33]

Historical Evolution of the German Healthcare System

The core component of the German healthcare system is the statutory sickness fund, whose precursor can be traced to the Middle Ages when guilds, trade associations, industries, and mutual-aid societies established private relief funds to help pay for health care, funerals, and other related expenses. The earliest record of such a relief fund dates back probably to the year 1300, during the reign of King Wenceslas II of Bohemia. At the time, a few early miner society funds (*Knappschaftskassen*) maintained hospitals for members and townsfolk in mining communities, but most aimed to care for widows and orphans of members killed in accidents.[34] By the end of the 17th century, five distinct types of relief funds had emerged in different regions across Germany: relief funds for journeymen, relief funds for craftsmen modeled after the mutual support systems of the guilds, factory relief funds founded by socially oriented entrepreneurs, relief funds founded by local authorities for workers

TABLE 12-2 Selected Major Reforms in the German Healthcare System[22,30,31]

Year	Reform
1977	- First law to address cost containment in health care (*Kostendämpfungsgesetz*) - Amended in 1982 (*Kostendämpfungs-Ergänzungsgesetz*)
Reunification	
1988	- Health Care Reform Act of 1989 (*Gesundheitsreformgesetz*)
1992	- Health Care Structure Act of 1993 (*Gesundheitsstrukturgesetz*)
1994	- Code of Social Law XI—Long-Term Care Insurance (social care) (*Sozialrecht—Sozial Pflegeversicherung*)
1996	- Health Insurance Contribution Rate Relief Act (*Beitragsentlastungsgesetz*)
1997	- First and Second Statutory Health Insurance (*Gesetzliche Krankenkenversicherung*, GKV) Restructuring Acts (*Neuordnungsgesetz*)
G1998	- Act to Strengthen Solidarity in Statutory Health Insurance of 1999 (*Solidaritätsstärkungsgesetz*)
1999	- Statutory Health Insurance Reform Act of 2000 (*GKV Gesundheitsreform 2000*) - Act to Equalize Statutory Provisions in Statutory Health Insurance of 2000 (*Gesetz zur Rechtsangleichung in der Gestzlichen Krnakenversicherung*)
2000	- Infection Protection Act (*Infektionsschutzgesetz*)
2001	- Code of Social Law IX (rehabilitation and participation of disabled people) (*Rehabilitation und Teilhabe behinderter Menschen*) - Reference Price Adjustment Act (*Festbetragsanpassungsgestz*) - Act to Reform the Risk Structure Compensation Scheme in Statutory Health Insurance (*Gesetz zur Reform des Risikostrukturausgleichs in der GKV*) - Act to Newly Regulate Choice of Sickness Funds (*Gesetz zur Neuregelung der Krankenkassenwahlrechte*) - Pharmaceutical Expenditure Limitation Act (*Arzneimittelbudget-Ablösungsgesetz*)
2002	- Pharmaceutical Expenditure Limitation Act (*Arzneimittelausgaben Begrenzungsgesetz*) - Case Fees Act (*Fallpauschalengestz*) - Long-Term Care Quality Assurance Act (*Pflegequalitätssicherungsgestz*)

TABLE 12-2 Selected Major Reforms in the German Healthcare System (*continued*)	
Year	**Reform**
2003	■ Twelfth Social Codebook V Amendment Act (*12. Sozialgesetzbuch V Änderungsgesetz*) ■ First Case Fees Amendment Act (*1. Fallpauschalenänderungsgesetz*) ■ Statutory Health Insurance Modernization Act (*GKV Modernisierungsgesetz*)
2004	■ Act to Adjust the Financing of Dentures (*Gesetz zur Anpassung der Finanzierung von Zahnersatz*) ■ Second Case Fees Amendment Act (*2. Fallpauschalenänderungsgesetz*)
2006	■ Act to Improve Efficiency in Pharmaceutical Care (*Gesetz zur Verbesserung der Wirtschaftlichkeit in der Arzneimittelversorgung*)
2007	■ Act to Strengthen Competition in Statutory Health Insurance (*GKV Wettbewerbsstärkungsgesetz*)
2009	■ Hospital Financing Reform Act (*Krankenhausfinanzierungsreformgesetz*)
2010	■ Statutory Health Insurance Reform Act (*GKV Änderungsgesetz*) ■ GKV Reform Act (*GKV Finanzierungsgesetz*) ■ Pharmaceutical Market Reform Act (*Arzneimittelmarktneuordnungsgestz*)
2011	■ Statutory Health Insurance Care Structures Act (*GKV Versorgungsstrukturgesetz*)
2012	■ Long-Term Care Realignment Act (*Pflege-Neuausrichtungsgesetz*) ■ Act to Reimburse Psychiatric Care (*Psych-Entgeldgesetz*)
2013	■ Patient Rights Act (*Patientenrechtegestz*)
2015	■ Act to Strengthen SHI Health Care Provisions (*Gesetz zur Stärkung der Versorgung in der GKV*) ■ Act to Strengthen Health Promotion and Prevention (*Gesetz zur Stärkung der Gesundheitsförderung und Prävention*)
2016	■ Hospital Care Structure Reform Act (*Krankenhausstrukturgesetz*)

Data from Busse R, Blümel M. Germany: health system review. *Health Systems in Transition*. 2014; 16(2):1–296; Bäcker G. Chronologie gesetzlicher Neuregelungen. Krankenversicherung und Gesundheitswesen, 1998-2015. Institut Arbeit und Qualifikation der Universität Duisburg-Essen. [website] http://www.sozialpolitik-aktuell.de/tl_files/sozialpolitik-aktuell/_Politikfelder/Gesundheitswesen/Dokumente/Chronologie_GKV_Gesundheitssystem.pdf. Published April, 2016. Accessed September 12, 2016; Obermann K, Müller P, Müller HH, Schmidt B, Glazinski B. Understanding the German health care system. Mannheim Institute of Public Health. [website] http://miph.umm.uni-heidelberg.de/miph/cms/upload/pdf/GHCS_Kap._3.pdf. n.d. Accessed September 15, 2016.

TABLE 12-3 Strengths and Weaknesses of the German Healthcare System

Strengths	Weaknesses
Ability to provide comprehensive, uniform, and universal coverage	Overconsumption of healthcare resources, due to generous benefits packages
Ability to cover almost every German citizen	Shifts escalating healthcare costs to employers and employees
Access to virtually cost-free outpatient, inpatient, and preventive care	Unresolved, ongoing tension between the forces of centralization and decentralization
Right to freely select a healthcare provider of choice or any physician within a given geographical area	Division of inpatient and outpatient care, leading to underutilization of outpatient care and significant inefficiencies
Simplified claims process	A dual financing system in which hospitals finance operational costs and state governments finance capital costs
An extremely patient-oriented healthcare system	Complex administrative system
Mandates that healthcare expenditures cannot rise faster than wages	Future demand for geriatric care will strain the sickness funds, as these funds are financed on a pay-as-you-go basis.

or trades people, and community relief funds for people who could not otherwise find insurance. Over the next one hundred or so years, this patchwork of coverage was expanded step by step to include a variety of occupations, so that ultimately no German would be without insurance. For example, farmers and forestry workers were enrolled in 1911, civil servants in 1914, unemployed people in 1918, housewives and daughters in 1919, all primary dependents in 1930, all retirees in 1941, people with physical disabilities in 1957, students in 1975, and artists in 1981.[22,35,36]

Throughout the 19th century, the emerging class of industrial workers continued the tradition of private and local assistance by establishing voluntary mutual-aid organizations specific to their various occupations. These organizations, along with similar mutual-aid schemes established by individual companies and local communities, augmented more formal assistance efforts given by municipalities and charitable institutions. By 1848, the German government had granted local municipalities the authority to recognize these voluntary funds and to make participation in them compulsory; for example, in Prussia—the largest of the German states—health insurance became compulsory for miners, and local communities could oblige employers and their employees to pay financial contributions toward health insurance.[34,35] In 1854, local authority was further expanded, allowing local communities to require that all uninsured local residents create insurance funds for mutual support. At the same time, a Prussian statute made membership compulsory and mandated employer contributions to be no less than half of that paid by workers. By 1876, over 850,000 citizens had insurance coverage through more than 5,000 sickness funds.[22,34–37] The private system developed around the turn of the 20th century, in tandem with the statutory system.[37]

By the end of the 19th century, it had become clear that the traditional systems of social support could no longer effectively address the social and health needs of a growing and industrialized citizenry. Even Pope Leo XIII raised the social question in a papal encyclical in 1891.[31] Just 15 years earlier, in 1876, the Ministry of Health (*Reichsgesundheitsamt*) was established, which laid the foundation for the modern system.[22] That same year, a formal law on relief funds (*Hilfskassengesetz*) was passed, stipulating that workers were to receive public financial support in case of illness or death. An imperial message (*Kaiserliche Botschaft*), delivered on November 17, 1881, by King Wilhelm I to parliament, recognized the importance of *material* protection (i.e., financial protection, *materielle Absicherung*) for all German citizens and announced pending laws regarding accidents, illness, disability, and retirement. It clearly announced the duty of the German government to ensure the welfare of the population, and it cleared the way for the creation of the modern German healthcare system, and with the passage of the Act on Health Insurance for Blue-Collar Workers (*Gesetz betreffend der Kranken-versicherung der Arbeiter*) signed into law on June 15, 1883, set the stage for the social health insurance system in place today (see **FIGURE 12-3**).[22,31]

The subsequent evolution of that system can be best described according to six major periods in recent German history: German industrialization and the introduction of a mandatory health insurance requirement at the national level in 1883; social conflict and the strengthening of the medical profession during the time of the German Empire up to the Weimar Republic (1871–1919); Hitler's Third Reich and World War II (1933–1945); the immediate post-war period (1945–1949) with a divided Germany; and the period following German reunification in 1990.[22]

German Industrialization and the National Health Insurance Act of 1883

The German healthcare system, as it exists in its modern form today, is unanimously credited to Otto von Bismarck, the first German chancellor (*Bundeskanzler*), who began implementing his Bismarck System in the early 1880s with a series of social policies. Bismarck, known as the *iron chancellor* (*Eiserne Kanzler*), had recently overseen the unification of Germany, thereby establishing the German Empire under the rule of the Prussian King Wilhelm I. Shortly thereafter, Bismarck introduced legislation that resulted in the now famous Health Insurance Act of 1883, making Germany the first country in Europe to offer compulsory social health insurance. Bismarck's motive for doing so, at least primarily, was not to help those in need or to further social justice but to deal a blow to the Social Democratic Party (*Sozialdemokratische Partei*, or SPD), which he considered a political threat, to maintain social order, and to win German workers over to the old imperial regime.[35,36]

At the time, Germany's blue-collar workers were very poor with little public support, and Bismarck sought to *buy* their loyalty in exchange for economic security and material benefits. Indeed, his motivations were not purely altruistic; rather, they reflected his *sugarbread and whip* approach to politics (*Politik von Zuckerbrot und Peitsche*) in his attempt to separate the working class from the increasingly popular Social Democratic Party. In his quest to win over the working class and to weaken socialism, Bismarck continued his efforts to establish what has come to be known as the Bismarck System—one of the most advanced systems of social insurance in the world, in modified form still in existence in Germany today. For example, the law for work-related accidents (workers' compensation, *Unfallversicherung*) that passed in 1884 included a mandate that employers must insure their employees against sickness; it also set up professional societies (*Berufsgenossenschaften*) and a disability pension (*Erwerbsunfähigkeits-rente*), the latter of which was to be paid for by employer contributions and federal subsidies.[22] Largely owing to his role in introducing social reform and despite his otherwise unwavering right-wing, nationalist views, Bismarck would later be called a socialist. Bismarck was not fazed; in his speech to Congress (*Reichstag*) during the 1881 debates, Bismarck remarked, "Call it socialism or whatever you like. It is the same to me." At the same time, he was quite frank about his political calculations. "Whoever has a pension for his old age," he said, "is far more content and far easier to handle than one who has no such prospect."[38]

In 1885, the Health Insurance Act covered only 26% of blue-collar workers (or 10% of the population); however, coverage through various sickness funds was subsequently expanded several more times to eventually include almost the entire German population. During the ensuing four decades, Statutory Health Insurance (SHI) was gradually extended to cover 51% of the population in 1925. After World War II, in West Germany, the percentage rose to 88%, while in East Germany almost everybody was covered from 1949 onward.[22] Between 2012 and 2015, about 70 million West Germans (85%) were covered through a sickness fund. In 2015, employed people (and other groups such as pensioners) earning less than €54,900 (US $69,760) per year were mandatorily covered by statutory insurance, while their non-wage-earning dependents were covered free of charge. Sickness funds continue to be funded by compulsory contributions levied as a percentage of gross wages; people whose gross wages exceed the annual threshold and those who are self-employed, civil servants, or working part-time and earning less than €450 per month can choose either to enroll in a sickness fund voluntarily—and 75% do—or to purchase substitutive public insurance. In 2015, 11% were covered through private schemes.[22,33] Because since 2009, being uninsured has become illegal and all private health insurers have been required to offer a standard basic insurance policy (*Basistarif*) that can be purchased if specific requirements are met, virtually all Germans are covered by some form of healthcare insurance.

Social Conflict and the Strengthening of the Medical Profession

The success of the newly created healthcare system is evidenced by the longevity of the policies and programs first developed and implemented under Bismarck. Even more remarkably, Bismarck was able to advance his political and social agendas with no input from individual physicians or medical organizations; in fact, the medical profession took scarcely any notice, and the new system was not even debated in professional journals until after it had already been adopted.[22,40] Bismarck was quite clever in introducing his system while at the same time avoiding the impression of making radical changes to the existing structure. In fact, the 1883 Health Insurance Act did not clearly define the relationship between sickness funds and physicians, nor did it address the qualification of healthcare professionals, leaving full authority to determine these matters to the sickness funds. By the 1890s, physicians had grown increasingly frustrated; they began to seek autonomy and to exert influence through several strikes and lobbying. In 1900, they formed a professional association, the Hartmann Union (*Hartmannbund*), and by 1910, 75% of all German physicians were members. Finally, in 1913, with intervention by the German government, sickness funds and physicians forged the Berlin Treaty (*Berliner Abkommen*), which significantly changed the relationship between physicians and sickness funds and established regular procedures for negotiating conflict; these procedures, in modified form, are still in practice today. For example, the treaty stipulated, for the first time, a physician-to-population ratio, thereby limiting the influence of the funds: at least one physician had to be available for every 1,350 insured.[31,40]

Hitler's Third Reich and World War II

The appointment of Adolf Hitler as chancellor on January 30, 1933, and the subsequent rise of the Third Reich marked the beginning of another, albeit not more progressive, phase in the German healthcare system. Soon after he was sworn in, Hitler began his stepwise process toward systematic and complete seizure of power and toward creating absolute and totalitarian rule of his regime. At the time, Germany was beset by widespread unemployment, and the German people felt a general sense of insecurity and intimidation. At the same time, many saw Hitler as a new leader (führer) who could restore Germany to its former glory. For example, Hitler's autobiographical manifesto, *Mein Kampf*, published in 1925, quickly became a bestseller. Some municipalities even gave the book to newlywed couples after they exchanged vows, and by the end of World War II, about 13 million copies were in print.[41]

Hitler immediately set out to adopt a system of totalitarian control, to create a permanent state of emergency (*Ausnahmezustand*), and to implement *forcible coordination* (*Gleichschaltung*)—synchronization and tight, centralized management by means of an invasive police force—of all aspects of government, society, and commerce.[42,43] In 1934, the Hitler regime appointed a director for sickness funds and one for other insurance programs; both reported directly to the regime.[17] In fact, between 1933 and 1935, the funds, community health services, other non-governmental organizations dealing with welfare and with health education, and health-related professional organizations came under centralized leadership in accordance with Hitler's leader principle (*Führerprinzip*). Just like the large numbers of Germans in general were, health professionals were swayed by Hitler's promises of a strong, stable, and unified Germany. In fact, after 1933, physicians joined the Nazi Party in greater numbers than any other profession. Between 1925 and 1944, the percentage of doctors in the party was almost three times as high as in the general population.[44,45]

One of Hitler's goals, perhaps even his ultimate purpose, was to create a master race (*Herrenrasse*) of racially and ethnically pure Germans. One of the intended consequences was to expel German citizens of Jewish decent and other stigmatized minorities from membership in the sickness funds and to deny them access to healthcare services. Ultimately, of course, Hitler sought to implement his *final solution* (*Endlösung*), which entailed the extermination of Jewish people (and any other people deemed by the Nazi regime as impure or unwanted) in the concentration camps (*Konzentrationslager*) and extermination camps. Increasingly, but especially with the onset of World War II in 1939, public funds formerly intended for social care, welfare, and health education were diverted toward satisfying the political targets of racial hygiene, eugenics, and social control.[4] The notion of racial hygiene in particular became the basis for many health-related and other laws. One of the first Nazi laws, the Law for the Prevention of Progeny of Hereditary Disease (*Gesetz zur Verhütung erbkranken Nachwuchses*) passed on July 14, 1933, prohibited reproduction by people defined as genetically inferior. In 1935, an adjunct law allowed forcible abortions in such cases up to the sixth month of pregnancy. It also allowed the misuse of private health information to perform compulsory sterilizations, primarily on people with mental handicaps, because they were deemed likely to have defective children. A total of 300,000 to 400,000 people were sterilized, and approximately 5,000 (nearly all women) died as a result of these operations.[29,45]

Despite the strongly centralized, totalitarian rule under the Hitler regime, several improvements in social and health insurance coverage were made between 1933 and 1945, simply because they served the political agenda of the Nazi regime. In 1938 artisans came to be covered under compulsory social insurance, and in 1941 public health insurance coverage was extended to pensioners. In 1942 all wage earners, regardless of occupation, were covered by accident insurance, health care became unlimited, and maternity leave was extended to 12 fully paid weeks with job protection.[46] Swayed by Hitler's push for racial hygiene, Germany's medical community held the belief that curing patients was worthwhile; however, *healing* the nation was eminently more important. A majority of German physicians participated in the systematic exclusion of their Jewish colleagues from the practice of medicine; they also willingly adhered to and promoted the ideas of racial hygiene. To a large degree, the medical profession was not politicized but politics became medicalized.[47,48]

The Post-War Period and Two German States

At the end of World War II and after the surrender of Hitler's army on May 8, 1945, the four main Allied Forces (the United States, Great Britain, the Soviet Union, and France) took control of Germany, and the country was divided into two separate states. Correspondingly, virtually all sectors of German society, including health care, were divided into two separate systems, each with its own economic, administrative, political, and social structures. The American, British, and French controlled the western portion of the country that became the Western Federal Republic of Germany (*Bundesrepublik Deutschland*, or *West Deutschland*) and Russia controlled the eastern portion of the country that became the Eastern German Democratic Republic (*Deutsche Demokratische Republik*. In the years immediately following World War II, health care in Germany was characterized by ad hoc public health interventions aimed at controlling and/or preventing outbreaks of epidemics and at distributing meager and often inadequate resources for health care.[22]

While under Allied control, and then after the end of the Allied occupation on March 20, 1948, the healthcare systems in the two German states developed in a very different fashion, resulting in two different German health systems. East Germany gradually moved toward a national socialist, state-financed health system, with the option to purchase private health insurance for additional treatment. This system was one of strong, centralized state control; it established a single sickness fund, managed by the Free German Trade Union Federation (*Freier Deutscher Gewerkschaftsbund*), a federation of trade unions that was subordinate to the Socialist Unity Party of Germany (*Sozialistische Einheitspartei Deutschlands*).[49] Socialist state ideology ruled these institutions: almost all hospitals were nationalized, and independent physician practices were forced out of business. In West Germany, the pre–World War II system was reestablished. As before, it was supervised by the government but was not government run, and it further developed into a highly decentralized corporate system in the face of modest parliamentary control. Political authority extended to benefits, eligibility, compulsory membership, covered risks (physical, emotional, mental, curative, and preventive), income maintenance during temporary illness, employer–employee contributions to the GKV, and other central issues. Healthcare coverage was expanded considerably, codified by social law (*Sozialgesetzbuch*) and by the GKV. More than 1,000 autonomous statutory sickness funds arose, which led to the broadest coverage within the free market system.[50,51]

For West Deutschland, the new Constitution, or Basic Law, was promulgated on May 23, 1949. In it, Germany was established as a democratic and social federal state (Article 20), in which *social rights* were defined by legislation. This legislation, with the exception of certain prescribed areas, came under the purview of state parliaments. When Germany was divided, West Germany consisted of 11 federal states (*Länder*); as is true today, each state had its own elected parliament (*Landtag*). Because health care is decentralized in Germany, its management is handled by three main bodies (see **TABLE 12-4**): the Federal Ministry of Health (*Bundesministerium für Gesundheit*, or BMG), established in 1961; the federal states; and the corporate bodies that comprise the sickness funds, the physicians associations, the hospital organizations, and patient representatives.[52] The BMG sets the legal framework of the system, with a primary focus on the drafting of bills, ordinances, and administrative regulations, including the principal benefits to be covered by the statutory health insurance system.[53] Within the legal framework set by the Ministry of Health, the Federal Joint Committee (*Gemeinsame Bundesausschuss*) functions as the central organ for self-administration; it has wide-ranging regulatory power to determine the services to be covered by sickness funds and to set quality measures for providers.[52,54]

TABLE 12-4 Number of Sickness Funds, by Type, 1993 and 2014

Type	Numbers 1993	Numbers 2014
General regional sickness funds	269	11
Company-based sickness funds	744	107
Substitute sickness funds	15	6
Guild sickness funds	169	6
Sickness funds for agricultural workers	22	1
Sailors' sickness fund	1	—
Miners' sickness fund	1	1
Total	1,221	132

Data from Busse R, Blümel M. Germany: health system review. *Health Systems in Transition*. 2014;16(2):1–296. http://www.euro.who.int/__data/assets/pdf_file/0008/255932/HiT-Germany.pdf?ua=1. Accessed January 12, 2017.

The federal states maintain the hospital infrastructure and supervise and monitor activities of public health personnel, goods, and diseases; undergraduate medical, dental, and pharmaceutical education; and regional physician and sickness fund organizations.[52] Today, all 16 states are also responsible for the implementation of federal health policy, but they have legislative power and considerable control in carrying out a wide range of tasks within their jurisdictions, as long as they do not violate federal mandate.[54]

The Fall of the Berlin Wall and a Reunified Germany

Twenty-eight years after construction began on the Berlin Wall on August 13, 1961, to formally demarcate the German Democratic Republic from the Federal Republic of Germany, German citizens from both states began scaling it and tearing it down on November 9, 1989. Eleven months later, on October 3, 1990, East Germany and West Germany were officially reunited. With the signing of the Treaty of Reunification (*Vereinigungsvertrag*), 17 million East German citizens became fully integrated into the system of the Federal Republic of Germany and thereby the political, economic, and social responsibility of the West German government. Although the public was extremely critical of what was perceived to be a totalitarian regime by the former East Germany's Socialist Unity Party (*Sozialistische Einheitspartei Deutschlands*), it regarded social welfare, health care, and educational systems much more positively.[55] Therefore, early in the reunification process, East Germans argued that they had made considerable achievements in the field of health and social policy that deserved to be preserved; they were particularly proud of the exclusion of commercialization from health care as a historic achievement.[56] Yet, although some (minor) compromises were made in the way in which health care was to be financed and delivered, East Germany's national health insurance system was quickly transformed to adopt the pluralist system of West Germany. In the process, almost all ideas from the German Democratic Republic healthcare system (e.g., polyclinics and public health initiatives) fell out of favor; however, today they are once again part of the debate on improving patient-centered care in the unified Germany.[31]

The extraordinary task of uniting and combining two formerly separate and distinct healthcare systems brought about unprecedented healthcare reforms in the late 20th century, which have continued into the 21st century. Over the course of the past 25 years since reunification, a large number of healthcare reforms have been introduced (see also Table 12-2). By the mid-1990s, healthcare benefits provided through the GKV were extensive and included, among other benefits, ambulatory care (care provided by office-based physicians), choice of office-based physicians, hospital care, full pay to mothers (from 6 weeks before to 8 weeks after childbirth), extensive home help, health checkups, sick leave to care for relatives, rehabilitation and physical therapy, medical appliances (such as artificial limbs), drugs, and stays of up to one month in health spas every few years. Particularly in the past two decades, reforms have included a focus on quality assurance, evidence-based medicine, and health technology assessment.[52] It is particularly noteworthy that the German healthcare system has embraced system-wide technological advances, such the health insurance smart card that has a chip encoded with a beneficiary's insurance information and basic personal health data. This specific technology has been used since the 1990s.

By the turn of the 21st century, there was a general feeling that reform was needed, most of all because of increasing SHI contribution rates (on average from 13.5% of gross wages in 2001 to 14.3% in 2003) and perceived deficiencies in the quality of care.[22]

By 2004, there was considerable pressure to adopt a major reform, including integration of inpatient and ambulatory care, which traditionally had been completely separate from one another in Germany.[57] In 2009, employers and employees began to pay the sickness fund premiums as a uniform percentage of gross wages or of income across all sickness funds. Sickness funds then would immediately pass those premiums to a central national fund (*Gesundheitsfonds*). Additionally, every German has since been required to have health insurance coverage for the basic benefit package.[57]

Reform efforts have been ongoing. To aid in the process, the German federal minister of health (*Gesundheitsminister*), Herman Gröhe, issued an invitation to the ministers of health of six leading industrial nations—the United States, Great Britain, France, Italy, Japan, and Canada—to join Germany for a meeting on October 8–9, 2015, during which leadership issued a declaration to address control of antimicrobial resistance and agreed to embrace responsibility for joint action toward ensuring global health.[58] On September 29, 2016, the Federal Ministry of Health passed amendments to the Second Long-Term Care Strengthening Act, active on January 1, 2017. These amendments introduce a new vision for long-term care in Germany to support self-reliance of people in need of care. To that end, regular benefits will be expanded by services for personal support and daily living assistance.[59]

At the time, reunification was not thought to cause significant problems. In fact, most everybody was initially very excited about the prospect of Germany being, once again, a unified nation. German citizens, in general, considered the West German welfare system to be one of the best and were eager to share it with their East German neighbors. However, in large part due to the seemingly never-ending reforms, attitudes about the social welfare system (and reunification itself) have undergone a pronounced change. Because of the speed with which it occurred, the reunification process was culturally very disorienting for many East Germans, while it left many West Germans frustrated over what they perceived to be a lack of appreciation for the sacrifices they made to help their "poor cousins in the land next door."[60(p462)] Not surprisingly, although 65% of East Germans rated their own social security system better than their own shortly after reunification, a short five years later, a whopping 92% favored their system, while only 3% preferred the Western system. Similarly, 65% of East Germans in 1990 thought that the healthcare system in West Germany was better than in the East; in 1995, 57% said the East German system was better.[61]

Solidarity and Subsidiarity: The Basis for the German Healthcare System

The modern German healthcare system has achieved a high degree of equity and justice, despite its fragmented federal organization: no single group is in a position to dictate the terms of service delivery, reimbursement, remuneration, quality of care, or any other important concerns. Access to health care is regarded as a right of all German citizens. That right reflects universality of coverage, comprehensive benefits, the principle of the healthy paying for the sick, and a redistributive element in the financing of health care. Healthcare provider reimbursement rates are negotiated with the federal government of Germany, health provider union organizations, and other stakeholder groups; this rate setting is done every few years. The structure of the German health insurance system is rooted in several assumptions about the nature of German society. First, it has been assumed that most Germans will have stable, long-standing connections to jobs, either through their own employment or through the employment of a spouse or parent. Second, it has been assumed that wage income would grow as quickly as the healthcare costs of the covered population. However, recent changes in German society have made these assumptions about the organizational structure of the German healthcare system much less valid.[62]

What does remain as two integral features of the system are the fundamental principles of solidarity and subsidiarity.[31,32,63] Both principles have been endorsed by the left, central, and right parties across the political spectrum and are secured in Germany's Basic Law of 1949. Solidarity refers to a shared commitment among members of society toward respect and mutual care; subsidiarity refers to their common understanding that social action should be transferred to the most appropriate level, with particular emphasis on the local and communal levels.[63] Both principles closely relate to the concept of generalized reciprocity, or the willingness to give to someone without expecting the person to return the benefit directly, but rather expecting that somehow, in some way, the benefit will be returned eventually. In the context of health care, it is the agreement among insured people to share health risks and to assess contributions commensurate with one's ability to pay[64] while at the same time to discharge government from any functions which could be solved better, or at least equally as well, via private efforts and responsibility.⁶³ In Germany, the belief in generalized reciprocity ultimately provides the conceptual basis for the evolution of the modern health insurance system.³¹

Description of the Current Healthcare System

Facilities

The current situation in the German healthcare system is marked by several recently implemented reform efforts. A central goal of such reforms by the German government has been to induce more competition in the healthcare marketplace, which in turn should lead to more efficiency. One result has been a steady decline, for years, in the number of general hospitals. In 2012, there were 2,017 hospitals with a total of 501,475 beds. Of these, 48% of beds were in publicly owned hospitals, 34% in private not-for-profit hospitals, and 18% in private for-profit hospitals.²² It is important to note that the number of private for-profit hospitals has been growing in recent years and has accounted for around one-sixth of all hospital beds.³³ Although the total number of acute hospital beds has been reduced substantially since 1991, it is still almost 60% higher than the EU average. The average length of stay also decreased steadily between 1991 and 2011, falling from 12.8 to 7.7 days.²² All hospitals are staffed principally by salaried doctors. They fall into four categories: basic service hospitals (usually up to 200 beds and 2–3 medical disciplines), regular service hospitals (up to 300 beds and 4–5 disciplines), central service hospitals (usually up to 500 beds and up to 8 different disciplines), and maximum care hospitals (big institutions, usually more than 1,000 beds, mostly university hospitals with a comprehensive spectrum of medical specialties and services, responsible for research, training, and hospital treatment).⁶⁶

One unique aspect of the German healthcare system is its well-developed rehabilitation sector. After patients have completed their stay in an acute care hospital, they often continue their treatment in a separate rehabilitation clinic to ensure, with the help of special procedures and facilities (e.g., physical therapy), the best possible outcome. This follow-up treatment must be booked separately, and a normal stay lasts about 21.0 days. In 2013, about 2.0 million patients were treated in all German rehabilitation clinics, with a mean duration of 25.3 days.⁶⁶

Although the number of pharmacies has decreased slightly since the early 2000s, it is still relatively high by international standards. In 2009 there were 21,548 pharmacies in Germany, of which 3,224 were branches (i.e., 26 pharmacies per 100,000 residents).²² For many years, German policymakers regulated public pharmacies in order to limit the increase in costs. However, they abandoned such restrictions in 2004 to encourage greater competition. Since then, it has been legal for individual pharmacists to own up to 4 pharmacies. In addition, mail-order pharmaceutical purchases became possible. However, the increased competition has not lead to a consolidation of pharmacies yet. The number of pharmacies has remained high with 20,441 in 2014.⁶⁷

Workforce

The German healthcare system is marked by a high number of healthcare personnel. By 2011, almost 5 million people were employed in the healthcare sector, accounting for 11.2% of all employment that year.²² Specifically, the number of physicians has steadily increased since the 1990s. In 2013, of more than 450,000 physicians, 326,945 were active, and of those, 174,829 practiced in hospitals, while 144,058 practiced in ambulatory care (about 123,000 as SHI-accredited physicians and about 21,000 as employed physicians in SHI physician practices). Another 29,808 physicians worked in the public healthcare sector, administration, government, and other sectors. In general, the density of physicians has remained above the EU average (but below the averages in Austria and Switzerland).²² The steady increase in the number of physicians in recent years is partly attributable to the increase in the number of foreign doctors, resulting in a steady, high supply of doctors in Germany. Yet, while the total number of physicians has continued to increase, the number of general practitioners has decreased. The discrepancy is in large part due to differences in earning potential; in 2013, specialists made over five times the average wage of general practitioners.²²,⁶⁸ **FIGURE 12-3** shows physicians by type.

The number of nursing professionals has also steadily increased since the 1990s. As is true for many countries of the OECD, nurses greatly outnumber physicians in Germany. In 2013, there were 883,000 nurses in Germany, or 1,086 per 100,000 residents. There were also 19,000 midwives, or 23 per 100,000 residents, and 161,000 nursing associate professionals, or 198 per 100,000 residents.⁶⁹ In contrast to nurses, who may work autonomously or in physician-led healthcare teams and assume

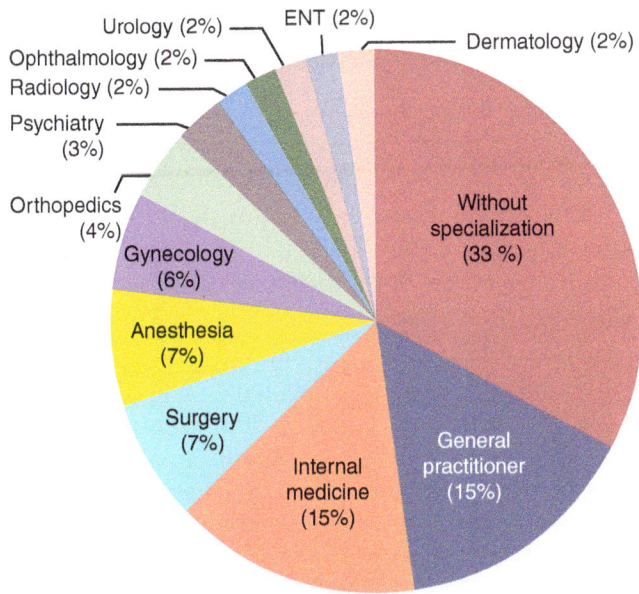

FIGURE 12-3 Proportions of Physicians, by Type

Reproduced from Obermann K (Hrsg.), Müller P(Hrsg.), Müller HH (Hrsg.), Glazinski B (Hrsg.). *The German Health Care System: Accessing the German Health Care Market*. 2nd ed. 2016. Used by permission of the publisher, medhochzwei, and the authors.

responsibility for the planning, management, and execution of total patient care, nursing associate professionals carry out basic nursing and personal care tasks and generally work under the supervision of, and in support of, the healthcare team. In Germany, as well as in many other countries, ongoing concerns linger about the current (and projected to be lasting) nursing shortage, as do ongoing concerns about the challenges of caring effectively for a graying society (especially for the baby boom generation). Therefore, Germany, as well as many other countries, has undertaken efforts to increase the training of new nurses and to retain practicing nurses in the profession. As a result, there has been a big increase in the number of nurse graduates in recent years, related at least in part to a greater offer of registered nurse training programs in several German universities, in addition to the traditional vocational nursing school programs.[70]

In contrast to the increasingly high number of physicians, the number of dentists in Germany continues to be much lower. As is true for several other OECD countries, it has remained fairly stable, although it did increase slightly, from 2008 to 2013, to 66,539 dentists, 82 dentists per 100,000 residents. In contrast, the number physiotherapist was much higher in 2013, at 167,000, or 205 per 100,000 residents. Moreover, the growth rate between 2008 and 2013 was also very high.[69] Physiotherapists assess, plan, and implement rehabilitative programs that improve or restore human motor functions, maximize movement ability, relieve pain syndromes, and treat or prevent physical challenges associated with injuries, diseases, and other impairments.

Technology/Equipment

With the passage of the Statutory Health Insurance Reform Act of 2000, the newly created Federal Joint Committee was given the responsibility for assessing new health technologies. Such technologies include a wide range of healthcare products to diagnose, monitor, and treat diseases and medical conditions affecting humans. Revenue from these products has increased dramatically; in 2003, the German medical industry revenue was US $19.0 billion. Within a decade, by 2013, the amount had more than doubled, to $42.4 billion. Germany is, with the United States and Japan, one of the largest manufacturers of medical technology worldwide. However, medical industry revenues in the United States continue to far exceed those elsewhere; in 2013, they totaled US $216.2 billion almost double the revenues of all European countries combined ($117.6 billion).[70] In Germany, as is true in other countries, the jump in medical industry revenues is directly related to the rapid proliferation in the availability of diagnostic technologies, such as computed tomography (CT) scanners, and magnetic resonance imaging (MRI) units. For example, the number of MRI units increased from about 1 per million population in 1992 to 12.20 in 2000 and 18.30 in 2011. By 2013, there was a total of 935.00 units in Germany, or 11.59 units per million residents in the country, although that number was still significantly below that of many other countries. In the same year, there were 46.87 units per million residents in Japan, 38.05 units per million residents in the United States, 22.55 units per million residents in South Korea, and 24.62 units per million residents in Italy.[69] The number of CT scanners in 2013 was much higher, with a total of 1,510.00, or 18.70 scanners per million residents. But similar to the rate of MRI units, the rate of CT scanners in Germany was much lower than the rate of 101.30 scanners per million residents in Japan and 43.50 scanners per million residents in the United States.[69]

▶ Evaluation of the Healthcare System

Cost

As is true for most of the Westernized countries, German citizens continue to pay relatively little out of pocket for their health care. With the GDP at US $3,355.77 billion in 2015, most SHI beneficiaries paid at a contribution rate of 0.9%—the same as in previous years, and their out-of-pocket per capita spending was $649. The remaining costs were assumed by social health insurance or by the government.[33] Yet, since the beginning of the new millennium, Germans pay more than ever for their health care. In a deeply unpopular reform, those enrolled in the statutory insurance plan have been required to pay €10 per yearly quarter since January 2004 to see a general practitioner. Individuals covered by private health insurance as well as youths were exempted from these co-payments. Beneficiaries now also must contribute toward the cost of, for example, prescription drugs, wound dressings, and bandages; they must assume 10% of the cost of prescriptions and of medical aids and supplies, with a €5 minimum and a €10 maximum. In addition, they must assume a share of the cost of inpatient preventive treatment and rehabilitation, outpatient rehabilitation, and inpatient hospital care (at €10 per day, for a maximum of 28 days annually). For dental prostheses, patients receive a lump sum, which on average covers 50% of actual costs.[49,72,73]

As mentioned before, healthcare coverage is universal for all legal residents of Germany, and employed citizens (and other groups such as pensioners) earning less than €54,900 ($69,760) per year as of 2015 are mandatorily covered by SHI, and their nonearning dependents are covered free of charge. Individuals whose gross wages exceed the threshold and those who were already previously SHI-insured or are self-employed can remain in the publicly financed scheme on a voluntary basis. Through chapter 3 of the Social Code Book V, the following types of benefits are currently legally included in the basic benefit package, usually in generic terms: preventive services, inpatient and outpatient hospital care, physician services, mental health care, dental care, prescription drugs, medical aids, rehabilitation, and sick leave compensation. SHI preventive services include regular dental checkups, child checkups, basic immunizations, checkups for chronic diseases, and cancer screening at certain ages.[33,73] Since 1995, long-term care has been covered by a separate insurance scheme, which is mandatory for the whole population. The contribution rate of 2.35% of gross salary is shared between employers and employees; people without children pay an additional 0.25%. Beneficiaries can choose between in-kind benefits and cash payments (around a quarter of Long Term Care Insurance expenditure goes to these cash payments). Both home care and institutional care are provided almost exclusively by private not-for-profit and for-profit providers. Since 2013, family caregivers also have been receiving financial support through payments of up to 50% of what professional providers would have received for that care.[33]

Total Healthcare Spending and Health Dollars Spent Per Capita

Germany continues to spend a large amount of its wealth on health. Overall, healthcare expenditures have been steadily on the rise since the passage of the National Health Insurance Act in 1883. In 1985, they accounted for 8.8% of GDP; by 1995, they had risen to 10.1%; and since 2005, they have continued to hover between 10.0% and 11.0%, despite ongoing efforts to curb spending. In 2014, total expenditures were US $492 billion; 58.5% were attributable to SHI spending.[4] By the latter part of the 20th century, and into the 21st century, dramatic increases in SHI spending occurred for physician services and ambulatory care; in contrast, and due to the strong ambulatory care sector, spending on acute hospital care has been relatively low.[22] SHI spending for pharmaceuticals has continued to fluctuate somewhat; it fell sharply between 1992 and 1994, rose slowly in 1996, fell in 1997, and then rose increasingly more quickly through 2003. By 2010, it had fallen again, largely due to the manufacturers' rebates for prescription-only drugs and drugs without reference prices being raised from 6.0% to 16.0% in mid-2010.[22] Total spending, by type of expenditure, as of 2012, is shown in **FIGURE 12-4**. Similar to overall healthcare expenditures, per capita expenditures have also been on the rise in Germany. In 1970, per capita

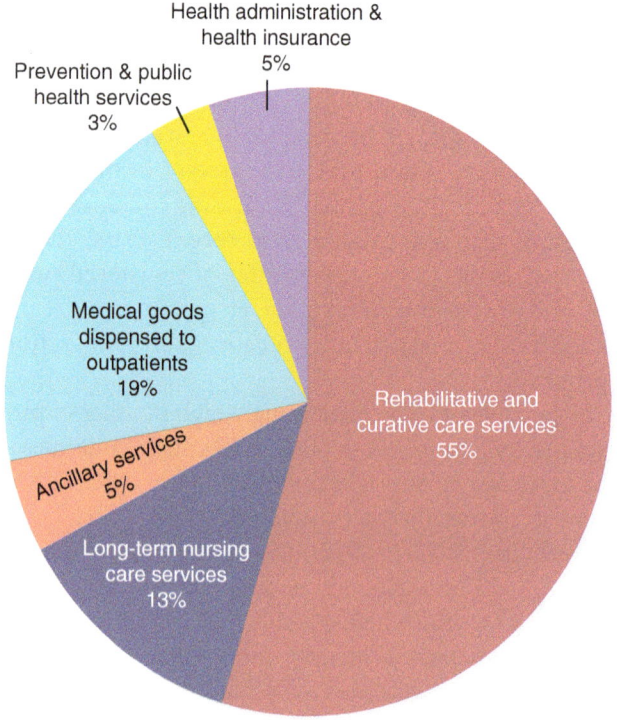

FIGURE 12-4 Total Healthcare Expenditures, by Type, 2012

Reproduced from European Commission. Eurostat Statistics Explained. Main page. http://ec.europa.eu/eurostat/statistics-explained/index.php/Main_Page. April 14, 2016. Accessed October 6, 2016.

healthcare spending was $663, accounting for 4.48% of the per capita GDP. By 2002, per capita spending had risen to $2,066, and in 2013, it was $4,819. The largest proportion of that amount was for public spending.[68,74]

Multiparty Payer System and Third-Party Distribution

At first glance, healthcare financing in Germany appears to be a rather straightforward process because almost all German citizens belong to statutory sickness funds and the remainder belong to private insurance plans. Therefore, one may assume—incorrectly—that the system has only two types of payers, or—because of the dominance of SHI, and again incorrectly—may go even further and classify it as a single-payer system. In fact, the German healthcare system is much more complex, and when, in 2006, Chancellor Angela Merkel proposed to reform the healthcare system by creating a centralized health fund (by shifting funding from payroll taxes to general revenues, trimming benefits, and increasing cost sharing), this proposal had to be quickly abandoned due to lack of public support and amidst political opposition.[75,76] Although it is true that the statutory sickness funds represent the most important type of payer in Germany's healthcare system and are the country's version of a "public" healthcare system, there are in fact a large number of these funds (see also Table 12-4). They make up a group of wholly private, nonprofit insurers that are heavily regulated but function independently of the government.

At the same time, it is important to note that sickness funds only perform the function of purchasing agents on behalf of a government-run central health fund and their patients. Specifically, Germans pay their health insurance premiums into a national, government-run central health fund that effectively performs the risk-pooling function for the entire system. This health fund (*Gesundheitsfonds*) is administrated by the Federal Social Insurance Office (*Bundesgesundheitsamt*), which determines how much of the fund will be allocated to each sickness fund, based on specific criteria.[77] It is really much more accurate to describe the German healthcare system as multipayer, compulsory, employer-based, highly regulated, and fee-for-service.

Much like the German education system, the German public health system is decentralized to the states and localities, although the federal government holds legislative authority. Public health remains principally the responsibility of the 16 federal states and covers issues such as surveillance of communicable disease and health promotion and education. As in the United States, the system is responsible for protecting public health, including water systems, sewer systems, other forms of environmental protection, food safety, and health promotion. The environmental protection measures have been quite successful in cleaning up major rivers and other forms of water pollution. Similarly, air quality has also markedly improved over the past 35 years.[78]

Unfortunately, public health promotion efforts have received considerably less attention. Historically, the states have resisted the influence of the federal government on public health, and although some elements of public health have been included in SHI in recent decades (such as cancer screening) and other interventions have separate agreements (e.g., immunizations), there have not been overarching public health guidelines in place, like the U.S. Office of Disease Prevention and Health Promotion's *Healthy People 2020*. But a few years ago, in September 2012, the 53 member states of the World Health Organization finally adopted a European health policy framework, *Health 2020*, that aims to "significantly improve the health and well-being of populations, reduce health inequalities, strengthen public health, and ensure people-centered health systems that are universal, equitable, sustainable, and of high quality."[79]

As a notable exception, from 1989 to 1996, health promotion measures were actually offered as a type of benefit by sickness funds directly to their members. This benefit was abandoned under the Second Social Health Insurance Restructuring Act; however, it has been partly reintroduced through the Reform Act 2000.

While the Social Code Book regulates preventive services and screening in considerable detail (e.g., concerning diseases to be screened for and intervals between screening), it leaves further regulations to the Federal Committee of Physicians and Sickness Funds (*Bundesausschuss der Ärzte und Krankenkassen*). This committee has remained one of the most important decision-making bodies on benefits in the ambulatory care sector. Established in 1923, it was the oldest joint institution in the system of joint self-government and has considerable latitude in defining the benefits catalogue for curative, diagnostic, and therapeutic procedures.[22] Additionally, the German Forum for Prevention and Health Promotion (*Deutsches Forum Prävention und Gesundheitsförderung*) was founded in July 2002 to actively strengthen prevention and health promotion, primarily via concerted health promotion activities in preschools, schools, and workplaces. For the elderly, a comprehensive program to prevent cardiovascular diseases was initiated. In 2007, it merged with the *Deutsche Bundesvereinigung Prävention und Gesundheitsförderung*.

Quality

Infant Mortality

In 2015, Germany recorded 737,575 live births, up from 683,000 live births in 2006 but still down from 747,000 in 2000.[4] Due to the advanced and comprehensive nature of the German healthcare system, infant mortality has remained very low. In 2006, it was 3.8 per 1,000 live births; in 2013, it had dropped even further, to 2.8 per 1,000 live births,[68] though it has since risen again just slightly, to 3.4 in 2016. The 2013 German infant mortality rate was lower than the OECD average of 3.8 but on par with other long-standing EU members, such as Italy (2.9) and Portugal (2.9), and it is higher than in Scandinavian countries, such as Iceland (1.3) and Finland (1.7).[68] Mortality for children under 5 years old has also declined. It was 8.5 per 1,000 live births in 1990, dropped to 5.0 per 1,000 live births in 2004, and has since dropped further to 3.1 per 1,000 live births in 2013. As such, it has remained well below the rates for the United States (11.2 per 1,000 live births in 1990, 8.1 per 1,000 live births in 2004, and 6.9 per 1,000 live births in 2013).[80] The main causes of deaths among children under 5 years of age appear to be unintentional; one of the leading causes is strangulation/choking.[81]

Two-Tiered Healthcare Systems (by Income)

The perception has long been that privately insured patients receive preferential treatment due to higher reimbursement to physicians by the private health insurance system. In other words, private health insurance offers benefits not available to those insured in the statutory health insurance system, such as single occupancy rooms during inpatient stays and treatment by senior physicians. In part, these perceptions may be fueled by the fact that health providers are able to charge a higher rate than the federally negotiated base rate, as outlined in the Fee Code for Doctors, for their privately insured beneficiaries. Although they must explain the higher charges in writing, physicians typically and as a matter of principle, charge fees between one and three times the base rate, depending on the extent and difficulty of the work involved.[82] In addition, there appear to be disparate wait times for elective treatment between privately insured and SHI patients, with those in the SHI waiting approximately three times longer for appointments for selected tests than the privately insured.[83] Similarly, it appears that sick adults with private health insurance may receive more health services than those with statutory insurance. They also tend to be more likely to see specialists, be admitted and have nonemergency surgery.[84] At the same time, some evidence exists that presence of the PHI system does not appear to have compromised quality of or access in the SHI system. For example, in 2010, two-thirds of SHI patients received same-day or next-day appointments with a doctor or nurse when sick or in need of care.[85]

Vaccination Coverage

By 2015, vaccination rates for German children rose to an all-time high level and were much improved from even 15 years ago. It should be noted that mandatory vaccinations were abolished with reunification in 1990. Consequently, there are some regional fluctuations in vaccination coverage, with East German states showing higher coverage. In general, vaccination rates for almost all common childhood diseases were at a high in 2015, with rates between 85.0% and 99.0%. For example, while rates for Diphtheria vaccinations were around 78.0% in 2000, they rose to 96.0% in 2016.[86] What remains of concern even today is the potential for measles outbreaks. For example, in 2011, although the measles vaccination rate was 96.1% for the East German state of Mecklenburg–Western Pomerania, it was only 89.8% in Bavaria.[87] However, measles outbreaks continue to be a problem. In 2006, Germany reported 2,307 cases of measles, up from 778 in 2005.[88] To date, Germany has not been able to meet the World Health Organization progress indicator—less than one notified case per million. Like many EU member countries, Germany also recommends influenza vaccination for adults ages 65 and older. In fact, Germany is one of four countries that recommend such vaccinations beginning at age 60 (the others are Greece, Iceland, and the Netherlands). In 2013, about 55.0% of the eligible population was immunized against influenza, as slight decrease from the year before.[89]

Quality Assurance

In Germany, quality assurance is addressed through a range of measures broadly defined by law, and in more detail by the Federal Joint Committee. In addition, in an advisory role, the Institute for Quality and Efficiency in Health Care, established in 2004, provides the committee with evidence-based evaluations of the benefits and cost benefits of health services and functions. Previously, quality assurance was carried out almost exclusively within one sector (in keeping with the deep divide between the hospital and ambulatory care sectors). Since 2007, with the passage of the Act to Strengthen Competition in SHI, multisector approaches to quality improvement have been encouraged. The law stipulates provisions for measuring quality of the following services:

- services that are provided in at least two different healthcare settings, both with a significant contribution to the treatment outcome (multisector procedures);
- services that can be provided in different sectors (procedures with sector equivalence);
- and services provided in one sector, with outcome quality measured in another sector (cross-sectoral follow-up procedures).[90]

In 2007, many of the previous regulations were combined to align quality requirements across all healthcare settings as much as possible. Further structural quality is assured by the requirement that providers have a quality management system, physicians continue their medical education, and health technology assessments are used for drugs and procedures. Although there is no revalidation requirement for physicians and hospital accreditation is voluntary,[33] hospitals participate in an external quality control process for acute care. This process is quite unique: for selected interventions (e.g., appendectomies), hospital treatment is documented for each patient based on a set of quality indicators specified in advance. Performance data are then transmitted to a central external agency (Institute for Applied Quality Improvement and Research in Health Care, or AQUA), as well as to the corresponding state offices for quality assurance where the data are evaluated.[90] The results are compiled in annual quality management reports that are discussed at regularly convened nationwide conferences on quality control, and they are incorporated into the day-to-day running of hospitals.

Patients' Rights

In 2004 Germany established a federal commissioner for patient issues in the health system (*Beauftragte der Bundesregierung für die Belange der Patientinnen und Patienten sowie Bevollmächtigter für Pflege*). The position is currently held by a political appointee; the commissioner is charged with ensuring that patient issues are considered at different levels in the health system. An analysis of the public inquiries received by the commissioner reveals that most complainants are older. Health insurance, especially medications, were a major topic as were concerns over communication with healthcare providers. Older complainants were more likely to mention anxiety, uncertainty, and feelings of injustice, and the personal financial burden of health services was featured prominently.[91] Further expansion of patients' rights occurred in 2013, with the passage of the Patients' Rights Act (*Patientenrechtegesetz*). This general law on patients' rights bundles several existing jurisdictions and gives detailed regulations (e.g., for complaints). The act created the *treatment contract*, a special contract that by law now governs every interaction between a person administering medical treatment and the patient. Although the law is aimed primarily at physicians, its scope also encompasses other healthcare professionals.[22,92]

▸ Access

Equity/Universality

As mentioned before, two of the main characteristics of the German healthcare system are free choice of providers and unrestricted access to all care levels. Such access is provided via near universal insurance coverage, with the majority of the population either mandatorily or voluntarily insured by statutory health insurance and with approximately 10% of the population insured privately. In theory, insured people have free choice of physicians, psychotherapists (since 1999), dentists, pharmacists, and emergency room services, but in reality, access to reimbursed care is available only upon referral by a physician.[22] In addition, there are differences in access between SHI insured people and privately insured people, with the latter generally having better access (see also discussion above on the two-tiered nature of the system). In addition, inequities regarding access to health care exist for migrants, asylum seekers, and refugees; in theory legal migrants are covered by the insurance system, asylum seekers can receive basic care as stipulated in the Asylum Seekers' Benefits Act (*Asylbewerberleistungsgesetz*), and undocumented immigrants who are ill are covered by social security.[33,93]

Uninsured Populations

Until the enactment of the U.S. Patient Protection and Affordable Care Act on March 23, 2010, by President Barack Obama, the number of uninsured people in Germany was far below that in the United States. And although that number had been increasing between 1999 and 2007, it has since declined drastically. Specifically, 145,000 people, or 0.2% of the population, were uninsured in 1999, and there were almost 200,000 people, or about 0.3%, uninsured during the first quarter of 2007, with some sources citing the number as high as 300,000. However, since then and as a result of the 2007 Health Care Reform Act, the number of uninsured people dropped to 137,000 by 2011, a 30.0% decline.[22,94] Today, despite the obligation to be insured, about 0.2% of employed people have no health insurance. The percentage is higher for foreign men aged 35 to 44 years (1.0%). The uninsured in Germany are mainly self-employed people who are unable or unwilling to pay the premiums after failed business ventures, self-employed people who take the risk of not buying coverage, privately insured people who are unable to continue to afford private coverage because of declining income or rising premiums, and long-term unemployed people who lost unemployment benefits (*Arbeitslosengeld II*) after introduction of the Hartz IV employment market reforms and therefore lost their entitlement for health insurance coverage. Low-income employees, divorced people, alien residents, university students, and people who did not graduate from school are also at risk.

▶ Current and Emerging Issues and Challenges

Cost Containment

Rooted in the Bismarck System of Social Health Insurance, the German healthcare system has always put more emphasis on free access and high numbers of providers and technological equipment than on cost-effectiveness or cost containment per se. Yet by the turn of the millennium, the German government had become extremely concerned with the ever-rising cost of health care and undertook efforts to curb spending. As mentioned before, in November 1999, the lower house of parliament passed the Reform 2000 bill, which was drafted to place severe limits on spending by physicians, dentists, and pharmacists and to impose heavy penalties on doctors who exceeded their budgets. The bill was rejected by the upper house of parliament only a month later. The era of cost containment actually started much earlier, with the introduction of the Cost Containment Act of 1977, and it did not stop then. Politicians and lawmakers have continued to introduce a number of measures designed to contain costs, including sectoral budgets, rational prescribing, price reductions, and downsizing. Yet, over recent years, the revenues from contributions have increased more slowly than health expenditures and the GDP. Such low revenues have led to repeated deficits and increasing debts, although sickness funds have attempted to counteract the trend by increasing their contribution rates.[73]

More recent cost containment strategies have been based on overall budgets for ambulatory physicians and hospitals, as well as on collective regional prescription caps for physicians. The Hospital Care Structure Reform Act of 2016 aims not only to link hospital payments to good service quality but also to reduce payments for low quality.[33]

Integration of Care

Some 25 years, ago, the challenge of an integrated system of care spoke directly to the need to combine the two healthcare systems in the two formerly separate German countries. At the time of reunification, the East German healthcare system could not have been more different from the West German system. It was a state-run system, with physicians as salaried state employees making an average of $10,000 annually. In contrast, physicians in the West were making an average of $100,000 annually.[75] Although the two systems roughly matched each other in numbers of physicians and hospital beds per capita, the characteristics and quality were quite different. Prior to reunification, East Germany had centralized, integrated, publicly financed, and provided health services. The great bulk of pharmaceutical, ambulatory medical care, and hospital services were organized under the state and were provided free of charge to patients. There was emphasis on ambulatory health centers ("polyclinics") and on occupational health services. Services were funded by a mixture of payroll taxes and general taxes. Although patients could choose their doctor, the doctors themselves were salaried and were very much under the thumb of the state. There was only a very small private sector: of the 20,840 active ambulatory care physicians, a mere 2% were in private practice.[56,96]

The major challenge of reunification of the two states along with the two healthcare systems can be summed up in one word: modernization. Many of the facilities in the former East were old substandard structures in great disrepair and were even obsolete. In a similar vein, health insurance coverage was provided primarily through company-based funds, in large part owing to the fact that many East German citizens were employees of state-run enterprises.[75] Shortly after the reunification, the West German government set out to bring the Eastern system more in line with its Western counterpart and to reflect better the Western (i.e., modern) image. But rather than to consider the strengths and weaknesses of both systems and to pursue a more strategic merger emphasizing the former, the Western system was rapidly introduced into the East, even eliminating resources that had proven to be cost effective, such as the policlinics with a defined referral system.[81] In review, reunification has had some positive consequences with respect to health. For example, life expectancy of East Germans rose dramatically. In 2015, it was identical for East and West German women, and it was nearly identical for East and West German men. In contrast, alcohol-related deaths remained much higher in East Germany. East Germans remained much more willing to be vaccinated.[97]

Today, integration and modernization refer to a much different challenge, namely to the urgent need to combine the traditionally strictly separate inpatient (stationäre), outpatient (ambulante), and rehabilitative sectors, thereby improving communication flow, economic efficiency, and quality of care. For the past 15 years, integration efforts, which aim to restructure and unify the health care Germans receive across these different sectors and providers, has taken center stage. In 2015, with the passage of the Health Care Strengthening Act, the German government has taken its latest steps in integrating the delivery of healthcare services within the SHI system. But integration efforts are nothing new. Integrated care programs (ICPs) were introduced as an important element of the Health Care Reform Act of 2000. The basic premise of ICPs is that providers from various sectors form an integrated care network (ICN), and the network (or the individual providers) then creates an integrated care contract (ICC) with a payer (a sickness fund), and then they begin providing the negotiated services.[98] To qualify as an integrated care network, at least two health providers from two different sectors and/or at least two different specialties have to collaborate within a program to qualify as integrated care (e.g., inpatient and outpatient sectors, general practitioners and cardiologists).[99] In 2004, the Health Care Modernization Act removed existing barriers to developing and implementing ICPs and provided financial incentives for both sickness funds and providers to proceed. Specifically, the government provided start-up financing to ICPs of up to 1% of the entire compensation of physicians and hospitals, which amounted to about €680 million.[100] As a result, between 2004 and 2008, when government start-up funding ran out, a total of 6,400 ICPs with 1,661,283 enrollees existed. Since, the number of ICPs has actually dropped slightly and enrollment has slowed considerably. In 2011, a total of 6,339 ICPs with 1,926,133 enrollees existed.[98]

Although there clearly has been movement toward integration of care, much remains to be done. Germany has taken steps to create a more fertile environment for integrated healthcare approaches, yet it continues to lag behind other European countries. One issue is that evaluative information regarding success (or lack thereof) of certain ICPs in terms of number of enrollees, degree of cooperation between providers, management capacity, and favorable/unfavorable outcomes is not publicly available. Mandatory reporting of a set of predefined and aligned quality indicators might improve the situation as integrated care efforts move ahead.[98]

The Aging Population

By the year 2050, one in three Germans will be older than 65.[101] The famous phrase coined in the 1950s by Chancellor Konrad Adenauer, in which he said that "people will always have children" could not have been more wrong. In increasing numbers, Germans have opted out of what is often referred to as a *generational contact*: taken in a societal context, those of working age provide the economic resources both for the young, in terms of family support and schooling, and for the old, in terms of pension and healthcare financing. In Germany, the aging of the population and concomitant increasing prevalence of chronic diseases and need for greater healthcare resources will continue to put significant pressure on the political and healthcare systems. The latest projections by the Federal Statistical Agency (*Statistisches Bundesamt*) suggest an inevitable decrease in the German population, from 80.8 million in 2013 to somewhere between 68.0 million and 73.0 million by 2060. In particular, the working-age population will shrink tremendously; the number of people aged 20 to 64, 49.0 million in 2013, will drop to between 34.0 and 38.0 million by 2060. At the same time, the number of people aged 65 and older will continue to grow, with an expected increase to between 22.0 and 23.0 million by 2060. In 2013, every 5th person belonged to this age group (21%); it will be every third person in 2060.[101]

A parliamentary commission described the anticipated picture as follows: a decreasing population will lead to decreasing population density with great regional variations. The shift in the age structure of the population is going to be greater than anticipated until recently, and although immigration may soften the impact it cannot reverse that shift, the average age of the population is going to increase considerably.[102] This trend is not limited to Germany but can be found in most developed countries and has effects beyond the healthcare system. Because of a number of factors, Germany is rated by the European Union to be at medium risk with regard to the sustainability of its public finances—aging of the population is prominent among the factors due to reforms of the pension system.[83]

The Refugee Crisis

In 2015, more than 1 million refugees crossed the borders into Europe, a massive movement of displaced people and families that has sparked political, economic, and social controversy. The largest number, more than 350,000, were Syrian refugees; the largest number of new asylum applications, more than 476,000, were in Germany.[103] One important aspect of the sudden and enormous influx of people in dire need of humanitarian aid into Germany has been the challenges to the German healthcare system. Many refugees arrive not only with infectious, communicable, noncommunicable, and/or chronic diseases but also with severe mental health needs due to stress and traumatic experiences.[104] According to the World Health Organization, effective response requires triage of refugees, followed by proper diagnosis and treatment, with full access to high-quality care for all refugees irrespective of their legal status. In the long-term, national healthcare systems must ensure that they are adequately prepared.[105] In Germany, access to health care happens in three stages: (1) in the first 6 to 12 weeks, asylum seekers are initially cared for in a centralized reception center run by one of the 16 federal states, where they undergo a comprehensive health assessment and receive vaccinations as necessary; (2) between 3 and 15 months, asylum seekers are transferred to the county where they receive basic benefits, such as food, clothing, housing, and limited access to health care; and (3) once asylum application are accepted (or after 15 months, regardless of application status). Of course, the current and most immediate concern is coping with the strain on the healthcare system caused by the rising number of asylum seekers.[105]

To respond more effectively to these challenges, Chancellor Angela Merkel spearheaded the passage of a new integration law (*Integrationsgesetz, Artikel 8, Absatz 6*) in July 2016 which was designed to proactively regulate the support refugees and asylum seekers will receive. However critics have dubbed it the *dis-integration law* because of what they see as demands and restrictions that make effective integration doubtful and that may in fact violate refugees' constitutional rights.[106] At the same time, as mentioned before, the public's attitudes regarding how the German government should address the challenges have become much more divided, with many Germans now believing that the country cannot and should not welcome new refugees and should send those already there back home. Over the past few years, a growing segment of frustrated Germans led to the formation of the Alternative for Germany party (*Alternative für Deutschland*) in 2013, a right-winged populist party with extremist tendencies and a hardline stance on immigration, and it has been spreading anti-Islamic, anti-Semitic, and anti-minority rhetoric.[107]

Clearly, responding to the refugee crisis in an economically viable manner while reflecting humanitarian and social justice principles will require ongoing careful attention, not only in Germany but also globally. In September 2016, Germany joined 51 other countries and international organizations, at the invitation of President Barack Obama, at the Leaders' Summit on the Global Refugee Crisis, to rouse renewed and significant new global commitments. Representatives agreed to (1) increase funding to humanitarian appeals and international organizations, (2) admit more refugees through resettlement or other legal pathways, and (3) increase refugees' self-reliance and inclusion through opportunities for education and legal work.[108]

Final Thoughts

Today, great challenges remain, not just for the healthcare system but also for German politics. The idea of solidarity in financing and providing access to health irrespective of means to pay—which is fundamental to the German healthcare system—will be severely tested, as Germans are being asked to provide. The heavy tax burden on German citizens, their ability to maintain a high standard of living and quality of life, and the push toward an equitable system of universal care may not be sustainable over the next decade without significant cost restructuring and reforms. The challenge for politicians and law makers is to make Germany's health care and social welfare systems sustainable. The first step is public debate. Fortunately, Germans seem to have got the message: some 80% of the population believe that the system will become worse if nothing happens during the next 10 years. Revealingly, people between the ages of 33 and 54 are the most concerned, as they now have to pay for themselves and for their retired fellow Germans.[109] One step toward addressing the challenges ahead was the formation of a national forum, termed National Health Targets (*Nationale Gesundheitsziele*) in 2000, as an initiative between the federal government and the 16 federal states. Together, they formulated seven national health targets, with the goal of establishing a coordinated joint strategy to prepare Germany's decentralized and pluralistic health system for the challenges and health risks ahead.[22,110] Since then, additional health targets have been formulated, and the forum has been seeking to anchor itself as a permanent body and comprehensive cooperation platform for the main stakeholders in the German healthcare system. Against the backdrop of a national debt of €2.1 trillion euros, with many federal states being heavily indebted and many municipalities being bankrupt, as well as the unabated refugee crisis during which Germany has been called upon to provide safe haven to migrants and refugees, it is clear that addressing the challenges will be both vital and incredibly complex for years to come.

References

1. Schulze H. *Kleine deutsche Geschichte. Erweiterte und aktualisierte Auflage.* München, Germany: C. H. Beck; 2007.
2. Kruse, W. *Das deutsche Kaiserreich. Sozialdemokratie zwischen Ausnahmegesetzen und Sozialreformen.* Bundeszentrale für politische Bildung. http://www.bpb.de/geschichte/deutsche-geschichte/kaiserreich/139650/sozialdemokratie-zwischen-ausnahmegesetzen-und-sozialreformen. Published September 27, 2012. Accessed September 15, 2016.
3. Military Education. 10 bloodiest battles of World War II. http://www.militaryeducation.org/10-bloodiest-battles-of-world-war-ii/. Published December 1, 2011. Accessed September 15, 2016.
4. Statistisches Bundesamt. Homepage. Facts and Figures. Destatis Statisches Bundesamt. https://www.destatis.de/EN/Homepage.html. Accessed September 5, 2016.
5. Statistisches Bundesamt. Land- ind Forstwirtschaft, Fischerei. Bodenfläche nach Art der tatsächlichen Nutzung. https://www.destatis.de/DE/ZahlenFakten/Wirtschaftsbereiche/LandForstwirtschaftFischerei/Flaechennutzung/Flaechennutzung.html. Published November, 25, 2015. Accessed September 5, 2016.
6. Deutscher Bundestag. Funktion und Aufgabe. http://www.bundestag.de/bundestag/aufgaben. Accessed September 8, 2016.
7. Bundesrat. Aufgaben des Bundesrates. http://www.bundesrat.de/DE/aufgaben/aufgaben-node.html. Accessed September 8, 2016.
8. Bundesverfassungsgericht. Das Gericht. Aufgaben. http://www.bundesverfassungsgericht.de/EN/Das-ericht/Aufgaben/aufgaben_node.html. Accessed September 12, 2016.
9. Der Bundesgerichtshof. Das Gericht. Stellung im Gerichtssystem. http://www.bundesgerichtshof.de/DE/DasGericht/StellungGerichtssystem/stellungGerichtssystem_node.html. Accessed September 8, 2016.
10. Rao S. German legal research guide. Government and political structure. Law Library. University of Wisconsin, Madison. http://law.wisc.libguides.com/c.php?g=125271&p=819917. Updated September 2, 2016. Accessed September 8, 2016.
11. European Union. About the EU. History of the European Union. https://europa.eu/european-union/about-eu/history/founding-fathers_en. Updated September 15, 2016. Accessed September 15, 2016.
12. Statistisches Bundesamt. Foreign Trade. Ranking of Germany's trading partners in foreign trade. https://www.destatis.de/EN/FactsFigures/NationalEconomyEnvironment/ForeignTrade/TradingPartners/Tables/OrderRankGermanyTradingPartners.pdf?__blob=publicationFile. Published September 11, 2016. Accesses September 6, 2016.
13. *The World Factbook*. Washington, DC: Central Intelligence Agency. https://www.cia.gov/library/publications/the-world-factbook/geos/gm.html. Accessed September 1, 2016.
14. Statistisches Bundesamt. Verkehr auf einen Blick. https://www.destatis.de/DE/Publikationen/Thematisch/TransportVerkehr/Querschnitt/BroschuereVerkehrBlick0080006139004.pdf?__blob=publicationFile. Published April 2013. Accessed September 10, 2016.
15. The German Way. The Autobahn. http://www.german-way.com/travel-and-tourism/driving-in-europe/driving/autobahn/. Accessed September 3. 2016.
16. Deutsche Bahn. Facts and Figures. http://www.deutschebahn.com/en/group/ataglance/facts_figures.html. Accessed September 6, 2016.
17. Statistisches Bundesamt.Fachserie 8, Serie 1.2. Verkehr im Überblick. https://www.destatis.de/DE/Publikationen/Thematisch/TransportVerkehr/Querschnitt/VerkehrUeberblick2080120147004.pdf?__blob=publicationFile. Published February 1, 2014. Accessed September 8, 2016.
18. Warner, MB. Traffic remains blocked after Rhine tanker accident. Der Spiegel ONLINE. http://www.spiegel.de/international/germany/the-shipwreck-and-the-lorelei-traffic-remains-blocked-after-rhine-tanker-accident-a-740322.html. Published January 19, 2011. Accessed September 8, 2106.
19. Deutsche Welle. Demographics. Germany reports highest fertility rate since reunification. http://www.dw.com/en/germany-reports-highest-fertility-rate-since-reunification/a-18920557. Published December 16, 2015. Accessed September 10, 2016.
20. Chu H. For Germany, refugees are a demographic blessing, as well as a burden. *The Los Angeles Times*. http://www.latimes.com/world/europe/la-fg-germany-refugees-demographics-20150910-story.html. Published September 10, 2015. Accessed September 9, 2016.
21. The force assaulting the euro; Free exchange. *The Economist*. June 6, 2015:70. *Biography in Context*. http://ic.galegroup.com/ic/bic1/MagazinesDetailsPage/MagazinesDetailsWindow?disableHighlighting=false&displayGroupName=Magazines&currPage=&scanId=&query=&prodId=BIC1&search_within_results=&p=BIC1&mode=view&catId=&limiter=&displayquery=&displayGroups=&contentModules=&action=e&sortBy=&documentId=GALE%7CA416514580&windowstate=normal&activityType=&failOverType=&commentary=&source=Bookmark&u=usclibs&jsid=d0bbd7aa465a15a9986cbe961d7c6102. Accessed September 20, 2016.
22. Busse R, Blümel M. Germany: health system review. *Health Systems in Transition*. European Observatory on Health Systems and Policies. 2014;16(2):1–296.
23. Statistisches Bundesamt. Households and families. https://www.destatis.de/EN/FactsFigures/SocietyState/Population/HouseholdsFamilies/HouseholdsFamilies.html. Published July 28, 2016. Accessed September 10, 2016.
24. Kultusminister Konferenz. Aufgaben. https://www.kmk.org/kmk/aufgaben.html. Accessed September 15, 2016.

25. Religionswissenschaftlicher Medien und Informationsdienst e.V. Religionen & Weltanschauungsgemeinschaften in Deutschland: Mitgliederzahlen. Gliederung. http://remid.de/info_zahlen/. Accessed September 10, 2016.
26. Ecumenical News. German Protestants and Catholics flee churches after compulsory taxes imposed. http://www.ecumenicalnews.com/article/german-protestants-and-catholics-flee-churches-after-compulsory-taxes-imposed/28183.htm. Accessed September 11, 2016.
27. Statistisches Bundesamt. Fact and figures. Press release. Number of deaths down by 2.8% in 2014. https://www.destatis.de/EN/PressServices/Press/pr/2015/12/PE15_465_232.html. Published December 15, 2015. Accessed September 16, 2016.
28. Björnberg A. *Euro Health Consumer Index 2015*. Health Consumer Powerhouse Ltd; 2016. http://www.healthpowerhouse.com/files/EHCI_2015/EHCI_2015_report.pdf. Published January 26, 2016. Accessed September 2, 2016.
29. Bundesverfassungsgericht. Erlassungen. Leitsätze. http://www.bundesverfassungsgericht.de/entscheidungen/ls20100209_1bvl000109.html. Published February 9, 2010. Updated 2016. Accessed September 18, 2016.
30. Bäcker G. *Chronologie gesetzlicher Neuregelungen. Krankenversicherung und Gesundtheitswesen, 1998-2015*. Institut Arbeit und Qualifikation der Universität Duisburg-Essen. http://www.sozialpolitik-aktuell.de/tl_files/sozialpolitik-aktuell/_Politikfelder/Gesundheitswesen/Dokumente/Chronologie_GKV_Gesundheitssystem.pdf. Published April, 2016. Accessed September 12, 2016.
31. Obermann K, Müller P, Müller HH, Schmidt B, Glazinski B. *Understanding the German healthcare system*. Mannheim Institute of Public Health. http://miph.umm.uni-heidelberg.de/miph/cms/upload/pdf/GHCS_Kap._3.pdf. Date unknown. Accessed September 15, 2016.
32. Green D, Irvine B, Clarke E, Bidgood E. *Health care systems: Germany*. Civitas. http://www.digitalezorg.nl/digitale/uploads/2015/03/germany.pdf. Updated January 2013. Accessed September 15, 2016.
33. Blümel M, Busse R, Osborn R, Sarnak D. The German healthcare system, 2015. In: Mossialos E, Wenzl M, eds. *2015 International Profiles of Health Care Systems*. New York, NY: The Commonwealth Fund; January 2015: 69–76.
34. Murray, JE. Health insurance in developed countries: History of. *Encyclopedia of Health Economics*. 2014;1:365–372. doi: 10.1016/B978-0-12-375678-7.00902-0.
35. Bump JP. The long road to universal health coverage: historical analysis of early decisions in Germany, the United Kingdom, and the United States. *Health Systems & Reform*. 2015;1(1):28–38.
36. Bärnighausen T, Suaerborn R. One hundred and eighteen years of the German health insurance system: are there any lessons for middle- and low-income countries? *Social Science & Medicine*. 2002;54:1559–1597.
37. Porter ME, Guth C. *Redefining German Health Care: Moving to a Value-Based System*. Berlin, Germany: Springer Verlag; 2012.
38. Silber K. From Bismarck to Bush. ThinkAdvisor. *Research Magazine*. http://www.thinkadvisor.com/2008/08/01/from-bismarck-to-bush. Published August 1, 2008. Accessed September 16, 2016.
39. Starr P. *The Social Transformation of American Medicine: The Rise of a Sovereign Profession and the Making of a Cast Industry*. New York: Basic Books; 1982.
40. Haffke D, ed. 100 Jahre Berliner Abkommen. *Niedersächsisches Ärzteblatt*. January 2014. http://www.haeverlag.de/nae/index.php?sheft=1&jgang=2014. Updated January 15, 2014. Accessed September 16, 2016.
41. What the Führer means for Germans today. *The Economist*. Christmas Specials section. Berlin: December 19, 2015. http://www.economist.com/news/christmas-specials/21683971-seventy-years-after-adolf-hitlers-death-how-germans-see-him-changing-what. Accessed September 16, 2016.
42. Evans R. *The Third Reich in Power*, 1933–1939. New York: The Penguin Press; 2006.
43. Jesse E. *Deutsche Geschichte: Vom Kaiserreich bis heute. Politik, Wirtschaft & Wissenschaft, Kunst & Kultur, Gesellschaft & Sport, Weltgeschichte. München*, Germany: Trautwein Lexikon Verlag; 2004.
44. Kater MH. *The Nazi Party: A Social Profile of Members and Leaders, 1919–1945*. Boston, MA: Harvard University Press; 1983. Dublin, Ireland: Albion Press Ltd; 2016.
45. Micozzi MS. National health care: medicine in Germany, 1918–1945. Foundation for Economic Education. https://fee.org/articles/national-health-care-medicine-in-germany-1918-1945/. Published November 1, 1993. Accessed September 16, 2016.
46. Solsten E. *Germany: a country study*. Collingdale, PA: DIANE Publishing; 1999.
47. Naas GE, Kretschmer R. Trauma nursing in the German healthcare system. *International Journal of Trauma Nursing*. 2007;8(1):9–14.
48. Ernst E. Commentary: The Third Reich—German physicians between resistance and participation. *International Journal of Epidemiology*. 2001;30:37–42.
49. Ryu, GC. Lessons from unified Germany and their implications for health care in the unification of the Korean peninsula. *Journal of Preventive Medicine & Public Health*. 2013; 46:127–133.
50. Arabin B, Raum E, Mohnhaupt A, Schwartz FW. Two types of health care systems and their influence on the introduction of perinatal care: An epidemiological twin model in Berlin from 1950 to 1990. *Maternal & Child Health Journal*. June 1999;3(2):81–91.
51. Wahner-Roedler DL, Knuth P, Juchems RH. The German healthcare system. *Mayo Clinic Proceedings*. 1997;72:1061–1068.
52. Perleth M, Gibis B, Göhlen B. A short history of health technology assessment in Germany. *International Journal of Technology Assessment in Health Care*. 2009;25(Suppl 1): 112–119.
53. Bundesministerium für Gesundheit. Ministerium. Aufgaben und Organisation. http://www.bmg.bund.de/ministerium/aufgaben-und-organisation.html. Published 2016. Accessed October 6, 2016.
54. Braasch P. *Das Gesundheitswesen in Deutschland*: Struktur, Leistungen, Weiterentwicklung. 4th ed. Köln, Germany: Deutscher Ärzte Verlag; 2007.
55. Stockemer D, Elder G. Germans 25 years after reunification: how much do they know about the German Democratic Republic and what is their value judgment of the socialist regime? *Communist and Post-Communist Studies*. 2015;48:113–122.
56. Ryu, GC. Lessons from unified Germany and their implications for healthcare in the unification of the Korean Peninsula. *Journal of Preventive Medicine & Public Health*. 2013;46:127–133.

57. Cheng TM, Reinhardt UE. Shepherding major health systems reform: a conversation with German health minister Ulla Schmidt. *Health Aff* (Millwood). 2008;27(3):204–213.
58. Bundesministerium für Gesundheit. Service. Publikationen. Shaping global health, taking joint action, embracing responsibility: the federal government's strategy paper. https://www.bundesgesundheitsministerium.de/fileadmin/dateien/Publikationen/Gesundheit/Broschueren/Screen_Globale_Gesundheitspolitik_engl.pdf. Published October 2013. Accessed October 6, 2016.
59. Bundesministerium für Gesundheit. Themen. Pflege. Pflegestärkungsgesetz. Fragen und Antworten zum PSGII. http://www.bmg.bund.de/themen/pflege/pflegestaerkungsgesetze/fragen-und-antworten-zum-psg-ii.html. Published January 29, 2016. Accessed October 6, 2016.
60. Dunbar RLM, Bresser RKF. Appreciating cultural differences: the case of German reunification. *Administration & Society*. 1997;29(4):440–470.
61. Dornberg J. Five years after reunification: Easterners discover themselves. *German Life*. 1995;December 1995/January 1996.
62. Amelung V, Glied S, Topan A. Health care and the labor market: learning from the German experience. *Journal of Health Politics, Policy, and Law*. 2003;28(4):693–714.
63. Schweigert FJ. Solidarity and subsidiarity: Complementary principles of community development. *Journal of Social Philosophy*. 2002;33(1):33–44.
64. Maarse H, Paulus A. Has solidarity survived? A comparative analysis of the effect of social health insurance reform in four European countries. *Journal of Health Politics, Policy, & Law*. 2003; 28(4):585–614.
65. von Krause JW. What types of hospitals are there in Germany? Hospital treatment in Germany. http://www.english.german-hospital-service.com/2005/01/what-type-of-hospitals-are-there-in.html. Published January 23, 2005. Accessed October 6, 2016.
66. Mau W. Structures and organization of services for medical rehabilitation in Germany. Presentation at the 9th World Congress of the International Society of Physical and Rehabilitation Medicine. http://www.dgrw-online.de/files/mau-german-rehab-isprm-2015.pdf. Published June 23, 2015. Accessed October 6, 2016.
67. ABDA—Federal Union of German Associations of Pharmacists. *German Pharmacies: Figures, Data, Facts 2015*. Berlin, Germany: Blueprint Berlin GmbH; 2015.
68. Organisation for Economic Co-operation and Development. *Health at a Glance 2015: OECD Indicators*. Paris, France: OECD Publishing; 2015.
69. European Commission. Eurostat Statistics Explained. Main page. http://ec.europa.eu/eurostat/statistics-explained/index.php/Main_Page. Updated April 14, 2016. Accessed October 6, 2016.
70. Cassier-Woidasky AK. *Nursing Education in Germany: Challenges and Obstacles in Professionalisation*, Stuttgart, Germany: DHBW; 2013.
71. EY. *Medical Technology Report 2015: Pulse on the Industry*. London, UK: Ernst & Young Global Ltd; 2015.
72. Böhm K. *The Transformation of the Social Right to Healthcare: Evidence from England and Germany*. New York, NY: Routledge; 2017.
73. Busse R. *Description of Health Care Systems: Germany and the Netherlands*. The Commonwealth Fund. http://www.allhealth.org/briefingmaterials/CountryProfiles-FINAL-1163.pdf. Accessed October 6, 2016.
74. Hagist C, Kotlikoff LJ. *Who's Going Broke? Comparing Healthcare Costs in Ten OECD Countries*. Cambridge, MA: National Bureau of Economic Research; 2005. Paper #11833.
75. Swami B. The German healthcare system. In: Thai KV, Wimberley ET, McManus SM, eds. *Handbook of International Health Care Systems*. New York: Marcel Dekker, Inc; 2002:333–358.
76. Shafrin J. Health care around the world: Germany. *Healthcare Ecomomist*. http://healthcare-economist.com/2008/04/24/health-care-around-the-world-germany/. Published April 24, 2008. Accessed October 6, 2016.
77. Döring A, Paul F. The German health care system. *Journal of the European Association for Predictive, Preventive and Personalised Medicine*. 2010;1:535–547.
78. Lassey ML, Lassey WR, Jinks MJ. *Health Care Systems Around the World: Characteristics, Issues, Reforms*. Upper Saddle River, NJ: Prentice-Hall; 1997.
79. World Health Organization. *Implementing Health 2020*. Brochure. https://euro.sharefile.com/document/#preview/fi62ac19-2b98-89aa-42bb-f96cfcbfd7d5/s73db1a792664325a. Accessed October 6, 2016.
80. Roser M. Child Mortality. *Our World in Data*. https://ourworldindata.org/child-mortality/#child-mortality-by-cause-of-death. Updated 2016. Accessed October 6, 2106.
81. European Child Safety Alliance. *Child Safety Country Profile 2012: Germany*. http://www.childsafetyeurope.org/reportcards/info/germany-country-profile.pdf. Published June 2012. Accessed October 6, 2016.
82. EU-Patienten De. Treatment in Germany. Planned treatment. After treatment. Bills. Questions about bills issued by healthcare providers. http://www.eu-patienten.de/en/behandlung_deutschland/nach_der_behandlung/rechnungen/fragen_zu_rechnungen.jsp. Updated June 24, 2016. Accessed October 6, 2016.
83. Lungen M, Stollenwerk B, Messner P, Lauterbach KW, Gerber A. Waiting times for elective treatments according to insurance status: A randomized empirical study in Germany. *International Journal of Equity in Health*. 2008;7:1.
84. Sawicki PT. Quality of health care in Germany. A six-country comparison. *Medizinische Klinik*. November 15, 2005;100(11):755–768.
85. Esmail N. *Health Care Lessons from Germany*. Lessons from Abroad: A Series on Healthcare Reform. Fraser Institute. https://www.fraserinstitute.org/sites/default/files/health-care-lessons-from-germany.pdf. Published May 2014. Accessed October 6, 2016.
86. World Health Organization. WHO vaccine-preventable diseases: monitoring system. 2016 global summary. http://apps.who.int/immunization_monitoring/globalsummary/countries?countrycriteria%5Bcountry%5D%5B%5D=DEU. Updated July 15, 2016. Accessed October 6, 2016.
87. Takla A, Wichmann O, Rieck T, Matysiak-Klose D. Measles incidence and reporting trends in Germany, 2007–2011. *Bulletin of the World Health Organization*. 2014;92(10):697–772.
88. Mette A, Reuss AM, Feig M, et al. Under-reporting of measles: an evaluation based on data from North Rhine-Westphalia. *Deutsches Ärzteblatt International*. 2011;108(12):191–6.
89. European Center for Disease Prevention and Control. *Seasonal Influenza Vaccinations in Europe: Overview of Vaccination Recommendations and Coverage Rates in the EU Member States For The 2012–13 Influenza Season*. Stockholm, Sweden: ECDC; 2015.

90. Gemeinsamer Bundesausschuss. Special topics. Quality assurance. Quality assurance and quality improvement across healthcare settings. http://www.english.g-ba.de/special-topics/quality/. Accessed October 6, 2016.
91. Schneider N, Dierks LM, Seidel G, Schwartz FW. The federal government commissioner for patient issues in Germany: initial analysis of the user inquiries. *BMC Health Services Research*. 2007; 7:24.
92. Palmer E. Germany: Patients' rights. Global legal monitor. Library of Congress. http://www.loc.gov/law/foreign-news/article/germany-patients-rights/. Published April 23, 2013. Accessed October 6, 2016.
93. Bundesamt für Migration und Flüchtlinge. Asyl und Flüchtlingsschutz. Ablauf des Asylverfahrens. Zuständige Aufnahmeeinrichtung. http://www.bamf.de/DE/Fluechtlingsschutz/AblaufAsylv/MeldungAE/meldung-aufnahmeeinrichtung-node.html. Published August 1, 2016. Accessed October 6, 2016.
94. Statistisches Bundesamt. Press release 285. Less people without health insurance. https://www.destatis.de/EN/PressServices/Press/pr/2012/08/PE12_285_122.html. Published August 20, 2012. Accessed October 6, 2016.
95. Greß S, Walendzik A, Wasem J. Persons without health insurance in Germany—who are they and what can be done. Presentation at the Annual Meeting of the European Public Health Association (EUPHA); November 16–18, 2006; Montreux, Switzerland.
96. Hurst JW. Reform of health care in Germany. *Health Care Financing Review*. 1991; 12(3):73–86.
97. Frankfurter Allgemeine Zeitung. Politik. 25 Jahre Wiedervereinigung: Noch immer große Unterschiede zwischen Ost und West. http://www.faz.net/aktuell/politik/inland/ost-west-unterschiede-nach-wiedervereinigung-deutschlands-13715180.html. Published July 22, 2015. Accessed October 6. 2016.
98. Milstein R, Blankhart CR. The health care strengthening act: the next level of integrated care in Germany. *Health Policy*. 2016;120:445:451.
99. Milstein R, Blankart CR. Special care in Germany. Country background note: Germany. Office of Economic Collaboration and Development. http://www.oecd.org/els/health-systems/Better-Ways-to-Pay-for-Health-Care-Background-Note-Germany.pdf. Published February 2016. Accessed October 12, 2016.
100. Amelung V, Hildebrandt H, Wolf S. Integrated care in Germany: a stony but necessary road. *International Journal of Integrated Care*. March 2012;12(27):1–8.
101. Statistisched Bundesamt. Press release 153. New projection of Germany's population by 2060. https://www.destatis.de/EN/PressServices/Press/pr/2015/04/PE15_153_12421.html. Published April 28, 2015. Accessed October 6, 2016.
102. Deutscher Bundestag. Schlussbericht der Enquête-Kommission Demographischer Wandel—Herausforderungen unserer älter werdenden Gesellschaft an den Einzelnen und die Politik (Drucksache 14/8800). Berlin: Deutscher Bundestag; March 28 2002. Drucksache 14/8800.
103. British Boradcasting Corporation. Migrant crisis: migration to Europe explained in seven charts. http://www.bbc.com/news/world-europe-34131911. Published March 4, 2016. Accesses October 12, 2016.
104. Hunter P. Science and society. The refugee crisis challenges nations health care systems. *EMBO reports*. April 2016; 17(4):492–495.
105. World Health Organization. Regional Office for Europe. *Migration and health: key issues.* http://www.euro.who.int/en/health-topics/health-determinants/migration-and-health/migrant-health-in-the-european-region/migration-and-health-key-issues. Accessed October 12, 2016.
106. Göpffart D, Bauhoff S. The public health dimension of Germany's refugee crisis. *Health Aff Blog*. http://healthaffairs.org/blog/2015/10/22/the-public-health-dimension-of-germanys-refugee-crisis/#one. Published October 22, 2015. Accesses October 12, 2016.
107. Deutsche Welle. Merkel presents new integration law as "mile stone." http://www.dw.com/en/merkel-presents-new-refugee-integration-law-as-milestone/a-19281722. Published May 25, 2016. Accessed October 12, 2016.
108. The White House. Office of the Press Secretary. Fact sheet on the Leaders' Summit on Refugees. https://www.whitehouse.gov/the-press-office/2016/09/20/fact-sheet-leaders-summit-refugees. Published September 20, 2016. Accessed October 12, 2016.
109. Disney H, Horn K, Hrobon P, et al. *Impatient for change: European attitudes to healthcare reform*. London, UK: The Stockholm Network; 2004.
110. Gesellschaft für Versicherungswissenschaft und—gestaltung e.V. Gesundheitsziele.de. W17(4): assind Gesundheitsziele? http://gesundheitsziele.de/. Accessed October 6, 2016.

CHAPTER 13

Ireland

Linda F. Dennard, John E. McDonough, and **Maria Creavin**

▶ Country Description

TABLE 13-1 Ireland	
Nationality	Noun: Irishman (men), Irishwoman (women), Irish (collective plural) Adjective: Irish
Ethnic groups	Irish 84.5%, other white 9.8%, Asian 1.9%, Black 1.4%, mixed and other 0.9%, unspecified 1.6% (2011 est.)
Religions	Roman Catholic 84.7%, Church of Ireland 2.7%, other Christian 2.7%, Muslim 1.1%, other 1.7%, unspecified 1.5%, none 5.7% (2011 est.)
Language	English, official, most widely spoken; Irish (Gaelic or Gaeilge), official, spoken mainly along the western seaboard by 38.7% of the population as a first or second language (2011)
Literacy	Definition: Age 15 and over can read and write. Total population: 99% Male: 99% Female: 99% (2003 est.)
Government type	Republic, parliamentary democracy
Date of independence	December 6, 1921 (from the United Kingdom by treaty)
Gross Domestic Product (GDP) per capita	$55,500 (2015 est.)

(continues)

TABLE 13-1 Ireland (continued)	
Unemployment rate	9.4% (2015 est.)
Natural hazards	—
Environment: current issues	Water pollution, especially of lakes, from agricultural runoff
Population	4,952,473 (July 2016 est.)
Age structure	0–14 years: 21.51% (male 544,506/female 520,934) 15–24 years: 11.80% (male 297,025/female 287,512) 25–54 years: 43.52% (male 1,082,577/female 1,072,721) 55–64 years: 10.33% (male 256,353/female 255,155) 65 years and over: 12.84% (male 293,577/female 342,113) (2016 est.)
Median age	Total: 36.4 years Male: 36.1 years Female: 36.8 years (2016 est.)
Population growth rate	1.2% (2016 est.)
Birth rate	14.5 births/1,000 population (2016 est.)
Death rate	397 deaths/100,000 population (2016 est.)
Disease burden	Communicable disease deaths: 22/100,000 population Noncommunicable disease deaths: 344/100,000 population Injury deaths: 32/100,000 population (2016 est.)
Net migration rate	4 migrant(s)/1,000 population (2016 est.)
Gender ratio	At birth: 1.06 male(s)/female 0–14 years: 1.05 male(s)/female 15–24 years: 1.03 male(s)/female 25–54 years: 1.01 male(s)/female 55–64 years: 1.00 male(s)/female 65 years and over: 0.86 male(s)/female Total population: 1.00 male(s)/female (2016 est.)
Infant mortality rate	Total: 3.7 deaths/1,000 live births Male: 4 deaths/1,000 live births Female: 3.3 deaths/1,000 live births (2016 est.)
Life expectancy at birth	Total population: 80.8 years Male: 78.5 years Female: 83.2 years (2016 est.)
Total fertility rate	1.98 children born/woman (2016 est.)
HIV/AIDS adult prevalence rate	0.28% (2014 est.)

TABLE 13-1 Ireland (continued)	
Number of people living with HIV/AIDS	8,000 (2014 est.)
HIV/AIDS deaths	100 (2014 est.)

Data from Central Intelligence Agency. The World Fact Book, 2016: Ireland. https://www.cia.gov/library/publications/the-world-factbook/geos/ei.html. Accessed April 19, 2016.

Introduction

One of the original members of the European Union and the furthest west of continental European countries, Ireland unearthed itself from three separate waves of invasion over a thousand years. The Irish then overcame the devastation of famine, poverty, civil war, and the limits of political isolation to become one of the wealthiest countries on the planet by the end of the 1990s. During the 21st century, it is again recovering, this time from the catastrophic effects of the global economic meltdown of 2007–2009. While not all agree that the deep cultural changes that have occurred in Ireland since the 1960s are all positive, no one denies that Ireland is no longer the rural, Catholic, and agrarian country of popular folklore.[1,2] Health care in Ireland has been part of the journey to a modernized society. But like many political issues in Ireland, healthcare policy is caught in a tide of populist sentiments arising from the revolution, the regulatory aegis of the European Union, and the demands of a free market economy.

Independence and Irish Identity

Following decades of attempted home rule and land reform, independence from Britain was secured by a contested treaty in 1922, which divided the country between the Free State in the south and Northern Ireland. The first Constitution of the Free State was approved in 1937. By 1948, the state had become the Republic of Ireland, although it is commonly referred to simply as Ireland.

At the core of the much publicized violence in both Ireland and Northern Ireland, particularly during the Troubles of the 1970s, were deep divisions, not merely between Catholics and Protestants, but more between those who favored the continued existence of the northern state and those who still hoped for a unified Ireland.[3] These conflicts have been ameliorated in recent years by a decommissioning of arms by paramilitary groups and other factors, including a demilitarization of the North by the British and improved economic growth in both states. However, both the Celtic Tiger and its subsequent demise have been accompanied by a growth in gang violence as a new source of social tension. These organizations are, at times, splinter groups of the Irish Republican Army, less engaged in political protest than they are in Mafia-style criminal activity. In the spring of 2016, seven people were killed in a gang shootout in Dublin.[4]

The Irish People

The people of the Republic of Ireland are largely of Celtic origin, although along the eastern borders families can trace their lineage to early Norse invaders and in the west to the Normans, who took on the Irish culture more readily than the Vikings. The Catholic Church is still the primary religion, having rewritten Celtic mythology with biblical themes in the 8th century. Yet the control the Church once had on politics is not as profound as it was before the Republic emerged from isolation in the late 1950s and before widespread allegations of sexual misconduct among priests surfaced.[5,6]

According to 2011 estimates, Irish are 84.5% white, 9.8% other white, 1.0% Asian, and 1.4% Black. With mixed and unspecified composing the remaining 2.4%.[6] About 85.0% of the population identifies as Roman Catholic, with the Church of Ireland claiming 2.7%, other Christians 2.7%, and Muslim 1.1%. Other religions account for 1.7% of the reporting population while 5.7% reported having no religion as of 2011. However, there has been a marked decrease in the religious observance in Ireland in the last 20 years. While the majority of people still report themselves as Catholic, the society has become noticeably more secular.[6,7] Changes in social mores, often encouraged by the European Union, have included more demands for equality of women, a lessening of the taboos on divorce, and a general thawing of society from the strictly regulated days of the early 20th century.[8]

Language

Ireland has two official languages and both are recognized by the European Union for translation purposes. English is spoken by the majority in Ireland. However, Gaelic or Gaeilge (Irish) is spoken by 38.7% of the population as a first or second language—mainly along the Gaeltracht along the western seaboard of Ireland. However, according to the 2011 census by the Central Statistics Office (CSO), Gaelic is now the third most spoken language in Ireland, falling behind Polish, which was brought by waves of immigrants at the turn of the last century.[5]

Population

In July 2015 the population of Ireland was estimated at 4,892,305. According to this estimate, 65.89% of the population fell between the ages of 15.0 and 64.0. Of these, 537,239 are male and 514,369 are female. The growing population of over 65.0 years comprised 12.61% of the population. Elderly males numbered at 284,399 while women numbered 332,666. The medium age for all was 36.1 in 2015—35.8 for males and 36.4 for females. Children aged 0–14.0 years comprised 21.50% of the population. Since the 1970s, Ireland's population has been increasing, displaying a turnaround for the country which experienced population decline and high levels of emigration for decades. In the years 2002 to 2011 the population jumped by 650,000 through heavy immigration.[8]

Immigration

Since 2013 the number of immigrants in Ireland has increased by about one-third per year. In 2014 an estimated 60,600 people immigrated to Ireland with an increase to 69,300 in 2015. However, this immigration has been offset by emigration statistics, 81,900 in 2014 and 80,900 in 2015. Of those emigrating in 2014, 29,300 were Irish nationals. This number decreased to 23,000 in 2015.[8] While there has been some backlash over the years to immigration of non-nationals to Ireland and nationalism is still an issue, there has been a gradual accommodation and less overt violence and racism than in other countries of Europe.[9]

Literacy and Education

The literacy rate in the Republic of Ireland is around 99.0% according to the CSO. The Irish education system is largely state-funded, and considerable emphasis has always been placed on education in national policy. The high education standards for nationals are a key factor in the economic promotion of the country internationally. One-third of the workforce aged 25–64 has third-level (university) qualifications. Among those who dropped out of school since the recession, the unemployment rate has been as high as 19.0%, compared to a rate of 8.2% among all others aged 18–24. Male dropouts are more likely to be unemployed than their female counterparts. The incidence of early school withdrawal is also more concentrated in areas with a lower socioeconomic profile. Since the recession, school completion numbers have increased slightly as individuals have returned to school in the face of unemployment. At the same time the rate of chronic unemployment among school dropouts has increased.[5,30]

Geography and Map

Comparatively, the area occupied by the Republic of Ireland is slightly larger than the U.S. state of West Virginia. Please refer to **FIGURE 13-1**. The Irish Republic is bound on the north by the North Channel, which separates it from Scotland, on the northeast by Northern Ireland, and on the east and southeast by the Irish Sea and St. George's Channel, which separate it from England and Wales. To the west, from north to south, the coast is washed by the Atlantic Ocean. The Irish coastline is 3,000 miles long and indented by numerous peninsulas. The coast is accentuated by mountains along much of its perimeter. Ireland's capital city, Dublin, is located on the Irish Sea coast.[10]

Climate Change

Global climate change is having a noticeable effect on the traditionally temperate maritime climate of Ireland. The Irish Environmental Protection Agency warns of rising sea levels, an increase in the severity of storms, an impact on fishing waters, flooding, and both water quality and water shortage issues. The island is already experiencing record high temperatures with an increase in rainfall in parts of the country and a decrease in frost days.[11]

Government and Political System

As a parliamentary democracy, Ireland has two houses. The Oireachtas (parliament) is composed of Dáil Éireann (the House of Representatives) and Seanad Éireann (the Senate). The Irish Constitution became law in 1937 and defines the powers and functions of the Oireachtas, the president and the government. The Constitution has been modified since. For example after a robust public debate, the Constitution was amended to allow a transfer of certain sovereign powers

FIGURE 13-1 Map of Ireland
© Rainer Lesniewski/Shutterstock

to the European Union. Member states are bound by the treaties they sign and therefore are also bound by the policies and directives of the European Union.[12]

The taoiseach (the prime minister) heads the government, the executive branch, with the support of the tánaiste (deputy prime minister). The taoiseach is elected by the Dáil as the leader of the political party, or coalition of parties, that wins the most seats in the national elections, which are conducted every five years unless called earlier. Executive power is vested in a cabinet whose ministers are nominated by the taoiseach and approved by the Dáil.

The Dáil's 166 members are known as TDs (teachta Dála) and are directly elected by the people. General elections take place at least once every five years. With the general election in February 2016, citizen dissatisfaction with the economy was high, and voter turnout was high at 61%.[12]

Ireland employs a proportional representation election system, the single transferable vote. This system is used to elect members to the Dáil, local councils, and the European Parliament. Electors indicate their most favored candidate by putting "1" beside the candidate's name on the ballot paper and can then go on to indicate their second, third, and lower preferences, which guarantees some representation in government by minority parties. Under the Constitution there must be at least one TD for every 20,000 to 30,000 people, and in 2016 there were 166 Members from 42 constituencies. These numbers are revised at least once every 12 years but are normally revised following each five-year census.

TDs are also often members of health boards, community groups, and vocational education committees. Deputies usually divide their time between their constituency and attendance at meetings of Dáil Éireann and its specialist committees. Dáil Éireann has its own committee system which offers advice on a wide range of legislative, social, economic, and financial issues. These committees also process legislation and examine government expenditure. Deputies also serve in international bodies, such as the Council of Europe, the British-Irish Inter-Parliamentary Body and other parliamentary associations, conduct research on issues, and influence policy at the national and international levels.[12]

Seanad has 60 members—11 are nominated by the taoiseach, and the remainder is elected from a number of vocational panels and by graduates of Irish universities. Seanad can initiate or revise legislation, but the Dáil has the power to reject these proposals or amendments. In theory, Seanad Éireann does not recognize party affiliations. However, voting trends tend to follow party lines. Seanad Éireann's main authority lies in revising legislation sent to it by the Dáil. However, in recent years the government has tended to make greater use of Seanad Éireann to initiate legislation. Under the Constitution it has the authority to both initiate and revise legislation. However, only the Dáil can initiate financial legislation. The Seanad can make recommendations but not amend such bills.[12]

The president, who serves as head of state in a largely ceremonial role, is elected directly by the people for a seven-year term and can be reelected only once. The president does not have an executive or policy role. The president does have absolute discretion to refuse the dissolution of the Dáil when the taoiseach has ceased to retain a majority in the house. The president can also refer a bill to the Supreme Court for a judgment on its constitutionality. Presidential candidates need the nominations of 20 members or ex-members of the Oireachtas or nomination by the councils of 4 administrative counties. Sitting presidents can nominate themselves but may only serve for 2 terms. Where there is more than one candidate, the people elect the president by direct vote.[12]

Government departments, 16 of them due to recent reorganization, are each headed by a minister. Health matters are primarily the responsibility of the Health Department (once the Health and Children's Department), accountable to a minister for health.[12]

Political Parties, of which there are six main ones, are active in Ireland. Irish politics, however, remain dominated by the two political parties that grew out of Ireland's bitter 1922-1923 civil war. Fianna Fáil has been the largest party in the Dáil since 1932. It is part of the Union for Europe group in the European Parliament. Fianna Fáil was formed by those who opposed the 1921 treaty that partitioned the island. Although treaty opponents lost the civil war, Fianna Fáil soon became Ireland's largest political party. Fine Gael, the second largest party, is part of the European People's Party. Fine Gael was formed by those forces in favor of the 1921 treaty that partitioned the island. Two smaller parties also exist. The Labour Party is a member of the Party of European Socialists in the European Parliament and the Progressive Democrats Party. The Green Party is associated with Green parties in over 30 other countries. Sinn Féin is an Irish Republican Party which has only begun contesting elections in the Republic in recent years. The party currently in power is Fine Gael, headed by Enda Kenny.[12]

The European Parliament holds 11 seats for Ireland, which are filled by election (usually at the same time as national elections). These members serve as Ireland's representatives under the terms of various treaties with the European Union, with which Ireland, as a member, is a partner.[12]

Democratic Ireland

Citizen participation and access to government has been a growing concern as local and national governments must respond to the demands of the European Union. However, the political landscape is active with an increasing number of interest groups, including for health care. TASC, the independent think tank on democracy, promotes citizen participation. It is also a highly visible and vocal advocate for more transparency in Irish government. TASC is a frequent critic of government, calling for more accountability in political appointments and more open meetings.[13]

Isolation and Emergence

Éamon De Valera, the first taoiseach (prime minister) of the Free State of Ireland (1922–1937) favored isolationist policies that kept "Ireland for the Irish" in response to centuries of subordination to other countries. Nationalist groups, like the Gaelic Athletic Association and the Gaelic League regulated Irish culture, producing standards for what was the "real Irish" in everything from hurling (the national sport) to dance, music, art, and religion. Of particular importance to these early nationalists was saving the Irish language. Also, during the years following the revolution, women were confined by the Church and the Irish Constitution to traditional roles. One of the marked changes in Irish culture in recent decades has been the rapid migration of women to the workforce and into key positions in business and government.[14]

Isolation kept Ireland poor and threatened to the point of producing another famine when the country did not become as self-sufficient as de Valera had hoped. In the late 1950s, Séan Lemass reversed the isolationist policies of his predecessor by reaching out to the world, encouraging involvement with the new European Market and actively soliciting investment from the United States and other countries. As an early member of the European Union (1973), Ireland benefitted from heavy investment in economic infrastructure by the European Union and foreign investors. By the late 1970s, the effects of this turn around were beginning to be felt in the Irish economy, and a short 20 years later, the economy was booming and the Celtic Tiger was born.[2]

The latest chapter in the Irish saga began with the collapse of world markets in 2007, produced by contingencies in the deregulated derivatives market. Like elsewhere, including the United States, Irish banks used the assurances of the derivative schemes to justify indiscriminate lending that led to a housing boom and subsequent bust. With the collapse of the Irish economy, unemployment rose dramatically while banks failed and the bond market Ireland depends on to sustain its economy disappeared. By 2013 Ireland was adjusting to the austerity demands of the Irish National Recovery Plan that accompanied an €85 billion bailout from the European Union and its global partners.[15]

Macroeconomics

The history of Irish economics is one of the most dramatic in Europe. Ireland's economy in the years preceding the 2007 economic collapse had become one of the worlds' most globalized, with extensive external trade and investment links. Until 2007, Ireland's rate of export growth outpaced world trade growth by a factor of 3, and Ireland's annual rate of real export growth in goods and services consistently ranked in the top 5 of the 30-member Organisation and Economic Co-operation and Development (OECD).[16]

Unprecedented economic growth began in the early 1990s. Between 1990 and 1995, the economy had an annual average growth rate of 4.8%, and between 1995 and 2000, it averaged 9.5%. Until the economic crash of 2007, growth rates were sustained at the 4.0–5.0% range, a level almost 5 times higher than the old 15-member EU average. The growth in the Irish economy was reflected in annual increases in national Gross Domestic Product (GDP), which in 2005 reached €160 billion. Measured on the basis of purchasing power, Ireland's level of economic activity, or GDP per inhabitant, in 2006 was almost 40.0% above the European Union average.[16]

When the Bubble Burst

Yet the boom that gave Ireland one of the strongest and fastest growing economies in Europe was not destined to last. Ireland fell into a deep recession in 2008 following the collapse of the Irish banking system. By 2010 Ireland was asking for a bailout from the European Union as its housing market collapsed, taking the banking system with it. The conditions that produced the crisis were similar to those in the United States and other countries, characterized by a rapid credit expansion, reduced nominal and real interest rates, and easy borrowing conditions that made the debt of the private sector unsustainable.[1,16] The housing prices had plummeted 37%, and by 2009 lending had simply stopped. During this time, GDP dropped by 9% and unemployment rate began its steady incline.[16]

Having few internal resources and an unstable tax base with which to support social programs like health, Ireland has relied heavily on outside sources of funding to remain economically buoyant. Although Ireland has no recurring property taxes to support it, social expenditures like health care doubled between 2000 and 2007. Ireland has attracted multinationals to Ireland in the past by keeping corporate taxes low, a policy which, especially in an economic turndown leaves the state vulnerable. During the economic downturn of 2010, foreign investments accounted for about 80% of national income, and foreign-owned companies accounted for the majority of exports and a substantial share of employment.[16,17] Both the European Union and Irish scholars have warned the government about the impact on the ability of the Irish domestic economy to improve if the government continues the practice of rewarding multinational corporations with hefty tax breaks, and they encourage creating a more stable domestic tax structure.[18]

But outside funding sources dried up in the crisis, leaving Ireland with both a failing banking systems and a sovereign debt problem. Although the flexible Irish market began to respond to the crisis as early the end of 2008, the government could not move fast enough within its own fragile economic infrastructure to avoid a bail out. With unemployment increasing to 15.1% in 2011, the Irish were again suffering. With the help of an EU bailout and a recovery of foreign investment, Ireland experienced a quick burst in economic growth. By 2015 it was once again Europe's fastest growing economy.[19]

Health Care and Economic Recovery

Although Ireland is on the road to full recovery, the European Union cautions that "despite a marked improvement in the economic outlook, risks related to the high levels of private and public sector indebtedness, remaining financial sector challenges such as the banks' profitability, and labor market adjustment marked by high structural unemployment, continue to deserve close attention." Despite rapid growth, there remain macroeconomic imbalances that could threaten the stability of the economy in the long term.[20] For health care this uncertainty is expressed in an uncomfortable gap between consumer expectations in Ireland and what the government can deliver.

With the EU recovery package came the need for austerity measures, and the impact on healthcare funding was felt almost immediately. HSE funding fell by 22% while staffing of public health services fell by over 12,000 full-time positions, or 10% of total from a peak in 2007. While public policy was pushing to redirect senior citizens from hospital wards to their homes to cut costs, the numbers of home healthcare workers were cut.[21]

Efficiency Issues

Some analysts say that austerity measures may have actually improved efficiencies in the Irish healthcare system in the short run. Despite long waiting lists for medical appointments and surgeries, once an individual is actually in a hospital bed, austerity measures seemed to result in shorter hospital stays as well as improved numbers of those served in emergency rooms. But these efficiencies may be a temporary phenomenon since waiting lists are increasing and the number of available beds is decreasing. A 2014 report on Irish health care refers to this as an *inflection point*: when further gains in efficiencies cannot be realized without structural changes in the healthcare system.[22]

Incremental Gains

Juggling a volatile political environment, the government did work to protect the most vulnerable during the economic crisis, and the improving economic conditions encouraged private insurance enrollment. The European Commission noted that Ireland responded quickly to the crisis and that steps toward increasing efficiency and access in the system have been made, although they also noted delays and inconsistent use of data.[22,45] By 2014 free family doctor access for children younger than five was offered. Medical cards were available that entitled qualified individuals to be seen by a family doctor for free with reduced costs for hospital care and low-cost medications. The number of people with health insurance increased by almost 100,000 in 2015 after declining during the recession. Young adult discounts and Lifetime Community Rating were introduced, and enrollments increased. An agreement with the Central Bank improved claims processing and accelerated payments for insured patients in public hospitals, according the Health Department's annual report in 2015.[25]

A Single-Tier System: Not Yet

Ireland is unique in the European Union system for having a two-tiered rather than a single-payer healthcare system. The Irish have struggled with the possibility of universal health insurance since postrevolutionary days with free health care seen as a legitimizing policy for the new government. However, this long-standing political promise has again been brought into question by a 2014 economic report that revealed what some feel are the prohibitive costs of the proposed program.[26] The report was prepared by the Fianna Fáil and was supported by a former Fine Gael health minister that, for the brief period of his tenure, made it seem like the government was backing down on its promise. However, even with a recent election and a health minister with a stronger commitment to the Fine Gael leadership, the uncertainty about universal health insurance will likely continue.[27]

While the European Union expects Ireland to eventually have a single-tier system, it mandates that it put in place building blocks to support such a system's sustainability. For now, the plan in Ireland is to create a hybrid of selected free care and general tax-supported social security and disability care. This "Future Health" section of the development plan lists these main features:

- equal access to health care based on need, not income;
- universal insurance for a standard package of health services;
- no difference between "public" and "private" patients;
- universal primary care, including GP care without fees for all;
- universal hospital care with independent, not-for-profit trusts and private hospitals.[28]

Poverty Rates and Healthcare

It has been the intention of government policy to reduce the rate of consistent poverty to prerecession levels by the end of 2016 and to 2% by 2020. However, with unemployment still high (8.6% in 2016) and despite significant improvement since 2013, even 2020 may not be an attainable goal. The consistent poverty rate (since 2010) has been around 8.0% for the general population, up from 4.2% in 2008, representing about 370,000 people. Those suffering from material deprivation have also risen despite economic gains since 2013. Those living in material insecurity rose from 13.7% in 2008 to 29% in 2014. Poverty for the unemployed reached 22.6%, up from 9.7% in 2008. The hardest hit have been children (11.2%) and single-parent families (22.1%.)[29,30] In relation to healthcare access in Ireland, the concern of EU observers is that those in danger of social exclusion in Ireland has risen from 25.0% in 2005 to 29.5% in 2014.[31] The role of the healthcare system in alleviating the conditions of poverty in Ireland is outlined as specifically deeper structural reforms to increase cost efficiency, progress toward a single-tier payer system on a par with the rest of the European Union, and effectively developing e-health tools, activity-based funding, and improved prescription services.[32]

General Health of the Population

According to the *Healthy Ireland Survey 2015*, 85% of the Irish population over 15 years old reported that their general health is good or very good. About 28%, or 1 in 4 citizens, reports having a chronic health condition. Around 19% of respondents reported that their daily activity was limited by a health concern, and 43% had experienced a health issue in the prior year. Around 73% of these individuals were over the age of 65. The average number of general practitioner consultations/visits per year for those over 15 years of age is 4.3, while the number of medical and/or surgical consultations/visits per year is 1.4. About 23% of the population aged 15 and older smoke. Of those, 19% smoke on a daily basis and 4% describe themselves as occasional smokers. Smoking levels are highest among the poor. Of smokers, 63% say they are trying to quit. More Irish adults are ex-smokers than smokers.[33,34]

Alcohol

Three-quarters of the population in Ireland drink, over half of whom do so weekly. Men drink more than women and almost 4 in 10 drinkers binge drink. Poorer residents drink less but are more prone to binging. About 22% of respondents feel they should reduce their drinking. In a 2014 report from the Health Department, alcohol cost the country US $3.5 billion in 2013 as a result of using healthcare and of traffic accidents.[33] In 2006 the National Crime Council of Ireland reported that alcohol-related crimes produced losses of $189 million and that nearly 40% of fatal accidents in Ireland were caused by drunk drivers. It is estimated that 70% of domestic violence in Ireland involves alcohol.[35,36]

In the boom years of the Celtic Tiger, the Irish drank more, almost double from the rates in 1984. The rate of consumption slowed some after the imposition of a stiffer alcohol tax just before the recession. It rose again until 2012 and then began declining, perhaps as the public became more educated on the effects of alcohol on the well-being of the Republic. However, Ireland remains in the top five of the EU28 membership in alcohol consumption, drinking around 10.6 liters per capita annually. Of particular concern in the steady increase in drinking among youth aged 15–17 who have been impacted by the development of impersonal "super pubs" that replace the more regulating locals.[36]

In 2015, the Public Health (Alcohol) Bill was published, which includes measures to reduce alcohol intake and addresses alcohol misuse in Ireland through initiatives like minimum unit pricing, health and calorie labeling, reducing availability and visibility in shops, and restrictions on marketing, advertising, and sponsorship.[37]

Suicide Prevention

The National Strategy to reduce suicide (2015–2020), Connecting for Life, seeks to reduce the level of suicide and self-harm by 10% in 5 years. This strategy arose from concern for the spike in suicide rates, especially among men, since the Celtic Tiger boom and bust cycle. According to figures from the National Suicide Research Foundation and the Central Statistics Office, the suicide rate in Ireland between the years 2000 to 2013 exceeds the norm in the rest of the European Union with an average of 11.8 per 100,000 population.[5] The rate for men is 5 times higher than for women, and in 2016, rates are 57% higher than would be expected in a recession.[36] A recession generally would not fully explain a high suicide rate in Ireland. Some experts point to the fact that suicide was decriminalized in 1993 and therefore carries less of a stigma. A telling statistic is that the suicide rates in Ireland, which were considerably lower in the decades before the economic boom, were at their highest from 2000–2004, at the peak of the boom. Some point to rapid social change in which the family and the relationship-based social structure of Ireland responded to the pressure of expanding market competition. Also, the population in Ireland grew by 650,000 between the years of 2002–2011, which may have contributed to the occurrence of more suicides.

Brief History of the Healthcare System

The Irish healthcare system began as a response to the poor. The first hospitals, funded by philanthropists, were started in Ireland in the early 18th century. Catholic religious orders were responsible for much of the early growth of hospitals and medical services. However, by the mid-19th century the British had institutionalized and politicized health care through the punitive workhouse system. Infirmaries, dispensaries, and medical staff provided minimal care in these houses of last resort for the Irish poor. In the colonialist mindset of the British at the time, helping the Irish too much would discourage them from working harder.[39]

After the revolution, the Free State government converted the dreaded workhouses into county homes for the poor in need of both shelter and medical care. Health services in the poorly funded new state, however, were not a financial priority, and hospital health care was delivered through the local network of county and city hospitals until 1970 through the Irish Hospitals' Sweepstakes lottery. However, the early state conducted a vigorous campaign to eradicate tuberculosis in the late 1940s. There were also some developments aimed at improving general public health, such as the provision of free milk to children and pregnant women in the early 1930s.[39]

Health and Social Solidarity in Ireland

As De Valera shepherded the Irish Free State into the era of the modern Republic, national government began to take a more active part in the delivery of health care. The new government published "Outline of Proposals for the Improvement of Health Services" and established the first Department of Health in 1947 with the intent of providing free health care at the point of use.[39] A system of universal health care was proposed in a second paper, "Social Security," in 1949, setting a course for the current dialogue for universally free health care.

However, the Roman Catholic Church, which retained a significant role in government policy process throughout much of the 20th century, was strongly opposed to the plans for state sponsored universal health care. Along with the Department of Finance and the medical community, the Church successfully defeated both the healthcare proposal and a social insurance proposal. The Finance Department argued that the new state could not afford a welfare state on a par with Britain and Northern Ireland. Health care was then subject to incremental changes based on existing service delivery rather than on more visionary planning.

One of the first such incremental measures was the 1953 Health Act, which provided funding to voluntary (nonprofit) agencies for health and related services. Health was broadly defined to include many social services. Section 65 funding became the largest source of funding for voluntary and community organizations in Ireland. Indeed, by 2001, Section 65 funding to voluntary and community groups was €486 million. The name was changed to Section 39 under the Health Act of 2004.[39]

Over time, this incremental approach to health care planning resulted in a patchwork of services, no clear channels for accountability, and an inconsistent pattern of healthcare delivery. A series of reorganizations have since attempted to centralize health care. The Health Care Act of 1970, for example, organized the country into eight regional health boards with similar governing structures. Each board had three programs areas (hospital services, special or psychiatric hospitals, and community care), each under a manager with broad authority. The health boards were made up of local authority councilors, representatives of the senior medical professions, and citizens nominated by the minister for health. There were frequent differences in the availability of services and facilities between health board regions. The Eastern Health Board was subdivided in the 1990s into 3 smaller boards (northern, southwestern, and east coast) increasing the number of regional boards to 11. Additionally, 40 semi-state agencies concerned with health care coevolved, each with specialized functions ranging from giving healthcare advice, health promotion, and health regulation.[39]

Centralizing Health Care

In 2004, the Oireachtas approved a major reorganization in the administration of health care that sought to separate the management of healthcare services from the more political nature of the evolving system and to clarify responsibility for the delivery of quality health care.[39] Today the Department of Health (once the Department of Health and Children) is technically accountable only for policy, while management of public health services falls to the Health Service

Executive Agency (HSE), administered by an executive board and general secretary. However, these two roles have been difficult to separate. The Department reorganization of 2015 sought to make this separation more profound by ultimately eliminating the HSE altogether.[40] Since 2004, however, the executive agency has operated 4 regional health offices, 32 local health offices, and a number of local healthcare centers. More significantly, the reorganization shifted health services from a decentralized federal system to a centralized system; one controlled more by management principles and conceivably less subject to local political pressures.[40]

2015 Reorganization: Restructuring in Three Phases

A new process of structural reform in the Irish Health system began in 2015 in part as a response to EU recovery mandates. The enabling law calls for three phases of development. As of 2016, the first phase is in process and focused on restructuring the management system with an emphasis on providing transparency and articulating specific values related to improved health outcomes. The Department has 10 divisions related to tasks and specific healthcare areas, 7 priority areas related to infrastructure and management improvements—including implementation of Activity-Based Funding—and a more patient-oriented approach to tracking and assigning costs. Within the department are 21 boards, commissions, and authorities related to various aspects of health care, healthcare policy, and their management. This hierarchy of people and ideas supports the implementation of the proactive Healthy Ireland agenda aimed at addressing the key areas of concern in Ireland, such as patient safety, alcohol use, obesity, and others.[40]

Phase II of the structural change will move the system toward a market model with the eventual dissolution of the HSE and a refocus of government activity on health policy and promotion. Phase III, Future Health, tackles healthcare insurance through proposed implementation of a hybrid universal health insurance for acute care and certain primary care services but would use a new general tax structure to support social care and disabilities.[28]

Healthcare Workforce

The overall ratio of physicians to 1,000 population was 2.67 in 2013. The ratio of general practitioners (GPs) employed per 1,000 people in Ireland has been the second lowest in the European Union in recent years. The EU average is approximately 1 GP per 1,000 population, although there is a higher than average number of nurses than the rest of the European Union. The Irish ratio is less than half of the EU average, 0.47 GPs per 1,000 people. There are almost 2,500 GPs in Ireland though not all are in full-time practice. Approximately 10% of these GPs see only private patients. Others see a mix of public and private patients.[22] In 2016 there were about 8,000 medical and dental personnel in Ireland, which represents an increase of about 9% since the end of 2005. The nursing population is 37,500, an increase of slightly less than 7% since 2005. The numbers of other healthcare specialists, such as speech and language therapists, have also increased since 2005 to 15,500 overall, an increase of about 210%.[22] In early summer 2016, the Health Department raised the ire of hospitals, healthcare workers, and citizens by instituting a hiring freeze for any new doctors, nurses, or midwives.[41]

Innovation

While the Irish system still feels unwieldy and overly politicized to some, there has been significant activity by government aimed at responding to pressure from both citizens and the European Union. Beginning in 2008, as economic recovery began, the Irish government authorized a €490 million budget for health information technology to improve access to timely health information. The money was also budgeted to develop electronic patient records to improve coordination of inpatient and outpatient records and for sustaining patient history. While some gains have been made, goals have not been met or have been delayed.[25]

In 2016, Health Innovation Hub of Ireland was granted €5 million over a period of 5 years to develop healthcare technologies. The project partners with private industry work through Enterprise Ireland to develop specific technologies to address web medicine, infection control, staffing and scheduling, among others. The program has funded over 20 projects to date. For example, Enterprise Ireland completed its first Maternity Strategy in 2015, which provides a framework for safer maternity service. This new model of care will provide more choice and personalized care for women and babies.[25]

The Air Ambulance Service was made permanent, and the National Emergency Operation Centre in Tallaght was opened in 2015. The government also approved an evidence-based multi-annual public health plan for the pharmaceutical treatment of patients with hepatitis C. The HSE established the National Hepatitis C Treatment Programme and in 2015 began treatment on almost 400 patients. The preliminary outcome data show high rates of sustained viral response and viral clearance according to government reports.[25]

New National Clinical Effectiveness Guidelines were published in conjunction with the Health Information and Patient Safety Bill. This bill establishes a new program of patient safety that includes a national patient advocacy service, measurement of patient experience, extending the clinical effectiveness agenda, and establishing a National Advisory Council of Patient Safety. Further, in 2015, a new HSE email service, Healthmail, was launched, enabling GPs to communicate securely with other parts of the health services, including all HSE hospitals and over 20 voluntary hospitals and agencies. It has the potential for more effective discharge processes.[25]

Pharmaceutical Regulation

Ireland, in common with the rest of the European Union, restricts advertising of prescription pharmaceuticals. Only over-the-counter drugs may be advertised. The reasons are unclear, but the Irish have a lower than average use of generic medicines despite being a major exporter of reduced cost prescriptions. In a recent review of the healthcare reorganization efforts in Ireland, the European Commission noted that Ireland has made some progress on getting control of high prescription costs in Ireland but has not yet negotiated with the Irish Pharmaceutical Healthcare Association to reduce the country's reliance on a single provider.[45]

▸ Evaluation of the Healthcare System

Cost of Health Care

Ireland is a striking example of the impact of the global recession on healthcare spending. Between 2005 and 2009, healthcare spending grew at an annual rate of 5.3%, the 7th highest rate among the 34 member nations of the OECD.[22] Irish spending on health care quadrupled between 1997 and 2007. But just as dramatically in the opposite direction, between 2009 and 2013, spending dropped at a rate of 4% annually, the 3rd steepest drop among OECD member states. Refer to **TABLE 13-2**. Between 2008 and 2013, approximately €2.3 billion was cut from the Irish health system, a drop of 22%, with more than 12,000 fewer HSE staff in 2013 as compared with 2007.[21]

On a per capita basis, in 2013, Ireland's spending was close to the OECD average, US $3,663 in Ireland vs. $3,453 for the OECD average. While overall spending has zigzagged during the first two decades of the 21st century and was reaching noticeably high levels by 2009, it is no longer a significant spending outlier within OECD norms (OECD includes nearly all member states of the European Union) nor does it appear to be an outlier on certain other measures of health system effectiveness. However, Ireland's measures relating to public and population health are less than exemplary and represent an important improvement opportunity for the physical and financial health of the nation.[22] **TABLE 13-3** outlines how the public health capital expenditures were allocated by program.

On basic measures of health system capacity and supply, Ireland does not appear as a wasteful system in comparison with other OECD nations: 2.8 physicians per 1,000 in 2014 versus 3.3 for the OECD; 2.8 hospital beds per 1,000 in 2013 versus 4.8 OECD; 3.8 doctor consultations per capita annually in 2010 versus 6.7 consultations for the OECD; hospital discharges at 13,532 per 100,000 people in 2013 versus 15,497 OECD; and average length of hospital stay at 5.6 days in 2013 versus 7.3 OECD. For some, these efficiencies appear to be a deficit when considered in light of how much Ireland spends on health care compared to most nations.

On major system capacity measures, Ireland exceeds the OECD average on nurses per 1,000 people at 12.4 versus 9.1 OECD. The Irish health system is facing many challenges, but oversupply does not appear to be one of them.[22] The European Union's concern has been that although Ireland spends above other OECD countries, there is not corresponding evidence of better health outcomes.

Access

While about 30% of the population in 2012 qualified for medical cards that allowed them free access to GP and hospital services, the numbers have dropped in more recent years as the Irish Health Service tightens its belt. Around 70% of the country is not eligible for the card, and eligibility requirements have, until recently, been tighter. A significant increase in cards was experienced as the unemployed received them. Without a card, consumers can get free or subsidized care based on their contributions to a mandatory Social Insurance Fund. Since 2015 some groups, especially children under five, have had a right to free access to family medicine, and heroin addicts have free access to methadone treatment. Since 2008 over €450 million in costs have been transferred to patients in the form of individual treatment user fees.[21,43]

The numbers covered by medical cards dropped by 65,000 because of tightened eligibility requirements in 2013. By 2013 more people were getting their

TABLE 13-2 Public Health Expenditure in Millions of Euros, 2006–2015

Change Percentage (in € millions)	2006	2007	2008	2009	2010	2011	2012	2013	2014	2015**	2006–2015	2014–2015
Total Public Noncapital Expenditure on Health	12,248	13,736	14,588	15,073	14,452	13,728	13,787	13,625	13,276	13,830	12.9	4.2
*Public Noncapital Expenditure on Health (excludes treatment *benefits*)	12,144	13,636	14,481	14,963	14,396	13,703	13,766	13,604	13,246	13,797	13.6	4.2
Total Public Capital Expenditure on Health	461	585	598	447	366	347	350	386	386	382	−17.1	−1.0
Total Public Expenditure	**12,709**	**14,321**	**15,186**	**15,520**	**14,818**	**14,075**	**14,137**	**13,662**	**13,662**	**14,212**	**11.8**	**4.0**

* Net noncapital expenditure excludes treatment benefits (funded by Office of the Minister for Children (2006–2008) and the Office of the Minister for Children & Youth Affairs (from 2009).
** Figures for 2015 are estimated.
Reproduced from An Roinn Sláinte Department of Health. Health in Ireland Key Trends 2015. http://health.gov.ie/wp-content/uploads/2015/12/Health_in_Ireland_KeyTrends2015.pdf. 2015.

TABLE 13-3 Capital Public Health Expenditure by Program in Millions of Euros, 2005–2014

Program	2005	2006	2007	2008	2009	2010	2011	2012	2013	2014	% Change 2005–2014	% Change 2013–2014
Acute hospitals	278	245	312	273	209	220	202	208	203	197	−29.1	−2.9
Community health	116	112	138	178	161	97	71	53	62	79	−31.9	26.1
Mental health	26	20	34	40	25	27	39	54	23	50	93.1	119.1
Disability services	32	42	45	69	27	5	11	6	8	6	−80.8	−21.0
ICT information & communications technology	58	25	30	20	13	7	16	22	41	41	−30.0	−0.3
Miscellaneous	6	17	26	18	12	10	8	7	11	14	135.9	28.8
Total public capital expenditure	**516**	**461**	**585**	**598**	**447**	**366**	**347**	**350**	**347**	**386**	**−25.1**	**11.1**

*Excludes capital expenditure by the Department of Children and Youth Affairs (2006–2010)

Revised estimates for public services and HSE reports on capital program.

Reproduced from An Roinn Slainte Department of Health. Health in Ireland Key Trends 2015. http://health.gov.ie/wp-content/uploads/2015/12/Health_in_Ireland_KeyTrends2015.pdf. 2015.

medical care through emergency rooms (ERs), which represented 83% of all admissions. Additionally, there has been a drop in the numbers of people who have private insurance, with 245,000 fewer in 2014 than in 2013.[21,22] Some gains were realized in 2015 as the economy improved and policies changed.

Transparency

There have been little data available before now on quality or healthcare outcomes in Ireland and even less data on the performance of government. The ESRI report on the costs of Universal Health Insurance, was concerned not only with the expense, but also with the capacity of government to manage a single-tier system, citing issues of transparency and data collection and use.

Transparency and trust of government continue to be issues with both healthcare professionals and citizens. Government has promoted the belief that it has capped maximum waiting time for an appointment for surgeries at 18 months, although many are scheduled earlier. While over 70% of patients are seen almost immediately, the access is not equitable for the other 30%. Furthermore, government estimates do not always align with consumer experience. In 2015, over 35,000 patients waited more than 18 months to be seen by a caregiver. This fact has led to disparities in the level of care people receive and horror stories about deaths of children who have had to wait too long.[21,22,29]

A frequent topic in the *Irish Times* is a new "trolley" story of someone who has been left in a hospital hallway for an extended time until a bed can be found. These stories have revealed that although the government collects daily metrics on every aspect of the system, in the past it has not published information about waiting lists and trolley problems. There seems to be a continued discrepancy between what hospitals and patients say they are experiencing and what the government is reporting.[44]

According to the European Health Consumer Index (EHCI) of 2015, waiting times in Irish emergency rooms are the worst in Europe, as is the waiting time for computed tomography (CT) scans. Ireland's rankings dropped from 14th place among 35 countries to 21st in 2014 because of waiting lists and wait. The EHCI observed that government estimates of wait times were not consistent with the high level of consumer complaints regarding wait times. On both CTs and magnetic resonance imaging machines (MRIs), Ireland's per capita supply of this advanced equipment is below the OECD median of 24.6 CT scanners per million population versus 17.8 in Ireland versus 24.6 among OECD nations, and 13.5 versus 14.3 for MRI machines. The use of waiting lists indicates deep inefficiencies in healthcare delivery. Waiting lists cost the system money and make it difficult to correlate the amount of money spent on health care and accessibility). The system ranks below the norm in providing access to a second opinion, providing no-fault malpractice insurance, and being up to speed on web-based health options, including e-prescriptions and direct access to specialists. Overall it ranks below the norm in healthcare equity.[24] While how complaints are handled by the system has improved, popular reports still describe the system as frequently hostile to complaints and as paternalistic.[27,29]

Health Outcomes

The bottom line for any health system's performance are measures of population health outcomes. In this category, the Irish track record is mixed with some clear opportunities for improvement. Ireland's life expectancy in 2013 was at 81.1 versus the OECD average at 80.5 years, tied for 17th among the 34 OECD member states. Life expectancy at age 65.0 was similarly close to the OECD average; 2.8 years for Irish females versus 21.1 for all of the OECD, and 18.1 for Irish males vs. 17.8 for all of the OECD. Infant mortality in Ireland is 3.5 per 1,000 live births as compared to the OECD average of 4.2.[78] Over the past decade Ireland has achieved a rapid improvement in life expectancy due in large part of significant reductions in circulatory diseases Likewise, Childhood vaccination rates have been increasing since 2005 and are now at 95.0% or above for most vaccinations.[22] By EU standards, Ireland ranks in about the middle third of OECD countries for health outcomes but in the bottom third for quality indicators like avoidable hospital admissions, cancer survival rates, and the volume of antibiotics used. The European Union's consistent complaint is that Ireland spends more than any country except Denmark on health care but without an attendant increase in quality.[45]

Certain unhealthy behaviors are standouts as opportunity for improvement, both physically and financially. Adult tobacco consumption at 24% in 2013 is much higher than the OECD average of 19.8%. Similarly, Irish alcohol consumption at 10.6 liters per capita per year is much higher than the OECD average at 8.8 liters. The Irish opportunity to extend life, to improve healthy living, and to save health system dollars, can be found in improved healthy behaviors by the Irish population.

Emerging Challenges

Any analysis of the Irish healthcare system at this point is made midstream. The Irish government is balancing multiple pressures—a major debt to the European Union being one. Balancing the recovery standards of the European Union with the needs of citizens and foreign investors is another. At the same time, Ireland is pressured to create a single-payer system that would meet the populist concerns for universal health insurance and EU expectations, and it must also find a more sustainable source of domestic tax dollars in order to fund it. Additionally, it must train itself to make effective use of data and to be transparent in political appointments and the use of public money.

Furthermore, the Irish population is aging. One-third is already on long-term medicine. Ireland has seen a growth in the elderly population aged over 65, with an increase of 20,000 people each year. This trend will have implications for future planning and health service delivery. Ireland will see large proportional increases in the population aged 85 years and older.[45] Ireland's fertility rates are still among the highest in Europe, but the birth rate has fallen to its lowest rate for the last decade. Ireland currently has the highest proportion of children and young people among EU countries. The total fertility rate has decreased slightly in recent years and now stands at 1.95. The EU average is 1.55.[34]

Prosperity and modernization have brought other problems to Ireland. The nation also suffers from a growing level of obesity, where one in four adults are considered obese.[34]

Technology poses yet another emerging challenge. As Ireland strengthens its primary care delivery system to lessen the load on the tertiary care system, a survey of 495 general practitioners (GP) found that one-third co-locate with other services (practice nurses, dieticians, physiotherapists), and 85% have ECG equipment in the practice. However, only 9% have ultrasound equipment and small numbers have X-ray equipment. Telemedicine facilities and orthopedic and specialized minor surgery facilities are still uncommon among the respondents. The evidence suggests that significant work needs to be done to ensure that all diagnostic testing can be undertaken at the primary care level.[44]

Of major concern is the medical brain drain that has plagued Ireland since the recession. A recent study revealed that 88% of medical students at Irish medical schools plan to migrate to the United States and other countries. The reasons involve working conditions, the unstable nature of the healthcare system, and a lack of career opportunities and lifestyle choices.[45] This condition affects the nation's ability to improve primary care.[45]

Perhaps the most difficult task for Irish politicians and the Health Care Department is the disappointment by the public in its healthcare system and the public wanting and expecting University Health Insurance. In meeting the demands of the National Recovery Plan and the European Union's insistence on a more rational and cost-effective system of healthcare delivery with more positive outcomes, the government has been easing away from the bold promise of Fine Gael in 2011 to provide universal healthcare insurance and free care for all to the citizens of Ireland within a decade. Indeed, universal health insurance has been replaced by the significantly different universal health care. Since 2014, in what some feel is a bureaucratic sleight of hand, the Department of Health policy has been to ration health care as needed and to pass on more of the cost of health care to the consumer. However, citizens are not simply clamoring for national health insurance but a more equitable and transparent system with improved health outcomes and safety.

Further challenges involve the government's ability to stick to the plan, in particular budget plans. Since 2010 the state has struggled to get control of the rising costs of health care and is plagued by systematic and increasingly high-cost overruns.[45] Politically committed to universal health insurance, the Irish government is dragging its feet, partially because there has been little progress in implementing a more sustainable tax system.[45]

Summary

The Health Ministry emphasizes its concern for patient safety and has written to its Medical Council an admonition to healthcare workers to advocate for better facilities if they work in a facility that is "not suitable for patients or for the treatment provided."[46] In 2015 reorganization of the management structure of the Irish health program, the emphasis has been on improving transparency of the health management process, which may go a long way in correcting the disconnect between patient experience and government predictions. This will be aided by cohesive attempts at understanding the system through improved data collection that is effectively employed in decision-making.

Coupled with attention to EU standards, attention to citizen concerns for transparency and accountability, as well as meeting structural reform goals to ease the inconsistencies in management and funding across the complex healthcare system, the Irish may be able to sustain gains made during the Celtic Tiger years. Yet as score cards for the Irish healthcare system indicate, the task of improving health in Ireland involves more than throwing money at the problem. The deep-rooted political significance of universal health coverage will continue to be an issue. Most importantly perhaps the Irish must be engaged in recovering healthy lifestyles while being provided meaningful opportunities to develop proactive relationships with healthcare givers.

References

1. Given B, Murphy G, eds. Continuity, change & crisis in contemporary Ireland. *Journal of Irish Politics*. 2008;23(4):457–474.
2. Fahey T, Whelen CT. Best of times? The social importance of the Celtic Tiger. Institute of Public Administration. Dublin, Ireland; 2007.
3. Ian GN. *Troubled Geographies: A Spatial History of Religion and Society in Ireland*. Bloomington, Ill. Indiana University Press; 2013.
4. Gangland feud claims seventh victim. *The Guardian*. May 24, 2016. http://www.theguardian.com/world/2016/may/24/dublin-gangland-feud-claims-seventh-victim. Accessed June 1, 2016.
5. Government of Ireland. An Phríomh-Oifig Staidrimh. Central Statistics Office. Population. http://www.cso.ie/en/statistics/population. Accessed June 2016.
6. Jean-Christophe P. From idealised moral community to secular Ireland to real tiger society: the Catholic Church in secular Ireland. *Journal of Irish Studies*. 2008(3):143–154.
7. Losada-Friend M, Jejedo C, Estevez-Saa JM, Huber W, eds. *Dreaming the Future: New Horizons / Old Barriers in 21st-Century Ireland*. Irish Studies in Europe. Vol. 3. 2012.
8. Government of Ireland. An Phríomh-Oifig Staidrimh. Central Statistics Office. Population and immigration statistics. http://www.cso.ie/en/releasesandpublications/er/pme/populationandmigrationestimatesapril2015/. Accessed May 2, 2016.
9. Fanning B. Immigration, the Celtic Tiger and the economic crisis. *Ir Stud Rev*. 24(1):9–20.
10. Means R. *Republic of Ireland*. NY: Great Neck Publishing. 2015.
11. Government of Ireland. Environmental Protection Agency. What is climate change? http://www.epa.ie/climate/communicatingclimatescience/whatisclimatechange/whatimpactwillclimatechangehavefo. Accessed May 10, 2016.
12. Government of Ireland. Department of Taoiseach. http://www.taoiseach.gov.ie/eng/Contacts/. Accessed April 29, 2016.
13. TASC. Open Government Toolkit. http://www.tasc.ie/researchpolicy/projects/open-government-toolkit/. Accessed May 29, 2016.
14. Changing roles of Irish women over past 50 years reflected in relationships. *TheJournal.ie*. https://www.thejournal.ie/changing-role-of-irish-women-over-past-50-years-reflected-in-relationships-382725-Mar2012/. May, 19, 2012. Accessed April 29, 2016.
15. Barrett SD. The EU/IMF Rescue Programme 2010–2013. *Econ Aff*. 2011;31(2):53–57.
16. European Commission. Ireland's economic crisis. How did it happen? What is being done? http://ec.europa.eu/ireland/economy/irelands_economic_crisis/index_en.htm. Published February 22, 2012. Accessed April 15, 2016.
17. Barnes S. Ireland's economic outlook. *OECD Observer*. http://www.oecdobserver.org/news/archivestory.php/aid/3129/Ireland_92s_economic_outlook.html. Published November 2009. Accessed May 25, 2016.
18. Taft M. Community Platform. *Paying Our Way: Progressive Proposals for Reforming the Irish Tax System*. http://communityplatform.ie/uploads/payingourway_preview%20(2).pdf. 2011. Accessed May 17, 2016.
19. The Irish economy: Celtic phoenix. Ireland shows there is economic life after death. *Economist*. http://www.economist.com/news/finance-and-economics/21678830-ireland-shows-there-economic-life-after-death-celtic-phoenix. November, 21, 2015. Accessed June 1, 2016.
20. European Commission. Directorate-General for Economic and Financial Affairs. *European Economy: Macroeconomic Imbalances. Country Report—Ireland 2015. Occasional Papers 215, June 2015*. Luxembourg: Publications Office of the European Union, 2015. http://ec.europa.eu/economy_finance/publications/. June 2015. Accessed May 22, 2016.
21. Burke S, Thomas S, Barry S, Keegan C. Indicators of health system coverage and activity in Ireland during the economic crisis 2008–2014—from "more with less" to "less with less." *Health Policy*. September 2014;117(3):275–278. doi: 10.1016/j.healthpol.2014.07.001.
22. Organisation for Economic Co-operation and Development. Health at a glance 2015. How does Ireland compare? https://www.oecd.org/ireland/Health-at-a-Glance-2015-Key-Findings-IRELAND.pdf. Accessed May 28, 2016.
23. Mesabbah M, Arisha A. Performance management of the public healthcare services in Ireland: a review. 2016. *Int J Health Care Qual Assur*. 2016;29(2):209–35. doi: 10.1108/IJHCQA-07-2014-0079.
24. Health Consumer Powerhouse. *Euro Health Consumer Index 2015*. http://www.healthpowerhouse.com/index.php?Itemid=55. Published January 26, 2016. December 6, 2016.
25. Government of Ireland. An Roinn Sláinte Department of Health. *Annual Report 2015. Progress on the First Year of our Three-Year Statement of Strategy 2015–2017*. http://health.gov.ie/wp-content/uploads/2016/04/Annual-Report-2015-080416.pdf.
26. Wren M, Connolly S, Cunningham C. *An Examination of the Potential Costs of Universal Health Insurance in Ireland*. Research Series # 45. September 2015. Department of Health and Economic and Social Research Institute. https://www.esri.ie/pubs/RS45.pdf. Accessed May 17, 2016.
27. Cullen P. Broken: Ireland's ailing health service. https://www.irishtimes.com/news/health/broken-ireland-s-ailing-health-service-1.2340468. September 8, 2015. Accessed May 12, 2016.
28. Government of Ireland. An Roinn Sláinte Department of Health. *Future Health—A Strategic Framework for Reform of the Health Service 2012–2015*. http://health.gov.ie/blog/publications/future-health-a-strategic-framework-for-reform-of-the-health-service-2012-2015/. Accessed May 21, 2016.
29. European Anti Poverty Network Ireland. Submission to National Reform Programme 2016. http://www.eapn.ie/eapn/submission-to-national-reform-programme-2016. Accessed May 17, 2016.
30. European Anti Poverty Network Ireland. Employment and Poverty. http://www.eapn.ie/eapn/policy/employment-overview. Accessed May 28, 2016.
31. European Commission. Expert Panel on Effective Ways of Investing in Health. Access to health services in the European Union. http://ec.europa.eu/health/expert_panel/opinions/docs/010_access_healthcare_en.pdf. September 29, 2015. Accessed June 5, 2016.

32. European Commission. Recommendation for a Council recommendation on the 2015 National Reform Programme of Ireland and delivering a Council opinion the 2015 Stability Programme of Ireland. Council Recommendation 10, Ireland Poverty, 2015. http://ec.europa.eu/europe2020/pdf/csr2015/csr2015_ireland_en.pdf. Accessed May 28, 2016.
33. Ipsos MRBL. *Healthy Ireland Survey 2015: Summary of Findings*. Dublin: The Stationery Office. https://www.ucd.ie/t4cms/Healthy%20Ireland%20Survey%202015%20-%20Summary%20of%20Findings.pdf. 2015. Accessed May 21, 2016.
34. Government of Ireland. An Roinn Sláinte Department of Health. Health in Ireland key trends 2015. http://health.gov.ie/blog/publications/health-in-ireland-key-trends-2015/. Accessed May 20, 2016.
35. Government of Ireland. An Roinn Sláinte Department of Health. *Alcohol Misuse Report 2014*. http://www.hse.ie/eng/health/az/A/Alcohol-misuse/. Accessed May 21, 2016.
36. Alcohol Action Ireland. How much do we drink? http://alcoholireland.ie/facts/how-much-do-we-drink/. Accessed May 23, 2016.
37. Government of Ireland. An Roinn Sláinte Department of Health. Alcohol measures announced. /blog/press-release/ministers-fitzgerald-reilly-and-white-announce-measures-to-deal-with-alcohol-misuse-minimum-unit-pricing-and-regulation-of-advertising-and-sponsorship-to-be-provided-for-in-a-public-health-bill/. 2013. Accessed May 23, 2016.
38. National Suicide Prevention Foundation. Suicide statistics. http://nsrf.ie/statistics/suicide/. Accessed May 24, 2016.
39. Combat Poverty IE. *Evolution of Health Services in Ireland*. http://www.combatpoverty.ie/publications/EvolutionOfHealthServicesAndHealthPolicyInIreland_2007.pdf. Accessed May 8, 2016.
40. Government of Ireland. An Roinn Sláinte Department of Health. http://health.gov.ie. Accessed May 11, 2016.
41. Recruitment suspension "will cost lives," INMO says. *Irish Times*. May 20, 2016. Accessed June 5, 2016.
42. Health Innovation Hub Ireland. http://hih.ie. Accessed May 25, 2016.
43. Health Product Regulatory Agency. Pharmaceutical regulations. https://www.hpra.ie/. Accessed May 25, 2016.
44. Wall M. Numbers on hospital trolleys 26% higher than a year ago. *Irish Times*. https://www.irishtimes.com/news/ireland/irish-news/numbers-on-hospital-trolleys-26-higher-than-a-year-ago-1.2493140. Published January 12, 2016. Accessed May 24, 2016.
45. European Commission. *Commission Staff Working Document: Country Report Ireland 2016*. http://ec.europa.eu/europe2020/pdf/csr2016/cr2016_ireland_en.pdf. Published February 2, 2016. Accessed June 4, 2016.
46. European Commission. *Ex Post Evaluation of the Economic Adjustment Programme: Ireland, 2010–2013*. Irish Health System. Institutional paper 004, July 2015. Luxembourg: Publications Office of the European Union, 2015. http://ec.europa.eu/dgs/economy_finance/evaluation/pdf/ex-post_ireland_en.pdf. Accessed May 12, 2016.
47. Government of Ireland. An Roinn Sláinte Department of Health. Analysis of potential measures to encourage the provision of primary care facilities. http://health.gov.ie/blog/publications/analysis-of-potential-measures-to-encourage-the-provision-of-primary-care-facilities. Published December 18, 2015. Accessed May 22, 2016.
48. Cullen P. 'Brain drain' of medical staff blamed on bad work conditions. *Irish Times*. https://www.irishtimes.com/news/health/brain-drain-of-medical-staff-blamed-on-bad-work-conditions-1.2217138. Published May 18, 2015. Accessed May 10, 2016.
49. Professional Ethics Medical Council of Ireland. *Guide to Professional Conduct and Ethics for Registered Medical Practitioners*. 7th edition. https://www.medicalcouncil.ie/News-and-Publications/Publications/Professional-Conduct-Ethics/Guide-to-Professional-Conduct-and-Behaviour-for-Registered-Medical-Practitioners-pdf.pdf. Published 2009. Accessed May 23, 2016.

CHAPTER 14

Russia

James H. Stephens, Alexander V. Sergeev, and Elena A. Platonova

▶ Country Description

TABLE 14-1 Russia

Nationality	Noun: Russian(s) Adjective: Russian
Ethnic groups	Russian 77.7%, Tatar 3.7%, Ukrainian 1.4%, Bashkir 1.1%, Chuvash 1.0%, Chechen 1%, other or unspecified 3.9% (2016)
Religions	Russian Orthodox 15%–20%, Muslim 10%–15%, other Christian 2% (2016)*
Language	Russian 85.7%, Tatar 3.2%, Chechen 1%, other 10.1% (2010 est.)
Literacy	Definition: Age 15 and over can read and write. Total population: 99.7% Male: 99.7% Female: 99.2% (2015 est.)
Government type	Semi-presidential federation
Date of independence	August 24, 1991 (from Soviet Union)
Gross Domestic Product (GDP) per capita	$25,400 (2015 est.)

(continues)

TABLE 14-1 Russia (continued)

Unemployment rate	5.4% (2015 est.)
Natural hazards	Siberian permafrost impeding development; volcanic activity in the Kuril Islands; volcanoes and earthquakes on the Kamchatka Peninsula; spring floods and summer/autumn forest fires throughout Siberia and parts of European Russia
Environment: current issues	Air pollution from heavy industry, coal-fired electric plants, and transportation in major cities; industrial, municipal, and agricultural pollution of inland waterways and seacoasts; deforestation; soil erosion; soil contamination from improper application of agricultural chemicals; scattered areas of sometimes intense radioactive contamination; groundwater contamination from toxic waste; urban solid waste management; abandoned stocks of obsolete pesticides
Population	142,355,415 (July 2016 est.)
Age structure	0–14 years: 16.94% (male 12,385,281/female 11,726,473) 15–24 years: 9.70% (male 7,071,489/female 6,754,928) 25–54 years: 45.16% (male 31,528,258/female 32,753,350) 55–64 years: 14.27% (male 8,727,233/female 11,591,221) 65 years and over: 13.92% (male 6,152,252/female 13,664,930) (2016 est.)
Median age	Total: 38.3 years Male: 35.1 years Female: 41.4 years (2008 est.)
Population growth rate	−0.06% (2016 est.)
Birth rate	11.3 births/1,000 population (2016 est.)
Death rate	13.6 deaths/1,000 population (2008 est.)
Net migration rate	1.7 migrant(s)/1,000 population (2016 est.)
Gender ratio	At birth: 1.06 male(s)/female 0–14 years: 1.06 male(s)/female 15–24 years: 1.05 male(s)/female 25–54 years: 0.96 male(s)/female 55–64 years: 0.75 male(s)/female 65 years and over: 0.45 male(s)/female total population: 0.86 male(s)/female (2016 est.)
Infant mortality rate	Total: 6.9 deaths/1,000 live births Male: 7.7 deaths/1,000 live births Female: 6.0 deaths/1,000 live births (2016 est.)
Life expectancy at birth	Total population: 70.8 years Male: 65.0 years Female: 76.8 years (2016 est.)
Total fertility rate	1.61 children born/woman (2016 est.)
HIV/AIDS adult prevalence rate	Not available

TABLE 14-1 Russia (continued)	
Number of people living with HIV/AIDS	Not available
HIV/AIDS deaths	Not available

*Religion estimates are of practicing worshipers; Russia has large populations of nonpracticing believers and nonbelievers, a legacy of over seven decades of Soviet rule.

Data from Central Intelligence Agency. The World Fact Book, 2016: Russia. https://www.cia.gov/library/publications/the-world-factbook. Accessed November 18, 2008.

History

Modern Russians are descendants of the Slavic tribes that settled in the contemporary Western part of the Russian Federation where the state of Kievan Rus' was established by the 9th century. In the 18th century, the Russian Empire was proclaimed under Czar Peter the Great (Peter I), who conducted "Westernization" reforms. Following abolishment of serfdom in 1861, the process of industrialization and urbanization began. The Revolution of 1905 resulted in some constitutional reforms. The Romanov dynasty was overthrown during the February Revolution of 1917, and the Bolsheviks led by Vladimir Lenin seized power during the October Revolution of 1917. In 1922, the Union of Soviet Socialist Republics was formed with the Russian Soviet Federated Socialist Republic, constituting the largest republic. Major industrialization and communist-style reforms in agriculture (collectivization) were underway in the 1920s and 1930s. The Soviet Union's war with Nazi Germany (the Great Patriotic War of 1941–1945) was a major theater of World War II. After the death of Joseph Stalin, some liberalization reforms were initiated by Nikita Khrushchev. Later, under Leonid Brezhnev, a period of economic stagnation emerged, followed by major economic and political reforms—*perestroika* (restructuring) and *glasnost* (openness)—under Mikhail Gorbachev. After the failed coup of August 1991, organized by Gorbachev's opponents, the Union of Soviet Socialist Republics was abolished. In 1991, the official name of the Russian state was changed from the Russian Soviet Federated Socialist Republic to the Russian Federation.

Size and Geography

Geographically, the Russian Federation (R.F.) is the world's largest country; the Russian Federation covers an area of 17.1 million square kilometers (6.6 million square miles), which is over one-eighth of the Earth's land area. The Russian Federation is located in two continents: Europe and Asia. Eight percent of the country's land is arable. The country's land border is about 12,500 miles and its coastline is about 26,100 miles. See **FIGURE 14-1**. The capital of the country is Moscow. The Russian Federation is composed of 85 federal subjects (constituent units). As of 2015, the population of the Russian Federation is 146.3 million[1]; it ranks the ninth largest in the world. There are more than 180 ethnic groups in the Russian Federation[2]; the largest ones (each comprising more than 1% of the total population) are Russian (80.0%), Tatar (3.8%), Ukrainian (2.0%), Bashkir (1.2%), and Chuvash (1.1%). The official state language of the Russian Federation is Russian.

Government and Political System

The Russian Federation is a federative state with a republican form of government. There are three branches of power: executive, legislative, and judicial. The president, the Federal Assembly (parliament), the Government (ministries), and the courts exercise state power in the Russian Federation. The head of the state is the president. The Federal Assembly consists of two chambers, the State Duma and the Federation Council (the upper chamber). The president is elected by universal and direct suffrage for a six-year term; the maximum number of consecutive presidential terms of office is two. The president appoints the prime minister, with State Duma approval.

The Constitutional Court consists of 19 judges. The Constitutional Court judges are nominated by the president and appointed by the Federation Council.[3] The Supreme Court is the highest appellate court in civil law, administrative law, and criminal law cases.

There are 77 political parties in the Russian Federation that are registered by the Ministry of Justice.[4] To be registered, a political party must have at least 500 members and have regional branches in at least half of the federal subjects, according to federal law.

Macroeconomics

The structure of the Russian economy is characterized by a significant prevalence of large companies and a relatively high proportion of extraction industry and

FIGURE 14-1 Map of Russia
© Bardocz Peter/Shutterstock

heavy industry. Foreign investment has been concentrated in nontradable sectors and extracting industries.[5] The major industries are machinery, ferrous and nonferrous metallurgy (the Ural economic region, Siberia, and the Far East economic region), chemicals and petrochemicals (the Central economic region, the Northwest economic region, and the Volga economic region), forestry, timber processing, paper and pulp (the North and Far East parts of the country), and food, as well as light industries (mostly the textile industry). The economic regions are not constituent units of the Russian Federation. The gas reserves of the Russian Federation are the world's largest, and its oil reserves are the ninth largest. The fuel and energy sector accounts for about 50% of R.F. exports.[6]

For the last 20 years, the economic policy of the Russian Federation has been oriented toward economic stabilization, liberalization of prices, and integration into the global economy.[7,8] Since the early 1990s, labor moved from low-productivity sectors (agriculture) to high-productivity sectors (manufacturing and service).[5]

Russian currency is the ruble (R); 1 ruble = 100 kopeks. In May 2016, the exchange rate was approximately R65 for US $1.

In 2014, the Russian Federation ranked 10th in the world with a GDP equivalent to US $1.861 trillion;[9] in 2007, the country ranked the 11th in the world with a GDP of $1.299 billion.[10] The GDP breakdown is as follows (given as percent of GDP at basic prices): industry 27.9%, trade 21.9%, other market services 17.9%, nonmarket services 10.6%, transportation and communication 8.6%, construction 7.2%, agriculture 5.0%, and other production of goods 0.8%.[11]

In recent years, annual inflation in the Russian Federation has been about 10%; it was 6.5% in 2013 and 11.4% in 2014.[5,12,13] The average monthly salary in 2015 was about R35,000 (about US $540).[14] In 2015, the average unemployment rate was 5.6%, a decrease from 7.3% in 2010.[15]

In 2010, there were a total of 1,450,300 kilometers (about 901,000 miles) of automobile roads, including 1,023,000 kilometers (about 636,000 miles) of concrete roads and macadam roads, and 86,300 kilometers (about 53,600 miles) of railroads.[16] The total length of the oil and gas pipelines was 232,200 kilometers (about 144,300 miles), and the total length of internal waterways was 102,000 kilometers (about 63,000 miles).[16]

Education

The Constitution of the Russian Federation (Article 43) guarantees the right to education for everyone. The legal regulations for the education system are laid down in federal law. Ethnic minorities have the right to be educated in their native languages. The learning of the state language, Russian, is a compulsory component of a secondary school curriculum.[17] The European Observatory on Health Systems and Policies states that the quality of education in the Russian Federation is high.[8]

The educational system consists of:

- Preliminary education (kindergarten for children 3–6 years old).
- Compulsory incomplete secondary education (grades 1–9).
- Complete secondary education (grades 10–11, equivalent to U.S. high school). After obtaining incomplete secondary education, students may enroll in complete general secondary education programs at secondary schools or in complete vocational secondary education at vocational schools (equivalent to U.S. community colleges).
- Higher education programs at universities (a.k.a. institutes and academies) leading to bachelor's degrees (4 years), specialist diplomas (additional year beyond a bachelor's degree), or master's degree (additional two years beyond a bachelor's degree).
- Higher medical education programs are six years long for MDs and 5 years long for DDMs; they are taught at medical institutes, medical academies, or medical universities (all these institutions are equivalent to medical schools in the United States). Professional preparation for nurses, physician assistants (*feldsher*), and midwives is conducted in medical colleges (secondary medical education programs).
- Postgraduate academic programs (*aspirantura*) are 3–4 years long, and they lead to PhDs (*Kandidat Nauk*) after conducting original research, publishing at least three original research articles based on the research results, passing candidate exams, and succeeding in defense of a dissertation. Those who have obtained master's, specialist's, or medical degrees (MDs or DDMs) are eligible for enrollment in PhD programs. Bachelor's degree holders and graduates of secondary medical education programs (nurses, physician assistants, and midwives) are not eligible for enrollment in PhD programs. The Russian *Kandidat Nauk* degree is equivalent to a PhD in the United States and western Europe.[18]

Demographics

Per the 2010 census, the largest age group was 20–24, followed by 25–29 and 50–54 (**TABLE 14-2**).

The R.F. Census 2010 reported that only 0.3% of the population age 15 and older was illiterate.[19] The Russian Federation had more academic graduates than any country in Europe. In recent years, a demand for commercially oriented education has emerged, resulting in an expansion of private institutions of higher education offering graduate degrees in law, business, and economics. As of the academic year 2015–2016, there were 4,061,400 students enrolled in 530 state institutions of higher education and 1,036,100 students enrolled in 446 private institutions of higher education in the Russian Federation.[19]

In 2012, the Gini index (ranging from 0, absolute equality of income distribution, to 100, absolute inequality) for the Russian Federation was relatively high at 41.6.[20] In terms of absolute poverty, 0.1% of the country's population reported living on no more than US $3.10 per day.[21]

Orthodoxy (the Russian Orthodox Church) constitutes the largest religious group (practiced by about 75% of respondents); the second largest group is Muslims (about 8%); other religious groups constitute less than 1%–2%.[22]

In the Russian Federation, the top five conditions contributing to total disability-adjusted life years are:[23]

- for males: cardiovascular disease, unintentional injuries, neuropsychiatric conditions, intentional injuries, and malignant neoplasms;
- for females: cardiovascular disease, neuropsychiatric conditions, unintentional injuries, malignant neoplasms, and digestive diseases.

The top three risk factors for males are alcohol, tobacco, and high blood pressure and for females high blood pressure, high serum cholesterol, and obesity (high BMI).[23]

▸ Brief History of the Healthcare System

Since 1991, the main focus of the healthcare system in the Russian Federation has been on transition from an integrated, hierarchical model of healthcare delivery to a more decentralized and insurance-based structure of public health care. Before the 1990s, the Soviet healthcare system was wholly financed by general government revenues.[24] The Soviet Union's total expenditure for medical care in 1960 was approximately 6.6% of GDP. It dropped to 6% in 1970 and to 5% by 1980. In principle, healthcare service was provided free to all citizens, and all health personnel were state employees. Socialized healthcare practices led to overutilization of

TABLE 14-2 Age Distribution of the Population

Population (by years of age)	People	% of total	Females per 1,000 males of a given age
Total	142,856,536	100	1,163
0–4	7,967,526	5.6	951
5–9	7,090,952	5.0	953
10–14	6,609,822	4.6	953
15–19	8,389,394	5.9	961
20–24	12,169,457	8.5	972
25–29	11,982,085	8.4	994
30–34	10,980,070	7.7	1,021
35–39	10,172,472	7.1	1,046
40–44	9,240,698	6.5	1,065
45–49	10,671,538	7.5	1,118
50–54	11,482,557	8.0	1,188
55–59	10,021,759	7.0	1,303
60–64	7,832,364	5.5	1,414
65–69	4,001,747	2.8	1,683
70–74	6,457,044	4.5	1,962
75–79	3,552,065	2.5	2,325
80–84	2,870,937	2.0	2,939
85 and older	1,329,740	0.9	4,557

Data from Federal State Statistics Service. http://www.gks.ru/free_doc/new_site/perepis2010/croc/Documents/Vol2/pub-02-02.xlsx. 2010. Accessed May 4, 2016.

hospital beds. Interestingly, control of epidemics and infectious diseases was the system's priority, which contributed to a large public health network to isolate infected patients. The Soviet system tended to underestimate the importance of primary care and placed enormous emphasis on specialists and hospital care. Despite such weaknesses, this model successfully dealt with infectious diseases, such as tuberculosis (TB), typhoid fever, and typhus. However, during the 1960s and 1970s, life expectancy and other health indicators stalled and some went into reverse. Despite doubling in the number of hospital beds and doctors per capita between 1950 and 1980, quality of care was in decline by the early 1980s. By 1991, many of the strengths of the old integrated state system had eroded as a result of general underinvestment and declining funding for prevention.[25]

Facing a deteriorating situation, Russian authorities decided to make the transition to an insurance-based system. In 1991, the Russian Federation created the

Federal Fund for Mandatory Medical Insurance (Federal'niy Fond Obayazatel'nogo Meditsinskogo Strakhovamiya, FFOMS), as well as territorial funds in each constituent region. Therefore, FFOMS funds were directed to healthcare providers through insurance companies and gave incentives both for quality patient care and efficiency.

President Vladimir Putin provided a boost to the healthcare system in the release of a report condemning inefficient healthcare delivery and mismanagement of the federal insurance fund. The report from the kremlin's government concluded that because Russia's health insurance fund received only a fifth of the funds needed to adequately sustain the system, patients are were denied "equal access to free medical services guaranteed by the state." Sergei Shishkin, senior researcher at Moscow's Institute for the Economy in Transition stated, "The Putin government is increasingly serious about overhauling health funding, which currently relies on an eclectic and inefficient mix of funds from government budgets and health insurance." Although the Russian Constitution still guarantees universal access to medical care, healthcare quality has declined since the Soviet collapse.

Anna Korotkova, head of healthcare quality research for the Russian Ministry of Health's Public Research Institute in Moscow, stated that inadequate health insurance funding is only part of the problem; recent research suggests that patients are hospitalized too long and too often for the wrong reasons. One reason is that drugs are more likely to be paid for if the patient is admitted to a hospital. Another reason is that there have not been previously effective utilization review systems to monitor lengths of stays in hospitals according to admitting diagnosis. Korotkova further stated, "Of course, we need more money for healthcare. But throwing more money at this won't solve the real problem if we don't also act to change clinical practice."[26]

The largest proportion of household spending on healthcare is payment for prescriptions. Russia's attempt to control rising prescription cost was originally designed with a combination of cost sharing and regulations. Ideally, drugs are provided to hospital patients free; however, it was intended that outpatients would have to pay for most of their prescriptions. This created a situation with unnecessary hospitalization to get prescriptions paid for. In practice, it is estimated that about 80% of inpatients pay a portion of the prescriptions. Generally hospitals, with their limited budgets, have to buy drugs through commercial contracts and therefore are very cautious with drug distribution for cost reasons. Combined with poorly enforced controls on wholesale and retail markups, this arrangement results in drugs often not being available for hospital patients unless they can pay. It is believed that a significant proportion of Russian drug needs go unmet for individuals who cannot pay for them.[8] Drugs account for an exceptionally large proportion of Russian healthcare expenditures, amounting to 30% of total healthcare spending. The high share of spending on drugs might also reflect an ingrained cultural expectation, left over from the Soviet period, that any consultation with a physician will result in a prescription.[8,27,28]

The Russian healthcare system still relies too much on specialist treatment and hospitalization. Hospital inpatient stays are common and too long. While there has been some success in changing this practice, progress has been slow. Starodubov reported that the share of healthcare expenditures devoted to inpatient services fell by only two percentage points over the preceding decade, and Russians still spend about twice as much on inpatient care as on outpatient services. About 30% of Russian physicians work in outpatient care settings, where 60% of them serve as specialists. It has been the history of Russia that primary care has been the least prestigious and least remunerated field of medicine, and the reputation of primary care physicians is low within the profession and the population. Recent substantial salary increase for primary care physicians in policlinics (about 4–6 times as much) and primary care nurses in policlinics (about 3–4 times as much) slowed down the flow of the workforce away from primary health care and helped to fill understaffed positions in policlinics.

▸ Description of the Current Healthcare System

Facilities

Russian laws passed in 1991 and 1993 transferred to local governments the federal government's responsibilities for all but a few dozen hospitals (top national centers) and established a mandatory medical insurance system.[19] There are few private providers of health care, except in large Russian cities like Moscow and Petersburg; although even there they are used by only a small elite group.

For most citizens of the Russian Federation, health care is provided by facilities managed by their regional/district administration. Most of these facilities have a service area with 15,000 to 50,000 people. A central district hospital is responsible for the administration of all facilities in the district with specialized divisions accountable to the regional health administration. The few tertiary-level facilities are owned by the federal Ministry of Health.[29] Facilities are generally not well maintained, and equipment tends to be seriously outdated. In rural areas, physicians' access to the Internet is limited.

Almost 95% of all active physicians work in the Ministry of Health while most of the remaining 5% are employed in various other ministries and industries. Most conditions of employment are defined for the whole public sector. Benefits include 24 to 36 paid holidays per year and up to 3 years of maternity leave. There are strict hierarchical regulations. Nurses are subordinate to physicians and have very little professional autonomy, while the hierarchy among physicians is even stricter, and decisions of heads of departments are hardly ever challenged.[30] While heads of hospital departments have the final say, they also have to carry the responsibility for the consequences if things go wrong.

Workforce

The Russian healthcare industry employed 7% of the working population, totaling 4.5 million people in 2000. According to RosStat, the National Committee on Statistics, medical facilities employed 3,563,000 people, rehabilitation facilities employed 300,000 people, and social care employed 372,000 people.[31]

There were 680,000 physicians in 1990, with a ratio of 4.07 per 1,000 population. Of these, 154,000 were internists, 89,000 surgeons, 69,500 pediatricians, 55,000 dentists, and 41,000 obstetricians and gynecologists. Only 1,500 physicians were trained in modern family medicine or general practice.[30] Males have been focused on the highest profile areas, such as surgery and other specialties, that earn significantly higher incomes, such as urology and gynecology, while females generally have secured positions in the first-level district facilities. The former Soviet system's medical education was rigid and centralized, lacking adequate teaching faculty familiar with world educational standards and a comprehensive vision of the role of medical education in the healthcare system and society.[32] Medical schools, even the most prestigious and high-quality ones in Moscow and Saint Petersburg, were generally freestanding institutions and not affiliated with a university.[33] The collapse of the Soviet Union left Russia unprepared to operate a system of medical education that would come close to Western educational standards. Various institutions from abroad are now being launched to help overhaul and modernize that outmoded system.[34]

Over the past couple decades, the countries from central and Eastern Europe have been discarding the Russian health system. Development of a new model of general practice began in the 1980s with pilot projects in Saint Petersburg, Kemerovo, and Samara.[35] A new training curriculum was developed at the federal level, allowing regional variations; training centers were established, often with the help from international donors. The first general practice cohort was trained in 1992. The adoption of the new model based on general practice sought to strengthen primary care to counteract excessive specialization,[36] although other factors were also at work. There was a political imperative to converge with western European models, which were somewhat influential, arguing that radical change would be easier than reforming the entrenched present model. The second stage of increasing the number of generalist was the transformation of existing specialists into generalists by retraining them in primary care medicine. However, some Russian critics argued that the transformation of specialists into generalists was problematic and demotivating, requiring a major investment in training and institutional change. Others stated that the newly trained staff often became isolated, leading to two disconnected models of care with fundamental structural problems being ignored.[37] On the other hand, family practice has been implemented successfully in some areas of Russia where there has been a coherent reform framework, with institutional support and consistent incentives.[38] Which model is best remains a subject of debate, although the general practice model has been universally implemented, with little testing of alternatives.

The organization of primary care in Russian cities and district levels is delivered in policlinics, whereas, in rural areas it is mostly delivered in small primary care practices staffed by *feldshers* (physician assistants). Russia has four categories of policlinics: for adults, mothers and children, women (*zhenskie konsuljtatsii*), and people with specific disorders (such as TB, sexually transmitted disease, mental disorders, and addiction). Policlinics are staffed by district physicians, both specialists and generalists, who are responsible for a geographically defined population of approximately 1,700 people. The clinic "specialists" are cardiologists, pulmonologists, gastroenterologists, pediatricians, obstetricians, gynecologists, otolaryngologists, etc. However, the patients are mostly seen by general practice physicians. There are also parallel systems serving the employees of some ministries and industries. The small private sector consists mainly of general practice and outpatient specialists. Policlinic staff provides only basic treatment and little gatekeeping or follow-up, and these clinics are often bypassed, with patients seeking hospital care through formal or informal channels.[39]

The largest share of new general practitioners (75%) returned to medical practice after training in traditional district policlinics and in outpatient facilities linked to industries (5%). Both types of facilities are mainly in urban areas. The real problem is that only 8% of the new general practitioners trained in policlinics and outpatient facilities returned to practice in rural facilities, although 27% of the population is rural.[40] One can see that the rural area is very much underserved by the number of new general practitioners seeking medical practice in this setting. Only 6% of the newly trained general practitioners went into independent practices or private facilities in suburban areas; and for another 6%, the destinations were unknown. New general practitioners reported that they faced major barriers in applying what they learned, faced opposition from senior physicians, unreformed financial structures and scarce equipment. Most general practitioners are paid salaries, although four regions are experimental sites that have introduced other methods. Many show enthusiasm for a shift to capitation payments and per procedure payments. Still, many comment on huge discrepancies between the average monthly income of general practitioners in state and private primary care facilities (a discrepancy of about 57 times).

A Soviet-style control still functions relating to salaries. Salaries are different by a unified salary scale regulating all salaries in the public sector. A distinguishing feature of the Russian healthcare system is that in reality physicians' one-full-time-effort (1.0 FTE) workday does not exceed 8.0 hours, and some specialists in policlinics have 6.5 hour workdays (1.0 FTE). Because of very low physician pay, this arrangement enables them to work in more than one place.[30] Some even subsidize their income by being taxi drivers at night. There was no noticeable decline in healthcare professionals from 1990 to 2000, except for nursing.

There was a significant decline of nurses in the 1990s from 1,844,000 to 1,611,700. Of these, 65.0% were general nurses, 10.0% midwives, 10.0% nurse practitioners, and less than 5.0% specialized in clinical operations. The Ministry of Health indicates that 99.0% of nurses in the Russian Federation are women. Most of these nurses (74.4%) work in inpatient facilities, and there is a disparity in number of nurses between rural and urban areas.

The health managers in the Russian health system are physicians. The director of regional and any major federal health management and financing organizations are almost exclusively physicians. Most often, they continue their clinical practice. There is only one regular health management program for nonphysicians, and it offers two years of training in health management and public health. However, many new graduates of the program are not attracted by working conditions in the government healthcare sector because they cannot compete for positions historically held by physicians.

Implementation of primary care reform in Russia has proven difficult and slow. The scale of the task has been underestimated, given the overwhelming estimated need for 90,000 general practitioners, with only about 2,500 trained so far,[41] which is only adequate for about 35% of the population. This demonstrates how difficult it will be for Russia to provide basic healthcare services both in suburban and rural areas in the future. Russia is not, however, unique in failing to understand the scale of the task and its long-term consequences. Their European counterparts have the same physician shortage issue, but not at the same scale as Russia. The broad, federal legislature framework provides no detailed guidance on the roles and responsibilities of general practitioners and their relationship with specialists. General practitioners have little opportunity to use their new skills. There is also little evidence of meaningful integration into the healthcare system, with the persisting hierarchy and hospital-dominated system leading to demoralization.[39] Yet the new model seems popular with patients, as has been noted in other former communist countries.[42]

Technology and Equipment

There is inadequate information related to technology and equipment in medical facilities both in suburban and rural areas of Russia. What is known is that there are significant disparities of high technology available in policlinics and hospitals throughout the country. Smaller policlinics and hospitals, particularly in rural areas, experience the greatest shortage of technology and medical equipment. However, EMI and CAT scanners are typically available in large healthcare facilities in the urban areas.

▸ Evaluation of the Health System

Cost

In the Soviet Union, the majority of healthcare services were constitutionally free of charge for its citizens.[43] In fact, the Soviet Union was the first nation that guaranteed a wide range of free medical care for the entire population.[8] The healthcare system was uniform, with the government responsible for managing and financing health care at every level (republic, oblast, and local), and it was funded from general revenues (state tax-financed model).[8] However, despite the stated goals of comprehensiveness and equitable access for the entire population, the Soviet Union did not have sufficient resources to implement the strategy. The system was hospital dominated, and policies were oriented toward expansion of medical services. For instance, budget allocations for hospitals were based on the number of beds and hospital personnel, thus creating an incentive to fill beds.[44] Consequently, the healthcare sector was severely underfunded, inefficient, and offered low-quality services.[8,45] At the beginning of the 1990s, the Russian Federation was the only industrialized country in which the population's life expectancy and other basic health indicators had significantly deteriorated.[46,47] There was a growing realization that Russia's healthcare system was in deep crisis and that it had to be reformed.[44,47–49]

Russian reformers decided to address the problem mainly through reform of healthcare financing and mandatory health insurance.[47,49,50] The key goals of the reform were to continue providing comprehensive medical coverage for the entire population by bringing additional nonbudgetary funds into health care and thus strengthening health care's financial basis; to shift away from the previous method of central government planning, management, and financing; and to improve healthcare efficiency and quality by introducing financial incentives for healthcare providers, insurers, and pateints.[8,35,47,49,51,52] The reform also intended to focus on primary health care by attracting the most competent doctors to this sector. The objective was to encourage primary care providers to treat patients on an outpatient basis in an ambulatory setting instead of giving referrals to hospitals,[8] thereby reducing hospitalizations, increasing efficiency, and improving quality of medical care.[35,53]

The law on Health Insurance of Citizens in the Russian Federation was passed in 1991, and mandatory health insurance was introduced in 1993. The law stipulated that the majority of healthcare funds were to be raised by regional/territorial governments.[24] It required employers and territorial governments to make contributions to one of the territorial mandatory health insurance funds (MHIFs) located in the oblasts/territories of the Russian Federation. MHIFs are not-for-profit, independent entities responsible for managing healthcare finance at the oblast (territory) level and accountable to the respective government. Employers had to contribute 3.6% of their payroll costs (with no matching employee contribution) to the MHIFs. From those funds, 3.4% was retained at the territorial level and was used mainly for the services provided by territorial and local health authorities (HAs). The remaining 0.2% was transferred to the Federal Mandatory Health Insurance Fund in Moscow for equalization purposes (to subsidize poorer territories). MHIFs had to transfer the retained funds (3.4%) to private health insurance companies (in the territories where they existed) based on a weighted capitation formula. Oblast/territorial governments had to cover medical expenses for the nonworking segments of the population, such as children, students, the retired or unemployed, and individuals on disability, by paying contributions to respective MHIFs. According to the law, mandatory health insurance could be supplemented with voluntary (private) insurance if patients wanted a higher level of healthcare services and could afford to purchase private insurance.[47] Employers could also purchase private health insurance for their employees for services not covered by mandatory health insurance.[8]

The system was intended to facilitate market mechanisms by introducing a third-party payer (health insurance companies) and by relying on competition between healthcare insurers and providers. Private health insurance companies had the incentive to select efficient healthcare health care providers who delivered high-quality health services; insurers had to compete for contracts with MHIFs, thus creating incentive to improve health service quality.[54] Physicians and healthcare facilities competed for contracts with health insurers and had the incentive to deliver high-quality, low-cost service; patients had freedom of choice among healthcare providers and insurers.[8]

The law allowed healthcare providers to supplement their income by redeploying some resources, selling services to private patients, and contracting with enterprises for the provision of services to their employees.[55] Hence, there were formal/legal payments (through a cash register) for privately delivered care and extra services (*chargeable* health services). Chargeable services could be provided by healthcare facilities only if they had special permission from a corresponding HA. Chargeable services could include some diagnostic and treatment services, as well as orthopedic and dental prostheses.[51]

However, Russia's implementation of universal health insurance was extremely challenging.[45,55] The key obstacle was the failure to get sufficient financial resources for reform implementation.[55] Government allocations to health care had been falling steadily since the introduction of the reform.[56] Between 2000 and 2012, government healthcare funding as a percentage of total government expenditures decreased from 12.7% to 8.9%.[57] Additionally, the proposed reform was structurally and managerially complex. A combination of old and new financial arrangements, wide variations in reform execution in different territories, poor coordination and ill-defined responsibilities among major stakeholders in healthcare finance, as well as failure to introduce competition among insurance companies, also contributed to slow and incomplete implementation.[50] Furthermore, in some territories the new financing mechanisms were not introduced at all, and in other territories the new system was introduced only in some districts. Finally, many Russians did not understand mandatory health insurance and were not motivated to participate in it.[58] According to a survey of practicing managers in the mid-1990s, the reform was unfinished and defective.[49]

At present, the healthcare system in Russia is characterized by a mixed structure of formal and informal (out-of-pocket) financing.[59] The formal funds come from two major sources: government revenues from general taxation (federal, territorial, and municipal governmental budgets) and employer contributions (percentage of gross salary) to MHIFs.[60] The Program of State Guarantees for Free of Charge Medical Care for Citizens provides a list of free services for the population. The Guaranteed Package has two parts: the basic MHIF package and the package financed from budgetary sources. Core federal programs, such as immunizations, TB, and medical technology development are financed nationally from the federal budget. Each year the Ministry of Health and the Ministry of Finance develop a national healthcare budget, revise, and update the Guaranteed Package for the following year.[59]

The second major source of financing is payments from MHIFs. MHIFs' budgets are developed using the insurance premiums from the employers. In January 2011 employer contributions increased to 5.1% of total gross salary with 2.1% going to the federal MHIF and 3% to territorial MHIFs.[61] The new law also provided for the centralization of MHIF contributions at the federal level; thus, all health insurance contributions from the territories for the nonworking populations now belong to the federal MHIF. A territorial MHIF only manages federal MHIF resources to implement the MHIF's basic program in that territory.[59] Territories pay contributions from their own budgets to their respective MHIFs for the nonworking populations.[61]

These two major funding sources are sometimes supplemented by direct contracts between companies and healthcare providers. Additionally, the healthcare system gets allocations from other state ministries: for instance, the Ministry of Finance does not only transfer budget funds to the Ministry of Health but also transfers funds for social purposes directly to oblasts/territories.[47] The territories then decide independently how much of the transfers to allocate to health care, education, and other social services. Territories subsequently transfer funds to regions, which also decide independently how to allocate the funds.[8] The funds transferred from the Ministry of Finance are typically used for capital investments for hospitals, such as facility repairs and buying equipment, for building special facilities such as psychiatric hospitals and maternal hospitals, and for funding federal healthcare facilities.[47]

The other significant funding source for health care is private payments from individuals.[56] A few studies confirm that there has been a dramatic increase in private payment for health services since the early 2000s. According to the *World Health Report 2015*, private payment for health, as a percentage of the total health expenditure in Russia, increased from 40.1% to 48.9% between 2000 and 2012. During the same time, out-of-pocket payments (as a proportion of the total private expenditure on health) increased from 74.7% to 92.0%.[57] A study found that the total costs for health care and medications represented 17.0% of the annual per capita GDP in Russia in 2010. While 19.0% and 5.7% of the study participants had to pay for outpatient and inpatient care (respectively), the out-of-pocket payment for drugs represented the largest expense for 70.4% of the participants.[62]

Vulnerable population groups are particularly at risk concerning high out-of-pocket expenses. A 2010 study found that Russians in poor health were at much higher risk of large out-of-pocket expenses compared with those in good health.[63] Specifically, 33% of study participants in poor health and 14% of respondents in good health had high out-of-pocket expenses. The high medication costs may be explained by the collapse of the Soviet pharmaceutical industry in 1991. Now Russia is dependent on imported Western brand drugs, which are often much more expensive.[64]

Some of the private payments are paid formally/legally (for chargeable services), while others are paid informally/illegally (under the table). Informal payments for health services are commonplace in Russia.[62,65] Paulina Aarva and colleagues reported in 2009 that 8.4% of their study respondents paid informally for primary care consultations and treatment services.[65] They concluded that the high level of informal payments (14.5% in the whole sample) could be explained by the lack of transparency in the current management system and clear payment rules. A recent study, by European and Russian researchers, of Russian pediatric hospitals found that although hospitalizations were officially free for admitted children, their parents often had to buy expensive medications and give them to attending physicians to treat their children, because hospitals did not have necessary medications.[66] The study found that hospital care was characterized by unnecessary use of multiple drugs and the costs were passed onto patients and their families. Hence, out-of-pocket expenditures for some allegedly free-of-charge healthcare services are becoming a common practice in Russia.[55,56,64,66] Interestingly, Russian patients consider gifts to doctors (flowers, alcohol, books, etc.) nothing more than necessary "little tokens of appreciation."[67]

The role of private health insurance is still negligible in Russia.[68] In fact, it decreased from 8.1% to 4.2% of the total private health expenditures between 2000 and 2012.[57] It is also significant that private health insurance policies are usually bought by employers and not by individuals.[59]

The exact amount of financial resources spent on health care in Russia is unknown because of incomplete reporting of financial flows.[8] It is also due to the fact that territories now have more control and independence in resource allocation. Territorial healthcare budgets amount to about 45% of healthcare financing and have also significantly declined since the inception of the reform.[8] According to a recent report, for the first time, MHIFs accounted for 51% of total health expenditures in 2015.[69]

According to the health insurance law, healthcare providers in Russia can be paid in a number of ways, including capitation, fee-for-service, diagnosis related groups (DRGs), global budgets, or a combination of methods. Each territory decides independently on a preferred method of payment.[56,59] Tariffs on healthcare services covered by mandatory health insurance are determined by territorial governments, insurance companies, and professional medical associations and are stipulated in the contracts between healthcare providers and MHIFs/insurance companies.[59] MHIFs transfer funds to competing insurance companies (in territories where they exist) using a weighted capitation formula to address the issue of different medical costs for different population groups. MHIFs make direct payments to healthcare providers in territories where insurance companies do not exist.[47]

In summary, despite an increase in healthcare spending in Russia,[70] it is still lagging behind industrialized countries in healthcare financing. Total pay and social insurance funds in Russia are 75%–83% less than the average in the Organisation for Economic Co-operation and Development countries; it is also estimated that the amount of money for medical care is 40%–50% less than the minimum necessary amount.[58] Continuous funding shortages and cost escalation resulted in higher out-of-pocket payments,[57] which have increased dramatically, especially payments for pharmaceuticals.[8]

Primary and Secondary Care Financing

Different payment methods may be used to reimburse providers, including capitation, number of visits, and payments for specific procedures, the complexity of which provides medical professional with incentive to treat patients on an outpatient basis instead of referring them to hospitals. Healthcare providers may or may not enter into contracts with local insurance companies to be compensated for the volume of provided services. Typically, they also receive considerable amounts of funding from the local government[8]; specifically, a local HA receives its budget from its respective government and allocates fixed budgets (on a per capita basis) to MHIFs for payment to policlinics.[47]

Hospital Financing

Budget allocations for hospitals have typically been based on the number of beds and hospital staff. However, hospitals are experimenting with various payment methods; according to one study,[71] in some territories at the time of the study hospitals were using five different payment methods simultaneously, such as DRGs and global budgets. Igor Sheiman analyzed trends in hospital payment in Russia and found that DRG payment had increased by 8% within a few previous years.[71] According to another study, new hospital payment methods in territories where they were introduced amounted to about one-third of hospital revenues. The remaining two-thirds comes from territories' budgets, is based on traditional payment methods, and still remains retrospective.[8]

In territories where insurance companies are active, they negotiate with hospitals a system of case payments (a type of DRG payments), which specify adequate lengths of stay, appropriate treatments, and procedures expected for each case for a given diagnosis. Insurers typically pay hospitals on a case-by-case basis and then retrospectively bill a respective MHIF for reimbursement for each item. Hence, insurers do not create incentives for inpatient facilities to reduce volume, cost of care, or unnecessary treatments. Thus, the insurers' role is claims processing, which may provide an incentive for insurers to collide with hospitals in billing MHIFs' maximum possible amounts.[8] There are some indications that Russian hospitals are persistently underfunded. For instance, a federal initiative to ban "chargeable services" in public hospitals failed to gain support from providers, as the majority of hospitals would go out of business. The amount of "chargeable" hospital services for the public is increasing and represents an estimated 50%–100% of budgetary funding.[72]

Healthcare Personnel Compensation

The vast majority of healthcare providers work in the public sector: they are employed by a respective level of government and paid salaries. Basic salary levels are determined by the hours or shifts to be worked, the number of patients, or the responsibilities. Basic salary levels may also reflect professional qualification and experience. Healthcare personnel are also paid performance-based bonuses.[8,59]

There is not much difference between how primary care doctors and specialists are reimbursed. However, there are more opportunities for specialists and hospitalists to improve their clinical expertise and have higher workloads. Thus, they tend to have slightly higher salaries.[8] Medical doctors and nurses continue to be underpaid: in 2001 the average pay was 61% of the national average and 54% of the hospital industry average.[56] However, official numbers may be quite misleading considering the extensive illegal payments to physicians and nurses; these under-the-table payments may considerably supplement their official salaries.[8]

The private healthcare sector appears to use a variety of approaches to reimburse physicians. They often pay a physician a share of profits in addition to a basic salary. Physicians offering private consultations charge a fee for service. If they work out of a clinic, they may keep a significant amount of the fee.[8,59]

Public Health in Russia

In the Soviet Union, public health service was based on the sanitary-epidemiological system that applied to the entire country. The system carried out traditional public health roles, such as environmental health and epidemiological control.[73] Public health was traditionally oriented toward curative health services, which still receive less attention and resources than funding of clinical care and healthcare providers. The majority of funds are allocated to clinical interventions, and health insurance companies pay mainly for hospitalizations and physician visits. In fact, 60% of all healthcare funding goes to hospitals.[72] Consequently, public health activities are often ill focused and underfunded.

Public health continues to be highly centralized and hierarchical.[74] Most of the activities related to disease prevention and health promotion are controlled and directly financed by the Ministry of Health. There are also other industries involved in public health financing. For instance, the Ministry of Labor and Social Development covers certain prevention activities for the working population. It provides vouchers for sanatoriums, health resources, and children's summer camps. The vouchers are then sold for a reduced price to employees and their families.[73]

Local public health agencies are severely understaffed with staff levels meeting 60%–70% of the demand.[53] HAs and health insurance companies are managed by physicians who sometimes may underestimate prevention requirements. Additionally, there is very limited collaboration between the curative and preventive parts of the healthcare system.[73]

Consequently, the healthcare system is not effective enough in addressing current health problems,[74] including the lowest male life expectancy in Europe,[46,75] low birth rates and high infant mortality rates, cardiovascular diseases, alcoholism, TB, HIV/AIDS, road accidents, suicides, and a resultant demographic crisis.[58] The grim situation is exacerbated by the reappearance of communicable diseases that were practically eliminated (e.g., syphilis and poliomyelitis) or effectively controlled in the former Soviet Union.[76]

Quality

According to the World Bank, infant mortality rate (the probability of dying under the age of one) was 8 per 1,000 live births between 2011 and 2015, an improvement compared with 19 deaths per 1,000 live births in the early 2000s.[77] Maternal mortality decreased from 40 to 25 per 100,000 during the same period.[77,78]

A study assessed quality of care in pediatric hospitals in Russia using a standard World Health Organization assessment tool and found that the quality of care is insufficient due to the lack of modern treatment technologies, facilities, and medications.[66] The study also found that the typical quality problems were over hospitalization, over diagnosis, and resultant overmedication. These conclusions are in line with Sheiman's estimate that about one-third of all hospitalized patients at any time could be treated on an outpatient basis.[71] Other major quality-related issues are a lack of evidence-based approaches in clinical decision making, organization of medical care, and disincentives for efficient medicine.[66]

Consequently, many Russians are dissatisfied with the accessibility and quality of medical care, the inability to choose a physician, long lines in outpatient facilities, insufficient compassion from healthcare personnel, and insufficient protection against low-quality health care. A recent study reported that only 47% of the surveyed geriatric patients were satisfied or highly satisfied with outpatient care.[79] For about 62% of respondents, it was difficult to get an appointment with a specialist; long waiting time in the clinic waiting area was an issue for 42% of respondents, and about 33% of participants were dissatisfied with poor registration and reception processes. According to another study, all respondents from different territories of Russia reported deterioration in quality of care.[80] The respondents also thought that the most important healthcare quality problems were high costs, unavailability of medications, quality of hospital facilities, and information given to patients. In the same study, about 25% of respondents were convinced that quality deteriorated after the reforms were introduced. Another patient survey shows that about 74% of the population believes that either the availability of medical care had decreased or there was no change in the situation since the inception of the reform.[81]

Some recent studies report that the quality of health services in Russia has improved since the early 2000s. For instance, Footman and colleagues found a significant reduction in the number of Russians who had to forgo medicines for financial reasons between 2001 and 2010.[64] Another study reported that one study participant who shared her recent birthing experience said, "I think that the health care in our country has gotten much better when I compare it to the stories of my mother and older relatives."[82(p241)] Vasquez and colleagues interviewed HIV-infected individuals in Saint Petersburg and found that about 88% of patients were satisfied with the quality of health services for HIV.[83]

Access

A recent empirical study conducted in eight countries of the former Soviet Union in 2010, found that access to primary care near patients' home was maintained in Russia.[62] The study also found that geographical access was not a barrier to access medical care, as transportation was usually very affordable. Another study suggested that there were some improvements between 2001 and 2010.[64] Another study found that access to inpatient care in Russian pediatric hospitals was generally good and that the majority of pregnant women had access to health care.[66]

Officially, high-quality free health care should be available for everyone in the nation. In reality, healthcare quality varies considerably. There are elite medical institutions that are typically accessible for a limited number of well-connected individuals; for the average patient, access to health care is notoriously poor.[56,58] There is also a widening gap among social groups regarding healthcare access and availability.

Additionally, the distribution of healthcare funds between rural and urban areas is worsening. While large urban areas are doing relatively well, rural areas are severely underfunded, and these inequities are getting worse.[8] For example, the number of healthcare facilities in rural locations decreased by more than 60% and the number of hospitals decreased by 86% from 2000 to 2008.[72] Wealthier urban households have much better access to affordable medications than poorer, rural households.[64] Many Russians have to pay under the table to get adequate medical assistance or necessary medication.[84]

It should be emphasized that access to health care and insurance mostly depends on employment status of an individual and on geographic location. While by Russian law no one can be denied urgent/hospital care, individuals must be registered with the territory of their residence to be assigned to a policlinic and have access to primary healthcare services. Consequently, marginalized and hard-to-reach groups—such as migrant, temporary, and informal workers—have inadequate or no access to primary health care.[54]

▸ Current and Emerging Issues and Challenges

Since the early 1990s, the Russian Federation has been undergoing major healthcare reforms. It became a challenge for many people to accept the adaptation of the field of medicine to the free market, which was the major goal of the reforms.[24,52,80,85] While some healthcare professionals believed that the reforms constituted a way to a sustainable health system, others believed that the reforms were ruining rather than strengthening Russian health care.

A growing demand for additional healthcare management education has been observed not only among administrators but also among practicing physicians.[86] Appropriate effort should be made to meet this demand.

Decentralization of healthcare regulation was supposed to make expenditures of healthcare budgets more effective. However, lack of federal control made it possible for some local authorities to spend money on building new expensive healthcare facilities and purchasing high-tech medical equipment based on political motivations, without considering availability of similar facilities and/or equipment already available in the geographic area. This resulted in heterogeneity of opinions expressed by major healthcare system stakeholders (including patients, healthcare professionals, hospital administrators, Federal and Territorial MHIFs, insurance companies, and employers), ranging from supporting the ongoing reforms to suggestions to return to previously existing system of socialized medicine.

Both chief medical officers (CMOs, a.k.a. chief doctors or head doctors—*glavniy vrach*—the top executive administrator, holding an MD, in charge of the hospital) and directors of regional MHIFs agreed that 3.6% employer payroll tax for health insurance was too low and should be increased up to about 8.0%.[45] Nevertheless, a 10.8% employers' contribution proposed in 1991 was not approved.[85]

As compared to hospital CMOs, regional MHIF directors tend to be stronger supporters of the healthcare reforms. Directors express stronger support to healthcare cost-decreasing measures, such as reduction of inpatient length of stay and shifting a substantial portion of inpatient health care to an outpatient basis.[45] While regional MHIFs directors tend to consider the mandatory health insurance system's performance as satisfactory, hospital CMOs are rather dissatisfied with the administrative expenses of the insurance system and tend to consider MHIFs and insurance companies as money-wasting middle men. CMOs are also unhappy about administrative limitations prohibiting them from shifting financial resources among designated hospital budget lines, such as medications, salaries, and utilities. While many CMOs are market minded, some of them are holdovers of Soviet-era socialized medicine.

The initiation of healthcare reform in the 1990s was accompanied with a substantial 33% decrease in expenditures on health care, observed from 1991 to 1998. In 1991, 100% of healthcare financing was from the state budget. Compared to 1991 (100%), by 2001 the level of healthcare financing dropped to 67%, of which 51% of financing was from the state budget and 16% was from mandatory health insurance contributions.[87] Generally, there has been a broad agreement among major stake holders that substantial improvement of the health system would require additional financial resources to supplement ongoing structural reforms.

Population decline remains a serious problem faced by the Russian Federation since the early 1990s. Male mortality in the Russian Federation is higher than in most other countries with similar per capita income.[88,89]

Emergence of infectious diseases, especially TB and HIV/AIDS, poses a challenge for the Russian health system. During the period of the last decade of the 20th century, TB rates in the country doubled, and multiple drug resistance has become a special concern.[90,91] The extent of the problem led to the federal law On Prevention of the Spread of TB in the Russian Federation, signed in 2001. Long-term inpatient TB treatment is still a common practice in the country, and the implementation of the Directly Observed Treatment Short Course (DOTS) is a challenging task, especially for remote regions of the Russian Federation.[92,93]

HIV/AIDS is another challenge. While only 2% of people living with HIV live in Russia (compared to 18% who live in South Africa and 4% who live in the United States), the UNAIDS's 2014 estimates of the proportion of new HIV infections by country indicate a higher proportion for Russia (4%) than for the United States (2%), while still much lower than for South Africa (16%).[94]

In the Russian Federation, HIV prevalence was estimated to be over 5% in the intravenous drug users group; it was estimated to be below 1% in pregnant urban women (2005).[95] Activities of NGOs working in the HIV/AIDS field are focused mostly on the problem of prevention among high-risk groups that are difficult for traditional public health institutes to contact.[95]

Noncommunicable diseases and injuries constituted the top ten causes of death in the country, accounting for about 70% of total mortality (2007).[89] Cardiovascular diseases, cancer, and injuries account for about 78% of mortality among the working-age population; as for the risk factors, high blood pressure, high serum cholesterol levels, and smoking constitute three leading risk factors contributing to over 75% of total mortality.[89,96]

The International Monetary Fund (IMF) report points out that the current system is excessively complicated for healthcare financing.[13] According to the IMF, the budget constraints for the MHIFs and the funds' incentives to monitor healthcare providers are compromised by a complicated financing system that combines federal and regional budget financing with the federal and regional health insurance funds. The competition among insurance companies is not sufficient because most of healthcare providers are operated by the local authorities, and insurers are typically chosen by employers without substantial consideration of the formers' performance by the latter. As a result, insurance companies bear relatively small risks while creating an extra 3% of administrative costs by acting as middle men.[13] The IMF report emphasizes that "healthcare financing could be simplified and made more incentive compatible" and points out that the Russian healthcare system could benefit from outcome-based (rather than input-based) financing and performance pay.[13]

Pharmaceutical shortage has been another challenge that emerged in the 1990s due to changes in the economic relationship between the Eastern European countries. Historically, the Soviet Union relied substantially on pharmaceuticals manufactured in those then communist countries; it did not develop its own large pharmaceutical industry. For commercial reasons, the Western drug companies that began expansion into the Russian pharmaceutical market in the early 1990s prefer to sell more expensive proprietary (brand) medications rather than lower priced generics. The IMF points out very high medication spending and recommends progressive co-payments to be put in place to control it.[13] Overall, citizens' advocacy groups and NGOs are less active in the Russian Federation than in Western countries.

Compared to other regions of the Russian Federation, the population health status situation in the North Caucasus region, where incidents of violent attacks against law enforcement occur, is more challenging. Access to health care in the region is limited, and the quality of health care compares unfavorably to other regions.[97] The WHO contributed to capacity building, especially to "primary health care in the areas of mother and child health, HIV/AIDS, TB, mental health services, and psychosocial rehabilitation."[97]

References

1. RosStat. Federal State Statistics Service. Population. 2015. http://www.gks.ru/free_doc/new_site/population/demo/demo11.xls. Accessed April 19, 2016.
2. Russian Census 2010, vol. 4. Nationality, languages, citizenship. http://www.gks.ru/free_doc/new_site/perepis2010/croc/perepis_itogi1612.htm. Accessed April 30, 2016.
3. Constitutional Court of the Russian Federation. 2016. http://www.ksrf.ru/ru/Info/Pages/default.aspx. Accessed April 28, 2016.
4. Ministry of Justice. Political parties. 2016. http://minjust.ru/nko/gosreg/partii/spisok. Accessed May 4, 2016.
5. World Bank. *Russian Economic Report No. 15*; 2007. http://siteresources.worldbank.org/INTRUSSIANFEDERATION/Resources/RER15_Eng.pdf. Accessed April 27, 2016.
6. Grinberg R. Russian fuel and energy sector: dynamics and prospects. In: Broadman H, Paas T, Welfens J, eds. *Economic Liberalization and Integration Policy: Options for Eastern Europe and Russia*. Berlin: Springer-Verlag. 2006:171–184.
7. Libman A. Russia's integration into the world economy: an interjurisdictional competition view. In: Broadman H, Paas T, Welfens J, eds. *Economic Liberalization and Integration Policy: Options for Eastern Europe and Russia*. Berlin: Springer-Verlag. 2006:334–348.
8. Tragakes E, Lessof S. *Healthcare Systems in Transition: Russian Federation*. The European Observatory on Health Systems and Policies. Copenhagen: 2003(5–3).
9. World Bank. World DataBank. Gross domestic product 2014. databank.worldbank.org/data/download/GDP.pdf. Published 2016. Accessed May 2, 2016.
10. World Bank. GDP at market prices (current U.S. dollars). 2007. http://data.worldbank.org/indicator/NY.GDP.MKTP.CD?order=wbapi_data_value_2007±wbapi_data_value&sort=desc&page=1. Published 2016. Accessed May 5, 2016.
11. International Monetary Fund. *Russian Federation: Statistical Appendix No*. Washington, DC; 2006.
12. World Bank. *Russia Economic Report No. 33*. Moscow; 2015.
13. International Monetary Fund. *Russian Federation: Selected Issues No. 07/352*. Washington, DC; 2007.
14. RosStat. Federal State Statistics Service. Wages. 2015. http://www.gks.ru/wps/wcm/connect/rosstat_main/rosstat/ru/statistics/wages/. Published 2016. Accessed April 18, 2016.
15. RosStat. Federal State Statistics Service. Labor Force. 2015. http://www.gks.ru/free_doc/new_site/population/trud/trud6.xls. Published 2016. Accessed April 16, 2016.
16. RosStat. Federal State Statistics Service. Transport and Communication. Length of transport lines. 2014. http://www.gks.ru/free_doc/new_site/business/trans-sv/prot.xls. Published 2015. Accessed April 25, 2016.
17. Schmidt G. Russian Federation. In: Horner W, Dobert H, Von Kopp B, Mitter W, eds. *The Education Systems of Europe*. Dordrecht, The Netherlands: Springer; 2007:646–668.
18. UNESCO. *Handbook on Diplomas, Degrees and Other Certificates in Higher Education in Asia and the Pacific*. 2nd ed. United Nations Educational, Scientific and Cultural Organization; 2004.
19. RosStat. Federal State Statistics Service. Education. 2010. http://www.gks.ru/free_doc/new_site/perepis2010/croc/Documents/Vol3/pub-03-01.xlsx. Accessed April 12, 2016.
20. World Bank. Gini Index. 2012. http://data.worldbank.org/indicator/SI.POV.GINI. Accessed May 4, 2016.
21. World Bank. Poverty gap at $3.10 a day. http://data.worldbank.org/indicator/SI.POV.GAP2/countries. Published 2011. Accessed May 5, 2016.
22. Russian Public Opinion Research Center. *Religion in Our Life Press-Release No. 789*. Moscow; 2007.
23. World Health Organization. Highlights on health in the Russian Federation. http://www.euro.who.int/__data/assets/pdf_file/0003/103593/E88405.pdf. Published 2005. Accessed April 30, 2016.
24. Burger E, Field M, Twigg J. From assurance to insurance in Russian health care: the problematic transition. *Am J Public Health*. 1998;88(5):755–758.
25. Schroeder G. Denton ME. An Index of Consumption in the USSR. In: *USSR: Measures of Economic Growth and Development*. Joint Economic Committee. Washington, DC; 1982.
26. Webster P. Russia hunts for funds for ailing health service. *The Lancet*. 2003;361(9356):498.
27. Karnitski G. *Health Care Systems in Transition: Belarus*. European Observatory on Health Care Systems. Copenhagen; 1997.
28. Hovhannisyan SG, Tragakes S, Lessof H, Aslanian H, Mkrtchayan A. *Health Care Systems in Transition: Armenia*. European Observatory on Health Care Systems. Copenhagen; 2001.
29. Chernichovsky D, Polapchik E. Genuine federalism in the Russian healthcare system: changing roles of government. *J Health Polit Polic*. 1999;24(1):115–144.
30. Danishevski K. Russian Federation. In: Rechel B, Dubois C, McKee M, eds. *The Health Care Workforce in Europe*. United Kingdom: Cromwell Press. 2006:101–114.
31. Goskomstat. *Zdravoohranenie v Rossii*. Moscow, National Committee on Statistics; 2001.
32. Barr DA, Schmid R. Medical education in the former Soviet Union. *Acad Med*. 1996;71(2).

33. Ryan M. *Doctors and the State in the Soviet Union*. New York, NY: St. Martin's Press; 1990.
34. Barr D, Field M. The current state of health care in the former Soviet Union: implications for health care policy and reform. *Am J Public Health*. 1996;86(3):307–312.
35. Sheiman I. New methods of financing and managing health care in the Russian Federation. *Health Policy*. 1995; 32(1–3): 167–180.
36. Reamy J, Gedik G. Health human resource reform in Tajikistan: part of a master plan for change. *Cah Sociol Demogr Med*. 2001;41:327–45.
37. Sharbarova Z. Primary health care in the NIS: history and current situation. An overview. *American International Health*. www.aiha.com/resource/Html/zoya.htm. Published 2001. Accessed December, 2007.
38. McEuen M. *The pilot process: case study on piloting complex health reforms in Kyrgyzstan*. Abt Associates. www.phrplus.org/Pubs/Tech036_fin.pdf. Published 2004. Accessed December, 2007.
39. Rese A, Balabanova D, McKee M, Sheaff R. Implementing general practice in Russia: getting beyond the first steps. *BMJ*. 2005;331(7510):204–207.
40. Goskomstat. *Population census of the Russian Federation*. Moscow: Goskomstat, www.perepis2002.ru/index.tml?id=11. Published 2002. Accessed December 2007.
41. Ministry of Health. *Indicators of health and health care*. MoH: Moscow; 2003.
42. Kersnik J. An evaluation of patient satisfaction with family practice care in Slovenia. *Int J Qual Health Care*. 2000;12:143–147.
43. Constitution of the Russian Federation. http://www.constitution.ru/en/10003000-01.htm. Published 1993. Accessed October 16, 2016.
44. Tkatchenko E, McKee M, Tsouros AD. Public health in Russia: the view from the inside. *Health Policy Plans*. 2000;15(2):164–169.
45. Twigg J. Health care reform in Russia: a survey of head doctors and insurance administrators. *Soc Sci Med*. 2002;55(12):2253–2265.
46. Atun R. The health crisis in Russia. *BMJ*. 2005;331(7530): 1418–1419.
47. Sinuraya T. Decentralization of the health care system and territorial medical insurance coverage in Russia: friend or foe? *Euro J Health L*. 2000;7:15–27.
48. Danishevski K, McKee M. Reforming the Russian health-care system. *Lancet*. 2005;365(9464):1012–1014.
49. Twigg JL. Obligatory medical insurance in Russia: the participants' perspective. *Soc Sci Med*. 1999;49(3):371–382.
50. Shishkin S. Problems of transition from tax-based system of health care finance to mandatory health insurance model in Russia. *Croat Med J*. 1999; 40(2):195–201.
51. Danishevski K, Balabanova D, McKee M, Atkins S. The fragmentary federation: experiences with the decentralized health system in Russia. *Health Policy Plans*. 2006;21(3): 183–194.
52. Chernichovsky D, Potapchik E. Health system reform under the Russian health insurance legislation. *Int J Health Plans Manage*. 1997;12(4):279–295.
53. Aris B. Money for health in Russia, at long last. *Lancet*. 2005;366(9493):1254–1255.
54. Balabanova D, Falkingham J, McKee M. Winners and losers: expansion of insurance coverage in Russia in the 1990s. *Am J Public Health*. 2003;93(12):2124–2130.
55. Shishkin S, ed. Bogatova T, Patapchik Y, Chernets V, Chirikova A, Shilova L. *Informal out-of-pocket payments for health care in Russia*. Moscow Public Scientific Foundation & Independent Institute for Social Policy. Moscow, Russia; 2003.
56. Rimashevskaia NM, Korkhova IV. Poverty and health in Russia. *Sociological Research*. 2004;43(3):5–30.
57. World Health Organization. *World Health Statistics 2015*. http://apps.who.int/iris/bitstream/10665/170250/1/9789240694439_eng.pdf?ua=1&ua=1. Published 2016. Accessed October 16, 2016.
58. Roik, VD. Ways to improve medical insurance in Russia. *Probl Econ Transit*. 2013; 55(12):50–60.
59. Popovich L, Potapchik E, Shishkin S, Richardson E, Vacroux A, Mathivet B. Russian Federation. Health system review. *Health Syst Transit*. 2011;13(7):xiii–xiv,1–190.
60. World Health Organization. Country Cooperation Strategy for the World Health Organization and the Ministry of Health of the Russian Federation: 2014–2020. http://www.euro.who.int/__data/assets/pdf_file/0003/249915/COUNTRY-COOPERATION-STRATEGY-for-the-WORLD-HEALTH-ORGANIZATION-and-the-MINISTRY-OF-HEALTH-OF-THE-RUSSIAN-FEDERATION-Eng.pdf. Published 2014. Accessed October 16, 2016.
61. Organisation for Economic Co-operation and Development. *OEDC Reviews of Health Systems: Russian Federation* 2012. Paris: OECD Publishing. http://dx.doi.org/10.1787/9789264168091-en
62. Balabanova D, Roberts B, Richardson E, Haerpfer C, and McKee M. Health care reform in the former Soviet Union: beyond the transition. *Health Serv Res*. 2012;47(2):840–863.
63. Baird K. The incidence of high medical expenses by health status in seven developed countries. *Health Policy*. 2016;120(1):26–34.
64. Footman K, Richardson E, Roberts B, et al. Forgoing medicines in the former Soviet Union: changes between 2001 and 2010. *Health Policy*. 2014;118; 118(2):184–192.
65. Aarva P, Ilchenko I, Gorobets P, Rogacheva A. Formal and informal payments in health care facilities in two Russian cities, Tyumen and Lipetsk. *Health Policy Planning*. 2009;24(5):395–405.
66. Duke T, Keshishiyan E, Kuttumuratova A, et al. Quality of hospital care for children in Kazakhstan, Republic of Moldova, and Russia: systematic observational assessment. *Lancet*. 2006;367(9514):919–925.
67. Aleksunin VA, Mit'kov SA. The social aspects of fee-based medical services. *Sociological Research*. 2007;46(3):71–77.
68. Wiesmeth H. Strengthening competitive forces in Russian mandatory health insurance. *Journal of Economic Policy of Emerging Economies*. http://gsem.urfu.ru/fileadmin/user_upload/site_48_4984/docs2/Eingereicht_Health_Insurance_Russia.pdf. Published 2015. Accessed October 16, 2016.
69. Zubarevich NV. Regional social expenditures: A country of contrasts. *Russian Economic Developments*. 2015;12:31–35.
70. Organisation for Economic Co-operation and Development. Focus on health spending: OECD health statistics 2015. https://www.oecd.org/health/health-systems/Focus-Health-Spending-2015.pdf. Published 2015. Accessed October 16, 2016.
71. Sheiman I. Paying hospitals in Russia. *Eurohealth*. 2001;7(3):79–81.
72. Bochkareva VK. Health-care reform and ensuring equal access to free medical services. *Problems of Economic Transition*. 2013;55(12):13–31.
73. Axelsson R, Bihari-Axelsson S. Intersectoral problems in the Russian Organization of public health. *Health Policy*. 2005;73(3):285–293.

74. Coker R, Atun R, McKee M. Health-care system frailties and public health control of communicable diseases on the European Union's new eastern border. *Lancet.* 2004;363(2):1389–1392.
75. Parfitt T. Russia's population crisis. *Lancet.* 2005;365(9461): 743–744.
76. Titterton M. Social policy in a cold climate: health and social welfare in Russia. *Soc Policy Admin.* 2006;40(1):88–103.
77. World Bank. Mortality rate, infant (per 1,000 live births). Published 2016. Accessed http://data.worldbank.org/indicator/SP.DYN.IMRT.IN?page=2. Published 2016. Accessed October 16, 2016.
78. Danishevski K, Balabanova D, Parkhurst J, McKee M. *Maternal Health Situation in Russia.* Health Systems Development Programme. http://missinglink.ucsf.edu/lm/russia_guide/Russia_Maternal_Situational_Analysis.pdf. Published 2002. Accessed October 16, 2016.
79. Novokreshchenova IG, Shevchenko IK. Quality of medical care for the elderly in out-patient conditions according to the sociological survey. *Russian Open Medical Journal.* 2015;4(1). doi: 10.15275/rusomj.2015.0101
80. Fotaki M. Users' perceptions of health care reforms: quality of care and patients' rights in four regions in the Russian Federation. *Soc Sci Med.* 2006;63(6):1637–1647.
81. Rimashevskaia N. The social vector of the development in Russia. *Russian Social Science Review.* 2005;46(6):4–51.
82. Callister L, Getmanenko N, Garvrish N, et al. Outcomes evaluation of St. Petersburg Russia Women's Wellness Center. *Health Care Women In.* 2009;30(3):235–248.
83. Vasquez C, Lioznov D, Nikolaenko S, et al. Gender disparities in HIV risk behavior and access to health care in St. Petersburg, Russia. *AIDS Patient Care and STDs.* 2013;27(5):304–310.
84. Osborn A. Half of Russia's doctors face sack in healthcare reforms. *BMJ.* 2004;328(7448):1092.
85. Field MG. Reflections on a painful transition: from socialized to insurance medicine in Russia. *Croat Med J.* 1999;40(2):202–209.
86. Rekhter N, Togunov IA. Needs sssessment for health care management education in Russia. *J Contin Educ Health Prof.* 2006;26(4):314–326.
87. Vienonen M, Vohlonen I. Integrated health care in Russia: to be or not to be? *Int J Integr Care.* 2001:1–7.
88. Anderson BA. Russia faces depopulation? Dynamics of population decline. *Popul Environ.* 2002;23(5):437–464.
89. Marquez P, Suhrcke M, McKee M, Rocco L. Adult health in the Russian Federation: more than just a health problem. *Health Aff.* 2007;26(4):1040–1051.
90. Balabanova Y, Ruddy M, Hubb J, et al. Multidrug-resistant tuberculosis in Russia: clinical characteristics, analysis of second-line drug resistance and development of standardized therapy. *Eur J Clin Microbiol Infect Dis.* 2005;24(2):136–139.
91. Spradling P, Nemtsova E, Aptekar T, et al. Anti-tuberculosis drug resistance in community and prison patients, Orel Oblast, Russian Federation. *Int J Tuberc Lung Dis.* 2002;6(9): 757–762.
92. Dimitrova B, Balabanova D, Atun R, Drobniewski F, Levicheva V, Coker R. Health service providers' perceptions of barriers to tuberculosis care in Russia. *Health Policy Plan.* 2006;21(4):265–274.
93. Marx FM, Atun RA, Jakubowiak W, et al. Reform of tuberculosis control and DOTS within Russian public health systems: An ecological study. *Eur J Public Health.* 2007;17(1):98–103.
94. UNAIDS. *The Gap Report.* Geneva. http://www.unaids.org/sites/default/files/media_asset/UNAIDS_Gap_report_en.pdf. Published 2014. Accessed May 4, 2016
95. Bobrik A. Combating HIV/AIDS, malaria, and other diseases. In: Bobylev S, Alexandrova A, eds. *Russia in 2015: Development Goals and Policy Priorities.* Moscow: United Nations Development Programee (UNDP); 2005:94–107.
96. Oganov R, Maslennikova G. Prevention of cardiovascular diseases—real way to improvement of demographic situation in Russia [In Russian]. Profilaktika serdechno-sosudistykh zabolevaniy - realjniy putj uluchsheniya demografichskoy situatsii v Rossii. *Kardiologiia.* 2007;47(1):4–7.
97. World Health Organization, Europe. *WHO Disaster and Preparedness Response Programme in the North Caucasus, Russian Federation, Annual Report 2006.* http://www.euro.who.int/__data/assets/pdf_file/0016/79000/NC_annualreport2006.pdf?ua=1. Accessed May 5, 2016.

CHAPTER 15

Turkey

Reyhan Ucku, Hatice Simsek, and **Omur Cinar Elci**

▸ Country Description

TABLE 15-1 Turkey

Nationality	Noun: Turk(s) Adjective: Turkish
Ethnic groups	Turkish 70–75%, Kurdish 18.0%, other minorities 7.0%–12.0%
Religions	Muslim 99.8% (mostly Sunni), other 0.2% (mostly Christians and Jews)
Language	Turkish (official), Kurdish, other minority languages
Literacy	Definition: Age 15 and over can read and write. Total population: 95.0% Male: 98.4% Female: 91.8% (2015 est.)
Government type	Republican parliamentary democracy
Date of independence	October 29, 1923 (successor state to the Ottoman Empire)
Gross Domestic Product (GDP) per capita (PPP)	$20,500 (2015 est.)
Unemployment rate	10.4% (2015 est.)

(continues)

TABLE 15-1 Turkey (continued)

Natural hazards	Severe earthquakes, especially in northern Turkey, along an arc extending from the Sea of Marmara to Lake Van. Limited volcanic activity; its three historically active volcanoes Ararat, Nemrut Dagi, and Tendurek Dagi have not erupted since the 19th century or earlier.
Environment: current issues	Water pollution from dumping of chemicals and detergents; air pollution, particularly in urban areas; deforestation; concern for oil spills from increasing Bosporus ship traffic
Population	80,274,604 (July 2016 est.)
Age structure	0–14 years: 25.4% (male 10,339,731/female 9,868,005) 15–64 years: 67.5% (male 27,128,739/female 26,446,696) 65 years and over: 7.1% (male 2,498,187/female 3,132,911) (2015 est.)
Median age	Total: 30.1 Male: 29.7 Female: 30.6 (2015 est.)
Population growth rate	1.26% (2015 est.)
Birth rate	16.33 births/1,000 population (2015 est.)
Death rate	638 deaths/100,000 population (2015 est.)
Disease burden	Communicable disease deaths: 44/100,000 population Noncommunicable disease deaths: 555/100,000 population Injury deaths: 39/100,000 population (2016 est.)
Net migration rate	2.16 migrant(s)/1,000 population (2015 est.)
Gender ratio	At birth: 1.05 male(s)/female 0–14 years: 1.05 male(s)/female 15–64 years: 1.03 male(s)/female 65 years and over: 0.80 male(s)/female Total population: 1.01 male(s)/female (2015 est.)
Infant mortality rate	Total: 18.87 deaths/1,000 live births Male: 20.13 deaths/1,000 live births Female: 17.55 deaths/1,000 live births (2015 est.)
Life expectancy at birth	Total population: 74.57 years Male: 72.26 years Female: 77 years (2015 est.)
Total fertility rate	2.05 children born/woman (2015 est.)
HIV/AIDS adult prevalence rate	Not available
Number of people living with HIV/AIDS	Not available
HIV/AIDS deaths	Not available

Data from Central Intelligence Agency. The World Fact Book, 2016: Turkey. https://www.cia.gov/library/publications/the-world-factbook/geos/tu.html. Accessed April 5, 2016.

History

In 1922, after World War I, the Ottoman Empire collapsed and the Anatolian peninsula was occupied by allied forces from the United Kingdom, Greece, Italy, and France. After the freedom war that was led by M. Kemal Ataturk, the modern Republic of Turkey was founded on October 29, 1923. Ataturk was also the first president of the country and held this post until his death in 1938. Ataturk initiated various social, cultural, political, linguistic, and economic reforms to establish the foundation of the new republic. From 1924 to 1946 there was a single-party government that focused on the modernization and Westernization of Turkey. Ataturk's ideology was based on secularism, nationalism, and modernization. It was during the same period of 1924–1946 that many of these reforms took place and the new republic turned toward the West. After World War II, which Turkey did not enter until the very end, Turkey was transformed from a single-party system into a multi-party system. Although this new parliamentary democracy was halted by military coups in 1960, 1971, and 1980, today Turkey is governed under a multi-party parliamentary democracy.[1]

After the 1960 and 1980 coups, the Constitution was changed, which had significant impacts on the health system in the country. In the 1961 Constitution, the state was identified as a social welfare state, and health was defined as a fundamental right for every citizen.[2] In the 1982 Constitution, however, the state was entitled to organize and supervise health services.[3] This significant transformation led the country into today's challenges.

Size and Geography

The Republic of Turkey is located in the northern hemisphere, at the crossroads of Asia and Europe (**FIGURE 15-1**). The majority of its 814,578 square kilometers of land is on the Asian peninsula called Anatolia, which is surrounded by the Black Sea to the north, the Mediterranean Sea to the south, and the Aegean Sea to the west. There is also an inland sea, called the Marmara Sea, that separates Asia and Europe to the northwest. Turkey's neighbors are Greece and Bulgaria to the northwest; Georgia, Armenia, Azerbaijan, and Iran to the east; and Iraq and Syria to the southeast. There are 7 geographical regions and 81 provinces in the country. The eastern Anatolia region consists of 21% of the area, although it has the lowest population density. The northwestern Marmara region has the highest population density, and Istanbul is the biggest city in the country. Istanbul has a unique location, as it has two sections, one on the continent of Europe and one on the continent of Asia. The capital of Turkey is Ankara, which is the second largest city and is located in central Anatolia. The third largest city, Izmir, is located in the western Ege region. The other two regions are Karadeniz in the north and Akdeniz in the south.[1,4]

Government and Political System

The government structure and the political system are described in the Constitution. As we discussed earlier, the 1924 Constitution was replaced by the 1961 and 1982 Constitutions. According to the current Constitution, the Republic of Turkey is

FIGURE 15-1 Map of Turkey
© Bardocz Peter/Shutterstock

a secular and democratic welfare state.³ The official language is Turkish and the capital city is Ankara. There are three governing bodies in Turkey. The Grand National Assembly of Turkey is the legislator, the president and the cabinet run the government, and independent courts are responsible for justice and the implementation of law. The Grand National Assembly of Turkey consists of 550 representatives, who are elected by the people every 4 years. The president is elected by the people every 5 years; each president can serve 2 terms.⁵ The governing cabinet includes the prime minister and other ministers. The president appoints the prime minister, who selects his cabinet members from among the members of the National Assembly. In November 2015, the 64th Cabinet began.

There are 81 provincial districts in the country. Besides the central city, each province has towns, townships, and villages. Each province is governed by governors, who are appointed by the central government. Local municipalities are run by mayors, who are elected by the people locally.

Macroeconomics

Because of the monetary policies applied during the 1990s, instability increased in Turkey's macroeconomics. Unstable growth, a high inflation rate, high public deficits, interest expenditures, and debt stock were the main problems in the economy during this period. The Turkish economy decreased by 6% in 1994 and 9.5% in the 2001 economic crisis. Tight fiscal and monetary policies were implemented after this crisis.⁶ At the beginning of 2016, an economic reform agenda was launched, aiming to raise productivity.⁷

Basic economic indicators from the 9th and 10th five-year development plans are shown after TABLE 15-2.⁶,⁷ The GDP was US $786.3 billion in 2012 and $719.9 billion in 2015.⁸,⁹ The GDP based on purchasing power parity was $11,394 per capita in 2005 and increased to $18,437 in 2012 and $20,300 in 2015.⁷,¹⁰ Annual GDP growth was 4.0% in 2015.⁹ The GDP was $786.3 billion in 2012 and $719.9 billion in 2015.⁸,⁹ In the 2014–2018 development plan, it is projected that GDP will increase by 5.5% annually during that period. Considering the decade from 2002 to 2012, the proportion of agricultural and industrial sectors in GDP has decreased, whereas the proportion of the service sector has increased. In 2015, the proportion of basic sectors in GDP was as follows: agriculture 7.6%, industry 23.4%, and service 57.4%.⁹ Deficit in trade balance was $63 billion, and the imports coverage by exports was 69.4% ¹¹.

TABLE 15-2 Basic Economic Indicators from the 9th and 10th Five-Year Development Plans

Economic indicators	2005	2012
GPD (US $billion)	363.4	786.3
Per capita GPD (PPP, $)	8,145	10,504
Growth (%)	7.4	2.2
Exports ($billion)	73.4	152.5
Imports ($billion)	116.5	236.5
Trade balance ($billion)	−32.8	−84.1
Labor force participation rate (%)	48.3	50.0
Employment level (people in millions)	22.1	24.8
Unemployment rate (%)	10.3	9.2

Data from Republic of Turkey Ministry of Development. The Ninth Development Plan (2007–2013). Official Journal, 2006; Republic of Turkey Ministry of Development. The Tenth Development Plan (2014–2018). Official Journal, 2014.

The 2015 inflation rate, based on the consumer price index, was 8.8%.¹²

The unregistered employment ratio was very high (39%) among the 24.8 million employed people in 2012. Unemployment, at 9.2% in 2012, is a significant problem, especially among the younger age group, whose figure was twice as high (17.5%).⁸

Demographics

After the first two censuses in 1927 and 1935, there have been *de facto* censuses every 5 years. In 2007, the last census was implemented based on household occupancies; the address-based population registration system (ABPRS) has been used since 2007. In 1927, the population was 13,648,278, and it increased to 78,741,053 in 2015.¹³,¹⁴ Until the 1960s, pronatalist demographic policies were in practice, and in 1960 the population growth rate reached its peak of 28.5 per 1,000 population. In 1965, the Population Planning Law initiated antenatalist policies, which decreased the demographic growth rate to 18.3 per 1,000 in 2000 and to 13.4 per 1,000 in 2015. According to the 2015 ABPRS, the population was

78,741,053, of which 92.1% were living in the urban areas. Women were 49.8% of the total population. The median age was 31. Turkey still has a relatively young population; 0- to14-year-old children constituted 24.0% of the population while elderly people age 65 years and over constituted 8.2% of the population. The dependent population was 48.0%.[13,14] The crude birth rate was 17.3 per 1,000 population and crude death rate was 5.1 per 1,000 population. Life expectancy was 77.0 years overall, with 74.8 years expected for men and 79.3 years expected for women.[15]

According to the health and demography survey in 2013,[16] the infant mortality rate was 13 per 1,000 live births, and the mortality rate for children under five was 15 per 1,000. Overall, total fertility was 2.26 children per women; it was higher in rural areas (2.73) than in urban (2.16) areas.

According to the tenth development plan, in 2006, 13.30% of the population had a daily income under US $4.3, this figure decreased to 2.80% in 2011.[7] According to the 2014 poverty survey, this proportion was 2.06% in 2013 and 1.62% in 2014.[17] The indicator of the disparity, the Gini index, also decreased, from 0.400 in the year 2006 to 0.397 in 2015.[13,18] The overall income of the richest 20% (46.50%) was 7.6 times higher than the poorest 20% of the people (6.10%) in 2015.[18]

▸ Brief History of the Healthcare System

The history of the healthcare system in Turkey can be summarized in three periods: (1) the period after the foundation of the Turkish Republic, from 1923 to 1960; (2) the period in which the socialization of health services began, 1961 to the 1980s; and (3) the period of health reform discussions, from the 1980s to the present.

The Period from 1923 to 1960

Before the foundation of the Turkish Republic, the Health Directorate in the Ministry of Interior Affairs was responsible for health services. At the provincial level, there were district health officers, whose responsibility was to provide preventive and curative health services. In 1920, before the Republic was founded, the Ministry of Health was established. Following the foundation of the Republic, in 1923, a new era began in which efforts were made to improve the health status of the population. At the beginning of this era, there was not only a shortage of health facilities and health manpower but also an inequality in distribution. The population was nearly 13 million in 1923. Although 78% of the population was living in rural areas, there were no accessible health services in the villages. The most significant health problems were communicable diseases, mainly malaria, syphilis, trachoma, and tuberculosis. There were only 554 physicians, and the number of population per physician was 22,500. The same shortage existed for hospital beds; there were approximately 5 beds per 10,000 population. The infant mortality rate was very high, with 250 infant deaths per 1,000 live births. The Ministry of Health budget was 2.21% of the general budget.[13,20–22]

In this period, providing health services was accepted as one of the main responsibilities of the government. Government health policy was aimed at the promotion of health, the prevention of disease, increasing the population, and struggling against communicable diseases. Dr. Refik Saydam, who was the Republic's first Minister of Health (MoH), was assigned to carry out these objectives. In his nearly 13 years as Minister, the objectives of the health policy were improving health organization; expanding health and social services to rural areas; increasing physician, midwife, and health technician numbers; struggling against malaria, tuberculosis, leprosy, trachoma, and syphilis; establishing a model hospital and maternal and children hospitals; enacting laws related to health; and founding the Hygiene Institute and School.[13]

During this period, the main priority was given to the preventive health services, especially to the control of highly prevalent communicable diseases. For this reason, vertical organizations were established, such as the malaria control dispensary and the syphilis and leprosy control dispensary, and their health services were taken to the villages. Malaria control was spread throughout the country, trachoma control was spread to the southern and southeast regions, and syphilis control was spread to the northern region. Tuberculosis control was first the responsibility of the non-governmental organizations supported by the Ministry of Health. Later it was administered by the ministry itself. In this period, it was believed that providing curative health services (hospitals) should be the responsibility of local governments, so the MoH's responsibility was limited to coordinating and guiding these services. Because of this, model hospitals were mostly established in the big cities. As a result, preventive and curative health services were not integrated, and they were administered by central and local governments separately. At the provincial level, there were only district health officers. Because of expanding health services to rural areas, dispensaries (diagnostic and treatment centers) were established in the districts. Dispensaries, which had 5–10 beds, were responsible for providing free-of-charge health care with a physician and a health technician. The number of dispensaries increased from 90 in 1933 to 180 in 1936. Other than dispensaries, there were also mobile physicians, whose responsibility was to provide preventive and curative health care to the rural population. These mobile physicians regularly visited villages for 20 days out of the month.[20]

As mentioned before, health manpower was insufficient at the beginning of this period. For this reason, priority was given to increasing the number of physicians and male nurses. Medical education was supported by scholarships and free dormitories. As a result, the number of physicians increased three-fold between 1923 and 1935. At the same time, compulsory service was introduced for physicians because of the shortage and unequal distribution of them. By giving top priority to preventive health services, doctors working in preventive healthcare services were paid more than those in curative services. The important characteristic of this period was the enactment of the main health legislations, consisting of 51 laws and 18 regulations, most of which are still in force.[13,20,21]

Unfortunately, accessible healthcare services to all people in the country could not be adequately implemented. After World War II, a new era commenced, and in 1946 the first national health plan was prepared. The objectives of this plan were not different from those accepted at the beginning of the Republic. The main difference was to establish a national health bank and health fund. According to this plan, the health services organization would be organized into seven different regions in the country. In each region, there would be a state hospital with 500 beds, special hospitals (including maternity, child, and mental hospitals and a sanatorium), and nursing/midwifery graduate schools. Unfortunately, this plan was not carried out as intended, and instead health centers were established with a new approach of integrated health services. A health center was established for every 40 villages (approximately 20,000 population), and it was responsible for the preventive and curative health care of this defined community. The health center, which had 10–25 beds, was staffed with 1–2 physicians and 11 other healthcare personnel (such as nurses, midwives, and male nurses). In this way, population-based, integrated healthcare services were intended to be accessible to the entire population.

Although the aim was to establish 1,000 health centers within 10 years, this was not implemented. The number of health centers increased from 16 in 1950 to 283 in 1960.[13,21,22]

In the postwar era, vertical organizations continued to serve as important centers for the control of communicable diseases because of active epidemics. In 1952, a new vertical organization for maternal and child health, serving a population of 30,000–50,000, was established under the MoH.[22] At the beginning of the 1950s, the MoH took over the hospitals run by local governments. Although this change was important for integrating preventive and curative services, curative health services were given high priority and preventive services were neglected. Even with this compromise, curative health services were not sufficiently improved due to the lack of health personnel.

In 1945, the Social Insurance Institution (SSK) was established to provide retirement benefits to workers. In 1952, SSK developed its own healthcare facilities, including hospitals and dispensaries, and assigned its own health personnel.[13]

The Period from 1960 to the 1980s

At the beginning of the 1960s, the population reached 27,755,000, 68.00% of whom were living in rural areas. There were 8,214 physicians; nearly half of them were specialists. Even though other health personnel increased in numbers over the years, there was still a shortage. The population per physician was 3,400, with 17,000 population per nurse, and 8,600 population per midwife. The annual population increase rate peaked at 2.90% in 1960; the infant mortality rate was also high, with 208 infant deaths per 1,000 live births. The Ministry of Health budget was 5.18% of the general budget in 1955 and reached its highest level of 5.27% in 1960.[17,22] At the provincial level, the healthcare system consisted of hospitals, health centers, district health officers, and vertically integrated organizations. Hospitals, not accessible to the entire population, were generally in the center of cities. The aim of establishing new health centers across the country could not be achieved completely. On the other hand, district health officers were busy with bureaucratic activities instead of health care. By 1960, it was apparent that the healthcare system and health status of the country would not improve with this model. Therefore, different healthcare policies started to be discussed, and a new law on socialization of health services was prepared by Dr. Nusret Fişek as an undersecretary of the Ministry of Health and was enacted in 1961. After 1960, five-year development plans began to be constructed, and programs regarding socialization policies were enacted in the First Five Year Development Plan. The implementation of the law was begun in 1963 and was gradually expanded to the whole country by 1984.[23]

The socialization law deals with the organization of all health services in the country, with the aim of providing health services to the entire population on an equitable basis. The basic principles of this law are the following: (a) to deliver equitable and continuous health services, (b) to integrate health services horizontally, (c) to organize a referral healthcare system, (d) to ensure community participation in health services decision making, (e) to implement a population-based healthcare system, (f) to deliver health services with a teamwork approach, and (g) to give top priority to preventive health services.[13,23]

According to the legislation, the Ministry of Health is responsible for health policy and health services. It is the main provider of primary and secondary health care and also partly of tertiary health care. The provincial health directorates are responsible for health services at the provincial level. The main primary healthcare settings are health centers (*sağlık ocağı*) and "health houses." Health centers are responsible for the health of a defined community, up to 10,000 people. With a holistic approach, they give preventive, curative, and rehabilitative health care to the community both in the health center as well as in people's homes. Health services provided by health centers and health houses are free for the entire population. In each health center works a team that consists of a physician, a nurse, midwives, a health technician, a medical secretary, and sometimes a pharmacist and a dentist.[13,23]

Since 1963, the number of health centers has gradually increased, reaching 6,377 in 2006, with 10,317 population per health center.[24] The smallest primary healthcare unit is called a *health house*, in which only one midwife works. Secondary and tertiary healthcare settings are hospitals. The Ministry of Health is mainly responsible for managing hospitals. The MoH runs state hospitals and also some specialist hospitals, such as maternity, psychiatric, children's, chest disease, bone disease, etc. University hospitals serve as referral centers, and there are also private hospitals. Although there were some hospitals that were administered by other ministries, SSK, or public institutions, in 2005 all of them were gathered under the Ministry of Health, with the exception of the military hospitals.[13,23]

There have been some problems in the implementation of this model despite the fact that it is a suitable model given the conditions of the country. The socialization law was put into practice successfully at the outset, but later, some changes were made to the implementation.[23] Some principles were neglected or not carried out, mainly because of lack of political stability. These neglected principles were as follows: having personnel working full time in each health center, free healthcare services, organizational unity of health services at the provincial level, and the two-way referral system. Instead, high priority was given to curative health services rather than preventive ones; qualified manpower for primary health care could not be trained; the shortage of buildings, supplies, and equipment for health care could not be adequately addressed; vertical organizations were not closed; and community participation, which is one of the most important principles, could not be achieved.

The Period after the 1980s

In the 1980s, the economic system of Turkey began to change toward liberalization, and at the same time health reform discussions commenced. A special unit for health reforms was created in the MoH after 1990, and several projects were carried out with the support of the World Bank. Two national health congresses were held to discuss the proposed reforms, which aimed to make changes to the organization (office-based family medicine services, instead of community-based health centers), funding (premiums instead of taxes), and manpower (contract-based work instead of civil servants). These proposals did not meet with general acceptance; there was also opposition from the Turkish Medical Association, health organizations, and some academics. Together with political changes, the reform proposal could not be put into practice, but in 2001, a rolling fund was implemented in health centers. In 2002, together with the new government, the reform discussions restarted with a different name, Health Transformation Programme (HTP), but with the same context.[22,25,26]

According to the newly established government program, the objectives of HTP were to organize, deliver, and finance the health services in effective, productive, and equal ways. The main components of HTP were reorganization of health services, universal health insurance, and skilled, motivated healthcare manpower. In terms of organization, its components were MoH as a planner and supervisor, strengthened primary health services and family medicine, referral chain, and public health facilities having financial autonomy. HTP was planned to take place in four stages: conceptualism, legitimization, controlled local practices, and spreading health services across Turkey. It began to be implemented gradually in 2003, and except for the referral chain, almost all components were carried out.[27]

Transformation of primary healthcare services began as a pilot project in a small province in 2005 with a law enacted in 2004, Pilot Implementation of the Law on Family Medicine; then it was extended to the entire country at the end of 2010. According to this law, family physicians (FP) are defined as primary care physicians who provide individual preventive and curative services. They are family medicine specialists or certificated general practitioners and are responsible for the health of 1,000–4,000 registered people. FPs are contracted for a period of 2 years. With this program, the concept of the primary healthcare team was transformed from a large team to a two-person team (a family physician and additional family health professional). After a few changes, the law on family medicine took its final form in 2014. At the beginning, there were no health facilities for the community primary healthcare services. In 2010, community health centers (CHC) were established by regulation for the first time. According to regulation in 2015, the responsibilities of CHCs are to determine public health risks; to plan interventions for these risks; to coordinate preventive, curative, and rehabilitative health services; to monitor, supervise, and assess primary health services; and to cooperate with other institutions.[28-30]

Another organizational component of HTP, public health facilities having administrative and financial autonomy, was carried out by Decree Law No. 663 in 2011. Before this transformation, all public hospitals were gathered under the roof of MoH. With the Decree Law No. 663, MoH's roles became planner and controller, and healthcare services—except emergency services—were transferred to affiliated institutions.[31]

At the beginning of HTP, priority was given to increasing health professionals, especially physicians and nurses, because on the ground there was a shortage and unequal distribution of them. Subsequently, obligatory health service for all physicians and full-time people working for physicians in public hospitals was accepted into practice in 2005, and it was accepted into university hospitals in 2010. It was planned to increase the salaries of health workers through a performance-based payment system, which tends to increase workload and disrupt workplace peace.[28]

Description of the Current Healthcare System

Description

Although the main responsible governmental body in Turkey for the planning and implementation of health services is the MoH, it is not the sole provider. Besides the MoH, universities, armed forces, regional and district municipalities, and the private sector provide health services. With Decree Law No. 663, enacted in 2011, MoH has been turned into a planner and controller position and the services have been transferred to affiliated institutions.[31]

MoH consists of central units, regional units, and affiliated institutions (see **FIGURE 15-2**). Among the central units, there are service units, the Supreme Council of Health, the Board for Medical Specialties, and the Health Professions Council. Regional units are provincial health directorates, and regional health services are organized as small models of national health services. Affiliated institutions are the Pharmaceuticals and Medical Devices Institution, Public Health Institution, Public Hospitals Institution, and General Directorate for Borders and Coastal Health.[31,32]

Public Health Institution is responsible for providing primary healthcare services, and its regional unit is the Provincial Public Health Directorate. The smallest service units are family health centers (FHC) and CHCs. Before the health transformation program, the main local health services units were health centers. The fundamental role of health centers was to provide primary, secondary, and, if necessary, tertiary health services with a holistic and team approach. With the program, health center services were divided into two parts: (1) individual preventive and curative services provided by FHCs and (2) community preventive services by CHCs.

FHCs consists of family health units (FHU); in each FHU, a family physician and a family health professional provide services. Family physicians are responsible for the health of a registered population, an average of 3,000–3,500 people. A midwife, nurse, male nurse, or an emergency medical technician can work with the physician in FHU.[33]

CHCs are responsible for the health services at the community level, determining public health risks; planning interventions for these risks; coordinating preventive, curative, and rehabilitative health services; monitoring, supervising, and assessing the primary health services, and cooperating with other institutions. In each district, regardless of population size, there is one CHC. Each CHC is administered by

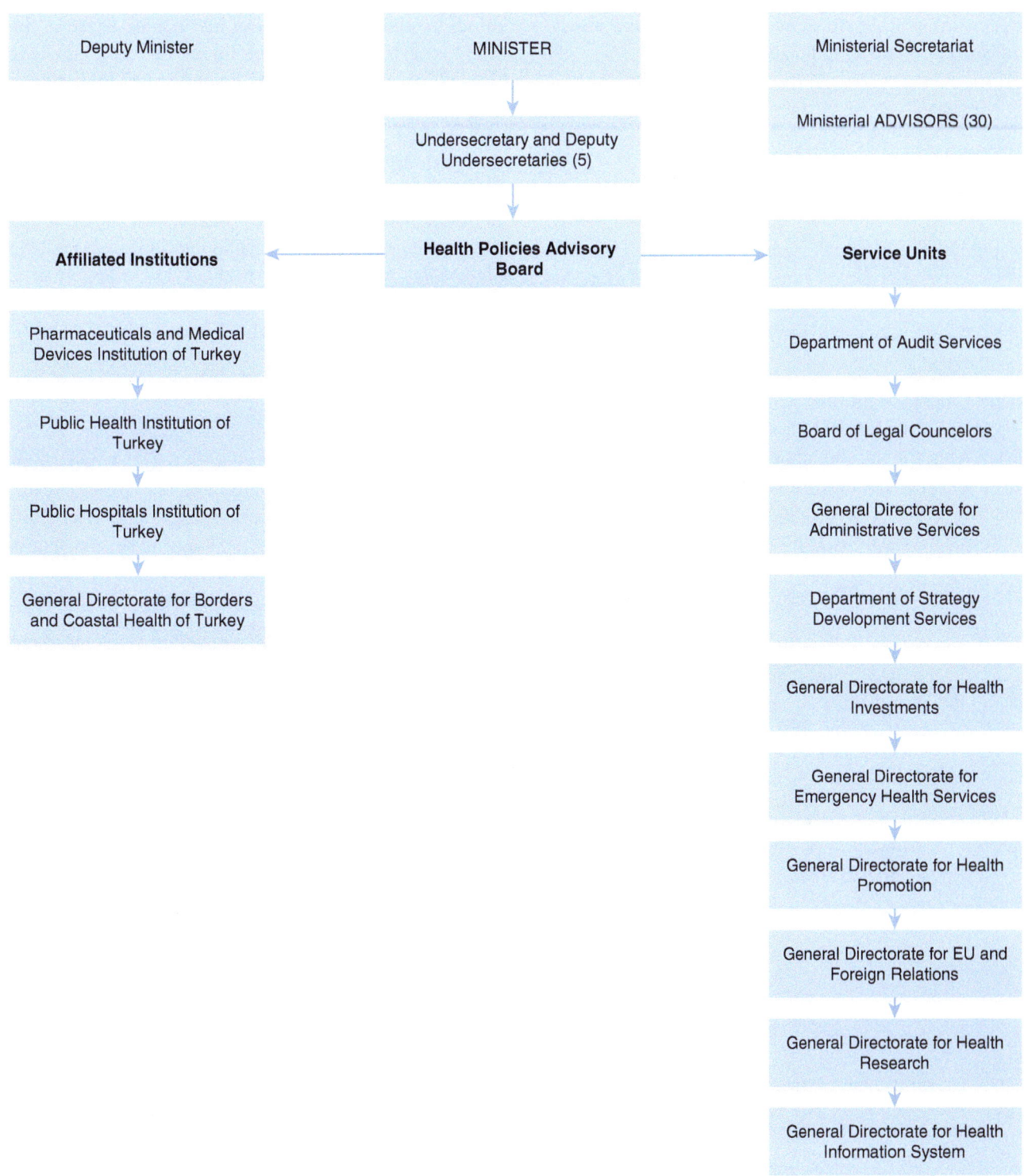

FIGURE 15-2 Structure of the Ministry of Health in Turkey

Data from T.C. Sa˘glık Bakanlı˘gı, Türkiye'de Sa˘glı˘ga Bakıs¸, Ankara 2007. The Ministry of Health of Turkey. *Health at a Glance: Turkey 2007*. Ankara; 2007.

the head of that CHC. Some CHCs have early cancer diagnosis; screening and training centers; maternity, child health, and family planning centers; tuberculosis control dispensaries; malaria control dispensaries; and/or health houses. Health houses, staffed with one health professional, provide preventive health services for small, remote communities, such as villages.[30]

Public Hospitals Institution is the second affiliated institution of MoH and is responsible for providing secondary and tertiary healthcare services. There is only one public health association in each province, except three in big cities. Each association has a general secretary and hospital administrators.[32]

Facilities

Primary Healthcare Facilities

In 2015, there were 21,284 PHUs, 6,092 PHCs, and 970 CHCs in Turkey; the average population per family physician was 3,633.[15,34] Distribution of these primary healthcare facilities are shown in **TABLE 15-3.**

Secondary and Tertiary Healthcare Facilities

In 2015, the total number of beds was 209,648 in 1,533 hospitals in Turkey.[19] Although there were regional differences, the number of beds per 10,000 population was 26.6. The number of beds per 10,000 population was 34.6 in the western Anatolia region and 20.5 in the southeastern Anatolia region in 2014.[10] In 2015 some 56.4% of hospitals and 58.4% of beds were administered by the MoH. The private sector provided 36.7% of all hospitals and 20.8% of all beds in Turkey.[19] In 2014, the total number of intensive care beds was 28,572, out of which 41.6% belonged to MoH, 40.5% belonged to the private sector, and 18.0% belong to universities.[10] **TABLE 15-4** presents the distribution of hospitals and beds in the country.[19,35]

In addition to these general hospitals, in 2014 there were specialty hospitals (134 hospitals with 22,314 beds), such as those for obstetrics, children, chest diseases, cardiovascular diseases, mental health, eye diseases, physical therapy and rehabilitation, oncology, venereal diseases, leprosy, emergency and traumatology, occupational diseases, and dentistry.[15]

Workforce

According to 2015 data, there were 141,259 physicians in Turkey. Some 54.5% of all physicians were specialists, 30.0% general practitioners, and 15.5% residents. Employed by the MoH were 50.0% of all specialist and 85.7% of all general practitioners; 29.2% of specialists worked in the private sector. **TABLE 15-5** shows distribution of healthcare professionals by sector.[19]

In 2014, While 94.0% of specialist physicians in the MoH work in hospitals, 62.1% of general practitioners work in FHUs. Nearly half of nurses and midwives work in hospitals.[15] In general, there were 179 physicians, 99 specialist physicians, 53 general practitioners, 32 dentists, 35 pharmacists, and 261 nurses and midwives per 100,000 population in 2015. There is a regional disparity in the distribution of health professionals; for example, in 2015, western Anatolia, there were 273 physicians per 100,000 population, while this figure was 131 in southeastern Anatolia.[19]

Technology

Medical technology is one of the areas that clearly demonstrates Turkey's dependency on foreign technology and finance. The main goal of investment in this area is to increase profit instead of technology development, research, or production. In 2015, the numbers of computerized tomography (CT) and magnetic resonance imaging (MRI) units were 1,119 and 794, respectively. There were 14.2 CT units and 10.1 MRI units per 1 million people in the country. Almost half of all CTs (44.9%) and of all MRIs (53.9%) were provided by the private sector.[19] (See **TABLE 15-6.**)

In 2014, out of the 849 hemodialysis centers in Turkey, there were 16,064 dialysis units. Regarding sectoral distribution, 51.7% of the hemodialysis centers and 30.8% of the dialysis units belonged to MoH;

TABLE 15-3 Distribution of Primary Healthcare Facilities in Turkey

Primary healthcare facilities	Number
Family health centers	6,902
Community health centers	970
Health houses	5,544
MCH-FP*	182
Tuberculosis control dispensaries	181
Malaria control dispensaries	37
Early cancer diagnosis, screening and training centers	156
Venereal disease control dispensaries	13
Hemoglobinopathy diagnostic unit	29
Trachoma control dispensaries	6
Authorized CHCs for occupational health and safety	116

*Maternity, child health, and family planning centers.
Data from Ministry of Health. 2015.

TABLE 15-4 Distribution of Hospitals and Beds in Turkey				
Administration	Hospitals		Beds	
Year	2006	2015	2006	2015
Ministry of Health	769	865	133,168	122,331
Universities	56	70	29,700	38,361
Private sector	305	562	13,707	43,645
Other	75	36	20,092	5,311
Total	1,205	1,528	196,667	209,648

Data from Sağlık Bakanlığı. Sağlık İstatistikleri Yıllığı 2014, Ankara 2014. The Ministry of Health of Turkey. *Health Statistics 2014*, Ankara 2015; Sağlık Bakanlığı. Yataklı Tedavi Kurumları Çalışma Yıllığı 2006, Ankara 2007.

41.1% of the hemodialysis centers and 61.8% of the dialysis units belonged to private sector; and 7.2% of the hemodialysis centers and 7.4% of the dialysis units belonged to university. In the whole country, there were 206.8 dialysis units per 1 million people in 2014.[15]

There has been significant improvement in the pharmaceutical industry in Turkey, especially since the 1950s. In 2015 there were 541 pharmaceutical companies.[36] The largest customers of these companies are the government facilities. While the number of domestically produced drugs was 7,457, the number of imported drugs was 3,159.[37]

Since before the foundation of the Republic, Turkey has been quite successful in vaccine production and vaccination programs. Until the mid-1990s, Turkey produced its own vaccines against smallpox, rabies, tuberculosis, pertussis, diphtheria, tetanus, typhoid fever, typhus, and cholera.[38] Unfortunately,

TABLE 15-5 Distribution of Healthcare Professionals by Sector						
Healthcare professionals (Çalışan)	Total	Ministry of Health	University	Private sector	Others	Number per 100,000 population
Physicians	141,259	82,589	28,810	28,384	1,476	179
Specialist physicians	77,622	38,783	14,972	22,655	1,212	99
General practitioners	41,794	35,833	216	5,729	16	53
Resident physicians	21,843	7,973	13,622	0	248	—
Dentists	24,834	8,683	1,698	14,291	162	32
Pharmacists	27,530	2,156	306	25,010	58	35
Nurses	152,803	101,722	22,526	25,941	2,614	2,611
Midwives	53,086	48,078	851	4,100	57	

Data from Sağlık Bakanlığı. Sağlık İstatistikleri Yıllığı 2014, Ankara 2014. The Ministry of Health of Turkey. *Health Statistics 2014*, Ankara 2015.

TABLE 15-6 Distribution of Medical Equipment in Turkey					
	Total	Per 1 million	Ministry of Health	University	Private
CT	1,119	14.2	4,484	133	502
MRI	794	10.1	2,267	99	428
Ultrasonography	5,518	70.1	22,843	661	2,014
Doppler ultrasonography	4,015	51.0	2,412	416	1,187
Echocardiography	1,897	24.1	983	234	680
Mammography	896	11.4	313	81	502

Data from Republic of Turkey Ministry of Health. Health statistics yearbook 2014. http://sbu.saglik.gov.tr/Ekutuphane/kitaplar/EN%20YILLIK.pdf. 2015.

privatization efforts in the late 1990s stopped national vaccination production and created an absolute dependence on imported vaccines.

Evaluation of the Health System

Cost

There are three main finance sources for healthcare services in Turkey: the state budget, the social security organizations' budget, and personal expenses. The general state budget is financed from tax revenues, which is the major source for health services finance in the country.

There are three different social security organizations in Turkey. The Civil Servants' Pension Fund (ES), the Social Insurance Institution (SSK), and the Social Security Organization for the Self-Employed (Bağ-Kur). ES is funded from state employee salaries and with state matching payments; this fund provides social and healthcare services for state employees, retirees, and their dependents. SSK provides the same healthcare services for workers who are employed in industry; this fund is supported by employers' payments as well as salary deductions. Bag-Kur, on the other hand, provides social and healthcare services for self-employed individuals, who pay funding premiums themselves. The Social Security Institution was established in 2006, and in 2008, the three social security institutions (ES, SSK, and Bağ-Kur) were united under one roof. In 2014, 82% of the population was covered by social security.[39] Although all state funds have prescription coverage, there was a 20% co-payment for active employees and 10% co-payment for retirees. Besides these state funds, there are also private retirement and health insurance systems that provide private health coverage.

In 2015, the total health expenditure took up 5.4% of the GDP, equivalent to US $38,537,000. Per capita health expenditure was equivalent to $496. And, 78.5% of the total health expenditure was for public health while 21.5% was for private health. The proportion of out-of-pocket expenses was also significant at 16.6% of all healthcare service expenses.[40]

In 2015, with respect to the use of health expenditure, the largest components of health spending were hospital services (48.9%), followed by medications (24.8%), outpatient services (11.8%), and public health programs (4.2%).[40] Over the years, total health expenditures, out-of-pocket expenses, and private sector expenses of the SSI have been increasing.

Quality

In 2015, primary health care, the number of annual outpatient services per person was 2.7 in family health centers throughout the country; this number was 5.7 in secondary and tertiary health care.[19] Hospital admissions were very high due to the lack of a referral system.

The one of the responsibilities of family physicians is to regularly monitor children aged 0–5 years, pregnant women, and reproductive age women. In 2014, the average number of visits per baby was 8.2, per child 2.2, and per pregnant woman 4.8.[15] Not only the quantity of home visits but also the quality of service, education, and prenatal care is important in primary health care. In Turkey, 97.0% of pregnant women received at least one prenatal care by a health professional.[15,16] At the same time, 97.0% of deliveries took place in health facilities. As expected, these numbers were lower in rural communities than in urban settings. Other important indicators of the quality of primary healthcare services are family planning, maternity, and child health services. The 2013 Turkish Demography and Health Survey demonstrated that 73.5% of reproductive age women aged 15–49 years used at least one family planning method. Although this number has increased over the years, only 47.4% of these women used a modern family planning technique in 2013.[16]

Nationwide vaccination services are provided by family health units and are free to all children and pregnant women. The routine vaccination schedule includes BCG, HepB, MMR, OPV, DTaP/IPV/Hib, and PCV (pneumococcal conjugate vaccine). In 2013, 75.0% of children under age 18 months were fully vaccinated. According to the 2015 Turkish Demography and Health Survey, vaccination rates were 94.4% for BCG, 86.4% for DTaP/IPV/Hib, 87.1% for the third dose of HepB, 89.8% for MMR, and 81.6% for the third dose of PCV among children 12–23 months old.[16] These vaccination rates are different from the data obtained from MoH statistics. The vaccine coverage was 97.0% for each vaccine according to 2015 MoH data.[19]

Annual admission to hospitals was 5.3 times per person in 2015. According to 2015 data, the national bed occupation rate was 69.6%, and the patient turnout rate was 65 patients with an average of 3.9 days of admittance.[19] These rates were the highest in university hospitals and the lowest in private hospitals. The crude mortality rate among hospital admittances is 17.0%.[15]

Access

In Turkey, the average annual hospital usage per person was 5.7 visits, and the average annual use of FHU per person was 2.7 visits.[19] There has been regional disparity in access to health care, with access higher in the western and northern regions compared to the middle eastern region. According to the Turkish Demography and Health Survey 2013, 11% of women were uncovered by a social security fund; this figure was higher among women living in rural areas (17%) and women in the lowest wealth quintile (22%).[16] These data show that people living in rural areas, who are in the lowest wealth status, and who are the least educated are disadvantaged in access to health services. Additionally, when receiving health care, individuals pay a certain amount of money called co-payment; this is also a disadvantage in access to health services.

In 2014, there were a total of 397 million outpatient and 13 million inpatient applications to hospitals in Turkey. Of these admittances, 1.2% were surgical operations. The number of surgical operation per 100,000 population was 61.8; 51.0% of all surgical operations were made in public hospitals, 16.0% were made in university hospitals, and 33.0% were made in private hospitals.[15]

Access to oral health services is a significant problem. The average annual service usage per person was only 0.49 in 2014; this figure was lower in the eastern region and higher in the western region.[15] The main cause of the access problem is that most oral health services are not covered by social insurance.

Regarding preventive healthcare services, in 2013, 79.0% of women of reproductive age had a need for family planning; the proportion of women who had an unmet need for family planning was 7.0%. The proportion of unwanted births increases with increasing birth order; 40.0% of fourth and higher births were unwanted pregnancy.[16] As mentioned before, the vaccination coverage was 97.0% for each vaccine according to MoH data in 2014; however, it ranged from 81.6% to 94.4% according to the Turkish Demography and Health Survey.[15,16]

Innovation

According to the Strategic Plan of MoH, the main objectives are to promote research, development, and innovation in health.[32] Strategies to achieve the objectives are: to support institutions that carry out healthcare service research and development (R&D) in cell, tissue, organ, and nerve engineering and in health nanotechnology and biotechnology; to support the foundation of clinical research and innovation centers; and to promote the production of vaccines in Turkey.

In 2011, the share of R&D expenditures on health within the total public sector R&D expenditures was 3%; it is estimated that this proportion will increase three-fold by 2017, and five-fold by 2023.[32]

Emerging Challenges

Regarding health services and quality of life, the most important challenges Turkey faces today are poverty and economic and social disparities. As discussed earlier, health expenditures are only a small percentage of the general budget. On the other hand, the private sector is getting stronger in the healthcare industry. Social security funds do not fully cover every citizen, and out-of-pocket expenses are also increasing significantly. A major challenge in access to health care is unequal distribution of healthcare facilities and human power throughout the country. When Turkey got involved in global policies with the Health Transformation Programme and healthcare services were transferred to affiliated institutions, it resulted in an increase in authority conflicts and multi-headed management conflicts.

Mainly, there were three objectives of HTP: transformation of the primary healthcare system, the hospitals, and universal health insurance; all of them were implemented. With the transformation of the primary healthcare system, the family health system was accepted instead of improving health centers, thereby providing holistic, accessible, free, population and district-based health services. At the same time, primary healthcare services were divided into two parts; family health centers for individual health care and community health centers for community health care. Furthermore, the salaries of physicians working in FHCs are higher than the salaries of CHC physicians; this has been a threat to harmonious and peaceful working environments. Another problem with primary healthcare services is that performance-based payment is part of health personnel compensation in FHCs.

In the transformation program, hospitals have become for-profit private enterprises. This has led health care into an expensive market economy, which increases the already excessive out-of-pocket expenses and exacerbates the problems with access to health care and the disparities in the community. At the same time, subcontracting in the health sector and precarious working conditions in hospitals have been increasing. While the private sector is making a growing contribution to health care, public-private partnership is becoming more prevalent because of incentives.

The third objective of HTP, a universal health insurance system, was also carried out, but it has only covered those who pay their insurance premiums. It also has created a new burden of unpaid insurance premiums. Social security institution incomes are less than SSI expenses, and there is an SSI budget deficit; one cause of this deficit is an increase in health spending. Therefore, we can expect insurance premium increases, a decrease in services covered by insurance, and increased out-of-pocket expenses.

After nearly 10 years of implementation of HTP, health indicators are not at a desirable level in Turkey. The Organisation for Economic Co-operation and Development (OECD) 2014 report stated that "despite universal health coverage, health indicators still remain among the lowest in the OECD" and emphasized that "the focus of ongoing reform should move from quantity to quality assurance."[41]

References

1. *Ana Britannica*. Turkish ed. Cilt 21, İstanbul; 1990.
2. T.C. Anayasası. *Resmi Gazete*. The Turkish Constitution. State Official Journal. July 09, 1961:334.
3. T.C. Anayasası. *Resmi Gazete*. The Turkish Constitution. State Official Journal. November 09, 1982-17863.
4. DİE. *Türkiye İstatistik Yıllığı 2004*. SIS. *Turkey's Statistical Yearbook 2004*. Ankara; 2005.
5. 6271 sayılı Cumhurbaşkanı Seçimi Kanunu. *Resmi Gazete*. January 26, 2012:28185.
6. Dokuzuncu Kalkınma Planı. Ninth Development Plan. *Resmi Gazete*. (2007–2013). State Official Journal. July 01, 2016.
7. Organisation for Economic Co-operation and Development. OECD Economic Surveys Turkey. OECD Publishing. http://www.keepeek.com/Digital-Asset-Management/oecd/economics/oecd-economic-surveys-turkey-2016_eco_surveys-tur-2016-en#page1. July 2016. Accessed January 28, 2016.
8. TC Kalkınma Bakanlığı. Onuncu Kalkınma Planı (2014–2018). *Tenth Development Plan (2014-2018)*. Republic of Turkey Ministry of Development. Ankara; 2013.
9. TÜİK. Haber Bülteni. http://www.tuik.gov.tr/PreHaberBultenleri.do?id=21511. Accessed November 23, 2016.
10. TÜİK. www.tuik.gov.tr/PreIstatistikTablo.do?istab_id=2218. Accessed November 23, 2016.
11. TÜİK. http://www.tuik.gov.tr/UstMenu.do?metod=temelist. Accessed November 23, 2016.
12. TÜİK. http://www.tuik.gov.tr/PreHaberBultenleri.do?id=21684. Accessed November 23, 2016.
13. Fişek NH. Halk Sağlığına Giriş. Unpublished speech at the Turkish Council, Ankara; 1985.
14. TÜİK. Adrese Dayalı Nüfus Kayıt Sistemi Sonuçları 2015. http://www.tuik.gov.tr/PreHaberBultenleri.do?id=21507. Accessed January 28, 2016.
15. Sağlık Bakanlığı. Sağlık İstatistikleri Yıllığı 2014. The Ministry of Health of Turkey. *Health Statistics 2014*. Ankara; 2015.
16. Hacettepe Üniversitesi Nüfus Etüdleri Enstitüsü. *Türkiye Nüfus ve Sağlık Araştırması 2013*. Hacettepe University Institute of Population Studies. *Turkey Demographics and Health Survey 2013*. Ankara; 2014.
17. TÜİK. Yoksulluk Çalışması 2014. http://www.tuik.gov.tr/PreHaberBultenleri.do?id=18690. Accessed December 2, 2015.
18. TÜİK http://www.tuik.gov.tr/PreHaberBultenleri.do?id=21584. Accessed November 23, 2016.
19. Sağlık Bakanlığı. Sağlık İstatistikleri Yıllığı 2015 Haber Bülteni. http://www.saglik.gov.tr/TR/dosya/1-107917/h/yillik.pdf?hfiqnahfiqesiqgd. Accessed November 23, 2016.
20. Aydın E. Türkiye'de Sağlık Teşkilatlanması Tarihi. Ankara; 2002.

21. Sağlık Bakanlığı, Dr. Refik Saydam Turkey *1881-1942*. Ankara:USDIK Press; 1982.
22. Soyer A. Sağlığın Öyküsü. Unpublished speech at the Turkish Council. İstanbul; 2004.
23. Öztek Z. Türkiye'de Sağlık Hizmetleri: Sorunlar ve Çözumler, HASUDER raporu. Ankara; 2007.
24. Sağlık Bakanlığı. Temel Sağlık Hizmetleri Genel Müdürlüğü Çalışma Yıllığı. 2006. Turkish Government Report. Ankara; 2007.
25. The Ministry of Health. Health Transition Program. Ankara; 2008.
26. T.C. Sağlık Bakanlığı. Türkiye'de Sağlığa Bakış. The Ministry of Health. *Health at a Glance: Turkey 2007*. Ankara; 2007.
27. Ministry of Health of the Republic of Turkey. Transformation in Health. December, 2003.
28. Sağlık Bakanlığı, Türkiye Sağlıkta Dönüşüm Programı Değerlendirme Raporu (2003–2011). Aralık; 2012.
29. Aile Hekimliği Pilot Uygulaması Hakkında Kanun. *Resmi Gazete*. December 9, 2004: 25665.
30. Toplum Sağlığı Merkezi ve Bağlı Birimler Yönetmeliği. *Resmi Gazete*. February 5, 2015:29258.
31. Sağlık Bakanlığı ve Bağlı Kuruluşlarının Teşkilat ve Görevleri Hakkında Kanun Hakkında Kararname. *Resmi Gazete*. November 2, 2011:28103.
32. Sağlık Bakanlığı. Stratejk Plan 2013–2017. Ankara; Aralık 2012.
33. Aile Hekimliği Uygulama Yönetmeliği. *Resmi Gazete*. January 2013:28539.
34. Türkiye Halk Sağlığı Kurumu. 2015 Faaliyet Raporu. Ankara; Şubat, 2016.
35. Sağlık Bakanlığı. Yataklı Tedavi Kurumları Çalışma Yıllığı 2006. Ankara; 2007.
36. Bilim, Sanayi ve Teknoloji Bakanlığı. Türkiye ilaç sektörü strateji belgesi ve eylem planı 2015–2018. Ankara; 2015.
37. Sağlık Bakanlığı. Türkiye İlaç ve Tıbbi Cihaz Kurumu 2013–2017 Stratejik Planı. Ankara; Aralık; 2013.
38. Toplum ve Hekim. Panel: Türkiye Aşı Üretmeli mi? Üretebilir mi? 2003;1885:398–400.
39. Sosyal Güvenlik Kurumu. Startejik Plan 2015–2019. Ankara; 2015.
40. TÜİK. Sağlık Harcamaları İstatistikleri, 2015. http://www.tuik.gov.tr/PreHaberBultenleri.do?id=21527. Accessed November 15, 2016.
41. Organisation for Economic Co-operation and Development. *OECD Reviews of Health Care Quality: Turkey 2014: Raising Standards*. OECD Publishing. 2014. doi: 10.1787/9789264202054-en.

CHAPTER 16

Jordan

Hani Michel Samawi, James E. Dotherow IV, and **Hala Madanat**

Country Description

TABLE 16-1 Jordan

Nationality	Noun: Jordanian(s) Adjective: Jordanian
Ethnic groups	Arab 98%, Circassian 1%, Armenian 1%
Religions	Sunni Muslim 97.2%, Christian 2.2% (majority Greek Orthodox, but some Greek and Roman Catholics, Syrian Orthodox, Coptic Orthodox, Armenian Orthodox, and Protestant denominations), other <1% (several small Shi'a Muslim and Druze populations) (2015 est.)
Language	Arabic (official), English widely understood among upper and middle classes
Literacy	Definition: Age 15 and over can read and write. Total population: 95.4% Male: 97.7% Female: 92.9% (2015 est.)
Government type	Constitutional monarchy
Date of independence	May 25, 1946 (from League of Nations mandate under British administration)
Gross Domestic Product (GDP) per capita	$12,100 (2015 est.)

(continues)

TABLE 16-1 Jordan (continued)

Unemployment rate	13% official rate; unofficial rate is approximately 30% (2015 est.)
Natural hazards	Droughts, periodic earthquakes
Environment: current issues	Limited natural freshwater resources, deforestation, overgrazing, soil erosion, desertification
Population	8,117,564 (July 2015 est.)
Age structure	0–14 years: 35.04% (male 1,470,865/female 1,397,057) 15–24 years: 20.12% (male 842,202/female 804,557) 25–54 years: 36.44% (male 1,491,855/female 1,491,302) 55–64 years: 4.46% (male 177,720/female 187,181) 65 years and over: 3.94% (male 151,071/female 171,574) (2016 est.)
Median age	Total: 22 years Male: 21.7 years Female: 22.4 years (2015 est.)
Population growth rate	0.83% (2015 est.)
Birth rate	25.37 births/1,000 population (2015 est.)
Death rate	746 deaths/100,000 population (2016 est.)
Disease burden	Communicable disease deaths: 53/100,000 population Noncommunicable disease deaths: 640/100,000 population Injury deaths: 54/100,000 population (2016 est.)
Net migration rate	−13.24 migrant(s)/1,000 population (2015 est.)
Gender ratio	At birth: 1.06 male(s)/female 0–14 years: 1.05 male(s)/female 15–24 years: 1.05 male(s)/female 25–54 years: 1 male(s)/female 55–64 years: 0.95 male(s)/female 65 years and over: 0.89 male(s)/female Total population: 1.02 male(s)/female (2016 est.)
Infant mortality rate	Total: 15.18 deaths/1,000 live births Male: 16.05 deaths/1,000 live births Female: 14.25 deaths/1,000 live births (2015 est.)
Life expectancy at birth	Total population: 74.35 years Male: 73 years Female: 75.78 years (2015 est.)
Total fertility rate	3.17 children born/woman (2015 est.)
HIV/AIDS adult prevalence rate	Less than 0.1% (2015)

TABLE 16-1 Jordan (continued)	
Number of people living with HIV/AIDS	325 (2015 est.)
HIV/AIDS deaths	Less than 100 (2015 est.)

Data from Central Intelligence Agency. The World Fact Book, 2016: Jordan. https://www.cia.gov/library/publications/the-world-factbook. Accessed June 2016; World Health Organization. Jordan: WHO statistical profile.

History

Jordan is a small Arab country that has limited natural resources. Its history, during and after World War I, is most relevant to understanding the current state of its healthcare system; however, historically, the land, known today as Jordan, was where major highways connecting the Middle East met and crossed.[1] Thus, its location has always been of great strategic importance to trade and communications.[1]

Since the mid-17th century, Jordan has been under the control of various Arab and Islamic dynasties, the last of these being the four centuries of Ottoman rule (1516–1918).[2] The Ottoman rule was generally seen as a period of limited development and much oppression. As World War I broke out, the Ottoman Empire sided with the Germans, and the Arabs saw a chance for liberation of their land. Sharif Hussein, great grandfather of King Hussein (the third king of Jordan) and leader of the Arab Nationalist Movement, negotiated with the British, who promised support for a unified Arab kingdom. Consequently, he initiated the Great Arab Revolt against the Ottoman rule; however, when the war ended, Britain and France denied Arabs their unified kingdom and had already divided the land into mandates and protectorates. The land of Jordan was now a British mandate, with Sharif Hussein's son Emir Abdullah being proclaimed ruler in 1921. That same year, he established the first centralized governmental system, in 'Amman (the capital of Jordan).[1,2]

The years that followed were all spent establishing modern Jordan and achieving independence. In 1928, a constitution was developed that provided for a parliament; it was known as the Legislative Council, and elections were held in February 1929. In 1946, Jordan received its full independence from the British and became known as the Hashemite Kingdom of Jordan, with King Abdullah named as the first king of the country. On the other side of the Jordan River, however, Palestine, which had been a British mandate but had been promised in the 1917 Balfour declaration as a Jewish homeland, became the state of Israel in 1948 as the British left it. This led to the first Arab-Israeli war, and over half a million displaced Palestinian refugees came to Jordan and were granted citizenship. The remainder of the Palestinian territories that were not under Israeli rule became part of the Kingdom of Jordan.[2]

In 1951, King Abdullah was assassinated in Jerusalem, and his eldest son, Crown Prince Talal, assumed the throne. King Talal abdicated the throne because of health reasons in 1952; however, during his short reign, King Talal was able to develop a new modern constitution that is still being used today. According to this constitution, King Talal's eldest son could not assume his duties as king until he had reached the age of 18 under the Muslim calendar (16 years of age). Thus, a council performed his functions until May 2, 1953, when King Hussein became the third king of Jordan.[2]

The years that followed had much political upheaval, and in 1967, Jordan and other Arab countries lost to Israel the remainder of the Palestinian territories. This led to an increase in the Palestinian refugees in Jordan, which were now estimated at over 1 million. This was followed by increased power by the Palestinian resistance groups in Jordan (known as *fedayeen*), and in 1970, this led to open fire between the Jordanian armed forces and the Palestinian fighters, who were expelled from Jordan in 1971.[2]

The years that followed were of much importance politically and economically. In 1973, the Arab nations were involved in another war with Israel. In 1974, King Hussein issued a royal decree dissolving the parliament, and in 1978, he replaced it with the National Consultative Council (until 1984).[3] In 1989, elections were reinstated, and the country initiated political and economic reforms. The Gulf War of 1990–1991, however, saw the return of many Jordanians working in the Gulf. This significantly decreased the income from worker remittances and further increased the population.[2]

In 1999, King Hussein died of cancer, and his eldest son King Abdullah II assumed the throne and continued his father's major economic reforms; however, the U.S.-led war in Iraq in 2003 led to an influx of 750,000 Iraqi refugees into Jordan, which further strained its economy.[4]

Size and Geography

Jordan has a coastline of 16 miles (26 kilometers). The land area is 34,318 square miles (88,884 square kilometers), and the water area is 127 square miles (329 square kilometers). Jordan's total area is 34,445 square miles (89,213 square kilometers). The land forms in Jordan are generally flat desert plateau, east and west. In the west, the Great Rift Valley (high hills and mountains) separates the East and West banks of the Jordan River. Significant bordering bodies of water include the Dead Sea, the Gulf of Aqaba, and the Sea of Galilee. The highest point, Jabal Rum, reaches 5,689 feet (1,734 meters), and the lowest point is the Dead Sea at −1,338.6 feet (408 meters) below sea level[5] (**FIGURE 16-1**).

Jordan is divided into 12 governorates, including Ajlun, Al 'Aqabah, Al Balqa', Al Karak, Mafraq,

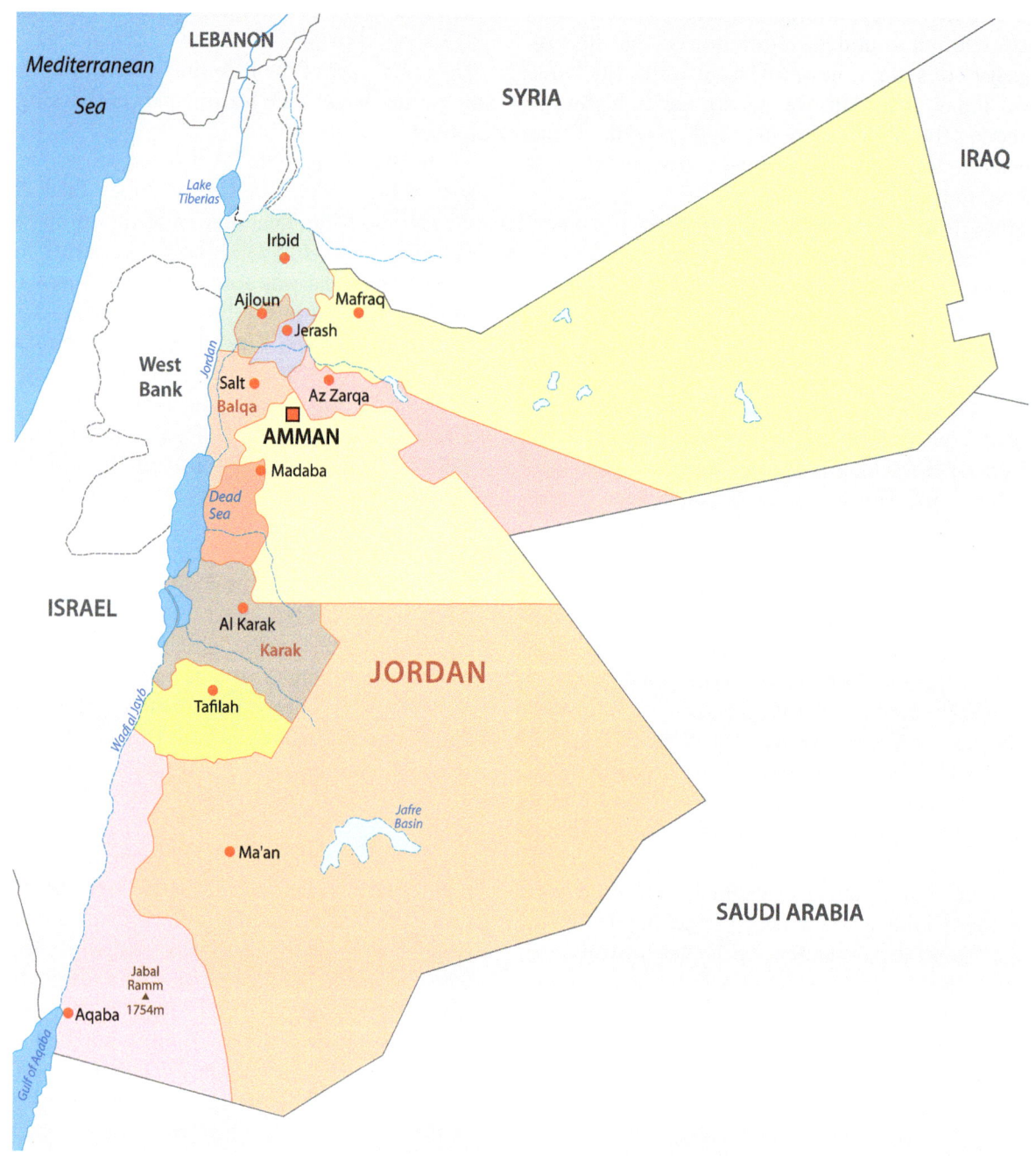

FIGURE 16-1 Map of Jordan
© Rainer Lesniewski/Shutterstock

'Amman, At Tafilah, Az Zarqa', Irbid, Jarash, Ma'an, and Madaba. Urbanization rates have increased drastically over the last 3 decades, and in 2015, 82.6% of the population lived in urban areas compared with 17.4% living in rural areas. More specifically, the population was concentrated in three main urban centers: 'Amman (38.8%), Az Zarqa' (14.9%), and Irbid (17.8%).[6]

Government and Political System

According to its constitution, the Hashemite Kingdom of Jordan is "parliamentary with a hereditary monarchy."[7] The king is the head of state, the chief executive, and the commander-in-chief of the armed forces. The king exercises his executive authority by appointing a prime minister, who then organizes a cabinet of ministers that has to be approved by the king. The prime minister and the cabinet must then be approved by the lower house of Parliament, the House of Deputies. If the House of Deputies votes against the prime minister, he and his entire cabinet must resign. The Lower House can also vote any individual minister out of office. The king also appoints all of the members of the upper house of Parliament, known as the Senate. The number of senators cannot exceed one half of the number of elected representatives.[7]

The cabinet is responsible before the elected House of Deputies, which along with the Senate constitutes the legislative branch of the government. The judicial branch, however, is an independent branch of the government.

The Constitution in Jordan specifically guarantees the rights of Jordanian citizens, including the freedoms of speech and press, association, academic pursuit, organization into political parties, religion, and the right to elect parliamentary and municipal representatives.[7]

Moreover, in the Constitution, the king must approve laws before they can take effect, although his authority can be overridden by a two-thirds majority vote of both houses of Parliament. He also authorizes the appointment and dismissal of judges, regional governors, and the mayor of 'Amman. He also approves constitutional amendments and declares war. As the commander-in-chief of the armed forces, the king ratifies treaties and agreements with the approval of the cabinet and parliament. The king is also entitled to grant special pardons and amnesties.[7]

Macroeconomics

Jordan's economic resources are based on phosphates, potash, and their fertilizer derivatives; tourism; overseas remittances; and foreign aids. These are Jordan's principal sources of hard-currency earnings. Jordan lacks forests, coal reserves, hydroelectric power, and commercially viable oil deposits.

In the late 1980s, Jordan went through a major economic crisis. In 1988, the Jordanian dinar depreciated by 48.5%. Unemployment rates reached an unprecedented 20%, and inequality and poverty increased dramatically.[8] During the first Gulf War, Jordan dealt with major reductions in its foreign aid, especially from the United States. Its trade was also largely affected because of the restrictions imposed on export of its agricultural products to Iraq, the primary location for export of its goods, and the rest of the Gulf countries. The number of refugees and returning workers from Iraq and the Gulf region further exacerbated the problem, especially with the large number of Palestinian refugees already in the country.[8]

The 1989 economic reforms were mainly geared toward liberalization, privatization, and removal of all trade barriers. In 2000, Jordan became the 136th member of the World Trade Organization and signed a free-trade agreement with the United States that same year. Furthermore, the private sector has been working closely with the government on development issues, such as the opening of export markets and attracting foreign and private investors into the country with hope of increasing job opportunities for Jordanians and decreasing the unemployment rates.[9]

Economically, Jordan is considered an upper middle-income country with a human development index of 0.748 and a Gini coefficient of 33.700.[33] Its per capita gross domestic product (GDP) increased from US $4,700 in 2007 to $11,406 in 2011; however, there has been a decline in real per capita income, increase in poverty, and decline in living standards. It was estimated that in 2015, 27% of families lived under the poverty line. This was a significant increase from 19% in 1987 and 21% in 1992.[11]

In 2015, Jordan's total GDP was US $37.52 billion, up from $30.94 billion in 2012. The estimated GDP growth rate was 2.4% in 2015 and 3% in 2016, and a growth of at least 3% is expected to continue until 2018. Moreover, in 2015, services (including finance, real estate, transport and communications, and government services) continued to dominate the economy, accounting for more than 66% of GDP. Industry contributed about 29.6% of GDP (including manufacturing, 17% of GDP). Agriculture provided just 4.2% of GDP.[32]

Demographics

Jordan faces a unique situation in terms of its demographic transition. In 1980, the population was 2.2 million, doubled by 1999, and is expected to double again by 2035.[6] In 2015, there was an estimated 8,117,564 people in Jordan, with a median age of 22 years, reflecting a young population.[6] These demographic changes are due to the influx of refugees from surrounding countries, as well as the healthcare reforms that are associated with decreased infant mortality rate and continued high fertility rates. Infant mortality rates have dropped from 160 per 1,000 live births in 1950 to only about 14 per 1,000 live births in 2016.[6,8] Although fertility rates have declined from 7.8 in 1970 to about 3.17 in 2015, they still remain higher than surrounding countries. Life expectancy has also dramatically changed, increasing from 54 years in 1970 to 74 years in 2015.

In 2015, the age distribution of the population was as follows: 35.42% were under the age of 15, 60.67% were between the ages of 15 and 64, and only 3.91% were 65 years of age or older. Approximately 48.5% of the population was female, and 51.5% was male.[13] The literacy for those 15 years of age or older was 95.4%, with 53.1% of the population having less than secondary education, 28.2% with a secondary education, 8.0% with an intermediate diploma, and 10.7% of the population with at least a bachelor's degree.[6] The religious distribution was as follows: Sunni Muslim (97.2%), Christian (2.2%), and others (0.6%).[13]

▸ Brief History of the Healthcare System

Pre–World War II

Jordan's healthcare system passed through two distinct phases. The first phase (1921–1946) was before Jordan was recognized as a kingdom. In 1921, Math'har Pasha Arsalan was recognized as the first health consultant to work in Jordan, and Dr. Rida Tawfiq was appointed as director of health. That same year, Jordan's first public hospital was established with 20 hospital beds. In 1923, Transjordan issued its first health law, which related to the practice of hospital medicine and was issued by the advisory council of the time. In 1924, the Italian Hospital in the city of Salt was approved by Prince Abdullah, and the city of Jerusalem established its first medical laboratory (the first laboratory to open in 'Amman was not until 1940). The following year, the first pharmacy opened in Transjordan, and Dr. Haleem Abu Rahmeh established the first health department, where he continued to work until 1939.[14] The first regulatory health law was decreed in Transjordan in 1926 and was used until 1971. About 28 male and female physicians were working in Transjordan by 1926, and the number increased to 39 by the end of the following year. That same year, the number of beds reached 60 in public hospitals and 99 in private hospitals.[14] By 1946, there were 7 hospitals in the capital city of 'Amman.

Since World War II

The second phase started in 1948 and has continued until the present. During this phase, the Arab-Israeli wars occurred, which added more burdens on the healthcare system because of the large influx of Palestinian refugees.[14] In 1950, however, the first ministry of health (MoH) was established and started its functions in 1951, followed by establishment of the physician union in 1954 and the central laboratory for medical tests in 1955.

Starting with opening of the first nursing school in 1953, health-related educational programs increased. In 1962, the Princess Mona nursing college opened, followed by the first medical school at the University of Jordan in 1970, the institute of allied health professions in 'Amman in 1973 and in Irbid in 1978, and the first pharmacy college in 1980.

The first health insurance system was implemented in 1963 for armed forces personnel, and the first public health insurance system for civilians was implemented in 1965. The King Hussein Medical Center was inaugurated in 1973 and is currently the largest referral and teaching hospital in Jordan and a part of the Royal Medical Services (RMS).

▸ Description of the Current Healthcare System

Jordan is considered as having one of the most modernized healthcare infrastructures in the region.[15] The healthcare system is also more complex, as it is composed of three sectors: public, private, and donors. The public sector is further divided into four groups: the MoH (see **FIGURE 16-2** for an organizational chart of the MoH), the RMS, the smaller university-based programs—the largest of which are the Jordan University Hospital (JUH) in 'Amman and the King Abdullah University Hospital (KAUH) in Irbid—and medical services linked to the ministries and public institutions.[16]

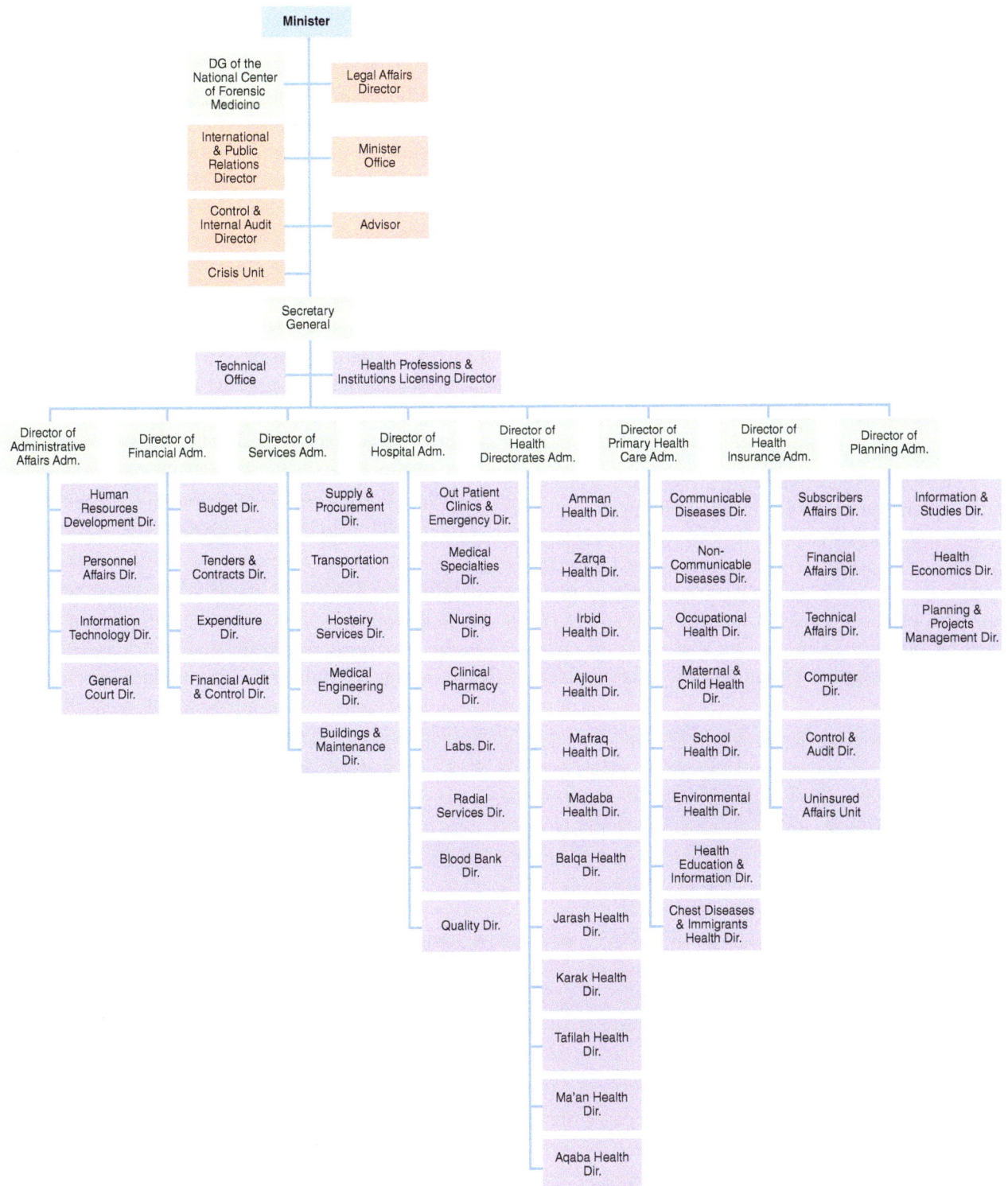

FIGURE 16-2 Organizational Chart for the Ministry of Health
Modified from Jordan Ministry of Health. http://www.moh.gov.jo/EN/AbouttheMinistryofHealth/Pages/Organizational-Chart.aspx

The MoH is considered the "single institution financer and provider of healthcare services in Jordan" and is the largest component of the healthcare delivery system compared with all other parts of the public and private sectors.[15] On the other hand, the RMS services are extended to all military and security personnel, as well as all uninsured patients referred from the MoH and the private sector.[15]

The private sector includes private hospitals, private clinics, and privately owned diagnostic facilities and allied health services.[16] A SWOT (strengths, weaknesses, opportunities, and threats) analysis of the private sector in Jordan reveals a need for better collaboration between the public and private sectors, as well as better regulation of its services.[15]

The donor sector includes services provided by the United Nations Relief and Works Agency for Palestine Refugees in the Near East (UNRWA) and other clinics and medical services provided by foreign non-governmental agencies (NGOs).[16]

Facilities

In 2015, there were 104 hospitals in Jordan, up from 95 in 2002, with 13,115 hospital beds, of which 38.3% were in MoH hospitals, 19.2% in RMS hospitals, 8.9% in the two university-based hospitals, and 33.6% in private hospitals. Thus, there was 1 hospital bed per 10,000 in the population. In addition to its hospitals, the MoH operated 99 comprehensive health centers, 378 primary health centers, 198 peripheral health centers, 460 maternal and child health centers, 12 chest disease centers, and 402 dental clinics.[29] Furthermore, the UNWRA provides care for more than 600,000 Palestinian refugees, many of whom are also covered by MoH and RMS. UNRWA operates 23 health and maternal and child health centers, but all inpatient services were provided through the MoH or RMS.[15] Although nursing homes exist in Jordan, the majority of the elderly population is cared for by family members. The health services (clinics and hospitals) are well distributed throughout the country. It is estimated that the average travel time to the nearest health center is 30 minutes.[15]

Workforce

In 2015, the private sector employed the majority of health professionals, with 71% of all physicians working in the private sector, 92% of all pharmacists, 85% of all dentists, and 22% of all nurses. It was estimated that the MoH and RMS hire 25% and 8% of all practicing physicians, respectively.[29]

Jordan has a large workforce of health professionals. The rate of health professionals per 10,000 population in 2015 was as follows: 27.30 physicians, 7.10 dentists, 12.70 pharmacists, 13.50 registered nurses, 5.24 associate degree nurses, 4.05 assistant nurses, and 2.02 midwives.[29] **TABLE 16-2** shows the health professionals by sector.

Technology and Equipment

Although Jordan's healthcare infrastructure is considered modern and better than many middle-income countries in the region, it continues to lag in production of medical

TABLE 16-2 Health Personnel by Selected Category and Health Sectors in Jordan, 2015

Category	Sector						Total	Rate per 10,000 population
	MoH	RMS	JUH	KAUH	Private	UNRWA		
Physicians	4,809	1,552	548	521	18,469	120	2,6019	27.30
Dentists	692	275	37	0	5,771	31	6,806	7.14
Pharmacists	622	286	22	28	11,116	2	12,076	12.67
Registered nurses	5,152	3,389	499	658	3,126	48	12,872	13.50
Associate degree nurses	2,170	2,633	154	38	0	0	4,995	5.24
Assistant nurses	2,017	0	59	42	1,549	194	3,861	4.05
Midwives	1,399	236	10	16	228	34	1,923	2.02

Data are from MOH, RMS, JUH, KAH, UNRWA, and doctors, dentists, pharmacists, and nurses associations. In Jordan Ministry of Health Annual Statistical Book 2007. Retrieved from http://www.moh.gov.jo/MOH/En/publications.php.

equipment, which is generally below international standards and limited to beds, medical dressing, plastic syringes, some optical products, and dental supplies.

In 2004, however, the MoH set a plan with public and private sectors to generate an annual US $1 billion in medical tourism by the year 2010. To reach this goal and to compete with neighboring countries that also have the ambition of becoming medical hubs in the region, there is a need to continuously upgrade and improve the medical services, facilities, and institutions, including the quality of hospital and clinic management and administration. Most of the medical equipment used is purchased from the United States and is exempt from custom duties.

Jordan's pharmaceutical industry was the second largest exporting industry in 2014 (80% of Jordanian production was exported, and Jordanian firms are the biggest pharmaceutical exporters by trade volume in the region). There were 22 factories in the pharmaceutical sector, with 5 major companies dominating the export business. The sector has modern plants, established regional marketing channels, and a skilled, low-cost workforce. Despite increasing local production, the demand for imported, patented medicines is expected to increase. U.S. pharmaceutical exports to Jordan totaled $308 million in 2014, and market opportunities for U.S. products are expected to increase.[15,39]

▶ Evaluation of the Healthcare System

Cost

Comparatively, Jordan spends a high percentage of its GDP on health. In 2014, 5.10% of GDP was spent on health by the public sector alone, down from 5.92% in 2010. No data on private health expenditures were found after 2001; however, in 2014, 2.26% of GDP was spent on health in the private sector. Thus, total health expenditures accounted for 7.45% of GDP in 2014.[30] The total healthcare expenditure in 2014 was approximately JD1.89 billion (US $2.7 billion), which translated into a per capita healthcare expenditure of JD255 ($359).[30]

One of the largest constraints of the healthcare system in Jordan has been the high cost of pharmaceuticals. In 2008 the pharmaceutical expenditure accounted for 35.9% of the total health expenditure, translating to JD32.6 (US $46) per capita, with 61.5% of these expenditures in the private health sector.[15,38]

Jordan's healthcare system is financed by three sources: (1) public funding (50% in 2015), such as general taxation and premiums paid by public firms; (2) household spending (42%), which refers to payroll deductions for insurance, direct expenditure on private healthcare services and pharmaceuticals, and premiums paid by private companies to insure their employees; and (3) donor contributions (8%), which includes the UNRWA and other NGOs.[34]

With the decline in public expenditure on health over the last couple decades (51% in 1990 to 5.1% in 2014), it appears that the private sector has risen as an important source of healthcare services in Jordan. An area of concern has been the weak investment in public health and health education. In 2015, 58% of public expenditure on health was spent on secondary and tertiary health care, 27% on preventive services and primary care, 5% on administrative activities, 3% on training, and 7% on miscellaneous activities.[15] It can be assumed that if Jordan does not increase its spending on prevention efforts, a higher percentage of its GDP will eventually be spent on health.[15] According to the Health Law of Jordan, the MoH is responsible not only for providing curative services but also preventative and surveillance programs. In addition, the MoH is in charge of supervising both the public and private health sectors, providing insurance for the citizens, and establishing and managing educational and training programs for health.[15]

Quality

According to the MoH's mortality statistics, chronic diseases are the leading cause of mortality in Jordan. The leading cause of death in 2012 was circulatory system diseases, attributed to 36.7% of deaths. Within this group, ischemic heart diseases rank first with 11.4%, followed by hypertensive diseases at 10.6% and cerebrovascular diseases at 9.1%. Neoplasms were the second leading cause of death at 16.2%. The leading causes within that group were throat and lung cancer, intestine cancer, and breast cancer. **TABLE 16-3** presents the 2012 mortality data for the leading causes of death. One alarming fact was the amount of external causes of mortality (9.37%), mainly caused by transport accidents.[35]

Furthermore, the age-adjusted death rates were highest among the older age groups. **TABLE 16-4** shows the numbers of deaths, death rates, and percentage of change in death rates by age and gender.[18] In addition, the under-five mortality rate in 2012 was 19 per 1,000, with life expectancy at 74 years. The total fertility rate in 2013 was 3.2.[31] Although Jordan seems to have accurate mortality data, morbidity data are inadequate with almost all non-MoH clinics and health centers and most hospitals not coding diseases.[15]

TABLE 16-3 2012 Mortality Data for Top 10 Leading Causes of Death in Jordan

Rank	Cause of death*	Deaths	% of total deaths	2012 crude rate	2012 age-adjusted rate
—	All causes	17,557	100.00	2.748	4.755
1	Circulatory system diseases (I00–I99)	6,436	36.66	1.008	2.006
2	Neoplasms (C00–D48)	2,845	16.20	0.445	0.811
3	External causes (V01–Y89)	1,645	9.37	0.258	0.299
4	Endocrine, nutritional, and metabolic diseases (E00-E89)	1,398	7.96	0.219	0.432
5	Respiratory system diseases (J00-J98)	1,030	5.87	0.161	0.288
6	Perinatal conditions (P00-P96)	958	5.46	0.150	0
7	Congenital malformations (Q00-Q99)	748	4.26	0.117	0.109
8	Genitourinary diseases (N00-N99)	544	3.10	0.085	0.162
9	Digestive system diseases (K00-K99)	523	2.98	0.082	0.155
10	Symptoms and signs not elsewhere classified (R00-R99)	512	2.92	0.080	0.158
—	Other (residuals)	918	5.24	0.060	—

*Cause of death is based on the International Classification of Diseases (ICD), 10th revision, 1992. The codes are the standard diagnostic tools for epidemiology, health management, and clinical purposes.[37]

Data from Jordan Ministry of Health. Mortality in Jordan, 2005. http://www.moh.gov.jo/EN/Pages/HealthStatisticsandIndicators.aspx

Jordan, however, has achieved universal child immunization since 1988. It has been polio free since 1995, and no diphtheria cases have been reported since 1993, with a small number of pertussis and tetanus cases reported. It is estimated that 97% of children have been immunized for polio, diphtheria, pertussis, and tetanus.[15]

The public sector programs are comprehensive and include access to pharmaceuticals with minimal cost to the patients. Although the uninsured are able to receive all public health services at highly subsidized prices, they have to pay full price for pharmaceuticals. On the other hand, private insurances vary widely in their comprehensiveness.

TABLE 16-4 Mortality Data by Age and Gender

Age	Both genders	Male	Female	Both genders	Male	Female	Both genders	Male	Female
	Deaths			Rate			Percentage change in rate, 2004–2005		
All ages	12,066	7,066	5,000	—	—	—	—	—	—
Crude	—	—	—	2.20	2.50	1.89	−3.5	−3.7	−3.3
Age adjusted	—	—	—	3.75	4.29	3.18	−4.3	−4.5	−4.0
Under 1 year	1,386	754	632	10.51	11.18	9.81	9.6	11.9	7.1
1–4 years	480	243	237	0.85	0.84	0.86	−9.4	−20.6	5.8
5–9 years	214	123	91	0.31	0.35	0.27	−7.0	−10.3	−2.3
10–14 years	148	98	50	0.23	0.29	0.16	−11.2	3.0	−30.2
15–19 years	196	134	62	0.33	0.43	0.21	−5.6	4.0	−21.3
20–24 years	267	183	84	0.46	0.61	0.30	−6.5	−5.3	−8.8
25–29 years	256	180	76	0.52	0.70	0.33	0.9	13.5	−20.1
30–34 years	237	154	83	0.55	0.69	0.40	−11.6	−10.9	−12.8
35–39 years	317	201	116	0.91	1.11	0.70	7.2	4.0	13.4
40–44 years	352	216	136	1.36	1.62	1.08	8.5	1.5	22.0
45–49 years	379	257	122	2.07	2.74	1.37	−2.2	−1.1	−4.6
50–54 years	439	280	159	3.19	4.03	2.33	0.0	−2.9	5.7
55–59 years	662	412	250	5.43	6.89	4.03	−12.7	−7.0	
60–64 years	1,087	676	411	10.26	12.10	8.20	−7.9	−10.5	−3.2
65–69 years	1,343	808	535	17.47	20.46	14.31	−2.4	−4.4	0.8
70–74 years	1,359	764	595	26.87	30.09	23.62	−4.9	−6.6	−2.6
75–79 years	1,222	733	489	45.97	51.95	39.21	−3.2	−0.4	−7.1
80–84 years	749	390	359	51.83	60.09	45.10	−7.9	−2.6	−13.0
85 years and older	931	440	491	113.68	111.39	115.80	−6.2	−11.2	−1.3
Not stated	42	20	22	—	—	—	—	—	—

Data from Jordan Ministry of Health. Mortality in Jordan, 2005. http://www.moh.gov.jo/EN/Pages/HealthStatisticsandIndicators.aspx

Access

Understanding the coverage provided by the healthcare system in Jordan is complicated largely because of the fact that often individuals are eligible for more than one insurance program, and many choose to pay out-of-pocket premiums to maintain private insurances. It was estimated that in 2015, 48% of the population was covered through the MoH or RMS, and an additional 20% was covered through private insurance or UNRWA. The remaining 32% that were not eligible for free health care through the public sector were still able to purchase all MoH facility services at highly subsidized prices; thus making it possible for everyone to receive health care.[15]

Although almost half of the population is covered through MoH and RMS, higher spending (58%) occurs in the private sector, indicating that a portion of those eligible for public sector services chooses to use the private sector instead. In reviewing the equity of the healthcare system, the World Health Organization (WHO) concluded the following:

> In assessing the "fairness" of the contribution/revenue base for financing the health system, one should consider whether individuals' contributions both through the general government revenue system and out-of-pocket are based on "ability to pay." The overall incidence of Jordan's general revenue structure is not progressive, since only a very limited proportion of revenues derive from progressive income taxes. In terms of individuals' contributions for services, while the Government, in effect, does potentially finance and provide subsidized care for the entire population, the structure of MoH and RMS eligibility and premiums as well as the higher payment levels required by the uninsured suggest that equity could be improved.[15]

Reproduced from World Health Organization. Health System Profile—Jordan. http://apps.who.int/medicinedocs/documents/s17296e/s17296e.pdf. Accessed June 5, 2008. Copyright 2006.

The report also indicates, however, that the government has taken significant measures to improve equity: (1) all government employees are eligible for the Civil Health Insurance Program (CHIP) regardless of their position; (2) children and husbands of female government employees are eligible for CHIP; (3) all children under the age of six years and people living in poverty pockets will have free health insurance; and (4) any citizen who wishes to enroll in CHIP can at the highly subsidized rates. The intent of these changes was to achieve coverage for all with minimal costs for the patient.[15]

In addition, the WHO report finds that Jordan has a "well-developed delivery system with a significant amount of capacity." WHO recognizes that there are differences among governorates and some groups, such as the near poor and those in rural geographic areas who have more difficulty accessing secondary and tertiary health services. However, the Royal Court clinics have devised a system in which these individuals can apply and be referred to the public hospitals for all needed health services, and the government reimburses these hospitals for the full cost of the services.[15]

▸ Current and Emerging Issues and Challenges

Noncommunicable Diseases

As Jordan has gone through both epidemiologic and demographic transitions, the expected declines in infant mortality, maternal mortality, total fertility rate, and infectious diseases have occurred, but these have given rise to an increase in noncommunicable diseases, such as cardiovascular diseases and cancer.[15] These changes have occurred at a fast rate, with the declines starting in the late 1970s, and have burdened the healthcare system, which was equipped to deal with the communicable diseases but not with the noncommunicable diseases, which often require more expensive diagnostics, treatments, and more training for the health professionals. It appears that Jordan's healthcare system has been able to catch up with many of those changes.[15]

It seems, however, that the current emerging health issues in Jordan are related to the increases in noncommunicable diseases. Jordan has observed dramatic increases in lifestyle-related diseases and conditions, such as lung cancer, cardiovascular diseases, obesity, and diabetes.[19] Ischemic heart disease (16.8%), stroke (10.7%), and hypertensive heart disease (4.3%) accounted for more than 30.0% of all deaths in 2012. Diabetes mellitus accounted for 6.7% of deaths, and kidney diseases accounted for 4.2%. While the crude death rates for ischemic heart disease and stroke have steadied and slightly declined over since 2008, death rates for diabetes mellitus, hypertensive heart disease, and kidney diseases have been rising (see **FIGURE 16-3**). The prevalence of noncommunicable diseases is affecting both men and women, and the probability of dying between the ages of 30 and 70 years from the four main ones is 20.0%.[31,36]

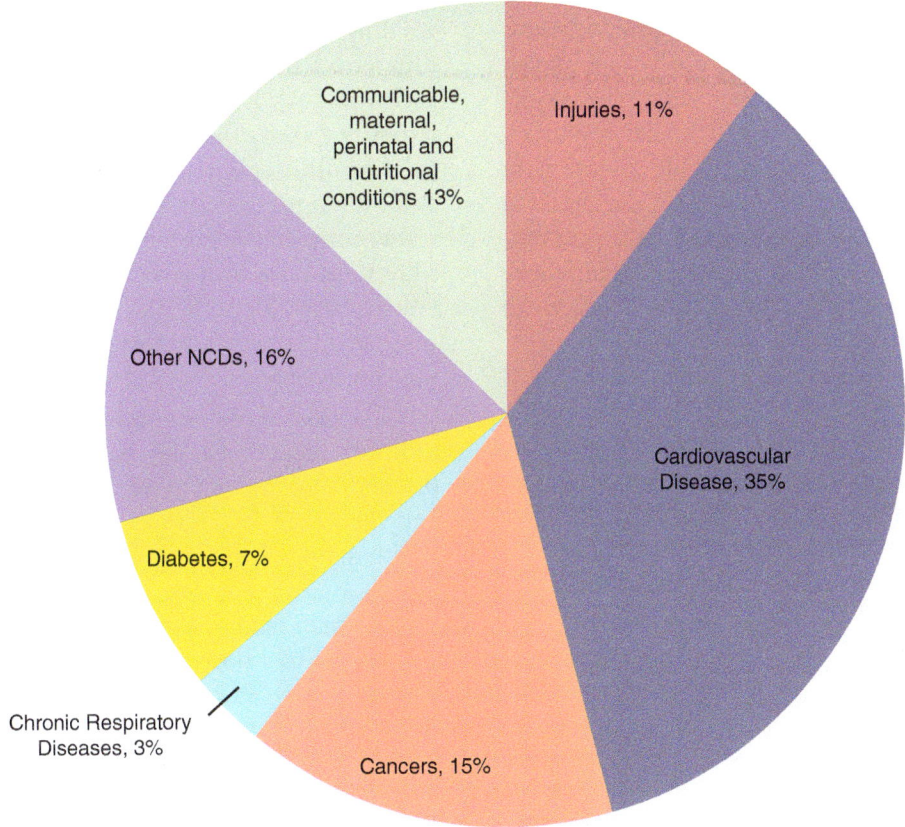

FIGURE 16-3 2014 Proportional Mortality

Reproduced from World Health Organization. Noncommunicable Diseases Country Profiles. http://who.int/nmh/countries/jor_en.pdf?ua=1. 2014. Copyright 2014.

For example, two studies found that the majority of women (54%) were overweight or obese, and approximately 42% fell in the normal range of body mass index.[19,20] Furthermore, in assessing the prevalence of risk factors associated with noncommunicable diseases in this population, the behavioral risk factor surveillance system found high levels of obesity, hypertension, high cholesterol, and diabetes in addition to high percentages of undiagnosed cases. Only 15.2% had been told they had hypertension compared with 30.2% who had hypertension; 8.5% had been diagnosed with high cholesterol compared with 23.1% who had high cholesterol; 22.4% thought that they were obese compared with 34.8% who were actually obese; and only 9.0% had been told they were diabetic compared with 16.9% who were. These high levels of underdiagnoses are alarming and require that a plan is developed and put into action to increase awareness, diagnosis, and early prevention or treatment.[17]

One study on the impact of Westernization on eating styles, body image, and the nutrition transition found that Jordanian women had high levels of overweight and obesity coupled with large levels of restrained eating, emotional eating, and disordered eating attitudes and behaviors; however, women had lower body dissatisfaction than is observed in other countries. It was argued that these women were caught between the traditional and modern societies, where the dietary patterns and eating habits were increasingly Westernized while the body esteem and body size preferences remained more traditional. Furthermore, the study highlighted the importance of assessing eating disorders in the population.[20]

Another important risk factor for noncommunicable diseases is tobacco use. Studies have shown alarming rates of smoking in the general population of Jordan. It was estimated that in 2011, 47% of adult males and 25% of boys ages 13 to 15 years smoked a tobacco product, whereas use for females was 6% of adults and 14.5% of girls ages 13 to 15 years.[21,31] Studies have also shown a high prevalence of smoking among medical professionals and students in 'Amman: 22.4% for male and 9.1% for female physicians, 42% for male nurses and 13% for female nurses, and 26% for male students and 7% for female medical students.[22–24] This unhealthy behavior has been of much concern, as lung cancer has become the third leading cancer in

Jordan.[25] Jordan has one of the oldest tobacco policies (1977) prohibiting smoking in public places; however, enforcement of this law remains low. Attempts to reduce consumption of tobacco products in developing countries has been problematic. The WHO identifies the "lack of adequate financial resources, inadequate commitment among some government sources, and lack of adequate studies on the smoking hazards" as Jordan's main obstacle in tobacco prevention. Understanding the factors that deter or influence tobacco consumption in this population is crucial to developing appropriate health education programs.[26]

Another cause for alarm is the number of deaths associated with road-traffic injuries. These deaths are easily preventable through the enforcement of traffic laws and the improvement of pedestrian walkways. Jordan has committed to reducing these deaths and injuries; however, this commitment is recent, and there are currently no data available on the changes in road-traffic deaths.[18]

Environmental Factors

Jordan is considered one of the world's 10 most water-stressed countries. In addition to the lack of water resources, pollution has made the situation worse. The majority of water pollution is linked to lack of management of domestic wastewater and disposal of industrial waste, which leaches from unsanitary solid waste landfills and agrochemical sources.[15]

Solid-waste collection and disposal has been inefficient largely because of budgetary constraints of the MoH and the Ministry of Environment, which are both in charge of its management. This problem is further exacerbated by the lack of trained professionals and low public awareness. The current design for collection of solid waste has been deemed environmentally unfriendly with severe impacts on ground water, air quality, and health. Furthermore, it is estimated that the annual use of chemicals has increased dramatically, leading to increases in chemical poisoning and detrimental environmental impacts, which can be attributed to lack of oversight and legislation. The decline in air quality has also been associated with the increased emission of pollutants—such as SO_2, NO_2, CO, and lead—linked to large increases in the number of automobiles and emissions from plants, mining, and other industries.[1]

Refugees in Jordan Adding a new Challenge to the Healthcare System

The large influx of refugee populations since Jordan's independence has affected its healthcare system. UNWRA data indicated that over 2.1 million Palestinian refugees were registered in the country in 2015, and the UNFPA estimated the number of Iraqis residing in the country to be 481,000.[4,27] There are differences in these two groups' health statuses and access to health. The UNWRA has been serving the majority (60%) of Palestinian refugees in Jordan, and their health status report for 2015 indicates that the Palestinian refugees have had generally similar health status compared with the Jordanian population. Fertility rates have dropped significantly for this population, largely because of UNWRA's family planning programs that were supported by the MoH in providing contraceptives.

The case of the Iraqi refugees is different because most of them have not been granted official status and thus do not have access to public services and resources. In addition, there are no data on the health status of this population. One study reported on breastfeeding among Iraqi refugees in Jordan that each woman who had given birth in the last year had given birth in a hospital but that the women had not received much information before or after delivery regarding the importance of breastfeeding or where to go for help regarding breastfeeding, even though the majority had been encouraged in the hospital to breastfeed every 2 to 3 hours. This study highlights the lack of existing information regarding Iraqi refugees and the difficulty in providing services to these individuals through a healthcare system that is already facing large budget concerns.[28]

Since 2011, close to 2,000 Syrians per day began pouring into Jordan to reside in the first refugee camp near Mafraq, created by the United Nations High Commissioner for Refugees (UNHCR). As a small, aid-dependent country already suffering from financial and environmental issues, the number of Syrians seeking refuge in Jordan has strained the country's resources, especially water, agriculture, and the healthcare system. The huge number of refugees has resulted in humanitarian aid organizations requesting more money and assistance from international powers. In November 2016, UNHCR reported that there were 655,716 Syrians registered as refugees in Jordan. In 2016, there were about 1.4 million Syrian refugees in Jordan, with only 22% living in the Za'atari, Marjeeb al-Fahood, Cyber City, and Azraq refugee camps. With the majority of the Syrian refugees interspersed throughout the state, especially in 'Amman, Irbid, Mafraq, and Jerash, environmental resources have been scarce for both Syrians and their Jordanian hosts. This has increased pressure on Jordan's infrastructure, specifically on the provision of health care, water supplies, sanitation facilities, housing, and energy.

In 2015, the true cost of hosting the refugees included electricity and water subsidies costing the Jordanian government around US $3,000 per year, per Syrian, as well as half of the Health Ministry's budget for medical care, or $350 million. According to the UN high commissioner's figures, the Azraq refugee camp had fewer than 23,000 refugees in August 2015, although its capacity is 50,000. The UN plans call for Azraq to hold more than 100,000 Syrians, making it the largest refugee camp in Jordan. The nearby Za'atari refugee camp had about 80,000 refugees, according to the UN agency.

Many of the refugees are elderly. Chronic diseases such as diabetes, lung disease, cancers, and cardiovascular disease have been discovered among a large number of the Syrians who fled across the border to safety in Jordan. This has led to a drop in supplies of medicines in some of the hospitals and healthcare centers. Therefore, "The pressure is beyond the health sector's strength to continue providing services for the refugees," Jordanian Health Minister Abdul Latif Wreikat said bluntly.

Moreover, International Medical Corps has been providing primary healthcare and psychosocial services through static and mobile clinics for the refugee population. However, it is not clear exactly how much aid the group has offered, working with its local partner, Jordan Health Aid Society, which also provides services to refugees and "vulnerable local populations." Clearly Jordan alone cannot sustain good quality health care for all refugee populations in Jordan, not because of a lack of good will but rather because of limited resources.

Health System Challenges

According to a 2002 Joint MoH/WHO report, Jordan's health system needs to deal with the following challenges:[15]

- The demographic changes representing an increase in population and higher life expectancy.
- Considerable changes in lifestyles favoring the development of determinants and risk factors for chronic diseases, accidents, injuries, and substance abuse.
- The epidemiological transition and changes in the pattern of disease characterized by a progressive increase in the magnitude of noncommunicable diseases like cardiovascular diseases, cancer, diabetes, and mental health problems as well as accidents and health of the elderly.
- Inefficiencies observed in the provision and financing of health services.
- The lack of a rigorous appraisal (and reorientation) of the current state of human resources development in health.
- The negative impact of poverty on accessibility to quality health care particularly in view of the high proportion of uninsured people.
- The increasing demands and expectations of the public for effective and accessible health care.
- The rapid advances in technology and rising healthcare costs.
- Inadequate coordination between the public sector and the increasingly significant private sector and the lack of effective systems for monitoring and auditing clinical practice.
- The emerging environmental health issues.

Reproduced from World Health Organization. Health System Profile—Jordan. http://gis.emro.who.int/healthsystemobservatory/main/Forms/CountryInfo.aspx?Country=JORDAN. Copyright 2006.

Although Jordan's healthcare system has undergone major reforms over the last 3 decades, it remains to be seen whether the MoH's commitment to improving coverage, reducing noncommunicable diseases, and maintaining and improving the quality of health care for its citizens can be achieved.

References

1. Salibi K. *The Modern History of Jordan*. New York: IB Tauris; 1998.
2. King Hussein website. Keys to the kingdom: history. http://www.kinghussein.gov.jo/history.html. Accessed June 3, 2008.
3. The Parliament. The Hashemite Kingdom of Jordan. *History of parliamentary life in Jordan*. http://www.parliament.jo/english/history_parliamentary_life.shtm. Accessed June 3, 2008.
4. United Nations Population Fund. Iraqis in Jordan. http://www.dos.gov.jo/sdb_pop/sdb_pop_a/index_o.htm. Accessed June 3, 2008.
5. Ministry of Tourism and Antiquities. Helpful facts about Jordan. http://www.tourism.jo/Inside/AboutJordan.asp. Accessed June 3, 2008.
6. Department of Statistics. Jordan in figures. http://www.dos.gov.jo/jorfig/2006/jor_f_a.htm. Accessed June 3, 2008.
7. The Parliament. The Hashemite Kingdom of Jordan. The Constitution of the Hashemite Kingdom of Jordan. http://www.parliament.jo/english/constitution_EN.shtm. Accessed June 3, 2008.
8. Bloom DE, Canning D, Huzarski K, et al. Demographic transition and economic opportunity: the case of Jordan. www.riverpath.com/library/pdf/jordan.pdf. Published 2001. Accessed June 4, 2008.
9. King Hussein website. Foreign Affairs. http://www.kinghussein.gov.jo/f_affairs3.html#The%20Economic%20Restructuring%20Program. Accessed June 4, 2008.
10. United Nations Development Programme. Jordan: the Human Development Index—going beyond income. http://hdrstats.undp.org/countries/country_fact_sheets/cty_fs_JOR.html. Accessed June 4, 2008.
11. Takruri H. *FAO—Nutrition Country Profile*: Jordan: Food and Agricultural Organization, 2003. Accessed June 4, 2008. ftp://ftp.fap.org/es/esn/nutrition/ncp/jormap.pdf.

12. World Bank. Country profiles: Jordan, Jordan data at a glance. http://data.worldbank.org/country/jordan. Accessed June 4, 2008.
13. Central Intelligence Agency's World Factbook. Jordan. https://www.cia.gov/library/publications/the-world-factbook/geos/jo.html. Accessed September 5, 2016.
14. Ministry of Health. *Focal point of health information: Jordan.* http://www.moh.gov.jo:7778/MOH/En/about.php. Accessed June 4, 2008.
15. World Health Organization. Health system profile—Jordan. http://gis.emro.who.int/healthsystemobservatory/main/Forms/CountryInfo.aspx?Country=JORDAN. Accessed September 7, 2016.
16. Ministry of Health. Ministry of Health Annual Statistical Book 2006. http://www.moh.gov.jo/MOH/En/publications.php. Accessed June 5, 2008.
17. Zindah M, Belbeisi A, Walke H, Mokdad AH. Obesity and diabetes in Jordan: findings from the behavioral risk factors surveillance system. *Prev Chronic Dis.* 2008;5(1):1–8.
18. Ministry of Health. Mortality in Jordan, 2005. http://www.moh.gov.jo/MOH/En/publications.php. Accessed June 5, 2008.
19. Demographic and Health Survey of Jordan. Nutritional status, prevalence of anemia, and micronutrient supplementation. www.measuredhs.com/pubs/pdf/FR138/10Chapter10.pdf. Accessed June 6, 2008.
20. Madanat HN, Brown RB, Hawks SR. The impact of body mass index and Western advertising and media on eating style, body image, and nutrition transition among Jordanian women. *Public Health Nutr.* 2007;10(10):1039–1046.
21. Global Youth Tobacco Survey Collaborating Group. Differences in worldwide tobacco use by gender: findings from the Global Youth Tobacco Survey. *Journal of School Health.* 2003;73(6):207–215.
22. Merrill RM, Madanat H, Kelley AT. Smoking prevalence, attitudes, and perceived smoking prevention and control responsibilities and practices among nurses in Amman, Jordan. *Int J Nurs Pract.*
23. Merrill RM, Madanat H, Layton JB, Hanson CL, Madsen CC. Smoking prevalence, attitudes, and perceived smoking prevention and control responsibilities and behaviors among physicians in Jordan. *Int Q Community Health Educ.* 2006–2007;26(4):397–413.
24. Merrill RM, Madanat HN, Cox E, Merrill JM. Perceived effectiveness of counselling patients about smoking among medical students in Amman, Jordan. Jordan. *East Mediterr Health J.* Sep-Oct 2009;15(5):1180–1191.
25. Ministry of Health. *Health News.* http://www.moh.gov.jo/MOH/arabic/health_newsdetails.php?newsid=343. Published 2004. Accessed February 15, 2008.
26. World Health Organization. EMRO Tobacco Free Initiative—country profile, 2000. http://www.emro.who.int/TFI/CountryProfile-JOR.htm. Accessed June 6, 2008.
27. United Nations Relief and Works Agency for Palestinian Refugees in the Near East. Where We Work: Jordan. http://www.unrwa.org/where-we-work/jordan. Accessed November 16, 2016.
28. Madanat H, Farrell H, Merrill R. Breastfeeding education, support, and barriers among Iraqi refugee women in Jordan. *Int Electron J Health Educ.* 2007;10:138–149.
29. Ministry of Health. Statistics and indicators. http://www.moh.gov.jo/EN/Pages/mainind.aspx?ind=http%3a//apps.moh.gov.jo/reports/headermain.jsp?firstjsp=populationmain&lang_parameter=english. Accessed September 7, 2016.
30. World Health Organization. Global health expenditure database. http://apps.who.int/nha/database/ViewData/Indicators/en. Accessed September 7, 2016.
31. World Health Organization. Jordan: WHO statistical profile. http://who.int/gho/countries/jor.pdf?ua=1. Accessed September 7, 2016.
32. World Bank. World development indicators: Jordan. http://databank.worldbank.org/data/reports.aspx?source=2&country=JOR. Accessed September 7, 2016.
33. United Nations Development Programme. Human development reports: Jordan. http://hdr.undp.org/en/countries/profiles/JOR. Accessed September 7, 2016.
34. World Health Organization. *Global health expenditure database.* Health system financing profile by country: Jordan. http://apps.who.int/nha/database/Country_Profile/Index/en. Accessed September 7, 2016.
35. Ministry of Health. Mortality data in Jordan 2012. http://www.moh.gov.jo/EN/Pages/Periodic-Newsletters.aspx. Accessed September 7, 2016.
36. World Health Organization. Noncommunicable diseases country profiles: Jordon. http://who.int/nmh/countries/jor_en.pdf?ua=1. Published 2014. Accessed September 5, 2016.
37. World Health Organizations. Classifications. http://www.who.int/classifications/icd/en/. Page updated 2016. Accessed November 16, 2016.
38. World Health Organization. Jordan Pharmaceutical Country Profile 2011. http://www.who.int/medicines/areas/coordination/Jordan_PSCPNarrativeQuestionnaire_27022012.pdf. Accessed November 14, 2016.
39. Oxford Business Group. Pharmaceuticals propel Jordan's economic diversification. September 26, 2014. http://www.oxfordbusinessgroup.com/news/pharmaceuticals-propel-jordan%E2%80%99s-economic-diversification. Accessed November 12, 2016.

CHAPTER 17

Israel

Sharon R. Elefant, Leonard Friedman, Osnat Levtzion-Korach, and **Harry Flaster**

▸ Country Description

TABLE 17-1 Israel

Nationality	Noun: Israeli(s) Adjective: Israeli
Ethnic groups	Jewish 75.0% (Israel-born 74.4%, Europe/America/Oceania-born 17.4%, Africa-born 5.1%, Asia-born 3.1%), non-Jewish 25% (mostly Arab) (2013 est.)
Religions	Jewish 74.8% (of which Israel-born 75.6%, Europe/America/Oceania-born 16.6%, Africa-born 4.9%, Asia-born 2.9%), non-Jewish 25.2% (mostly Arab) (2015 est.)
Language	Hebrew (official), Arabic (officially used for Arabic speakers), English (most commonly used foreign language)
Literacy	Definition: Age 15 and over can read and write. Total population: 97.8% Male: 98.7% Female: 96.8% (2011 est.)
Government type	Parliamentary democracy
Date of independence	May 14, 1948 (from League of Nations mandate under British administration)
Gross Domestic Product (GDP) per capita	$34,300 (2015 est.)
Unemployment rate	5.3% (2015 est.)

(continues)

TABLE 17-1 Israel (continued)

Natural hazards	Sandstorms may occur during spring and summer; droughts; periodic earthquakes
Environment: current issues	Limited arable land and natural freshwater resources pose serious constraints; desertification; air pollution from industrial and vehicle emissions; groundwater pollution from industrial and domestic waste, chemical fertilizers, and pesticides
Population	8,049,314* (July 2015 est.)
Age structure	0–14 years: 27.95% (male 1,151,247/female 1,098,632) 15–24 years: 15.50% (male 637,758/female 609,597) 25–54 years: 37.13% (male 1,528,271/female 1,460,772) 55–64 years: 8.57% (male 336,662/female 353,352) 65 years and over: 10.85% (male 389,401/female 483,622) (2015 est.)
Median age	Total: 29.6 years Male: 28.9 years Female: 30.2 years (2015 est.)
Population growth rate	1.56% (2015 est.)
Birth rate	18.48 births/1,000 population (2015 est.)
Death rate	363 deaths/100,000 population (2015 est.)
Disease burden	Communicable disease deaths: 31/100,000 population Noncommunicable disease deaths: 311/100,000 population Injury deaths: 21/100,000 population (2016 est.)
Net migration rate	2.24 migrant(s)/1,000 population (2015 est.)
Gender ratio	At birth: 1.05 male(s)/female Under 15 years: 1.05 male(s)/female 15–24 years: 1.05 male(s)/female 25–54 years: 1.05 male(s)/female 55–64 years: 0.95 male(s)/female 65 years and over: 0.81 male(s)/female Total population: 1.01 male(s)/female (2015 est.)
Infant mortality rate	Total: 3.55 deaths/1,000 live births Male: 3.51 deaths/1,000 live births Female: 3.58 deaths/1,000 live births (2015 est.)
Life expectancy at birth	Total population: 82.27 years Male: 80.43 years Female: 84.21 years (2015 est.)
Total fertility rate	2.68 children born/woman (2015 est.)
HIVE/AIDS adult prevalence rate	—

TABLE 17-1 Israel (continued)

Number of people living with HIV/AIDS	—
HIV/AIDS deaths	—

* Population number includes residents of the Golan Heights (approximately 20,500 Israelis) in the Golan subdistrict and of East Jerusalem (211,640 Israelis) (2014 est.), which was annexed by Israel after 1967. East Jerusalem was annexed by Israel, unlike the West Bank and Gaza. Though this annexation has not necessarily been recognized by the rest of the world, Israelis in East Jerusalem are not viewed as settlers.

Data from Central Intelligence Agency. The World Factbook, 2016: Israel. https://www.cia.gov/library/publications/the-world-factbook/geos/is.html.

History of Country

Background

Israel is an ancient land that has been inhabited by many different peoples, nations, and empires since the dawn of Western civilization. Although Jewish people have resided in Israel since about 1300 BCE when Israelite communities started multiplying in the northern hills area of Canaan, the first unified nation was in the era of King David (1000 BCE). The Northern Israel kingdom was destroyed by the Assyrians in 710 BCE, and the Southern Kingdom of Judah was destroyed by the Babylonians in approximately 500 BCE. The Jews returned to Israel when Persian rule was crushed (538–516 BCE) and rebuilt what is known as The Second Temple, which was originally built by King Solomon (960 BCE). In a revolt led by Judah Maccabee, Jewish independence from Macedonia (Greek rule) was reestablished in 166 BCE, which is commemorated by the holiday of Hanukkah. Under King Herod's Roman rule (64–63 BCE), King Solomon's second temple was declared a world wonder.[1] Visitors to Israel today can touch the Western Wall of the Second Temple and see its foundation in underground tunnels. The Roman Empire ended Jewish rule of Israel in approximately 70 CE. The Jewish Diaspora to the Iberian Peninsula and Europe followed, though a small population remained in Israel. Hundreds of years, the Inquisition, thousands of pogroms, and The Holocaust would mark the suffering of an exiled people longing to return to their homeland, Israel. The creation of the modern state of Israel was not dependent on the history of suffering, but surely anti-Semitism was a trigger for Zionism and the creation of a Jewish homeland in Israel.

In 1917, the Balfour Declaration by Great Britain validated Jewish historical claim to Israel, endorsing the claim of the First Zionist Congress to establish a nation in what was then called Palestine under the British Mandate. At the end of World War II, on November 29, 1947, the United Nations General Assembly recommended partition of Palestine into a Jewish and an Arab state; the recommendation was accepted by the Zionist leadership but was totally rejected by the Arab leadership.[1]

On May 14, 1948, David Ben-Gurion proclaimed the creation of Israel. In that proclamation, key values highlighted were liberty, democracy, justice, and peace with Arab neighbors.

Healthcare organizations are a bridge to peace. Bringing advanced medical care to all, regardless of race, ethnicity, or nationality, earned Hadassah's two hospitals in Jerusalem—Mount Scopus and Ein Kerem—a nomination for a Nobel Peace Prize in 2005. Notably, the three areas cited for the nomination included treating terrorists, having a diverse staff, and building bridges to peace through collaborating on medical activities with physicians.

Today's visitor to Israel will notice that the cultural universal in Israel is *carpe diem*. One must seize the day because the threat to life is ubiquitous. Everyone has lost someone; Yom HaZichron, the Day of Remembrance, is marked nationwide by an early morning siren, during which Israelis stop whatever they are doing, including driving, and remember those who have fallen. But, after sunset, which is considered the next day according to Jewish tradition, Yom HaAtzmaut, Independence Day, is marked by public and private celebrations. In a land continually under siege, people know how to live life to the fullest.

Israel's history of accomplishments in its brief 68 years as a modern nation speaks to the industriousness and determination of the people to succeed and make significant, positive contributions to the modern world. In 2000, Israel invented the Pill Cam, an ingestible video camera used to noninvasively diagnose digestive diseases. Israel is known as the start-up nation; in *Start-Up Nation:*

The Story of Israel's Economic Miracle (2009), "Technology companies and global investors are beating a path to Israel and finding unique combinations of audacity, creativity, and drive everywhere they look. Which may explain why, in addition to boasting the highest density of start-ups in the world (a total of 3,850 start-ups, one for every 1,844 Israelis)."[2] In January 2016 Professor Dimitrios Karussis, MD, PhD, of Hadassah Medical Organization, conducted the world's first clinical trial using patients' own bone marrow stem cells to treat amyotrophic lateral sclerosis (ALS). Using identical protocols, the Mayo Clinic, Massachusetts General Hospital (a Harvard affiliate) and the University of Massachusetts Memorial Medical Center are conducting expanded stem cell trials in the United States. In modern Israel, medical care and world-class medical researchers continue to make significant contributions to the world.

▶ Size and Geography

Slightly larger than New Jersey, Israel is located in the Middle East between Egypt and Lebanon and is surrounded by the Gaza Strip, Jordan, Syria, the West Bank, and the Mediterranean Sea. See **FIGURE 17-1**. Due to the geopolitics of hostile bordering countries, Israel is a nation constantly under siege, which impacts the healthcare system. Terrorism and mass casualties make Israeli medical personnel the world experts in mass casualty trauma care. As a matter of fact, just prior to the terrorist incident at the April 2013 Boston Marathon, Hadassah's Dr. Avi Rivkind conducted a mass casualties workshop at Massachusetts General Hospital, the result of which enabled first responders and hospitals to save many lives after the attack.[3]

Israel is a land of geographical extremes with the lowest point 408 meters below sea level in the Dead Sea and the highest elevation 1,208 meters on Har Hermon. One can ski on Har Hermon and swim in the Dead Sea, all on the same day in December when it might be raining in Haifa. The desert areas of the South and East are hot and dry. The *khamsin*, a hot, sandy wind, blows grit from the east onto streets, into houses, and into eyes and lungs. When the khamsins blow, those with respiratory illnesses, the elderly, and the very young are vulnerable. During the spring, though, which is in late February–April, the climate is mild, especially in the northern Upper Galilee, down through the coastal plains, and east to Jerusalem. During the hot, humid summers, one can often find cool relief in Jerusalem. Israel's very diverse population is over 8 million people spanning 20,700 square kilometers.[4]

Israel is not rich in natural resources; most of the timber was logged over 1,000 years ago. Today, Israeli homes and buildings are mainly stone, stucco, and concrete. Agriculture used to be Israel's prime income source; however, in the early 1980s the agricultural income base transitioned to manufacturing, industry, technology, and medicine. The forests that do exist in Israel today are predominantly part of the Jewish National Fund forests, and, as such, are forest reserves not timberlands for harvest.

Lake Kinneret (sometimes known as the Sea of Galilee) is one of the main freshwater sources, as is the water table in Samaria. Water use and water rights were some of the primary underlying issues in the region. With part Mediterranean and part desert climate, Israel has suffered water shortage and drought issues. However, since 2005, desalination plants—the largest of which can be seen along the Haifa–Tel Aviv highway—have significantly improved water issues in Israel, to the extent that some agronomists feel that water issues no longer exist. Says Shaul Ben-Dov, an agronomist at Ramat Rachel, "Now there is no problem of water. The price is higher, but we can live a normal life in a country that is half desert."[5] Even so, others argue that specific regions in Israel are at risk for water shortages; therefore, residents are constantly vigilant and conserving water.

▶ Government and Political System

Israel is the only democracy in the Middle East. Citizens are exceptionally active in their democracy and vote on all levels: local, regional, and national. The voter percentage in Israel is extraordinarily high. In the 2013 election, 71.8% of the electorate voted.[6]

Like the United States, the Israeli government has an executive, legislative, and judicial branch. Separation of power is secured because the independence of the judicial branch is guaranteed by law and the executive branch is dependent on the confidence of the legislature.

The Israeli Congress is a parliamentary democracy, which means that political parties have historically been organized around political beliefs and world views. On a national level, citizens vote for party lists, members of whom then become Knesset members based on the percentage of votes their

FIGURE 17-1 Map of Israel
© Bardocz Peter/Shutterstock

party receives. All citizens may vote, and each vote is equally counted. Citizens vote for the political party that most closely represents the citizen's values, although that seems to be in transition as Israelis debate about both candidates and issues. In the 2015 election, 26 parties submitted a list of candidates to the General Elections Committee.[4] The political parties then are represented in the Knesset (Congress) in proportion to how many votes the party receives. The prime minister is the person whose political party (a) gets the most votes and (b) can create a coalition in the Knesset.

Elections are usually held every 4 years, but they can be held earlier if the Knesset votes to dissolve before the end of the term, if it fails to pass a budget within 3 months, if the prime minister dissolves the Knesset because the Knesset members object to the coalition government, or if the prime minister fails to form a coalition government. Currently, the Likud party, with Benjamin Netanyahu as its head, had the controlling percentage of Knesset seats; therefore, Netanyahu is the prime minister of Israel. His term of office, though, depends on the stability of the coalition he put together; currently it is scheduled until 2019. Coalitions are frequently fragile and depend on the support and cooperation of Knesset members from other parties. Opposing coalitions are often formed and present formidable opposition to the majority party.

▸ Macroeconomics

Israel has a technologically advanced, mixed economy. Much of the economy is free market. However, agriculture is heavily subsidized and food product prices are controlled. High-technology equipment and pharmaceuticals are among its leading exports. Its major imports include crude oil, grains, raw materials, and military equipment. Israel's trade deficits are offset by tourism and technology exports.[7] There is a significant inflow of foreign investment into Israel. The newest and upcoming Israeli industry is medical tourism. Israel is cited in the top three countries by the Medical Tourism Index.[8] Patients seek Israeli medical care for its services and top-quality patient care. According to the *International Medical Travel Journal*, Hadassah University Hospital in Jerusalem had revenues totaling NIS 108 million.[9]

Recently discovered natural gas fields discovered off Israel's coast promise a potential boost to the economy via energy independence. However, political and regulatory issues have delayed the development of one of the largest fields. Production from a smaller field has yielded a "0.8% boost to Israel's GDP in 2013 and a 0.3% boost in 2014."[10]

Housing prices, income disparities, and a growing poverty rate are becoming major concerns in Israel. Most young Israelis seeking to purchase a home still rely on parents to do so. In spite of a call for government reforms, the actual response has been slow and ineffective.

Recent changes in educational opportunities for the ultraorthodox and Arab Israeli communities are starting to result in a growing labor sector among these communities. For example, in Nazareth, TRI/O Tech entrepreneurship hub provides education and services for Arab start-ups and participation in the technology sector. In Jerusalem, Hadassah Academic College provides gender-separate curriculum for Jewish Orthodox men and women, without which those community members could not attend classes due to religious law.

Israelis have had to rely on brain power in the modern world to create a viable economic base. There was a time in Israel, not too long ago, in the 1980s, when items on grocery store shelves did not have price tags. The price list was kept up at the cashier's stand. Daily inflation was well over 30%. In 2016 agriculture has been almost replaced by clean industry. Israel is a nation of innovation. Today, Israel's economic strengths lie in two areas, technology and medical research. The middle class is strong and growing.

▸ Demographics

Israeli culture is as rich and diverse as its people. On Independence Day 2016, "Israel's population stood at

Ethnic Groups in Israel[11]	
Jews	75.0%
Muslims	17.5%
Christians	2.0%
Druze	1.6%
Not classified by religion	3.9%

Data from Rosen B, Waitzberg R, Merkur S. Israel: Health System Review. Copenhagen: European Observatory on Health Systems and Policy; 2015.

a record 8,522,000."[4] Overall, the total population of Israel "experienced a growth rate of 2%,"[4] and by 2025 Israel is projected to have 10 million. Israel is the 99th most populous country in the world, not counting the 250,000 refugees from Sudan and the illegal foreign workers. The ethnic breakdown in Israel roughly matches the breakdown in religions. According to the Israel Ministry of Foreign Affairs, the majority of the religious groups which are also the ethnic groups are as follows:

In 2014, 75% of the population were sabras, native-born Israelis. However, "between Independence Day 2015 and 2016, 25% of the new immigrants arrived from France and 24% from Ukraine."[4] These data are not surprising, considering the terrorist activities in both countries. This recent immigration wave and increase in terrorism has impacted hospitals both in terms of additional patients needing services and in terms of patients and medical staff needing translators.

Jewish people immigrated to Israel from many lands around the world. They came from Europe, Russia, Latin America, and many Arab and North African countries. Jews are native to and have continued to reside on this land for thousands of years. Arab Christians and Arab Muslims have also resided on this land and are now citizens in Israel. Tel Aviv, the economic center of Israel, received a top World Smart City Award in 2014 for taking advantage of the potential of technology to increase public engagement.[12] Jerusalem is a major spiritual center, with sites that are spiritually significant to Jews, Christians, and Muslims.

Israel provides substantial benefits and services to women including maternity leave and job protection. Under qualifying conditions, Israeli women can be paid 100% of their salary for 14 weeks of maternity leave and are granted significant extensions for multiple births.[13] In addition, a spouse may be eligible to receive the maternity leave benefits if the woman wishes to return earlier to work or in the case of multiple births or disabled children. The National Insurance Institute of Israel sets the policy and establishes salary payouts. Additionally, a woman who is in vocational training may receive maternity benefits. According to the CIA's *The World Factbook*, Israel's global healthy life expectancy ranked 11th out of 188 countries; Israel's overall life expectancy is 82.4 years.[10]

About 25.2% of Israeli citizens are Arabs.[10] As citizens of Israel, they have full and equal voting rights. Furthermore, Israel is one of the few nations in the Middle East where women have full voting rights. Additionally, Arab Israelis have "their own political parties, serve on the Israeli Knesset, Cabinet, and Supreme Court"[14]

National Service and Security

Israel requires compulsory national service for all citizens, both men and women, commencing at 18 years old. Most serve in the Israel Defense Forces (IDF): men are required to serve in the military for 3 years of active duty and women for 2 years of active duty. Men are also required to serve in the army reserves for a number of years after active duty; women are welcome to do so if they choose. Women also may be combatants and fighter pilots. Options for types of service are available: based on eligibility, some people may do community service. One area of controversy involves what kind of service certain ultra-Orthodox men must do. Currently, they are allowed to study in a yeshiva; however, bills are constantly proposed to the Knesset to change this option for required service. Druzes serve with distinction and can be officers in the IDF; however, Muslim Arab Israelis do not serve in Israel's military. Christian Arab Israelis occasionally serve. This is a sensitive topic.

The IDF protects citizens and borders and serves in defense capacity. Terrorist attacks occur inside Israel proper as well as in Judea and Samaria, often referred to by Western journalists as The West Bank. Men and women serve in areas of high conflict.

Israeli citizens consider serving in the IDF not only an obligation to the nation but also an honor. When seniors graduate from high school and receive notification of their assignments, there are usually congratulations expressed and family gatherings to honor the inductees; after boot camp, family members attend the induction ceremonies at Masada or at the Western Wall in Jerusalem. IDF personnel make significant, crucial lifelong contacts that can result in important business connections, which often lead to start-up businesses and employment opportunities.

▸ Healthcare System in Israel: Organization, Financing, and Delivery

While the nation of Israel was founded in 1948, it was not until 1995 that a National Health Insurance (NHI) program was put into place.[15] Since the start of the NHI, Israel has become a world-class example of how to provide highly effective health care to all citizens at a price significantly below that of the other OECD member nations.[16] According to 2013 data, Israel spent 7.5% of GDP on health services compared to the OECD average of 8.9%. In contrast, the United States spent 16.4% of GDP on health services. Life expectancy of those living in Israel was 82 years (81 for males and 84 for females). In contrast, life expectancy in the United States was 79 years (76 for males and 81 for females).[17] Life expectancy is but one measure of the overall success of the efforts throughout the healthcare system to keep people healthy and productive throughout their life spans.

Before examining the organization, financing, and delivery of health services in Israel, it is useful to briefly explore how health services were delivered prior to the passage of the National Health Insurance Law in 1995. Prior to the founding of the nation, health services were delivered by a number of *sick funds* in addition to a number of nonprofit entities.[18] These sick funds ultimately morphed into the present payer groups. One of the more interesting organizations was the Hadassah Medical Organization—founded in 1912 by Henrietta Szold, an American—which established the Tipat Halav system (well-baby clinics, literally *drop-of-milk clinics*).[18] Today, Hadassah operates two hospitals in Jerusalem. Government hospitals provide more than half of all acute beds in Israel, along with most psychiatric facilities. A number of these hospitals are located in buildings abandoned by British Army camps, left over from the War of Independence in 1947–1948.[18]

As is noted earlier in this chapter, Israel is not a homogenous nation in any sense of the word. A healthcare system that proposes to provide coverage to all citizens must account for multiple religious and cultural norms. Israel is a diverse nation and all Israeli citizens and residents, "have access to basic healthcare from the State, through their HMO."[19] Health indices suggest that disparities between Arabs and Jews living in Israel. For example, differences exist in "infant mortality, at 3 per 1,000 live births for Jews and 7 per 1,000 for Arabs; a gap in life expectancy with Jews living longer, which increased from 2 years in 1998 to 3.7 years in 2008."[19]

While a small nation in terms of both geographic size and population, and a young nation, having been established in 1948, Israel has succeeded in crafting a universal health system based on the principle of provision of health services to all people without discrimination.[20] As a matter of fact, Hadassah hospitals were nominated in 2005 for a Nobel Peace Prize because, by policy and deed, they serve all people, regardless of race, creed, religion, or ethnicity. In order to develop a clear understanding of health services in Israel, the remainder of this section will focus on the organization, financing, and delivery of health services.

Organization

Since 1995, health services in Israel have been organized under the National Health Insurance Law. The NHI is structured in a manner as to provide health services to every citizen and permanent resident of the nation. Every eligible person elects to be part of one of four not-for-profit health insurance plans (Kupot Cholim). These plans are: Clalit Health Services, Leumit Health Fund, Maccabi Healthcare Services, and Meuhedet Health Fund.[21] The 2009 membership in each of the four health plans is shown in **TABLE 17-2**.

According to Dr. Bruce Rosen, the director of the Smokler Center for Health Policy Research at the Meyers-JDC-Brookdale Institute, "Clalit was founded by the Labor Party–affiliated General Federation of Labor and, as such, historically had a decidedly Socialist orientation. Leumit was founded by the Nationalist Workers Association, which was affiliated with Israel's right wing parties; thus, while it did not share Clalit's Socialist origins, both approached health care as a service to be provided within the context of broader national goals. Maccabi and Meuhedet, in contrast, were founded by physicians with a liberal, free-market orientation."[20] All of the four Health Plans are

TABLE 17-2 Health Plan Membership, 2009[22]

Health Plan	Membership (thousands)	Market Share (%)
Clalit	3,863	53
Maccabi	1,781	24
Meuhedet	978	13
Leumit	677	9
Total	7,300	100

Reproduced with permission from Rosen B. (2011). *How Health Plans in Israel Manage the Care Provided by Their Physicians*. Jerusalem: Myers-JDC-Brookdale Institute; 2011.

completely computerized; 100% of the physicians, and most of the other healthcare professionals, use an electronic medical record that is either connected online to, or is an integral part of, the health plan's central medical record.[23]

Other significant differences among the plans include size; the mix of members in terms of age, income, and geographic location; the extent of reliance on salaried physicians (as opposed to independents); the extent of reliance on group practices (as opposed to solo practitioners); and whether they own acute care hospitals.[22]

The Ministry of Health (MoH) requires that each of the health plans provide to their members a basic *basket of health services* that are available at either no cost or a heavily discounted rate. The elements of the basket include:[20]

- Clinic visits for consultation, diagnosis and treatment by primary care and specialty physicians
- Prescription drugs
- Routine vaccinations
- Hospitalization and emergency room services
- Certain durable medical equipment
- Diagnostic services (including X-rays and imaging procedures)
- Mental health services
- Rehabilitation
- Fertility treatments (including genetic testing)
- Certain modalities of physical therapy
- Elective surgeries
- Organ transplants
- Critical cancer care
- Ambulatory services
- Dental care for children under 14 years old

It should be noted that at the present time, dental services are not a covered benefit in the basic basket, with the exception of pediatric dental care up to age 14. However, the costs are significantly lower than they are in the United States. The basket of services is provided to all eligible citizens and permanent residents who live in Israel at least 183 days of the calendar year. Unlike preferred provider organizations (PPOs) in the United States, care from specialty physicians in Israel is available only with a referral from a primary care physician.

Supplemental health insurance (including long-term care insurance) is available for purchase through the four Kupot Cholim. While there are a number of supplemental health plans available, coverage through these plans includes:[24]

- Access to a broader range of medications
- Ability to choose surgeons and hospital locations
- Options for overseas treatment that may include innovative procedures not yet available in Israel
- Other components, such as new pioneering cancer management packages, critical illness coverage, and personal accident coverage.

Without question, the most important stakeholder in the NHI system is the MoH, which has overall responsibility for the organization and functioning of the system. In addition to assuring the efficient operation of the overall system, the Ministry is involved with technology assessment, prioritization of new technology, health plan regulation, quality monitoring of community-based care, and support for population health initiatives.[18]

In summary, the NHI system is organized in a way to assure all citizens and permanent residents of Israel a basic basket of services that are focused on primary and preventive care. Specialty care is available but requires a referral from the primary care provider. Hospitalization, pharmaceuticals, diagnostic testing, durable medical equipment, mental health, and rehabilitation services are all covered benefits. It should be noted that people can switch health plans annually if desired.[21]

Financing

According to data from the OECD, health spending in Israel accounted for 7.5% of GDP in 2013, below the average of 9.4% in other OECD countries. In comparison, in the same year the United States spent 17.3% of its GDP on health.[25] The public sector is the main source of health funding in nearly all OECD countries.[16] In Israel, 60.0% of health spending was funded by public sources in 2012, well below the average of 72.0% in OECD countries (see **FIGURE 17-2**).[26] Per

Outpatient/ambulatory physician services	36.6%
Inpatient hospital care, including psychiatric and chronic care	32.7%
Pharmaceuticals, medical supplies, and medical equipment	13.8%
Outpatient/ambulatory dental services	7.7%
Health administration	4.4%
Fixed capital formation	3.1%
Health research and development	1.2%
Public health and prevention	0.4%

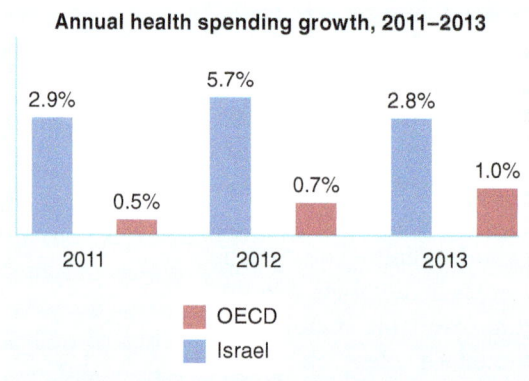

FIGURE 17-2 Percentage of Total Health Expenditures
Reproduced from OECD. OECD Health Policy Overview: Health Policy in Israel. http://www.oecd.org/health/bycountry/. 2016. Accessed June 26, 2016.

capita health expenditures in Israel for 2013 was US $2,428 in contrast to the OECD average of US $3,453 and $8,713 in the United States.[16] In 2012, as a fraction of total health expenditures in Israel, spending on health services were:

The overall NHI system is financed primarily by a health tax and general tax revenue. Over a third of Israel's national health expenditures are covered by households, through a mix of out-of-pocket payments and supplemental insurance packages.

Payments by households cover co-payments for certain services included in the NHI benefits package (such as visits to specialists and pharmaceuticals), as well as services not included in that package (such as dental and optometric care).[27] See **FIGURE 17-3**. The health tax is 3% of the gross monthly income for employees earning up to 60% of the average wage (€1850 per month in 2014) (US $1,965) and 5% of the gross monthly income for those earning above the average wage.[19] Income above 5 times the average wage is not taxed for NHI purposes. Failure to pay the required health tax will result in government action to enforce payment but does not jeopardize the individual's right to NHI benefits. The tax is paid to the National Insurance Institute. Health taxes are supplemented by funds from the national budget that are also transferred to the

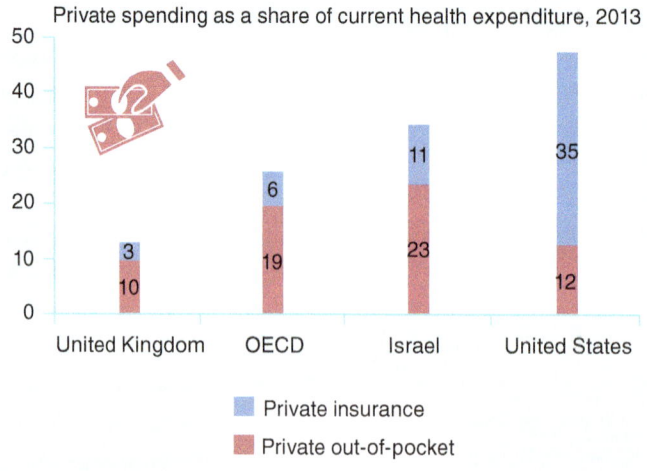

FIGURE 17-3 Private Health Spending as a Share of Health Expenditures (2013)
Reproduced from OECD. OECD Health Policy Overview: Health Policy in Israel. http://www.oecd.org/health/bycountry/. 2016. Accessed June 26, 2016.

Institute. Combined, these funds must equal the "cost of the basket of services" as defined by the National Health Insurance Law. They are distributed to the four health plans via a capitation formula based primarily on age, sex, and geographic region.[28] Since 1998, the Ministry of Finance has indexed inflationary increases for the basket of services to the standard national inflation rate and eliminated the previous practice of recognizing a separate and substantially higher inflation rate for the medical industry.[15]

According to the NHI, payment of health insurance premiums is mandatory for every person over 18 years of age. The level of payment is set on a progressive scale that varies according to income. People who work for an employer have their health insurance premiums deducted by their employer. Self-employed individuals or the unemployed must make arrangements directly with the National Insurance Institute. Certain categories of individuals are exempt from paying premiums or pay at a significantly reduced rate. These include married women who do not work outside of the home, soldiers in regular compulsory service and recipients of specific types of National Insurance Institute allowances.[20]

Along with the low and decreasing public expenditure on health, there has been a constant increase in private spending. The voluntary health insurance (VHI) market is one of the largest in OECD countries with about 87% of Israel's adult population covered with a voluntary health plan and 53% covered with commercial insurance. Household spending on VHIs has increased over the past decade. Out-of-pocket expenditures are also high relative to many other countries (26% of total health expenditures, compared to a European Union average of 21%), and have increased somewhat over time. There are large differences in household expenditures on health by income quintile, which indicates the existence of inequalities.[18]

Hospital revenue is generated primarily through the provision of health services, with approximately 80% coming from the four health plans. Payment to public hospitals in Israel is based on a combination of fee-for-service, per diem fees, and case payments, which are subject to a revenue cap.[18] The revenue capping system's goal has been to eliminate incentives for hospitals to overprovide inpatient care and to constrain the growth in expenses, particularly that related to hospital services.

Despite the reimbursement mechanisms, the MoH subsidizes retrospectively almost all public hospitals. Subsidies have more than doubled from around €75 million in 2006 to €170 million (US $79 million to $180 million) in 2012.[29] Nevertheless, both public and nonprofit hospitals have faced growing deficits in recent years. The extreme case of this was the near bankruptcy of the private nonprofit Hadassah Medical Center in 2014. The hospital did not dissolve because the MoH provided massive financial aid and increased the cap ceiling.[18] In addition, Hadassah, the Women's Zionist Organization, committed to a multimillion-dollar payment via fundraising efforts in order to retain ownership. From a symbolic perspective and considering their role in delivering inpatient hospital services, the closure of Hadassah Medical Center would have resulted in uncounted negative outcomes.

In Israel, payment for physician services is the largest component of total health expenditures. Most physicians are paid employees of one of the four health plans or the public hospitals. As in the United States, physicians may choose to practice as an independent contractor and function as an independent business entity. A collective bargaining agreement between the Israel Medical Association and the major employers governs the payment terms for employed physicians in the health plans and hospitals. Physicians working independently are not covered by the agreement.[18] Physicians employed by the health plans are paid a combination of straight monthly salary plus a capitation fee for the panel of patients in the plan depending on how the particular health plan operates.

It should be noted that physicians (both primary care and specialists) are well paid in comparison to their counterparts throughout other OECD countries. While there are certainly differences in tax rates from one nation to the next, physicians in Israel appear to be fairly compensated for their work product.

In summary, financing of health services in Israel consists of a combination of public and private funds that serves as the foundation for a comprehensive set of services made available to all citizens and permanent residents. The majority of citizens pay an income-indexed health tax and are also responsible for an increasing level of out-of-pocket spending for co-payments and health services not covered in the basic basket.

Delivery

In this segment of the chapter, the delivery of health services in Israel is examined. Health services are divided between public health services and private health services, including hospitals and physicians. Delivery of health services to women and men in active duty of the military is not addressed because soldiers receive routine care through the Israel Defense Forces Medical Corps.[30]

Public Health

Public health in Israel is coordinated through the Health Division within the MoH.[31] The Health Division is made up of six subordinate units:

- Department of Emergencies
- Medical Administration
- Medical Institute for Road Safety
- Medical Technologies and Infrastructure
- Public Health
- Quality, Service, and Safety Administration

Language from the MoH specific to public health services states, "The Public Health Services concentrate on the healthy individual from the personal, community, and environmental preventive medicine perspectives through assimilation of the innovative concept of health promotion. The Public Health Services are committed to promoting health and disease prevention among the citizens of Israel, starting with family health stations, health services for school children, district health offices, through to the professional administrative staff."[31]

The range of public health services provided by the Health Division includes:

- Community Genetics
- Community Rehabilitation
- Employees' Health
- Environmental Health
- Epidemiology
- Health Education and Promotion
- Mother, Child and Adolescent Health
- National Food Service
- National Institute for Studying the Implications of Scalp Ringworm Treatment
- Nutrition
- Public Health Laboratories
- Public Health Nursing
- Tuberculosis and AIDS

Public health services are delivered through 18 health bureaus (roughly equivalent to local and county health departments) spread throughout the country.

Physicians

Access to physicians is made available through enrollment in one of the four health plans. According to Rosen et al., in 2014, there were approximately 7,000 primary care physicians (PCPs) working with the health plans.[18] Data from the World Bank enable comparison of a global ratio of 1.53 physicians to 1,000 people to Israel's 3.35 physicians per 1,000 people.[32] These PCPs work primarily in outpatient clinics throughout the nation, with higher concentrations of these clinics located in larger population centers. Access to primary care physicians is good, with most community clinics run by the health plans offering same-day visits.

Specialty care is provided through a network of over 17,000 board-certified specialty physicians. These specialty physicians are employed by the various hospitals or operate independently in community-based clinics. As might be expected, the four health plans are beginning to employ specialty physicians directly as a way of better controlling their expenses.[18] This effort by the health plans to bring more specialty care under their direct control has resulted in an increasing level of competition with hospitals and ambulatory clinics in the hospitals. According to Rosen et al., hospitals have reacted by making access to specialty care quicker and less cumbersome than in health plan sponsored community settings.[18] Waiting times for specialists appear to be reasonable. In 2012, among people who visited a specialist in the preceding 3 months, 45% reported waiting 1 week or less, 16% waited 1 to 2 weeks, and 36% waited more than 2 weeks.[33]

Specialty physicians employed by the hospitals are salaried members of the hospital staff and are prohibited from billing patients or health plans for additional services. This system of physician employment by hospitals is similar to what is currently in place in the United States, given the substantial growth of physician-hospital organizations (PHOs).[34] Generally speaking, patients in Israeli hospitals cannot select which specialist will care for them. They are assigned a physician according to the rotation schedule determined by department heads and their assistants. The exception is the private medical service in Jerusalem's nonprofit hospitals where, in return for an additional fee, the patient can choose a physician.[18]

Acute Care Hospitals

There are 28 acute care hospitals currently available in Israel.[35] The majority of hospitals in Israel have in excess of 100 beds each, and all are operated as not-for-profit organizations.[35] Hospital services are available across the country with the largest concentration of hospitals in the major population centers. At the center of Israel there are 9 acute care hospitals, and Jerusalem is the home to 3 major hospitals. According to data from the OECD, Israel has one of the lowest ratios of acute care hospital beds to 1,000 people of any of the member states. See **FIGURE 17-4**. In 2012, there were 3.1 beds per 1,000 people. In comparison, the OECD average in 2012 was 4.8 acute care hospital beds per 1,000 people.[26]

As is the case in the United States, hospitals in Israel are operated as public and private organizations. Public hospitals are required to accept payment from the four health plans leaving patients with only their co-payment. Private hospitals can accept payment from the health plans but can also bill separately for services. Among the largest hospitals in Israel as measured by number of beds are:

- Chaim Sheba–Academic Medical Center (1,200 beds)
- Hadassah Medical Organization: Ein Karem and Mount Scopus (1,100 beds)
- Rabin Medical Center (1,300 beds)
- Shaare Zedek Medical Center (1,000 beds)
- Tel Aviv Sourasky Medical Center (1,300 beds)

Medical tourism is an important activity made available by most of the private hospitals in Israel. A wide variety of medical and surgical procedures are accessible through medical tourism, including oncology, orthopedics, cardiology, cardiac surgery, neurosurgery, neurology, ear, nose and throat surgeries, endocrinology, gastroenterology, general surgery, pediatrics, urology, plastic and aesthetic surgery, ophthalmology, vascular surgery, bone marrow transplants, pulmonology, and fertility treatment (including IVF and complex dental procedures).[37] The medical tourism was mainly from Russia. The financial crisis in Russia resulted in a decrease in medical tourism. The advantage to offering medical tourism services is the ability to charge patients a predetermined rate and not have to be concerned with reimbursement through one of the four health plans. For the patient, high-quality clinical care is available on demand at typically a lower cost than might be available in their home country.

Rehabilitation Services

Rehabilitation is included in the NHI benefits package and responsibility for its provision, therefore, lies with the health plans. Rehabilitation services are provided in the general hospitals, in designated rehabilitation hospitals, in geriatric hospitals and in the community. Outpatient services include clinics for child development and rehabilitation, clinics for general rehabilitation and daycare rehabilitation. All these services are provided in community facilities of the health plans. All rehabilitation services incur a co-payment.[18]

In mid-2014, there were 732 general rehabilitation beds in Israel. Of these, 37% were in two large rehabilitation hospitals, 35% in 10 rehabilitation wards in general hospitals and 28% in 6 geriatric rehabilitation centers. Approximately one third (31%) of the beds were for neurological rehabilitation, 25% for people comatose for an extended period, 18% for general rehabilitation, 13% for children and 13% for orthopedic rehabilitation.[38]

Long-Term Care Services

The vast majority of elderly people in Israel live or are cared for at home, with only 3.5% residing in any kind of institutional setting (with some 2.5% in a skilled nursing home). Even among the disabled elderly, nearly 80% still live in the community because of the extensive care provided by families and the development of formal services intended to reinforce this social support and to help families to cope with the burden of care.[18]

In addition to some 1,400 social clubs that provide a framework for activities and facilitate interpersonal contact and socialization for the elderly population who are in good health, a network of

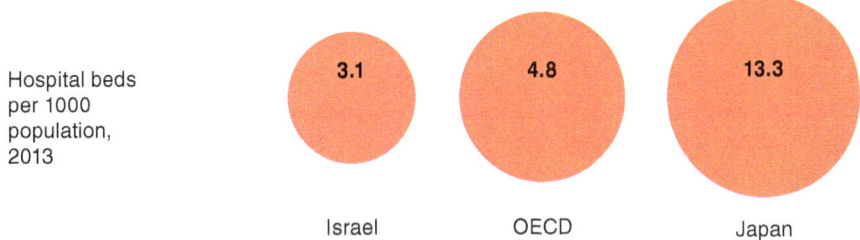

FIGURE 17-4 Hospital Beds per 1,000 Persons (2013)

Reproduced from OECD. OECD Health Policy Overview: Health policy in Israel. Oecd.org. https://www.oecd.org/health/health-systems/Health-Policy-in-Israel-March-2016.pdf. March 2016. Accessed June 26, 2016.

daycare centers for the disabled elderly has been developed. Daycare centers contribute significantly to the ability of the disabled elderly to remain in the community. The service also improves the quality of their lives and releases the family from caregiving duties during the day, freeing them to work and attend to other tasks.[18]

If institutional long-term care services are required, there are more than 400 care homes available across the country providing a continuum of services, similar to those in the United States, starting with senior housing and moving up to traditional nursing homes. Payment for skilled nursing services is also managed in a way similar to the United States in that residents and/or their family members are expected to pay a large monthly fee (approximately US $3,000 per month). To help offset these costs, the MoH provides a subsidy that is pegged to the annual income of the elderly person and/or their family.[18]

Summary

The organization, financing, and delivery of health care in Israel is based on the principle of universal, comprehensive care for each and every citizen, regardless of religion, gender, or ethnicity. Despite being a small nation in a highly dangerous and volatile part of the world, the National Health Insurance Law established in 1995 has created a system in which the Iron Triangle[39] of health care—high quality, universal access and (comparatively) low cost—has been achieved. While improvements are needed to help reduce health disparities—particularly among Arab Israelis and Palestinians living in Israel—and to help continue to manage costs and deal with discontent among physicians regarding their salaries, Israel serves as a beacon for nations around the world in making health care affordable and universally accessible.

▶ Emerging Challenges and Opportunities

The State of Israel was established in 1948, but the current healthcare system has been developing since the beginning of the 20th century with the establishment of the Clalit Sick Fund in 1911 for the treatment of the workers. The system was built on the foundation of Otto Von Bismarck's principles of equality and social responsibility. Equality and social responsibility are the key values that have been preserved throughout the development of the Israeli healthcare system, and they remain its hallmarks.

Two other important players in the establishment of the healthcare systems were the generous Rothschild family and Hadassah, the Women's Zionist Organization of America. Starting in 1912, Hadassah built and operated hospitals, medical clinics, pharmacies, and *drop-of-milk clinics* (mother and child welfare clinics that concentrated on child development and were responsible for vaccinations) across the State of Israel, clinics that are still active today.

The population size of Israel in 1948 was 870,000, and at the time, medical insurance was voluntary, and only 53% of the population were insured. With the immigration waves after World War II, the population of Israel doubled in 4 years. The Clalit Sick Fund became the main insurer and supplier for the majority of citizens.

"Israel has established one of the most enviable healthcare systems among OECD countries in the 15 years since it legislated mandatory health insurance," stated the OECD report published in 2012.[40]

The healthcare system is mainly public, with 28 general acute care hospitals. Ownership varies: 11 are government owned, 8 are owned by the Clalit Sick Fund, and 7 are privately owned public hospitals (e.g., Hadassah owned by HWZOA), and 2 are private hospitals (1 privately owned, and 1 owned by the Maccabi Sick Fund).[41]

The primary care is excellent, with a high level of clinical care, as seen in the national quality measures program, with the advantage of full electronic medical records. There have been national quality measures for hospitals since 2012. Over 90% of Israelis are satisfied with the system.[42] The ability of Israel to contain the costs and to maintain some of the low-cost health expenditure is due to:

1. Tight regulation both on hospital beds and on advanced expensive equipment, such as MRI and CT scans, to limit the supplier-induced demand phenomenon.
2. The simple and transparent reimbursement system; the tariff is published by the MoH after it is decided upon in a committee composed of all stakeholders (the ministers of finance and health as well as hospital and sick fund stakeholders). There are annual discussions and updates about the tariff.
    a. There is only one bill per hospital admission. The basis is fee for service;

surgeries and other procedures are reimbursed by Diagnosis Related Group (DRG), which means there is an all-inclusive payment; for other hospitalizations, such as pneumonia, when the patient is in Internal Medicine, the reimbursement is "per diem."
3. The capping system between hospitals and the sick funds; there is a defined amount of money (which is calculated based on the activity in the previous three years) above the capped amount, and the goal is to limit the hospital's incentive to increase activity.

Although Israeli health care is considered very good; the system is facing significant challenges.

Shortage of Resources

Financially, both the sick funds and the hospitals have deficient budgets. The sick funds are undercompensated for the rising costs of the basket of benefits and the salary increases that are part of national union agreements.

Hospitals are crowded because there is a bed shortage, with 3.1 beds per 1,000 inhabitants (compared to the average of 5.0 in OECD countries) including 1.9 acute care beds (higher only than Mexico's 1.6 beds per 1,000 inhabitants). The average occupancy rate is 97% (usually much higher in the winter time), compared to the OECD average of 75%. The length of stay of 4.3 days on average is shorter than the OECD average by 2.2 days.[26]

Without enough staff, quality of care can be diminished and patients and staff can experience frustration.

There is a shortage of advanced technology in remote rural areas—a limited number of MRIs and a severe shortage of radiotherapy—as part of the cost containment.

Public vs. Private Expenditure

There is significant activity with private medicine in Israel outside the public hospitals (only a few hospitals have permission to practice both private and public medicine). Although there is physical separation of private and public systems, there is overlapping with physicians working in both systems and patients moving in both directions between the private and public systems. The physicians usually direct the less complicated cases to private medicine, thus retaining the more complicated patients in the public hospitals. This often presents a challenge in that if patients see a private physician who also works at a hospital, billing is often incorrect or confusing.

Comparatively, the waiting times for office visits and surgeries are shorter in the private system. The private system is readily affordable due to the fact that 75% of the population carries complementary insurance; however, this also presents a challenge in that many citizens cannot afford the complementary insurance that the sick funds sell for about a US $100 per family per month.[42]

The benefits of these insurances are mainly the ability to be treated in a private hospital and the coverage of treatments that are not in the basket of benefits. The difficulty is that Israel's care system is part socialism and part capitalism, so access is a challenge.

In recent years there is a significant increase in the consumption of private medicine, with an increase in out-of-pocket payments. There is a significant ministerial effort to limit private medicine and bring back patients to the public system. The challenge is that this effort could result in a large tax increase to provide a revenue stream or, to the contrary, it could result in a reduction of private services, which would be unacceptable to most of the public.

Workforce

During the 1990s there was a large wave of immigration from the former Soviet Union, which increased the population size as well as the number of physicians. However, these physicians from Russia do not all speak Hebrew nor do they have licenses to practice medicine in Israel. Sometimes there was a knowledge gap, but the largest barrier was language, which was addressed in the *ulpan*, Hebrew language school. Currently the ratio of active physicians is 3.4 per 1,000 inhabitants, compared with the OECD average of 3.5. Partly due to the aging of these physicians who came in the Russian immigration wave, in future years the shortage of physicians will be worse. In Israel all hospital physicians are hospital employees. The nursing situation is worse, with 4.9 nurses per 1,000 inhabitants, compared with the OECD average of 9.8.[26] Many factors contribute to the nursing shortage: overcrowded wards with inability to provide proper care, comparatively low salaries, the stereotype that nursing is a feminine profession, the tendency for nurses to decrease their work hours or shift to less demanding nursing positions outside hospitals, and early professional retirement.

Geographical Inequality

Although the National Health Insurance Law ensures that everyone has medical insurance, the access to high-quality medical care differs geographically, with much better access in urban centers compared to suburban or rural areas. In recent years, the inequality has improved due to significant financial incentives that were given to physicians working in the geographic periphery, but shortages and inequities still exist.

The Conflicting Roles of the Ministry of Health

The MoH is responsible for the whole healthcare system: for the licensing of institutions and health professionals, for the functionality of the sick funds and hospitals, and for the provision of directives and regulations. In addition, the MoH owns many hospitals—acute care, psychiatric care, and geriatric care—thus there are conflicting interests. This anomaly was recognized from the inception of the Israeli healthcare system, with many suggestions over the years for correction, but, practically speaking, the anomaly was not resolved.

Nursing Care

Long-term nursing care is currently not in the basket of benefits; there is limited financial assistance from the National Insurance Institute, but still the financial burden falls on the families. There have been recent suggestions to include nursing care in the basket of benefits in return for the health tax increases.

▸ An Integrated Healthcare System

> "I am an Israeli Arab, this is my country, I feel the same as Yochi (Doctor Schiffman) feels. It's my country and I'm doing my job, I try to do my best. This is the way I look at that. So, I don't wake up in the morning and start thinking 'I'm an Arab not a Jew' and such things, I am focused on patient treatment, that's all."[43]
>
> —Professor Ahmed Eid, Chief of the Department of Surgery, Hadassah Hospital, Mount Scopus.

The Israeli healthcare system is well known in Israel for providing health care for the entire population, regardless of a patient's ability to pay, ethnicity, or religion. In contrast to other government institutions, such as public education, where separate, publically funded schools may provide services to distinct, often segregated, populations, the Israeli healthcare system is a single integrated system where Arab and Jewish Israelis, religious and secular, all experience the same level of care and are treated by the same physicians regardless of their background. Despite years of conflict in the region between Arabs and Jews, in Israel you will find Arab doctors and nurses treating Jewish patients and vice versa, even in the context of ongoing violence between their two respective communities.[43,44,45] The Arab Israeli minority is well integrated at all levels of the Israeli healthcare system, and Arab Israelis run prominent academic medical departments at Israel's most prestigious hospitals in addition to serving as CEOs and medical directors for entire hospitals.[46,47,48] Indeed, one particular Israeli-Arab community of Arraba in the lower Galilee has more than 6 doctors per 1,000 inhabitants, one of the highest numbers of doctor per capita in the world.[49]

This remarkable success is no accident. Even before the founding of the State of Israel, health care was protected from the many divisions in Israeli society. Hadassah, the Women's Zionist Organization of America, which founded many of the hospitals and clinics in Israel many decades before the State of Israel was formally declared, has always had a mission to provide care to all, "regardless of race, ethnicity, or nationally."[50] The culture of medicine naturally serves such a humanitarian cause. The Abraham Fund Initiatives, a nonprofit organization with a mission to "promote coexistence and equality among Israel's Jewish and Arab-Palestinian citizens," found that Israeli healthcare employees state that a "patient's identity and cause of illness or injury are of no relevance in the ER or on the operating table, and the caretaker's identity or ethnic origin are similarly irrelevant."[48] This guiding ethos is formally stated in Israeli law. The Patient's Rights Act of 1996 includes a prohibition against discrimination, "no medical facility or clinician shall discriminate between patients on grounds of religion, race, sex, nationality, country of birth, or other such grounds."[51]

This close integration, which can go without notice or comment in a typical day at any Israeli hospital or clinic, can sometimes reveal itself in a dramatic fashion. One example, among many, occurred on August 4 when an Arab gunman on a motorbike opened fire on an Israeli soldier, Chen Schwartz. Schwartz was rushed to Hadassah's Mount Scopus hospital, where the chair of the surgery department, Professor Ahmed Eid, an Arab Israeli, saved the soldier's life. Asked later by the media about his role in the event, Professor Eid answered as almost any Israeli healthcare provider would, "I was doing my job. That's what I do…. We don't really think about who we are treating. We are focused on saving lives of patients. Preventing death."[43,44]

The Israeli humanitarian drive does not stop with Israeli citizens but extends to Palestinians from the West Bank and Gaza Strip. In 2015, according to the Palestinian Ministry of Health, 10,300 patients were sent from the West Bank and Gaza Strip to hospitals in Israel for advanced treatment.[52] This kind of patient transfer is supported by various governmental and philanthropic agencies in Israel, the Palestinian Authority, and the international community. Perhaps most remarkable is the ongoing cooperation between the Palestinian Ministry of Health and the Israeli Ministry of Health in securing the safe medical transfer of thousands of Palestinians from the Gaza Strip, which has been controlled by Hamas since 2007. Hamas is a militant Islamic fundamentalist organization that openly calls for the destruction of the State of Israel by any means.[53] That thousands of Gazans depend on the State of Israel for advanced health care is an irony seemingly lost on the Hamas leadership, who personally benefit from Israeli health care. Indeed, shortly following the 2014 war between Israel and Gaza, which cost over 2,000 lives, a daughter of Ismail Haniyeh, an important leader of Hamas in Gaza and a former prime minister, was urgently transferred to an Israeli hospital after suffering complications from a surgical procedure in Gaza.[54] Despite the well-documented integration of the Israeli and Palestinian healthcare system, a series of articles in 2009 on Palestinian health care published in the prominent British medical journal *The Lancet* failed to mention this cooperation at all, perhaps in part because it failed to include a single Israeli physician among its many authors and its steering committee.[55,56]

In a Middle East divided by ethnic and religious divisions that fuel violence, the cooperation in the Israeli healthcare system between Arabs and Jews, and between Palestinian physicians and Israeli physicians, is an inspiring and overlooked example of humanity and reason persevering in a region where humanity is too easily silenced in the name of religion, ethnicity, or nation state.

Israeli Leadership in Global Health

Despite its small size and recent founding, Israel has had a disproportionately positive impact on health care in the Middle East and around the globe and is often among the first nations to respond to humanitarian crises. According to the Israel Ministry of Foreign Affairs, Israel has sent humanitarian teams to 140 nations around the world.[60] Both Israeli governmental and non-governmental organizations have played decisive roles in providing emergency health care in humanitarian crises. Examples include the Israeli response to the devastating 2010 earthquake in Haiti and more long-term healthcare partnerships, such as infectious disease surveillance and healthcare capacity building in the Middle East and in Africa. This altruistic role predates the existence of the State of Israel and is in keeping with the priorities of the Zionist movement, which sought not just to create a Jewish state but also an exemplary moral state, in keeping with the biblical prophecy of Isaiah, to be "a light to the nations."[61] While its small size and many wars may at first glance seem to be a hindrance to Israel coming to the aid of other nations, it is these very challenges that give Israel the expertise to assist in a crisis. As the Israeli prime minister Golda Meir stated following her visit to postcolonial Africa, "We have been forced to find solutions to problems that large, wealthy, powerful states have never encountered."[62]

Remarkably, Israel's international development arm, MASHAV, began in 1958, a mere decade after the creation of the State of Israel and prior to the founding of the U.S. Agency for International Development in 1961. In the area of emergency medical response, Israel has an unrivaled track record. In partnership with IDF, MASHAV has quickly established field hospitals around the world in response to humanitarian crises. One notable example includes Israel's response to the Rwandan refugee crisis in 1994. A 120-bed field hospital with operating rooms and specialty care was established in Zaire, now the Democratic Republic of Congo. The decision was made on July 22 to establish the hospital, and the first patients were being treated on July 26—an incredibly rapid response. In the first 12 days, the hospital received 1,215 patients, of whom 723 required admission to the hospital, and 16 required emergency surgery.[63] This experience was repeated following earthquakes in Turkey (1999) and in India (2001), as well as in humanitarian missions to Kosovo (1999).[64]

For Haiti's devastating earthquake in 2010 that killed an estimated 230,000 and injured approximately 250,000 people,[65] Israeli medical personnel were among the first on the ground. Within hours of the earthquake, Israel sent its initial response team, via one passenger plane and one cargo plane. The planes were in the air before Haiti's only international airport, which was damaged by the earthquake, was declared operational. As a result, only the passenger plane managed to land initially, while the cargo plane, due to its larger size, was delayed for 8 hours, unable to land until the runway was declared safe.[66] Despite these logistical hurdles and the fact that Haiti is 6,500 miles away from Israel (in comparison, the distance from Miami to Port au Prince, Haiti's capital, is 700 miles), the Israeli field hospital was operational 89 hours after the earthquake, providing advanced care days before any other nation was able to accomplish this feat. During the 10 days that the hospital was operational, it treated 1,111 patients, of which 737 required admission, and performed 244 operations on 203 patients.[65]

Critics of the Israeli government have maintained that such relief work, while commendable, is actually motivated by a cynical desire to "divert attention away from their behavior toward the Palestinians."[67] Such criticism is misleading because it ignores the extensive resources that Israel devotes to Palestinian health care, and indeed, to health care throughout the Middle East. Representatives of the Palestinian authority and even the militant terrorist group Hamas cooperate with Israel in order to ensure healthcare delivery to Palestinian civilians and combatants. Every month, hundreds to thousands of Palestinian civilians are transferred out of the Gaza Strip and the West Bank to be treated in Israeli hospitals.[68] In the context of the ongoing violence between Hamas and Israel, this degree of cooperation is unprecedented in its scope and perseverance and provides needed inspiration in a seemingly intractable conflict.

Indeed, Israel's role in coordinating infectious disease surveillance and vaccine deployment extends to its current and former enemies, and it quietly predates the peace accords with Egypt and Jordan. Extensive polio monitoring and vaccine deployment, with the goal of eradication, began before the 1967 war in which Israel gained control of the Gaza Strip and the West Bank and continues despite the Hamas takeover of Gaza. This cooperation, even during conflict, ultimately resulted in the eradication of the disease from these territories.[69] Cooperation with Egyptian and Jordanian governments, expedited through the World Health Organization, has enabled early detection of outbreaks and coordinated responses. Though understated and often under the radar, Israeli leadership in global health extends not just to nations thousands of miles away but also to its enemies, even those whose stated goal is the destruction of Israel.

▶ Summary

The Israeli healthcare system, large, complex, and multifaceted, is currently undergoing changes that the MoH started implementing in 2015. According to the OECD Health Policy Overview, "While the Israel population enjoys good health outcomes and the health system performs fairly well, there are specific areas—health workforce and hospital care, in particular—where policy attention is needed."[57]

The Israeli government is in the process of standardizing the supplementary insurance packages across all of the four sick fund organizations. Drugs not currently reimbursed in the supplementary insurance packages will be reimbursed under the new regulations. In addition, the government is exploring and planning to implement ways to pay the premiums for poor populations who cannot currently afford supplementary health insurance. The impact on pharmaceutical companies is unclear; however, if the government increases payment benefits on unreimbursed drugs, the pharmaceutical companies might experience financial gains. Additionally, a government increase in payments to accommodate the needs of the poor have the potential to increase the flow of funds into the four insurance systems.[58]

The good news for Israelis is that one need not travel abroad for world-class medical care. Medical personnel, research facilities, and hospitals are among the best in the world. Additionally, patients benefit from Israel's translational (lab to bedside) medical practice, which quickly "brings the benefits of science back to the patient, with better technology to create improved infrastructure."[59] For example, in 2015 Hadassah received a US $6.5 million grant to create the Wohl Centre for Translational Medicine, which will focus on cancers, ALS, Parkinson's, and other degenerative diseases.[59]

The Israeli healthcare system, with its cutting-edge research in Israel and its partnerships with many medical research centers throughout the world (for example, Massachusetts General Hospital in the United States and clinics in Kenya), serves not only Israeli citizens but also demonstrates its ability to improve the health and care for people around the world.

References

1. Moses J. My Jewish learning: Israel before the State. http://www.myjewishlearning.com/article/israel-before-the-state/. Accessed June 26, 2016.
2. Senor D, Singer S. *Start-Up Nation: The Story of Israel's Economic Miracle*. New York: Twelve; 2009: 18.
3. Werman M, Bell M. Israeli doctor paved the way for emergency response in Boston. Public Radio International. http://www.pri.org/stories/2013-04-26/israeli-doctor-paved-way-emergency-response-boston. Aired April 26, 2013. Accessed June 26, 2016.
4. Israel government and politics: how does the Israeli government work? Jewish Virtual Library. https://www.jewishvirtuallibrary.org/jsource/Politics/how_govt_works.html. Published 2016. Accessed June 26, 2016.
5. Kershner I. Aided by the sea, Israel overcomes an old foe: drought. *The New York Times*. http://www.nytimes.com/2015/05/30/world/middleeast/water-revolution-in-israel-overcomes-any-threat-of-drought.html?_r=0. Published 2015. Accessed June 26, 2016.
6. Final voter turnout at 71.8%, four percent more than 2013 election. *The Jerusalem Post*. http://www.jpost.com/Israel-News/Voter-turnout-at-10-am-higher-than-in-2013-election-394166. Published March 17, 2015. Accessed June 26, 2016.
7. The State: political structure. Ministry of Foreign Affairs. http://www.mfa.gov.il/mfa/aboutisrael/state/pages/the%20state-%20political%20structure.aspx. Accessed June 26, 2016.
8. Country ranking. Medical Tourism Index 2014. http://www.medicaltourismindex.com/2014-mti/country-ranking/. Accessed June 26, 2016.
9. Israel's medical tourism at the crossroads. *IMTJ*. http://www.imtj.com/news/israels-medical-tourism-crossroads/. Published November 29, 2013. Accessed June 26, 2016.
10. *The World Factbook* 2016. Washington, DC: Central Intelligence Agency, 2016. https://www.cia.gov/library/publications/the-world-factbook/geos/is.html. Accessed June 26, 2016.
11. Facts about Israel: history. Israel Ministry of Foreign Affairs. http://mfa.gov.il/MFA/AboutIsrael/History/Pages/Facts%20about%20Israel-%20History.aspx. Published 2010. Accessed June 26, 2016.
12. Awards 2014. Smart City Expo World Congress. http://www.smartcityexpo.com/awards-2014. Accessed June 26, 2016.
13. Maternity allowance. National Insurance Institute of Israel. https://www.btl.gov.il/English%20Homepage/Benefits/Maternity%20Insurance/Maternity%20Allowance/Pages/default.aspx. Accessed June 26, 2016.
14. 10 Facts About the Arab-Israeli Conflict. Fact #2: one quarter of Israeli citizens are not Jewish. http://arabisraeliconflict.info/arab-israel-facts/fact-2-arab-israeli-citizens. Accessed November 11, 2016.
15. Chinitz D. An overview of Israel's universal health care system. http://ldi.upenn.edu/news/overview-israels-universal-health-care-system. Published August 2014. Accessed June 26, 2016.
16. OECD. *Focus on Health Spending: OECD Health Statistics 2015*. http://www.oecd.org/health/health-systems/Focus-Health-Spending-2015.pdf. Published July 2015. Accessed June 26, 2016.
17. *World Health Statistics 2016*. Geneva: World Health Organization.
18. Rosen B, Waitzberg R, Merkur S. *Israel: Health System Review*. Copenhagen: European Observatory on Health Systems and Policy; 2015.
19. Southern J, Roizin H, Daana M, et al. Varied utilisation of health provisions by Arab and Jewish residents in Israel. *International Journal for Equity in Health*. 2015;14(1). http://dx.doi.org/10.1186/s12939-015-0193-8.
20. Ministry of Aliyah and Immigrant Absorption. *Health Services in Israel*. Jerusalem: The Publications Department; 2015.
21. Kupot Cholim. Nefesh B'Nefesh. http://www.nbn.org.il/aliyahpedia/government-services/health-care-national-insurance/kupot-cholim-health-plans/. Accessed June 26, 2016.
22. Rosen B. *How Health Plans in Israel Manage the Care Provided by Their Physicians*. Jerusalem: Myers-JDC-Brookdale Institute; 2011.
23. Telemedicine in Israel: Israel's health and care system organisation. Momentum. http://www.telemedicine-momentum.eu/israel/. Published 2012. Accessed June 26, 2016.
24. Goldfus Insurance and Investments. (2016). *Private Health Insurance*. http://www.goldfus-ins.co.il/logic_eng.asp?id=25.
25. National health expenditure data. Centers for Medicare and Medicaid Services. CMS.gov. https://www.cms.gov/research-statistics-data-and-systems/statistics-trends-and-reports/nationalhealthexpenddata/nationalhealthaccountshistorical.html. Modified December, 3, 2015. Accessed June 26, 2016.
26. OECD. *OECD Health Statistics 2014*. Paris: OECD Publishing; 2014.
27. Rosen B, Kanel K. *Healthcare in the US and Israel: Comparative Overview*. Jerusalem: Brookdale Institute; 2010.
28. Telemedicine in Israel: Israel's health and care system organisation. Momentum. http://www.telemedicine-momentum.eu/israel/. Published 2012. Accessed June 26, 2016.
29. Financial report 2012 for the governmental general. State of Israel Ministry of Health. http://www.health.gov.il/English/Pages/HomePage.aspx. Accessed May 24, 2016.
30. *Israel Defense Forces: Medical Corps*. Jewish Virtual Library. http://www.jewishvirtuallibrary.org/jsource/Society_&_Culture/medical.html. Accessed June 1, 2016.
31. Health Division. State of Israel Ministry of Health. http://www.health.gov.il/English/MinistryUnits/HealthDivision/Pages/Default.aspx. Accessed June 2, 2016.
32. The World Bank. Physicians (per 1,000 people). http://beta.data.worldbank.org/indicator/SH.MED.PHYS.ZS?end=2011&start=2008. Accessed June 2, 2016.
33. Brammli-Greenberg S, Waitzberg R, Guberman D. (2015). *Waiting Times for (Non-Urgent) Ambulatory Services from Patient's Perspective*. Jerusalem: Myers-JDC Brookdale Institute; 2014.

34. Bader B. (2009). Clinically Integrated Physician-Hospital Organizations. *Great Boards*. Winter 2009. Baltimore: Bader and Associates.
35. Hospitals and medical centers. Israel Science and Technology Homepage. http://www.science.co.il/Hospitals.asp. Accessed June 5, 2016.
36. Shirom A. Private medical services in acute-care hospitals in Israel. *Int J Health Plann Manage*. 2001;16(4):325-345.
37. *Medical Tourism to Israel*. Health-tourism.com. https://www.health-tourism.com/medical-tourism-israel/. Accessed June 5, 2016.
38. Haklai Z. *Inpatient institutions and day care units in Israel: 2013*. Jerusalem: Ministry of Health; 2014.
39. Kissick W. *Medicine's Dilemmas*. New Haven: Yale University Press; 1994.
40. OECD. *OECD Reviews of Health Care Quality: Israel 2012: Raising Standards*. Paris: OECD Publishing; 2012. http://dx.doi.org/10.1787/9789264029941-en.
41. National Insurance Institute of Israel. https://www.btl.gov.il/English%20Homepage/Pages/default.aspx. Accessed 2015.
42. Israeli Ministry of Health. N Keidar & R Plotnik Planning & Strategy Division; May 2015. http://www.health.gov.il/PublicationsFiles/OECD_2012.pdf
43. Jerusalem doctors treat terrorists and victims alike, identities unknown. *Jerusalem Post*. http://www.jpost.com/Arab-Israeli-Conflict/Jerusalem-doctors-treat-terrorists-and-victims-alike-without-knowing-identities-431904. Accessed November 17, 2016.
44. Horovitz D. Arab doctor saves Jewish soldier hit by Arab bullets. No big deal? *The Times of Israel*. http://www.timesofisrael.com/arab-doctor-saves-jewish-soldier-hit-by-arab-bullets-no-big-deal/. Accessed November 17, 2016.
45. Mitnick J. For Israeli-Palestinian interaction, a new venue: the Arab doctor's office. *Christ Sci Monit*. http://www.csmonitor.com/World/Middle-East/2016/0201/For-Israeli-Palestinian-interaction-a-new-venue-the-Arab-doctor-s-office. February 2016. Accessed November 17, 2016.
46. Avraham R. Arab Doctor to Head Emergency Medicine at Hadassah. United With Israel. http://unitedwithisrael.org/arab-muslim-to-head-emergency-medicine-at-hadassah/. Published April 20, 2013. Accessed November 19, 2016.
47. The Abraham Fund Initiatives. Research and publications. http://www.abrahamfund.org/10862. Accessed November 19, 2016.
48. Reznik R. *Integrating Israel's Arab Citizens in the Healthcare System: A Success Story?* The Abraham Fund Initiatives. http://www.abrahamfund.org/webfiles/fck/Integration%20in%20the%20Healthcare%20System%20-%20English.pdf. Published April 2011. Accessed November 17, 2016.
49. Press VS. The small Israeli village where everyone's a doctor. Israel21c. http://www.israel21c.org/the-small-israeli-village-where-everyones-a-doctor/. Accessed November 17, 2016.
50. History. Hadassah, The Women's Zionist Organization of America. http://www.hadassah.org/about/history.html. Accessed November 19, 2016.
51. Patient's Rights Act, 1996. http://waml.haifa.ac.il/index/reference/legislation/israel/israel1.htm. Accessed November 19, 2016.
52. تقارير الأحصائية. وزارة الصحة الفلسطينية. http://www.moh.ps/index/Books/BookType/2/Language/ar. Accessed November 19, 2016.
53. The Avalon Project. Hamas covenant 1988: the covenant of the Islamic resistance movement. Lillian Goldman Law Library. Yale Law School. http://avalon.law.yale.edu/20th_century/hamas.asp. Published August 18, 1988. Accessed November 19, 2016.
54. Newman M, AP. Hamas leader's daughter receives medical care in Israel. *The Times of Israel*. http://www.timesofisrael.com/hamas-leaders-daughter-said-to-receive-medical-care-in-israel/. Accessed November 19, 2016.
55. Horton R. The occupied Palestinian territory: peace, justice, and health. *Lancet*. 2009;373(9666):784-788. doi:10.1016/S0140-6736(09)60100-8.
56. Chalmers I, Leaning J, Shannon HS, Zurayk H. Lancet Steering Group on the occupied Palestinian territory. *Lancet*. 2009;373(9666):788–790. doi:10.1016/S0140-6736(09)60102-1.
57. OECD. Health policies and data. Health policy in your country. Israel. Paris: OECD Publishing; April 2016. http://www.oecd.org/health. Accessed June 26, 2016.
58. IHS Markit. Israel to conduct major overhaul of health insurance system. https://www.ihs.com/country-industry-forecasting.html?ID=1065999186. Published August 5, 2015. Accessed June 26, 2016.
59. Hadassah receives $6.5 million grant to create Translational Medicine Institute. Hadassah, the Women's Zionist Organization of America. http://www.hadassah.org/news-stories/hadassah-receives-65.html?referrer=https://www.google.com/. Published February 2, 2015. Accessed June 26, 2016.
60. Israeli humanitarian relief operations: MASHAV-Israel's Agency for International Development Cooperation. http://mfa.gov.il/MFA/ForeignPolicy/Aid/Pages/Israeli%20Humanitarian%20Relief-%20MASHAV%20-%20the%20Israel%20F.aspx. Accessed August 18, 2016.
61. Jewish Values Online. Multiple Jewish perspectives on morals and ethics. 2016. http://www.jewishvaluesonline.org/665. Accessed August 18, 2016.
62. Africa's development needs: state of implementation of various commitments, challenges and the way forward. Address by Mr. Aaron Abramovich, Director-General of the Israel Ministry of Foreign Affairs, to the United Nations General Assembly High-Level Meeting on Development. Israel Ministry of Foreign Affairs. http://mfa.gov.il/MFA/InternatlOrgs/Speeches/Pages/MFA_Dir-Gen_Abramovich_Address_UN_General_Assembly_High-Level_Meeting_Development_22-Sep-2008.aspx. Published September 22, 2008. Accessed August 18, 2016.
63. Operation 'Interns for Hope': Israeli medical aid for Rwandan refugees in Zaire. Israel Ministry of Foreign Affairs. http://mfa.gov.il/MFA/PressRoom/1994/Pages/ISRAELI%20MEDICAL%20AID%20FOR%20RWANDAN%20REFUGEES%20IN%20ZAIRE.aspx. Published July 26, 1994. Accessed August 18, 2016.
64. Summary of Israeli humanitarian relief operations: 1997–1999. Israel Ministry of Foreign Affairs. http://mfa.gov.il/MFA/MFA-Archive/1999/Pages/Summary%20of%20Israeli%20Humanitarian%20Relief%20Operations-.aspx. Published December 26, 1999. Accessed August 18, 2016.
65. Bar-On E, Abargel A, Peleg K, Kreiss Y. Coping with the challenges of early disaster response: 24 years of field hospital experience after earthquakes. *Disaster Med Public Health Prep*. 2013;7(5):491–498. doi:10.1017/dmp.2013.94.

66. Israel's medical operation in Haiti—Anderson Cooper 360°. CNN.com. Blogs. http://ac360.blogs.cnn.com/2010/01/21/israels-operation-in-haiti/. Published January 21, 2010. Accessed August 18, 2016.
67. Freedman S. Israel's double standards over Haiti. *The Guardian*. https://www.theguardian.com/commentisfree/2010/jan/22/israel-haiti-relief-palestine. Published January 22, 2010. Accessed August 18, 2016.
68. World Health Organization Regional Office for the Eastern Mediterranean. WHO monthly reports on referral of patients from the Gaza Strip. http://www.emro.who.int/pse/publications-who/monthly-referral-reports.html. Accessed August 18, 2016.
69. Tulchinsky TH, Ramlawi A, Abdeen Z, Grotto I, Flahault A. Polio lessons 2013: Israel, the West Bank, and Gaza. *Lancet Lond Engl. 2013*;382(9905):1611–1612. doi:10.1016/S0140-6736(13)62331-4.

CHAPTER 18

Ghana

Umar Haruna and **Musah A. Sugri**

▸ Country Description

TABLE 18-1 Ghana	
Nationality	Noun: Ghanaian(s) Adjective: Ghanaian
Ethnic groups	Akan 47.5%, Mole-Dagbon 16.6%, Ewe 13.9%, Ga-Dangme 7.4%, Gurma 5.7%, Guan 3.7%, Grusi 2.5%, Mande-Busanga 1.1%, other 1.6% (2010 est.)
Religions	Christian 71.2% (Pentecostal/Charismatic 25.1%, Protestant 19.0%, Catholic 16.1%, other 11%), Muslim 17.6%, traditional 5.2%, other 0.7%, none 3.3% (2010 est.)
Language	Asante 16%, Ewe 14%, Fante 11.6%, Boron (Brong) 4.9%, Dagomba 4.4%, Dangme 4.2%, Dagarte (Dagaba) 3.9%, Kokomba 3.5%, Akyem 3.2%, Ga 3.1%, other 31.2%; English (official) (2010 est.)
Literacy	Definition: Age 15 and over can read and write. Total population: 76.6% Male: 82% Female: 71.4% (2015 est.)
Government type	Constitutional democracy
Date of independence	March 6, 1957 (from the United Kingdom)

(continues)

TABLE 18-1 Ghana (continued)	
Gross Domestic Product (GDP) per capita	$4,300 (2015 est.)
Unemployment rate	5.2% (2013 est.)
Natural hazards	Dry, dusty, northeastern harmattan winds occur from January to March; droughts
Environment: current issues	Recurrent drought in north severely affects agricultural activities; deforestation; overgrazing; soil erosion; poaching and habitat destruction threatens wildlife populations; water pollution; inadequate supplies of potable water
Population	26,908,262* (July 2016 est.)
Age structure	0–14 years: 38.2% (male 5,164,505/female 5,113,185) 15–24 years: 18.66% (male 2,498,185/female 2,522,353) 25–54 years: 34.05% (male 4,445,321/female 4,716,311) 55–64 years: 4.91% (male 642,984/female 678,784) 65 years and over: 4.19% (male 520,589/female 606,045) (2016 est.)
Median age	Total: 21 years Male: 20.5 years Female: 21.5 years (2016 est.)
Population growth rate	2.18% (2016 est.)
Birth rate	30.8 births/1,000 population (2016 est.)
Death rate	1,222 deaths/100,000 population (2014 est.)
Disease burden	Communicable disease deaths: 476/100,000 population Noncommunicable disease deaths: 670/100,000 population Injury deaths: 76/100,000 population (2016 est.)
Net migration rate	−1.9 migrant(s)/1,000 population (2016 est.)
Gender ratio	At birth: 1.03 male(s)/female 0–14 years: 1.01 male(s)/female 15–24 years: 0.99 male(s)/female 25–54 years: 0.94 male(s)/female 55–64 years: 0.95 male(s)/female 65 years and over: 0.86 male(s)/female Total population: 0.97 male(s)/female (2016 est.)
Infant mortality rate	Total: 36.3 deaths/1,000 live births Male: 40.2 deaths/1,000 live births Female: 32.2 deaths/1,000 live births (2016 est.)
Life expectancy at birth	Total population: 66.6 years Male: 64.1 years Female: 69.1 years (2016 est.)

TABLE 18-1 Ghana (continued)

Total fertility rate	4.03 children born/woman (2016 est.)
HIV/AIDS adult prevalence rate	1.61% (2015 est.)
Number of people living with HIV/AIDS	274,600 (2015 est.)
HIV/AIDS deaths	12,600 (2015 est.)

* Estimates for this country explicitly take into account the effects of excess mortality caused by AIDS; this can result in lower life expectancy, higher infant mortality, higher death rates, lower population growth rates, and changes in the distribution of population by age and gender than would otherwise be expected.

Data from Central Intelligence Agency. The World Factbook, 2016: Ghana. https://www.cia.gov/library/publications/resources/the-world-factbook/geos/gh.html.

History

The Republic of Ghana was named after the medieval Ghana Empire of West Africa in Ancient Ghana. Geographically, Ancient Ghana was approximately 500 miles (800 kilometers) north of the present Ghana and occupied the area between the rivers Ankobra and Volta. The actual name of the Empire was Ouagadougou. Ghana was the title of the kings who ruled the kingdom. The word *ghana* means warrior king.[1] Ancient Ghana was controlled by Sundiata in 1240 CE and absorbed into the larger Mali Empire, which reached its peak of success under Mansa Musa in approximately 1307. Around 1235, a Muslim leader named Sundiata united warring tribes. He then brought neighboring states under his rule to create the Mali Empire. Its capital city was called Kumbi-Saleh. Ancient Ghana derived power and wealth from gold and the camel, introduced through trans-Saharan trade. The Islamic community at Kumbi-Saleh remained a separate community quite a distance away from the king's palace. It had its own mosques and schools, but the king retained traditional beliefs. He drew on the bookkeeping and literary skills of Muslim scholars to help run the administration of the territory.[2]

On March 6, 1957, when the leaders of the former British colony of the Gold Coast sought an appropriate name for their newly independent state, the first African nation to gain its independence from colonial rule, they named their new country after ancient Ghana. The choice was more than merely symbolic because modern Ghana, like its namesake, was equally famed for its wealth and trade in gold. The growth of trade stimulated the development of early Akan states located on the trade route to the gold fields in the forest zone of the south.[3]

The Europeans arrived on the Gold Coast in the late 15th century. The Portuguese were the first to arrive. By 1471, under the patronage of Prince Henry the Navigator, they had reached the area that is now known as the Gold Coast because Europeans knew the area as the source of gold that reached Muslim North Africa by way of trade routes across the Sahara.[4] The initial Portuguese interest in trading for gold, ivory, and pepper increased so much that in 1482 the Portuguese built their first permanent trading post on the western coast of present-day Ghana. This fortress, Elmina Castle, constructed to protect Portuguese trade from European competitors and hostile Africans, still stands. With the opening of European plantations in the New World during the 1500s, which suddenly expanded the demand for slaves in the Americas, trade in slaves soon overshadowed gold as the principal export of the area. During the 17th and 18th centuries, other European adventurers emerged on the Gold Coast. First Dutch and later English, Danish, and Swedish were granted licenses by their governments to trade overseas. On the Gold Coast, these European competitors built fortified trading stations and challenged the Portuguese. Sometimes they were also drawn into conflicts with local inhabitants, as Europeans developed commercial alliances with local chiefs.[5]

The principal early struggle was between the Dutch and the Portuguese. With the loss of Elmina in 1642 to the Dutch, the Portuguese left the Gold Coast permanently. The next 150 years saw drastic changes and uncertainty, marked by local conflicts and diplomatic maneuvers, during which various European powers struggled to establish or to maintain a position of dominance in the profitable slave trade. There were short-lived ventures by the Swedes and the Prussians.[6] The Danes remained until 1850, when they withdrew from the Gold Coast. The British gained possession of all Dutch coastal forts by the end of the 19th century, thus making them the dominant European power on the Gold Coast until March 6, 1957, when the new republic of Ghana was born with Osagyefo "liberator" Dr. Kwame Nkrumah as its first president. It was during the first republic that healthcare facilities were built to take care of the indigenous Ghanaian population.

Size and Geography

Until March 1957, Ghana was known to the world as the Gold Coast. The Portuguese who came to Ghana in the 15th century found so much gold between the rivers Ankobra and Volta that they named the place Mina, meaning mine. English colonists later adopted the Gold Coast. The Republic of Ghana occupies an area of 239,460 square kilometers (92,440 square miles), and it borders Côte d'Ivoire (also known as Ivory Coast) to the west, Burkina Faso to the north, Togo to the east, and the Gulf of Guinea to the south. (See **FIGURE 18-1**.)

Ghana is composed of 10 administrative regions and 216 administrative districts with a decentralized system of administration. Within this arrangement, the national level is responsible for policy and strategy development. The regional level is the intermediate level responsible for translating national policy into regional strategies and coordinating district actions. The district is the level at which all government policies are implemented. The district assemblies are the highest political and administrative authority at the local level. The district assemblies, through their subcommittees, harmonize and coordinate plans and activities of all decentralized ministries. They also facilitate grassroots participation and community involvement in socioeconomic development programs and activities. The district assemblies are generally supportive of decentralized departments. Undoubtedly, the district assemblies are very important in the implementation and sustainability of a multisectoral response to healthcare systems.[7]

Economy

Ghana's economy has been strengthened by a quarter century of relatively sound management, a competitive business environment, and sustained reductions in poverty levels. In late 2010, Ghana was recategorized as a lower middle-income country. Ghana is well endowed with natural resources, and agriculture accounts for roughly one-quarter of GDP and employs more than half of the workforce, mainly small landholders. The services sector accounts for 50% of GDP. Gold and cocoa production and individual remittances are major sources of foreign exchange. Oil production at Ghana's offshore Jubilee field began in mid-December 2010 and is producing close to target levels. Additional oil projects are being developed and are expected to come on line in a few years. Estimated oil reserves have jumped to almost 700 million barrels, and Ghana's growing oil industry is expected to boost economic growth as the country faces the consequences of 2 years of loose fiscal policy, high budget and current account deficits, and depreciating currency.[8]

Demographics

Ghana has a population of 26.9 million, of which 52% are female and 48% are male (2016 estimates). Life expectancy of the total population is 66.6 years, with males at 64.1 years and females at 69.1 years. The illiteracy rate is 76.6%.[17] More than half live in rural settings. English is the official language of business and instruction. Local dialects include Akan (majority), Ga, and Ewe: Akan 47.5%, Mole-Dagbon 16.6%, Ewe 13.9%, Ga-Dangme 7.4%, Gurma 5.7%, Guan 3.7%, Grusi 2.5%, Mande-Busanga 1.1%, other 1.6% (2010 census). The Christian population is 71.2%, with the following distributions by denominations: Pentecostal/Charismatic 28.3%, Protestant 18.4%, Catholic 13.1%, and other 11%; Muslim is 17.6%, traditional African religion 5.2%, other 0.7%, and none 3.3% (2010 census).[9]

▸ Brief History of the Healthcare System

Pre–World War II

Until October 19, 1923, when the Korle Bu Teaching Hospital, formerly known as the Gold Coast Hospital, was opened by the Gold Coast governor at that time, Sir Gordon Guggisberg, health services were solely for Europeans. There were only European physicians who treated only the settlers. The majority of the indigenous Ghanaian population practiced traditional African medicine. After the opening of the Gold Coast Hospital, the indigenous population of Accra was able to receive European health care at a minimal cost. Korle Bu Hospital had less than 200 beds and treated up to 200 patients daily.[10] At that time, Korle Bu was described as the finest hospital in Africa, on account of its impressive array of fine buildings and a cadre of competent staff, who provided excellent medical services to the population of

FIGURE 18-1 Map of Ghana
© Rainer Lesniewski/Shutterstock

Ghana in general and the city of Accra in particular. Korle Bu Hospital, from its inception, has been used for the training of practical nurses, nurse anesthetists, dispensers, midwives, and other paramedical staff.

Since World War II

In 1946, a nurses' training college was opened at Korle Bu to train a higher level of staff registered nurses for the hospital and for the entire country. In April 1963, the government made Korle Bu Hospital the teaching hospital for the University of Ghana Medical School.[11] After independence, medical services became free to all citizens of Ghana and were financed by the government. Under the leadership of Dr. Kwame Nkrumah, Ghana set up a national health service, which was fully financed from state revenue. Still, during this time, because of the lack of facilities in rural areas, the quality of care received there was very poor; however, the concept during that time was concentrated on vaccine-preventable diseases, and everybody (including the rural areas) had access to available vaccinations. It was the belief of the Nkrumah administration that health before wealth was more than just an old adage; it developed programs that aim to protect and improve the health of people to help in the battle against poverty.[12] The government was committed to the objective of health for all. Good health boosts labor productivity, educational attainment, and income and thus reduces poverty. A country's economic development is closely interrelated with the health status of its population, so an efficient and equitable healthcare system is an important instrument in breaking the vicious circle of poverty and ill health. Until 1983, Ghana's health system was financed mainly out of the national budget.[13]

By the early 1980s, Ghana was experiencing a balance of payments crisis, which was soon generalized into an economic crisis that affected all sectors of the economy. Thus, Ghana not only experienced a general decline in agricultural productivity and exports, which included declining world prices for cocoa and gold, but also a shortfall in foreign exchange earnings, which negatively impacted import-dependent manufacturing firms. Furthermore, consumer goods shortages, inflationary pressures, and unemployment gradually built up and resulted in deficit financing via external borrowing, making the situation worse. By this time, Ghana's balance of payments was in disarray; budget deficits were ballooning, and foreign investment flows had nearly dried up.[14]

In Ghana and across Africa, structural adjustments were foisted on one country after the other, and efforts were made to dismantle agricultural marketing boards; to privatize, commercialize, and liquidate state-owned enterprises; to deregulate various aspects of the economy; to reduce the size of state bureaucracy through civil service retrenchments; to encourage the private sector; and to promote the market. Structural adjusters were very concerned about balancing budgets and servicing public debt, both domestic and external. To do this, there were budget cuts on social spending, with education and health taking the heaviest brunt. Slowly but surely, in 1978, the government was forced to introduce cost recovery into the health system in Ghana.[15] This was popularly known as *cash and carry*. This system was a product of the structural adjustment program that the International Monetary Fund and the World Bank had prescribed and that Ghana readily adopted. It involved the wholesale withdrawal of government subsidies on health delivery. Under the cash-and-carry system, patients were asked to pay for the full cost of medication and care. Because of economic crises and mismanagement, the government had to reduce spending on health and social affairs. Less money was available for health. The government was not able to finance the health system via general taxation. The Bamako Initiative reform (1988) also instituted the introduction of user fees in government health facilities, the joint management of the resources generated by health staff and the community, and the decentralization of the health sector. The rationale behind full cost recovery was that there would be an increase in resources for the healthcare facilities, which would allow them to expand and upgrade their services, improve access to health care, improve patient care, and achieve better efficiency because of the increased revenue from charges. Furthermore, there was the presumption that cost recovery would help reduce unnecessary visits by patients who were abusing the system because it was free. The evidence gathered thus far suggests that none of these assumptions materialized. Since its introduction, the cash-and-carry system appeared to have carried away health services from the people. The system could best be described as "stinking and dehumanizing" because patients who did not have the ability to pay for medical services were turned away from hospitals only to die at home. The disabled, poor, and accident victims were being asked to pay on the spot before getting medical attention.[16] To make matters worse, cost recovery was introduced at a time when many people had been laid off from the public sector and income levels were extremely low. Many poor people were turned away from health centers for lack of funds.[17]

Unfortunately, the poor were simply priced out of hospital care, and a two-tiered healthcare system came into operation with better facilities for those who could afford to pay. Once again, women and children bore the brunt of such harsh policies. The introduction of user fees further impoverished the majority of Ghanaians, and for a long time it devastated their ability to sustain livelihoods. Some people, especially those living below the poverty line, had to borrow money, take out loans, sell their animals or furniture, dissolve their little savings, cut down on buying food, and even stop sending their children to school in order to pay for health care. The process of borrowing money from extended family delayed treatment and, in many cases, caused deterioration of health and even death. In other cases, people did not seek medical treatment because they could not afford it, which often increased morbidity and mortality.[18]

It was welcome news when in 2004 the government rekindled social equity as a key part of healthcare policy by establishing the National Health Insurance Scheme (NHIS) to replace the cash-and-carry system.

▸ Description of the Current Healthcare System

There are four main categories of healthcare delivery systems in Ghana: the public, private for profit, private not for profit, and traditional systems.[19] The public health system, centered around the Ministry of Health (MoH), has a hierarchical organizational structure disseminating from the central headquarters in Accra to the regions, districts, and subdistricts. Services are delivered through a network of facilities, with health centers and district hospitals providing primary healthcare services, regional hospitals providing secondary health care, and four teaching hospitals—the Korle Bu Hospital, the Komfo Anokye Teaching Hospital (KATH), the Tamale Teaching Hospital (TTH), and the Cape Coast Teaching Hospital—at the apex providing tertiary services. The four teaching hospitals play a key role in teaching and research, offering facilities for the training of doctors and other health professionals and for medical and public health research. KATH and TTH serve about half of the people of Ghana and serve as the main tertiary referral center for neighboring Burkina Faso and Côte d'Ivoire.

Ghana's health system is composed of a variety of facility types and affiliations, ranging from government-owned to private facilities. Approximately one-third of Ghana's health facilities are operated under private ownership, and a 2008 McKinsey study indicated that more than 50% of health service provision in Ghana is delivered by the private sector.[20] However, consistently collected information on private sector performance and delivery mechanisms is sparse at best. Data on private facility medical supplies, expenditures, and interventions are not routinely captured or included in Ghana's health information systems,[21] and thus data on service delivery successes and challenges experienced by Ghana's private sector are not easily ascertained.[22]

Facilities

There are many different categories of hospitals in Ghana. Generally the agglomerations are served better than the rural areas. Rural areas have very limited access and archaic health institutions. This is the reason why a lot of people still rely on self-medication, especially in rural Ghana. Private facilities number around 1,294. Private hospitals usually provide better quality of treatment and have more modern equipment than public institutions. Public hospitals number around 1,818. They tend to be overcrowded and lacking in quality, especially compared to developed countries. Both public and private institutions are generally located in urban areas. Religious institutions, generally Christian or Muslim, number around 204. These are found predominantly in rural areas.[23]

Regional hospitals provide secondary health care, whereas four teaching hospitals are at the apex providing tertiary services. Health care is structured in a four-tiered system. Level A is composed of health systems at the community level, including trained birth attendants and community health workers. Level B is composed of health posts and health centers at the subdistrict level. Level C is composed of hospitals that function as district referral units. Regional and teaching hospitals comprise level D and provide tertiary services at the national, regional, district, and subdistrict levels.

National

The national level is made up of the MoH, where health policy is formulated, the health system is monitored, and evaluation of progress in achieving targets is conducted. The second entity within the national level is Ghana Health Services, which is responsible for resource allocation and the creation of partnerships with the private sector.

Regional

There are 10 regional health administrations that serve as links between the national and district levels and allocate resources within the region. Regional and district hospitals are set up as part of a national policy that is supposed to ensure that every region and district has a befitting health facility; however, not all regions and districts in the country have such facilities, especially now that new districts are springing up in conformity with the decentralization policy. The regional hospitals depend on district hospitals for their patient load. The majority (68%) of the dentists in Ghana work in public regional hospitals. On-site, there are usually a dentist, two or three dental surgery assistants, and one or more dental laboratory technicians, depending on the size of the catchment area. The dentist works under the chief medical officer of the hospital. Unlike the medical profession, dentistry has no representation at the regional, district, or community levels.

District

The focal point of the healthcare system is at the district level, where the implementation of the national healthcare strategy takes place. The district level is concerned with operational planning and implementation of service within the district. It is responsible for the construction of health facilities: hospital, health centers, and community health clinics. This is the key level of management of the primary healthcare system and provides leadership in district health care. The attempt to provide middle, paradental personnel to provide oral health services in the district and rural areas, especially to school children, was defeated when 15 dental therapists trained overseas in the late 1970s ended up in schools within Accra, the capital.

Subdistrict

Community-Level Health Centers These provide outpatient services to relieve the district and regional hospitals of all but their most specialized functions. Health centers usually serve a catchment area of about 8 square kilometers and provide the first point of contact with health personnel from the MoH. There is no dental equivalent to the delivery system at this level, except for the odd outreach program by an already understaffed dental team from one of the regional hospitals.[24]

Health Centers, Health Posts, and Rural Clinics
This is the smallest unit at the broad base of the three-tiered system. Minor cases like cuts and wounds are treated, and serious cases are referred to the health centers or the district hospitals. These stations are run by community clinic attendants and function as first-aid stations and health observational posts. There is no equivalent oral health delivery system at this level.

Community-Level Health Planning and Services
This is a new system of healthcare delivery introduced to the country a few years ago based on research by the Navrongo Health Research Centre. It is similar to the primary healthcare concept, but a qualified health worker, called community health officer, normally minds this program. Community health nurses are mostly reoriented to assume this position. Now it has been integrated into their training program. This system is operated on a zonal basis in a given subdistrict. The requirement for setting up the community-based health planning and services zone is similar to that of the health center. One distinct feature is that community-based health planning and services zones are normally established in remote areas composed of a number of communities with a total population of between 3,000 and 4,000. The emphasis is more on health promotion (preventive health) than curative health.

Workforce

The nation has four medical schools that are responsible for training physicians. They are the University of Ghana Medical School in Accra, Kwame Nkrumah University of Science and Technology Medical School in Kumasi, the University for Development Studies Medical School in Tamale and the University of Cape Coast School of Medical Sciences in Cape Coast.

Besides these four teaching institutions, there are a number of other institutions, with links to the MoH, located at Korle Bu, that are also involved in training the healthcare workforce in Ghana. These are as follows: Nurses Training School, Public Health Nurses Training School, Midwifery Training School, School of Hygiene, Disease Control Division of the MoH, Health Education Unit of the MoH, and Center for Health Statistics of the MoH. In addition, the University of Allied Health Sciences and the public nursing training colleges across the ten regions have joined the public institutions tasked with training Ghana's health workforce. These institutions have been able to train adequate workforce for the system; hence, workforce training has not been the issue in Ghana—the issue has been retention. The lack of ability of the system to craft adequate compensation and pay structures to retain the trained workforce has led to the migration of the healthcare workforce to developed countries for greener pastures.[25]

A World Health Organization (WHO) report on international migration stated that by the end of 2005 Ghana lost over 50% of her highly skilled labor. Of this, 90% were healthcare professionals. Ghana was the only country to lose most of its professionals during the 1980s. Currently Ghana's doctor-patient ratio and nurse-patient ratio have seen improvement over the past years. According to the deputy minister of health, the doctor-patient ratio is 1 to 10,000, while nurse-patient ratio is 1 to 1,251.[26]

Technology and Equipment

The provision of equitable, quality, and efficient health care requires an extraordinary array of properly balanced and managed resource inputs. Physical resources such as fixed assets and consumables, often described as healthcare technology, are among the principal types of these inputs. Technology is the platform on which the delivery of health care rests and is the basis for provision of the majority of health interventions. Technology generation, acquisition, and utilization require massive investment, and related decisions must be made carefully to ensure the best match between the supply of technology and the health system needs, to ensure the appropriate balance of capital and recurrent costs, and to ensure the capacity to manage technology throughout its life. There is a large need for new medical equipment for the new facilities that are being built and for the existing facilities that are being expanded and/or refurbished.

Much of the existing equipment is also obsolete or broken and cannot be repaired locally because of a lack of spare parts or maintenance expertise. This need is expected to increase as more of the planned projects are started. Future demand will increase as there has been a recognized need to improve the health service in Ghana, and this is being addressed as funds become available.[27]

Doctors try to improve information in various ways, frequently by prescribing tests. An ideal test is cheap, produces no adverse side effects, and is accurate in two senses: it always identifies pathology when present and confirms absence when not present. Even accurate and safe tests can be worthless—for instance, when no effective treatment is available. If resources dedicated to health care are limited, something has to be sacrificed (rationing), and this is the case in Ghana when it comes to diagnostic or treatment procedures that require pieces of high-tech equipment that are either not available or scarce in the nation. Other nations have rationed health care for years by setting healthcare budgets or regulating fees, effectively controlling the numbers of hospitals or the amount of medical equipment or other devices.

The country depends on Ghanaians in the diaspora, non-governmental organizations (NGOs), and bilateral and multilateral donors for donations of pieces of technological equipment in the medicine field. The technological donations have been in the form of new, used, refurbished, and/or rehabilitated medical equipment and mobile medical services and equipment, as was the case on October 3, 2007, when GE vice president of corporate citizenship visited the KATH in Kumasi to commission the product donations, which provide the much-needed infrastructure and technology to enable lifesaving health care. These included a fluoroscopy unit for radiology, ultrasounds, incubators, monitors, lighting, electrical distribution equipment, water purification, and Internet connectivity.[28]

▸ Evaluation of the Healthcare System

Cost

The cost of health service delivery can be grouped simply into two categories: the capital cost and the recurrent cost. The capital cost is the hardware cost that includes the provision of healthcare facilities—such as the cost of building hospitals, maintaining healthcare facilities, and training health service providers. These costs have always been borne by government under the previous health financing schemes. The health insurance system that is currently being implemented falls short of taking care of these costs.

The other cost is the recurrent cost—the cost associated with the consumables and other supplies such as medical supplies (disinfectants, surgical masks, syringes, etc.), drugs, laboratory inputs, ambulance fuel, and servicing of equipment. This is the cost, or probably part of the cost, that users of health services are usually asked to pay. It must be mentioned here that the cost passed on to the "ordinary Ghanaian" is usually not the full recurrent cost. The average cost of hospital admission varies tremendously from region to region and among districts.

According to an ABCE study, average expenditure at the health facility level grew 38%, from GH¢818,420 (US $511,513) in 2007 to ¢1,130,154 ($706,346) in 2011. Most of this growth appears to be driven by increases in service and personnel expenditures. Regional referral hospitals and public hospitals spent the most among health facility types. Private clinics documented the strongest growth between 2007 and 2011. Across and within facility types, the average facility cost per patient visit varied substantially in 2011. An outpatient visit was generally the least expensive output to produce for most facilities. The average facility cost per outpatient visit ranged from ¢14 ($4) per outpatient visit at maternity clinics to ¢33 ($10) at regional referral hospitals. Births accounted for the highest facility cost per visit for all facilities, ranging from an average of ¢120 ($38) at maternity clinics to ¢445 ($139) at regional referral hospitals. All fees associated with delivery have been covered by NHIS since 2008, so the relatively high facility costs per birth have substantial financial implications for Ghana's nationwide insurance program.[29]

However, in comparison with Kenya, Uganda, and Zambia, the average facility cost per patient in Ghana in 2013 was generally higher, especially for average facility costs per birth. Ghana had slightly lower average costs per inpatient bed-day (¢62, US $39) than those found in Kenya and Uganda (both ¢66, $41).[29]

Finance

Identifying and quantifying the variety of health finance flows are challenging exercises. Where data are available, they are not collected or managed systematically because Ghana lacks a central entity responsible for carrying out these tasks. Accordingly, even the MoH acknowledges that its figures must be treated with care.[30] Often, particularly in the case of flows that bypass the Ministry's budget, data are not even available. Rising allocations from the central government have allowed Ghana to reach the 2001 Abuja Declaration target of allocating 15% of the annual budget to improvements in the health sector. Derived mostly from national sources, these allocations are augmented by three foreign sources.

To begin, a number of donors (including the World Bank, the United Kingdom, the European Union, and the African Development Bank) have begun using general budget support as an aid modality through the Multi-Donor Budget Support initiative. Because budget support has generally not been tied to specific sectors, measuring the extent of its use for health is practically impossible. The share of health finance channeled through central government is likely to increase in the future because several donors are currently considering a move to budget support. Other sources of central government allocations to the health sector include commercial lending (15%) and debt relief (0.2%, from the Heavily-Indebted Poor Country initiative).

The budget of the MoH distinguishes three sources of funding: allocations from central government (which accounted for 59.20% of the Ministry's total budget of US $435 million in 2005), support from bilateral and multilateral donors (27.20%), and internally generated funds from private households (13.60%). Similarly, in 2014 the total health expenditure was funded as follows: 40.00% was from central government allocations to public health, 30.00% from the National Health Insurance Fund, 17.00% from international donors, 11.00% from private households, and 1.06% from private employers. In 2015, out of a total of GH¢4.456 billion, ¢1.34 billion came from the NHIS fund, ¢1.4 billion from the Ministry's appropriations from parliament, an estimated ¢1 billion from internally generated funds, donor support of about ¢712.8 million, and loans of about ¢575 million.[31] The distinction between the three sources of health finance used in most government documents paints a simplified picture that does not capture adequately the various financing channels and actors in Ghana's health sector.

First, it is important to understand that funds from the central government are derived from different sources, including foreign ones. Second, donors use diverse channels to achieve health outcomes. Third, a large degree of private finance bypasses the MoH's budget. Finally, new actors such as foundations, global funds, and NGOs have important roles to play in financing health. (See **FIGURE 18-2**.)

Donors have an important stake in the healthcare sector in Ghana, providing between 25% and 35% of the Ministry's budget.[32] Their support for health increased six-fold between 1999 and 2003, from US $30.7 million to $192.5 million. This can be seen as part of a larger global shift of official development assistance toward the social sectors, encouraged by the adoption of the Millennium Development Goals and the Poverty Reduction Strategy Initiative of the World Bank; however, the volumes actually disbursed in Ghana may differ from those pledged and reported to the Development Assistance Committee.

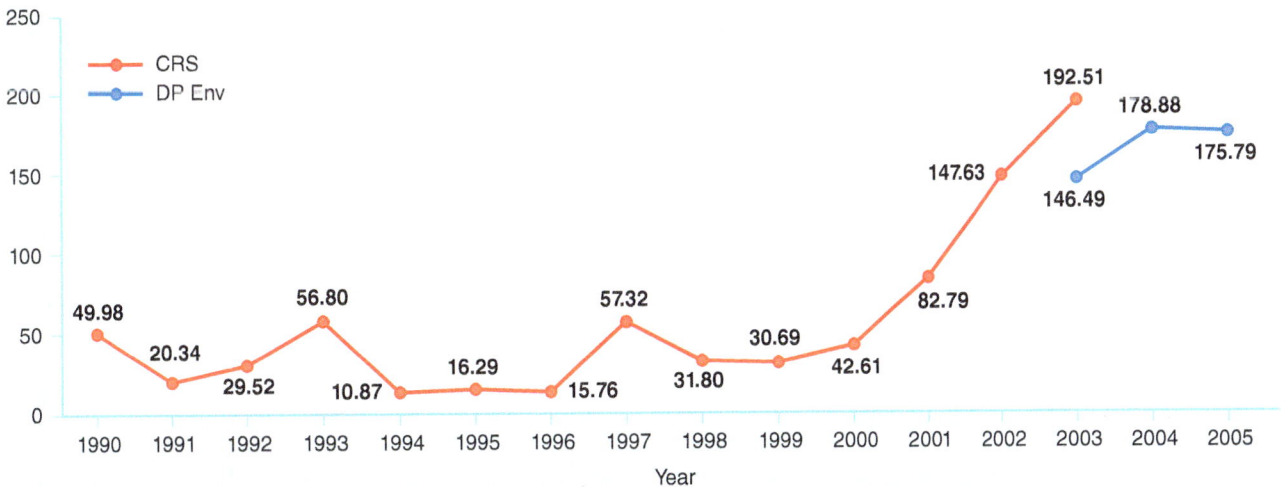

FIGURE 18-2 Official Development Assistance to Ghana's Health Sector
Author calculations based on data from DAC Creditor Reporting System (CRS) 2006 and Ghana Development Partner Envelope Overview (DP Env) 2006 on health in Ghana compared to the public sector's contribution of 35 percent.

Although the use of private capital inflows cannot be determined with certainty, evidence from Ghana suggests that remittances help households cover emergency expenses, for example, in the case of major illnesses.[32] New actors that have begun financing health in Ghana are NGOs, global funds, private donors, the pharmaceutical industry, and private foundations, as well as private commercial capital flows. (See **FIGURE 18-3**.)

Non-Governmental Organizations

As estimated by the National Coalition of Health NGOs in 2015, 400 NGOs are active in the Ghanaian health sector, with a large majority acting as implementing agencies for donor-funded projects. This means that their self-generated financial contribution to the sector is minimal. Nevertheless, their proximity to local institutions and marginalized individuals, especially in remote areas, renders them a crucial part of the healthcare system. Faith-based NGOs, such as the Catholic Secretariat representing the Catholic Church and the Christian Health Association of Ghana, are particularly important in Ghana.

Global Funds

Global funds have had a tremendous impact on health sector finance in recent years. The two largest global funds in the Ghanaian health sector are the Global Fund and Gavi, the Vaccine Alliance. Between 2000 and 2015, the former has disbursed US $42 million of the $93.4 million pledged in its grant agreement with Ghana, directing funds to fighting malaria (44%), HIV/AIDS (36%), and tuberculosis (20%). Gavi has disbursed around $20 million to Ghana since 2000, targeting hepatitis B (a total of $45 million pledged) and yellow fever ($4.5 million) in a multiyear vaccination plan (2002–2006) and providing cash support for vaccination services ($3.6 million) and injection safety ($855,000).[33]

Private Donors

It is particularly difficult to determine an exact figure for private donations. They are neither recorded systematically nor captured by national statistics. According to the MoH, it administered a total of US $176 million in financial and in-kind donations between 2004 and 2005. Although these numbers must be treated with caution, they show that private donations constitute a considerable inflow to the sector, especially bearing in mind that the Ministry's total annual budget (excluding donations) amounted to only $435 million in 2005. Some private donors use informal financing channels, meaning that the magnitude of Ghana's total receipts is almost certainly even larger. The Catholic Secretariat, for example, reported donations of $160,000 in 2004.

The Pharmaceutical Industry

Of the 14 pharmaceutical companies contacted, only one (Pfizer) provided details of program support through in-kind contributions. In 2005, the company delivered US $1.6 million worth of Zithromax to fight trachoma (International Trachoma Initiative) and $320,000 worth of Diflucan to fight opportunistic infections, that is, infections that predominantly affect people with a poorly functioning or suppressed immune system (Diflucan Partnership Program).[34]

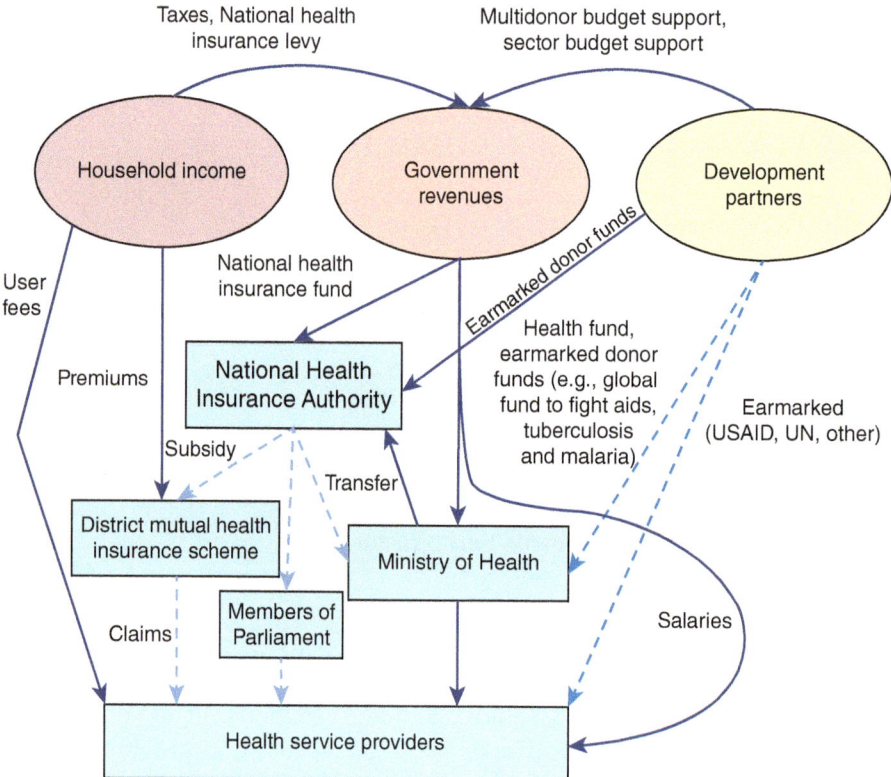

FIGURE 18-3 A Complex Picture of Actors, Channels, and Flows
Data from Appiah-Denkyria, Nartey, and Enemark. 2005.

Pfizer also engages in Ghana through the Pfizer Foundation, which provides grants for training and capacity-building activities in the health sector. Other pharmaceutical industry activities have been captured by the International Federation of Pharmaceutical Manufacturers and Associations (2004 and 2005).[35] Thus, GlaxoSmithKline supports malaria prevention in Ghana through the African Malaria Partnership, and Merck & Co. has supported the dissemination of healthcare materials, together with the International Council of Nurses and Elsevier Science. Finally, Abbott Laboratories and Boehringer Ingelheim have donated Viramune and Determine within the framework of their joint initiative for the prevention of mother-to-child transmission of HIV.

Private Foundations

Information on the activities of foundations in Ghana remains incomplete. Among the 11 foundations contacted, the Gates Foundation appears to be the largest sponsor of health-related projects. It granted US $16.4 million between 2000 and 2005. The Rockefeller Foundation reported $3.4 million in grants to Ghana between 1999 and 2005, including projects by the MoH, the Forum of African Women, and the University of Ghana. European foundations are also gaining in importance. The U.K.-based Wellcome Trust, for example, granted $903,000 to Ghanaian health projects between 2000 and 2006.[36]

Private Commercial Capital Flows

Like many other low-income countries, Ghana has not yet attracted large amounts of private commercial capital. Although the importance of foreign direct investment is gradually growing, these investments have concentrated predominantly on the mining and manufacturing industries, with a few investment projects identified in the health sector. Commercial bank loans, on the other hand, are important when used to finance health infrastructure projects. In 2015, they constituted 13% of the total budget of the MoH.

National Health Insurance Scheme

Households in many developing countries face the constant risk of having to finance the treatment of serious illnesses directly out of pocket. Health insurance systems, both public and private, based on prepayment and risk pooling, could help alleviate the exposure to these risks significantly.[37] The Ghanaian government in 2005 introduced the NHIS to replace the cash-and-carry system in the hope of easing the overall burden borne by private households. The law underpinning the NHIS makes membership of an insurance scheme compulsory, with households expected to make premium payments in line with their ability to pay.[38] Medical informatics would help create standards for electronic exchange of financial and administrative data and also standards for unique identifiers, code sets, security, and privacy; however, this would require a tremendous investment in technology. This well-intended initiative is not founded on solid grounds, with doubts having been voiced regarding its financial sustainability.[39] Further information would allow the government to make a better distinction between those who could pay higher contributions for quality packages and those who must remain exempt from payments, which currently includes the poor indigenous people and children with insured parents.

The National Health Insurance Levy was introduced on August 1, 2004, to provide seed money for the NHIS. The levy is a disguised value-added tax (VAT) of 2.5% on some goods and services, and thus, consumers in Ghana are paying the levy. VAT is a consumption tax administered in Ghana. The tax regime that started in 1998 had a single tax rate, but in September 2007, Ghana entered into a multiple tax rate regime. The 1998 tax rate was 10%, and 2000 was 12.5%; however, with the passage of Act 734 of 2007, a 3% VAT Flat Rate Scheme began to operate for the retail distribution sector. This allows retailers of taxable goods under Act 546 to charge a marginal 3% on their sales and account the same to the VAT service. People under 18 years old, those over 70 years old, and the indigent are exempt from premium payment. An entire family unit must enroll in the plan. The benefits package covers 95% of disease burden in Ghana, and there are no co-payments or deductibles. The NHIS is funded by premiums, sales tax, and social security contributions.

A 2014 study on the NHIS reveals that there are emerging issues that have threatened its financial sustainability. They include corruption, delay in release of identity cards, and many other issues. According to the study, while many of these issues are not new, their intensity and impact pose a fundamental challenge to the scheme.[40] Prominent among the challenges is a lack of funds that has led to the persistent indebtedness to service providers by the NHIA (National Health Insurance Authority). The lack of funds has been blamed on escalating claims payment by the NHIA. The findings of this research show that claims payment is the major cost driver of the scheme. Claims payments increased from GH¢7.60 million in 2005 to ¢549.77 million in 2011, representing 76.2% of the total expenditure of the NHIA.[40] This figure shot up to ¢787.24 million by the end of 2015.

A number of changes have been implemented to improve the NHIS: there are plans to roll out capitation payments to all providers of primary care; the electronic processing of claims is being extended countrywide; free-of-charge care available to NHIS members is being broadened to include all cancer services; and the NHIA is aiming to almost double NHIS membership, up from 33% to 60% of the population.

Quality

Effective health service delivery not only depends on being able to pay for drugs and other consumables but also requires state-of-the-art facilities that effectively promote diagnosis, treatment, and recovery from illness. It also requires well-qualified and motivated health personnel to use and manage those facilities. The ideal is to have an environment that shields people from falling ill, which means having the appropriate environment to reduce infections and other noncommunicable diseases. Ghana needs massive capital investments in the health and social service sectors to ensure such an ideal health environment. Ghanaians deserve good health facilities; indeed, all of the regional hospitals and district hospitals should be like those of Sunyani, Ho, and the Cape Coast hospitals. (For those who have not been to any of these hospitals, the facilities can be compared with any standard hospital in the United States and western Europe.) Because of the lack of diffusion of the state-of-the-art technology in the country and because treatment of tertiary diseases is not up to par with the developing standard, the country's preventive care methods are top quality. There is an unequal distribution of healthcare delivery across the country. There are severe disparities between regions and districts and between rural and urban areas in terms of healthcare quality and access to services.

Access

Ghana lacks adequate infrastructure to care for its citizens. There is also a disparity in the availability of healthcare facilities between rural and urban areas. As a result, access to health care in rural areas is difficult, and rural care lacks the standard of quality deserved. With the introduction of NHIS advertising, more people are signing on to the concept of insurance that has open access to most people, including those who otherwise could not afford to visit the hospital.

The potential effects of insurance enrollment on access to health care and to costs of health care have implications for the NHIS. One concern often raised in connection with prepayment schemes is whether the premiums would be affordable for the target population. The data from one study offer arguments for and against the premiums set by the government of Ghana for the NHIS. Although exemption policies and practices would need to be flexible to respond to the needs of a given community, the NHIS premium structure and rates seem to be within reach of the majority of Ghanaians.[41]

▸ Current and Emerging Issues and Challenges

In addition to significant disparities in service between north and south and between rich and poor, factors such as cultural and religious beliefs, poor physical infrastructure, and limited resources all work together to hamper the provision of equitable healthcare services. Malaria continues to be the major cause of high morbidity as well as mortality. Poor sanitation and the apparent unpreparedness of the healthcare system to prevent or management potential epidemics creates challenges for planners and policymakers.[42]

A major challenge for Ghana's health sector is the unequal distribution of healthcare delivery across the country. There are severe disparities between regions and districts and between rural and urban areas in terms of healthcare quality and access to services. In Ghana there has long been a north-south divide, with those in the Northern, Upper East, and Upper West regions (an area containing around 17% of the population and covering around 40% of Ghana's land mass) having significantly less than those in the south. When compared with those in the south, the people living in the Northern, Upper East, and Upper West regions have very limited access to secondary healthcare facilities but are somewhat better served by community services. Perhaps as a reflection of the inequitable distribution of facilities, the northern regions are also poorly served in the number of clinical staff; for example, just 90 medical professionals covered the whole region in 2011.[43]

There are many ingrained cultural and religious practices traditionally undertaken by Ghanaian groups and tribes that have an adverse impact on health, including early marriage of females, polygamy, female genital mutilation, and the elaborate "cleansing" of widows (whereby a widow must have sexual intercourse with a stranger to "purify" herself). Some of these practices are against the law, but they continue to be practiced in more rural areas.

Early marriage is common in some parts of the country. Although the legal age for girls to marry is 18, nearly 6% of girls between the ages of 12 and 17 are married. These practices are often related to gender discrimination. If women have the same rights to education, employment, and health care as men they are better empowered to make decisions and to stand up for their rights. Ghana's achievements in this respect are measured against the third Millennium Development Goal (MDG): to promote gender equality and the empowerment of women. Although Ghana appears to be on track for achieving gender parity in primary school and junior high school, female representation in parliament currently stands at just 27 out of 275 total positions.[44]

Ghana suffers from a chronic shortage of health workers and from inequities in the distribution and skills mix of workers; this severely restricts access to services and hampers achievement of national health objectives. The country has just over 11 doctors, nurses, and midwives per 10,000 population, less than half the number (23 per 10,000) deemed necessary by the WHO for achievement of the health MDGs.[45] The health workforce shortage is not really caused by the lack of numbers since the various training institutions keep churning out relatively skilled workforce. The problem has to do with refusal to accept postings and the recent freeze on employment in an attempt to curtail the ballooning wage bill, at the insistence of the IMF. Many health workers have not been employed years after completing their education.

Rural areas are particularly poorly served with access to health care. In 2009, for example, there was 1 doctor for every 5,103 people in Greater Accra, but in the Northern Region, there was 1 doctor for every 50,751 people.[46] Some of the many reasons physicians give for preferring employment in urban areas is that rural facilities lack career development opportunities (no opportunity to specialize, seek mentoring support, or obtain study leave); offer limited promotional opportunities; require longer working hours and carrying a heavier workload; lead to professional isolation; present difficulties in referring patients who are often not prepared to travel; require physicians to be jacks of all trades, leading to concerns about quality of care; provide no opportunities to supplement income through local work; do not have adequate local housing; suffer from delayed insurance payments, which adversely affects supplies; and have inadequate infrastructure/broken equipment.

The government has introduced a number of schemes to try to address this problem, including the Deprived Area Incentive Scheme, which offered an additional allowance of 20%–35% of basic salary (this has been discontinued), the Health Staff Vehicle Hire Purchase Scheme, and various housing schemes, but none has proven particularly successful. The Single-Spine Pay Policy, aimed at rationalizing salaries of public sector workers, has not solved the numerous agitations among the health workforce. Indeed, there appears to be a widening disparity in the pay structure of health workers, leading to numerous industry-wide actions by almost all categories of health workers.

As a result, diseases such as malaria are significantly more prevalent in rural than in urban areas. Malaria remains the main cause of mortality and morbidity in Ghana, accounting for about 21% of the under-five mortality rate and 40% of outpatient morbidity. Over 60% of hospital admissions of children under the age of five and 8% of hospital admissions of pregnant women are related to malaria. As the disease particularly affects pregnant women and children, interventions such as promoting chemoprophylaxis for pregnant women and the use of Insecticide Treated Nets (ITNs) are often aimed at these groups.

The government has been tackling this problem by making efforts to reduce the burden of malaria. It launched a Malaria Drug Policy in 2005 and, under its Intermittent Prevention Treatment strategy for malaria, adopted the amodiaquine–artesunate drug combination that was new at the time for prevention and treatment. In 2006, the Ghana Health Service changed the recommended dose of this drug combination after controversy over side effects also scaled-up ITN distribution across the country. Over 5 million ITNs were procured for distribution, and ITN utilization increased by 40.5% for pregnant women and 31.0% for children under 5 years old in 2008. A target was set of achieving universal coverage of ITNs by 2015 with 80.0% of the population sleeping under a net. There were many challenges in achieving this target, however, including running out of stock, distribution problems, and cultural barriers.[46]

In Ghana, a lack of access to clean water and sanitation systems is a central public health concern, contributing to 70% of diseases. There is substantial variation in access to clean, affordable water and sanitation, depending on income, rural or urban area, and region. According to the Ghana Water Sector Restructuring Secretariat, in 2005, only 46% of the total population had access to piped water.[47] The figure fell to 22% for those classified as poor. Uninterrupted access to treated and piped water only occurs in some urban areas. Average urban access is 46%, whereas in rural areas, only 35% of the population has access. Access to proper sanitation is equally dismal. Again, according to the Water Sector Restructuring Secretariat, the percentage of the population with access to improved sanitation facilities is approximately 40% in urban areas and 35% in rural areas. This poor state of water and sanitation in both urban and rural areas has been one of the most significant causes of many diseases. For instance the perennial deadly outbreaks of cholera, particularly in the greater Accra Region, has claimed many lives. This has put a lot of strain on the healthcare system and has left many healthcare officials sleepless.

Finally, related to this is the unpreparedness of the healthcare system in Ghana to prevent and or to manage an outbreak of any potential disease. In October 2015, a strand of meningitis broke out in a remote area in the middle belt of the country. Health officials were severely challenged in controlling its spread. By February 2016, the Brong Ahafo recorded the highest number of cases, 359 with 52 deaths; the Northern Region had 62 with 15 deaths; the Upper East recorded 47 cases with 2 deaths; while the Upper West had 44 with 9 deaths; the Ashanti Region recorded 18 cases with 8 deaths; the Volta Region had 7 cases with 1 death; while the Eastern Region registered 4 cases with 3 deaths; and the Western Region recorded 2 cases with 1 death. Indeed, only 1 region did not record a single incident of the pneumococcal meningitis disease.[48]

Admittedly Ghana lies in the meningitis belt of Africa, so such outbreaks are not uncommon. However, the spread rate and the mortality rate of this strain alarmed health workers and the citizenry at large. This called into questions the preparedness of the health system to deal with public health concerns, bearing in mind the lurking threats of Ebola and Zika viruses.

In response to the many health system challenges, the government over the past few years has attempted to solve infrastructure and equipment deficits. There are attempts to add 6,000 hospital beds to the existing 1,200. As such, a number of hospitals and health centers are under construction. There is also an attempt to reequip various health facilities to make them more functional. The bottom line is that funding for the sector continues to dwindle, healthcare costs are increasing, and donor support continues to shrink. The NHIS has been strained to a point of distress, and the government must find a way to tackle all these issues in a holistic and comprehensive manner.

References

1. Jackson JG. *Introduction to African Civilizations*. 2nd ed. Chaleston, SC: Kensington Publishing Corp, Citadel Press; 2001.
2. Stearns PN, Langer WL. *The Encyclopedia of World History: Ancient, Medieval, and Modern*. 6th ed. New York: Houghton Mifflin; 2001.
3. Buah FK. *History of Ghana*. London: Macmillan; 1980.
4. Nkrumah K. *Revolutionary Path*. New York: International Publishers; 1973.
5. MacLean I. *Rational Choice and British Politics: An Analysis of Rhetoric and Manipulation from Peel to Blair*. Oxford: Oxford University Press; 2001.
6. Ghana Information Services Department. *Ghana: A Brief Guide*. Accra: GIS Publication; 1994.
7. Ghana Statistical Service (GSS), Ghana Health Service (GHS), and ICF International. *Ghana Demographic and Health Survey 2014*. Rockville, Maryland: GSS, GHS, and ICF International; 2015.
8. Ghana Statistical Service. 2010 population and housing census. Summary report of final results. http://www.statsghana.gov.gh/docfiles/2010phc/Census2010_Summary_report_of_final_results.pdf. Published 2012. Accessed February 13, 2013.
9. Ghana Ministry of Health. *The Ghana Health Sector 2005 Programme of Work. Bridging the Inequality Gap: Addressing Emerging Challenges with Child Survival*. Accra: Ghana Ministry of Health; 2005.
10. Twumasi PA. *Medical Systems in Ghana: A Study in Medical Sociology*. Accra: Ghana Publishing Corp; 1975.
11. Bossert TJ, Beauvais JC. Decentralization of health systems in Ghana, Zambia, Uganda and the Philippines: a comparative analysis of decision space. *Health Policy and Planning*. 2002;17:14–31.
12. Agyapong IA. Reforming health service delivery at the district level in Ghana: the perspective of a district medical officer. *Health Policy and Planning*. 1999;14:59–69.
13. Gaines K. *On Nkrumah Assassination by CIA: American Africans in Ghana, Black Expatriates and the Civil Rights Era*. Chapel Hill, NC: The University of North Carolina Press; 2006.
14. Bonsi SK. *Studies on an Appropriate Mechanism for Exemptions from Charges for Drugs and Curative Care in Government Health Facilities in Ghana*. Accra: Ghana Ministry of Health; 2001.
15. World Health Organization Commission on Macroeconomics and Health. *Macroeconomics and Health: Investing in Health for Economic Development*. Geneva: World Health Organization; 2001.
16. Sikosana PL, Dlamini N, Issakov A. *Health Sector Reform in Sub-Saharan Africa: A Review of Experiences, Information Gaps and Research Needs*. Geneva: World Health Organization; 1997.
17. Asante AD, Zwi AB, Ho MT. Equity in resource allocation for health: a comparative study of the Ashanti and Northern Regions of Ghana. *Health Policy*. 2006;78:135–148.
18. Reporters Without Borders. Worldwide Press Freedom Index 2006. https://rsf.org/en/worldwide-press-freedom-index-2006. November 3, 2016.
19. Adjei S. Assessing the effect of primary health on mortality in Ghana. *J Biosoc Sci Suppl*. 1989;10:115–125.
20. Institute for Health Metrics and Evaluation. *Health Service Provision in Ghana: Assessing Facility Capacity and Costs of Care*. Seattle: IHME; 2015.
21. Multiple Indicator Cluster Survey. *Ghana-Accra Multiple Indicator Survey in 5 High Density Populated Localities, 2010–2011*. Geneva: MICS/UNICEF; 2012.
22. Saleh K. *The Health Sector in Ghana: A Comprehensive Assessment*. Washington, DC: World Bank; 2012.
23. Quaicoe-Duho R. Ghana reports general improvement in doctor ratio. http://www.politicosl.com/articles/ghana-reports-general-improvement-doctor-ratio-0. Published January 7, 2015. Accessed November 3, 2016.
24. Dubbeldam R, Witter S, Silimperi D, et al. *Health Sector Five-Year Programme of Work: 2002–2006*. Accra: Ghana Ministry of Health; 2007.
25. Adusei K, Akor SA, Oppong-Mensah D. *Ministry of Health Oral Health Policies and Medium Term Strategic Plan*. Accra: Oral Health Unit, Ministry of Health; 2000.
26. Bampoe AV. The state of healthcare delivery in Ghana. A paper delivered in Atlanta, Georgia; 2014.
27. Adams O, Stilwell B. Health professionals and migration. *Bulletin of the World Health Organization*. 2004;82:550–558.
28. Business Wire. GE expands healthcare initiative to hospitals in Ghana: partner initiative to provide medical and infrastructure equipment across Africa. http://findarticles.com/p/articles/mi_m0EIN/is. Published October 3, 2005. Accessed March 1, 2008.
29. Addae-Korankye A. Challenges of financing health care in Ghana: the case of National Health Insurance Scheme (NHIS). *International Journal of Asian Social Science*. 2013;3(2):511–522.
30. Organisation for Economic Co-operation and Development. Creditor reporting system. Paris: Development Assistance Center Report; 2006.
31. Anemana S. Current health financing issues in the health sector. A paper delivered at GIMPA. http://www.moh.gov.gh/wp-content/uploads/2016/02/2015-Summit-Health-Financing-Strategy-Final-Presentation.pdf. Accessed May 23, 2016.
32. African Development Bank. African Development Report. Natural resources for sustainable development in Africa. http://www.afdb.org/en/documents/. Published 2007. Accessed March 12, 2008.
33. United States AID for International Development. *Private Remittances Flows to Ghana*. Washington, DC: Country Report; 2005.
34. Hudson Institute. *A Review of Pharmaceutical Company Contributions—HIV/AIDS, Tuberculosis, Malaria, and Other Infectious Diseases*. Washington, DC: Center for Science in Public Policy Report. Hudson Institute; 2004.
35. International Federation of Pharmaceutical Manufacturers Associations. *Building Healthier Societies through Partnerships*. Geneva: International Federation of Pharmaceutical Manufacturers Associations Report; 2005.
36. World Health Organization Commission on Macroeconomics and Health. *Macroeconomics and Health: Investing in Health for Economic Development*. Geneva: World Health Organization; 2001.
37. United Nations Development Program. *International Cooperation at a Crossroads: Aid, Trade and Security in an Unequal World*. New York: United Nations Development Program Human Development Report; 2005.

38. Drechsler D, Jütting J. Is there a role for private health insurance in developing countries? *German Institute for Economic Research*. 2005;15:123–138.
39. Dubbeldam R, Witter S, Silimperi D, et al. *Health Sector Five-Year Programme of Work: 2002 2006*. Accra: Ghana Ministry of Health; 2007.
40. Owusu-Sekyere E, Bagah, DA. Towards a Sustainable Health Care Financing in Ghana: Is the National Health Insurance the Solution? *Public Health Research*. 2014;4(5):185–194. doi: 10.5923/j.phr.20140405.06.
41. Schieber, G., Cashin, C., Saleh, K. and Lavado, R. *Health Financing in Ghana*. Washington, DC: World Bank. http://uhcforward.org/sites/uhcforward.org/files/718940PUB0PUBL067869B09780821395660.pdf. Published 2012. Accessed May 23, 2016.
42. The Association of Chartered Certified Accountants. *Key Health Challenges in Ghana*. London: ACCA; 2013.
43. Ghana Ministry of Health. The Health Sector in Ghana: Facts and Figures 2010. https://s3.amazonaws.com/ndpc-static/CACHES/NEWS/2015/07/14//2010±GHS±Facts±and±Figures.pdf. Published 2012. Accessed November 3, 2016.
44. Government of Ghana, National Development Planning Commission and the United Nations Development Programme Ghana, 2010. Ghana Millennium Development Goals Report. https://s3.amazonaws.com/ndpc-static/CACHES/NEWS/2015/07/11//Ghana±MDGs±Report±2008.pdf. Published 2010. Accessed March 6, 2013.
45. International Organization for Migration. National Profile of Migration of Health Professionals—Ghana. http://www.mohprof.eu/LIVE/DATA/National_profiles/national_profile_Ghana.pdf. Published 2011. Accessed March 7, 2013.
46. World Health Organization. *Ghana Health Profile*. http://www.who.int/gho/countries/gha.pdf. Published May 2012. Accessed March 7, 2013.
47. Water and Sanitation Program. *Economic Impacts of Poor Sanitation in Africa: Ghana*. http://siteresources.worldbank.org/INTGHANA/Resources/ghana-economic-impacts-of-poor-sanitation-in-africa.pdf. Published 2012. Accessed March 7, 2013.
48. Agbenyega P. 93 people die of meningitis in Ghana so far. News Ghana. https://www.newsghana.com.gh/93-people-die-of-meningitis-in-ghana-so-far/. Published February 16, 2016. Accessed May 27, 2016.

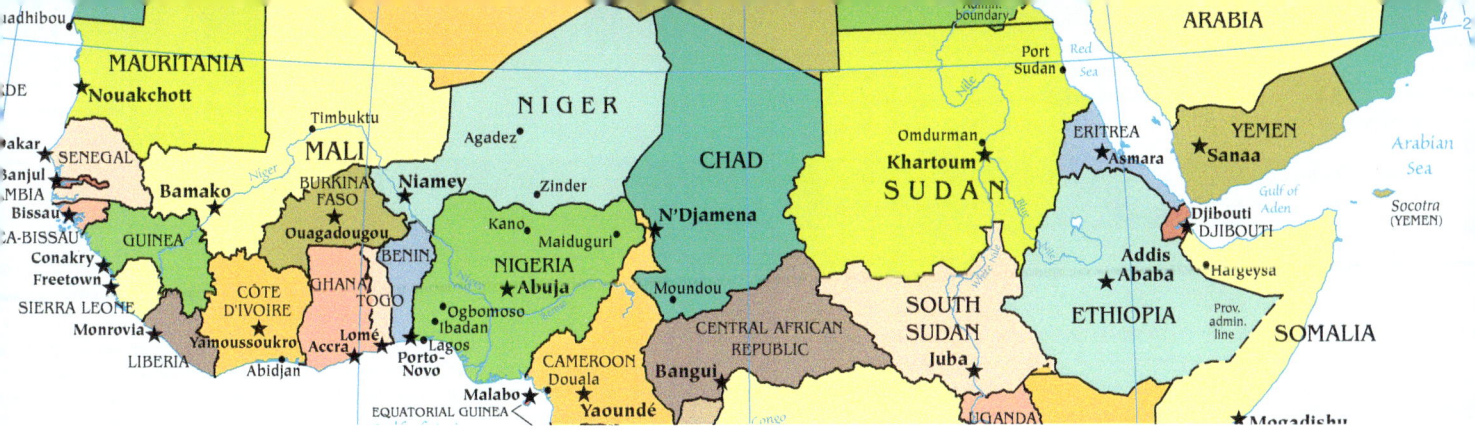

CHAPTER 19

Nigeria

Yetunde Ogunneye, Qwolabi Ogunneye, and **Kalu Kalu**

▶ Country Description

TABLE 19-1 Nigeria	
Nationality	Noun: Nigerian(s) Adjective: Nigerian
Ethnic groups	More than 250 ethnic groups; the most populous and politically influential: Hausa and Fulani 29%, Yoruba 21%, Igbo (Ibo) 18%, Ijaw 10%, Kanuri 4%, Ibibio 3.5%, Tiv 2.5%
Religions	Muslim 50%, Christian 40%, indigenous beliefs 10%
Language	English (official), Hausa, Yoruba, Igbo (Ibo), Fulani
Literacy	Definition: Age 15 and over can read and write. Total population: 59.6% Male: 69.2% Female: 49.7% (2015 est.)
Government type	Federal republic
Date of independence	October 1, 1960 (from the United Kingdom)
Gross Domestic Product (GDP) per capita	$6,100 (2015 est.)
Unemployment rate	23.9% (2011 est.)

(continues)

353

TABLE 19-1 Nigeria (continued)	
Natural hazards	Periodic droughts; flooding
Environment: current issues	Soil degradation; rapid deforestation; urban air and water pollution; desertification; serious damage from oil pollution, oil spills—water, air, and soil; loss of arable land; rapid urbanization
Population	186,053,386 (July 2016 est.)*
Age structure	0–14 years: 42.79% (male 40,744,956/female 38,870,303) 15–24 years: 19.48% (male 18,514,466/female 17,729,351) 25–54 years: 30.65% (male 29,259,621/female 27,768,368) 55–64 years: 3.96% (male 3,595,293/female 3,769,986) 65 years and over: 3.12% (male 2,754,040/female 3,047,002) (2016 est.)
Median age	Total: 18.3 years Male: 18.2 years Female: 18.4 years (2016 est.)
Population growth rate	2.44% (2016 est.)
Birth rate	37.3 births/1,000 population (2016 est.)
Death rate	1,685 deaths/100,000 population (2016 est.)
Disease burden	Communicable disease deaths: 866/100,000 population Noncommunicable disease deaths: 674/100,000 population Injury deaths: 146/100,000 population (2016 est.)
Net migration rate	−0.2 migrant(s)/1,000 population (2016 est.)
Gender ratio	At birth: 1.06 male(s)/female Under 15 years: 1.05 male(s)/female 15–24 years: 1.04 male(s)/female 25–54 years: 1.05 male(s)/female 55–64 years: 0.95 male(s)/female 65 years and over: 0.91 male(s)/female Total population: 1.04 male(s)/female (2016 est.)
Infant mortality rate	Total: 71.2 deaths/1,000 live births Male: 76.0 deaths/1,000 live births Female: 66.2 deaths/1,000 live births (2016 est.)
Life expectancy at birth	Total population: 53.4 years Male: 52.4 years Female: 54.5 years (2016 est.)
Total fertility rate	5.13 children born/woman (2016 est.)
HIV/AIDS adult prevalence rate	3.17% (2014 est.)

TABLE 19-1 Nigeria (continued)	
Number of people living with HIV/AIDS	3,391,600 (2014 est.)
HIV/AIDS deaths	174,300 (2014 est.)

*Population estimates for Nigeria explicitly take into account the effects of excess mortality caused by AIDS; this can result in lower life expectancy, higher infant mortality, higher death rates, lower population growth rates, and unusual distribution of population by age and gender.

Data from Central Intelligence Agency. The World Fact Book, 2016: Nigeria. https://www.cia.gov/library/publications/the-world-factbook. Accessed November 15, 2016.

History

Nigeria's independence from Britain was achieved on October 1, 1960, but from the outset, the new nation was challenged by regional and ethnic divisiveness that made it difficult to establish a common foundation for constitutional governance. The complications arose partly as a result of British colonial policy but more fundamentally because of the lack of regional consensus on the viability of independence as well as general unpreparedness by the indigenous elite to transform the anticolonial rhetoric into a wholesome nationalist culture. Although British colonial rule in Nigeria lasted for nearly a century, its duration and persistence depended largely on the ability of British colonialists to play one ethnic group against the other. The 1914 amalgamation by the British of the Northern, Southern, and Lagos Protectorates (which were up until then a collection of disjointed and virtually independent groups) into what is today's Nigeria set the stage for latter events that would exploit the deep-seated tensions that became the bane of the emergent postcolonial state.

In northern Nigeria, there existed a monolithic class system that distinguished the ruling oligarchy from the ordinary people. The dominant ethnic groups in the north were the Hausas and Fulanis, who could trace their origins to northern Africa. An opportune mix of itinerant and nomadic culture created the dynamic for a theocratic conquest of much of northern Nigeria by the Hausa-Fulani. The existent class system provided the British colonialists with a judicial and administrative infrastructure that facilitated a sort of "indirect rule" in the North. Because the emirs and other lower ranking officials in the emirate system were simply designated as colonial officers ruling their subjects on behalf of the British colonial state,[1(pp69–71)] it created an additional privilege and authority that they were unwilling to give up easily, even at the price of independence. To secure the consent of northern leaders for independence, much of the feudal authority system in the region was left intact. This meant that, in the formative years of Nigeria's independence, two parallel authorities operated side by side, a paternalistic feudal authority in the north and a federal parliamentary authority for the rest of the country.

In the south, there was the relatively egalitarian society of the Igbos.[1] In order to replicate the system of indirect rule within the ethnic group—characteristically disposed to a decentralized, communal, and less paternalistic form of traditional governance—it became necessary for the British to impose their own stratification system by inventing a system of warrant chiefs who, in addition to British military force, were used to enforce colonial rule and authority.[1] Among the functions of the warrant chiefs or native officials were the collection of taxes for colonial administration, provision of cheap native labor for colonial public works, and the enforcement of colonial regulations and ordinances.

In western Nigeria's Yorubaland, especially within the Ile-Ife, Oyo, and Ibadan principalities, the semi-feudal structure of chiefs and councils of elders also provided the British the opportunity to use the existing traditional authority to implement a *de facto* system of indirect rule, but not to the extent possible in the north. More than anything, the system of indirect rule and the compromise to allow a quasi-autonomous authority in the north retarded the process of national political integration, as well as sectionalized consequent efforts at developing a truly Nigerian citizenship. From then on, the evolution of "national" political parties was regionalized. Political leadership became personalized, and objective government policy yielded to the allure of self-serving inclinations.

Size and Geography

The population of Nigeria is about 186,053,386 people (2016 est.)—the largest on the African continent and the seventh most populous in the world.[2] Nigeria (officially the Federal Republic of Nigeria) is located in West Africa on the Gulf of Guinea (part of the Atlantic Ocean). It is bounded by four other countries: Niger to the north, Chad and Cameroon in the east, and the Benin Republic to the west. Human habitation of the area now known as Nigeria dates back archaeologically to at least 9000 bce.[3] **FIGURE 19-1** shows the national borders and states in the country.

Government and Political System

Nigeria is a federal republic with a president, a national assembly consisting of a Senate and a House of Representatives, and a judicial system headed by a Supreme Court. With a modified system of federal government with 36 states and a federal capital territory, spread across 6 geopolitical zones (southeast, south-south, southwest, northeast, northwest, north central), the central government in the capital city of Abuja has a great deal of authority over allocation of values, national policy, resource distribution, and infrastructural development. With nonexistent or ineffective state constitutions (if they exist), the central government holds sway in matters of program development, national security, and finance. Nigeria's brand of federalism has, in fact, come to reflect an awkward hybrid between popular consent and authoritarian regimentation. Much of this had not evolved as an accident of fate but rather as a lingering consequence of the disagreements and compromises that befell the country for much of its 56 years of existence.

Macroeconomics

With an estimated −2.2% industrial production growth rate,[4] 90% of Nigeria's export income comes

FIGURE 19-1 Map of Nigeria
© Rainer Lesniewski/Shutterstock

from petroleum and petroleum-related products, whereas the rest comes from cocoa, ships, textiles, cotton, and aluminum.[5] As a result of the country's indigenization decree of the late 1970s and the consequent privatization schemes, the private sector has become more prominent in the ownership and management of key industrial facilities. This, however, has continued to create a situation in which a sizable proportion of the nation's wealth is concentrated in the hands of a narrow and select economic oligarchy.

The petroleum economy has remained the principal source of the country's wealth and foreign exchange earnings, especially since the end of the civil war, which lasted from 1967 to 1970. Although the first oil well was drilled in Oloibiri (Niger Delta) in 1956, it took major shifts in the international supply and demand of oil in the early 1980s to generate an overwhelming reliance on the oil sector for the revenue needed to support the nation's developmental programs. Nigeria's former military rulers failed to diversify the economy away from its overdependence on the oil sector, which accounts for about 35% of gross domestic product (GDP) and over 90% of total export revenue.[6]

The largely subsistence agriculture sector has failed to keep up with rapid population growth, and the country, once a large net exporter of food, now must import food to feed its growing population.

After the signing of an International Monetary Fund (IMF) standby agreement in August 2000,[7] Nigeria received a debt-restructuring deal from the Paris Club and a US $1 billion credit from the IMF, both contingent on economic reforms. Nigeria pulled out of its IMF program in April 2002, after failing to meet spending and exchange rate targets, making it ineligible for additional debt forgiveness from the Paris Club. In later years, the government began showing the political will to implement the market-oriented reforms urged by the IMF, such as to modernize the banking system, to curb inflation by blocking excessive wage demands, and to resolve regional disputes over the distribution of earnings from the oil industry. In 2003, the government began deregulating fuel prices, announced the privatization of the country's four oil refineries, and instituted the National Economic Empowerment Development Strategy, a domestically designed and run program modeled on the IMF's Poverty Reduction and Growth Facility for fiscal and monetary management. In November 2005, Nigeria won Paris Club approval for a debt-relief deal that eliminated $18 billion of debt in exchange for $12 billion in payments—a total package worth $30 billion of Nigeria's total $37 billion external debt. The deal required Nigeria to be subject to stringent IMF reviews.

In 2015, GDP real growth rate was 2.7% with a GDP per capita (PPP) of US $6,100; agricultural sector accounted for 20.3% of Nigeria's GDP, whereas industry and services accounted for 23.6% and 56.1%, respectively.[4] Despite oil revenues, Nigeria remains essentially an agriculture-based economy, with the agricultural sector accounting for 70% of the labor force, industry 10%, and services 20%.[4] By August 2016, foreign exchange reserves were at their lowest point for the year, $27 billion.[8]

Because of the centrality of oil in the macroeconomy, serious market failures have become more salient. The role of the state in mediating between public ownership (property rights) and private capital in the free market creates a situation where politics, not markets, determine the incentives of ownership. Hazem and Luciano wrote that because "the state receives revenues which are channeled to the economy through public expenditure, the allocation of these public funds between alternative uses has great significance for the future development pattern of the economy."[9(p12)] Because most public infrastructures are not profitmaking, they must be supported by continuous appropriation of public funding generated through external rents, despite the performance of other sectors of the domestic macroeconomy.

Even though state expenditures on public sector infrastructures can help to create jobs, thereby reducing unemployment, it can also provide additional sources for extracting legal and illegal rents (corruption) from the public treasury. Although Nigeria is heavily dependent on oil-related rents (income received by a country for use of its natural resources by outside parties), the vast majority of this wealth benefits a tiny fraction of the population.[10] Nigeria's ruling classes, exploiting their influence on and dominance of the government, are able to appropriate oil rents for their own benefit. This points to an important factor in the development process—that is, renter economies rarely spread the wealth but rather concentrate it in the hands of those who control political power.

With a total land mass of about 923,768 square kilometers (356,667 square miles), the country operates a total of 28,980 kilometers of paved road network and 164,220 kilometers of unpaved road network.[4] There are three major seaports with terminals in Port Harcourt, Calabar, and Lagos. The railways system with a total line of about 3,798 kilometers[4] has suffered maintenance problems over the years. This is due partly to the fact that land and air traffic have become the predominant means of transportation since the end of the civil war in 1970 and affluence and occupational mobility rose, attributable to the oil economy. The country maintains about 54 airports, with 40 having fully paved runways (2013 estimate).[4]

Demographics

The annual population growth rate was 2.44% in 2016.[4] The median age of the population was about 18.3 years (2016),[4] with a literacy rate of 69.2% for males, 49.7% for females, and 59.6 for both genders (2015).[4] Between 2008 and 2012, primary school net enrollment ratios were 60.1% for males and 54.8% for females.[12] Some 58% of the population lived under 140% of the poverty line (2013 est.), which is close to $2 per day if converted into internationally comparable PPP terms.[13]

The gross national income per capita in 2015 was US $5,800.[14] The two major religions in Nigeria are Christianity (mainly in the southern region) and Islam (northern region). The World Bank in 2015 estimated that the population density was 200 people per square kilometer,[15] with 48% living in the urban centers and 52% residing in rural areas.[16]

Although three major ethnic groups (Igbo, Hausa, and Yoruba) constitute over 40% of the population, there are also numerous subethnic, tertiary groups that complement the more than 250 ethno-lingual distinctions in the country. The official language in Nigeria is English, but it has been estimated that 521 different languages are spoken across the country. The three major indigenous languages spoken in Nigeria are Hausa, Yoruba, and Igbo. See **TABLE 19-2** for the demographics of Nigeria.

▸ Brief History of the Healthcare System

Pre–World War II

The beginning of modern medical and health services in Nigeria has a historical precedent that predates the Amalgamation Decree of 1914 that united the Northern and Southern Protectorates to form what is today's Nigeria. As pointed out in the United States Library of Congress Country Studies[17] Western medicine was not formally introduced into Nigeria until 1860, when the Sacred Heart Hospital was established by Roman Catholic missionaries in Abeokuta. For much of the colonial period, modern healthcare facilities in Nigeria were provided through religious missions.

Although Roman Catholic missions predominated (accounting for about 40% of the total number of mission-based hospital beds by 1960), there were a total of 118 mission hospitals compared with 101 government hospitals in 1960.[18(p2)] Roman Catholic missions were concentrated in the southeastern and midwestern parts of the country, whereas the Sudan United and the Sudan Interior missions focused on the Middle Belt region and the Islamic North, respectively. Together, they operated 25 hospitals or other facilities in the northern half of the country, and many of the mission hospitals remained an important component of the healthcare network into the 1990s.

The missions also played an important role in medical training and education, providing training for nurses and paramedical personnel and sponsoring basic education as well as advanced medical training (often in Europe) for many of the first generation of Western-educated Nigerian doctors. This helped to lay the foundation for a wider distribution and

TABLE 19-2 Comparison of Demographics of Nigeria with the United States, 2016

Country	Population						
	Total (000)	< 15 years (%)	15–64 years (%)	> 65 years (%)	Population growth (annual%)	Male (%)	Female (%)
Nigeria	186,053,386	42.79	54.09	3.12	2.44	50.90	49.10
United States	323,995,000	18.84	65.91	15.25	0.81	49.60	50.40

Data from Central Intelligence Agency. The World Factbook, 2016. https://www.cia.gov/library/publications/the-world-factbook/. Accessed November 15, 2016.

acceptance of the efficacy of modern medical care with a majority of the indigenous population. The British colonial government began providing formal medical services with the construction of several clinics and hospitals in Lagos, Calabar, and other coastal trading centers in the 1870s. The hospital in Jos (Plateau state) was built in 1912 after the beginning of tin mining in that part of the country and partly because the temperate climate in that region made habitation for Europeans much more appealing than in the more arid savannah region in the north. Unlike the missionary facilities, the colonial hospitals were initially for the sole use of Europeans, and this privilege was later extended to African employees of European establishments.

World War I had a detrimental effect on medical services in Nigeria because of the large number of medical personnel (both European and African) who were pulled out to serve in Europe. After the war, medical facilities were expanded substantially, and a number of government-sponsored schools for the training of Nigerian medical assistants were established. Although a number of Nigerian physicians were trained in Europe, they were not permitted to practice in colonial government hospitals unless they were there specifically to treat an African patient. This practice led to protests and to the frequent involvement of doctors and other medical personnel in the nationalist movements of the period.

Since World War II

The end of World War II brought about a dramatic shift in the attitude of the colonial government toward indigenous health care. In 1946, a 10-year health development plan was announced. The health plan established the federal Ministry of Health (MoH) to coordinate health services throughout the country, including those provided by the government, private companies, and missions. The plan also allocated funds for hospitals and clinics, most of which were concentrated in the main cities; however, little funding was appropriated for rural health centers, and there was also a strong imbalance between the allocation of facilities to southern areas compared with those in the north.[19(p3)] In 1948, the University of Ibadan was established, with the country's first full faculty of medicine and the first university hospital. Before 1948, the University of Ibadan had sub-university status, and equipment was transferred to the university from its sub-university predecessors, the Yaba Higher College, (established in 1932, formally opened in 1934), and the Yaba Medical School (established in 1930). In addition, a number of nursing schools were established, as were two schools of pharmacy. By 1960, the country had 65 government nursing or midwifery training schools.

The problems of geographic maldistribution of medical facilities among the regions and of the inadequacy of rural facilities persisted into the 1980s. There were also significant disparities within each of the regions. For example, in 1980, there was an enormous discrepancy between Lagos, with 2,600 people per physician, and the extremely rural region of Ondo, with 38,000 people per physician.[20(p4)] Across the urban-rural divide, many of the specialized physicians preferred to establish their practices in the urban areas, and few moved to the rural areas. The few doctors who did work in the rural areas did so as part of their requirement to serve in the National Youth Service Corps[20(p4)]—a national Peace Corps–type program established in 1973.

▸ Description of the Current Healthcare System

The three tiers of care stipulated under the National Health Policy are primary, secondary, and tertiary levels. These levels are supervised respectively by the three tiers of government (local, state, and federal), with some overlap in responsibilities.[21,22]

The federal government launched its primary health care (PHC) plan in August 1987, which the president at the time, Ibrahim Babangida, announced as the cornerstone of the country's health policy.[23] The policy also spells out the functions of each tier of government and provides for the establishment of the advisory National Council on Health, chaired by the federal minister of health.[24] Other bodies set up by the policy include the State Health Advisory Committees and Local Government Health Committees.[24] Their main objectives were to accelerate healthcare personnel development, to improve collection and monitoring of health data, to ensure availability of essential drugs in all areas of the country, to implement an Expanded Programme on Immunization, to improve nutrition and promote health awareness, to develop a national family health program, and to develop oral rehydration therapy for treatment of diarrheal disease in infants and children. The MoH, in collaboration with participating local government councils, was charged with the implementation of these programs.

The national health policy was revised in 1996 and later in 2003.[22] This policy is based on the fundamental principles of the second National Development Plan (1970–1974), which describes five national goals:

a free and democratic society; a just and egalitarian society; a united, strong, and self-reliant nation; a great and dynamic economy; and a land of full opportunities for all citizens.[22-25] This policy states that health development shall be seen not solely in humanitarian terms but also as an essential component of the package of social and economic development as well as an instrument of social justice.

The 2003 reform was a purposeful reform of the national healthcare delivery system in the context of the National Economic Empowerment and Development Strategy. A health reform was also necessary because Nigeria has struggled to meet only three of the eight Millennium Development Goals (MDGs): basic education, HIV/AIDS prevalence, and global partnership for development. This prompted the government to develop a policy framework to address these fundamental shortfalls, particularly the number one MDG, poverty reduction.

Further, with so much disease burden on the population, evidenced by health indicators below country's targets and internationally-set benchmarks, it was obvious that the human capital required to achieve the country's economic growth were simply unhealthy. This prompted the national development plans; initiation of the Vision 20:2020 document (focused on transforming Nigeria into one of the top 20 global economies by 2020) and the revision of the national health policy (the National Health Sector Reform Programme (2003-2007). At its final evaluation, the National Health Sector Reform Programme (HSRP) was successful in helping the system to develop a viable policy basis upon which a strategic plan could be constructed. This led to the development of a comprehensive plan, the National Strategic Health Plan (NSHP), 2010–2015. The aim was to improve on the previous initiative, to accelerate the process of achieving the MDGs before 2015, to fulfill the "new international commitments for improved efficiency in health systems and to meet certain international health indicators."[26] However, considering the need to integrate the NSHP initiatives with Vision 20:2020, the NSHP was expanded and later developed into a National Strategic Health Development Plan (NSHDP). NSHDP, with its national results framework, serves as the overarching reference document for local actions in health to ensure transparency and mutual accountability. The NSHDP has eight priority areas: leadership and governance; health service delivery; human resources for health; financing for health; a national health management information system; partnerships for health; community participation and ownership; and research for health.[26]

Facilities

Through the NSHDP, the federal government is responsible for formulation, strategic guidance, coordination, supervision, monitoring, and evaluation of healthcare services at all levels.[26] It also has operational responsibility for disease surveillance, essential drug supply, vaccine management, and for the provision of specialized care through tertiary institutions such as university teaching hospitals and federal medical centers.[26] Some state governments also provide tertiary care through state-owned teaching hospitals.[26] These tertiary centers serve as referral institutions for secondary health facilities but may also provide some primary healthcare services through their general outpatient departments (**FIGURE 19-2**).

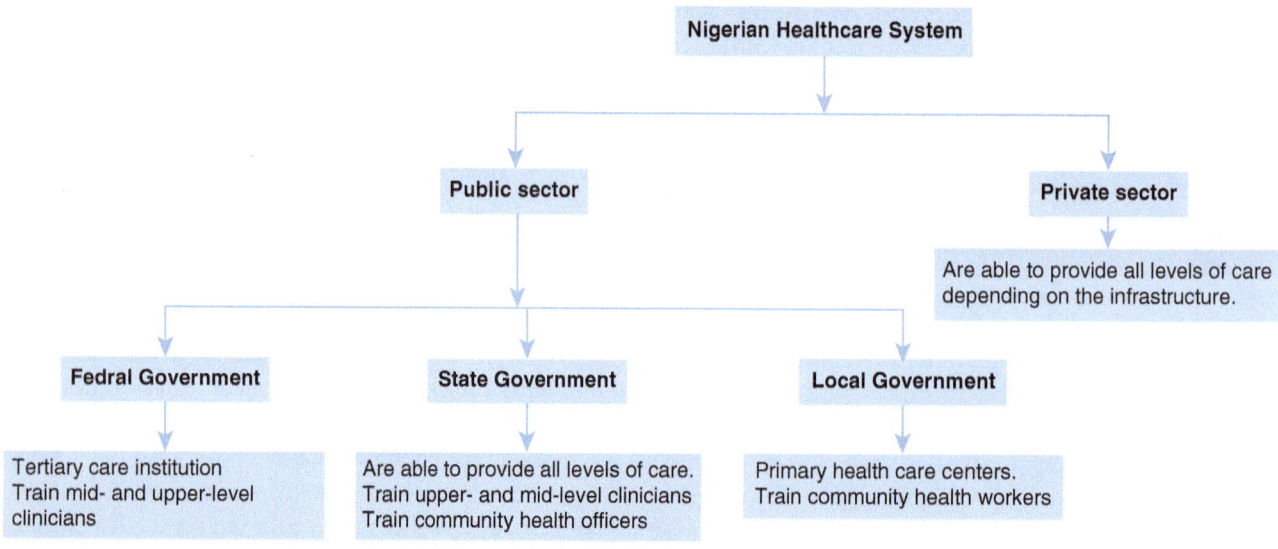

FIGURE 19-2 Overview of the Nigerian Healthcare System

Service delivery is through PHC centers, health clinics, and health posts. The Library of Congress Country Studies[19(p3)] pointed out that in 1979 in Nigeria there were 562 general hospitals, supplemented by 16 maternity and pediatric hospitals, 11 armed forces hospitals, 6 teaching hospitals, and 3 prison hospitals. In addition, general health centers were estimated to number slightly less than 600, general clinics 2,740, maternity homes 930, and maternal health centers 1,240. In addition to the public health sector, the private health sector plays a major role in healthcare delivery in Nigeria. Private providers (including voluntary and missionary agencies) are broadly divided into for-profit and not-for-profit categories.[27,28] These private providers offer a mixture of services ranging from primary to tertiary care, depending on infrastructure and staffing levels. There is also the informal healthcare system, consisting of unregistered healthcare providers and operating outside of the organized and monitored formal healthcare system.[29,30] Most Nigerians resort to the informal system for common ailments, usually because of financial constraints.

According to available data from the MoH, in 1999, there were 18,258 registered PHC facilities, 3,275 secondary facilities, and 29 tertiary facilities across the country.[24] The public sector accounted for 67% of PHC facilities, 25% of secondary facilities, and 97% of tertiary facilities.[24] A nationwide survey of health facilities showed that less than 4% of existing facilities in 1991 were owned by missionary and other voluntary agencies.[28] The MoH's 2005 data revealed a total of 23,640 health facilities in Nigeria: 20,278 primary (85.7%), 3,303 secondary (14%), and 59 tertiary (0.2%) care facilities.[26]

Currently, 38% of the health facilities in Nigeria are owned by the private sector, providing 60% of the health care in the country.[26] About 60% of the public primary healthcare facilities are located in the northern zones of the country, and they are mainly health posts and dispensaries that provide only basic curative services.[26]

Although there has been an overall increase in the number of facilities, there has not been much change to the proportion of ownership when compared with equivalent 1999 figures.

Primary health centers are present in every district of each of the 774 local government council areas,[29] and the local government authorities are directly responsible for them; however, the MoH—through the NSHDP 2010–2015—supervises the standard operating procedures and guidelines for delivery of services at all levels.[26] Characteristically, hospitals are divided into general wards, which provide both outpatient and inpatient care on a fee-for-service basis, and amenity wards, which charge higher fees but offer better aesthetic and therapeutic conditions. The general wards are usually crowded and require long waits for registration as well as for treatment. Inpatient hospitalization in the general wards can be sometimes quite challenging. Patients frequently do not see a doctor but only a nurse or other practitioner.

Because of limited space, beds are put in corridors, and some patients even sleep on the floors, regardless of whether they themselves or others around them are contagious. Although some family members offer to bring food to their relatives in the hospital, the hospital provides food, but mostly in the tertiary facilities. Most of the Nigerian elite do not have to see or witness these conditions; they usually travel abroad to the West for medical care, either for periodic medical checkups or when a serious or recurrent medical ailment exists.

Workforce

The objective of primary health care is the provision of inexpensive and simple treatments of everyday ailments that do not require specialist care, as well as preventive medicine for the promotion of health.[29] Referrals are made, when needed, to secondary and tertiary health centers. General practitioners, community health doctors, registered nurses, and community health officers staff these health centers. Community health extension workers head the smaller health clinics and health posts in villages. They are assisted by voluntary village health workers and traditional birth attendants.[29] These healthcare workers receive training for varying lengths of time, often from tertiary facilities, on basic preventive health and maternity services. The 36 state governments and the federal capital territory are also responsible for the provision of the secondary level of care through general hospitals.[21] The general hospitals are managed by the state health management boards.[29]

Nigeria, like many African countries, is facing a serious shortage of health workers. According to the World Health Organization (WHO) *World Health Statistics* 2010 report, there were 55,376 physicians in Nigeria (4 per 10,000 population) and 224,943 midwives and nurses (16 per 10,000 population). Comparable 2010 figures for the United States were 793,648 active physicians (27 per 10,000 population) and 2,927,000 midwives and nurses (98 per 10,000 population).[31] **TABLE 19-3** shows some selected health occupations and rates per 10,000 population.

TABLE 19-3 Comparative Healthcare Professionals/Workforce

Indicators	Nigeria (2009)	United States (2009)
Physicians	55,376	793,648
Physicians per 10,000 population	4.0	27.0
Nurses and midwifery personnel	224,943	2,927,000
Nurse and midwifery personnel per 10,000 population	16.0	98.0
Dentists	3,781	463,663
Dentists per 10,000 population	0.5	16.0
Pharmacists	18,682	249,642
Pharmacists per 10,000 population	1.0	9.0

Data from World Health Organization. World Health Statistics 2010. Geneva: WHO. http://www.who.int/whosis/whostat/2010/en/. 2010. Accessed July 25, 2016.

One of the factors contributing to this shortage is the emigration of healthcare professionals from the country. Thousands of Nigerian-trained doctors continue to migrate annually for various reasons, including poor remuneration, limited spaces for postgraduate medical residency training, dilapidated medical infrastructure, and poor job satisfaction.[32,33] The state of the healthcare system has been worsened by this progressive shortage of doctors and nurses. In 2005, there were 2,392 Nigerian doctors practicing in the United States and 1,529 in the United Kingdom.[34] Even Nigerian doctors who have completed their postgraduate medical residency training overseas are unwilling to return to the country because of limited incentives.[35]

Medical training in Nigeria is also in dire need of reform. The undergraduate medical education terminates with a Bachelor of Medicine and Bachelor of Surgery Degree after six years of study (3 years spent in premedical/basic medical sciences training and 3 years in medical/clinical training). Immediately after completion of the medical training is a one-year internship, or housemanship, in an accredited teaching hospital or general hospital. After the internship is completed, a doctor begins a one-year service to the nation, usually in a rural area in dire need of medical personnel (the National Youth Service Corps). Postgraduate training or private practice can then commence after the completion of the National Youth Service Corps.

Since 1948, when the University College Hospital in Ibadan was established as a branch of the University of London, there has not been substantial modification to the curriculum. Efforts made to reform the curriculum regionally and nationally have failed. There are also varying levels of compliance by the different medical schools to the minimum standards set by the regulatory bodies (the National Universities Commission and the Medical and Dental Council of Nigeria).[36] There are currently about 27 accredited medical schools in Nigeria, most of which were established by the federal government.[37]

Technology and Equipment

In the early 1980s, expensive medical equipment could not be operated because of shortages in electricity and equipment spare parts. As the cost of imported goods skyrocketed, public healthcare facilities became unable to handle the healthcare needs of the population. At this time, private facilities, although largely unregulated, began to fill the void left by the public healthcare sector.[20(p4)] As the demand for modern medical care far outstripped its availability and government hospitals deteriorated, medical personnel, drugs, and equipment were increasingly provided by the private sector.[38(pp4–5)]

Today, Nigeria has several pieces of technologically advanced diagnostic equipment. A significant proportion of this equipment is still owned by private hospitals, and their services are always too expensive for the average citizen because such health care is largely funded out of pocket. Consequently, mostly high-income individuals and highly compensated government officials can afford to pay for expensive medical tests. The government hospitals offer diagnostic services at a relatively cheaper price, but the equipment is obsolete and still too expensive for the low-income citizens. Besides, services are very erratic because of poor management, inadequate accountability, and interrupted power supply. Even when the equipment is functioning, the waiting period is often too long. For these reasons people prefer to patronize the private facilities, and the poor often rely on money borrowed from friends and families to offset the cost of the services. In extreme cases some sell property.

Evaluation of the Current Healthcare System

The National Health Insurance Scheme (NHIS) was first introduced in Nigeria in 1962 as a compulsory scheme for public service workers. In 1999, the scheme was modified to cover more people and was introduced by NHIS Act 35 of 1999.[22] This scheme includes mandatory payroll deductions and allows each insured person to decide at which health center to register. A healthcare provider registered under the scheme provides a defined range of services as needed for a capitation for each patient.[39] Health maintenance organizations are also expected to play a major role in coordination of the health centers, while the overall regulation of the scheme rests with the NHIS Council. The major objectives of the scheme are to ensure that every Nigerian has access to adequate healthcare services, to protect families from financial hardship caused by huge medical bills, and to limit the rise in the cost of and to ensure efficiency in healthcare services.[22,39]

Cost

Health care is financed in Nigeria through a variety of sources, including budgetary allocations from government at all levels (federal, state, and local), loans and grants, private sector contributions, and out-of-pocket expenses.[24] The public health sector is financed with an allocation from the Federation Account's general revenue. This allocation is made to the various levels of government based on a preagreed revenue allocation formula. The general mechanism for mobilization of revenue includes royalties and fees from the oil sector; general tax revenue, including a value-added tax; social health insurance; cost recovery, including user fees in public health facilities; and external aid in terms of loans, donations, and grants.[22] The allocation by the government to the health sector had always been about 2%–3% of the national budget,[22] and this has remained low in spite of the declaration among the African heads of state and the Nigerian government at a conference in Abuja, Nigeria, in 2001 to allocate at least 15% of their national budgets to the health sector. Health expenditure as a percentage of total Nigerian government expenditure was 5.7% in 2010, 7.4% in 2011, 7.4% in 2012, 6.5% in 2013, and 8.3% in 2014.[40] **TABLE 19-4** shows the core health expenditure comparison between Nigeria and the United States.

TABLE 19-4 Core Health Expenditure Indicators

Country	Total expenditure on health as % of GDP		Government expenditure on health as % of total expenditure on health		Private expenditure on health as % of total expenditure on health		Expenditure on health as % of total government expenditure		Per capita total expenditure on health (PPP in US $)	
	2010	2014	2010	2014	2010	2014	2010	2014	2010	2014
Nigeria	3.5	3.7	26.2	25.1	73.8	74.9	5.7	8.3	174	217
United States	17.0	17.1	47.5	48.3	52.5	51.7	19.0	21.3	8,269	9,403

UNAIDS. HIV and AIDS estimates (2015). http://www.unaids.org/en/regionscountries/countries/nigeria/. Accessed November 16, 2016.

Estimates from the WHO database reveal Nigeria's per capita total expenditure (PPP Intl. $) of $178 in 2012, $208 in 2013, and $217 in 2014.[40] This source shows that Nigeria's public expenditure on health hovered around 3.5% of GDP between 2010 and 2014. The private health sector is mainly financed through out-of-pocket expenses and also through donations from voluntary and missionary agencies (local and international).

Some employers, such as oil companies and other large organizations, have also financed health care by establishing company-owned clinics where employees receive primary- and secondary-level health care. Other employers engage in *retainership* with private providers.[27] Retainership is a financing mechanism whereby employees can benefit from health services up to a prescribed monthly limit through a contracted private provider. The provider is reimbursed retrospectively at agreed intervals. In some scenarios, the employees pay the bills up front and are later reimbursed by their employers. In other cases, employees are paid medical allowances as part of their fringe benefits. They are at liberty to spend these allowances in whichever facility they choose. These various forms of employee medical benefit schemes are an important part of private health insurance in Nigeria.

In 2014, private expenditure on health add up to 74.9% of total health expenditure, whereas government spending covers the remainder of total health expenditure.[40] Of the total private expenditure, out-of-pocket payments account for 95.5%, whereas prepaid plans account for 3.1%.[40] The total expenditure on health as a percentage of GDP was 3.7% in 2013 and 2014. The corresponding figures for the United States were 16.9% of GDP in 2013 and 17.1% in 2014.[40]

Quality

Among the various health-related ailments that affect the most Nigerians, communicable diseases exert a great toll. Notable are malaria, tuberculosis, diarrhea, and HIV/AIDS (**TABLE 19-5**). The incidence of these diseases is so high that it earns Nigeria recognition as the country with the third highest burden of infection in the world, including an estimated 3,500,000 people living with HIV (2015).[41]

The average life expectancy at birth is 53 years for males and 55 years for females.[43] The adult mortality rate (probability of dying between 15 and 60 years) is 357 per 1,000 population for males and 325 per 1,000 population for females.[43] The infant mortality rate is 69.4 per 1,000 live births, and the total under-five mortality for both genders is 108.8 per 1,000 live births.[43] Needless to say, the maternal and child health statistics in Nigeria remain abysmal. The maternal mortality ratio is 560 per 100,000 live births, one of the worst in the world.[42] Some of the common causes of maternal mortality are obstetric hemorrhage, sepsis, and preeclampsia/eclampsia.[46,47] The high maternal mortality rate may be because only approximately 35% of births are attended by skilled health personnel.[42] In addition, prenatal coverage is low, with about 51% of women attending at least four prenatal visits per year.[42] **TABLE 19-6** shows the various primary health indicators.

TABLE 19-5 Infectious Disease Morbidity Statistics and the United States

Indicator	Nigeria (Year)	United States (Year)
Tuberculosis prevalence per 100,000 population[42]	326.0 (2013)	4.1 (2013)
Tuberculosis incidence per 100,000[42]	338.0 (2013)	3.3 (2013)
Reported polio cases[43]	35 (2014)	0 (2014)
Malaria incidence cases (per 100,000)[42]	28,430 (2013)	0 (2013)
People living with HIV/AIDS[41,44]	3,500,000 (2015)	1,218,400 (2014)
HIV: estimated pediatric infections, 0–14 years[41,45]	260,000 (2015)	209 (2014)
HIV: estimated children orphaned by AIDS, 0–17 years[41]	1,800,000 (2015)	—

UNAIDS. HIV and AIDS estimates (2015). http://www.unaids.org/en/regionscountries/countries/nigeria/. Accessed November 16, 2016.

TABLE 19-6 Primary Health Indicators

Year	Life expectancy at birth		Life expectancy at 60 years		Adult mortality (per 1,000 population)		Neonatal mortality rate (per 1,000 live births)	Under-five mortality rate (per 1,000 live births)	Infant mortality ratio (per 1,000 live births)	Maternal mortality ratio (per 100,000 live birth)
	Male	Female	Male	Female	Male	Female				
2012	51.8	53.5	13.8	14.3	371.0	346.0	36.5	121	76.2	—
2013	52.2	54.2	13.8	14.3	357.0	325.0	35.8	117	73.8	560.0
2014	52.6	54.7	13.9	14.4	—	—	35.0	113	71.5	—
2015	53.4	55.6	13.9	14.5	—	—	34.3	108	69.4	814.0

Data from World Health Organization. Global Health Observatory Data Repository. apps.who.int/gho/data/node.main; World Health Organization. World Health Statistics, 2015. http://apps.who.int/iris/bitstream/10665/170250/1/9789240694439_eng.pdf?ua=1. 2015.

Access

In Nigeria, access to quality health care is dictated by the ability to pay. Because of this, many individuals and families are unable to engage in the kinds of preventive medicine and practices (such as early vaccination) necessary to avoid future, more expensive hospitalization. For instance, in 2014, 51% of 1-year-olds in Nigeria got measles vaccines, 66% got DPT vaccines, and 66% got hepatitis B vaccines.[43] During the same period in the United States, 91% of 1-year-olds received the measles vaccine, 94% had the DPT vaccine, and 90% had the hepatitis B vaccine (TABLE 19-7).[43] Payment to the various provider groups and for different services (such as private and government hospitals, general practitioners, specialists, maternity services, and vaccinations) is mainly by fee-for-service, and very few can afford to pay.

Before 1986, free medical services, including food for hospitalized patients, were provided in public hospitals; however, because of the economic recession in the 1980s, the ill-fated SAP was introduced with the support of the IMF and the World Bank.[27] Some of the requirements of SAP included the rationalization and introduction of user fees in public health facilities.

TABLE 19-7 Health Service Coverage

Indicator	Nigeria% (Year)	United States% (Year)
Measles vaccination among 1-year-olds	51 (2014)	91 (2014)
DPT* vaccination among 1-year-olds	66 (2014)	94 (2014)
Hepatitis B** vaccination among 1-year-olds	66 (2014)	90 (2014)
Prenatal coverage (at least 1 visit)	61 (2014)	—
Prenatal coverage (at least 4 visits)	51 (2014)	97 (2014)
Births attended by skilled health personnel	35 (2014)	99 (2014)
Contraceptive prevalence rate	15 (2013)	76 (2013)

*Three doses of diphtheria, pertussis and tetanus toxoid vaccine.

**Three doses of hepatitis B vaccine.

*Data from World Health Organization. Global Health Observatory Data Repository. http://apps.who.int/gho/data/node.home. n.d.; **Data from World Health Organization. World Health Statistics 2015. http://apps.who.int/iris/bitstream/10665/170250/1/9789240694439_eng.pdf.

Whether these user fees were paid by individuals, with or without reimbursement by their employers, or by the employers directly, payments were made on a fee-for-service basis.

Such fees were usually set arbitrarily by providers, and in general, fees accessed by public health facilities were much cheaper than those accessed by private providers. In 1992, however, the Guild of Medical Directors introduced new billing guidelines and fee schedules for provider reimbursement in the private health sector in order to harmonize fees across the country and reduce price competition to levels that would pose a minimal threat to ethical medical practice.[28] Nevertheless, the policy remains highly unregulated.

The Bamako Initiative was introduced by the African ministers of health who met in 1987, with financial support from several organizations, including the WHO, the United Nations International Children's Emergency Fund, and the United Kingdom's Department of International Development.[30,48] It was adopted by the Nigerian government in 1988. The main aim of the initiative was to strengthen the primary healthcare infrastructure through the introduction of user fees. The revenue generated was to be used to improve the availability and affordability of essential drugs and to improve health center infrastructures; however, this initiative has been criticized as placing too much emphasis on drugs to the detriment of other aspects of the health system.[48] The introduction of the user fees in public healthcare facilities and the subsequent rise in healthcare costs limited access and made it prohibitive for many citizens to seek needed healthcare services in a timely manner. Many sought relief through unregulated private health facilities, drug vendors, and traditional healers,[30] thereby worsening their health status.

▸ Current and Emerging Issues and Challenges

Despite the receding influence of such endemic diseases as yellow fever, health problems in Nigeria remain acute. In the adult population, communicable disease accounts for 866 deaths per 100,000 population versus 674 death per 100,000 population caused by noncommunicable disease.[42] This is in sharp contrast to statistics reported for the United States, where communicable disease accounts for 31 deaths per 100,000 population and noncommunicable disease caused 413 deaths per 100,000 population.[42] Although death from malaria is showing a downward trend, it has remained the most common cause of death among children under 5 years old and accounted for 21% of registered deaths in 2013.[42] Diarrhea and HIV combined caused less than 15% of under-five mortality during the same period.[42] In parts of northern Nigeria, there have also been major outbreaks of cerebrospinal meningitis, a potentially fatal inflammation of the membranes of the brain and spinal cord.[49(p3)]

Nigerians also experience high rates of schistosomiasis, guinea worm, trachoma, yaws, and river blindness (onchocerciasis).[49] Over the last couple of years, a program for the eradication of river blindness and malaria has been undertaken in cooperation with the WHO. The River Blindness Programme has maintained remarkable success in Nigeria. The most recent epidemiological assessment in 2013 revealed a prevalence rate of less than 1% in all the inflicted states except Taraba, which had a prevalence rate of 7.8%.[50] In December 2006, the World Bank approved a US $180 million Malaria Control Booster Project. This project was billed as Africa's largest and was expected to support national coverage of malaria control interventions in 7 of the 36 states of the federation. Sadly, the control interventions have not caused any remarkable change as statistics has confirmed "no change in confirmed malaria cases, admission, and deaths across all age groups."[51]

In March 1987, the presence of AIDS was officially confirmed in the country. Since then, the infection rate reached its epidemic peak in 2001, with a prevalence rate of 5.8%, and then it gradually declined to 3.4% in 2012.[52] According to 2015 statistics, an estimated 3.5 million Nigerians were living with HIV/AIDS, and approximately 180,000 deaths were attributable to HIV/AIDS.[41] The government is working to control the spread of HIV/AIDS and other sexually transmitted diseases through public education and behavior change. External stakeholders are also part of the fight against the transmission of HIV in Nigeria.

The United States National Intelligence Council study highlighted the rising HIV/AIDS problem through 2010 in five countries that had large populations at risk for HIV infection: Nigeria, Ethiopia, Russia, India, and China. In response, Nigeria was designated as 1 of 15 countries worldwide to be assisted under the U.S. President's Emergency Plan for AIDS Relief. The United States Agency for International Development has been working with the Nigerian government to make antiretroviral treatment available to approximately 350,000 people living with HIV/AIDS, as well as to provide health and social services to close to 2 million HIV-positive people. This partnership is also making efforts toward prevention and care of people with a co-morbidity of HIV and tuberculosis.[53]

So far, the joint effort of external stakeholders and the Nigerian government have steadily reduced the annual number of new HIV infections from 270,667 in 2010 to 253,506 in 2012 and to 227,518 in 2014.[52]

Malnutrition also remains a serious crisis among children in Nigeria. In 2014, 36% of Nigerian children under the age of 5 years were stunted and 31% were underweight. The same statistics for American children were 2% for stunted growth and 0.5% for underweight.[42] Solving this problem in Peru has been a major challenge because of the activities of insurgents that are so prevalent in the affected region of the country.

In addition to the "brain drain" of professional health workers in Nigeria, counterfeit drugs have posed a major challenge to the health of Nigerians. Factors that have facilitated drug counterfeiting in Nigeria include corruption, poor drug control systems, and poor interagency cooperation. The extent of the corruption overwhelmed the ability of the National Drug Regulatory Agency to police. As a result, in 1993, a new agency was formed with autonomy and extra powers.[54] This new agency, the National Agency for Food and Drug Administration and Control, has taken major strides to reduce the counterfeit drug problem and has made tremendous progress initially unthinkable in the Nigerian system. In collusion with corrupt government and customs officials, the subterranean economy that traffics in the importation of illegal pharmaceuticals and drugs has continued to undermine National Agency for Food and Drug Administration and Control efforts to achieve an overwhelming sense of regulatory efficacy.

Nigeria has a great need to address the issue of lack of clean drinking water. Millions of Nigerians are afflicted annually by various waterborne diseases, worms, and parasites. As a serious public health issue, water provides a common link—either through drinking or bathing—for the transmission of infectious diseases and provides a breeding ground for harmful pathogens.

Nigeria also suffers from a rising level of e-waste (a litany of used electronic gadgets such as computers, radios, cell phones, and televisions) that are indiscriminately discarded around cities, with some ending up in dumpsites where they are burned. Among them are millions of used cell phone SIM cards. To date, very little or no testing has been done regarding the chemical decomposition of these types of materials and their implication for the integrity of the groundwater as well as public health.

Nigeria today could also be termed a "plastic society." The streets of the major cities and urban centers are littered with little plastic sachets used for packaging and selling drinking water. After use, people dispose of them in the streets. When it rains, the plastic sachets block the drains and clog the gutters causing the drains to overflow, flooding streets and homes. Because these polyethylene plastic products are essentially nonbiodegradable, they litter the ground for years. In most cases, they are scooped up and burned in open incinerators, further emitting harmful toxic fumes into the air.

Cherry Picking: A Two-Tiered System

One of the most critical problems confronting the delivery of health care in Nigeria is the perennial low level of government commitment to the healthcare sector. Although the budgetary allocations for healthcare average 2%–3%, in some specific instances, because of corruption and other factors, statistics indicate that the actual amount released from the national budget is as low as 30%–40% of the budgeted amount.[22] Hence, beyond budgetary allocations, a concern in funding the healthcare sector in Nigeria is the growing gap between budgeted figures and the actual funds released from the treasury for health activities. Although much of the expenditures go into administering the health personnel system, a sizable proportion of the funds are lost as a result of waste, mismanagement, and official malfeasance. The government also needs to take a more proactive role in ensuring a competitive patient cost-sharing system while regulating arbitrary cost increases and insurance risk exposure. According to Laurence A. Graig, "Such competition should be regulated in the sense that a risk equalization fund ensures that insurance funds compete for members on factors other than risk status."[55(p178)]

The WHO, in the year 2000, ranked Nigeria 187th of 191 countries in overall health systems performance.[56] In the area of responsiveness to people's nonmedical expectations—i.e., respect for people (respect for dignity, confidentiality, autonomy) and client orientation (prompt attention, quality of amenities, access to social support networks, choice of provider/facility)—Nigeria ranked 149th. For comparison, the United States ranked 37th in overall systems performance and 1st in terms of responsiveness. In a satisfaction study involving 250 inpatients at a teaching hospital in the state of Edo, Nigeria, the authors found that only 93 of the 250 patients (37.2%) claimed to have received adequate information concerning their disease condition.[57] Concerning friendliness, 136 of the patients (54%) evaluated the doctors as very friendly, whereas 6 patients (2.4%) perceived the doctors to be unfriendly. In contrast, 32 patients (12.8%) judged the nurses very friendly, whereas 76 (30.6%) felt that the nurses were unfriendly.

Another problem worth mentioning is that there are few or no long-term care facilities or professionals needed to provide that service. Also, mental care is very rudimentary in Nigeria. The majority of mental health services are concentrated in only eight regional psychiatric centers and psychiatric departments of medical schools and in a few general hospitals. Because of the local belief systems, these formal systems face competition from native herbalists and faith healing centers. The ratio is less than 0.5 psychiatrist per 100,000 population.[42] In Nigeria, there is a clear demarcation between the health-seeking behavior of the haves and have-nots. Wealthier individuals usually seek health care in well-equipped hospitals and private clinics. On the other hand, those who are financially challenged are more likely to use the "informal" private health sector or, at best, the primary health centers, which are usually chronically understaffed. Traditional medicine healers, drug peddlers, and others who practice in the informal sector usually prescribe "mixtures" of drugs without relaying appropriate dosage regimens or manufacturers' safety standards. Treatments prescribed are usually based on conjectured diagnoses without any form of laboratory workup.[30]

Equally troublesome is the lack of a safety net system for the poor. In a system in which health care is mainly paid for out of pocket, there is no safety net for individuals who are below the poverty line (which is arbitrarily defined as earning less than US $275 annually).[29] Few public health facilities and even fewer private health facilities accommodate patients who cannot afford to pay for treatment. Some missionary-run health facilities occasionally hold medical outreaches to provide a wide range of services (such as outpatient services, general surgery, and eye clinics) free of charge or for very minimal fees. Many poor patients bear their illnesses without seeking medical attention while waiting for the next free medical outreach; however, if the government succeeds in its effort to initiate a social health insurance scheme, this would allow cross-subsidization in the health sector—in the sense that the scheme would give healthcare access to people who cannot afford it—provided by the contribution of members who are financially able.[58]

Apart from the healthcare system, several other supporting systems—such as road, transportation, electricity, water, and sewage—have inadequate infrastructure. According to the WHO, in 2015, 81% of the urban population and 57% of the rural population had access to improved drinking water sources.[59] The proportion of the population with access to improved sanitation was 33% and 25% for the urban and rural areas, respectively.[59] There have also been several ethnic and religious uprisings in the country, which have led to the loss of lives and property and to an overburdening of the fragile healthcare system. These instability and security issues have discouraged potential investors, thereby negatively impacting growth in the economic and health sectors.[60] Hence, for meaningful progress to be made in the healthcare system, there have to be equivalent improvements in other related sectors of Nigerian society and economy.

At the Nigerian National Health Conference held in November 2006,[61] participants representing stakeholders from within and outside the country identified priorities to sustain the current health reforms. The goal of this conference was to develop a health agenda for Nigeria in the 21st century. Some of the observations endorsed at the conference were that Nigeria still has one of the worst health indices in the world, as it accounts for 10% of the world's maternal deaths but 2% of the world's population (2000 figures). In addition, the health system was still underfunded, with per capita expenditure of US $9.44 on health, and key correlates of ill health—such as hunger, poverty, illiteracy, poor sanitation, gender inequalities, and unemployment—are still prevalent in the society.

Following these observations, several resolutions and recommendations were made and endorsed by the conference: the establishment of a special system of social welfare for the disadvantaged and vulnerable groups, promotion and legitimization of public-private partnership in all aspects of the health system to ensure sustainability, and an increase in Nigeria's per capita expenditure on health from US $ 9.44 to the WHO-recommended $34. In addition, the conference endorsed a new, competitive welfare and compensation package for healthcare practitioners in the private and public health sectors.[61]

Reviewing some health indicators a few years after the conference, some improvements were observed. For instance, the number of new HIV infections has steadily declined from 270,667 in 2010 to 253,506 in 2012 and to 227,518 in 2014.[52] The under-five mortality rate per 1,000 population dipped from 121 in 2012 to 108 in 2015.[43] Similarly, economic indicators revealed some increase. Per capita expenditure on health grew from US $81 in 2007 to $118 in 2014, and the expenditure on health as a percentage of GDP rose from 2.8% in 2000 to 4.5% in 2007, but it dipped to 3.7% in 2014.[40]

Successfully managing health promotion and education must be seen as a collective responsibility among citizens, the government, and the medical and health research centers. To the extent that a healthy population is an active population, the negative effects of disease and illness can be offset by an active and energetic workforce fully engaged in the nation's productive process. Rather than speaking in broad generalities, the nation's health policy must speak to the specifics—the need to isolate chronic epidemiological issues (such as malaria, HIV/AIDS, sexually transmitted diseases, yellow fever, and waterborne parasites) and to exercise the political will necessary to address the specific needs of marginalized groups or at-risk populations. There should be an increased commitment of resources to understanding the environmental conditions and cultural and biological circumstances that make certain types of pathologies more prevalent or chronic in the Nigerian context so that intervention or preventive measures can be taken to mitigate their more costly and public health effects.

The ongoing shift toward social health insurance is welcome in principle, but the means to achieving an optimal public-private sector mix in the design of health plans will remain a major challenge as long as the triple issues of cost, access, and quality are not taken seriously. Affordable health care on demand is a key objective that should inform government healthcare policymaking.

References

1. Badru Padre. *Imperialism and Ethnic Politics in Nigeria, 1960–1966*. Trenton, NJ: Africa World Press; 1998.
2. United Nations. Department of Economic and Social Affairs. Population Division. *World Population Prospects*. 2015 revision. https://esa.un.org/unpd/wpp/publications/files/key_findings_wpp_2015.pdf. New York: United Nations; 2015. Accessed August 4, 2016.
3. McIntosh SK, McIntosh RJ. Current directions in West African prehistory. *Annual Review of Anthropology*. 1983;12:215–258.
4. *The World Factbook 2016*. Washington, DC: Central Intelligence Agency, 2016. https://www.cia.gov/library/publications/the-world-factbook/geos/ni.html. Accessed August 4, 2016.
5. Michigan State University. Global Edge. Nigeria: trade statistics. http://globaledge.msu.edu/countries/nigeria/tradestats/. UN Comtrade 2014 data. Accessed August 16, 2016.
6. Organization of the Petroleum Exporting Countries. Nigeria facts and figures 2016. http://www.opec.org/opec_web/en/about_us/167.htm. Accessed November 15, 2016.
7. *The World Factbook 2008*. Nigeria. Washington, DC: Central Intelligence Agency, US General Printing Office, 2008.
8. Central Bank of Nigeria. The movement in reserves. https://www.cbn.gov.ng/IntOps/Reserve.asp?MoveDate=8/4/2016%2010:11:55%20PM. Accessed August 5, 2016.
9. Hazem B, Luciano G, eds. *The Rentier State*. Vol. 2. New York: Croom Helm; 1987.
10. Omeje K. Oil conflict and accumulation politics in Nigeria. Report from Africa: population, health, environment, and conflict. ECSP Report. 2007;12:45:44–49. http://www.eia.doe.gov/emeu/cabs/orevcoun.html. Accessed January 10, 2008.
11. Nigeria National Bureau of Statistics. The National Literacy Survey. http://www.nigerianstat.gov.ng/pdfuploads/National%20Literacy%20Survey,%202010.pdf. Published June 2010. Accessed July 23, 2016.
12. UNICEF. At a glance: Nigeria. https://www.unicef.org/infobycountry/nigeria_statistics.html. Accessed November 13, 2016.
13. World Bank. 2014. *Nigeria economic report*. Nigeria economic report; no. 2. Washington, DC: World Bank Group. http://documents.worldbank.org/curated/en/2014/07/19883231/nigeria-economic-report-no-2. Accessed July 23, 2016.
14. World Bank. World Development Indicators database. Gross national income per capita 2015, Atlas method and PPP. http://databank.worldbank.org/data/download/GNIPC.pdf. Published October 11, 2016. Accessed July 23, 2016.
15. World Bank. Food and Agriculture Organization and World Bank population estimates. Population density (people per square kilometer of land area). http://data.worldbank.org/indicator/EN.POP.DNST?locations=NG. Accessed July 23, 2016.
16. World Bank. United Nations, World Urbanization Prospects. Urban population (% of total) 2015. http://data.worldbank.org/indicator/SP.URB.TOTL.IN.ZS?locations=NG. Accessed July 23, 2016.
17. Library of Congress Country Studies, CIA *World Factbook 1991*. Nigeria: History of Modern Medical Services; 1991. http://www.photius.com/countries/nigeria/society/nigeria_society_history_of_modern_me~10005.html. Accessed March 30, 2008.
18. Library of Congress Country Studies, CIA *World Factbook 1991*. http://www.photius.com/countries/nigeria/society/nigeria_society_history_of_modern_me~10005.html. Data as of June 1991. Accessed March 30, 2008.
19. Library of Congress Country Studies, CIA *World Factbook 1991*. http://www.photius.com/countries/nigeria/society/nigeria_society_history_of_modern_me~10005.html. Data as of June 1991. Accessed March 30, 2008.
20. Library of Congress Country Studies, *CIA World Factbook 1991*. http://www.photius.com/countries/nigeria/society/nigeria_society_history_of_modern_me~10005.html. Data as of June 1991. Accessed March 30, 2008.
21. Onwujekwe O, Uzochukwu B. Socio-economic and geographic differentials in costs and payment strategies for primary healthcare services in Southeast Nigeria. *Health Policy*. 2005;71(3):383.
22. Petu A. Health financing reforms: the Nigerian experience. *African Health Monitor*. 2005;6(1):33–34.
23. Library of Congress Country Studies, *CIA World Factbook 1991*. http://www.photius.com/countries/nigeria/society/nigeria_society_primary_health_care_~10006.html. Data as of June 1991. Accessed February 18, 2008.
24. World Health Organization. *WHO Country Cooperation Strategy: Federal Republic of Nigeria, 2002–2007*. Geneva, Switzerland: WHO; 2007.
25. World Health Organization. *Health Systems Policies and Service Delivery*. Nigeria: Ministry of Health; 2006.
26. Federal Ministry of Health. *National Strategic Health Development Plan (NSHDP) 2010-2015*. http://www.health.gov.ng/doc/NSHDP.pdf. Published November 2010. Accessed July 24, 2016.

27. Alubo O. The promise and limits of private medicine: health policy dilemmas in Nigeria. *Health Policy Plan.* 2001;16(3):313–321.
28. Ogunbekun I, Ogunbekun A, Orobaton N. Private health care in Nigeria: walking the tightrope. *Health Policy Plan.* 1999;14(2):174–181.
29. Akanji BO, Ogunniyi A, Baiyewu O. Healthcare for older persons, a country profile: Nigeria. *J Am Geriatr Soc.* 2002;50(7):1289–1292.
30. Uzochukwu BS, Onwujekwe OE. Socio-economic differences and health seeking behavior for the diagnosis and treatment of malaria: a case study of four local government areas operating the Bamako initiative programme in south-east Nigeria. *Int J Equity Health.* 2004;3(1):6.
31. World Health Organization. *World Health Statistics 2010.* Geneva, Switzerland: WHO. http://www.who.int/whosis/whostat/2010/en/. Published 2010. Accessed July 25, 2016.
32. Arah OA, Ogbu UC, Okeke CE. Too poor to leave, too rich to stay: developmental and global health correlates of physician migration to the United States, Canada, Australia, and the United Kingdom. *Am J Public Health.* 2008;98(1):148–154.
33. Clark DA, Clark PF, Stewart JB. The globalization of the labour market for health-care professionals. *International Labour Review.* 2006;145.
34. Mullan F. The metrics of the physician brain drain. *N Engl J Med.* 2005;353(17):1810–1818.
35. World Health Organization. *Managing Brain Drain and Brain Waste of Health Workers in Nigeria, 2006.* Geneva, Switzerland: WHO; 2006.
36. Ibrahim M. Medical education in Nigeria. *Med Teach.* 2007;29(9):901–905.
37. Medical and Dental Council Of Nigeria. Medical and dental schools accredited by the Medical and Dental Council of Nigeria. https://www.mdcn.gov.ng/page/accredited-medical-schools. Accessed July 25, 2016.
38. Library of Congress Country, *CIA World Factbook.* www.ciafactbook.gov. Accessed October 23, 2008.
39. Federal Republic of Nigeria. *National Health Insurance Scheme Decree 1999.* Nigeria: Ministry of Health; 1999.
40. World Health Organization. Table of key indicators for all the Member States. http://apps.who.int/nha/database/Key_Indicators/Index/en. Accessed July 26, 2016.
41. UNAIDS. HIV and AIDS estimates (2015). http://www.unaids.org/en/regionscountries/countries/nigeria/. Accessed November 16, 2016.
42. World Health Organization. *World Health Statistics 2015.* Geneva, Switzerland: WHO. http://apps.who.int/iris/bitstream/10665/170250/1/9789240694439_eng.pdf. Published 2015. Accessed July 27, 2016.
43. World Health Organization. Global Health Observatory data repository. http://apps.who.int/gho/data/node.home. Accessed November 16, 2016.
44. Centers for Disease Control and Prevention. HIV among people aged 50 and over, 2014. http://www.cdc.gov/hiv/group/age/olderamericans/index.html. Accessed November 16, 2016.
45. Centers for Disease Control and Prevention. *HIV Surveillance Report. Diagnoses of HIV Infection in the United States and Dependent Areas, 2014.* Vol. 26. http://www.cdc.gov/hiv/pdf/library/reports/surveillance/cdc-hiv-surveillance-report-us.pdf. Published November 2015. Accessed November 16, 2016.
46. Onah HE, Okaro JM, Umeh U, Chigbu CO. Maternal mortality in health institutions with emergency obstetric care facilities in Enugu State, Nigeria. *J Obstet Gynecol.* 2005;25(6):569–574.
47. Aboyeji AP, Ijaiya MA, Fawole AA. Maternal mortality in a Nigerian teaching hospital: a continuing tragedy. *Nigeria Health.* 2007;37(2):83–85.
48. Uzochukwu BS, Onwujekwe OE, Akpala CO. Effect of the Bamako-Initiative drug revolving fund on availability and rational use of essential drugs in primary health care facilities in south-east Nigeria. *Health Policy Plan Trop Doct.* 2002;17(4):378–383.
49. The Library of Congress Country Studies, U.S. Central Intelligence Agency *World Factbook* 1991. www.ciafactbook.org. Accessed November 23, 2008.
50. World Health Organization. Weekly epidemiological record. http://www.who.int/wer/2014/wer8949.pdf?ua=1. Published December 5, 2014. Accessed July 28, 2016.
51. World Health Organization. *World Malaria Report 2014.* http://www.who.int/malaria/publications/world_malaria_report_2014/wmr-2014-no-profiles.pdf. Published 2014. Accessed July 28, 2016.
52. National Agency for the Control of AIDS (NACA). Global AIDS Response: Country Progress Report, 2015. http://www.unaids.org/sites/default/files/country/documents/NGA_narrative_report_2015.pdf. Accessed July 27, 2016
53. U.S. Agency for International Development. Nigeria: USAID Strategy in Nigeria. http://www.usaid.gov/locations/sub_saharan_africa/countries/nigeria. Accessed February 18, 2008.
54. World Health Organization. *Report of Pre Eleventh ICDRA Satellite Workshop on Counterfeit Drugs,* Madrid, Spain, February 13–14, 2004. Geneva, Switzerland: WHO; 2004.
55. Graig LA. *Health of Nations.* Washington, DC: CQ Press; 1999.
56. World Health Organization. Health Systems: Improving Performance. *World Health Report 2000.* Geneva, Switzerland: WHO; 2000.
57. Ofovwe CE, Ofili AN. Indices of patient satisfaction in an African population. *Public Health.* 2005;119(7):582–586.
58. Okonkwo A. Nigeria set to launch health insurance scheme. *Lancet.* 2001;358(9276):131.
59. World Health Organization. Progress on sanitation and drinking water: 2015 update and MDG assessment. http://apps.who.int/iris/bitstream/10665/177752/1/9789241509145_eng.pdf?ua=1. Accessed August 2, 2016.
60. Okafor C, Follen M, Adewole I. Opportunities to improve health systems in Africa: a comparative overview of healthcare challenges for stakeholders and strategic planners. *Gynecol Oncol.* 2007;107(1 Suppl 1):S86–S93.
61. Federal Republic of Nigeria. Federal Ministry of Health. Conference Communiqué: Nigerian National Health Conference (NHC2006), November 28–29, 2006. Abuja, Nigeria: Ministry of Health; 2006.

CHAPTER 20

Botswana

Styn M. Jamu and **Lesego Gabaitiri**

▶ Country Description

TABLE 20-1 Botswana

Nationality	Noun: Motswana (singular), Batswana (plural) Adjective: Motswana (singular), Batswana (plural)
Ethnic groups	Tswana linguistic groups 79% (including 8 major tribes: Bangwato, Bakgatla, Bakwena, Bangwaketsi, Bakgatla, Barolong, Batlokwa, Bamalete), Bakalanga 11%, Basarwa 3%, other minority ethnic groups 7% (including Babirwa, Bakgalagadi, Wayeyi, Hambukushu, Batswapong, Ova, Herero, and non-African) (2016 est.)
Religion	Christians 79.1%, Badimo 4.1%, Others 1.4% (including Baha'i, Hindu, Muslim, Rastafarian), unspecified 0.3%, and no religion 15.2% (2011 est.)
Languages	English (official) 2.8%, Setswana 77.3%, Sekalanga 7.4%, Shekgalagadi 3.4%, Zezuru/Shona 2%, Sesarwa 1.7%, Sembukushu 1.6%, Ndebele 1%, other 2.8% (2011 est.)
Literacy	Definition: Age 15 and over can read and write. Total population: 88.5% Male: 88.0% Female: 89.9% (2015 est.)
Government type	Constitution/parliamentary republic
Date of independence	September 30, 1966 (from the United Kingdom)

(continues)

TABLE 20-1 Botswana (continued)	
Gross Domestic Product (GDP) per capita	$17,700 (2015 est.)
Unemployment rate	17.5% (2015 est.)
Natural hazards	Recurrent drought, overgrazing, veldt fires, seasonal August winds that can obscure visibility
Environment: current issues	Limited freshwater resources, desertification
Population	2,209,208 Female: 1,084,458 Male: 1,124,750 (2016 est.)
Age structure	0–14 years: 32.4% (male 364,807/female 350,888) 15–24 years: 21.3% (male 234,251/female 236,650) 25–54 years: 37.6% (male 444,290/female 386,622) 55–64 years: 4.6% (male 45,186/female 55,272) 65 years and over: 4.1% (male 36,216/female 55,026) (2016 est.)
Median age	Total: 23.2 years Male: 23.4 years Female: 23.1 years (2016 est.)
Population growth rate	1.19% (2016 est.)
Birth rate	20.7 births/1,000 population (2016 est.)
Death rate	1,255 deaths/100,000 population (2016 est.)
Disease burden	Communicable disease deaths: 555/100,000 population Noncommunicable disease deaths: 612/100,000 population Injury deaths: 88/100,000 population (2016 est.)
Net migration rate	4.5 migrant(s)/1,000 population (2016 est.)
Gender ratio	At birth: 1.03 male(s)/female Under 15 years: 1.04 male(s)/female 15–24 years: 0.99 male(s)/female 25–54 years: 1.15 male(s)/female 55–64 years: 0.82 male(s)/female 65 years and over: 0.66 male(s)/female Total population: 1.04 males/female (2016 est.)
Infant mortality rate	8.6 deaths/1,000 live births (2016 est.)
Life expectancy at birth	Total population: 54.6 years Male: 56.3 years Female: 52.6 years (2016 est.)

TABLE 20-1 Botswana (continued)	
Total fertility rate	2.3 children born/woman (2016 est.)
HIV/AIDS adult prevalence rate	22.2% (2015 est.)
Number of people living with HIV/AIDS	370,850 (2016 est.)
HIV/AIDS annual deaths	5,528 (2016 est.)

Data from Central Intelligence Agency. The World Factbook, 2016: Botswana. https://www.cia.gov/library/publications/the-world-factbook/.; Statistics Botswana. Botswana AIDS impact survey IV (BAIS IV). Gaborone, Botswana: Statistics Botswana; 2014; World Health Organization, Botswana Country Profile. http://www.who.int/countries/bwa/en/ Accessed 1/25/2017.

History and Culture

Botswana gained her independence from Britain in 1966. Between 1885 and 1966, Botswana was the poor and peripheral British Protectorate known as Bechuanaland. The country was named after its dominant ethnic group, the Tswana, and the national language was Setswana (Parsons, 1999). The citizens of Botswana are referred to as Batswana (which is plural, and singular is Motswana).[1]

The original inhabitants of Botswana were the San, followed by the Khoi and Bantu speakers. Therefore, the history and culture of Botswana can be traced among these groups. The San and the Khoi are often referred to as the Khoisan. It was around the late 18th and early 19th centuries when other Tswana groups evolved, and consequently different tribes were established. In 1885, when Botswana's national security was under threat from the Boers of Transvaal and the Ndebele of today's Zimbabwe, the Bangwato leader, Khama III, and other Tswana chiefs, Bathoeng Gaseitsiwe of the Bangwaketsi and Sebele I of the Bakwena, sought the British protection through the support of the missionaries. British protection was established on March 31, 1885, and the area was named Bechuanaland. At that time, the country was divided into two parts such that the northern part of Botswana was put under the direct administration of the British while the southern part became a part of the Cape Colony.[1]

During the years when Botswana was under the British protection, there was political freedom, no war of liberation, and more importantly there were very few differences between Botswana's leaders and the Bechuanaland Protectorate administrators. Between the late 1950s and early 1960s, there were political developments which motivated the desire for self-rule.[2] After some requests for self-government, in 1964, Britain acceded to the requests, paving the way for Botswana's preparation to self-government. Political parties were formed; the first was the Bechuanaland People's Party founded in 1960, followed by the Bechuanaland Democratic Party (which is now called Botswana Democratic Party) in 1962. The Constitution of Botswana, which led to the first general elections, was drawn in 1965, and the Botswana Democratic Party won the first elections. Sir Seretse Khama, its leader, was named Botswana's first president. The country's independence was officially declared on September 30, 1966, and the name was changed from Bechuanaland to Botswana, with Gaborone as the capital city.[2]

Size and Geography

Botswana is a landlocked, semiarid country, covering about 581,730 square kilometers, about the size of France or the state of Texas in the United States. The land mass constitutes 566,730 square kilometers, and the remaining 15,000 are composed of water bodies. It is located in the center of southern Africa and shares borders with South Africa in the south and east, Namibia in the west, and Zimbabwe and Zambia in the north (**FIGURE 20-1**).

It is located in the subtropical high-pressure belt of the southern hemisphere, away from the oceanic front; as a result, the temperatures are high. There is high interannual viability of rainfall, and drought is recurrent, which adversely affects farming and seriously impairs the rural economy and sociocultural structures. Summers are hot, with an average temperature of 39°C (89.6°F). Rains are usually from October to April. The winter season runs from May through July and is cold and dry at night and warm during the day.[3]

Botswana has dry and sandy soils, which accounts for the varied population distribution, with the majority

FIGURE 20-1 Map of Botswana
© Rainer Lesniewski/Shutterstock

of the population concentrated in the eastern belt of the country, where there are relatively arable soils for agriculture. The Okavango Delta in the northwestern part of the country is one of the country's major water bodies. The combination of high temperatures and moderate amounts of rainfall in the Okavango Delta area creates an optimal environment for the breeding of mosquitoes that transmit malaria. The most common natural hazards for Botswana are overgrazing, drought, and veldt fires.[3] The terrain is predominately flat with gentle undulation and occasional rocky outcrops. The Kalahari Desert occupies most of the southwestern part of the country. The country has an elevation of 531 meters above sea level at the lowest point (at the junction of the Limpopo and Shahe rivers) and 1,489 meters at the highest point (Tsodilo Hills).[4]

Government and Political System

Botswana attained self-rule from the United Kingdom after 80 years under the British Protectorate in 1965 and became an independent country on September 30, 1966. The country is a republic constitution, based on a unicameral Westminster parliamentary system of government with a "first-past-the-post" (FPTP), or "the-winner-takes-all," electoral system. The FPTP is based on a single-member constituency system, in which a candidate with the plurality of vote is elected a Member of Parliament. The United Kingdom and India also practice the FPTP electoral system.[5] Botswana has three distinct branches: executive, legislative, and judiciary.

The president is the head of state, commander-in-chief of the armed forces, and in charge of the government. The president presides over the cabinet of ministers, who are all drawn from the national assembly.[1] The vice president of the country is second in command. Parliament consists of a National Assembly of elected members from multiple political parties and six specially elected members from the ruling party. The first multiparty national election was held in 1965. Since then, the country has held multiparty elections every five years, and the last elections were held in October 2014.[1]

The Botswana judicial system consists of four branches: the Court of Appeals, the High Court, magistrate courts, and the customary courts. The Court of Appeals is the highest legal branch of the judicial system and deals with appeals from the High Court. The High Court is the appeals court for magistrate and customary courts and has jurisdiction over capital offenses, such as murder and treason. The magistrate courts handle all offenses except for capital offenses, and the customary courts deal with offenses concerning property, inheritance, and personal arbitration in rural areas.[3] Botswana has also a *Ntlo ya Dikgosi* (House of Chiefs) composed of 8 permanent members representing major ethnic groups (Tswana-speaking ethnic groups) and 27 representatives from other ethnic groups. The chiefs advise government on matters affecting custom and tradition, including draft bills, which they review before consideration by Parliament.[3]

Administrative Structure of the Central Government

Permanent secretaries in each government ministry manage administrative structures of the central government, with a permanent secretary to the president as the head of the civil service. The civil service falls under the Directorate of Public Service Management. Botswana is divided into sixteen administrative districts that are composed of two city councils, four town councils, and ten district councils. The central government is represented in each district by a district commissioner. At the political level, the city/town council is headed by a mayor, while the central government is represented by a city/town clerk. In a district council, the council chairperson heads the political side while the council secretary heads the central government side. Botswana has 16 administrative districts, with Gaborone as the capital city.[3]

Macroeconomics

The World Bank classifies Botswana as an upper middle-income country, and it has one of the fastest growing economies. The discovery of mineral deposits soon after independence in 1967, combined with prudent management of the economy, transformed Botswana into one of the richest countries in southern Africa. The country has a relatively better infrastructure for social services, such as better health and education than most other countries in the Southern African Development Community region. Before the discovery of mineral wealth, Botswana was one of the poorest countries in the world and depended on beef exports and migrant labor remittance from Batswana men who worked in the South African mines.[3] Botswana has resource-intensive production that is dominated by diamond mining, which contributes more than one-third of the gross domestic product (GDP) (TABLE 20-2).

Botswana is a member of the Southern African Customs Union (SACU), which provides a standard tariff regime and revenue sharing among participating countries based on an agreed formula. Other major GDP sectors are shown in Table 20-2.[6] Botswana's economic policy rests on a budget sustainability ratio that is measured by the extent to which government's non-investment, recurrent expenditures are being financed by recurring sustainable revenues to ensure macroeconomic stability. The policy is instrumental in planning and guiding budgetary prudence, particularly given the unsustainability of mineral revenues. Fiscal rules limit government expenditures to 40% of GDP and outstanding public loans and guaranteed public loans to 20% of GDP each for internal and external debt. Botswana's tax system is considered robust and nondistortionary. The value-added tax of 12% in 2016 is lower than other countries in the SACU region. Income tax rates are progressively applied to income levels, ranging from 5% to 25% for the high-earning brackets. Nonetheless, Botswana needs to enhance its tax administration system.[6]

The Botswana monetary policy is aimed at achieving an inflation rate within the range of 3% and 6%. Since 2007, the inflation rate has, however, consistently overshot the upper band of the target. The annual inflation rate in October 2016 averaged 2.7%.[7] One of the major macroeconomic challenges that Botswana faces is the high level of poverty, inequality, and unemployment, as well as the high HIV/AIDS prevalence rate.[6]

Demographics

The 2016 population estimates based on the *2011 Housing and Population Census* give a population of 2,209,208 in Botswana, showing an intercensal annual growth rate of 1.2%. Females accounted for 49.1% of the national population, reflecting a gender ratio of 1.04 males per 100 females (see TABLE 20-1). The population density increased from 1 person per square kilometer in 1971 to 3.5 people per square kilometer in 2011.[7]

Population Age Structure

Botswana's population has remained relatively young, with 53.7% under 25 years old in 2016. About 32.4% of the population is under 15 years old, and 4.1% are aged 65 years and above (FIGURE 20-2). However, the population age structure suggests that Botswana is gradually becoming older. For example, in the 1971 census, Botswana's median age was 15 years, compared to 23.2 years in the 2016 projected population. The 2011 census data showed a resurgence of the 0–4 year age group, which had declined in the 2001 census as a result of HIV-related mortality. The changing pattern in this age group reflects the success of the antiretroviral therapy and the programs to prevent mother to child transmission, ensuring survival of infants and children, most of whom are born without the virus.[7]

TABLE 20-2 General Domestic Product by Sector

Sector	2006	2011
Agriculture, forestry, fishing, and hunting	1.9	2.6
Mining and quarrying	46.1	34.7
Manufacturing	3.5	4.2
Electricity, gas, and water	2.7	3.1
Construction	4.3	5.7
Wholesale and retail, hotels and restaurants	11.1	14.4
Transport, storage, and communication	3.9	4.9
Finance, real estate, and business services	6.2	7.4
General government services	16.4	18.4
Other services	3.9	4.6
GDP at basic price/cost factor	**100**	**100**

Data from AfDB, OECD, UNDP. Botswana. In *African Economic Outlook 2015: Regional Development and Spatial Inclusion*. Paris: OECD Publishing; 2015.

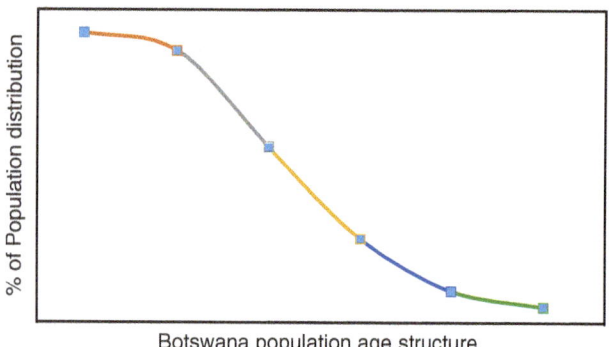

FIGURE 20-2 The Distribution of Botswana Population by Age Categories

Data from Ministry of Finance and Development Planning, Central Statistics Office. Project document: 2011 population and housing census. http://unstats.un.org/unsd/Demographic/sources/census/wphc/Botswana/census%20project.pdf. August 2009.

Fertility Rate

In 2011, 54.4% of the women in Botswana were childbearing age (15–49 years old), representing 27.8% of the population. However, these statistics indicate rapid decline in the total fertility rate (the average number of children likely to be born to a woman over her lifetime). For example, in 1991, the total fertility rate was 6.6 children per woman compared to 2.7 in 2011[7] and 2.3 in 2016 (see Table 20-1).

Growth and Crude Deaths Rates

The 2016 annual growth rate has also been declining, probably due to the slowdown in natural increase and in net migration. One of the threats to industrialization and economic diversification is the country's small population size. Decreasing fertility and short life expectancy are a threat to the realization of a critical population mass to sustain industrialization and economic growth.[7] Between 1991 and 2001, the level of mortality went up, mainly as a result of the increased number of deaths associated with the HIV/AIDS epidemic. As a result of the introduction of free antiretroviral (ARV) drugs, mortality declined over the intercensal period between 2001 and 2016. This demographic change has resulted from socioeconomic change and investment in public health and other social services by the government of Botswana.[7]

Urbanization

Urbanization has been increasing since 2001. Between 2010 and 2015, for example, urbanization increased at a rate of 1.3% and was estimated to be 57.4% in 2015.[8] Urbanization in Botswana is a product of three factors, namely reclassification of previously rural settlements, migration, and natural increase. Botswana reclassified some of the villages to urban status, once they exceeded a certain population size threshold and attained a minimal functional characteristic. This is a positive development because the new urban villages will now be entitled to the allocation of better infrastructure and social services, commensurate with their populations, functions, and status in the settlement hierarchy.[9]

Economically Active Population

In 2016, the working-age population (15–64 years) was 1.2 million. The dependency ratio (children aged under 15 years and people aged 65 years and over), on the other hand, decreased from 71.5 in 2001 to 56.7 in 2011. The decline reflects an increase in the size of the economically active cohort and a decline in the children and infant category, as well as a decline in the population of the elderly.[9]

Poverty

Although there has been a decline in the percentage of people living below the national poverty line, the poverty level is still high in Botswana. The country experiences an unemployment rate of around 17.5% coupled with vast income inequality (with a Gini coefficient of 0.6), among the highest in the world. More than 30% of the youth, particularly the girls, are unemployed. The unemployment rate is linked to a mismatch of education quality with market demands.[5]

▸ Brief History of the Healthcare System

Pre-Independence Health System

There was little development of the health system in Bechuanaland under the British Protectorate. Having reluctantly assumed responsibility of the high commission territories of Botswana, Swaziland, and Lesotho, the British colonial government grossly neglected these countries politically, socially, and economically for 50 years.[10] The development of the pre-independence health system is accredited to the missionaries (Seventh Day Adventists, London Missionary Society, and Dutch Reformed Church) in Bechuanaland. The Dutch Reformed Church started to unofficially administer simple drugs as early as 1887. However, it was not until 1922, when the Seventh Day Adventist missionaries constructed the first mission hospital, that the beginning of today's Botswana health system can be marked.[10] The first colonial government hospital was constructed in 1930 and another one was in 1931. The colonial medical services were concentrated in the eastern part of the country close to the railway line, which provided means of communication for a small fraction of the population. Consequently, the majority of the citizens were largely neglected.[10]

During this period, the Batswana population was largely rural and preferred traditional doctors for their medical care because modern Western medicine was too expensive, too inaccessible, and too untested for most rural people. Traditional medicine was well known and believed in, and it was more accessible and affordable. When Botswana gained independence in 1966, there were five mission hospitals and four government hospitals in the country. There was only a skeleton of qualified staff, and the country did not have a ministry responsible for health.[11]

Description of the Current Healthcare System

Leadership and Governance

The Botswana health system has significantly evolved since the establishment of the Ministry of Health and Wellness (MoHW) in 1975 into one of the relatively more advanced health systems in southern Africa. The MoHW has the responsibility for the overall delivery, improvement, and maintenance of national health. It sets broad policy directions, goals, and strategies for health development and delivery under the political leadership of the minister of health and her/his assistant. The permanent secretary and three deputies for health/clinical services, technical support services, and corporate services head the executive arm of the ministry. Under the deputy permanent secretaries are six directors for these departments:

- Policy, Planning, Monitoring and Evaluation
- AIDS Prevention and Care
- Clinical Services
- Public Health
- Health Inspectorate
- Corporate Services[12]

Following the reorganization of the MoHW's operations, all primary healthcare services that had been provided by the Ministry of Local Government and Rural Development migrated to the MoHW, with an exception of environmental health services at the district level. The responsibility for all public health facilities at the district level lies with the 27 district health management teams, each of which has a designated geographical area; this is the decentralized model of health service delivery (**FIGURE 20-3**). The district health management teams are organized into curative, preventive, and corporate services. The teams develop plans aligned to the national health strategies and negotiate budgetary allocation with the MoHW annually.[12]

Model of Service Delivery

The Botswana health system is modeled on the primary healthcare perspective. The current Botswana

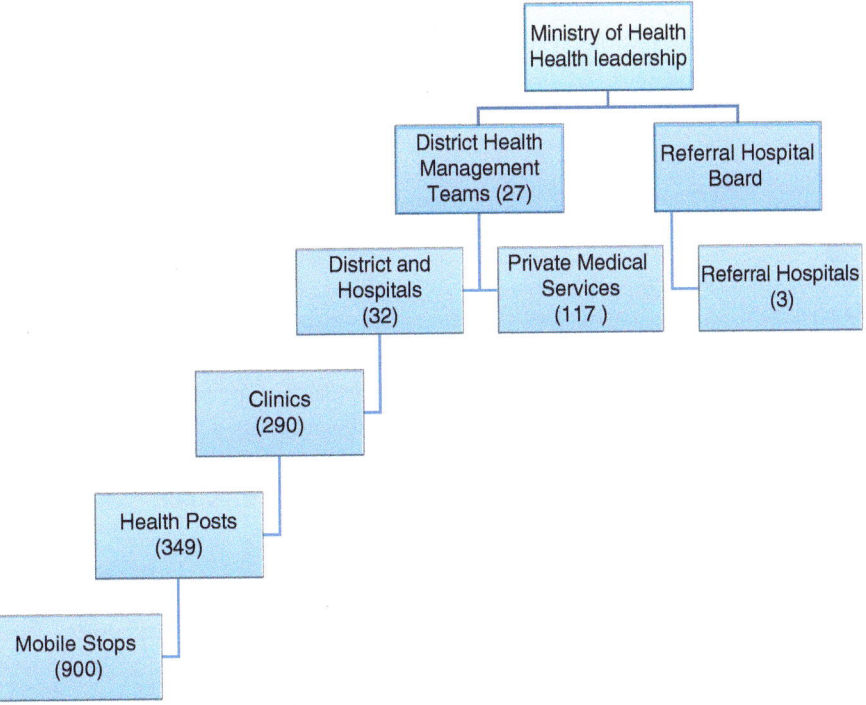

FIGURE 20-3 Botswana's Decentralized Health Service Delivery System

health system policies and strategies show that the country is making progressive reforms toward achieving evidence care and the values of equity in health.[13]

Policy development is guided by Vision 2030 with health goals set in the National Development Plan 11 (2017–2022). The Integrated Health Services Plan (2010–2020) and the revised National Health Policy (2011) are the flagship documents of the MoHW. Other key policy documents put in place to advance health service delivery include the HIV policy, an accelerated child survival and development strategy; the national road map for reduction of maternal and newborn mortality; the noncommunicable disease policy and strategic plan; the national cervical cancer strategy; the health promotion strategy; the accountability framework on women and children's health; the Libreville declaration on health and environment; and the malaria elimination strategic plan.[13]

Corporation for Health

The country adopted the sector-wide approach to improve collaboration and coordination of health services.[13] The MoHW and its partners have been discussing better ways to support the harmonization and alignment of health services. These partners include the Ministry of Local Government and Rural Development, the National AIDS Coordination Agency (NACA), bilateral organizations (such as the U.S. government, through United States Aid for International Development), the President's Emergency Plan for AIDS Relief, Centers for Disease Control and Prevention (CDC), the European Union, multilaterals agencies (such as the United Nations family), local and international NGOs, academia, and public and private medical aid societies.[13]

Health Facilities

The Botswana health system consists of public, private for-profit, faith-based, and private nonprofit medicine practices. In 2016, the public sector was the primary provider of health services and operated 80.0% of the health facilities. The services are decentralized to the district level and delivered through a hierarchical network of public, mission, mine and private medical services.[14] The master list of health facilities published in 2015, effective until March 2017, reported that Botswana had 697 public and private (including mission and mine) facilities composed of 3 referral hospitals, 15 district hospitals, 17 primary hospitals, 318 clinics, and 347 health posts. In addition, there were 128 private medical practices in most urban health districts. In 2016, the government operated 973 mobile stops in hard to reach rural areas.[14]

Health Workforce

The MoHW is the major health human resource training agency in the country, training healthcare providers in the field for nursing, midwifery, pharmacy, medical laboratory, dental therapy, health education, and more. The University of Botswana offers both undergraduate and graduate degrees in nursing, medical laboratory, environmental health, and medicine. The medical school was established in 2007, and the first group of medical students was admitted in 2009. Prior to 2009, all doctors were trained outside the country. The development priority has been aimed at increasing both the numbers and the skill mix of the healthcare workforce and has steadily progressed over time. The density of doctors and nurses per 10,000 population increased to 4.0 and 42.0, respectively by 2014.[15]

In 2014, there were 13,713 health workers in clinical practice registered with the Botswana Health Professional Council (BHPC) and the Nurses Midwifery Council of Botswana (NMCB). Batswana made up 41% of all health professionals registered with BHPC and 84% of the nurses registered with NMCB. There were 1,820 doctors, of whom only 21% were Batswana. Batswana accounted for 39% of physiotherapists, 13% of radiographers, and 35% of optometrists registered as professional healthcare workers.[15] Despite heavy investments in human resource development, about 69% of the medical doctors practicing in Botswana are foreign nationals, largely from Zimbabwe, the Democratic Republic of Congo, and other African nations.[15]

In 2014, 47% of the registered doctors and 25% of the registered nurses worked in the country's two cities (Gaborone and Francistown). Data suggest that about 4 in every 10 healthcare professionals work in Botswana in the 2 referral hospitals in Gaborone and Francistown and that about 26% of nurses were working in primary, district, and referral hospitals. Botswana has yet to devise strategies for luring externally trained Botswana doctors back to their country to serve their people.[15]

Technology and Equipment

The country and the donor community has made strides in technology and equipment for health. From a policy platform, under the Clinical Services Department, the country has a policy on health technology and has a national drug list and an essential drug list.[16,17] The overall aim is to provide medical equipment and drugs of acceptable safety, efficacy, and quality; to make them available and affordable to all who need them; and to ensure their rational use by providers, dispensers, and users. The management of medical drugs is computerized to keep up with the need to process drug procurement and distribution efficiently.[17]

However, current national technology policy is not part of the national health policy, and the country does not have an approved list of medical devices. Analysis of selected medical equipment (0.495 per 1 million population for magnetic resonance imaging, 0.990 per 1 million for computerized scanners, and 19.1 per 1 million population for mammograms for females aged 50–69 years) indicate the lack of critical equipment to improve the diagnostic quality for chronic respiratory diseases and breast cancer in the country.[17] The WHO Country Office in Botswana noted that the availability of health information that is necessary for planning, timely interventions, and monitoring and evaluation remains a big challenge in the health sector.[18] While remarkable progress has been made in some programs, particularly in HIV/AIDS laboratory diagnosis, there are still major gaps in articulation and use of data, which result in a lack of proper monitoring and assessment frameworks. In addition, there are inconsistencies in health information, particularly related to the main indicators, reported by different programs and partners, including United Nations agencies. Botswana also suffers from the shortage of skilled staff in areas such as radiology.[18]

Evaluation of the Healthcare System

Cost

Health financing is one of the major factors used to evaluate whether the health system has adequate funding to enable citizens to have access to health services. Botswana is one of the few African countries that has achieved the target set in the Abuja Declaration, which called for dedicating about 15% or more of the government expenditure to health care and to spending over US $44 per capita on health care.[19] The 2010 government expenditure on health, $444.70 per capita, provided a high level of financial risk protection for its population. The 2010 national health account showed an increase in health expenditure, as a percentage of GDP, from 5.3% in 2007/2008 to 6.3% in 2009/2010 (TABLE 20-3).

The 2010 health data showed that 70.2% of health expenditure was allocated to curative/clinical services, of which 51.0% was spent on inpatient services. The World Health Organization states that more spending on prevention and public health services is an efficient allocation of resources because the benefits of curative care accrue to the individual and not to the general population (i.e., curative care is less of a public good than prevention or public health). In 2010, hospitals were the largest recipient, consuming an average of 26.6% of THE, and the general health administration consumed 17.1% of THE. Preventive and public health programs received an average of 8.7%.[19]

TABLE 20-3 Botswana Health Expenditure and Health Outcome Performance Indicators Compared with Other Upper Middle-Income Countries

Countries	THE* per capita (US$)	Health outcome performance indicators			
		IMR** per 1,000 live births	MMR*** per 100,000 live births	Life expectancy
Botswana	444.7	43	190	54.4
Mauritius	377.5	13	36	73.0
Namibia	258.0	34	18	57.0

* THE = Total health expenditure
** IMR = Infant mortality rate
*** MMR = Maternal mortality rate
Data from Botswana Ministry of Health of Health. National health accounts.

The major health financing agent in Botswana is the national government, which controls an average of 43.6% of THE followed by the medical aid schemes. Other financing agents include NACA, the donor community, and household direct out-of-pocket payments at an average of 4.2%. The major sources of the private health funds (65%) are contributions to medical aid schemes, while private companies and parastatal organizations contribute an average of 35%. These findings reinforce the government's desire to introduce social health insurance and mandate all employers to provide health insurance for their employees and to fund other healthcare activities as part of their social responsibility.[19]

Current cost data underscore two fundamental health issues. First, given the low percentage of out-of-pocket financing, cost may not be a universal barrier to access basic healthcare services in Botswana. Second, with a high THE spent in hospitals and fewer resources going to preventive services, the Botswana health system can be characterized as hospital-based. With the changing epidemiological profile with noncommunicable diseases emerging as major public health threats, there will be a need to shift some resources toward community-based health extension programs.[19]

Quality

The Health and Medicine Division (HMD) defines the quality of care as the extent to which health services for individuals and populations increase the likelihood of desired results.[20] The definition underscores the need for evidence-based approaches that meet desired health outcomes. Improved quality of care improves the use of limited resources, reduces costs, and strengthens healthcare leadership, governance, and accountability.[21]

Botswana has some of the world's most successful and high-quality health programs. The aggressive national response and the country's leadership commitment have resulted in successes in the use of antiretroviral therapy (ART) and prevention of mother to child transmission of HIV (PMTCT). The national PMTCT program has provided ART to 96.8% of HIV pregnant mothers, which has contributed to the decline of infants born HIV-infected to 2.2%.[31] The national Antiretroviral Treatment Program, which made treatment available to all eligible Batswana, has significantly reduced premature deaths among HIV-infected parents and improved the health outcomes.[22]

Despite the remarkable successes in the quality of care in the HIV/AIDS programs, quality improvement studies suggest the Botswana health system lacks the culture of quality improvement. Studies on the pneumoconiosis-based chronic care model found that the primary healthcare settings lacked a reasonably good enough standard of care to provide quality of care for pneumoconiosis patients.[23] In a performance assessment study of the health system, it was found that the government hospitals lacked quality improvement structures to foster care.[24] In a root-cause analysis of maternal deaths in referral hospitals, researchers found that most professional healthcare workers failed to recognize the seriousness of patients' conditions and in most instances failed to follow recommended clinical practice guidelines, policies, and protocols. The study found that most of the maternal deaths in referral hospitals could have been avoided with improved quality of care.[25]

Studies suggest that although Botswana spends more on health than Mauritius and Namibia, some of the core health systems health outcomes have remained poor. Health outcome indicators, such as infant mortality rate, maternal mortality rate, and life expectancy are lower than Namibia and Mauritius, probably due to low quality of care (Table 20-3).

Access

Strong health systems are fundamental to maintaining good health throughout the life cycle.[26] Between 1966 and 2016, Botswana made enormous efforts to increase access to health service. The 2015 estimates suggest that 95% of the urban population lived within 5 kilometers of a health facility, and in rural areas 72% of the population lived within 8 kilometers of the nearest public health facility. There were 828 health delivery points (public, private, mission, faith-based, and parastatal) with an additional 973 mobile stops in hard to reach rural areas.[14] In addition, health services among citizens are free in the public health sector. With the low out-of-pocket rate, factors other than cost may be the major barrier to health service access among most of the disadvantaged population in the country.

However, it is important to note that availability of health infrastructure alone may not promote access to health services. Studies suggest that some of the barriers to equitable access to health services in Botswana include a lack of professionally specialized healthcare workers, especially in rural areas. There is also distance to hospitals, low health literacy, patients' demographic characteristics, and a lack of technology and equipment (in most clinics and health posts where the majority of the population live).[23] There are, therefore, still pockets of Batswana who lack equal access to preventive, diagnostic, and curative services in the country. The curative-based nature of service is another major barrier to access of health services, especially for noncommunicable diseases and neglected diseases, such as pneumoconiosis among the elderly population in rural areas.

Innovation

The healthcare industry has experienced a proliferation of innovations aimed at enhancing life expectancy, quality of life, diagnostic and treatment options, as well as efficiency and cost effectiveness. Information technology (IT) has played a vital role in the innovation of healthcare systems.[27]

Innovative approaches to enhance health services in Botswana started as early as 2003 with the introduction of a computer-based patient tracking system in Botswana's national antiretroviral program in Gaborone. The program was replaced a year later with an integrated patient management system to centralize health data. The effectiveness of the computer-based tracking systems was limited due to the short time the system was used.[28] In 2010, the Botswana–University of Pennsylvania Partnership piloted mobile technology for telemedicine in the specialties of women's health (cervical cancer screening utilizing visual inspection with acetic acid), radiology, oral medicine, and dermatology. The results suggest that the innovation improved access to healthcare resources. However, the innovation faced both technical and social challenges, such as unreliable IT infrastructure and cultural misalignment between IT and healthcare providers.[29] Studies in the health informatics suggest technological innovations have not fully penetrated the health sector in Botswana because most facilities are still using paper-based health record management systems. The 2015 study suggests that there are several (but fragmented) technological initiatives in the health system. The study found that the challenges in harnessing innovation are due to weak leadership, lack of regulatory framework, and inadequate resources to advance innovations in the health sector.[30]

▸ Current and Emerging Challenges

Current Challenges

Despite political and health leadership demonstrated in the fight against HIIV/AIDS, Botswana still faces the most severe HIV/AIDS burden in the world, with the national HIV prevalence estimated at 18.5%. HIV/AIDS remains a leading health, economic, social, and developmental challenge.[31] Botswana also suffers from a high prevalence of TB, childhood diseases, and high maternal morbidity and mortality rates. As a result, the health system is oriented toward clinical care for communicable diseases rather than noncommunicable care.[32] The health sector lacks adequate professional healthcare workers as well as equipment and drugs, especially in rural areas. The health information system remains weak, and the capacity to use information for program planning lags behind in several areas.

Emerging Challenges

Botswana has been experiencing a steady increase in noncommunicable diseases. A countrywide survey of people aged 50 years and above seeking health services revealed that 67.0% had hypertension and 12.4% had diabetes. The survey also revealed the increasing trend of cardiovascular diseases, cancers, and chronic respiratory diseases.[32] Botswana, along with other southern African countries, bears a disproportionately high burden of chronic respiratory diseases among men who worked in the South African mines. The 2015 study in Botswana suggests pneumoconiosis (silicosis, asbestosis, and coal worker's pneumoconiosis) is neglected in the primary healthcare settings due to lack of clinical structure and process to address the problem.[23] To these emerging disorders and conditions, Botswana will need to develop a response using community-based partnerships and resources to promote preventive and health promotion services. Addressing noncommunicable diseases will also need committed leadership and a responsive, prepared, and committed health workforce.

References

1. Parsons QN. Botswana history index. University of Botswana. Department of History. http://ubh.tripod.com/bw/index.html. Published 1999. Accessed May 20, 2016.
2. Fawcus P, Tilbury A. *Botswana: The Road to Independence*. Gaborone, Botswana: Pula Press and The Botswana Society; 2000.
3. Ministry of Finance and Development Planning. *National Development Plan* 10. April 2009–March 2016. Gaborone, Botswana: Government Printing and Publishing Services; 2009.
4. Central Intelligence Agency. *The World Factbook 2016*. Botswana. Washington, DC: 2016. http://www.cia.gov/library/publication/the-world-factbook/index.html. Accessed November 19. 2016.
5. Molomo MG. In search of an alternative electoral system for Botswana. *Botswana Journal of African Studies*. 2000;14(1):109–121.
6. African Development Bank, OECD Development Centre, and United Nations Development Program. *African Economic Outlook 2016*. doi: http://dx.doi.org/10.1787/aeo-2016-en
7. Gwebu TD, Mphetolang G, Baakile T. Population distribution, density and policy implication in Botswana. In: *Statistics Botswana. Population and Housing Census Analytical Report*. Gaborone, Botswana: Statistics Botswana; 2014:2–16.

8. Gwebu TD. Urbanization patterns and processes and their policy implication in Botswana. In: *Statistics Botswana. Population and Housing Census Analytical Report*. Gaborone, Botswana: Statistics Botswana; 2014:168–181.
9. Mmopelwa D, Lekobane KR. Assessing household wealth status: an asset based approach. In: *Statistics Botswana: Population and Housing Census Analytical Report*. Gaborone, Botswana: Statistics Botswana; 2014:17–25.
10. Molefi, RK. *Medical History of Botswana*. Gaborone, Botswana: Botswana Society; 1996.
11. Ministry of Health. *Financing of the Health Services and Activities in Botswana: Second Study*. Gaborone, Botswana: Government Printers; 1979.
12. Personal communication [Styn Jamu] with the principal health officer in the Department of Policy, Planning, Monitoring and Evaluation in the Ministry of Health on May 20, 2016.
13. World Health Organization. *Botswana Country Corporation Strategy at a Glance*. Gaborone, Botswana: World Health Organization, Country Office; 2014.
14. Ministry of Health. *Master Health Facility List for 2015–2017*. Gaborone, Botswana: Ministry of Health; 2015.
15. Nkomazana O, Peersman W, Willcox M, et al. Human resources for health in Botswana: the results of in-country database and reports analysis. *Afr J Prm Health Care Fam Med*. 2014;6(1):E1–8. doi:10.4102/phcfm.v6i1.716
16. Ministry of Health. *Botswana National Drug Policy*. Gaborone: Botswana: Ministry of Health; 2005.
17. World Health Organization. *Global Atlas of Medical Devices 2014. Botswana. Country Indicators*. Geneva, Switzerland: World Health Organization, 2014.
18. Botswana Ministry of Health. *Botswana Country Progress Report 2013*. Gaborone, Botswana: National AIDS Coordinating Agency; 2014.
19. Ministry of Health. (2012). *National Health Accounts: Financial Years*. 2007/2008, 2008/2009, and 2009/2010. Bethesda, Maryland: Abt Associates.
20. Institute of Medicine (IOM). *Performance Measurement: Accelerating Improvement*. Washington, DC: National Academies Press; 2006.
21. Leatherman S, Ferris TG, Berwick D, et al. The role of quality improvement in strengthening health systems in developing countries. *Int J Qual Health Care*. 2010;22(4):237–243.
22. National AIDS Coordinating Agency. *Progress Report of the National Response to the 2011 Declaration of Commitments on HIV and AIDS*. Gaborone, Botswana: National AIDS Coordinating Agency; 2014.
23. Jamu SM. Systems *Approach to Managing Chronic Occupational Respiratory Disorders: Shared Path to Improving the Pneumoconiosis Screening Program for South African Ex-Miners in Botswana* [dissertation]. Mount Pleasant: Central Michigan University; 2015.
24. Seitio-Kgokgwe O, Gauld RDC, Hill PC, et al. Assessing performance of Botswana's public hospital system: the use of the World Health Organization health system performance assessment framework. *Int J Health Policy Manag*. 2014;3(4):179–189.
25. Madzimbamuto FD, Ray SC, Magobe KD, et al. A root-cause analysis of maternal deaths in Botswana: towards developing a culture of patient safety and quality improvement. *BMC Pregnancy Childbirth*; 2014;14:231. doi: 10.1186/1471-2393-14-231
26. World Health Organization. Regional Office for Africa. *WHO Country Cooperation Strategy 2008–2013*. Botswana. Brazzaville, Republic of Congo: World Health Organization; 2009.
27. Omachon VK, Einspruch NG. Innovation in healthcare delivery systems: A conceptual framework. *The Innovation Journal*. 2010;15(1):Article 2.
28. Bussmann H, Wester WC, Ndwapi N, et al. Hybrid data for capturing patients on highly active retroviral therapy (HAART) in urban Botswana. *Bulletin of the World Health Organization*. 2006;84(2):127–131.
29. Littman-Quinn R, Mibenge C, Antwi C, et al. Implementation of m-health applications in Botswana: telemedicine and education on mobile devices in a low resource setting. *Journal of Telemedicine and Telecare*; 2013. doi: 10.1177/1357633X12474746
30. Seitio-Kgokgwe O, Gauld RDC, Hill PC, et al. Development of the National Health Information Systems in Botswana: pitfalls, prospects, and lessons. *Online Journal of Public Health Informatics*. 2015;7(2):e210.
31. Statistics Botswana. *Botswana AIDS Impact Survey IV (BAIS IV)*. Gaborone, Botswana: Statistics Botswana; 2014.
32. Ministry of Health. (2011). *National Health Policy: Towards a Healthier Botswana*. Gaborone, Botswana: Bay Publishing (Pty) Ltd.

CHAPTER 21

Bangladesh

Amal K. Mitra and **Manzoor Hussain**

▶ Country Description

TABLE 21-1	Bangladesh
Nationality	Noun: Bangladeshi(s) Adjective: Bangladeshi
Ethnic groups	Bengali about 99%, at least 54 ethnic groups 1.1%
Religions	Muslim 89.1%, Hindu 10.0%, other (Buddhist and Christian) 0.9%
Language	Bangla (or Bengali) 98.8%, other 1.2%
Literacy	Definition: Age 15 and over can read and write. Total population: 61.5% Male: 64.6% Female: 58.5%
Government type	Parliamentary republic
Date of independence	December 16, 1971
Gross Domestic Product (GDP) per capita	$3,600 per capita (2015 est.)
Unemployment rate	4.9% (2015 est.)
Natural hazards	Droughts, cyclones, much of the country routinely inundated during the summer monsoon season

(continues)

TABLE 21-1 Bangladesh (*continued*)	
Environment: current issues	Many people landless and forced to live on and cultivate flood-prone land; waterborne diseases prevalent in surface water; water pollution from commercial pesticides, especially an issue in fishing areas; ground water contaminated by naturally occurring arsenic; intermittent water shortages due to falling water tables in northern and central parts of the country; soil degradation and erosion; deforestation; severe overpopulation
Population	156,186,882 (July 2016 est.)
Age structure	0–14 years: 28.27% (male 22,456,564/female 21,695,491) 15–24 years: 19.53% (male 15,261,363/female 15,247,635) 25–54 years: 39.39% (male 29,565,250/female 31,951,537) 55–64 years: 6.77% (male 5,232,828/female 5,342,822) 65 years and over: 6.04% (male 4,493,557/female 4,939,835) (2016 est.)
Median age	Total: 26.3 years Male: 25.6 years Female: 26.9 years
Population growth rate	1.05% (2016 est.)
Birth rate	19 births/1,000 population
Death rate	847 deaths/100,000 population
Disease burden	Communicable disease deaths: 235/100,000 population Noncommunicable disease deaths: 549/100,000 population Injury deaths: 64/100,000 population (2016 est.)
Net migration rate	−3.1 migrant(s)/1,000 population
Gender ratio	At birth: 1.04 male(s)/female Under 14 years: 1.04 male(s)/female 15–24 years: 1.0 male(s)/female 25–54 years: 0.93 male(s)/female 55–64 years: 0.98 male(s)/female 65 years and over: 0.97 male(s)/female Total population: 0.97 male(s)/female (2016 est.)
Infant mortality rate	Total: 32.9 deaths/1,000 live births Male: 35.2 deaths/1,000 live births Female: 30.4 deaths/1,000 live births
Life expectancy at birth	Total population: 73.2 years Male: 71.02 years Female: 75.48 years
Total fertility rate	2.19 children born/woman
HIV/AIDS adult prevalence rate	0.01% (2014 est.)
Number of people living with HIV/AIDS	9,600 (2015 est.)
HIV/AIDS deaths	900 (2015 est.)

Data from Central Intelligence Agency. The World Fact Book, 2016: Bangladesh. https://www.cia.gov/library/publications/the-world-factbook/.

History

Bangladesh became an independent country through a nine-month war against the regime of Pakistan in 1971. Bangladesh, formerly known as East Pakistan, was a part of Pakistan but is physically separated from West Pakistan by 1,600 kilometers of Indian land. In 1952 Mohammad Ali Jinnah, the national leader of Pakistan, declared Urdu as the official language of the entire country. The people in East Pakistan, who speak Bengali, protested the declaration and broke out in violence, which led to the language movement of the country in 1952. This incidence sparkled a feeling that the Bengali people of East Pakistan were deprived of their rights and were being oppressed by the rulers of West Pakistan. In 1969, there was a mass movement in East Pakistan against the military ruler Ayub Khan. The following year in a general election, the political party of Awami League, led by the sheikh Mujibur Rahman, made a landslide victory, winning 167 of 169 seats from East Pakistan and thus secured an absolute majority in the 313-seat parliament of Pakistan. Unfortunately, the military presidents Yahya and Khan did not want to hand over the power to the sheikh Mujibur Rahman. Rather, the military forces of West Pakistan launched a sudden attack on the general public on the night of the 25th of March, which eventually led to the liberation war of Bangladesh. The Indian army became directly involved in the war for liberation of Bangladesh from Pakistan. They provided training and ammunition to the soldiers of Bangladesh, Mukti Bahini (freedom fighters). The Indian government provided shelter, food, and health care for nearly 10 million refugees from East Pakistan. Finally, Bangladesh got the victory on December 16, 1971, and became an independent country.

The culture of Bengal evolved through several phases. The first phase was dominated by Buddhism, followed by Buddhism and Jainism in the third century BCE. Bangladesh remains the establishment of Buddhist educational centers, with residential facilities from the 8th to 12th centuries CE, in Moinamoti in the district of Comilla. From the 12th century, under royal patronage of the Sena rulers, there was a revival of Brahmanical Hinduism. Vaishnavism grew to be popular under the leadership of Sri Sri Chaitanya Mahaprobhu, from the end of the 15th century onward. Islam first arrived in Bengal during the 8th century CE. Bengal first came under Muslim rule in the early 13th century, under the ruler Mohammad Bin Bakhtiyar Khilji. Christianity first arrived in the 16th century and spread with the efforts of the Portuguese missionaries. During the British rule in the 18th century, many prominent Bengalis converted to Christianity.

The official language is Bangla (or Bengali), which is spoken by 98% of the people in Bangladesh, by more than 85% in Kolkata, West Bengal, and by about 67% of the people in the Tripura district of India. English is the second language and is widely used in higher education, law, and across many government activities. Approximately 3 million indigenous people, belonging to at least 54 different ethnic groups in northern and southeastern Bangladesh, speak a variety of native languages; the major tribes are Chakmas, Marmas, Mizos, Santals, Garos, Manipuri, Tripuri, Khasis, Khajons, Tanchangya, and Mros.[1]

Size and Geography

The People's Republic of Bangladesh (in short Bangladesh) is situated on the apex of the Bay of Bengal in South Asia and is bordered by India and by Myanmar in the southeast. See Figure 21.1. The country's area is 148,460 square kilometers, which is slightly bigger than the state of Iowa (**FIGURE 21-1** map). It has 580 kilometers of coastline and is situated between India and Myanmar. The population size of Bangladesh is estimated at 156,186,882 million people as of July 2016. This makes Bangladesh the 9th most populous country in the world. With an estimated population density of 10,520 people per square kilometer.[2]

It is divided into six administrative divisions: Dhaka, Chittagong, Khulna, Barisal, Rajshahi, and Sylhet. The capital city, Dhaka (formerly spelled Dacca), is located in the central part of the country on the river Buriganga. About 700 rivers, including tributaries, flow through the country constituting a waterway with a total length of around 24,140 kilometers (15,000 miles). The major rivers are Padma, Meghna, Jamuna, Bramhaputra, Teesta, Karnaphuli, and Surma. The Ganges enters the northwestern part of Bangladesh where it is renamed Padma; then it unites with Jamuna (the main channel of Brahmaputra), later joins Meghna, and then finally flows into the Bay of Bengal.

Urbanization has been rapid and largely imbalanced in recent decades in Bangladesh. Because of population pressure and poverty, a huge number of population are moving to big cities, such as Dhaka and Chittagong. A quarter of the population now lives in urban areas, while in 1960 the number was just 5%. Urbanization has been skewed toward Dhaka, making it among the fastest growing metropolises in the world. According to the 2014 census, the number of slum population in Dhaka and in other urban cities increased 60% from 1.39 million to 2.23 million since 1997. The increase of slum population means additional strains on already inadequate infrastructure, public services,

FIGURE 21-1 Map of Bangladesh
© PeterHermesFurian/iStock/Getty Images Plus/Getty

and basic health care, including an inadequate supply of pure drinking water, poor sanitation, lack of electricity and paved roads, and poor housing.[3]

Bangladesh's climate is tropical, with three main seasons, namely a hot and humid summer from March to June, a monsoon (or rainy) season from June to September, and a mild winter from October to February. Bangladesh is prone to floods, tornados, and cyclones because of its low deltaic location. The natural disasters of 1970, 1987, 1988, 1998, 1999, 2004, and 2010 were of catastrophic consequences in recent years. Some waterborne diseases, especially cholera outbreaks, occur immediately after cyclones and floods, due to a disruption of the drinking water system and increased survival of vibrios in saline water. A similar cholera outbreak after a devastating cyclone that occurred in a coastal area of Swandip, Chittagong, in 1988 was intervened and reported.[4]

Government and Political System

Bangladesh follows the parliamentary system of democracy, whereby the prime minister is the head of government and the president is the head of state. The president is now a largely ceremonial post elected by the members of the parliament (MPs) in an open ballot. The MPs are elected by general election. According to the Constitution, the president appoints the prime minister, who must be the leader of the majority party that wins the general election. The cabinet is composed of ministers selected by the prime minister and appointed by the president. At least 90% of the ministers must be MPs elected by the general people. The other 10% may be non-MP experts or *technocrats* who are selected by the prime minister. There are three branches of the Bangladesh government: executive, judicial, and legislative. As the executive head, the president can dissolve parliament upon the written request of the prime minister. However, the Constitution allows the president to act only upon the advice of the prime minister and the cabinet. The prime minister is collectively accountable for the policies and actions to the parliament, to their political party, and ultimately to the electorate. The MPs make the laws which are executed by the judicial branch. The Supreme Court is the highest judicial power. Supreme Court judges are appointed by the president. There are 300 MPs in the legislative branch of the government. They are elected for 5 years by popular vote from single territorial constituencies. The number of seats in parliament is to be raised to 345, of which 45 (15%) will be reserved for women. The seats will be allocated to parties in proportion to their overall share of the vote.

Administratively, the central government is divided into 6 administrative divisions, which are further subdivided into 64 districts. Each district in Bangladesh is subdivided into *upazila* (or subdistricts). Each police service area, except for those in metropolitan areas, is divided into several unions, with each union consisting of multiple villages. Direct elections are held for each union (or ward), electing a chairperson and a number of members. In 1997, a parliamentary act was passed to reserve 3 seats (out of 12) in every union for female candidates. In Bangladesh, the rural/regional local governments have three tiers: *zila parishad* (or district council), *upazila parishad* (or subdistrict council), and union *parishad* (union council, which is made up of nine villages). There are 508 *upazila parishads* and 4,498 union *parishads*.[5]

In the metropolitan areas, police service areas are divided into wards, which are further divided into *mahallas*. There are 10 city corporations, which have mayoral elections: Dhaka South, Dhaka North, Chittagong, Khulna, Sylhet, Rajshahi, Barisal, Rangpur, Comilla, and Gazipur.[5]

Macroeconomics

The economic growth of Bangladesh has been strong and relatively stable over the past five years. However, the country is facing a number of challenges that are hindering its full potential of growth. The overall entrepreneurial activity is disadvantaged by an uncertain regulatory environment, poor infrastructure, and the absence of effective long-term institutional support for private-sector development. Recent unrest and political instability, poor enforcement of rule of law, and corruption are among big challenges. Despite those challenges, the 2015 estimated Gross Domestic Product (GDP) of the country increased to US $209 billion, up from $150 billion in 2013, with an international reserve of $18.088 billion, according to the World Bank.[6] Bangladesh's economy is the second fastest growing major economy of 2016, with a rate of more than 6% growth.[7] In 2016, per capita income stood at $3,840 (PPP) and $1,466 (nominal). In recent years, Bangladesh has seen a major surge in exports from its garment industry, the second largest in the world, along with that of the emerging pharmaceutical and information technology industries. The country's exports are projected to exceed $50 billion by 2021. Being situated in one of the most fertile regions of Earth, agriculture plays a crucial role, with the principal cash crops including rice, jute, tea, wheat, cotton, and sugarcane.[8]

Demographics and Health Indicators

Most of the population in Bangladesh are young. According to a 2015 estimate, nearly one-third of the population (28.27%) was under age 15, and about 6.00% were 65 years or older, making a total dependency ratio of approximately 52.50%.[9] The population growth rate was 1.06% per year. Urbanization between 2010 and 2015 was at a rate of 3.55% per year and 34.30% of the population lived in urban areas.

The percentage of GDP spent on health (3.7%) was comparable to that of India and slightly better than that of Pakistan, two neighboring countries (TABLE 21-1). The life expectancy of the total population is 70.7 years, with 71.2 years for males and 75.4 years for female. The infant mortality rate is 32.9 per 1,000 live births. Child mortality rate over the past 2 decades have decreased significantly, with under-five mortality falling from 144 to 38 per 1,000 live births from 1990 to 2015. Maternal mortality also decreased from 322 to 176 for every 100,000 live births during the period from 2001 to 2015.[9] Still, with the present mortality rate Bangladesh is considered to be a riskier place for mothers and newborns than countries like Vietnam, the Philippines, and Cambodia. On the other hand, Bangladesh has progressed in reducing maternal mortality rates in comparison to neighboring countries like India, Pakistan, Nepal, and Bhutan. In Bangladesh, over three-quarters of births still take place at home, but women are increasingly choosing to admit themselves into clinics and hospitals. The current literacy rate of the total population is only 61.5%, and is slightly lower for females. As education levels among women improve, these mortality rates are likely to decrease further.[10]

According to the international standards, access to safe drinking water and improved sanitation is poor in Bangladesh. About 85% of the total population have access to improved sources of drinking water, and only 57% of people use improved sanitation facility. These are some of the reasons for increased rates of infectious and communicable diseases and parasitic infections in the country. See TABLE 21-2 for comparison of demographic and health statistics between Bangladesh, India, and Pakistan.

TABLE 21-2 Comparative Demographics and Health Profiles of Bangladesh, India, and Pakistan

	Bangladesh	India	Pakistan
Population	166,280,712	1,236,344,631	196,174,380
Age (years)	% of population		
0–14	32.3%	28.5%	33.3%
15–24	18.8%	18.1%	21.5%
25–54	38.0%	40.6%	35.7%
55–64	5.9%	7.0%	5.1%
≥65	5.0%	5.8%	4.3%
Dependency ratio (total)	52.2%	51.8%	60.4%
Population growth rate	1.6%	1.25%	1.49%
Urbanization rate	28.4%	31.3%	36.2%
% of GDP spent on health	3.7%	3.9%	2.5%
Birth rate	21.61/1,000	19.89/1,000	23.19/1,000
Death rate	5.64/1,000	7.35/1,000	6.58/1,000

TABLE 21-2 Comparative Demographics and Health Profiles of Bangladesh, India, and Pakistan (*continued*)

	Bangladesh	India	Pakistan
Infant mortality rate	45.67/1,000 live births	43.19/1,000 live births	57.48/1,000 live births
Maternal mortality rate	170/100,000 live births	200/100,000 live births	260/100,000 live births
Life expectancy at birth (years)			
Total	70.7	67.8	67.0
Male	69.1	66.7	65.2
Female	71.6	69.1	69.0
Literacy rate			
Total	57.7%	62.8%	54.9%
Male	62.0%	75.2%	68.6%
Female	53.4%	50.8%	40.3%
Improved source of drinking water			
Total	84.8%	92.6%	91.4%
Urban	85.8%	96.7%	95.7%
Rural	84.4%	90.7%	89.0%
Improved sanitation facility			
Total	57.0%	36.0%	47.4%
Urban	55.2%	60.2%	71.8%
Rural	57.8%	24.7%	33.6%

Data from World Bank. World Bank Open Data. http://www.data.worldbank.org. n.d.

Status of Infectious Diseases

Tuberculosis (TB) has been a major public health problem in Bangladesh for a long time. According to 2014 revised estimates by the World Health Organization (WHO), the prevalence of all forms of TB was 404 per 100,000 people, with a mortality rate of 51/100,000 people.[12]

Malaria is another important health problem in Bangladesh. Out of the 64 districts in the country, 13 districts in the east and northeast that border the eastern states of India and Myanmar have reported about 98% of total cases in Bangladesh. A total of 54,132 *Plasmodium falciparum* cases and 3,348 *Plasmodium vivax* cases were identified in the 2014.[13]

In 2014, a total of 2,135,220 diarrhea cases were reported. Death due to diarrhea drastically decreased by 2007 and further decreased in 2014.[13] Strategies like early oral rehydration at the household level seems to be highly effective in the treatment and reduction of diarrhea-related deaths.

Bangladesh has experienced dengue infection since 2000, after an earlier outbreak in the 1960s known as Dhaka fever. The reemergence of dengue viruses has been dreadful. In 2014, a total of 375 cases of dengue fever were reported, without any mortality.[13] Bangladesh is one of the most endemic areas of kala-azar (leishmaniasis). About 31 million people are at risk with 26 endemic districts. The National Kala-Azar Elimination Programme in Bangladesh set the target for elimination of kala-azar by 2017. Filariasis is prevalent all over the country, with the highest endemicity in the northern part. About 20 million have been suffering from the disease. Mass Drug Administration was introduced in 2001 for the control of filaria in 19 endemic districts.[13]

Bangladesh is still considered a low-prevalence country for HIV/AIDS, but it remains vulnerable to an HIV epidemic because of the high prevalence in neighboring countries. Inadequacy in correct knowledge about HIV and AIDS due to illiteracy, ignorance, and gender inequity may aggravate the vulnerability. In 2014 a total of 433 new cases were diagnosed, and about 9,500 people were living with HIV; 563 people died.[14]

Based on the report from the Infectious Disease Hospital (IDH), cases of neonatal tetanus pose a high rate of mortality and unsatisfactory outcome. In a study of all cases of neonatal tetanus admitted over a one year period from May 2008 to April 2009, the overall mortality was 52.9%.[15] Low socioeconomic conditions, mothers' illiteracy, lack of antenatal care, involvement of untrained people during delivery of babies, and unclean cord care practices were important factors contributing to neonatal tetanus.[15,16] However, the number of cases with neonatal tetanus admitted to IDH dropped to 16–20 cases per year from 2009 to 2014 due to the introduction of safe delivery services and training of traditional birth attendants (**FIGURE 21-2**).

The number of chickenpox cases ranged from 103 to 180 per year, with a total of 761 cases between 2009 and 2014 (**FIGURE 21-3**). Rabies, a zoonotic infectious disease, is transmitted mainly due to infected dog bites. Annually about 30,000 bite cases are attended to in outpatient departments, with administration of rabies vaccines; over 90% have been due to dog bites. Most cases of rabies (143 out of 170, 84%) were with people who had not been vaccinated, and 99% did not receive wound care.[17] The total number of rabies cases treated in the hospital was 598 (ranging from 85 to 115 per year) from 2009 to 2014. The number of hospitalizations due to complicated cases of measles, diphtheria, and whooping cough has been drastically reduced due to the success of a high rate of vaccination coverage in the country.[16]

Vaccination

Many infectious diseases are vaccine-preventable. The WHO initiated the Expanded Program on Immunization (EPI) in May 1974 with the objective to vaccinate children throughout the world against six vaccine-preventable diseases: TB, diphtheria, whooping cough (pertussis), tetanus, measles, and poliomyelitis. Currently, vaccines against nine diseases are being administered to children under one year old.[13]

Tremendous progress has been made over the past 20 years toward development of an effective national immunization program. The full coverage is more than 85%, an achievement that helped Bangladesh to become 1 of the 6 countries in the world that achieved the Millennium Development Goal (MDG) for child mortality before the 2015 deadline.[13] Bangladesh was also a

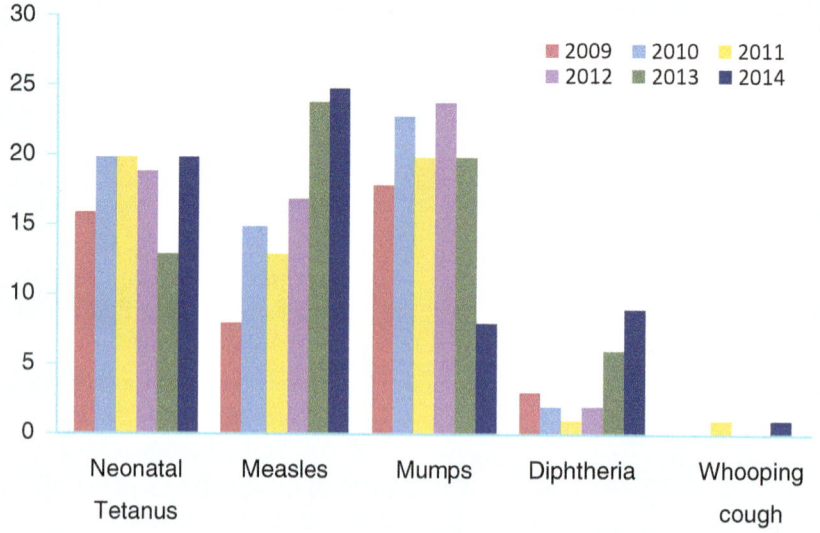

FIGURE 21-2 Number of Cases with Neonatal Tetanus, Measles, Mumps, Diphtheria, and Whooping Cough Seen at the Infectious Disease Hospital, Bangladesh, 2009–2014.

Data from Infectious Disease Hospital, Bangladesh, hospital records, 2009–2014.

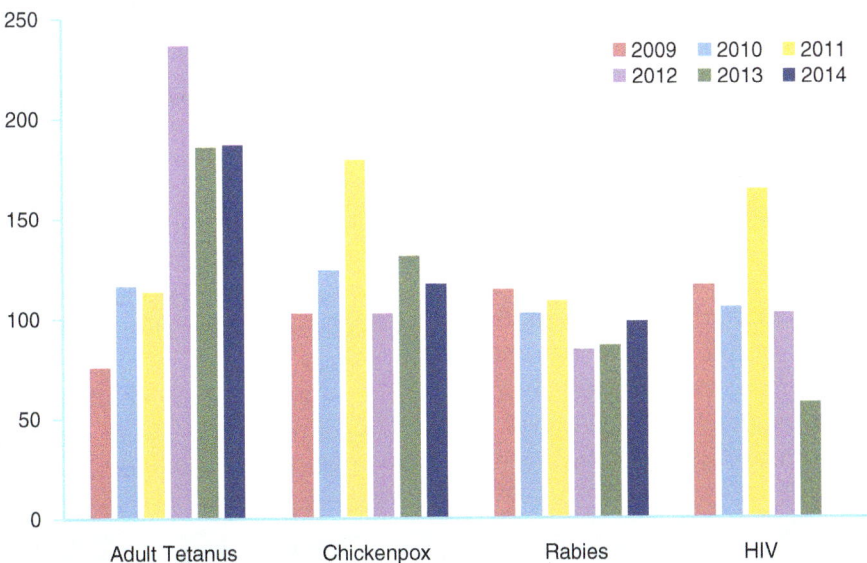

FIGURE 21-3 Number of Cases of Adult Tetanus, Chickenpox, Rabies, and HIV Infection Seen at the Infectious Disease Hospital, Bangladesh, 2009–2014.

Data from Infectious Disease Hospital, Bangladesh, hospital records, 2009–2014.

success story about polio eradication. The country has been polio-free since 2000, with 18 exceptional cases of wild polio virus imported from neighboring India in 2006. Despite being polio-free since March 2007, Bangladesh could not achieve a polio-free certificate because of the delay in eradication of polio in neighboring countries. Finally, Bangladesh, along with 11 other countries in the region (including India), became certified polio-free in March 2014.[18] As per the global Polio Eradication and Endgame Strategic Plan 2013–2018, Bangladesh introduced an inactivated polio virus vaccine in March 21, 2015, for the prevention of vaccine-derived polio viruses. Now the country's plan is to switch from trivalent oral polio vaccine (tOPV) to bivalent oral polio vaccine (bOPV) in 2016 for the prevention of outbreak due to the type 2 component of OPV.[13]

The country is also satisfactorily progressing toward achieving the WHO's goal for measles elimination in Southeast Asia by 2020. The measles and rubella vaccine was introduced on August 7, 2012, with current coverage of 86.6%.[13] Pneumonia is the leading cause of death in under-five children. WHO estimates that *Haemophilus influenzae* type b (Hib) and pneumococcus together accounted for more than 50% of pneumonia deaths among children aged 1 month to 5 years.[19] Because pneumonia causes more deaths in under-five children every year, a Hib vaccine was introduced on January 15, 2009, with coverage of 93%, and a pneumococcal vaccine was introduced on March 21, 2015. Bangladesh has yet to introduce a *Rotavirus* vaccine as part of the routine vaccination schedule. A monovalent (RV1) and a pentavalent (RV5) vaccine have been found to be highly effective against severe *Rotavirus* infection in children.[20]

Nutritional Status

There is a vicious cycle between nutritional status and infections. Malnutrition has been a long-standing public health problem in Bangladesh. Approximately 41% of children under 5, equivalent to more than 9.5 million children, suffer from moderate to severe stunting, an indicator of chronic malnutrition. Micronutrient deficiency, especially due to deficiency of iron, zinc, iodine, and vitamin A, is highly prevalent among children. Iron deficiency is the most common micronutrient deficiency disorder among children in the developing world.[21] In Bangladesh, iron deficiency affects about half of all children and more than 70% of all women. The main cause of iron deficiency in Bangladesh is chronic inadequate dietary intake. Worm infestation, particularly rampant among young children, can aggravate the situation of malnutrition and anemia. WHO recommends periodic deworming of all children in countries such as Bangladesh, where more than 20% of children have worm infestations.

Bangladesh has made remarkable progress in periodic distributions of high doses of vitamin A supplementation for small children. In a nationally representative survey of 10,500 households selected from 361 clusters throughout Bangladesh,[22] the coverage of periodic vitamin A capsules among children aged 18–59 months was 86.4% within the past 6 months. Lower maternal education was significantly associated with children who missed the vitamin A distribution program.

Use of iodized salt has shown sustainable progress in reducing the iodine deficiency disorder rate from 47% in 1993 to 6.2% in 2004–2005.[23] However, the households with adequate coverage of iodized salt is slightly over 51%.

The malnutrition rate for women is also high. While overweight and obesity is rapidly becoming a major public health problem in the form of an epidemic in many parts of the world, in Bangladesh the amount of women with body mass indexes (BMI) less than 18.5 kg/m^2 (undernutrition) range from 47.6% in the southern district of Khulna to 59.6% in the northeastern district of Sylhet.[24] About 60 million people in Bangladesh suffer from food shortage and food insecurity, mainly due to unemployment or underemployment, inadequate access to land for cultivation, and vulnerability to natural disasters. Women and girls in particular often face additional challenges that increase food and nutrition insecurity. According to the government's National Strategy for Accelerated Poverty Reduction, the key elements in the fight against hunger include strengthening social safety nets and welfare programs, improving the status of women, ensuring modern and child nutrition, increasing school enrollment and expanding school feeding programs in schools, and preparing for the impacts of natural disasters and climate change.[25]

▸ Brief History of the Healthcare System

Despite success stories of Bangladesh in health care in the last two decades, there are huge disparities with the quality of healthcare services provided for urban and rural population. Almost all of the referral hospitals are located in the capital of Dhaka. Many private clinics and hospitals and state-of-the-art diagnostics laboratories also flourished in Dhaka. A large number of people, therefore, rush to the capital city every day for treatments of complications, and sometime for illnesses that could have otherwise been managed in large district hospitals. This creates long waiting times for patients to get specialist appointments. The burden of this centralized healthcare system is aggravated partly due to the lack of proper diagnostic facilities in rural health centers and partly due to the shortage of qualified (and specialized) doctors in remote villages.

Community Clinics

Realizing these facts, in 2009 the government of Bangladesh initiated a massive plan to revitalize community clinics (one clinic for every 6,000 population) to bring primary healthcare services at the doorstep of the village people. Community clinics are the first level, one-stop service centers that provide the following services:[13]

- Maternal and neonatal healthcare services
- Integrated management of childhood diseases
- Reproductive health and family planning services
- Vaccination
- Nutrition education and micronutrient supplements
- Health education and counseling
- Screening for chronic and noncommunicable diseases
- Treatment of minor ailments, common diseases, and first aid
- Referrals to higher facilities, such as union health centers or *upazila* (subdistrict) health complexes.

The community clinic is a unique example of public-private partnership because the land for the clinic is donated by the community people, the clinic building is constructed by the government, the clinic is managed by a team of community support groups and the government, and the logistics and services are provided by the government and some non-governmental organizations (NGOs). The number of service seekers in the community clinics drastically increased (586%) in five years, from 14,627,416 in 2009 to 100,408,157 in 2013.[26]

Public Sector Health Services

FIGURE 21-4 shows that health services in Bangladesh are provided by publically funded health facilities at

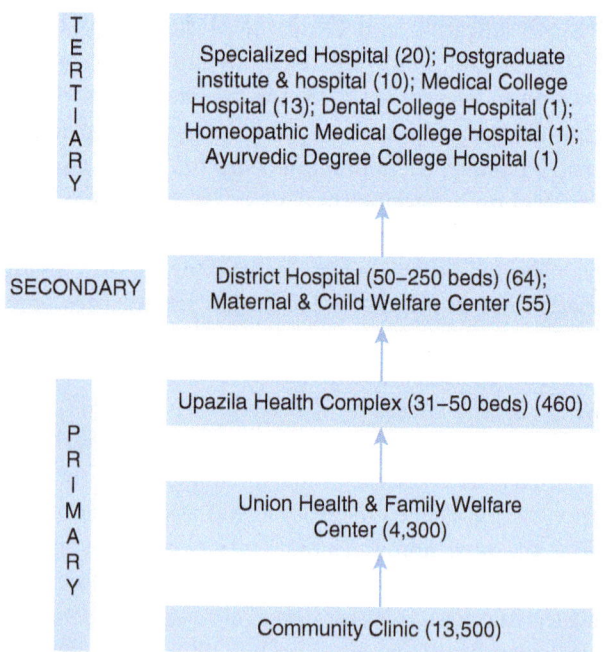

FIGURE 21-4 Hierarchy of Public Sector Health Services from the Primary Level to the Tertiary Level in Bangladesh

Data from Government of the People's Republic of Bangladesh. Directorate General of Health Services. Ministry of Health and Family Welfare. Health Bulletin 2015. http://www.dghs.gov.bd/index.php/en/home/3631-dghs-health-bulletin-2015. December 2015. Accessed August 12, 2016.

three levels: (1) primary level—about 13,500 community clinics, 4,300 union health and family welfare centers, and about 460 *upazila* (subdistrict) health complexes; (2) secondary level—district hospitals and maternal and child welfare centers; and (3) tertiary level—a number of specialized and referral hospitals, medical college hospitals, dental college hospitals, and other hospitals.[13]

Role of Non-Governmental Organizations

Involvement of NGOs in health services has run parallel to the public health services. According to the *NGO Monitor: Annual Report 2015*, there are 2,333 NGOs registered in Bangladesh. With the aid from a number of donor agencies, these NGOs deliver a variety of services, including delivery of essential health care and health education, women's empowerment, advocacy for social rights, and financing through microcredit.[27] Much of the NGO support has been in the form of health education, training, and facilitating links with rural health centers. For example, the Slum Improvement Project in Bangladesh employs NGOs to train local community health workers and sanitary workers. The Bangladesh Integrated Nutrition Project uses participatory, community-based nutrition activities through NGOs. Rangpur-Dinajpur Rural Service (RDRS), supported by the Lutheran World Federation/Department for World Service, has been working to empower the rural poor in 10 northern districts of Bangladesh, including Panchagarh, Thakurgaon, Dinajpur, Rangpur, Nilphamari, Lalmonirhat, Kurigram, Jamalpur, Moulvibazar, and Habiganj. RDRS also provides high-quality preventive and curative services to mothers and children and provides care for leprosy and TB patients through its community-based health services. Gono Shasthaya Kendra (Peoples' Health Center, popularly known as GK) emerged as a field hospital to treat injured soldiers during the liberation war of 1971. Eventually, GK expanded its healthcare services, covering almost 1.2 million rural population in 631 villages, 28 *upazilas* of 19 districts across the country through 43 primary healthcare centers and 5 referral hospitals.

Among others, two NGOs play a vital role in the health services delivery in the country—they are the Bangladesh Rural Advancement Committee (BRAC)[28] and the International Centre for Diarrhoeal Disease Research, Bangladesh (ICDDRB).[29] BRAC, the largest NGO in the world, helps the government of Bangladesh in service delivery and training from the grassroot level to the district level in the fields of health, nutrition, and population control. In addition, BRAC has expanded its service in other health-related fields, including disaster management; water, sanitation, and hygiene; education; gender equality; and community empowerment. BRAC employs over 100,000 people, roughly 70% of whom are rural women, to reach more than 126 million people.[28]

ICDDRB is the largest health research institution in the Asian region and the largest research and service center for diarrheal diseases in the world. Major sources of funding for the research and services of the center include the government of Bangladesh, the U.S. Agency for International Development, the Bill and Melinda Gates Foundation, the Department of Foreign Affairs, Trade and Development of Canada, the Department of International Development, the United Kingdom, Centers for Disease Control and Prevention, the United States, the Global Fund for AIDS, TB and Malaria, the National Institutes of Health, Johns Hopkins University, Sida, Sweden, and Grand Challenges, Canada.[29] The Center is located in Mohakhali, Dhaka, and has rural branches at Matlab Upazila of Comilla District, Teknaf Upazila of Cox's Bazar District, and in some other parts of the country. Among many achievements in health research, the discovery and implementation of the oral rehydration solution for the treatment of diarrheal diseases has been considered "potentially the most important medical advance of this century" and has saved over 40 million people worldwide. Each year, more than 100,000 diarrheal patients are treated at this center. The center works with the government of Bangladesh in combatting diarrheal disease epidemics throughout the country, providing training on diarrheal disease management, running a two-year medical residency program, and offering short courses on areas of public health (epidemiology and biostatistics), family planning, disease surveillance, nutritional management, and child survival strategies.[29]

Specialized Hospitals

Most of the specialized hospitals are located in the city of Dhaka (**TABLE 21-3**). However, there are chest disease hospitals, infectious disease hospitals, diabetic clinics, and some other specialized hospitals in most of the big cities.

Diabetic Association of Bangladesh

The Diabetic Association of Bangladesh has been a member of the International Diabetes Federation since 1959. According to a report published in 2014,[38] 8.4 million cases (or 10% of the population) suffered from diabetes, and another 23% were prediabetic in Bangladesh. According to the International Diabetes Federation, the prevalence will be 13% by 2030. The number of cases of type 2 diabetes has doubled

TABLE 21-3 Specialized Hospitals Operated in Bangladesh: Location and Number of Beds

Specialty	Name	Location	Number of beds
Heart diseases	National Institute of Cardiovascular Diseases	Sher-e-Bangla Nagar, Dhaka	414
	National Heart Foundation of Bangladesh	Mirpur, Dhaka	300
	National Center for Control of Rheumatic Fever and Heart Diseases	Sher-e-Bangla Nagar, Dhaka	—
Tuberculosis and other lung diseases	National Institute of Diseases of the Chest and Hospital	Mohakhali, Dhaka	660
	Tuberculosis Hospital	Shyamoli, Dhaka	250
	National Asthma Center	Mohakhali, Dhaka	100
Infectious diseases	Infectious Diseases Hospital	Mohakhali, Dhaka	100
Childhood diseases	Dhaka Shishu (Children's) Hospital	Sher-e-Bangla Nagar, Dhaka	640
Diabetes and other endocrine diseases	Bangladesh Institute of Research and Rehabilitation in Diabetes, Endocrine and Metabolic Disorders	Shahbag, Dhaka	700
Orthopedics	National Institute of Traumatology and Orthopaedic Rehabilitation	Sher-e-Bangla Nagar, Dhaka	500
Kidney diseases	National Institute of Kidney Diseases and Urology	Sher-e-Bangla Nagar, Dhaka	100
Mental health diseases	National Institute of Mental Health, Dhaka	Sher-e-Bangla Nagar, Dhaka	100
	National Institute of Mental Health, Pabna	Pabna	500
Eye diseases	National Institute of Ophthalmology and Hospital	Sher-e-Bangla Nagar, Dhaka	250
	Islamia Eye Institute and Hospital	Farm Gate, Dhaka	—
Cancer	National Institute of Cancer Research and Hospital	Mohakhali, Dhaka	150
Leprosy	Leprosy Hospital	Mohakhali, Dhaka	30
Spinal cord injury and paralysis	Centre for the Rehabilitation of the Paralysed (CRP)	Savar, Dhaka	100

Data from Secondary and tertiary level hospitals all over the country. Specialized hospitals in Bangladesh. Available at http://www.hsmdghs-bd.org/Govt_Hospital.htm. Accessed August 12, 2016; Diabetic Association of Bangladesh. Available at http://www.dab-bd.org/birdem.php; Dhaka Shishu (Children) Hospital. Available at http://dhakashishuhospital.org.bd/; National Heart Foundation of Bangladesh. Available at http://www.nhf.org.bd/; National Institute of Traumatology & Orthopaedic Rehabilitation. Available at http://nitorbd.com/; Ispahani Islamia Eye Institute & Hospital, Bangladesh. Available at http://islamia.org.bd/

over the past decade, making diabetes a major public health problem in the country. It is alarming that 56% of diabetics were unaware of their condition, and only 40% were receiving treatment regularly.[38] The Diabetic Association of Bangladesh has been monitoring a countrywide surveillance of cases of diabetes and has been offering treatment, dietary advice, and preventive health services through its district satellite clinics and a central referral hospital, known as Bangladesh Institute of Research and Rehabilitation in Diabetes, Endocrine and Metabolic Disorders (BIRDEM).[31]

Infectious Disease Hospital

Infectious Disease Hospital (IDH) is the only referral hospital for infectious diseases located in Mohkhali, Dhaka. Patients with common infectious diseases—including diphtheria, whooping cough, tetanus, rabies, chickenpox, measles, mumps, rubella, viral hepatitis, enteric fever, and HIV infection—are treated in this hospital.[16]

Dhaka Shishu (Children's) Hospital

Dhaka Shishu (Children's) Hospital is a 640-bed referral hospital that was established in 1972 as an autonomous institution, with the help of the Save the Children Fund of the United Kingdom and World Vision of Bangladesh, and is run by a management board formed by the Ministry of Health and Family Welfare of Bangladesh. The objectives of the institution include health care for poor children, maintenance of a clinic for vaccination of children, education of mothers in feeding and elementary hygiene, motivation of parents for family planning, promotion of research in child heath, and training of doctors, nurses, and paramedics. In 2015, 225,309 patients attended OPD with an average 700–800 patients each day, and 38,221 patients were admitted in different units of the hospital. Bangladesh Institute of Child Health conducts postgraduate pediatric courses, such as FCPS (Fellow of the College of Physicians and Surgeons), MD (Doctor of Medicine), MS (Master of Surgery), DCH (Diploma in Child Health), and various certificate courses in pediatrics. So far, 489 students graduated with MD in pediatrics, 310 with DCH, 20 with FCPS in pediatrics, and 74 completed MS in pediatric surgery from this institute.[32]

National Heart Foundation

National Heart Foundation Hospital and Research Institute is an example of a large public-private partnership healthcare hospital which hosts state-of-the-art cardiac care facilities in the country. The hospital provides free care for 30% of the patients who are poor. In addition to outpatient care, emergency services, and cardiac surgery, the institute offers postgraduate degrees (MD in cardiology and MS in cardiothoracic surgery). Nurse training for cardiac care and diplomas in cardiac nursing, and a number of training programs for doctors on cardiovascular diseases are offered. The National Heart Foundation of Bangladesh has spread its outreach activities and heart camps through its 33 affiliated bodies in different places in the country. In 2015, 88,343 outpatients and 21,704 inpatients were treated at this hospital. Of the procedures, 13,921 required cardiac catheterization and 3,419 had coronary angioplasty (PTCA) done at the hospital in 2015.[33]

National Institute of Traumatology and Orthopaedic Rehabilitation

The National Institute of Traumatology and Research (NITOR) was established in 1972 with the dedication of a philanthropist and a friend of Bangladesh during the liberation war, Doctor R. J. Garst, who used to help treat the wounded freedom fighters from the war of liberation. NITOR is now a 500-bed tertiary center, receiving referral patients from all over the country. There are 12 units in the hospital, offering specialized services in the fields of arthroscopy, arthroplasty, hand surgery, pediatric orthopedics, musculoskeletal tumor surgery, spinal surgery, reconstructive deformity correction surgery, plastic surgery, and physiotherapy. The institute runs postgraduate degree programs (an MS in orthopedics and a diploma in orthopedics) and a bachelor degree in physiotherapy.[34]

Ispahani Islamia Eye Institute and Hospital

Founded in 1960 as a nonprofit organization, Ispahani Islamia Eye Institute and Hospital has emerged as the leading eye-care hospital in the country by providing services through its main hospital, located at the heart of the Dhaka City in Farm Gate, and three branch hospitals located in Barisal, Jamalpur, and Naogaon districts. Over the last 13 years, Ispahani Islamia Eye Institute and Hospital has shown tremendous growth by offering outpatient care to 153,872 patients in 2001 and 662,802 patients by 2014, and inpatient surgical care to 6,910 patients in 2001 to 44,192 patients in 2014. In addition to clinical services, the institute offers training to postgraduate students, including physicians, nurses, and paramedics in ophthalmology.[35]

Medical and Dental Colleges and Hospitals

In Bangladesh, there are 93 recognized medical colleges, 30 of which are public, 57 private, and 6 semipublic. The 87 public and private medical colleges are governed under the jurisdiction of the Ministry of Health and Family Welfare, and 6 semipublic medical colleges are run by the Bangladesh Armed Forces and are under the Ministry of Defense. Bangladesh Medical and Dental Council is the statutory body of the government entrusted with the responsibilities for maintaining the standard of medical education and healthcare services in the country. Annually, 3,222 students are admitted to the public medical college, 375 to the armed forces medical colleges, and more than 5,000 students in private medical colleges.[36]

There are 9 public and 16 private dental colleges that offer a graduate course known as Bachelor of Dental Surgery. More than 1,300 dental surgeons graduate each year from these dental colleges.[36]

The medical colleges are attached to a general hospital. Dhaka Medical College Hospital is the largest hospital in the country, with 2,300 beds. It provides outpatient services to about 3,000 patients daily at a very nominal fee. The hospital has 34 departments and 42 wards, 234 doctors, 140 interns, 560 nurses, and more than 1,100 staff to ensure 24-hour health service. Sir Salimullah Medical College Hospital (formerly known as Mitford Hospital) is the second largest public hospital, having 600 beds and serving more than 2,000 outpatients daily. Hospital beds of most other medical college hospitals range from 250 to 600. Bangabandhu Sheikh Mujib Medical University (BSMMU) is the only medical university in Bangladesh. Popularly known as PG Hospital, it hosts a 1,500-bed tertiary care hospital and offers postgraduate degrees in various fields, including MD, PhD, MPhil, MS, MDS, Diploma, and FCPS. The university is an autonomous body governed by a 24-member syndicate. BSMMU is composed of 36 departments under 4 faculties.[30]

Nursing Training Institutes

The Directorate of Nursing Services under the Ministry of Health and Family Welfare is responsible for the delivery of nursing services and education. There are 43 nursing institutes in the government sector and 5 private ones offering a three-year diploma in nursing science and a one-year diploma in midwifery. The total intake of students is 2,580 each year. In addition, there are 1,200 more nurses with four-year bachelor of science degrees in nursing or two-year bachelor of science degrees in public health nursing that are graduated each year from 11 nursing colleges. There are approximately 22,000 registered nurses, out of which 14,689 are working in the public sector. In the public sector, there are 171 positions of managerial level first-class nursing officers, and 470 instructor level second-class nursing positions available. The government has created another 17,798 second-class nursing positions for supervisors, public health nurses, staff nurses, and senior nurses in the public sector.[37]

Workforce

Human Resources for Health, the backbone of the healthcare delivery system, is in a crisis situation in Bangladesh, with a critical shortage of health workers. Presence of a huge body of unskilled providers, including *palli chikitshaks* (village practitioners), homeopathic medicine practitioners, ayurvedic practitioners, *kabiraji* (herbal) medicine practitioners, and traditional birth attendants of unknown quality make the situation worse. Homeopathic, ayurvedic, and *kabiraji* (herbal) medicines are type of complementary and alternative medicine. According to the General Medical Council, as of April 2016, there are 273,761 registered medical practitioners in the country, 86,729 (31.7%) of which are specialists, and 66,330 (24.2%) are general practitioners.[36]

The density of formally qualified registered Healthcare Providers (HCP), (i.e., doctors, nurses, and dentists), in Bangladesh is 7.7 per 10,000 population, and it constitutes only about 5% of the total health workforce. This is lower than all other countries in Southeast Asia, and it falls far short of the WHO projected needs.[39] In Bangladesh, both the number of nurses per 1,000 population and the nurse-doctor ratio are among the lowest in the world. There are around 5 physicians and 2 nurses per 10,000 population, making the nurse-doctor ratio in Bangladesh only 0.4. There is an overwhelming bias toward urban areas in the distribution of HCPs. The doctor-population ratio is 1 to 1,500 in urban areas and 1 to 15,000 in rural areas. The nursing profession is an indispensable piece of the health system. As of January 2011, Bangladesh had 26,644 registered nurses. Bangladesh has a population-nurse ratio of 5,000 to 1, a bed-nurse ratio of 13 to 1, and a doctor-nurse ratio of 2.5 to 1. These fall far short of the international standard for a bed-nurse ratio of 4 to 1 and a doctor-nurse ratio of 1 to 3.[39,40]

Healthcare Financing

The government of Bangladesh has adopted a healthcare financing strategy that aspires to move toward universal health coverage for its population by 2032.

The strategy has three objectives to mobilize resources for health: improve equity of healthcare services, improve access to healthcare services, and enhance the efficiency of the health system. The strategy prioritizes protecting not only the poor from the financial burden related to healthcare costs but also providing coverage for the entire population.

Approximately 35% of the health sector funding from the government is coordinated through a large consortium of donors and aid agencies. Some 500 NGOs (mentioned earlier) operate in the health, nutrition, and population sectors in Bangladesh. A less apparent but important source of private spending is informal or out-of-pocket payments by patients to private-sector providers. For large medical procedures, payment can be quite high, which indicates that people are willing to pay for better care to supplement the resource-starved and ineffective public health sector. Channeling this money into an organized health insurance scheme would reduce payment at time of illness and spread the cost of care across time and individuals.

In a quasi-experimental case-control study, the Community-Based Health Insurance (CBHI) offered through local cooperative organizations was found to be an effective option in healthcare utilization from qualified providers.[41] More studies are needed for an affordable health insurance plan for the people.

Health Budget

Based on a report published in 2015, total health expenditure (THE) in Bangladesh was ৳325.1 billion (US $4.1 billion) in 2012. In recent years, THE grew at an annual average of approximately 8%.[42]

The development budget of the Ministry of Health and Family Welfare (MoHFW) and its agencies comes from the Health, Population and Nutrition Sector Development Program (HPNSDP) 2011–2016. The total allocation and expenditure under the revised annual development program of 2014–2015 fiscal year among 17 operational plans of the Directorate General of Health Services (DGHS) are shown in TABLE 21-4.

TABLE 21-4 Allocation, Expenditure, and Utilization of FY2014–2015 Revised Annual Development Program for HPNSDP, Directorate General Health Services, Bangladesh

Program	Allocation (US $ in millions)	Expenditure ($ in millions)	Utilization rate (%)
Maternal, neonatal, child, and adolescent health	92.48	66.55	71.96
Essential services delivery	8.71	4.08	46.84
Community-based health care	35.05	23.00	65.62
Tuberculosis and leprosy control	9.13	7.51	82.26
National AIDS/STD program	5.35	2.82	52.71
Communicable disease control	14.00	13.60	97.14
Noncommunicable diseases	2.40	1.60	66.67
National eye care	0.70	0.53	75.71
Hospital services management and safe blood transfusion	48.10	46.83	97.36
Alternative medical care	1.53	1.38	90.20
In-service training	4.40	3.15	71.59
Pre-service education	19.82	19.35	97.63

(continues)

TABLE 21-4 Allocation, Expenditure, and Utilization of FY2014–2015 Revised Annual Development Program for HPNSDP, Directorate General Health Services, Bangladesh (continued)

Program	Allocation (US $ in millions)	Expenditure ($ in millions)	Utilization rate (%)
Planning, monitoring, and research (health)	1.22	0.96	78.69
Health information system and eHealth	11.10	11.00	99.10
Health education and promotion	3.50	3.44	98.29
Procurement, logistics, and supplies management	16.19	15.30	94.50
National nutrition services	14.07	10.30	73.21
Total	282.41	231.40	81.94

Data from Government of the People's Republic of Bangladesh. Directorate General of Health Services. Ministry of Health and Family Welfare. Health Bulletin 2015. http://www.dghs.gov.bd/index.php/en/home/3631-dghs-health-bulletin-2015. 2015. Accessed August 12, 2016.

Emerging Challenges

1. Shortage of health manpower: There is an acute shortage of health manpower, including doctors, nurses, and paraprofessionals in Bangladesh. Nursing services are probably the weakest of all the healthcare provider services in the country. Along with the challenge of meeting the shortage of nurses, the question of quality is key. Establishment of new nurse training institutes will provide skilled and qualified nurses to meet the existing acute shortage of nurses in Bangladesh. In addition, nursing colleges need to strengthen the postgraduation program. Similarly, BSMMU, the premier postgraduate medical institution in the country, and other specialized medical institutions must produce more qualified specialist doctors.
2. Maldistribution of existing manpower: The population in Bangladesh is predominantly rural, with almost 80% of the population living in rural areas. Many people live in remote areas that lack healthcare facilities at their doorstep. Lack of transport and proper road links to the nearest health centers are causes of many avertable deaths. Most of the large and specialized hospitals are located in Dhaka and big cities only.
3. Blooming of private medical colleges and private clinics: In recent years, a huge number of private medical colleges were established in the country without much supervision and maintaining standards of education. There are also private clinics growing like mushrooms. The quality of services provided by these private clinics need close monitoring.
4. Integration of services: The health and family welfare services are integrated at the top administrative level but not so much at the *upazila* level or down to the village level workers. Because of lack of coordination between *upazila* health administrators (medical doctors) and *upazila* family planning officers (nonmedical administrators), there is always a parallel of dual administration existing at the rural level, hindering necessary proper care for the people.
5. Health care for the poor: 32% of the Bangladesh population live under the national poverty line of US $2 per day, according to the World Bank. Because of the growing cost of health care, many people cannot afford to get the basic healthcare services. The Bangladesh government introduced the National Drug Policy in 1982. Since then the pharmaceutical industries in the country have been in competition, resulting

in increased output of essential drugs and considerable reduction of costs of drugs. The policy of community clinic is another step toward reaching the poor with basic health services. It remains a challenge to see the success of the community clinics and the services provided by community health workers at the village level.

6. Lack of health insurance: Most people does not perceive health as a commodity to be purchased. As such, the concept of health insurance is not very popular in the country, and government and private sectors have not come up with a health insurance plan. Only a few business facilities and large organizations offer healthcare costs to their employees. Well-planned affordable health insurance is very much needed.

7. Disease burden: In upcoming years Bangladesh will have to confront the challenges of the newly set Sustainable Development Goals. The country is still facing a huge burden of infectious and communicable diseases, including diarrhea, pneumonia, dengue fever, malaria, and TB. Malnutrition and infection is a vicious cycle affecting the health of the children. Because of the rapid increase of noncommunicable diseases, such as heart disease and diabetes, in addition to the existing problem of infectious diseases, the country is facing the challenges of a double burden of diseases.

Over the last few years, Bangladesh has made tremendous progress in the health sector. Global leaders lauded the progress of Bangladesh in the health sector saying "Bangladesh is a development surprise."[43] These achievements are the results of planning, careful implementation, and good monitoring and evaluation of health interventions. After internationally recognized successes in achieving the targets of the MDGs even with limited resources, it is now time for Bangladesh to focus on the upcoming Sustainable Development Goals set by the United Nations as the post-2015 agenda.

References

1. International Work Group for Indigenous Affairs. Indigenous peoples in Bangladesh. http://www.iwgia.org/regions/asia/bangladesh. Accessed August 12, 2016.
2. World Population Review. Bangladesh population 2016. http://worldpopulationreview.com/countries/bangladesh-population/. Accessed May 5, 2016.
3. Bangladesh Bureau of Statistics. *Preliminary Report on Census of Slum Areas and Floating Population 2014*. Dhaka: BBS; 2015.
4. Siddique AK, Islam Q, Akram K, et al. Cholera epidemic and natural disaster: where is the link. *Trop Geogr Med*. 1989;41:377–382.
5. Bangladesh Bureau of Statistics. *Statistical Year Book Bangladesh 2014*. Dhaka: BBS; 2016.
6. World Bank. Bangladesh poverty assessment: a decade of progress in reducing poverty, 2000–2010. http://www.worldbank.org/en/news/feature/2013/06/20/. Published in 2013. Accessed May 13, 2016.
7. World Bank. Bangladesh development update: economy requires focus on sustainable and inclusive growth. http://www.worldbank.org/en/news/feature/2016/04/30/bangladesh-development-update-bangladesh-economy-requires-focus-on-sustainable-and-inclusive-growth-moving-forward. Published April 30, 2016. Accessed June 2, 2016.
8. Food and Agriculture Organization of the United Nations. *Statistical Pocket Book*. World Food and Agriculture, 2015.
9. National Institute of Population Research and Training, Mitra and Associates, and ICF International. *Bangladesh Demographic and Health Survey 2014*. Dhaka, Bangladesh, and Rockville, Maryland, USA; 2016. http://dhsprogram.com/pubs/pdf/FR311/FR311.pdf. Accessed June 2, 2016
10. Karlsen S, Say L, Souza JP, et al. The relationship between maternal education and mortality among women giving birth in health care institutions: analysis of the cross sectional WHO Global Survey on Maternal and Perinatal Health. *BMC Public Health*. 2011;11:606. doi:10.1186/1471-2458-11-606
11. World Bank. Open data. http://www.data.worldbank.org.
12. Global Tuberculosis Report 2015. 20th ed. http://www.who.int/tb/publications/global_report/en.
13. Government of the People's Republic of Bangladesh. Directorate General of Health Services. Ministry of Health and Family Welfare. *Health Bulletin 2015*. http://www.dghs.gov.bd/index.php/en/home/3631-dghs-health-bulletin-2015. Accessed August 12, 2016.
14. Country Progress Report Bangladesh. Global AIDS response progress reporting 2015, UNAIDS. http://aidsdatahub.org/bangladesh-global-aids-response-progress-report-2015.
15. Dey AC, Saha L, Shahidullah M. Risk factors, morbidity and mortality of neonatal tetanus. *Mymensingh Med J*. 2011;20(1):54–58.
16. Ehsan A, Akhter S, Salam F. Neonatal tetanus, yet not gone: Infectious Disease Hospital experience. *Journal of Enam Medical College*. 2015;5:161–165.
17. Haque SM, Yeasmin T, Islam MM. Epidemiologic characteristics of human rabies at Infectious Disease Hospital, Dhaka. *Bangladesh J Child Health*. 2011;35(3):102–107.
18. Bahl S, Kumar R, Menabde N, et al. Polio-free certification and lessons learned—South-East Asia Region, March 2014. *MMWR Morb Mortal Wkly Rep*. 2014;63:941–946.
19. GAVI support for Bangladesh immunization: GAVI; 2013.
20. Cortese MM, Immergluck LC, Held M, et al. Effectiveness of monovalent and pentavalent rotavirus vaccine. *Pediatrics*. 2013;132:e25-33. doi:10.1542/peds.2012–3804
21. Mitra AK, Akramuzzaman SM, Fuchs GJ, Rahman MM, Mahalanabis D. Long-term oral supplementation with iron is not harmful for young children in a poor community of Bangladesh. *J Nutr*. 1997;127:1451–1455.

22. Semba RD, de Pee S, Sun K, Akhter N, Bloem MW, Raju VK. Coverage of vitamin A capsule program in Bangladesh and risk factors associated with non-receipt of vitamin A. *J Health Pop Nutr*. 2010;28(2):143–148.
23. Pandav C. Breakthroughs in Bangladesh boost iodized salt quality. IDD Newsletter 2013.
24. Food and Agriculture (2010). Nutrition country profile: Bangladesh. http://www.fao.org/ag/agn/nutrition/bgd_en.stm. Accessed March 13, 2016.
25. World Food Programme. Fighting hunger worldwide. Bangladesh. https://www.wfp.org/countries/bangladesh/food-security. Accessed May 13, 2016.
26. Nargis M. *Scaling-up Innovations: Community Clinic in Bangladesh*. http://www.who.int/pmnch/about/governance/partnersforum/4a_nargis.pdf. Accessed May 17, 2016.
27. Zohir, S. *NGO Sector in Bangladesh: An Overview*. http://sajjadz.net/document_library/admin/upload/epw%20ngo-20140206-131909.pdf. Accessed May 24, 2016.
28. BRAC. http://www.brac.net.
29. ICDDRB. http://www.icddrb.org/.
30. Secondary and tertiary level hospitals all over the country. Specialized hospitals in Bangladesh. http://www.hsmdghs-bd.org/Govt_Hospital.htm. Accessed August 12, 2016.
31. Diabetic Association of Bangladesh. http://www.dab-bd.org/birdem.php.
32. Dhaka Shishu (Children) Hospital. http://dhakashishuhospital.org.bd/.
33. National Heart Foundation of Bangladesh. http://www.nhf.org.bd/.
34. National Institute of Traumatology and Orthopaedic Rehabilitation. http://nitorbd.com/.
35. Ispahani Islamia Eye Institute and Hospital, Bangladesh. http://islamia.org.bd/.
36. Bangladesh Medical and Dental Council. The regulatory authority in Bangladesh. http://bmdc.org.bd/.
37. Directorate of Nursing Services. Government of People's Republic of Bangladesh. http://dns.gov.bd/.
38. Akter S, Rahman MM, Abe SK, Sultana P. Prevalence of diabetes and prediabetes and their risk factors among Bangladeshi adults: a nationwide survey. *Bulletin of the World Health Organization*. 2014;92:204–213A. doi: http://dx.doi.org/10.2471/BLT.13.128371
39. Mahmud S. Health workforce in Bangladesh. 2013. http://opinion.bdnews24.com/2013/03/24/health-workforce-in-bangladesh/. Accessed May 30, 2016.
40. Islam A, Biswas T. Health system in Bangladesh: challenges and opportunities. *American Journal of Health Research*. 2014;2(6):366–374.
41. Khan J, Ahmed S. Healthcare financing—challenges and opportunities for achieving universal health coverage in Bangladesh. https://kiedit.ki.se/en/lime/calendar/healthcare-financing-challenges-and-opportunities-for-achieving-universal-health. Accessed August 12, 2016.
42. Government of Bangladesh. Summary Bangladesh National Health Accounts, 1997–2012. http://www.slideshare.net/policyadda/summary-bangladesh-national-health-accounts-19972012. Accessed August 12, 2016.
43. Al-Muti SA. Bangladesh's development surprise: a model for developing countries. http://asiafoundation.org/2014/06/25/bangladeshs-development-surprise-a-model-for-developing-countries/. Accessed August 12, 2016.

CHAPTER 22

India

Puneet Misra, Kapil Yadav, Neelam Sharma, and **Sudha Xirasagar**

▸ Country Description

TABLE 22-1 India	
Nationality	Noun: Indian(s) Adjective: Indian
Ethnic groups	Indo-Aryan 72%, Dravidian 25%, Mongoloid, other 3% (2000)
Religions	Hindu 79.8%, Muslim 14.2%, Christian 2.3%, Sikh 1.7%, Buddhist 0.7%, Jain 0.4%, others 0.8%, unspecified 0.2% (2011 est.)
Language	Hindi (official national language, primary for 30%); English (most widely used for official political and commercial communication); 21 other official: Assamese, Bengali, Bodo, Dogri, Gujarati, Kannada, Kashmiri, Konkani, Maithili, Malayalam, Manipuri, Marathi, Nepali, Oriya, Punjabi, Sanskrit, Santhali, Sindhi, Tamil, Telugu, Urdu; Hindustani (variant of Hindi/Urdu) in northern India but not official
Literacy	Definition: Age 15 and over can read and write. Total population: 71.2% Male: 81.3% Female: 60.6% (2015 est.)
Government type	Federal republic
Date of independence	August 15, 1947 (from Great Britain)

(continues)

TABLE 22-1 India (continued)

Gross Domestic Product (GDP) per capita	$1,498.9 (2013 est.)
Unemployment rate (15–24 age group)	10.7% (2012 est.)
Natural hazards	Droughts, flash floods, destructive flooding from monsoon rains, severe thunderstorms, occasional earthquakes
Environment: current issues	Deforestation, soil erosion, overgrazing, desertification, air pollution from industrial effluents and vehicle emissions, water pollution from raw sewage and agricultural pesticide runoff, tap water not potable throughout the country, huge growing population overstraining natural resources
Population	1,251,695,584 (2015 est.)
Age structure	0–14 years: 27.71% (male 186,420,229/female 164,611,755) 15–24 years: 17.99% (male 121,009,850/female 106,916,692) 25–54 years: 40.91% (male 267,203,029/female 251,070,105) 55–64 years: 7.30% (male 46,398,574/female 46,105,489) 65 years and over: 6.09% (male 36,549,003/female 40,598,872) (2016 est.)
Median age	Total: 27.3 years (2015 est.) Male: 26.7 years Female: 28.0 years
Population growth rate (annual)	1.22% (2015 est.)
Birth rate	19.55 births/1,000 population (2015 est.)
Death rate	1,051 deaths/100,000 population (2016 est.)
Disease burden	Communicable disease deaths: 253/100,000 population Noncommunicable disease deaths: 682/100,000 population Injury deaths: 116/100,000 population (2016 est.)
Net migration rate	−0.04 migrant(s)/1,000 population (2015 est.)
Gender ratio	At birth: 1.12 male(s)/female Under 15 years: 1.13 male(s)/female 15–24 years: 1.13 male(s)/female 15–54 years: 1.06 male(s)/female 55–64 years: 1.01 male(s)/female 65 years and over: 0.90 male(s)/female Total population: 1.08 male(s)/female (2015 est.)
Infant mortality rate	Total: 41.81 deaths/1,000 live births Male: 40.56 deaths/1,000 live births Female: 43.22 deaths/1,000 live births (2015 est.)

TABLE 22-1 India (continued)	
Life expectancy at birth	Total population: 68.13 years Male: 66.97 years Female: 69.42 years (2015 est.)
Total fertility rate	2.48 children born/woman (2015 est.)
HIV/AIDS adult prevalence rate	0.26% (2015 est.)
Number of people living with HIV/AIDS	2,079,700 (2013 est.)
HIV/AIDS deaths	127,200 (2013 est.)

Data from Central Intelligence Agency. The World Fact Book, 2016: India. https://www.cia.gov/library/publications/the-world-factbook. Accessed April 28, 2016.

History

India is the second most populous country in the world, with 1,251 million people (about 3.5 times that of the United States, with a land area of about a third of that of the USA).[1] It has 22 officially recognized languages spoken in 844 different dialects rooted in two indigenous languages, Sanskrit and Tamil, with elements of Persian, Arabic, and English imbibed in the course of trade relations and armed conquests. English is one of two official national languages, the other being Hindi. The major religious-cultural identity is Hinduism (80%), followed by Islam (14%) and Christianity (3%).

The Indo-Gangetic Plain is a large area encompassing most of northern and eastern India and is possibly the world's oldest surviving civilization to this day, dated as a mature civilization at about the 7th millennium BCE.[2] Evidence of sewage systems and public baths are found in archeological excavations dated to about 4,000 BCE. The earliest Vedic treatises and scriptures transmitted in the oral tradition (that can be dated by astronomical events recorded within them) reflect a culture with a strong hygiene orientation; a pastoral lifestyle and lactovegetarian preference; economic systems that included weights and measures; and use of copper, iron, and barley.[2]

The Vedic civilization laid the foundation of Hinduism's approach of an integrated physical, mental, social, civic, and spiritual way of life, which continues to influence subtly the attitudes and lifestyles related to education, health, illness, treatment, death, and dying. In addition to Hinduism, with its many philosophical schools, India birthed two other ancient religions: Buddhism, founded by Buddha (1887 to 1807 BCE),[2] and Jainism. In the 16th century, Sikhism emerged. These traditions share with Hinduism the core doctrines of the sacredness of all life (therefore a bias toward vegetarianism), introverted pursuit of enlightenment for liberation from the cycle of rebirth, self-sacrifice and self-denial to attain enlightenment, belief in rebirth and karma, and a shared heritage of yoga and Ayurveda. As a result of the shared philosophy of life, there has been fluid interchange, including intermarriage, conversions, and cross-identification of these religions. Hinduism identifies Buddha as its 10th avatar (God taking human form). Currently, a small percentage of population identifies with these religions (2%), in contrast to the widespread prevalence of Buddhism into and beyond the Himalayas up to Japan.

Two major spinoffs from the Vedic culture's focus on knowledge and spiritual enlightenment were yoga and Ayurveda (knowledge, or science of life). The surgical branch of Ayurveda gained much momentum in the post-Buddha era because of Buddhism's focus on a practical version of spirituality and real-time compassion (in contrast to the ritual and other-worldly focus of Hinduism). Together, these two health systems prescribe a way of healthful life and healing, based on a premise that the self (and self-discipline) is the root of health and healing. Many elements of yoga and Ayurveda are intimately woven into the prescribed (and for the most part, ritually practiced), daily personal lifestyle, civic norms, and social traditions. Ayurveda, Yoga, and Siddha (a South Indian system of medicine that is several millennia old) continue to provide the foundation of many indigenous health and healing practices in modern India, particularly among the rural population. Together with Unani and homeopathy, alternative systems of medicine are offered through AYUSH care by trained doctors of these systems. AYUSH care is offered in both the public and private sector, with the public services funded by the AYUSH ministry of the central government and offered through a large number of primary health centers in the country. In recent years many new initiatives are being launched by the central government in India to ramp up awareness and to mainstream the AYUSH system of medicine.

The Indian subcontinent—known since ancient times for its riches, driven by trade in spices, gold, and precious stones—experienced many invasions, from Alexander of Greece, through the Islamic invasions (from the 8th century CE onward, through the Persian Moghul invasion and rule between the 15th and 19th centuries), and British rule (consolidated in 1757, lasting up to 1947). These historic events triggered much religious and cultural diversity, particularly the widespread conversions to Islam, and the birth of Sikhism. Christianity entered the subcontinent through the west coast almost during the time of Jesus Christ and has a significant present in the western coastal states.

The British colonial period marked a political milestone by initiating a crucial shift from a variegated administration pattern across nearly 500 dynastic kingdoms to adoption of system-based institutional structures and the rule of law. Other contributions of British colonial rule further enabled the modern nation-state, grounded in the norm of political stewardship of public resources for public good, implemented through political processes rooted in a democratic framework. Critical contributions included modern communications, such as railroads, the postal system, and the telegraph, and the implicit unifying effects of a universal single language of English. Parallel with these modernizing effects, however, British colonialism also led to the disappearance of many local arts, crafts, economic activities, Ayurvedic and other indigenous medicinal treatises, and local medicinal traditions and knowledge.[2]

After World War II, the Indian subcontinent's nonviolent struggle for independence led to freedom from British rule on August 15, 1947, concurrent with partition into the Islamic state of Pakistan (East and West) and an explicitly secular India with a predominantly Hindu population. (In 1971, East Pakistan seceded to form Bangladesh.) Other neighboring nation-states, Afghanistan and Myanmar (Burma), were also created at this time. Within India, the indigenous, universal civic institution of decentralized village self-rule (*panchayati raj*) was overlaid with the new nation-states identity and governance. Its new Western-educated, progressive political leaders determined that parliamentary democracy was best suited to govern India's diverse people with a multitude of caste, religious, and language identities. However, these identities continue to play an important role in social and political life, including voting patterns in political elections.

For millennia, the Hindu caste system defined individuals' place in the occupational and social hierarchy. The millennia-old major castes with the associated vocations are Brahmins (responsible for priestly, spiritual, and intellectual pursuits and asserted to be closest to final enlightenment from the cycle of rebirth), Kshatriyas (warriors), Vaishyas (businessmen), and Shudras (farmers/artisans/other labor occupations). Outside of this mainstream caste system were the untouchables, or dalits or scheduled caste (previously known as Harijans), who experienced much discrimination, often severe exploitation, and exclusion from all development and governance roles in preindependent India. The caste system became entrenched as a hereditary hierarchy sometime during the first millennium BCE, when it was asserted that one's birth in a caste was the result of karma (deeds) in previous births. If each individual fulfilled their role dutifully, all human beings would eventually attain spiritual enlightenment through successive rebirths into higher order castes. The caste system persists to this day, defining boundaries for marriage and cultural associations and dietary patterns (such as meat-eating, permitted by the scriptures only for the physically laboring castes, kshatriyas, shudras, and dalits). The Indian Constitution, promulgated in 1950, abolished untouchability (making it a felony) and established affirmative action, providing scholarships and living expenses for education, and reserving 22.5% of all educational and job opportunities in government and public sector industries for the dalits and tribals (forest-dwelling aboriginal peoples). Over the past seven decades, these constitutional guarantees, along with economic and educational development, have enabled much upward social and economic mobility for dalits, tribals, and lower castes, significantly reducing caste-based social and economic disparities, particularly in urban areas.

Size and Geography

India is a land of 3,287,263 square kilometers (approximately a third of the U.S. land area); it is bound by the Himalayan mountains to the north and northeast, with its peninsular part surrounded by oceans (the Indian Ocean, Arabian Sea, and Bay of Bengal). It has a land frontier of 15,200 kilometers and a coastline of 7,516 kilometers (**FIGURE 22-1**). The northernmost state of Jammu and Kashmir remains disputed, with Pakistan occupying a third of this state after a post-independence war.

FIGURE 22-1 Map of India
© Bardocz Peter/Shutterstock

Government and Political System

In 1950, promulgation of the Indian Constitution conferred sovereign, secular, and democratic republic status, with a multiparty, parliamentary system of democratic governance, similar to Britain.[3] Within this governance structure, its mixed economic model (public and private sector) was premised on the concept of a welfare state for much of its post-independent history. The central government led the charge for improving socioeconomic and health conditions by establishing large public sector industries (heavy engineering, coal, steel, power, etc., the "commanding heights of the economy") to serve as the engines of economic development and social equalization of the traditionally oppressed castes. Most developmental infrastructure, including health and education, has been funded by the central government through successive five-year plans, which have ensured consistency in the pattern, as well as speed of development of the public health infrastructure across India's diverse states.

The central government has three wings: the legislature (two houses of parliament), executive (prime minister and cabinet of ministers), and the judiciary (Supreme Court to deal with constitutional law). Superimposed on these is the Lok Ayukta, with jurisdiction to indict any public functionary of any level or wing in government in matters of governance and breach of the respective codes of conduct. The country is divided into 550 electoral districts that directly elect their representative (universal suffrage, all citizens aged over 18 years) to the Lower House or Lok Sabha (literally, People's Council, equivalent to Britain's House of Commons), who in turn elect the prime minister. Elections to the Lok Sabha are held every 5 years, unless advanced by political shifts or major national crises. Multiple parties are represented, and either the majority party or a coalition assumes power and chooses the prime minister. The prime minister is the nation's chief executive, sharing responsibility and power with the cabinet. The prime minister selects cabinet members (ministers) to lead the departments, based on the electorate represented in the ruling party and political exigencies. The cabinet provides political leadership to the departments run by career civil servants.

The key lawmaking agency is the Lok Sabha, with ratification from the Upper House or Rajya Sabha (literally governing council). The latter is composed of indirectly elected members, a third each elected by state legislators, nation's college graduates, and teachers. The president is the titular head of government, chief of the armed forces, and serves a reserve executive governance function during national emergencies or parliamentary deadlocks. India has a semifederalist structure with 29 states (divided mostly on linguistic bases, and a few on cultural basis) and 7 union territories. States are further divided into 630 administrative districts.[3] Each state government is modeled along similar lines as the central government, with subject jurisdictions laid out under central (e.g., defense), state (e.g., education), or concurrent lists. Since independence, except for a two-year period of national emergency declared by the prime minister for 1975 to 1977, the country has been governed under constitutionally elected governments by the people.

States do not levy income taxes; they derive revenues from sales and excise taxes, as well as their share of income and other central tax revenues based on a combination of formulas and discretionary disbursements that are driven by political, natural disaster, and national interest considerations. Below the state level, local governments are governed by directly elected councils on local issues (district councils, called *zillaparishads*, municipalities, and over a half-million village *panchayats*). Functioning of sub-state entities is greatly restrained by wide and growing gaps between revenues and infrastructure/service needs of a growing population.

Macroeconomics

The major economic sectors by contribution to gross domestic product (GDP) (2010) are agriculture, forestry, and fishing (16.8%); manufacturing, mining, and construction (27.1%); financial, information technology (IT), and other services (15.8%); and trade, hotels, transport, and communication (24.8%).[4] The currency is the Indian rupee (exchange rate approximately Rs66.7 = US $1 in 2016).

Since independence, India has pursued a mixed economy model with public and private sector participation in industrial development. In the early postindependent years, a socialist model of public sector investment in large-scale industries (particularly steel, coal, oil, heavy engineering, defense, and power generation), with tight controls on foreign direct investment, served important purposes in nation building. These were: (1) emergence of a significant, salaried, middle class (from a preindependent situation of over 90% of population either at or near starvation levels of existence), (2) nominal universalization of the idea of caste equality, including the untouchables, (3) generation of significant domestic purchasing power for goods and services, and (4) generation of a well-educated and professional workforce fueled by the emerging middle class. To recall a metaphor by Swaminathan S. Aiyar, a prominent Indian economist, India graduated from "mass famine (starvation deaths by the tens of thousands) in British India to mass starvation in the sixties" (chronic caloric deficiency; not a single famine recorded in postindependent democratic India). Then one observes the onward progress to mass malnutrition in the 1970s and 1980s (calorie sufficient but nutrient deficient), and since then, a rising middle class coexists with significant micronutrient malnutrition among the poor. The 21st century has been characterized by a significant growth of overweight and obesity among the affluent (both urban and rural).

Soon, however, the utility of public sector-driven economic development became hamstrung by poor accountability, low productivity, large-scale deficit financing, and politician–civil servant corruption in the name of bureaucratic controls, ostensibly to "regulate" the greedy and exploitative for-profit sector. Bureaucracy, corruption, and unbridled populism (the latter fueled by a multiparty democratic setup within a socially, linguistically, and religiously fragmented electorate, dominated by the poor and near poor) began to stymie economic growth. In 1991, a situation approaching bankruptcy propelled major economic liberalization reforms favoring the free market, gradual privatization, dismantling dysfunctional regulation, and the silent, unfettered rise of the IT industry.

The reforms unleashed a dramatic economic revolution, lifting millions out of poverty. In 2007, it produced an estimated total GDP of PPP US $2.965 trillion (in purchasing power parity) or $3,460 per capita in 2007,[5] logging over 7% annual growth rate since 1997 (8.5% in 2007),[6] led by IT or IT-enabled services and by industrial manufacturing. Between 2007 and 2015, GDP of PPP grew to $7,965 trillion.[7] On the other hand, economic liberalization has led to large and rapidly widening income/wealth gaps between the haves and have-nots, poised to threaten the social and civic fabric particularly in urban areas. According to international statistics from 2012, agriculture accounted for 49% of the total estimated workforce and only 17% of GDP.[7] The Gini index of distribution of family income was 33.6 (2012), the lowest 10.0% by household income consume/earn 3.6% of GDP, and the top 10% earn 31.1% of GDP.[7] An estimated 23.1% of the population lived in poverty in 2011, down from 30% in 2010, and compared to 49.4% in 1993.[7-9] Unemployment in 2015 stood at 8.7% (with a significant, indeterminate number underemployed).[7] The female labor participation rate was 43.0%; among them 59.0% were agricultural workers and 7.0% (similar to the percentage of male workers) in professional, technical, administrative, and managerial occupations.[10]

A major issue for civic infrastructure and healthcare financing has been the distribution of its employed population: among the total employed population, 20% have been employed in the formal sector of industry and have accounted for 30% of GDP.[11] The remaining 31% of the population have been engaged in service industries or self-owned enterprises but have accounted for 45% of GDP. Thus, the income tax base for government revenues is limited largely to the employed population.[12,7] Major industries are textiles, chemicals, food processing, steel, transportation equipment, cement, mining, petroleum, and heavy machinery, with IT assuming a major role since the mid-1990s. Although IT and IT-enabled services are mostly limited to the major metropolitan cities, the remaining industries are widely distributed.

Agricultural production, led by the green revolution since 1951, has made major strides, moving the country from being a net food importer at independence to a net food exporter.[10] India also became the world's leading milk producer (overtaking the United States) in 2002, a status that sustained through 2015, with 18.5% of world milk production.[13] Despite this, malnutrition continues to be widespread, with pulses and legumes (the major source of protein for its largely vegetarian population) declining in per capita availability from 60.0 grams (gm) in 1951 to 36.0 gm in 2004.[10] The per capita net daily availability of cereals and pulses has decreased from 468.8 gm in 1971 to 401.4 gm in 2013.[14] These numbers obscure major inequalities in actual consumption because of poor purchasing power of the lowest income decile of population.

Major shortages prevail in the areas of electricity, energy, and transportation, with seasonal shortages of water. Major infrastructure shortages are also faced in roads, sanitation, water supply, and so forth. In 2015, 94% of households had access to improved drinking water sources. But only 47.0% of households had a water source within the house, and 70.6% of the urban population had access to in-house piped water with the remaining urban population using hand pumps fitted to borewells or similar sources.[15] Of greater concern is the rapidly diminishing water resource availability per capita, expected to fall by 2025 below what is classified as a water stress level (with many areas already under stress/scarcity conditions). Experts predict a grave water crisis in the near future, attributable entirely to the increasing population. Deteriorating water quality further compounds the issue. In 2015, it was reported that of the entire population only 39.6% had access to sanitation facilities, mostly in urban areas.[7] Water and sanitation deficiencies will continue to be key challenges because of significant population with very low purchasing power. Less than 30.0% of the population without these facilities was prepared to pay for even community-based facilities.[16] The National Family Health Survey reported that in 2005 to 2006, 68.0% of households had electricity, but this increased to 79% by 2013.[7,9]

Transportation is largely road and rail based, with 65% of freight and 80% of passenger traffic transported by road,[17] while the rest is by rail. In total in 2015, India had 4,699,000 kilometers of roadways and 68,000 kilometers of railways.[7] Inadequate road length and width and poor quality are a major drag on industrial productivity. Poor connectivity in rural areas also directly hampers rapid medical attention. Road infrastructure is a key infrastructural weakness (along with water, sanitation, and electricity) that will limit India's current upward spiral in development and global economic participation.[18] There are 12 major ports developed and maintained by the central government and 200 minor ports.[19]

Education is another area of concern, particularly for the rural and urban poor. According to the 2011 census, the literacy rate among the population aged 7 years and older was 74% (82% among males and 65% among females), an increase of 13% over the 2001 census rate. There has been a modest improvement, and in 2015, India reported a 71% literacy rate. This disparity in literacy is mostly between males (80% literacy rate) and females (60% literacy rate). Both genders spend between 11 and 12 years in school.[7] Most illiteracy is now accounted for by the elderly. During recent years, children show near-universal primary school enrollments, although dropout rates are high. Despite laws requiring primary school enrollment of age-appropriate children, a combination of economic factors, distance barriers, inadequate teachers, a lack of accountability in teacher attendance, poor transportation and school infrastructure, and poor quality schooling results in rural children receiving poor quality education. They drop out early (particularly girls) to turn to domestic or economically productive activities such a farming and petty economic activities.

The Gross Enrolment Ratio (GER) represents the ratio of actual enrolled students at several different grade levels (like elementary, middle school, and high school) to the population in the age group that qualifies for enrollment at each level. A higher GER implies children of older ages than the expected age group being enrolled, and lower GER implies corresponding drop out of children of the age group. GER for females at the primary level stood at 102.65 compared with 100.20 for males in 2013–2014. At the middle school level, the GER for females has been reported as 92.75 against 86.31 for males, and at the higher secondary level, 51.58 and 52.70, respectively, during 2013–2014.[20]

There was a seven-fold increase in school enrollment from the time of independence (1950–1951 census) to 2011–2012, from 19.2 million to 139.9 million, while the population increased four-fold in the same period. Total enrolment in the upper primary grades increased by 55.4% from 2000–2001 to 2013–2014. The primary school dropout rate decreased from 64.9 in 1960–61 to 22.3 in 2011–2012, being higher at 23.4% for boys and 21.4% for girls.[21]

These factors have major implications for communicable diseases, maternal and child health, general population health, healthcare access, affordability, power relations among the economic and health haves versus have-nots, healthcare financing mechanisms, and service delivery.

Demographics

India's population profile and vital statistics are presented in **TABLE 22-2**.[1,22–24] India has 16.70% of the world's population living on 2.40% of the world's land area.[23] India's population continues to be predominantly rural with 67% of the population living in rural areas.[7] As of 2015, it is estimated that the urban

TABLE 22-2 India's Demographic Profile and Vital Statistics

Indicator	Current status
Total population	1,266,883,000 (2016 est.)[23]
Crude birth rate	19.3/1,000 (2016 est.)
Crude death rate	7.3/1,000 (2016 est.)
Life expectancy at birth	Total population: 68.13 years (2015 est.) Male: 66.97 years Female: 69.42 years
Annual growth rate	1.19% (2016 est.)
Population doubling time at current growth rate	41.2 years[17]
Population rural	67.3% (2016 est.)[23]

TABLE 22-2 India's Demographic Profile and Vital Statistics (*continued*)

Indicator	Current status
Adult literacy rate	71.2% of total population 60% of females 15 years and older 80% of males 15 years and older (2016 est.)
Age-appropriate school attendance	72.0% for primary school 51.0% for high school (2005–2006)
Population younger than 15 years	27.71 (2016)[23]
Population older than 60 years	6.09% (2016)[23]
Average household size	4.8 (2011)
Female mean age at marriage	21.2 years 17.2 years (median) (2012)[17]
Annual per capita GDP (PPP)	$6,200 (2016)[26]
Percent below poverty line	30% (2016)[27]
Age dependency ratio (% of working age population)	52.4% (2015)[28]
Infant mortality rate	Total: 40.5/1,000 live births (2016)[29] Rural: 44/1,000 live births (2013)[28] Urban: 27/1,000 live births (2013)[28]
Maternal mortality rate	16.3/1,000 births (2007–2009) and 17.4/1,000 births (2015)
Life expectancy at birth	68.5 years (2016) 67.3 years (male)[30] 69.8 years (female)[29]
Total fertility rate (per woman)	2.45 (14% decline over the previous 7 years) (2016)
Desired total fertility rate	1.99 per woman (2005–2006)
Labor force participation per 1,000 by gender	Female: rural 181, urban 134 Male: rural 547, urban 560 (2012)[31]
Regular exposure to mass media (television, newspapers, radio, cinema)	Female: 65% (2005–2006)[10] Male: 82% (2005–2006)[10]

All 2005–2006 data are from the National Family Health Survey 3, 2005–2006, sampling a nationally representative sample of 109,041 households interviewing 198,744 women and men of reproductive age group.

population increases each year by over 2%. The rural sector of the population has consistently attracted strong policy and public investment emphasis from successive governments.[25] Except for the 5 largest cities of 6 million or more—Delhi, the capital city; Mumbai, the most densely populated city; Kolkata; Chennai; and Bangalore—India's urban population is widely distributed: 56.60% of its urban population lives in 322 cities of more than 100,000 population, and 43.40% in 4,293 towns of 1,000 to 100,000 population.[10]

Population growth, outpacing civic and infrastructure growth, remains the chief concern, causing an ever-increasing gap between the need and availability of water, sanitation, housing, health care, agricultural land, law enforcement, primary and secondary education institutions (both quality and quantity), and other basic needs of development. The current population and expected short-term growth are widely agreed to be India's "fundamental social, economic, and environmental problem[s]."[6] Population concerns have long guided India's domestic policies: India was the world's first government to sponsor a state-promoted, voluntary, family planning program in 1952, based on mass media and couples education, financial incentives for women choosing family planning, and provision of a widely accessible network of facilities with family planning service capability within 5 kilometers of every household.[21]

Major Morbidity and Its Distribution

The major health problems can be classified as communicable diseases, environmental and sanitation-related problems, nutritional problems, and noncommunicable diseases. These issues are fueled by rapid population growth, which arose after independence out of the rapidly falling death rates caused by eradication of famines and massive reductions in communicable disease mortality (notably malaria, plague, smallpox, and diarrheal disease) and infant mortality. From a crude death rate of about 35 per 1,000 and an infant mortality rate of 160 per 1,000 live births at independence,[32] these rates fell to 15 per 1,000 and 129 per 1,000 live births respectively, from 1971 through 1981, and further to 7 per 1,000 and 40 per 1,000 in 2013.[23] Despite high contraception prevalence levels (56% among currently married women), early marriage of a very large youth population from the population expansions of the 1970s and 1980s has continued to fuel large population increases in the 1990s and will continue up to 2020.[9] Marriage is near universal, and out-of-wedlock births are rare. Demographic pressures seriously undermine the impact of significant additions to public health and healthcare infrastructure achieved through massive investments, causing the percentage of population with access to health, water, and sanitation facilities to improve modestly or even stagnate in some sectors.

Despite mandatory birth and death registration, rural vital statistics have relied upon the Sample Registration System, covering a nationally representative sample (1.5 million households in 2013).[28] While communicable diseases continue to be a major concern, the composition and salience of diseases have changed significantly. The incidence and mortality due to malaria have declined steeply, with 0.88 million cases and 440 deaths identified in 2013 having declined more than 50% over the prior decade.[33] The malaria situation has remained at low-grade endemic levels following the early dramatic reductions from an estimated 75 million malaria cases out of 350 million population at the time of independence to about 1 million cases among an expanded population of about 550 million in 1976, and now there are about 0.88 million in a 1.25 billion population, primarily because of the National Malaria Eradication/Control Program.[21] Environmental sanitation deficiencies and climatic conditions favoring mosquito propagation permit endemic low-grade transmission, particularly in the rainy season.

Two endemic, chronic diseases with long latent periods and a low lifetime probability of disease are tuberculosis and leprosy. The tuberculosis incidence has remained stagnant since first measured in the 1960s, at 4 sputum-positive (infectious) tuberculosis cases per 1,000 population and 16 per 1,000 X-ray–positive cases, and 30% of the population is infected. An estimated 240,000 tuberculosis deaths take place every year, reduced by about 45% over the prior decade.[34] Leprosy continues to cause morbidity, with 125,785 new cases in 2014–2015 (58.9% of the world's cases). Of the total, 9.04% are children, 4.61% have deformity of grade II and above, and 52.82% are multibacillary (infectious) cases.[35] The latter figure indicates that, like tuberculosis, leprosy transmission continues, with newly infected people carrying the latent potential of breaking down to active disease for the rest of their lifetimes. Widespread implementation of multidrug therapy since 1983 under the National Leprosy Eradication Program has substantially reduced the deformity rate and number of chronic cases.

Other major public health problems are diarrheal disease—responsible for 700,000 deaths each year, mostly children under 5 years of age, predisposed by nutritional deficiencies (vitamin A, protein energy malnutrition, and anemia)—and filariasis, with at least 6 million cases of acute filarial infection each year, with a cumulative number of at least 45 million having chronic residual damage.[4,21] Other communicable diseases include visceral leishmaniasis, typhoid and related enteric fevers, and intestinal parasitic infestations, which are not notifiable and are therefore difficult to estimate because the majority of cases are treated in the private sector. Dengue fever with large scale urban transmission has replaced malaria as the major communicable disease of concern to health policymakers and the population, especially because of dengue hemorrhagic fever, which carries a high mortality rate.

The population-based prevalence of HIV was assessed for the first time in 2005–2006,[9] covering 105,477 women and men in the reproductive age group (15–49 years). The test participation rate was 94.50% among 111,616 eligible samples. This established a nationwide HIV-positive rate of 0.28% in these age groups (0.22% among women and 0.36% among men), translating to a total of 1.7 million cases nationally among adults aged 15 to 49 in 2006. According to the 2014–2015 annual report, the number of people living with HIV is estimated to be 2.9 million in 2011 among the age group of 15–49 years, 39.0% being women. As with other diseases, there is much variation across states within this overall figure. The survey also found near universal awareness of major routes of HIV transmission and prevention. Most men and women (63% and 82%, respectively) wanted HIV/AIDS to be a part of the school curriculum.[10]

Widespread nutritional deficiencies directly and indirectly impact the population's health by mediating maternal health risks and children's susceptibility to infections and succumbing to disease. In 2007 children aged 6 months to 5 years, almost 70% are anemic (40% moderately anemic and 3% severely anemic).[9] Anemia levels have not been reduced in recent years and, in fact, have increased in the past few years, the reasons for which are not clear.[9] In 2013, 55.3% women aged 15–49 years were anemic, 1.8% severely anemic. In 2015 children under the age of 5 years, 38.7% are stunted, and 42.5% are underweight, with 19.8% of these showing wasting.[36] According to a 2009 survey to determine vaccination coverage, the full number of doses and all recommended vaccines among children aged 12–23 months was 61.0%, largely because of dropouts after one or two doses of DPT or polio vaccine.[32] The pattern of under-five mortality causes reflects that these major health problems, coupled with water and sanitation infrastructure deficiencies, and the maternal health and perinatal care deficiencies, confer significant mortality risk on infants and young children.

Despite major strides in maternal health care, much remains to be done. In 2005–2006, 76.0% of women with a live birth in the previous 5 years received antenatal care, with only two-thirds of them receiving 3 or more antenatal visits.[9] Some 49.7% of pregnant women aged 15–49 had 3 or more prenatal care visits (2013–2014). Responding to the dismal maternal and child health scenario, several groundbreaking initiatives were launched in recent years. The Janani Suraksha Yojana offers all pregnant women a Mother and Child Protection card that entitles them to personalized healthcare navigation to institutional prenatal care and delivery at a private or government health facility. These facilities are village- or neighborhood-level female auxiliary health activists who are incentivized to enroll and retain pregnant women in antenatal care throughout pregnancy and to personally transport mothers to a health facility for delivery. Each mother is also provided financial assistance contingent upon undergoing delivery at an institution. Private facilities are reimbursed fixed service charges for providing services to women with the card. This initiative has doubled the rate of institutional deliveries and prenatal care, and it has greatly improved postnatal follow-up visits with infants, including timely vaccinations. These services are documented to have reached the most underserved sections of the population and the poorest states. Other effects on contraception prevalence among traditionally low-use geographic regions and population subgroups, and the use of other maternal and child health services, are expected to fructify in the near future.

The contraception prevalence rate in 2012–2013 was 54.8% (35.8% female, with the terminal method, tubal ligation).[32] The contraception rate has steadily increased and accelerated among traditional nonusers in the last few years. Fertility has been reduced significantly to 2.45 per woman, although still well above the replacement level of 2.1 per woman.[32] Of concern is the fact that contraception is inversely related to poverty and female low education level (increasing the maternal and child mortality risk of these groups). The good news is that reduction in family size (with increasing contraception) is expanding to subgroups with persistent high fertility in the past,[10] which bodes well for maternal and child health, as well as population control.

Infant mortality, child mortality, malnutrition, and long-term growth and educational-economic prospects for children are inversely related to maternal health and nutrition. The total under-five child mortality rate of 85% is accounted for by neonatal conditions, diarrheal diseases, and pneumonia, all closely linked to maternal/child nutritional status or maternal health issues.[5] In turn, these factors are linked to low interpregnancy interval/early childbearing or deficient prenatal/intrapartum/postnatal care.

The maternal mortality rate, although significantly reduced from preindependence levels, continues to be unacceptably high.[5] It has decreased significantly from about 5.4 per 1,000 live births in the 1990s to 2.12 in 2007, and further to 1.67 in 2014 due to various government programs, a major facilitator being the Janani Suraksha Yojana.

The previously mentioned communicable diseases that were characteristic of the "age of receding pandemics"[37] are typically readily controlled by public health interventions, health education, and nutritional changes (relatively cheap public health interventions). Concurrent with these receding diseases, there are unfolding problems of noncommunicable diseases requiring expensive secondary and tertiary care, largely cardiovascular disease, mental illness, diabetes, and cancer. Cardiovascular disease is a major silent killer, causing 25% of deaths among adults in the 30- to 50-year-old group.[38] Bronchial asthma affects an estimated 15 to 20 million (about 1.5% of population). Population-wide prevalence rates of mental illness and cancer are not available.

▸ Brief History of the Healthcare System

Pre–World War II

Before World War II, the British set up hospitals in the major cities with British officers and troops stationed to administer the colonial functions and local administration. British India's government (under the governor-general) had the surgeon general oversee the development and administration of medical care facilities (largely in cities and towns) and had the public health commissioner oversee public health functions, largely from a colonial perspective: control of epidemics and prevention during large scale fairs and pilgrim events, sporadic water and sanitation activities, and communicable disease (malaria and gastroenteritis) research.

As for rural primary health care based on modern medicine, the first primary health centers (PHCs) were established by the maharajah (king) of Mysore (in South India) in the 1920s, financed from the royal treasury, providing grassroots services such as sanitation education, purification of wells, physician services, and family planning advice. These PHCs may be some of the earliest publicly financed PHCs in the world, with integrated public health and primary care orientation. Generally, however, in the preindependent era, PHCs remained occasional curios in princely states with progressive kings.

Use of Traditional Medicine as Part of the Culture

Ayurveda (in North India) and Siddha (in South India) are two indigenously derived systems of medicine, well established before 1000 BCE,[39] constantly accruing new knowledge over time. Other alternative systems are Unani (rooted in traditional Arab medicine) and homeopathy. Sushruta, placed somewhere between 600 and 1000 BCE, was the founder of surgery in the Ayurvedic medical system.[39] Charaka was the founder of medicine. Many texts and pharmacopeias developed through the ages were lost through the various invasions in northern and middle India, and during the British colonial period. Currently, Ayurveda and Siddha are practiced at two levels: the household level, where common knowledge, herbs, and practices passed on by word of mouth are a part of people's routine response to prevent and treat certain illnesses; and the professional level, with formal college education for 4.5 years plus a year of internship (similar to physicians of modern medicine). The formal Ayurvedic system uses pharmacopeias to systematically treat diseases, particularly chronic diseases (such as rheumatoid arthritis). Many medical colleges and other government hospitals, as well as large, financially self-sustained nonprofit establishments, operate in South India and some parts of north India. It is impossible to quantify the magnitude of use because much consulting (including advice on household herbs) takes place at an informal level. Since the 1980s, Ayurvedic medicine manufactured on an industrial scale has been accelerating with a large clientele, both urban and rural.

Since World War II

After achieving independence, the Indian government integrated the functions of the surgeon general and the public health commissioner into the Office of the Director General of Health Services and faced up to the extremely inadequate healthcare infrastructure and manpower. The Health Survey and Development Committee reported to the outgoing British government in 1947[31] that 1 in every 4 Indians were affected by malaria, 1% of the population suffered from plague in the prior year, the maternal mortality rate was 20 per 1,000 live births, and the crude death rate was about 35 per 1,000 (nearly balancing the crude birth rate of 44 per 1,000). Yet the hospital bed availability was 3 per 10,000 population; physicians were 1 per 10,000, and nurses were 5 per 100,000.[8] Importantly, although 80% of the population was rural, almost no inpatient beds were available in rural areas.[31]

In successive five-year plans since 1951, the government systematically expanded the health infrastructure with an emphasis on rural PHCs, urging PHC medical officers to provide clinical care services as well as logistic and supervisory support to the public health programs that were led by district program officers. All public health programs except family planning (e.g., malaria, leprosy, and tuberculosis) are funded jointly by the central government and state governments, with family planning funded by the central government.[21]

Public medical care institutions (hospitals and clinics) are funded by state governments. The district civil surgeons/chief medical officers (chiefs of all government funded curative services in each district) and medical officers at primary and community health centers (CHCs) are responsible for primary and first-level referral medical care, as well as public health programs. Each district also has a chief medical superintendent and specialists at district hospitals who are concerned with secondary-level medical care.

In 1977, when smallpox was declared eradicated in India and malaria moved from epidemic status to low-grade endemic, the government officially adopted family planning as its chief public health concern. It established the National Institute of Health and Family Planning and launched the Rural Health Scheme to systematically establish rural PHCs (1 for every 30,000 population).[21] Each PHC served as the ultimate implementation unit and hub for all public health programs, led by medical officers, and powered by health workers trained for malaria surveillance and control; diarrheal disease control through chlorination of wells; providing safe delivery and maternal health services; and teaching traditional birth attendants in hygienic delivery, health education, and under-five children's health. This development received further impetus in 1978 by the historic Alma-Ata declaration of Global Strategy for Health for All by the Year 2000, signed by 126 countries under the aegis of the World Health Organization. The HFA declaration called for a population-based network of PHCs in rural and urban areas to provide "essential health care to individuals, families, and communities (preventive and essential health care), in a culturally and socially acceptable manner, at a cost that the country and community could afford."[40]

During the following two decades, the Indian government systematically expanded PHCs in rural and remote tribal/hilly areas (1 per 20,000 tribal/hill population), with a male and a female medical officer, one male and female health worker, field supervisory staff, a basic obstetric facility (for vaginal delivery), and a basic laboratory facility with microscopy for major communicable disease detection (malaria, tuberculosis, and leprosy). Under each PHC are six subcenters, 1 per 5,000 rural population (3,000 in tribal areas) with 1 resident female health worker (auxiliary nurse midwife, ANM, additionally trained in public health) and 1 male health worker. Both male and female health workers visit households in their care. The male health worker is responsible for door-to-door surveillance; presumptive treatment; possibly compliance monitoring of malaria, filariasis, tuberculosis, and leprosy; regular chlorination of wells; and demonstration of sanitary pit latrines and environmental sanitation.

The female health worker is primarily responsible for fortnight visits of all households in her area to provide prenatal and postnatal care, motivate couples for temporary and permanent family planning methods, organize child vaccination clinics, conduct surveillance for diarrheal disease and respiratory infection among children, and conduct home treatment of common ailments, including intestinal parasites.

To provide inpatient and surgical referral care for medical, surgical, and obstetric patients in rural areas, government-run CHCs were established with 30 beds each to serve the area of four PHCs, or 120,000 rural population. CHCs are located in semiurban towns, with an internist, general surgeon, and obstetrician/gynecologist, along with an anesthesiologist at selected CHCs. The next level of publicly funded curative facilities is the district level, with additional specialties, including ear-nose-throat, ophthalmology, psychiatry, and other specialties. Expansion of infrastructure is carried out with a combination of central five-year plan funds and multilateral/bilateral agency loans (e.g., World Bank, Overseas Development Assistance—United Kingdom). Most maintenance, including salaries and administration/supervision, is the responsibility of the state governments, with health being a state subject.

Description of the Current Healthcare System

The health system is a mosaic of institutions that can be viewed through several lenses: government/private ownership, rural/urban distribution, public access/closed insurance facilities, and different medical science systems (allopathic and Indian systems of medicine).

Facilities
Government Health Facilities

In line with the welfare state approach that ruled India's politics until recently, the government health infrastructure is the most widely available, universally accessible, and well documented in number and distribution. Because of disproportionate vulnerability and poverty among the rural population, successive governments have focused more heavily on rural primary health care, leading to much of the government health infrastructure located in rural areas, particularly a multi-tiered primary care system.

TABLE 22-3 shows the present status of healthcare infrastructure in India, including primary care

TABLE 22-3 Primary Health Care and Secondary/Tertiary Health Infrastructure

Institutional type	Number
Allopathic medicine/public health (government/public)	
Primary health centers	25,308 (2015: 1/33,840 population)
Subcenters	153,655 (1/5,480 population) (2015)
Community health centers	5,396 (inpatient and surgery)
Other rural hospitals	884
CHCs in urban locations	433
Other urban hospitals (including tertiary-care centers)	2,256
Total hospitals with bed capacity	20,306 hospitals with 6,75,779 beds (2014)
Hospitals with bed capacity in urban areas	3,490 hospitals with 4,92,177 beds (2014)
Hospital with bed capacity in rural areas	16,816 hospitals with 1,83,602 beds (2014)
Total publicly funded rural hospital bed capacity	111,872 beds (1 bed/7,000 population)*
Total publicly funded urban hospital bed capacity	292,813 beds
Total government-funded bed capacity open to public	469,672 beds (1 bed/2,336 population) (2005)
Medical care facilities under AYUSH (government)	
AYUSH dispensaries[32]	26,102 (2014)
AYUSH hospitals[32]	3,631 (2014)
Hospital beds	24,880 (at 450 medical college hospitals)
Closed-panel government-owned facilities for insured populations	
Employees State Insurance Corporation (ESIC)	
Covered beneficiaries[42]	758,000
Total dispensaries	1,418 (2015)
Total hospitals	166
Total hospital beds	19,089
Central Government Employees Insurance (CGHS)	
Covered beneficiaries	3,191,131
Number of impaneled hospitals under CGHS[43]	498
Wellness centers under CGHS[42]	337

TABLE 22-3 Primary Health Care and Secondary/Tertiary Health Infrastructure (continued)

Institutional type	Number
Polyclinics under CGHS[42]	19
Dental units under CGHS[42]	19
Inpatient care (purchased from government and private hospitals)	—
Medical facilities (privately owned) for workers of hazardous industries (mica, iron ore, limestone, etc.)	
Covered beneficiaries	—
Outpatient clinics and onsite first aid clinics	275
Hospital beds	525
Indian Railways Health Service	
Covered beneficiaries[44]	6,400,000
Outpatient clinics and onsite basic clinics	661
Total number of hospitals	125
Hospital beds	13,702
Private closed-panel (in-house) / contracted health care: public sector industries/undertakings	
Employees (central, state, local government)	18.1 million
Covered beneficiaries	72 million (approximate estimate)
Outpatient clinics/hospitals/beds	—
Closed-panel (in-house) facilities: private sector large industries	
Employees	1.034 million (computed from Central Bureau of Health Intelligence)[8]
Covered beneficiaries	4.13 beneficiaries (estimated)
In-house facilities: armed forces personnel	
Covered beneficiaries	4.4 million (estimated from 1.1 million personnel)[9]
Private sector facilities open to the public	
Hospitals	3,327
Beds	265,137 (1/3,536 population)
Total bed capacity open to the public (government and private)	734,809 (0.7 bed/1,000 uninsured population)

infrastructure and hospital bed capacity in the government and private sectors. It also shows the healthcare infrastructure classified by open-access versus closed panel facilities that cover specific employer-based population subgroups. The rural healthcare system has integrated public health and curative care at the PHC and subcenter (SC) level, both serving as the first point of contact with the healthcare system. Secondary health care provides for internal medicine, surgical, and obstetrics/gynecology care at the CHC level. These facilities are constructed with central government funding and are administered/maintained by state governments under state directorates of health services. Starting the count with the first 725 rural PHCs established in 1951 to 1958, there are 5,396 CHCs, 25,308 PHCs, and 153,655 SCs functioning in India as of March 2015, per the *Rural Health Statistics Report* 2014–2015.[41] There are 20,306 hospitals with 6,75,779 beds in the country. In rural areas, there are 16,816 hospitals with 183,602 beds, and 3,490 hospitals are urban with 492,177 beds.[32]

Although PHCs and subcenters were established based on population ratios, the establishment of CHCs, small 30-bed hospitals in rural areas, has not been achieved at the expected ratio of 1 for every 4 PHCs. This is due to complex reasons: availability of other urban government hospitals, such as district and *taluk* (state-owned) hospitals for referral cases, the need for substantial investments (equipment and consumables) beyond just building the facility, a proliferation of small private inpatient and surgical facilities in the private sector that compete for patients, the lack of consistent piped water supply and electricity in semirural areas, the lack of critical support infrastructure, such as blood banks, the need for complex management roles among government-employed physicians to plan and manage materials and manpower, and resistance of government-employed specialists rooted in the potential competition posed by CHCs for their own parallel private practices/private hospitals.

Above the level of CHCs are government medical facilities with specialists, including taluk hospitals (subdistrict level), district hospitals, and medical college hospitals. These are administered and maintained by state governments under directors of medical services. In addition, there are municipal hospitals (mostly maternity centers). There are a total of 3,490 such urban hospitals with a combined bed capacity of 492,177 beds. There are 16,816 rural government hospitals with a total bed capacity of 183,602. Combining urban and rural bed capacity in the government sector, an estimated 1,833 population is served per bed in allopathic medicine facilities in the government sector.[32]

In 2014, there were 3,631 hospitals and 26,102 dispensaries of Indian systems of medicine and homeopathy, both government and private (mostly Ayurveda and homeopathy clinics, some Unani clinics based on an Arab traditional medicine system, and Siddha clinics). Separate from these professionally staffed institutions, herbal medicines and preventive practices are widely used in rural and semiurban areas, as an integral part of lifestyle and through informal consulting with local scholars of traditional texts.

In addition to a publicly accessible health infrastructure, there is a large network of closed panels of hospitals and outpatient clinics for employees and their dependents in most of the formal sector of the economy. Eligible dependents include all individuals residing in an extended family household. The major populations covered by closed-panel provider networks are central government employees, armed forces, Indian Railways employees, small industries with more than 25 workers, and hazardous small industries (such as privately owned mines and large industries, both public and private).

Table 22-3 also shows the availability of health facilities under health insurance or other closed-panel schemes for such defined population groups. As shown, central government employees are covered by the Central Government Health Scheme, a combination of a closed panel of outpatient clinics and purchased inpatient care from approved public and private hospitals.[10] The health system for armed forces and defense employees is also a closed system with primary, secondary, and tertiary care fully provided within the Ministry of Defense health facilities. The tripartite—the mandatory Employee State Insurance Scheme, funded by the state governments, employers, and nominal employee contributions—provides comprehensive health care to employees of all private industries employing between 25 and 1,000 employees. This is also a closed system with outpatient clinics and secondary-level hospital beds with all basic specialties. They are located in major small-scale industry hubs in all states. Tertiary care is purchased from other public or private hospitals.

The Indian Railways has its own in-house network of clinics and hospitals throughout the country; it is limited to railway employees and their dependents, and for victims of railway accidents. Another closed-panel system covers employees of hazardous, privately owned, small industries (mainly mining); it provides outpatient care close to the mining/residential sites. There is also a large network of in-house comprehensive healthcare facilities that are mandated for any large manufacturing or mining industry with more than 1,000 employees, public or private. Based on employee numbers, large industries have to comply with regulations regarding in-house outpatient and inpatient facilities. Industries that do not opt to own facilities have to provide comprehensive healthcare coverage under a social insurance plan.

Medical Care Facilities in the Private Sector

Current data on hospitals and beds in the private sector are not available, except for data on the 368 accredited hospitals by the National Accreditation Board for Hospitals and Healthcare Providers.[45]

Care of the Elderly

There are few institutional facilities specifically established for the care of the elderly, and little information is available. It is the cultural norm that children or other relatives take care of parents until their death. Regardless of medical conditions, the elderly live with their children or relatives, getting sporadic medical care.[46] For the indigent elderly population, there are social security funding provisions to support non-governmental organizations (NGOs) managing group homes. Recent legislation obligates children to take care of elderly parents or face prosecution.

In 2010, the government of India launched the "National Program for the Health Care of Elderly" to address various health problems of the elderly. It provides for promotive, preventive, curative, and rehabilitative services to the elderly through a community-based primary healthcare approach. The spectrum of services includes home visits by female auxiliary nurses or male health workers to bedridden elderly people and offers geriatric clinics at primary health centers once weekly and at community health centers twice weekly, as well as a daily geriatric clinic and geriatric wards at district and state level hospitals. Progress under this program has been modest. Currently under this program, geriatric outpatient departments are functioning at 8 geriatric centers, institutional care is provided at 6 geriatric centers, 65 geriatric wards are established at various district hospitals, biweekly geriatric clinics are provided at 2 CHCs, and weekly geriatric clinics at 15 PHCs are functional.[47]

Workforce

TABLE 22-4 presents the availability of medical, paramedical, and nursing personnel, as well as rural health workers.[32] Fashioned after Britain's medical

TABLE 22-4 Health Workforce Statistics

Category	Number
Doctors of allopathic medicine	938,861 (2014)
Nurses / registered midwives	1,780,006 (2014)
Auxiliary nurse midwives (public health)	786,061 (2014)
General nurse midwives (hospital trained)	839,862 (0.78/1,000) (2003)
Female health visitor	55,914 (2014)
Dentists*	154,436 (2014)
Pharmacists	664,176 (2014)
Doctors of Indian systems of medicine (AYUSH)**	736,538 (2014)

* Dentists undergo a four-year program of study plus six months of internship to earn the bachelor of dental surgery degree. The master's program in dental surgery consists of advanced training in specialized fields for an additional two years. A nurse can be a registered nurse (RN) with either an associate's degree or a bachelor's degree. RNs undergo a three-and-a-half-year program of study, including practice internships in hospitals. Nurses who earn a bachelor's degree get four years of training, including a clinical internship. There are masters- and doctoral-level trained individuals for academic nursing positions. Male and female health workers (the latter trained as auxiliary nurse-midwives) are trained at Rural Health and Family Welfare training centers located in each state. Female health workers are trained as auxiliary public health nurses/midwives. Allopathic medical, dental, nursing, and Indian Systems of Medicine teaching institutions are regulated and accredited by national councils (Medical Council, Dental Council, Nursing Council, and Central Council of Indian Medicine).

** These doctors are graduates of recognized Indian systems of medicine and homeopathy medical colleges.

Data from World Health Organization. The Health Workforce in India. http://www.who.int/hrh/resources/hwindia_health-obs16/en/. 2016. Accessed on January 12, 2017.

education system, physicians are trained at the first level to be general family medicine doctors through a four-and-a-half-year academic program, followed by one year of clinical internship rotations through the basic specialty departments in hospitals, and three months of supervised, rural primary care facility service. Similar to the U.K. educational system, Indian doctors are awarded a bachelor's degree in medicine and surgery and are licensed by the Indian Medical Council to practice independently as doctors of medicine. For specialty training, there are three-year postgraduate programs (residency and additional academic preparation), leading to a physician's specialty degree (MD) or surgeon's specialty degree (MS).

NGOs in Health Care

There are over 10,000 NGOs primarily focused on health promotion or medical care activities in India, with most organizations pursuing health as part of a larger community-based development project in rural and tribal areas, as well as urban slums. These include the church-associated organizations (3,226 member institutions of the Catholic Health Association of India in 2008[48] and 330 member institutions of the [Protestant] Christian Medical Association of India)[49] and approximately 4,500 members of the secular Voluntary Health Association of India.[50] There are countless other NGOs that are not members of associations. Many church-associated hospitals are self-financed through fees and hospital charges. Most community health and development NGOs are funded by foreign aid agencies, collectively estimated to account for 0.5% of total health expenditures.[5] These NGOs have significantly impacted the most disadvantaged communities, providing health education and facilitating improved nutrition, income, water sanitation, liaison for underserved populations accessing government healthcare institutions, and community development. Recognizing NGOs' contributions to health, India's National Health Policy of 2002 called for a 10% allocation of public health program funds for NGO involvement.[8]

Technology and Equipment

Given the overwhelming preponderance of communicable diseases, maternal and child health problems, and other primary healthcare issues since independence, successive governments have heavily focused on primary care infrastructure and personnel. With significant increases in sedentary lifestyles, increased consumption of dietary fat with increasing prosperity, and increasing life expectancy, cardiovascular disease and cancer incidence is increasing, causing increased demand for tertiary-care services using advanced technology. While hospital bed strength data are available, there are no data on healthcare technology. Generally it can be stated that most of the population's high-technology care needs are served largely by the private sector, industrial hospitals, and both public and private sector industry hospitals. The premier central government medical institutions and government medical college hospitals also have considerably advanced technology, which is often used in providing "free" care to the poor and lower middle-class population. An important recent initiative is the central government's insurance coverage for major noncommunicable disease treatment at any hospital, public or private, for families with below-poverty income.

Basic, Publicly Sponsored Health Insurance for the Poor

The Rashtriya Swasthya Bima Yojana (RSBY) was launched in 2008, and enrollment targets were given to government health staff to recruit beneficiaries for coverage: below-poverty-line households, and certain defined categories of unorganized workers. These included construction workers registered with the Welfare Boards, licensed railway porters, street vendors, certain National Rural Employment Guarantee Program workers, biri (*beedi*, hand-rolled crude cigarette) workers, domestic workers, sanitation workers, private mine workers, rickshaw pullers, rag pickers, and auto rickshaw/taxi drivers. The beneficiaries under RSBY are entitled to hospitalization coverage up to R30,000 per year for up to five members of the family, which includes the head of household, spouse, and up to three dependents. Additionally, transportation expenses up to R100 per hospitalization are covered, subject to a maximum of R1,000 per year per family. Beneficiaries are required to pay only R30 (less than US $0.50) as an annual registration fee. The premium cost for enrolled beneficiaries under the scheme is shared by the national and state governments.[51]

▸ Evaluation of the Healthcare System

Cost

The estimated total per capita expenditure on health (public and private spending combined) is US $196 (PPP). Public health expenditure (all government) amounts to 1.08% of GDP, and personal health care accounts for 4.10% for a total of about 5.20% of GDP spent on health care.[52] Government spending on prevention and health promotion services as a percentage of total government spending on health is lower than that of neighboring China and Sri Lanka, which spend two-thirds of their public expenditures on public health services.[42] Their population health indicators mirror these differences. In India, the total government expenditure on health as a percentage of total government expenditures is 30.50%. Out-of-pocket expenditure as a percentage of expenditure on personal healthcare services is 87.20%.[53] The distribution of out-of-pocket expenditures is extremely regressive. Most of the middle class, particularly those employed by private sector industry, spend a negligible proportion out of pocket because of comprehensive coverage, including prescription drugs, under social insurance plans fully funded by their employers, or the government, or both. Despite considerable government healthcare infrastructure, particularly in rural areas, informal payments for care that are often required by clinical providers and paramedical staff may result in out-of-pocket expenditures in public and private facilities being similar.[49] Health expenditure is the leading cause of family debt among the poor.[45] Both the rural population and urban poor face significant risk of overwhelming debt from any surgical or major medical event. According to the World Health Organization in 2106, financial barriers to care are major drivers of the wide gap between life expectancy at birth (66.97 years and 69.42 years for men and women, respectively) and healthy life expectancy at birth (59.50 years).[54]

There is much disparity in health services across states, rural/urban residence, and socioeconomic status. Of total government expenditure, approximately 33% is spent on public health programs (vaccination; antenatal, maternal, and postnatal care; contraceptives and other family planning measures; community-based services, such as spraying for malaria; and health education). Of the two-thirds spent on curative care, 75% is spent on secondary and tertiary hospitals, primarily located in urban areas.[42] Thus, a tiny fraction of publicly funded curative services is available in rural areas, requiring most rural residents to travel to nearby towns for health care.

In absolute terms, the cost of medical care is very modest compared to other countries. This is because of low average income of most of the population and provision of services by salaried physicians in government institutions or system-owned institutions for the insured population, with no incentives to induce demand. No data are available on quality indicators. However, the health indicators, including morbidity and mortality statistics, suggest that the technical quality of care may be good, but responsiveness and interpersonal aspects are very inadequate, particularly for poor and disadvantaged populations.

Quality

Population Health Outcomes, Utilization, and Disparities

Reflecting the regressive nature of health financing that disproportionately challenges poor and rural populations, rural-urban public health indicators show significant disparities.[5] As per the Sample Registration System 2014 report, the under-five child mortality rate (probability of dying before the fifth birthday) is 49 per 1,000 live births. The WHO Statistics 2007 provides a breakdown by wealth quintile, revealing that the under-five mortality varies by a ratio of 3 to 1 between the bottom and top quintile. By educational level of the mother (no education, to high school, or more), the under-five mortality ratio is 2.5 per 1,000 live births. These disparities are consistent with disparities in infrastructure/personnel, regressive health expenditure burden, and access to personal healthcare services.

Annual morbidity estimates show a little less than two episodes of illness per year, higher in rural populations and in females in the reproductive age group.[42] Of those reporting illness, approximately 10% did not seek treatment (higher proportion for rural populations, females, elderly, and never married individuals). Treatment was mostly outpatient care (93%), largely at private clinics, and inpatient care (7%), mostly at public hospitals. There is also disproportionately higher use of public facilities for catastrophic and serious illnesses, such as tuberculosis, complicated pregnancy and childbirth, injury, and sexually transmitted diseases. People in hilly and impoverished areas, the *dalit*, castes, and tribal populations rely almost fully on public facilities. Surveys show that the morbidity rate increases with increased health or development level, showing higher morbidity in the wealthiest state, Punjab, and demographically most advanced state, Kerala, compared with poorer or demographically less advanced states.[42]

Access

Apart from closed-panel health facilities (funded by employers and limited to those employed in the formal sector) and a large network of private facilities, there is a nominally large network of government healthcare facilities, funded by tax revenues. Because health care is a state subject, the infrastructure (built by the central government using revenues from income taxes and excise duties) suffers considerable financial difficulties after the built facilities are turned over to the state governments for maintenance. Finances of these institutions are meager, barely meeting the mandatory salary expenditures, with little left for equipment, drugs, consumables, and maintenance. States have no state income tax revenues; they rely on sales/value-added taxes (which are low or uncertain because much trade is informal and undocumented), and a share of the central income taxes and excise taxes (subject to political and exigent situations). Therefore, state health facilities tend to be chronically underfunded and have decrepit equipment, and consumables and drugs are woefully inadequate. The public, mostly the poor and underserved who access care from government hospitals, has to purchase many care items and drugs out of pocket,[47] in addition to informal payments.[49] Government curative services are weighted in favor of the nonpoor, with the ratio of care accessed by the poor versus the richest quintile being 1:4.[47] Hospitalized Indians spend, on average, 58% of their total annual income, and over 40% of them borrow heavily or sell assets to cover hospital expenses, so 25% fall into poverty.[47]

In the wake of the recent economic boom fueled by the IT and technology sector, several innovations have been initiated, funded by buoyant tax revenues, to address the most refractory problems affecting the rural, poor, women, and children. The National Rural Health Mission (NRHM) launched in 2005 took a significant change of direction from earlier initiatives in allocating public money for services provided by private facilities to rural and poor families for maternal and child health care.[47] Services include transportation, facilitation services by trained female activists in each village, and outpatient/inpatient care. The NRHM has initiated training (in a phased manner) of community-based female activists (Accredited Social Health Activists, ASHAs, meaning hope) in each village, who are compensated based on units of services delivered to promote and facilitate maternal and child healthcare utilization at public or private facilities. The facilities are reimbursed from district health budgets. The NRHM also recognizes and mainstreams effective local health traditions. Several state governments are underwriting comprehensive maternal and child health care for the rural and urban poor, reimbursing the private sector on a fee-for-service.

Encouraged by the success of the NRHM, the National Urban Health Mission was launched in May 2013 to improve the health status of the urban poor by facilitating equitable access to quality care by strengthening the existing capacity of the urban health delivery system. The model is to create community-based women's health committees (Mahila Arogya Samiti), one for every 50–100 households, establish community health activists, ASHAs or Link Workers (LWs) in urban poor settlements (one ASHA for 1,000–2,500 population, covering about 200 to 500 households), and establish one urban ANM for every 10,000 population, one urban PHC for every 50,000 population, and one urban CHC for every 250,000 population (0.5 million population in metropolitan cities). This mission would enhance provision of quality care for urban poor population.[55]

Current and Emerging Challenges and Opportunities

Despite significant proactive involvement of the central and state governments in health development since independence, prominent challenges remain. Challenges remain in the areas of (1) ensuring consistent onsite availability of physicians and support personnel at PHCs and specialists at CHCs; (2) inability to address the issue of informal payments that have become the norm at many government facilities or the parallel private practices (moonlighting) by government doctors; (3) grossly inadequate water and sanitation infrastructure that directly and indirectly impacts women's and children's health; (4) a virtual epidemic of noncommunicable diseases that is barely addressed for the majority of the population employed in the informal sector of the economy; (5) limitations of innovative initiatives by the central and state governments due to bureaucracy and corruption dominating the process; and (6) potential slowdown of the booming tax collections from a rapidly growing economy that have fueled innovations thus far. In such a scenario, the fragile reform process is likely to stall, especially because incentivizing care access and utilization has been the bulwark of recent reforms.

Opportunities

Some opportunities are notable. One is the recent government initiative to facilitate care navigation through paid local activists (ASHA workers) and government underwriting of care provided by private facilities. This initiative should substantially change the health situation in the coming years for rural and poor people who previously depended on "free" care at government health facilities. A second major development is the engagement of NGOs. Recognizing the significant contribution of NGOs, the National Health Policy 2002 directed disease control programs to allocate at least 10% of implementation funds for activities suitable for the NGO sector. The Policy also advocated, for the first time, handing over public health service outlets to well-regarded NGOs, along with transfer of funds earmarked for public health activities to enable better management and service delivery.[8] There has also been an enormous nationwide resurgence in the practice of yoga, Ayurveda, Siddha, and other indigenous health systems, as well as healthful traditions including local herbal use, with much potential to reduce morbidity and extend healthy life expectancy, both in rural and urban areas. This movement has been massively aided by the accelerated penetration of television, Internet, and mobile phones in recent decades.

Another opportunity is the large stock of subspecialty beds and high-technology care services in the private sector, providing state-of-the-art care at a fraction of the prevailing cost in the West. The National Health Policy 2002 explicitly offered financial incentives and the status of deemed exports (as with other service exports) for providers of medical services to overseas patients. A third technology-driven transformation is the instantaneous communication though cheap Internet and mobile phones that has shrunk distances and dramatically increased public officials' and physicians' responsiveness to individual and public health crisis situations. Thus, clinical care responses tend to be timely, before severe consequences, including death, supervene and generate adverse press. A critical mass of public awareness and assertiveness has been created by decades of developmental and health activism by tens of thousands of local NGOs, and this may have stimulated some of the recent innovations by government to extend them to target populations. The massive upsurge in demand for education in rural areas will also advance the cause of health. The National Rural Health Mission, launched in 2005, and the National Urban Health Mission, launched in 2013, represent a major break from past preoccupation with supply-side interventions (mainly expanding government infrastructure and personnel postings) to demand-side interventions, providing financial teeth to rural populations to access health care regardless of private or public provider classification. Compensated village facilitators (ASHAs) can potentially ensure that the most disadvantaged are not left behind. Finally, a kit for the mainstream Indian system of medicine AYUSH (Ayurveda, Yoga, Unani, Siddha, and Homeopathy system) is provided to health workers who encourage the population to use AYUSH-trained medical doctors when appropriate.[47]

The health status and challenges are daunting; however, many developments that have recently fructified, after dormancy for decades, represent a novel break from traditional conceptualizations of health development in the developed countries. The current Western paradigm of illness and medical care calls for multiplicative increases in health infrastructure and investments to meet the population's healthcare needs. This predicts a gloomy outlook for India, considering the 1.25 billion population to be "provided" for. However, unforeseen and little understood, grassroots phenomena have the potential to generate an unprecedented dynamic of population health development without traditional healthcare investments. These include the rising popularity of health and medicine practices rooted in self-driven health behaviors and low-cost indigenous sciences (yoga, meditation, Ayurveda, etc.), rise of volunteerism through NGOs, and other developments. In 2015, sales of a single manufacturer of Ayurvedic medicines, supplements, and healthy lifestyle products of daily use exceeded US $750 million, a volume that is at least matched by other manufacturers in this sector combined. The practice of yoga has taken on a life of its own on a large scale, spurred by mass media and Internet-driven mass communications by religious and nonprofit gurus. Although the dynamic of profit- and illness-driven modern medicine flowing from specialists and pharmaceuticals/bioengineering will continue to provide value for many illnesses, its magnitude is being significantly toned down by these new developments, whose implications are yet unfolding. Time will tell whether India's health culture will blend with the globally surging, pill-popping culture, engaging in an endless struggle to keep up with the never-satiable demand/need for medical care, or whether it will evolve into a locally, self-determined, health-enhancing, route to trim the need for care at the source.

References

1. Government of India. Know India: Population Commission. New Delhi. http://populationcommission.nic.in/content/932_1_Tables MapsAndBarCharts.aspx. Published 2016. Accessed April 28, 2016.
2. Lakshmikantham V. *The Origin of Human Past*. Mumbai, India: Bharatiya Vidya Bhavan Press; 1988.
3. Government of India. 2008. *Know India: Profile*. http://www.india.gov.in/knowindia/profile.php. Accessed February 2008.
4. Government of India. Central Statistical Organization, 2008. Summary Data Real Sector 2010. Ministry of Statistics and Program Implementation. http://mospi.gov.in. Updated March 12, 2010. April 26, 2016.
5. World Health Organization. *World Health Statistics 2007*. Geneva, Switzerland.
6. U.S. Department of State. Background Note: India. Bureau of South and Central Asian Affairs, 2007. http://www.state.gov/r/pa/ei/bgn/3454.htm. Accessed February 17, 2008.
7. *The World Factbook*. Washington, DC: Central Intelligence Agency, 2016. https://www.cia.gov/library/publications/the-world-factbook. Accessed 28 April, 2016.

8. Government of India. Ministry of Health and Family Welfare. National Health Policy 2002. http://mohfw.nic.in. Accessed March 3, 2008.
9. Millennium Development Goals Indicators. http://mdgs.un.org/unsd/mdg/Data.aspx.
10. International Institute for Population Sciences and Macro International. National Family Health Survey Three, 2005–2006: India: Vol. I. Mumbai: IIPS, 2007. http://rchiips.org/nfhs/nfhs3.shtml. Accessed February 19, 2008.
11. Government of India, Central Bureau of Health Intelligence. Health Information of India 2005. http://www.cbhidghs.nic.in/hia2005/content.asp. Published 2006. http://www.cbhidghs.nic.in/hia2005/9.01.htm. Accessed February 15, 2008.
12. Government of India. Ministry of Finance. Union Budget and Economic Survey 2007–2008. http://indiabudget.nic.in. Accessed March 5, 2008.
13. Press Information Bureau. GoI, Ministry of Finance. http://pib.nic.in/newsite/mainpage.aspx. Published February 26, 2008. Accessed May 12, 2016.
14. Economic Survey 2015–2016. Technical Appendix. http://indiabudget.nic.in/es2015-16/estat1.pdf. Accessed May 10, 2016.
15. CensusInfoIndia2011.Houses.Householdamenitiesandassets. http://www.dataforall.org/dashboard/censusinfo/website/index.php/pages/drinking_water/total/withinthepremises/IND. Accessed May 10, 2016.
16. Government of India. Planning Commission. Midterm appraisal of water resources in the 10th Five Year Plan. https://india.gov.in/outerwin.htm?id=http://planningcommission.nic.in/midterm/english. Accessed February 18, 2008.
17. Government of India. Department of Road Transport and Highways. *Annual Report 2005–2006*. http://morth.nic.in/writereaddata/sublinkimages/chapter12109984519.pdf. Published 2007. Accessed March 3, 2008.
18. Singh YP. 2016 unpublished Google Books preview. *Geography: Class XII*. Chapter 2: Population: Trends, Patterns, Composition and Demographic Study. VK (India) Enterprises. https://books.google.co.in/books?id=vOSsuOpmiVMC&lpg=PA28&dq=Population%20doubling%20time%20at%20current%20growth%20rate%2C%20india&pg=PA28#v=onepage&q=Population%20doubling%20time%20at%20current%20growth%20rate,%20india&f=false. Accessed July 2016.
19. Government of India. Ministry of Shipping. *Annual Report 2015–2016*. http://shipping.nic.in/showfile.php?lid=2266. Accessed June 1, 2016.
20. Government of India. Ministry of Statistics and Programme Implementation. 2015. Men and women in India, 2015. http://mospi.nic.in/publication/women-and-men-india-2015. Accessed June 2, 2016.
21. Government of India. Ministry of Human Resource Development. *Statistics of School Education 2011–12*. http://mhrd.gov.in/sites/upload_files/mhrd/files/statistics/SSE1112.pdf. Published 2014. Accessed May 12, 2016.
22. Park K. *Textbook of Preventive and Social Medicine*. Jabalpur, India: Banarasidas Bhanot Publishers. 2007.
23. Government of India. Ministry of Health and Family Welfare. Bulletin on Rural Health Statistics in India. Published 2007. http://mohfw.nic.in. Accessed March 2, 2008.
24. Census of India 2011. http://www.dataforall.org/dashboard/censusinfo/. Accessed May 10, 2016.
25. Government of India. Planning Commission. *Towards Faster and More Inclusive Growth: An Approach to the 11th Five Year Plan*. http://planningcommission.gov.in/plans/planrel/app11_16jan.pdf. Published 2006. Accessed March 13, 2008.
26. World Bank. International Comparison Program database. GDP per capita, PPP (current international $). http://data.worldbank.org/indicator/NY.GDP.PCAP.PP.CD. Accessed June 1, 2016.
27. Government of India, Planning Commission. *Report of the Expert Group to Review the Methodology for Measurement of Poverty*. http://planningcommission.nic.in/reports/genrep/pov_rep0707.pdf. Published 2014. Accessed June 1, 2016.
28. World Bank. Age dependency ratio (% of working-age population). http://data.worldbank.org/indicator/SP.POP.DPND Accessed May 12, 2016,
29. Government of India. Office of the Registrar General. Sample Registration System. *SRS Bulletin*. September 2014;49(1).
30. Government of India. *Economic Survey 2014–15: Statistical Appendix. A139*. Interstate comparison of India. http://indiabudget.nic.in/es2014-15/estat1.pdf. 2015. Accessed November 24, 2016
31. Government of India. Planning Commission. *Labour force participation*. https://data.gov.in/catalog/labour-force-participation-rate-work-force-participation-rate-and-unemployment-rate. Published July 09, 2015. Accessed May 11, 2016.
32. Government of India. *Report of the Health Survey and Development Committee*. Simla, India: Government of India Press; 1946.
33. Universal Immunization Program. http://www.mohfw.nic.in/WriteReadData/l892s/5628564789562315.pdf. Accessed June 17, 2016.
34. Ministry of Health and Family Welfare. Central TB Division. *TB India 2015, Annual Status Report*. Revised National Tuberculosis Control Programme.
35. Central Leprosy Division. Directorate General of Health Services. *NLEP—Progress Report for the Year 2014–15*. New Delhi, India: National Leprosy Eradication Programme.
36. Raykar N, Majummdar M, Laxminarayan R, Menon P. 2015. *India Health Report Nutrition 2015*. New Delhi, India: Public Health Foundation of India.
37. Omran AA. The epidemiological transition: a theory of epidemiology of population change. *Milbank Memorial Fund Quarterly*. 1971;49:509–538.
38. Government of India. Ministry of Health and Family Welfare. National Program for Prevention and Control of Diabetes. Cardiovascular Diseases and Stroke. http://www.mohfw.nic.in/for%20websitediabetes.htm. Published 2007. Accessed March 2, 2008.
39. Chari PS. Susruta and our heritage. *Indian J Plast Surg*. 2003;36:4–13.
40. World Health Organization. *Targets for Health for All: 2000*. http://www.euro.who.int/__data/assets/pdf_file/0006/109779/WA_540_GA1_85TA.pdf. 1978. Accessed March 11, 2008.
41. Government of India. Ministry of Health and Family Welfare. Rural Health Statistics 2014–15.
42. Government of India. Ministry of Labour and Employment. Employees' State Insurance Corporation. http://www.esic.nic.in/coverage.php. 2013. Accessed June 3, 2016.
43. *Annual Report 2012–13*. Medical relief and supplies. http://www.mohfw.nic.in/WriteReadData/l892s/CHAPTER%2013.pdf. Accessed June 3, 2016.
44. *Hospital Management in Indian Railways*. http://www.cag.gov.in/content/report-no-28-2014-performance-audit-hospital-management-indian-railways-union. 2014. Accessed June 3, 2016.

45. National Accreditation Board for Hospital and Healthcare Providers. http://nabh.co/frmViewAccreditedHosp.aspx. Accessed June 3, 2016.
46. Gumber A. Structure of the Indian healthcare market: implications for the health insurance sector. *Regional Health Forum*. 2000;4(3). http://www.searo.who.int/publications/journals/seajph/issues/whoseajphv3n3-4/en/. Accessed November 24, 2016.
47. Government of India. Ministry of Health and Family Welfare. *Annual Report 2013–14*. National Programme for the Health Care of the Elderly. New Delhi, India: 147–148.
48. Catholic Health Association of India. http://www.chai-india.org. Accessed March 11, 2008.
49. Christian Medical Association of India. http://www.cmai.org/index.html. Accessed February 11, 2008.
50. Voluntary Health Association of India. http://www.vhai.org/htm/index.asp. Accessed February 21, 2008.
51. Rashtriya Swasthya Bima Yojana. http://www.rsby.gov.in/about_rsby.aspx. Accessed June 3, 2016.
52. Government of India. National Rural Health Mission. Ministry of Health and Family Welfare. http://www.mohfw.nic.in/NRHM. Published 2005. Accessed March 4, 2008.
53. World Health Organization. *World Health Statistics 2015*. http://apps.who.int/iris/bitstream/10665/170250/1/9789240694439_eng.pdf. Published 2015. Accessed May 12, 2016.
54. World Health Organization. Global Health Observatory data repository. Life expectancy data by country. http://apps.who.int/gho/data/node.main.688. Accessed June 3, 2016.
55. Government of India. Ministry of Health and Family Welfare. Department of Health and Family Welfare. *National Urban Health Mission*. http://www.pbhealth.gov.in/NUHM_Framework.pdf. Published October 2012. Accessed on June 16, 2016.

CHAPTER 23

China

Ning Lu, Kuo-Cherh Huang, and Hua Xu

▸ Country Description

TABLE 23-1 China

Nationality	Noun: Chinese (singular and plural) Adjective: Chinese
Ethnic groups	Han Chinese 91.6%, Zhuang 1.3%, other (includes Hui, Manchu, Uighur, Miao, Yi, Tujia, Tibetan, Mongol, Dong, Buyei, Yao, Bai, Korean, Hani, Li, Kazakh, Dai, and other nationalities) 7.1% (2010 est.)*
Religions	China is officially atheist. Buddhist 18.2%, Christian 5.1%, Muslim 1.8%, folk religion 21.9%, Hindu < 0.1%, Jewish < 0.1%, other 0.7% (includes Taoist), unaffiliated 52.2% (2010 est.)
Language	Standard Chinese or Mandarin (a.k.a. Putonghua; based on the Beijing dialect), Yue (Cantonese), Wu (Shanghainese), Minbei (Fuzhou), Minnan (Hokkien–Taiwanese), Xiang, Gan, Hakka dialects, minority languages (see "Ethnic groups" row)**
Literacy	Definition: Age 15 and over can read and write. Total population: 96.4% Male: 98.2% Female: 94.5% (2015 est.)
Government type	Communist state
Date of independence	January 1, 1912 (Qing Dynasty replaced by the Republic of China); October 1, 1949 (People's Republic of China established)

(continues)

TABLE 23-1 China (continued)	
Gross Domestic Product (GDP) per capita	$19.39 trillion (2015 est.)
Unemployment rate	4% (2015 est.)***
Natural hazards	Frequent typhoons (about five per year along southern and eastern coasts); damaging floods; tsunamis; earthquakes; droughts; land subsidence; volcanism****
Environment: current issues	Air pollution (greenhouse gases, sulfur dioxide particulates), from reliance on coal, producing acid rain; water shortages, particularly in the north; water pollution from untreated wastes; deforestation; estimated loss of one-fifth of agricultural land since 1949 to soil erosion and economic development; desertification; trade in endangered species
Population	1,373,541,278 (July 2016 est.)
Age structure	0–14 years: 17.1% (male 126,732,020/female 108,172,771) 15–24 years: 13.27% (male 97,126,460/female 85,135,228) 25–54 years: 48.42% (male 339,183,101/female 325,836,319) 55–64 years: 10.87% (male 75,376,730/female 73,859,424) 65 years and over: 10.35% (male 67,914,015/female 74,205,210) (2016 est.)
Median age	Total: 37.1 years Male: 36.2 years Female: 38.1 years (2016 est.)
Population growth rate	0.43% (2016 est.)
Birth rate	12.4 births/1,000 population (2016 est.)
Death rate	7.7 deaths/1,000 population (2016 est.)
Net migration rate	−0.4 migrant(s)/1,000 population (2016 est.)
Gender ratio	At birth: 1.15 male(s)/female 0–14 years: 1.17 male(s)/female 15–24 years: 1.14 male(s)/female 25–54 years: 1.04 male(s)/female 55–64 years: 1.02 male(s)/female 65 years and over: 0.92 male(s)/female Total population: 1.06 male(s)/female (2016 est.)
Infant mortality rate	Total: 12.2 deaths/1,000 live births Male: 12.4 deaths/1,000 live births Female: 12 deaths/1,000 live births (2016 est.)
Life expectancy at birth	Total population: 75.5 years Male: 73.5 years Female: 77.9 years (2016 est.)
Total fertility rate	1.6 children born/woman (2016 est.)
HIV/AIDS adult prevalence rate	0.1% (2012 est.)

TABLE 23-1 China (continued)	
Number of people living with HIV/AIDS	780,000 (2012 est.)
HIV/AIDS deaths	—

*The Chinese government officially recognizes 56 ethnic groups.

** Zhuang is official in Guangxi Zhuang, Yue is official in Guangdong, Mongolian is official in Nei Mongol, Uighur is official in Xinjiang Uygur, Kyrgyz is official in Xinjiang Uygur, and Tibetan is official in Xizang (Tibet).

*** Official data are for urban areas only; there is substantial unemployment and underemployment in rural areas. Including migrants may boost total unemployment to 9%.

**** China contains some historically active volcanoes including Changbaishan (also known as Baitoushan, Baegdu, or P'aektu-san), Hainan Dao, and Kunlun although most have been relatively inactive in recent centuries.

Data from Central Intelligence Agency. The World Fact Book, 2010: China. http://www.cia.gov/library/publications/the-world-factbook. Accessed January 5, 2010.

History

The People's Republic of China (hereinafter referred to as China) is one of the world's oldest civilizations. The written records of China's history can be traced back to as early as 1500 BCE.[1] There are three distinctive eras of Chinese history: the ancient era (2100–220 BCE), the imperial era (221 BCE–1911 CE), and the modern era (since 1912).

The earliest dynasties of the ancient era were Xia (2100–1600 BCE), Shang (1600–1046 BCE), and Zhou (1045–256 BCE), followed by the Warring States period (256–221 BCE). The imperial era began with the Qin Dynasty (221–206 BCE) after the Qin conquered all of the Warring States and unified China in 221 BCE. This period represented the first unified nation in Chinese history.[1] It was well known for the terra cotta warriors unearthed in Xi'an in Shaanxi province, and the initial construction of the Great Wall. Following the Qin Dynasty, the ancient China discovered the Four Great Inventions of papermaking, gunpowder, printing, and compass that made a significant impact on the civilization development of the world. The last imperial dynasty was Qing (1644–1911). At its zenith, the Qing Empire held the largest economy in the world and ruled more than one-third of the world's population.[2]

Toward the end of the more than 2,000 years of imperial dynasty, the Qing Empire was internally stagnant and externally threatened by Western powers. The Opium War (1839–1842), which ended in a victory for British colonists, plunged China into a semicolonial and semifeudalist society.[3] Infuriated by the Qing government's impotence and its resistance to reform, the movement of overthrowing the Qing Empire and creating a republic was intensified among students, militaries, and young officials. The revolutionary military uprising known as the Wuchang Uprising of October 1911 marked the ending of the imperial era and the beginning of the Republican era, with the formation of the Republic of China in March 1912.[3] Sun Yat-Sen, who played an instrumental role in overthrowing the Qing Empire, was appointed the president of the Republic of China.

The Republican period (1912–1949) underwent several significant eras, including the warlord era (1915–1928) signified by the political and military power struggles of warlord generals, the Sino-Japanese war period (1937–1945), and the Chinese Civil War period (1927–1949).[3] Sun Yat-Sen, the leader of the Nationalist Party, or Kuomintang (KMT), resigned from his post as the president of the Republic of China two years after the overthrow of the Qing Empire, due to the pressure from the Beiyang Army, a Western-style Imperial Chinese Army founded by the Qing government in the late 19th century. The subsequent warlord factions known as the Beiyang cliques ushered in a period of regional divisions. With the help of the Soviet Union and the Chinese Communist Party (CCP) founded in 1921, the KMT led by Chiang Kai-Shek launched the Northern Expedition in 1926 to bring the warlords under the control of KMT, and they ended the warlord era in 1928.[3] By this time the Chinese Civil War fought between the Nationalist Party and the Communist Party was already underway.

In 1937 Japan invaded China with an exchange of gunshots, known as the Marco Polo Bridge Incident, near Beijing. The Incident marked the beginning of the Second Sino-Japanese War (1937–1945).[3] By 1938 the Japanese occupied most major cities, the eastern and northeastern regions, and much of the southeast of China. To resist the invasion of Japan, the CCP led by Mao Zedong and the KMT led by Chiang Kai-Shek formed a united front to fight against Japan. At the end of the World War II, in September 1945, Japan surrendered to Allied forces following the atomic bombings of Hiroshima and Nagasaki.

The end of the war against Japan also brought the end of the united front of the CCP and the Nationalist Party. Despite the attempts to negotiate a peace agreement, the two parties resumed a full-scale civil war in 1946. The war ended four years later with the Communist Party reuniting mainland China and with the Nationalist Party retreating from mainland China to the island of Taiwan.

In October 1949 Mao Zedong declared the founding of the People's Republic of China. Following the Soviet Union's model, China was transformed into a socialist country. Its development was impacted by multiple economic, social, and political campaigns, including the Great Leap Forward (1958–1961) and the Cultural Revolution (1966–1976). In 1978 after the death of Mao Zedong, Deng Xiaoping, who was considered the paramount leader of China led the country through numerous market economy reforms. China since then has developed into one of the fastest growing economies in the world for more than three decades.

Size and Geography

China, located in Southeast Asia, is the third-largest country in the world, with a coastline of 18,000 kilometers and an area of 9.6 million square kilometers. As shown in **FIGURE 23-1**, China is bordered by Russia and Mongolia to the north; Kazakhstan, Kyrgyzstan, Tajikistan, and Afghanistan to the west; Pakistan, Nepal, India, Myanmar, Laos, Thailand, and Vietnam to the south; and North Korea to the east. Southeastward, China is bordered by an arched coastline of 5,774 kilometers, with the sea separating the country from Japan in the east and the Philippines, Malaysia, Brunei, Indonesia, and Singapore in the south.

FIGURE 23-1 Map of China
© Bardocz Peter/Shutterstock

The diverse geography of China encompasses high plateaus and mountains, such as Tibet and the Himalayas in the west and the basins and plains in the east. Plateaus, mountains, and hills jointly make up about 67% of the total land area. The Yangtze River and the Yellow River are the two main waterways that run eastward. China's highest population densities are found in the Yangtze River delta area, Pearl River delta area, Sichuan Basin area, and the Huang-Huai Plain.

China consists of 23 provinces (including Taiwan, which is traditionally claimed as China's province by the Chinese government), 5 ethnic minority autonomous regions, 4 municipalities directly under the central government (CAMs), and 2 special administrative regions (SARs). The four CAMs are Beijing, Tianjin, Shanghai, and Chongqing. The two SARs are Hong Kong and Macau, returned to China from the British and the Portuguese, respectively, in the late 20th century.

Based on traditional economic classifications, China is divided into three economic zones: Eastern China, Central China, and Western China. There is enormous economic disparity among the zones. Eastern China is more developed economically and socially than Central and Western China. Since 1999, as a national development strategy, the central government has implemented policies to expand the economic and social development of the western economic zone.

Government and Political System

China is a socialist country led by a single party, the CCP. Shortly after the CCP founded the People's Republic of China in the mainland in 1949, socialism was instituted in the country and the new constitution was created. The Chinese government system is highly centralized with a hierarchical structure of central government and local governments of five levels: village, township, county, city, and province. In the centrally administered cities, the corresponding levels of government are municipal, district, subdistrict, and resident community.

The structure of Chinese central government is similar to Western parliamentary systems, consisting of an executive branch, the State Council, and 28 central ministries or commissions; the legislative branch, the National People's Congress (NPC); and the judicial branch, the Supreme People's Court and the Supreme People's Procuratorate. (See **FIGURE 23-2** for an illustration of the Chinese central government structure.) The People's Liberation Army (PLA) is the military branch of the government via the Central Military Commission. Under the Constitution of China, the NPC is the highest organ of state power. The State Council is the chief administrative authority, synonymous with the central government of China. The Supreme People's Court is the highest court in the judicial system of China. The Central Military Commission supervised by the Standing Committee of the NPC controls and commands the PLA of China. The central government structure allows a certain degree of separation of power among the executive, legislative, and judiciary branches. The leader of the country, currently Xi Jingping, is the president of China, the general secretary of the Communist Party and the Central Committee, and the chairman of the Central Military Commission. The Communist Party of China, the Central Committee, and the Central Military Commission form three interlocking branches of power. In other words, the president of China controls the Chinese Communist Party, the state, and the military. The provincial and local governments have a similar three-branched administrative structure.

The political system of China is developed in the framework of a socialist republic run by the CCP. Since the branches of the central government, and in fact, of all governments in China are dominated by the members of the CCP, checks and balances are difficult to achieve in practice. The NPC is the only legislative house in China. It is rare for the NPC to overthrow a proposal put before them, but the NPC has grown into a forum in which legislation is debated before being put to a vote. The president is elected by the NPC for up to two five-year terms. The State Council consists of the heads of each governmental department and agency, is appointed by the NPC, and is chaired by the premier of China.

The Communist Party of China is the founding and ruling political party in China. The National Congress of the Communist Party is held about once every five year. When the National Congress is not in session, the Central Committee is the highest body of the CCP. The CCP is the sole governing party in China. It is supplemented by the Chinese People's Political Consultative Conference, which consists of eight minority parties in political participation. These eight parties are the Revolutionary Committee of the Chinese Kuomintang, China Democratic League, China Democratic National Construction Association, China Association for Promoting Democracy, China Peasants and Workers' Democratic Party, China Zhigong Party, Jiu San Society, and Taiwan Democratic Self-Government League.[5]

The economic reforms in China since the late 1970s have pushed for political reform and a democratic system. In 1980, Deng Xiaoping suggested that three parallel central committees "mutually

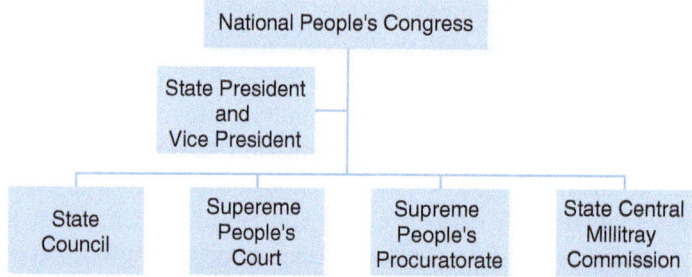

FIGURE 23-2 Central Government Structure

Data from Publicity CL. The composition, power and function of the State Council. State Organs. Available at http://english.moj.gov.cn/State-Organs/content/2009-02/03/content_1028259.htm. Accessed August 8, 2016.

supervise and impose constraints on each other" and that "the work of the Party should be separated from the work of administrative organs, in enterprises and businesses, and enterprise management should be democratized."[6] Deng's political reforms would change the political system in China into a system with "checks and balances" between various political institutions. Although many policy reforms and organizational administrative reforms have taken place in China, they are mostly the changes made within the political system rather than the changes of the political system itself.[7]

Macroeconomics

In line with communist ideology and following the former Soviet Union's model, China's economy was highly centralized and planned without any private entities from 1949 until 1978. All industries and enterprises were owned and controlled by the government. Workers were employees of government or state-owned enterprises (SOEs). In 1978 China launched economic reforms aimed at converting the planned economic system to a market-based one. Since then, many policies that were in favor of a market economy have been implemented. In rural areas, the household responsibility system replaced the communes. In urban areas, the SOEs were given autonomy and responsibilities for their profits and losses. Special economic zones in southern China were created with economic autonomy. Such economic autonomy was extended eventually to the rest of the country. These reforms have created market competition and consequently improved economic performance. Between 1979 and 2014, the national Gross Domestic Product (GDP) had an average annual growth rate of 9.75%, with a per capita GDP of 8.90%. According to the World Bank, China's GDP at market prices reached US $10.9 trillion in 2015, becoming the world's second largest economy after the United States ($17.9

trillion).[8] The breakdown of China's GDP in 2014 indicated that the agricultural sector, the industrial sector, and the service sector accounted for 9.20%, 42.70%, and 48.10% of the economy, respectively.[9]

In the financial market, the People's Bank of China is the central bank in China. It plays an important role in designing and implementing monetary policies and regulating the financial sector along with the China Bank Regulatory Commission. Varied ownership of banking institutions exists, including state-owned commercial banks, joint-stock commercial banks, policy-oriented banks, city commercial banks, rural and urban credit cooperatives, foreign-owned banks, etc. Traditionally, saving and lending were dominated by four major state-owned commercial banks: the Industrial and Commercial Bank of China, China Construction Bank, Agricultural Bank of China, and the Bank of China, which jointly constituted over half of the financial market. The Rural Credit Cooperative has been the key financial institution in rural China. To fulfill the requirements of the World Trade Organization (WTO), the financial sector opened up to foreign competition in 2001 when China joined the WTO. The state ownership is reduced as the shares of some of the major commercial banks are listed and traded in the stock markets. Major Chinese banks are now partners with major banks overseas, such as Citibank and HSBC. In contrast, the bond market assumes a minimal role in the Chinese financial sector. Stock exchange did not exist in China until 1991 when the first two stock markets were introduced in Shenzhen and Shanghai. Since then, the equity market has experienced several cycles of boom-and-bust beset by speculative market investment. Chinese stock markets have high turnover rates compared with other stock markets, such as the New York Stock Exchange.

In the labor market, China has experienced a large-scale farmer migration from agriculture to the industrial and manufacturing sectors, and from rural to urban areas. Major heavy industries include mining and ore processing, aluminum, coal, iron and steel, cement, machinery, automobiles, armaments, petroleum, chemicals, fertilizers, telecommunications, and transportation equipment such as ships, aircrafts, locomotives, and rail cars. Light industries include textiles and apparel, food processing, and consumer products such as footwear, electronics, and toys. The information technology industry has undergone rapid developments and has become an important component of the Chinese economy. Thanks to economic reforms and opening-up policies, more jobs have been created in the private sector. The registered urban unemployment rate was 4.05% by the end of 2015.[10]

As for international trade, the total exports of goods and services from China equaled 22.4% of GDP in 2015, up from 4.3% in 1960, and the total imports accounted for 18.8% of GDP, up from 4.5% in 1960.[11,12] Electronic equipment had the highest percentage of shares of the import market (25.7%) and the export market (26.3%) in 2015. The Chinese economy, self-contained before 1978, now relies heavily on exports. Labor-intensive processing industries, such as electronic equipment, footwear, and clothing, are highly concentrated in coastal provinces and fuel the export of Chinese products. Major trade partners of China include the United States, Japan, South Korea, Russia, Taiwan, Singapore, and European Union countries including Germany and the Netherlands. In addition, the share of the regional trade with other Asian countries has become an important economic component for China. In recent years, due to the global economic recession, the demand for goods from China has reduced significantly, adversely impacting the nation's economy. In reaction to the decline in exports, the Chinese government implemented a massive stimulus plan to increase domestic demand.

Over the past three decades, China has experienced phenomenal growth in international trade and has maintained a high level of foreign exchange reserves as a result of the sustained favorable trade balance. To maintain the yuan's *de facto* pegging to the U.S. dollar constant and to prevent the yuan from appreciating, China keeps a huge foreign exchange reserve of US $3.3 trillion.[13] The government's preferential industrial development policies and its proximity to Hong Kong and Taiwan have made China an attractive destination for foreign direct investment (FDI), which has fueled economic growth over the past three decades. China is the second largest recipient of FDI, with more than $100 billion in recent years, compared to near zero in the early 1980s. In 2015, China attracted a total of $249.9 billion in FDI, according to the World Bank.[14]

China's sustained economic growth of the past few decades has significantly improved the living conditions in China and lifted millions of Chinese people out of poverty. Despite its rapid economic growth, China remains a developing country, with a per capita GDP of US $7,924.7 in 2015 compared to a per capita GDP of $55,836.8 in the United States.[15]

Demographics

China is the most populous country in the world, with a population of over 1.3 billion. According to the World Bank,[16] the Chinese population aged over 60 years was 14% and under 15 was 18% in 2013. The age dependency ratio (% of working-age population) in China was about 36% in 2014, compared to 77% in 1960. Although the number of children increased rapidly between the 1950s and the 1970s, it has declined significantly since the 1980s, partially due to China's one-child policy that began to be formally phased out in 2015. For 2014, the population's natural growth rate currently was 5.21% with a birth rate of 12.37% and a death rate of 5.31%.[9] In the next few decades, China is expected to experience the serious economic and social challenges of an aging population.

According to the National Bureau of Statistics of China,[9] by the end of 2014, the total population in China was 1,367,820,000, with 51.2% male and 48.8% female. The urban population increased dramatically to 749,160,000 (54.8%) of the total population in 2014 from only 172,450,000 (17.9%) in 1978. The number for rural population was 618,660,000 (45.2%) in 2014 down from 790,140,000 (82.1%) in 1978. There are 56 ethnicities, with Han as the majority accounting for 92% of the total population.

Buddhism is the most influential religion in China. Other major religions include Taoism, Confucianism, Islam and Christianity. Buddhism, Confucianism, and Taoism have played significant roles historically in shaping Chinese culture. Some scholars prefer not to use the term "religion" in reference to Confucianism or Taoism, believing they are "thought systems" or "philosophies."[17] The largest religious group is the Chinese popular religion with elements of Taoism, Buddhism, and Confucianism. The traditional practice of these religions includes paying respect for the forces of nature, gods, ancestors, and figures from Chinese mythology. The Chinese government formally and institutionally recognizes five religions in China: Buddhism, Taoism, Islam, Protestantism, and Catholicism. There has been more institutional recognition for Confucianism and the Chinese popular religion in recent years. In addition, Christianity has gained popularity due to the influence of missionary and economic exchanges with the Western world since the 19th century. As of China's last census in 2010, about 52% of the population was unaffiliated with any religion, and the other 48% was distributed among the officially recognized religions, popular religions, and very small proportion of Jewish and Hindu religions.[18]

Education

Since the foundation of the People's Republic of China in 1949, the Chinese government has placed priority on developing and reforming the education system. In 1986, the Compulsory Education Law of the People's Republic of China took effect to provide at least nine years of free education for all school-age children. Since the 1990s, China has had a comprehensive state-owned public education system without any private schools. Today a few private schools have entered China's education system.

The education system of China contains preschool, primary school, secondary school, high school, college and university, and graduate school.[19] The nine-year compulsory education law covers primary school (six years) and secondary school (three years). High school education lasts three years for students who pass the high school entrance examination. Higher education at the undergraduate level includes two- and three-year colleges (also called short-cycle colleges) and four-year colleges and universities (five years for medical universities) leading to bachelor's degrees. Universities also offer graduate programs leading to master's and doctorate degrees. Admission to a university or college is largely dependent on the results of the highly competitive national higher education entrance examination (Gao Kao), which takes place in June each year. There were 9.42 million students taking the examination in June 2015.[20]

The college-age population significantly increased from 1.4% in 1978 to over 20% in 2015.[20] As a result, China experienced an explosive growth in annual college enrollment. In addition, the number of college students pursuing studies overseas has increased considerably. The most favored destinations are North America, Australia, the United Kingdom, and several other European countries.

Poverty

Along with the rapid economic growth, the living conditions in China have improved dramatically. The number of people living in poverty has reduced significantly largely due to the economic growth and government-sponsored poverty intervention programs since the late 1970s. According to the World Bank, more than 500.0 million people were lifted out of poverty as China's poverty rate fell from 88% in 1981 to 6.5% in 2012.[21] Traditionally, poverty in China is concentrated in remote rural areas in the southwestern and northwestern regions where natural conditions are harsh and transportation infrastructure is not well established. Despite China's significant improvement in poverty, there were 70.2 million people living in poverty in rural areas in 2014, based on China's current poverty standard (annual per capita rural net income of ¥2,300 or below, approximately US $371).[21] In addition, the income disparity between the rural and urban areas has widened, resulting in rural-urban inequalities in access to and quality of healthcare services.

Brief History of the Healthcare System

Description

The health system in China has gone through three major phases since the founding of the People's Republic of China in 1949. Before 1949, China did not have an organized health system. Most health care was provided by private healers, private clinics, and religious institutions. The first phase started with the founding of China and lasted until the early1980s. During this phase, the government created a health system that was modeled similarly to that of the Soviet Union with the government owning, financing, and operating the health and healthcare sector. The government and state enterprises provided health insurance to nearly 90% of the Chinese population, and the health system provided free or near-free health services. The second phase began in 1978 with the initiation of the remarkable economic reform in China. During this phase, the role of government in health and the healthcare sector was reduced drastically as China converted to the free market economy. The health system was largely left to the forces of the free market economy, which resulted in a vast majority of the Chinese population being without health insurance, created an inefficient healthcare delivery system, and bred public discontent toward the health system. Confronted with increasing healthcare problems and the severe acute respiratory syndrome (SARS) outbreak that spread from China to 37 countries worldwide in 2003,[22] the Chinese government launched the health reform that marked the beginning of the third phase. During this phase, the central government reasserted its role in the health and healthcare sector with unprecedented funding and with the socialist ideology to promote equity and social stability. This resulted in universal health insurance coverage for 1.3 billion Chinese people in 2012 and an ongoing reform of its health delivery system.

Evolution of the Chinese Health System

Before 1949: Private and Unorganized Health Delivery

Although the practice of traditional Chinese medicine existed for several thousand years, China did not have an organized health or healthcare system until the mid-20th century. Most healthcare services were provided by private healers, small clinics, and religious and charity institutions. The earliest contemporary hospitals, mostly run by Western churches in the form of missionary hospitals, began to emerge in China in the mid-19th century. Before the establishment of the new China in 1949, there was little effort made to improve public health. Outbreaks of epidemics, such as typhoid, cholera, malaria, and tuberculosis, were frequent and rampant during the 19th century and first half of the 20th century in China. During this period, China was one of the least healthy countries in the world.[23,24]

Phase I (1950–1978): A Government Owned, Funded, and Operated Health System

Since the Communist Party took control of China in 1949, the modern health system was developed under the planned economy of China. The private practice and private ownership of health facilities disappeared completely. The Ministry of Health as an executive agency of the national government was established in 1954 to coordinate health resources, ensure the accessibility of health services, monitor the quality of health services provided to the public, and establish and supervise health policies. The health system that consisted of hospitals, outpatient clinics, maternal and child care stations, and epidemic prevention centers was owned, funded, and run by the government at various administrative levels. The system was designed to provide affordable care to every member of the population, regardless of the ability to pay, by controlling and coordinating the distribution of financial resources, healthcare personnel, equipment, and technology.[25] All healthcare personnel—including physicians, nurses, pharmacists, and administrators—were government employees and paid a fixed salary. The prices for all healthcare services, including medications, were set and regulated by the central government.[25]

To provide universal coverage for healthcare services for all, China established three socialist health insurance schemes in rural and urban areas throughout China. In rural areas, the Rural Cooperative Medical System (RCMS) was implemented in the 1950s to cover health service for rural populations. The RCMS consisted of a three-tiered healthcare delivery system and a community-based insurance scheme. The three-tiered system was composed of the village health clinics that provided basic health care by barefoot doctors (the first tier), township health centers consisting of outpatient clinics and small hospitals that provided care for the most common illnesses (the second tier), and county or higher level hospitals that were utilized for treating severe illnesses (the third tier).[25] The township health centers played an essential role in of providing health care for rural populations by supervising the care delivered at the village clinics and referring patients to the higher level of hospitals, equipped with more advanced medical equipment and sophisticated technologies. In addition, township health centers were responsible for the organization and delivery of preventive care in rural areas. The insurance scheme of RCMS was a prepayment pool consisting of individual contributions, a village collective welfare fund, and subsidies from the government. The RCMS members received health services free or at a reduced cost.[25]

In urban areas, there were two main health insurance schemes to cover urban populations for health services. One was the Labor Insurance Scheme (LIS) and the other was the Government Employee Insurance Scheme (GIS), established in 1951 and 1952, respectively. The LIS covered healthcare costs for employees (and their dependents) of state-owned or collectively owned enterprises and their dependents. The GIS covered healthcare costs for government employees, government retirees, and college students.[25] Similar to the three-tiered delivery system for the rural population, health care in urban areas was provided through public facilities at three levels: workplace or neighborhood clinics (the first level) that provided basic health services by mostly barefoot doctors; district hospitals (the second level) that provided primary care and treatment for common illnesses; and the city hospitals (the third level) that were utilized for treating complicated illnesses. Both LIS and GIS provided open-ended healthcare coverage at no cost or at very minimal cost (i.e., registration fee) to individuals. Urban employees enjoyed essentially free outpatient and inpatient care, with little or no concerns about the cost.

Payment for health services was fee-for-services, based on a predetermined fee schedule set by the government. To ensure that health care was affordable to all members of the population, the government set the prices for the medical services below their costs. By the end of 1975 the insurance provided by the RCMS, LIS, and GIS covered nearly 90% of the population, including almost all the urban population and 85% of the rural population.[25,26]

To improve the nation's health, the Chinese government focused on the control and prevention of infectious diseases and rural health improvement. In 1954 the Ministry of Health introduced an epidemic prevention system, known as Epidemic Prevention Service (EPS), that consisted of epidemic prevention stations and 25 million workers. By the end of 1965, all provinces and municipalities had established the EPS system that was responsible for monitoring, reporting, preventing and controlling infectious diseases, providing vaccination, and improving environmental sanitation.[27] The Chinese government engaged its population in a mass undertaking known as "patriotic health campaigns" in its efforts to improve the environmental sanitation and to control infectious diseases.[27,28] The campaigns targeted major epidemics of cholera, diarrhea, hookworm, typhoid fever, typhus, meningitis, malaria, diphtheria, smallpox, tuberculosis, schistosomiasis, and other infectious diseases. Various forms of vector controls and sanitation programs, such as latrine improvement, mosquito extermination, and draining swaps were carried out. Free vaccinations were provided to the public. Maternal and child health programs, such as midwife training, were widely implemented. These government measures and mass efforts sharply reduced infectious diseases and nearly eliminated parasitic disease of schistosomiasis. The mass campaign approach proved particularly successful in controlling syphilis, which was eliminated by the end of 1960s.[27–29]

This period in Chinese history has seen a remarkable achievement in improving population health and health services delivery in China. The life expectancy at birth increased from 35 years in 1952 to 68 years in 1985, and the infant mortality rate dropped from 250 to 34 per 1,000 live births for the same period.[30] In addition to the remarkable health gains, the health delivery system contained costs. According to the World Bank, in 1981 healthcare costs in China were only 3% of its GDP.[24]

Phase II (1978–2002): Health System in the Era of Economic Reforms

Beginning in 1978, the government-owned health system started to crumble as the Chinese government introduced radical economic reforms that transformed China from a centrally planned economy to a market-oriented system. The economic reform involved opening up to foreign investment, privatization of state-owned industry, and decentralization of the fiscal system and decision-making power, including policies and price controls of the government. With these changes the government monopolized purchases and sales were abolished. The industry was given more power and independence in production and marketing. The state-owned enterprises paid taxes to the government instead of turning over profit. Every industrial unit was responsible for its own losses and profits. Most government-owned factories and commercial units were either contracted out for management or transformed into privately owned businesses or joint-stock operations, or they closed doors.

Whatever the government could not finance, it left to the private market. The private sector grew drastically, accounting for nearly 70% of China's GDP by 2005.[29] These economic reforms had profound effects on China's health system, including substantial changes in its finance and delivery of health services.

In rural areas, the remarkable economic reform was the introduction of the Household Production Responsibility System (HPRS). Before the economic reform, the villages were called production brigades. A brigade was divided into several production teams, and the team leaders directed production and product distribution. The farmers' work and other contributions were recorded as working points by the production teams. The distribution of the products was based on the total working points and the number of heads in each household. After paying tax to the government in the form of agricultural products, the production teams would keep some for the Rural Cooperative Medical Fund (usually 30%–50%). The remainder was distributed to the households. Due to the implementation of HPRS as part of the economic reform in rural areas, the collective economy of agriculture collapsed. Under HPRS, the arable land is distributed to individual households by capitation. The households assume the sole responsibility of their gains and losses. Every household directly pays a certain amount of the tax in the form of agricultural products to the government and keeps the remainder. Consequently, the villages no longer had collective funds for RCMS to use to finance the village clinics or to provide income to barefoot doctors. Coupled with the decline in government funding to RCMS, most village clinics were closed, and some transformed into private practices. Barefoot doctors became private providers or changed to other professions. Most RCMS disappeared in rural areas.[31] Although various forms of voluntary health insurance programs were developed since the mid-1980s, less than 1% of the rural population was enrolled. By 1998 only 5% (down from 85% in 1975) of the rural population was covered by the RCMS, mostly in more developed and rich areas. As a result, approximately 900 million rural populations, including poor farmers in relatively richer rural localities, had to pay out of pocket for virtually all health services.[25]

In urban areas, alongside the privatization of state-owned industry, the government funding of healthcare facilities declined considerably, forcing healthcare facilities and professionals to rely on user fees for supporting their operations. Many healthcare professionals who were state employees became private entrepreneurs.[25] At the same time, the moral hazard effect inherited in the GIS and LIS schemes started to emerge, such as overutilization of free health care that drove up healthcare cost. As a result, the healthcare cost rose four times faster than the fiscal income of the government.[32] Neither GIS nor LIS can be financially sustained. Since the mid-1980s both insurance schemes were greatly altered. Considerable co-payment, co-insurance, deductible, and expenditure ceilings were introduced into both insurance schemes, with a significant decline in their coverage and benefit. By 1989, the direct patient pay through fee-for-service accounted for 36% of the total health expenditure; the GIS, LIS, and RCMS health insurance schemes accounted for 44%; and the remaining 20% came from government funding.[33]

The decline of government funding to public health insurance coupled with nonexisting private insurance left the vast majority of the Chinese population without health insurance coverage. By 1998, the health insurance rate fell to 36% and 5% in urban and rural areas, respectively.[34] The lack of access to health care and the shift of disease patterns to the increasingly costly illnesses of cancer, cerebrovascular, and cardiovascular diseases left the Chinese population largely at risk of medically caused financial catastrophe. The out-of-pocket payments increased to 18 times what they were in 1990. The average cost of a single hospitalization was more than double the average annual income of the lowest 20% of the population. More than 35% of rural households and 43% of urban households could not afford healthcare costs; many were left with no choice but to avoid care or became impoverished.[35]

In addition to the profound effect of the free market economy on the health system, several government decisions and measures during this period also affected the cost, quality, and equality of health care. One of which was government's skewed hospital pricing policy. Since the beginning of the economic reform, the central government gradually reduced its funding to hospitals that provided comprehensive healthcare services, including outpatient, inpatient, diagnostic testing, pharmaceutical supplies, and traditional Chinese medicine. By the end of 2000, government funding accounted for only approximately 10% of hospital revenue, forcing hospitals to generate the rest of their revenue from health services and drug sales.[36] However, the price for certain health services, such as doctor visits and surgical procedures were regulated by the government, with 90% of the services having prices set below their costs. The policy was supposedly to ensure equitable access to affordable health care.[37] Meanwhile, the price for prescription drugs and high-technology diagnostic tests, such as advanced imaging, was largely left to a free market. The government allowed healthcare facilities to profit as much as a 15%–20% markup on prescription medicines and use of high-end technologies.[38] To offset the losses on underpriced services and to make profits, hospitals that operated much like for-profit enterprise increased the use of profitable pharmaceuticals and high-technology services.

During the same period, the government also modified the salary-based compensation of hospital professionals to allow bonuses.[39] The size of the bonuses was based on a hospitals' overall revenue, which relied heavily on profitable prescription drugs and diagnostic services. The compensation modification by the government further provided financial incentives for hospitals and healthcare professionals to overprescribe drugs and high-technology services to bring in additional income.[40] In 1993, drug and high-technology spending had exploded. The pharmaceuticals alone accounted for more than half (52%) of China's health spending, with 85% of pharmaceutical sales taking place in hospital settings. Nearly 44% of hospital income was generated through drug sales. The investment in high-end medical equipment by hospitals increased quickly. One typical example was the Computerized Tomography (CT). By 2003, almost 31% of all Chinese hospitals owned CT machines, more than the United States and major European countries.[37-41] The results were ill-allocated healthcare spending, a distorted healthcare delivery system, and compromised quality of patient care. In addition, the healthcare cost rose sharply. The total health spending increased 8% per year from 1978 to 1986 and 11% per year from 1986 to 1993, exceeding GDP growth of 7.7% per capita for the same periods.[24] The inflated healthcare costs deprived millions of uninsured people access to health care and robbed the core competency of the health system to provide quality care. Hospitals and healthcare professionals, when faced with financial pressure and incentives, put profit before the interest of patients they serve, resulting in increased public distrust and anger toward the shealth system.[25]

From 1980 to 2000, the disparity in healthcare access and quality between rural and urban areas grew significantly due to several factors.[38] First, the local government funding to health care through taxations was more than four times higher in urban areas than in rural areas.[42] Second, a disproportionately large amount of healthcare resources was concentrated on large urban hospitals, resulting in more than 80.0% health expenditures allocated to urban areas, despite the fact that 70.0% of the population lived in rural areas.[43] Third, the rural-urban income gap grew wider. By 2005, the rural-urban income difference hit its highest point, with rural per capita income being only 39.0% of urban per capita income.[44] As a result, the rural-urban inequality in healthcare delivery and utilization was escalated. In 2003, the number of beds per 1,000 population in urban areas was 3.67 versus only 1.50 in rural areas, and the number of health professionals per 1,000 population was 4.84 in urban areas versus only 2.19 in rural areas.[45,46] According to the Third National Health Services Survey, conducted in China in 2003, healthcare utilization measured by hospitalization rate was 11.0% in urban areas and only 7.0% in rural areas.[45] Furthermore, the annual inpatient days per 1,000 population increased by12.8% for urban residents, compared to a 10.3% decline for rural residents from 1985 to 1993. In 1993, nearly 40.0% of the rural population who did not seek necessary hospital care reported inability to pay as the main reason, and 30.0%–50.0% of poor rural households became impoverished due to illness, according to various estimates.[46] The provision of preventive care was also reduced significantly in rural areas. For example, in 1999, only 84.0% of rural children received recommended vaccinations compared to 96.0% of urban children. In 2000, the infant mortality rate per 1,000 live births was 37.0 in rural areas, compared to 11.8 in urban areas. The situation was even worse in rural areas of western China, a traditionally poor region, with the infant mortality rate of as high as 52.3 per 1,000 live births.[47]

Due to the decline in government funding and the decentralization of decision-making power of the central government, China's public health programs were severely weakened. Between 1978 and 1993, the financing of EPS dropped from 0.11% of GDP to only 0.04% of GDP, forcing EPSs to cut back in providing and coordinating public health programs.[24] Public health workers and village barefoot doctors became independent practitioners charging for public health programs. For example, the vaccinations against tuberculosis, diphtheria, pertussis, tetanus, polio, and measles charged fees in many areas that created major financial barriers for rural and poor households who needed the services the most.

The decentralization of public health system and central government's fiscal system also resulted in the diminished responsibility and ability of the Ministry of Health to organize and control its disease prevention and surveillance system. The infectious disease reporting and surveillance system was not updated regularly. For example, reporting was not required for SARS, and the information was not shared across health and healthcare organizations horizontally or vertically during the initial occurrence, which quickly turned into an epidemic in 2003.[48] Besides SARS, China had seen other emerging and reemerging infectious diseases, such as AIDS, gonorrhea, syphilis, and an alarming upward trend of tuberculosis that was typically related to worsened living conditions and poverty in rural areas.[23]

The weakened public health system also largely ignored health education, promotion, and disease prevention. According to China's national surveys, the smoking rate reached 67% for adult males and 1.5% for females in 2002.[49] About 66% of diabetics had no idea of their diabetic condition, 27% of diabetics took medication, and only 10% of those who took medication gained control of their condition. By the end of the 1990s, 20 million people were overweight, 160 million had hypertension, and about 200 million cases of cancer were diagnosed each year.[50]

Phase II period has seen a remarkable economic growth and improved living standards of China. But the economic growth did not lead to a better health system, and the health improvement did not progress what the economic growth could have afforded. The decentralization and marketization of China's health system during this period resulted in an ineffective and inefficient delivery system, a vast population without access to health care, increased rural-urban and affluent-poor inequalities, and a weakened public health system for disease control and prevention.

Phase III (2003–ongoing): Rebuilding the Health System

The SARS outbreak in 2003 and other healthcare problems associated with the decentralization and marketization of China's health system have led to growing concerns and resentments of the general public toward the health system. The Chinese government, led by socialist ideology, realized that health is a sector that cannot simply be left to market forces,[24] and it started shifting its development strategy from prioritizing economic expansion to promoting equity and social stability. In 2003, within several months of the SARS outbreak, the Chinese government decided to reinstate its role in the health sector with a massive investment in public health programs, which marked a new era of health reform in China.[51]

Between 2003 and 2008 of the third phase, the government focused on health insurance reform by implementing three main public insurance schemes: (1) the New Rural Cooperative Medical Scheme (NRCMS) launched in 2003 to cover the rural population; (2) the Urban Resident Basic Medical Insurance (URBMI) introduced in 2007 to provide insurance coverage for children, students, and the unemployed in urban areas; and (3) the Urban Employee Basic Medical Insurance (UEBMI), an employment-based insurance program launched in 1998.

The NRCMS is the successor of the RCMS, which had almost completely collapsed since the economic reforms in 1978. The initial coverage of NRCMS was quite shallow, with a goal to reduce the financial burden of inpatient costs for rural residents. The NRCMS is overseen by the Chinese National Health and Family Planning Commission (formerly the Ministry of Health) and is managed by the local governments who are allowed to design and implement the NRCMS according to their local needs and condition, provided that three specific central government's guidelines are met: voluntary participation, coverage for catastrophic illnesses, and county level administration.[32]

The financing of NRCMS comes from the central government, local government, and individual households. At its inception, the amount of financial contribution was equally split three ways among the central, local government, and individual household. Gradually, the government increased its share. For example, in 2008, the annual contributions from the central and local governments each reached ¥80 (about US $10.7) per person, an 800% increase from 2003, and ¥20 (about $2.7) from each participating household.[32] In order to encourage the local governments in poor areas to promote the NRCMS, the central government matches the contribution of the local government only when its enrollment reaches 80% of the target population. In the meantime, governments subsidize 100% of the premiums for poor households who cannot afford health insurance through the Medical Financial Assistance (MFA) program, which was established in 2002.[52] Another unique feature of NRCMS financing is related to its household participation instead of individual participation and therefore to avoid potential adverse selection and to generate a better risk pool. By 2008, in just a few years, the NRCMS enrollment reached 90% of the rural population.[53]

Unlike its predecessor (RCMS) that provided coverage for basic and preventive care, the NRCMS focused on covering expensive inpatient care. The reimbursement rate was between 30% and 60% for inpatient services in 2008, with higher reimbursement rates for services received from lower level facilities. Deductibles and expenditure ceilings are commonly applied across all counties. In recent years, many NRCMS have started to cover outpatient care. Currently, four main NRCMS coverage models exist: (1) covering both inpatient and outpatient care; (2) covering inpatient and high-cost outpatient care; (3) covering inpatient care only; and (4) covering inpatient care with pooled government contributions and covering outpatient care using household contributions as savings accounts.

The NRCMS, as one of the major public insurance programs, has made significant progress in improving access to health care for China's vast rural population. Yet, several challenges remain to be addressed. First, the benefit of the NRCMS has been quite narrow and shallow, with a focus on inpatient cost. Thus its protection against the financial burden of its enrollees is quite limited. Although the majority of rural residents have participated in the NRCMS, the utilization of the NRCMS has been low.[54,55] Only recently the general outpatient services were added to the NRCMS with the increase of government funding.[56] Second, the portability of NRCMS has been restricted and there is no cross-county subsidizing. As a result, millions of migrant workers who have drifted from rural areas to work in urban areas have fallen through the insurance cracks. According to the National Bureau of Statistics of China, the number of rural workers in urban areas reached more than 225 million in 2008.[57] These migrant workers, although they work and live in urban areas, were still registered as rural residents due to the *Hukou* system, a residence registration system that classifies residents according to their hometown locations. The reimbursement for healthcare costs outside an individual's registered county was seldom realized, leaving millions of migrant workers without health insurance.

In urban areas, China launched two basic health insurance schemes, the UEBMI and the URBMI. The UEBMI is an employment-based insurance program that evolved from LIS and GIS, which were established in the 1950s during the planned economy era. The UEBMI was officially launched in 1998 to expand the insurance coverage to private sector employees. The financing of UEBMI comes from the contributions of employers and employees, with each contributing 6% and 2% of employee wages.[58] The enrollment in UEBMI is mandatory, with risk pooled at the municipal level. The pooled funds are divided into two parts: socially pooled funds to pay for inpatient stays with deductibles and medical savings accounts to pay for outpatient visits.[59] Although the UEBMI is overseen by the national government's Ministry of Human Resources and Social Security (MOHRSS), the municipal governments have the flexibility to determine the premium contributions for their UEBMI. For example, in more affluent areas, such as in Shanghai, the premium contributions were as high as 14% of annual salaries of employees. By the end of 2008, the enrollment of UEBMI rose to 81% of the total urban population from only 5% in 1998.[60,61]

Prior to 2007, about 420 million urban residents outside formal employment were left out of public health insurance schemes. With the government's new emphasis on social stability and promoting equity, providing basic healthcare service to everyone became one of the top priorities of China's new development strategy.[62,63] In 2007, a large-scale pilot of the URBMI program was carried out in 79 cities. By the end of 2010, the program was extended to all cities in China.[64]

URBMI mainly covers urban children, students, and residents without formal employment. Similar to the NRCMS, the enrollment in URBMI is voluntary and at the household level. The program pools the premiums at the city level and is administered by the local governments and overseen by the MHRSS. The local governments develop and implement the URBMI according to their specific local needs. The finance of URBMI comes from individual contributions and subsidies from both local and central governments. On average, individual participants contribute a larger proportion of the funds. Governments provide certain amounts of predetermined and guaranteed subsidies required by the central government. For example, in 2007, the central government required an annual government subsidy of no less than ¥40 (about US $7) per year per enrollee. For individuals with financial difficulties, the government provides an additional subsidy, of which 50% comes from the central government.[64]

The URBMI fund is primarily used to cover inpatient costs and costs for certain outpatient visits for chronic or critical diseases, such as diabetes and heart disease. Preventive services are not covered by the URBMI. The URBMI's reimbursement policy and premium level differ from city to city. As a result, the deductibles, co-payments, and expenditure ceilings vary across cities.[64] In general, the reimbursement rate for healthcare expenses is higher for services received from lower level facilities.[61] At the end of 2011, the enrollment rate of URBMI was 93% of the eligible population, equivalent to 221 million urban residents.[51]

URBMI has played a significant role in closing the health insurance gap by providing coverage to millions of Chinese who otherwise would have no financial access to healthcare services. Together with UEBMI and NRCMS, China has been making impressive progress toward providing universal insurance coverage for all of its citizens. In the meantime, many published studies suggest that to provide affordable health care for 1.3 billion people, the health insurance reform needs to go deeper and the healthcare delivery system needs a fundamental transformation.[26,34,35,55]

In 2009, the Chinese government released a comprehensive health reform plan with unprecedented funding of ¥850 billion for three years (about US $204 billion, adjusted for purchasing power parity) to improve five key areas with a goal of providing affordable basic health care for everyone by 2020: (1) expand health insurance to cover more than 90% of the total population; (2) establish a national essential drug system to ensure the safety, quality, access, and supply of essential medicine; (3) improve the primary care delivery system to enhance disease prevention and health promotion; (4) strengthen public health services; and (5) reform public hospitals.[51,65] The Chinese government formally reinstated its role in the health sector and abandoned market-based health reform. The year 2009 marked the beginning of a comprehensive and historical health reform in China.[26]

By 2012, China achieved near-universal health insurance coverage, with more than 95% of 1.3 billion population covered by some form of health insurance, including rural migrant workers who could enroll in either the NRCMS in their hometowns or the URBMI where they work. Building up to that, to reduce excessive drug prescription and improve access to safe and effective essential medicines, the Ministry of Health published the "National Essential Drug List" in late 2009 that consists of more than 300 Western and traditional Chinese medicines, with a policy of zero-markup national retail prices for drugs on the list. The list is for primary healthcare facilities to use and will be extended to hospitals.[66] In 2011, to strengthen public health and primary care, the government increased funding per person for primary care providers to deliver a predefined package of basic public health services. In addition, the government directed its funding to building the primary care infrastructure with a focus on improving the healthcare workforce distribution. The efforts include waiving tuition fees for medical graduates who would work at township health centers for at least three years. The reform of public hospitals has been challenging.[67] The main goal of public hospital reform is to make inpatient care affordable and cost effective by prohibiting the increase of drug prices, reducing medical test costs, and increasing prices for medical services, such as surgeries. The government has invested over US $10 billion in pilot projects that are expected to expand to 200 cities in 2016. The result of public hospital reform, however, is less clear. Several recent studies have demonstrated that although the medication cost was reduced, total out-of-pocket spending increased significantly.[68–69] In addition, many hospitals, mostly tertiary public hospitals, resisted the reform efforts. To counter the resistance, the government once again sought market forces by inviting private investors to own up to 20% of China's hospitals by 2015 in the hope of creating competition that would bring the public hospital sector in line with the health system.[26]

Description of the Current Healthcare System

In China, socialism is the official ideology. Guided by the principle that every Chinese citizen is entitled to basic healthcare services, the central government is responsible for designing national health law and policy, planning and budgeting resource allocation, and supervising healthcare services and health professionals. Local governments of four administrative levels (provincial, city, county, and township) are responsible for providing healthcare services according to their local situation. The NHFPC was created by merging the former Ministry of Health with the National Population and Family Planning Commission in 2013, and the local Health and Family Planning Commissions have the primary responsibility for the health and healthcare sector.[70] The State Administration of Traditional Chinese Medicine, subordinated to NHFPC, undertakes the responsibility of health service management of traditional Chinese medicine. The China Food and Drug Administration is responsible for supervising food and drug industries. Other central government agencies also play important roles in organizing and developing healthcare services. For example, the National Development and Reform Commission (NDRC) is jointly leading China's health system reform with the NHFPC. The NDRC is specifically responsible for pricing rules and regulations, grassroots healthcare services, personnel education, and the national reimbursement drug list.[71] The Ministry of Finance provides funding for government subsidies and health insurance contributions. The Ministry of Human Resources and Social Security runs both UEBMI and URBMI programs. **FIGURE 23-3** illustrates the organization of health administration in China.

Both central government and local governments own public hospitals. For example, the NHFPC directly owns several hospitals in Beijing, the capital of the country. In addition, national universities administered by the Ministry of Education own affiliated hospitals. Local governments at the provincial, city, and county levels may have similar structure and may own hospitals at their administrative levels.

Facilities

Health services in China are mainly provided by the public system, which consists of facilities that provide primary care, outpatient specialist care, inpatient care, and mental health care. Primary care is provided in village clinics, township and community hospitals, and

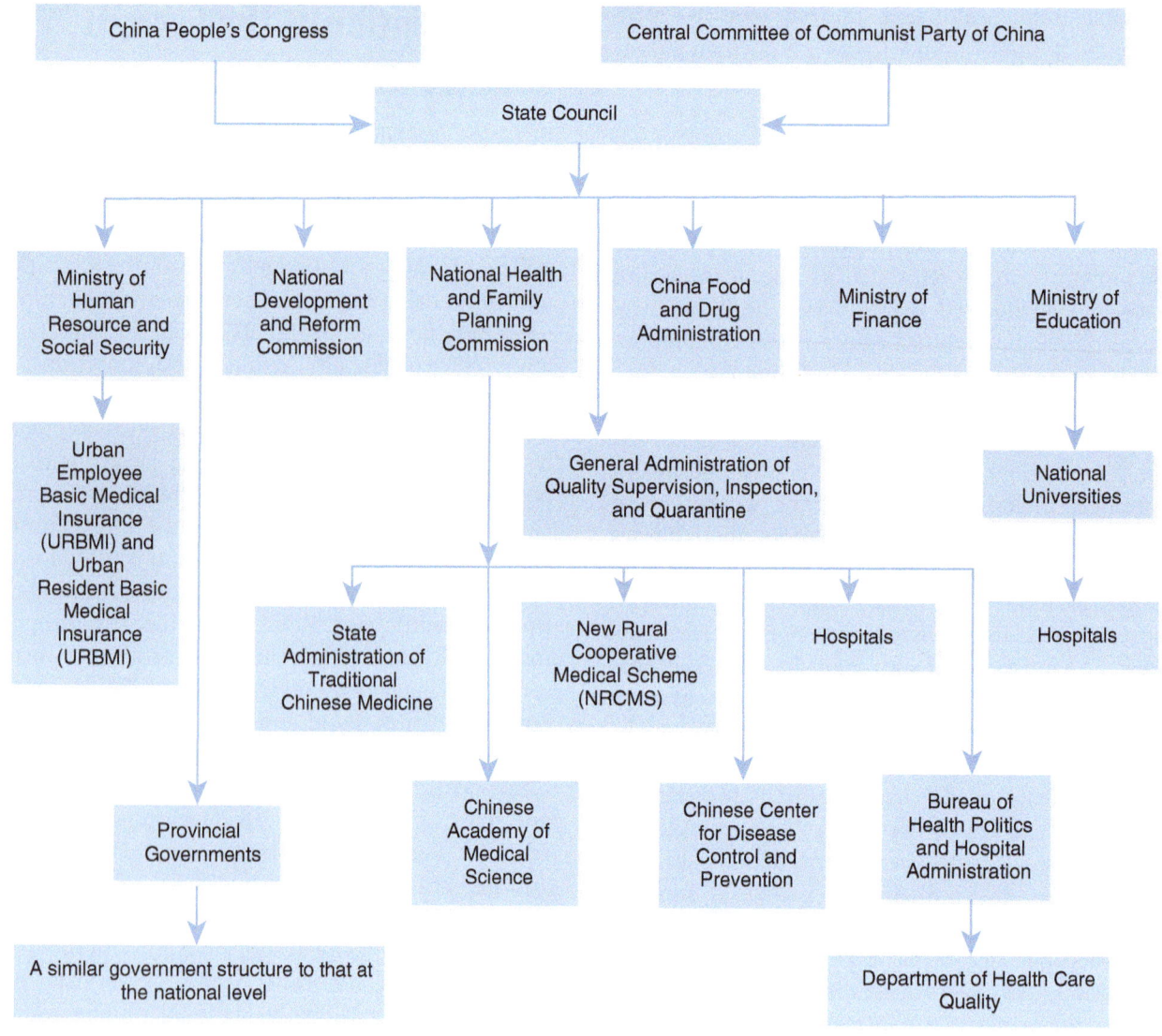

FIGURE 23-3 Organization of Health Administration in China

Modified from Fang H. China. In: Mossialos E, Wenzl M, Osborn R, Sarnak D, eds. *2015 International Profiles of Health Care Systems*. The Commonwealth Fund; 2016.

in secondary and tertiary hospitals. Outpatient specialist care is typically delivered in hospital outpatient settings. Patients usually can see outpatient specialists without general practitioner referral. **TABLE 23-2** summarizes the type of the facility and services provided.

The health system in China is dominated by public hospitals that provide comprehensive healthcare services, including primary care, outpatient specialist care, and inpatient care. They also play a vital function in providing emergency services. The number of hospitals increased significantly, with an annual average growth rate of 2.5%; specialized hospitals increased the fastest, at an annual rate of 9.4% since the 1980s.[9] In addition, hospitals are growing in size. Currently, 16 hospitals in China have more than 3,000 beds. The supersized hospitals are mostly university affiliated and are located in the center of big cities, including Beijing, Shanghai, and Chengdu.

The largest hospital in the world, of more than 7,000 beds, is located in Henan province, one of the most populous provinces in China. As the number of hospitals has increased, the number of township health centers and village clinics have decreased.[9] **FIGURE 23-4** and **FIGURE 23-5** demonstrate these changes in the number of facilities.

In recent years, more private hospitals have entered the healthcare market. By the end of 2010, the percentage of private hospitals had increased from 33% to 17% in 2005. Despite the increase in the number of private hospitals, public hospitals still account for nearly 90% of total hospital beds and 92% of outpatient visits.[9] Traditional Chinese medicine is an integral part of healthcare services in China. Most hospitals have a department of traditional Chinese medicine. Public traditional Chinese medicine hospitals are arranged along four administrative levels.

TABLE 23-2 Health Service Facilities (2011)

Hospitals type	Number of hospitals	Hospital services provided
Hospitals		
General hospitals	14,328	General services including outpatient and inpatient, all kinds of physical examination and diagnosis, etc.
Traditional Chinese medicine hospitals	3,308	General services including outpatient and inpatient, all kinds of physical examination and diagnosis, etc.
Specialist hospitals	4,283	Outpatient and inpatient; examination services; specialized in oral, eye, tumor, cardiovascular, pediatrics, mental health, OB/GYN, skin, infectious diseases
Grassroots healthcare facilities		
Community health service centers	32,860	General diagnosis services and treatment of common diseases, acute care, rehabilitation, consultation, referrals, preventive care, hygiene, vaccination, health education, family planning, etc.
Township hospitals	37,962	Health services at township level in urban areas including diagnosis and treatment of common diseases, acute care, rehabilitation, consultation, referrals, preventive care, hygiene, vaccination, health education, family planning, etc.
Village clinics	662,894	Public health services including preventive care, maternal and child hygiene, and primary diagnosis and treatment of common diseases
Outpatient clinics affiliated with hospitals but not located in hospitals	9,218	General outpatient services
Clinics and infirmaries	175,069	Simple health facilities affiliated with factory or agency providing diagnosis and treatment of common diseases under the supervision of hospitals or community health centers.
Specialized public health institutions		
Diseases prevention and control	3,484	Diseases prevention and control, public health emergency preparedness and response, behavior risk factor surveillance and intervention, clinical laboratory inspection and evaluation, health education and promotion, health service management, scientific research.
Specialist preventive care institutions	1,294	Preventive health in oral diseases, mental health, skin diseases, sexually transmitted diseases, tuberculosis, occupational diseases, endemic diseases, schistosomiasis, drug rehabilitation, etc.
Health education institutions	147	Health promotion and health education and related policy advocacy, technical consultation and promotion, staff training, information management and disclosure, surveillance and evaluation

(continues)

TABLE 23-2 Health Service Facilities (2011) (*continued*)

Hospitals type	Number of hospitals	Hospital services provided
Maternal and child healthcare institutions	3,216	Basic health services, health promotion, health education, and preventive care for women and children
Emergency centers (ambulance services)	270	Emergency services, rescue and treatment on site, and transportation
Blood center	525	Collecting, testing, and supplying blood to medical facilities.
Health inspection and supervision	3,022	Enforcement of health law, inspection and supervision of food safety, public area sanitation, occupational health and medical appliances, etc.
Other institutions	2,629	Sanatoria, clinical testing centers, medical scientific institutions, medical on-the-job training institutions, medical examinations councils, rural water hygiene centers, human talent exchange centers, bureau of health statistics, etc.

Data from National Bureau of Statistics of China. China Statistical Yearbook 2015. Beijing: National Bureau of Statistics of China; 2015.

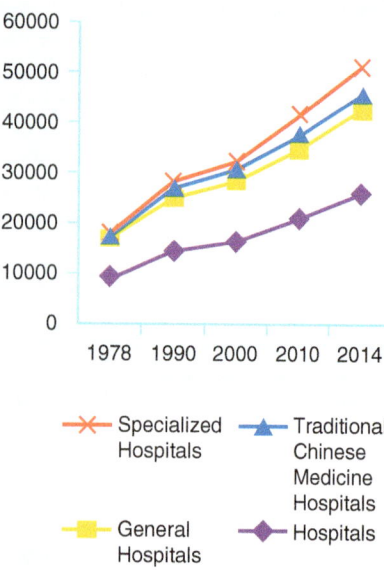

FIGURE 23-4 Number of Hospitals, 1978–2014
Data from China Statistical Yearbook. 2015.

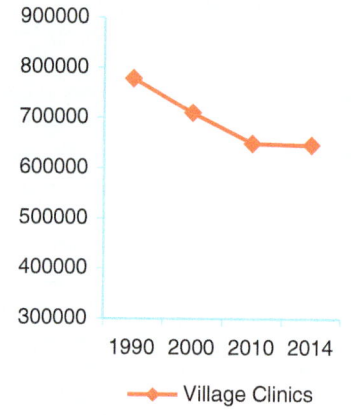

FIGURE 23-5 Number of Village Clinics, 1990–2014
Data from China Statistical Yearbook, 2015.

The number of acute care hospital beds per 1,000 population in China is the third highest (4.55), after Japan (7.92) and Germany (5.34), of Organisation for Economic Co-operation and Development countries.[73] Compared with the United States, both the number of hospital discharges per 1,000 population (China's 140 versus United States' 125) and the average length of hospital stays for curative care (China's 8.9 versus United States' 5.4) are much higher in China than in the United States.[73] China's health delivery system is typically centered on hospitals that reward volumes of services and sales of medicines and high-technology procedures. The success of health delivery reform is largely dependent on if the government can reform public hospitals to build a primary-care-centered delivery system that provides high-quality and cost-effective health services.

Mental health service is primarily hospital based and is provided in special psychiatric hospitals or psychological departments of tertiary hospitals. Most mental health professionals are psychiatrists and psychiatric nurses, with few clinical psychologists or social workers. Mental health care has been separated from primary care. Mild mental health problems are treated at home or untreated. Only severely mentally ill patients are treated in psychiatric hospitals. The funding for the mental health system is complex and small. According to the World Health Organization (WHO), only 2.35% of the total health budget was spent on mental health, and less than 15.00% of the population had health insurance that included coverage for psychiatric disorders in 2005. The number of psychiatrists working in the mental health sector was only 1.53 per 100,000 population in 2011.[74,75]

Long-term care facilities in China are virtually nonexistent. Thus, long-term care is mostly provided by family members at home with few formal long-term care providers. Family care givers are not paid formally, and long-term care insurance benefits are virtually absent from any health insurance scheme. There are some government efforts to develop a long-term care system, but there is no specific structure for delivering long-term care yet in place.[76]

Workforce

There has been a significant growth in the quantity of health human resources in the past decade in China. The number of professional health workers per 1,000 population has increased to 5.56 in 2014 from 3.50 in 2005.[9] Similar to most countries, the composition of the professional health workforce in China consists of medical practitioners, nurses, medical technicians, pharmacists, and other professionals. TABLE 23-3 illustrates the composition of professional health workers.

In 2014, there was a total of 10,234,213 health workers, among which 7,589,790 were medical technical personnel (licensed doctors, nurses, and other medical personnel), 1,058,182 were village doctors and health workers, and 1,586,241 were nonprofessional workers (administrators, logistical workers, etc.).[9] There have been insufficient nurses and other health professionals compared to the number of doctors. Unlike most other countries, China has had more doctors than nurses, with a national average ratio of 1.4 to 1 until 2014.[77] In addition, grassroots and rural health facilities, such as township hospitals and community health centers, have been experiencing shortages of health professionals. Doctor density in urban areas is more than twice that in rural areas; nursing density is 3.3 times higher in urban areas than in rural areas.[9] The Chinese government has started to take measures to redistribute health human resources. Such measures include increasing the income of health professionals in township and community health centers, waiving tuition for medical students who are willing to work in rural health facilities, and requiring regular staff exchange between community health centers and hospitals.[77]

Higher education for professional health workers in China includes clinical medicine, preventive medicine, public health, traditional Chinese medicine, dentistry, medical laboratories, nursing, medical technology, and pharmacy. Currently there are 159 higher education institutions in medicine.[78] Medical education in China involves undergraduate, graduate,

TABLE 23-3 Composition and Distribution of Health Workers in China (2014)

Profession	Number	Percentage	Total density	Urban density	Rural density
Medical practitioner	2,374,917	31.3%	2.12*	3.54*	1.51*
Assistant medical practitioner	517,601	6.8%			
Registered nurse	3,004,144	39.6%	2.20	4.30	1.31
Pharmacist	409,595	5.4%	0.27**	—	—
Technician	379,740	5.0%	0.26**	—	—
Other	903,793	11.9%	0.58**	—	—
Total	7,589,790	100.0%	5.56	9.60	3.77

* Density data include assistant medical practitioners.
** Density data are from 2011.

Data from National Bureau of Statistics of China. *China Statistical Yearbook 2015*. Beijing: National Bureau of Statistics of China; 2015.

postgraduate education, and in-service training. The system is complicated. But in general, to obtain a medical doctorate degree in clinical medicine or medical technology, it requires five years of undergraduate study at a medical university, two to three years of master's degree study, and three years of postgraduate study consisting of six months at a medical university and two and a half years of medical research, or six months of curriculum study and one and a half years of clinical training in a hospital and one year of medical research. To major in nursing or pharmacy, it usually takes four years of study for a bachelor's degree and seven years for a master's degree.[79] Of all health workers, a little over 22.0% have a bachelor's degree and only 3.4% hold a master's degree or higher. A sizable 74.0% have an education level below bachelor's degree.[80] Using education level as a proxy for health workforce quality—such as technical competency, knowledge, and skills—it presents a picture of inadequate quality of China's health workforce.

Technology

The remarkable economic growth for the past three decades has led to the proliferation of health technology in supporting specialized healthcare services in diagnosis and treatment in China. For example, in 2011, the number of pieces of high-technology medical equipment that cost above ¥500,000 (US $77,414) owned by health institutions was 144,971, equivalent to 0.11 per 1,000 population. The number of pieces of equipment costing ¥1,000,000 ($154,828) was 61,249, or 0.05 per 1,000 population. The number of PET-CTs owned by hospitals was more than 100, CT was 6,456, and MRI was 2,322.[80] Most high-technology medicine is concentrated in urban hospitals and inefficiently used. For example, in 2013, the number of MRI exams per 1,000 population was 42.7, compared to 106.9 in the United States.[73] High-technology medicine is a double-edged sword. It provides high-quality care but also drives up healthcare costs, in addition to its potential side effects. The unbalanced distribution of high technology is manifested in the growth of urban high-technology medicine at the expense of rural primary care. China has also become one of the top countries for biomedical technology development. Government policies favoring biomedical development combined with massive investments in health technology make China an emerging leader in the biomedical technology sector.[81]

In recent years, China has launched a series of aggressive campaigns to accelerate the adoption of Health Information Technologies (HIT) in order to improve the quality of care, control costs, and enable regional and national information sharing for public health (e.g., disease outbreak surveillance) and other secondary-use purposes (e.g., research and policy making). To date, almost all healthcare providers have established electronic health record (EHR) systems. However, due to the variations in EHR systems and the lack of coordination, EHR systems can only be operated within their own systems of an organization. The problem leads to low meaningful use of HIT for patients, diminishing HIT value in quality improvement and cost control.[72]

The most remarkable HIT achievement in China is perhaps the rapid establishment of a nationwide real-time disease reporting information network, which is the world's largest: the China Information System for Disease Control and Prevention (CISDCP). Recognizing the importance of the timely collecting, processing, and reporting of epidemic information following the 2003 SARS crisis, the CHFPC mobilized tremendous resources within a very short period of time to create an integrated information-sharing network that links China's hospitals and clinics at all levels. The system, launched on January 1, 2004, has been implemented in 93.5% of medical facilities at the county level and 70.3% of medical facilities at the district level, resulting in a reduction of the average number of days needed for data reporting from 4.9 days to 0.8. In 2005, a total of 4,428,548 cases covering 37 common types of infectious diseases were processed through CISDCP.

Another use of technology in China is digital health care and telemedicine, which have promoted the growing number of distance healthcare cases in China. The use of telemedicine, digital health care, or eHealth can channel advanced health services available in large cities to grassroots rural areas.[82] Private investors have invested over a billion dollars in digital health care ranging from e-commerce to online physician consultation services to health promotion and disease management applications. There are a number of challenges, though. For example, no clear regulation exists regarding eHealth or health technology applications, such as remote consultation, an issue that the government must address. It is also not clear as to the quality, safety, and acceptance of using eHealth or digital health care.[82,83]

▸ Evaluation of the Current Healthcare System

Cost

Health spending in China in recent decades has increased significantly, driven primarily by rapid economic growth, health insurance reforms, an aging population, health technology advancement, and a surge in noncommunicable diseases, such as cancer, diabetes, and heart disease. According to the National Bureau of Statistics of China, the country's health expenditure increased from ¥510 (US $82.2) per capita in 2003 to ¥2,582 ($416) per capita in 2014.[84] For the same period, government health spending as a percentage of total health expenditure rose from 17.8% to 30%. Health expenditure as a percentage of GDP rose from 4.8% to 5.6%.[84] It is projected that if the current hospital-centered delivery model that rewards volume and sales continues, health spending increases will average 8.4% per year. More than 60% of the projected growth in health spending will be due to increased inpatient services in hospitals.[85]

Some efforts have been made recently to control rising healthcare costs, such as the introduction of diagnosis-related groups (DRGs), global budgets, capitation to replace the fee-for-service provider payment system, and the release of the essential drug list of zero markups for retail price. In addition, the central government placed constraints on new hospital buildings, hospital beds, and the purchase of high-technology equipment.[70] China needs further health system reform to meet the growing needs of the population and to control health costs, suggested a two-year study conducted jointly by the World Bank, the WHO, the Ministry of Finance, the National Health and Family Planning Commission, and the Ministry of Human Resources and Social Security of China.[85] The study pointed out that despite the remarkable achievements in universal health coverage from the government's 2009 health reforms, deeper health reform is needed for China to build a value-based health service delivery system that provides high-quality and cost-effective care.

Quality

In 2000, the World Health Organization conducted a study to measure the overall health system performance for 191 member countries using 5 key measures: disability-adjusted life expectancy; responsiveness of the health system, including speed of service, protection of privacy, and quality of amenities; and fairness of financial contribution. China was ranked 144th.[86] Since then China has instituted major health reforms and made significant progress toward improving health and healthcare quality. The health of the Chinese has improved significantly, with life expectancy at birth increasing from 72 years in 2000 to 76 years in 2015. The maternal mortality ratio decreased from 58 per 100,000 live births in 2000 to 27 per 100,000 live births in 2015. The infant mortality rate dropped from 30.0 to 10.9 per 1,000 live births, and the under-five mortality rate dropped from 37.0 to 12.7 per 1,000 live births from the year 2000 to 2013. In many parts of the country the under-five mortality rate now is lower than the United State or Canada.[87,88] **FIGURE 23-6** presents child mortality rate decrease since 1980 in China.

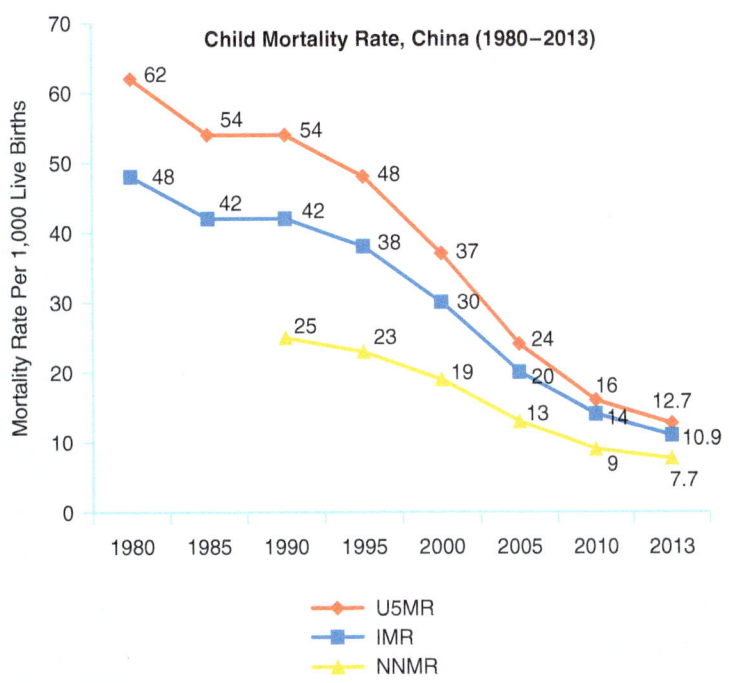

FIGURE 23-6 Mortality Rate, China, 1980–2013

Modified from World Health Organization. China: Neonatal and Child Health Profile. http://www.who.int/maternal_child_adolescent/epidemiology/profiles/neonatal_child/chn.pdf?ua=1. Copyright 2014.

Despite the improvements in major health indicators, the profound rural-urban disparities in health and healthcare quality persist. In a study conducted in a province of China, the neonatal mortality in rural areas is more than twice that in urban areas (17.8 per 1,000 live births in rural compared to 7.5 per 1,000 live births in urban areas). The chances of neonatal death due to birth asphyxia, preterm low birth weight, and pneumonia is 2.2 to 2.6 higher for rural babies than for urban babies. These differences largely reflect poor access to prenatal health services and poor quality of care provided in rural areas.[89] The authors of the study pointed out that most neonatal death in rural areas were caused by preventable or treatable conditions. In other words, those deaths could be avoided if timely and appropriate health care were provided.[89]

The quality of health workers, such as village doctors and facilities in rural areas is generally low. Most village doctors are descended from barefoot doctors who were undertrained, had a low level of education, and had limited experience. In addition, there is no systematic strategy to monitor and evaluate village doctors.[90] A study of quality in rural areas of China concluded that the quality of care provided in rural clinics is poor.[91] On average, only 26% of the clinicians' diagnoses are correct; 64% of the prescriptions provided by the clinicians are either unnecessary or even harmful; and only 18% of the items on a clinical checklist of recommended questions or physical exams are performed.[91] Most quality hospitals are located in urban areas where health professionals are better trained and technology is more advanced.

The central government has implemented some measures to improve the quality of health services in general and reduce rural-urban inequity in particular. For example, in 2009 the former Ministry of Health released clinical pathways that are now regulated nationally. Governments sponsor training for rural doctors in urban hospitals, provide financial incentives for new medical graduates to work in rural hospitals, and require new graduates to work as residents in rural health facilities.

Access

China achieved near universal health coverage in 2012 with three main publically financed health insurance programs: NRCMS (for rural residents), UEBMI (for urban employed), and URBMI (for urban unemployed). The coverage rate reached more than 95% of the entire population of China.[51] All three programs cover primary, specialist, emergency, hospital, and mental health care, as well as traditional Chinese medicine and prescription drugs. Dental care and vision care in most cases are not covered. All three insurance programs require deductibles, co-payments, and reimbursement ceilings with different amounts. **TABLE 23-4** summarizes the key features of three insurance programs. In addition, for individuals who cannot afford insurance premiums or out-of-pocket costs, governments provide subsidies through medical financial assistance programs. Approximately 6.6% of China's population received such medical financial assistance for paying insurance premiums or health expenses.[73]

There is no limitation on a patient's choice and no general practitioner gatekeeping role for specialist or hospital services, although patients are encouraged to seek primary care in grassroots clinics and lower level healthcare facilities. The reimbursement is usually higher for the services received from lower level healthcare facilities.

The World Health Organization defines universal health coverage as "attained when people actually obtained the health services they need and benefit from financial risk protection" and universal access as "the opportunity or ability to do both of these things."[92] Despite China's universal health insurance coverage, two major problems of access to health care remain. One is the availability problem with urban major hospitals (particularly tertiary hospitals) and academic health centers being crowded with long waiting lines, and rural areas suffering from poor quality of health providers and hospitals. The other is the financial burden of using health services. Out-of-pocket costs for co-payments and deductibles, coupled with low reimbursement ceilings, make the healthcare cost still too high for many to afford. In 2013, out-of-pocket expenses per capita were US $216, representing about 34% of the total health expenditure.[73] High out-of-pocket costs are major barriers for rural residents and poor families seeking needed health services. The financial protection offered by universal coverage is widely believed inadequate. In 2015, a special health insurance program that supplements the three main public insurances was introduced to provide coverage for severe diseases—such as cancers, kidney disease, and acute myocardial infarction—by reimbursing expenses beyond the rather low reimbursement ceilings of the three regular insurances. The program is mostly government financed and run by local governments. In addition, private insurance programs have entered the health insurance market to provide mostly supplemental coverage to the three main public insurance programs.

TABLE 23-4 Summary of China's Three Main Publically Financed Health Insurance Programs (2013)

	UEBMI	URBMI	NRCMS
Target population	Urban employees	Urban children, students, unemployed, disabled	Rural residents
Year launched	1998	2007	2003
Enrollment rate (%)*	99	98	97
Number of enrollees (million)	274.2	299	802
Unit of enrollment	Individuals	Households	Households
Premium per person per year (US $)**	240	21	24
Risk-pooling unit	Urban	Urban	Rural
Government subsidy (US $)**	0	18	18
Benefit coverage			
Inpatient reimbursement rate (%)	68	48	44
Countries or cities covering general outpatient care (%)	100	58	79
Countries or cites covering outpatient care for major and chronic diseases (%)	100	83	89
Annual reimbursement ceiling	6 times the average wage of urban employees	6 times the disposable income of local residents	6 times the income of local farmers
Overseeing government	MOHRSS	MOHRSS	NHFPC

*Total enrollment rate is 98.7%.

**2011 data. MOHRSS: Ministry of Human Resources and Social Security; NHFPC: National Health and Family Planning Commission

Modified from Yu H. Universal health insurance coverage for 1.3 billion people: What accounts for China's success. Health Policy. 2015; 119(9): 1145-1152. Copyright 2015, with permission from Elsevier

Innovation

While writing about China's health system, one of the questions we are asked frequently is how China could provide near universal coverage (98.7% enrollment in 2014) for its enormous population of 1.3 billion in such a short period of time whereas the United States cannot? There are many factors, including strong government financial and political commitment, the rapid economic growth backing the Chinese government's ambitious move, the strong public support of government intervention in the health sector, and the socialist ideology endorsing health as a right of all.[51] Many of these factors are unique to China and altogether created the right timing and opportunity. But without one innovative strategy, universal coverage might not be realized in such a short time: first provide shallow coverage for all, then gradually expand benefits to cover the specific needs of the population, then reduce out-of-pocket money as more government financing becomes available, and involve private insurers to provide complementary coverage. This innovative strategy may provide a model for other countries that pursue universal health coverage.

Another innovation in China's health sector is manifesting itself in digital health developments, including telemedicine, that can bridge the rural-urban gap in health and health care.

Current and Emerging Issues and Challenges

China has embarked on a systematic health reform to provide affordable basic health care for all of China's population by 2020. Despite the impressive accomplishments of the ongoing health reform since 2009, such as successfully launching and implementing universal coverage for 1.3 billion Chinese people, China is facing a number of challenges. Some of these challenges are common to other countries, such as aging populations and an epidemiological transition from infectious diseases to noncommunicable chronic diseases (NCDs); others reflect China's progress toward its goal of building a high-quality, value-based healthcare delivery system, and of becoming a wealthy and harmonious society.

Burden of Noncommunicable Chronic Diseases and an Aging Society

China is living through a rapid epidemiological transition from infectious diseases to NCDs.[93] According to China's CDC, the sharp increase in NCD incidences accounted for 85% of all deaths and 70% of the total number of years lost due to ill health, disability, or premature death. The leading causes of death in China now are cancers, cardiovascular diseases, and chronic respiratory diseases.[94,95] The burden of NCDs is compounded with the aging population. It is estimated that about 250 million Chinese will be 65 years of age or older by 2020, accounting for 18% of China's population.[94] The unhealthy lifestyles associated with urbanization, such as smoking, excessive drinking, physical inactivity, and a diet high in fat, sugar, and salt, are prevalent in China. For example, as high as 67% of Chinese men smoke, contributing to more than one million smoking-related deaths every year. If the current trend continues, the number of smoking-related death will double to 2 million by 2030, making it the number one cause of preventable death.[96]

Inequity in Health and Healthcare

The disparities and inequities in health and health care will be a crucial challenge for China into the future. There are significant variations in access to health care and healthcare outcomes between rural and urban areas, rural migrants and city dwellers, and geographic areas such as the Eastern and Western regions. Although the Chinese government has made efforts to tackle the inequities, they continue to widen and most likely will worsen into the future as the society experiences substantial changes associated with the economic growth of the past three decades. Changes in living conditions, lifestyles, individual values, and consumer behaviors will confound the issues of inequities and disparities.

Air Pollution and Health

China is confronted with severe and extensive air pollution, with the highest concentrations in and near urban areas. The physical and psychological effects of air pollution have been recognized as having serious negative impacts on the health and wellbeing of people. Outdoor air pollution contributes to an estimated 1.6 million deaths in China annually.[97] About 38% of the Chinese population breathes air that would be rated unhealthy by United States standards. The most dangerous pollutants are the fine airborne particles, less than 2.5 microns in diameter, which can be breathed deep into lungs and absorbed into the bloodstream to cause a host of health problems, including asthma, strokes, lung cancer, and heart attacks.[97] The Chinese government will allocate US $2.57 billion to improve air quality in 2016. In addition, the government issued a policy to increase renewable energy production to 15% of total energy by 2020,[98] which requires a long-term coordination of many sectors at central and local levels.

Inefficient Healthcare Delivery

Despite the significant progress made in improving healthcare financing, China's healthcare delivery system faces a number of challenges with providing affordable and high-quality care for the whole population of China. Such challenges include an inefficient healthcare delivery model and inadequate quality of care.

China's healthcare delivery model is heavily centered on hospitals that have been utilized as one-stop shopping for all health services. The increase in China's total health expenses is mainly due to rapid economic growth, increased healthcare demands, an aging population, increased noncommunicable diseases, and an inefficient healthcare delivery model. To control health spending and provide value-based quality care, the health delivery model needs to be transferred from expensive hospital-focused care to cost-effective, grassroots-based primary care. The transfer requires building a strong primary care infrastructure that is coordinated and integrated with tertiary care and with referral systems. Such transformation poses several main challenges:

1. Improving the quality of primary care providers at the grassroots level and improving the distribution of the health workforce.
2. Modifying provider payment mechanisms, including disconnecting financial incentives from service volumes and prescription drugs.
3. Increasing health resources in areas where the greatest gains are.
4. Improving the efficiency of hospitals.
5. Fostering healthcare professionalism to put patients' interests first.
6. Developing a systematic strategy to monitor, evaluate, and control the quality of health services across the delivery system.

The success of the transformation is largely dependent on the success of public hospital reform that is currently underway. China still has a long way to go to delivering value-based and affordable quality care for all.

References

1. Murphey R. *East Asia: A New History*. 5th ed. New York: Longman-Pearson; 2010.
2. Ho PT. The significance of the Ch'ing Period in Chinese history. *J Asian Stud*. 1967;2(26):189–195.
3. Blunden C, Elvin M. *Cultural Atlas of China*. Revised ed. New York: Checkmark Books; 1998.
4. Publicity CL. The composition, power and function of the State Council. *State Organs*. http://english.moj.gov.cn/State-Organs/content/2009-02/03/content_1028259.htm. Accessed August 8, 2016.
5. The Composition of CPPCC. *Chinese People's Political Consultative Conference*. http://www.cppcc.gov.cn/zxww/2012/07/03/ARTI1341301498421103.shtml. Accessed June 29, 2016.
6. Li C. *China's Leaders: The New Generation*. New York: Rowman & Littlefield Publishers, Inc; 2001.
7. Hieyeon K, Campbell JR. The price of change: policy reform and leadership transitions in post 1978 Chinese politics with comparison to Gorbachev's Soviet Union. *J East Asian Aff*. 1994;8(1).
8. World Bank. GDP (current US $). World Bank national accounts data and OECD National Accounts data files. http://data.worldbank.org/indicator/NY.GDP.MKTP.CD?view=chart. Published 2016. Accessed July 13, 2016.
9. National Bureau of Statistics of China. *China Statistical Yearbook 2015*. Beijing: National Bureau of Statistics of China; 2015.
10. National Bureau of Statistics of China. Statistical communique of the People's Republic of China on the 2015 national economic and social development. http://www.stats.gov.cn/english/PressRelease/201602/t20160229_1324019.html. Published 2015. Accessed July 13, 2016.
11. World Bank. Exports of goods and services (% of GDP). World Bank national accounts data, and OECD National Accounts data files. http://data.worldbank.org/indicator/NE.EXP.GNFS.ZS. Published 2016. Accessed July 14, 2016.
12. Bank TW. Imports of goods and services (% of GDP). World Bank national accounts data, and OECD National Accounts data files. http://data.worldbank.org/indicator/NE.IMP.GNFS.ZS. 2015. Accessed July 14, 2016.
13. China's State Administration of Foreign Exchange. The scale of China's foreign exchange reserves (1950–2015). http://www.safe.gov.cn/. Accessed July 14, 2016.
14. World Bank. Foreign direct investment, net inflows (BoP, current US $). International Monetary Fund, Balance of Payments database, supplemented by data from the United Nations Conference on Trade and Development and official national sources. http://data.worldbank.org/indicator/BX.KLT.DINV.CD.WD. Accessed July 15, 2016.
15. World Bank. GDP per capita (current US $). World Bank national accounts data, and OECD National Accounts data files. http://data.worldbank.org/indicator/NY.GDP.PCAP.CD. Accessed July 15, 2016.
16. World Bank. Age dependency ratio (% of working-age population). http://data.worldbank.org/indicator/SP.POP.DPND. Accessed June 30, 2016.
17. Taylor RL. Proposition and praxis: the dilemma of neo-Confucian syncretism. *Philos East West*. 1982;32(2).
18. China's population mix. http://www.china.org.cn/e-groups/shaoshu/mix.htm. Accessed June 30, 2016.
19. The Central People's Government of the People's Republic of China. China's education system. http://english1.english.gov.cn/2005-08/27/content_26661.htm. Published 2016. Accessed July 26, 2016.
20. Center of Education China. China education. http://www.chinaeducenter.com/en/cedu.php. Published 2016. Accessed July 26, 2016.
21. World Bank. China Overview. www.worldbank.org/en/country/china/overview. Updated April 6, 2016. Accessed August 6, 2016.
22. World Health Organization. Summary of probable SARS cases with onset of illness from 1 November 2002 to 31 July 2003. http://www.who.int/csr/sars/country/table2004_04_21/en/. Data as of December 31, 2003. Accessed 2016.
23. Zhang D. *The Social History of Disease in Modern China*. Shandong, China: Shandong Education Publishing House; 2006.
24. World Bank. *Financing Health Care: Issues and options for China*. China 2020 Series. Washington, DC: World Bank; 1997.
25. Blumenthal D, Hsiao WW. Privatization and its discontents—the evolving Chinese health care system. *N Engl J Med*. 2005;353(11):1665–1670.
26. Blumenthal D, Hsiao W. Lessons from the East—China's rapidly evolving health care system. *N Engl J Med*. 2015;372(14):1165–1170.
27. Yuanli Liu. China's public health-care system: facing the challenges. *Bulletin of the World Health Organization*. 2004;82:532–538.
28. Zhang SN, Liu ZB, Gu ZW. Disease control and prevention in China in the 20th century and prospects. *Environ Health Prev Med*. July 2002(7):132–137.
29. Ma J, Lu M, Quan H. From a national, centrally planned health system to a system based on the market: lessons from China. *Health Aff*. 2008;27(4):937–948.

30. World Bank. Life expectancy at birth, total (years). http://data.worldbank.org/indicator/SP.DYN.LE00.IN. Accessed July 7, 2016.
31. Liu G, Liu X, Meng Q. Privatization of the medical market in socialist China: a historical approach. *Health Policy*. 1994;27:157–174.
32. Barber SL, Lan Y. Health insurance systems in China: a briefing note. *World Health Report 2010: Background Paper*, No 37. World Health Organization; 2010.
33. Hillier S, Shen J. Health care systems in transition: People's Republic of China. Part I: an overview of China's health care system. *J Public Health Med*. 1996;18(3):258–265.
34. Meng Q, Tang S. Universal health care coverage in China: challenges and opportunities. *Social and Behavioral Sciences*. 2013;77:330–340.
35. Hu S, Tang S, Liu Y, Zhao Y, Escobar ML, Ferranti D. *Health System Reform in China 6*. World Health Organization. www.who.int/management/district/6.Financing.pdf. Published October 20, 2008. Accessed July 28, 2016.
36. Tao D, Hawkins L, Wang H, et al. *Fixing the Public Hospital System in China*. Washington, DC: World Bank; 2010.
37. Liu X, Liu Y, Chen N. The Chinese experience of hospital price regulation. *Health Policy Plan*. June 2000;2(15):157–163.
38. Hesketh T, Zhu W. Health in China: The healthcare market. *BMJ*. 2004;314:1616–1618.
39. Daemmrich A. The political economy of healthcare reform in China: negotiating public and private. *SpringerPlus*. 2013;2(448):1–13.
40. Liu X, Mills A. The influence of bonus payments to doctors on hospital revenue: results of a quasi-experimental study. *Appl Health Econ Health Policy*. 2003;2(2):91–98.
41. Healthcare in China—IBM. 2010. www-935.ibm.com/services/us/imc/pdf/g510-62. Accessed July 24, 2006.
42. Shi L. Health care in China: a rural urban comparison after the socioeconomic reforms. *Bulletin of the World Health Organization*. 1993;71(6):723–736.
43. Shi G, Gong S. Analysis about China's health investment since market open and reform. *China Development Review*. 2005.
44. Park A. *Rural—Urban Inequality in China*. World Bank; 2010.
45. Liu M, Zhang Q, Lu M, Kwon CS, Quan H. Rural and urban disparity in health services utilization in China. *Medical Care*. 2007;45(8):767–774.
46. Liu Y, Hsiao WC, Eggleston K. Equity in health and health care: the Chinese experience. *Social Science & Medicine*. 1999;49:1349–1356.
47. Hsiao WC. *Disparity in Health: The Underbelly of China's Economic Development*. 2004;1(5):64–70.
48. Liu Y. China's public health-care system: facing the challenges. *Bulletin of the World Health Organization*. July 2004;82(7):532–538.
49. Jiang Y, Jin S. Social economic burden attributed to smoking in China. Paper presented at: Proceedings from the National Conference on Policy Development of Tobacco Control in China in the 21st Century, 2000; Beijing.
50. Ma J, Lu M, Quan H. From a national, centrally planned health system to a system based on the market: lessons from China. *Health Aff*. 2008;27(4):937–948.
51. Yu H. Universal health insurance coverage for 1.3 billion people: What accounts for China's success. *Health Policy*. 2015;119:1145–1152.
52. Ma X, Zhang J, Meessen B, et al. Social health assistance schemes: the case of Medical Financial Assistance for the rural poor in four counties of China. *Int J Equity Health*. 2011;10(44):1–13.
53. Yip WCM, Hsiao WC, Chen W, Hu S, Ma J, Maynard A. Early appraisal of China's huge and complex health-care reforms. *Lancet*. March 2012;379:833–841.
54. Li C, Hou Y, Sun M, Lu J. An evaluation of China's new rural cooperative medical system: achievements and inadequacies from policy goals. *BMC Public Health*. 2015;15(1079):1–9.
55. Long Q, Xu L, Bekedam H, Tang S. Changes in health expenditures in China in 2000s: has the health system reform improved affordability. *Int J Equity Health*. 2013;12(40):1–8.
56. You X, Kobayashi Y. The new cooperative medical scheme in China. *Health Policy*. 2009;91:1–1.
57. China National Bureau of Statistics. Statistical communiqué of the People's Republic of China on the 2010 national economic and social. http://www.stats.gov.cn/was5/web/search?channelid=250710&andsen=migrant±workers. Accessed 2016.
58. Guo B. China's Urban Health Care System. *Asian Survey*. 2003;43(2):385–403.
59. Liu Y. Reforming China's urban health insurance system. *Health Policy*. 2002(2):133–150.
60. James CA. Reform plans promise significant change, but what does that mean for foreign healthcare players? *China Business Review*. 2009.
61. Dong K. Medical insurance system evolution in China. *China Economic Review*. 2009;20(4):591–597.
62. Central Committee of the Communist Party. The standing conference of the State Council of China's adopted guidelines for furthering the reform of the healthcare system in principle. In *Chinese*. http://news.xinhuanet.com/newscenter/2009-04/06/content_11138803.htm. Accessed July 28, 2016.
63. Agency XN. Hu Jintao: Building up a basic health care system to cover both urban and rural residents—a speech at the 35th study session of the 16th Central Committee's Political Bureau, October, 24 2006. In *Chinese*. http://politics.people.com.cn/GB/1024/4954631.html. Accessed July 28, 2016.
64. Lin W, Liu GG, Gang C. The urban resident basic medical insurance: A landmark reform towards universal coverage in China. *Health Economics*. 2009;18(Suppl 2):S83–S96.
65. Zhu C. Launch of the health-care reform plan in China. *Lancet*. 2009;373:1322–1324.
66. Ministry of Health. National essential medicines list for primary health institutions. The Central People's Government of People's Republic of China. In *Chinese*. http://www.gov.cn/gzdt/2009-08/18/content_1395524.htm. September 21, 2009. Accessed July 28, 2016.
67. Cheng TM. Early results of China's historical health reforms: the view from Minister Chen Zhu. *Health Aff*. 2012;31(11):2536–2544.
68. Zhang Y, Ma Q, Chen Y, Gao H. Effects of public hospital reform on inpatient expenditures in rural China. *Health Economics*. 2016. doi: 10.1002/hec.3320.
69. Guan X, Qi L, Liu L. Controversy in public hospital reforms in China. *Lancet Global Health*. 2016;4(4 e420):1.
70. National Health and Family Planning Commission of the PRC. What we do. http://en.nhfpc.gov.cn/2014-05/07/c_46917.htm. Updated 2014. Accessed July 30, 2016.
71. Kahler C. China's healthcare reform: how far has it come? *China Business Review*. 2011.
72. Fang H. China. In: Mossialos E, Wenzl M, Osborn R, Sarnak D, eds. *2015 International Profiles of Health Care Systems*. The Commonwealth Fund; 2016.
73. Mossialos E, Wenzi M, Osborn R, Sarnak D. *2015 International Profiles of Health Care Systems*. The Commonwealth Fund; 2016.

74. Liu J, Ma H, He YL, et al. Mental health system in China: history, recent service reform and future challenges. *World Psychiatry*. October 2011;10(3):210–216.
75. World Health Organization. Psychiatrists working in mental health sector, per 100,000. Global Health Observatory (GHO) data. http://apps.who.int/gho/indicatorregistry/App_Main/view_indicator.aspx?iid=2954. Accessed August 3, 2016.
76. Du P. Long-term care for older persons in China: United Nations Economic and Social Commission for Asia and the Pacific; 2015. Working paper.
77. Anand S, Fan V, Zhang J, et al. China's human resources for health: quantity, quality, and distribution. *Lancet*. 2008;372(9651):1774-1781.
78. Xu D, Sun B, Wan X, Ke Y. Reformation of medical education in China. *Lancet*. 2010;375(10):1502–1504.
79. Lijuan W, Wang Y, Peng X, et al. Development of a medical academic degree system in China. *Medical Education Online*. 2014;19:1–7.
80. Center CNHDR. *Health Service Delivery Profile—China*. Beijing: China National Health Development Research Center; 2012.
81. Chicago, University of Illinois. The 4 top countries for health tech development. http://healthinformatics.uic.edu/resources/articles/the-4-top-countries-for-health-tech-development/. Accessed August 2, 2016.
82. Zhao N, Wu B, Samples C, Sh RJ. Mobile technology for health care in rural China. *International Journal of Nursing Sciences*. 2014;1:323–324.
83. Chaua PY, Hu PJH. Investigating healthcare professionals' decisions to accept telemedicine technology: an empirical test of competing theories. *Information & Management*. 2002;39:297–311.
84. National Bureau of Statistics of People's Republic of China. National Bureau of Statistics of People's Republic of China. In Chinese. http://www.stats.gov.cn/. Accessed June 29, 2016.
85. World Bank Group, World Health Organization, Ministry of Finance P, National Health and Family Planning Commission P, Ministry of Human Resources and Social Security P. *Healthy China: Deepening Health Reform in China, Building High-Quality and Value-Based Service Delivery*. World Bank Group; 2016.
86. The World Health Organization. *World Health Report 2000: Health Systems—Improving Performance*. Geneva, Switzerland: World Health Organization; 2000.
87. The World Health Organization. *Neonatal and Child Health Profile*. The World Health Organization. http://www.who.int/maternal_child_adolescent/epidemiology/profiles/neonatal_child/chn.pdf?ua=1. Accessed August 3, 2016.
88. Horton R. Offline: China—the triumph (and danger) of transition. *Lancet*. Nov 2015;387.
89. Yi B, Wu L, Liu H, Fang W, Hu Y, Wang Y. Rural-urban differences in neonatal mortality in a poorly developed province of China. *BMC Public Health*. 2011;11(477):1–7.
90. Tang S, Ehiri J, Longcorrespo Q. China's biggest, most neglected health challenge: non-communicable diseases. *Infect Dis Poverty*. 2013;2(1):7.
91. *Survey using incognito standardized patients shows poor quality care in China's rural clinics*. Rural Education Action Program. Stanford University. reap.fsi.stanford.edu. 2014. Accessed August 3, 2016.
92. Evans D, Hsu J, Boerma T. Universal health coverage and universal access. *Bulletin of the World Health Organization*. 2013;91:546-546A. doi: http://dx.doi.org/10.2471/BLT.13.125450
93. Yang G, Kong L, Zhao W, et al. Emergence of chronic non-communicable disease in China. *Lancet*. 2008;372(9650):1679–1705.
94. China CDC. China national plan for NCD prevention and treatment (2012–2015). http://www.chinacdc.cn/en/ne/201207/t20120725_64430.html. Accessed August 4, 2016.
95. Wang L, Kong L, Wu F, et al. Preventing chronic diseases in China. *Lancet*. 2005;366(9499):1821–1824.
96. Koplan J, Eriksen. Smoking cessation for Chinese men and prevention for women. *Lancet*. 2015;386:1422–1423.
97. Rohde R, Muller R. Air pollution in China: mapping of concentrations and sources. *PLOS ONE*. 2015;10(8):e0135749. http://dx.doi.org/10.1371/journal.pone.0135749.
98. Liping G. Beijing to spend 16.5 billion yuan for cleaner air in 2016. CCICED special policy study report. http://www.ecns.cn/m/2016/01-25/196934.shtml. Published January 25, 2016. Accessed August 5, 2016.

CHAPTER 24

Japan

Mikiyasu Hakoyama

▶ Country Description

TABLE 24-1 Japan

Nationality	Noun: Japanese (singular and plural) Adjective: Japanese
Ethnic groups	Japanese 98.5%, Korean 0.5%, Chinese 0.4%, other 0.6% (2004)*
Religions	Shintoism 79.2%, Buddhism 66.8%, Christianity 1.5%, other 7.1% (2012 est.)**
Language	Japanese
Literacy	Definition: Age 15 and over can read and write. Total population: 99% Male: 99% Female: 99% (2002)
Government type	Parliamentary constitutional monarchy
Date of independence	660 BCE (traditional founding by Emperor Jimmu)
Gross Domestic Product (GDP) per capita	$38,100 (2015 est.)
Unemployment rate	3.3% (2015 est.)

(continues)

TABLE 24-1 Japan (continued)

Natural hazards	many dormant and some active volcanoes; about 1,500 seismic occurrences (mostly tremors but occasional severe earthquakes) every year; tsunamis; typhoons; volcanism***
Environment: current issues	Power plant emissions resulting in air pollution and acid rain; acidification of lakes and reservoirs degrading water quality and threatening aquatic life; Japan's exceptionally large consumption of fish and tropical timber contributing to depletion of these resources in Asia and elsewhere; nuclear disaster****
Population	126,702,133 (July 2016 est.)
Age structure	0–14 years: 12.97% (male 8,472,869/female 7,963,782) 15–24 years: 9.67% (male 6,436,935/female 5,813,222) 25–54 years: 37.68% (male 23,593,194/female 24,145,406) 55–64 years: 12.4% (male 7,867,611/female 7,840,141) 65 years and over: 27.28% (male 15,080,738/female 19,488,235) (2016 est.)
Median age	Total: 46.9 years Male: 45.6 years Female: 48.3 years (2016 est.)
Population growth rate	−0.19% (2016 est.)
Birth rate	7.8 births/1,000 population (2016 est.)
Death rate	319 deaths/100,000 population (2016 est.)
Disease burden	Communicable disease deaths: 34/100,000 population Noncommunicable disease deaths: 244/100,000 population Injury deaths: 41/100,000 population (2016 est.)
Net migration rate	0 migrant(s)/1,000 population (2016 est.)
Gender ratio	At birth: 1.06 male(s)/female 0–14 years: 1.06 male(s)/female 15–24 years: 1.11 male(s)/female 25–54 years: 0.98 male(s)/female 55–64 years: 1 male(s)/female 65 years and over: 0.77 male(s)/female Total population: 0.77 male(s)/female (2016 est.)
Infant mortality rate	Total: 2 deaths/1,000 live births Male: 2.3 deaths/1,000 live births Female: 1.8 deaths/1,000 live births (2016 est.)
Life expectancy at birth	Total population: 85 years Male: 81.7 years Female: 88.5 years (2016 est.)
Total fertility rate	1.41 children born/woman (2016 est.)

TABLE 24-1 Japan (continued)	
HIV/AIDS adult prevalence rate	—
Number of people living with HIV/AIDS	—
HIV/AIDS deaths	—

*Up to 230,000 Brazilians of Japanese origin migrated to Japan in the 1990s to work in industries; some have returned to Brazil (2004).
**The total of adherents exceeds 100% because many people practice both Shintoism and Buddhism.
***Unzen (elevation 1,500 meters) and Sakura-jima (elevation 1,117 meters) are decade volcanoes with explosive history and close proximity to human populations; other historically active volcanoes include Asama, the most active volcano on Honshu Island, Aso, Bandai, Fuji, Iwo-Jima, Kikai, Kirishima, Komaga-take, Oshima, Suwanosejima, Tokachi, Yake-dake, and Usu.
****After the Fukushima nuclear disaster in 2011, Japan planned to phase out nuclear power, but since then it implemented a new policy to restart nuclear power plants that meet new, strict safety standards.
Data from Central Intelligence Agency. The World Fact Book, 2008: Japan. https://www.cia.gov/library/publications/the-world-factbook. Accessed November 18, 2008.

History

Archaeological evidence indicates that the current inhabitants of Japan may have been there continuously for the last 30,000 years. The first period of Japanese prehistory is from approximately 10,000 BCE to 300 BCE, which is known as the Jomon era. The name *Jomon* is derived from design patterns found on clay vessels that are created by pressing a rope. It is assumed that Jomon people lived a simple nomadic life consisting of hunting, fishing, and picking edibles. The Yayoi era began at approximately 300 BCE. During this period, residents of Japan developed a more sophisticated lifestyle. They adopted wet field or water-irrigated rice cultivation, which ensured them a steady food supply. This adoption of agriculture made it possible for the early Japanese to stop being nomadic and to form permanent communities.[1]

For over 1,000 years from the Yamato era to the Azuchi-Momoyama era, Japan's history has been characterized by continuous civil wars. It was not until the Edo era that began in the beginning of the 17th century that Japan became a peaceful country. It was at this time that the Dutch began to visit Japan for trading. Being afraid of strong foreign influences, especially of the spread of Christianity, the Japanese government promulgated Sakoku-rei (an isolationist policy) in the mid-17th century, which protected Japan from being Westernized by an influx of foreign influences. This isolationist policy prohibited any interactions with foreign countries except China and the Netherlands. Trading with the Dutch was allowed only in Dejima, a manmade island in Nagasaki. This arrangement continued for nearly 230 years.[2]

It was during the Meiji Era (1868–1912) that Japan passionately adopted Western technology to establish a modernized and militaristic nation. At the end of the 19th century, Japan used its military force to gain new territories successfully, including Korea and part of China. Japan's military invasions continued into the mid-20th century. This eventually led to a war against the United States with a surprise attack by Japanese aircrafts on the U.S. Pacific Fleet in Pearl Harbor, Hawaii, on December 7, 1941. Japan's militaristic ambition was finally forced to end in August 1945 when the United States detonated two atomic bombs in Japan, the first on Hiroshima on August 6, 1945, and the second on Nagasaki three days later. The U.S. occupation that followed immediately after Japan's unconditional surrender and lasted until 1952 immensely impacted the construction of modern Japan in various areas from economy to politics. During this period of U.S. occupation, a framework for a democratic government was established. Based on a British model, Japan established a parliamentary system and an independent judiciary. The emperor was retained as a symbol of the state.[1]

The current educational system was also restructured during this period by adopting the American system of a six-year elementary school, a three-year junior high, and a three-year high school.[1] The Japanese are nearly 100% literate, and their level of educational attainment is high.[3]

Size and Geography

Japan, the nation of the rising sun, lies off the coast of the Eurasian continent in the Far East, or in the western end of the northern Pacific Ocean. The Japanese Archipelago consists of four large islands and several thousand small islands that stretch 1,200 miles from northeast to southwest. The four main islands are, from the north to the south, Hokkaido, Honshu, Shikoku, and Kyushu. Honshu is the largest. It is narrow and long in shape, and the widest point is only 160 miles. Unlike many other islands and continents, Japan did not break off from the Eurasian continent. Instead, the Japanese islands were formed as a result of volcanic eruptions. Approximately 60 volcanoes remain active in Japan.[4]

The total land area of Japan is approximately 145,379 square miles, which is larger than Great Britain or Italy. Because of the great majority of its land area being extremely mountainous, nearly all of the population inhabits approximately one-sixth of its total land area. Japan is, therefore, more crowded than the population density per square mile indicates.[1] See **FIGURE 24-1**.

Government and Political System

The foundation of Japan's current democratic government was also laid during the U.S. occupation. The present constitution was written and adopted in 1947, which provides for universal suffrage for both genders and also for an independent judicial system. The Diet consists of two houses. The upper house, or the House of Councilors, has 242 members who are elected for six-year terms. The lower house, or the House of Representatives, has 475 members who serve four-year terms. Terms in the lower house can be shortened, however, if opposing parties call for a reelection because of a vote of no confidence. Whenever the election takes place, the prime minister must be elected again.

A great deal of political power remains in the lower house, however, because a bill, once defeated by the upper house, can still be passed and become law if the lower house passes it for a second time with a two thirds majority.[1] The prime minister is elected by the House of Representatives from among its members; therefore, the support of the majority party becomes essential in the selection of the prime minister, who, in

FIGURE 24-1 Map of Japan
© Bardocz Peter/Shutterstock

turn, appoints the members of his cabinet.[3] The cabinet members are composed of heads of ministries and other government agencies.[1]

The Japanese political world is composed of multiple parties, the majority leading party and several minority opposition parties. The Liberal Democratic Party (LDP), which is conservative and pro-business, was the majority leading party for most of the second half of the 20th century, during which time Japan strived for and achieved its goal of becoming an economic giant. Structural change within Japanese political dynamics took place in the mid-1990s when the Japanese economy faced a serious economic crisis. With the burst of the bubble economy, the LDP was no longer able to maintain the majority; however, the LDP maintained its control by forming a coalition with other minority parties. At this time, the LDP has successfully regained its members and currently holds the majority on its own.

Macroeconomics

Japan experienced rapid and acute economic growth during the 1960s and 1970s, during which time Japan was reconstructed as a modernized nation. Japan's economy slowed down in the 1980s, and the growth rate of the gross domestic product (GDP) decreased. Japan's economy suffered severely during the 1990s as a result of the abrupt ending of the bubble economy.

Japan's real GDP in recent years, when compared globally, maintained second place, following the United States, until 2008. However, it fell to third place, following the United States and China, in 2009 and has remained third since then. In 2014, 22.0% of the world's GDP was generated by the United States, 13.1% by China, and 5.8% by Japan.[5]

Demographics

Japan's population as of July 2016 was estimated to be approximately 126.7 million, consisting of slightly more females (over 2.5 million more) than males; this gap increased slightly since 2008. The population aged 15 to 64 years makes up slightly less than two-thirds (61.3%) of the total population. The population aged 65 and over constitutes approximately 26.0% of the total population, which is a considerable increase from 20.8% in 2006. Conversely, the current young population (aged 0 to 14 years) declined to 12.8% from 13.6% in 2006. As these statistics indicate, an aging population has become a persistent concern for today's Japan.[6]

Statistics indicate that Japan is relatively safe society compared with many of its counterparts in the world. Rates of violent crime, theft, and drug abuse in Japan are among the lowest in the world. A statistical comparison between Japan and the United States revealed that despite the fact that Japan has one-third as many police per capita as the United States, it has only 37 prisoners for every 100,000 people, 7% of the number of prison inmates (519) per 100,000 in the United States.[1]

Poverty

Poverty has become an urgent concern for the Japanese in recent years. According to the report by the Organisation for Economic Co-operation and Development (OECD), among 34 OECD nations for which the data were available, Japan ranked the sixth worst in relative poverty, defined as earning less than one-half of the median household disposable income. In fact, Japan is the sole OECD country in which the lowest income decile has faced an absolute decline in their real income since the mid-1980s.[7] The poverty level has kept rising since the mid-1980s, and the proportion of the population living in relative poverty rose to 16.0% in 2014, a considerable rise from 13.5% in 2000.[8] Furthermore, the number of welfare recipients has risen to over 2 million people in 2012; more shocking, however, is the fact that 31.6% of single household women aged 20 to 63 live in relative poverty.[9] For women aged 65 years and older who live alone and for single mothers, those who live in poverty are even more prevalent, reaching nearly 50.0%, subsequently impacting their children's wellbeing.[9]

Religion

The two major religions in Japan are Shinto and Buddhism. Shinto is an indigenous, shamanic religion of Japan that venerates kami (superior beings) whose spirits are believed to inhabit objects or plants temporarily. The central tenets of Shinto are thought to have originated in the Yayoi era (300 BCE to 300 CE). It was not until the seventh century, however, that these beliefs became recognized as a coherent religion called Shinto, primarily in order to differentiate these existing beliefs from those of Buddhism, the newly introduced religion.[10] Shinto is a nonexclusive religion that has no founder, doctrines, or texts. The kami, often translated as deity, are numerous and frequently applied to objects such as mountains, big trees, and large rocks, which is very dissimilar to the transcendent deities of Western religions.[11]

Since the seventh century, Buddhism has constantly been supported by the Japanese government and has come to be the major religion, along with Shinto.[11] Both Shinto shrines and Buddhist temples are found throughout Japan and are visited by people on numerous occasions every year. Although approximately 90% of Japanese report that they are Buddhists, they also visit Shinto shrines.[1] Religion to Japanese, whether it is Shinto or Buddhism, is an important aspect of their traditional lifestyle and is qualitatively different from what it means to be religious for Christians, Muslims, Hindus, or Jews. Many Japanese marry and christen babies at Shinto shrines and gather for funerals at Buddhist temples. At the same time, more young people are choosing Christian churches as the place to get married. It is perhaps more accurate to conclude that most Japanese are much more secular than their American counterparts.[1]

It has long been debated whether Confucianism is a religion or philosophy. There is no doubt, however, that it has profoundly influenced northeast Asian nations, including Japan. Although Confucian teachings have long been influential, their influence was enhanced when Confucianism was incorporated into the nation's legal system more than 300 years ago. Teachings of Confucius are deeply integrated into Japanese life, teachings that emphasize appropriate virtue and conduct in this world, such as hard work, education, obligation, and reciprocity. Japanese society is status conscious, one of the characteristics of the Confucian influence. Vertical relationships are clearly structured, and superiors and subordinates owe each other certain obligations, including protection, loyalty, and good teamwork. Many Japanese, however, do not connect these values imbedded in Japanese culture to Confucianism.[1]

▸ Brief History of the Healthcare System

Pre–World War II

Foreign influences on Japanese health care and medicine began in the 6th century when traditional Chinese medicine was introduced, treatment of which featured the use of acupuncture and herbal medicines. Both are still popular in Japan.[12] A thousand years after the Chinese influence, the Japanese were exposed to Western medical practices by Portuguese missionaries. This influence was minimal, however, because of the isolation policy the Tokugawa government issued in the 17th century, effectively barring the Portuguese from Japan. Besides the Chinese, only the Dutch were allowed to trade with Japan during the centuries of this isolation period. Because of this, the influence of Dutch medical care practices on the development of Japan's healthcare system has been profound.[13]

During the Meiji Era that began in the late 19th century, the Japanese were willing to open themselves up to a variety of Western influences.[12] Although the Japanese accepted various Western concepts and technologies for the modernization of their nation, they expressed a particular interest in the German healthcare system, which was regarded as the best in Europe at that time.[14] The Japanese constructed its nationwide health insurance system based heavily on the German model.[12]

Japan's health insurance system improved gradually from the 1920s to the 1960s. The Health Insurance Law enacted in 1922 was designed to direct employers to provide health insurance coverage mainly for their blue-collar workers, such as factory workers and miners.[15] In 1938, the Ministry of Public Health and Social Welfare was established, and the National Health Insurance Law was enacted, which required local governments to offer health insurance coverage to those who were not subject to the 1922 law, such as those engaged in fishing, farming, and forestry.[16] It is estimated, however, that as many as one-third of the citizens were uninsured in 1955. It was not until 1961 when health insurance coverage was extended to every citizen.[16]

In 1931 when the population was 64.5 million, Japan had 3,710 hospitals, and by 1940, they had increased to 4,732 with an approximate ratio of 1 doctor and 2 nurses per 1,000 Japanese. These conditions worsened, however, during the early 1940s when Japan was at war and the number of hospitals and clinics as well as doctors, nurses, and beds per 1,000 decreased sharply. In 1945, when World War II ended, all these conditions began to improve again.[16]

Since World War II

One of the public health issues during the U.S. occupation immediately after the end of World War II was to deal with infectious diseases such as smallpox, cholera, and diphtheria. The most feared disease was smallpox. Some 17,000 cases were reported during the first year of the occupation. Immediate measures were taken that included production and inoculation of sufficient vaccines for the total population, as a result of which the epidemic subsided. Tuberculosis was also a major threat to the Japanese during the 1930s and 1940s. It had been the leading cause of death, and in the year 1945 alone, more Japanese died from tuberculosis than by all the fire raids and bombings, including the two atomic bombs. When the U.S. occupation first took place, it was estimated that there were 1 to 2 million clinical cases of tuberculosis. The Public Health and Welfare officials, concluding that vaccination was the best approach, developed a dried BCG vaccine and successfully vaccinated 30 million people under 30 years old. Although vaccination contributed to the drop in mortality and morbidity, it was not until 1960 that streptomycin became available to treat those who were already infected and that tuberculosis was no longer the number one cause of death in Japan.[16]

Another challenge in reestablishing healthcare systems after World War II was rebuilding the physical infrastructure of costly healthcare facilities. Because of successful reduction in the rates of infectious disease, hospital resources could be reallocated for other purposes. The quality of care provided by these hospitals, however, was in need of improvement. In order to cope with issues related to quality care, a model hospital was set up in each prefecture that was to serve as a benchmark for cleanliness and efficient management. A legal step was taken in 1948 to improve healthcare quality by reinspecting and classifying hospitals. Small hospitals that had fewer than 10 beds were downgraded to clinics and were limited in patient care as they lacked sufficient operating rooms and laboratory services. Although the number of doctors in Japan was adequate, their quality was questioned, as more than 60% of the 77,000 doctors were graduates of second-class medical schools that required only 4 years of medical education beyond high school. Based on the new standards established, all the medical schools were inspected, as a result of which schools not meeting the standards were closed. By the early 1950s, the quality of doctors in Japan improved significantly. The quality of nursing was also improved in a similar fashion during this period.[16] Currently all physicians, dentists and pharmacists must attend 6 years of college beyond high school and pass the national exam to be certified. This allows Japanese to practice medicine at a younger age than their American counterparts.

The number of physicians in relation to population steadily increased, and by the end of 1992, there were approximately 220,000 physicians (1.77 physician per 1,000 population). More than 95% of these physicians were in medical practice, about 27% of which were owners of medical care facilities such as hospitals or clinics, whereas the rest were employed in medical care facilities.[17]

▸ Description of the Current Healthcare System

Facilities

Japan has 13.3 healthcare facilities per 1,000 population, ranking first out of 41 OECD countries. As of October 1, 2014, the number of healthcare facilities in operation in Japan was 177,546, an increase of 2,602 (1.5%) from 2006 but a decrease of 223 (0.1%) facilities from the previous year. Of the 177,546 facilities, 8,493 (4.8%) were hospitals (20 or more beds), 100,461 (56.6%) were clinics (19 or fewer beds), and 68,592 (38.6%) were dental clinics.[18]

Whereas 87.4% (7,426) of hospitals were general hospitals in 2014, the rest were mental hospitals (1,067). When these hospitals were classified according to sponsorship, 5,721 (67.4%) were medical corporations, followed by 1,231 (14.5%) hospitals run by the public (governmental) medical organizations. Of the 100,461 clinics, 91.7% (92,106) were clinics with no beds. As for the sponsorship of these clinics, 43.6% (43,863) were individually owned, followed by medical corporations (39,455).[18]

In 2014, the total number of beds was 1,568,261. More than one-half of these beds (894,216) belonged to general hospitals. There were 1,234 beds per 100,000 inhabitants. A little more than one-half (703.6 beds per 100,000) were for general patients whereas about a quarter (266.1 per 100,000) were psychiatric beds and another quarter (258.2 per 100,000) were for long-term care.[18] Considering Japan's fast-growing elderly population, demands for beds, especially long-term care beds, were expected to rise.[18]

Workforce

By 2015, the number of physicians was 311,205; 79.6% were males and nearly two-thirds (194,961) belonged to the hospitals. The average age of these physicians was 49.8 years (51.4 years for males and 43.5 years for females). The number of physicians to 100,000 population was 233.6, a slight improvement from 212.9 of 2008.[19] The number of dentists by 2015 was 103,972; more than three quarters (77.5%) of whom were males; the average age was 50.5 years (52.2 years for males and 44.8 years for females). A great majority (85.4%) of these dentists were engaged in clinics. The number of dentists per 100,000 population was 79.4, an improvement from 75.7 of 2008.[19]

The number of pharmacists was 288,151 by 2015; 62.9% (161,151) were engaged in pharmacies and 19.0% (54,879) in hospitals and clinics; 15.1% (43,608) belonged to pharmaceutical corporations. Unlike physicians and dentists, a majority (61.0%) of pharmacists were females. The average age of the pharmacists was 45.9 years (45.9 years for males and 45.8 years for females). The number of pharmacists per 100,000 population was 170.0, a significant improvement from 145.7 in 2008.[19] Six years of education beyond high school are required to become a pharmacist.

There were 1,086,779 nurses and 340,153 assistant nurses working in 2015. The number of nurses increased significantly (54.7% increase) since 2002, whereas that of assistant nurses decreased from 393,413 in 2002.[18] Also, there were 48,452 public health nurses and 33,956 midwives. There were 855.2 nurses, 267.7 assistant nurses, 38.1 public health nurses, and 26.7 midwives per 100,000 population.[19] Disparity in distribution of these medical professionals from prefecture to prefecture is apparent. For instance, compared to the 304.5 physicians of Tokyo and the 307.9 of Kyoto per 100,000 population, only 152.8 physicians were available in Saitama. Similarly, the number of dentists per 100,000 population in Tokyo (118.4) was twice as large as some other prefectures, such as Fukui (52.9) and Shiga (55.4).[19] The number of nurses per 100,000 population also indicates disparity, varying from 1,314.4 in Kochi to 625.1 of Chiba and that of assistant nurses from 608.8 of Kagoshima to 109.8 of Tokyo. Distribution disparity is equally extreme for public health nurses, varying from 70.7 per 100,000 population of Yamanashi to 22.8 of Kanagawa, whereas it is less apparent for midwives, varying from 40.9 of Shimane to 19.5 of Saitama.[19]

Technology and Equipment

Computed tomography (CT), also called computed axial tomography (CAT) scanners, magnetic resonance imaging (MRI) units, mammography, and radiation therapy equipment are major modern medical technologies. CT scanners and MRI units are both used to produce cross-sectional views of the inside of the patient's scanned body, which can assist physicians in making a prompt diagnosis. There were 101.3 CT scanners per 1 million population in Japan in 2014, which was by far the highest number among the OECD countries. There were 46.9 MRI units per 1 million population currently available in Japan, far less than that of CT scanners. However, it was also the highest number among all the OECD countries. There were 6.8 pieces of radiation therapy equipment per 1 million population in Japan; this is less than one-half of Switzerland's, and Japan ranked 11th among OECD countries. These figures suggest that Japan's healthcare focuses more on preventive and diagnostic aspects than therapeutic aspects.[20] See **TABLE 24-2**.

TABLE 24-2 Medical Technologies in OECD Countries, Number per Million Population, 2014 (or Latest Available)

Rank	CT scanners		MRI units		Radiation therapy equipment	
	Country	Per million	Country	Per million	Country	Per million
1	Japan	101.28	Japan	46.87	Switzerland	16.49
2	Australia	55.94	United States	38.05	Denmark	13.40
3	United States	40.97	Korea	25.66	United States	12.47
4	Iceland	40.53	Italy	24.62	Iceland	12.47
5	Denmark	38.06	Finland	22.06	New Zealand	12.31
6	Korea	37.09	Iceland	21.83	Slovak Republic	12.19
7	Switzerland	36.15	Austria	19.22	Australia	10.54
8	Greece	35.17	Denmark	15.39	Finland	9.56
9	Italy	33.29	Spain	15.34	Ireland	9.11
10	Austria	29.60	Australia	15.18	Czech Republic	7.99
11	Portugal	27.56	Ireland	13.45	Italy	6.99
12	Finland	21.70	Luxembourg	12.59	Japan	6.83
13	Luxembourg	21.58	Netherlands	11.49	Slovenia	5.82

TABLE 24-2 Medical Technologies in OECD Countries, Number per Million Population, 2014 (or Latest Available) (*continued*)

Rank	CT scanners		MRI units		Radiation therapy equipment	
	Country	Per million	Country	Per million	Country	Per million
14	Estonia	18.97	Estonia	11.38	Portugal	5.78
15	Spain	17.59	New Zealand	11.18	Greece	5.75
16	New Zealand	17.55	Turkey	10.48	Korea	5.63
17	Poland	17.17	Chile	9.43	Luxembourg	5.40
18	Ireland	16.70	Portugal	9.28	United Kingdom	4.99
19	France	15.43	Slovenia	8.74	Austria	4.95
20	Slovak Republic	15.33	Czech Republic	7.42	Spain	4.89
21	Czech Republic	15.03	Slovak Republic	6.65	Hungary	4.75
22	Chile	14.76	Poland	6.44	Poland	4.68
23	Canada	14.67	United Kingdom	6.16	Estonia	3.79
24	Turkey	14.18	Hungary	3.03	Turkey	2.52
25	Slovenia	13.09	Israel	2.81	Chile	2.50
26	Netherlands	11.54	Mexico	2.06	Mexico	1.71
27	Israel	9.53			Israel	0.37
28	United Kingdom	8.10				
29	Hungary	7.88				
30	Mexico	5.31				

Data from OECD. OECD Health Statistics 2015.

Evaluation of the Healthcare System

Cost

Japan is the first nation in Asia to have introduced a comprehensive social insurance program, and the program features universal coverage by mandating everyone to join the plan, available at either a place of employment or a place of residence. It is mandatory for all companies employing five or more workers to contribute to a health insurance plan for their employees. Those not covered by their employers join the National Health Insurance (NHI) program administered by municipal governments and NHI associations.[12] Both the Employee's Health Insurance (EHI) and the NHI plans cover dependent family members in the same household. Premiums for the EHI plan are determined based on the employee's monthly income, which is adjusted periodically according to the medical expenditure. The employer is required to contribute 50% of the cost. While the premiums vary from union to union as well as location to location, in 2016, the monthly payment for the EHI plan was approximately 10% of the employee's monthly income for those who were under 40 years of age; those who were

40 years old and older paid slightly more per month due to added responsibility to cover long-term care insurance.

The average income over a three-month period (April–June) is calculated to determine the EHI payment, which is applied for the coming year starting September 1. This includes every form of income, such as overload pay and commuting expenses covered by the employer. For example, if a 39-year-old man employed in the Tokyo district with an average income for the three-month period ¥300,000 (approximately US $2,739, based on the May 31, 2016 exchange rate of ¥109.53 to the dollar), the EHI payment will be ¥29,910 ($273) per month (¥300,000 x 9.97%), half of which (¥14,955 = $136.5) is covered by the employer and the rest (¥14,955) by the employee himself. The EHI premium is adjusted annually. A 40-year-old in the same condition will also be required to pay long-term care insurance, which is 1.58%, therefore, his monthly payment will be ¥17,325 (¥300,000 × 11.55% [9.97% + 1.58%] / 2). Retired people who are no longer eligible for the EHI plans switch to the NHI plans or become dependents of other family members, such as their adult children who are covered with the EHI plans.

Monthly payment for the NHI plan also depends on the resident's income. Because the NHI is administered by local governments and each government utilizes its own system in calculating the cost, the figure varies widely depending on residence. The difference could be more than double between the two neighboring cities. It is likely to be around 5% to 10% of the resident's income. The maximum amount of premium per year per household for the NHI is ¥510,000 (US $4,656). Because the employer does not cover any of the premiums, Individuals insured by the NHI may pay more than those insured by the EHI. Individuals insured by both NHI and EHI are responsible for 30% of their medical expenses as the NHI covers 70%. Therefore, if a doctor's visit costs $100, the NHI covers $70 and the patient is responsible for $30. Individuals insured by the EHI also share 30% of the cost. Individuals aged 70 to 74 are responsible for 20% and those aged 75 and older are responsible for 10% of their medical expenses.[21]

The nation's medical expenditure has gradually increased over the past decade, as did the ratio of the nation's medical expenditure in relation to its national income (NI). In 2006, the medical expenditure per capita was ¥259,300 (US $2,367.4), accounting for 8.76% of NI, which went up to ¥314,700 ($2873.2), 11.08% of NI in 2013.[21] According to the latest OECD data available, Japan's health expenditure per capita is $3,713, ranking 14th out of 44 OECD nations. This is slightly higher than the OECD average of $3,453 and less than one-half of the highest ranked expenditure, that of the United States ($8,713).[22] Japan's health expenditure as a share of GDP is 10.2%, ranking 8th out of 44 OECD nations, which is considerably higher than the OECD average of 8.9%.[22]

Japan's annual average growth rate in per capita health expenditure since 2009 is 3.9%, which is much higher than the OECD average (0.6%) or that of the United States (1.5%), and it is the 3rd highest across 34 OECD nations.[22] Although health insurance premiums keep increasing, and each citizen's share of the medical cost has also increased, every citizen has access to decent medical care at a reasonable cost.

Quality

Detailed licensing regulations for hospitals, including the structure, the equipment, and the number of staff are provided by the Medical Service Law, which contributes to the quality of health care available to citizens. All the hospitals must meet these standards before they are given permission from the prefectural governor to operate. The prefectural government sends medical inspectors periodically to ensure that all the hospitals abide by the regulations.[17]

Because the number of medical schools is limited and only so many seats are available each year, it is very competitive to become a physician in Japan. There are only 80 medical schools throughout Japan, 43 of which are national schools and 8 of which are public school (e.g., prefectural schools). Those who wish to be admitted to medical school study very hard throughout their high school years. Many of the students who fail to be admitted to medical school spend one or more years just studying for the following year's entrance exam. Although it is not very costly to attend public medical school, it is much more costly to attend private medical school. After successfully completing 6 years of medical school education, all medical school students must pass the national medical examination administered by the Ministry of Health, Labour and Welfare before they are licensed to practice medicine.[17] While it had been customary for new physicians to be engaged in residency training for at least 2 years in the medical school hospitals or in those hospitals designated by the Ministry of Health, Labour and Welfare, this 2-year residency training was mandated in 2004.[23] This law ought to increase confidence in the ability to practice in novice physicians, which, in turn, contributes to the quality of medical care made available.

Assessment of health care quality is by no means simple and easy, as many elements are intertwined.

One way of assessing healthcare quality is to examine current health status, including life expectancy and other outcomes, such as the mortality rate and the survival rate following cardiac arrest. Life expectancy at birth for Japanese in 2013 was 83.4 years, ranked at the top of 44 OECD nations. This is a remarkable accomplishment considering that the life expectancy in 1960 was 67.8 years, ranked 1 of the bottom 5. When focusing on the gender difference, women live longer than men in every OECD country; while the life expectancy at birth of Japanese women is 86.6 years, the top in the OECD nations; that of men is 80.2 years, ranking fifth. This gender difference is due partially to the greater tendency among men to engage in risky behaviors such as tobacco and alcohol use.[22]

Life expectancy at age 65 is 21.5 years for Japanese (24 years for women and 19 years for men), ranked at the top among the OECD nations. This gain of nearly 8 years since 1970 is the highest among OECD countries. Life expectancy at age 65 also highly correlates with that at age 80. Based on the data in 2013, for women in Japan, along with those in France, life expectancy at age 80 was the highest; they can expect to live an additional 11.5 years.[22]

Cardiovascular diseases remain the leading cause of mortality among OECD countries, accounting for a third (32.3%) of deaths in 2013. While cardiovascular diseases include a wide range of circulatory-related illnesses, ischemic heart disease (IHD), commonly known as heart attack, accounts for 20% and stroke accounts for 7% of mortality in 2013.[22] Japan's mortality from IHD is the lowest in the OECD countries. See **FIGURE 24-2**. Mortality from cancer remains high, accounting for 25% of all deaths in 2013; cancer is the second leading cause of deaths in OECD countries following cardiovascular diseases. Japan's age-standardized rate per 100,000

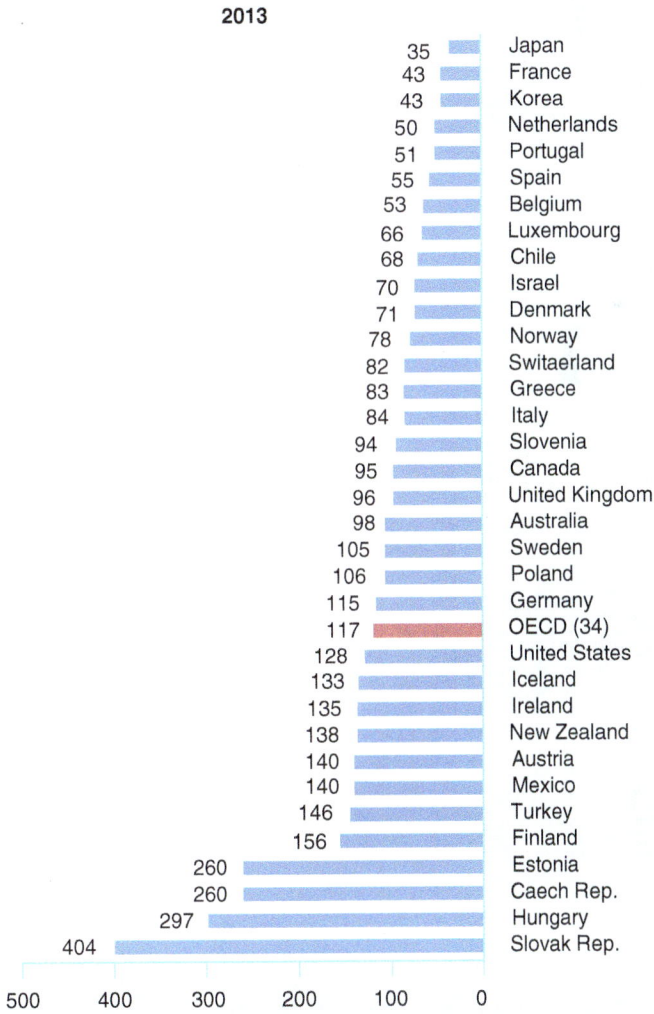

FIGURE 24-2 Ischemic Heart Disease Mortality, 2013

Reproduced from OECD. Mortality from cardiovascular diseases. In *Health at a Glance 2015: OECD Indicators*. Paris: OECD Publishing; 2015:50–51.

population for cancer mortality in 2013 was 179.0, ranked the 5th lowest of 34 OECD countries.[22] See **FIGURE 24-3**.

In addition to mortality, the 30-day acute myocardial infarction (AMI) case-fatality rate—deaths occurring in the same hospital within 30 days of admission for AMI—is also a good indicator of care quality, which includes effective medical interventions as well as timely transport of patients. Among OECD countries, Australia has the lowest rate at 4.1%. On the other hand, Mexico's AMI case-fatality rate is the highest at 28.2%, indicating that AMI patients do not have access to timely recommended care. Japan's AMI case-fatality rate is 12.2%, more than 3 times greater than that of Australia, and ranks 29th among 32 OECD countries While Japanese are less likely to die from heart disease, when compared to other OECD countries, they are more likely to die once hospitalized for AMI. See **TABLE 24-3**. One possible reason for this can be attributed to the patients' severe AMI conditions at the time of hospital admission. Japan's case-fatality rate within 30 days of admission for ischemic stroke, however, is 3.0%, the lowest among 31 OECD countries.[22] See **TABLE 24-4**.

Vaccination rates are a reliable indicator for assessing quality of care for communicable diseases. Although influenza is a common infectious disease that affects individuals of all ages, the elderly and those with chronic medical conditions are at higher risk for complications, including death. Effective vaccination, therefore, is a recommended way to prevent illness, hospitalization, and mortality among this at-risk population. Based on the latest OECD available data (2013 or nearest, depending on the nation), Japan's influenza vaccination rate in people aged 65 years and over is not very high. While more than 75% of the elderly received influenza vaccination in Mexico, Korea, Chile, and the United Kingdom, only 50% of Japanese elderly people were vaccinated. This is not much different from that of 48% in 2005, an indication that more efforts are needed to promote vaccination.[22]

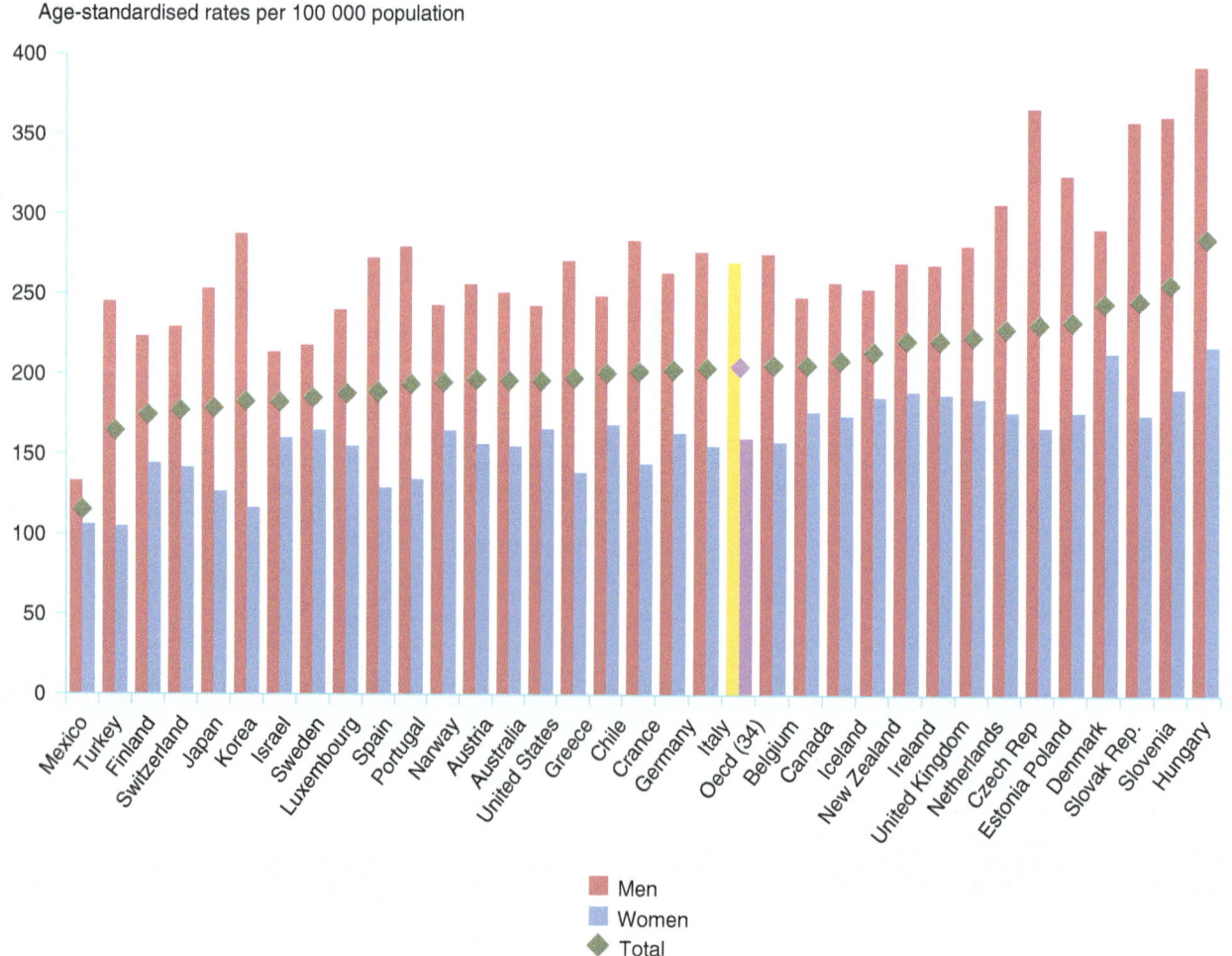

FIGURE 24-3 Age-Standardized Cancer Mortality Rate

Reproduced from OECD. Mortality from cancer. In *Health at a Glance 2015: OECD Indicators*. Paris: OECD Publishing; 2015:52–53.

TABLE 24-3 In-Hospital Case Fatality Rates Within 30 Days of Admission for AMI, 2013

Country	Age-gender standardized rate	95% CI	Country	Age-gender standardized rate	95% CI
Australia	4.1	0.1	Slovak Republic	7.2	0.6
Sweden	4.5	0.2	Belgium	7.3	0.3
Poland	4.7	0.3	Netherlands	7.6	0.5
Slovenia	5.2	0.9	United Kingdom	7.6	0.2
Italy	5.5	0.2	Switzerland	7.7	0.4
United States	5.5	0.1	Spain	7.8	0.2
Denmark	5.7	0.4	Korea	8.3	0.4
Ireland	6.4	0.6	Germany	8.7	0.1
Finland	6.5	0.4	Portugal	9.4	0.6
New Zealand	6.6	0.6	Austria	10.0	0.5
Canada	6.7	0.2	Estonia	11.5	1.3
Czech Rep.	6.7	0.4	Japan	12.2	0.9
Israel	6.7	0.5	Hungary	—	—
Norway	6.7	0.4	Chile	14.0	0.9
Iceland	6.9	2.6	Latvia	15.4	1.2
Luxembourg	7.0	1.4	Mexico	28.2	0.7
France	7.2	0.2	**OECD**	**8.0**	—

Data from OECD Health Statistics 2015

Children are also vulnerable to communicable diseases. Appropriate vaccination is one of the most cost-effective health policy interventions. Effective vaccination successfully eradicated polio and diphtheria across OECD countries. Vaccination against measles and diphtheria, tetanus and pertussis (DTP) has also been promoted; as a result, vaccination rates for these diseases reached beyond 90% in most OECD countries, reaching the OECD average of 95% for DTP and 94% for measles. Based on 2013 data, Japan's vaccination rate for DTP was 98%, ranking 10th among 34 OECD countries, and for measles ranking 18th at 95%. Vaccination against hepatitis B has also been promoted in many OECD countries resulting in the vaccination rate reaching higher than 90% in 26 OECD countries. However, numerous OECD countries do not include hepatitis B in their infant vaccination programs; Japan is one of six such countries.[22]

The majority of patients in Japan, both inpatients and outpatients, were satisfied with the overall hospital care they received in 2010; 58.0% of the outpatients were satisfied with nursing care and 57.4% were satisfied with communication with doctors. Among inpatients, 71.0% were satisfied with nursing care and 69.9% were satisfied with medical treatment. For both inpatients and outpatients, high quality of nursing care is playing an important role in patients' positive

TABLE 24-4 In-Hospital Case Fatality Rates Within 30 Days of Admission for Ischemic Stroke, 2013

Country	Age-gender standardized rate	95% CI	Country	Age-gender standardized rate	95% CI
Japan	3.0	0.2	Luxembourg	9.1	1.4
Korea	3.2	0.2	United Kingdom	9.2	0.2
United States	3.6	0.0	Australia	9.3	0.3
Finland	5.1	0.3	Belgium	9.3	0.4
Norway	5.4	0.4	Czech Republic	9.6	0.3
Israel	6.0	0.5	Hungary	—	—
Italy	6.2	0.1	Ireland	9.7	0.8
Austria	6.4	0.3	Spain	9.7	0.2
Germany	6.4	0.1	Canada	10.0	0.3
Sweden	6.4	0.3	Portugal	10.2	0.4
Switzerland	6.9	0.4	Slovak Republic	10.8	0.4
Netherlands	7.1	0.4	Estonia	13.0	1.2
France	7.9	0.2	Slovenia	13.2	1.2
Iceland	8.0	3.0	Latvia	18.4	1.0
New Zealand	8.0	0.7	Mexico	19.5	0.9
Chile	8.9	0.9	**OECD**	**8.4**	—
Denmark	9.1	0.6			

Data from OECD. Mortality following stroke. In *Health at a Glance 2015: OECD Indicators*. Paris: OECD Publishing; 2015:140–141.

experiences. Two major dissatisfactions outpatients express are long waiting time and medical expenditure. Dissatisfactions expressed by inpatients are content of meals and quality of facilities such as hospital rooms and bathrooms.[24]

Patient-reported experience measures are also used in many OECD countries in assessing quality of medical care. As for doctors providing easy-to-understand explanations and giving opportunity to ask questions or raise concerns, the majority of patients report positive experiences across countries. For both aspects of experiences, almost 98% of the patients in Belgium report positive experiences, ranking at the top of 19 OECD countries. A great majority of patients in Japan (96.3%) also reports that doctors provide easy-to-understand explanations, ranking 4th in 19 OECD countries in 2015. However, concerning doctors giving patients opportunity to ask questions or raise concerns, only 69.8% reported positive experiences, ranking 18th across 19 OECD countries. While doctors in Japan provide patient-friendly explanations, they do not provide patients with sufficient opportunity to ask questions, a clear indication that doctors are authoritative figures who provide one-way communication. More education may be needed to urge doctors to engage in two-way communication with patients.[22]

Access

One factor that influences patients' access to high-quality medical care is the supply of well-trained and geographically well-distributed health professionals such as physicians and nurses. This can be assessed by examining physician density (the number of practicing doctors per capita). In 2013, there were 2.3 physicians per 1,000 inhabitants in Japan, which was way below the OECD average of 3.3 per 1,000 and ranked 32nd out of 43 OECD nations.[22] It is common in many countries to have a greater density of physicians in urban areas than in rural regions, which reflects the concentration of specialized services, including surgery. This gap in distribution of physicians between urban and rural areas is much smaller in Japan than in many other OECD countries.[22] However, access to medical care in Japan varies depending on residence due to an apparent disparity in physician density across prefectures. For instance, in 2010, there were 279.2 physicians per 100,000 population in Kyoto prefecture and 277.4 per 100,000 in Tokyo, while there were only 139.9 per 100,000 in Saitama, one of Tokyo's neighboring prefectures.[24] Disparity in dentist density was also apparent across prefectures. There were 75.7 dentists per 100,000 in Japan but 117.9 dentists per 100,000 in Tokyo, however, this number dropped to 49.5, less than a half, in Fukui.[24] Nurse shortages have become an issue for some countries, and it is expected to continue to be an issue especially in aging countries such as Japan. In 2010, the number of practicing nurses per 1,000 population in Japan was 10.5, ranking 13th out of 43 OECD countries; this was slightly higher than the OECD average of 9.1. Disparity in nurses were equally apparent across prefectures; while there were 1,854.8 nurses and assistant nurses in Kochi prefecture, there were only 765.5 in Saitama prefecture.[24]

In addition to the overall number of doctors, the age and gender composition of the doctors influences the supply of medical services. The higher age of Japan's doctors raises concerns that there may be shortage of doctors in the near future due to lack of new recruits to replace those who retire. The increase of female doctors may affect the availability of doctors as they are likely to work shorter hours than men. In Japan in 2015, 33% of doctors were 55 years and older, ranking 15th in the 29 OECD countries. In regard to gender, only 20% of doctors were females; this was the smallest share of female doctors across 33 OECD countries. This may be an access issue for patients who prefer female doctors.[22]

Another important element in assessing quality of care, especially in aging countries like Japan, is access to long-term care beds in hospitals and nursing homes, beds that are mostly used to care for the elderly with chronic illness or disability. Japan's number of long-term care beds ranked 27th out of 31 OECD nations in 2015. There were 35.1 long-term care beds per 1,000 people aged 65 years and over in Japan, which was far fewer than the OECD average of 49.7, less than one-half of the rate in Belgium, and only one-third of the rate in Switzerland. It is preferred by most OECD countries to have more long-term care beds in nursing homes where services are more care oriented than treatment oriented and also more cost saving than hospitals; however, only two-thirds of the long-term care beds in Japan belonged to nursing institutions in 2015. This was far fewer than most OECD countries.[22]

Access to emergency medical care in Japan varies across disciplines. Although 53.2% of facilities specializing in internal medicine accepted emergency patients during night hours in 2010, only 17.4% of those specializing in pediatrics were available for nighttime emergencies, while 15.4% of obstetricians were, and 11.0% of psychiatric care services were.[24]

Because medical cost is an issue for most individuals, one of the factors that influence access to healthcare services is health insurance coverage. Lack of coverage frequently discourages many people from having access to appropriate medical care in a prompt manner. Lack of coverage also restricts those in need from having access to innovative treatments, as well as preventive services such as screening and vaccination. Along with the majority of the OECD nations, 100% of Japanese have public health insurance coverage for a core set of services. One advantage of the Japanese health insurance system is that practically every clinic and hospital accepts any type of health insurance. All one has to do is to present an insurance card at the window at the time of the first visit.

The majority of hospitals are privately owned, and most clinics and small hospitals are physician-owned. Practically all medical facilities provide primary care services, and individuals can select any facility of their choice. Although there are people who have their own home doctor, there are many others who do not. Depending on their health conditions, many individuals select one of the clinics nearby for primary care. If the patient's health condition is diagnosed to be more serious than the clinic can manage, the physician refers the patient to a larger hospital where appropriate treatment can be provided. In large hospitals, treatment is more costly, and outpatient visits are frequently limited to the morning hours. Except for those who live in extremely isolated areas, access to medical care is not a big issue in Japan. Access to high-quality care, however, may depend on each individual's attention to their local doctor's reputation for high quality.[14]

Current and Emerging Issues and Challenges

Care for the Elderly Population

Japan is one of the world's most rapidly aging societies, with 23% of the population aged 65 years and over in 2015, the highest across all OECD countries (the OECD average was 15% and the United States average was 13%). It is projected that in Japan this proportion will increase to 39% in 2050 while that of the United States will be 21%. Shares of adults aged 80 years and over in Japan was 6% in 2015, also ranked the highest across all OECD countries. This is projected to increase to 16% in 2050.[22] It is not only the increased proportion of the elderly population in Japan that requires attention but the rapid speed with which this demographic change is occurring. Projected share of adults aged 65 years and over and also for aged 80 years and over in Japan is the greatest across OECD countries. This trend of increased share of elderly adults is expected to rapidly accelerate in the coming decades (**FIGURE 24-4**).[22]

Furthermore, while Japan's longevity ranks the highest, its fertility rate is one of the lowest in OECD countries (28th out of 34).[25] These trends clearly indicates the importance of healthcare services for the elderly population in Japan. The number of elderly people in need of medical care has increased over the past few decades. In 2010, of the 6,843,000 outpatients per day, 1,484,500 (21.7%) were 65 to 74 years old and 1,592,300 (23.3%) were 75 or older, indicating that nearly one-half of all outpatients were 65 or older. Of all the inpatients per day in Japan, 20.0% were aged 65 years and over and 46.9% were aged 75 years and over; more than two-thirds (66.9%) of all inpatients were elderly.[24]

National medical care expenditure has kept increasing, and its share of the national income now is more than 10%. National medical care expenditure per capita constantly increases with age, and the higher the age, the more apparent the increase. Furthermore, much of the increase in expenditure from one age group to the next for the elderly is due clearly to an increase in inpatient expenses.[24]

Because of continuously increasing medical costs, the premiums for each insured individual, as well as the patient's share of his/her medical cost, have increased. In order to cope with the extra medical expenditure related to nursing home care for the elderly, everyone aged 40 to 64 years pays an additional premium. This system intends to lighten the financial burden of those who are in need of long-term care; however, for this system to efficiently support those in need, there are many remaining issues to be dealt with, such as accessibility and sufficient number of providers.

Traditionally Japanese families formed extended families consisting of three generations. The family's eldest son would keep living with his parents after marriage, and his wife was expected to take care of her

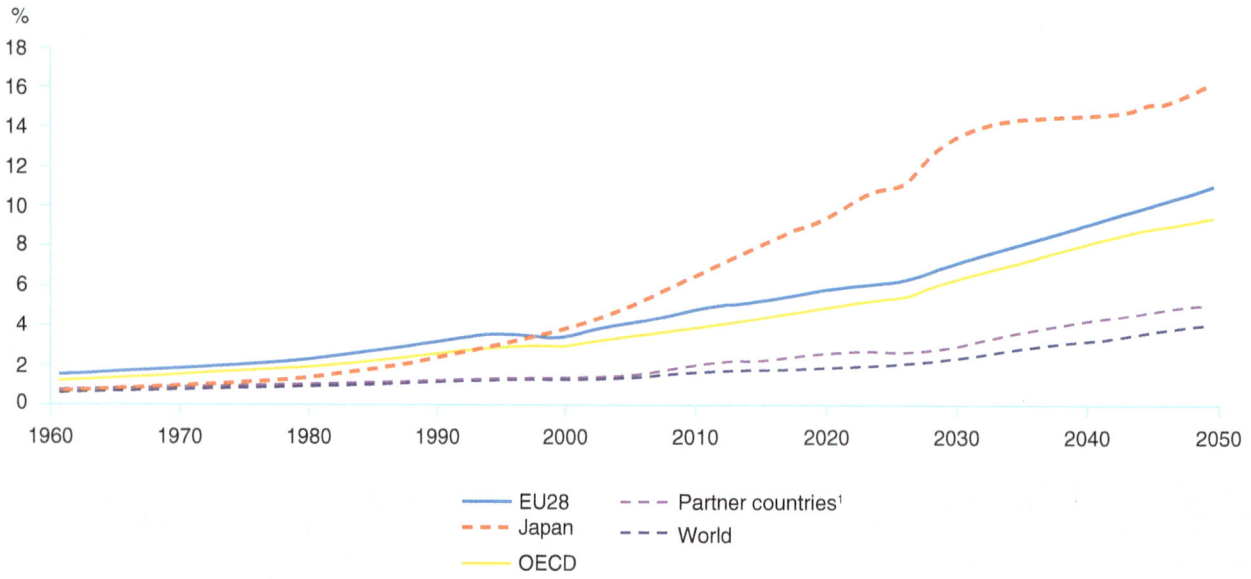

1. Partner countries include Brazil, China, India, Indonesia, Latvia, Lithuania, Russia and South Africa.

FIGURE 24-4 Trends in the share of the population aged over 80 years, 1960–2050

Reproduced from OECD. Demographic trends. In *Health at a Glance 2015: OECD Indicators*. Paris: OECD Publishing; 2015:192–193.

husband's aging parents; therefore, each family was expected to be self-sufficient in caring for the elderly in the family. However, this type of family structure is no longer common even in conservative rural areas. Frequently, adult children of elderly adults are not able to live close enough to their parents to make regular visits, or to be available for their aging parents when the help is needed. Many Japanese women are hesitant to marry a man if there is a possibility that they will have to live with their husband's parents in the future.

In order to cope with the healthcare needs of an ever-increasing elderly population in Japan, an innovative healthcare system must be quickly developed to ensure an adequate number of facilities and workforce, effective methods of delivering nursing care, and sufficient funds for the system to be smoothly sustained.

Antismoking Campaigns

In the arena of public health, smoking continues to be an issue in Japan. Smoking is known to be the single largest preventable cause of disease and premature death. It has been documented that smoking can lead to heart disease, stroke, lung disease, and cancer of many types. Tobacco causes almost 6 million deaths each year; sadly, more than 600,000 of such victims are nonsmokers exposed to second-hand smoke. Further, smoking during pregnancy leads to low birth weight and illness among infants. Smoking still is the largest avoidable health risk factor worldwide.[22]

Although the number of smokers in Japan decreased more than 30% in the past two decades, it remains high among developed countries. In 2013, 19.5% of Japanese adults were daily smokers; this is only slightly better than the OECD average of 21.1%. Only 8.4% of Japanese women are daily smokers, ranking the 7th lowest among 41 OECD countries. However, 32.2% of Japanese men remain daily smokers, ranking the 9th highest across 41 OECD countries.[26]

According to the World Health Organization, Japan's antitobacco laws are weaker than other developed nations (i.e., providing fewer smoke-free public environments). Japanese people tend to be tolerant of smoking. Anti-smoking campaigns have been implemented and the number of daily smokers has decreased. However, it is still customary to allow smoking during work hours in many offices and many hospitals have not yet implemented no-smoking policies for their entire facilities, a clear indication that Japanese people are quite tolerant of smoking.

Diabetes Prevention

Along with many other nations, diabetes has become one of the most important public health concerns in Japan. It is estimated that over 380 million people were affected worldwide in 2014, and the number is projected to increase to almost 600 million in 2035.[22] Diabetes can lead to blindness as well as renal failure. While it is difficult to accurately estimate the number of diabetics, it is estimated that 7.9% (approximately 10.7 million) of adults aged 20 to 79 years in Japan are diabetic.[27]

More men than women in Japan tend to be diabetic. Also, the higher the age, the higher the risk of becoming diabetic. For both men and women, the incidence rate greatly increases for those aged 50 years and over; in 2014, for men 14.3% of those aged 50 to 59 years, 23.0% of those aged 60 to 69 years, and 24.2% of those aged 70 years and over were diabetic; for women, 9.4% of those aged 50 to 59 years, 15.0% of those aged 60 to 69 years, and 18.0% of those aged 70 and over were diabetic.[28] In order to improve health quality, as well as to lighten the financial burden of the nation, effective preventive approaches, including promotion of physical activity and proper diet, must be promptly implemented.

Breast Cancer Screening: Promoting Mammography

Considering the high prevalence of breast cancer (the most common cancer among women in all OECD countries, affecting one in nine women at some point in life), a serious approach toward prevention should be adopted throughout the world. Japanese women, along with other women in Far Eastern countries, are at a lower risk of developing breast cancer than their Western counterparts. Japan's breast cancer age-standardized mortality rate was 14.2 per 100,000 women in 2015 and was the third lowest among all the OECD countries.[22] Although breast cancer is the most common cancer amongst women in Japan, breast cancer mortality is relatively small, ranking fifth among all cancer deaths.[29]

Regardless of type of cancer, early detection is the key to higher survival rates, and the effectiveness of breast cancer screening has been documented repeatedly. Along with other nations, mammography screening has become popular in Japan; mammography screening rate in women aged 50 to 69 years has almost doubled in the past decade and reached 41.0% in 2013. However, it is lower than the OECD average; Considering 5 OECD countries exceed 80% (Finland, Slovenia, Denmark, the United States, and the Netherlands), much more effort is needed in promoting mammography screening.[22] Public campaigns that encourage women aged 50 years and older to receive annual mammography screenings are bound to increase the rate of early breast cancer detection, which, in turn, should contribute to a higher survival rate.

Suicide Prevention

Suicide is a significant cause of death worldwide, accounting for more than 150,000 deaths across OECD countries. High suicide rates are a very serious issue in Japan as well. Numerous factors are associated with attempting and committing suicide, including low income, alcohol and drug abuse, unemployment, social isolation, and psychiatric disorders, such as severe depression, bipolar disorder, and schizophrenia.[22] Since 1990, the OECD average of the age-standardized suicide rate has constantly declined from 16.2 per 100,000 in 1990 to 11.2 per 100,000 in 2013; however, Japan's has been constantly high, only declining slightly in the past few years, 18.7 per 100,000 in 2013. This was the third highest in all OECD countries, following 29.1 per 100,000 in Korea and 19.4 per 100,000 in Hungary. Gender difference is apparent in all OECD countries; men's rate is significantly higher than that of women; the OECD average for men was 19.3 per 100,000 in 2013 while for women it was 5.5 per 100,000. In Japan the men's rate was 27.2 per 100,000 and the women's rate was 10.6 per 100,000.[22] According to the statistics by the Ministry of Health, Labour and Welfare, suicide is the leading cause of death for individuals aged 15 to 39 years and the second leading cause for those aged 10 to 14 years and 40 to 49 years. Some gender differences are observed; among men suicide is the leading cause of death for those aged 10 to 44 years, the second for those aged 45 to 49 years, the third for those aged 50 to 54 years, fourth for 55 to 59 years, and fifth for 60 to 64 years. See **FIGURE 24-5**. Among women, suicide is the leading cause of death for those aged 15 to 34 years, the second for those aged 35 to 49 years, the third for those aged 50 to 54 years, and the fourth for those aged 55 to 64 years. See **FIGURE 24-6**. It is a disturbing fact that suicide remains a leading cause of death for teenagers (of both genders). Stigmas related to mental illness must also be dealt with more effectively, and mental healthcare services must be made

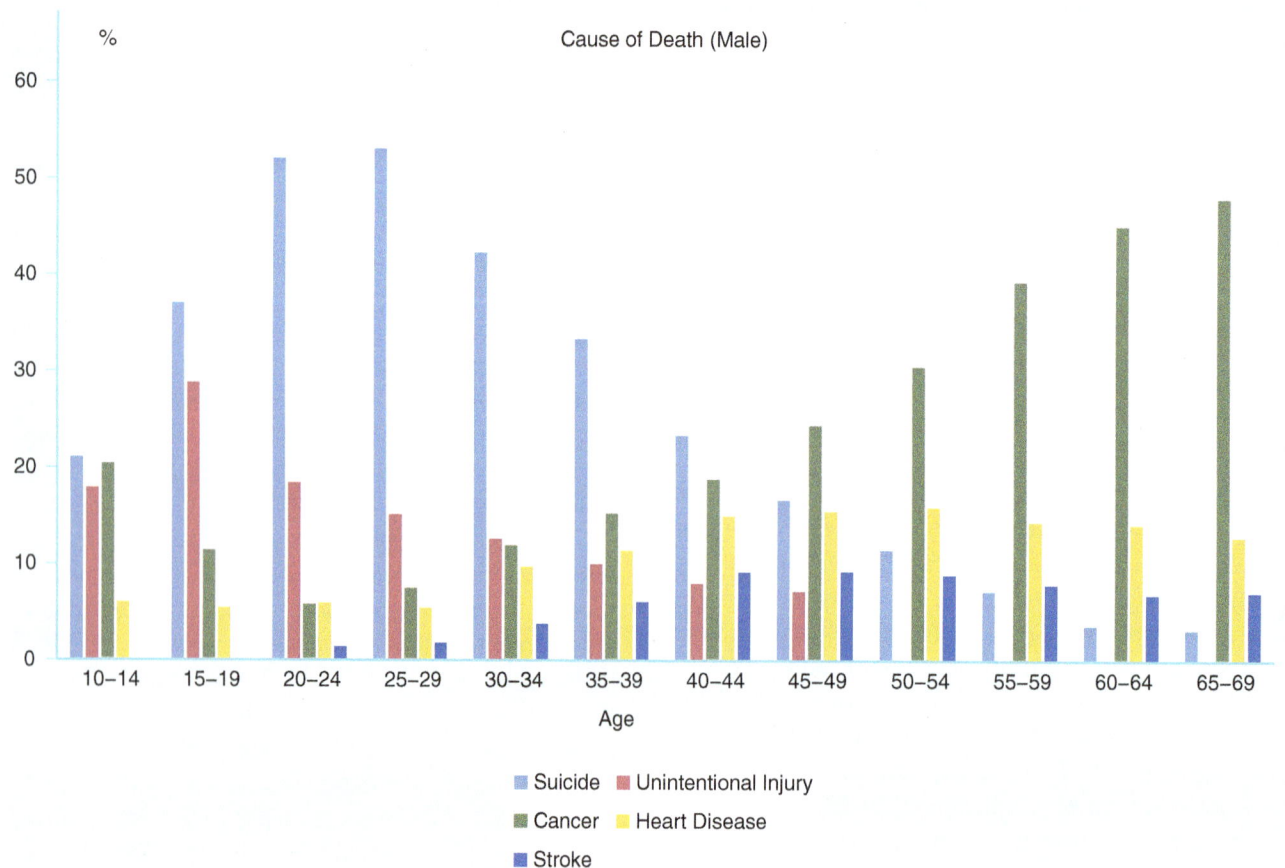

FIGURE 24-5 Cause of Death, Japan, 2014 (Male).
Data from Japanese Ministry of Health, Labor and Welfare.

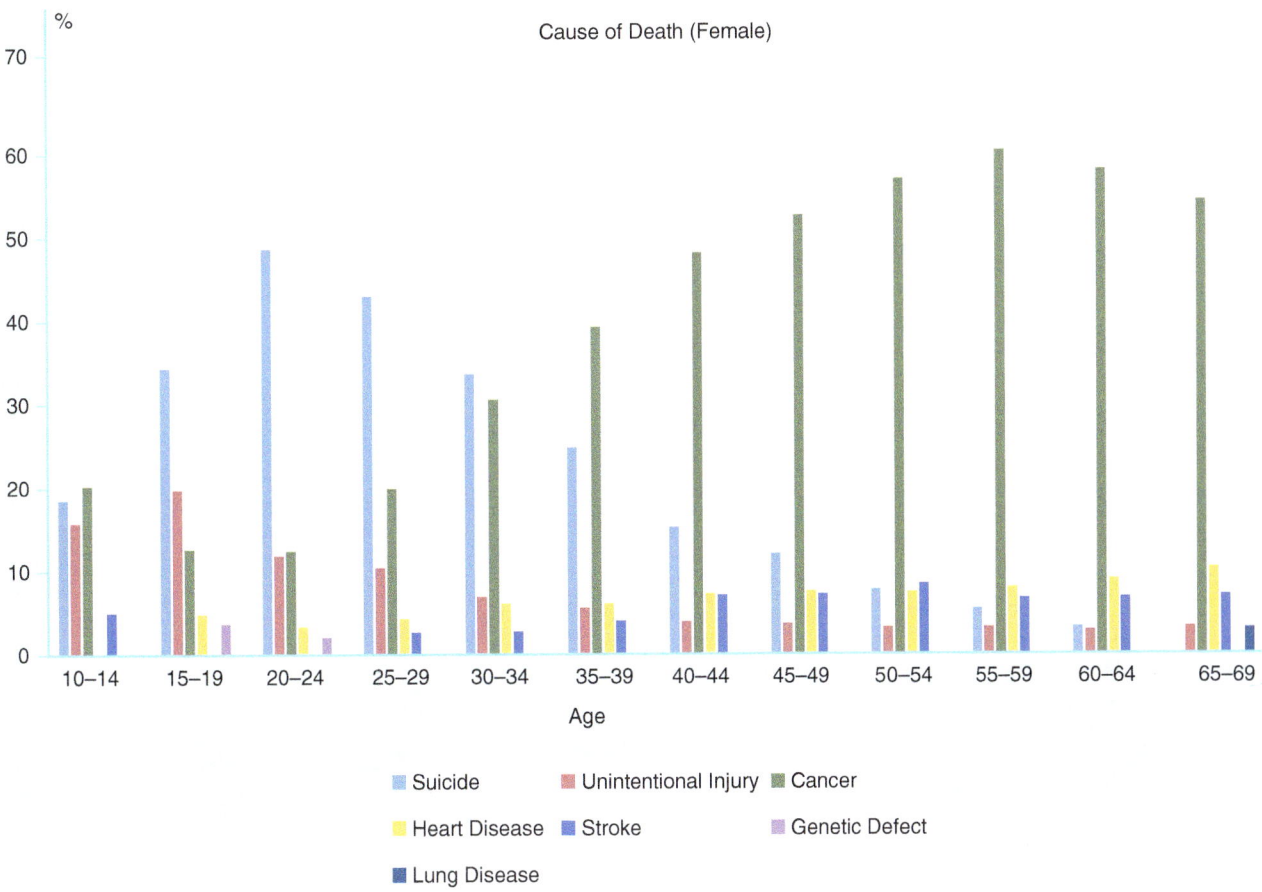

FIGURE 24-6 Cause of Death, Japan, 2014 (Female).
Data from Japanese Ministry of Health, Labor and Welfare.

more accessible. More attention has been paid to mental health in recent years, and campaigns are carried out that focus on mental health;[30] however, considering that suicide is the number one cause of death for people of varying ages, both men and women, continuous and consistent efforts are needed to enhance the mental health of the nation.

Dementia Care

It is estimated that more than 47 million people live with dementia worldwide; with population aging and lack of effective preventive measures, this number is expected to keep rising, and so is the cost associated with dementia. Because dementia is strongly associated with the elderly, countries with a greater share of older adults, including Japan, are likely to be greatly affected by dementia. In 2015, it was estimated that 21.0 Japanese population per 1,000 were affected by dementia, ranking second out of all OECD nations, following 21.8 per 1,000 in Italy. However, this number in Japan is projected to rise to 36.6 per 1,000 in 2035, ranking first and surpassing that of Italy; these figures indicate that dementia care and treatment are one of the most serious and pressing health and medical issues in Japan.[22]

Of the 30,790,000 Japanese population aged 65 years and over, approximately 4,620,000 (15%) are estimated to suffer from dementia; an additional 4 million adults aged 65 years and over are estimated to be dementia suspects who are already affected by or at risk for developing dementia. To cope with the increasing prevalence of dementia, the Japanese Ministry of Health, Labour and Welfare launched a five-year comprehensive dementia support plan in 2012, which includes promoting dementia screening for early detection, providing support for family members and caregivers, enhancing medical services, and increasing long-term care providers. With accelerated population aging, all these measures against dementia are bound to be critically important in improving quality of late life of the elderly in Japan.[31]

References

1. Ellington L. *Japan: A Global Studies Handbook*. Santa Barbara, CA: ABC-CLIO; 2002.
2. Frederic L. *Japan: Encyclopedia*. Cambridge, MA: Harvard University Press; 2002.
3. Richie D. *Introducing Japan*. New York: Kodansha International; 1996.
4. Woolley PJ. *Geography and Japan's Strategic Choices: From Seclusion to Internationalization*. Washington, DC: Potomac Books; 2005.
5. Government of Japan. GDP: international comparison. Economic and Social Research Institute Cabinet Office website. In Japanese. http://www.esri.cao.go.jp/jp/sna/menu.html. Accessed April 26, 2016.
6. Statistics Bureau. *Statistics: Result of the Population Estimates*. Japanese Ministry of Internal Affairs and Communications website. http://www.stat.go.jp/english/data/jinsui/2.htm. Accessed April 26, 2016.
7. Organisation for Economic Co-operation and Development. OECD Economic Surveys: Japan. April 2015 overview. Executive summary. http://www.oecd.org/eco/surveys/Japan-2015-overview.pdf. Accessed April 26, 2016.
8. Japan's working poor: struggling. *The Economist*. http://www.economist.com/news/asia/21647676-poverty-worsens-more-japanese-work-non-permanent-contracts-struggling. Published April 4, 2015. Accessed April 27, 2016.
9. Aoki M. Poverty a growing problem for women. *Japan Times*. April 19, 2012. http://www.japantimes.co.jp/news/2012/04/19/national/poverty-a-growing-problem-for-women/#.VyBHy0orJdg Accessed April 27, 2016.
10. Frederic L. *Japan: Encyclopedia*. Cambridge, MA: Harvard University Press; 2002.
11. Richie D. *Introducing Japan*. New York: Kodansha International, Limited; 1996.
12. Graig LA. *Health of Nations: An International Perspective on U.S. Health Care Reform*. 3rd ed. Washington, DC: Congressional Quarterly; 1999.
13. Iglehart JK. Japan's medical care system. *New England Journal of Medicine*. 1988; 319:807–812.
14. Hashimoto M. Health services in Japan. In: Raffel MW, ed. *Comparative Health Systems*. University Park, PA: The Pennsylvania State University Press; 1984.
15. Steslicke WE. Development of health insurance policy in Japan. *Journal of Health Politics, Policy and Law*. 1982;7:197–226.
16. Jones SG, Hilborne LH, Anthony RC, et al. Securing Health: Lessons from Nation-Building Missions. Santa Monica, CA: RAND Corp; 2006.
17. Nakahara T. The health system of Japan. In: Raffel MW, ed. *Health Care and Reform in Industrialized Countries*. University Park, PA: Pennsylvania State University Press. 1997;105–133.
18. Statistics. Summary of health care facilities 2014. Japanese Ministry of Health, Labour and Welfare website. In *Japanese*. http://www.mhlw.go.jp/toukei/saikin/hw/iryosd/14/. Accessed April 29, 2016.
19. Statistics. Chapter 2 Healthcare Report 2015. Japanese Ministry of Health, Labour and Welfare website. In *Japanese*. http://www.mhlw.go.jp/toukei/youran/indexyk_2_2.html. Accessed April 30, 2016.
20. Organisation for Economic Co-operation and Development. OECD health statistics 2015. http://stats.oecd.org/index.aspx?queryid=30184. Accessed April 30, 2016.
21. Japanese Ministry of Health, Labour and Welfare. Health insurance. http://www.mhlw.go.jp/bunya/iryouhoken/index.html and http://www.mhlw.go.jp/english/wp/wp-hw6/dl/02e.pdf. Accessed June 10, 2016.
22. Organisation for Economic Co-operation and Development. Health at a glance 2015: OECD Indicators. http://www.oecd.org/health/health-systems/health-at-a-glance-19991312.htm and http://www.oecd-ilibrary.org/social-issues-migration-health/health-at-a-glance-2015_health_glance-2015-en. Accessed June 12, 2016.
23. Japanese Ministry of Health, Labour and Welfare. Medical care. In Japanese. http://www.mhlw.go.jp/english/index.html. Accessed June 11, 2016.
24. Japanese Ministry of Health, Labour and Welfare. Health statistics in Japan 2010. http://www.mhlw.go.jp/english/database/db-hss/index.html. Accessed June 18, 2016.
25. Organisation for Economic Co-operation and Development. Society at a glance 2014. OECD iLibrary. http://www.oecd-ilibrary.org/social-issues-migration-health/society-at-a-glance_19991290. Accessed June 18, 2016.
26. Organisation for Economic Co-operation and Development. Smoking. OECD iLibrary. http://www.oecd-ilibrary.org/sites/factbook-2013-en/12/02/01/index.html?itemId=/content/chapter/factbook-2013-98-en. Accessed June 18, 2016.
27. Organisation for Economic Co-operation and Development. Diabetes—health at a glance. Asia/Pacific 2012. OECD iLibrary. http://www.oecd-ilibrary.org/social-issues-migration-health/health-at-a-glance-asia-pacific-2012/diabetes_9789264183902-15-en. Accessed June 18, 2016.
28. Japanese Government. Health and Nutrition Survey. e-Stat website. In Japanese. http://www.e-stat.go.jp/SG1/estat/eStatTopPortal.do. Accessed June 18, 2016.
29. Japan Cancer Society. About cancer and checkup. http://www.jcancer.jp/. Accessed June 20, 2016.
30. Ministry of Health, Labour and Welfare. Summary of population changes statistics 2014. In Japanese. http://www.mhlw.go.jp/toukei/saikin/hw/jinkou/kakutei14/index.html. Accessed June 20, 2016.
31. Dementia Measures. Japanese Ministry of Health, Labour and Welfare. In Japanese. http://www.mhlw.go.jp/stf/seisakunitsuite/bunya/0000076236.html. Accessed June 20, 2016.

CHAPTER 25

Korea

Hailun Liang, Whiejong M. Han, and Leiyu Shi

▶ Country Description

TABLE 25-1 Korea

Nationality	Noun: Korean(s) Adjective: Korean
Ethnic groups	Homogeneous (except for about 20,000 Chinese)
Religions	Christian 31.6% (Protestant 24.0%, Roman Catholic 7.6%), Buddhist 24.2%, other or unknown 0.9%, none 43.3% (2010 survey)
Language	Korean, English widely taught in junior high and high school
Literacy	Definition: Age 15 and over can read and write. Total population: 97.9% Male: 99.2% Female: 96.6% (2002)
Government type	Republic
Date of independence	August 15, 1945 (from Japan)
Gross Domestic Product (GDP) per capita	$36,700 (2015 est.)
Unemployment rate	3.5% (2015 est.)
Natural hazards	Occasional typhoons with high winds and floods; low-level seismic activity common in the southwest

(continues)

TABLE 25-1 Korea (continued)

Environment: current issues	Air pollution in large cities, acid rain, water pollution from the discharge of sewage and industrial effluents, drift net fishing
Population	50,924,172 (July 2016 est.)
Age structure	0–14 years: 13.45% (male 3,535,137/female 3,315,510) 15–24 years: 13.08% (male 3,515,779/female 3,146,084) 25–54 years: 45.93% (male 12,008,399/female 11,379,261) 55–64 years: 14.01% (male 3,521,569/female 3,611,481) 65 years and over: 13.53% (male 2,918,156/female 3,972,796) (2016 est.)
Median age	Total: 41.2 years Male: 39.7 years Female: 42.8 years (2016 est.)
Population growth rate	0.53% (2016 est.)
Birth rate	8.4 births/1,000 population (2016 est.)
Death rate	5.8 deaths/1,000 population (2016 est.)
Disease burden	Communicable disease deaths: 34/100,000 population Noncommunicable disease deaths: 302/100,000 population Injury deaths: 53/100,000 population (2016 est.)
Net migration rate	Not available
Gender ratio	At birth: 1.07 male(s)/female Under 15 years: 1.07 male(s)/female 15–24 years: 1.12 male(s)/female 25–54 years: 1.06 male(s)/female 55–64 years: 0.98 male(s)/female 65 years and over: 0.71 male(s)/female Total population: 0.73 male(s)/female (2016 est.)
Infant mortality rate	Total: 3.86 deaths/1,000 live births Male: 4.05 deaths/1,000 live births Female: 3.66 deaths/1,000 live births (2015 est.)
Life expectancy at birth	Total population: 80.04 years Male: 76.95 years Female: 83.34 years (2015 est.)
Total fertility rate	1.25 children born/woman (2015 est.)
HIV/AIDS adult prevalence rate	Less than 0.1% (2003 est.)
Number of people living with HIV/AIDS	8,300 (2003 est.)
HIV/AIDS deaths	Less than 200 (2003 est.)

Data from Central Intelligence Agency. The World Fact Book, 2016: Korea. https://www.cia.gov/library/publications/the-world-factbook/geos/ks.html. Accessed April 15, 2016.

Introduction

Owing to continuous economic growth and social progress, the healthcare system in Korea has undergone many important developments and reforms, and has experienced rapid improvement in health outcomes over the past decades. Korea achieved universal health coverage through the National Health Insurance (NHI) system in 1989 in a record 12 years of rapid coverage expansion, which was quite unique in the history of countries' transitions to universal coverage. Korea started to adopt a single-payer approach in 2000, with government-run health insurance financing, claims processing, quality controlling, and fee-negotiation. Korea's single-payer system, while quite similar to other countries' single-payer systems in many respects, has not been able to control the rate of growth in health spending as well. Among Organisation for Economic Co-operation and Development (OECD) countries, Korea has been the country with the highest rate of health spending growth. In contrast to public health financing, healthcare delivery in Korea is characterized by the dominance of private providers, with approximately 90% of total medical institutions being private facilities. Moreover, the wide use of complementary and alternative medicine makes the Korean healthcare system unique. In recent years, the rapid increase of population is the major challenge facing the Korean healthcare system. The implementation of Korea's long-term care insurance scheme is aimed at improving access for elderly people to long-term care and reducing their socioeconomic burden. However, the coordination among long-term care facilities and hospitals remains a crucial issue in Korea. Moreover, the role of primary care in gatekeeping is relatively weak. Policy to increase efficiency across the continuum of care should be a priority for future reforms.

The main objective of this chapter is to provide a general overview of Korea as a nation and its healthcare delivery system. We will also describe the content, process, and implementation of healthcare policies and will highlight areas and challenges that require more in-depth reforms.

History

Korea is located in eastern Asia and has one of the oldest histories in the world. Throughout the establishment and collapse of many dynasties through 5,000 years of history, Korea developed its own distinctive culture. Under the last dynasty, Joseon, before modernization, Korea became known as the Land of Morning Calm because the name *Joseon* in Korean means morning calm. With Confucianism and Buddhism in its long history, Korea is also known as the country of courtesy in the East.

From 1910 to 1945, Korea was under Japanese rule. During this period, many different groups inside and outside Korea fought for independence. The Korean Provisional Government was established at that time to fight for independence. It declared war on Japan and provided close cooperation with Allied powers during World War II. In 1945 Japan surrendered to the Allies, ending war in the Pacific, and withdrew from the Korean Peninsula.

Soon after, Korea was divided into two parts along the 38th parallel, South and North Korea, because of ideological conflicts among various groups. A communist form of government came into power in North Korea (Democratic People's Republic of Korea), and the United States turned its authority over to South Korea (Republic of Korea). On Sunday morning, June 25, 1950, North Korea invaded South Korea (Korea hereafter) without declaration of war. It was the beginning of the Korean War, which lasted for about three years. With military support from the United Nations, the Korean War ended with an armistice on July 27, 1953.

The war destroyed the country and yielded many economic, political, and social problems. In the aftermath, the Korean government focused on rebuilding the country. Under the leadership of the third president, Jeong-Hee Park, Korea achieved dramatic economic growth. During the Park administration, the human and natural resources of the nation were effectively organized for the first time in modern history. The economy began to grow at an annual rate of 9.2%. Per capita gross domestic product (GDP) increased from a mere US $87 in 1962 to $1,503 in 1980, and exports rose by 32.8% per year from $56.7 million in 1962 to $17.5 billion in 1980.[1] Continuous efforts by the Korean government after the Park administration resulted in Korea becoming a modern and developed country. In 1996, Korea joined the OECD, marking its advancement into the ranks of developed nations. As of 2015, GDP of Korea was $1.39 trillion, and GDP per capita was $36,600.[5] In the presidential election of 2013, Ms. Geun-hye Park, the daughter of former president Chung-hee Park, was elected. She is the first woman to be elected as president in Korea. President Park began her term in office in February 2013.

Size and Geography

FIGURE 25-1 shows the map of the Korean Peninsula. The Korean Peninsula lies in East Asia, adjacent to China and Japan. The west coast of the Korean Peninsula borders the Korean Bay to the north and the Yellow Sea to the south. The east coast faces the East

FIGURE 25-1 Map of Korea
© Rainer Lesniewski/Shutterstock.

Sea, and the south coast faces the South Sea. Because of the long north-south stretch and topographic character, Korea has several distinct regions with significantly different climates, although Korea is a geographically small country. The total area of the Korean Peninsula, including South Korea (Korea) and North Korea, is approximately 223,600 square kilometers, and it includes 3,300 scattered islands. The land area of Korea, which occupies about 45% of the Korean Peninsula, is 99,720 square kilometers, with a population of 49.1 million, as of 2015. The area of Seoul, the capital city of Korea, is 605 square kilometers. The distance between South Korea's two major cities, Seoul and Busan, one in the very northwest and the other in the very southeast, is only 210 miles.[3]

Rapid industrialization and urbanization in the 1960s and 1970s has been accompanied by continuing migration of rural residents into the cities, particularly Seoul. The administrative divisions of Korea consist of nine providences and seven metropolitan cities. In 2015, more than 83% of the entire population lived in metropolitan areas.[1] In recent years, however, an increasing number of people have been moving to suburban areas.

Government and Political System

Korea has a democratic form of government based on the separation of powers. The Constitution was first adopted in 1948 when the Republic was established, and it has been revised nine times as the country has struggled to make democracy work effectively. The most recent revision of the Constitution provided, among other things, for the direct election of the president for a single five-year term and for the institution of a system of local autonomy for the first time in 30 years. These two provisions are keys to the strengthening of democratic institutions in the Republic. The revision also reinstated the right of the National Assembly to inspect all aspects of state affairs on a regular basis, as a check on the power of the executive branch. Finally, it charges the government to seek to reunify the nation.

The political system of Korea is based on a republic form of government, with the president as chief of the state and the prime minister as the head of government. The government consists of three branches: (1) the legislature, in the form of a unicameral National Assembly; (2) the judiciary, consisting of district and appellate courts and the Supreme Court; and (3) the executive, headed by the president. The president is also commander-in-chief of the armed forces, and the president is assisted by the prime minister and the State Council.

Macroeconomics

Korea has achieved exponential economic growth since the mid-20th century. Referred to as the "Miracle of the Han River," the economy of Korea grew dramatically, and it ranked 11th in the world in terms of GDP in 2015. Over decades, Korea enjoyed an average of 5.0% in GDP growth per year. For 2015, GDP of Korea was US $1.39 trillion, and GDP per capita was $36,600, which showed dramatic growth in less than 45 years.[2,5] The amount of exports reached $548.8 billion, and imports were about $428.50 billion. For exports, major partners in trading were China (26.0%), the United States (13.3%), and Hong Kong (5.8%), whereas imports were mainly from China (20.7%), Japan (10.5%), and the United States (10.1%).[5]

In the 1970s and 1980s, the Korean economy emphasized heavy industry and the automotive industry. Hyundai, Samsung, LG, and POSCO are Korean-based global companies that have a strong reputation in the world. In the 1980s, the Korean economy started to divert into the service industry. Since then, service industries have grown to 57% of GDP, whereas manufacturing has accounted for 37% of GDP.[5] In the 1990s, Korea entered into the information technology business, starting the information technology project with strong government support. Within a few years, Korea became a world leader in information technology.

In 1998, the Korean economy, like other Asian countries, faced financial crisis. All industries and citizens suffered from the crisis. With well-planned government strategies and financial support from the International Monetary Fund, Korea overcame the financial difficulty and bounced back in a few years. After the crisis, the government attempted financial reform to restore economic stability. The economic growth rate again reached 9% in 2000, and by 2006 the unemployment rate started to decline from 6.0% to 3.5%.[6] In the 2007–2008 global economic downturn, Korea's export-focused economy experienced decreases, but it rebounded rapidly with over 6% growth in 2010. Between 2012 and 2015, the economy experienced slow growth, 2%–3% per year, due to sluggish domestic consumption and investment.[5]

A well-developed infrastructure, including transportation, roads, and communication, facilitated expansion of industries. Rapid improvement in transportation and road systems increased mobility. More than 100 of the airports and ports support industries' business activities. Because of the topographical characteristics of Korea, most industries are in the northwest or southeast of the country. Services and manufacturing are located in the northwest, whereas heavy industry is located in the southeast.

Koreans believe that education is a critical key to success, and thus, much energy is put into learning. Learning a second language, particularly English and Chinese, is believed to be a stepping stone for future success in the trend of globalization. For this reason, English is taught as a required subject starting in elementary school. Many people, especially in the business sectors, are voluntarily learning Chinese as well. A large number of high school and college-level students go to advanced countries, particularly to the United States, to study for years. According to U.S. statistics, 87,384 Korean students were studying in the United States in December 2015. Korea ranked second in terms of the number of active students in the United States from abroad.[7]

Demographics

According to the data from the Economically Active Population Survey, administrated by Statistics Korea (KOSTAT) (formerly named as National Statistical Office of Korea), the population in Korea was estimated in July 2016 to be 50.9 million. Of those, 43.4 million (85.3%) were age 15 years and older. Almost 27.6 million were economically active. Among them 26.6 million were employed, and the labor participation rate in economic activities was 63.5% in July 2016. Because of a low birth rate and aging society, however, KOSTAT projects that economically active people will decrease from 2016 and the total population will start to decline in 2019.[4] By age group, the number of those less than 15 years old has steadily decreased since 1970, whereas the population that is aged 65 years and over is increasing. The population growth rate in Korea was 0.48 in 2010–2015.[8]

One problem in the population structure of Korea is population density in city areas. In 2015, 50.3% of the total population lived in the Seoul metropolitan area, including Incheon and Gyeonggi provinces. Seoul, by itself, had more than 10 million people (19.4%) living in it. The population density in Seoul was 16,700 people per square kilometer.[1] This unequal population distribution creates many problems, such as housing shortages, high prices of commodity, pollution, unequal education opportunity, and even the availability of medical services.

In 2010, each Korean household had an average of 3.7 people. Average annual income per house was US $41,576. Among the 43.0 million people aged 15 and over in 2015, 32.2 million people (74.0%) had at least a high school diploma. Of those who were employed, 84.2% were high school graduates or above.[4]

Religion

In terms of religious groups, the major religions in Korea are Christianity, Buddhism, and Confucianism. According to the Korean National Statistical Office, it is estimated that more than 40.0% of Koreans profess these three religions.[4] Because of influences from China in the history of Korea, Buddhism and Confucianism were dominant religion groups until the late 19th century. Still, Buddhism is one of the major religions in Korea, and it is estimated that 24.0% of Koreans are Buddhists.[5] With the beginning of modernization and industrialization, however, Confucianism rapidly declined, and it is estimated that only 0.2% of Koreans fall under Confucianism. Because of the influence of Buddhism and Confucianism, the morality of Koreans still gives high value to family, relationships, respect, and cooperation.

Arriving Catholic and Protestant missionaries in Korea in the 19th century changed religious affiliation in Korea. Christianity and Catholicism spread rapidly, and a significant number of Koreans converted. Currently, more than 30% of Koreans are Christians.[5] Methodism, Presbyterianism, and Catholicism are the most popular in Korea.

▶ Brief History of the Healthcare System

Pre–World War II

Throughout the long history of Korea, Koreans have used traditional Korean medicine and remedies, including acupuncture and herbal medicine. Korean traditional medicine has its focus on prevention as well as treatment of diseases. People often visit traditional medicine clinics, which typically are family inherited, to preserve their health or to cure sickness. This long-held tradition was almost destroyed when Japan annexed Korea in the early 20th century.

During the period of occupation, the Japanese prohibited Koreans from using traditional medicine. Instead, the Japanese put their own healthcare system in Korea, which included Westernized medicine.

Since World War II

National liberation in 1945 brought back these revered Korean traditional medicine practices. Since then, both Westernized medicine and traditional medicine have coexisted in Korea. After World War II, Korea experienced Western culture and medicine at an accelerating pace. Rapid development of the economy in the 1960s pushed the Korean government to consider the welfare and health of its citizens.

In 1963, the Korean government enacted the Medical Insurance Law, permitting voluntary health insurance. After this first step, however, development of a healthcare system was slow because of the government's devotion to economic expansion. Health insurance corporations, such as Busan Blue Cross Plan, offered individual policies, but they did not become a major source of health insurance coverage because of the very low participation from citizens.[9]

In 1977, the government passed a law mandating employers with more than 500 employees to provide health insurance to their employees and families. This requirement of health insurance coverage has been gradually increased over time. In 1979, all companies with 300 or more employees were required to provide health insurance. The same year, the government expanded mandatory health insurance coverage to government employees and private school teachers. It was expanded again in 1981 to companies with more than 100 workers and to the self-employed. In addition, the government started demonstration programs in some rural areas to provide health insurance coverage. These step-by-step expansions finally achieved universal coverage in 1989.[10] A year before, the Korean government mandated health insurance coverage to all residents in rural areas, and in 1989, the government mandated coverage to all residents in urban areas, no matter what their employment status was. At that time, the government controlled three different medical insurance societies: (1) the medical insurance society for employees, (2) a regional medical society of the self-employed, and (3) a society for government employees and private school employees.

Since then, the Korean government implemented two major reforms, integration reform in 1998 and separation reform in 2000. In October 1998, the first integration reform integrated two medical insurance societies into one. With the establishment of the National Health Insurance Corporation (NHIC) in 2000, the second initiative of integration was implemented, where all medical insurance societies were integrated under the control of the NHIC.[11,12]

The separation reform in July 2000 was for specialization and quality improvement. Before this reform, both physicians and pharmacists could prescribe and dispense drugs for outpatient services. This resulted in overuse and misuse of drugs. The reform separated the function of prescribing and dispensing drugs between doctors and pharmacists.

In 2000, the Health Insurance Review and Assessment Service (HIRA) was established to assess effectiveness and efficiency of clinical services in order to improve quality of care. Moreover, the Hospital Service Evaluation Program was launched in 2004 to ensure high quality of services.

Description of the Current Healthcare System

Facilities

In 2014, the total number of hospitals and clinics, including specialized ones, in Korea was 86,629. **TABLES 25-2** and **25-3** indicate the total number of

TABLE 25-2 The Number of Hospitals and Clinics by Type, 2010–2014

Year	Hospital			Dental facility		Oriental medicine facility	
	General hospital	Hospital	Clinic	Hospital	Clinic	Hospital	Clinic
2010	274	2,181	27,469	191	14,681	168	12,061
2011	275	2,363	27,837	199	15,058	184	12,401
2012	278	2,524	28,033	202	15,365	199	12,705
2013	281	2,683	28,328	203	15,727	212	13,100
2014	287	2,811	28,883	205	16,172	231	13,423

Data from Ministry of Health and Welfare, Healthcare Resources Team. http://www.medicalkorea.or.kr/content.do?method=getContent&gcd=G1001&cmscd=CM9015; and http://kosis.kr/eng/statisticsList/statisticsList_01List.jsp?vwcd=MT_ETITLE&parmTabId=M_01_01#SubCont.

TABLE 25-3 Number of Specialized Hospitals and Clinics by Type, 2010–2014

Year	Long-term care hospital	Tuberculosis hospital	Mental hospital	Midwifery
2010	450	5	39	46
2011	411	1	35	40
2012	—	2	27	33
2013	—	—	28	34
2014	—	5	—	35

Data from Ministry of Health and Welfare, Healthcare Resources Team. http://www.medicalkorea.or.kr/content.do?method=getContent&gcd=G1001&cmscd=CM9015; and http://kosis.kr/eng/statisticsList/statisticsList_01List.jsp?vwcd=MT_ETITLE&parmTabId=M_01_01#SubCont.

hospitals and clinics. Total numbers have been gradually increasing over time, and the ratio of each type of facility has been steady. The ratio of clinics to the total number was 33.3%, and 18.9% of all facilities were dental hospitals and clinics. Oriental medicine hospitals and clinics, however, have rapidly increased since 2002. In 2014, there were a total of 13,654 oriental medicine facilities in Korea, and they accounted for 15.8% of all types of hospitals and clinics.[6]

In terms of specialized hospitals and clinics, long-term care hospitals have remarkably increased over the past decades. This was mainly due to the increasing needs and demands of an aging society. There were no regulations for long-term care facilities, and in a hypercompetitive market, healthcare providers with financial difficulties simply diverted into long-term care as a niche market for their business. In July 2008, the long-term care insurance scheme was launched with the aim of controlling healthcare expenditure, which was high due to using acute hospital for long-term care. Therefore, the expansion of long-term care facilities was persistent in past years. The number of midwifery facilities significantly decreased due to more women going to hospital maternity wards to deliver their babies.

Most healthcare facilities in Korea are owned and operated by the private sector. TABLE 25-4 provides the types and numbers of providers. All citizens have freedom in the selection of healthcare providers. Insurance beneficiaries, however, are required to receive

TABLE 25-4 Number of Medical Institutions by Type of Establishment, as of the End of 2014

Classification	Hospital*	Clinic	Dental facility**	Oriental medicine facility**
Public	82	34	10	9
School foundation	84	22	14	34
Social welfare foundation	43	48	2	11
Medical corporation	1,033	151	31	77
Individual	1,650	28,116	16,212	13,353
Others***	186	337	89	137

* *Hospital* includes tertiary hospitals, general hospitals, hospitals, medical care hospitals, long-term care, and mental hospitals.
** Both dental facilities and oriental medicine facilities include hospital-based and clinic-based settings.
*** Others include Religious Foundation, Special Juridical Corporation, Corporation Aggregate, and Military.

Data from Korean National Health Insurance Corporation and Health Insurance Review & Assessment Service. *2013 National Health Insurance Statistical Yearbook*. Seoul, Korea: NHIC and HIRA; December 2014.

TABLE 25-5 Number of Beds by Type of Institutions, in Selected Years

Year	Hospital*	Long-term care hospital	Dental facility**	Oriental medicine facility**
2007	238,232	66,727	266	8,700
2009	304,204	90,775	317	8,694
2011	324,984	124,512	554	12,635

* Hospital includes general hospitals, hospitals, and mental hospitals.
** Both dental and oriental medicine facilities include hospital-based and clinic-based settings.

Data from Ministry of Health and Welfare, Healthcare Resources Team. http://www.medicalkorea.or.kr/content.do?method=getContent&gcd=G1001&cmscd=CM9015; and http://kosis.kr/eng/statisticsList/statisticsList_01List.jsp?vwcd=MT_ETITLE&parmTabId=M_01_01#SubCont.

initial treatments from first-level healthcare providers. All providers in Korea, except specialized hospitals, are endowed as first-level providers. When patients need to have specialized care, they can be referred to the second-level providers. This two-level provider system not only serves to use the limited medical resources efficiently but also prevents the tendency of preferring general hospitals. The first-level hospitals or clinics, therefore, play the role of gatekeeper for health services.

Korea is the only nation among the OECD countries that has an increase in inpatient beds. According to OECD health data published in 2014, the number of beds per 1,000 population in Korea was 11.7, which was higher than the average of 4.7 beds among other OECD countries. Korea ranked second, after Japan (13.2 beds/1,000 population) in terms of the number of beds per 1,000 population. Between 2000 and 2013, the number of beds in Korea increased by 80.3%, whereas the average number of beds among OECD countries during the same period decreased by 14.3%.[13,14] All types of facilities experienced an increase in the number of beds except in oriental medicine hospitals/clinics. The growing demand and supply of dental surgeries, such as for dental implants, also made the number of beds available increase in dental hospitals/clinics.[6] TABLE 25-5 demonstrates the number of beds in Korea, by types of institution.

Because the majority of healthcare facilities is owned and managed by the private sector, many medical services providers target mass markets. More than 86% of hospitals were concentrated in urban areas in 2012. This unequal distribution of medical services created a problem in accessibility. Citizens living in rural areas have difficulty accessing medical services, especially specialty care. With a great safety net system, however, delivery of primary care has done well for citizens in rural areas. TABLE 25-6 shows healthcare facilities by geographic locations, and TABLE 25-7 represents the number of safety net providers available in Korea.

Health centers, subhealth centers, and primary healthcare posts are mostly located in rural areas in Korea. As safety net providers, these government-subsidized facilities mainly provide primary care services to citizens in rural areas and those who cannot afford the high cost of care in hospitals or clinics.

TABLE 25-6 Healthcare Facilities by Type and Geographic Location, 2012

	Hospital*		Long-term care hospitals and clinics		Dental hospitals		Oriental medicine hospitals	
	Urban	Rural	Urban	Rural	Urban	Rural	Urban	Rural
Number	2,460	342	898	189	199	3	194	5
Percentage	87.8%	12.2%	82.6%	17.4%	98.5%	1.5%	97.5%	2.5%

* Hospitals includes general hospitals and hospitals.

Data from Ministry of Health and Welfare, Healthcare Resources Team. http://www.medicalkorea.or.kr/content.do?method=getContent&gcd=G1001&cmscd=CM9015; and http://kosis.kr/eng/statisticsList/statisticsList_01List.jsp?vwcd=MT_ETITLE&parmTabId=M_01_01#SubCont.

TABLE 25-7 Health Centers, Subhealth Centers, and Primary Healthcare Posts, 2010–2014

Year	Total	Health center	Subhealth center	Primary Healthcare post
2010	3,459	253	1,294	1,912
2011	3,466	253	1,305	1,908
2012	3,464	254	1,315	1,895
2013	3,476	253	1,323	1,900
2014	3,497	254	1,339	1,904

Data from Ministry of Health and Welfare, Healthcare Resources Team. http://www.medicalkorea.or.kr/content.do?method=getContent&gcd=G1001&cmscd=CM9015; and http://kosis.kr/eng/statisticsList/statisticsList_01List.jsp?vwcd=MT_ETITLE&parmTabId=M_01_01#SubCont.

A total of 3,497 facilities are health centers, subhealth centers, or primary healthcare post. Subhealth centers and primary healthcare posts are considered as branches of health centers that supervise these facilities. These providers also act as gatekeepers. For patients who need complex care, they refer patients to a higher level of medical institution or to specialty physicians.[15]

Workforce

TABLES 25-8 and 25-9 indicate the number of licensed healthcare professionals and qualified medical specialists, respectively. The number of licensed healthcare professionals in Korea has grown fast over the last decades. The average overall growth rate for healthcare professionals is approximately 4%. The number of nurses has increased the most, an average of 5%, followed by oriental medicine doctors, who have an average growth rate of 4%. In spite of this fast-growing workforce, the number of practicing physicians per 1,000 population in Korea was 2.1 in 2012, which was 32 out of 34 among OECD countries. Similar to the ratio of practicing physicians, practicing nurses per 1,000 population was 4.8. This ratio was 29 out of 34 among OECD countries. The average number of practicing nurses per 1,000 population in OECD countries was 8.8 in 2012. Like other countries, Korea faces a nursing shortage. The ratio of nurses to physicians in 2013 was 2.4, which was lower than the OECD countries' average ratio of 2.8.[6,13,16]

TABLE 25-10 shows the number of healthcare professionals in health centers, subhealth centers, and primary healthcare posts. To increase accessibility caused by the unequal distribution of services, the Korean government forced medical college/university

TABLE 25-8 Number of Licensed Healthcare Professionals, 2010–2014

Year	Physician (MD)	Dentist	Oriental medicine doctor	Pharmacist	Nurse
2010	82,137	20,936	16,156	60,564	116,071
2011	84,544	21,410	16,826	62,988	118,711
2012	86,761	21,888	17,353	60,699	120,491
2013	90,710	22,482	18,199	60,586	134,748
2014	92,927	22,952	18,767	60,733	147,210

Data from Ministry of Health and Welfare, Healthcare Resources Team. http://www.medicalkorea.or.kr/content.do?method=getContent&gcd=G1001&cmscd=CM9015; and http://kosis.kr/eng/statisticsList/statisticsList_01List.jsp?vwcd=MT_ETITLE&parmTabId=M_01_01#SubCont.

TABLE 25-9 Number of Qualified Medical Specialists by Type of Specialty, 2010–2014

Year	Primary care	General surgery	Orthopedics	Radiology	Others
2010	25,083	5,096	4,603	2,641	24,423
2011	26,065	5,237	4,793	2,756	25,610
2012	27,334	5,400	5,007	2,910	26,923
2013	28,475	5,559	5,206	3,065	28,304
2014	29,486	5,675	5,339	3,186	29,424

Data from Ministry of Health and Welfare, License Information System of MOHW. http://www.medicalkorea.or.kr/content.do?method=getContent&gcd=G1001&cmscd=CM9015; and http://kosis.kr/eng/statisticsList/statisticsList_01List.jsp?vwcd=MT_ETITLE&parmTabId=M_01_01#SubCont.

TABLE 25-10 Healthcare Professionals in Health Centers, Subhealth Centers, and Primary Healthcare Posts, 2008–2011

Year	Physicians*	Dentists*	Oriental medical doctors*	Nurses**
2008	2,357	897	899	8,226
2009	2,473	860	1,025	8,173
2010	2,418	772	1,072	8,277
2011	2,362	629	1,034	8,123

* Includes medical officers and public health doctors.
** Includes nursing assistants.

Data from Ministry of Health and Welfare, Healthcare Resources Team. http://www.medicalkorea.or.kr/content.do?method=getContent&gcd=G1001&cmscd=CM9015; and http://kosis.kr/eng/statisticsList/statisticsList_01List.jsp?vwcd=MT_ETITLE&parmTabId=M_01_01#SubCont.

graduates to serve in rural areas. By serving in rural areas as public health doctors, they can waive service in the army, which is mandatory for all Korean males. Most medical college graduates take this option as a replacement of military service.

Technology and Equipment

In terms of medical technology and equipment, Korea is a country with rapid adoption of new medical technology. According to the OECD, the number of computed tomography scanners per million population in Korea increased rapidly from 12.2 in 1990 to 35.9 in 2011, which makes Korea a leading country among OECD member countries. Similarly, the number of magnetic resonance imaging machines per million population also dramatically increased, from 1.4 in 1990 to 21.3 in 2011. Again, Korea was a leader among OECD member countries concerning this medical technology.[13,17]

Evaluation of the Healthcare System

Cost

Over the decades, Korea has experienced fast economic growth and rapid industrialization. As a result of the profoundly developing economy, Korea joined the OECD in 1996, becoming the 29th member country and the second country in Asia. Economic development has dramatically improved the health of the population, particularly with the inception of national health insurance.

National health insurance was introduced in Korea in 1977. Through the gradual coverage of additional population groups, Korea could provide universal health coverage to all of its citizens by 1989, only 12 years after its first introduction. Since then, healthcare expenditure has increased rapidly.

Healthcare expenditure in Korea was 7.2% of GDP in 2015, which was 1.8% lower than the OECD average. Medical spending per capita in Korea was US $2,488 in the same year. It is also ranked below the OECD average of $3,814 in 2015.[13] The rate of growth in health spending was three times greater (6.8%) than the average of the OECD countries in 2005–2015 (2.1%) as the result of the increase in public spending. Public spending on health accounted for 55.6% of the total healthcare expenditure in 2015, which showed a dramatic increase from 30.0% in 1985.[13,18] Another factor affecting the rise of health spending is pharmaceutical spending. Although the growth of pharmaceutical spending has slowed, it still comprises a large part of the healthcare expenditure. Spending on pharmaceuticals in 2014 was 20.6% of total healthcare expenditure, which was higher than the OECD average of 16.3%.[19]

NHIC of Korea provides health coverage to citizens by their employment status. Two medical insurance societies for industrial workers and the self-employed are under the Korean National Health Insurance (NHI) program, which covers approximately 97.0% of citizens. The Medical Aid program, which is under local government control, provides health coverage to low-income and indigent people. **TABLE 25-11** shows the enrollment of NHI and Medical Aid programs, which cover all citizens. In 2014, more than 51 million (97.2%) were insured with NHI, and the remaining 1.4 million (2.8%) were covered by Medical Aid.[6]

Financing of health care comes from three sources: the mandatory health insurance contribution (premium), government subsidies, and patients' out-of-pocket payments. The mandatory health insurance contribution is set by and includes a contribution from both the employer and employee. The contribution rate for industrial workers is based on income and their personal properties. Employers are responsible for paying 50.00% of the contribution of their employees. As of 2011, the contribution rate was about 5.64% of salaried income. Although this rate is one of the lowest among OECD countries, many Koreans feel that it is a heavy financial burden for them. According to a national survey, only 19.00% said that the contribution rate was appropriate for the offered benefits.[4,15] For the self-employed, the contribution is set by economic activity, income, and property.

Government subsidy accounts for a small portion of total financing. The government's share, however, has been increasing since 2002, to give financial relief to the NHI. The subsidy comes from tax revenue, both general taxation and cigarette tax in accordance with the Special Act for Financial Stabilization. This act was legislated to solve the financial crisis of the NHI that has rapidly deteriorated since 1999.[10,20]

One of the distinct features of the Korean healthcare system is the domination of the private sector

TABLE 25-11 People Covered by Health Insurance, by Category of Insured (Unit: 1,000 Population, Percentage)

Classification	Total*,**	Health insurance for industrial workers**,***	Health insurance for self-employed**	Health insurance for indigent group (medical aid)**
2011	50,909 (100)	33,257 (65.3)	16,043 (31.5)	1,609 (3.2)
2012	51,169 (100)	34,106 (66.7)	15,556 (30.4)	1,507 (2.9)
2013	51,448 (100)	35,006 (68.0)	14,984 (29.1)	1,459 (2.8)
2014	51,757 (100)	35,602 (68.8)	14,715 (28.4)	1,441 (2.8)

* All numbers include dependents.
** Numbers in parentheses are proportion of enrollments.
*** Industrial workers include government employees and private school teachers.

Data from MOHW, Health Insurance Policy Team/National Health Insurance Corporation. http://www.medicalkorea.or.kr/content.do?method=getContent&gcd=G1001&cmscd=CM9015; and http://www.nhic.or.kr/static/html/wbd/g/a/wbdga0704.html.

in healthcare delivery and even in healthcare financing. The relatively high private share (about 42%) of healthcare financing is related to substantial out-of-pocket payments.[21,22] Private providers supply the majority of healthcare services, with public providers playing a residual role. More than 90% of hospitals and clinics are privately owned. In most cases, therefore, physicians both own and manage the facilities. Physician clinics have inpatient facilities, and most hospitals operate large outpatient centers, which promotes competition between hospitals and clinics. All pharmacies are owned and operated by individual pharmacists as well.

Cost sharing is controlled by one insurer, the NHIC of Korea. Insurance allowance is also controlled, with strong government intervention; however, it is difficult to control the costs for services that are not covered by NHI. Since adoption of the NHI system, administration costs have been managed with strong governmental regulation. With expansion of benefit coverage and increasing demands from customers, however, it has been rapidly increasing in recent years.

The reimbursement mechanism in Korea is traditional fee-for-service, which calculates medicine, material, and treatment costs separately and reimburses under a predetermined fee schedule.[10] Many medical examinations and treatments are done competitively under fee-for-service. To create demand and to secure more patients, providers excessively purchase new and advanced technologies. Providers induce demand by prescribing more drugs, requiring that patients have more visits for care, and encouraging treatments which are not included in the NHI's benefit package. This results in increases in customers' out-of-pocket costs and total healthcare expenditure.

For medical services, patients are responsible for paying some portion of the medical cost, in the form of either a deductible or coinsurance. Deductibles and coinsurance are predetermined by the NHIC in annual negotiations with organizations representing providers, such as the Korean Medical Association, the Korean Dental Association, and the Korean Physicians Association. Deductibles are applied only to people in medical aid programs. Depending on the patient's income level, a patient can use medical services either at no cost or for a small charge (about US $1–2).

Coinsurance rates vary by types of services (inpatient or outpatient care) and types of healthcare facilities (clinic, hospital, and general hospital). For outpatient services in clinics, patients are responsible for 30% of the total charges. The rate is 50% for services in hospitals and 55% in general hospitals. For inpatients, the coinsurance is 20% of total medical charges.[10,15]

Other than deductibles and coinsurance, some patients pay an extra fee for outpatient services from certain physicians. When patients want services from certain doctors who have more experience and an exceptional reputation, those patients are required to pay this special fee on top of regular medical charges. Typically, senior medical staff in general hospitals are in this category.

To control increasing healthcare expenditures, the NHIC introduced diagnosis-related groups in 1997 as a pilot program. It was planned to apply to all providers after three years. Because of the strong opposition from providers, however, only a few providers voluntarily participate in this system, which is currently applied to eight selected procedures. In 2001, a Resources-Based Relative Value Scale payment system was implemented in Korea. The payments to providers increased, but without a mechanism to control the volume and expenditure.[20]

The flow of medical claims is important to understand. After providers provide medical services to insurance beneficiaries, they send medical claims to both the NHIC and the HIRA. The HIRA reviews claims submitted by providers for appropriateness of medical procedures provided and the claim costs. After the HIRA evaluates claims, the NHIC makes payments to providers in accordance with the review results.[10]

For certain chronic diseases and serious illnesses, for example, diabetes and cancer, the NHI cuts patients' out-of-pocket costs for the elderly. The benefit package of the NHI has been expanded over time.

Even with separation of dispensing authority from medical practices, antibiotics are still overused because of the practice patterns of physicians. Most primary care and preventive services, which are critical for public health, are still not included in the NHI's benefit package. Complaints from customers regarding preventive services are growing.

Overutilization, low reimbursement rates, addition of preventive services in the benefit package, and duplication of medical shopping services are issues to be solved by the Korean government. These factors yield high administrative costs and eventually will increase in healthcare expenditure.

Quality

Rapid economic development in Korea was paralleled by unprecedented achievements in the health of the population. Dramatic improvements have been attained in life expectancy, and infant mortality rates have been steadily reduced. Mortality and morbidity patterns have changed from communicable diseases to chronic and lifestyle-related diseases. The infant mortality rate per 1,000 live births has decreased to 3.0 in 2016 from 45.0 in 1970, whereas life expectancy at birth reached 82.2 years (males, 79.0 years; females, 85.5 years) in 2014. Both figures are about average for OECD countries, 77.9 and 83.3 years, respectively.[6,13]

One factor in the improvement of population health is due to a regulated healthcare system in Korea. Because the fee-for-service system in Korea is strongly regulated, healthcare providers do not compete with others in price. To secure more patients, providers compete with quality of service. Providers realize that patient-centered care, high quality with advanced medical technologies, and friendly services are essential for success in their businesses. This phenomenon in a hypercompetitive market contributes to improving continuously the quality of health services. On the other hand, indiscreet provider-induced demand in some areas yields overutilization. In addition, the areas with poor populations still have limited access and poor quality of care because of risk pooling.

For the year 2012, the 10 leading causes of death in Korea accounted for 70.5% of total deaths and were malignant neoplasms, heart diseases, cerebrovascular diseases, intentional self-harm, diabetes mellitus, pneumonia, chronic lower respiratory diseases, diseases of the liver, transport accidents, and hypertensive diseases.[6] Accidents are the primary cause of early death, and smoking still remains a major health risk factor in Korea. For cancer, major cancer incidents in Korea in 2012 were stomach, colorectal, lung, liver, and prostate, which accounted for 66.8% of all cancer incidents. The 5-year relative survival rate of patients diagnosed in the 5 years (2008–2012), however, increased by 26.9% compared with those from 1993 to 1995.[6,16]

According to results of Social Survey, which was done by KOSTAT in 2014, the majority of people who used medical services responded that they were satisfied with those medical services. TABLE 25-12 shows the level of satisfaction for medical services by types of healthcare facilities.[6,15]

2014 Social Survey

For those who were dissatisfied with medical services, the reasons of dissatisfaction were high medical charges (24.7%), unsatisfactory treatment (20.7%), and long waiting times (20.2%).

Healthcare expenditure depends not only on price but also on the volume of services provided. Under the fee-for-service system, which strictly regulates fees, physicians have perverse incentives to increase the frequency of office visits and hospital admissions, as well as the intensity of services. The high rate of caesarean sections in Korea is one good example of provider-induced demands. Although the rate of caesarean operations has declined in recent years, it is still higher than the average rate of OECD countries.[13,16]

Obesity is one of the growing health issues in many countries. As demonstrated in TABLE 25-13, the prevalence of obesity among those age 20 years and older in Korea was 31.5% in 2014, which was the lowest among the OECD countries. This prevalence has increased over decades. Since the year 2001, however, the growth has slowed.[13] Interestingly, the overall increase was due to the increase of overweight in the male population, whereas the prevalence of obesity in women declined slightly during the same time.[1,6]

Access

The Korean NHI achieved a goal to cover all citizens for medical care. With freedom of choice, citizens can access medical services any time of the year and from whom they want. When NHI was introduced in Korea,

TABLE 25-12 Level of Satisfaction for Medical Services, by Type of Healthcare Facility

Facility type	% very satisfied	% moderately satisfied	% acceptable	% moderately dissatisfied	% very dissatisfied
General hospital	18.8	35.7	33.4	10.8	1.4
Hospital/clinic	11.7	36.2	44.8	6.8	0.5
Public health center	29.4	38.9	27.7	3.6	0.4

Data from Statistics Korea (KOSTAT). http://kostat.go.kr/portal/eng/pressReleases/11/5/index.board

TABLE 25-13 The Prevalence of Obesity Among Those 20 Years and Older, in Selected Years

Classification	2001	2005	2010	2014
Total	30.6	31.8	31.4	31.5
Men	32.4	35.2	36.5	37.7
Women	29.4	28.3	26.4	25.3

Obesity is defined as a body mass index equal to or greater than 25.0.

Data from Ministry of Health and Welfare, Health Investment Planning Team. http://www.medicalkorea.or.kr/content.do?method=getContent&gcd=G1001&cmscd=CM9015; and http://kosis.kr/eng/statisticsList/statisticsList_01List.jsp?vwcd=MT_ETITLE&parmTabId=M_01_01#SubCont.

it initially allowed citizens to use medical services for only 180 days per year, but by 2006, this service limitation was removed. According to OECD health data, the number of physician visits per citizen in Korea was 14.6 in 2013, exceeding the average number of visits of OECD member countries. In addition, length of stay in hospitals in Korea was 16.5 days as compared with the OECD average of 8.1 days. This is mainly because the Korean NHI does not have a prospective payment system that could help to contain costs. Moreover, many hospitals tend to increase capacity for the same reason. Korea is the only country among the OECD countries that has an increasing number of beds over time.[6,13,23]

Accessibility to medical care in Korea is considered high overall, but like many countries, accessibility is less in rural areas. The distribution of medical services is not even. Because most of the healthcare facilities are privately owned, they tend to be concentrated in cities where there are many customers and where a lifestyle for healthcare providers' families can be realized. The limited availability of healthcare services in rural areas with small populations is a problem for Korea.

Current and Emerging Issues and Challenges

Along with a rapid expansion of the economy, health care in Korea improved remarkably in a short period. Every citizen has healthcare coverage since the introduction of NHI. With strong government regulation, NHI has been successful in both cost containment and quality improvement. Some statistics, however, indicate that the growth of healthcare expenditures in Korea is fast and that it is above the average of OECD countries, although healthcare expenditures in terms of GDP in Korea still remain below the OECD average. Moreover, rapidly changing environments, such as increasing demand, seeking high quality of care, and hypercompetitive healthcare markets put more burdens on the insurer (NHIC), providers, and even citizens. Growing distrust of the NHIC caused by increasing cost of care and out-of-pocket payment is one of the current issues in Korea. Government may need to conduct the payment reform based on a prospective payment mechanism, and expand the role of public hospitals to reduce the disparities in health care and health outcomes.[24]

Second, the number of long-term care providers is growing. Since 2003, the number of long-term care facilities has dramatically increased because of an aging society and increasing demands. There are many new long-term care facilities, and many existing healthcare providers are diverting their focus to long-term care as a market niche strategy in a hypercompetitive market. In July 2008, the long-term care insurance scheme was launched with the aim of controlling healthcare expenditure on acute hospitals for long-term care. Therefore, the expansion of long-term care facilities has been persistent since then. The implementation of the long-term care insurance scheme is targeted to improve access for elderly people to long-term care and to reduce the socioeconomic burden. However, the coordination among long-term care facilities and hospitals remains an unresolved issue in Korea.[25]

Third, the structure of the healthcare industry in Korea is changing. One distinct characteristic in Korea is that the private sector, particularly small hospitals and clinics, dominates the healthcare market. In a competitive market, these providers undergo financial difficulty because of increasing costs. To survive, many providers are moving toward integration in order to achieve economies of scale, increased quantity to reduce per unit cost. Either horizontal or vertical integration activities through networking, franchising, or partnerships among providers are becoming prevalent in Korea's healthcare market.

On December 2006, the Korean government announced Service Industry Development Plans for the healthcare sector. The government proposed (1) to encourage providers to adopt practice guidelines and clinical pathways in order to improve quality of care, (2) to allow the establishment of management service organizations (MSO) to provide management services for healthcare providers, (3) to consider having in the healthcare market for-profit hospitals, which are still illegal in Korea, (4) to introduce private health insurance for healthcare services, and (5) to give governmental support to providers to attract customers from abroad (medical tourism).

After the government's plans were announced, several MSOs were established to provide management services to healthcare providers. Typically, hospitals/clinics in Korea are owned and managed by physicians. By contracting with MSOs, physicians at hospitals and clinics can focus more on delivering care and can gain efficient management; nevertheless, private health insurance and for-profit hospitals are controversial. These proposed changes will face strong opposition from stakeholders.

Finally, for medical tourism, a few big hospitals in Korea are preparing to have patients from other countries. Because the quality of care and services are the main concern in medical tourism, those hospitals are making every effort to improve performance. One of these hospitals is now accredited by Joint Commission International.

Like many developed countries, Korea must face the challenge of growing healthcare costs, as the portion of GDP going to healthcare continues to increase. Because healthcare spending exceeds economic growth, there is cause for concern in the long run. This problem is not unique to Korea. The government may be considering moving to a prospective payment system or to global budgeting to control utilization. It may be that Korea must revisit their benefit package and include more preventive care services.

Continuous quality improvement will remain a challenge. The government will make every effort to improve and monitor quality of care, especially for long-term care. There is no systemized control system to monitor and evaluate long-term care services. Government should strengthen the accreditation process for long-term care facilities.

Third, an appropriate method to incentivize providers to use resources effectively and efficiently should be considered. Even with strong government regulation and a relatively low reimbursement rate to providers, there is overutilization and misuse. These are resources that could better be used elsewhere in the system. Future reforms of incentive structures for providers should focus on healthcare quality and efficiency, such as implementing the pay-for-performance scheme to reward providers for achieving specified performance targets.

Fourth, the NHI should maintain its financial status in balance. Since the beginning of the 2000s, the NHI suffered from financial difficulty with huge deficits. Consideration might be given to raising contributions rates and tight cost control. The contribution rate (premium) from citizens is relatively low when compared with other countries, even though Koreans enjoy high-quality and technology-driven medical services. Although the NHIC could face opposition from citizens, it is noted that the NHI contribution rates have been gradually increasing. One of the mechanisms being used effectively now is implementation of the electronic data interchange (EDI) system to ensure more stable resource collection.

Finally, the NHI in Korea has been remarkably successful in the past. Since the 2010s began, however, the NHIC has been facing not only financial burdens, but also complaints from both providers and citizens. Reestablishing trust in the NHI system and reinforcing the NHIC's accountability will be another challenge. The Korean government should improve public relations and be more responsive to the increasing demands of its citizens.

It will be crucial to build a transparent policy process for greater trust in the government's decision making. Stakeholder discussions and raising public awareness can play influential roles in convincing citizens that there is a need for reforms.[26] Consistent and continuous efforts to reach consensus, to contain cost, and to build social solidarity around the objectives of equity, efficiency, and quality will be the ultimate task for future growth of the Korean healthcare system.

References

1. Korea National Statistical Office. Korean Statistical Services. http://kosis.kr/eng/. Accessed April 18, 2016.
2. International Monetary Fund. World Economic Outlook Database. https://www.imf.org/external/pubs/ft/weo/2015/02/weodata/index.aspx. October 2015. Accessed April 18, 2016.
3. Korean Government. About Korea: geography. http://www.korea.net/AboutKorea/Society/South-Korea-Summary. Accessed April 18, 2016.
4. Korea National Statistical Office. Economically Active Population Survey. http://kostat.go.kr/portal/eng/surveyOutline/4/1/index.static. Accessed April 18, 2016.
5. Government of the United States. Central Intelligence Agency. The World Factbook. https://www.cia.gov/library/publications/the-world-factbook/geos/ks.html. Updated 2016. Accessed April 18, 2016.

6. Korean Government. Ministry of Health and Welfare. *Yearbook of Health and Welfare Statistics, 2014*. Seoul, Korea: Ministry of Health and Welfare. October 2014;60.
7. US Department of Homeland Security. US Immigration and Customs Enforcement. Student and Exchange Visitor Information System. *General Summary Quarterly Review*. Published February 2015. Accessed April 18, 2016. https://www.ice.gov/sites/default/files/documents/Document/2015/by-the-numbers.pdf.
8. United Nations. Department of Economic and Social Affairs. Population Division. *World Population Prospects*. 2015 Revision. http://esa.un.org/unpd/wpp/Download/Standard/Population/. Accessed April 18, 2016.
9. Anderson GF. Universal health care coverage in Korea. *Health Aff*. 1989;8(2):24–34.
10. Korean National Health Insurance Corporation. *National Health Insurance Program in Korea*. Seoul, Korea: National Health Insurance Corporation; 2004.
11. Kwon SM. *Changing Health Policy Process: Politics of Health Care Reform in Korea*. https://cdn1.sph.harvard.edu/wp-content/uploads/sites/114/2012/10/RP206.pdf. Accessed April 19, 2016.
12. Lee JC. Health care reform in South Korea: Success of failure? *Am J Public Health*. 2003;93(1):48–51.
13. Organisation for Economic Co-operation and Development. *OECD Health Data 2015*. Paris, France: OECD; 2016.
14. Kwon S, Lee TJ, Kim CY. Republic of Korea: health system review. *Health Systems in Transition*. 2015; 5(4):1–102.
15. Korean Government. Ministry of Health and Welfare. *The White Paper on Health and Welfare 2006*. In Korean. Seoul, Korea: Ministry of Health and Welfare; July 2007.
16. Korean National Health Insurance Corporation, Health Insurance Review and Assessment Service. *2013 National Health Insurance Statistical Yearbook*. Seoul, Korea: NHIC and HIRA; December 2014.
17. Bae SI, Kim YS, Tae YH, Lee CJ. *The Current Condition and Prospect of Health Care in Korea: View from International Statistics*. In Korean. Research Paper Series. Korea: National Health Insurance Corporation; December 2007: 2007–2027.
18. Center for Health Policy Research. *Lessons Learned from the South Korean Health Care System*. Tulsa, Oklahoma: Oklahoma Medical Research Foundation; February 1992.
19. Organisation for Economic Co-operation and Development. How does Korea compare? *OECD Health Statistics 2014*. http://www.oecd.org/els/health-systems/Briefing-Note-KOREA-2014.pdf. Accessed April 20, 2016.
20. Kwon SM. Payment system reform for health care providers in Korea. *Health Policy Plan*. 2003;18(1):84–92.
21. Shin Y. Health care systems in transition II. Korea, part I: an overview of health care systems in Korea. *J Public Health Med*. 1998;20(1):41–46.
22. Yang BM. The role of health insurance in the growth of the private health sector in Korea. *Int J Health Plan Manage*. 1996;11(3):231–251.
23. Anderson GF, Poullier JP. Health spending, access, and outcomes: trends in industrialized countries. *Health Aff*. 1999;18(3):178–192.
24. Mathauer I, Xu K, Garrin G, Evans Db. An analysis of the health financing system of the Republic of Korea and options to strengthen health financing performance. http://www.who.int/health_financing/documents/hsfr_e_09-korea.pdf. Published September 2009. Accessed April 20, 2016.
25. World Health Organization. Korea Ministry of Health and Welfare. *Health Service Delivery Profile: Republic of Korea 2012*. http://www.wpro.who.int/health_services/service_delivery_profile_republic_of_korea.pdf. Accessed April 20, 2016.
26. Chun CB, Kim SY, Lee JY, Lee SY. Republic of Korea: health system review. *Health Systems in Transition*. 2009; 11(7):1–184.

CHAPTER 26

Australia

Gary E. Day and **Bernard J. Kerr Jr.**

▶ Country Description

TABLE 26-1 Australia	
Nationality	Noun: Australian(s) Adjective: Australian
Ethnic groups	English 25.9%, Australian 25.4%, Irish 7.5%, Scottish 6.4%, Italian 3.3%, German 3.2%, Chinese 3.1%, Indian 1.4%, Greek 1.4%, Dutch 1.2%, other 15.8% (includes Australian aboriginal .5%), unspecified 5.4%
Religions	Protestant 30.1% (Anglican 17.1%, Uniting Church 5.0%, Presbyterian and Reformed 2.8%, Baptist, 1.6%, Lutheran 1.2%, Pentecostal 1.1%, other Protestant 1.3%), Catholic 25.3% (Roman Catholic 25.1%, other Catholic 0.2%), other Christian 2.9%, Orthodox 2.8%, Buddhist 2.5%, Muslim 2.2%, Hindu 1.3%, other 1.3%, none 22.3%, unspecified 9.3% (2011 est.)
Language	English 76.8%, Mandarin 1.6%, Italian 1.4%, Arabic 1.3%, Greek 1.2%, Cantonese 1.2%, Vietnamese 1.1%, other 10.4%, unspecified 5% (2011 est.)
Literacy#	Below Level 1: 3.7% Level 1: 10% Level 2: 30% Level 3: 38% Level 4: 14% Level 5: 1.2%
Government type	Federal parliamentary democracy

(continues)

TABLE 26-1 Australia (continued)

Date of independence	January 1, 1901 (federation of UK colonies)
Gross Domestic Product (GDP) per capita	$65,400 (2015 est.)
Unemployment rate	6.2% (2015 est.)
Natural hazards	Cyclones along the coast; severe droughts; forest fires
Environment: current issues	Soil erosion from overgrazing, industrial development, urbanization, and poor farming practices; soil salinity rising because of the use of poor-quality water; desertification; clearing for agricultural purposes threatens the natural habitat of many unique animal and plant species; the Great Barrier Reef off the northeast coast, the largest coral reef in the world, is threatened by increased shipping and its popularity as a tourist site; limited natural freshwater resources
Population	23, 940,333 (Dec. 2015 est.)
Age structure	0-14 years: 17.9% (male 2,089,561/female 1,982,719) 15-24 years: 13.14% (male 1,533,526/female 1,455,870) 25-54 years: 41.67% (male 4,822,083/female 4,658,371) 55-64 years: 11.82% (male 1,333,924/female 1,355,347) 65 years and over: 15.47% (male 1,628,108/female 1,891,505) (2015 est.)
Median age	Total: 38.4 years Male: 37.7 years Female: 39.2 years (2015 est.)
Population growth rate	1.07% (2015 est.)
Birth rate	12.15 births/1,000 population (2015 est.)
Death rate	7.14 deaths/1,000 population (2015 est.)
Net migration rate	5.65 migrant(s)/1,000 population (2015 est.)
Sex ratio	At birth: 1.06 male(s)/female 0-14 years: 1.05 male(s)/female 15-24 years: 1.05 male(s)/female 25-54 years: 1.04 male(s)/female 55-64 years: 0.98 male(s)/female 65 years and over: 0.86 male(s)/female Total population: 1.01 male(s)/female (2015 est.)
Infant mortality rate	Total: 4.37 deaths/1,000 live births Male: 4.67 deaths/1,000 live births Female: 4.04 deaths/1,000 live births (2015 est.)
Life expectancy at birth	total population: 82.15 years male: 79.7 years female: 84.74 years (2015 est.)
Total fertility rate	1.77 children born/woman (2015 est.)

TABLE 26-1 Australia (continued)	
HIV/AIDS adult prevalence rate	0.17% (2015 est.)
Number of people living with HIV/AIDS	28,200 (2013 est.)
HIV/AIDS deaths	Less than 100 (2013 est.)

Data from Central Intelligence Agency. The World Fact Book, 2016: Australia. https://www.cia.gov/library/publications/the-world-factbook/geos/as.html. Accessed December 4, 2016; Australian Bureau of Statistics. Programme for the International Assessment of Adult Competencies, Australia, 2011–2012. Catalogue No. 4228.0. http://www.abs.gov.au/ausstats/abs@.nsf/Lookup/4228.0Main+Features202011-12. September 10, 2013. Accessed 2016.

History

Australia is a vast, ancient island continent. It was first settled more than 50,000 years ago by migrating tribes making the short trip across from Southeast Asia to the northern parts of the continent. These Aboriginal and Torres Strait Islander peoples spread across the land, including the island of Tasmania to the south, and are thought to have numbered around 350,000 at the time of first European contact in the 17th century.[1]

After a period of exploration by Dutch, French, and English explorers, the eastern parts of Australia were claimed in 1770 by Captain James Cook in the name of Great Britain. Initial settlement quickly followed. The first fleet of 11 ships carrying 700 convicts and 400 guards and officials arrived in January 1788 to establish the penal colony of New South Wales. Five more self-governing British crown colonies were then established during the early part of the 19th century. On January 1, 1901, after a countrywide referendum, the six colonies federated, and the Commonwealth of Australia was formed.

Australia's history since British settlement in 1788 has been marked by several important events. The discovery of gold in the early 1850s brought many immigrants to Australia from Britain, Ireland, Europe, North America, and China. This and subsequent gold discoveries heralded a period of considerable prosperity, population growth, and spread. Involvement in two world wars and in other major conflicts of the 20th century, notably Korea and Vietnam, while creating a large loss of life (mainly young men) and a strain on national resources, helped create a sense of national unity and identity.

Colonization, however, severely disrupted Aboriginal society and economy—epidemic disease caused an immediate loss of life, and the occupation of land by settlers and the restriction of Aboriginal and Torres Strait Islanders to reserves disrupted their ability to support themselves. Over time, this combination of factors had such an impact that by the 1930s only an estimated 80,000 of this population remained in Australia.[1]

A massive program of European immigration after World War II—some 2 million people arriving between 1948 and 1975—saw Australia's population grow substantially, helping to fuel a lengthy period of economic prosperity and growth. Discovery and exploitation of the country's natural and mineral resources have underpinned Australia's development and wealth and encouraged rapid development of agricultural, mining, and manufacturing industries up until 2009.

Most recently, a downturn in global commodities has seen sharp falls in the export earnings from Australia's natural resources, putting pressure on revenues that underpin the national economy. Similarly, Australia is at a nexus in terms of large scale manufacturing due to the relatively small size of the Australian market and cost of local salaries and wages compared to less expensive imports. With large-scale industries, such as motor vehicle manufacturing, ceasing in 2017, Australia is looking to redefine its economy with new markets and approaches to manufacturing and exports.

Size and Geography

Australia has a land area of some 7.7 million square kilometers. This is about twice the size of the European Union and is close to the size of the United States (excluding Alaska). Situated in the southern hemisphere between the Indian and Pacific oceans, a large proportion of the continent (around 40%) lies within the tropics (see map in **FIGURE 26-1**). Distances are huge, some 4,000 kilometers from west (Steep Point in Western Australia) to east (Byron Bay in New South Wales) and 3,680 kilometers from north (Cape York in Queensland) to south (Wilson's Promontory in Victoria).

Beyond its continental shores, Australia also has jurisdiction over a large number of islands, most notably the island of Tasmania, but also many others such as Melville Island (off the Northern Territory), Kangaroo Island (South Australia), King and Flinders Islands (Tasmania), the Torres Strait Islands (Queensland), and more distant islands including Macquarie Island (well south of Tasmania), Christmas Island (off Western Australia, and Lord Howe Island (off New South Wales).

Government and Political System

Since achieving nationhood in 1901, Australia has had a federal system of government whereby power is divided among the Commonwealth Government and the governments in each of Australia's six states and two territories. The form of government reflects the country's British heritage, a constitutional monarchy with the British sovereign as head of state (currently Queen Elizabeth II). The monarch is represented federally by the governor-general and at state levels by state governors.

FIGURE 26-1 Map of Australia
© Bardocz Peter/Shutterstock

Separation of powers—legislative, executive, and judicial—is embedded in the system of government. This is well described by Healy et al.[2]

> The Parliament makes the laws, the Government implements and supervises, and the Courts interpret them. The legislative power of the Commonwealth is vested in a Federal Parliament. The executive power is vested in the Queen and is exercisable by the Governor-General as the Queen's representative. Judicial power is exercised by the High Court of Australia and the Federal Court of Australia, and other state courts exercising federal jurisdiction.
>
> Healy et al.[2]

The Commonwealth Parliament, located in the nation's capital, Canberra (in the Australian Capital Territory), is bicameral. Elections for the two chambers, the House of Representatives (the lower house) and the Senate (the upper house), take place every three years. Electorates in the 150-seat lower house are allocated by population size, and members are elected for 3 years with a preferential voting system. Senators in the upper house are allocated equally across the states. Each state is represented by 12 senators and each territory by 2, elected for 6 years by proportional representation. Through a system of rotation, half of the Senate retires every 3 years and is replaced (or reelected) at the time of a general election for House of Representatives members.[3]

The political party that wins the majority of seats in the lower house is empowered to form a government. Since 1944, when the Liberal Party was formed by Robert Menzies, successive Commonwealth Governments have been formed by the Australian Labor Party and by a coalition of the Liberal and National parties. Over the last nine years there has been a succession of prime ministers and changes of government from Coalition to Labor and now back to Coalition. Over this time Australia has seen six changes of prime minister (1996–2007 John Howard, 2007–2010 Kevin Rudd, 2010–2013 Julia Gillard, 2013 Kevin Rudd, 2013–2015 Tony Abbott, and since 2015 Malcolm Turnbull). While the current federal government is led by the Coalition (Liberal and National Parties), there is a mix of Labor Party and Coalition governments across the seven states and territories. Another interesting and unusual feature of Australia's system of government is that voting is compulsory for all enrolled citizens aged 18 years and over, in each state and territory and at the federal level.

Macroeconomics

During the 1990s and early 2000s, Australia's economy performed particularly well, boasting one of the Organisation for Economic Co-operation and Development's (OECD) fastest growing economies during that period. Significant reforms since the 1980s, including financial deregulation, floating the exchange rate, free trade agreements, stronger trade ties with Asia, lowering of tariffs, and changes to the tax system, have helped to produce a diversified and internationally competitive economy with per capita gross domestic product (GDP) (A$50,026/US $37,828 in 2016) on par with several major European economies, such as the United Kingdom, Germany, and Canada.

An abundance of natural resources has enabled Australia to become a major exporter of agricultural products, minerals, metals, and fossil fuels. Much of Australia's economic focus has been on the economies of the Asia-Pacific region. The boom in mining exports in recent years, driven largely by China's rapid growth, has now slowed substantially, placing pressure on natural resource revenues and national balance of payment emergence as an economic force in the world economy.

A short summary of Australia's most recent economic statistics reveals that (1) inflation has remained steady at 1.30% per year through June 2016, (2) unemployment has been climbing slowly in line with slowing economic growth (5.70% in June 2016), (3) the exchange rate has been around A$0.74 to US $1, and (4) cash rates have been at a historically low level of 1.75%. The Reserve Bank of Australia has tightened monetary policy by reducing interest rates in an attempt to stimulate the domestic economy.[4] As to the future, the Australian economy is entering a phase of significant international uncertainty. The global economy, and in particular the Asian economies that Australia trades with, is slowing, and this is substantially affecting all Australians with borrowings. In addition, rising unemployment, nationwide droughts affecting agricultural production, falling commodity prices, and major shifts in large-scale local manufacturing are all creating economic issues for the national government. As a result, Australia's strong economic footing will be at risk. Australia's economic growth has slowed considerably over the last eight years, and with the government carrying larger burdens of national debt, there will be pressure on our national credit ratings.

Demographics

Australia's population was close to 24.0 million in December 2015,[5] a 1.0% increase over the previous year. Around half of this increase is due to natural increase (births less deaths) and half to net overseas migration. Since federation in 1901,[6] the population has increased by just over 20.0 million people; in the decade from 2006 to 2016, the population increased by around 2.4 million.[5,7]

The majority of Australians are of European descent, a reflection of early settlement from the British Isles during the colonial era and to post-federation immigration from Europe. More recently, an increasing number of immigrants to Australia are from Asia and Oceania. Australia has one of the largest proportions of immigrant populations in the world. More than 23% of Australians were born overseas.[5]

The mainland Aboriginal and Torres Strait Islander population was 669,900 (3.0% of the total population) in 2011.[8] In 2001 this population was estimated at 534,770. Over the decade to 2011 there has been an annual growth rate in population of between 2.0% and 2.3% per year.[8]

Australia's population is highly urbanized with two-thirds living in major cities around the coastal fringe. The state capitals are all coastal: Sydney, Melbourne, Brisbane, Adelaide, Perth, and Hobart. The exception is the nation's capital, Canberra, which is inland from Sydney but still within 100 kilometers from the coast.

Although Australia has no official state religion, the 2011 census provides a snapshot of the religious beliefs of the population. Results show that 61.0% of Australians called themselves Christian, of which 25.0% identified themselves as Roman Catholic and 17.0% as Anglican. Followers of non-Christian religions numbered 7.2% (Buddhism, Islam, Hinduism) and 22.0% were categorized as having "no religion" (which includes nontheistic beliefs, such as humanism, atheism, agnosticism, and rationalism).[9]

▸ Brief History of the Healthcare System

Pre–World War II

A range of influences have shaped the complex system of health care now in place in Australia. From early beginnings as a convict settlement in the colony of New South Wales in 1788, health services in Australia have evolved into a mix of public and private delivery, based largely on British and American models and shaped inevitably by unique political, economic, and social events.

The first 100 or so years of European settlement were characterized by a somewhat haphazard mix of private medical services and government-funded hospitals for convicts, paupers, and the impoverished. Support for health costs was also forthcoming from a range of benevolent and charitable organizations and friendly societies. During the 19th century, colonial governments across the country also assumed responsibility for the maintenance of public health, such as sanitation and the control of infectious diseases, through the passage of comprehensive public health acts modeled on British legislation of the time.[10]

The coming of nationhood in 1901 brought with it a federal system of government under which responsibility for the provision of health services was shared among the Commonwealth Government and the governments of the six states and two territories.

Since World War II

Initially, the Commonwealth's health responsibilities were restricted to quarantine matters only, but an amendment to the Constitution in 1946 enabled the Commonwealth to make laws with respect to (among other things) "pharmaceutical, sickness and hospital benefits, medical and dental services, but not so as to authorize any form of civil conscription." This latter clause was inserted into the amendment following pressure from the medical profession, a response no doubt to the perceived threat of a British-style National Health Service being introduced in Australia.

Prohibition of civil conscription, interpreted to mean that medical practitioners could not be compelled to work for the government, not only helped to entrench the predominant fee-for-service payment system for medical services but also played a part in delaying the introduction of the Commonwealth-funded prescription insurance system under which all Australians have access to subsidized life-saving medicines. As a result, the Pharmaceutical Benefits Scheme (PBS), as it is known, first mooted in 1945, was not fully implemented until the Pharmaceutical Benefits Act passed through Federal Parliament in 1948. Passage of this act had not been easy. It was passed twice and overturned once; it was the subject of a national referendum, constitutional change, and fierce public debate on the powers of the Commonwealth Government.

The 1946 constitutional amendment also enabled the Commonwealth Government to enter into funding agreements with the states for the provision of free public hospital care for patients in public wards. This arrangement, intended to protect patients from the high cost of hospital care, has remained the basis of hospital financing agreements between the Commonwealth and the states ever since.

The other main features of the health system (given effect through the 1953 National Health Act) were the pensioner medical services arrangements and the medical benefits scheme. The former ensured the provision of free health services to aged and invalid pensioners through agreements with the Australian Medical Association, whereas the latter subsidized medical costs for members of nonprofit health insurance schemes.

These four pillars of Australia's health system—(1) subsidized medicines, (2) Commonwealth funding for state hospitals, (3) subsidized health care for pensioners, and (4) subsidized private health insurance—remained in place largely unaltered for the next 20 years, until the introduction of a national health insurance scheme known as Medibank in 1975. Not surprisingly, the move from a system funded predominantly through subsidized private insurance to one funded predominantly by government was met with strident opposition from vested interests and political opponents alike. After rejection of the necessary legislation by the opposition-controlled Senate in 1973 and 1974, dissolution of both houses of Parliament and a subsequent general election, Medibank was finally enacted in July 1974 and came into operation a year later. The major elements of the new scheme were subsidized medical services for patients and free access to public hospital care through hospital cost-sharing arrangements among the Commonwealth and the state and territory governments.

From 1975, a period of conservative government ensued (the Fraser-led Liberal-National Coalition), during which several changes were made to Medibank, which saw a gradual return to greater reliance on private health insurance for medical services.[10] Election of a Labor Party government in 1983 then heralded the return of a universal tax-funded national health insurance scheme known as Medicare. The subsequent change of government in 1996 did not materially affect these arrangements, which now enjoy bipartisan political support and widespread public support.

▶ Description of the Current Healthcare System

The Australian healthcare system is complex with numerous providers of services, funding arrangements, and regulatory mechanisms. The overall aim of the system is to provide all Australians with ready access to healthcare services at low cost or no cost at all. Service providers include medical practitioners (physicians), various health professionals, private and public hospitals, and government and nongovernment agencies.

Responsibility for funding is shared among all levels of government and the nongovernment sector, such as private health insurers and individual consumers.

The Commonwealth Government is responsible for funding the provision of medical services, pharmaceutical benefits, aged residential care services, and disability services, as well as public health, research, and national information management. The state and territory governments are responsible for delivery and management of a range of health services, such as public hospital services, mental health programs, community support programs, and women's and children's services.

Facilities

Medicare is the centerpiece of Australia's health system. It is a universal, publicly funded health insurance system that allows all Australians to access affordable high-quality health care. In place in its present form since 1984, Medicare is financed by general taxation revenue and a Medicare levy based on taxable income. Medicare provides free or subsidized treatment by medical practitioners (physicians) and grants to the states and territories to assist with the cost of running public hospitals. The Commonwealth jointly funds public hospitals with the states so that these services are provided free of charge to patients. In 2011–2012, there were 1,345 acute care hospitals throughout Australia, of which 753 were public hospitals containing a total of 56,582 beds.[11] In that same year, there were 592 private hospitals in Australia (**TABLE 26-2**), with a total of 24,362 beds.[11] There were also a small number of public psychiatric hospitals containing a total of 1,705 beds.

Workforce

In common with many other countries around the world, Australia is experiencing significant shortages of health professionals across the spectrum of occupations. This is despite significant growth in the overall health workforce in recent years. Between 2006 and 2011, the total number of people employed in health occupations grew by 22.1% from 956,150 to 1,167,633.[11] **TABLE 26-3** shows total numbers employed in selected health occupations, as well as rates per 100,000 population. Australia has a similar number of practicing medical practitioners per capita as the OECD average and a higher per capita number of practicing nurses.[11]

Health workforce shortages will continue into the future due in part to an aging population and lower numbers coming into the health workforce due to falling fertility rates in the 1980s and 1990s. For comparison, the two largest components making up the

TABLE 26-2 Australia's Hospitals and Available Beds, 2011–2012

	Public acute	Public psychiatric	Private hospitals	Total
Hospitals	753	17	592	1,362
Available beds	56,582	1,838	24,362	82,782
Available beds per 1,000 population	2.6	0.1	1.3	4.0

Data from Australian Institute of Health and Welfare. *Australia's Health 2014*. Canberra; 2014.

TABLE 26-3 Australia's Health Workforce, Selected Occupation, 2012

Occupation	Number	Per 100,000 population
Nurses and midwives	290,144	1,124
Medical practitioners	79,653	374
Pharmacists	21,331	89
Physiotherapists	20,081	80
Dental practitioners	17,283	74
Occupational therapists	7,231	45

Data from Australian Institute of Health and Welfare. *Australia's Health 2014*. Canberra; 2014.

health workforce are nurses and midwives and doctors; almost two out of five nurses and midwives are 50 years or older, with one in four medical practitioners being 55 or older.[12]

Technology and Equipment

Australia's fortunate status as a wealthy developed nation has enabled it to build and foster a health system with access to advanced, up-to-date medical and surgical technologies and health facilities. Although direct measures of the stock and spread of these technologies and equipment are not available, it is possible to identify particular technologies—new pharmaceutical listings for example—and to measure their impact on health costs and (in some instances) health outcomes.

The scale of the medical technology industry in Australia is immense, with an annual turnover of approximately A$10.0 billion (US $7.6 billion) in 2012, imported goods to the value of A$4.4 billion (US $3.3 billion), and exported goods worth A$1.9 billion (US $1.4 billion).[13] From these figures alone, regulation and monitoring has been necessary to keep health expenditure in check and to ensure that only the most effective and efficient technologies are approved for use. An earlier study by the Productivity Commission (a Commonwealth Government agency) into the impacts of advances in medical technology in Australia[14] concluded that (1) advances in medical technology in Australia have brought large benefits but have also been a major driver of increased health spending in recent years and that (2) overall, advances in medical technology arguably have provided value for money, particularly as people highly value improvements in the quality and length of life.

The predominance of public funding in Australia's health system brings with it various rationing and gate-keeping mechanisms aimed at controlling the cost impact of new technologies. The underlying philosophy of these mechanisms is for evidence-based health care. New drugs and medical procedures, for example, must be assessed as cost-effective before they can be subsidized for listing on the PBS or the Medicare Benefits Schedule. Indeed, Australia was the first country in the world to require drug manufacturers seeking to have a new drug listed on the PBS to demonstrate its cost-effectiveness.

Another feature of Australia's system is the drive to increase the diffusion and use of information technology at all levels of health care. There is high-level commitment from all levels of government to encourage the uptake of information technology to improve clinical and medical practice. Most physician practices are computerized both for clinical and administrative purposes, and the introduction of a national electronic medical record is currently being implemented, albeit with a slow uptake. This is mainly due to an opt-in system for patients. This national electronic medical record is intended to reduce errors, adverse events, and duplication of services, reduces the incidence of inappropriate treatments, and allows for access across Australia. There remains considerable scope for progress in this area, which to date has been delayed by understandable concerns about patient privacy, confidentiality and cost.

Evaluation of the Healthcare System

Over the last decade there has been an awareness of and emphasis on health system performance in Australia. An indication of this was the establishment in 2011 of the National Health Performance Authority (NHPA). The NHPA was responsible for monitoring, reporting, and benchmarking hospital performance and a range of other health performance measures, including national reporting on *MyHospital* and *MyHealthyCommunities*. In 2016, the NHPA ceased operations, and its role and functions were taken up by the Australian Institute of Health and Welfare and the Australian Commission on Safety and Quality in Health Care.[15] The performance criteria cover a wide range of indicators, including equity, effectiveness, appropriateness, efficiency, responsiveness, accessibility, safety, continuity, capability, and sustainability. Also high on the list in any evaluation of health system performance are measures of health status and health outcomes.

Cost

Health spending in Australia totaled nearly A$155 billion (US $117 billion) in 2013–2014 or A$6,639 (US $5025) per person.[16] This represents 9.7% of Australia's GDP, which puts Australia around the average in comparison with other OECD countries, including Norway, Finland, and Greece; below countries, such as the United States, Canada, Japan, and New Zealand; and above the United Kingdom. **TABLE 26-4** shows how spending on health services in Australia has progressed in the past decade.

In the ten years from 2003–2004 to 2013–2014, total health expenditure tended to grow faster in real terms than GDP, with an average annual real growth of 5.0% being 2.2 percentage points higher than the 2.8% for GDP. In 2013–2014, growth in real health expenditure was just 0.6 of a percentage point higher than GDP (3.1% compared with 2.5%, respectively). In the previous year, real health expenditure growth was 1.4 percentage points lower than GDP growth (1.1% compared with 2.5%).[16(p8)]

Funding and responsibility for Australia's health system is a complex blend of purchasers and providers and is funded predominantly from taxation sources with federal, state, and territory governments, contributing close to 70% of all health spending (see **FIGURE 26-2**).

Nongovernment funding is drawn mainly from out-of-pocket payment by individuals and health insurance funds, which help to cover the cost of treatment in private hospitals and a range of other medical and ancillary health services.

Funding from governments, individuals, private insurance, and other sources remained relatively proportional until 2006 (see **FIGURE 26-3**), when the Australian government started to bear a larger percentage of overall funding. In recent times, funding for health has become an area for strong debate among the Commonwealth and the states and territories. There has been strong disagreement about the adequacy of health funding from the Commonwealth, particularly in a time where the economy is shrinking and the population is ageing. Attempts to curb the growth

TABLE 26-4 Trends in Health Spending in Australia, 2003–2014

	2003–2004	2008–2009	2013–2014
Total health expenditure, current prices (A$ million) (US$ million)	94,932 38,864	125,705 55,029	154,633 82,633
Total health expenditure as a percentage of GDP	8.53	9.09	9.78
Total per capita health expenditure, current prices (A$) (US$)	3,708 2,026	5,328 2,854	6,639 3,990
Public share of total health expenditure (%)	67.3	68.8	67.8

Data from Australian Institute of Health and Welfare. *Health Expenditure Australia 2013–2014*. Canberra; 2015.

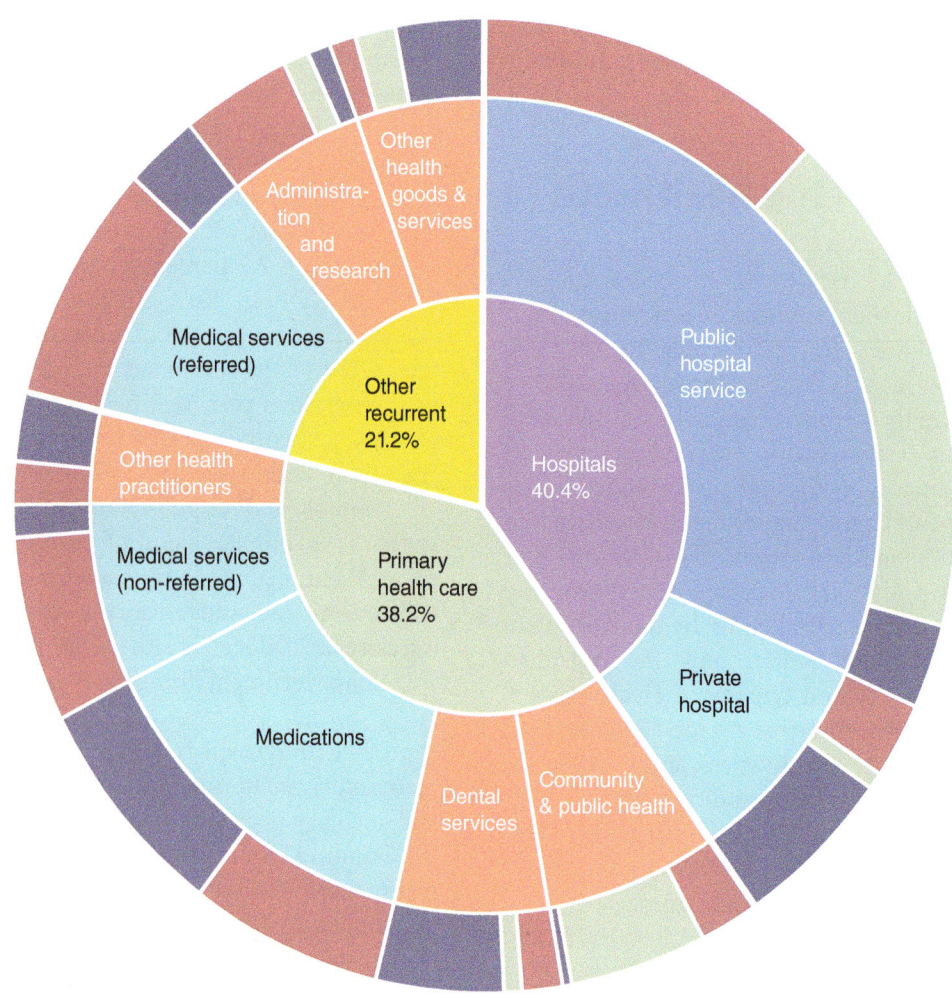

FIGURE 26-2 Health Services—Funding and Responsibility, 2014

Reproduced from Australian Institute of Health and Welfare. Australia's Health 2014. Canberra; 2014. http://www.aihw.gov.au/australias-health/2014/health-system/#t2. Creative Commons license available at https://creativecommons.org/licenses/by/3.0/au/

in health funding in recent years have been largely unsuccessful.

The public share of health spending has varied markedly over the years, reflecting the major policy changes of the federal government. The introduction of Medibank in 1975 saw the public share jump from 57.0% to 73.0%; this share then declined to 63.0% in the late 1970s with the gradual dismantling of Medibank by the Fraser Coalition government. The public share of health spending jumped to 72.0% after the introduction of Medicare by Hawke's Labor Party government in 1984. In 2013–2014, the public share of health funding was 67.8%, with the nongovernment sector (insurance funds, individuals, and other) accounting for 32.2% of funding.[16]

FIGURE 26-4 shows that the greatest proportion of health funding in 2011–2012 was spent on hospitals, followed by primary health care and other recurrent costs. Component costs, public hospitals, medications, and medical services were the single largest contributors to health expenditure.[16]

Under Medicare, patients are entitled to access public hospital care at no charge. This includes free medical and surgical care from physicians and surgeons, accommodation, meals, and other health services while in the hospital if they are admitted as public patients.

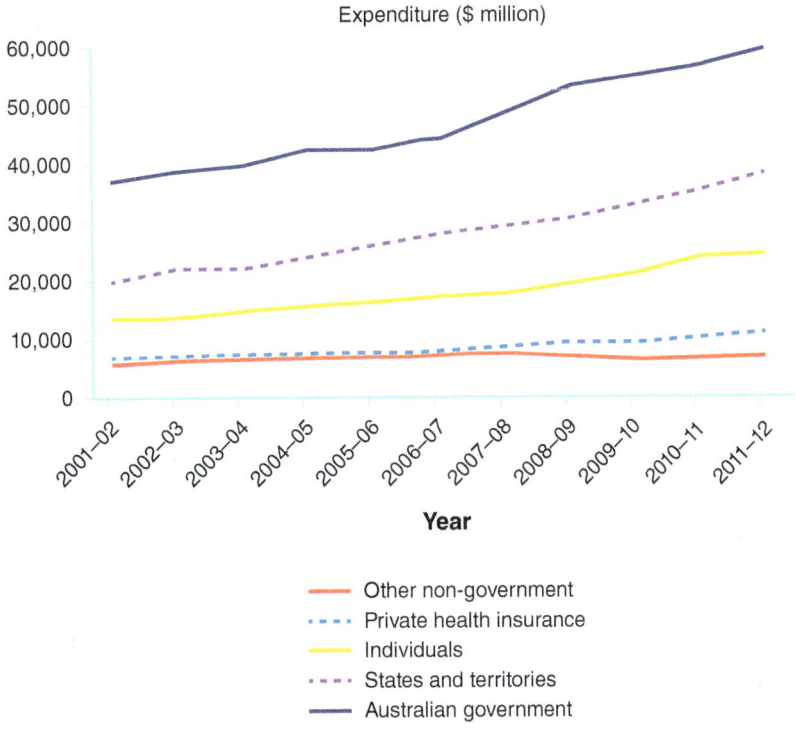

FIGURE 26-3 Source of Funds for Health, 2001–2002 to 2011–2012

Reproduced from Australian Institute of Health and Welfare. Australia's Health 2014. Canberra; 2014. http://www.aihw.gov.au/australias-health/2014/health-system/#t2. Creative Commons license available at https://creativecommons.org/licenses/by/3.0/au/

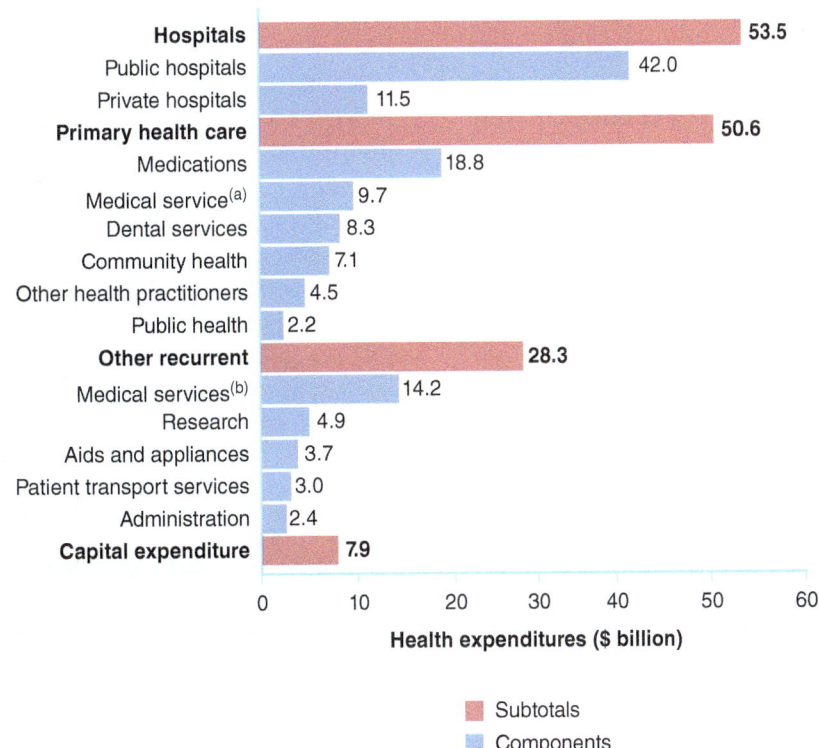

FIGURE 26-4 Proportion of Health Funding in Australia, 2013–2014

Reproduced from Australian Institute of Health and Welfare. Australia's Health 2014. Canberra; 2014. http://www.aihw.gov.au/australias-health/2014/health-system/#t2. Creative Commons license available at https://creativecommons.org/licenses/by/3.0/au/

In addition to having a publicly funded social health insurance scheme (Medicare), Australians can also subscribe to private health insurance. If privately insured patients choose to be admitted as private patients, then additional fees and charges are likely. In these instances, the patient can choose their own physician/surgeon. When in private hospitals, patients are charged fees for accommodation, nursing care, and other hospital care. They are also charged separately for any medical and surgical treatment. Private health insurance is available to cover such expenses (and ancillaries, such as optical, dental and allied health) if people wish to subscribe. Any premiums are additional to the Medicare levy (2.0% of income, with some reductions and exclusions), which all Australian taxpayers are obliged to pay.[17] In recent years, the government has introduced a number of policies to reduce the pressure on the public health system penalizing higher earning taxpayers with an additional Medicare surcharge if they do not take out private insurance.

Under Medicare, the government pays a flat rate per physician consultation. A physician can choose to charge the patient either that amount or more. A patient pays any difference. Other services funded through Medicare include services from participating optometrists and services delivered by a practice nurse on behalf of a general practitioner and for certain services from eligible dentists and allied health practitioners. Claims can be made by post or over the counter at Medicare offices, or the physician can "bulk bill" patients. In this case, physicians send accounts directly to Medicare and accept the Medicare rebate as full payment for the service. There is no cost to the patient. Just over 8 of 10 physicians "bulk billed" the government for their patient consultations in 2013–2014.[18]

In 2015, there were 373.4 million Medicare services, an average of 15.4 services per person, at a total cost of A$20.5 billion (US $15.7 billion).[19] The main services were general practitioner consultations, followed by pathology tests, diagnostic imaging, and specialist physician attendances.

As with Medicare, the PBS is also a central and unique feature of Australia's health system. Since its inception in 1948, the PBS has consistently provided reliable, timely, and affordable access to important medicines for all Australians. In so doing, the PBS has proven itself to be one of the best systems in the world. Medicines on the Australian market are not only of high quality but also are less costly than in most other countries. Under the scheme, consumers can access more than 2,300 brands of prescription medicines that they are assured have been rigorously tested and found to be cost-effective. These medicines are available from a network of 5,000 independently owned community pharmacies spread across all parts of Australia.

Currently, most of the population (general consumers) pay a maximum of A$38.30 (US $28.97) for any one prescription item. Concessional patients and pensioners pay only A$6.20 (US $4.70) per item. There are two safety net thresholds—one for general patients and the other for concessional patients. From January 1, 2016, the general patient safety net threshold was A$1,475.00 (US $1,126.00). When patients and/or their families reach this amount, they can apply for a Safety Net Concession Card and pay only A$6.00 (US $4.52) per prescription for the rest of the calendar year. The concessional safety net threshold is A$372.00 (US $284.00). Once patients and/or their families reach this amount, they can apply for a Safety Net Entitlement Card and receive items free of charge for the rest of the calendar year.[20]

The cost of the scheme has risen significantly over the years. In 2005, its first year of operation, around 300,000 prescriptions for PBS medicines were dispensed, at a cost to the Commonwealth Government of A$150,000 Australian dollars (US $113,000). By 1960, this had grown to 24 million prescriptions at a cost of A$44.00 million (US $33.10 million). In 2006–2007, the PBS covered 170.00 million prescriptions at a total cost (government and private) of A$6.70 billion (US $5.04 billion). By 2014, this had risen to A$9.10 billion (US $6.85 billion). The total PBS prescription volumes increased by 6.3% from 2013 to a total of 209.80 million in 2014. Government expenditure amounted to 82.5% of the total cost of PBS prescriptions. The remainder was patient contributions that amounted to A$1.50 billion (US $1.13 billion). The average dispensed price per prescription of PBS medicines decreased to A$42.20 (US $31.80) for the year ending June 2014. The average government cost of these scripts was A$34.83 (US $26.23) for the same period.[19]

There are several reasons for this increasing cost. First, the number of available medicines continues to grow. As new drugs come onto the market and get approved, they are added to the list of subsidized medications. Second, the new generation drugs listed on the PBS are more costly and doctors tend to prescribe the newer, more potent, and more effective products. Thus, the mix of drugs being prescribed by doctors is increasing in cost. Third, Australia's aging population and chronic disease profile is driving the use of more medications. The number of prescriptions dispensed per person increases with age as medicines play an important role in improving the quality and longevity of people's lives. Fourth, the number of people eligible for concessional and pensioner pharmaceutical benefits is increasing, which in turn adds to the cost for the PBS.

Quality

Quality of care is but one of a number of factors, in addition to socioeconomic, environmental, behavioral, biomedical, and genetic factors, that help to determine the health and well-being of the population. Quality is difficult to define and even more difficult to measure. It can be subjective, such as an individual patient's view of the quality of a particular encounter with the health system or the wider public's view of the performance of their local hospital or ambulance service.

A key biennial government publication, *Australia's Health*, outlines the health improvement of the nation over time. Since *Australia's Health* was first published over 25 years ago, Australia's ranking among comparable countries has improved on most measures: (1) Australia's life expectancy at birth (84.8 years for females and 79.8 years for males in 2016) placed Australia among the top 6 nations in the world. (2) Marked improvements in ranking are evident for mortality rates from coronary heart disease, stroke, lung cancer, and transport accidents. (3) Rates of smoking continue to fall, moving Australia into the "best third" of OECD countries on this measure. (4) Australia also scores well and has improved rankings on self-rated health, dental health, various mortality measures, and lower alcohol consumption.

On the downside, Australia's ranking has fallen on measures of mortality from suicide, diabetes, respiratory diseases, and infant mortality. The ranking for obesity has not changed, with 63% of Australians classified as overweight or obese.[11] Australia is among the "worst third" group of OECD countries on this measure.

Australia's health system has also been compared to other developed health systems worldwide. Australia had mixed results when compared internationally, including:

- Ranked 4th out of 11 for access to care on the same or next day appointment with a doctor when sick (behind Germany, New Zealand, and the Netherlands),
- Ranked 4th worst when waiting four or more months for surgery (behind Norway, Canada, and New Zealand),
- Ranked 5th out of 11 for experiencing a medical/medication or lab error in the last two years (19%),
- Ranked 5th out of 11 for experiencing a gap in discharge planning in the last two years (55%), and
- Ranked 4th out of 11 for a health system that works well with only minor changes required (behind the United Kingdom, Switzerland, and the Netherlands).[22]

Access

Equity of access to health services is one of the main objectives of Australia's health system. In particular is one of the underpinning principles of the universal taxpayer funded Medicare and Pharmaceutical Benefits (PBS) systems. Both are funded through general taxation as well as by a 2% Medicare levy on income. Patients also contribute through a system of structured co-payments for prescription medicines. For physician services, patients pay any gap between the amount that the physician charges and the Medicare rebate for the service.

Access to public hospital services is available for Australian citizens who can elect to have free accommodation, medical and nursing care, as well as necessary medicines as public patients. Patients can also choose, if they wish, to be treated in a private hospital, or as a private patient in a public hospital. They are then required to meet the associated medical, surgical, and accommodation costs with the assistance of private health insurance and some assistance from Medicare.

Access to a wide range of prescription medicines is made possible through the PBS. As described earlier, patients are required to contribute to the cost of their medicines through a system of co-payments. In addition, a safety net is in place that provides further protection for individuals and families against the financial burden associated with high use of medicines. Access to pharmaceutical services is also facilitated through a set of regulations that govern where Australia's nearly 5,000 community pharmacies are located. This is particularly important in rural and remote parts of Australia where population density is low and communities are few and far between.

In 2013, the federal government commenced the centrally funded National Disability Insurance Scheme. Currently under trial in multiple sites across Australia, this scheme will provide all Australians under the age of 65 (who have a permanent, significant disability) with reasonable and necessary supports to be as active as possible in the community. Over 460,000 Australians with disabilities, families, and caregivers will have access to the scheme.

Current and Emerging Issues and Challenges

Australia is fortunate to have a health system that features a sophisticated infrastructure, advanced medical technologies, and highly trained health professionals, all of which have helped to deliver high levels of health across most sectors of the population. Several challenges and emerging issues are apparent in the early years of the 21st century. The final section of this chapter focuses on four of these: (1) the challenges of an aging population, (2) the inequality of Aboriginal and Torres Strait Islander health, (3) the twin health challenges of increasing levels of obesity and diabetes, and (4) the organizational and structural challenges that the government faces with a publicly funded healthcare system.

An Aging Population

"Demography shapes destiny" was one of the catchcries of former Australian treasurer, Peter Costello, referring to the inevitability of the aging of the population in the country, described elsewhere as "a quiet transformation, because it is gradual, but also unremitting and ultimately pervasive."[23] Falling fertility, the aging of the baby-boomer generation, declining mortality, and increased life expectancy are combining to increase the number and proportion of the population that is older, that is, those aged 65 years or more. Over recent decades population growth has been stronger among older age groups compared with younger age groups. Between 1973 and 2013, the number of people aged 65 and over tripled, from 1.1 million to 3.3 million. There was a six-fold increase in the number of people aged 85 and over, from 73,100 to 439,600. Over the same period, the number of children and young people (aged under 25) rose by just 22% from 6.1 million to 7.5 million people. To highlight this point, in 2013, people aged 65 and over comprised 14% of the population compared with 9% in 1973. People aged under 25 comprised one-third (32%) of the population in 2013 compared with almost half (45%) 40 years earlier.[11(p11)]

The implications of an aging population for healthcare costs have been the focus of much analysis and commentary in the past two decades. The upward pressure on health costs applied by an aging population results both from the fact that older people tend to have a greater need for health services and that they use those services more often than other age groups. The other major drivers of rising health costs are the increasing cost and availability of new health technology, as well as burgeoning consumer demands and expectations. Consumers increasingly expect and demand the latest and best, whether it is the latest medical/surgical advance or the latest "miracle" drug.

Growing older is accompanied by an increasing incidence of nonfatal diseases of aging and chronic degenerative diseases. These include arthritis, diabetes, heart disease, cancer, and dementia. Such diseases can severely impact the quality of life and independence of older people. They also bring with them markedly increased utilization of health services, such as medications, doctor consultations, and hospital admissions.

Although there are many who believe an aging population is a crisis in the making, the prevailing view is not so pessimistic. Population aging is gradual. Governments, health planners, and administrators have plenty of time to develop new policy approaches to address the challenges ahead. The Productivity Commission, for example, points out[23] that future productivity growth will ensure that Australians are much richer and are better able to afford the costs associated with aging. Moreover, although people are living longer, they are generally healthier than previous generations. In the last few years more discussion has focused on healthy aging and contributing to the workforce in later life.

The government's *Intergenerational Report*[24] concluded that Australians will live longer and continue to have one of the longest life expectancies in the world. For 2054–2055, life expectancy at birth is projected to be 95.1 years for men and 96.6 years for women. "Not only will Australians live longer, but improvements in health mean they are more likely to remain active for longer. 'Active ageing' presents great opportunities for older Australians to keep participating in the workforce and community for longer, and to look forward to more active and engaged retirement years. There will be fewer people of traditional working age compared with the very young and the elderly. This trend is already visible, with the number of people aged between 15 and 64 for every person aged 65 and over having fallen from 7.3 people in 1974–1975 to an estimated 4.5 people today. By 2054–2055, this is projected to nearly halve again to 2.7 people."[24(pviii)]

Aboriginal and Torres Strait Islander Health

One of the major challenges for all levels of government, but particularly the federal government, is the state of health of Australia's Aboriginal and Torres Strait Islanders.

This population (there were approximately 73,600 in Australia in 2014) dies on average 10 years earlier (10.6 years for males and 9.5 years for females) than other Australians.[25] While the life expectancy gap has decreased over the last decade, by any measure it is still unacceptable. On almost every measure of health, the gap between indigenous and nonindigenous people in Australia is significant. In terms of health disparity, Aboriginal and Torres Strait Islanders have:

- Twice the rate of hospitalization for injury or poisoning,[25]
- Ten times the rate for dialysis,[25]
- Five times the likelihood of dying from endocrine, nutritional, and metabolic conditions (including diabetes)
- Three times the likelihood of dying from digestive conditions,[11]
- Age-standardized death rates that are five times as high for the 35–44 age group,[11]
- 1.5 times the rate of death from cardiovascular disease,[25]
- Twice the death rate for children aged 0–4,[11] and
- 1.5 times the likelihood of becoming obese, twice the likelihood of smoking, of being physically inactive, and of having poor nutrition (10% higher).[11]

Much of this disparity in health status is due to a range of social conditions that affect health, including the inadequate and overcrowded living conditions of many Aboriginal and Torres Strait Islander peoples that do not satisfy the basic requirements of shelter, safe drinking water, and adequate waste disposal.

Around A$4.6 billion (US $3.5 billion) was spent on health services for this population in 2010–2011, about 3.7% of all health spending.[25] This equates to approximately A$7,995 (US $6,093) per Aboriginal and Torres Strait Islander, compared with A$5,437 (US $4,114) for each nonindigenous person. Between 2008–2009 and 2010–2011, government health expenditure for indigenous peoples increased by A$847 per person (US $646, adjusted for inflation)—an average annual growth rate of 6.1%. The corresponding growth rate for nonindigenous people was 2.6%.[25(p150)]

In many regards, health services for Aboriginal and Torres Strait Islanders are often more costly to deliver, both because of the remoteness of many communities and because many of the health services are provided in different ways. A much higher proportion of health dollars for indigenous peoples is spent on hospital services, and proportionately much less on primary health care, particularly Medicare and the PBS. Average Medicare and PBS spending for each indigenous Australian in 2011 was around 20%–30% less than for other Australians.[25] Average spending per indigenous person on dental, private hospital, and other professional health services was also much lower than for other Australians.

Obesity and Diabetes

Two significant and related health challenges for Australia in the early years of the 21st century have been obesity and diabetes. In common with many other developed nations, Australia has been experiencing an increasing prevalence of obesity in recent years. Described by the World Health Organization as a global epidemic, obesity (or excess body fat) is associated with an increased risk of type 2 diabetes, cardiovascular disease, high blood pressure, certain cancers, sleep apnea, osteoarthritis, psychological disorders, and social problems.[25,6]

The latest statistics[27] on the prevalence of overweight and obesity in Australia shows that (1) nearly two-thirds (63%) of all adults (or 7.4 million people aged 18 years and over) are either overweight or obese, up from 44% in 1995; (2) the rate of overweight adults increased from 32% in 1995 to 35% in 2012; and (3) the rate of obesity in adults increased from 12% to 28% over the same period.

These rates of adult obesity in Australia are well above OECD averages, ranking 4th out of 16 countries. Australia sits behind the United States, Mexico, and Hungary for obesity rates, well ahead of New Zealand, Canada, and the United Kingdom. Apart from the well-documented health and social consequences of obesity, the associated costs are significant and growing. A recent study by Obesity Australia found that if left unchecked, the direct and indirect economic impact of obesity would reach A$88.0 billion (US $67.1 billion) and affect one-third of Australians by 2025.[28]

Policy options abound, but successful outcomes are few and far between. Imposing a tax on food products considered likely to contribute to obesity is not widely favored, as it targets food products consumed by obese and nonobese alike. While a sugar tax on soft drinks has been adopted overseas, this is yet to gain traction among Australian law makers. It also cannot be assumed that higher tax on certain foods will necessarily shift consumption away from them toward healthier alternatives. Pressure on the government to impose advertising restrictions, such as bans on food advertisements for children, has also been rejected to date. Instead, there is a voluntary code of practice in place for advertising to children that aims to not encourage or promote an inactive lifestyle combined with unhealthy eating or drinking habits.[29]

While there has been much made of self-control or government regulation of the food industry, the government's preferred approach in recent times has been to fund awareness, health promotion, and prevention campaigns.

Diabetes is a significant and growing chronic disease in Australia. The latest statistics show that:

- About 1 in 20 (approximately 917,000) have been diagnosed with diabetes.
- In 2014, nearly 30,000 people started using insulin to treat their diabetes.
- Around 9% of all hospital admission in 2013–2014 were attributable to diabetes.
- Approximately 1 in 10 deaths in 2012 were attributable to diabetes.
- Diabetes death rates among the Aboriginal and Torres Strait Islander population due to diabetes are three times higher than the nonindigenous population.[30]

Diabetes can cause diseases of the eyes, kidneys, nerves, and cardiovascular system, which can lead to a reduced quality of life and premature death. Type 2 diabetes, the most common form, has increased in prevalence in Australia since the 1980s, and further increases in obesity and physically inactive lifestyles and increases in the aging of the population have the potential to continue this increase. Diabetes has been among conditions of concern to Australia's health ministers (federal, state, and territory) for some time and continues to be a focus of the Council of Australian Governments' broader commitment to reducing the prevalence of avoidable chronic diseases and their risk factors.

There is also much concern about the financial burden of diabetes. Recent assessments suggest health care that is directly attributable to diabetes costs approximately A$1.7 billion (US $1.3 billion) per year, while the total cost of diabetes annually has been estimated to be as high as A$14.0 billion (US $10.7 billion). Annual direct costs for people with diabetes complications are more than twice as much as for people without complications; A$9,600 (US $7,328) compared with $3,500 (US $2,672).[31]

Structural and Organizational Issues

International comparisons suggest that Australia has a health system that produces high levels of health at reasonable cost (close to the OECD average). The predominantly publicly funded system provides universal access to high-quality health and hospital services, ensuring that Australians are ahead of most other comparable countries on most measures of health. Despite these successes, Australia's historical, political, and societal characteristics, in particular the complexities associated with its federal/state structure, have given rise to some fundamental and somewhat intractable fiscal and organizational problems. Five-year Health Care Agreements between the Commonwealth and state/territory governments determine the amount of federal funding to be allocated to the states and territories to help cover the costs of running public hospitals. Funding for the current agreement (from 2016–2017 to 2019–2020) is likely to exceed A$95.0 billion (US $72.4 billion).[32] Tensions inevitably arise between federal and state governments concerning the adequacy and distribution of this funding. Accusations of cost shifting among different levels of government, of inefficiencies, systems growth and of overlap and duplication of services are commonplace and make for ongoing public controversy and debate.

In 2008, Australia's Labor Party government was determined to address these problems, to improve the way health care was delivered, and to make it sustainable for the future. To this end, the National Health and Hospitals Reform Commission was established and charged with developing "a blueprint for tackling future challenges in Australia's health system, including: (1) the rapidly increasing burden of chronic disease; (2) the aging of the population; (3) rising health costs; and (4) inefficiencies exacerbated by cost shifting and the blame game."[33] Following the release of the National Health and Hospitals Reform Commission Report in 2009, the Commission was disbanded. Since this time, successive governments have implemented and later disbanded bodies charged with reviewing, advising, and monitoring current health performance. This role has now been largely taken up by the Australian Institute of Health and Welfare and the Australian Commission on Safety and Quality in Health Care.

Similarly, successive governments in recent years have taken approaches to addressing primary healthcare needs across Australia. With an emphasis on regional general practice, chronic disease management, community mental health services, nurse primary care, and after hours medical services, Rudd's Labor Party government established Medicare Locals in 2010. These were disbanded by Abbott's Liberal-National Coalition government in 2015 to be replaced by Primary Health Networks (PHNs). The primary distinction between the Medicare Local approach and PHNs is that the role of the general practitioner was strengthened and there was an emphasis on coordinating and purchasing services rather than being a healthcare provider that competes with other local healthcare services. It is currently too early to assess the success in the change in approach in terms of patient outcomes, particularly in regional and rural area.

The Australian healthcare system is large and complex, approaching A$155 billion (US $117 billion) in cost and close to 10% of GDP. Despite the relatively favorable health outcomes and life expectancies of Australians, there will be much political and philosophical debate about the sustainability, efficiency, and equity of the system going forward. With pressures on the national budget due to a changing economy and an aging population, the future funding and subsidization of the health system will continue to be a source of discussion. Future governments will need to carefully consider the funding of healthcare as it takes up an increasing larger proportion of the overall national budget.

References

1. Smith L. *The Aboriginal Population of Australia*. Canberra, Australia: Australian National University Press; 1980.
2. Healy J, Sharman E, Lokuge B. Australia: health system review. *Health Systems in Transition*. 2006;8:9.
3. Parliament of Australia. About the Senate. Canberra, Australia. http://www.aph.gov.au/About_Parliament/Senate/About_the_Senate. Accessed July 2016.
4. Reserve Bank of Australia. Australian economic snapshot. http://www.rba.gov.au/snapshots/economy-snapshot/. Published November 2, 2016. Accessed July 2016.
5. Australian Bureau of Statistics. 3101.0—Australian demographic statistics. http://www.abs.gov.au/AUSSTATS/abs@.nsf/mf/3101.0. Published Dec. 2015. Accessed July 2016.
6. Australian Bureau of Statistics. 2001 Census of population and housing—00 1901 Australian snapshot. http://www.abs.gov.au/websitedbs/D3110124.nsf/24e5997b9bf2ef35ca2567fb00299c59/c4abd1fac53e3df5ca256bd8001883ec!OpenDocument. Accessed July 2016.
7. Australian Bureau of Statistics. 3235.0—population by age and sex, Australia, 2006. http://www.abs.gov.au/ausstats/abs@.nsf/Previousproducts/3235.0Main%20Features32006?opendocument&tabname=Summary&prodno=3235.0&issue=2006&num=&view=. Published July 24, 2007. Accessed July 2016.
8. Australian Bureau of Statistics. 3238.0—Estimates and projections, Aboriginal and Torres Strait Islander Australians, 2001 to 2026. http://www.abs.gov.au/ausstats/abs@.nsf/Products/C19A0C6E4794A3FACA257CC900143A3D?opendocument. Published April 30, 2014. Accessed July 2016,
9. Australian Bureau of Statistics. 2071.0—reflecting a nation: stories from the 2011 Census, 2012–2013. Canberra, Australia. http://www.abs.gov.au/ausstats/abs@.nsf/Lookup/2071.0main±features902012-2013. Published June 21, 2012. Accessed in July 2016.
10. Sax S. *A Strife of Interests*. Sydney, Australia: Allen & Unwin; 1984.
11. Australian Institute of Health and Welfare. *Australia's Health 2014*. Canberra, Australia: AIHW; 2014.
12. Australian Institute of Health and Welfare. Workforce. Health workforce. http://www.aihw.gov.au/workforce/. 2016. Accessed July 2016.
13. *Medical Technology in Australia: Key Facts and Figures 2013*. Occasional Paper Series. Sydney, Australia: Medical Technology Association of Australia; 2013. http://www.mtaa.org.au/docs/key-documents/mtaa-factbook-2013-final.pdf?sfvrsn=0. Accessed July 2016.
14. Australian Government. Productivity Commission. *Impacts of Advances in Medical Technology in Australia*. Research report. Melbourne, Australia: Productivity Commission; 2005.
15. National Health Performance Authority. http://www.nhpa.gov.au/internet/nhpa/publishing.nsf/Content/home-1. Published April 2016. Accessed in July 2016.
16. Australian Institute of Health and Welfare. *Health Expenditure Australia 2013–14*. Health and welfare expenditure series. Canberra, Australia: AIHW. 54(Cat. HWE 63); 2015.
17. Australian Taxation Office. Medicare levy. https://www.ato.gov.au/Individuals/Medicare-levy/. Accessed in July 2016.
18. Australian Government. Department of Health. Annual Medicare statistics. http://www.health.gov.au/internet/main/publishing.nsf/Content/Annual-Medicare-Statistics. Updated August 28, 2014. Accessed July 2016.
19. Australian Government. Department for Human Services. Annual Report 2014–15. https://www.humanservices.gov.au/corporate/annual-reports/annual-report-2014-15. Published June 25, 2015. Accessed July 2016.
20. Pharmaceuticals Benefits Scheme. About the PBS. http://www.pbs.gov.au/info/about-the-pbs. Updated July 2016. Accessed July 2016.
21. Australian Government. Department of Health. PBS Information Management Section Pharmaceutical Policy Branch. *Expenditure and prescriptions twelve months to 30 June 2014*. http://www.pbs.gov.au/statistics/2013-2014-files/expenditure-and-prescriptions-12-months-to-30-june-2014.pdf. Accessed July 2016.
22. Mossialos E, Wenzl M, Osborn R, Anderson C, eds. *International Profiles of Health Care Systems, 2014*. The Commonwealth Fund. http://www.commonwealthfund.org/~/media/files/publications/fund-report/2015/jan/1802_mossialos_intl_profiles_2014_v7.pdf. Published January 2015. Accessed July 2016.
23. Australian Government. *Economic Implications of an Ageing Australia*. Research Report. Canberra, Australia: Productivity Commission; 2005.
24. Australian Government. The Treasury. *2015 Intergenerational Report: Australia in 2055*. http://www.treasury.gov.au/PublicationsAndMedia/Publications/2015/2015-Intergenerational-Report. Published March 5, 2015. Accessed July 2016.
25. Australian Institute of Health and Welfare. *The Health and Welfare of Australia's Aboriginal and Torres Strait Islander Peoples 2015*. http://www.aihw.gov.au/WorkArea/DownloadAsset.aspx?id=60129551281. 2015. Accessed in July 2016.
26. World Health Organization. *Obesity: Preventing and Managing the Global Epidemic*. Report of a WHO Consultation. WHO Technical Report Series 894. Geneva, Switzerland: WHO; 2000.
27. Australian Institute of Health and Welfare. Overweight and obesity. http://www.aihw.gov.au/overweight-and-obesity/.2016. Accessed July 2016.
28. Obesity Australia. *No Time to Weight 2, Obesity: Its Impact on Australia and a Case for Action*. http://www.obesityaustralia.org/resources. Accessed July 2016.

29. Barr E, Magliano DJ, Zimmet PZ, et al. *The Australian Diabetes, Obesity and Lifestyle Study*. Melbourne, Australia: International Diabetes Institute; 2006.
30. Australian Institute of Health and Welfare. How many Australians have diabetes? http://www.aihw.gov.au/how-common-is-diabetes/. Accessed July 2016.
31. Australian Government. *Nation's Largest Diabetes Conversation*. Media release. Canberra, Australia: Minister for Health and Minister for Sport; April 15, 2015.
32. Australian Government. Department of Health. Budget 2016–17. *Public Hospitals— New Funding Arrangements*. Media release. http://www.health.gov.au/internet/budget/publishing.nsf/Content/CA4F2762AA873875CA257FA80010E5C8/$File/06_Hosp_PublicHospitals_3May16_PRINT_v2.pdf. Accessed July 2016.
33. Australian Government. National Health and Hospitals Reform Commission. http://www.health.gov.au/internet/nhhrc/publishing.nsf/Content/home-1. Accessed July 2016.

PART III
Challenges, Innovations, and Opportunities

CHAPTER 27 Small Country Innovations

CHAPTER 28 Health Systems in Crisis and Disaster

CHAPTER 29 Comparative Global Challenges and Opportunities

Chapter 27
Small Country Innovations

Sheyna Gifford and James A. Johnson

▸ Introduction

As discussed in the first chapter of this book, health systems around the world are challenged to focus on cost, quality, and access. Furthermore, there is a greater need than ever to also focus on innovation. As shown in Figure 1-2, "Innovation Diamond" in that chapter, innovation forms a strong linkage to cost, quality, and access. Effectiveness in all four of these dimensions is essential to health system sustainability. This was discussed further in Chapter 4 where critical success factors were elaborated on. A climate of innovation is seen as one such critical factor and a national integrated health information system being another. Likewise, a national political consensus and social agreement on the importance of at least some basic level of guaranteed health care is essential for health system sustainability.

A lot can be learned from a little country. When compared to the largest nations in the world—Russia, Canada, and the United States—in terms of square kilometers, Cuba, Costa Rica, Singapore, Taiwan, are indeed small. As you are about to discover, in terms of heath care systems, these countries are only comparatively and superficially diminutive. Cuba boasts the highest population in the region as well as the best healthcare outcomes.[1] Singapore is extremely large by population density yet has, by some accounts, the most efficient healthcare system in the world.[2,3] Taiwan has achieved tremendous strides in the use of technology to improve health care, far more so than almost any country in the world of any size, tracking every citizen's health from birth to death. The Netherlands introduced enviable cost containment policies that have kept critical drugs available and affordable, while Costa Rica, which has been centrally managing its health care for more than 70 years, is one of the few middle-income countries to have successfully implemented universal health coverage.[4–6] Each of these five small nations has a variety of healthcare needs and a distinct set of resources with which to attempt to meet them. Here we will examine how these countries leveraged the available resources to meet their needs. With this information in hand, we can then make valid and interesting comparisons between and among them and lay the foundations for meaningful comparisons to other systems discussed in this book.

To understand the factors affecting the efficiency and effectiveness of these healthcare systems, we'll begin by examining the single greatest resource, as well as the single greatest resource consumer in any nation: the people. In approaching populations as both a resource and a responsibility, we need to know not just how many people are in each country but also other factors that affect overall health, such as respective age clusters. That demographic feature leads to an important determinant of current and future health in any country: dependency ratios.[7] The ability of a population to economically support its healthcare system provides a sense of the current resource base available to fund these systems today and gives us a glimpse of the logistical challenges they may face in the future. To put the efficiency of these systems in perspective, we'll need to know how much they cost the nation and the individual user and what services can be expected for that investment. Coupled in terms of importance to how many people support and depend on a system is where those people are located in physical space. The geography of a nation tells us how available the known resources are to what percentage of the population. It also informs us about how far someone many have to travel to receive care.

While efficiency of a healthcare system can be understood by looking at the cost for population located over a certain area to receive a specific set of services, to understand system effectiveness, we need to integrate information about clinical outcome. Factors affecting clinical outcome include the numbers of doctors, and in some cases nurses and pharmacists, available to attend to a population. Naturally, once a patient has reached a point of care staffed by a provider, we want to know about how he or she fares. One of the measures that we use to determine system efficiency at this level is mortality rate. However, clinical outcome is about far more than the number of people who live and die in a country per year. How long people live before they die is a significant factor, as is information about the primary causes of death in a country. The morbidity caused by acute diseases like HIV/AIDS, chronic diseases like diabetes and heart disease, and lifestyle choices like smoking prior to and leading up to the end of life are all aspects of system effectiveness. Morbidity, or disease burden, reflects not only a system's ability to treat disease but also a nation's public health approach to disease mitigation and prevention. In order to put health outcomes into the proper perspective, in these chapters, numbers representing disease burdens will be presented along with examples of proactive attempts by national public health to decrease those burdens are essential.

In modern healthcare systems, effectiveness and efficiency are often linked to use of healthcare technology. We want to understand what technological options the populations of these five countries have in terms of getting their needs met. In this chapter, we will ask: How is health monitored? In terms of information management, are there electronic medical records? Is there eHealth available from every patient's home? Along the same lines, implementation of technology often reflects an individual country's level of development. Development comes with both benefits *and* costs. We'll want to know about the perks of more integrated systems—such as tracking chronic diseases and increased access—and also the downsides, including increased pollution and higher costs of health care.

As we're about to see, many of these smaller countries have expanded medical access to their citizens while, to some extent, containing costs. Some, like Taiwan, have succeeded by integrating and deploying new technologies nationwide. Others, like Costa Rica, have chosen physical expansion as the best route to reach their needier populations. One country—Singapore—allows the free market to drive costs down while improving quality, while another, Cuba, effectively bans competition in favor of standardization. By methods reflective of their unique social values and assets, all five of these nations have strived for and achieved some level of universal health coverage, demonstrating that, when it comes to medical systems, country size does not matter so much as national dedication to universal health coverage.

▸ Cuba

Economic disadvantage and political isolation have worked somewhat to Cuba's advantage in terms of health and health care. Cuba's historical and political circumstances drove the development of a unique, low-cost, high-efficiency, low-technology healthcare system. This system's current success is contingent on some shifting variables, including a large working-age population and very high doctor–patient ratio, which, in the future, may not always be available.

Population and Geography

In December 2014, the WHO listed Cuba's population as 11.3 million, making it the most populous country in the Caribbean.[8] One-third of all citizens of Caribbean nations and territories can be found in Cuba. This is likely a consequence of being the largest island in the region. Geographically, Cuba is the 106th largest country in the world, with more territory than Hungary, Ireland, Portugal, Austria, or Guatemala.[9] Additionally, Cuba has a higher population density than all of these countries except for Guatemala.[9] Cuba's island population, with roughly 101 people per square kilometer, is the 78th densest in the world.[9] As might be intuited, the highest population concentration is in and around Havana, which is home to 2.7 million people. The other 8.5 million are distributed over Cuba's 109,820 square kilometers. The population itself is fairly uniform. A majority are Caucasian (64%), with the remainder being mostly Mestizo. There is only one official language: Spanish.[14] This uniformity of culture and diffuse geographic distribution of the majority of Cuba's citizens heavily influenced the healthcare system that developed to serve them.

History of the System and Distribution of Stakeholders and Resources

The development of the modern Cuban medical system effectively began in 1959. From 1959 to 1970, in the postrevolutionary period, attempts to expand care to as much of the population as possible began. The number of rural hospitals was increased from 1 to 59, bringing millions of Cubans into close proximity to emergency health services for the first time. In 1970, health care became a constitutional right. In the 1970s and 1980s, emergency services were established in many communities, followed by medical training and primary care. Today, virtually every significantly inhabited area in Cuba has comprehensive health services ranging from obstetrics to dental care, provided by doctors and nurses who trained in that community, many of whom even live in the buildings where the care is provided.[11]

System Affordability, Healthcare Quality, and Health Outcomes

Owing to the vastly distributed network of doctors and clinics, Cuba's healthcare resources are extremely accessible. The next things we want to know are: how affordable is the system and how well does it perform? Performance is measured by health outcomes taken in the context of Cuba's economic means, its past and present health issues, infrastructure, and social commitment to healthcare services. To address the question of system affordability, we must first examine the cost of health care, Cuba's average personal income, and what percentage of the population is working.

Statistics regarding the average annual income in Cuba vary substantially. Average in-country income in 2014 was close to US $18,000 according to the World Health Organization (WHO) and closer to $10,000 per year according to the Central Intelligence Agency.[12,13] Whatever the exact number may be, two things are known. First, as shown in **FIGURE 27-1**, Cuba's GDP per capita is significantly lower than the average for developing nations in the region; and second, in spite of this, owing to a comparatively large tax base and low cost of care—$1,828 per person per year—Cuba's working population is currently able to pay for the medical care for system dependents: full pension for those who are over the age of retirement (rising from 65 years of age to 70 in 2017), and for those under 20.[8,9]

Via tax-based governmental financing, all basic health services are prepaid.[14] By expending 8.8% of its GDP directly on health care, Cuba furnishes preventive care, testing, and medications to hospitalized patients (when such medications are available) at no direct cost to the individual.[8,15] Health adjuncts like hearing aids and glasses, drugs, and devices such as crutches and wheelchairs are available for purchase at government-subsidized stores for those who can afford to purchase them; these items are provided for free to low-income citizens.[15]

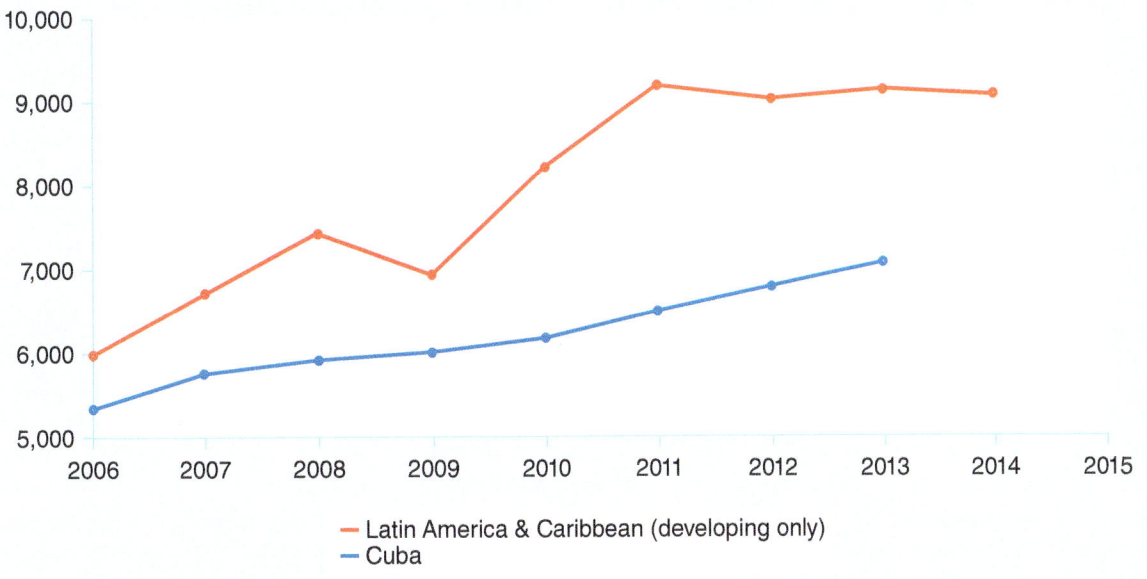

FIGURE 27-1 Plot of Cuba vs. Latin America and the Caribbean

Data from The World Bank. GDP per capita (current US$). Plot of Cuba vs. Latin America and the Caribbean. http://data.worldbank.org/indicator/NY.GDP.PCAP.CD/countries/xj-CU?display=graph. 2016.

In spite of making comparatively modest expenditures on their system, health in Cuba has been on an upward trajectory for the last half century. In 1962, they were the first country in the world to eliminate polio.[16] In 1996, Cuba eliminated measles, a feat that many developed nations have been unable to accomplish.[16(p818)] Life expectancy has been increasing steadily over the past decade. A child born today in Cuba can expect to live to the age of 79, on average slightly longer than the child born in the United States and 5 years longer than the Caribbean child.[17]

A major contributor to these outcomes is the omnipresence of free or highly subsidized preventive and routine health maintenance services, particularly prenatal care and childhood care. In 2015, Approximately 95% of women who gave birth in Cuba received prenatal care.[18] Standard childhood vaccination rates were at 98%.[34] Maternal mortality rate was down to 38 per 100,000 births. While that level of maternal mortality was higher than many developed nations, it was substantially lower than average for the Caribbean, which was 43.1 deaths per 100,000 live births, and was a far superior outcome than could be seen on any of the neighboring islands of Jamaica (110 per 100,000), the Dominican Republic (150 per 100,000), or Haiti (350 per 100,000).[20,21] By contrast, in the United States, maternal mortality had increased from 27 to 28 per 100,000 between 2010 and 2015.[22]

Cuba's countrywide healthcare system focuses on prevention and early detection. It includes sustained national efforts to tightly control chronic diseases like diabetes and aggressively treat acquired diseases like cancer. In 2009, Cuba's National Cancer Control Unit set a goal of cutting mortality from all forms of cancer by 15% in 2015.[23] As a result of these efforts, Cuba's ranking in health care has risen dramatically. In the WHO's most recent ranking of countries by healthcare performance (2000), Cuba came in 36th in the world in terms of healthcare outcomes, and 39th in terms of system performance.[24]

How does a Caribbean island, where the average income is less than US $19,000 per year, manage to provide better health care (by certain measures) than Germany and better life expectancy than the United States?[25] Again, the answer, according to multiple sources, is prevention and attention. By way of prevention, Cuba emphasizes bringing free preventive care directly to the population where they live: literally to their door. Everyone under treatment by a physician, which is virtually everyone in the country, receives at least one blood pressure screening annually.[18] If patients do not appear for appointments, for whatever reason, Cuban medical staff make house calls. In some part of the country, house calls are scheduled as part of normal practice procedures. This level of attention paid to each patient is only possible because, at 6.7 physicians per 1,000 people, Cuba has far and away the highest doctor–patient ratio of the region, and, in fact, has more doctors per person than any other country in the world except for Monaco and Qatar.[26] With only 11.7 million people to oversee, Cuba's 76,000 doctors can afford to make a house call to every patient on their roster once a year.[27]

This right-to-your-door approach is emblematic of Cuba's policies, which for reasons of efficacy and cost savings, focus largely on community-level health behavior and illness prevention. Providers organize their patients into health risk levels.[27] A healthy person with no risks is a Risk Level 1; a smoker is a Level 2; with chronic but stable diseases Level 3; and so on.[27(p297)] Treatment is planned and executed accordingly. Those with chronic diseases are seen more often.

As of 2015, of the 48 Millennium Goal measures, Cuba had already met the following: universal primary education, promotion of gender equality, and reduction in child mortality. It was on track to meet several more of these goal, including eradication of hunger and poverty, improvements in mental health, combating HIV/AIDS and malaria, and developing global partnerships to promote and increase health coverage.

Apropos of HIV, owing to Cuba's strict policies of testing and treatment, it boasts one of the lowest prevalences of HIV in the world. Among those aged 15–45, the average prevalence of HIV is 0.1%–0.2%.[30,31] More than 95% of the affected population with advanced HIV is on antiretroviral therapy, as shown in **FIGURE 27-2** this makes Cuba's ART program far and away one of the most successful programs in the world.[32]

Initially, these outstanding outcomes were achieved via a draconian system of cloistering HIV-positive members of society in sanatoriums.[33] In the mid-1990s, after lobbying from patients and their families, policies were altered, and HIV-positive members of society were permitted to return to their jobs, homes, and families under the strict care of local physicians who were given supplemental training in how to monitor their health.[34]

One health issue that Cuba has yet to successfully address is its national tobacco-use crisis. Smoking is still allowed inside cafés, restaurants, government facilities, offices, and workplaces.[35] Due to severe funding limitations, smoking cessation products including nicotine replacement therapy (gum and patches) and cessation-assisting pharmaceuticals

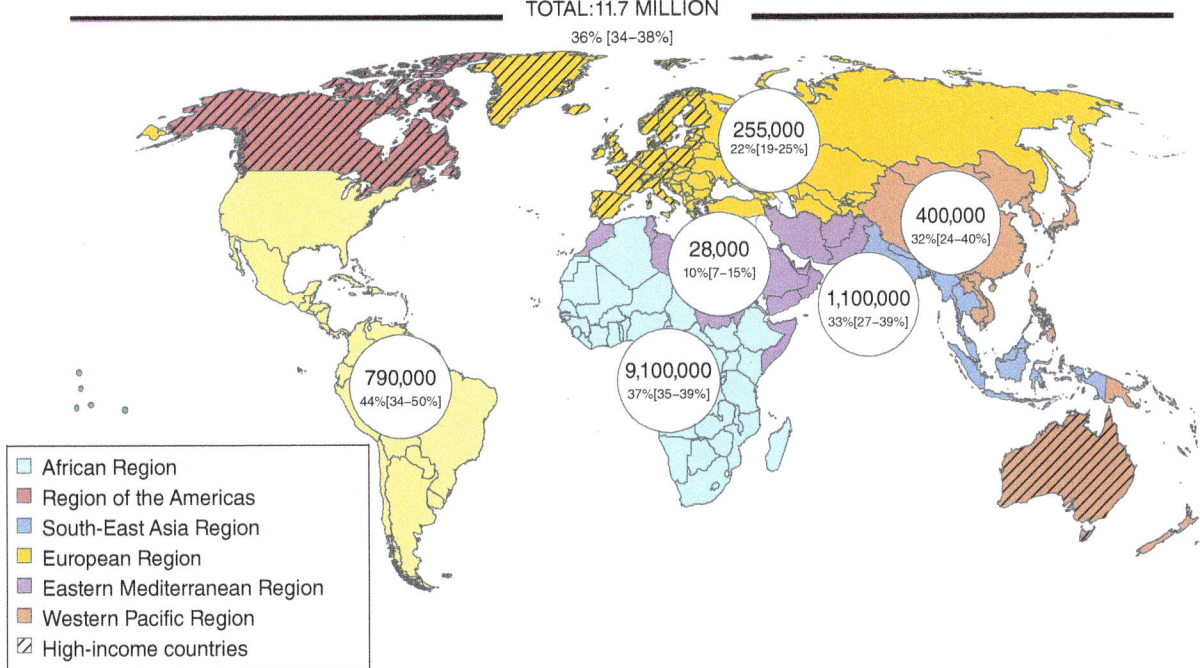

FIGURE 27-2 Number of People Receiving ART and Percentage Living with HIV

Reproduced from World Health Organization. Number of people receiving ART and percentage of all people living with HIV receiving ART in low- and middle-income countries overall and by WHO region, 2013. http://www.who.int/hiv/data/artmap2014.png. n.d. Copyright 2013.

are not available. Promotion of tobacco products to all ages in all mediums is legal and common, as is free sample distribution of tobacco products at public events. Tobacco companies are not required by law to contribute to antismoking campaigns. One-quarter of the men in Cuba are daily tobacco users, as are nearly 20% of the woman and 17% of children aged 13–15.[35] As a result of having the third highest rate of smoking in the world, in the recent past, lung cancer accounted for up to 30% of all deaths in Cuba.[36]

Technology and the Future of Health Care in Cuba

It is important to note that Cuba has not achieved excellent overall health and health care by means of increasing technology. In Cuba, pencil and paper charting is common; CT scanners are uncommon; and medical students have limited, dialup Internet access.[27] This reliance on paper charts and avoidance of expensive test by no means implies that cutting edge treatments are unavailable. On the contrary, Cuba has developed a reputation for excellence in regenerative medicine and is a major center of stem-cell-related clinical trials.[37] Bone marrow transplants are done on an outpatient basis at 10% of the cost for the same procedure in the United States, where these same types of patients often spend weeks in the hospital.[37] This approach arises not from evidence-based medicine so much as from financial necessity. However, this minimalist, outpatient approach often has excellent outcomes; some of which, at least in the case of bone marrow transplant, are superior to the expensive inpatient routes common in more technologically heavy medical systems. The same can be said of Cuba's approach to pharmaceuticals. In order to provide affordable treatments for rare diseases, Cuban health care often turns to natural remedies. In the case of hemophilia, a disease where the blood cannot properly clot, Cuba uses components from scorpion toxin and pig milk as an anti-inflammatory and clotting factor replacement, respectively, which cost on the order of tens of U.S. dollars per treatment. Clotting factor replacement in the United States can exceed $50,000 per year.[38]

The recent end of the U.S. embargo against Cuba may well change the levels of available medical technology. Doubtlessly, development across the board will increase in the coming years. Hand-in-hand with that technological progress, Cuba may face worsening health outcomes. Increases in the number of vehicles and the amount of industry will no doubt impact the environment. As with many rapidly developing nations, Cuba already faces a future in which increased levels of carbon dioxide production and other associated industrial pollutants are a growing concern. Until recently, Cuba was below average in terms of greenhouse gas emissions in the Caribbean. Then, as Cuba grew to resemble an upper income country, its pollution levels rose. In 2008, well before the end of the embargo, Cuba's carbon dioxide emissions had already risen to average pollution levels allowable locally.[39] Then, in 2010, it quickly surpassed them. Cuba's ability to mitigate pollution-related diseases and to bring its smoking standards in alignment with the rest of the developed world will be tested in the years to come.

Conclusion

The Lancet recently noted that, "Cuba's health system has been able to solve some issues that other countries have not."[27] Truly, Cuba's current healthcare system is seemingly well adjusted, well organized, and well attuned to the general needs of its current population. Universal primary care, a high doctor–patient ratio, and excellent education of both doctors and lay people have reduced the burden of chronic diseases and increased compliance, lowering costs, and expanding access without investing heavily in technology.

However, it is important to bear in mind that populations are never static and that policies often change when leadership does. Health in Cuba began to improve after the 1959 revolution. The same government has been in power ever since. This situation has brought consistency of healthcare policy, which in turn has improved health continuously and dramatically at the cost of personal liberty. Outcomes have also been partly achieved by recruiting medical students from Latin America and Africa.[16] Lured by free education, those newly trained doctors often remain in Cuba. This improves Cuba's doctor-patient ratio but drains other countries of their physician populations. To compensate, as of 2015, Cuba had placed 34,000 doctors in 52 poorer countries.[16] It should be noted that Cuban doctors both at home and abroad are required to work for the government and receive government-dictated pay, with no real possibility of advancement or employment in the private sector.[40]

Lastly, although Cuba attempts to make up for medical brain drain by sending doctors abroad, there is another drain that might be more difficult to ameliorate: population drain. Cuba's population is the fastest aging in the Caribbean.[41] The bulk of the working population in Cuba will reach retirement age by 2020. Within a generation, the 30% of the population now under age 30 in Cuba will end up supporting the remainder of the population. This is the source of Cuba's low potential support ratio: 5.2% as of 2015.[9] Other, currently poorer Caribbean nations have far greater potential to support their young and old populations: Haiti, 13.31%, Dominican Republic 12.78%, and Barbados 12.78%.[42] Possibly in anticipation of this epoch of a smaller tax base, Cuba has already begun closing hospitals and cutting services. In 2011, Cuba shut down 54 hospitals and shuttered at least 400 clinics, resulting in public health expenditure savings in the realm of 7.7%.[43] On the other hand, with the end of the U.S. embargo and the reopening of political relations, Cuba may be able to make up somewhat for the shrinking tax base with profit from U.S. medical tourism.[44] Whatever the future holds, with a fraction of the United States' GDP, Cuba currently claims the title of one of the most efficient and effective healthcare systems in the world. Whether this trend can be sustained in the face of a growing economy, expanding industry, and shifting population dynamics, as shown in **FIGURE 27-3**, remains to be seen.

▶ Singapore

Fifty years ago, Singapore was a poor nation with even poorer health outcomes. Today, it is among the wealthiest nations in the world.[45] Sudden wealth afforded Singaporeans the opportunity to create whatever healthcare system they wanted. The one that they eventually established ranks sixth in the world in health outcomes and reflects the circumstances that brought them economic success: open competition and constant innovation. However, as we are about to see, its true costs to the country as a whole and to its citizens as individuals are also on the rise.

Population and Geography

At 697 square kilometers, Singapore is the physically smallest nation that we will be discussing in this chapter. In the spectrum of all of the nations in the world, it is the 192nd smallest out of 257 countries (including the Holy See in Italy).[45] It can reasonably be thought of as a large city-state—one with a long history of occupancy by a European power.

When Singapore gained independence from Great Britain in 1959, it had a population of 2 million. As of 2014, the island nation boasted a population of up to 5.6 million. At more than 8,000 people per square kilometer, Singapore is the most

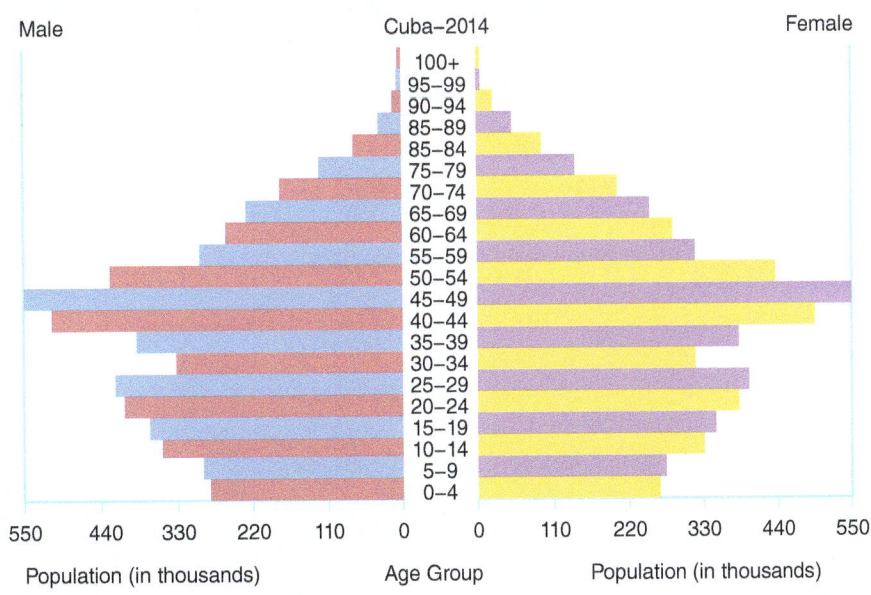

FIGURE 27-3 Cuba's Population Pyramid as of 2014
Reproduced from Central Intelligence Agency. The World Factbook, 2016: Cuba. https://www.cia.gov/library/publications/the-world-factbook/geos/cu.html

densely populated nation in our set. Singapore is also the most culturally diverse, hosting four official languages—Mandarin (36.3%), English (29.8%), Malay (11.9%), and Tamil (4.4%)—and four major religions (Buddhism, Islam, Taoism, and Christianity).[45,46,*] This diversity and rapid population growth has both supported and complicated the Singaporean healthcare system. More than anything else, it has provided a large base of working age people to financially support it, who, as of yet, have not begun to draw extensively upon its resources.

History of the System and Distribution of Stakeholders and Resources

Singapore has been an independent nation for less than 60 years. When it achieved independence, the nation's first priority was not to establish an excellent healthcare system but rather to safeguard its newfound freedom by virtue of a strong defense program, a strong economy, and international recognition.[47(p18)] Though some initial attention was given to improving housing, sanitation, and vaccination, health care as a national priority was delayed until 1983.[47(p18)] At that point, the Singaporean economy was deemed highly successful, and the same government that had been leading the country since independence finally turned its full attention to constructing a new healthcare system. The new Singaporean National Health Plan (NHP) provided no free services to any person who could pay for their own care, though, in solidarity with the former British-style system, it continued to fund free or low-cost services for the poor, the young, and those beyond the age of retirement.[47(p22)]

In 2016, the ratio of workers contributing to the healthcare system versus system dependents was quite favorable. In contrast to many Western countries, Singapore's population is predominantly young.[46] With less than 10% of the population over the age of 65, Singapore's total dependency ratio was 37% in 2016—meaning that for every 1 person who needed to be supported by social services, there were about 3 working-age people contributing support.[45]

Geography significantly contributes to the efficiency and cost-effectiveness of the Singaporean healthcare system. While countries like Cuba and Costa Rica must find ways to deliver care over broad and sometimes sparsely populated regions, the entire nation of Singapore is readily and rapidly accessible. A tightly regulated system of trains and buses over 171 kilometers connects all populated parts of the country and allows patients to easily travel from their homes to doctors, hospitals, and pharmacies offering the best arrangement of desired services. With roughly 2 doctors per 1,000 people, access to a physician in Singapore is substantially better than it is in neighboring China, and it is on par with other Western Pacific nations such as Japan and the Republic of Korea.[48]

System Affordability, Healthcare Quality, and Health Outcomes

As of 2013, Singapore was expending approximately 4.6% of its GDP on health care.[49] No other developed nation in the world spends so little at the national level.[50] In the same year every country in Europe spent between 5.1% and 10%, and the United States spent more than 13% of its GDP on health care.[51]

This grand achievement must be taken in context, however. Cost containment has been achieved by dividing financial responsibility for health care in Singapore three ways. The most heavily responsible party consists of the subscribers themselves. Working citizens in Singapore are legally required to contribute to their current and future health by maintaining health savings accounts.[49] These tax-exempt funds are then available to pay for medical needs as they arise. Corporations operating within the country's borders contribute to these funds in a tax-exempt way as well.[52]

This system of MediSave accounts (MSA) has functioned as the first-line source of economic support for Singaporean health care since 1984. Today, out-of-pocket expenditure pays for approximately 57% of the cost of the system.[53] The average Singaporean can expect to pay around US $2,500 per year out of pocket for their health care. This cost is generally lower than in the other developed nations in the western Pacific (see TABLE 27-1) and certainly below the out-of-pocket costs of health care in the United States (approximately $3,800), Canada (approximately US $5,700), and some parts of Europe. Of course, it is substantially higher than what we observed in Cuba, where the government generally bares the cost of healthcare delivery.[54] One of the most common uses for MSA money is in fact to buy health insurance. Many kinds are available, including the public option, government-sponsored MediShield: a low-cost, catastrophic coverage type that kicks in when MSA funds have been depleted.

In Singapore, the government's contribution largely comes into play for those who cannot pay into the system due to age, disability, or sudden disaster. When MSA funds have run out and MediShield has been depleted, the government steps in to assist with Medifund: a pool of money set aside to bail out Singaporeans in dire financial straits for medical reasons. Lastly, for the elderly and chronically ill, the government provides a long-term, low-cost insurance scheme called Eldershield. However, Eldershield, too, comes with premiums. Subscribers are expected to pay in cash or with MSA funds.[47(p24)] In this way, the healthcare system in Singapore is a combination of pre- and post-paid publicly and privately funded system.

Because the system is largely privately funded, it is highly user driven. Subscribers can choose to take their MSA money to any provider and to pay, or not, for any given service or arrangement of services. As a

TABLE 27-1 Western Pacific: Per Capita Total Expenditure on Health at Average Exchange Rate (U.S. $) 2013

Country	Data
Vietnam	14
Lao People's Democratic Republic	32
Vanuatu	43
Cambodia	76
Tonga	87
Papua New Guinea	94
Solomon Islands	100
Tuvalu	102
Philippines	122
Kiribati	156
Fiji	189
Mongolia	244
Samoa	271
China	367
Micronesia (Federated States of)	407
Malaysia	423
Cook Islands	526
Marshall Islands	630
Nauru	718
Brunel Darussalam	974
Palau	1,008
Niue	1,260
Republic of Korea	1,880
Singapore	2,507

TABLE 27-1 Western Pacific: Per Capita Total Expenditure on Health at Average Exchange Rate (U.S. $) 2013 (continued)

Country	Data
Japan	3,966
New Zealand	4,063
Australia	6,110

Data from World Health Organization. Per capita total expenditure on health at average exchange rate (US$): 2013. http://gamapserver.who.int/gho/interactive_charts/health_financing/atlas.html. Accessed August 20, 2015.

result, most primary care services (80%) are provided by private practitioners, who compete for clients and affordability with government-run clinics. Private hospitals, too, are available, but because they are paying for their own care, when it comes to hospitalizations, Singaporeans typically choose admission to lower cost government-run hospitals. Once admitted, they have a choice of accommodations that reflect their desire and ability to pay, ranging from open wards to single-bed rooms.[55] Those choosing the open wards will be given significant financial assistance by the government, to the tune of an 80% subsidy. Those opting for privacy bear the full cost of their stay.[55] A similar range of user-paid, government-assisted service options exist when it comes to chronic care, nursing homes, home care, and day care for the elderly.[55] When it comes to medications, rather than regulate drug prices or availability, the government publishes drug costs and lists of drugs it has deemed essential. Essential drugs are government subsidized.[55]

The health outcomes in this user-driven, government-aided-as-needed system are outstanding. Life expectancy is the third best in the world at 84.68 years.[45] Expectant women have continuous access to some of the world's most skilled routine and emergency care. As a result, infant mortality ratios and maternal mortality ratios are extremely low: 1.7 per 1,000 live births and 10 per 100,000 live births in 2015, respectively.[56,57]

Unlike infant and maternal mortality, smoking is an insufficiently controlled issue in Singapore. Though smoking is not as prevalent overall as it is in Cuba, 25% of men in Singapore are daily smokers. The result is a high proportion of smoking-related cancers and death. Death from lung, bronchial, or tracheal cancer is substantially more common in Singapore than death from any other kind of cancer in men, including prostate cancer. Attempts to stem the tide of smoking and smoking-related illness include national bans on cigarette advertising and a steep tobacco tax, up to 75% of retail cost. Graphics photographs of the effects of smoking have been placed on cigarette packaging.[58] Nicotine replacement therapy is listed and priced as a necessary drug.[59]

In spite of the restriction, stigmatization, and cost, smoking is on the rise in Singapore, especially among the youth.[60] Singapore's National Smoking Control Programme, which has been attempting to police the situation since 1984, has launched a multimedia campaign called the "28-day countdown," complete with online registration, a hashtag, and a way to post to social media that you have quit, in the hopes of gaining ground on this issue in the most affected demographic.[61]

Since 1992 another separate public health campaign has been underway in Singapore: the battle against obesity, a problem first identified by the military. Military service in Singapore is mandatory. In 1991, so many overweight recruits reported for duty that the Singaporean government was forced to take action.[62] Since then, the National Healthy Lifestyle Program has taken steps to quell the obesity epidemic in Singapore's youth. Every school in the country was equipped with indoor and outdoor sport facilities. School food was improved; cooks were educated about healthy food choices; fried options were limited in quantity and frequency. As a result, from 1993 to 2006, the percentage of students passing the national physical fitness test rose from approximately 60% to approximately 80%.[62] Over the same period, student obesity dropped into the single digits, but some grade levels still suffer from up to 16% obesity.[63]

Technology and the Future of Health Care in Singapore

Home to the world's busiest port (by tonnage), Singapore is also home to world-market-level industries in health care and healthcare technology.[64] In stark contrast to Cuba, Singapore not only embraces every possible form of healthcare technology but also the government has made an active effort to drive its creation. Open competition between hospitals, care groups, and individual providers is encouraged. Consumer choice about where to spend the funds from their private savings accounts is widespread and aided by publicly published market rates for services, devices, and pharmaceuticals.[45,65] This system generates a tremendous profit for individuals and private hospitals, to the tune of US $15 billion in 2015.[66]

Singapore hosts its own e-Health Service Development Programme (HSDP), which was established by the Health Ministry with the specific objective of developing new health services and medical capabilities. It does so by funding three types of pilot projects: (1) cutting edge medical technology that has yet to be evaluated in the market; (2) well-established, advanced treatments, which, due to cost, are offered on a subsidized basis only to those patients who are most likely to benefit from them; and (3) significant improvements in the current management capability for certain diseases.[55]

In keeping with its diverse culture, Singapore publicly funds and provides e-Health services in multiple languages. A National EHR system was introduced in 2011 and is used by all primary, secondary, and tertiary care facilities. Billing and supply chain management is electronic, as is laboratory, pathology, pharmacology, and radiology information. Interestingly, Singapore does not have an automated vaccine alert system, but it does have electronic medical appointment reminders, mobile telehealth, and a national policy regarding the use of social media to promote public health. Singapore is one of the few countries in the world (5%) that can claim to have a strategy for using social media in this way.[67]

On the whole, Singapore views technology as an indispensable adjunct to the provision of optimal health care. This was never more apparent than during the SARS outbreak of 2003. At the time of the outbreak, accurate diagnostic testing for SARS was lacking; the only option for containing the outbreak was to engender immediate and complete cooperation from healthcare practitioners as well as the public.[68] Nearly overnight, the Singaporean government set up an electronic SARS surveillance and control system that, once in place, was completely successful in preventing any cases of SARS from being important into or exported from the country.[69] The linchpin of the national SARS surveillance system was the Internet-based SARSWeb. Via SARSWeb, every relevant institution in Singapore had access to real-time information about all current and suspected SARS cases, locations of home quarantines, and the hospital records of patients who had been recently treated at any healthcare facility in the country for any reason. Via SARS web, all probable or even possible cases were identified and isolated. While public health efforts were coordinated by SARSWeb, the public itself was being educated and kept up to date with a newly launched SARS TV Channel that continuously ran information, updates, and relevant educational programs.[70] The result of these efforts was an effective outbreak response that is believed to have reduced that number of in-country cases by many hundreds, and the probably spread to other locations by many thousands.[70] Other countries, such as neighboring Taiwan, were not as proactive nor comprehensive in their use of technology-based public health measures, and were not nearly as successful in containing the outbreak.[71]

Conclusion

A few special circumstances supported Singapore's meteoric rise in terms of economy and health standards. First, the same political party has been in power in Singapore for fifty years, virtually since their independence.[72] As was the case in Cuba, this effective one-party system in Singapore provided an ideal political climate for the unopposed and uninterrupted pursuit of various proactive healthcare policies over the last half-century.[73] Another precondition for Singapore's healthcare success was this: within 20 years of independence, Singapore attained tremendous financial success. The massive influx of wealth into the country facilitated the achievement of its stated principle needs: national security, job creation, housing, and education. The focus was then switched to health care, where it has remained ever since.[73(p112)] Importantly, the new economic circumstances dictated the terms of the healthcare system that was ultimately created, which involves a fairly high, but currently sustainable, out-of-pocket cost to the user. Lastly, when the healthcare system was established, it was created as a mirror to Singapore's free market economy. The same economic forces that had brought the country its financial success were brought to bear on health care: active competition, transparency, and choice.

While these factors have performed well so far, they will have to be flexible if they are to continue to serve Singapore's health system as they have in the recent past. While wealth has brought good short-term health to Singaporeans, high socioeconomic status has a downside—or, at least, a broadside.[74] In Singapore, economic gain and weight gain have gone hand-in-hand. With the availability and affordability of sweetened beverages and snacks and processed meat on the rise in the region, type 2 diabetes has dramatically increased in prevalence across Southeast Asia during the past three decades in all age and demographic groups.[75] As the wealthiest nation in the region, Singapore has seen a five-fold increase in diabetes in the last 40 years.[76] This trend is seen even in disadvantaged segments of Singapore's population and persists in spite of all the aforementioned public health endeavors, including technology-heavy efforts that have recruited tens of thousands of Singaporeans to start using diet and exercise trackers on smartphones.[63,77]

Wealth is not the only harbinger of an increased chronic disease burden; time contributes its fair share as well. Singapore is home to one of the fastest-aging populations in Asia. As the population ages, the rate of chronic diseases increases commensurately, as does the frequency of healthcare system utilization.[78] Although today's population over the age of 65 is only 10%, by the 2030s, Singapore's aged population will double to nearly 20%.[79]

There are three general approaches to supporting an aging population while controlling costs: add working-age people into the system; increase the age of retirement; and alter available services. In contrast to some European countries, the population in Singapore is still growing, but only a little. Fertility rates are low at around 1.2 children born per woman.[79] In addition to creating a new population base, Singapore could reasonably count on inheriting one. This wealthy nation with good services is an attractive local for immigrants. Additionally, since the 1990s, Singapore's government has been deliberately and successfully encouraging certain foreign nationals to relocate to its "global city" in the hopes of growing its intellectual economy.[80] However, the system has a few snags. Three types of people are granted immigration rights: foreign students, foreign talent, and foreign workers. While the first two are given substantial benefits upon arrival, the last group, foreign workers, are forbidden by law from marrying locals, subject to required health screenings, and severely limited in their ability to obtain housing and permanent residency.[80] In spite of this strict regulation, immigration—specifically Singaporean opposition to it—has become a hot-button political topic. In recent elections, locals opposing the influx of foreigners made their voices heard by withdrawing their support of the long-standing ruling political party.[80] As a result, immigration has declined, and population growth in Singapore has slowed to the lowest in a decade: 1.2%.[81]

With limited options in terms of increasing the population, and with no desire to reduce services, Singapore has turned to increasing the age of retirement as the third and final means of balancing the healthcare books. In the 1990s, the legal age of retirement in Singapore was 60. In 1999, the age of retirement was raised to 62; in 2012, it became 65. It will be increasing to 67 in 2017. The Singaporean Ministry of Social and Family Development has even put forth the notion of doing away with retirement age entirely.[82] So, as Singaporeans age, they will be expected to continue to work and to pay out of pocket for the ever-increasing cost of their health care.[52]

Taiwan

More than 20 years after its first democratic presidential election, Taiwan's political status remains contentious.[83,84] However, no one debates that over the last 50 years, this island of 36,188 square kilometers (13,972 square miles) has given rise to a national health system that tops the charts for quality and affordability.[85] Today, Taiwan's technology-heavy National Health Insurance (NHI) program covers all citizens at all levels of care, from first-world dentistry to traditional Chinese medicine.[86]

Population and Geography

With 23.4 million in-country residents as of 2015, Taiwan is by far the most heavily populated country in our set and is, in fact, more heavily populated than the continent of Australia.[84] The 157th country in the world in terms of size, Taiwan is an island in the Philippine Sea, southeast of mainland China, with about as much land area as the North American states of Maryland and Delaware combined, but with 3.5 times the population.[84,87,88] To boot, two-thirds of Taiwan is not especially inhabitable. The entire interior of the island consists of either tall mountains or high plateaus. With more than 23 million people inhabiting 37% of the land area of an already small nation, it becomes obvious why Taiwan is the second most densely populated country in the world.[89]

Although less diverse than Singapore, Taiwan has a substantial subpopulation of ethnic Chinese, millions of whom fled to the island in the wake of the 1949 Communist victory in mainland China. The local population lived under either Chinese or Japanese rule until the year 2000, when the military government peacefully ceded power to Taiwan's first democratic party.

History of the System and Distribution of Stakeholders and Resources

A generation before it became a democracy, the Taiwanese legislature began work on the development of what eventually become Taiwan's national healthcare system. At the end of World War II, the morbidity and mortality in Taiwan was typical of an undeveloped nation: infant mortality was high (45 per 1,000), and the main killer was infectious disease.[90] In a pattern typical of the relationship between wealth and health, between 1951 and 2006 as the Gross National Product per capita in Taiwan increased from US $145 to $16,471 per year, infant mortality dropped to 5 per

1,000, and the leading causes of death in the country became chronic illnesses. These achievements were the result not only of economic gain, but also of a deliberate two-part development process that took place at the national level.

In the first phase, lasting from 1971 to 1995, universal health care was enacted. Although 24 years may seem like a long period of time to implement a policy, Taiwan's initial state was one of rampant malaria, low vaccination rates, few hospitals, and very few doctors per capita. In 1970 when universal health care began, Taiwan had less than 0.5 doctors per 1,000 people. Those few doctors were heavily concentrated in big cities. As we know, due to geographical limitations, the Taiwanese people are largely restricted to the coastline and a few dozen major cities and countries that ring the island.[91] However, with 22% of the land dedicated to agricultural activities, there remained a significant inland population whose medical needs were unmet. As soon as country-wide vaccination had been achieved and each of Taiwan's 21 counties had at least one public hospital, the government turned its attention to training and redistributing doctors and increasing the over effectiveness of the system.[90]

In 1995, once coverage for the entire population was in place, the second phase for national health care began. In the phase, Taiwanese government made a conscious effort to increase the number of medical schools. Between 1957 and 2010, the physician density in Taiwan rose from 0.54 physicians per 1,000 population to 1.67 per 1,000. By way of comparison, Taiwan's neighbors Korea, China, and Japan have 2.14, 1.49, and 2.30 physicians per 1,000 population, respectively; the United States has 2.45 per 1,000.[92]

After increasing the number of physicians to serve the population, the NHI expanded the equality of the system by subtly encouraging doctors to redistribute themselves to more rural areas. Rather than offering direct incentives such as higher pay or forcibly reassigning physicians to needy areas, the NHI simply set reimbursement rates at clinics higher than at hospitals. Taiwanese physicians practicing in hospitals, most of which are urban, must split their salaries with the facilities in which they practice. Clinic physicians, who own their practices and who are the main providers of care in medically underserved areas, may keep the full amount that they are reimbursed for their services. Also, as is true in most countries, the cost of living is far lower outside the city limits. The NHI made their reimbursements to physicians approximately 30% taxable, regardless of location. So physicians operating in less expensive areas not only receive more money for their services, they also get to keep more of it in the end.[86] Lastly, to tackle both the physician shortage and the maldistribution, the Taiwanese Department of Health established physician training group practice centers (GPCs) in underserved areas. Physicians who choose to work in GPCs keep 80% of the profits.[90]

These maneuvers managed to increase the availability of physicians to the entire population. Between March 1, 1995, the day that National Health Insurance become compulsory, and today, Taiwan's mandatory universal health insurance scheme has raised the health standards in Taiwan to historically high levels at a fraction of the cost of other healthcare systems.

System Affordability, Healthcare Quality, and Health Outcomes

In terms of financing, Taiwan's system of universal health care lies somewhere in between Singapore's and Cuba's. Like Cuba, Taiwan centrally funds its system—in this case, via a payroll tax. Like Singapore, it also integrates cost sharing.[93] However, the cost-sharing aspect of the system in Taiwan is much more moderate than in Singapore. Rather than having individual subscribers put money away and spend it as needed, Taiwan's single-payer scheme contracts physicians at a fixed rate and sets costs uniformly across the system. Unlike Singapore, there is no open market for healthcare goods and services. Users in Taiwan pay low set rates for services, which are known in advance thanks to the government-mandated fee schedule. The schedule lists prices for all reimbursable treatments and diagnostic services. At the national level, a certain amount of funding is set aside every year for each kind of drug, treatment, and service. This allows the government to contract the correct number of provider services, prepay for goods, and buy in bulk. Hence, in Taiwan, economics and health care do meet in the sense that, as more people use a drug, procedure, or service, the cost of that drug, procedure, or service drops.[93]

The net result of this prepaid approach is an extremely affordable system. In 2010, Taiwan spent 6.2% of its GDP on health care.[94] In that same year, the United Kingdom spent 8.3%, Germany spent 10.7%, and the United States spent 17.7% of its GDP on health care.[95] Additionally, Taiwan's system supports an extremely wide range of services. Reimbursable services include all hospital services, primary care services, dental care, traditional Chinese medicine, and others. Unlike Cuba, where primary care is emphasized, 65.0% of Taiwan's recent national budget for health went to hospital services, while 22.0% was allocated to primary care services. The remainder of

Taiwan's US $11 billion budget that year was divvied up between Chinese medicine, dentistry, home care, day care for the mentally ill, dialysis, and vision care. Rather than have hospitals or individual practices compete for their share of the budget, Taiwan distributes funds to regions. This encourages the hospitals and clinics within each region to cooperate in order to treat patients with maximum efficiency at minimal cost.[96]

In terms of the cost of the system as a whole and who pays for it, out-of-pocket expenditures by users covers a little over 35% of the cost of maintaining the system. The residual is covered by the payroll tax, taxes on extra personal income (professional fees, investment dividends, rental income, etc.), and financial investments made by the government on behalf of the system. In exchange for their out-of-pocket expenditures, which vary by ability to pay, users of the system can take their insurance cards to any provider in any location for any reason without preapproval. Taiwanese who cannot pay for insurance due to poverty, illness, or age are given government subsidies to cover the cost of their premiums.[97] The cost to the users of the system is fairly constant. Unlike Singapore, where different levels of services can be purchased, Taiwan's single-payer premiums generally afford all citizens the same level of health care.

To date, national satisfaction with the care that the NHI system provides is in the 80% range. This reported high satisfaction with the system has a lot to do with its quality and availability. Diversity of services is great, and there are few if any restrictions placed upon the users of the system in terms of when, where, and from whom they receive their care. The NHI and other government interventions have improved the standard of living such that average life expectancy in Taiwan is very high: 83.25 years at birth for women and 76.69 years for men.[98,99] Maternal mortality is low at 12.6 per 100,000.[100] Infant mortality is low for the region, and falling, at 4.4 per 1,000 live births.[101] By contrast, neighboring China's infant mortality rate is three times as high.

While Taiwanese life expectancy is already high, it would likely be even higher if the country did not feature a large number of smokers. At the beginning of the millennium, nearly half the adult male population consumed an average of 17 cigarettes per day, making smoking as serious of an issue in Taiwan as it is in Singapore and Cuba.[102] Since 2001, half the population of Taiwan either smokes or was exposed to secondhand smoke at home.[102] As a direct result, cancer is one of the leading preventable causes of death in Taiwan. Between smoking and liver disease, Taiwan has some of the highest incidence and prevalence rates of cancer in the world (incidence 244 per 100,000, mortality 120 per 100,000, age-adjusted).[103] Next to smoking, the other leading preventable cause of death in Taiwan is diabetes.

The Taiwanese health service has been intervening on both fronts with some positive results. In 2015, the prevalence of diabetes was nearly 10% with impaired glucose tolerance, or prediabetes, measured in just over 15.00% of the population.[104] Emphasizing standards such as tight glucose control, blood pressure less than 130/80 (considered normal), and lowering lipid profiles, Taiwan lowered the proportion of premature mortality due to diabetes almost 7% between 2002 and 2012 (36.88% to 29.99%), and kept the percentage of their population with diabetes at near year 2000 levels.[105,106] In terms of smoking cessation, Taiwan passed the Tobacco Hazards Prevention Act, which banned smoking in indoor public places and many workplaces. A major media advertising campaign for Smoke-Free Environments in 2007 brought national smoking level from 17.00% in all genders and ages down to 10.00% in 2010.[107,108] To measure the effectiveness of this and other campaigns, Taiwan conducts frequent population surveys via an online and telephone-based Adult Smoking Behavior Surveillance System (ASBS). The ASBS indicates that positive gains seem to have reversed, and as of 2013, it has shown that in some places 47.00% of men and 4.00% of women still smoke.[109]

Technology and the Future of Health Care in Taiwan

The smoking epidemic notwithstanding, Taiwan has accomplished excellent outcomes with low expenditure on the national and personal levels. This has been accomplished primarily by setting prices for health-related goods and services at the national level and prepaying for these, in bulk where possible. The rest of the system efficiency is generally attributed to low levels of litigation, nonexistence of marketing expenses (since there is only one system, there is no need to advertise it), and, finally, an incredibly powerful information technology (IT) system.[110] IT provides cost savings in several ways. One is improved efficiency. Information on everything from public health emergencies to system utilization to daily expenditures on drugs in every facility in the Taiwan is readily available.[97] The rapid availability of information on patients leads to decreased administrative costs, or what is referred to in the industry as the medical loss ratio. That loss ratio can be as high as US $0.20

for every $1 spent by insurers in the United States.[111] By contrast, administrative costs were 1% of the total NHI expenditures in 2015. This feat of information tracking and utilization is only possible because every one of Taiwan's 23 million citizens has a unique identification number, to which their individual healthcare outcomes are associated; which the government uses en masse to understand the health behavior and for public health planning purposes.[100]

One public health issue that the country of Taiwan has begun using this data to try and plan its way around is a serious pollution problem. The exquisite availability of data has allowed the Taiwanese government to pinpoint the expected age that air-pollution-induced allergic rhinitis begins in school children (10% by preschool age), to backtrack to the level of pollutants in the areas of those preschools, and to recommend that car traffic in those areas be reduced.[112] Similar analyses of health data have turned up positive correlations between air pollutants and deaths in people of retirement age living in Taiwanese cities, as well as increased incidents of respiratory diseases and hospital admissions.[113]

Conclusion

Since the beginning of Taiwan's move toward universal health care in the 1950s, quality has soared, costs have been regulated, resources have been better distributed, all-cause mortality has shifted from infectious disease to chronic disease like diabetes, and the birth rate has plummeted. In the last 50 years, the rate of live births in Taiwan has dropped from 50 per 1,000 to 9 per 1,000.[90] Of course, more children are surviving into adulthood and more adults are living longer, healthier lives. However, as is true with many highly developed and technologically advanced societies, Taiwan is facing a significant population shortage. Due to a birth rate that only barely exceeds the death rate, and relatively low levels of immigration, the population growth rate is only 0.23%.[84] Unless the fertility or immigration rates are altered, in 20 years Taiwan is likely to experience significant labor shortages and declining tax revenues, both of which would threaten in the well-being of the healthcare system and the aging population that it supports.[84] For the moment at least, the population percentage headed for retirement is balanced by the population percentage slated to enter the workforce.[84] This allows for some breathing room in which Taiwan can contemplate its other major challenges: resource allocation, physician satisfaction, and environmental catastrophe.

As opposed to Singapore's mostly free market system but similar to Cuba's, Taiwan's state-run approach dictates physicians' levels of pay. Since the implementation of the NHI program, Taiwanese physicians have seen a decrease in their annual pay. At least one study suggests that Taiwanese physicians value their professional dignity more highly than they do economic incentives; news reports regarding malpractice suits and fraud cases have increasingly marred doctors' professional images in this country, leading to adverse changes in the medical profession.[114,115] In the future, low pay may collude with decreased doctor satisfaction to reverse the hard-earned, positive trend in physician density. Meanwhile, physician allocation, while much improved since the 1950s, is still not perfected. Studies show that in spite of overall improvement, geographical disparity persists, leading to a resource imbalance that still favors North Taiwan.[116]

Lastly, unlike Singapore, Taiwan's neighbor, trading partner, and fellow high-population-density country, Taiwan has an abundance of open land, and thus it is contending with the ongoing effects that climate change is bringing to its more mountainous regions. Some 22% of the country's land is dedicated to agriculture, most of which resides on steep slopes. As much as Taiwan's healthcare future rests on finding ways to sustain its healthcare system in the wake of a waning population, its food supply hinges upon winning an ongoing battle with soil erosion and finding sustainable solutions for soil and water conservation.[89]

▶ The Netherlands

The Netherlands is one of a small handful of European countries that follows a Bismarck model of statutory health insurance, also known as social insurance.[117] In contrast to Taiwan's NHI model, funded by the central government, in the Bismarck scheme, three parties bear the burden of maintaining mandatory, universal health coverage for their respective populations: corporate entities, private insurance companies, and individual users.[118] In this way, the Netherlands has created a unique model of managed competition, wherein basic services are guaranteed by the government, yet private companies contract with private citizens as to where and how those services will be utilized.

Population and Geography

The Netherlands, a constitutional monarchy that has been variously occupied by Spain, France, and Germany, is currently home to approximately 17 million people.[119] The population is fairly uniform, with just over 75% being of Dutch extraction and other European, and the remainder consists of immigrant groups, largely from the Middle East and from the Caribbean, where the Dutch occupied and still assist in the administration of various islands. See **FIGURE 27-4** for other population characteristics. The main region of the Netherlands itself is around 41,500 square kilometers, approximately 34,000 square kilometers of which is land.[119] The abundance of waterways is one of the reasons the Netherlands has such a successful shipping industry. Its powerful network of ports supports the exportation of locally sourced agricultural and petroleum resources, which have made this small country one of the largest economies in Europe. The ensuing trade surplus has been instrumental in funding the establishment of the Netherlands' system of universal health care.

History of the System and Distribution of Stakeholders and Resources

The Netherlands began its journey toward establishing universal health care in 1904. After four decades of various unsuccessful political attempts, in 1941 the Netherlands enacted compulsory health insurance for lower income and middle-income citizens.[120] High-income individuals were not required to buy private insurance, though most did. Until 2005, the central government took responsibility only for some amount of cost containment and for ensuring that physicians were licensed, that all persons had access to essential medical services, and that no citizen was ever brought to financial arrears by medical expenses, not even by mental or physical disability.

This state of affairs was successful in that 98.5% of the population purchased coverage.[120] However, ongoing issues with efficiency and cost containment lead to a new system being established in 2006. At that point, the Netherlands migrated to its current mandatory, regulated, private health insurance system with competing schemes.[117] Every person working in the Netherlands must subscribe to the private insurer of their choice. Insurers must accept all applicants—exclusion for preconditions is prohibited—and provide an essential service package regulated by the government. In return, all citizens pay premiums. In addition, all employers pay into a national medical fund. If a certain patient is high risk, the government compensates their insurer for the extra costs using that national fund; hence the name of this pool of money, the Risk Equalization Fund (REF).

Like Taiwan, the vast majority of healthcare system stakeholders in the Netherlands are located in cities. Also similar to Taiwan, agricultural activities occupy large portions of the geography; but, due to high levels of mechanization, only 2% of the population is able to farm just over 50% of the country's land.[119] With more than 90% of the population concentrated in urban areas like Amsterdam and Rotterdam, it stands to reason that the majority of healthcare resources would be concentrated there as well. That is true, but regardless of the physician concentration and location, every Dutch citizen is registered with

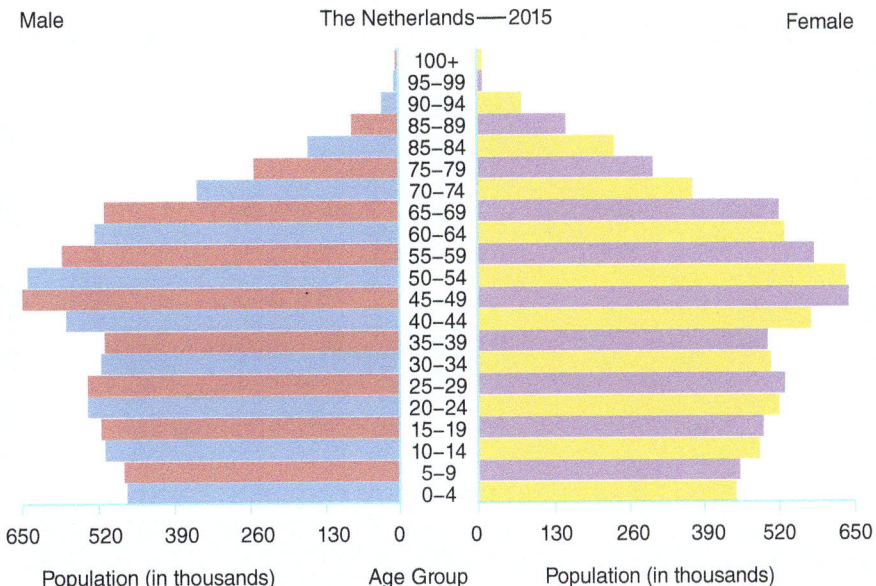

FIGURE 27-4 The Population Pyramid for the Netherlands, Demonstrating How the Bulk of the Population Is at or Near Retirement Age

Reproduced from Central Intelligence Agency. The World Factbook, 2016: Netherlands. https://www.cia.gov/library/publications/the-world-factbook/geos/nl.html.

a general practitioner (GP).[121] In order to ensure adequate numbers of GPs, the central government measured the near-term population increase and recruited physicians to ensure physician density of approximately 3 per 1,000 people.[122] This is projected to be sufficient for each personal living in each Dutch municipality to have adequate access to a GP, but, as we will discuss later, increased service demands due to population aging may decrease the functional capacity of physicians in the Netherlands.[121]

System Affordability, Healthcare Quality, and Health Outcomes

In the Netherlands, demand for healthcare services is high. In 2015 the Netherlands spent almost 13% of its GDP on health care.[123] While that is less than is spent in the United States (which expends 17% of its GDP on health care), as shown in **FIGURE 27-5**, the amount spent by the Netherlands at the national level is more than any other country in Europe, and by far the most of any country in our set of small countries.

The system is not only expensive on the national level but also on the level of the individual user. In general, out-of-pocket costs of health care in northern Europe are among the highest anywhere. In terms of out-of-pocket costs to the subscriber, the Netherlands in particular has one of the top five most expensive systems in the world. This is partially due to mandatory health insurance premiums. Though rates are set at a level considered affordable to the local community, adult subscribers pay an average of US $1,600 per year in premiums for the most basic level of health insurance.[124] For any health care beyond basic services—including dental care, vision care, physical therapy, elective procedures, and alternative medicine—additional insurance may be purchased, or costs can be paid out of pocket.[120] To help cover these additional costs, the majority of the households in the Netherlands receive US $2,200 in government healthcare subsidies. Even with these subsidies and corporate contributions, the cost of health care in the Netherlands has been steadily on the rise.[125] Users can expect to pay approximately $6,145 per year for their health care, including basic insurance premiums, before applying the government subsidy.

While the healthcare system in the Netherlands is very expensive, especially when compared to countries like Singapore, that cost must be viewed in the context of what the country can bear. The Netherlands' healthcare system is supported by a sizable economy, which, thanks to trade surpluses and immense agricultural exports, is the sixth largest in Europe.[119] As an oil-rich nation, the Netherlands is in the top 30 for purchasing power—its ability to buy goods and services, including health care. Additionally, the Netherlands supports a far smaller population than most of the other countries that exceed it in terms of purchasing power.[119]

On the other hand, the average per capita income in the Netherlands is substantially lower than it is in Singapore—US $50,000 versus $85,000—while the cost of health care is substantially higher and

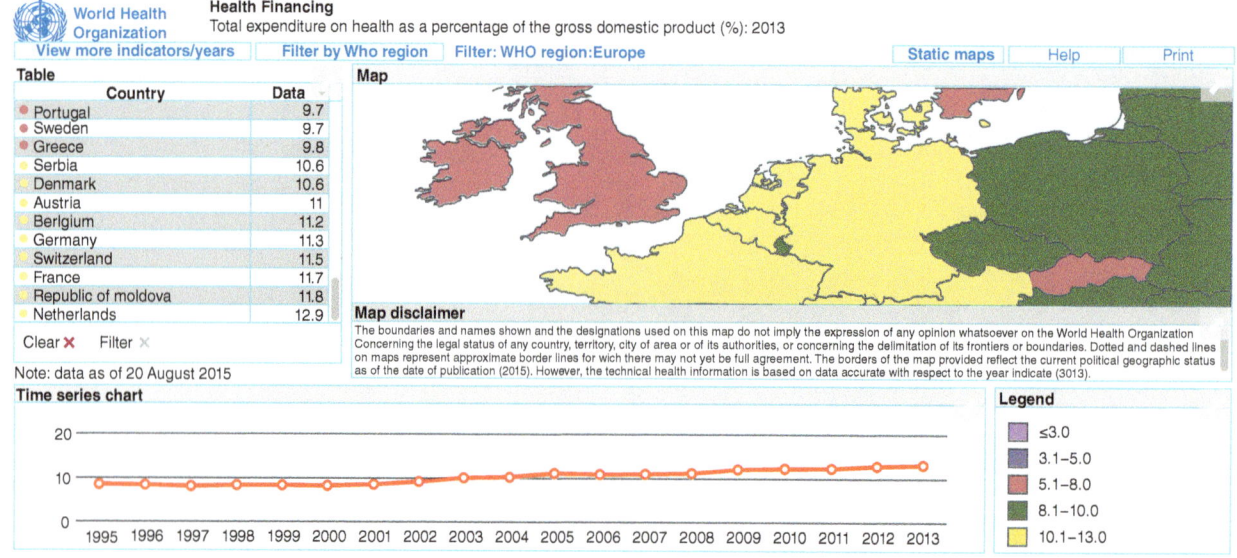

FIGURE 27-5 Total Expenditure on Health as a Percentage of GDP of the Netherlands

Reproduced from World Health Organization. Total expenditure on health as a percentage of the gross domestic product (%): 2014. The Netherlands. http://gamapserver.who.int/gho/interactive_charts/health_financing/atlas.html. Copyright 2014.

climbing steadily.[119] This trend has led to serious self-examination of priorities and a systematic restructuring of the country's services.[126] In recent years, the Netherlands has focused its efforts on controlling costs and improving service to citizens with chronic healthcare problems.[117]

In reaction to the rising cost of their postpaid healthcare system, the Netherlands has instituted cost-containment measures on some goods and services, especially pharmaceuticals. These measures are based on drug interchangability.[5] Similar in principle to Singapore's "essential drugs" list, the preferred drug list in the Netherlands emphasizes use of generics to lower costs to the user and the system.[127] By 2013, this policy had saved the country almost a billion euros.[128]

As is true in Cuba, primary care services are seen as a source of cost savings and are therefore readily available to all residents in the Netherlands—even undocumented immigrants living in the country.[129] Though doctor-patient interviews are short by U.S. standards—10 minutes in the Netherlands compared to 17 in the United States—Dutch physicians do more listening than talking and tend to socialize more with their patients.[130] This socialization is somewhat necessary, for, as we will see shortly, GPs work very closely with their chronically ill patients to create individualized healthcare plans that are the bases of disease management.

In return for their substantial financial investment, as of 2015 the Dutch have an impressive life expectancy of 81.23 years.[119] Maternal mortality is on par with the rest of Europe at 6 deaths per 100,000 live births.[20] Infant mortality, on the other hand, is at 3.6 infant deaths per 100,000 live births in the Netherlands. This is substantially higher in than many other European countries, but still below the European Union average of 4 per 1,000.[101] Some scholars attribute the higher rate of infant mortality in the Netherlands to large immigrant groups, who suffer from more congenital abnormalities and have more perinatal illnesses, respectively, than the native Dutch.[131] Ethnic minorities also have a higher incidence of smoking and smoking-related illnesses than the native population.

Smoking in the Netherlands is closely linked to socioeconomic status, with higher prevalence of use in more disadvantaged socioeconomic groups across the board.[132] Smoking as a social phenomenon was on the downturn in the Netherlands for many years, even through the 2008 global financial crisis when smoking markedly increased in hard-hit regions like Ireland and Spain.[132] On the public health level, Dutch smokers desirous of quitting received free behavioral counseling through their basic medicine plans. However, until recently, pharmacologic smoking-cessation aids such as the nicotine patch were not covered by insurance and were expensive to obtain.[133] Then, in 2011, as the positive gains made against smoking to reverse, the Dutch government embarked on a national reimbursement policy for smoking cessation. Any smoker who signed up to quit received counseling, group support, and free pharmacologic aids. This program ran for one year, was very successful, and was reintroduced in 2013 in an attempt to curb the current national smoking rate, which is up to 16% for men and 31% for women.[134] With the exception of designated smoking rooms typically reserved for cannabis consumption, smoking is banned in Dutch workplaces in the public and private sector, including hospitality.[135,136] Compliance is high, but not universal.[135] Smoking bans have served to notably reduce smoking during pregnancy in the Netherlands, from 13% down to 6.3%.[137]

Because of the high rate of smoking, especially for Dutch women, mortality from lung cancer is projected to be an ongoing issue in northern Europe through at least 2050.[134] Skin cancer, too, is projected to rise precipitously due to locally high levels of UV radiation and the population's fair complexion.[138] Due to public health measures, mortality from other forms of cancer, including prostate and colon cancer, are waning and years of survival are increasing.[139] Since the introduction of regular breast cancer screening in the Netherlands in the 1980s, morbidity and mortality have rapidly declined.[140] However, it should be noted that, partially due to the aging population and partially due to continual issues of smoking and sun exposure, the incidence of cancer diagnosis was noted to be increasing by 5% a year, and it is predicted to continue to do so.[138,139] This has important consequences for the healthcare system in terms of cost and resource utilization and therefore to the country as a whole.

Healthcare systems, even universal ones, vary in terms of how the outcomes of individual subscribers are followed. Unlike in Taiwan, where every citizen has a number, the Netherlands is divided into healthcare regions. These reflect the political system in the country, which is subdivided into provincial and regional governments.[141] Each Dutch region is its own health district, responsible for the health of the citizens within that region. How this plays out in practice is that preventive care services, like pap smears, take place when the regional system invites the women of the pertinent age group—in this case, women ages 30–60—living in the region to receive their preventive care.[142] While the schedule of preventive services is regulated at the national level, invitations to care are offered regionally, and services are rendered locally. Locally oriented management has also been promoted by the government as the preferred method for dealing with chronic diseases such as diabetes, the prevalence of which, at 5.5%, is the lowest in our set of small countries.[143]

As a cost-saving measure, private insurers in the Netherlands are keen to migrate care for diabetes away from hospitals and toward GPs.[144] GPs, in turn, are financially incentivized to detect diabetes and to treat it by making a plan with each patient and following through. In this scheme, responsibility for improvements and outcomes ultimately lies with the individual patient. As mentioned previously, the current standard of care for diabetes and other chronic diseases in the Netherlands is for each patient to have a personalized, written treatment plan; the patient can use it to monitor the progress and adequacy of her or his own care.[144]

Technology and the Future of HealthCare in the Netherlands

The Netherlands takes a conservative approach to integrating new technologies wholesale into their healthcare system. Prior to integration, the technology in question undergoes multiple assessments: first for medical effectiveness, then for cost effectiveness and clinical acceptability.[145] The assessment and integration of breast cancer screening is a paradigm exemplar of this effect. When mammography was first shown to be a potentially useful tool for breast cancer screening in the United States, the Netherlands ran its own series of clinical trials to prove that there was not only cost savings associated with the procedure but also life savings —not only in years, but also in quality adjusted life years. When these were proven, the public was then asked to comment on making mammography a free, standard procedure in which all women in the Netherlands ages 50–69 would be invited to participate. After public debate ensued, political debate began. Before breast cancer screening was fully integrated in 1993, the Minister of Health had to personally guarantee that the quality of the screenings would be high, that access would be made equally available and free to all, and that, while invitations would be issued to all eligible women, freedom of choice would be respected.[145]

While the Netherlands may be initially cautious in their adoption of healthcare policies and technologies, once vetted, policies are generally well supported with practical tools for implementation and continual utilization, typically in the form of complementary technology.

The success of the interchangeable pharmaceutical policy is just one example. After deciding to pursue cost containment via interchanging drugs whenever possible, the Netherlands distributed software that actively encourages healthcare providers to prescribe less costly, generic drug equivalents.[146] In addition, the Netherlands introduced financial incentives for pharmacists. Paying the dispensers of the drugs based on performance induced many in the field to dispense lower cost prescriptions whenever possible. These systems of prescriber encouragement and pharmacist incentivization are only possible thanks to special tracking software. When it comes to most services, from preventive care like pap smears to expensive options like assisted reproduction, the Netherlands takes a similar approach to healthcare technology: conducting assessments before, during, and after integration to ensure quality, equivalency, and cost effectiveness.[147] Often, in the wake of these extensive assessments, resource utilization is optimized while quality is maintained.[148]

Rather than investing in healthcare information technology as a country, as Singapore and Taiwan have, the Netherlands sees innovation as the purview of private companies and individuals. Industries likely to generate helpful products in fields such as pharmaceuticals or information technology are given warm welcomes and economic incentives. Tools that promote self-management are especially encouraged. These fit into the government's policy of personal responsibility for disease management—vis-à-vis individual treatment plans—as opposed to collective organization and central management for the prevention of disease, as was seen in Cuba.[144]

Naturally, as individuals are held responsible for their health and health care is rendered at the local level, e-health has been slow in coming to the Netherlands. Though the nation is digitally mature, and Dutch hospitals all subscribe to a common electronic medical record system, not many patients have home access to their own medical data.[149] In 2015, to further their goals of personal, and personalized, care for chronic diseases, the Dutch government announced that before 2020 the majority of chronic disease patients will be able to monitor their health status via online access to their medical data, and that recipients of home care will have access to video consultations at any time of day or night.[150]

The other side of the coin in a system such as this one, in which individual users are empowered to manage their own health, is that users sometimes demand that certain recourses be made available, irrespective of the level of evidence for—or even the most basic utility of—the resource in question. Such was the case in the

Netherlands when it came to the da Vinci machine, a high-end robotic-assisted surgical device. Though the clinical outcomes and cost-effectiveness of this device were uncertain at the time of implementation, enthusiasm by system stakeholders rapidly resulted in integration of this costly device into an otherwise fairly conservative system.[151] Apart from a few high-end technologies like the da Vinci, the Dutch are more likely to embrace assessment tools that provide a picture of system performance and pinpoint areas for improvement than they are to buy cutting-edge equipment. However, in 2006 the Netherlands became one of the first countries to begin using such a tool. The Dutch Health Care Performance Report (DHCPR) gives subscribers and the government an up-to-date tool for holding the system accountable and for planning how to better utilize healthcare resources in the future.[152]

Surveys using the DHCPR and private health insurance data have indicated that judicious utilization of physical resources will be critical to the future of health care in the Netherlands.[153] Ecological resource management will be important as well. Much of the country not actively engaged in agriculture is heavily industrialized. Due to the industrialization and a profusion of waterways, the Netherlands contends with significant issues of water pollution, industrial and agricultural runoff, and air pollution from vehicles and the resulting acid rain.[119] In an attempt to improve their circumstances, the Netherlands has ratified dozens of international ecological agreements. Efforts are complicated by the fact that the country lies at the mouth of three major European rivers, and pollution from everywhere along the Rhine, the Maas, and the Scheide arrives on the Netherlands' doorstep, effecting the health of the population.

Conclusion

The Netherlands needs to be especially careful to protect what population it has. As with many developed countries, in spite of immigration, the overall population is in decline. From nearly 17 million in 2016, the Netherlands population is projected to stabilize through 2030 and then fall to just under 16 million in 2060.[154] Although most of the countries in our set face somewhat similar scenarios, in the Netherlands, the dependency ratio is already 53.3%.[119] As a result, planning for the aging population has been an important aspect of the Netherlands' political agenda since 1996, when the Dutch population forecast was published and demonstrated that the population of older cohorts was set to increase dramatically through 2020.[155,156] Healthcare costs were projected to rise concomitantly and have done so, but aging alone cannot explain the overall cost increases that have occurred in areas ranging from CT scan utilization to use of expensive drugs in the last years of life.[153,157] As aging alone cannot fully explain cost increases, potential other explanations—including staff training, litigation aversion, and increased utilization due to availability—must be recognized and mitigated appropriately if the Netherlands is going to successfully maintain a high standard of care in the face of increasing demands and a waning economic base supporting its health system.[127]

▶ Costa Rica

Although slightly smaller than the state of West Virginia in the United States, the country of Costa Rica has made tremendous strides toward reaching its goals of universal health coverage.[158] Popular social support, continuous support at the highest government levels, and ongoing national investment have ensured that these rights were enacted into policies and that the policies have been applied uniformly throughout the system for the last 40 years.[159] The results are some of the highest standards of living, education, and health care, not only in the region but in all of the Americas.

Population and Geography

At 4.8 million people, Costa Rica has the smallest population in our group of small countries and has the largest geography.[158] Though not as heavily urbanized as Singapore, Taiwan, or the Netherlands, approximately 78% of the Costa Rican population resides in cities, and that number is increasing at nearly 3% per year.[158] Roughly one-quarter of the country's residents already reside in the capital of San José. The remainder of the largely Caucasian and mestizo population is distributed over 51,100 square kilometers and is actively engaged in agricultural, animal husbandry, and tourism. The age distribution in Costa Rica is roughly divided into 40-40-20: working age people, those near or just below working age, and the elderly. This distribution makes Costa Rica's total dependency ratio approximately 45%, which is more favorable than that of the Netherlands, and makes the potential support ratio of 7.7% the highest of any country in this set

History of the System and Distribution of Stakeholders and Resources

Efforts toward universal health coverage for this geographically widely distributed population began almost 70 years ago in the form of universalization of social security for all workers in the country. The legal right of all residents to health care was codified in 1973 by the Costa Rican General Law of Health, which grants all subscribers an extensive set of right as patients. These rights include access to information about the education that their doctors have received, complete disclosure of risks and benefits inherent to each treatment and procedure, treatment with dignity irrespective of personal traits (including ability to pay for care), emergency care, access to copies of all of one's own personal health records, and confidentiality of healthcare information; and lastly, to receive a detailed bill explaining all expenses incurred.[160]

Achieving these rights on a practical level required a number of changes, including transferring ownership of all hospitals—many of which had been established by private businesses to ensure the health of the population of agricultural workers—to the national social security administration and, similar to the Netherlands, the establishment of district healthcare regions.[161] Within these regions, certain needs had to be functionally met before primary and emergency healthcare services could be established. For example, well into the 1980s, the southern-most healthcare region in Costa Rica, Heutar Atlantic, which shares a border with Panama, had few paved roads.[162] Paving those roads allowed the influx of not only electricity, sanitation, and medical services but also economic improvement via increases in tourism. In this way, a few investments in essential infrastructure made a generation ago have led to significant improvements in health in Costa Rica, where administration of health care to the entire population is severely complicated by the fact that the majority of the country's land is forested, and the remaining 48% is largely agricultural.[158]

These geographic facts exacerbate the issue of physician density. Of all the countries we have looked at in these chapters, Costa Rica has the lowest ratio of physicians to population, approximately 1 per 1,000, as well as a low-per-person number of hospital beds.[122] To compensate for the relative paucity of physicians, Costa Rica has established an extensive network of pharmacies and clinics. Costa Rican pharmacists can issue medications for routine issues, from birth control to migraine headaches and high cholesterol; Costa Rica's own public website encourages people to go straight to their neighborhood pharmacy for any nonemergency health issues.[163] To counterbalance the lack of hospitals, particularly in rural areas, Costa Rica created 105 health regions, subdivided into areas of 3,500–4,000 residents. Each subdivision has its own health clinic called an EBAIS, an acronym meaning Basic Equipment for Integrated Health Assistance. The purpose of these approximately 1,000 EBAIS clinics, each of which is staffed with one doctor, one nurse, and one technician, is to administer initial care.[164] If more comprehensive care is needed—extensive emergency services, simple surgery, outpatient consultations, or diagnostics—the patient is referred to a regional level major clinic or hospital.[160] From those clinics, if still more comprehensive care is needed, the patient is sent to one of seven national hospitals. This system affords the appropriate level of care for patients while avoiding an excess of unused or poorly allocated resources. **FIGURE 27-6** provide useful data pertaining to the health system.

System Affordability, Healthcare Quality, and Health Outcomes

While the cost of this system of health care in Costa Rica is on the high end of our set—approximately 10% of GDP—that level of expenditure is on par with the other countries in that region in the Americas.[123] Additionally, these costs have been held relatively steady over the last few years, likely through a combination of drug price regulation, local health center utilization, and a system that favors visits with pharmacists rather than with physicians for routine healthcare needs. These cost-saving measures notwithstanding, historically, the Costa Rican government has intentionally spent around 20% of its annual GDP on health care and education.[165] Putting that cost into perspective, Costa Rica, with an annual GDP of US $50 billion, expends an average of $1,311 per person per year on health services.[166] This covers 70% of the cost of the postpaid system.

The rest of the system is supported either by employees or by the system users themselves, largely in the form of payments to the Caja Costarricense de Seguro Social (Caja), Costa Rica's social security system. For approximately 11% of an individual's personal income, the Caja fully covers primary care, preventive care, and major medical incidents, including hospitalizations.[167] Those who cannot pay for insurance due to socioeconomic circumstances can register to receive state-insured Caja benefits.[168] As is true in many countries, private medical insurance is available, though only through the government-owned National Health Insurance (INS). For US $60–$130 per month, the INS covers 80%–100% of the cost of prescriptions, dental and vision care, checkups, hospitalizations, and surgery.[169] Interestingly, though health care is universally offered and available, it is not legally required. Although all those working in the country pay into the

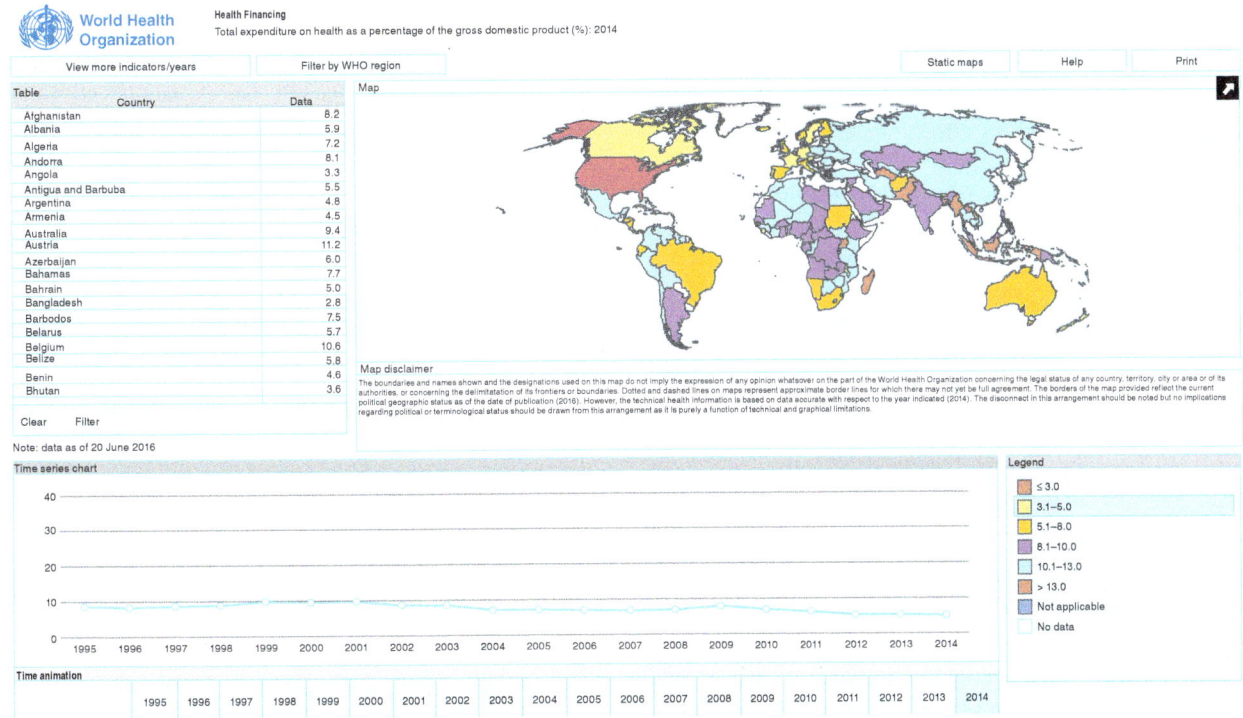

FIGURE 27-6 Expenditures on Health, the Americas
Reproduced from World Health Organization. Total expenditure on health as a percentage of the gross domestic product (%): 2014. The Americas. http://gamapserver.who.int/gho/interactive_charts/health_financing/atlas.html. Copyright 2014.

system via social security, individuals may choose to not participate in either the one public or one private health insurance scheme. Such persons pay cash for services and receive their care via the local pharmacies or the emergency departments. Unlike in Singapore, where different levels of service may be purchased, by law all persons must receive equal care.

In return for their income-based monthly investments, the people of Costa Rica enjoy a life expectancy on par with the United States and Cuba at 78.4 years.[158] Though that is not as high as it is in Singapore or the Netherlands, it is among the highest in the Americas. Maternal deaths per live births is high for our set—40 per 100,000—but very low for Central America, where maternal mortality is more typically between 92 and 120 per 100,000.[20] Infant deaths in Costa Rica are also the highest in our set at approximately 8.5 per 1,000 live births.[101] Again, this figure must be taken in context with region and GDP. Infant mortality in the most developed countries in the Americas—the United States and Canada—are 7 per 1,000 and 4.7 per 1,000, respectively.[101] At approximately US $9,400 per year in earnings, Costa Rica shares a GDP bracket with its neighbor, Mexico, where GDP per capita is approximately 8,400 and the infant mortality is 24 per 1,000 live births.[170]

Although mosquito control and other public health measures have decreased the incidence and prevalence of many infectious and parasitic diseases, owing to Costa Rica's extensive ecology and to its close proximity to other nations with worse standards of health, acute infectious diseases continue to plague the country. Dengue, for example, is an issue in urban areas due to importation by travelers from other regions.[171] Hepatitis A vaccination is recommended for travelers headed to Costa Rica as is typhoid. Visitors to more rural regions must be vigilant for Chagas disease.

As for chronic disease, in contrast to Singapore, Taiwan, and most countries in the Americas, at 8.5%, diabetes prevalence is low.[143] This figure stands out against the large number of patients on renal replacement therapy (RRT). RRT is often the end product of poorly controlled diabetes causing chronic kidney disease (CKD). In countries with the technology to support it, RRT comes in two forms: dialysis and renal transplant. Compared to its neighbors, Costa Rica has a low prevalence of CKD. This is likely due to superior primary health care in Costa Rica and to the high availability of dialysis, which prolongs the lives of CKD patients. In accordance with the needs of the population and its technological level of development, Costa Rica provides RRT to all those in the system who require the treatment to survive.[164] This has resulted in an influx of patients from poorer countries where dialysis is not available, and from wealthier countries like the United States, where the treatment is available but expensive.

The second form of renal replacement therapy is also notably affordable and accessible in Costa Rica. In 2002, 56% of all patients on dialysis received kidney transplants, 70% from living donors, for a total of 24.81 transplants per million persons.[164] The United States, which has 87 times the population of Costa Rica, barely achieved that number of living donors in the same year.[173] That discrepancy may be explained by two economic disparities. First, the cost of renal replacement therapy in the United States is around $250,000 per year, compared to $6,000 in Costa Rica.[164,174] Second, GDP in Costa Rica is around $10,000–15,000, thus adding to the inducement of locals to become living donors.[158,175] Although cash payments for organ donation have been illegal in Costa Rica since 1994, owing to the short waiting list of only 100–200 people and the excellence of the kidney transplant centers, the nation is a highly attractive destination for nonresidents seeking kidneys.[176,177]

Given how progressive Costa Rica is in terms of primary care and kidney care, it is somewhat surprising that until very recently, the country made relatively little progress on controlling smoking. Early on in Costa Rica's healthcare reform, smoking was banned on buses and in the workplace except in designated areas.[178] After the 1980s, little changed. While other Central and South American countries, even those growing hundreds of thousands of hectares of tobacco, like Brazil, built smoke-free zones, Costa Rica, which produces less tobacco by the ton than any other Latin American country, continued to allow smoking virtually everywhere.[179] In 2001, ads were banned within 200 meters of schools and were removed from movie theaters, but they were allowed to remain on television. Even in 2009, when Costa Rica's National Anti-Tobacco network demonstrated that smoking was costing the country almost US $300,000 dollars in health-related expenses every year, and it was costing 10 Costa Rican lives every day, a smoke-free law failed to materialize.[178] Scholars attribute Costa Rica's failure to mature on this issue to interference from large tobacco companies, which have, since the mid-1980s, used lobbying to prevent enactment of smoke-free bills even after they have been voted on and passed by the national legislature, as the last bill was in 2012.[180]

The result of this social stagnation on the issue of smoking is lifetime prevalence of tobacco consumption of over 40% in Costa Rica.[181] Also, Costa Rica has one of the highest asthma rates in the world. National studies have shown that one-third of the children and adolescents who wheeze are active smokers. This pattern persists in spite of a hefty cigarette tax, in place since the 1960s, which Costa Rica uses to finance the healthcare system.[159] It persists in spite of a graphic antismoking campaign aimed at depicting the dire outcomes of habitual tobacco intake. The 2014 Costa Rican Tobacco Free Initiative includes the slogans "Smokers die young," "Smoking kills," and "Smoking causes heart attack," with accompanying photographs, and "Your smoke harms me," an antisecondhand-smoke campaign.[182-185] Nonetheless, more than 25,000 Costa Ricans die every year of smoking-related illnesses: 0.6% of the population.[186] In other public health measures, Costa Rica has been far more successful. Malaria control is one example. Almost 4,000 new in-country cases in 2005 were decreased to zero in 2011. The level of success has been sustained through the most recent report (2014).[187]

Technology and the Future of HealthCare in Costa Rica

Thanks to international assistance, particularly from the United States, Costa Rica has had a national telehealth strategy since 1996.[188] Owing to the remoteness of many of the EBAIS clinics and second-level clinics, Costa Rica has cultivated the WHO's intermediate levels of teleradiology, teledermatology, and telepsychiatry.[189] As part of fulfilling its legal obligation to the users to provide access to medical health records, Costa Rica developed a national e-health policy and a national health information system in 2012.[189] All of the primary, secondary, and tertiary healthcare centers mentioned earlier in this chapter utilize government-legislated electronic health records.[189] Medical billing systems are electronic, as is supply-chain management, pharmacy systems, laboratory information systems, and the radiology imaging system.[189] Both medical students and medical professionals have access to e-learning systems, in which national-level information, tools, and databases are available.[189] While technologically advanced in some areas, such as e-health and kidney transplant, Costa Rica is severely limited in other areas, such as advanced medical equipment. There are only 4 MRIs in the entire country, 25 CT scanners, and 60 mammography machines.[190]

Health care in Costa Rica faces many upcoming challenges, some of which it shares with the other countries in this set. As was true in Singapore and Taiwan, the prevalence of diabetes is steadily on the rise.[191] As is true of most developed nations, and of all the nations in this set, the birth rate is below replacement level. By 2020, almost 10% of the population will be over the age of 65. This is a more positive population growth outlook than in Singapore and is certainly less daunting than the situation in the Netherlands. Nonetheless, if current birth, death, and immigration rates continue along their projected course, the population of Costa Rica will begin to decline between 2050 and 2060.[192] Immigration from less well-developed countries in the region—including Panama, Nicaragua, and El Salvador—provides Costa Rica with a source of unskilled labor for its agricultural and ranching endeavors, and, as it is in Singapore, is a source of political and social tension.[193] In Costa Rica, these groups tend not only to be poorer socio-economically but also are heavily disadvantaged in terms of health and are subject to varying levels of restriction and strong regulation.

Challenges unique to Costa Rica include very high rates of neuropsychiatric disorders in 2015 (2.3 per 1,000 people, with 3.0 per 1,000 being the highest in the world) and, as previously mentioned, very high rates of asthma (2.3 per 1,000, with 2.8 per 1,000 being the highest in the world).[194] Because so much of its economy is pinned on ecotourism, erosion of the ecology threatens Costa Rica in particular. In an attempt to improve health as well as preserve their ecology, Costa Rica has ratified dozens of environmental treaties. Impressively, the country has managed to keep its carbon dioxide emissions at close to 1997 levels and has protected 11% of its land in a national parks system.[39,195] Costa Rica was also one of the first countries to trade in carbon bonds and to begin discussions of sustainable development. However, as is true for the cigarette companies, interested groups including cattle, lumber, and farming regimes that continuously lobby to expand their rights to access lands for exploitation. Furthermore, poor farmers and sharecroppers continue to work whatever land they can find, irrespective of legal protections.

Conclusion

For a country still in the process of addressing basic issues, such as undernourishment in its population, Costa Rica has made remarkable strides toward achieving population-wide health coverage.[196,*] This has been possible due to a favorable political climate—more than a century of uninterrupted democracy—as well as a consistently growing economy that has not expended resources on a military since 1949.[158] It has also been possible largely because of intermittent but significant international support. International support from the United States and the WHO set off the positive changes of the 1970s that lead to the excellent trends visible today.[197]

That same international support, with new emphasis on healthcare privatization, is seen by some scholars as a direct threat to the current and future success of the Costa Rican system, which is almost entirely public, is socially funded, and is outperforming the United States in terms of healthcare outcomes in the poorest quartile of their respective populations.[198,199] Support for experiments in first-world style policies, such as paying doctors for performance, have had paradoxical effects in Costa Rica, leading to a worse quality of care and an increased consumption of healthcare resources.[200]

Looking back on the last 70 years of health care in Costa Rica, scholars seem to agree that vast improvements in life expectancy, infectious diseases, and infant mortality were achieved by internal measures, such as extending primary care services at local levels via a network of staffed and supplied health outposts, not by the externally mandated doctrines, such as community participation in health, that were insisted upon by the WHO then rapidly discarded when they proved to be untenable and unproductive.[197] Still, if history is any teacher, Costa Rica, as a middle-income country surrounded by other less developed nations, will once again need to rely upon international assistance, financially and politically, in order to continue to render the world-class care that has put it on par with the other fully developed, technologically advanced, wealthy and/or independently successful small nations in this set that offer universal health care.

▸ Concluding Commentary

This chapter makes a clear case for the opportunity to learn from small nation states and provinces. Health systems have many expressions, wide ranging attributes, and are embedded in a diversity of cultures and political contexts. Sometimes, best practices arise in smaller systems that can embrace innovation or can be more adaptable to changing circumstances. These health systems can in turn inform larger, more complex systems. Furthermore, as with smaller units of government, like states in the United States or provinces in Canada, there are potential laboratories for experimentation in the small countries. As students of public health, health policy, and health administration, you are encouraged to keep informed about the activities, practices, and policies of the countries discussed in this chapter, while also seeking other examples for yourself. As future leaders and policy makers, we encourage you to bring these innovations into the national dialogue wherever you may be in your professional career.

References

1. *The World Factbook*. Central American and the Caribbean: Cuba. Washington, DC: Central Intelligence Agency. https://www.cia.gov/library/publications/the-world-factbook/geos/cu.html.

2. *The World Factbook*. East and Southeast Asia: Singapore. Washington, DC: Central Intelligence Agency. https://www.cia.gov/library/publications/the-world-factbook/geos/sn.html.
3. Bloomberg Visual Data: Most Efficient Healthcare 2014. The Bloomberg Report. http://www.bloomberg.com/visual-data/best-and-worst/most-efficient-health-care-2014-countries.
4. World Health Organization. Drugs and money—prices, affordability and cost containment, development of national systems. http://apps.who.int/medicinedocs/en/d/Js4912e/3.3.html.
5. International Society for Pharmacoeconomics and Outcomes Research. Global healthcare systems road map. The Netherlands: description of healthcare system. Updated December 2007. http://www.ispor.org/HTARoadMaps/Netherlands.asp.
6. Rocío Sáenz M, Bermúdez JL, Acosta M. Universal Coverage in a Middle Income Country: Costa Rica. *World Health Report 2010*, background paper 2011. The World Health Organization. http://www.who.int/healthsystems/topics/financing/healthreport/CostaRicaNo11.pdf.
7. World Bank. Age dependency ratio (% of working-age population). Data table. http://data.worldbank.org/indicator/SP.POP.DPND. 2015. Accessed August 6, 2015.
8. World Health Organization. Countries: Cuba. http://www.who.int/countries/cub/en/.
9. *The World Factbook*. Central America: Cuba https://www.cia.gov/library/publications/the-world-factbook/geos/cu.html. Published 2015. Accessed August 6, 2015.
10. *The World Factbook*. Central America and Caribbean: Cuba. https://www.cia.gov/library/publications/the-world-factbook/geos/cu.html. Accessed February 2016.
11. Feinsilver JM. *Healing the Masses: Cuban Health Politics at Home and Abroad*. Los Angeles, CA: University of California Press; 1993.
12. World Health Organization. Global Health Observatory county views. Cuba statistics summary (2002–present). http://apps.who.int/gho/data/node.country.country-CUB?lang=en. Published 2015. Accessed August 6, 2015.
13. *The World Factbook*. Central America and the Caribbean: Cuba. https://www.cia.gov/library/publications/resources/the-world-factbook/fields/2004.html#tw. Published 2004.
14. Garrett L, Chowdhury A, Pablos-Méndez A. All for universal health coverage. *Lancet*. 374(9697): 1294–1299. doi:10.1016/S0140-6736(09)61503-8.
15. Spiegel JM, Yassi A. Lessons from the margins of globalization: appreciating the Cuban health paradox. *Journal of Public Health Policy*. 2004;25(1):97. doi:10.1057/palgrave.jphp.3190007.
16. Cooper RS, Kennelly JF. Orduñez-Garcia P. Health in Cuba. *International Journal of Epidemiology*. 35(4):818. doi:10.1093/ije/dyl175. Published 2006.
17. World Bank. http://www.worldbank.org.
18. Perez C. *Caring for Them from Birth to Death*. Lanham, MD: Rowman & Littlefield; 2008.
19. Más Lago P. Eradication of poliomyelitis in Cuba: a historical perspective. *Bull World Health Organ*. 1999;77(8):681–7.
20. *The World Factbook*. Country Comparison: Maternal Mortality Rate. https://www.cia.gov/library/publications/the-world-factbook/rankorder/2223rank.html.
21. Gorry C. Cuban maternity homes: a model to address at-risk pregnancy. *MEDICC Rev*. 2011 July;13(3):12–15.
22. World Bank. Maternal mortality ratio (modeled estimate, per 100,000 live births). Data table. http://data.worldbank.org/indicator/SH.STA.MMRT. Published 2015. Accessed August 15, 2015.
23. Johnson D. Cancer control in Cuba: the national cancer control unit. *Lancet Oncol*. 2010;11(11):1024–1025. doi:10.1016/S1470-2045(10)70252-7
24. World Health Organization. *The World Health Report 2000—Health Systems: Improving Performance*. http://www.who.int/whr/2000/en/. Geneva, Switzerland: WHO; 2000.
25. World Health Organization. Global Health Observatory Data Repository. http://apps.who.int/gho/data/node.country.country-CUB?lang=en. 2015. Accessed August 6, 2015.
26. World Health Organization. Health Workforce. Density of physicians per 1,000 population. http://www.who.int/gho/health_workforce/physicians_density/en/. 2010.
27. Campion EW, Morrissey S. A different model—medical care in Cuba. *New England Journal of Medicine*. 2013;368(4):297–299. doi:10.1056/NEJMp1215226.
28. Gorry C. MDGs and health equity in Cuba. http://www.medicc.org/publications/medicc_review/0905/spotlight.html. Accessed August 15, 2015.
29. World Health Organization. Millennium Development Goals. Accessed August 15, 2015. http://www.who.int/topics/millennium_development_goals/en/.
30. World Health Organization. *Global Health Observatory*. Cuba: HIV prevalence. http://apps.who.int/gho/data/node.country.country-CUB?lang=en.
31. Celentano DD, Beyrer C. *Public Health Aspects of HIV/AIDS in Low and Middle Income Countries: Epidemiology, Prevention and Care*. New York: Springer;2008–2009:605. doi:10.1007/978-0-387-72711-0
32. Merson M, O'Malley J, Serwadda D, Apisuk C. HIV prevention 1—the history and challenge of HIV prevention. *Lancet*. 2008;372(9637):475–488. doi:10.1016/S0140-6736(08)60884-3
33. Gorry C. Cuba's national HIV/AIDS program. *MEDICC Rev*. 2011;13(2):5-8.
34. Pérez J. The human dimension of AIDS in Cuba: Jorge Perez, MD, MS, Director, Pedro Kouri Tropical Medicine Institute. Interviewed by Gail Reed. *MEDICC Rev*. 2011;13(2):14–16.
35. World Health Organization. Prevalence of tobacco use. Country Profile: Cuba. http://www.who.int/tobacco/surveillance/policy/country_profile/cub.pdf. December 2014.
36. Colditz G. Encyclopedia of cancer and society. *Choice*. Middletown: American Library Association dba CHOICE. 2007;45:1130. doi: http://dx.doi.org/10.4135/9781412953979.n173.
37. Calabro, A. Cuba on "cutting edge" of many areas in health care. *HEM/ONC Today*. 2013; 14(2):16.
38. Blankenship CS. To manage costs of hemophilia, patients need more than clotting factor. *Biotechnology Healthcare*. 2008;5(4):37–40.
39. World Bank. Country Data: Costa Rica. CO_2 emissions (metric tons per capita). http://data.worldbank.org/country/costa-rica.
40. Frehywot S, et al. Compulsory service programmes for recruiting health workers in remote and rural areas: do they work? Department of Health Policy, George Washington University. January 2010. http://www.who.int/bulletin/volumes/88/5/09.
41. Herrera-Valdes R, Almaguer-Lopez M. Strategies for national health care systems and centers in the emerging world: Central America and the Caribbean—the case

42. Knoema. Dependency ratios—potential support ratio (ratio of population aged 15–64 per population 65+)—ranking. http://knoema.com/atlas/topics/Demographics/Dependency-Ratios/Potential-support-ratio-15-64-per-65. 2015. Accessed August 6, 2015.
43. Xinhua News Agency—CEIS. Cuba trims health care sector to cut costs. http://libproxy.usc.edu/login?url=http://search.proquest.com.libproxy2.usc.edu/docview/1097354909?accountid=14749. October 11, 2012.
44. Neuman W. Cuba's health care could be a lure; low cost but high quality of treatment may appeal to U.S. medical tourists. *International New York Times*. 2015.
45. World Factbook. East and Southeast Asia: Singapore. https://www.cia.gov/library/publications/the-world-factbook/geos/sn.html.
46. World Health Organization. Western Pacific Region. Countries: Singapore. http://www.wpro.who.int/countries/sgp/en/. 2016.
47. Haseltine WA, Ebrary I. *Affordable Excellence: The Singapore Healthcare Story*. 1st ed. Washington, DC: Brookings Institution Press; 2013.
48. World Health Organization. Health workforce. Density of Physicians (total number per 1,000 population). http://gamapserver.who.int/gho/interactive_charts/health_workforce/PhysiciansDensity_Total/atlas.html2013.
49. Tan KB, Tan WS, Bilger M, Calvin WL Ho. Monitoring and evaluating progress towards universal health coverage in Singapore. *PLoS Medicine*. 2014;11(9). doi:10.1371/journal.pmed.1001695
50. World Health Organization. Total expenditure on health as a percentage of gross domestic product (US$): Situation and trends as at 20 August 2015. http://www.who.int/gho/health_financing/total_expenditure/en/.
51. World Health Organization. Global Health Observatory. World: total expenditure on health as a percentage of the gross domestic product. http://gamapserver.who.int/mapLibrary/Files/Maps/TotPercentGDP_2013.png. 2013. August 20, 2015.
52. Chia N, Tsui AKC. Medical savings accounts in Singapore: how much is adequate? *Journal of Health Economics*. 2005;24(5):855–875. doi:10.1016/j.jhealeco.2005.01.005
53. World Health Organization. Global Health Observatory. Expenditures on health. Out-of-pocket expenditure on health as a percentage of total expenditure on health (%). http://www.who.int/gho/health_financing/total_expenditure/en/. 2013. August 20, 2015.
54. World Health Organization. Global Health Observatory. Expenditures on health. Western Pacific: per capita total expenditure on health at average exchange rate (US$). http://gamapserver.who.int/gho/interactive_charts/health_financing/atlas.html. 2013. August 20, 2015.
55. Pwee KH. Health technology assessment in Singapore. *International Journal of Technology*. Assessment in Health Care. 2009;25(S1):235. doi:10.1017/S0266462309090692
56. Singapore Department of Statistics. Latest Data. Births and Deaths. http://www.singstat.gov.sg/statistics/latest-data#18. 2015.
57. World Health Organization, UNICEF, UNFPA, World Bank Group, and United Nations Population Division Maternal Mortality Estimation Inter-Agency Group. *Maternal mortality in 1990–2015*: Singapore. http://www.who.int/gho/maternal_health/countries/sgp.pdf.
58. World Health Organization. Media Centre: Tobacco. http://www.who.int/mediacentre/factsheets/fs339/en/. July 2015.
59. World Health Organization—Cancer Country Profiles, 2014. Singapore. http://www.who.int/cancer/country-profiles/sgp_en.pdf.
60. Subramaniam M, Shahwan S, Fauziana R, et al. Perspectives on Smoking Initiation and Maintenance: A Qualitative Exploration among Singapore Youth. *International Journal of Environmental Research and Public Health*. 2015;12:8956–8970.
61. Singapore Health Promotion Board. Go one step closer to a smoke-free life. http://www.hpb.gov.sg/HOPPortal/health-article/11946. February 2016.
62. Yin LK. The fight against obesity in Singapore. *Southeast Asian Journal of Tropical Medicine and Public Health*. 2014;45(Suppl 1):158.
63. Foo LL, Vijaya K, Sloan RA, Ling A. Obesity prevention and management: Singapore's experience. *Obesity Reviews*. 2013;14:106–113.
64. Hashim et al. Health and healthcare systems in Southeast Asia. United Nations University. http://unu.edu/publications/articles/health-and-healthcare-systems-in-southeast-asia.html. April 2012.
65. World Health Organization. Assesses the world's health systems. World Health Report. http://www.who.int/whr/2000/media_centre/press_release/en/. 2000.
66. Health care providers industry profile: Singapore. Market line industry profile. Industry overview. London, UK: Progressive Digital Media; February 2012.
67. World Health Organization. Publications: Altas, Singapore. http://www.who.int/goe/publications/atlas/2015/sgp.pdf.
68. Hsieh Y, Chen CWS, Hsu S. SARS outbreak, Taiwan, 2003. *Emerging Infectious Diseases*. 2004;10:201–206.
69. Lai AY, Tan TB. Combating SARS and H1N1: insights and lessons from Singapore's public health control measures. *Austrian Journal of South-East Asian Studies*. 2012;5:74.
70. James L, Shindo N, Cutter J, Ma S, Chew SK. Public health measures implemented during the SARS outbreak in Singapore, 2003. *Public Health*. 2006;120:20–26.
71. Hsieh Y, King C, Chen CWS, et al. Impact of quarantine on the 2003 SARS outbreak: a retrospective modeling study. *Journal of Theoretical Biology*.
72. Specifically, independence from Malaysia. Singapore achieved independence from Great Britain in 1959.
73. Okma KGH, Crivelli L, Klein R. *Six Countries, Six Healthcare Reform Models*. Hackensack, N.J: World Scientific; December 2009:111.
74. George PP, Heng BH, De Castro M, et al. Self-reported chronic diseases and health status and health service utilization—results from a community health survey in Singapore. *International Journal for Equity in Health*. 2012;11(1):44. doi:10.1186/1475-9276-11-44.
75. Odegaard AO, Koh W, Butler LM, et al. Dietary patterns and incident type 2 diabetes in Chinese men and women: the Singapore Chinese health study. *Diabetes Care*. 2011;34(4):880–885. doi:10.2337/dc10-2350
76. Soh S, Chong Y, Kwek K, et al. Insights from the growing up in Singapore towards healthy outcomes (GUSTO). Cohort study. *Annals of Nutrition and Metabolism*. 2014;64:218–225.
77. Sabanayagam C, Shankar A, Saw SM, et al. The association between socioeconomic status and overweight/obesity in a Malay population in Singapore. *Asia-Pacific Journal of Public Health*. 2009;21:487–496.

78. Smith GD, Blane D, Bartley M: Explanations for socio-economic differentials in mortality. *European Journal of Public Health*. 1994;4(2):131–144.
79. World Health Organization. Countries: Singapore. http://www.wpro.who.int/countries/sgp/en/. 2016.
80. Ortiga YY. Multiculturalism on its head: unexpected boundaries and new migration in Singapore. *Journal of International Migration and Integration*. 2015;16(4):947–963. doi:10.1007/s12134-014-0378-9.
81. Singapore Government National Population and Talent Division. Singapore population in brief 2015. http://www.nptd.gov.sg/Portals/0/Homepage/Highlights/population-in-brief-2015.pdf.
82. Singapore Government. Ministry of Social and Family Development. Possibility of doing away with retirement age. http://app.msf.gov.sg/Press-Room/Possibility-of-Doing-Away-with-the-Retirement-Age. August 16, 2010.
83. BBC. Taiwan profile. http://www.bbc.com/news/world-asia-16164639. Published September 2013. Accessed March 5, 2015.
84. *World Factbook*. East and Southeast Asia: Taiwan. Washington, DC: Central Intelligence Agency. https://www.cia.gov/library/publications/resources/the-world-factbook/geos/tw.html. March 31, 2016.
85. Taiwan tops the expat health care charts. *The Telegraph*. http://www.telegraph.co.uk/news/health/expat-health/11190870/Taiwan-tops-the-expat-health-care-charts.html. 2014. Accessed January 3, 2015.
86. Yang C, Huang YA, Hsueh YA. Redistributive effects of the National Health Insurance on physicians in Taiwan: A natural experiment time series study. *International Journal for Equity in Health*. 2013;12:13.
87. U.S. Department of Commerce. *United States Census*. Quickfacts: Maryland. http://www.census.gov/quickfacts/table/AGE295213/24.
88. U.S. Department of Commerce. *United States Census*. Quickfacts: Delaware. http://www.census.gov/quickfacts/map/PST045214/10.
89. Huang W, Lee Y. Strategic planning for land use under extreme climate changes: A case study in Taiwan. *Sustainability* (Switzerland). 2016;8:1–17.
90. Rachel Lu J, Chiang T. Evolution of Taiwan's health care system. *Health Economics, Policy and Law*. 2011;6:85-107.
91. Chou T, Chang J. Urban sprawl and the politics of land use planning in urban Taiwan. *International Development Planning Review*. 2008;30:67–92.
92. *World Factbook*. Physicians Density. Washington, DC: Central Intelligence Agency. https://www.cia.gov/library/publications/the-world-factbook/fields/2226.html.
93. Chiang T. Taiwan's 1995 health care reform. *Health Policy*. 1997;39:225–239.
94. Wu, T. Majeed, A. Kuo, K. An overview of the healthcare system in Taiwan. *London Journal of Primary Care*. 2010;3:115–19. http://www.radcliffehealth.com/sites/radcliffehealth.com/files/ljpc_articles/3_2_12.pdf.
95. World Bank. Health expenditure, total (% of GDP). http://data.worldbank.org/indicator/SH.XPD.TOTL.ZS. Accessed March 5, 2015.
96. Peng TA, Lo F, Lin C, Yu CJ. Benefiting from networks by occupying central positions: an empirical study of the Taiwan health care industry. *Health Care Management Review*. 2006;31:317–327.
97. Cheng T-M. Taiwan's health care system: the next 20 years. *Taiwan-U.S. Quarterly Analysis*. May 2015 (17 of 20). http://www.brookings.edu/research/opinions/2015/05/14-taiwan-national-healthcare-cheng.
98. Taiwan Department of Budget, Accounting and Statistics. *Statistical Yearbook*. Table 8. Population by sex, rate of population increase, average persons per household, density and natural increase rate. http://eng.dgbas.gov.tw/public/data/dgbas03/bs2/yearbook_eng/y008.pdf. Accessed March 5, 2015.
99. Taiwan Department of Budget, Accounting and Statistics. *Statistical Yearbook*. Table 16. Life expectation. http://eng.dgbas.gov.tw/public/data/dgbas03/bs2/yearbook_eng/y016.pdf.
100. Wu T, Liang F, Huang Y, Chen L, Lu T. Maternal mortality in Taiwan: a nationwide data linkage study: e0132547. *PLoS One*. 2015;10.
101. *World Factbook*. Country comparison: infant mortality rate. Washington, DC: Central Intelligence Agency. https://www.cia.gov/library/publications/the-world-factbook/rankorder/2091rank.html#nl.
102. Wen C, Levy DT, Cheng TY, Hsu CC, Tsai SP. Smoking behaviour in Taiwan, 2001. Tobacco Control. 2005;14:i51–i55.
103. 2008 Taiwan Cancer Registry. 2008 Statistics of Major Causes of Death.
104. Chang C, Lu F, Yang YC, et al. Epidemiologic study of type 2 diabetes in Taiwan. *Diabetes Res Clin Pract*. October 2000(50 Suppl); 2:S49–59. PubMed PMID: 11024584.
105. Yu NC, Chen IC. A decade of diabetes care in Taiwan. *Diabetes Res Clin Pract*. December 2014;106(Suppl 2):S305–8. doi: 10.1016/S0168-8227(14)70734-X
106. International Diabetes Federation. *IDF Diabetes Atlas*. 6th ed. Brussels, Belgium: International Diabetes Federation. http://www.idf.org/diabetesatlas. 2013.
107. Smoking cessation treatment outcomes in men and women in Taiwan: implications for interpreting gender differences in smoking cessation. *The Open Addiction Journal*. 2013;6:1–5. http://benthamopen.com/contents/pdf/TOADDJ/TOADDJ-6-1.pdf.
108. Wu T, Chie W, Lai M, et al. Knowledge of the new tobacco hazards prevention act is associated with smokers' behavior of seeking help in smoking cessation in Taiwan. *Asia-Pacific Journal of Public Health*. 2015;27:NP212-NP222.
109. Health Surveillance Health promotion infrastructure, Taiwan. http://www.hpa.gov.tw/BHPNet/English/Class.aspx?Sub=application&No=201401280001. January 29, 2014. Accessed March 3, 2015.
110. Liu L. The health heterogeneity of and health care utilization by the elderly in Taiwan. *International Journal of Environmental Research and Public Health*. 2014;11:1384–1397.
111. U.S. Centers for Medicare and Medicaid Services. Medical Loss Ratio (MLR). https://www.healthcare.gov/glossary/medical-loss-ratio-MLR/.
112. Chung H, Hsieh C, Tseng C, Yiin L. Association between the first occurrence of allergic rhinitis in preschool children and air pollution in Taiwan. *International Journal of Environmental Research and Public Health*. 2016;13:1.
113. Liang W, Wei H, Kuo H. Association between daily mortality from respiratory and cardiovascular diseases and air pollution in Taiwan. *Environmental Research*. 2009;109:51–58.
114. Chen MS, Lee CB. Between professional dignity and economic interests—evidence based on a survey of Taiwan's

primary care physicians. *International Journal of Health Planning and Management*. 2013; 28(2):153–171. doi:10.1002/hpm.2126.
115. Chang YM, Bair H, Pai J. (2013). The changing image of physician in Taiwan. *Asian Social Science*. 9(4):32–41. doi:10.5539/ass.v9n4p32.
116. Kreng VB, Yang C. The equality of resource allocation in health care under the National Health Insurance System in Taiwan. *Health policy*. 2011;100:203–210.
117. Nolte E, Knai C, Hofmarcher M, et al. Overcoming fragmentation in health care: chronic care in Austria, Germany and the Netherlands. *Health Economics, Policy and Law*. 2012;7(1):125-146. doi:10.1017/S1744133111000338.
118. Reeves A, Gourtsoyannis Y, Basu S, et al. Financing universal health coverage-effects of alternative tax structures on public health systems: cross-national modelling in 89 low-income and middle-income countries. *Lancet*. 2015;386:274–280.
119. *World Factbook*. Europe: The Netherlands. Washington, DC: Central Intelligence Agency. https://www.cia.gov/library/publications/resources/the-world-factbook/geos/nl.html. March 14, 2016.
120. van de Ven WP, Schut FT. Universal mandatory health insurance in the Netherlands: a model for the United States? *Health Affairs*. 2008;27:771–781.
121. Schäfer W, Kroneman M, Boerma W, et al. The Netherlands: health system review. Health systems in transition. 2010;12:v. The European Observatory on Health Systems and Health Policy. http://www.euro.who.int/__data/assets/pdf_file/0008/85391/E93667.pdf.
122. World Health Organization. Global Health Observatory data. Density of physicians (total number per population, 2003). http://www.who.int/gho/health_workforce/physicians_density/en/.
123. World Health Organization. Global Health Observatory. Expenditures on health. Total expenditure on health as a percentage of the gross domestic product, 2013. http://www.who.int/gho/health_financing/total_expenditure/en/. August 20, 2015.
124. Kulesher R, Forrestal E. International models of health systems financing. *Journal of Hospital Administration*. 2014;3(4). doi: 10.5430/jha.v3n4p127.
125. World Health Organization. Global Health Observatory. Expenditures on health. Per capita total expenditure on health at average exchange rate (US$), 2013. http://www.who.int/gho/health_financing/total_expenditure/en/.
126. Stolk EA, Poley MJ. Criteria for determining a basic health services package: recent developments in the Netherlands. *European Journal of Health Economics*. 2005;6(1):2–7. doi:10.1007/s10198-004-0271-0.
127. Simoens S. Creating sustainable European health-care systems through the increased use of generic medicines: a policy analysis. *Journal of Generic Medicines*. 2010;7:131–137. doi:10.1057/jgm.2010.8.
128. Steketee M, Oesterle S, Jonkman H, et al. Transforming prevention systems in the United States and the Netherlands using communities that care. *European Journal on Criminal Policy and Research*. 2013;19:99–116.
129. Rechel et al., eds. European Observatory on Health Systems and Policies Series. Migration and health in the European Union. New York: McGraw-Hill Open University Press; 2011.
130. Roter DL, Bensing J, Hulsman RL. Communication patterns of primary care physicians in the United States and the Netherlands. *Journal of General Internal Medicine*. 2003;18:335–342.
131. Troe EWM, Bos V, Deerenberg IM, et al. Ethnic differences in total and cause-specific infant mortality in the Netherlands. *Paediatric and Perinatal Epidemiology*. 2006;20:140–147.
132. Benson F, Kuipers M, Nierkens V, et al. Socioeconomic inequalities in smoking in the Netherlands before and during the Global Financial Crisis: a repeated cross-sectional study. *BMC Public Health*. 2015;15:469.
133. Willemsen MC, Segaar D, van Schayck CP. Population impact of reimbursement for smoking cessation: A natural experiment in the Netherlands: Reimbursement for smoking cessation. *Addiction*. 2012:n/a.
134. Stoeldraijer L, Bonneux L, van Duin C, et al. The future of smoking-attributable mortality: the case of England and Wales, Denmark and the Netherlands: The future of smoking-attributable mortality. *Addiction*. 2015;110:336–345.
135. Verdonk-Kleinjan WMI, Rijswijk PCP, de Vries H, Knibbe RA. Compliance with the workplace-smoking ban in the Netherlands. *Health Policy*. 2013;109:200–206.
136. Sheldon T. Netherlands bans smoking in enclosed public places but allows closed smoking rooms. *BMJ*. 2007;334:1292–1293.
137. Lanting C, Wouwe JV, Burg Ivd, et al. 127 trends in smoking in pregnancy in the Netherlands (2001–2010). *Archives of Disease in Childhood*. 2012;97:A35-A35.
138. de Vries E, van de Poll-Franse LV, Louwman WJ, et al. Predictions of skin cancer incidence in the Netherlands up to 2015. *British Journal of Dermatology*. 2005;152:481–488.
139. Stirbu I, Kunst AE, Vlems FA, et al. Cancer mortality rates among first and second generation migrants in the Netherlands: Convergence toward the rates of the native Dutch population. *International Journal of Cancer*. 2006;119:2665–2672.
140. Fracheboud J, Broeders MJM, Otto SJ, et al. Decreased rates of advanced breast cancer due to mammography screening in the Netherlands. *British Journal of Cancer*. 2004;91:861–867.
141. Van Steen, Paul J. M, Pellenbarg PH, Groote PD. Population Growth of Cities in the Netherlands. *Journal of Economic and Social Geography*. 2016;107:126–128.
142. Habbema D, de Kok IMCM, Brown ML. cervical cancer screening in the United States and the Netherlands: a tale of two countries. *Milbank Quarterly*. 2012;90:5–37.
143. World Bank. Data by Country. Diabetes prevalence (% of population ages 20 to 79). http://data.worldbank.org/indicator/SH.STA.DIAB.ZS/countries/1W-NL?display=graph. 2015.
144. Rogers A, Portillo MC, Koetsenruijter J, et al. Emerging trends in diabetes care practice and policy in the Netherlands: a key informants study. *BMC Research Notes*. 2014;7:693–693.
145. Boenink M. Debating the desirability of new biomedical technologies: lessons from the introduction of breast cancer screening in the Netherlands. *Health Care Analysis*. 2011;20:84–102.
146. Dylst P, Vulto A, Simoens S. Demand-side policies to encourage the use of generic medicines: An overview. *Expert Review of Pharmacoeconomics and Outcomes Research*. 2013;13:59–72.
147. Bos M. Health technology assessment in the Netherlands. *International Journal of Technology Assessment in Health Care*. 2000;16:485–519.

148. Habbema D, de Kok IM, Brown ML. Cervical cancer screening in the United States and the Netherlands: a tale of two countries. *Milbank Quarterly*. 2012;90(1):5–37. doi:10.1111/j.1468-0009.2011.00652.x
149. Aalbers T, Baars MA, Qin L, et al. Using an eHealth intervention to stimulate health behavior for the prevention of cognitive decline in dutch adults: a study protocol for the brain aging monitor. Eysenbach G, ed. *JMIR Research Protocols*. 2015;4(4):e130. doi:10.2196/resprot.4468
150. Verhoeven F, Tanja-Dijkstra K, Nijland N, et al. Asynchronous and synchronous teleconsultation for diabetes care: a systematic literature review. *Journal of Diabetes Science and Technology*. 2010;4(3):666–684.
151. Abrishami P, Boer A, Horstman K. Understanding the adoption dynamics of medical innovations: affordances of the da Vinci robot in the Netherlands. *Social Science & Medicine*. 2014;117:125–133.
152. van den Berg M, Kringos D, Marks L, Klazinga N. The Dutch health care performance report: seven years of health care performance assessment in the Netherlands. *Health Research Policy and Systems*. 2014;12:1.
153. Tariq L, Bisschop C, Mohammad G, et al. Health care resource utilization and expenditures of incident breast cancer patients in the Netherlands: retrospective Analysis of health insurance data. *Value in Health*. 2013;16:A426-A426.
154. Pardee Center for International Futures. *Population Forecast for the Netherlands*. University of Denver. Denver, Colorado, USA. http://www.ifs.du.edu/ifs/frm_CountryProfile.aspx?Country=NL.
155. Veenman SA. Futures studies and uncertainty in public policy: a case study on the ageing population in the Netherlands. *Futures*. 2013;53:42–52.
156. Joung IMA, Kunst AE, Van Imhoff E, Mackenbach JP. Education, aging, and health: to what extent can the rise in educational level relieve the future health (care) burden associated with population aging in the Netherlands? *Journal of Clinical Epidemiology*. 2000;53:955–963.
157. Bijwaard H, Pruppers M, de Waard-Schalkx I. The Influence of Population Aging and Size on the Number of CT Examinations in the Netherlands. *Health Physics*. 2014;107:80–82.
158. World Factbook. Central America and Caribbean: Costa Rica. Washington, DC: Central Intelligence Agency. https://www.cia.gov/library/publications/resources/the-world-factbook/geos/cs.html. 2/25/2016.
159. Vargas JR, Muiser J. Promoting universal financial protection: a policy analysis of universal health coverage in Costa Rica (1940–2000). *Health Research Policy and Systems*. 2013;11:28-28.
160. Saenz MR, Bermudez JL, Acosta M. Universal coverage in a middle income country: Costa Rica. World Health Organization Report (2010). Background Paper 11. Health System Financing. http://www.who.int/healthsystems/topics/financing/healthreport/CostaRicaNo11.pdf.
161. Mesa-Lago C. Health care in Costa Rica: boom and crisis. *Social Science & Medicine*. 1985;21:13–21.
162. Hill CE. National and Cultural Influences on Economic Development. Political Decision Making, and Health Care Changes in the Rural Frontier of Costa Rica. *Human Organization*. 1994;53:361–371.
163. Costa Rica National website. Health Care. Pharmacies. http://costarica.com/relocation/health-care/. Jun 24, 2015.
164. Cerdas M. Chronic kidney disease in Costa Rica. *Kidney International*. 2005;68:S31–S33.
165. World Bank. Latin American and the Caribbean: Costa Rica. GDP at market prices (current US$). http://data.worldbank.org/country/costa-rica.
166. World Health Organization. Global Health Observatory (GHO) data. Costa Rica: country profiles. Health systems: Essential health technologies. http://www.who.int/gho/countries/cri/country_profiles/en/.
167. Costa Rica National website. Health Care. Public Health Care—Caja Costarricense de Seguro Social (CCSS). http://costarica.com/relocation/health-care/#sthash.3ECV7Pds.dpuf.
168. World Health Organization. Universal Health Coverage in a Middle Income Country: Costa Rica. World Health Report 2011. http://www.who.int/healthsystems/topics/financing/healthreport/CostaRicaNo11.pdf.
169. Costa Rica National website. Health Care. Private Insurance. http://costarica.com/relocation/health-care/. Jun 24, 2015.
170. Unger JP, De Paepe P, Buitrón R, Soors W. Costa Rica: Achievements of a heterodox health policy. *American Journal of Public Health*. 2008;98(4):636–643. doi:10.2105/AJPH.2006.099598
171. Centers for Disease Control. Health Information for Travelers to Costa Rica. Clinician View http://wwwnc.cdc.gov/travel/destinations/clinician/none/costa-rica.
172. Wesseling C, van Wendel de Joode, Berna, Crowe J, et al. Mesoamerican nephropathy: geographical distribution and time trends of chronic kidney disease mortality between 1970 and 2012 in Costa Rica. *Occupational and Environmental Medicine*. 2015;72:714–721.
173. Cecka JM. Kidney transplantation in the United States. *Clinical Transplantation*. 2008:1–18. PMID: 19711510.
174. National Foundation for Transplants. How Much Does a Transplant cost?. http://www.transplants.org/faq/how-much-does-transplant-cost. September, 2010.
175. World Bank. Country Data: Costa Rica. http://data.worldbank.org/country/costa-rica. 2014.
176. Dyer Z. New organ donation law in the wings as Costa Rica's Caja distances itself from private transplants. *McClatchy-Tribune Business News*. 2013.
177. Kane C. Would-be donors reveal details of organ trafficking ring linking Costa Rica and Israel. *McClatchy-Tribune Business News*. 2014.
178. Levin M. For Costa Rica, smoking laws have proven elusive. *McClatchy-Tribune Business News*. 2012.
179. Müller F, Wehbe L. Smoking and smoking cessation in Latin America: a review of the current situation and available treatments. *International Journal of Chronic Obstructive Pulmonary Disease*. 2008;3(2):285–293.
180. Crosbie E, Sebrié EM, Glantz SA. Tobacco industry success in Costa Rica: the importance of FCTC Article 5.3. *Salud Publica De Mexico*. 2012;54(1):28–38.
181. Esquiel, LS. Smoke-free spaces in Costa Rica. World Health Organization. WHO/NHM/TFI/05.5 http://www.who.int/tobacco/training/success_stories/TfiR3hrCRs.pdf
182. World Health Organization. WHO FCTC Health Warnings Database. Costa Rica: Smokers Die Young. http://www.who.int/tobacco/healthwarningsdatabase/tobacco_large_Costa_Rica_Death_01/en/.
183. World Health Organization. WHO FCTC health warnings database. Costa Rica: smoking kills. http://www

.who.int/tobacco/healthwarningsdatabase/tobacco_large_Costa_Rica_Death_02/en/.
184. World Health Organization. WHO FCTC health warnings database. Costa Rica: smoking causes health attack. http://www.who.int/tobacco/healthwarningsdatabase/tobacco-large-Costa-Rica-heart-01/en/.
185. World Health Organization. WHO FCTC health warnings database. Costa Rica: your smoking harms me. http://www.who.int/tobacco/healthwarningsdatabase/tobacco-large-Costa-Rica-children-01/en/.
186. World Health Organization. Costa Rica smoking prevalence tobacco economy. http://www.who.int/tobacco/media/en/Costa_Rica.pdf.
187. World Health Organization. Global observatory for eHealth: Costa Rica. Malaria. http://www.who.int/malaria/publications/country-profiles/profile_cri_en.pdf.
188. de Fatima dos Santos, Alaneir, DAgostino M, Bouskela MS, Fernandez A, Messina LA, Alves HJ. An overview of telehealth initiatives in Latin America/Uma visao panoramica das acoes de telessaude na America Latina. *Revista Panamericana de Salud Publica*. 2014;35:465.
189. World Health Organization. Global Observatory for eHealth: Costa Rica. http://www.who.int/goe/publications/atlas/2015/cri.pdf.
190. World Health Organization. Medical devices by country. Costa Rica. http://www.who.int/medical_devices/countries/cri.pdf. 2013.
191. World Health Organization. Global Observatory for eHealth: Costa Rica. http://www.who.int/goe/policies/countries/cri/en/.
192. United Nations. Economic Commission for Latin America and the Caribbean Costa Rica. Estimated and projected indicators of population growth, selected Quinquenniums, 1950–2100 [Fertility, births, mortality, life expectancy by sex, and migration.] 84 (Table 26); 2013 IIS 3230-S1. 2013.
193. Gradín C. Race, ethnicity, immigration, and living conditions in Costa Rica. *Review of Income and Wealth*. 2015.
194. World Health Organization. Country profile of environmental disease burden: Costa Rica. 2011. http://www.who.int/quantifying_ehimpacts/national/countryprofile/costarica.pdf.
195. Brockett CD, Gottfried RR. State policies and the preservation of forest cover: lessons from contrasting public-policy regimes in Costa Rica. *Latin American Research Review*. 2002;37:7–40.
196. Human Development Report 2003. Millennium Development Goals: A compact among nations to end human poverty. New York: United Nations Development Programme; 2003.
197. Morgan LM. International politics and primary health care in Costa Rica. *Social Science & Medicine*. 1990;30:211–219.
198. Escobar M, Griffin CC, 1951, Shaw RP, Brookings Institution. *The Impact of Health Insurance in Low- and Middle-Income Countries*. Washington, DC: Brookings Institution Press; 2010.
199. Rosero-Bixby L, Dow WH. Exploring why Costa Rica outperforms the United States in life expectancy: a tale of two inequality gradients. *Proceedings of the National Academy of Sciences*. 2016;113:1130–1137.
200. Soors W, De Paepe P, Unger J. Management commitments and primary care: another lesson from Costa Rica for the world? *International Journal of Health Services*. 2014;44:337–353.

CHAPTER 28

Health Systems in Crisis and Disaster

Caren Rossow and **James A. Johnson**

▸ Introduction

Health systems in all countries face challenges that come from beyond the system itself. These challenges can be in the form of threats, disasters, conflicts, environmental events, epidemics, or terrorism. Any of these are likely to be disruptions in a health system's ability to function effectively and efficiently. Given the fact that no country or health system is immune to disruptive events, it becomes imperative for any such system to engage in preparedness and to become more resilient. In this chapter, to demonstrate the incredible range of events and locales that can be affected, we profile several countries that are included in the earlier chapters of this book, including India, China, Canada, Botswana, Japan, Brazil, and the United States. Additionally, we discuss the earthquake in Haiti and the Ebola outbreak in the West Africa region, both of which severely challenged the health systems of those areas.

Natural Disasters

The International Federation of the Red Cross and Red Crescent defines natural disasters as naturally occurring phenomena, physical in nature, caused by geophysical, hydrological, climatological, meteorological, and biological reasons. Geophysical natural disasters are best described as earthquakes, landslides, tsunamis, and volcanic activity; hydrological—floods and avalanches; climatological—weather extremes (hot and cold), drought, and wildfires; meteorological—severe storms, cyclones, wave surges; and biological—epidemics and plagues. In addition, technological or human generated hazards due to conflicts, famine, displaced populations, industrial, and large transport accidents are events usually close to communities. Other critical factors include climate change, population growth, unplanned urbanization, uncontrolled building on flood plains, poverty and threats of pandemics, and increased human vulnerability to complexity and severity of disasters.

According to the Centre for Research on the Epidemiology of Disasters (CRED), in the last 20 years, 6,457 weather-related disasters were recorded, attributing to 606,000 deaths and over 4 billion injures (2016). Annual economic losses from the disasters are estimated by the United Nations Office for Disaster Risk Reduction to be US $250–300 billion.[1]

In the last two decades, approximately 90% of disasters have been triggered by storms, floods, heat waves, and other weather events. According to CRED, "Flooding alone accounted for 47% of all weather-related disasters (1995–2005), affecting 2–3 billion individuals, the majority of whom (95%) lived in Asia."[1]

Flooding was more frequent, and storms were more deadly, attributing to the deaths of 242,000 individuals. Nearly 89% of these deaths occurred in low-income countries. Drought impacted approximately 1.1 billion individuals between 1995 and 2005, primarily in Africa. Economic and human impact included water shortages, hunger, spread of diseases, and loss of jobs, homes, crops, and livestock.

Extreme temperature changes account for 27% of all deaths between 1995 and 2005, with the majority being heatwaves in Europe's high-income countries. During the same decade, extreme cold temperatures were reported in the Americas (Central and South) impacting millions of individuals, attributing to death, property damage, and economic loss.

Geophysical Disasters

Japan—Earthquake and Tsunami

On Friday March 11, 2011 at 2:49 pm the Great East Japan Earthquake struck off the cost of Japan. The 9.0 magnitude double earthquake, centered 130 kilometers off shore under the city of Sendai on the eastern coast of Honshu Island, triggered a horrendous tsunami, the largest in Japan's history. The large tsunami waves hit the eastern coast and peaked at 37.88 meters, flooding an area of 560 square kilometers, causing severe costal damage to towns, and destroying over a million buildings. Approximately 130,927 individuals were displaced, and the infrastructure of 2,126 roads, 56 bridges, and 26 railways were damaged or destroyed. The resulting death toll exceeded 19,000 (see **TABLE 28-1**).[2]

According to the World Nuclear Association, at the time of quake, 11 reactors at 4 nuclear power plants were in operation, and all shut down when the quake hit.[3] Initial inspection of the nuclear power plants led to the conclusion that there was no significant damage to the reactors. However, Tokyo Electric Power Company's Fukushima-Daiichi nuclear power plant lost power an hour after the quake when the entire site was flooded by 15-meter tsunami waves. This rendered the backup generators useless, resulting in a situation in which four of the nuclear reactors had no workable instrumentation to regulate reactor cooling.[4] Three of the reactors quickly heated up due to reactor decay, leading to a series of explosions, causing radiological contamination to spread into areas of the environment, as described by the International Atomic Energy Agency. This led to radioactive contamination of large areas of farmland, inhabited areas, and forest. Five years after the event, tens of thousands of individuals who were evacuated from their homes have still not been able to return.[5]

Haiti—Earthquake

On January 12, 2010, the 7.0 magnitude Haiti earthquake occurred in the boundary region separating the Caribbean plate and the North America plate.

TABLE 28-1 Lives Lost, People Injured or Affected, and Damages Due to Earthquakes in 2005–2015

Year	Loss of life	People injured	People affected	Damage in US $1,000
2005	1	793	4,430	400,000
2007	10	1,371	55,228	12,750,000
2008	24	648	918	277,000
2009	1	319	25,319	400,000
2010	316,000	300,000	1,300,000	
2011	19,848	6,065	368,952	210,000,000
2013		32	8,438	
2014		46	2,611	

Modified from Guha-Sapir D, Below R, Hoyois Ph. EM-DAT: The CRED/OFDA International Disaster Database. www.emdat.be. Université Catholique de Louvain–Brussels–Belgium; 2016.

The Port-au-Prince area and much of southern Haiti were devastated. Official estimates include 316,000 individuals killed, 300,000 injured, 1.3 million displaced, 97,294 houses destroyed, and 188,383 structures damaged (USGS, 2016). The Haitian people lost family members, means of employment and income, and their basic ways of life. In the immediate aftermath, the country's medical capacity, infrastructure, economic sustainability, and housing were destroyed.

Consequently, one of the most severe cholera outbreaks in modern history began. Between October 2010 and June 2014, there were 705,207 cases with 8,559 reported deaths. The total medical cost to eradicate the cholera epidemic is estimated at US $82 million, plus another $310 million to cover the cost of health and water sanitation through 2017, according to the World Bank. Despite humanitarian efforts from around the world, Haiti remains one of the poorest countries in the western hemisphere, with $846 GDP per capita, ranking 163 out of the 188 countries covered by the United Nations' Human Development Index.[6]

Reconstruction programs are in the process of repairing and/or building safer housing, allowing 1.4 million individuals who were living in camps to relocate to permanent housing. Over the 10 years after the earthquake, extreme poverty dropped from 31% to 24% in urban areas and foremost in Port-au-Prince.[7] Quality education remains a challenge; however, access and participation from school-age children has risen to 90%. Although considerable challenges remain, Haiti has seen positive developments since the earthquake.

▸ Biological Events

Botswana—HIV

Human immunodeficiency virus (HIV) attacks the immune system and diminishes the body's defense system to fight infections and some cancers. As the process continues, the body gradually becomes immune deficient (measured by CD4 cell or T cells), leaving the individual susceptible to infections and diseases. Once these opportunistic infections and/or diseases occur, the individual is diagnosed with acquired immune deficiency syndrome (AIDS).

The cause of the virus is unknown but scientists believe that the chimpanzee version of the virus (*Simian immunodeficiency virus*, or SIV) was most likely the cause. Transmitted from chimpanzees to humans, it mutated into HIV when humans hunted for their meat and came in contact with the chimpanzees' infected blood. Research suggests that this may have occurred as early as the late 1800s. Transmission of HIV in humans is through body fluids from infected individuals: blood, semen, vaginal secretions, and breast milk.

As reported by the World Health Organization (WHO), in 2016, there were an estimated 36.8 million people worldwide diagnosed with HIV.[8] According to The Henry J. Kaiser Family Foundation, approximately half (51%) of all adults living with HIV worldwide are women.[9] Currently it is the leading cause of death among women of childbearing age. These disparities are attributed to gender inequalities, access to service, sexual violence, and younger women being biologically more susceptible to HIV exposure and infection.

Africa's sub-Saharan region has been enormously impacted, with more than 25.6 million individuals living with the disease in 2016, according to the WHO. Currently, two-thirds of all newly diagnosed cases occur in this region. Nowhere is this as apparent as in Botswana, Africa. According to the U.S. Centers for Disease Control and Prevention (CDC), Botswana is one of few countries where the HIV epidemic has passed "the tipping point." In 2015, there were approximately 350,000 people living in Botswana with HIV. The prevalence rate among individuals 15 to 49 year of age is 22.2%. Individuals 15 years of age and older with HIV is estimated at 340,000; women 15 years and older are an estimated 190,000; children 14 years and younger are 8,500. Currently there are 60,000 children orphaned due to the epidemic. In 2015 there were 3,200 deaths in Botswana.

Collaboration between the CDC and government of Botswana began in 1995 to decrease the prevalence of Tuberculosis through prevention and expanded to HIV. From an initial emergency response, the HIV prevention, care and treatment program has become a sustainably shared model focusing on evidence-based, high-impact interventions. A successful combination approach has been used focusing on antiretroviral therapy, prevention of mother-to-child transmission, the use of condoms, and voluntary male circumcision to maximize epidemic impact.

Brazil—Zika Virus

Zika virus is a mosquito-borne flavivirus that was first detected in a rhesus monkey in the Zika forest of Uganda in 1947. In 1952, Zika virus was identified in humans in Uganda and Tanzania. Periodic outbreaks during the latter half of the century have been confirmed in Africa, the Americas, Asia, and the Pacific. Those infected with the disease normally report only mild symptoms, including mild fever, skin rash, conjunctivitis, muscle and joint pain, malaise, and headache; symptoms normally last 2–7 days. In February 2015, Brazil reported a cluster of individuals in the northeastern part of the country complaining of febrile rash related to the virus. Then in October 2015, Bahia, a single state in the northeast, reported 56,318 suspected cases.[10]

Brazil reported in July 2015 an association between Zika virus infection and Guillain-Barré syndrome and in October 2015 an association between the virus and microcephaly.[11] Guillain-Barré syndrome is a rare condition in which the body's immune system attacks part of the peripheral nervous system, which may result in muscle weakness and loss of sensation. Complications can cause permanent paralysis that controls breathing, requiring mechanical ventilation. Microcephaly is an uncommon birth defect with which a newborn's head circumference and brain are significantly smaller than expected for the age and weight. Symptoms vary by degree of severity, with long-term prognosis unknown. Infants may go on to develop epilepsy, cerebral palsy, hearing and vision problems, and learning disabilities requiring long-term medical care.

Authorities in Brazil estimate that between 497,593 and 1,482,701 cases of Zika virus infection have occurred since the outbreak began. Once established in Brazil, the virus spread rapidly within the country and then throughout Latin America and the Caribbean. Within a year, the virus had been detected in nearly every country or territory infested with *Aedes aegypti*, the principal mosquito species that transmits Zika. Since 2015, 65 countries and territories have documented cases of the vector borne illness, and the virus is considered a public health emergency of international concern.[12]

The Zika Response Plan is a global initiative focusing on prevention by decreasing the risk of exposure by vector control measures, promotion of personal protective measures, and management of medical complications. Special attention is aimed at ensuring women of childbearing age, pregnant women, and their partners have the necessary information and materials to reduce the risk of exposure. Expansion of the current health systems' capabilities and an estimated US $122.1 million are necessary to effectively implement the Zika Strategic Response Plan through 2017.[13]

Guinea, Liberia, and Sierra Leone—Ebola

Ebola virus disease (EVD), formerly known as Ebola hemorrhagic fever, is a severe and often fatal disease in humans, with a case mortality rate of approximately 50%. EVD can be found in humans and nonhumans.

According to the CDC, there are five identified Ebola virus species: *Zaire ebolavirus*; *Sudan ebolavirus*; *Taï Forest ebolavirus*, formerly *Côte d'Ivoire ebolavirus*; and *Bundibugyo ebolavirus*. Four are known to cause disease in humans, and one causes disease in nonhumans. A natural reservoir host of Ebola virus remains unknown. However, researchers suspect that the virus is animal-borne and that bats are the most likely reservoir.

Humans get EVD through direct contact (through broken skin and membranes, eyes, and oral cavities) with contaminated blood, body fluids (possibly including semen from an infected male), needles, and syringes and with infected fruit bats and primates. Signs and symptoms may appear anywhere from 2 to 21 days after exposure and include fever, severe headache, muscle pain and weakness, fatigue, diarrhea, vomiting, abdominal pain, and unexplained hemorrhaging.

Vaccines are currently under development with some early success. At present, treatment is supportive care with intravenous fluids, maintaining oxygen levels and blood pressure, and treating other symptoms as needed.

The first EVD cases appeared in 1976 with two outbreaks, one near the Ebola River in the Democratic Republic of the Congo and the other in South Sudan. Since its discovery, periodic outbreaks have ensued. In March 2014, the largest and most complex Ebola outbreak occurred, causing more deaths than all others outbreaks combined.[14]

The most severely affected countries—Guinea, Liberia, and Sierra Leone—have very weak healthcare systems. Liberia has only one academic referral hospital, which was severely damaged during the years of civil war. The hospital suffers from frequent floods and electrical fires. As in Sierra Leone, some of Liberia's healthcare workers who strived to heal the sick, while working in minimally equipped hospitals, became infected with EVD themselves and died. During the peak of the epidemic in Liberia, the overwhelmed healthcare systems had diminished capacity to deliver basic care, treatment, or emergency services. In some facilities desperate families and their ill loved ones were turned away in large numbers. In addition, years of conflict and instability in the region have diminished infrastructure and human resources. Although they were rebuilding prior to the epidemic, businesses shut down, impacting the availability of food and fuel, which added to the plight of the infirmed and their families. The Ebola outbreak required getting essential health services back up and running and addressing the weaknesses of the health system. On August 8, 2014, the WHO declared the epidemic to be an international public health emergency. Supported by the WHO, United Nations, World Food Programme, CDC, USAID, and other humanitarian agencies, Liberia received aid in the form of Ebola clinics (stationary and mobile) to provide supportive care, laboratories for diagnosis, medical supplies, healthcare workers, and food. Several countries sent doctors, nurses, and other essential healthcare personnel.

On March 29, 2016, the WHO inspector director-general declared the end of the public health emergency of international concern in West Africa. A total of 28,616 confirmed, probable, and suspected cases have been reported in Guinea, Liberia, and Sierra Leone, with 11,310 deaths and over 10,000 survivors of Ebola.[15]

Canada—SARS

Severe acute respiratory syndrome (SARS) emerged in Guangdong, China, in November of 2002 with outbreaks occurring in early 2003 in Hong Kong, Hanoi, Toronto, and Singapore.[16(pp325-326)] Overall 30 countries were affected and reported 8,098 probable cases with 774 deaths during the outbreak.[16] SARS is a viral respiratory illness caused by a coronavirus, called SARS-associated coronavirus (SARS-CoV). Normally, SARS begins with a fever greater than 100.4°Fahrenheit (38°Celsius), headache, body aches, and general feelings of discomfort. Mild respiratory symptoms occur at the onset, with a dry cough that usually develops into pneumonia.

SARS was first found in Toronto, Canada, in a woman who returned from Hong Kong on February 23, 2003.[17] Transmission to other individuals occurred, resulting in an outbreak among 257 individuals in several Greater Toronto area hospitals (Public Health Agency of Canada). SARS continued to spread in Toronto among patients, staff, and visitors at one local hospital, forcing the hospital to close its emergency and intensive care services and to divert new admission and potential transfers to other facilities. The local healthcare sector was in crisis. Strict public health isolation measures were implemented to lessen the transmission of the disease. The government designated SARS as a reportable, communicable, and virulent disease under the Health Protection and Promotion Act of March 25, 2003, allowing authorities to restrict individuals from engaging in activities that allowed for the spread of the disease, including isolation and quarantine. Anyone who had visited local hospitals was asked to adhere to a ten-day home quarantine.

On March 26, the Ontario Ministry of Health declared a medical state of emergency in the province.[18] It was lifted on May 17 when the outbreak was thought to be over. Seven days later, several more cases of SARS were discovered in four of the local hospitals in Toronto. Again, intensive protective measures were implemented throughout the healthcare sector. On July 2, 2003, the state of emergency ended, with a total of 250 people diagnosed and 38 dead from the outbreak. The healthcare sector was radically impacted by the outbreak. Approximately 40% of the SARS cases in the Toronto outbreak were healthcare workers. Of them, two nurses and one family physician died.

China—Avian Influenza

The A(H5N1) virus subtype is a highly pathogenic avian influenza virus; it first infected humans in 1997 during a poultry outbreak in Hong Kong, China. Since then, widespread outbreaks have occurred in 2003 and 2004. A total of 851 confirmed human cases of A(H5N1) were reported to the WHO between January 2003 and 2016 from Canada and a number of countries in Asia, the Near East, Africa, and Europe.

The virus is particularly aggressive, with rapid deterioration and high morbidity and mortality. Commonly seen symptoms include the development of flu-like symptoms with high fever, leading to respiratory distress, a hoarse voice, and a crackling sound on inhalation. Complications of A(H5N1) and now the A(H7N9) infection include hypoxemia, multiple organ dysfunction, and secondary bacterial and fungal infections.

The virus seems limited to poultry workers and has shown an inability to spread from human to human. In domestic poultry, the A(H5N1) outbreaks have been a catastrophe for agriculture. The outbreaks have affected the very backbone of subsistence farming in rural areas where large numbers of people depend on poultry for livelihood and food. The widespread nature of A(H5N1) in domestic poultry, the risk of it spreading to water fowl, and the possibility of mutations over time has raised fears that the virus will become communicable between humans, with disastrous consequences.

On March 13, 2013, China reported a strain of the virus, A(H7N9), which previously had not been seen (WHO, 2014). This new strain is of great concern because those infected become severely ill. According to the United Nations Food and Animal Organization (FAO), the cumulative number of A(H7N9) human cases since February 2013 is 795, with 308 deaths. The virus does not seem to transmit easily, and no sustained human-to-human transmission has been reported. Similar to A(H5N1), most of the new cases of A(H7N9) have reported recent exposure to domestic poultry or potentially contaminated environments, including markets where birds have been sold. Of great concern is that the infected poultry show few or no clinical signs. In fact, A(H7N9) surveillance relies on targeted sampling, and only laboratory tests can confirm infection. The Chinese government's public health response includes enhancing surveillance and control measures, medical treatment, and risk communication to the public.

Climate Events

India—Cyclones, Droughts, and Floods

India is extremely susceptible to a variety of significant natural disasters, primarily cyclones, droughts, earthquakes, and floods, as shown in **TABLE 28-2**. A nation with varied climate and elevations, India's land is 68% drought prone, 60% earthquake prone, 12% flood prone, and 8% cyclone prone.[19] Approximately 85% of the land mass is vulnerable to natural hazards, with 22 states designated as hazard prone. Research suggests that natural disaster losses in India are equal to 2% of the country's GDP and up to 12% of federal government's revenues. Approximately 50 million people are affected yearly with destruction of personal belongings, property, human suffering, and loss of life.

Population growth and urbanization have forced individuals to live on marginal lands or in overpopulated cities that are at great disaster risk. Millions of individuals are affected on India's coastline (5,700 kilometers), which is subject to severe cyclones, and approximately 40% of India's population lives within 100 kilometers of the coastline. These natural disasters impact India's economy as well as the infrastructure, food and water supply, sanitation, public health, and agriculture. In 2010, the Government of India and the World Bank initiated the National Cyclone and Risk Mitigation Program to reduce the vulnerability of coastal communities to cyclone and other hydrometeorological hazards. Initial goals include development of an Early Warning Dissemination System (EWDS) and shelters for coastal communities. On October 12, 2013, the system was tested when the severe cyclone Phailin reached the coast. The cyclone resulted in 44 deaths, damaged about 256,600 homes and impacted 13.2 million people in over 18,370 villages. Damages were due to high winds of up to 220 kilometers per hour, followed by flooding ensued by torrential rains. The storm surge was up to about 3.5 meters above normal. Casualties were minimized due to preparedness planning and evacuation of nearly 1 million individuals and rescue teams. From this experience, an improvement plan for disaster risk reduction and management capabilities has been devised.

Phase II of the National Cyclone Risk Mitigation Program was approved in May 2015. A goal was to enhance disaster preparedness by improving capacity and access to emergency shelters and evacuation routes and by protecting critical infrastructure against cyclones and hydrometeorological hazards to mitigate potential loss of life, property, and infrastructure and to ensure continuation of services. Preparedness planning has helped to mitigate loss of life in India. Community members, government organizations, academic and research institutions, armed forces, and non-governmental organizations have joined forces to contribute to disaster preparedness and management in India.

United States—Hurricane

Hurricane Katrina was one of the costliest and most devastating natural disasters in the history of the United States and was responsible for 1,833 deaths and approximately US $108 billion in damages. On August 23, 2005, tropical storm Katrina formed off the coast of the southeast Bahamas. Tracking west the storm intensified, and on August 25th it reached landfall along the southeast Florida coast as a Category 1 hurricane (80 mph) on the Saffir-Simpson Hurricane Wind Scale. Moving southwest across the Gulf of Mexico, the hurricane strengthened significantly, reaching winds of 175 miles per hour, which classified it as a Category 5 hurricane. Katrina turned northwest, diminishing in strength to a Category 3 hurricane with 125 mph winds reaching landfall on August 29 near Buras, Louisiana.

Although the hurricane was destructive, the devastation in New Orleans was not directly from the hurricane but rather from the breaching of the levee system used to restrict the flow of waters from rivers, estuaries, and most importantly Lake Ponchatrain.[20] The intense storm surge overflowed the levee system in Orleans and St. Bernard parishes, leading to extensive levee failures and flooding of the parishes. Flooding of 80% of the city of New Orleans ensued at depths up to 20 feet.[21] The destruction from the storm left a wake of devastation and destroyed homes, businesses, and city infrastructure. Those who could afford to did evacuate before the storm hit, and those who stayed waited for days for rescue. Approximately

TABLE 28-2 Deaths, Injuries, Homelessness, People Affected, and Damage Due to Natural Disasters in India, 2005–2015

Year	Disaster type	Occurrence	Loss of life	Injured	Homeless	Total affected	Total damage in USD × 1,000
2005	Earthquake	1	1,309	6,622	150,000	156,622	1,000,000
2005	Flood	17	2,129	71	256,500	28,281,571	6,190,000
2005	Storm	4	82	90	57,500	68,590	
2006	Flood	17	1,194	178	4,000,000	7,234,178	3,390,000
2006	Storm	2	190	300	150,000	150,300	
2007	Flood	16	2,051	8		38,143,008	376,151
2007	Storm	1					
2008	Flood	8	1,590		2,400,000	13,989,018	145,000
2008	Storm	1	111	50		50	25,000
2009	Flood	6	1,500	8		5,986,008	2,434,000
2009	Storm	6	218	85	4,000	5,109,085	300,000
2010	Flood	8	690	225	400,000	3,772,408	2,149,000
2010	Storm	7	287	80	507,000	507,080	
2011	Earthquake	1	112	200	75,000	575,200	
2011	Flood	7	608			12,004,069	1,657,000
2011	Storm	3	106	50	250,000	250,050	375,625
2012	Flood	6	279			4,210,860	244,000
2012	Storm	1	40			70,000	
2013	Earthquake	1	3	70		59,350	120,000
2013	Flood	5	6,453	4,473		3,419,473	1,360,000
2013	Storm	5	106	4		13,230,004	895,471
2014	Flood	7	622		650,000	5,222,500	16,263,000
2014	Storm	5	111	84		931,564	7,000,000
2015	Earthquake	3	89	10		10	
2015	Flood	10	839	1,025	54,097	16,413,459	2,880,000
2015	Storm	6	212	100		135,100	1,069,000

Modified from Guha-Sapir D, Below R, Hoyois Ph. EM-DAT: The CRED/OFDA International Disaster Database. www.emdat.be. Université Catholique de Louvain–Brussels–Belgium; 2016.

1 million individuals were displaced.[22] Several of the healthcare facilities sustained primary damage from the storm. Hospitals were evacuated, and the remaining healthcare system was overwhelmed with attempting to care for those with chronic conditions and immediate injuries. Patients with preexisting health conditions worsened as they were cut off from access to essential medications and treatments, such as oxygen, insulin, and kidney dialysis. Hospitals that did not evacuate prior to the storm found themselves and their patients in dismal circumstances when rising floodwaters made it difficult, with shortages of medical supplies, to maintain standards of care. Communications with the outside world were minimal to nonexistent in the hard-hit areas. When possible, critically ill patients were evacuated to a triage center, which then became overwhelmed itself. Patients were sent for treatment to various permanent and temporary healthcare facilities across of the south central United States, separating them from family and loved ones. Public health emergencies were declared in nine parishes, and local states became hosts to large numbers of evacuees needing healthcare.

Basic needs of fresh water, food, and sewage handling were concerns. Public health challenges included keeping responders and victims safe, preventing diseases in temporary shelters, safely storing food supplies, and controlling mosquitoes. The short- and long-term behavioral health needs of victims, first responders, and healthcare providers had to be addressed.[22] Psychological problems—including acute stress disorder, posttraumatic stress disorder, depression, substance abuse, and anxiety—are some of the behavioral health problems that can result from exposure to natural disasters.[24] Federal, state, and local governments, the community at large, the faith community, and volunteers worked tirelessly to provide relief to Katrina's victims. Years later, there are still challenges, especially in the impoverished areas.

In disaster situations, a quick response must be achieved. Damage can be considerably minimized with adequate disaster planning and preparedness. The four phases of emergency management (see **FIGURE 28-1**) can be used by national, state, and local governments as well as business organizations. Cyclical in nature, they include mitigation, preparedness, response, and recovery.[23] Mitigation is the cornerstone of disaster management and includes activities to decrease the potential loss of life and property by lessening the impact of disasters.[25] Mitigation should start early, long before a disaster occurs, involving all key stakeholders. The focus of preparedness is to enhance the capacity to respond to an incident. Taking steps to ensure who, what, where, when, and how people and resources are available before an event occurs. Preparedness involves development of training programs for the community, public awareness, logistical support, and communications, early warning, with ongoing monitoring. Response is the implementation of the time-critical plan in order to take action to save lives and to prevent further damage. The recovery phase incorporates actions necessary to maintain and/or return the community to normal after the disaster.[26] Recovery may include repairing buildings, streets, railways, and other infrastructure damaged during the disaster.

▸ Health Systems Response

Several critical success factors for all communities should be considered. As described by Johnson and Johnson,[27] they include training and education; mitigation of confusion, fear, and panic; time management, building response capacity, and economic empowerment. Health systems and public health leaders need to take responsibility for addressing concerns about the possibility of any of the disruptors described in this chapter. Awareness is the key. Leaders should inform all their key stakeholders that preventive and response policies and programs are under way. This may take place in the form of briefings, in-service workshops, simulations and mock exercises, security enhancements, and coordination with local health facilities. Health systems will want to develop disaster plans and crisis management initiatives that help victims and their families remain in the information loop or in some cases to evacuate affected areas. Additionally, the private sector will need to have contingency plans and backup systems to deal with business downtime. A robust communication plan for the public will

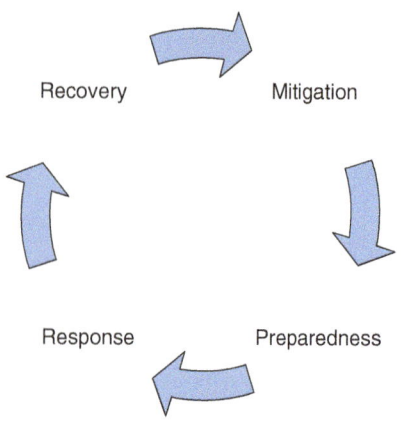

FIGURE 28-1 The Four Phases of Disaster

also be essential. There are several critical success factors for a health system to consider, and these should include the following:

1. Health system workforce training
2. Mitigation of confusion
3. Time management (time is critical)
4. Building a response capacity
5. Economic constraints
6. Coordination with local health agencies
7. Mitigation of fear and panic

Training

Training is essential for all health personnel. This could be in the form of awareness enhancement or actual training in disease detection and early intervention. Additionally, the training of disaster coordinators would be important. These individuals can serve as resource people, advisors, counselors, and/or organizers. They also could have the responsibility for staying informed and maintaining contact networks with local health agencies. Ideally, these coordinators would receive continuing education for periodic updates on skills and knowledge needed to be effective in this role.

Mitigation of Confusion

Mitigation of confusion is a critical success factor in managing any crisis. The natural tendency of humans in a state of confusion is to panic. If this occurs, more harm can result. Training, preparedness, and prior discussion of the range of possibilities and response scenarios all help to mitigate confusion. Fast, clear communication to all personnel is essential. Some organized protocols for testing and prophylaxis will help provide much needed reassurance that the organization cares for its people and is taking appropriate steps. Finally, a key to avoiding confusion is the development of roles and responsibilities that are clearly understood and communicated widely.

Time Management

Time is critical in all matters pertaining to infectious disease. Early signs, early diagnosis, early warning to the noninfected, and early intervention all have positive implications for the decreased spread and eventual decreased impact of the disease.

Response Capacity

Response capacity may be in the form of trained personnel, along with needed equipment and proper training. It also includes working with local health agencies to develop quick response to a crisis. There are financial considerations, such as cost of training, supplies, equipment, and down time that should be part of the capacity building within the organization. Some might even consider a "health crisis reserve" for contingency planning.

Mitigation of Fear and Panic

There is no better way to decrease stress and anxiety in anticipation of a possible disruptive event, and likewise no better way to control for panic, than putting in the requisite time and resources to properly train the workforce and larger community. This should include the design of a disaster-control command center where all communications originate. When there are but a few people directing the response, it tends to minimize panic and maximize effective distribution of information.

Importance of Planning

All health systems, regardless of size and geographic location, should have a disaster plan or crisis management plan for the populations they serve. See **BOX 28-1** for a generic overview with key elements for consideration in plan development and implementation. There will be wide variation in the plans according to local culture, political structure, and economics.

▶ Conclusion

Health systems and societies everywhere will continue to be challenged by disasters and crises of many types. As profiled in the examples in this chapter, there is every indication that there will be no two events that are completely the same.[28] However, health systems and the communities they serve can prepare for likely events, and by working with international agencies, such as the World Health Organization, we can better anticipate the unexpected. One example of this is the Global Health Security Agenda, a 30-plus nation initiative to promote global health security by strengthening countries' ability to prevent, detect, and respond to health threats.[29] Furthermore, if we are to achieve the Sustainable Development Goals[30] being promulgated by the United Nations, we will certainly have to develop and maintain robust health systems that have the capacity to effectively manage crises. Hopefully, with adequate planning and surveillance, events and disasters, can become less disruptive to health systems.

BOX 28-1 A General Preparedness Plan for Health Systems

Address the following areas in the plan:

- A collaboration plan, including area health care; public health; veterinary, physician, and medical group practices; and law enforcement with specific preparation action steps (training, stockpiling appropriate levels of material, etc.) and with the local hospital(s)
- Reporting of incidents and possible incidents and how they can be handled
- Infection control practices and procedures and decontamination procedures
- A postexposure management plan for employees (prophylactics, vaccines, and a plan to prevent secondary infections)
- An offsite contingency operation plan
- An education plan (prospective and concurrent to an attack) and a public relations plan

Components of an Effective Response

- Establish protocols
- Establish a response command and control structure with which critical decisions can be made (should be community-based)
- Develop and implement a training and awareness program with local healthcare, public health, and law enforcement officials
- Ensure surveillance systems are in place

Cost Considerations (consider when preparing a budget)

- Cost of detection devices
- Cost of personal protection devices, such as masks and body covering
- Cost of vaccines and prophylaxis (antibiotics, etc.)
- Cost of training: training professionals, resources, and personnel hours
- Cost of constructing evacuation avenues, decontamination sites, and "safe rooms"
- Cost of temporary or permanent loss of business and government functionality
- Cost of securing substitute personnel in case of temporary or permanent loss of regular personnel

References

1. Centre for Research on the Epidemiology of Disasters, United Nations Office for Disaster Risk Reduction: 1995–2005. The Human Cost of Weather Related Disasters. http://cred.be/HCWRD.
2. Guha-Sapir D, Below R, Hoyois, P. EM-DAT: The CRED/OFDA International Disaster Database. www.emdat.be. Université Catholique de Louvain. Brussels, Belgium; 2016.
3. World Nuclear Association. Fukushima Accident. http://www.world-nuclear.org/information-library/safety-and-security/safety-of-plants/fukushima-accident.aspx. 2016.
4. Johnson JA, Johnson JA. Applied social sciences and public health disaster response: Comparative analysis of New Orleans, Haiti, and Japan. *National Social Science Journal.* January 2013; 39(2):52–59. http://www.nssa.us/journals/pdf/NSS_Journal_39_2.pdf. Accessed March 7, 2016
5. Jawerth, N. Five years after Fukushima: making nuclear power safer. International Atomic Energy Agency. Published March 2016. Accessed June 1, 2016. https://www.iaea.org/newscenter/news/five-years-after-fukushima-making-nuclear-power-safer.
6. United Nations Development Programme. Human Development Index. http://hdr.undp.org/en/content/human-development-index-hdi. Published 2015. Accessed June 1, 2016.
7. World Bank Group. Clean Water, Improved Sanitation, Better Health. Haiti Conference. Washington, DC. https://www.worldbank.org/content/dam/Worldbank/document/book_haiti_6oct_print.pdf. Published October 2014. Accessed July 6, 2016.
8. World Health Organization. Media Centre: HIV/AIDS. http://www.who.int/mediacentre/factsheets/fs360/en/. 2016. Accessed July 3, 2016.
9. The Henry J. Kaiser Family Foundation. Global Health Policy. The global HIV/AIDS epidemic. http://kff.org/global-health-policy/fact-sheet/the-global-hivaids-epidemic/. Published. 2015. Accessed June 26, 2016.
10. World Health Organization. Zika situation report: neurological syndrome and congenital abnormalities. http://apps.who.int/iris/bitstream/10665/204348/1/zikasitrep_5Feb2016_eng.pdf. Published 2016. Accessed July 6, 2016.
11. World Health Organization. The history of Zika virus. http://www.who.int/emergencies/zika-virus/history/en/. Updated 2016. Accessed July 6, 2016.
12. World Health Organization. Microcephaly. http://who.int/mediacentre/factsheets/microcephaly/en/. Published 2016. Accessed July 6, 2016.
13. World Health Organization. Epidemiological update. http://www.who.int/emergencies/zika-virus/situation-report/14-july-2016/en/. Published 2016. Accessed July 14, 2106.
14. World Health Organization. Ebola virus disease. http://www.who.int/mediacentre/factsheets/fs103/en/. Published 2016. Accessed June 20, 2016
15. World Health Organization. Emergency preparedness, response: six months after the Ebola outbreak was declared. What happens when a deadly virus hits the destitute?

http://www.who.int/csr/disease/ebola/ebola-6-months/en/. Published 2016. June 23, 2016.
16. Haagmans BL, Osterhaus A. SARS: From Zoonosis to Pandemic Threat. In: Lashley FR, Durham JD, eds., *Emerging Infectious Diseases*. 2nd ed. 2016; New York, NY: Springer.
17. Varia M, Wilson S, Sarwal S, et al. Investigation of a nosocomial outbreak of severe acute respiratory syndrome. *Canadian Medical Association Journal*. Toronto, Canada: August 2003; 169(4):285–292.
18. Silverman A, Simor A, Loutfy, ML. Toronto emergency medical services and SARS. *Emerging Infectious Diseases*. September 10, 2004; 10(9). doi: 10.3201/eid1009.040170.
19. Sharma VK, Ashtutosh DK. Natural disaster management in India. *Yojana*. 30–36. http://insightsonindia.com/wp-content/uploads/2013/09/natural-disaster-management-in-india.pdf. March 2012. Accessed June 1, 2016
20. Graumann A, Houston T, Lawrimore J, et al. Hurricane Katrina: a climatological perspective. In: *National Oceanic and Atmospheric Administration*. Published August 2006. http://www1.ncdc.noaa.gov/pub/data/techrpts/tr200501/tech-report-200501z.pdf. Accessed June 30, 2016.
21. Johnson JA. *Health Organizations: Theory Behavior, and Development*. Sudbury: Jones and Bartlett Publishers; 2009.
22. Lister, SA. Hurricane Katrina: The public health and medical response. In: Congressional Research Service. Washington, DC: Library of Congress; 2006:1–23. http://fpc.state.gov/documents/organization/54255.pdf. Published 2006. Accessed June 24, 2016
23. Martin, JR. Disaster phases and earthquake policies. https://training.fema.gov/emiweb/downloads/earthquakeem/session%2008/session%208%20-%20disaster%20phases%20final_01.pdf. Published 2008. Accessed June 24, 2016
24. Pan American Health Organization, World Health Organization. Zika—epidemiological update. http://www.paho.org/hq/index.php?option=com_docman&task=doc_view&Itemid=270&gid=35262&lang=en. Published June 30, 2016. Accessed August 6, 2016.
25. Federal Emergency Management Agency. What is mitigation? https://www.fema.gov/what-mitigation. July 1, 2016.
26. Lindsay, BR. *Federal Emergency Management: A Brief Introduction*. Washington, DC: Library of Congress; 2012:1–5. https://training.fema.gov/hiedu/highref/federal%20em-a%20brief%20introduction-r42845%20-%20lindsay.pdf. Accessed June 24, 2016
27. Johnson. JA, Johnson A. Community preparedness and response. *National Social Science Perspectives Journal*. 2006; 33(1):27–30.
28. Dowell SF, Tappero JW, Frieden TR. Public health in Haiti—challenges and progress. *NEJM*. January 27, 2011:300–301. http://www.nejm.org/doi/pdf/10.1056/NEJMp1100118 Accessed June 15, 2016.
29. Kanji L. Hidden dangers: the implications of the global security agenda. *Harvard International Review*. 2016;37(2):8–12.
30. Rosenbaum, B. Making the millennium development goals sustainable: the transition from MDG's to SDG's. *Harvard International Review*. 2015;37(1):58–62.

CHAPTER 29
Comparative Global Challenges and Opportunities

James A. Johnson and **Carleen H. Stoskopf**

▸ Introduction

Health systems in the 21st century are facing many new challenges as they seek to provide health care for growing populations with increasingly complex medical conditions. There is a global labor shortage of skilled professionals, especially nurses and physicians. Facilities are in need of repair or upgrading; improvements in efficiency, effectiveness, and equity remain elusive in many cases; and financial resources are often in short supply.

As described in previous chapters of this book, there are many aspirations and opportunities for improving the scope and effectiveness of health systems within the overall agenda for global health. The United Nations has approved goals that will help achieve this. These Sustainable Development Goals (SDGs) are designed to support well-being at all levels of society. However, there is one that is specifically focused on health. This is referred to as SDG 3 and has 13 targets, as summarized here:

- By 2030, reduce the global maternal mortality ratio to less than 70 per 100,000 live births.
- By 2030, end preventable deaths of newborns and children under 5 years of age, with all countries aiming to reduce neonatal mortality to at least as low as 12 per 1,000 live births and under-five mortality to at least as low as 25 per 1,000 live births.
- By 2030, end the epidemics of AIDS, tuberculosis, malaria, and neglected tropical diseases and combat hepatitis, waterborne diseases and other communicable diseases.
- By 2030, reduce by one-third premature mortality from noncommunicable diseases through prevention and treatment and promote mental health and well-being.
- Strengthen the prevention and treatment of substance abuse, including narcotic drug abuse and harmful use of alcohol.
- By 2020, halve the number of global deaths and injuries from road traffic accidents.
- By 2030, ensure universal access to sexual and reproductive healthcare services, including for family planning, information and education, and the integration of reproductive health into national strategies and programs.
- Achieve universal health coverage, including financial risk protection, access to quality essential healthcare services, and access to safe, effective, quality, and affordable essential medicines and vaccines for all.
- By 2030, substantially reduce the number of deaths and illnesses from hazardous chemicals and air, water, and soil pollution and contamination.
- Strengthen the implementation of the WHO Framework Convention on Tobacco Control in all countries.

- Support the research and development of vaccines and medicines for the communicable and noncommunicable diseases that primarily affect developing countries and provide access to affordable essential medicines and vaccines.
- Substantially increase health financing and the recruitment, development, training, and retention of the health workforce in developing countries, especially in least developed countries and small island developing states.
- Strengthen the capacity of all countries for early warning, risk reduction, and management of national and global health risks.

Concurrent with these aspirations and the requisite work that will be done to achieve the goals and meet targets, there are other opportunities described in the remainder of this chapter. There are also challenges and perhaps a few barriers, that will require robust health systems and strong leadership.

International Health Policy, Globalization, and Privatization

It is the policy of most international funding organizations, such as the World Bank and the International Monetary Fund, to encourage developing countries to move to privatization of their healthcare systems. The World Bank furthers this agenda by having privatization as an objective of many of their funded projects in developing countries, by funding priorities of the International Funding Corporation, and by providing investment guarantees through the Multilateral Investment Guarantee Agency. The International Funding Corporation invests only in the private sector and is targeting areas such as water, transportation systems, education, health care, and the environment. The Trade-Related Aspects of Intellectual Property Rights group works actively on a global scale to ensure that pharmaceutical companies and their patents are protected in developing countries, keeping the cost of drugs high worldwide, contributing to the profits of those countries, and preventing countries from making their own drugs and providing them at cost to their own citizens. The International Monetary Fund has as its policy to privatize public services, including healthcare systems, a condition of their loans.

Second, the multinational corporations are marketing to developing countries. The World Trade Organization has spent a decade promoting privatization of healthcare systems as well. Through the General Agreement on Trade in Service, privatization is promoted as a core principle of the World Trade Organization. Adding to this trend is the role that NAFTA (North American Free Trade Agreement) and the European Union are playing. Both work to open the markets of developing counties to private companies of the developed world. These groups are seen as treating health care worldwide as a marketing opportunity. What is being promoted in developing countries is an expansion of their sales for diagnostic and therapy services, such as dialysis, blood products, and magnetic resonance imaging scans. Also, these treaties work to open markets to Health Maintenance Organizations and other insurers to operate in developing countries.[1-3]

The policies of the organizations outlined previously are consistent with that of creating competition in economies and consistent with their push for free trade across countries. These policies are also consistent with the belief that competition provides the best product or service at the lowest price. Competition also creates an environment conducive to innovation in what services are provided and how they are delivered. In regard to healthcare organizations, a privately financed healthcare system would rely on a third-party payer and health insurance premiums paid by individuals or paid in conjunction with employers. When services are delivered, the healthcare practitioner would be reimbursed for his or her services by the health insurance plan. There have been some attempts by U.S. groups to move their financing and delivery services for health care into other countries, but so far, this effort has been weak. Also, U.S. hospitals have not been successful in expanding into other countries. What has been successful is the expansion and privatization of such healthcare services as cleaning, laundry, and food service; however, as we move further into the 21st century, it is believed that multinational companies and their subsidiaries will try to continue their expansion and that they hope that as more free trade agreements emerge, profitable opportunities will grow.

There are several problems with privatization and competition in healthcare services. First, most people do not want to purchase this service. Second, people purchasing health care do so with serious information inequality (information asymmetry) regarding the services they are purchasing. How does a patient know whether he or she has purchased the best appendectomy? Comparison shopping is not easily done for most healthcare services, especially emergency services. Third, where individual healthcare services are concerned, no one wants a bargain. Everyone wants premium services, whereas with other services the purchaser may not actually buy the most expensive product for a variety of rational reasons. Consumers are irrational when it comes to purchasing health services. Fourth, other services are not bought through a third-party payer, a situation that removes the individual from the purchasing process. Finally, outcomes are difficult to measure. A quote from the Public Services International Research Unit at the University of Greenwich is this: "Health care industry goods and services differ significantly from those of other industries in one very particular way: the product or output of the industry is not often as tangible or measurable. From a producer's perspective, and even more so from that of a consumer, health care is an unpredictable industry with a hard-to-define output."[4]

Although it is understandable that governments want and need employers to assist in paying for healthcare services, this type of system can lead to inequities in healthcare access and services and to a two-tiered system of care—those with insurance and those without. In some countries described in this book, Russia and Turkey, those without health insurance partially paid by an employer are left to access a public healthcare system that often has limited resources and substandard government facilities. Not only are these systems poorly funded but also healthcare practitioners migrate to the private systems that serve the privately insured, as the potential for increased incomes is much greater, especially in high-technology, specialized medicine. This leaves only a few practitioners, who often are not specialized, to care for "the other half of society" in public systems with limited equipment and administrative support, poor infrastructure, limited resources such as laboratories and pharmacies, and reduced nursing care; therefore creating a government network available for those without employment-based insurance often forces the most vulnerable (the elderly and the poor) to use only safety net providers and have little access to higher quality care.

Barriers to privatization of healthcare systems in developing countries include installation and maintenance of advanced information systems. Privatization with insurance companies or health maintenance organizations requires that health information is collected on patients, access and utilization information is captured, billing information can be made available, and financing can be tracked. There are also issues of unionized workers in countries where unions have been a tradition, understanding local and culture-specific healthcare needs and marketing to those groups, providing high-technology equipment and maintaining it while making a profit, and providing pharmaceuticals at a price that can be afforded in these markets.[5]

One solution to this problem can be seen when those who are not working have their health insurance premiums paid by the government. This places these vulnerable populations in the health insurance risk pool with the entire population and gives them access to the same quality of health services the working population has. It also allows for privatization. This approach reduces the probability of creating a two-tiered system and promotes the concept of a true risk pool, where risk is truly spread across an entire population. South Korea is a country that engages in this type of health insurance coverage for all of its population.

▶ Decentralization

Most countries are attempting to decentralize their healthcare systems. By *decentralization* we mean "a political reform, designed to reduce the extent of central influence and promote local autonomy."[6] The level of decentralization used in healthcare systems is a continuous issue of concern. Decentralization is praised as an instrument for improving efficiency and quality. Theoretically, when decisions are made locally, people who have more knowledge of local conditions will have better input for the services needed, can give more immediate feedback on the quality of care, and are more attuned to what actual healthcare services cost. This approach is good from the perspective that those making decisions are closer to the problems in their jurisdiction. Local administrators and politicians do tend to have a better understanding of local problems and populations and therefore should be able to use resources in the most efficient manner for that locale. Local officials can be held accountable for poor quality by the people who live in their communities. The downside of decentralization is that the needed funding and other resources do not necessarily accompany the responsibility or mandate for providing appropriate health care in local areas. Rather, a noticeable trend is for central governments to put demands on local governments to provide part of the funding for the healthcare system, something that many are not prepared to do. The local governments now have the responsibility but not the money. They have the authority to raise money but a population who cannot afford to be further taxed. The health systems in some countries have given much responsibility to regional and local governments for the provision of health care but without providing the means to do so. The local governments are unable to raise the money from their poor populations to provide quality health care, and thus, the demand for health goes unmet.

Some of the other issues that are raised, especially in developing countries, are information asymmetry, local politics, capability of local officials, poor local tax base, keeping the same values between the central and local administrations (congruence), and difficulty in coordinating services. Perhaps the biggest hurdle to successful decentralization is ensuring that local leaders, especially healthcare leaders, have the training necessary to carry out the complex activities of finding resources, deciding on their use, and providing a range of health services while meeting the hugely diverse needs of the population being served. Should resources be spent on preventive care, primary care, or care of elderly people? A major difference seen between the United States and some other developed countries and less developed countries is the use of specially trained healthcare management professionals who are educated specifically in business. To be successful at all levels of healthcare system management, the people doing the administering must understand financing, work design, information systems, policy, and human resources, to name a few, as well as the basics of medicine and science. The melding of the skills of business managers, politicians, and medical practitioners is not easy to achieve at any level, but especially not in small, local arenas.

The quality of decision making at these lower levels of the healthcare system may not be as good. The complexities of providing health care at a local level often result in healthcare systems that are ineffective and wasteful. The person making the healthcare decisions must work within the framework of local politics. Local politicians may have their own reasons for providing certain types of healthcare services, such as owning hospitals or long-term care facilities. Local healthcare administrators may actually work for the politicians. Unfortunately, in developing countries, funds that are put into the hands of local administrators or officials are not always used for the intended purpose. The issues of graft in developing countries among government officials at all levels seriously contribute to ongoing poverty.

Health Care as an Increasing Portion of GDP

Nearly all countries are reporting that their healthcare expenditures are continuing to increase as a percentage of GDP. The question is how high can these percentages go before the opportunity costs are too high? Although this trend is seen virtually everywhere, this situation is a problem primarily for the many developed countries where the percentage is inching over 10%. Countries including Japan, South Korea, Germany, Switzerland, the United Kingdom, and certainly the United States are struggling to control their healthcare expenditures as the percentage of GDP that they represent continues to creep upward. The United States is seeing its healthcare costs, as the highest percentage of its GDP, topping 16%. The crucial question is what could we be spending our money on instead? Could it be infrastructure, education, or manufacturing? Should some of this money be better directed toward eliminating, or at least addressing, poverty, inequity, and social injustices?

Is there such a thing as too much health care? On the other hand, the healthcare industry itself is very desirable for many communities. In the United States, for example, small hospitals in rural areas are often the major employers in that community. The majority of jobs in healthcare systems are well paid, and for those that are not (food service, custodial care), there are good employment benefits. Healthcare workers as a group perhaps form the most educated industry overall. The jobs are often highly technical and highly credentialed and require a fair amount of education, even in supporting roles such as administrative. These healthcare workers have higher salaries, pay more taxes, own more homes, purchase more, and make major contributions to their communities. The future appears to promise continuing increases in healthcare expenditure, especially among the developed countries.

Injuries and Violence

There is an increase in injuries, trauma, and death caused by violence globally. Violence is defined as "the intentional use of physical force or power, threatened or actual, against oneself, another person, or against a group or community … that either results in injury, death, psychological harm, maldevelopment or deprivation."[7] Although vital statistics and surveillance are inadequate in so many areas of the world, there is still evidence of increases in injuries and violence. Injuries increase as more people in developing countries purchase automobiles while safety laws lag behind. Inadequate preparation of new drivers, poorly maintained vehicles, and a lack of traffic signs and laws make roads in many parts of the world unsafe. Second, there are areas where violence from cartels, smuggling, and gangs is common (Latin America), and other areas of the world experience violence caused by wars and political/tribal unrest (sub-Saharan Africa and the Middle Eastern crescent). In our chapters on Mexico and Nigeria, these concerns are voiced.

In the later part of the 20th century, death caused by violence emerged as a serious threat to the public's health. Using data from the Global Burden of Disease, over 1.8 million people died of violence (35 per 100,000 population). Death from violence included suicide, homicide, and deaths caused by war.[8] Homicides were highest in sub-Saharan Africa, followed by Latin American countries, whereas suicide was the highest in China and countries whose economies were formerly socialist. Death from wars was highest in sub-Saharan Africa, followed by the Middle Eastern crescent.[9]

In addition to deaths from the three previously mentioned causes, there is a tremendous amount of violence that does not end in death but instead results in extensive injury and disability. Included in this category are spousal and child abuse, neglect by caregivers, elderly abuse, sexual violence, self-directed abuse, and collective violence.

Acts of violence and their consequences put considerable strain on healthcare systems and divert resources from other pressing healthcare needs. Incidents of violence often have long-term consequences, not only physically but also for mental health. In fact, psychological violence can cause extensive disruption to individuals, families, and communities. Another type of violence is deprivation, under which individuals can be deprived of basic needs, such as shelter, food, and water, or deprived of emotional support. Violence is often enabled by the presence of alcohol and drugs, availability of firearms, and social and economic inequities or injustices. Consequences of violence include behavioral problems, depression and/or anxiety, drug and alcohol abuse, and reproductive health problems.[10] Causes of violence can be categorized into four levels: (1) personal/biological factors, (2) close relationships, (3) community, and (4) broad societal factors.

In response to violence, countries provide adequate and appropriate services to the victims of violence, engage in legislative reform, perform better data collection and research on the causes of violence and successful interventions, and have organizations responsible for monitoring violence. Most needed to carry out these activities are a commitment to funding nationally, community empowerment so that individuals feel ownership of the behavior in their communities, and a global commitment to reducing wars and conflicts.

▶ Mental Illness

Necessary to health and well-being is good mental health. Generally about 15% of the burden of illness is from mental illness, the most prevalent of these being depression, substance abuse, and anxiety disorders. Also of importance is that mental illness is closely associated with a variety of physical illness, both chronic and communicable, as well as increased injury. Depression is of special concern as social and economic conditions worsen, such as overcrowding, increased war and refugees, decreased access to food and water due to climate change, competition for fuel, and greater disparity between the world's rich and poor.[11]

The challenge for the future is for healthcare providers, insurers, and policymakers to put mental health on a par with physical illnesses in terms of early diagnosis and correct diagnosis, as well as treatment. More importantly is that the causes of mental illness, in particular the causes of depression and substance abuse, must be recognized and addressed. Once again, the conversation turns to social determinants of health status, especially those associated with mental illness. Such factors as socioeconomic development, educational attainment, technological advances, environmental hazards, and how they are distributed in populations continue to be major contributors to morbidity and mortality.[12]

Globally, resources for mental health are well below those provided for other types of illness, in both developed and developing countries. The least developed countries put the fewest resources in mental health, and the care that is available is usually institutionally based. Coupled with cultural views of the mentally ill among many populations, services are poorly funded and provided and not considered a priority.

Most countries lack qualified health practitioners in numbers adequate to diagnose, treat, and care for mentally ill people. The inability to address mental illness will impact treatment of other illnesses. Given that today many mental illnesses are treatable, this is difficult to witness. Even in developed countries, where identification and treatment of mental illness is more advanced, there is inequity in access, treatment, and outcomes among varying groups in these populations.[13] Furthermore, those who are mentally ill face many difficulties in their communities where mental illness may be associated with "bad spirits," the supernatural, or an embarrassment to family and friends and the community as a whole.

▶ Aging Population

All developed countries, and to a lesser extent developing countries, are facing the issues of aging population. These issues include (1) increasing healthcare costs/fewer young people to spread the risk, (2) an inability to replace the elderly in the workforce, (3) inadequate planning for long-term care solutions/facilities, (4) how to finance health care and pensions, and (5) end-of-life costs. The older population is generally defined as people aged 65 and older. Since 1950, the numbers of older people have increased from 4% of the world population to nearly 7% in 2000. This trend is expected to continue, especially as the baby boomers enter this age group. In addition, those in the 65-and-older category are aging, and more people are living to age 85 and older. Europe and North America lead in the percentage of older people, but all countries, including developing countries, are experiencing population aging.

Although in some areas of the world, aging is not occurring as fast, it is nevertheless occurring. In some of the world, such as in sub-Saharan Africa, the governments are the least able to deal with these shifting demographics. As populations age, the need for more healthcare services rises, and those services needed by the older population are often different from the ones provided to the younger part of the population, such as chronic disease management versus vaccinations and infectious disease management. Aging also puts more strain on other types of services provided by caregivers, case managers, and other groups that support finding adequate shelter, food, protection, and support/social networks for older people.[14]

A second problem that arises with an increase in the percentage of the older population is that there are fewer individuals in the workforce to support pensions, to share in the risk pool of health insurance, and to provide a tax base for all government functions. Fertility has declined worldwide, even in developing countries, and the aging of the population will be a problem. At the same time, those who reach age 60 have a longer predicted life span from that time forward than ever before. This is especially true in developed countries where modern medicine and improvements in lifestyle have created the highest proportions of older people. As less developed countries continue to move forward in the world economy, the life expectancy of their older people will grow as well. The rate of older people grows at a rate of 2.6% per year, whereas the population as a whole grows at a rate of 1.1% per year. In developing countries, the fastest growth among those 65 and older is among those in the lowest socioeconomic groups, who are already vulnerable due to many other factors. **TABLE 29-1** shows the changes in age demographics between 1950, 2000, and estimations for 2050 worldwide. The ratio of those in the workforce to older people declines. The median age increases. The absolute numbers of those 60 and older increases dramatically, and among the older population, the number of those 85 and older in relation to those aged 50 to 64 increases.[15(xxv–xxix)] All of these demographic changes have consequences on many levels, and much work is needed to ensure that those 65 and older have quality health care available, adequate pensions, affordable housing and food, social networks and support, and quality of life and well-being.

▸ Environmental Impact/Climate Change

As climate change proceeds, there is considerable evidence that the world is getting warmer and drier. This has resulted in an increase in droughts in North America, Africa, and China. The overall impact of climate change contributes to food scarcity and political destabilization. Unfortunately, despite the efforts of many international groups and the high-profile work of people like Nobel Laureate Al Gore, there still is no

TABLE 29-1 Global Demographic Changes from 1950 to 2050

Statistic	1950	2000	2050
Support ratio: people in the workforce per person age 65 and older	12:1	9:1	4:1
Median age	—	28	38
People aged 60 and older	200 million	600 million	2 billion
People aged 85 and older to people aged 50–64	2:100	4:100	12:100

Data from United Nations Department of Economic and Social Affairs, Population Division. Executive Summary: World Population Aging 2007. http://www.un.org/esa/population/publications/WPA2007/wpp2007.htm. 2007.

grand consensus on how to best deal with an impending global crisis. Some countries, such as Germany, have worked hard to reduce carbon emissions whereas others, like the United States, have a mixed approach. The Olympics in China underscored the need for China and other rapidly developing countries to control air and water pollution better. An increasing incidence of respiratory disorders furthers the urgency of addressing this problem. Furthermore, the Intergovernmental Panel on Climate Change (established by the United Nations and the World Meteorological Society) issued a report in 2007 concluding that without a dramatic reduction in human-induced carbon dioxide emissions, climate change may bring "abrupt or irreversible" effects on air, oceans, glaciers, land, coastlines, and species.[16] Climate change also contributes to an increase in infectious disease because the range of disease vectors increases with the warming of various regions of the world. Climate change has also been associated with changes in weather patterns that have resulted in increases in storms and floods. Hurricane Katrina in the United States provided a glaring example of how ill-prepared even the wealthy nations are in dealing with such disasters. As we have seen, health systems are often vulnerable during times of disaster, thus leaving people unserved at a time of greatest need. Many health systems are already functioning on limited budgets and are currently understaffed. The extra stressors of natural disaster is often enough to cause a serious disruption in even the most basic services.

There is a slow but vibrant movement to create sustainable health systems (**BOXES 29-1**, **29-2**, and **29-3**) that can generate their own electricity and be independent of local power grids. Others have ongoing disaster training exercises and contingency plans to address the challenges of natural disaster.

▶ Refugees, Displaced People, and Humanitarian Crises

The number of people who are displaced forcibly has never been higher. The United Nations High Commission on Refugees estimates that there are 65.3 million people who have been forcibly displaced worldwide due to war and violence, sustained droughts, earthquakes, and severe weather events. Of those, 21.3 million are categorized as refugees and over half of those are under the age of 18. Ten million people are considered stateless, which means that they have "been denied a nationality and access to basic human rights that include education, health care, employment, and freedom of movement."[17] According to the World Health Organization, "A refugee is someone who fears being persecuted for reasons of race, religion, nationality, membership of a particular social group, or political opinion. A refugee is outside the country of his or her nationality, and is unable to, or unwilling to be protected by that country."[18] More than half (54%) of refugees come from just three countries: Somalia, Afghanistan, and Syria.[19]

The medical challenges of refugees include many common problems but with a higher incidence and prevalence. The most prevalent are accidental injuries, hypothermia, burns, cardiovascular events, pregnancy and delivery complications, diabetes, and hypertension. Women experience problems related to maternal, newborn, and child health, sexual and reproductive health, and violence. Refugee children have high rates of respiratory infections, diarrhea, and skin infections due to poor hygiene.[18]

The poor health status of refugees occurs for a variety of reasons. Most importantly is lack of hygiene facilities (adequate toilets, sewage disposal, and bathing areas) and clean water supplies, which contribute to diarrhea and skin infections. Furthermore, refugees experience an increase in psychosocial disorders associated with the complete disruption in their lives, which increases the rates of alcohol and drug abuse and can lead to increased violence. Refugees lose all continuity in their health care, especially among those with chronic diseases; incidences of heart disease, diabetes, and hypertension are greatly increased among refugees due to disruption in their care and medications. Many of these chronic health issues are made worse by the stress and conditions endured by people who find themselves in this most untenable situation. Although health care may be available, it is generally not enough care, the right care, or provided in a timely manner. The refugee healthcare "system" is dependent upon donors and the ability of the host nation to provide healthcare services. Food supplies are uncertain for most refugees, both in camps and during the process of fleeing their countries, resulting in a higher incidence of malnutrition, especially among children. Finally, refugees, who are already compromised in so many ways, fall victim to violence by those who find these situations opportunities for crime. The health of refugees creates health challenges and crises that health systems in host countries, international health agencies, and non-governmental organizations (NGOs) must work to meet. The challenges are daunting.[20]

At any given time, many healthcare systems in countries worldwide are challenged by humanitarian crises and require humanitarian assistance

BOX 29-1 Sustainability in Health Systems

Dr. George Velez

Sustainability uses the *triple bottom line* of financial viability, social responsiveness, and environmental responsibility and applies systems thinking to the strategic development of sustainability efforts. This is a critical component for health systems to integrate holistic strategic processes to support sustainability efforts of initiatives, services, and the mission of the organization as a whole. A healthcare organization is a microcommunity living within a larger community. Hence, the sense of culture and community, stewardship, and neighborliness are essential components of most healthcare system sustainability strategies. Healthcare systems in the near future will confront several critical issues on multiple levels. These issues are not unique to health care but certainly will drive urgencies and opportunities in the years to come. Some examples of these critical issues are significant changes in the aging of the population, in family structure, and in employment patterns that will influence reimbursement schemes and change traditional healthcare benefits. In view of these challenges, health systems cannot be sustained without addressing the trade-off between restricted resources (financial, people, environmental) and reaching overall health policy goals within the context of community and environmental stewardship. It will be crucial to generate new strategies for controlling the complex mechanisms that affect expenditure and performance of healthcare sustainability while striving for the achievement of core objectives of healthcare policies, such as universal access, high-quality standards, efficiency and effectiveness, adequate funding, and satisfaction of patients.

BOX 29-2 Community Health Centers

Dr. Neil Steven Gardner

The community health center (CHC) movement in the United States began in the mid-1960s, an outgrowth of the neighborhood health clinics that were part of the early social programs of that period. The CHC model reflects the pioneering work done in South Africa in the 1940s by Drs. Sidney and Emily Kark. The early centers in the United States were sometimes established more on social/political considerations than with the objective of delivering primary health care. This was also the case with the Community Health Program (CHP) centers established in South Australia. The current CHC model in the United States, more specifically the Federally Qualified Health Centers, provides primary healthcare services to people who otherwise would not have access to such services. Many CHCs are housed in state-of-the-art clinical facilities providing professional and pleasant family-oriented health care. In the case of South Australia, the CHP centers have been used as part of a national program to provide universal access to health care. The Australian model was initially supported by the Commonwealth Government, but with subsequent revisions to the program, the centers became the responsibility of the Australian states.

India has a three-tiered system of public healthcare delivery that includes community health centers. In that nation, the CHCs receive cases from the basic primary health centers, which are the foundation of health services serving some 25,000 in the rural areas of India. The CHCs refer cases to the 30-bed hospitals and higher level hospitals at the district level as necessary.

In the United States, there is collaboration between the federal government and the communities that are being served. The federal funding to a CHC never represents the total budget. There is the expectation for the CHC to leverage the federal dollars through enhanced Medicaid reimbursement, additional sources of funding, and private insurance reimbursements, as well as self-payment by users of the center based on a sliding fee scale that determines an individual's ability to pay.

In both the United States and Australia, there has been an emphasis on community involvement; an aspect that may be a factor contributing to the sustainability of the CHC model. This community involvement includes a U.S. requirement of 51% user representation on the governing board of the center.

In addition to well visits, specialty care services are often available in community health centers in the United States or through paid referral for services. The model has emphasized wellness and prevention. Under the current models, no one is denied access to care. After care is sought, there is the opportunity to promote wellness and prevention through the services offered by the center. Although most of the current users in the United States are below 200% of the federal poverty level and are without health coverage, there are a number of center users who have private commercial health insurance coverage. In the United States, especially in rural areas where there are no other healthcare facilities available, insured and self-paying users make up a significant portion of the patient mix of the CHC. This is also the case in centers that are established around a culturally specific community, the attraction being culturally sensitive care.

BOX 29-3 Health System Designs for the 21st Century

Dr. Glenn A. Croxton

A series of papers related to the design of hospitals for the 21st century was presented by the Center for Health Design and Health Care Without Harm at a conference sponsored by the Robert Wood Johnson Foundation, September 2006. The Center for Health Design is a nonprofit research and advocacy organization. Its mission is to transform healthcare settings into healing environments. The healing environment is seen as a vital part of therapeutic treatment and where design of healthcare setting contributes to health rather than adding to the burden of stress.

Health Care Without Harm is an international coalition of 440 groups in 55 countries working to transform the healthcare industry so that it is ecologically sustainable and no longer of harm to people and the environment.

First, Do No Harm

Gary Cohen discussed how healthcare institutions that support the Hippocratic Oath have a special responsibility to ensure that their operations are not major sources of chemical exposure and environmental harm. Until recently, healthcare professionals and hospital administrators were unaware of their contributions to chemical contaminants and broader societal disease burdens according to Cohen.

Chronic diseases and disabilities now affect more than 90 million men, women, and children in the United States alone. In spite of much advancement in medical practice, the best available data show an increase in the incidence of asthma, autism, birth defects, childhood brain cancer, acute lymphocytic leukemia, endometriosis, Parkinson's disease, and infertility. The economic costs of these diseases by 2020 will exceed US $1 trillion yearly in healthcare cost and lost productivity.

The field of environmental health is attempting to link each of these diseases and disorders to exposure to toxic chemicals. The old way of looking at chemical risk and safety would have missed these links, as they are not as simple as single cause and single effect. Through the new lens of science, we have learned that exposure to toxic chemicals, at levels thought to have been safe, is increasing the chronic disease burden of millions of Americans.

Green Hospitals

The second paper, "Values-Driven Design and Construction: Enriching Community Benefits through Green Hospitals," was presented by Robin Guenther, Gail Vittori, and Cynthia Atwood. They discussed how many hospitals are successfully reaching beyond measures that have economic payback and are achieving community benefits beyond their four walls. Healthcare leaders recognize the high costs of inaction on matters of the environment—such as climate change and chemical contamination on the health of our families, neighbors, and communities at hand and globally. By embedding sustainable design in a broader vision of leadership and mission, these projects and organizations are succeeding in delivering the first generations of sustainable healthcare projects.

Ted Schettler, MD, MPH, identified three tiers of operational environmental performance evolving in hospitals.

- Tier 1: minimum local, state, and national environmental performance
- Tier 2: beyond compliance to measures that save money
- Tier 3: informed by inextricable link between environment and human health and moving beyond both compliance and monetary savings with a long-term plan to reduce environmental footprints

He contended that applying *triple bottom line* approaches to pollution-prevention initiatives—that is, measuring economic, social, and environment benefits—would deliver significant benefits for healthcare organizations and the communities they serve. Early tier 3 hospitals supported this notion. Named one of the state's top four recyclers, the University of Michigan Health System described its program's social benefit as an institution-wide initiative that engages everyone.

As building initiatives accelerate, it is clear that we can apply the same system-tiered performance to organizations engaged in sustainable building. Tier 1 organizations will not undertake green building until they are mandated to do so through legislative policy initiatives. They will not make the link or the organizational leap between the health of their facilities and the patients they serve.

Creating Safe and Healthy Spaces: Selecting Materials That Support Healing

Mark Rossi, PhD, and Tom Lent outlined the relationship of the materials and products used in healthcare facilities to the chemicals to which our communities are exposed. Rossi and Lent further described the opportunities available to healthcare organizations to help society break from its dependence on toxic materials and define the path to healthier, sustainable materials that benefit patients, communities, nature, and the organizational bottom line.

(continues)

> **BOX 29-3** Health System Designs for the 21st Century *(Continued)*

Kaiser Permanente, for example, framed its environmental goals for building design in terms of community health in March 2002 in the "Kaiser Permanente Position Statement on Green Buildings."

Kaiser Permanente's mission is to improve the health of the communities served. In recognition of the critical linkages between environmental health and public health, it is Kaiser's desire to limit adverse impacts upon the environment resulting from the siting, design, construction, and operation of our health facilities. We will address the life cycle impacts of facilities through design and construction standards, selection of material and equipment, and maintenance practices. Additionally, KP will require architects, engineers, and contractors to specify commercially available, cost-competitive materials, products, technologies, and processes—where appropriate—that have positive impact or that limit negative impact on environmental quality and human health.

Preventive Medicine for the Environment: Developing and Implementing Environmental Programs that Work

Laura Brannen suggested moving from the theoretical aspects of why healthcare facilities should adopt green principles to how to do it. According to Brannen, healthcare facilities alone generate a tremendous variety and quantity of waste—at least 2 million tons of waste per year—that may represent real occupational and environmental health threats. Healthcare facilities are the fourth largest consumer of energy, spending US $6.5 billion on energy cost alone and accounting for 11% of all commercial energy use. Water consumption and discharge to public sewer systems are excessive. Wastewater contains toxic laboratory and cleaning chemicals and pharmaceutical compounds, many of which are not broken down in sewage treatment plants and are disposed of in landfills, resulting in sewage sludge applied to farmland and released in rivers and streams.

Finally, Brannen sees healthcare facilities of the future that are high-performance buildings that use less energy and less water, require fewer chemicals to maintain, and are designed for maximum operational waste management systems: where materials are purchased with health and environmental considerations, where materials are used efficiently and staff take responsibility for and participate in waste minimization programs, where end-of-life considerations are maximized, and where reuse and recycling are effective.

Redefining Healthy Food: An Ecological Health Approach to Food Production, Distribution, and Procurement

The fifth paper in this series was presented by Jamie Harvie, who discussed the ecological health approach to food production. According to Harvie, food production, distribution, and procurement intersect with a wide variety of issues. Economics, immigration policy, spirituality, agriculture and trade, culture, environment, and nutrition are but several of the myriad concerns associated with the food we grow and eat. There is perhaps no issue that has such a wide depth of actively involved interest. The complexity of interest requires a system, or ecological, approach. Such an approach is challenging because it is not linear and requires observation of the whole context while seeking to understand the connections between the parts.

Hospital food is big business. In 2004 alone, the top healthcare group purchasing organizations purchased approximately US $2.75 billion worth of food. Although patient food receives considerable attention in the media, it is cafeteria and catered food that make up the largest percentage of the food budget, accounting for approximately 55% to 70% of hospital volume.

Hospital and health systems are not only changing procurement practices to support healthy food systems, they are explicitly identifying the link between healthy food systems and healthy patients, communities, and the planet in their policies and programs. These systems are pioneers in an ecological approach to preventive medicine.

Toward an Ecological View of Health: An Imperative for the 21st Century

The final paper presented at the conference was by Ted Schettler, MD, MPH. Schettler began by discussing the relationship between human and environmental health. In 2005, the United Nations released the largest assessment ever undertaken of the health of the earth's ecosystems. More than 1,000 experts from 95 countries prepared the report, which was then reviewed by a large independent board of editors and commented on by hundreds of experts and governments before being released.

The Green Building Council of Australia's environmental rating system, Green Star, has now developed tools to assess buildings in the education, retail, and healthcare sectors. The Green Star—Healthcare rating tool, in particular, aims to address the unique qualities, constraints, and opportunities within hospitals and other medical facilities.

However, it remains much harder to measure the true value of a green hospital because the productivity and operation have different measures and often different management. The majority of hospitals will look at patient

> **BOX 29-3** Health System Designs for the 21st Century *(Continued)*
>
> recovery time, bed turnover, and staff retention to estimate their attributes and performance. The truly green hospital can look at benefits in all of these areas and more, but the situation requires true, holistic investment in people's health.
>
> Finally, Changi General Hospital is Singapore's first purpose-built, multidisciplinary regional hospital, providing healthcare services to approximately 750,000 people in the eastern and northeastern parts of Singapore. Changi General Hospital instilled several green practices within these grounds. Some of these were waste composting from water conservation (the first hospital to use NewWater), increased energy efficiency of their hospital building and installations, waste-minimization methods to control the generation of unnecessary waste in both the administration and day-to-day running of the hospital, and participation in community grassroots education and staff enrichment programs.
>
> Reproduced by permission of Dr. Glenn A. Croxton.

from outside their borders. It is incumbent on donor nations, international agencies, and NGOs to meet these challenges. Some humanitarian crises go on for years, and others are episodic. It is the challenge of the 21st century to be prepared to react swiftly and in unison to meet the basic needs of people in terms of water, food, shelter, safety, and health care. The WHO has identified a number of countries that are in crises as of the summer of 2016. Many humanitarian crises are the result of violence and include northeast Nigeria and the countries that are part of the Lake Chad Basin (Mali and Niger), South Sudan, Yemen, Syria (Allepo), Iraq, Central African Republic, Libya, and Ukraine. These nations are under siege of violence, creating conditions that require immediate humanitarian assistance. These situations are the impetus for people migrating and adding to the problems associated with displaced people and refugees. Other nations are experiencing humanitarian crises of a different nature that deserve and need the attention of the international community. Cameroon is experiencing a measles and monkey pox outbreak; Ethiopia has a severe drought, and it is estimated that 1.7 million people are malnourished as a result; Zanzibar (Tanzania) is experiencing a severe cholera epidemic; Ecuador is recovering from an earthquake that destroyed major infrastructure; and Fiji is recovering from a major typhoon (Winston).[21]

The need for humanitarian aid is varied and unrelenting. Currently the coordination of international relief and health services is, at best, piecemeal and has little coordination. A challenge of the future is to be able to better respond to the crises as they begin. There is a need for quick assessment, movement of appropriate materials and personnel, protection, and the expertise to build and rebuild infrastructure, maintain health services and public health systems, and mitigate damage.

Responding to the challenges of the 21st century and recognizing the need to respond to emergencies quickly, the World Health Organization (WHO) is building a new Health Emergencies Program. This program will be available to member states and is designed to help nations build their capacities to manage health emergency risks, assist when national capacities are overwhelmed, and lead and coordinate the international health response in collaboration to contain outbreaks, provide effective relief, and assist in recovery. WHO will "work with countries and partners to prepare for, prevent, respond to, and recover from all hazards that create health emergencies, including disasters, disease outbreaks, and conflicts." The new Health Emergencies Program will change the way WHO handles emergencies worldwide. It will not be primarily a technical and normative organization but rather will be an agency of its own, with a common structure across the organization, its own budget and planning mechanism, a single workforce, and its own standards and processes. Accountability will be clearly defined. Its goals are to plan for and rapidly deploy expertise and materials to effectively and predictably respond to health emergencies worldwide.

While health systems will continue to be challenged, they will also adapt and continue to move toward greater sustainability.

In conclusion, it can be said that health systems around the globe will be challenged in ways never before considered. The governments and private sectors in these countries will have to work in partnership to ensure the sustainability of vital health services. Additionally, health systems will need to realize their interconnectedness with the rest of the world as we face global pandemics and macro problems, such as climate change. Likewise, at the micro level, health systems will need to reduce bureaucracy by streamlining management, increasing cost-effectiveness, improving efficiency through reorganized services, decentralizing services, and allocating resources to better address the needs of the population.

References

1. Hall D. *Globalization, Privatization and Healthcare—A Preliminary Report*. Public Services International Research Unit. School of Computing and Mathematical Sciences, University of Greenwich. Greenwich: University of Greenwich; 2001.
2. Pollock AM, Price D. Rewriting the regulations: how the World Trade Organization could accelerate privatization in the health care system. *Lancet*. 2000;356(9246):1995–2000.
3. OXFAM America. http://www.oxfamamerica.org/whatwedo/issuesweworkon/trade/newspublications/trips/art5391.html. Accessed June 23, 2008.
4. 2nd Annual Global Healthcare Expansion Congress. Dubai, UAE. 2007.
5. Lethbridge J. A global review of the expansion of multinational healthcare companies. Public Services International Research Unit, University of Greenwich; September 2007. www.psiru.org.
6. World Bank. Decentralization. http://go.worldbank.org/MUFMCLWJR1. Accessed November 2016.
7. La Vecchia C, Lucchini F, Levi F. Worldwide trends in suicide mortality, 1955–1989. *Acta of Psychiatry Scandinavia*. 1994;90:53–64.
8. Murray CJL, Lopez AD, eds. *The Global Burden of Disease*. Cambridge, MA: Harvard University Press; 1996.
9. Reza Q, Mercy JA, Krug E. Epidemiology of violent deaths in the world. *Injury Prevention*. 2001;7:104–111.
10. Krug EG, Mercy JA, Dahlberg LL, Zwi AB. The world report on violence and health. *Lancet*. 2002;360(9339):1083–1088.
11. Prince M, Patel V, Saxena S, et al. Global mental health 1: no health without mental health. *Lancet*. 2007;307(9590):859–878.
12. Murray CJL, Lopez AD. Alternative projections of mortality and disability by cause 1990–2020: the global burden of disease study. *Lancet*. 1997;349(9064):1498–1504.
13. Saxena S, Thorniroft G, Knapp M, Whiteford H. Global mental health 2: resources for mental health: scarcity, inequity, and inefficiency. *Lancet*. 2007;370(9590):878–890.
14. Rand Corporation. Preparing for an aging world. http://www.rand.org/pubs/research_briefs/RB5058/index1.html. Accessed November 2016.
15. United Nations Department of Economic and Social Affairs. Population Division. *Executive Summary: World Population Aging 2007*. New York: United Nations; 2007.
16. Friedman T. *Hot, Flat, and Crowded*. New York: Farrar Strauss & Giroux; 2008.
17. United Nations High Commission on Refugees. Figures at a Glance. www.unhcr.org/en-us/figures-at-a-glande/html. 2015. Accessed September 27, 2016.
18. World Health Organization. Health topics: refugees. www.who.int/topics/refugees/en. Accessed September 26, 2016.
19. United Nations High Commission on Refugees. Figures at a Glance. September 27, 2016.
20. World Health Organization, September 2015, Features Q & A: Refugees. www.who.int/features/qa/88/en/. Accessed 9/27/2016.
21. World Health Organization, 2016. Emergencies. www.who.int/emergencies/en/. Accessed 9/27/2016.

Glossary of Health Systems Terms[1]

A

Access An individual's ability to obtain appropriate healthcare services. Barriers can be financial (insufficient monetary resources), geographic (distance to providers), organizational (lack of available providers), and sociological (e.g., discrimination, language barriers). Efforts to improve access often focus on providing/improving health coverage.

Accreditation A process whereby a program of study or an institution is recognized by an external body as meeting certain predetermined standards. For facilities, these standards are usually defined in terms of physical plant, governing body, administration, and medical and other staff. This recognition process is often carried out by organizations created to assure the public of the quality of the institution or program. The state or federal government can grant this recognition in lieu of, or as the basis for, licensure or other mandatory approvals. Public or private payment programs often require such recognition as a condition of payment for covered services. This recognition may be permanent or may be given for a specified period of time.

Activities of daily living (ADL) An index or scale which measures a patient's degree of independence in bathing, dressing, using the toilet, eating, and moving from one place to another.

Acute care Medical treatment rendered to individuals whose illnesses or health problems are of a short-term or episodic nature. Providers of this treatment are hospitals that mainly serve people with short-term health problems.

Affordable Care Act of 2010 Often referred to as Obamacare; this U.S. legislation was a major reform of the health care system that seeks to improve access, improve quality of care, and reduce costs. Under this legislation, 20 million uninsured people were able to get healthcare insurance.

Acute disease A disease that is characterized by a single episode of a relatively short duration from which the patient returns to his or her normal or previous level of activity. Although these diseases are frequently distinguished from chronic diseases, there is no standard definition or distinction. It is worth noting that a short, severe episode of a chronic disease (e.g., an episode of diabetic coma in a patient with diabetes) is often treated as this.

Adverse event In a medical context, an injury resulting from a medical intervention.

Adverse selection A tendency for utilization of health services in a population group to be higher than average. From an insurance perspective, this tendency occurs when people with poorer than average health status apply for, or continue, insurance coverage to a greater extent than do people with average or better health expectations.

Affiliation An agreement (usually formal) between two or more otherwise independent entities or individuals that defines how they will relate to each other. These agreements between hospitals may specify procedures for referring or transferring patients from one facility to another, joint faculty and/or medical staff appointments, teaching relationships, sharing of records or services, or provision of consultation between programs.

Agency for Healthcare Research and Quality (AHRQ) This agency was created in December 1989 as the Agency for Healthcare Policy and Research (AHCPR), a public health service agency within the U.S. Department of Health and Human Services reporting to the Secretary. This agency was reauthorized in December 1999 under the new name. Its mission is to support research designed to improve the outcomes and quality of health care, reduce its costs, address patient safety and medical errors, and broaden access to effective services. The research sponsored, conducted, and disseminated by this agency provides information that helps people make better decisions about health care.

All patient diagnosis-related groups (APDRG) An enhancement of the original DRGs designed to apply to a population broader than that of Medicare beneficiaries, who are predominately older individuals. The APDRG set includes groupings for pediatric and maternity cases as well as services for HIV-related conditions and other special cases.

Allied health personnel Specially trained and licensed (when necessary) health workers other than physicians, dentists, optometrists, chiropractors, podiatrists, and nurses. The term has no constant or agreed-on detailed meaning; it is sometimes used synonymously with paramedical personnel, sometimes meaning all health workers who perform tasks that must otherwise be performed by a physician, and at other times referring to health workers who do not usually engage in independent practice.

Allowable costs Items or elements of an institution's costs that are reimbursable under a payment formula. Both Medicare and Medicaid reimburse hospitals on the basis of only certain costs. These reimbursements may exclude, for example, luxury accommodations and costs that are not reasonable expenditures or that are unnecessary for the efficient delivery of health services to people covered under the program in question.

All-payer system A system in which prices for health services and payment methods are the same, regardless of who is paying. For instance, in this system, federal or state government, a private insurer, a self-insured employer plan, an individual, or any other payer could pay the same rates. The uniform fee bars healthcare providers from shifting costs from one payer to another (see cost shifting).

Ambulatory care All kinds of health services that are provided on an outpatient basis, in contrast to services provided in the home or to people who are inpatients. Although many inpatients have traveled for care, this term usually implies that the patient must travel to a location to receive services that do not require an overnight stay (see also *ambulatory setting* and *outpatient*).

Ambulatory payment classification (APC) The basis for payment for care in the outpatient prospective payment system. This classification is used similarly to the way Diagnosis-Related Groups (DRGs) are used for payment for inpatients. Both are intended to represent groups of patients that are similar clinically and that also have roughly the same resource consumption. The significant difference between them is that this classification depends on the procedures performed, whereas DRGs depend on the diagnoses treated.

Ambulatory care setting A kind of institutional, organized health setting in which health services are provided on an outpatient basis. This kind of setting may be either mobile (when the facility is capable of being moved to different locations) or fixed (when the person seeking care must travel to a fixed service site).

American Association of Health Plans (AAHP) This association, located in Washington, DC, represents more than 1,000 HMOs, PPOs, and other network-based plans. Together they care for close to 140 million Americans nationwide. This association was created by the merger of the Group Health Association of America (GHAA) and the American Managed Care and Review Association (AMCRA). The merger of the two groups created a new organization that delivers a unified message about the modern style of healthcare delivery pioneered by HMOs, PPOs, and similar health plans.

Ancillary services Supplemental services, including laboratory, radiology, physical therapy, and inhalation therapy, that are provided in conjunction with medical or hospital care.

Antitrust A legal term encompassing a variety of efforts on the part of government to ensure that sellers do not conspire to restrain trade or fix prices for their goods or services in the market.

Any willing provider laws Laws that require managed care plans to contract with all healthcare providers that meet their terms and conditions.

Appropriateness Appropriate health care is care for which the expected health benefit exceeds the expected negative consequences by a wide enough margin to justify treatment.

Assignment A process in which a Medicare beneficiary agrees to have Medicare's share of the cost of a service paid directly to a doctor or other provider and the provider agrees to accept the Medicare approved charge as payment in full. Medicare pays 80% of the cost and the beneficiary 20%, for most services.

Assisted living A broad range of residential care services that includes some assistance with activities of daily living and instrumental activities of daily living but does not include nursing services, such as administration of medication. Assisted-living facilities and in-home assisted-living care stress independence and generally provide less intensive care than that delivered in nursing homes and other long-term care institutions.

Association A term signifying a relationship between two or more events or variables. Events are said to be associated when they occur more frequently together than one would expect by chance. This term does not necessarily imply a causal relationship. Statistical significance testing enables a researcher to determine the likelihood of observing the sample relationship by chance if in fact no association exists in the population that was sampled. This term is often used interchangeably with "relationship."

Average wholesale price (AWP) of prescription drugs Relates to the price that wholesalers charge pharmacies and is often used by pharmacists to price prescriptions. Drug manufacturers and labelers commonly publish suggested wholesale prices for their products. Price surveys of wholesalers are also available.

B

Bad debts Income lost to a provider because of failure of patients to pay amounts owed. This lost income may sometimes be recovered by increasing charges to paying patients. Some cost-based reimbursement programs reimburse for certain lost income. The impact of the loss of revenue may be partially offset for proprietary institutions by the fact that income tax is not payable on income not received.

Balance billing In Medicare and private fee-for-service health insurance, the practice of billing patients for charges that exceed the amount that the health plan will pay. Under Medicare, the excess amount cannot be more than 15% above the approved charge.

Behavioral health An umbrella term that includes mental health and substance abuse and frequently is used to distinguish from "physical" health. Healthcare services provided for depression or alcoholism would be considered this kind of care, whereas setting a broken leg would be physical health.

Behavioral Risk Factor Surveillance System (BRFSS) The world's largest telephone survey. This system tracks risk behaviors related to chronic diseases, injuries, and death in the United States. Administered and supported by the Division of Adult and Community Health, National Center for Chronic Disease Prevention and Health Promotion, and Centers for Disease Control and Prevention, this system is an ongoing data collection program. By 1994, all states, the District of Columbia, and three territories were participating in this system.

Benchmark A level of care set as a goal to be attained. This kind of internal goal is derived from similar processes or services within an organization. Competitive goals of this kind are comparisons with the best external competitors in the field. Generic goals of this kind are drawn from the best performance of similar processes in other industries.

Beneficiary An individual who receives benefits from, or is covered by, an insurance policy or other healthcare financing program.

Biased selection The market imperfection that results from the uneven grouping of risks among competing subscribers. This includes favorable selection (attracting good risks and repelling bad ones) as well as adverse selection (the reverse). This can occur naturally, according to historical or accidental patterns, or it can occur strategically, according to conscious choices by either subscribers or insurers.

Bioterrorism The unlawful use, or threatened use, of micro organisms or toxins derived from living organisms to produce death or disease in humans, animals, or plants. The act is intended to create fear and/or intimidate governments or societies in the pursuit of political, religious, or ideological goals.

Board certified Status granted to a medical specialist who completes a required course of training and experience (residency) and passes an examination in his or her specialty. Individuals who have met all requirements except examination are referred to as *board eligible*.

C

Capital Fixed or durable nonlabor inputs or factors used in the production of goods and services, the value of such factors, or the money specifically allocated for their acquisition or development. Such costs include, for example, the buildings, beds, and equipment used in the provision of hospital services. Such assets are usually thought of as permanent and durable as distinguished from consumables, such as supplies.

Capital costs Expenditures for land, facilities, and major equipment. They are distinguished from operating costs, which include such items as labor, supplies, and administrative expenses.

Capital expenditure An expenditure for the acquisition, replacement, modernization, or expansion of facilities or equipment that, under generally accepted accounting principles, is not properly chargeable as an expense of operation and maintenance.

Capitation A method of payment for health services in which an individual or institutional provider is paid a fixed amount for each person served, without regard to the actual number or nature of services provided to each person in a set period of time. This is the characteristic payment method in certain health maintenance organizations. It also refers to a method of federal support of health professional schools. Under these authorizations, each eligible school receives a fixed payment, called a *capitation grant*, from the federal government for each student enrolled.

Carrier A private organization, usually an insurance company, that finances health care.

Carve out Regarding health insurance, an arrangement whereby an employer eliminates coverage for a specific category of services (e.g., vision care, mental health/psychological services, and prescription drugs) and contracts with a separate set of providers for those services according to a predetermined fee schedule or capitation arrangement. This term may also refer to a method of coordinating dual coverage for an individual.

Case based Refers to a single patient or case.

Case management The monitoring and coordination of treatment rendered to patients with specific diagnoses or requiring high-cost or extensive services.

Case mix A measure of the various kinds of patients being treated by a particular healthcare provider that is intended to reflect the patients' different needs for resources. This measure is generally established by estimating the relative frequency of various types of patients seen by the provider in question during a given time period and may be measured by factors, such as diagnosis, severity of illness, utilization of services, and provider characteristics.

Case severity A measure of intensity or gravity of a given condition or diagnosis for a patient.

Catastrophic health insurance Health Insurance that provides protection against the high cost of treating severe or lengthy illnesses or disability. Generally, such policies cover all, or a specified percentage of, medical expenses above an amount that is the responsibility of another insurance policy up to a maximum limit of liability.

Catchment area A geographic area defined and served by a health program or institution, such as a hospital or community mental health center, that is delineated on the basis of such factors as population distribution, natural geographic boundaries, and transportation accessibility. By definition, all residents of the area needing the services of the program are usually eligible for them, although eligibility may also depend on additional criteria.

Causality Relating causes to the effects they produce. Most of epidemiology concerns this relationship, and several types of causes can be distinguished. A cause is termed *necessary* when a particular variable must always precede an effect. This effect need not be the sole result of the one variable. A cause is termed *sufficient* when a particular variable inevitably initiates or produces an effect. Any given cause may be necessary, sufficient, neither, or both.

Centers for Disease Control and Prevention (CDC) This agency, based in Atlanta, Georgia, is charged with protecting the nation's public health by providing direction in the prevention and control of communicable and other diseases and responding to public health emergencies. Within the U.S. Public Health Service, this is the agency that led efforts to prevent such diseases as malaria, polio, smallpox, toxic shock syndrome, Legionnaire's disease, and, more recently, acquired immunodeficiency syndrome (AIDS) and tuberculosis. This agency's responsibilities evolve as the agency addresses contemporary threats to health, such as injury, environmental, and occupational hazards, behavioral risks, and chronic diseases.

Centers for Medicare and Medicaid Services (CMS) The government agency within the Department of Health and Human Services that directs the Medicare and Medicaid programs (Titles XVIII and XIX of the Social Security Act) and conducts research to support those programs. It was formerly the Health Care Financing Administration (HCFA).

Charity care Generally refers to physician and hospital services provided to people who are unable to pay for the cost of services, especially those who are low income, uninsured, and underinsured. A high proportion of the costs of this care is derived from services for children and pregnant women (e.g., neonatal intensive care).

Chronic care Care and treatment rendered to individuals whose health problems are of a long-term and continuing nature. Rehabilitation facilities, nursing homes, and mental hospitals provide this kind of care.

Chronic disease A disease that has one or more of the following characteristics: is permanent; leaves residual disability; is caused by nonreversible pathological alternation; requires special training of the patient for rehabilitation; or may be expected to require a long period of supervision, observation, or care.

Clinic A facility, or part of one, devoted to diagnosis and treatment of outpatients. "Clinic" is irregularly defined. It may either include or exclude physicians' offices, may be limited to describing facilities that serve poor or public patients, and may be limited to facilities in which graduate or undergraduate medical education is done.

Clinical condition A diagnosis (e.g., cerebrovascular hemorrhage) or a patient state that may be associated with more than one diagnosis (such as paraplegia) or that may not be diagnosed yet (such as low back pain).

Clinical event Services provided to patients (items of history taking, physical examination, preventive care, tests, procedures, drugs, advice) or information on clinical condition or on patient state used as a patient outcome.

Clinical performance measures Instruments that estimate the extent to which a healthcare provider: delivers clinical services that are appropriate for each patient's condition; provides them safely, competently, and in an appropriate time frame; and achieves desired outcomes in terms of those aspects of patient health and patient satisfaction that can be affected by clinical services.

Clinical practice guidelines Systematically developed statements to assist practitioners and patients' decisions about health care to be provided for specific clinical circumstances.

Coinsurance A cost-sharing requirement under a health insurance policy. It provides that the insured party will assume a portion or percentage of the costs of covered services. The health insurance policy provides that the insurer will reimburse a specified percentage of all, or certain specified, covered medical expenses in excess of any deductible amounts payable by the insured. The insured is then liable for the remainder of the costs until their maximum liability is reached.

Community-based care The blend of health and social services provided to an individual or family in their place of residence for the purpose of promoting, maintaining, or restoring health or minimizing the effects of illness and disability.

Community rating A method of calculating health plan premiums using the average cost of actual or anticipated health services for all subscribers within a specific geographic area. The premium does not vary for different groups or subgroups of subscribers to reflect their specific claims experience or health status. Under such *modified* rating (the most common form), rates may vary based on subscribers' specific demographic characteristics (such as age and gender), but rate variation based on individuals' health status, claims experience, or policy duration is prohibited. Under such *pure* rating, variation based on demographic as well as health factors is prohibited, and all subscribers in an area pay the same rate.

Community rating by class (CRC, class rating) For federally qualified HMOs, this is the adjustment of community-rated premiums on the basis of such factors as age, family size, and tobacco use. These health plan premiums reflect the experience of all enrollees of a given class within a specific geographic area, rather than the experience of any one employer group.

Co-morbidities Conditions that exist at the same time as the primary condition in the same patient (e.g., hypertension exists at the same time as diabetes, ischemic heart disease, and end-stage renal disease).

Competition A characteristic of market economics in which buyers choose from among alternative goods and services made available in the market by two or more sellers. In a classic competitive market, there are many buyers and many sellers.

Consumer A person who purchases or receives goods or services for personal needs or use and not for resale.

Continuum of care Clinical services provided during a single inpatient hospitalization or for multiple conditions over a lifetime. It provides a basis for evaluating quality, cost, and utilization over the long term.

Contractual allowance The difference between what hospitals bill and what they receive in payment from third-party payers, most commonly government programs. Also known as contractual adjustment.

Coordination of benefits (COB) Procedures used by insurers to avoid duplicate payment for losses insured under more than one insurance policy. A coordination of benefits clause, or nonduplication clause, in either policy prevents double payment by making one insurer the primary payer and assuring that not more than 100% of the cost is covered. Standard rules determine which of two or more plans, each having COB provisions, pays its benefits in full and which becomes the supplementary payer on a claim.

Co-payments A fixed amount of money paid by a health plan enrollee (beneficiary) at the time of service. For example, the enrollee may pay a $10 co-pay at every physician office visit and $5 for each drug prescription filled. The health plan pays the remainder of the charge directly to the provider. This is a method of cost-sharing between the enrollee and the plan and serves as an incentive for the enrollee to use healthcare resources wisely. An enrollee might be offered a lower price benefit package in return for a higher co-payment.

Cost Expenses incurred in the provision of services or goods. Many different kinds of expenses are defined and used. The charge, the price of a service or amount billed to an individual or third party, may or may not be equal to the service cost.

Cost-based reimbursement Payment made by a health plan or payer to healthcare providers based on the actual costs incurred in the delivery of care and services to plan beneficiaries. This method of paying providers is still used by some plans; however, it is being replaced by prospective payment and other payment mechanisms.

Cost-benefit analysis An analytic method in which a program's cost is compared with the program's benefits for a period of time, and is expressed in dollars, as an aid in determining the best investment of resources. For example, the cost of establishing a vaccination service might be compared with the total cost of medical care and lost productivity that will be eliminated as a result of more people being vaccinated. This method can also be applied to specific medical tests and treatments.

Cost center An accounting device whereby all related costs attributable to some *financial center* within an institution, such as a department or program, are segregated for accounting or reimbursement purposes.

Cost-effectiveness analysis A form of analysis that seeks to determine the costs and effectiveness of a medical intervention compared with similar alternative interventions to determine the relative degree to which they will obtain the desired health outcome(s). This analysis can be applied to any of a number of standards, such as median life expectancy or quality of life after an intervention.

Cost of illness analysis An assessment of the economic impact of an illness or condition, including treatment costs.

Cost sharing Any provision of a health insurance policy that requires the insured individual to pay some portion of medical expenses. The general term includes deductibles, co-payments, and co-insurance.

Cost-shifting Recouping the cost of providing uncompensated care by increasing revenues from some payers to offset losses and lower net payments from other payers.

Coverage The guarantee against specific losses provided under the terms of an insurance policy. This term is sometimes used interchangeably with *benefits* or *protection* and is also used to mean *insurance* or *insurance contract*.

Covered entity Refers to three kinds that must comply with federal health information privacy regulations (i.e., HIPAA Privacy Rule): healthcare providers, health plans, and healthcare clearinghouses. For these purposes, healthcare providers include hospitals, physicians, and other caregivers, as well as researchers, who provide health care and receive, access, or generate individually identifiable healthcare information.

Covered services Healthcare services covered by an insurance plan.

Credentialing The recognition of professional or technical competence. This process may include registration, certification, licensure, professional association membership, or the award of a degree in the field. Certification and licensure affect the supply of health personnel by controlling entry into practice and influence the stability of the labor force by affecting geographic distribution, mobility, and retention of workers. This process also determines the quality of personnel by providing standards for evaluating competence and by defining the scope of functions and how personnel may be used.

Critical access hospital (CAH) A rural hospital designation established by the Medicare Rural Hospital Flexibility Program (MRHFP) enacted as part of the 1997 Balanced Budget Act. Rural hospitals meeting criteria established by their state may apply for this status. Designated hospitals are reimbursed based on cost (rather than prospective payment), must comply with federal and state regulations for this status, and are exempt from certain hospital staffing requirements.

Crowd out A phenomenon whereby new public programs or expansions of existing public programs designed to extend coverage to the uninsured prompt some privately insured people to drop their private coverage and take advantage of the expanded public subsidy.

Cultural competence A practitioner's or institution's understanding of and sensitivity to the cultural background and primary language of patients in any component of service delivery, including patient education materials, questionnaires, office or healthcare organization setting, direct patient care, and public health campaigns.

Current population survey (CPS) A national survey conducted annually by the U.S. Department of Commerce's Census Bureau to gather information on the noninstitutionalized population of the United States. This survey is the most commonly reported source for the number of people without health insurance and other information about this population.

Current Procedural Terminology (CPT) A manual that assigns five-digit codes to medical services and procedures to standardize claims processing and data analysis.

Customary charge One of the factors determining a physician's payment for a service under Medicare. Calculated as the physician's median charge for that service over a prior 12-month period.

D

Debt service Required payments for interest on and retirement of a debt. The amount needed, supplied, or accrued for meeting such payments during any given accounting period. A budget or operating statement heading for such items.

Deductible The amount of loss or expense that must be incurred by an insured or otherwise covered individual before an insurer will assume any liability for all or part of the remaining cost of covered services. This loss or expense may be either a fixed-dollar amount or the value of specified services (such as two days of hospital care or one physician visit). This loss or expense is usually tied to some reference period over which it must be incurred, for example, $100 per calendar year, benefit period, or spell of illness.

Defined benefit Funding mechanisms for pension plans that can also be applied to health benefits. Typical pension approaches include pegging benefits to a percentage of an employee's average compensation over his or her entire service or over a particular number of years; calculation of a flat monthly payment; and setting benefits based upon a definite amount for each year of service, either as a percentage of compensation for each year of service or as a flat dollar amount for each year of service.

Deidentification A process whereby information that could identify the clinician, the reporter, the healthcare institution, or another organization involved in a medical error are removed from an error report after it is received. This process is used to maintain records of factors that could cause errors, but it assures those who report errors that their reports will not be used in civil lawsuits against them.

Deinstitutionalization Policy that calls for the provision of supportive care and treatment for medically and socially dependent individuals in the community rather than in an institutional setting.

Demand In health economics, the amount of a good or service consumers are willing and able to buy at varying prices, given constant income and other factors. This amount should be distinguished from utilization (the amount of services actually used) and need (which has a normative connotation and relates to the amount of goods or services that should be consumed based on professional value judgments).

Denominator For a performance measure, the sample of cases that will be observed (e.g., the number of patients discharged alive with a confirmed diagnosis of acute myocardial infarction, excluding patients with bleeding or other specified conditions).

Diagnosis-related groups (DRGs) Groupings of diagnostic categories drawn from the International Classification of Diseases and modified by the presence of a surgical procedure, patient age, presence or absence of significant co-morbidities or complications, and other relevant criteria. These groupings are the case-mix measure used in Medicare's prospective payment system.

Direct cost A cost that is identifiable directly with a particular activity, service, or product of the program experiencing the costs. These costs do not include the allocation of costs to a cost center that are not specifically attributable to that cost center.

Direct patient care Any activities by a health professional involving direct interaction, treatment, administration of medications, or other therapy or involvement with a patient.

Disability Any limitation of physical, mental, or social activity of an individual as compared with other individuals of similar age, gender, and occupation. Frequently refers to limitation of a person's usual or major activities, most commonly vocational. There are varying kinds (functional, vocational, learning), degrees (partial, total), and durations (temporary, permanent) of limitation. Public programs often provide benefits for specific limitations, such as total and permanent.

Discharge The release of a patient from a provider's care, usually referring to the date when a patient checks out of a hospital.

Disease May be defined as a failure of the adaptive mechanisms of an organism to counteract adequately, normally, or appropriately to stimuli and stresses to which it is subjected, resulting in a disturbance in the function or structure of some part of the organism. This definition emphasizes that the failure is multifactorial and may be prevented or treated by changing any or a combination of the factors. This term is a very elusive and difficult concept to define, being largely socially defined. Thus, criminality and drug dependence are presently seen by some as such, whereas they were previously considered to be moral or legal problems.

Disease burden A term that refers to the amount, or level, of disease in a specific population. It is quantified using morbidity rates for specific diseases, various mortality rates, injury rates, and nutritional status. Disease burden is important for planning and operating healthcare systems.

Disease management The process of identifying and delivering within selected patient populations (e.g., patients with asthma or diabetes) the most efficient, effective combination of resources, interventions, or pharmaceuticals for the treatment or prevention of a disease. This process could include team-based care where physicians and/or other health professionals participate in the delivery and management of care. It also includes the appropriate use of pharmaceuticals.

Drug risk-sharing arrangements Healthcare provider organizations may be at partial, full, or no risk for drug costs. Provider groups at partial risk share in a proportion of savings and/or cost overruns. The group can share in savings if it prescribes less than the budgeted amount (*upside risk*), and it may also share in any over-expenditures (*downside risk*). Groups at full risk realize all of the savings or absorb all of the losses. Groups at no risk absorb none of the losses and profits (typically, risks are absorbed by the HMO or other managed care organization).

Drug utilization review (DUR) A formal program for assessing drug prescription and use patterns. This program typically examines patterns of drug misuse, monitors current therapies, and intervenes when prescribing or utilization patterns fall outside preestablished standards. This program is usually retrospective but can also be performed before drugs are dispensed. Such programs were established by the Omnibus Budget Reconciliation Act (OBRA) in 1990 and are required for Medicaid programs.

E

Electronic claim A digital representation of a medical bill generated by a provider or by the provider's billing agent for submission using telecommunications to a health insurance payer.

Emergency medical services (EMS) Services used in responding to the perceived individual need for immediate treatment for medical, physiological, or psychological illness or injury.

Epidemic A group of cases of a specific disease or illness clearly in excess of what one would normally expect in a particular geographic area. There is no absolute criterion for using the term—as standards and expectations change, and based on the specific disease, so might the definition (e.g., of violence).

Epidemiology The study of the patterns of determinants and antecedents of disease in human populations. This study uses biology, clinical medicine, and statistics in an effort to understand the etiology (causes) of illness and/ or disease. The ultimate goal of such a practitioner is not merely to identify underlying causes of a disease but to apply findings to disease prevention and health promotion.

Etiology Cause. This term is used by epidemiologists.

Evidence-based decision making In a health policy context, this means the application of the best available scientific evidence to policy decisions about specific medical treatments or changes in the delivery system. The goals are to improve the quality of care, increase the efficiency of care delivery, and improve the allocation of healthcare resources.

Evidence-based medicine The conscientious, explicit, and judicious use of current best evidence in making decisions about the care of individual patients. This approach must balance the best external evidence with the desires of the patient and the clinical expertise of healthcare providers.

Exclusive provider arrangement (EPA) All indemnity or service plans that provide benefit only if care is rendered by the institutional and professional providers with which they contract (with some exceptions for emergency and out-of-area services).

Experience rating A method of adjusting health plan premiums based on the historical utilization data and distinguishing characteristics of a specific subscriber group.

F

Family practice A form of specialty practice in which physicians provide continuing comprehensive primary care within the context of the family unit.

Favorable selection A tendency for utilization of health services in a population group to be lower than expected or estimated.

Federal poverty level (FPL) The amount of income determined by the federal Department of Health and Human Services to provide a bare minimum for food, clothing, transportation, shelter, and other necessities; reported annually and varies according to family size. Public assistance programs usually define income limits in relation.

Fee-for-service Method of billing for health services under which a physician or other practitioner charges separately for each patient encounter or service rendered. It is the method of billing used by the majority of U.S. physicians. Under this kind of payment system, expenditures increase if the fees themselves increase, if more units of service are provided, or if more expensive services are substituted for less expensive ones. This system contrasts with salary, per capita, or other prepayment systems where the payment to the physician is not changed with the number of services actually used.

Fee schedule An exhaustive list of physician services in which each entry is associated with a specific monetary amount that represents the approved payment level for a given insurance plan.

Financial feasibility The projected ability of a provider to pay the capital and operating costs associated with the delivery of a proposed healthcare service.

Formulary A list of drugs, usually by their generic names, and indications for their use; intended to include a sufficient range of medicines to enable physicians, dentists, and, as appropriate, other healthcare practitioners to prescribe all medically appropriate treatment for all reasonably common illnesses. An *open* kind allows coverage for almost all drugs whereas a *closed* kind provides coverage for a limited set of drugs. A *managed* kind includes a list of preferred drugs that the health plan prefers to use because they cost less or are more effective or for other reasons. A *tiered* kind financially rewards patients for using generic and formulary drugs by requiring the patient to pay progressively higher co-payments for brand-name and non-formulary drugs.

G

Gatekeeper The primary care practitioner in managed care organizations who determines whether the presenting patient needs to see a specialist or requires other nonroutine services. The goal is to guide the patient to appropriate services while avoiding unnecessary and costly referrals to specialists.

General practice A form of practice in which physicians without specialty training provide a wide range of primary healthcare services to patients.

Generic substitution In cases in which the patent on a specific pharmaceutical product expires and drug manufacturers produce generic versions of the original branded product, the generic version of the drug (which is theorized to be identical to the product manufactured by a different firm) is dispensed even though the original product is prescribed. Some managed care organizations and Medicaid programs mandate generic substitution because of the generally lower cost of generic products. There are state and federal regulations regarding generic substitutions.

Genomics The study of genomes, which includes gene mapping, gene sequencing, and gene function.

Global budgeting A method of hospital cost-containment in which participating hospitals must share a prospectively set budget. Methods for allocating funds among hospitals may vary but the key is that the participating hospitals agree to an aggregate cap on revenues that they will receive each year. This method may also be mandated under a universal health insurance system.

Global fee A total charge for a specific set of services, such as obstetrical services that encompass prenatal, delivery, and postnatal care.

Globalization[2,3] The process whereby national and international policymakers promote domestic deregulation and external liberalization; the removal of barriers to international trade, foreign direct investments, and short-term financial flows. Globalization impacts health in many ways as world markets are opened. Access to world markets affects national economies and politics, which in turn affect the health-related sectors of the economy. These changes then affect each country's healthcare system, population level health, and individual risks. Globalization also has an impact on the economies of countries and the economies of households. In turn, the wealth of individuals and countries are highly correlated with the health status of populations.

Graduate medical education (GME) Medical education after receipt of the Doctor of Medicine (MD) or equivalent degree, including the education received as an intern, resident (which involves training in a specialty), or fellow, as well as continuing medical education. Centers for Medicare and Medicaid Services (CMS) partly finances this education through direct and indirect Medicare payments.

Gross domestic product (GDP) The market value of all goods and services produced by labor and property within a single country during a particular period of time. Income from overseas operations of a domestic corporation would not be included in this value, but activities carried on within a country's borders by a foreign company would be. This value measures how the country's economy is doing.

Group practice A formal association of three or more physicians or other health professionals providing health services. Income from the practice is pooled and redistributed to the members of the group according to some prearranged plan (often, but not necessarily, through partnership). Groups vary a great deal in size, composition, and financial arrangements.

Guaranteed issue Requirement that insurance carriers offer coverage to groups and/or individuals during some period each year. HIPAA states that insurance carriers, for all products to small groups (2–50), must meet this requirement. Some state laws exceed HIPAA's minimum standards and require carriers to guarantee issue to additional groups and individuals.

Guaranteed renewal HIPAA requirement that insurance carriers renew existing coverage for all products to all groups and/or individuals.

H

Handicapped As defined by Section 504 of the Rehabilitation Act of 1973, any person who has a physical or mental impairment that substantially limits one or more major life activity, has a record of such impairment, or is regarded as having such an impairment.

Health The state of complete physical, mental, and social well-being and not merely the absence of disease or infirmity. It is recognized, however, that this state has many dimensions (anatomical, physiological, and mental) and is largely culturally defined. The relative importance of various disabilities will differ depending on the cultural milieu and the role of the affected individual in that culture. Most attempts at measurement have been assessed in terms or morbidity and mortality.

Health consumer One who may receive or is receiving health services. Although all people at times use health services, a consumer, as the term is used in health legislation and programs, is usually someone who is not associated in any direct or indirect way with the provision of health services.

Health education Any combination of learning opportunities designed to facilitate voluntary adaptations of behavior (in individuals, groups, or communities) conducive to health.

Health facilities Collectively, all physical establishments used in the provision of health services—usually limited to establishments that were built for the purpose of providing health care, such as hospitals and nursing homes. An office building that includes a physician's office would not be included. Classifications include hospitals (both general and specialty), long term care establishments, kidney dialysis treatment centers, and ambulatory surgical establishments.

Health insurance Financial protection against healthcare costs arising from disease or accidental bodily injury. Such protection usually covers all or part of the costs of treating the disease or injury. Financial protection may be obtained on either an individual or a group basis. Although the term is often used by policymakers to refer to comprehensive coverage, insurers and regulators also use it to refer to other forms of coverage such as long-term care, supplemental, specific disease, and accidental death and dismemberment.

Health maintenance organization (HMO) An entity with four essential attributes: (1) an organized system that provides health care in a geographic area and that accepts the responsibility to provide or otherwise assure the delivery of (2) an agreed-upon set of basic and supplemental health maintenance and treatment services to (3) a voluntarily enrolled group of people and (4) for which services the entity is reimbursed through a predetermined fixed, periodic prepayment made by, or on behalf of, each person or family unit enrolled. The payment is fixed without regard to the amounts of actual services provided to an individual enrollee. Individual practice associations involving groups or independent physicians can be included under the definition.

Health manpower shortage area (HMSA) An area or group which the U.S. Department of Health and Human Services designates as having an inadequate supply of healthcare providers. This may be an urban or rural geographic area; a population for which access barriers prevent individuals from using local providers; or medium- or maximum-security correctional institutions and public or nonprofit, private residential facilities.

Health personnel Collectively, all people working in the provision of health services, whether as individual practitioners or employees of health institutions and programs. They may be professionally trained or not, and may be subject to public regulation or not.

Health plan An organization that provides a defined set of benefits. This term usually refers to an HMO-like entity, as opposed to an indemnity insurer.

Health planning Planning concerned with improving health, whether undertaken comprehensively for a whole community or for a particular population, kind of health service, institution, or health program. The components include data assembly and analysis, goal determination, action recommendation, and implementation strategy.

Health policy An insurance contract consisting of a defined set of benefits.

Health promotion Any combination of health education and related organizational, political, and economic interventions designed to facilitate behavioral and environmental adaptations that will improve or protect health.

Health-related quality of life (HRQL) In public health and in medicine, this concept refers to a person or group's perceived physical and mental health over time. Physicians have often used such indicators to measure the effects of chronic illness in their patients in order to better understand how an illness interferes with a person's day-to-day life. Similarly, public health professionals use such indicators to measure the effects of numerous disorders, short- and long-term disabilities, and diseases in different populations. Tracking these indicators in different populations can identify subgroups with poor physical or mental health and can help guide policies or interventions to improve their health.

Health risk factors Chemical, psychological, physiological, or genetic factors and conditions that predispose an individual to the development of a disease.

Health service area Geographic area designated on the basis of such factors as geography, political boundaries, population, and health resources for the effective planning and development of health services.

Health services research The multidisciplinary field of scientific investigation that studies how social factors, financing systems, organizational structures and processes, health technologies, and personal behaviors affect access to health care, the quality and cost of health care, and ultimately our health and well-being. Its research domains are individuals, families, organizations, institutions, communities, and populations.

Health status The state of health of a specified individual, group, or population. It may be measured by obtaining proxies such as people's subjective assessments of their health, by one or more indicators of mortality and morbidity in the population, such as longevity or maternal and infant mortality, or by using the incidence or prevalence of major diseases (communicable, chronic, or nutritional). Conceptually, this is the proper outcome measure for the effectiveness of a specific population's medical care system, although attempts to relate effects of available medical care to variations in health status have proved difficult.

Healthcare cost and utilization project quality indicators (HCUP QIs) Comprise a set of 33 clinical performance measures that inform hospitals' self-assessments of inpatient quality of care as well as state and community assessments of access to primary care. Developed by the Agency for Healthcare Research and Quality (AHRQ) as quick and easy-to-use screening tools, these measures are intended as starting points in identifying clinical areas appropriate for further, more in-depth study and analysis. These measures span three dimensions of care: potentially avoidable adverse hospital outcomes, potentially inappropriate utilization of hospital procedures, and potentially avoidable hospital admissions.

Healthcare paraprofessional Home health aides, certified nurse's aides, and personal care attendants who provide direct care and personal support services in hospitals, nursing homes, and other institutions, as well as home-based care to the disabled, the elderly, and the infirm.

High-risk pool A subsidized health insurance pool organized by some states as an alternative for individuals who have been denied health insurance because of a medical condition or whose premiums are rated significantly higher than the average because of health status or claims experience; commonly operated through an association composed of all health insurers in a state. HIPAA allows states to use these pools as an *acceptable alternative mechanism* that satisfies the statutory requirements for ensuring access to health insurance coverage for certain individuals.

Holism Refers to the integration of mind, body, and spirit of a person and emphasizes the importance of perceiving the individual (regarding physical symptoms) in a *whole* sense. This integration teaches that the healthcare system must extend its focus beyond solely the physical aspects of disease and consider the whole person and the interrelationships between the emotional, social, spiritual, and physical elements of disease and health.

Home- and community-based services (HCBS) Any care or services provided in a patient's place of residence or in a noninstitutional setting located in the immediate community. These services may include home health care, adult day care or day treatment, medical equipment services, or other interventions provided for the purpose of allowing a patient to receive care at home or in the community.

Home health care Health services rendered in the home to elderly, disabled, sick, or convalescent individuals who do not need institutional care. The services may be provided by a visiting nurse association (VNA) home health agency, county public health department, hospital, or other organized community group and may be specialized or comprehensive. The most common kinds are the following nursing services: speech, physical, occupational, and rehabilitation therapy; homemaker services; and social services.

Horizontal integration Merging of two or more firms at the same level of production in some formal, legal relationship (see *vertical integration*).

Hospice A program that provides palliative and supportive care for terminally ill patients and their families, either directly or on a consulting basis with the patient's physician or another community agency. Originally a medieval name for a way station for crusaders where they could be replenished, refreshed, and cared for, this term is used here for an organized program of care for people going through life's "last station." The entire family is considered the unit of care, and care extends through their period of mourning.

Hospital An institution whose primary function is to provide inpatient diagnostic and therapeutic services for a variety of medical conditions, both surgical and nonsurgical. In addition, most of these institutions provide some outpatient services, particularly emergency care. These institutions may be classified by length of stay (short- or long-term), as teaching or nonteaching, by major type of service (general, psychiatric, tuberculosis, and other specialties such as maternity, pediatric, or ear, nose, and throat), and by type of ownership or control (federal, state, or local government; for-profit and nonprofit). Such short-term, general, nonprofit community institutions are often called *voluntary* and dominate the sector.

Iatrogenic Caused by medical treatment, such as a drug side effect or a postoperative infection.

Incidence In epidemiology, the number of cases of disease, infection, or some other event having their onset during a prescribed period of time in relation to the unit of population in which they occur; measures morbidity or other events as they happen over a period of time. Examples include the number of accidents occurring in a manufacturing plant during a year in relationship to the number of employees in the plant, or the number of cases of mumps occurring in a school during a month in relation to the number of pupils enrolled in the school. It refers only to the number of new cases.

Incurred but not reported (IBNR) Claims that have not been reported to the insurer as of some specific date for services that have been provided. The estimated value of these claims is a component of an insurance company's current liabilities.

Indemnity Health insurance benefits provided in the form of cash payments rather than services. Such a contract usually defines the maximum amounts that will be paid for covered services.

Independent practice association (IPA) An organized form of prepaid medical practice in which participating physicians remain in their independent office settings, seeing both enrollees in this form of organization and private-pay patients. Participating physicians may be reimbursed by the organization on a fee-for-service basis or a capitation basis.

Indicator A quantitative or statistical measure or gauge for monitoring clinical care.

Indigent care Health services provided to the poor or those unable to pay. Because many of these patients are not eligible for federal or state programs, the costs that are covered by Medicaid are generally recorded separately from these care costs.

Indirect cost A cost that cannot be identified directly with a particular activity, service, or product of the entity incurring the cost. These costs are usually apportioned among an entity's services in proportion to each service's share of direct costs.

Individually identifiable health information A subset of health information that includes demographic information collected from an individual and that is created or received by a healthcare provider, health plan, employer, or healthcare clearinghouse; relates to the past, present, or future physical or mental health or condition of an individual, the provision of health care to an individual, or the past, present, or future payment for the provision of health care to an individual.

Infectious disease An illness resulting from the presence of a pathogenic biological agent in a host, human, or animal. The pathogen may or may not be able to be transmitted to other humans or animals.[4(p7)]

Inpatient A person who has been admitted at least overnight to a hospital or other health facility (which is therefore responsible for his/her room and board) for the purpose of receiving diagnostic treatment or other health services.

Institutional health services Delivered on an inpatient basis in hospitals, nursing homes, or other inpatient institutions. This term may also refer to services delivered on an outpatient basis by departments or other organizational units of, or sponsored by, such institutions.

Instrumental activities of daily living (IADL) An index or scale that measures a patient's degree of independence in aspects of cognitive and social functioning, including shopping, cooking, doing housework, managing money, and using the telephone.

Integrated services network (ISN) A network of organizations, usually including hospitals and physician groups, that provides or arranges to provide a coordinated continuum of services to a defined population and is held both clinically and fiscally accountable for the outcomes of the populations served.

Intermediate care facility (ICF) An institution that is licensed under state law to provide on a regular basis, health-related care and services to individuals who do not require the degree of care or treatment that a hospital or skilled nursing facility is designed to provide. Public institutions for care of the mentally retarded or people with related conditions are also included in the definition. The distinction between *health-related care and services* and *room and board* has often proven difficult to make but is important because these institutions are subject to quite different regulations and coverage requirements than institutions that do not provide health-related care and services.

International Classification of Diseases (ICD) A publication of the World Health Organization (WHO), revised periodically. The full title is *International Statistical Classification of Diseases and Related Health Problems*. This classification, which originated for use with deaths, is used worldwide for that purpose. In addition, it has been used widely in the United States for hospital diagnosis classification since about 1955, with various adaptations and modifications.

International medical graduate (IMG) A physician who graduated from a medical school outside of the United States, usually Canada. U.S. citizens who go to medical school abroad are classified as international medical graduates, as are foreign-born people who are not trained in medical school in the United States. U.S. citizens represent only a small portion.

Internist A physician who focuses his or her practice on the care of critically ill and injured patients. After initial training in internal medicine, anesthesiology, or surgery, additional training in critical care is required to become board certified.

Intervention strategy A generic term used in public health to describe a program or policy designed to have an impact on an illness or disease. For example, a mandatory seat belt law is designed to reduce automobile-related fatalities.

Inventory A detailed description of quantities and locations of different kinds of facilities, major equipment, and personnel that are available in a geographic area and the amount, type, and distribution of services these resources can support.

J

Joint Commission on Accreditation of Healthcare Organizations (JCAHO) A national private, nonprofit organization whose purpose is to encourage the attainment of uniformly high standards of institutional medical care; establishes guidelines for the operation of hospitals and other health facilities and conducts survey and accreditation programs.

L

License/licensure A permission granted to an individual or organization by a competent authority, usually public, to engage lawfully in a practice, occupation, or activity; the process by which the permission is granted. It is usually granted on the basis of examination and/or proof of education rather than on measures of performance. This permission is usually permanent but may be conditioned on annual payment of a fee, proof of continuing education, or proof of competence.

Long-term care A set of health care, personal care, and social services required by people who have lost, or never have acquired, some degree of functional capacity (e.g., chronically ill, elderly, disabled, or retarded people) in an institution or at home for a long time. The term is often used more narrowly to refer only to ongoing institutional care, such as provided in nursing homes, homes for the retarded, and mental hospitals. Ambulatory services such as home health care and assisted living, which can also be provided on a long-term basis, are seen as alternatives.

M

Magnetic resonance imaging (MRI) This relatively new form of diagnostic radiology is a method of imaging body tissues that uses the response or resonance of the nuclei of the atoms of one of the bodily elements, typically hydrogen or phosphorus, to externally applied magnetic fields.

Malpractice Professional misconduct or failure to apply ordinary skills in the performance of a professional act. A practitioner is liable for damages or injuries caused by this kind of misconduct or failure. For some professions, such as medicine, insurance can cover the costs of defending suits instituted against the professional and/or any damages assessed by the court, usually up to a maximum limit; a patient must demonstrate some injury and must prove that the injury was caused by the professional's negligence.

Managed behavioral health organization Assumes the responsibility for managing the behavioral health benefit for an employer or payer organization under a *carve-out* arrangement. The management may range from utilization management services through its own organization or provider network. Reimbursement may be on a fee-for-service, shared risk, or full-risk basis. This is a specialty managed care organization (MCO).

Managed care The body of clinical, financial, and organizational activities designed to ensure the provision of appropriate healthcare services in a cost-efficient manner. Its techniques are most often practiced by organizations and professionals that assume risk for a defined population (e.g., health maintenance organizations).

Management services organization (MSO) Provides administrative and practice management services to physicians; typically owned by a hospital, hospitals, or investors. Large group practices may also establish this kind of organization to sell management services to other physician groups.

Mandatory reporting A system under which physicians or other health professionals are required by law to inform health authorities when a specified event occurs (e.g., a medical error or the diagnosis of a certain disease).

Maximum allowable actual charge (MAAC) A limitation on billed charges for Medicare services provided by nonparticipating physicians. For physicians with charges exceeding 115% of the prevailing charge for nonparticipating physicians, this limit increases in actual charges to 1% per year. For physicians whose charges are less than 115% of the prevailing, the limit on actual charge increases so they may not charge more than 115%.

Measure set A collection of measures with a common purpose and developer (see *clinical performance measures*).

Medicaid (Title XIX) A U.S. federally aided, state-operated and administered program that provides medical benefits for certain indigent or low-income people in need of health and medical care. The program, authorized by Title XIX of the Social Security Act, is basically for the poor. It does not cover all of the poor, only people who meet specified eligibility criteria. Subject to broad federal guidelines, states determine the benefits covered, program eligibility, rates of payment for providers, and methods of administering the program.

Medical audit Detailed retrospective review and evaluation of selected medical records by qualified professional staff; used in some hospitals, group practices, and occasionally in private, independent practices for evaluating professional performance by comparing it with accepted criteria, standards, and current professional judgment; usually concerned with the care of a given illness and undertaken to identify deficiencies in that care in anticipation of educational programs to improve it.

Medical error An error or omission in the medical care provided to a patient; can occur in diagnosis, treatment, preventive monitoring, or in the failure of a piece of medical equipment or other component of the medical system; often, but not always, results in adverse events, such as injury or death.

Medically indigent People who cannot afford needed health care because of insufficient income and/or lack of adequate health insurance.

Medical informatics The systematic study, or science, of the identification, collection, storage, communication, retrieval, and analysis of data about medical care services that can be used to improve decisions made by physicians and managers of healthcare organizations.

Medically necessary A treatment or service that is appropriate and consistent with a patient's diagnosis and that, in accordance with locally accepted standards of practice, cannot be omitted without adversely affecting the patient's condition or the quality of care.

Medically needy People who are categorically eligible for Medicaid and whose income, less the accumulated medical bills, is below state income limits for the Medicaid program.

Medically underserved population A population group experiencing a shortage of personal health services. This group may or may not reside in a particularly medically underserved area or be defined by its place of residence. Thus, migrants, American Indians, or prison inmates, or mental hospital residents may constitute such a population. The term is defined and used to give priority for federal assistance (e.g., the National Health Service Corps).

Medical management information system (MMIS) A data system that allows payers and purchasers to track healthcare expenditure and utilization patterns.

Medical review criteria Systematically developed statements that can be used to assess the appropriateness of specific healthcare decisions, services, and outcomes.

Medical savings account (MSA) An account in which individuals can accumulate contributions to pay for medical care or insurance. Some states give tax-preferred status to contributions to this kind of account, but such contributions are still subject to federal income taxation. This kind of account differs from medical reimbursement accounts, sometimes called flexible benefits or Section 115 accounts, in that it does not need to be associated with an employer. It is not currently recognized in any federal statute.

Medicare (Title XVIII) A U.S. health insurance program for people aged 65 and over, for people eligible for Social Security disability payments for 2 years or longer, and for certain workers and their dependents who need kidney transplantation or dialysis. Monies from payroll taxes and premiums from beneficiaries are deposited in special trust funds for use in meeting the expenses incurred by the insured. It consists of two separate but coordinated programs: hospital insurance (Part A) and supplementary medical insurance (Part B).

Medicare+Choice A Medicare program created by the 1997 Balanced Budget Act; allows the Centers for Medicare and Medicaid Services (CMS) to contract with a variety of different managed care and fee-for-service entities offering greater flexibility to Medicare participants. People eligible for Medicare parts A and B are also eligible for this program (Medicare Part C).

Medicare Payment Advisory Commission (MedPAC) An independent federal body that advises the U.S. Congress on issues affecting the Medicare program. It was established by the Balanced Budget Act of 1997 (P.L. 105-33), which merged the Prospective Payment Assessment Commission (ProPAC) and the Physician Payment Review Commission (PPRC).

Medicare Rural Hospital Flexibility Program (MRHFP) A limited service hospital program created by the Balanced Budget Act of 1997 and modified by the Balanced Budget Refinement Act in 1999. Under this program, rural hospitals meeting criteria specified by their state can apply to become critical access hospitals. This program provides regulatory relief and a cost-based payment option for smaller, low-volume facilities that lack the resources needed to meet hospital staffing and other requirements under Medicare.

Medigap policy A private health insurance policy offered to Medicare beneficiaries to cover expenses not paid by Medicare. This policy is strictly regulated by federal rules. It is also known as Medicare supplemental insurance.

Mental health The state of being of the individual with respect to emotional, social, and behavioral maturity. Although the term is often used to mean *good mental health*, it is a relative state, varying from time to time in the individual, with some people more healthy than others in this regard.

Morbidity The extent of illness, injury, or disability in a defined population. It is usually expressed in general or specific rates of incidence or prevalence.

Mortality Death. This term is used to describe the relation of deaths to the population in which they occur. This rate of death expresses the number of deaths in a quantified population within a prescribed time and may be expressed as a *crude death rate* (e.g., total deaths in relation to total population during a year) or as death rates specific for diseases and sometimes for age, gender, or other attributes (e.g., number of deaths from cancer in white males in relation to the white male population during a given year).

N

National Committee for Quality Assurance (NCQA) A national organization founded in 1979, composed of 14 directors representing consumers, purchasers, and providers of managed health care. It accredits quality assurance programs in prepaid managed healthcare organizations and develops and coordinates programs for assessing the quality of care and service in the managed care industry.

National Health Service Corps (NHSC) A program administered by the U.S. Public Health Service that places physicians and other providers in health profession shortage areas by providing scholarship and loan repayment incentives. Since 1970, the corps members have worked in community health centers, migrant centers, Indian health facilities, and in other sites targeting underserved populations.

National Pharmaceutical Stockpile (NPS) Program The mission of this program, with the Centers for Disease Control and Prevention (CDC), is to ensure the availability and rapid deployment of lifesaving pharmaceuticals, antidotes, and other medical supplies and equipment necessary to counter the effects of nerve agents, biological pathogens, and chemical agents. This program stands ready for immediate deployment to any U.S. location in the event of a terrorist attack using a biological toxin or chemical agent directed against a civilian population.

Network An affiliation of providers through formal and informal contracts and agreements. Networks may contract externally to obtain administrative and financial services.

Numerator For a performance measure, the cases in the denominator group that experience events specified in a medical review criterion (e.g., the number of patients discharged alive with a confirmed diagnosis of acute myocardial infarction, excluding patients with bleeding or other specified conditions, who were discharged on aspirin) (see *denominator*).

Nurse An individual trained to care for the sick, the elderly, or the injured; can be defined as a professional qualified by education and authorized by law to practice nursing. There are many different types, specialties, and grades within this profession.

Nurse practitioner A registered nurse qualified and specially trained to provide primary care, including primary health care in homes and in ambulatory care facilities, long-term care facilities, and other healthcare institutions. These professionals generally function under the supervision of a physician but not necessarily in his or her presence. They are usually salaried rather than reimbursed on a fee-for-service basis, although the supervising physician may receive fee-for-service reimbursement for their services.

Nursing home Includes a wide range of institutions that provide various levels of maintenance and personal or nursing care to people who are unable to care for themselves and who have health problems that range from minimal to very serious. The term includes free-standing institutions or identifiable components of other health facilities that provide nursing care and related services, personal care, and residential care. This kind of facility includes skilled nursing facilities and extended care facilities but not boarding homes.

O

Occupancy rate A measure of inpatient health facility use, determined by dividing available bed days by patient days. It measures the average percentage of a hospital's beds occupied and may be institution-wide or specific for one department or service.

Occupational health services Health services concerned with the physical, mental, and social well-being of an individual in relation to his or her working environment and with the adjustment of individuals to their work. The term applies to more than the safety of the workplace and includes health and job satisfaction. In the United States, the principal statute concerned with this field is the Occupational Safety and Health Act administered by the Occupational Safety and Health Administration (OSHA) and the National Institute of Occupational Safety and Health (NIOSH).

Office of Public Health Preparedness (OPHP) Directs the Department of Health and Human Services' (HHS) efforts to prepare for, protect against, respond to, and recover from all acts of bioterrorism and other public health emergencies that affect the civilian population, and it serves as the focal point within HHS for these activities. This office is headed by a director, who reports directly to the secretary, and serves as the secretary's principal advisor on HHS activities relating to protecting the civilian population from acts of bioterrorism and other public health emergencies. This office was created in January 2002.

One Health The study of the relationships among humans, animal, and ecosystems and the how the interconnectedness of these three impact human health; the health of all living things.[4(p1)]

Open enrollment A method for ensuring that insurance plans, especially prepaid plans, do not exclusively select good risks. With this requirement, a plan must accept all who apply during a specific period each year.

Operating cost Necessary expenses to operate an activity that provides health services. These expenses normally include personnel, materials, overhead, depreciation, and interest.

Operating margin Revenues from sales minus current cost of goods sold. A measure of operating efficiency that is independent of the cost flow assumption for inventory. Sometimes called *current (gross) margin*.

Opportunity cost The cost of foregone outcomes that could have been achieved through alternative investments.

Outcome Refers to the finding of a given diagnostic procedure. It may also refer to the cure of the patient, restoration of function, or extension of life. When used for populations or the healthcare system, it typically refers to changes in birth or death rates, or some similar global measure.

Outcomes research Research on measures of changes in patient treatment results, that is, patient health status and satisfaction resulting from specific medical and health interventions. Attributing changes in results to medical care requires distinguishing the effects of care from the effects of the many other factors that influence patients' health and satisfaction.

Outpatient A patient who is receiving ambulatory care at a hospital or other facility without being admitted to the facility. Usually, it does not mean people receiving services from a physician's office or other program that also does not provide inpatient care.

Overhead The general costs of operating an entity that are allocated to all the revenue producing operations of the entity but that are not directly attributable to a single activity. For a hospital, these costs normally include facility maintenance, occupancy costs, housekeeping, administration, and other factors.

P

Parity Equality or comparability between two things. Associated legislation, usually applicable to mental health conditions, such as depression or schizophrenia, requires that health insurers adhere to a principle of equal treatment when making decisions regarding mental health benefits compared with other kinds of medical benefits. *Data parity* is a term used by researchers to describe the degree to which different data measures are equivalent.

Participating physician A physician who agrees by contractual arrangement to accept the rules, terms, and fee schedule of a given health plan or provider network. In Medicare, a physician who signs an agreement to accept assignment on all Medicare claims for one year (see *assignment*).

Pathological Indicative of or caused by a disease or condition.

Peer review Generally, the evaluation by practicing physicians or other professionals of the effectiveness and efficiency of services ordered or performed by other members of the profession. Frequently, this term refers to review of research by other researchers.

Performance measures Methods or instruments to estimate or monitor the extent to which the actions of a healthcare practitioner or provider conform to practice guidelines, medical review criteria, or standards of quality.

Per member per month (PMPM) A unit of measure referring to health plan costs, revenues, hospital days, or patient visits.

Pharmaceutical assistance program A public program to provide pharmaceutical coverage to those who cannot afford or have difficulty obtaining prescription drugs. Several states operate such state-funded programs primarily to provide benefits to low-income elderly people or people with disabilities who do not qualify for Medicaid.

Pharmaceutical care system A strategy that attempts to use drug therapy more efficiently to achieve definite outcomes that improve a patient's quality of life. This kind of system requires a reorientation of physicians, pharmacist, and nurses toward effective drug therapy outcomes. It is a set of relationships and decisions through which pharmacist, physicians, nurses, and patients work together to design, implement, and monitor a therapeutic plan that will produce specific therapeutic outcomes.

Pharmacoeconomics The study of the costs and benefits associated with various pharmaceutical treatments.

Pharmacy benefit manager (PBM) Many insurance companies, HMOs, and self-insured employers contract with these managers to manage drug benefit coverage for employees and health plan members. Common tools employed by these managers for drug benefits include management of pharmacy networks, implementation of generic substitution and mail order programs, negotiation of rebates with drug manufacturers, formulary management, and clinical programs such as for disease management.

Physician assistant (PA) Also known as a physician extender; a specially trained and licensed or otherwise credentialed individual who performs tasks that might otherwise be performed by a physician, under the direction of a supervising physician.

Physician-hospital organization (PHO) A legal entity formed by a hospital and a group of physicians to further mutual interests and to achieve market objectives; generally combines physicians and a hospital into a single organization for the purpose of obtaining payer contracts. Doctors maintain ownership of their practices and agree to accept managed care patients according to the terms of a professional services agreement with the entity. The entity serves as a collective negotiating and contracting unit. It is typically owned and governed jointly by a hospital and shareholder physicians.

Point of service A health insurance benefits program in which subscribers can select between different delivery systems (i.e., HMO, PPO, and fee-for-service) when in need of healthcare services, rather than making the selection between delivery systems at time of open enrollment at place of employment. Typically, the costs associated with receiving care from HMO providers are less than when care is rendered by PPO or noncontracting providers.

Population A set of individual people, objects, or items from which samples are taken for statistical measurement—for example, all of the patients with a disease or condition that are of interest for a particular study, such as all of the cases of myocardial infarction occurring within a given year.

Population-based services Health services targeted at populations of patients with specific diseases or disorders (e.g., patients with asthma or diabetes). The concept that the health care can be better administered if patients are examined as populations as well as specific cases is one basis for disease management and managed care.

Portability Requirement that health plans guarantee continuous coverage without waiting periods for people moving between plans.

Postacute care Also called *subacute care* or *transitional care*; a kind of short-term care provided by many long-term care facilities and hospitals that may include rehabilitation services, specialized care for certain conditions (such as stroke and diabetes), and/or postsurgical care and other services associated with the transition between the hospital and home. Residents on these units often have been hospitalized recently and typically have more complicated medical needs. The goal is to discharge residents to their homes or to a lower level of care.

Potentially preventable adverse outcomes Complications of a condition that may be modified or prevented with appropriate treatment (e.g., permanent hearing loss as an outcome of otitis media with effusion).

Practice guidelines, parameters Standards used to guide providers based on accepted clinical treatment protocols for typical cases.

Preadmission certification A process under which admission to a health institution is reviewed in advance to determine need and appropriateness and to authorize a length of stay consistent with norms for the evaluation.

Preexisting condition A medical condition developed prior to issuance of a health insurance policy. Some policies exclude coverage of such conditions for a period of time or indefinitely.

Preferred drug list (or drug formulary) A list of prescription drugs which are covered by a health plan (or other payer, e.g., Medicaid). Some drugs may be subject to a prior authorization mechanism, whereby the physician or other prescriber must justify why the patient would need a particular brand-name product (see *prior authorization*).

Preferred provider arrangement (PPA) Selective contracting with a limited number of healthcare providers, often at reduced or prenegotiated rates of payment.

Preferred provider organization (PPO) Formally organized entity generally consisting of hospital and physician providers. The entity provides healthcare services to purchasers, usually at discounted rates, in return for expedited claims payment and a somewhat predictable market share. In this model, consumers have a choice of using providers in network or out of network; however, financial incentives are built in to benefit structures to encourage utilization of in-network providers.

Prepayment Usually refers to any payment to a provider for anticipated services (such as an expectant mother paying in advance for maternity care). Sometimes this kind of payment is distinguished from insurance as referring to payments to organizations that, unlike insurance companies, take responsibility for arranging for and providing needed services as well as paying for them (such as health maintenance organizations, prepaid group practices, and medical foundations).

Prevailing charge One of the factors determining a physician's payment for a service under Medicare, set at a percentile of customary charges of all physicians in the locality.

Prevalence The number of cases of disease, infected people, or people with some other attribute, present at a particular time and in relation to the size of the population from which drawn. It can be a measurement of morbidity at a moment in time (e.g., the number of cases of hemophilia in the country as of the first of the year).

Preventive medicine Care that has the aim of preventing disease or its consequences. It includes healthcare programs aimed at warding off illnesses (e.g., vaccinations), early detection of disease (e.g., Pap smears), and inhibiting further deterioration of the body (e.g., exercise or prophylactic surgery). This kind of care developed after the discovery of bacterial diseases and was concerned in its early history with specific medical control measures taken against the agents of infectious diseases. This care is also concerned with general preventive measures aimed at improving the healthfulness of the environment. In particular, the promotion of health through altering behavior, especially using health education, is gaining prominence as a component of preventive care.

Primary care Basic or general health care focused on the point at which a patient ideally first seeks assistance from the medical care system. This kind of care is considered comprehensive when the primary provider takes responsibility for the overall coordination of the care of the patient's health problems, be they biological, behavioral, or social. The appropriate use of consultants and community resources is an important part of effective care. Such care is generally provided by physicians but is increasingly provided by other personnel, such as nurse practitioners or physician assistants.

Primary care case management (PCCM) The use of a primary care physician to manage the use of medical or surgical care. This kind of program usually pays for all care on a fee-for-service basis.

Primary care provider (PCP) A generalist physician (family practice, general internal medicine, general pediatrics, and sometimes obstetrics/gynecology for women patients) who provides primary care services.

Primary payer The insurer obligated to pay losses before any liability is assumed by other, secondary insurers. Medicare, for instance, is a primary payer with respect to Medicaid.

Prior authorization A formal process requiring a provider to obtain approval to provide particular services or procedures before they are done. This is usually required for nonemergency services that are expensive or likely to be abused or overused. A managed care organization will identify those services and procedures that require this process, without which the provider may not be compensated.

Probability (P value) The likelihood that an event will occur. When looking at differences between data samples, statistical techniques are used to determine whether the differences are likely to reflect real differences in the whole group from which the sample is drawn or whether they are simply the result of random variation in the samples.

Proprietary Owned and operated for the purpose of making a profit, whether or not one is actually made.

Prospective payment Any method of paying hospitals or other health programs in which amounts or rates of payment are established in advance for a defined period (usually a year). Institutions are paid these amounts regardless of the costs they actually incur. These systems of payment are designed to introduce a degree of constraint on charge or costs increases by setting limits on amounts paid during a future period. In some cases, such systems provide incentives for improved efficiency by sharing savings with institutions that perform at lower than anticipated costs. This kind of payment contrasts with the method of payment originally used under Medicare and Medicaid (as well as other insurance programs) where institutions were reimbursed for actual expenses incurred.

Provider Hospital or licensed healthcare professional or group of hospitals or healthcare professionals that provide healthcare services to patients. This may also refer to medical supply firms and vendors of durable medical equipment.

Public good A good or service whose benefits may be provided to a group at no more cost than that required to provide it for one person. The benefits of the good are indivisible and individuals cannot be excluded. For example, a public health measure that eradicates smallpox protects all, not just those paying for the vaccination.

Public health The science dealing with the protection and improvement of community health by organized community effort. Such activities are generally those that are less amenable to being undertaken by individuals or are less effective when undertaken on an individual basis and do not typically include direct personal health services. Such activities include administering vaccination; sanitation; preventive medicine, quarantine, and other disease-control activities; occupational health and safety programs; assurance of the healthfulness of air, water, and food; health education; and epidemiology.

Q

Quality-adjusted life years (QALYs) Years of life saved by a medical technology or service, adjusted according to the quality of those years (as determined by some evaluative measure); the most commonly used unit to express the results in some types of cost-effectiveness analysis.

Quality improvement The sum of all the activities that created a desired change in quality. In the healthcare setting, this kind of improvement requires a feedback loop that involves the identification of patterns of the care of patients (or of the performance of other systems involved in care), the analysis of those patterns to identify opportunities for improvement (or instances of departure from standards of care), and then action to improve the quality of care for future patients.

Quality of care The degree to which delivered health services meet established professional standards and judgments of value to the consumer; may also be seen as the degree to which actions taken or not taken maximize the probability of beneficial health outcomes and minimize risk and other outcomes, given the existing state of medical science and art; frequently described as having three dimensions: quality of input resources (certification and/or training of providers), quality of the process of services delivery (the use of appropriate procedures for a given condition), and quality of outcome of service use (actual improvement in condition or reduction of harmful effects).

R

Rate A measure of the intensity of the occurrence of an event. For example, for mortality, this measure equals the number of those who die in one year divided by the number at risk of dying. This measure is usually expressed using a standard denominator, such as 1,000 or 10,000 people. It may also be expressed as a percentage.

Rate band The allowable variation in insurance premiums as defined in state regulations. Acceptable variation may be expressed as a ratio from highest to lowest, as a percentage of the index rate (e.g., ± 20%). It is used to limit variation for individual factors (such as age, gender, occupation, or geographic region) or to limit variation for all of these factors together (composite).

Rate review Evaluation by a government or private agency of a hospital's budget and financial data, performed for the purpose of determining the reasonableness of the hospital's charges and proposed increases of them.

Rate setting A method of paying healthcare providers in which the federal or state government established payment rates for all payers for various categories of health services.

Reference-based drug pricing Has been adopted both within Canada (in British Columbia and Nova Scotia) and in other countries (including the United States, Australia, New Zealand, and Germany) as a means of limiting expenditures for drug subsidy and insurance programs; limits reimbursement for a group of drugs with similar therapeutic application but different active ingredients to the price of the lowest cost drug within the group (the reference standard). Patients have the option of purchasing drugs that are partially subsidized, in which case they pay the difference between the retail price and the reference price.

Referral The process of sending a patient from one practitioner to another for healthcare services. Health plans may require that designated primary care providers authorize coverage of specialty services.

Rehabilitation The combined and coordinated use of medical, social, educational, and vocational measures for training or retraining individuals disabled by disease or injury to the highest possible level of functional ability. Several different types of training are distinguished: vocational, social, psychological, medical, and educational.

Reimbursement The process by which healthcare providers receive payment for their services. Because of the nature of the healthcare environment, providers are often paid by third parties who insure and represent patients.

Reinsurance The resale of insurance products to a secondary market, thereby spreading the costs associated with underwriting.

Relative risk The rate of disease in one group exposed to a particular factor (e.g., a toxic spill) divided by the rate in another group which is not exposed; indicates that the two groups have the same rate of disease.

Reliability The extent to which a measurement can be replicated with low levels of random error in measurement.

Respite care Care given to a hospice patient by another caregiver so that the usual caregiver can rest.

Retrospective reimbursement Payment made after-the-fact for services rendered on the basis of costs incurred by the facility (see also *prospective payment*).

Revenue The gross amount of earnings received by an entity for the operation of a specific activity. It does not include any deductions for such items as expenses, bad debts, or contractual allowances.

Risk Responsibility for paying for or otherwise providing a level of healthcare services based on an unpredictable need for these services.

Risk adjustment A process by which premium dollars are shifted from a plan with relatively healthy enrollees to another with sicker members. It is intended to minimize any financial incentives health plans may have to select healthier than average enrollees. In this process, health plans that attract higher risk providers and members would be compensated for any differences in the proportion of their members that require high levels of care compared with other plans.

Risk-based capital formula A method of establishing the minimum amount of capital appropriate for an insurance company to support its overall business operations in consideration of its size, structure, and risk profile. It is used to assess a managed care organization's financial viability and help prevent insolvency.

Risk-bearing entity An organization that assumes financial responsibility for the provision of a defined set of benefits by accepting prepayment for some or all of the cost of care; may be an insurer, a health plan or self-funded employer, or a physician-hospital organization (PHO) or other form of PSN.

Risk A term used by epidemiologists to quantify the likelihood that something will occur.

Risk factor Something which either increases or decreases an individual's chance of developing a disease; however, it does not mean that, if exposed, an individual will definitely contract a particular disease.

Risk selection Occurs when a disproportionate share of high or low users of care join a health plan.

Risk sharing The distribution of financial risk among parties furnishing a service. For example, if a hospital and a group of physicians from a corporation provide health care at a fixed price, this kind of arrangement would entail both the hospital and the group being held liable if expenses exceed revenues.

Root cause analysis A process for identifying the basic or causal factor(s) that underlies variations in performance, including the occurrence or possible occurrence of an error.

S

Safety net The network of providers and institutions that provide low-cost or free medical care to medically needy, low-income, or uninsured populations. This network can include (but is not limited to) individual practitioners, public and private hospitals, academic medical centers, and smaller clinics or ambulatory care facilities.

Safety net providers Providers that historically have had large Medicaid and indigent care caseloads relative to other providers and are willing to provide services regardless of the patient's ability to pay.

Sample In statistical analysis, a finite subset of a statistical population whose properties are studied to gain information about the whole population or universe.

Screening The use of quick procedures to differentiate apparently well people who have a disease or a high risk of disease from those who probably do not have the disease. It is used to identify high-risk individuals for more definitive study or follow-up. *Multiple screening* is the combination of a battery of tests for various diseases performed by technicians under medical direction and applied to large groups of apparently well people.

Secondary care Services provided by medical specialists who generally do not have first contact with patients (e.g., cardiologist, urologists, dermatologists). In the United States, however, there has been a trend toward self-referral by patients for these services, rather than referral by primary care providers. This is quite different from the practice in England, for example, where all patients must first seek care from primary care providers and are then referred to secondary and/or tertiary providers, as needed.

Secondary payer An insurer obligated to pay losses above or beyond losses that are assumed by a primary payer.

Secondary prevention Early diagnosis, treatment, and follow-up. These activities start with the assumption that illness is already present and that primary prevention was not successful. The goal is to diminish the impact of disease or illness through early detection, diagnosis, and treatment (e.g., blood pressure screening, treatment, and follow-up programs).

Self-funding, self-insurance An employer or group of employers sets aside funds to cover the cost of health benefits for their employees. Benefits may be administered by the employer(s) or handled through an administrative service-only agreement with an insurance carrier or third-party administrator. Under this arrangement, it is generally possible to purchase stop-loss insurance that covers expenditures above a certain aggregate claim level and/or covers catastrophic illness or injury when individual claims reach a certain dollar threshold.

Sensitivity A high rate of detection of *true positives* (the fraction of patients who actually received good care who are classified as recipients of good care).

Sentinel event An unexpected occurrence or variation involving death or serious physical or psychological injury, or the risk thereof. Serious injury specifically includes loss of limb or function. The event sends a signal or sounds a warning that requires immediate attention, hence the term.

Service period Period of employment that may be required before an employee is eligible to participate in an employer-sponsored health plan, most commonly one to three months.

Severity of illness A risk prediction system to correlate the seriousness of a disease in a particular patient with the statistically expected outcome (e.g., mortality, morbidity, efficiency of care). Most effectively, the seriousness is measured at or soon after admission, before therapy is initiated, giving a measure of pretreatment risk.

SF-12 A shorter version of the SF-36 (one-page, 2-minute) survey form that has been shown to yield summary physical and mental health outcome scores that are interchangeable with those from the SF-36 in both general and specific populations. This shorter version of the SF-36 was published in early 1995 and is one of the most widely used surveys of health status.

SF-36 A comprehensive short-form health status questionnaire with only 36 questions that yields an eight-scale health profile as well as summary measures of health-related quality of life. As documented in more than 750 publications, this questionnaire has proven useful in monitoring general and specific populations, comparing the burden of different diseases, differentiating the health benefits produced by different treatments, and screening individual patients. This questionnaire is a standard measure of healthcare quality used by health services researchers and others who monitor quality of care. The survey is produced by Quality Metric, Inc.

Skilled nursing facility (SNF) A nursing care facility participating in the Medicaid and Medicare programs that meets specified requirements for services, staffing, and safety.

Solo practice Lawful practice of a health occupation as a self-employed individual; by definition a private practice but not necessarily general practice or fee-for-service practice (this kind of practice may be paid by capitation, although fee-for-service is more common); common among physicians, dentists, podiatrists, optometrists, and pharmacists.

Specialist A physician, dentist, or other health professional who is specially trained in a certain branch of medicine or dentistry related to specific services or procedures (e.g., surgery, radiology, pathology), certain age categories of patients (e.g., geriatrics), certain body systems (e.g., dermatology, orthopedics, cardiology), or certain types of diseases (e.g., allergy, periodontics); these health professionals usually have advanced education and training related to their specialties.

Specificity A high rate of detection of *true negatives* (i.e., the fraction of patients who actually received bad care who are classified as recipients of bad care).

Spend down The amount of expenditures for healthcare services, relative to income, that qualifies an individual for Medicaid in states that cover categorically eligible, medically indigent individuals. Eligibility is determined on a case-by-case basis.

Standard error In statistics, defined as the standard deviation of an estimate. That is, multiple measurements of a given value will generally group around the mean (or average) value in a normal distribution. The shape of this distribution is known by this term.

State Children's Health Insurance Program (SCHIP) This program was enacted as part of the Balanced Budget Act of 1997, which established Title XXI of the Social Security Act to provide states with $24 billion in federal funds for 1998–2002 targeting children in families with incomes up to 200% of the federal poverty level.

Substance Abuse and Mental Health Services Administration (SAMHSA) The mission of this administration is to provide, through the U.S. Public Health Service, a national focus for the federal effort to promote effective strategies for the prevention and treatment of addictive and mental disorders. This is primarily a grant making organization, promoting knowledge and scientific state-of-the-art practice. It strives to reduce barriers to high-quality, effective programs and services for individuals who suffer from or are at risk for these disorders, as well as for their families and communities.

Survey An investigation in which information is systematically collected. For a population, this may be conducted by face-to-face inquiry, by self-completed questionnaires, by telephone, by postal service, or in some other way. Each method has its advantages and disadvantages. The generalizability of results depends on the extent to which those surveyed are representative of the entire population.

Supply In health economics, the quantity of services provided or personnel in a given area.

Swing-bed hospital A hospital participating in the Medicare program that allows rural hospitals with fewer than 100 beds to provide skilled post-acute care services in acute care beds.

Systems approach A school of thought evolving from earlier systems analysis theory, propounding that virtually all outcomes are the result of systems rather than individuals. In practice, this school of thought is characterized by attempts to improve the quality and/or efficiency of a process through improvements to the system.

Systems error An error that is not the result of an individual's actions, but the predictable outcome of a series of actions and factors that comprise a diagnostic or treatment process.

T

Technology assessment A comprehensive form of policy research that examines the technical, economic, and social consequences of technological applications. It is especially concerned with unintended, indirect, or delayed social impacts. In health policy, the term has come to mean any form of policy analysis concerned with medical technology, especially the evaluation of efficacy and safety.

Telehealth The use of telecommunications technologies and electronic information to support long-distance clinical health care, patient and professional health-related education, or public health and health administration.

Telemedicine The use of telecommunications (i.e., wire, radio, optical or electromagnetic channels transmitting voice, data, and video) to facilitate medical diagnosis, patient care, and/or distance learning.

Tertiary care Services provided by highly specialized providers (e.g., neurologists, neurosurgeons, thoracic surgeons, and intensive care units). Such services frequently require highly sophisticated equipment and support facilities. The development of these services has largely been a function of diagnostic and therapeutic advances attained through basic and clinical biomedical research.

Tertiary prevention Prevention activities that focus on the individual after a disease or illness has manifested itself. The goal is to reduce long-term effects and to help individuals cope better with symptoms.

Third-party administrator (TPA) A fiscal intermediary (a person or an organization) that serves as another's financial agent. This intermediary processes claims, provides services, and issues payments on behalf of certain private, federal, and state health benefit programs or other insurance organizations.

Third-party payer Any organization, public or private, that pays or insures health or medical expenses on behalf of beneficiaries or recipients. An individual pays a premium for such coverage in all private and in some public programs; the payer organization then pays bills on the individual's behalf. These payments are distinguished by the separation among the individual receiving the service (the first party), the individual or institution providing it (the second party), and the organization paying for it (third party).

Title XVIII (Medicare) The title of the part of the Social Security Act that contains the principal legislative authority for the Medicare program and therefore a common name for the program.

Title XIX (Medicaid) The title of the part of the Social Security Act that contains the principal legislative authority for the Medicaid program and therefore a common name for the program.

U

Uncompensated care Service provided by physicians and hospitals for which no payment is received from the patient or from third-party payers. Some costs for these services may be covered through cost shifting. Not all uncompensated care results from charity care. It also includes bad debts from people who are not classified as charity cases but who are unable or unwilling to pay their bill.

Underinsured People with public or private insurance policies that do not cover all necessary healthcare services, resulting in out-of-pocket expenses that exceed their ability to pay.

Underwriting In insurance, the process of selecting, classifying, evaluating, and assuming risks according to their insurability. Its purpose is to make sure that the group or individual insured has the same probability of loss and probable amount of loss, within reasonable limits, as the universe on which premium rates were based. Because premium rates are based on an expectation of loss, the underwriting process must classify risks into groups with about the same expectation of loss.

Uninsurables High-risk people who do not have healthcare coverage through private insurance and who fall outside the parameters of risks of standard health underwriting practices.

Uninsured People who lack public or private health insurance.

Unit (of analysis) The unit to which a performance measure is applied (e.g., patients, clinician, group of clinicians, institution).

Usual, customary, and reasonable (UCR) fees The use of fee screens to determine the lowest value of physician reimbursement based on the physician's usual charge for a given procedure, the amount customarily charged for the service by other physicians in the area (often defined as a specific percentile of all charges in the community), and the reasonable cost of services for a given patient after medical review of the case.

Utilization Use; commonly examined in terms of patterns or rates of use of a single service or type of service (e.g., hospital care, physician visits, prescription drugs). Use is also expressed in rates per unit of population at risk for a given period.

Utilization review Evaluation of the necessity, appropriateness, and efficiency of the use of healthcare services, procedures, and facilities. In a hospital, this includes review of the appropriateness of admissions, services ordered and provided, length of a stay, and discharge practices, both on a concurrent and retrospective basis. This evaluation can be done by a peer review group or a public agency.

V

Validity The ability of a performance measure to capture what it purports to measure (e.g., a particular aspect of clinical care).

Vertical integration Organization of production whereby one business entity controls or owns all stages of the production and distribution of goods or services.

Vital statistics Statistics relating to births (natality), deaths (mortality), marriages, health, and disease (morbidity). For the United States, these are published by the National Center for Health Statistics.

Voluntary reporting A medical error reporting system where the reporter chooses to report an error to prevent similar errors from occurring in the future. One theory of this kind of system is that they allow reporters to focus on a set of errors broader than just those that cause serious harm and that they help to detect system weaknesses before the occurrence of serious harm.

W

Wellness A dynamic state of physical, mental, and social well-being. A way of life that equips the individual to realize the full potential of his or her capabilities and to overcome and compensate for weaknesses. A lifestyle that recognizes the importance of nutrition, physical fitness, stress reduction, and self-responsibility. Wellness has been viewed as the result of four key factors over which an individual has varying degrees of control: human biology, environment, healthcare organization (system), and lifestyle.

Withhold A form of compensation whereby a health plan does not pay a provider until the end of a value-based purchasing period, at which time the plan distributes any remaining funds based on provider performance. Provider performance can include measures, such as the number and appropriateness of referrals to specialists, or the number of patients who receive preventive screenings (i.e., measures of cost efficiency and/or quality of care). Value-based purchasing brings together information on the quality of health care, such as patient outcomes and health status, with data on the dollar outlays going toward health. It focuses on managing the use of the healthcare system to reduce inappropriate care and to identify and reward the best performing providers. This strategy can be contrasted with more limited efforts to negotiate price discounts, which reduce costs but do little to ensure that quality of care is improved.

Working capital The sum of an institution's short-term or current assets, including cash, marketable (short-term) securities, accounts receivable, and inventories. Net working capital is defined as the excess of total current assets over total current liabilities.

World Bank[5,6] This organization is a vital source of financial and technical assistance to developing countries around the world. Its primary focus is on helping the poorest people and countries. Two unique development institutions owned by 185 member countries—the International Bank for Reconstruction and Development (IBRD) and the International Development Association (IDA)—comprise this organization. The IBRD focuses on middle income and creditworthy poor countries, whereas

IDA focuses on the poorest countries in the world. This organization provides low-interest loans and interest-free credit and grants to developing countries for education, health, infrastructure, communications, and many other purposes.

World Health Organization (WHO)[7] This organization is the directing and coordinating authority for health within the United Nations system. Established in 1948, this organization has grown to have 193 member countries. It is responsible for providing leadership on global health matters, shaping the health research agenda, setting norms and standards, articulating evidence-based policy options, providing technical support to countries, and monitoring and assessing health trends.

World Trade Organization (WTO)[8] This organization is the only global international organization that deals with the rules of trade between nations. Led by the General Agreement on Tariffs and Trade (GATT), this organization was created January 1, 1995. At the heart of the system, known as the multilateral trading system, are the organization's agreements, negotiated and signed by a large majority of the world's trading nations and ratified in their parliaments. These agreements are the legal ground rules for international commerce and cover trade in services and in traded inventions, creations, and designs (intellectual property). The goal is to help producers of goods and services, exporters, and importers conduct their business and thereby improve the welfare of the peoples of the member countries.

References

1. All terms, unless otherwise indicated, are from *Glossary of Terms Commonly Used in Health Care*, 2004 edition, published by AcademyHealth. A more expansive glossary is available on their website, www.academyhealth.org.
2. Cornia GA. Globalization and health: results and options. *Bull World Health Organ*. 2001;79(9):834–841.
3. Woodward D, Drager N, Beaglehole R, Lipson D. Globalization and health: a framework for analysis and action. *Bull World Health Organ*. 2001;79(9):875–881.
4. Riegelman R, Kirkwood B. *One Health: From Aids to Zika*. Burlington, MA: Jones and Bartlett; 2018.
5. World Bank. About the World Bank. http://web.worldbank.org/WBSITE/EXTERNAL/EXTABOUTUS/0,pagePK:50004410~piPK:36602~theSitePK:29708,00.html.
6. World Bank. *World Bank Group: Working for a World Free of Poverty*. http://siteresources.worldbank.org/EXTABOUTUS/Resources/wbgroupbrochure-en07.pdf.
7. World Health Organization. About WHO. http://www.who.int/about/en/. Accessed December 4, 2016.
8. World Trade Organization. *The World Trade Organization....* http://www.wto.org/english/res_e/doload_e/inbr_e.pdf. Published 2014. Accessed December 4, 2016.

Index

A

Abbott, Tony, 495
Abdullah, Emir, 299
Abdullah, King, 299
Abdullah, King II, 299
Abdullah, Prince, 302
accountability, 93–94
Acumen, 70
advocacy NGOs, 69
African Union, 68
aging population, 557–558
air quality, 17
Aiyar, Swaminthan S., 406
alcohol, 25, 253, 255, 463
Alma-Ata Declaration (Saint Lucia), 413
amenable mortality, 180
American Hospital Association, 50
American Red Cross, 70–71, 541
American Revenue Act (1764), 80
Amnesty International, 70
aneurysm, 26
Arm's length bodies (ALB) (United Kingdom), 177, 178
arrhythmias, 27
Arsalan, Math'har Pasha, 302
Ataturk, Kemal, 283
Atwood, Cynthia, 561
Australia
    country description, 491–493
    current and emerging issues and challenges, 504–507
    demographics, 495–496
    description of current healthcare system, 497–499
    evaluation of healthcare system, 499–503
    government and political system, 494–495
    history, 493
    history of healthcare system, 496–497
    macroeconomics, 495
    size and geography, 493–494
avian influenza, 44
    in China, 545–546

B

Babangida, Ibrahim, 359
Bag-Kur (Turkey), 292
Bamako Initiative (Nigeria), 340, 366
Bangladesh
    country description, 383–384
    demographics and health indicators, 388–389
    emerging challenges, 398–399
    government and political system, 387
    history, 385
    history of healthcare system, 392–397
    macroeconomics, 387
    size and geography, 385–387
    status of infectious diseases, 389–392
Basic Law of 1949 (Germany), 231
behavioral model for vulnerable populations, 7–8
biological events
    avian influenza, 545–546
    ebola virus disease (EVD), 544–545
    human immunodeficiency virus (HIV), 543
    severe acute respiratory syndrome (SARS), 545
    Zika virus, 543–544
Bismarck, Otto von, 217, 223, 227, 228
Botswana
    administrative structure of central government, 374
    country description, 371–373
    current challenges, 381
    demographics, 375–376
    description of current healthcare system, 377–379
    emerging challenges, 381
    evaluation of healthcare system, 379–381
    government and political system, 374
    history and culture, 373
    history of healthcare system, 376–377
    human immunodeficiency virus (HIV), 543
    macroeconomics, 374–375
    size and geography, 373, 374
BRAC, 70
brain drain, 260, 367
Brannen, Laura, 562
Brazil
    country description, 149–151
    demographics, 153–154
    description of current healthcare system, 158–160
    emerging issues and challenges, 163–165
    evolution of healthcare system, 160–163
    government and political system, 151–152
    history, 151
    history of healthcare system, 154–158
    macroeconomics, 153
    size and geography, 151, 152
    Zika virus, 543–544
breast cancer, 103, 131, 469–470
Brezhnev, Leonid, 26
Bush, George W., 56

C

Cabot, John, 79, 99
Cambodia, 388
Canada
    country description, 97–99
    current and emerging issues and challenges, 114–117
    demographics, 102–103
    description of current healthcare system, 106–107
    evaluation of healthcare system, 111–114
    facilities, 107–108
    government and political system, 100–102
    history, 99–100
    history of healthcare system, 103–106
    macroeconomics, 102
    SARS, 545
    size and geography, 100
    technology and equipment, 110–111
    workforce, 108–110
Canada Health Act (1984), 106, 117
cancer, 27
    in Brazil, 154
    in Canada, 104
    cervical, 25, 38, 378
    in Mexico, 131
    in United Kingdom, 183
capital cost, 343
CARE International, 70
Cartier, Jacques, 79
cash-and-carry system, 340, 347
Center for Health Design, 561
Centre for Research on the Epidemiology of Disasters (CRED), 541
cerebrospinal meningitis, 366

Charaka, 412
CHC. See community health center (CHC)
China
   avian influenza, 545–546
   country description, 425–427
   current and emerging issues and challenges, 448–449
   demographics, 431–432
   description of current healthcare system, 439–444
   education, 432
   evaluation of current healthcare system, 444–448
   government and political system, 429–430
   history, 427–428
   history of healthcare system, 433–439
   macroeconomics, 430–431
   poverty, 432
   safety problems in, 57
   size and geography, 428–429
cholera, 34–35
chronic disease, 25
Civil Servants' Pension Fund (Turkey), 292
climate change, 558–559
   in Ireland, 248
Clinton, Bill, 52
Clinton, Hillary, 56
Coaching Association of Canada, 72
Coercive Acts (1774), 80
Cohen, Gary, 561
Columbus, Christopher, 79
Commission on Future of Healthcare in Canada, 114
Community health center (CHC), 560
Confucius, 458
Constitution Act of 1867 (Canada), 100, 112
Constitution of the United States, 81
convergence of policy problems, 52–56
   access to care, 53–54
   cost containment, 53
   impact of new technologies, 54
   measuring health outcomes, 54
   quality of care considerations, 54
Cook, James, 493
CORECO, 72
coronary artery disease, 26
Costa Rica
   population and geography, 529
   system affordability, healthcare quality, and health outcomes, 530–532
   system and distribution of stakeholders and resources, 529–530
   technology, 532–533
cost containment, 53
Cost Containment Act of 1977 (Germany), 238
Costello, Peter, 504

country description
   of Australia, 491–493
   of Bangladesh, 383–384
   of Botswana, 371–373
   of Brazil, 149–151
   of Canada, 97–99
   of China, 425–427
   of France, 187–189
   of Germany, 215–217
   of Ghana, 335–337
   of India, 401–403
   of Ireland, 245–247
   of Israel, 313–315
   of Japan, 453–455
   of Jordan, 297–299
   of Korea, 473–474
   of Mexico, 121–123
   of Nigeria, 353–355
   of Peru, 133–134
   of Russia, 263–265
   of Turkey, 281–282
   of United Kingdom, 169–171
   of United States, 77–78
CRED. See Centre for Research on the Epidemiology of Disasters (CRED)
Crisis Housing Caring Support, 72
Croxton, Glenn A., 561
Cuba
   population and geography, 512
   system affordability, healthcare quality, and health outcomes, 513–515
   system and distribution of stakeholders and resources, 513
   technology, 515–516
Currency Act (1764), 80
cyclical process, 51
cyclones, 546
   India, 546

D

death. See also mortality/morbidity
decentralization, 555–556
demographics
   of Australia, 495–496
   of Bangladesh, 388–389
   of Botswana, 375–376
   of Brazil, 153–154
   of Canada, 102–103
   of China, 431–432
   of France, 193–194
   of Germany, 221
   of Ghana, 338
   of India, 408–412
   of Israel, 318–319
   of Japan, 457
   of Jordan, 302
   of Korea, 478
   of Nigeria, 358

   of Peru, 139
   of Russia, 267, 268
   of Turkey, 284–285
   of United Kingdom, 174
   of United States, 83–84
dentists
   in Brazil, 160
   in Canada, 110
   in France, 208, 209
   in Germany, 233, 238
   in India, 417
   in Japan, 459, 467
   in Jordan, 304
   in Nigeria, 362
   in Russia, 270
   in Turkey, 290
   in United States, 85–86
Department of Health
   in Ireland, 254–255
   in United Kingdom, 175–176
   in United States, 82
deprivation, 556, 557
de Soto, Hernando, 59
Deutscher Musikrat, 72
De Valera, Êamon, 250, 251
diabetes, 28
   gestational, 28
   prediabetes, 28
   type 1, 28
   type 2, 28
diarrheal disease, 33–34
digital backbone, 55–56
Direct Relief International, 72
disaster, phases of, 548
displaced people, 559, 563
distributive justice, 58–59
Doctors Without Borders, 71
drought, 542, 546
   in India, 546
drug-resistant bacteria, 42
drugs, administering, 45

E

Early Warning Dissemination System (EWDS), 546
earthquake
   Haiti, 542–543
   Japan, 542
Eastern Health Board (Ireland), 254
ebola hemorrhagic fever virus, 43
ebola virus disease (EVD), 544–545
Economic and Social Council, 66
economic marketplace, 50
economy
   of Ghana, 338
   of Ireland, 251–252
   of Mexico, 123–125
education
   in China, 432

in Germany, 221
in Mexico, 125
in Russia, 266–267
egalitarian view of justice, 59
Eiriksson, Leifur, 99
Elizabeth II, 101, 172, 494
Emergency Medical Treatment and Labor Act of 1986 (USA), 91
emerging challenges
  of Australia, 504–507
  of Bangladesh, 398–399
  of Botswana, 381
  of Brazil, 163–165
  of Canada, 114–117
  of China, 448–449
  of Germany, 238–241
  of Ghana, 348–349
  of India, 420–421
  of Ireland, 252
  of Israel, 326–328
  of Japan, 468–471
  of Jordan, 308–311
  of Korea, 487–488
  of Nigeria, 366–369
  of Russia, 277–278
  of Turkey, 294
  of United Kingdom, 184
emigration, 79, 135, 248, 362
Employee's Health Insurance (EHI) plan (Japan), 461
Enabling factors, in health systems, 6
environment, 270, 558–559, 562
environmental impact/climate change, 558–559
environmental programs, 562
equity/universality, Peru, 146
ethics, 57–59
EVD. *See* ebola virus disease (EVD)
e-waste, 367
EWDS. *See* Early Warning Dissemination System (EWDS)

F

facilities of health care
  in Australia, 497
  in Botswana, 378
  in Brazil, 159
  in Canada, 107–108
  in China, 439–443
  in France, 200–201
  in Germany, 232
  in Ghana, 341–342
  in India, 414–417
  in Japan, 459
  in Jordan, 304
  in Korea, 479–482
  in Mexico, 129
  in Nigeria, 360–361
  in Peru, 142–143
  in Russia, 269–270
  in Turkey, 290
  in United Kingdom, 181
  in United States, 85
fairness, 59
Federal Commission for Protection against Health Risks (Mexico), 345–131
Federal Committee of Physicians and Sickness Funds (Germany), 235
Federal Fund for Mandatory Medical Insurance (Russia), 269
fertility
  in Australia, 497, 504
  in Botswana, 376
  in Brazil, 154
  in France, 193–194
  in Germany, 221
  in India, 411
  in Ireland, 260
  in Israel, 325
  in Japan, 468
  in Jordan, 302, 310
  in Mexico, 128
  in Peru, 145
  in Taiwan, 521
  in Turkey, 285
  in United States, 83
Fine Gael, 250, 252, 260
flooding, 542, 546
  in India, 546
food, 562. *See also* nutritional deficiencies
foreign-born population (United States), 83
France
  Capitalism à la Française, 193
  country description, 187–189
  demographics, 193–194
  description of current healthcare system, 200–205
  evaluation of healthcare system, 205–209
  government and political system, 192
  health status of population, 194–195
  history, 189–191
  history of healthcare system, 195–200
  issues in healthcare, 210–212
  macroeconomics, 192–193
  poverty, 194
  religion, 194
  size and geography, 191–192
free markets, 82, 91–92, 116, 140, 193, 247, 276
funding, 128, 499–500

G

Gardner, Neil Steven, 560
GAVI Alliance, 345
GDP, 556
  healthcare as portion of, 556
General Assembly, 66
General Health Law of 2003 (Mexico), 130
Geophysical disasters, 541–543
George, David Lloyd, 175
Germany
  access, 237–238
  country description, 215–217
  culture and religion, 221–222
  demographics, 221
  description of current healthcare system, 232–233
  educational system, 221
  emerging issues and challenges, 238–241
  in European Union, 218–220
  evaluation of healthcare system, 233–236
  government and political system, 218, 219
  history, 217–218
  history of healthcare system, 222–232
  macroeconomics, 220–221
  map of, 219
  mortality and morbidity, 222
  quality, 236–237
  size and geography, 218
Gesetzliche Krankenversicherung (GKV), 223
Gesundheitsfonds, 231, 235
GG. *See Grundgesetz* (GG)
Ghana
  country description, 335–337
  demographics, 338
  description of current healthcare system, 341–343
  economy, 338
  emerging issues and challenges, 348–349
  evaluation of healthcare system, 343–348
  history, 337–338
  history of healthcare system, 338–341
  size and geography, 338, 339
Gingrich, Newt, 56
GKV. *See Gesetzliche Krankenversicherung* (GKV)
global funds, 39, 344, 345
global health, 21–22
  burden of disease, 22–23
  cancer, 27
  causes of death in 2016, 27
  diabetes (*See* diabetes)
  functions, 22
  indicators, 22, 23
  infectious disease (*See* infectious disease)
  mental illness, 28–29
  noncommunicable/chronic diseases (*See* noncommunicable/chronic diseases)

global health (*continued*)
  public health and healthcare services, 44–46
  respiratory infections (*See* respiratory infections)
  sexually transmitted infections (STIs) (*See* sexually transmitted infections (STIs))
  vector-borne diseases (*See* vector-borne diseases)
  waterborne diseases (*See* waterborne diseases)
  zoonotic infections (*See* zoonotic infections)
globalization, 554–555
Gorbachev, Mikhail, 265
Gore, Al, 558
government
  of Australia, 494–495
  of Bangladesh, 387
  of Botswana, 374
  of Brazil, 151–152
  of Canada, 100–102
  of China, 429–430
  of France, 192
  of Germany, 218, 219
  of India, 405–406
  of Ireland, 248–250
  of Israel, 316–318
  of Japan, 456–457
  of Jordan, 301
  of Korea, 477
  of Mexico, 123
  of Nigeria, 356
  of Russia, 265
  of Turkey, 283–284
  of United Kingdom, 172
  of United States, 81–82
green hospitals, 561, 563
Green Star, 562
Grundgesetz (GG), 218
Guenther, Robin, 561
Guggisberg, Gordon, 338
Guild of Medical Directors (Nigeria), 366

H

Haiti, 542–543
Hartmann Union, 228
Harvie, Jamie, 562
health
  definition of, 3
  ecological view of, 562–563
  social determinants of, 8–10
healthcare quality
  in Costa Rica, 530–532
  in Cuba, 513–515
  in The Netherlands, 526–528
  in Singapore, 517–519
  in Taiwan, 522–523

healthcare system
  in Australia, 496–503
  in Bangladesh, 392–397
  in Botswana, 376–381
  in Brazil, 154–163
  in Canada, 103–107, 111–114
  in China, 433–448
  in France, 195–209
  in Germany, 222–236
  in Ghana, 338–348
  in India, 412–420
  in Ireland, 252, 254–261
  in Israel, 319–326
  in Japan, 458–468
  in Jordan, 302–308
  in Korea, 478–483, 486–487
  in Mexico, 126–132
  in Nigeria, 358–366
  in Peru, 140–142, 144
  in Russia, 267–276
  in Turkey, 285–292
  in United Kingdom, 174–184
  in United States, 84–94
Healthcare Without Harm, 561
"Health For All by 2000" (India), 413
health indicators, 213
Health Insurance Act (Germany), 227
Health Insurance Contribution Rate Exoneration Act (1996) (Germany), 224
Health Insurance Law (Japan), 458
Health Insurance Review and Assessment Service (HIRA) (Korea), 481
Health Maintenance Organization (HMO) Act of 1973 (USA), 85
health outcomes
  in Costa Rica, 530–532
  in Cuba, 513–515
  in Singapore, 517–519
  in Taiwan, 522–523
Health Savings Account (HSA), 55, 92
health status of population (France), 194–195
health system, 3–6, 553
  behavioral model for vulnerable populations, 7–8
  building blocks of, 6
  cost, quality, access triangle, 6
  designs for 21st century, 561–563
  determinants influence population health, 7–8
  financial input data, 4
  general preparedness plan for, 550
  global health and disease, 12–13
  healthcare resources for selected countries, 5–6
  importance of planning, 549
  within larger social systems, 6–16
  mitigation of confusion, 549
  mitigation of fear and panic, 549
  response, 548–549

  social determinants of, 9–10, 14–16
  sustainability in, 560
  time management, 549
  training, 549
  in Turkey, 292–293
  word health trends and implications, 16
Healthy People 2020, 11
heart attack, 26
heart failure, 26
Henry the Navigator, 337
high blood pressure, 26
Hilfskassengesetz, 226
Hippocratic Oath, 561
history (countries)
  of Bangladesh, 385
  of Botswana, 373
  of Brazil, 151
  of Canada, 99–100
  of China, 427–428
  of France, 189–191
  of Germany, 217–218
  of Ghana, 337–338
  of India, 403–404
  of Israel, 315–316
  of Japan, 455
  of Jordan, 299–300
  of Korea, 475
  of Mexico, 123
  of Nigeria, 355
  of Peru, 135
  of Russia, 265
  of Turkey, 283
  of United Kingdom, 171–172
  of United States, 79–80
Hitler, Adolf, 217–218, 228–229
HIV/AIDS, 51, 543
  in Australia, 493
  in Bangladesh, 384, 390
  in Botswana, 373, 543
  in Brazil, 151, 157
  in Canada, 99
  in China, 426–427
  in France, 189
  in Germany, 217
  in Ghana, 337
  in India, 403, 411
  in Ireland, 246–247
  in Israel, 314–315
  in Japan, 455
  in Jordan, 298
  in Korea, 474
  in Mexico, 123
  in Nigeria, 354–355
  in Peru, 134
  in Russia, 264–265, 277
  in Turkey, 282
  in United Kingdom, 171
  in United States, 364
hospitals
  in Brazil, 156–157, 163–164
  in Canada, 104–108, 112, 113

in France, 195–202
green, 561, 563
health food system, 562
in Mexico, 126 127, 129
in Peru, 140–144
in United Kingdom, 174–180
in United States, 84, 86–90
Hospital Services Plan, 105
Howard, Jon, 495
HSA. *See* Health Savings Account (HSA)
Hudson, Henry, 79
humanitarian crises, 559, 563
Human Rights Watch, 70
Hurricane Katrina, 546–548
Hussein, King, 299–300
Hussein, Sharif, 299

I

ICC. *See* International Criminal Court (ICC)
ICRC. *See* International Committee of the Red Cross (ICRC)
IDS. *See* integrated delivery system (IDS)
IGOs. *See* intergovernmental organizations (IGOs)
IHD. *See* ischemic heart disease (IHD)
IMF. *See* International Monetary Fund (IMF)
immigration, Ireland, 248
immunization
    in Bangladesh, 390
    in Brazil, 161
    in Canada, 112, 113
    in Germany, 234
    in Jordan, 306
    in Nigeria, 359
    in Russia, 273
    United Kingdom, 179
IMSS. *See* Mexican Institute for Social Security (IMSS)
IMSS-Oportunidades Program (Mexico), 128, 129
incidence, 22
independence, Ireland, 247
India
    country description, 401–403
    current and emerging challenges and opportunities, 420–421
    cyclones, 546
    demographics, 408–412
    description of current healthcare system, 413–418
    droughts, 546
    evaluation of healthcare system, 418–420
    floods, 546
    government and political system, 405–406
    history, 403–404

history of healthcare system, 412–413
    macroeconomics, 406–408
    size and geography, 404, 405
Indian Health System, 89
indigenous health, 359, 403
individual autonomy, 59
infancy, social determinants of health and, 11
infant mortality. *see* mortality/morbidity
infectious disease, 29–30
    in Bangladesh, 389–392
    climate change, 41
    drug-resistant infectious bacteria, 41
    examples, 43–44
    globalization, 43–44
    lack of infrastructure, 43
    population migration, 41
    poverty, 41
influenza, epidemics and new strains in humans, 37–38
infrastructure
    in Peru, 139
    in United Kingdom, 174
injuries, 17, 556–557
inpatient institutions, 86
inputs, 4
insurance, 50–52, 59
    in Bangladesh, 397
    in Brazil, 156–157, 164–165
    in Canada, 102, 104–106, 110–116
    in China, 433–435, 437
    in France, 193–201
    in Germany, 217, 223, 224, 227–234
    in Ghana, 343, 347
    in India, 416–419
    in Ireland, 252, 254, 255, 259–261
    in Israel, 320–323
    in Jordan, 302, 305, 308
    in Mexico, 128–129, 131
    in Nigeria, 363–364, 367
    in Peru, 140–142, 146
    in Russia, 268–269, 272–278
    in Turkey, 288–289, 292–293
    in United Kingdom, 182, 183
    in United States, 84–94
integrated delivery system (IDS), 89
integrated healthcare system (Israel), 328–329
integration, 90
intergovernmental organizations (IGOs), 65–66
    African Union, 68
    International Criminal Court (ICC), 68
    Organisation for Economic Co-operation and Development (OECD), 68
    United Nations System, 66–68
    World Trade Organization (WTO), 68
International Committee of the Red Cross (ICRC), 70–71

International Court of Justice, 67
International Criminal Court (ICC), 68
International Federation of the Red Cross and Red Crescent, 541
International Funding Corporation, 554
international health policy, 554–555
International Monetary Fund (IMF), 67–68, 357, 554
International Trachoma Initiative, 345
Ireland
    alcohol, 253
    climate change, 248
    country description, 245–247
    democratic, 250
    economies, 251–252
    efficiency issues, 252
    evaluation of healthcare system, 257–261
    general health of population, 253
    geography and map, 248, 249
    government and political system, 248–250
    health care and economic recovery, 252
    history of healthcare system, 254–256
    immigration, 248
    independence and Irish identity, 247
    Irish people, 247
    isolation and emergence, 250–251
    language, 248
    macroeconomics, 251
    population, 248
    poverty rates and healthcare, 253
    single-tier system, 252
    suicide prevention, 253–254
ischemic heart disease (IHD), 183
Islamic Relief, 72
Israel
    challenges and opportunities, 326–328
    country description, 313–315
    demographics, 318–319
    government and political system, 316–318
    healthcare system in, 319–326
    history, 315–316
    integrated healthcare system, 328–329
    leadership in global health, 329–330
    macroeconomics, 318
    national service and security, 319
    size and geography, 316, 317

J

Japan
    country description, 453–455
    current and emerging issues and challenges, 468–471
    demographics, 457
    description of current healthcare system, 459–461

Japan (continued)
  evaluation of healthcare system, 462–468
  government and political system, 456–457
  history, 455
  history of healthcare system, 458–459
  macroeconomics, 457
  poverty, 457
  religion, 457–458
  size and geography, 455–456
Jefferson, Thomas, 80
Joint Commission on Accreditation of Healthcare Organizations (USA), 86, 130
Jordan
  country description, 297–299
  demographics, 302
  description of current healthcare system, 302–305
  emerging issues and challenges, 308–311
  evaluation of healthcare system, 305–308
  government and political system, 301
  history, 299–300
  history of healthcare system, 299–300, 302
  macroeconomics, 301
  size and geography, 300–301
justice, distributive, 58, 59

K

Kaiser Permanente, 562
Kark, Sidney and Emily, 560
Kokkyo naki Kodomotachi, 72
Korea
  country description, 473–474
  current and emerging issues and challenges, 487–488
  demographics, 478
  description of current healthcare system, 479–483
  evaluation of healthcare system, 486–487
  government and political system, 477
  history, 475
  history of healthcare system, 475, 478–479
  macroeconomics, 477–478
  size and geography, 475–477
Korean Association for Suicide Prevention, 72
Korotkova, Anna, 269

L

Lasswell, Harold, 50
Law 'On Health Insurance of Citizens in the Russian Federation,' 272
Leadership in Israel, 329–330
Lemass, Séan, 251
Lenin, Vladimir, 265
Lent, Tom, 561
Leprosy, 394, 410
Lymphatic Filariasis Elimination Program, 45

M

macroeconomics
  of Australia, 495
  of Bangladesh, 387
  of Botswana, 374–375
  of Brazil, 153
  of Canada, 102
  of China, 430–431
  of France, 192–193
  of Germany, 220–221
  of India, 406–408
  of Ireland, 251
  of Israel, 318
  of Japan, 457
  of Jordan, 301
  of Korea, 477–478
  of Nigeria, 356–358
  of Peru, 138–139
  of Russia, 265–266
  of Turkey, 284
  of United Kingdom, 172
  of United States, 82
macro policymaking, 51–52
malnutrition of Peru, 145
mammography screenings, 292, 469–470, 532
managed care system (USA), 87–88
Mandatory Health Insurance Funds (MHIF) (Russia), 272–274, 277
mapping, 45
market justice, 93
marketplace model of policymaking, 50
Materielle Absicherung, 226
Médecins Sans Frontières (Doctors Without Borders), 71
Medibank (Australia), 497, 500
Medicaid (USA), 84, 88–90
Medical Aid (Korea), 484
Medical Care Insurance Act (Canada), 105
Medical Service Law (Japan), 462
medical services
  in postindustrial America, 84–85
  in preindustrial America, 84
Menéndez, Pedro, 79
mental illness, 557
  burden of, 16
Methicillin-resistant *Staphylococcus aureus*, 44
Mexican Institute for Social Security (IMSS), 126, 128–131

Mexico
  access, 131
  business and economic environment, 123–125
  causes of death, 127
  challenges facing, 131–132
  components of healthcare system, 128, 129
  cost of health care, 130
  country description, 121–123
  education, 125
  facilities, 129
  government and political system, 123
  history, 123
  history of healthcare system, 123, 126–132
  mortality and morbidity, 126, 127
  organizations, 128–129
  poverty and economic equality in, 125, 126
  public health services, 131
  quality, 130–131
  size and geography, 123, 124
micro policymaking, 50–51
military medical care system, 86, 88
Millennium Development Goals, 344, 348, 360, 390
mitigation
  of confusion, 549
  of fear and panic, 549
mortality/morbidity
  in Germany, 222
  in Mexico, 126, 127
  in Peru, 144–145
multicausation disease model, 25

N

NAFTA (North American Free Trade Agreement), 554
National Agency for Food and Drug Administration and Control (Nigeria), 367
National Development Plan (Nigeria), 359
National Health Council (Mexico), 130
National Health Insurance Act (United Kingdom), 175
National Health Insurance Act of 1883 (Germany), 277
National Health Insurance Corporation (NHIC) (Korea), 479
National Health Insurance Levy (Ghana), 347
National Health Insurance Scheme (NHIS) (Ghana), 341
National Health Insurance Scheme (NHIS) (Nigeria), 363
National Health Policy 2002 (India), 420, 421

National Health Service (NHS)
United Kingdom, 171, 174–177
National Health Service (NHS) (United Kingdom), 171, 174–177
National Rural Health Mission (India), 420
national service and security (Israel), 319
natural disasters, 541–542
    geophysical, 541
need factors, in health systems, 7
neglected tropical disease (NTDs), 45
The Netherlands
    population and geography, 524–525
    system affordability, healthcare quality, and health outcomes, 526–528
    system and distribution of stakeholders and resources, 525–526
    technology, 528–529
New Zealand, 499
NGO. See nongovernmental organization (NGO)
NHS. See National Health Service (NHS)
Nigeria
    country description, 353–355
    demographics, 358
    description of current healthcare system, 359–363
    emerging issues and challenges, 366–369
    evaluation of current healthcare system, 363–366
    government and political system, 356
    history, 355
    history of healthcare system, 358–359
    macroeconomics, 356–358
    size and geography, 356
Nigerian National Health Conference, 368
Nixon, Richard, 84
Nkrumah, Kwame, 338, 340, 342
noncommunicable/chronic diseases, 23–25
    aneurysm, 26
    arrhythmias, 27
    cardiovascular disease, 25–26
    congenital heart disease, 26
    coronary artery disease, 26
    heart failure, 26
    high blood pressure, 26
    stroke, 27
nongovernmental organization (NGO), 68–69
    Acumen, 70
    Amnesty International, 70
    BRAC, 70
    CARE International, 70
    classifying, 69
    with country-specific missions, 72
    diversity by country, 71–72
    Human Rights Watch, 70
    International Committee of the Red Cross (ICRC), 70–71

Médecins Sans Frontières (Doctors Without Borders), 71
    Oxfam International, 71
    Save the Children International, 71
    World Vision International, 71
North American Free Trade Agreement (NAFTA), 65
No to Alcohol and Drug Abuse, 72
NTDs. See neglected tropical disease (NTDs)
nutritional deficiencies, 156, 410, 411

O

Okun, Arthur, 57
Operation Smile, 72
Organisation for Economic Co-operation and Development (OECD), 68
Oxfam International, 71
OzGREEN, 72

P

Parkinson's Disease Society, 72
Partners in Health (PIH), 71
Peru
    age and sex distribution of population, 139–140
    country description, 133–134
    demographics, 139
    description of healthcare system, 141–142
    equity/universality, 146
    evaluation of healthcare system, 144
    facilities, 142–143
    fertility rate, 145
    government/political system, 137–138
    history, 135
    history of healthcare system, 140–141
    infrastructure, 139
    macroeconomics, 138–139
    malnutrition, 145
    mortality and life expectancy, 144–145
    population and annual average growth rate in, 137
    population centers, 137
    religion, 140
    size and geography, 135–137
    technology and equipment, 143
    uninsured population, 146–147
    vaccination, 146
    workforce, 143
Peter the Great, 265
Pharmaceutical Benefits Scheme (PBS) (Australia), 496, 498, 502, 503, 505
pharmaceuticals, 51–55
    in Bangladesh, 387, 398

    in Brazil, 159–160
    in Canada, 97, 112
    in China, 435
    in France, 193, 198, 209
    in Germany, 220, 230
    in Ghana, 345–346
    in India, 421
    in Ireland, 255, 256
    in Israel, 322
    in Jordan, 304
    in Mexico, 129
    in Nigeria, 367
    in Peru, 144
    in Russia, 273, 274
    in Turkey, 291
    in United Kingdom, 183
    in United States, 85, 92
PIH. See Partners in Health (PIH)
policlinics (Russia), 269, 270
policy making
    around world, 60–61
    convergence of policy problems, 52–57
    macro, 51–52
    micro, 50–51
    national health tradeoffs, ideology and ethics, 57–59
    worldwide challenge of, 49–50
policy process
    implementation, 52
    outcomes, 52
    policy formulation, 51
    policy outputs, 51–52
    recognition of inputs, 51
polio, 33, 68
political symbolism, 52
political system
    of Australia, 494–495
    of Bangladesh, 387
    of Botswana, 374
    of Brazil, 151–152
    of Canada, 100–102
    of China, 429–430
    of France, 192
    of Germany, 218
    of India, 405–406
    of Ireland, 248–250
    of Israel, 316–318
    of Japan, 456–457
    of Jordan, 301
    of Korea, 477
    of Mexico, 123
    of Nigeria, 356
    of Russia, 265
    of Turkey, 283–284
    of United Kingdom, 172
    of United States, 81–82
Ponce de León, Juan, 79
population
    aging, 16
    of Costa Rica, 529
    of Cuba, 512

population (*continued*)
 of Ireland, 248, 253
 of The Netherlands, 524–525
 of Peru, 137, 139–140
 of Singapore, 516–517
 of Taiwan, 521
poverty
 in China, 432
 in France, 194
 in Ireland, 253
 in Japan, 457
 in Mexico, 125
Poverty Reduction Strategy Initiative, 344
Powell, Tia, 58
PPO model, 93
prediabetes, 28
predisposing factors, in health systems, 7
prevalence, 22
preventive medicine, 562
Primary Healthcare Approach (Saint Lucia), 417
primary medical service (PMS) (United Kingdom), 179
privatization, 554–555
public health, 87, 131
Putin, Vladimir, 269

R

Rahmeh, Haleem Abu, 302
Raleigh, Walter, 79
Rawls, John, 59
recurrent cost, 343
Reform Act 2000 (Germany), 235
Reform 2000 bill (Germany), 238
refugees, 559, 563
Reichsgesundheitsamt, 226
Relief International (RI), 72
religion
 in France, 194
 in Japan, 457–458
 in Peru, 140
respiratory infections, 35
 influenza, 36
 tuberculosis, 35–36
response capacity, 548–549
Revolutionary War (USA), 80
RI. *See* Relief International (RI)
Rice, Thomas, 59
Romanow Commission (Canada), 114
Roosevelt, Franklin D, 66
Rose decision of 1704 (United Kingdom), 175
Rossi, Mark, 561
Rudd, Kevin, 495, 506
Russia
 country description, 263–265
 demographics, 267, 268
 description of current healthcare system, 269–271
 education, 266–267
 emerging issues and challenges, 277–278
 evaluation of health system, 271–276
 government and political system, 265
 history, 265
 history of healthcare system, 267–269
 macroeconomics, 265–266
 size and geography, 265

S

SARS. *See* severe acute respiratory syndrome (SARS)
Save the Children International, 71
Saydam, Refik, 285
Schettler, Ted, 561, 562
Schiavo, Terri, 59
Schwartz, William, 49, 61
Section 65 Funding (Ireland), 254
Security Council, 66
severe acute respiratory syndrome (SARS), 43, 545
 Canada, 545
sexually transmitted infections (STIs), 36–39
 to global public health, 38
 HIV/AIDS, 39
Shishkin, Sergei, 269
Singapore
 population and geography, 516–517
 system affordability, healthcare quality, and health outcomes, 517–519
 system and distribution of stakeholders and resources, 517
 technology, 519–520
single-tier system in Ireland, 252
size and geography
 of Australia, 493–494
 of Bangladesh, 385–387
 of Botswana, 373
 of Brazil, 151
 of Canada, 100
 of China, 428–429
 of France, 191–192
 of Germany, 218
 of Ghana, 338, 339
 of India, 404, 405
 of Israel, 316, 317
 of Japan, 455–456
 of Jordan, 300–301
 of Korea, 475–477
 of Mexico, 123, 124
 of Nigeria, 356
 of Peru, 135–137
 of Russia, 265, 266
 of Turkey, 283
 of United Kingdom, 172, 173
 of United States, 80–81
social accumulation, 11
social/community organizations, 49
Social Health Insurance Restructuring Act (Germany), 235
Social Insurance Institution (SSK) (Turkey), 286, 292
social justice, 93
Social Security Act (USA), 84, 88
Social Security Organization for the Self-Employed (Turkey), 292
social systems, 6–16
Soto, Hernando de, 59
Special Act for Financial Stabilization (Korea), 484
Stalin, Joseph, 265
Stamp Act (1765), 80
State Children's Health Insurance Program (SCHIP) (USA), 86
State Health Services (Mexico), 128
STIs. *See* sexually transmitted infections (STIs)
Strategic Health Authorities (SHA) (United Kingdom), 179
Sugar Act (1764), 80
suicide prevention, 72
 in Ireland, 253–254
Sundiata, 337
Sushruta, 412
Sustainable Development Goals (SDGs), 17, 553–554
symbolic politics, 52
system affordability
 in Costa Rica, 530–532
 in Cuba, 513–515
 in Singapore, 517–519
 in Taiwan, 522–523
system and distribution of stakeholders and resources
 in Costa Rica, 529–530
 in Cuba, 513
 in The Netherlands, 525–526
 in Singapore, 517
 in Taiwan, 521–522
system for vulnerable populations, 88–89
SYSTEM of Social Protection in Health (Mexico), 128, 131

T

Taiwan
 population and geography, 521
 system affordability, healthcare quality, and health outcomes, 522–523
 system and distribution of stakeholders and resources, 521–522
 technology, 523–524
Talal, King, 299
Tawfiq, Rida, 302
Tea Act (1773), 80
Teachta Dàla, 249

technology
  in Canada, 110–111
  in Costa Rica, 532–533
  in Cuba, 515–516
  in The Netherlands, 528–529
  in Peru, 143
  in Singapore, 519–520
  in Taiwan, 523–524
  in United States, 90–91
technology-driven delivery system, 89–90
Third Reich, 227, 228–229
time management, 549
tobacco, 25, 27
  in France, 194, 211
  in Ireland, 259
  in Japan, 469
  in Jordan, 309–310
  in United States, 80
Townshend Revenue Act (1767), 80
trachoma, 72
tradeoffs, 57–59
training of health systems, 549
Treaty of Reunification, 230
TriCare (USA), 88
Tsunami, Japan, 542
Turkey
  country description, 281–282
  demographics, 284–285
  description of current healthcare system, 288–292
  emerging challenges, 294
  evaluation of health system, 292–293
  government and political system, 283–284
  history, 283
  history of healthcare system, 285–288
  macroeconomics, 284
  size and geography, 283

U

UN Charter, 66
UNICEF, 32, 34, 67
uninsured population (Peru), 146–147
United Kingdom
  country description, 169–171
  demographics, 174
  description of current healthcare system, 179–182
  emerging issues and challenges, 184
  evaluation of healthcare system, 182–184
  government or political system, 172
  history, 171–172
  history of healthcare system, 174–179
  infrastructure and transportation development, 174
  macroeconomics, 172
  size and geography, 172, 173

United Nations (UN), 17, 35, 66–68
United Nations Charter, 66
United Nations Children Fund (UNICEF), 32, 34, 67
United Nations Conference on International Organization, 66
United Nations Development Programme (UNDP), 67
United Nations High Commissioner for Refugees (UNHCR), 67
United Nations System, 66–68
United States, 79
  components of, 82
  cost, unequal access, and mixed outcomes, 91
  country description, 77–78
  current healthcare system, 85–89
  demographics, 83–84
  evaluation of healthcare system, 89–94
  facilities, 85
  foreign-born population, 83
  government and political system, 81–82
  government as subsidiary, 92–93
  healthcare system, 84–85
  health care under imperfect market conditions, 91–92
  history, 79–80
  hurricane, 546–548
  integration and accountability, 93–94
  integration and coordination, 90
  macroeconomics, 82
  map of, 81
  market *vs.* social justice, 93
  multiple players and balance of power, 93
  racial/ethnic mix, age categories, and gender mix of, 83
  size and geography, 80–81
  technology-driven delivery system, 90–91
U.S. healthcare delivery, 87

V

vaccination. *See also* immunization
  Peru, 146
vector-borne diseases, 30–31
  malaria, 31–33
  by type of pathogen, 31
  Zika virus, 33
Velez, George, 560
Vereinigungsvertrag, 230
Verrazano, Giovanni da, 79
Vespucci, Amerigo, 79
Veterans Administration (USA), 86
violence, 556–557
  causes of, 557
Vittori, Gail, 561

W

Washington, George, 80
waterborne diseases, 33
  cholera, 34–35
  diarrheal disease, 33–34
water pollution, 235
water quality, 17
West Nile virus, 43
Wilhelm I, 217, 227
workforce
  in Australia, 497–498
  in Bangladesh, 396
  in Botswana, 378
  in Brazil, 159–160
  in Canada, 108–110
  in China, 443–444
  in France, 201–204
  in Germany, 232–233
  in Ghana, 342–343
  in India, 417–418
  in Israel, 327–328
  in Japan, 459–460
  in Jordan, 304
  in Korea, 482–483
  in Nigeria, 360–361
  in Peru, 143
  in Russia, 270–271
  in Turkey, 290
  in United Kingdom, 182
  in United States
    Indian Health System, 89
    inpatient institutions, 86
    integrated delivery system (IDS), 89
    managed care system, 87–88
    military and veterans systems, 88
    outpatient settings, 86–87
    public health, 87
    subsystems of U.S. healthcare delivery, 87
    system for vulnerable populations, 88–89
World Bank, 68
World Food Programme (WFP), 67
World Health Organization (WHO), 3, 68
World Trade Organization (WTO), 68
World Vision, 69, 71, 395

Z

Zika virus, 44, 543–544
  Brazil, 543–544
zoonotic infections, 39
  avian influenza, 40
  ebola virus, 40